D1195335

Your Hit Parade

&

American Top Ten Hits

IN MEMORIAM

To all of those whose help and knowledge
added so much to these pages,
but who didn't live to see this work complete,
this is for you....

Andre Baruch
Dorothy Collins
Chuck Connors
Snooky Lanson
Don Vinson

Your Hit Parade

&
American
Top Ten Hits

A Week-by-Week Guide
to the Nation's
Favorite Music,
1935-1994

Fourth Edition

by
Bruce C. Elrod

60th Anniversary Edition,
Charted Music in America

Popular Culture, Ink.
1994

American Top Ten Hits is based on the
BILLBOARD® Hot 100 charts, 1958-1994.

The BILLBOARD® chart information used herein is
copyright © 1955-1991 by BPI Communications Inc.
and 1992-1994 by BPI Communications Inc.,
Soundscan Inc., and Broadcast Data Systems
and is used with courtesy of BILLBOARD®.
All Rights Reserved.
Used under license of VNU Business Press
Sydnication International B.V.

Cover art is copyright © 1994 by
Popular Culture, Ink.
All Rights Reserved.

Book design and layout by
Alex Przebienda and Tom Schultheiss.
Cover design by Diane Bareis.

ISBN 1-56075-037-5
LC 94-68618

Published by
Popular Culture, Ink.
P.O. Box 1839
Ann Arbor, MI 48106

PCI Collector Editions
are published especially for discerning collectors and libraries.
Each Collector Edition title is released in limited quantities
identified by edition, printing number, and number of copies.
Unlike trade editions, they are not generally available in bookstores.

10 9 8 7 6 5 4 3 2
(Fourth edition, second printing: 500 copies)

Printed in the United States of America

Home of
``The best rock-and-roll books in the world!''

Contents

Preface

My first recollections involving music go back to my fourth year. It was 1953, and I was at my grandparents' house on "N" Street in Cayce, South Carolina. I remember my grandmother singing "Powder Your Face With Sunshine," which came out around the time I was born in February 1949.

I remember spending many such weekends with my grandparents—always a fun place to be when you're four years old. They had a little cement storage shed in the backyard, inside of which were stacks of 78's that belonged to my Uncle Charlie, who was stationed in Korea at the time. He had been a local disc jockey in the Columbia, South Carolina, area and was also a disc jockey in the military. The 78's were fun to look at, but I soon found out that they were very easy to break. Minor catastrophes aside, I first heard some of them play on my Aunt Billie's record player. The ones I remember most are "Rudolph" and "Peter Cottontail."

All through my early years I thoroughly enjoyed radio. TV was something new, and most of the time you could only get one station anyway. To get UHF, you had to attach a little box to your television set, and then you had to keep adjusting it. One show worth the trouble—one of my favorites—was called "Your Hit Parade"; another one was Mitch Miller's "Sing Along With Mitch." "American Bandstand" came along in 1957, and—at least for people in the South—there was the "Grand Ole Opry" as well. Good musical diversity.

In my teen years, my Dad bought our first stereo system from Western Auto. I remember my Mom got all excited about the purchase, and went to Sears where she proceeded to buy twenty or thirty LP's. My brother and I bought 45's. It was 1962, and each of us had our personal favorites. My brother Ricky liked Elvis, I liked country and rock-and-roll, my Dad was a Johnny Cash fanatic, and my Mom loved Sonny James and Andy Williams. I remember spending hours in front of that stereo.

My brother and I grew up in a time of great musical change. Elvis gave way to the Beatles, and the Walkmans of today were born under the name "transistor radios." Ever ride in a car with no radio except your handy transistor? To get the best AM reception—there was no FM at the time—you had to hang an antenna out the window. We had two great disc jockeys in our area at the time. One, Handy Andy, played country, while Woody With The Goodies played the Top 60 in Dixie. Woody liked to rhyme.

Throughout my teens, I continued to collect records, mainly 45's. A cost-conscious shopper, I recall vividly when they went from 39 cents to 69 cents a piece. If you were patient and could wait six months, however, stores would punch holes in the sleeves and sell them ten-for-a-dollar. Yes, old-time 45's are still pressed today, although few places sell them, especially at old-time prices. As an example, I recently bought a new Garth Brooks single—it cost me five dollars.

In 1967-68, when I graduated from high school, my parents opened a record shop. We were ahead of our time for the area we lived in; you don't make much profit selling records, mainly 45's. Albums sold for $3.88, and folks just wouldn't buy them. Although the store lasted for only two years, they were valuable years that furthered my musical education. I recall that our big-

Bruce Elrod

ix

gest seller was Bobby Goldsboro's "Honey," followed by Jeannie C. Riley's "Harper Valley P.T.A." I did the ordering for the shop, and I remember how our distributor once tried to sell me a box (25 LP's) of a new Beatles album called "Yesterday...And Today." I took one look at that "Butcher Cover" and knew—being from the heart of the Bible Belt—there was No Way! If only I knew then what I know now: those pristine, sealed albums would later be worth over $100,000.

When we closed our little shop, I went out on my own, roaming through 22 states, living for a time in Colorado, Arizona, and finally settling in Atlanta, Georgia. I always made it a point to find out where the good record shops were, and my collection kept on growing all through these years. In Georgia, where I worked for Peach's record chain, I got to meet some fine collectors, two of whom helped with this book—Charlie Kaufman and Esmer Daniel. Esmer got me hooked again on the old Hit Parade, and Charlie is an expert on the music of the thirties and forties.

Esmer, bless his heart, had actually kept a weekly listing of the songs aired on the Hit Parade. To our knowledge, no similar listing existed, so Charlie and I put together the first edition of this book on St. Patrick's Day, 1977. We printed 800 copies and quickly sold out, thanks in large part to the enterprising record shops—mainly Jim Salle and Clark Music—that backed our efforts and stocked the book. While I continued to work at Peach's and make my weekly rounds of area record shops, Charlie had bigger fish to fry: he opened a used record shop called Record Heaven.

One vivid memory from this period reminds me just how crazy record collectors can be. One of my good friends, whose name—Marty Feldman—most serious collectors know well, lived in the "elite" section of Atlanta. On this occasion, he had conned me into going with him to look at a record collection that was for sale. I spent the night at his home, and he got me up early the next morning—one of the coldest mornings Atlanta had ever experienced, maybe -1° F! Inside, though, we had put on our summer shorts, t-shirts, and flip-flops, and we just jumped into Marty's old VW "bug" and took off. Pretty soon, I was freezing. Marty waited until we were fifteen miles from his house to tell me—looking at me with those big, moon-shaped eyes—that the car heater didn't work. Well, we ended up buying the record collection, but not before we convinced the seller that, yes, we did actually have to climb *inside* his roaring fireplace for just a bit.

In 1981, I finally moved back home to South Carolina where, in 1985, I opened up my own record shop with three partners: "Your Hit Parade" Golden Oldies. We sold 78's, LP's and 45's. As president of the local Youth Development Foundation, the shop allowed me a forum through which to pass along my love of music and the many joys of record collecting; hopefully, my own enthusiasm has helped foster a new generation of "musicologists." Two more editions of this book were also published in this period, the second in 1982, and the third in 1985. Much as with this edition, I added more and more information to accommodate the tastes of a larger and more diverse audience.

In 1986, the same year I enjoyed the distinction of being listed in *Who's Who in Entertainment*, I started my own record label, Lost Gold Records. This year, 1994, with partner Tommy Overstreet, I also entered the field of music licensing with the discovery of some forgotten Patsy Cline masters—just the kind of "lost gold" which forms our namesake. My inspiration to continue in the music business during all these latter years has been my best friend, retired attorney John O. Ehrenclou, and my original partner in C & E Records and Lost Gold Records, Lewis T. "Chappy" Chapman.

All of the above has been an effort on my part to acquaint readers with my background in recorded music—my "credentials," so to speak—and my reasons for doing yet another edition of this book. Spanning sixty years as it does, this volume includes songs and stars which, from my point of view, should not be lost—*cannot* be lost—to the young people of the current generation. To be sure, they have and enjoy their own music (which is included in this book, by the way), and probably do so to the exclusion of much that has come before. Likewise, the older generation continues to enjoy its own music, largely to the exclusion of many of the tunes enjoyed by the current generation. My hope is that all generations will be able to draw from this volume an appreciation of the full panorama of American music, its traditions, the tapestry of its many aspects, faces, rhythms and themes.

With tolerance as a starting point, however, I hope the reader will permit me a few more moments to editorialize—that is, to candidly express my opinions about some things musical. In the past forty-five years, I have been witness to a great many changes in American music—changes in the music, and changes in the mediums developed to carry that music into the various settings of our lives. Just think of the formats we've been through: 78's, 45's, 12-inch LP's, EP's, quad LP's, 8-track tapes, cassette tapes, reel-to-reel tapes, compact discs and, most recently, DAT's and computer-based systems.

Even though limited pressings still occur, I'm someone who misses the old LP's and 45's. Call me old fashioned. CD's and DAT's sound beautiful, but they're cold to me. Gone is the warmth of a hiss, a pop, a scratch—some indication that this is a product of faulty human beings, part of the whole fabric of our "wax" heritage and memories. Also, with our main source of music now being cassettes and CD's, singles and albums as an "art form" have all but vanished from the American scene. Gone are the record sleeves—examples of a past we will never see again—of the type pictured in this book, and gone are liner notes that could actually be read without a microscope. A handful of executives at record labels simply decided at some point that all the millions of turntables didn't matter any more, and proceeded to ram their new formats down our throats. To my knowledge and pleasure, my little record label was the last to issue a four-color picture sleeve—"Star Of Bethlehem" by Tony Sands.

Sadly, from my perspective, our musical tastes have dramatically changed as well. The music of my generation was rock-and-roll. Most "older" people of the time hated it. True, it was the original "Devil's music." To me, however, the fun "message" behind classic rock-and-roll of the fifties and sixties—even the defiant independence distilled into the half-serious, parent-freaking chant of seventies "sex,drugs & rock-and-roll"—has been replaced with the dismally earnest, mirthless music which fixates on violence and death, perversity, drugs, body parts and functions, and Satan.

What is frightening is that kids today take it seriously, and act upon the "message" they are hearing. A lot of it is not worth listening to, much less remembering. I shudder to think that in fifty years some of the sleaze that passes for music today will be considered "classic," and will air daily to the exclusion of truly classic rock, country, rhythm-and-blues, etc. To be sure, my tastes and judgments are very subjective—they are my own. Now, I am "older" people. Before calling me too much to task, though, please note that I did include Heavy Metal and Rap in this new edition. I even like *some* of it—remember, I said I felt that "a lot" of it was trash, not all.

Music is not just entertainment. It is our heritage, lyrical threads woven into the fabric of the history of our nation. The changes I have mentioned have motivated the politically correct among us to attempt to ban certain songs and types of music. I've always "pulled the plug" on music to which I did not want to listen, but I certainly haven't made a complete *ass* of myself by judging what music others were entitled to hear. The world will not come to an end because you or anybody else heard the time-honored, Old English "f-word" in a Rap song. Slang is just slang. Vulgarity has always been with us. Human beings are vulgar. Hell, how do you think all of us got born into this world! (Besides, can you really see the young artists of our time trying to rhyme the word "copulate"?)

Today's parents should take heed. They should listen to the music of their children, if only to gauge the extremes to which that generation feels it has to go to be listened to. It's all there in their music, just as it was in our own. The loss of your child to a particular lifestyle that includes a particular type of music is not the fault of the music; it is the fault of parents who raise their children in such a way that they are not equipped with values that put the messages of such music into perspective. Music might open a door or close it, but it is a door that a youngster is already disposed to pass through, based on the time, attention, treatment, love and understanding given them by their parents.

I realize that this conclusion will not sit well with some groups. Those on the Christian Right, of course, have long been embarked on a campaign to silence the voices of Heavy Metal and Rap music, instead of simply stopping their own ears. It seems now that the "joyful noise" which the Bible encourages us to make unto the Lord must be both joyful and judged beforehand. Similarly, there are those on the Radical Left who feel it is their mandate to regulate what you may hear, see, read, and say. Doubtless there are even those who will take exception to the reproduction of a pack of "Lucky Strikes" cigarettes (the sponsor of "Your Hit Parade") in this volume. (Don't you have anything better to do with your time?)

The goals at all such extremes are certainly similar: they wish to create a "perfect" world, a "perfect" society—at least as perfect as they can imagine, one which conforms to their view of perfection, one made in their own image. If they succeed, there will be no room in it for you or me, rest assured. As this book goes to press, there is an effort within the state of South Carolina, for example, to forever eradicate the

Confederate flag and the song "Dixie"—probably one of the most harmless songs ever written, a favorite of none other than Abraham Lincoln—from the history and heritage of the citizens of this state.

To this writer, such advocacy is the height of short-sighted censorship in the name of immediate political goals. Within the pages of this book you will find a list of the favorite songs of the Confederacy during the Civil War, a list which includes the song "Southern Cross," written in 1862 about the Confederate flag. It also happens to be the same tune—from a popular English melody called "To Anacreon In Heaven," and played widely in this country prior to 1862 as a "patriotic air" known as "The Star-Spangled Banner"—to which the words of Francis Scott Key's 1814 poem were set, a combination adopted as our own national anthem by Congress in 1931. Should we not now disavow this clear link between our nation and the Confederacy?

Think about it. If groups like these have their way with our heritage, musical and otherwise, just what will the future of music be like? Antiseptic and inoffensive, no doubt—and nothing to do with human beings. When such a new anthem is played, conceived and judged acceptable by such groups, who among us—good Americans all—will be able to rise and stand in the certain knowledge that in time the faults and foibles of our past will be forgiven us, and that things of value will not be cast on the garbage heap because they remind us of our human failings? Perhaps another Biblical admonition is appropriate here: "If thine eye offend thee, pluck it out and cast it from thee." Nothing literal intended, of course. Merely a suggestion: if a song offends you, don't buy the record or tape, turn off the radio, change the channel. American music must remain uncensored if we as a nation wish to remain free.

This book chronicles the complete cavalcade of American music, music that is forever changing. Probably the one area that never changes, though, is Christmas. Classic songs really do last forever. "White Christmas" is one of them.

I hope you enjoy this book. Thousands of hours went into its preparation. Please feel free to write to me with your thoughts and reactions: c/o Lost Gold Records, P.O. Box 10, Ridgeway, SC 29130.

—**Bruce Elrod**

My
Hit Parade

Research Associates

The expert guidance of these four individuals is directly responsible for the thoroughness of this edition.

ESMER DANIEL

From Clarkdale, Georgia, Esmer, an avid record collector for more than 60 years, was instrumental in providing advice and information in all sections of the book.

ROBERT ZUNDEL

From Medford, Oregon, Robert is an avid Hit Parader and the proud owner of countless radio shows and transcriptions from that era. Robert helped supply photos and numerous trivia tips.

CHARLIE KAUFMAN

My partner in the first edition of this book in 1977, Charlie was the former owner of Record Heaven in Atlanta. He is very knowledgeable about the Hit Parade era and classic hits, and is responsible for the Big Band trivia section.

JON E. JOHNSON

Jon, from Avondale, Minnesota, is Associate Editor for *DISCoveries* magazine. He supplied additional photos and is responsible for the rhythm-and-blues trivia section.

Acknowledgments

I would like to thank the following collectors and orga-
nizations for their love of music and for the many
man-hours of assistance given to me to make this
book possible:

Charlie Kaufman (Atlanta, GA)
Esmer Daniel (Clarkdale, GA)
Jon Johnson (Avondale, MI)
Robert Zundel (Medford, OR)
Alice Rogers (Demming, NM)
Sy Sussman (Las Vegas, NV)
Harold Sherrick (Van Nuys, CA)
Jerry Osborne (Port Townsend, WA)
Tony Mastrianni (Albany, NY)
Dennis Pettit (Collectables; Philadelphia, PA)
Ronnie Pugh (Country Music Foundation; Nash-
    ville, TN)
Chris Golden (Billboard; New York, NY)
Terri Harak (Billboard; New York, NY)
The Wax Museum (Charlotte, NC)
Seaco Music (Sumter, SC)
Rebel Music (Roanoke, VA)
Jimmie Rodgers Museum (Meridian, MS)
John McKenna (American Tobacco Co.)
Rose DeRusha (American Tobacco Co.)
Rhino Records
Collectable Records
Terry Rosen (Jazz singles)
Stan Lewis (Paula Records; Shreveport, LA)
Treis Williams (Irmo, SC)
Jim Quirin (Chartmasters; Covington, LA)
Barry Cohen (Chartmasters; Covington, LA)
Warner Mack (Hendersonville, TN)
Wendy Cruzan (Blythewood, SC)
Rex Pratt (Ridgeway, SC)
Express Printing (Lugoff, SC)
Ken McLeod (Winnsboro, SC)
Strawberry Skyes Recording Studio (West Co-
    lumbia, SC)
John O. Ehrenclou (Columbia, SC)
Lewis "Chappy" Chapman (Camden, SC)
Tommy Overstreet (Springfield, MO)
Glenn Ballard (Lexington, SC)
Shelly Liebowitz (Ft. Lauderdale, FL)
Richard Kaufman (Atlanta, GA)

John LaMonte (Albuquerque, NM)
Steve Miller (Nashville, TN)
Bernie Wayne (Los Angeles, CA)
Fairfield Printers (Winnsboro, SC)
Ernest Yarborough (Winnsboro, SC)
Bea Wain (Beverly Hills, CA)
Andre Baruch (Beverly Hills, CA)
Snooky Lanson (Nashville, TN)
Gisele MacKenzie (N. Hollywood, CA)
Russell Arms (Palm Springs, CA)
Dorothy Collins (Vero Beach, FL)
Skeeter Davis (Nashville, TN)
Marion Carter (Elliott, SC)
Merle Kilgore (Paris, TN)
Melba Montgomery (Nashville, TN)
Norma Jean (Nashville, TN)
Billy Deaton (Nashville, TN)
Hubert Stroud (Shreveport, LA)
Justin Tubb (Nashville, TN)
Ray Ruff (W. Columbia, SC)
Chuck Connors (Los Angeles, CA)
Dee Presley (Nashville, TN)
Johnny Sea (Cleibourne, TX)
Nick Shaffran (New York, NY)
Jim Shaw (Bakersfield, CA)
Jan Kurtis (Leavenworth, WA)
Walter Smith (Glen Allen, VA)

Special thanks go to:

My Mom, Betty Elrod, and my son Chris for their help.

To the town of Ridgeway, a quaint little village of 400 in
    Fairfield County, South Carolina—a beautiful set-
    ting to write this book.

To The Bear & Missy.

To the recording artists of Lost Gold Records, whose
    patience allowed me the time to finish this book:
    Tony Sands, Lyndia Ann Tarlton, Flipside, Argie
    Darnell, Shannon McConnell, Roz Bowie, Don Vinson,
    Warner Mack, Art Buchanan, David Bell, About Face,
    and Dennis Price.

Your Hit Parade
1935-1958

``Be Happy, Be Happy,
Be Happy, Go Lucky Strike.
Be Happy, Go Lucky,
Go Lucky Strike Today!''

Lucky Strike Presents...

...Your Hit Parade.
"The Top Tunes All Over America
As Determined By The 'Your Hit Parade' Survey
—Sheet Music, Phonograph Records,
Songs Most Played On The Air,
And The Songs Played On Automatic Coin Machines.
An Authentic Tabulation Of America's Taste In Popular Music."

Andre Baruch and Bea Wain

"And now, the Lucky Seven songs of the week..."

by Andre Baruch

Why this book?

"Your Hit Parade" was a magnificent hallmark in the history of radio and television broadcasting. Its impact on the public and the music industry needs to be kept alive for future generations as a reminder to those who reveled in its original presentation.

When it first started on the air—April 20, 1935—sounds were still coming out of clumsy, clunky wooden boxes with panels and ridges and knobs and dials and a little eye that never blinked and a big webbed mouth that looked like it was making a perfect "O."

As the years went by, radio technology became more advanced and so did the presentations of "Your Hit Parade." However, in the Golden Days of Radio (and even TV, for that matter), the sponsor was the "Big Brother" of the broadcasting industry. He had the authority to determine what could be aired on his program and how it was to be broadcast. "Your Hit Parade" was no exception, especially when the president of the American Tobacco Company, George Washington Hill, was its lord and master. This is not to say that he could dictate the actual songs that had attained the honor of being listed on the Hit Parade Survey, however. What he could demand was that they be played in a bright, exciting tempo regardless of whether they were ballads or blues.

The "Your Hit Parade" survey was compiled by tabulating the sales of records and sheet music, the number of times records were played on the air by disc jockeys, and by querying band leaders as to their most often requested songs. The information was combined to produce the song ratings. Mr. Hill did have some leeway if he cared to act outside the ratings, though, by choosing what were called "Lucky Strike Extras." For example, a song that had been in the Top Ten for eleven weeks, a song which he loved—"The Lady In Red"—suddenly dropped off the survey. When he didn't hear it any more, he started the special category called "Extras." This enabled him to add any tune that tickled his fancy.

"Your Hit Parade" remained a musical portrait of the Golden Age of popular music during the thirties, forties and fifties. These were the decades of wonderful singers, of "live" radio and TV, and the Big Bands. What was your pleasure—swing, sweet, or jazz? Whatever your preference, it could always be heard on that program because it was truly the People's Choice. We should know because Bea Wain, Mrs. Baruch, was a star of the show for four years and I was its announcer for most of its run during nearly a quarter of a century. How well I remember saying time and again: "And now...here it is...the song the survey finds in first place on 'Your Hit Parade'...Song NUMBER ONE!," followed by the song title.

How well I recall working with some of America's greatest talents, who contributed so much to the show: Barry Wood, Lawrence Tibbett, Johnny Mercer, Doris Day, Eileen Wilson, Buddy Clark, Snooky Lanson, Gisele MacKenzie, Russell Arms, Mark Warnow, Dorothy Collins and so many others whom you see listed in the pages of this book.

To this very day, "Your Hit Parade" is being heard throughout the U.S. via syndication in a re-creation of this fabulous show. Although no longer a live presentation, it does emulate the original authentic surveys that helped make the songs hit the charts.

No musical program has ever attained the longevity or popularity of "Your Hit Parade," and perhaps none ever will. Therefore, it is entirely fitting that another volume be dedicated to recording its history.

Dorothy Collins

◄ Dorothy Collins circa 1955. Dorothy started singing in the forties with Raymond Scott, then joined "Your Hit Parade" in the early fifties. During the same period, her biggest hits were "My Boy—Flat Top" in 1955, and "Seven Days" in 1956. Both reached the Top 20.

A Letter from Dorothy Collins

Dear Bruce:

Thanks so much for my copy of "Your Hit Parade"—it's filled with wonderful memories...

...of the years when I had no idea that I would one day be a part of the actual show (years when I would sit glued to the radio, waiting for "this week's Top Ten") to the songs that I had the pleasure—the joy—of singing on TV's "Your Hit Parade," with Snooky, Gisele, and Russell....

I've often referred to the years on the show as my "Alma Mater Years." I learned so much that stood me in good stead for every other working experience: Discipline...adaptability...being able to learn lines, dance routines, vocal routines quickly. Oh, how lucky we were—and to be able to "study" with such "Brilliant" men that made up the production staff.

All good, happy, wonderful years!!

Thanks again,
    Dorothy

Snooky Lanson

▲ Snooky Lanson circa 1955.
Snooky started with Ray
Noble in the forties before
coming to the "Your Hit Parade"
show. Snooky's biggest hit was
"The Old Master Painter" in 1949.
During his Hit Parade years,
Snooky had a Top 20 hit with
"It's Almost Tomorrow" in 1955.

An Interview with Snooky Lanson

[Some years before his death, I interviewed Snooky Lanson about his Hit Parade memories, an interview which was first published in the Nov.1988 issue of *DISCoveries* magazine. Snooky was a remarkable personality, and his answers give a great deal of insight into what made "Your Hit Parade" an American institution. —Bruce Elrod]

BRUCE: "Snooky"—is that your real name or a stage name?

SNOOKY: No, my real name is Roy Landman. I was born in 1914 in Memphis Tennessee. Snooky came from an early cartoon called "Snookums," and Lanson from the Irving Berlin song "All Night Long." It developed into Snooky Lanson.

BRUCE: Lucky Strikes put on "Your Hit Parade." Did you endorse the product?

SNOOKY: I sure did. A stipulation in our contract said we could only smoke Lucky Strikes. Till I quit smoking recently, the wife and I received two cartons every week from American Tobacco. I still like to nip every once in a while. It's good for the body.

BRUCE: Are you still active in recording or television work?

SNOOKY: No, I'm retired.

BRUCE: When did you actually begin recording, and what was your first record?

SNOOKY: I started with Ray Noble in 1940. My first record was "By The Light Of The Silvery Moon" as vocalist for Ray Noble. It sold a million and a half copies. Ray's royalties were $75,000; mine was $25. You see, vocalists were paid only a set fee back then. My biggest hit record by myself was "The Old Master Painter," which entered the "Your Hit Parade" charts January 7, 1950, and peaked at number two. It stayed in the Top Ten for eight weeks. In the rock era, beginning in 1955, I had a Top Twenty hit on Dot Records, "It's Almost Tomorrow."

BRUCE: When did "Your Hit Parade" begin its television broadcast? When did you sign on?

SNOOKY: I signed on July 1, 1950. There were three experimental shows during the summer of 1950. Eileen Wilson was the other singer signed. There were only two of us during the first year of "Your Hit Parade," which became a regular series around September 15, 1950.

The roster then went from Eileen, who was replaced by June Valli for one year, to Gisele [MacKenzie], then to Dorothy [Collins], who was on a short time during the early years due to pregnancy. Polly Bergen replaced Dorothy. Russell Arms came on doing commercials in 1953, and was allowed to become a regular cast member in 1955.

BRUCE: For those too young to know, how was a variety show like "Your Hit Parade" done in those days?

SNOOKY: "Your Hit Parade" was done live. We would learn our songs and took direction from the choreographer. We rehearsed Tuesday through Saturday, two hours a day except for Friday and Saturday, which was all-day rehearsal. Each of us learned two songs and maybe a duet each week. Any mistakes you made or misfortunes that may happen on the set were telecast intact for all America to see. There was no editing or video tape in those days.

BRUCE: Did you ever meet any of the early rock stars, such as Bill Haley or Elvis?

SNOOKY: No, and I didn't care to. Not that I had anything against them, but our music was worlds apart.

BRUCE: Who did you meet and work with that impressed you the most?

SNOOKY: Bing Crosby, Frank Sinatra, Mary Martin, Jack Teagarden, Clifton Faddamon, and most of all, Kate Smith. She was one of my favorites. Her mother kind of adopted me and looked after me. One year I had a crewcut haircut, and Kate's mother told me to grow my curly hair back.

BRUCE: What did you think of your co-stars?

SNOOKY: They were all wonderful people. We had no conflicts and had a great time doing the show.

BRUCE: Now Snooky, what's this I've heard about your incidents with one of Gisele's dogs?

SNOOKY: Gisele had two of the lousiest, dirtiest, stinkingest dachshunds you ever saw. She would bring them to work, and when she got to the eighth floor she would drop their leashes and the dogs would go wild and run into the studio. They were not house trained, and during my final dress rehearsal for, of all things, "How Much Is That Doggie In The Window," that mutt of her's let up a curl and s**t right at my feet. I looked over at Gisele and said, "Is that an opinion?"

BRUCE: What about the Hit Parade dancers? Is it true that male dancers had to be "gay"?

SNOOKY: The Hit Parade dancers were good people. Bob Fosse was the original Hit Parade dancer. To the last part of your question, I'll take the fifth and answer: "No comment."

BRUCE: Did you have a favorite "Your Hit Parade" show?

SNOOKY: I'll have to be truthful. I loved every show I did. We did forty shows a year for eight years—three hundred and twenty shows—and I loved 'em all.

BRUCE: What were your favorite songs on "Your Hit Parade"?

SNOOKY: My favorites were "Too Young," "Sixteen Tons," and "Mr. Sandman."

BRUCE: Your least favorite?

SNOOKY: I absolutely despised "Come On To My House." I recall I had to open the show with this song, and being that I hated the song so much, I wrote the words and lyrics in chalk on the floor at dress rehearsal where I was to stand to sing. We took a five-minute break and they called me on, the camera light came on, and the janitor had mopped up my words. I had to ad-lib two-and-a-half minutes of that dumb song.

BRUCE: Why did "Your Hit Parade" end?

SNOOKY: Contrary to popular belief, rock and roll did not play a major role in the demise of "Your Hit Parade." American Tobacco decided to put out a new brand of cigarettes called "Hit Parade." They wanted a completely new cast and image. So we (the old cast) were let go. Hell, the new cast was awful and the cigarettes even worse!

BRUCE: I see that in the sixties you returned to Nashville and recorded an LP and several country singles for the Starday label. Did you always have an interest in country music?

SNOOKY: No, I never had an interest in country music. They called me over to Starday to do what they called "middle of the road country." Needless to say, my career as a country singer flopped. I did these sessions and no more. I do like some Brenda Lee, Loretta Lynn, Tennessee Ernie Ford, Red Foley and Hank [Williams] Sr. though.

BRUCE: Do you ever hear from your co-stars?

SNOOKY: Three years ago, Gisele, Russell and I took a cruise on the U.S.S. Constitution in Hawaii. As far as I know, Gisele and Russell live in California. Dorothy [Collins] lives in Florida, and called me a couple of years ago on my birthday. I heard a week or so ago, or so I thought, on the Jerry Lewis telethon, that Dorothy had been in an auto accident in Texas.

BRUCE: I hear Bea Wain and Andre Baruch have revived the radio version of "Your Hit Parade."

SNOOKY: They sure did. It's run several times in Nashville and they've done a wonderful job because they have all the original records.

BRUCE: To what do you owe your longevity?

SNOOKY: For those entering the music or entertainment fields, just have fun. I had no aspiration to be a superstar. Just to have fun and support my family. I've been married for forty-nine years, have three kids and eight grandchildren.

9

Gisele MacKenzie

▼ Gisele MacKenzie circa 1988.
Gisele had several hits during the fifties (all reaching the Top
20). Among them were "Adios," "La Fiacre," and "Don't Let The Stars
Get In Your Eyes." Her biggest—"Hard To Get"—officially reached
#4, but got #1 Hit Parade status in 1955 as a personal tribute.

Gisele MacKenzie's Fond Memories

The Hit Parade was a time of magic, of promise of the future kind of entertainment that was mind-boggling to both the performers and production staff, but also to the audience. It represented romance and spontaneous fun with American music. The fact that the audience waited every week to find out what the number one song would be created an expectancy of fun, excitement and glamour a bit like the old movies used to do.

I was privileged and proud to be part of giving that kind of entertainment to the public. What a thrill the night Andre Baruch announced my own hit record as the number one song in the country. It was a moment I'll never forget.

The Hit Parade was a show much ahead of its time in presentation, fast-paced comedy and drama. The actors, dancers and singers had to learn to act, dance and do anything the writers would throw at them...a challenge, indeed.

The Hit Parade was an inspiration for the videos of today.

Good days, fun days, learning days—they were the Hit Parade.

—Gisele MacKenzie

11

Russell Arms

Russell Arms
Remembers

My entrance to the Hit Parade was through the back door.

When the show went on TV, it was designed as a three-star show for Dorothy Collins, Snooky Lanson, and Eileen Wilson, who had come over from radio. I started doing live commercials, which consisted of a singing-dancing group who performed each week. One week I did a particular character in one of the commercials, it caught the eye of the producers, and I was signed to a contract to be the general understudy of the show, as well as to continue doing the commercials. On the last show of that season, I was allowed to sing a song, and the fan mail was considerable over the summer hiatus, all asking the same question..."Who was THAT?!"

Seeing the interest I had created, the producers decided to incorporate me into the show the following year. I got to sing duets, plus an occasional solo, and the fan mail continued to grow! The following season, it was decided to make it a four-star show consisting of Dorothy Collins, Snooky Lanson, Gisele MacKenzie, and (at last!) Russell Arms! Two more years followed with this highly successful grouping, and the show received just about every award that TV gave out...the Emmy, the Peabody, etc.

I was very proud to be associated with the show, especially when I would go to another town to do a local guest spot. The production staff of the local station would inevitably come around and ask about the technical aspect of the Hit Parade because it was, indeed, far ahead of its time in production values. It was a great learning experience!

Happily, through the intervening years since the HP left the air, we four "stars" have maintained contact. We have done some special reunion shows, cruises, and, at the very least, have exchanged Xmas cards each year. The six years I spent connected with the show were a very big part of my show biz life, and I'm happy to have been there in live TV!

—Russell Arms

▲ Russell Arms circa 1988. Russell was the last of the four major Hit Parade stars. He had a big hit with "Cinco Robles"—it peaked at #22—in 1957.

"Your Hit Parade" Cast (circa 1955)

(Second row, starting third from left: Gisele MacKenzie, Snooky Lanson, Dorothy Collins, and Russell Arms.)

"Your Hit Parade" Stars Charted Hits

RUSSELL ARMS
CINCO ROBLES ∗   Era 1026   1957

DOROTHY COLLINS
MY BOY—FLAT TOP ∗   Coral 61510   1955
SEVEN DAYS ∗   Coral 61562   1956
BACIARE BACIARE   Top Rank 2024   1959
BANJO BOY   Top Rank 2052   1960

SNOOKY LANSON
ON A SLOW BOAT TO CHINA ∗   Mercury 5191   1948
THE OLD MASTER PAINTER ∗   London 555   1949
WHY DON'T YOU WRITE ME   Dot 15385   1955
IT'S ALMOST TOMORROW ∗   Dot 15424   1955

GISELE MACKENZIE
LA FIACRE ∗   Capitol 1907   1952
ADIOS ∗   Capitol 2156   1952
WATER CAN'T QUENCH THE FIRE   Capitol 2266   1952
    OF LOVE ∗
DON'T LET THE STARS GET IN   Capitol 2256   1952
    YOUR EYES ∗
LIPSTICK-A-POWDER-N PAINT   Capitol 2404   1953
HARD TO GET ∗   X 0137   1955
PEPPER HOT BABY   X 0172   1955
THE STAR YOU WISHED UPON   Vik 0233   1956
    LAST NIGHT

    ∗Biggest hits.

The Thirties

April 20, 1935
1. SOON   Bing Crosby
2. LULLABYE OF BROADWAY   Dorsey Brothers Orch. (VR: Bob Crosby)
3. LOVELY TO LOOK AT   Eddy Duchin Orch. (VR: Lew Sherwood)
4. I WON'T DANCE   Eddy Duchin Orch. (VR: Lew Sherwood)
5. WHEN I GROW TOO OLD TO DREAM   Glen Gray Orch. (VR: Kenny Sargent)
6. ISLE OF CAPRI   Ray Noble Orch. (VR: Al Bowlly)
7. EVERY DAY   Victor Young Orch.
8. I WAS LUCKY   Benny Goodman Orch. (VR: Helen Ward)
9. EVERYTHING'S BEEN DONE BEFORE   Freddy Martin Orch. (VR: Elmer Feldkamp)
10. IT'S EASY TO REMEMBER   Bing Crosby
11. IT'S AN OLD SOUTHERN CUSTOM   Eddy Duchin Orch. (VR: Lew Sherwood)
12. HERE COMES COOKIE   Henry Busse Orch. (VR: Marion Holmes)
13. IF THE MOON TURNS GREEN   Paul Whiteman Orch. (VR: Ramona Davies)
14. WHAT'S THE REASON?   Guy Lombardo Orch. (VR: Carmen Lombardo)
15. SOLITUDE   Duke Ellington Orch.

April 27, 1935
1. LOVELY TO LOOK AT   Eddy Duchin Orch. (VR: Lew Sherwood)
2. LULLABYE OF BROADWAY   Dorsey Brothers Orch. (VR: Bob Crosby)
3. WHEN I GROW TOO OLD TO DREAM   Glen Gray Orch. (VR: Kenny Sargent)
4. SOON   Bing Crosby
5. ISLE OF CAPRI   Ray Noble Orch. (VR: Al Bowlly)
6. I WAS LUCKY   Benny Goodman Orch. (VR: Helen Ward)
7. I WON'T DANCE   Eddy Duchin Orch. (VR: Lew Sherwood)
8. EVERY DAY   Victor Young Orch.
9. IT'S EASY TO REMEMBER   Bing Crosby
10. HERE COMES COOKIE   Henry Busse Orch. (VR: Marion Holmes)
11. IT'S AN OLD SOUTHERN CUSTOM   Eddy Duchin Orch. (VR: Lew Sherwood)
12. FLOWERS FOR MADAME   Ray Noble Orch. (VR: Al Bowlly)
13. WHOSE HONEY ARE YOU?   Fats Waller Orch. (VR: Fats Waller)
14. SHE'S A LATIN FROM MANHATTAN   Victor Young Orch. (VR: Hal Burke & Tune Twisters)
15. ONCE UPON A MIDNIGHT   Hal Kemp Orch. (VR: Bob Allen)

May 4, 1935
1. LULLABYE OF BROADWAY   Dorsey Brothers Orch. (VR: Bob Crosby)
2. SOON   Bing Crosby
3. LOVELY TO LOOK AT   Eddy Duchin Orch. (VR: Lew Sherwood)
4. I WON'T DANCE   Eddy Duchin Orch. (VR: Lew Sherwood)
5. LIFE IS A SONG   Ruth Etting
6. ISLE OF CAPRI   Ray Noble Orch. (VR: Al Bowlly)
7. WHEN I GROW TOO OLD TO DREAM   Glen Gray Orch. (VR: Kenny Sargent)
8. I WAS LUCKY   Benny Goodman Orch. (VR: Helen Ward)
9. EVERY DAY   Victor Young Orch.
10. YOU'RE A HEAVENLY THING   Benny Goodman Orch. (VR: Helen Ward)
11. EVERYTHING'S BEEN DONE BEFORE   Freddy Martin Orch. (VR: Elmer Feldkamp)
12. LOVE AND A DIME   Jan Garber Orch. (VR: Fritz Heilbron)
13. IT'S EASY TO REMEMBER   Bing Crosby
14. IT'S AN OLD SOUTHERN CUSTOM   Eddy Duchin Orch. (VR: Lew Sherwood)
15. WHAT'S THE REASON?   Guy Lombardo Orch. (VR: Carmen Lombardo)

May 11, 1935
1. LULLABYE OF BROADWAY   Dorsey Brothers Orch. (VR: Bob Crosby)
2. SOON   Bing Crosby
3. WHEN I GROW TOO OLD TO DREAM   Glen Gray Orch. (VR: Kenny Sargent)
4. LIFE IS A SONG   Ruth Etting
5. LOVELY TO LOOK AT   Eddy Duchin Orch. (VR: Lew Sherwood)
6. ABOUT A QUARTER TO NINE   Ozzie Nelson Orch. (VR: Ozzie Nelson)
7. I WON'T DANCE   Eddy Duchin Orch. (VR: Lew Sherwood)
8. SHE'S A LATIN FROM MANHATTAN   Victor Young Orch. (VR: Hal Burke & Tune Twisters)
9. EVERY DAY   Victor Young Orch.
10. WHAT'S THE REASON?   Guy Lombardo Orch. (VR: Carmen Lombardo)
11. YOU'RE A HEAVENLY THING   Benny Goodman Orch. (VR: Helen Ward)
12. FLOWERS FOR MADAME   Ray Noble Orch. (VR: Al Bowlly)
13. WOULD THERE BE LOVE   Guy Lombardo Orch. (VR: Carmen Lombardo)
14. IT'S EASY TO REMEMBER   Bing Crosby
15. ONCE UPON A MIDNIGHT   Hal Kemp Orch. (VR: Bob Allen)

May 18, 1935
1. WHAT'S THE REASON?   Guy Lombardo Orch. (VR: Carmen Lombardo)
2. I WON'T DANCE   Eddy Duchin Orch. (VR: Lew Sherwood)
3. WHEN I GROW TOO OLD TO DREAM   Glen Gray Orch. (VR: Kenny Sargent)
4. LULLABYE OF BROADWAY   Dorsey Brothers Orch. (VR: Bob Crosby)
5. LOVELY TO LOOK AT   Eddy Duchin Orch. (VR: Lew Sherwood)
6. SHE'S A LATIN FROM MANHATTAN   Victor Young Orch. (VR: Hal Burke & Tune Twisters)
7. LIFE IS A SONG   Ruth Etting
8. TELL ME THAT YOU LOVE ME TONIGHT   Freddy Martin Orch.
9. ABOUT A QUARTER TO NINE   Ozzie Nelson Orch. (VR: Ozzie Nelson)
10. LOVE AND A DIME   Jan Garber Orch. (VR: Fritz Heilbron)

15

11 FLOWERS FOR MADAME   Ray Noble Orch. (VR: Al Bowlly)
12 IT'S EASY TO REMEMBER   Bing Crosby
13 YOU'RE A HEAVENLY THING   Benny Goodman Orch. (VR: Helen Ward)
14 LADY IN RED   Xavier Cugat Orch. (VR: Don Reid)
15 IN A LITTLE GYPSY TEA ROOM   Bob Crosby Orch. (VR: Frank Tennille)

May 25, 1935
1 WHAT'S THE REASON?   Guy Lombardo Orch. (VR: Carmen Lombardo)
2 WHEN I GROW TOO OLD TO DREAM   Glen Gray Orch. (VR: Kenny Sargent)
3 SHE'S A LATIN FROM MANHATTAN   Victor Young Orch. (VR: Hal Burke & Tune Twisters)
4 ABOUT A QUARTER TO NINE   Ozzie Nelson Orch. (VR: Ozzie Nelson)
5 LULLABYE OF BROADWAY   Dorsey Brothers Orch. (VR: Bob Crosby)
6 LIFE IS A SONG   Ruth Etting
7 I WON'T DANCE   Eddy Duchin Orch. (VR: Lew Sherwood)
8 TELL ME THAT YOU LOVE ME TONIGHT   Freddy Martin Orch.
9 WAY BACK HOME   Victor Young Orch. (VR: Milton Watson)
10 LOVELY TO LOOK AT   Eddy Duchin Orch. (VR: Lew Sherwood)
11 LOVE AND A DIME   Jan Garber Orch. (VR: Fritz Heilbron)
12 FLOWERS FOR MADAME   Ray Noble Orch. (VR: Al Bowlly)
13 EVERYTHING'S BEEN DONE BEFORE   Freddy Martin Orch. (VR: Elmer Feldkamp)
14 SOON   Bing Crosby
15 IN THE MIDDLE OF A KISS   Hal Kemp Orch. (VR: Bob Allen)

June 1, 1935
1 LIFE IS A SONG   Ruth Etting
2 LULLABYE OF BROADWAY   Dorsey Brothers Orch. (VR: Bob Crosby)
3 WHAT'S THE REASON?   Guy Lombardo Orch. (VR: Carmen Lombardo)
4 SHE'S A LATIN FROM MANHATTAN   Victor Young Orch. (VR: Hal Burke & Tune Twisters)
5 ABOUT A QUARTER TO NINE   Ozzie Nelson Orch. (VR: Ozzie Nelson)
6 IN THE MIDDLE OF A KISS   Hal Kemp Orch. (VR: Bob Allen)
7 IN A LITTLE GYPSY TEA ROOM   Bob Crosby Orch. (VR: Frank Tennille)
8 TELL ME THAT YOU LOVE ME TONIGHT   Freddy Martin Orch.
9 FLOWERS FOR MADAME   Ray Noble Orch. (VR: Al Bowlly)
10 EVERYTHING'S BEEN DONE BEFORE   Freddy Martin Orch. (VR: Elmer Feldkamp)
11 I WON'T DANCE   Eddy Duchin Orch. (VR: Lew Sherwood)
12 LOVE AND A DIME   Jan Garber Orch. (VR: Fritz Heilbron)
13 RESTLESS   Hal Kemp Orch. (VR: Maxine Gray)
14 LOVELY TO LOOK AT   Eddy Duchin Orch. (VR: Lew Sherwood)
15 WAY BACK HOME   Victor Young Orch. (VR: Milton Watson)

June 8, 1935
1 LIFE IS A SONG   Ruth Etting
2 WHAT'S THE REASON?   Guy Lombardo Orch. (VR: Carmen Lombardo)
3 TELL ME THAT YOU LOVE ME TONIGHT   Freddy Martin Orch.

4 CHASING SHADOWS   Dorsey Brothers Orch. (VR: Bob Eberly)
5 ABOUT A QUARTER TO NINE   Ozzie Nelson Orch. (VR: Ozzie Nelson)
6 LULLABYE OF BROADWAY   Dorsey Brothers Orch. (VR: Bob Crosby)
7 IN A LITTLE GYPSY TEA ROOM   Bob Crosby Orch. (VR: Frank Tennille)
8 IN THE MIDDLE OF A KISS   Hal Kemp Orch. (VR: Bob Allen)
9 SEEIN' IS BELIEVIN'   Guy Lombardo Orch. (VR: Carmen Lombardo)
10 SHE'S A LATIN FROM MANHATTAN   Victor Young Orch. (VR: Hal Burke & Tune Twisters)
11 LOVELY TO LOOK AT   Eddy Duchin Orch. (VR: Lew Sherwood)
12 EVERYTHING'S BEEN DONE BEFORE   Freddy Martin Orch. (VR: Elmer Feldkamp)
13 I'LL NEVER SAY 'NEVER AGAIN' AGAIN   Ozzie Nelson Orch. (VR: Ozzie Nelson)
14 WAY BACK HOME   Victor Young Orch. (VR: Milton Watson)
15 LADY IN RED   Xavier Cugat Orch. (VR: Don Reid)

June 15, 1935
1 IN A LITTLE GYPSY TEA ROOM   Bob Crosby Orch. (VR: Frank Tennille)
2 LIFE IS A SONG   Ruth Etting
3 WHAT'S THE REASON?   Guy Lombardo Orch. (VR: Carmen Lombardo)
4 IN THE MIDDLE OF A KISS   Hal Kemp Orch. (VR: Bob Allen)
5 ABOUT A QUARTER TO NINE   Ozzie Nelson Orch. (VR: Ozzie Nelson)
6 LULLABYE OF BROADWAY   Dorsey Brothers Orch. (VR: Bob Crosby)
7 LOVELY TO LOOK AT   Eddy Duchin Orch. (VR: Lew Sherwood)
8 CHASING SHADOWS   Dorsey Brothers Orch. (VR: Bob Eberly)
9 SHE'S A LATIN FROM MANHATTAN   Victor Young Orch. (VR: Hal Burke & Tune Twisters)
10 LADY IN RED   Xavier Cugat Orch. (VR: Don Reid)
11 SEEIN' IS BELIEVIN'   Guy Lombardo Orch. (VR: Carmen Lombardo)
12 THRILLED   Hal Kemp Orch. (VR: Maxine Gray)
13 FLOWERS FOR MADAME   Ray Noble Orch. (VR: Al Bowlly)
14 FOOTLOOSE AND FANCY FREE   Richard Himber (VR: Stuart Allen)
15 EVERY LITTLE MOMENT   Dorsey Brothers Orch. (VR: Kay Weber)

June 22, 1935
1 CHASING SHADOWS   Dorsey Brothers Orch. (VR: Bob Eberly)
2 IN A LITTLE GYPSY TEA ROOM   Bob Crosby Orch. (VR: Frank Tennille)
3 ABOUT A QUARTER TO NINE   Ozzie Nelson Orch. (VR: Ozzie Nelson)
4 IN THE MIDDLE OF A KISS   Hal Kemp Orch. (VR: Bob Allen)
5 WHAT'S THE REASON?   Guy Lombardo Orch. (VR: Carmen Lombardo)
6 LADY IN RED   Xavier Cugat Orch. (VR: Don Reid)
7 LIFE IS A SONG   Ruth Etting
8 I'LL NEVER SAY 'NEVER AGAIN' AGAIN   Ozzie Nelson Orch. (VR: Ozzie Nelson)

Bing Crosby—who had over 350 career hits
—landed the first #1 song
of the Hit Parade era (April 20).
``Soon'' was from the film ``Mississippi.''

Bob Crosby
In mid-1935, the younger brother of Bing (inset) hits #1 with ``In A Little Gyspy Tea Room.''
(Toni Tennille—of Captain & Tennille fame—is the daughter of Bob Crosby's vocalist, Frank Tennille.)

9   TELL ME THAT YOU LOVE ME TONIGHT   Freddy Martin Orch.

10   LOVE AND A DIME   Jan Garber Orch. (VR: Fritz Heilbron)

11   FLOWERS FOR MADAME   Ray Noble Orch. (VR: Al Bowlly)

12   SEEIN' IS BELIEVIN'   Guy Lombardo Orch. (VR: Carmen Lombardo)

13   THRILLED   Hal Kemp Orch. (VR: Maxine Gray)

14   LET'S SWING IT   Ray Noble Orch. (VR: Al Bowlly)

15   EAST OF THE SUN   Tom Coakley Orch. (VR: Carl Ravazza)

June 29, 1935

1   CHASING SHADOWS   Dorsey Brothers Orch. (VR: Bob Eberly)

2   IN A LITTLE GYPSY TEA ROOM   Bob Crosby Orch. (VR: Frank Tennille)

3   IN THE MIDDLE OF A KISS   Hal Kemp Orch. (VR: Bob Allen)

4   ABOUT A QUARTER TO NINE   Ozzie Nelson Orch. (VR: Ozzie Nelson)

5   LIFE IS A SONG   Ruth Etting

6   WHAT'S THE REASON?   Guy Lombardo Orch. (VR: Carmen Lombardo)

7   LADY IN RED   Xavier Cugat Orch. (VR: Don Reid)

8   THRILLED   Hal Kemp Orch. (VR: Maxine Gray)

9   AND THEN SOME   Ozzie Nelson Orch. (VR: Ozzie Nelson)

10   PARIS IN THE SPRING   Ray Noble Orch. (VR: Freshmen)

11   I'LL NEVER SAY 'NEVER AGAIN' AGAIN   Ozzie Nelson Orch. (VR: Ozzie Nelson)

12   LOVE AND A DIME   Jan Garber Orch. (VR: Fritz Heilbron)

13   I'M LIVIN' IN A GREAT BIG WAY   Louis Prima Orch. (VR: Louis Prima)

14   SEEIN' IS BELIEVIN'   Guy Lombardo Orch. (VR: Carmen Lombardo)

15   KISS ME GOODNIGHT   Richard Himber Orch. (VR: Stuart Allen)

July 6, 1935

1   CHASING SHADOWS   Dorsey Brothers Orch. (VR: Bob Eberly)

2   IN A LITTLE GYPSY TEA ROOM   Bob Crosby Orch. (VR: Frank Tennille)

3   LADY IN RED   Xavier Cugat Orch. (VR: Don Reid)

4   I'LL NEVER SAY 'NEVER AGAIN' AGAIN   Ozzie Nelson Orch. (VR: Ozzie Nelson)

5   WHAT'S THE REASON?   Guy Lombardo Orch. (VR: Carmen Lombardo)

6   LIFE IS A SONG   Ruth Etting

7   THRILLED   Hal Kemp Orch. (VR: Maxine Gray)

8   IN THE MIDDLE OF A KISS   Hal Kemp Orch. (VR: Bob Allen)

9   ABOUT A QUARTER TO NINE   Ozzie Nelson Orch. (VR: Ozzie Nelson)

10   FOOTLOOSE AND FANCY FREE   Richard Himber (VR: Stuart Allen)

11   EAST OF THE SUN   Tom Coakley Orch. (VR: Carl Ravazza)

12   AND THEN SOME   Ozzie Nelson Orch. (VR: Ozzie Nelson)

13   EVERY LITTLE MOMENT   Dorsey Brothers Orch. (VR: Kay Weber)

14   TELL ME THAT YOU LOVE ME TONIGHT   Freddy Martin Orch.

15   LET'S SWING IT   Ray Noble Orch. (VR: Al Bowlly)

July 13, 1935

1   IN A LITTLE GYPSY TEA ROOM   Bob Crosby Orch. (VR: Frank Tennille)

2   CHASING SHADOWS   Dorsey Brothers Orch. (VR: Bob Eberly)

3   LADY IN RED   Xavier Cugat Orch. (VR: Don Reid)

4   IN THE MIDDLE OF A KISS   Hal Kemp Orch. (VR: Bob Allen)

5   AND THEN SOME   Ozzie Nelson Orch. (VR: Ozzie Nelson)

6   I'LL NEVER SAY 'NEVER AGAIN' AGAIN   Ozzie Nelson Orch. (VR: Ozzie Nelson)

7   ABOUT A QUARTER TO NINE   Ozzie Nelson Orch. (VR: Ozzie Nelson)

8   PARIS IN THE SPRING   Ray Noble Orch. (VR: Freshmen)

9   THRILLED   Hal Kemp Orch. (VR: Maxine Gray)

10   LIFE IS A SONG   Ruth Etting

11   EAST OF THE SUN   Tom Coakley Orch. (VR: Carl Ravazza)

12   GOT RHYTHM IN YOUR FEET   Benny Goodman Orch. (VR: Helen Ward)

13   I'M LIVIN' IN A GREAT BIG WAY   Louis Prima Orch. (VR: Louis Prima)

14   LET'S SWING IT   Ray Noble Orch. (VR: Al Bowlly)

15   I COULDN'T BELIEVE MY EYES   Freddy Martin Orch.

July 20, 1935

1   CHASING SHADOWS   Dorsey Brothers Orch. (VR: Bob Eberly)

2   IN A LITTLE GYPSY TEA ROOM   Bob Crosby Orch. (VR: Frank Tennille)

3   LADY IN RED   Xavier Cugat Orch. (VR: Don Reid)

4   IN THE MIDDLE OF A KISS   Hal Kemp Orch. (VR: Bob Allen)

5   AND THEN SOME   Ozzie Nelson Orch. (VR: Ozzie Nelson)

6   LET'S SWING IT   Ray Noble Orch. (VR: Al Bowlly)

7   ABOUT A QUARTER TO NINE   Ozzie Nelson Orch. (VR: Ozzie Nelson)

8   I'LL NEVER SAY 'NEVER AGAIN' AGAIN   Ozzie Nelson Orch. (VR: Ozzie Nelson)

9   PARIS IN THE SPRING   Ray Noble Orch. (VR: Freshmen)

10   LOVE AND A DIME   Jan Garber Orch. (VR: Fritz Heilbron)

11   STAR GAZING   Kay Kyser Orch.

12   THRILLED   Hal Kemp Orch. (VR: Maxine Gray)

13   LOVE ME FOREVER   Russ Morgan Orch.

14   EAST OF THE SUN   Tom Coakley Orch. (VR: Carl Ravazza)

15   EVERY LITTLE MOMENT   Dorsey Brothers Orch. (VR: Kay Weber)

July 27, 1935

1   IN THE MIDDLE OF A KISS   Hal Kemp Orch. (VR: Bob Allen)

2   CHASING SHADOWS   Dorsey Brothers Orch. (VR: Bob Eberly)

3   AND THEN SOME   Ozzie Nelson Orch. (VR: Ozzie Nelson)

4   IN A LITTLE GYPSY TEA ROOM   Bob Crosby Orch. (VR: Frank Tennille)

5   LADY IN RED   Xavier Cugat Orch. (VR: Don Reid)

6   EAST OF THE SUN   Tom Coakley Orch. (VR: Carl Ravazza)

7   I'LL NEVER SAY 'NEVER AGAIN' AGAIN   Ozzie Nelson Orch. (VR: Ozzie Nelson)

8   PARIS IN THE SPRING   Ray Noble Orch. (VR: Freshmen)

9   THRILLED   Hal Kemp Orch. (VR: Maxine Gray)

10   EVERY LITTLE MOMENT   Dorsey Brothers Orch. (VR: Kay Weber)

11   LET'S SWING IT   Ray Noble Orch. (VR: Al Bowlly)

12   YOU'RE ALL I NEED   Eddy Duchin Orch. (VR: Lew Sherwood)

13   LULU'S BACK IN TOWN   Fats Waller Orch. (VR: Fats Waller)

14 I'M LIVIN' IN A GREAT BIG WAY   Louis Prima Orch. (VR: Louis Prima)

15 EVERY SINGLE TINGLE OF MY HEART   Dorsey Brothers Orch. (VR: Kay Weber)

August 3, 1935

1 CHASING SHADOWS   Dorsey Brothers Orch. (VR: Bob Eberly) *

2 I'LL NEVER SAY 'NEVER AGAIN' AGAIN   Ozzie Nelson Orch. (VR: Ozzie Nelson) **

3 IN A LITTLE GYPSY TEA ROOM   Bob Crosby Orch. (VR: Frank Tennille)

4 YOU'RE ALL I NEED   Eddy Duchin Orch. (VR: Lew Sherwood)

5 IN THE MIDDLE OF A KISS   Hal Kemp Orch. (VR: Bob Allen)

6 LADY IN RED   Xavier Cugat Orch. (VR: Don Reid)

7 LOVE ME FOREVER   Russ Morgan Orch.

8 EAST OF THE SUN   Tom Coakley Orch. (VR: Carl Ravazza)

9 PARIS IN THE SPRING   Ray Noble Orch. (VR: Freshmen)

10 LULU'S BACK IN TOWN   Fats Waller Orch. (VR: Fats Waller)

11 THRILLED   Hal Kemp Orch. (VR: Maxine Gray)

12 I COULDN'T BELIEVE MY EYES   Freddy Martin Orch.

13 AND THEN SOME   Ozzie Nelson Orch. (VR: Ozzie Nelson)

14 LET'S SWING IT   Ray Noble Orch. (VR: Al Bowlly)

15 I'M LIVIN' IN A GREAT BIG WAY   Louis Prima Orch. (VR: Louis Prima)

Note: * Tied for first place.
  ** Tied for first place.

August 10, 1935

1 PARIS IN THE SPRING   Ray Noble Orch. (VR: Freshmen)

2 AND THEN SOME   Ozzie Nelson Orch. (VR: Ozzie Nelson)

3 EAST OF THE SUN   Tom Coakley Orch. (VR: Carl Ravazza)

4 IN A LITTLE GYPSY TEA ROOM   Bob Crosby Orch. (VR: Frank Tennille)

5 YOU'RE ALL I NEED   Eddy Duchin Orch. (VR: Lew Sherwood)

6 IN THE MIDDLE OF A KISS   Hal Kemp Orch. (VR: Bob Allen)

7 LOVE ME FOREVER   Russ Morgan Orch.

8 CHASING SHADOWS   Dorsey Brothers Orch. (VR: Bob Eberly)

9 LADY IN RED   Xavier Cugat Orch. (VR: Don Reid)

10 I'LL NEVER SAY 'NEVER AGAIN' AGAIN   Ozzie Nelson Orch. (VR: Ozzie Nelson)

11 I COULDN'T BELIEVE MY EYES   Freddy Martin Orch.

12 STAR GAZING   Kay Kyser Orch.

13 EVERY LITTLE MOMENT   Dorsey Brothers Orch. (VR: Kay Weber)

14 LULU'S BACK IN TOWN   Fats Waller Orch. (VR: Fats Waller)

15 PAGE MISS GLORY   Hal Kemp Orch. (VR: Skinnay Ennis)

August 17, 1935

1 AND THEN SOME   Ozzie Nelson Orch. (VR: Ozzie Nelson)

2 EAST OF THE SUN   Tom Coakley Orch. (VR: Carl Ravazza)

3 IN A LITTLE GYPSY TEA ROOM   Bob Crosby Orch. (VR: Frank Tennille)

4 PARIS IN THE SPRING   Ray Noble Orch. (VR: Freshmen)

5 I COULDN'T BELIEVE MY EYES   Freddy Martin Orch.

6 I'M IN THE MOOD FOR LOVE   Little Jack Little (VR: Little Jack Little)

7 LOVE ME FOREVER   Russ Morgan Orch.

8 YOU'RE ALL I NEED   Eddy Duchin Orch. (VR: Lew Sherwood)

9 IN THE MIDDLE OF A KISS   Hal Kemp Orch. (VR: Bob Allen)

10 CHASING SHADOWS   Dorsey Brothers Orch. (VR: Bob Eberly)

11 YOU'RE SO DARN CHARMING   Hal Kemp Orch. (VR: Bob Allen)

12 LULU'S BACK IN TOWN   Fats Waller Orch. (VR: Fats Waller)

13 STAR GAZING   Kay Kyser Orch.

14 MAD ABOUT THE BOY   Ray Noble Orch. (VR: Al Bowlly)

15 DOUBLE TROUBLE   Ray Noble Orch. (VR: Freshman & Ray Noble)

August 24, 1935

1 EAST OF THE SUN   Tom Coakley Orch. (VR: Carl Ravazza)

2 AND THEN SOME   Ozzie Nelson Orch. (VR: Ozzie Nelson)

3 IN A LITTLE GYPSY TEA ROOM   Bob Crosby Orch. (VR: Frank Tennille)

4 PARIS IN THE SPRING   Ray Noble Orch. (VR: Freshmen)

5 YOU'RE ALL I NEED   Eddy Duchin Orch. (VR: Lew Sherwood)

6 LOVE ME FOREVER   Russ Morgan Orch.

7 I COULDN'T BELIEVE MY EYES   Freddy Martin Orch.

8 I'M IN THE MOOD FOR LOVE   Little Jack Little (VR: Little Jack Little)

9 I'LL NEVER SAY 'NEVER AGAIN' AGAIN   Ozzie Nelson Orch. (VR: Ozzie Nelson)

10 ROSE IN HER HAIR   Russ Morgan Orch.

11 SWEET AND SLOW   Fats Waller (VR: Fats Waller)

12 THAT'S WHAT YOU THINK   Will Osborne Orch. (VR: Will Osborne)

13 PAGE MISS GLORY   Hal Kemp Orch. (VR: Skinnay Ennis)

14 LULU'S BACK IN TOWN   Fats Waller Orch. (VR: Fats Waller)

15 LET'S SWING IT   Ray Noble Orch. (VR: Al Bowlly)

August 31, 1935

1 YOU'RE ALL I NEED   Eddy Duchin Orch. (VR: Lew Sherwood)

2 IN A LITTLE GYPSY TEA ROOM   Bob Crosby Orch. (VR: Frank Tennille)

3 EAST OF THE SUN   Tom Coakley Orch. (VR: Carl Ravazza)

4 I'M IN THE MOOD FOR LOVE   Little Jack Little (VR: Little Jack Little)

5 PARIS IN THE SPRING   Ray Noble Orch. (VR: Freshmen)

6 AND THEN SOME   Ozzie Nelson Orch. (VR: Ozzie Nelson)

7 LOVE ME FOREVER   Russ Morgan Orch.

8 I COULDN'T BELIEVE MY EYES   Freddy Martin Orch.

9 ROSE IN HER HAIR   Russ Morgan Orch.

10 CHEEK TO CHEEK   Fred Astaire

11 THAT'S WHAT YOU THINK   Will Osborne Orch. (VR: Will Osborne)

12 PAGE MISS GLORY   Hal Kemp Orch. (VR: Skinnay Ennis)

13 LOAFIN' TIME   Johnny "Skat" Davis Orch.

14 DOUBLE TROUBLE   Ray Noble Orch. (VR: Freshman & Ray Noble)

15 TRUCKIN'   Fats Waller Orch. (VR: Fats Waller)

September 7, 1935

1 EAST OF THE SUN   Tom Coakley Orch. (VR: Carl Ravazza) *

19

2 YOU'RE ALL I NEED   Eddy Duchin Orch. (VR: Lew Sherwood) **

3 I'M IN THE MOOD FOR LOVE   Little Jack Little (VR: Little Jack Little)

4 IN A LITTLE GYPSY TEA ROOM   Bob Crosby Orch. (VR: Frank Tennille)

5 ACCENT ON YOUTH   Duke Ellington Orch.

6 AND THEN SOME   Ozzie Nelson Orch. (VR: Ozzie Nelson)

7 CHEEK TO CHEEK   Fred Astaire

8 PAGE MISS GLORY   Hal Kemp Orch. (VR: Skinnay Ennis)

9 LULU'S BACK IN TOWN   Fats Waller Orch. (VR: Fats Waller)

10 ROSE IN HER HAIR   Russ Morgan Orch.

11 RHYTHM AND ROMANCE   Fats Waller Orch. (VR: Fats Waller)

12 TOP HAT   Fred Astaire

13 I WISHED ON THE MOON   Bing Crosby

14 I COULDN'T BELIEVE MY EYES   Freddy Martin Orch.

15 FROM THE TOP OF YOUR HEAD   Bing Crosby

Note: * Tied for first place.
      ** Tied for first place.

September 14, 1935

*

Note: * YHP troupe enroute to Hollywood. Program of "Big Broadcast" stars airs instead.

September 21, 1935

1 I'M IN THE MOOD FOR LOVE   Little Jack Little (VR: Little Jack Little)

2 YOU'RE ALL I NEED   Eddy Duchin Orch. (VR: Lew Sherwood)

3 CHEEK TO CHEEK   Fred Astaire

4 EAST OF THE SUN   Tom Coakley Orch. (VR: Carl Ravazza)

5 WITHOUT A WORD OF WARNING   Bing Crosby

6 ACCENT ON YOUTH   Duke Ellington Orch.

7 I COULDN'T BELIEVE MY EYES   Freddy Martin Orch.

8 PAGE MISS GLORY   Hal Kemp Orch. (VR: Skinnay Ennis)

9 RHYTHM AND ROMANCE   Fats Waller Orch. (VR: Fats Waller)

10 I'M ON A SEE SAW   Ambrose Orch.

11 TOP HAT   Fred Astaire

12 DOUBLE TROUBLE   Ray Noble Orch. (VR: Freshman & Ray Noble)

13 ISN'T THIS A LOVELY DAY   Fred Astaire

14 NO STRINGS   Fred Astaire

15 I WISHED ON THE MOON   Bing Crosby

September 28, 1935

1 CHEEK TO CHEEK   Fred Astaire

2 I'M IN THE MOOD FOR LOVE   Little Jack Little (VR: Little Jack Little)

3 ACCENT ON YOUTH   Duke Ellington Orch.

4 RHYTHM AND ROMANCE   Fats Waller Orch. (VR: Fats Waller)

5 YOU'RE ALL I NEED   Eddy Duchin Orch. (VR: Lew Sherwood)

6 FROM THE TOP OF YOUR HEAD   Bing Crosby

7 ISN'T THIS A LOVELY DAY   Fred Astaire

8 PAGE MISS GLORY   Hal Kemp Orch. (VR: Skinnay Ennis)

9 EVERY NOW AND THEN   Ramona

10 TOP HAT   Fred Astaire

11 I WISHED ON THE MOON   Bing Crosby

12 ROSE IN HER HAIR   Russ Morgan Orch.

13 NO STRINGS   Fred Astaire

14 YOU'RE SO DARN CHARMING   Hal Kemp Orch. (VR: Bob Allen)

15 PICCOLINO   Fred Astaire

October 5, 1935

1 CHEEK TO CHEEK   Fred Astaire

2 TOP HAT   Fred Astaire

3 I'M IN THE MOOD FOR LOVE   Little Jack Little (VR: Little Jack Little)

4 ISN'T THIS A LOVELY DAY   Fred Astaire

5 I'M ON A SEE SAW   Ambrose Orch.

6 THAT'S WHAT YOU THINK   Will Osborne Orch. (VR: Will Osborne)

7 I WISHED ON THE MOON   Bing Crosby

8 WITHOUT A WORD OF WARNING   Bing Crosby

9 FROM THE TOP OF YOUR HEAD   Bing Crosby

10 NO STRINGS   Fred Astaire

11 I WISH I WERE ALADDIN   Bing Crosby

12 EVERY NOW AND THEN   Ramona

13 RHYTHM AND ROMANCE   Fats Waller Orch. (VR: Fats Waller)

14 BROADWAY RHYTHM   Guy Lombardo Orch. (VR: Carmen Lombardo)

15 DOUBLE TROUBLE   Ray Noble Orch. (VR: Freshman & Ray Noble)

October 12, 1935

1 CHEEK TO CHEEK   Fred Astaire

2 I'M IN THE MOOD FOR LOVE   Little Jack Little (VR: Little Jack Little)

3 YOU ARE MY LUCKY STAR   Eddy Duchin Orch. (VR: Lew Sherwood)

4 I'M ON A SEE SAW   Ambrose Orch.

5 TOP HAT   Fred Astaire

6 ISN'T THIS A LOVELY DAY   Fred Astaire

7 I WISHED ON THE MOON   Bing Crosby

8 TRUCKIN'   Fats Waller Orch. (VR: Fats Waller)

9 FROM THE TOP OF YOUR HEAD   Bing Crosby

10 WITHOUT A WORD OF WARNING   Bing Crosby

11 DOUBLE TROUBLE   Ray Noble Orch. (VR: Freshman & Ray Noble)

12 THE GENTLEMAN OBVIOUSLY DOESN'T BELIEVE   Dorsey Brothers Orch. (VR: Kay Weber)

13 RHYTHM AND ROMANCE   Fats Waller Orch. (VR: Fats Waller)

14 EVERY NOW AND THEN   Ramona

15 I'VE GOT A FEELIN' YOU'RE FOOLIN'   Dorsey Brothers Orch. (VR: Bob Eberly)

October 19, 1935

1 CHEEK TO CHEEK   Fred Astaire

2 I'M IN THE MOOD FOR LOVE   Little Jack Little (VR: Little Jack Little)

3 YOU ARE MY LUCKY STAR   Eddy Duchin Orch. (VR: Lew Sherwood)

4 I'M ON A SEE SAW   Ambrose Orch.

5 ISN'T THIS A LOVELY DAY   Fred Astaire

6 ROSE IN HER HAIR   Russ Morgan Orch.

7 ON TREASURE ISLAND   Tommy Dorsey Orch. (VR: Edythe Wright)

8 WITHOUT A WORD OF WARNING   Bing Crosby

9 TOP HAT   Fred Astaire

10 BROADWAY RHYTHM   Guy Lombardo Orch. (VR: Carmen Lombardo)

11 PICCOLINO   Fred Astaire

12 I WISHED ON THE MOON   Bing Crosby

Astaire hit #1 again in the fall of 1936
(Oct. 24) with ``The Way You Look Tonight''

Fred Astaire
The greatest dancer in American musical history, Fred Astaire hits #1 with ``Cheek To Cheek'' (Sep 28.)

13 FROM THE TOP OF YOUR HEAD   Bing Crosby
14 DOUBLE TROUBLE   Ray Noble Orch. (VR: Freshman & Ray Noble)
15 ACCENT ON YOUTH   Duke Ellington Orch.

October 26, 1935
1 CHEEK TO CHEEK   Fred Astaire
2 YOU ARE MY LUCKY STAR   Eddy Duchin Orch. (VR: Lew Sherwood)
3 I'VE GOT A FEELIN' YOU'RE FOOLIN'   Dorsey Brothers Orch. (VR: Bob Eberly)
4 I'M ON A SEE SAW   Ambrose Orch.
5 ISN'T THIS A LOVELY DAY   Fred Astaire
6 I'M IN THE MOOD FOR LOVE   Little Jack Little (VR: Little Jack Little)
7 WITHOUT A WORD OF WARNING   Bing Crosby
8 TOP HAT   Fred Astaire
9 I FOUND A DREAM   Enric Madriguera Orch. (VR: Tony Sacco)
10 RED SAILS IN THE SUNSET   Guy Lombardo Orch. (VR: Carmen Lombardo)
11 FROM THE TOP OF YOUR HEAD   Bing Crosby
12 THE GENTLEMAN OBVIOUSLY DOESN'T BELIEVE   Dorsey Brothers Orch. (VR: Kay Weber)
13 I WISHED ON THE MOON   Bing Crosby
14 LULU'S BACK IN TOWN   Fats Waller Orch. (VR: Fats Waller)
15 EVERY NOW AND THEN   Ramona

November 2, 1935
1 YOU ARE MY LUCKY STAR   Eddy Duchin Orch. (VR: Lew Sherwood)
2 I'M IN THE MOOD FOR LOVE   Little Jack Little (VR: Little Jack Little)
3 CHEEK TO CHEEK   Fred Astaire
4 ON TREASURE ISLAND   Tommy Dorsey Orch. (VR: Edythe Wright)
5 HERE'S TO ROMANCE   Enric Madriguera Orch. (VR: Tony Sacco)
6 I'M ON A SEE SAW   Ambrose Orch.
7 RED SAILS IN THE SUNSET   Guy Lombardo Orch. (VR: Carmen Lombardo)
8 I'VE GOT A FEELIN' YOU'RE FOOLIN'   Dorsey Brothers Orch. (VR: Bob Eberly)
9 TOP HAT   Fred Astaire
10 BROADWAY RHYTHM   Guy Lombardo Orch. (VR: Carmen Lombardo)
11 WITHOUT A WORD OF WARNING   Bing Crosby
12 ISN'T THIS A LOVELY DAY   Fred Astaire
13 I WISH I WERE ALADDIN   Bing Crosby
14 TRUCKIN'   Fats Waller Orch. (VR: Fats Waller)
15 IT NEVER DAWNED ON ME   Enric Madriguera Orch. (VR: Tony Sacco)

November 9, 1935
1 YOU ARE MY LUCKY STAR   Eddy Duchin Orch. (VR: Lew Sherwood)
2 RED SAILS IN THE SUNSET   Guy Lombardo Orch. (VR: Carmen Lombardo)
3 ON TREASURE ISLAND   Tommy Dorsey Orch. (VR: Edythe Wright)
4 CHEEK TO CHEEK   Fred Astaire
5 ISN'T THIS A LOVELY DAY   Fred Astaire
6 I'VE GOT A FEELIN' YOU'RE FOOLIN'   Dorsey Brothers Orch. (VR: Bob Eberly)
7 I'M ON A SEE SAW   Ambrose Orch.

8 I FOUND A DREAM   Enric Madriguera Orch. (VR: Tony Sacco)
9 ROLL ALONG PRAIRIE MOON   Smith Ballew Orch. (VR: Smith Ballew)
10 HERE'S TO ROMANCE   Enric Madriguera Orch. (VR: Tony Sacco)
11 TWENTY FOUR HOURS A DAY   Teddy Wilson Orch. (VR: Billie Holiday)
12 I'D RATHER LISTEN TO YOUR EYES   Jacques Renard
13 FROM THE TOP OF YOUR HEAD   Bing Crosby
14 NO OTHER ONE   Benny Goodman Orch. (VR: Helen Ward)
15 RHYTHM AND ROMANCE   Fats Waller Orch. (VR: Fats Waller)

November 16, 1935
1 YOU ARE MY LUCKY STAR   Eddy Duchin Orch. (VR: Lew Sherwood)
2 RED SAILS IN THE SUNSET   Guy Lombardo Orch. (VR: Carmen Lombardo)
3 I'VE GOT A FEELIN' YOU'RE FOOLIN'   Dorsey Brothers Orch. (VR: Bob Eberly)
4 ON TREASURE ISLAND   Tommy Dorsey Orch. (VR: Edythe Wright)
5 HERE'S TO ROMANCE   Enric Madriguera Orch. (VR: Tony Sacco)
6 CHEEK TO CHEEK   Fred Astaire
7 ISN'T THIS A LOVELY DAY   Fred Astaire
8 I FOUND A DREAM   Enric Madriguera Orch. (VR: Tony Sacco)
9 I'M ON A SEE SAW   Ambrose Orch.
10 DON'T GIVE UP THE SHIP   Tommy Dorsey Orch. (VR: Cliff Weston)
11 ROLL ALONG PRAIRIE MOON   Smith Ballew Orch. (VR: Smith Ballew)
12 NO OTHER ONE   Benny Goodman Orch. (VR: Helen Ward)
13 THANKS A MILLION   Paul Pendarvis Orch. (VR: Marjorie Beatty)
14 TAKE ME BACK TO MY BOOTS AND SADDLE   Tommy Dorsey Orch. (VR: Cliff Weston)
15 I'M SITTIN' HIGH ON A HILLTOP   Guy Lombardo Orch. (VR: Carmen Lombardo)

November 23, 1935
1 RED SAILS IN THE SUNSET   Guy Lombardo Orch. (VR: Carmen Lombardo)
2 ON TREASURE ISLAND   Tommy Dorsey Orch. (VR: Edythe Wright)
3 YOU ARE MY LUCKY STAR   Eddy Duchin Orch. (VR: Lew Sherwood)
4 I'VE GOT A FEELIN' YOU'RE FOOLIN'   Dorsey Brothers Orch. (VR: Bob Eberly)
5 TWENTY FOUR HOURS A DAY   Teddy Wilson Orch. (VR: Billie Holiday)
6 NO OTHER ONE   Benny Goodman Orch. (VR: Helen Ward)
7 TOP HAT   Fred Astaire
8 HERE'S TO ROMANCE   Enric Madriguera Orch. (VR: Tony Sacco)
9 TAKE ME BACK TO MY BOOTS AND SADDLE   Tommy Dorsey Orch. (VR: Cliff Weston)
10 I'M SITTIN' HIGH ON A HILLTOP   Guy Lombardo Orch. (VR: Carmen Lombardo)
11 ROLL ALONG PRAIRIE MOON   Smith Ballew Orch. (VR: Smith Ballew)

Guy Lombardo
The greatest band leader of all time peaks at #1 with ``Red Sails In The Sunset'' (Nov. 23).
Despite over 200 hits and 100 million record sales, Lombardo's New Year's Eve trademark song
—``Auld Lang Syne''—remains his primary claim to fame for succesive generations of Americans.

12 DON'T GIVE UP THE SHIP   Tommy Dorsey Orch. (VR: Cliff Weston)

13 I FOUND A DREAM   Enric Madriguera Orch. (VR: Tony Sacco)

14 CHEEK TO CHEEK   Fred Astaire

15 A LITTLE BIT INDEPENDENT   Fats Waller Orch. (VR: Fats Waller)

November 30, 1935

1 RED SAILS IN THE SUNSET   Guy Lombardo Orch. (VR: Carmen Lombardo)

2 ON TREASURE ISLAND   Tommy Dorsey Orch. (VR: Edythe Wright)

3 I FOUND A DREAM   Enric Madriguera Orch. (VR: Tony Sacco)

4 TAKE ME BACK TO MY BOOTS AND SADDLE   Tommy Dorsey Orch. (VR: Cliff Weston)

5 YOU ARE MY LUCKY STAR   Eddy Duchin Orch. (VR: Lew Sherwood)

6 DON'T GIVE UP THE SHIP   Tommy Dorsey Orch. (VR: Cliff Weston)

7 NO OTHER ONE   Benny Goodman Orch. (VR: Helen Ward)

8 I'VE GOT A FEELIN' YOU'RE FOOLIN'   Dorsey Brothers Orch. (VR: Bob Eberly)

9 THANKS A MILLION   Paul Pendarvis Orch. (VR: Marjorie Beatty)

10 I'M SITTIN' HIGH ON A HILLTOP   Guy Lombardo Orch. (VR: Carmen Lombardo)

11 TWENTY FOUR HOURS A DAY   Teddy Wilson Orch. (VR: Billie Holiday)

12 ROLL ALONG PRAIRIE MOON   Smith Ballew Orch. (VR: Smith Ballew)

13 A LITTLE BIT INDEPENDENT   Fats Waller Orch. (VR: Fats Waller)

14 I'D LOVE TO TAKE ORDERS FROM YOU   Phil Harris Orch. (VR: Phil Harris)

15 I'D RATHER LISTEN TO YOUR EYES   Jacques Renard

December 7, 1935

1 RED SAILS IN THE SUNSET   Guy Lombardo Orch. (VR: Carmen Lombardo)

2 ON TREASURE ISLAND   Tommy Dorsey Orch. (VR: Edythe Wright)

3 A LITTLE BIT INDEPENDENT   Fats Waller Orch. (VR: Fats Waller)

4 ROLL ALONG PRAIRIE MOON   Smith Ballew Orch. (VR: Smith Ballew)

5 DON'T GIVE UP THE SHIP   Tommy Dorsey Orch. (VR: Cliff Weston)

6 I FOUND A DREAM   Enric Madriguera Orch. (VR: Tony Sacco)

7 TAKE ME BACK TO MY BOOTS AND SADDLE   Tommy Dorsey Orch. (VR: Cliff Weston)

8 I'M SITTIN' HIGH ON A HILLTOP   Guy Lombardo Orch. (VR: Carmen Lombardo)

9 NO OTHER ONE   Benny Goodman Orch. (VR: Helen Ward)

10 THANKS A MILLION   Paul Pendarvis Orch. (VR: Marjorie Beatty)

11 TRUCKIN'   Fats Waller Orch. (VR: Fats Waller)

12 EENIE MEENIE MINY MO   Benny Goodman Orch. (VR: Helen Ward)

13 I'VE GOT A FEELIN' YOU'RE FOOLIN'   Dorsey Brothers Orch. (VR: Bob Eberly)

14 TWENTY FOUR HOURS A DAY   Teddy Wilson Orch. (VR: Billie Holiday)

15 WHERE AM I?   Little Jack Little (VR: Little Jack Little)

December 14, 1935

1 RED SAILS IN THE SUNSET   Guy Lombardo Orch. (VR: Carmen Lombardo)

2 A LITTLE BIT INDEPENDENT   Fats Waller Orch. (VR: Fats Waller)

3 ON TREASURE ISLAND   Tommy Dorsey Orch. (VR: Edythe Wright)

4 THANKS A MILLION   Paul Pendarvis Orch. (VR: Marjorie Beatty)

5 TAKE ME BACK TO MY BOOTS AND SADDLE   Tommy Dorsey Orch. (VR: Cliff Weston)

6 ROLL ALONG PRAIRIE MOON   Smith Ballew Orch. (VR: Smith Ballew)

7 EENIE MEENIE MINY MO   Benny Goodman Orch. (VR: Helen Ward)

8 I'VE GOT A FEELIN' YOU'RE FOOLIN'   Dorsey Brothers Orch. (VR: Bob Eberly)

9 I'M SITTIN' HIGH ON A HILLTOP   Guy Lombardo Orch. (VR: Carmen Lombardo)

10 WHERE AM I?   Little Jack Little (VR: Little Jack Little)

11 YOU ARE MY LUCKY STAR   Eddy Duchin Orch. (VR: Lew Sherwood)

12 DON'T GIVE UP THE SHIP   Tommy Dorsey Orch. (VR: Cliff Weston)

13 TWENTY FOUR HOURS A DAY   Teddy Wilson Orch. (VR: Billie Holiday)

14 NO OTHER ONE   Benny Goodman Orch. (VR: Helen Ward)

15 WITH ALL MY HEART   Hal Kemp Orch.

December 21, 1935

1 ON TREASURE ISLAND   Tommy Dorsey Orch. (VR: Edythe Wright)

2 RED SAILS IN THE SUNSET   Guy Lombardo Orch. (VR: Carmen Lombardo)

3 A LITTLE BIT INDEPENDENT   Fats Waller Orch. (VR: Fats Waller)

4 TAKE ME BACK TO MY BOOTS AND SADDLE   Tommy Dorsey Orch. (VR: Cliff Weston)

5 TWENTY FOUR HOURS A DAY   Teddy Wilson Orch. (VR: Billie Holiday)

6 EENIE MEENIE MINY MO   Benny Goodman Orch. (VR: Helen Ward)

7 I'M SITTIN' HIGH ON A HILLTOP   Guy Lombardo Orch. (VR: Carmen Lombardo)

8 I FOUND A DREAM   Enric Madriguera Orch. (VR: Tony Sacco)

9 THANKS A MILLION   Paul Pendarvis Orch. (VR: Marjorie Beatty)

10 WITH ALL MY HEART   Hal Kemp Orch.

11 DON'T GIVE UP THE SHIP   Tommy Dorsey Orch. (VR: Cliff Weston)

12 ONE NIGHT IN MONTE CARLO   Freddy Martin Orch.

13 NO OTHER ONE   Benny Goodman Orch. (VR: Helen Ward)

14 WHERE AM I?   Little Jack Little (VR: Little Jack Little)

15 IT'S DANGEROUS TO LOVE LIKE THIS   Hal Kemp Orch.

December 28, 1935

1 A LITTLE BIT INDEPENDENT   Fats Waller Orch. (VR: Fats Waller)

2 ON TREASURE ISLAND   Tommy Dorsey Orch. (VR: Edythe Wright)

3 RED SAILS IN THE SUNSET   Guy Lombardo Orch. (VR: Carmen Lombardo)

4   WHERE AM I?   Little Jack Little (VR: Little Jack Little)
5   WITH ALL MY HEART   Hal Kemp Orch.
6   I'M SITTIN' HIGH ON A HILLTOP   Guy Lombardo Orch. (VR: Carmen Lombardo)
7   TAKE ME BACK TO MY BOOTS AND SADDLE   Tommy Dorsey Orch. (VR: Cliff Weston)
8   THANKS A MILLION   Paul Pendarvis Orch. (VR: Marjorie Beatty)
9   MOON OVER MIAMI   Eddy Duchin Orch. (VR: Lew Sherwood)
10   EENIE MEENIE MINY MO   Benny Goodman Orch. (VR: Helen Ward)
11   ROLL ALONG PRAIRIE MOON   Smith Ballew Orch. (VR: Smith Ballew)
12   WHY SHOULDN'T I?   Johnny Green Orch.
13   NO OTHER ONE   Benny Goodman Orch. (VR: Helen Ward)
14   ALONE   Tommy Dorsey Orch. (VR: Cliff Weston)
15   QUICKER THAN YOU CAN SAY 'JACK ROBINSON'   Ozzie Nelson Orch. (VR: Ozzie Nelson)

January 4, 1936

1   A LITTLE BIT INDEPENDENT   Fats Waller Orch. (VR: Fats Waller)
2   ON TREASURE ISLAND   Tommy Dorsey Orch. (VR: Edythe Wright)
3   RED SAILS IN THE SUNSET   Guy Lombardo Orch. (VR: Carmen Lombardo)
4   MOON OVER MIAMI   Eddy Duchin Orch. (VR: Lew Sherwood)
5   THANKS A MILLION   Paul Pendarvis Orch. (VR: Marjorie Beatty)
6   EENIE MEENIE MINY MO   Benny Goodman Orch. (VR: Helen Ward)
7   THE MUSIC GOES 'ROUND AND 'ROUND   Tommy Dorsey Orch. (VR: Edythe Wright) *
8   WITH ALL MY HEART   Hal Kemp Orch.
9   TAKE ME BACK TO MY BOOTS AND SADDLE   Tommy Dorsey Orch. (VR: Cliff Weston)
10   I'M SITTIN' HIGH ON A HILLTOP   Guy Lombardo Orch. (VR: Carmen Lombardo)
11   NO OTHER ONE   Benny Goodman Orch. (VR: Helen Ward)
12   ALONE   Tommy Dorsey Orch. (VR: Cliff Weston)
13   LIGHTS OUT   Eddy Duchin Orch. (VR: Lew Sherwood)
14   IF I SHOULD LOSE YOU   Richard Himber Orch. (VR: Stuart Allen)
15   I FEEL LIKE A FEATHER IN THE BREEZE   Jan Garber Orch. (VR: Lee Bennett)
    Note: * Another version by: Riley-Farley Orch. (VR: Riley & Farley).

January 11, 1936

1   THE MUSIC GOES 'ROUND AND 'ROUND   Tommy Dorsey Orch. (VR: Edythe Wright) *
2   A LITTLE BIT INDEPENDENT   Fats Waller Orch. (VR: Fats Waller)
3   RED SAILS IN THE SUNSET   Guy Lombardo Orch. (VR: Carmen Lombardo)
4   WITH ALL MY HEART   Hal Kemp Orch.
5   TAKE ME BACK TO MY BOOTS AND SADDLE   Tommy Dorsey Orch. (VR: Cliff Weston)
6   MOON OVER MIAMI   Eddy Duchin Orch. (VR: Lew Sherwood)
7   THE BROKEN RECORD   Guy Lombardo Orch. (VR: Carmen Lombardo)
8   ON TREASURE ISLAND   Tommy Dorsey Orch. (VR: Edythe Wright)

9   ALONE   Tommy Dorsey Orch. (VR: Cliff Weston)
10   EENIE MEENIE MINY MO   Benny Goodman Orch. (VR: Helen Ward)
11   THANKS A MILLION   Paul Pendarvis Orch. (VR: Marjorie Beatty)
12   LIGHTS OUT   Eddy Duchin Orch. (VR: Lew Sherwood)
13   I FEEL LIKE A FEATHER IN THE BREEZE   Jan Garber Orch. (VR: Lee Bennett)
14   I'M SITTIN' HIGH ON A HILLTOP   Guy Lombardo Orch. (VR: Carmen Lombardo)
15   NO OTHER ONE   Benny Goodman Orch. (VR: Helen Ward)
    Note: * Another version by: Riley-Farley Orch. (VR: Riley & Farley)

January 18, 1936

1   THE MUSIC GOES 'ROUND AND 'ROUND   Tommy Dorsey Orch. (VR: Edythe Wright) *
2   MOON OVER MIAMI   Eddy Duchin Orch. (VR: Lew Sherwood)
3   RED SAILS IN THE SUNSET   Guy Lombardo Orch. (VR: Carmen Lombardo)
4   WITH ALL MY HEART   Hal Kemp Orch.
5   A LITTLE BIT INDEPENDENT   Fats Waller Orch. (VR: Fats Waller)
6   THE BROKEN RECORD   Guy Lombardo Orch. (VR: Carmen Lombardo)
7   ALONE   Tommy Dorsey Orch. (VR: Cliff Weston)
8   I FEEL LIKE A FEATHER IN THE BREEZE   Jan Garber Orch. (VR: Lee Bennett)
9   DINNER FOR ONE, PLEASE JAMES   Ray Noble Orch. (VR: Al Bowlly)
10   ON TREASURE ISLAND   Tommy Dorsey Orch. (VR: Edythe Wright)
11   EENIE MEENIE MINY MO   Benny Goodman Orch. (VR: Helen Ward)
12   RHYTHM IN MY NURSERY RHYMES   Tommy Dorsey Orch. (VR: Edythe Wright)
13   NO OTHER ONE   Benny Goodman Orch. (VR: Helen Ward)
14   THANKS A MILLION   Paul Pendarvis Orch. (VR: Marjorie Beatty)
15   TAKE ME BACK TO MY BOOTS AND SADDLE   Tommy Dorsey Orch. (VR: Cliff Weston)
    Note: * Another version by: Riley-Farley Orch. (VR: Riley & Farley).

January 25, 1936

1   THE MUSIC GOES 'ROUND AND 'ROUND   Tommy Dorsey Orch. (VR: Edythe Wright) *
2   MOON OVER MIAMI   Eddy Duchin Orch. (VR: Lew Sherwood)
3   ALONE   Tommy Dorsey Orch. (VR: Cliff Weston)
4   WITH ALL MY HEART   Hal Kemp Orch.
5   I FEEL LIKE A FEATHER IN THE BREEZE   Jan Garber Orch. (VR: Lee Bennett)
6   THE BROKEN RECORD   Guy Lombardo Orch. (VR: Carmen Lombardo)
7   RED SAILS IN THE SUNSET   Guy Lombardo Orch. (VR: Carmen Lombardo)
8   LIGHTS OUT   Eddy Duchin Orch. (VR: Lew Sherwood)
9   PLEASE BELIEVE ME   Wingy Manone (VR: Wingy Manone)
10   DINNER FOR ONE, PLEASE JAMES   Ray Noble Orch. (VR: Al Bowlly)
11   I'M SHOOTIN' HIGH   Jan Garber Orch. (VR: Lew Palmer)
12   EENIE MEENIE MINY MO   Benny Goodman Orch. (VR: Helen Ward)

13 BEAUTIFUL LADY IN BLUE   Jan Garber Orch. (VR: Lew Palmer)
14 RHYTHM IN MY NURSERY RHYMES   Tommy Dorsey Orch. (VR: Edythe Wright)
15 TAKE ME BACK TO MY BOOTS AND SADDLE   Tommy Dorsey Orch. (VR: Cliff Weston)
   Note: * Another version by: Riley-Farley Orch. (VR: Riley & Farley).

February 1, 1936
1 MOON OVER MIAMI   Eddy Duchin Orch. (VR: Lew Sherwood)
2 ALONE   Tommy Dorsey Orch. (VR: Cliff Weston)
3 WITH ALL MY HEART   Hal Kemp Orch.
4 THE MUSIC GOES 'ROUND AND 'ROUND   Tommy Dorsey Orch. (VR: Edythe Wright) **
5 DINNER FOR ONE, PLEASE JAMES   Ray Noble Orch. (VR: Al Bowlly)
6 THE BROKEN RECORD   Guy Lombardo Orch. (VR: Carmen Lombardo)
7 RED SAILS IN THE SUNSET   Guy Lombardo Orch. (VR: Carmen Lombardo)
8 I FEEL LIKE A FEATHER IN THE BREEZE   Jan Garber Orch. (VR: Lee Bennett)
9 LIGHTS OUT   Eddy Duchin Orch. (VR: Lew Sherwood)
10 RHYTHM IN MY NURSERY RHYMES   Tommy Dorsey Orch. (VR: Edythe Wright)
11 CLING TO ME   Richard Himber Orch. (VR: Stuart Allen)
12 PLEASE BELIEVE ME   Wingy Manone (VR: Wingy Manone)
13 BEAUTIFUL LADY IN BLUE   Jan Garber Orch. (VR: Lew Palmer)
14 I'M BUILDING UP TO AN AWFUL LETDOWN   Fred Astaire
15 EENIE MEENIE MINY MO   Benny Goodman Orch. (VR: Helen Ward)
   Note: * Another version by: Riley-Farley Orch. (VR: Riley & Farley).

February 8, 1936
1 ALONE   Tommy Dorsey Orch. (VR: Cliff Weston)
2 MOON OVER MIAMI   Eddy Duchin Orch. (VR: Lew Sherwood)
3 I FEEL LIKE A FEATHER IN THE BREEZE   Jan Garber Orch. (VR: Lee Bennett)
4 LIGHTS OUT   Eddy Duchin Orch. (VR: Lew Sherwood)
5 THE BROKEN RECORD   Guy Lombardo Orch. (VR: Carmen Lombardo)
6 THE MUSIC GOES 'ROUND AND 'ROUND   Tommy Dorsey Orch. (VR: Edythe Wright) *
7 YOU HIT THE SPOT   Richard Himber Orch. (VR: Stuart Allen)
8 CLING TO ME   Richard Himber Orch. (VR: Stuart Allen)
9 DINNER FOR ONE, PLEASE JAMES   Ray Noble Orch. (VR: Al Bowlly)
10 WITH ALL MY HEART   Hal Kemp Orch.
11 I'M SHOOTIN' HIGH   Jan Garber Orch. (VR: Lew Palmer)
12 RED SAILS IN THE SUNSET   Guy Lombardo Orch. (VR: Carmen Lombardo)
13 I'M BUILDING UP TO AN AWFUL LETDOWN   Fred Astaire
14 ALONE AT A TABLE FOR TWO   Guy Lombardo Orch. (VR: Carmen Lombardo)
15 I'M GONNA SIT RIGHT DOWN AND WRITE MYSELF A LETTER   Boswell Sisters **
   Note: * Another version by: Riley-Farley Orch. (VR: Riley & Farley).
      ** Another version by: Fats Waller Orch. (VR: Fats Waller)

February 15, 1936
1 ALONE   Tommy Dorsey Orch. (VR: Cliff Weston)
2 MOON OVER MIAMI   Eddy Duchin Orch. (VR: Lew Sherwood)
3 LIGHTS OUT   Eddy Duchin Orch. (VR: Lew Sherwood)
4 I FEEL LIKE A FEATHER IN THE BREEZE   Jan Garber Orch. (VR: Lee Bennett)
5 CLING TO ME   Richard Himber Orch. (VR: Stuart Allen)
6 I'M BUILDING UP TO AN AWFUL LETDOWN   Fred Astaire
7 I'M SHOOTIN' HIGH   Jan Garber Orch. (VR: Lew Palmer)
8 I'M GONNA SIT RIGHT DOWN AND WRITE MYSELF A LETTER   Boswell Sisters *
9 BEAUTIFUL LADY IN BLUE   Jan Garber Orch. (VR: Lew Palmer)
10 DINNER FOR ONE, PLEASE JAMES   Ray Noble Orch. (VR: Al Bowlly)
11 WITH ALL MY HEART   Hal Kemp Orch.
12 YOU HIT THE SPOT   Richard Himber Orch. (VR: Stuart Allen)
13 PLEASE BELIEVE ME   Wingy Manone (VR: Wingy Manone)
14 IT'S BEEN SO LONG   Benny Goodman Orch. (VR: Helen Ward)
15 RHYTHM IN MY NURSERY RHYMES   Tommy Dorsey Orch. (VR: Edythe Wright)
   Note: * Another version by: Fats Waller Orch. (VR: Fats Waller)

February 22, 1936
1 ALONE   Tommy Dorsey Orch. (VR: Cliff Weston)
2 MOON OVER MIAMI   Eddy Duchin Orch. (VR: Lew Sherwood)
3 LIGHTS OUT   Eddy Duchin Orch. (VR: Lew Sherwood)
4 I'M BUILDING UP TO AN AWFUL LETDOWN   Fred Astaire
5 I'M SHOOTIN' HIGH   Jan Garber Orch. (VR: Lew Palmer)
6 I FEEL LIKE A FEATHER IN THE BREEZE   Jan Garber Orch. (VR: Lee Bennett)
7 IT'S BEEN SO LONG   Benny Goodman Orch. (VR: Helen Ward)
8 DINNER FOR ONE, PLEASE JAMES   Ray Noble Orch. (VR: Al Bowlly)
9 PLEASE BELIEVE ME   Wingy Manone (VR: Wingy Manone)
10 BEAUTIFUL LADY IN BLUE   Jan Garber Orch. (VR: Lew Palmer)
11 CLING TO ME   Richard Himber Orch. (VR: Stuart Allen)
12 RHYTHM IN MY NURSERY RHYMES   Tommy Dorsey Orch. (VR: Edythe Wright)
13 YOU HIT THE SPOT   Richard Himber Orch. (VR: Stuart Allen)
14 SING AN OLD FASHIONED SONG TO A YOUNG SOPHISTICATED LADY   Fats Waller (VR: Fats Waller)
15 I'M GONNA SIT RIGHT DOWN AND WRITE MYSELF A LETTER   Boswell Sisters *
   Note: * Another version by: Fats Waller Orch. (VR: Fats Waller)

February 29, 1936
1 ALONE   Tommy Dorsey Orch. (VR: Cliff Weston)
2 LIGHTS OUT   Eddy Duchin Orch. (VR: Lew Sherwood)
3 I'M GONNA SIT RIGHT DOWN AND WRITE MYSELF A LETTER   Boswell Sisters *
4 MOON OVER MIAMI   Eddy Duchin Orch. (VR: Lew Sherwood)
5 YOU HIT THE SPOT   Richard Himber Orch. (VR: Stuart Allen)
6 I'M SHOOTIN' HIGH   Jan Garber Orch. (VR: Lew Palmer)

Tommy Dorsey
His seventh solo hit after separating from brother Jimmy, ``Alone'' hits #1 (Feb. 8).

7   PLEASE BELIEVE ME   Wingy Manone (VR: Wingy Manone)
8   I'M BUILDING UP TO AN AWFUL LETDOWN   Fred Astaire
9   CLING TO ME   Richard Himber Orch. (VR: Stuart Allen)
10   BEAUTIFUL LADY IN BLUE   Jan Garber Orch. (VR: Lew Palmer)
11   LITTLE RENDEZVOUS IN HONOLULU   Tommy Dorsey Orch. (VR: Jack Leonard)
12   I FEEL LIKE A FEATHER IN THE BREEZE   Jan Garber Orch. (VR: Lee Bennett)
13   DINNER FOR ONE, PLEASE JAMES   Ray Noble Orch. (VR: Al Bowlly)
14   SING AN OLD FASHIONED SONG TO A YOUNG SOPHISTI-CATED LADY   Fats Waller (VR: Fats Waller)
15   WAH HOO   Paul Whiteman Orch. (VR: Durelle Alexander)
     Note: * Another version by: Fats Waller Orch. (VR: Fats Waller)

March 7, 1936
1   LIGHTS OUT   Eddy Duchin Orch. (VR: Lew Sherwood)
2   I'M GONNA SIT RIGHT DOWN AND WRITE MYSELF A LETTER   Boswell Sisters *
3   ALONE   Tommy Dorsey Orch. (VR: Cliff Weston)
4   PLEASE BELIEVE ME   Wingy Manone (VR: Wingy Manone)
5   I'M SHOOTIN' HIGH   Jan Garber Orch. (VR: Lew Palmer)
6   IT'S BEEN SO LONG   Benny Goodman Orch. (VR: Helen Ward)
7   BEAUTIFUL LADY IN BLUE   Jan Garber Orch. (VR: Lew Palmer)
8   CLING TO ME   Richard Himber Orch. (VR: Stuart Allen)
9   MOON OVER MIAMI   Eddy Duchin Orch. (VR: Lew Sherwood)
10   WEST WIND   Fats Waller Orch. (VR: Fats Waller)
11   ALONE AT A TABLE FOR TWO   Guy Lombardo Orch. (VR: Carmen Lombardo)
12   YOU HIT THE SPOT   Richard Himber Orch. (VR: Stuart Allen)
13   DINNER FOR ONE, PLEASE JAMES   Ray Noble Orch. (VR: Al Bowlly)
14   WAH HOO   Paul Whiteman Orch. (VR: Durelle Alexander)
15   LET YOURSELF GO   Fred Astaire
     Note: * Another version by: Fats Waller Orch. (VR: Fats Waller)

March 14, 1936
1   ALONE   Tommy Dorsey Orch. (VR: Cliff Weston)
2   LIGHTS OUT   Eddy Duchin Orch. (VR: Lew Sherwood)
3   I'M SHOOTIN' HIGH   Jan Garber Orch. (VR: Lew Palmer)
4   PLEASE BELIEVE ME   Wingy Manone (VR: Wingy Manone)
5   LET'S FACE THE MUSIC AND DANCE   Fred Astaire
6   I'M GONNA SIT RIGHT DOWN AND WRITE MYSELF A LETTER   Boswell Sisters *
7   BEAUTIFUL LADY IN BLUE   Jan Garber Orch. (VR: Lew Palmer)
8   LET YOURSELF GO   Fred Astaire
9   I'M PUTTIN' ALL MY EGGS IN ONE BASKET   Fred Astaire
10   YOU HIT THE SPOT   Richard Himber Orch. (VR: Stuart Allen)
11   IT'S BEEN SO LONG   Benny Goodman Orch. (VR: Helen Ward)
12   CLING TO ME   Richard Himber Orch. (VR: Stuart Allen)
13   MOON OVER MIAMI   Eddy Duchin Orch. (VR: Lew Sherwood)
14   GOODY GOODY   Benny Goodman Orch. (VR: Helen Ward)

15   WEST WIND   Fats Waller Orch. (VR: Fats Waller)
     Note: * Another version by: Fats Waller Orch. (VR: Fats Waller)

March 21, 1936
1   LIGHTS OUT   Eddy Duchin Orch. (VR: Lew Sherwood)
2   GOODY GOODY   Benny Goodman Orch. (VR: Helen Ward)
3   ALONE   Tommy Dorsey Orch. (VR: Cliff Weston)
4   IT'S BEEN SO LONG   Benny Goodman Orch. (VR: Helen Ward)
5   LET YOURSELF GO   Fred Astaire
6   I'M PUTTIN' ALL MY EGGS IN ONE BASKET   Fred Astaire
7   I'M SHOOTIN' HIGH   Jan Garber Orch. (VR: Lew Palmer)
8   CLING TO ME   Richard Himber Orch. (VR: Stuart Allen)
9   PLEASE BELIEVE ME   Wingy Manone (VR: Wingy Manone)
10   BEAUTIFUL LADY IN BLUE   Jan Garber Orch. (VR: Lew Palmer)
11   MOON OVER MIAMI   Eddy Duchin Orch. (VR: Lew Sherwood)
12   SING AN OLD FASHIONED SONG TO A YOUNG SOPHISTI-CATED LADY   Fats Waller (VR: Fats Waller)
13   LOST   Guy Lombardo Orch. (VR: Carmen Lombardo)
14   WHAT'S THE NAME OF THAT SONG   Paul Whiteman Orch. (VR: John Hauser)
15   LOVELY LADY   Tommy Dorsey Orch. (VR: Buddy Gately)

March 28, 1936
1   GOODY GOODY   Benny Goodman Orch. (VR: Helen Ward)
2   IT'S BEEN SO LONG   Benny Goodman Orch. (VR: Helen Ward)
3   LET'S FACE THE MUSIC AND DANCE   Fred Astaire
4   I'M PUTTIN' ALL MY EGGS IN ONE BASKET   Fred Astaire
5   LET YOURSELF GO   Fred Astaire
6   LIGHTS OUT   Eddy Duchin Orch. (VR: Lew Sherwood)
7   BEAUTIFUL LADY IN BLUE   Jan Garber Orch. (VR: Lew Palmer)
8   ALONE   Tommy Dorsey Orch. (VR: Cliff Weston)
9   WAH HOO   Paul Whiteman Orch. (VR: Durelle Alexander)
10   WHAT'S THE NAME OF THAT SONG   Paul Whiteman Orch. (VR: John Hauser)
11   LOST   Guy Lombardo Orch. (VR: Carmen Lombardo)
12   WAKE UP AND SING   Bob Howard Orch. (VR: Bob Howard)
13   PLEASE BELIEVE ME   Wingy Manone (VR: Wingy Manone)
14   CLING TO ME   Richard Himber Orch. (VR: Stuart Allen)
15   LOVELY LADY   Tommy Dorsey Orch. (VR: Buddy Gately)

April 4, 1936
1   GOODY GOODY   Benny Goodman Orch. (VR: Helen Ward)
2   I'M PUTTIN' ALL MY EGGS IN ONE BASKET   Fred Astaire
3   LET YOURSELF GO   Fred Astaire
4   IT'S BEEN SO LONG   Benny Goodman Orch. (VR: Helen Ward)
5   LET'S FACE THE MUSIC AND DANCE   Fred Astaire
6   BEAUTIFUL LADY IN BLUE   Jan Garber Orch. (VR: Lew Palmer)
7   LOST   Guy Lombardo Orch. (VR: Carmen Lombardo)
8   LIGHTS OUT   Eddy Duchin Orch. (VR: Lew Sherwood)
9   ALONE   Tommy Dorsey Orch. (VR: Cliff Weston)
10   WAH HOO   Paul Whiteman Orch. (VR: Durelle Alexander)
11   PLEASE BELIEVE ME   Wingy Manone (VR: Wingy Manone)

12 THE TOUCH OF YOUR LIPS   Bing Crosby *
13 I'M SHOOTIN' HIGH   Jan Garber Orch. (VR: Lew Palmer)
14 YOU STARTED ME DREAMING   Tommy Dorsey Orch. (VR: Joe Dixon)
15 YOURS TRULY IS TRULY YOURS   Leo Reisman Orch. (VR: Benny Davis)
    Note: * Another version by: Hal Kemp Orch. (VR: Skinnay Ennis)

April 11, 1936
1   GOODY GOODY   Benny Goodman Orch. (VR: Helen Ward)
2   I'M PUTTIN' ALL MY EGGS IN ONE BASKET   Fred Astaire
3   LET YOURSELF GO   Fred Astaire
4   LOST   Guy Lombardo Orch. (VR: Carmen Lombardo)
5   WHAT'S THE NAME OF THAT SONG   Paul Whiteman Orch. (VR: John Hauser)
6   BEAUTIFUL LADY IN BLUE   Jan Garber Orch. (VR: Lew Palmer)
7   LIGHTS OUT   Eddy Duchin Orch. (VR: Lew Sherwood)
8   THE TOUCH OF YOUR LIPS   Bing Crosby *
9   IT'S BEEN SO LONG   Benny Goodman Orch. (VR: Helen Ward)
10 LET'S FACE THE MUSIC AND DANCE   Fred Astaire
11 WAH HOO   Paul Whiteman Orch. (VR: Durelle Alexander)
12 A MELODY FROM THE SKY   Jan Garber Orch. (VR: Lee Bennett)
13 ALONE   Tommy Dorsey Orch. (VR: Cliff Weston)
14 LOVE IS LIKE A CIGARETTE   Duke Ellington Orch. (VR: Ivie Anderson)
15 YOU STARTED ME DREAMING   Tommy Dorsey Orch. (VR: Joe Dixon)
    Note: * Another version by: Hal Kemp Orch. (VR: Skinnay Ennis)

April 18, 1936
1   GOODY GOODY   Benny Goodman Orch. (VR: Helen Ward)
2   LOST   Guy Lombardo Orch. (VR: Carmen Lombardo)
3   I'M PUTTIN' ALL MY EGGS IN ONE BASKET   Fred Astaire
4   LET YOURSELF GO   Fred Astaire
5   IT'S BEEN SO LONG   Benny Goodman Orch. (VR: Helen Ward)
6   A MELODY FROM THE SKY   Jan Garber Orch. (VR: Lee Bennett)
7   YOU STARTED ME DREAMING   Tommy Dorsey Orch. (VR: Joe Dixon)
8   WHAT'S THE NAME OF THAT SONG   Paul Whiteman Orch. (VR: John Hauser)
9   TORMENTED   Richard Himber Orch. (VR: Stuart Allen)
10 WAH HOO   Paul Whiteman Orch. (VR: Durelle Alexander)
11 BEAUTIFUL LADY IN BLUE   Jan Garber Orch. (VR: Lew Palmer)
12 YOU   Tommy Dorsey Orch. (VR: Edythe Wright)
13 LIGHTS OUT   Eddy Duchin Orch. (VR: Lew Sherwood)
14 LET'S FACE THE MUSIC AND DANCE   Fred Astaire
15 ALL MY LIFE   Fats Waller Orch. (VR: Fats Waller)

April 25, 1936
1   LOST   Guy Lombardo Orch. (VR: Carmen Lombardo)
2   I'M PUTTIN' ALL MY EGGS IN ONE BASKET   Fred Astaire
3   GOODY GOODY   Benny Goodman Orch. (VR: Helen Ward)
4   A MELODY FROM THE SKY   Jan Garber Orch. (VR: Lee Bennett)
5   LET YOURSELF GO   Fred Astaire
6   THE TOUCH OF YOUR LIPS   Bing Crosby *

7   YOU STARTED ME DREAMING   Tommy Dorsey Orch. (VR: Joe Dixon)
8   IT'S BEEN SO LONG   Benny Goodman Orch. (VR: Helen Ward)
9   LET'S FACE THE MUSIC AND DANCE   Fred Astaire
10 BEAUTIFUL LADY IN BLUE   Jan Garber Orch. (VR: Lew Palmer)
11 YOU   Tommy Dorsey Orch. (VR: Edythe Wright)
12 LIGHTS OUT   Eddy Duchin Orch. (VR: Lew Sherwood)
13 YOURS TRULY IS TRULY YOURS   Leo Reisman Orch. (VR: Benny Davis)
14 WHAT'S THE NAME OF THAT SONG   Paul Whiteman Orch. (VR: John Hauser)
15 ALL MY LIFE   Fats Waller Orch. (VR: Fats Waller)
    Note: * Another version by: Hal Kemp Orch. (VR: Skinnay Ennis)

May 2, 1936
1   LOST   Guy Lombardo Orch. (VR: Carmen Lombardo)
2   GOODY GOODY   Benny Goodman Orch. (VR: Helen Ward)
3   A MELODY FROM THE SKY   Jan Garber Orch. (VR: Lee Bennett)
4   YOU STARTED ME DREAMING   Tommy Dorsey Orch. (VR: Joe Dixon)
5   IT'S BEEN SO LONG   Benny Goodman Orch. (VR: Helen Ward)
6   WHAT'S THE NAME OF THAT SONG   Paul Whiteman Orch. (VR: John Hauser)
7   ALL MY LIFE   Fats Waller Orch. (VR: Fats Waller)
8   YOU   Tommy Dorsey Orch. (VR: Edythe Wright)
9   LET YOURSELF GO   Fred Astaire
10 THE TOUCH OF YOUR LIPS   Bing Crosby *
11 TORMENTED   Richard Himber Orch. (VR: Stuart Allen)
12 I'M PUTTIN' ALL MY EGGS IN ONE BASKET   Fred Astaire
13 BEAUTIFUL LADY IN BLUE   Jan Garber Orch. (VR: Lew Palmer)
14 LOVE IS LIKE A CIGARETTE   Duke Ellington Orch. (VR: Ivie Anderson)
15 LET'S FACE THE MUSIC AND DANCE   Fred Astaire
    Note: * Another version by: Hal Kemp Orch. (VR: Skinnay Ennis)

May 9, 1936
1   LOST   Guy Lombardo Orch. (VR: Carmen Lombardo)
2   YOU   Tommy Dorsey Orch. (VR: Edythe Wright)
3   A MELODY FROM THE SKY   Jan Garber Orch. (VR: Lee Bennett)
4   GOODY GOODY   Benny Goodman Orch. (VR: Helen Ward)
5   THE TOUCH OF YOUR LIPS   Bing Crosby *
6   I'M PUTTIN' ALL MY EGGS IN ONE BASKET   Fred Astaire
7   ALL MY LIFE   Fats Waller Orch. (VR: Fats Waller)
8   LOVE IS LIKE A CIGARETTE   Duke Ellington Orch. (VR: Ivie Anderson)
9   YOU STARTED ME DREAMING   Tommy Dorsey Orch. (VR: Joe Dixon)
10 IT'S BEEN SO LONG   Benny Goodman Orch. (VR: Helen Ward)
11 LET YOURSELF GO   Fred Astaire
12 TORMENTED   Richard Himber Orch. (VR: Stuart Allen)
13 LET'S FACE THE MUSIC AND DANCE   Fred Astaire
14 IS IT TRUE WHAT THEY SAY ABOUT DIXIE   Jimmy Dorsey Orch. (VR: Bob Eberly)
15 I DON'T WANT TO MAKE HISTORY   Hal Kemp Orch. (VR: Maxine Gray)
    Note: * Another version by: Hal Kemp Orch. (VR: Skinnay Ennis)

May 16, 1936
1. A MELODY FROM THE SKY   Jan Garber Orch. (VR: Lee Bennett)
2. LOST   Guy Lombardo Orch. (VR: Carmen Lombardo)
3. GOODY GOODY   Benny Goodman Orch. (VR: Helen Ward)
4. YOU   Tommy Dorsey Orch. (VR: Edythe Wright)
5. ALL MY LIFE   Fats Waller Orch. (VR: Fats Waller)
6. YOU STARTED ME DREAMING   Tommy Dorsey Orch. (VR: Joe Dixon)
7. TORMENTED   Richard Himber Orch. (VR: Stuart Allen)
8. THE TOUCH OF YOUR LIPS   Bing Crosby *
9. IS IT TRUE WHAT THEY SAY ABOUT DIXIE   Jimmy Dorsey Orch. (VR: Bob Eberly)
10. I DON'T WANT TO MAKE HISTORY   Hal Kemp Orch. (VR: Maxine Gray)
11. LOVE IS LIKE A CIGARETTE   Duke Ellington Orch. (VR: Ivie Anderson)
12. ROBINS AND ROSES   Bing Crosby
13. THERE'S ALWAYS A HAPPY ENDING   Rudy Vallee
14. IT'S A SIN TO TELL A LIE   Fats Waller Orch. (VR: Fats Waller)
15. WOULD YOU   Henry King Orch. (VR: Joe Sudy)
    Note: * Another version by: Hal Kemp Orch. (VR: Skinnay Ennis)

May 23, 1936
1. YOU   Tommy Dorsey Orch. (VR: Edythe Wright)
2. A MELODY FROM THE SKY   Jan Garber Orch. (VR: Lee Bennett)
3. LOST   Guy Lombardo Orch. (VR: Carmen Lombardo)
4. THE TOUCH OF YOUR LIPS   Bing Crosby *
5. IS IT TRUE WHAT THEY SAY ABOUT DIXIE   Jimmy Dorsey Orch. (VR: Bob Eberly)
6. YOU STARTED ME DREAMING   Tommy Dorsey Orch. (VR: Joe Dixon)
7. ALL MY LIFE   Fats Waller Orch. (VR: Fats Waller)
8. ROBINS AND ROSES   Bing Crosby
9. SHE SHALL HAVE MUSIC   Lud Gluskin Orch. (VR: Buddy Clark)
10. LOVE IS LIKE A CIGARETTE   Duke Ellington Orch. (VR: Ivie Anderson)
11. GOODY GOODY   Benny Goodman Orch. (VR: Helen Ward)
12. TORMENTED   Richard Himber Orch. (VR: Stuart Allen)
13. WOULD YOU   Henry King Orch. (VR: Joe Sudy)
14. LET YOURSELF GO   Fred Astaire
15. CHRISTOPHER COLUMBUS   Andy Kirk Orch. (VR: Pha Terrell)
    Note: * Another version by: Hal Kemp Orch. (VR: Skinnay Ennis)

May 30, 1936
1. LOST   Guy Lombardo Orch. (VR: Carmen Lombardo)
2. A MELODY FROM THE SKY   Jan Garber Orch. (VR: Lee Bennett)
3. YOU   Tommy Dorsey Orch. (VR: Edythe Wright)
4. ALL MY LIFE   Fats Waller Orch. (VR: Fats Waller)
5. ROBINS AND ROSES   Bing Crosby
6. IS IT TRUE WHAT THEY SAY ABOUT DIXIE   Jimmy Dorsey Orch. (VR: Bob Eberly)
7. GOODY GOODY   Benny Goodman Orch. (VR: Helen Ward)
8. YOU STARTED ME DREAMING   Tommy Dorsey Orch. (VR: Joe Dixon)
9. TORMENTED   Richard Himber Orch. (VR: Stuart Allen)
10. LOVE IS LIKE A CIGARETTE   Duke Ellington Orch. (VR: Ivie Anderson)

11. THE TOUCH OF YOUR LIPS   Bing Crosby *
12. SHE SHALL HAVE MUSIC   Lud Gluskin Orch. (VR: Buddy Clark)
13. WOULD YOU   Henry King Orch. (VR: Joe Sudy)
14. IT'S A SIN TO TELL A LIE   Fats Waller Orch. (VR: Fats Waller)
15. THE GLORY OF LOVE   Benny Goodman Orch. (VR: Helen Ward)
    Note: * Another version by: Hal Kemp Orch. (VR: Skinnay Ennis)

June 6, 1936
1. IS IT TRUE WHAT THEY SAY ABOUT DIXIE   Jimmy Dorsey Orch. (VR: Bob Eberly)
2. ALL MY LIFE   Fats Waller Orch. (VR: Fats Waller)
3. YOU   Tommy Dorsey Orch. (VR: Edythe Wright)
4. ROBINS AND ROSES   Bing Crosby
5. LOST   Guy Lombardo Orch. (VR: Carmen Lombardo)
6. A MELODY FROM THE SKY   Jan Garber Orch. (VR: Lee Bennett)
7. THE TOUCH OF YOUR LIPS   Bing Crosby *
8. SHE SHALL HAVE MUSIC   Lud Gluskin Orch. (VR: Buddy Clark)
9. WOULD YOU   Henry King Orch. (VR: Joe Sudy)
10. TORMENTED   Richard Himber Orch. (VR: Stuart Allen)
11. IT'S A SIN TO TELL A LIE   Fats Waller Orch. (VR: Fats Waller)
12. THERE'S A SMALL HOTEL   Hal Kemp Orch. (VR: Maxine Gray)
13. THE GLORY OF LOVE   Benny Goodman Orch. (VR: Helen Ward)
14. YOU STARTED ME DREAMING   Tommy Dorsey Orch. (VR: Joe Dixon)
15. LOVE IS LIKE A CIGARETTE   Duke Ellington Orch. (VR: Ivie Anderson)
    Note: * Another version by: Hal Kemp Orch. (VR: Skinnay Ennis)

June 13, 1936
1. IS IT TRUE WHAT THEY SAY ABOUT DIXIE   Jimmy Dorsey Orch. (VR: Bob Eberly)
2. ROBINS AND ROSES   Bing Crosby
3. SHE SHALL HAVE MUSIC   Lud Gluskin Orch. (VR: Buddy Clark)
4. ALL MY LIFE   Fats Waller Orch. (VR: Fats Waller)
5. IT'S A SIN TO TELL A LIE   Fats Waller Orch. (VR: Fats Waller)
6. YOU   Tommy Dorsey Orch. (VR: Edythe Wright)
7. THE TOUCH OF YOUR LIPS   Bing Crosby *
8. A MELODY FROM THE SKY   Jan Garber Orch. (VR: Lee Bennett)
9. LOST   Guy Lombardo Orch. (VR: Carmen Lombardo)
10. THE GLORY OF LOVE   Benny Goodman Orch. (VR: Helen Ward)
11. TORMENTED   Richard Himber Orch. (VR: Stuart Allen)
12. WOULD YOU   Henry King Orch. (VR: Joe Sudy)
13. YOU STARTED ME DREAMING   Tommy Dorsey Orch. (VR: Joe Dixon)
14. THERE'S A SMALL HOTEL   Hal Kemp Orch. (VR: Maxine Gray)
15. CHRISTOPHER COLUMBUS   Andy Kirk Orch. (VR: Pha Terrell)
    Note: * Another version by: Hal Kemp Orch. (VR: Skinnay Ennis)

June 20, 1936
1. IS IT TRUE WHAT THEY SAY ABOUT DIXIE   Jimmy Dorsey Orch. (VR: Bob Eberly)

30

Jimmy Dorsey
Absent brother Tommy, Jimmy hits #1 with ``Is It True What They Say About Dixie'' (June 6).

2 ROBINS AND ROSES   Bing Crosby
3 ALL MY LIFE   Fats Waller Orch. (VR: Fats Waller)
4 YOU   Tommy Dorsey Orch. (VR: Edythe Wright)
5 SHE SHALL HAVE MUSIC   Lud Gluskin Orch. (VR: Buddy Clark)
6 IT'S A SIN TO TELL A LIE   Fats Waller Orch. (VR: Fats Waller)
7 YOU CAN'T PULL THE WOOL OVER MY EYES   Benny Goodman Orch. (VR: Helen Ward)
8 TAKE MY HEART   Eddy Duchin Orch. (VR: Jerry Cooper)
9 A MELODY FROM THE SKY   Jan Garber Orch. (VR: Lee Bennett)
10 LOST   Guy Lombardo Orch. (VR: Carmen Lombardo)
11 THE GLORY OF LOVE   Benny Goodman Orch. (VR: Helen Ward)
12 THE TOUCH OF YOUR LIPS   Bing Crosby *
13 WOULD YOU   Henry King Orch. (VR: Joe Sudy)
14 ON THE BEACH AT BALI-BALI   Connee Boswell
15 THERE'S A SMALL HOTEL   Hal Kemp Orch. (VR: Maxine Gray)
   Note: * Another version by: Hal Kemp Orch. (VR: Skinnay Ennis)

June 27, 1936

1 IS IT TRUE WHAT THEY SAY ABOUT DIXIE   Jimmy Dorsey Orch. (VR: Bob Eberly)
2 ROBINS AND ROSES   Bing Crosby
3 SHE SHALL HAVE MUSIC   Lud Gluskin Orch. (VR: Buddy Clark)
4 ALL MY LIFE   Fats Waller Orch. (VR: Fats Waller)
5 IT'S A SIN TO TELL A LIE   Fats Waller Orch. (VR: Fats Waller)
6 WOULD YOU   Henry King Orch. (VR: Joe Sudy)
7 THE GLORY OF LOVE   Benny Goodman Orch. (VR: Helen Ward)
8 YOU   Tommy Dorsey Orch. (VR: Edythe Wright)
9 THESE FOOLISH THINGS   Benny Goodman Orch. (VR: Helen Ward)
10 TAKE MY HEART   Eddy Duchin Orch. (VR: Jerry Cooper)
11 A MELODY FROM THE SKY   Jan Garber Orch. (VR: Lee Bennett)
12 ON THE BEACH AT BALI-BALI   Connee Boswell
13 THERE'S A SMALL HOTEL   Hal Kemp Orch. (VR: Maxine Gray)
14 THE TOUCH OF YOUR LIPS   Bing Crosby *
15 LOST   Guy Lombardo Orch. (VR: Carmen Lombardo)
   Note: * Another version by: Hal Kemp Orch. (VR: Skinnay Ennis)

July 4, 1936

1 THE GLORY OF LOVE   Benny Goodman Orch. (VR: Helen Ward)
2 IS IT TRUE WHAT THEY SAY ABOUT DIXIE   Jimmy Dorsey Orch. (VR: Bob Eberly)
3 ROBINS AND ROSES   Bing Crosby
4 THERE'S A SMALL HOTEL   Hal Kemp Orch. (VR: Maxine Gray)
5 WOULD YOU   Henry King Orch. (VR: Joe Sudy)
6 THESE FOOLISH THINGS   Benny Goodman Orch. (VR: Helen Ward)
7 TAKE MY HEART   Eddy Duchin Orch. (VR: Jerry Cooper)
8 IT'S A SIN TO TELL A LIE   Fats Waller Orch. (VR: Fats Waller)
9 ALL MY LIFE   Fats Waller Orch. (VR: Fats Waller)
10 YOU CAN'T PULL THE WOOL OVER MY EYES   Benny Goodman Orch. (VR: Helen Ward)
11 SHE SHALL HAVE MUSIC   Lud Gluskin Orch. (VR: Buddy Clark)

12 LET'S SING AGAIN   Fats Waller Orch. (VR: Fats Waller)
13 A MELODY FROM THE SKY   Jan Garber Orch. (VR: Lee Bennett)
14 YOU   Tommy Dorsey Orch. (VR: Edythe Wright)
15 CROSS PATCH   Fats Waller Orch. (VR: Fats Waller)

July 11, 1936

1 IS IT TRUE WHAT THEY SAY ABOUT DIXIE   Jimmy Dorsey Orch. (VR: Bob Eberly)
2 WOULD YOU   Henry King Orch. (VR: Joe Sudy)
3 THESE FOOLISH THINGS   Benny Goodman Orch. (VR: Helen Ward)
4 TAKE MY HEART   Eddy Duchin Orch. (VR: Jerry Cooper)
5 THERE'S A SMALL HOTEL   Hal Kemp Orch. (VR: Maxine Gray)
6 ROBINS AND ROSES   Bing Crosby
7 THE GLORY OF LOVE   Benny Goodman Orch. (VR: Helen Ward)
8 IT'S A SIN TO TELL A LIE   Fats Waller Orch. (VR: Fats Waller)
9 SHE SHALL HAVE MUSIC   Lud Gluskin Orch. (VR: Buddy Clark)
10 YOU CAN'T PULL THE WOOL OVER MY EYES   Benny Goodman Orch. (VR: Helen Ward)
11 ALL MY LIFE   Fats Waller Orch. (VR: Fats Waller)
12 STOMPIN' AT THE SAVOY   Benny Goodman Orch.
13 ON THE BEACH AT BALI-BALI   Connee Boswell
14 WHEN I'M WITH YOU   Hal Kemp Orch. (VR: Skinnay Ennis)
15 A MELODY FROM THE SKY   Jan Garber Orch. (VR: Lee Bennett)

July 18, 1936

1 TAKE MY HEART   Eddy Duchin Orch. (VR: Jerry Cooper)
2 THESE FOOLISH THINGS   Benny Goodman Orch. (VR: Helen Ward)
3 YOU CAN'T PULL THE WOOL OVER MY EYES   Benny Goodman Orch. (VR: Helen Ward)
4 IS IT TRUE WHAT THEY SAY ABOUT DIXIE   Jimmy Dorsey Orch. (VR: Bob Eberly)
5 THE GLORY OF LOVE   Benny Goodman Orch. (VR: Helen Ward)
6 IT'S A SIN TO TELL A LIE   Fats Waller Orch. (VR: Fats Waller)
7 WOULD YOU   Henry King Orch. (VR: Joe Sudy)
8 THERE'S A SMALL HOTEL   Hal Kemp Orch. (VR: Maxine Gray)
9 ROBINS AND ROSES   Bing Crosby
10 ON THE BEACH AT BALI-BALI   Connee Boswell
11 STOMPIN' AT THE SAVOY   Benny Goodman Orch.
12 LET'S SING AGAIN   Fats Waller Orch. (VR: Fats Waller)
13 NO REGRETS   Tommy Dorsey Orch. (VR: Jack Leonard)
14 CROSS PATCH   Fats Waller Orch. (VR: Fats Waller)
15 SHE SHALL HAVE MUSIC   Lud Gluskin Orch. (VR: Buddy Clark)

July 25, 1936

1 TAKE MY HEART   Eddy Duchin Orch. (VR: Jerry Cooper)
2 THE GLORY OF LOVE   Benny Goodman Orch. (VR: Helen Ward)
3 THESE FOOLISH THINGS   Benny Goodman Orch. (VR: Helen Ward)
4 YOU CAN'T PULL THE WOOL OVER MY EYES   Benny Goodman Orch. (VR: Helen Ward)
5 IS IT TRUE WHAT THEY SAY ABOUT DIXIE   Jimmy Dorsey Orch. (VR: Bob Eberly)

6 IT'S A SIN TO TELL A LIE   Fats Waller Orch. (VR: Fats Waller)
7 THERE'S A SMALL HOTEL   Hal Kemp Orch. (VR: Maxine Gray)
8 ON THE BEACH AT BALI-BALI   Connee Boswell
9 WOULD YOU   Henry King Orch. (VR: Joe Sudy)
10 LET'S SING AGAIN   Fats Waller Orch. (VR: Fats Waller)
11 CROSS PATCH   Fats Waller Orch. (VR: Fats Waller)
12 ROBINS AND ROSES   Bing Crosby
13 WHEN I'M WITH YOU   Hal Kemp Orch. (VR: Skinnay Ennis)
14 AFTERGLOW   Leo Reisman Orch.
15 SHE SHALL HAVE MUSIC   Lud Gluskin Orch. (VR: Buddy Clark)

August 1, 1936
1 THESE FOOLISH THINGS   Benny Goodman Orch. (VR: Helen Ward)
2 YOU CAN'T PULL THE WOOL OVER MY EYES   Benny Goodman Orch. (VR: Helen Ward)
3 TAKE MY HEART   Eddy Duchin Orch. (VR: Jerry Cooper)
4 WOULD YOU   Henry King Orch. (VR: Joe Sudy)
5 THE GLORY OF LOVE   Benny Goodman Orch. (VR: Helen Ward)
6 CROSS PATCH   Fats Waller Orch. (VR: Fats Waller)
7 IS IT TRUE WHAT THEY SAY ABOUT DIXIE   Jimmy Dorsey Orch. (VR: Bob Eberly)
8 THERE'S A SMALL HOTEL   Hal Kemp Orch. (VR: Maxine Gray)
9 ON THE BEACH AT BALI-BALI   Connee Boswell
10 IT'S A SIN TO TELL A LIE   Fats Waller Orch. (VR: Fats Waller)
11 WHEN I'M WITH YOU   Hal Kemp Orch. (VR: Skinnay Ennis)
12 LET'S SING AGAIN   Fats Waller Orch. (VR: Fats Waller)
13 NO REGRETS   Tommy Dorsey Orch. (VR: Jack Leonard)
14 STOMPIN' AT THE SAVOY   Benny Goodman Orch.
15 A RENDEZVOUS WITH A DREAM   Johnny Green Orch.

August 8, 1936
1 THESE FOOLISH THINGS   Benny Goodman Orch. (VR: Helen Ward)
2 TAKE MY HEART   Eddy Duchin Orch. (VR: Jerry Cooper)
3 ON THE BEACH AT BALI-BALI   Connee Boswell
4 THE GLORY OF LOVE   Benny Goodman Orch. (VR: Helen Ward)
5 WHEN I'M WITH YOU   Hal Kemp Orch. (VR: Skinnay Ennis)
6 YOU CAN'T PULL THE WOOL OVER MY EYES   Benny Goodman Orch. (VR: Helen Ward)
7 IT'S A SIN TO TELL A LIE   Fats Waller Orch. (VR: Fats Waller)
8 WOULD YOU   Henry King Orch. (VR: Joe Sudy)
9 THERE'S A SMALL HOTEL   Hal Kemp Orch. (VR: Maxine Gray)
10 DID I REMEMBER   Shep Fields Orch. (VR: Charles Chester)
11 CROSS PATCH   Fats Waller Orch. (VR: Fats Waller)
12 NO REGRETS   Tommy Dorsey Orch. (VR: Jack Leonard)
13 STOMPIN' AT THE SAVOY   Benny Goodman Orch.
14 IS IT TRUE WHAT THEY SAY ABOUT DIXIE   Jimmy Dorsey Orch. (VR: Bob Eberly)
15 A RENDEZVOUS WITH A DREAM   Johnny Green Orch.

August 15, 1936
1 WHEN I'M WITH YOU   Hal Kemp Orch. (VR: Skinnay Ennis)

2 THESE FOOLISH THINGS   Benny Goodman Orch. (VR: Helen Ward)
3 TAKE MY HEART   Eddy Duchin Orch. (VR: Jerry Cooper)
4 YOU CAN'T PULL THE WOOL OVER MY EYES   Benny Goodman Orch. (VR: Helen Ward)
5 ON THE BEACH AT BALI-BALI   Connee Boswell
6 IT'S A SIN TO TELL A LIE   Fats Waller Orch. (VR: Fats Waller)
7 DID I REMEMBER   Shep Fields Orch. (VR: Charles Chester)
8 THE GLORY OF LOVE   Benny Goodman Orch. (VR: Helen Ward)
9 A RENDEZVOUS WITH A DREAM   Johnny Green Orch.
10 NO REGRETS   Tommy Dorsey Orch. (VR: Jack Leonard)
11 WOULD YOU   Henry King Orch. (VR: Joe Sudy)
12 A STAR FELL OUT OF HEAVEN   Hal Kemp Orch.
13 YOU'RE NOT THE KIND   Fats Waller Orch. (VR: Fats Waller)
14 CROSS PATCH   Fats Waller Orch. (VR: Fats Waller)
15 ME AND THE MOON   Hal Kemp Orch.

August 22, 1936
1 WHEN I'M WITH YOU   Hal Kemp Orch. (VR: Skinnay Ennis)
2 THESE FOOLISH THINGS   Benny Goodman Orch. (VR: Helen Ward)
3 DID I REMEMBER   Shep Fields Orch. (VR: Charles Chester)
4 ON THE BEACH AT BALI-BALI   Connee Boswell
5 YOU CAN'T PULL THE WOOL OVER MY EYES   Benny Goodman Orch. (VR: Helen Ward)
6 TAKE MY HEART   Eddy Duchin Orch. (VR: Jerry Cooper)
7 IT'S A SIN TO TELL A LIE   Fats Waller Orch. (VR: Fats Waller)
8 KNOCK, KNOCK, WHO'S THERE?   Ted Weems Orch. (VR: Chorus)
9 THE GLORY OF LOVE   Benny Goodman Orch. (VR: Helen Ward)
10 YOU'RE NOT THE KIND   Fats Waller Orch. (VR: Fats Waller)
11 A RENDEZVOUS WITH A DREAM   Johnny Green Orch.
12 BYE, BYE, BABY   Fats Waller (VR: Fats Waller)
13 WOULD YOU   Henry King Orch. (VR: Joe Sudy)
14 NO REGRETS   Tommy Dorsey Orch. (VR: Jack Leonard)
15 UNTIL TODAY   Fletcher Henderson Orch.

August 29, 1936
1 DID I REMEMBER   Shep Fields Orch. (VR: Charles Chester)
2 WHEN I'M WITH YOU   Hal Kemp Orch. (VR: Skinnay Ennis)
3 THESE FOOLISH THINGS   Benny Goodman Orch. (VR: Helen Ward)
4 NO REGRETS   Tommy Dorsey Orch. (VR: Jack Leonard)
5 A RENDEZVOUS WITH A DREAM   Johnny Green Orch.
6 A STAR FELL OUT OF HEAVEN   Hal Kemp Orch.
7 UNTIL THE REAL THING COMES ALONG   Andy Kirk Orch. (VR: Pha Terrell)
8 ON THE BEACH AT BALI-BALI   Connee Boswell
9 TAKE MY HEART   Eddy Duchin Orch. (VR: Jerry Cooper)
10 IT'S A SIN TO TELL A LIE   Fats Waller Orch. (VR: Fats Waller)
11 WOULD YOU   Henry King Orch. (VR: Joe Sudy)
12 BYE, BYE, BABY   Fats Waller (VR: Fats Waller)
13 KNOCK, KNOCK, WHO'S THERE?   Ted Weems Orch. (VR: Chorus)

14 THE GLORY OF LOVE   Benny Goodman Orch. (VR: Helen Ward)
15 SING, BABY, SING   Ruby Newman Orch (VR: Barry McKinley)

September 5, 1936
1   DID I REMEMBER   Shep Fields Orch. (VR: Charles Chester)
2   WHEN I'M WITH YOU   Hal Kemp Orch. (VR: Skinnay Ennis)
3   A STAR FELL OUT OF HEAVEN   Hal Kemp Orch.
4   UNTIL THE REAL THING COMES ALONG   Andy Kirk Orch. (VR: Pha Terrell)
5   TAKE MY HEART   Eddy Duchin Orch. (VR: Jerry Cooper)
6   THESE FOOLISH THINGS   Benny Goodman Orch. (VR: Helen Ward)
7   NO REGRETS   Tommy Dorsey Orch. (VR: Jack Leonard)
8   ON THE BEACH AT BALI-BALI   Connee Boswell
9   A RENDEZVOUS WITH A DREAM   Johnny Green Orch.
10 BYE, BYE, BABY   Fats Waller (VR: Fats Waller)
11 YOU'RE NOT THE KIND   Fats Waller Orch. (VR: Fats Waller)
12 IT'S A SIN TO TELL A LIE   Fats Waller Orch. (VR: Fats Waller)
13 KNOCK, KNOCK, WHO'S THERE?   Ted Weems Orch. (VR: Chorus)
14 ME AND THE MOON   Hal Kemp Orch.
15 I'M AN OLD COWHAND   Bing Crosby with Jimmy Dorsey Orch.

September 12, 1936
1   DID I REMEMBER   Shep Fields Orch. (VR: Charles Chester)
2   UNTIL THE REAL THING COMES ALONG   Andy Kirk Orch. (VR: Pha Terrell)
3   WHEN I'M WITH YOU   Hal Kemp Orch. (VR: Skinnay Ennis)
4   A STAR FELL OUT OF HEAVEN   Hal Kemp Orch.
5   BYE, BYE, BABY   Fats Waller (VR: Fats Waller)
6   THESE FOOLISH THINGS   Benny Goodman Orch. (VR: Helen Ward)
7   A RENDEZVOUS WITH A DREAM   Johnny Green Orch.
8   ME AND THE MOON   Hal Kemp Orch.
9   KNOCK, KNOCK, WHO'S THERE?   Ted Weems Orch. (VR: Chorus)
10 WHEN DID YOU LEAVE HEAVEN   Guy Lombardo Orch. (VR: Carmen Lombardo)
11 UNTIL TODAY   Fletcher Henderson Orch.
12 NO REGRETS   Tommy Dorsey Orch. (VR: Jack Leonard)
13 I CAN'T ESCAPE FROM YOU   Bing Crosby with Jimmy Dorsey Orch.
14 I'M AN OLD COWHAND   Bing Crosby with Jimmy Dorsey Orch.
15 YOU'RE NOT THE KIND   Fats Waller Orch. (VR: Fats Waller)

September 19, 1936
1   DID I REMEMBER   Shep Fields Orch. (VR: Charles Chester)
2   UNTIL THE REAL THING COMES ALONG   Andy Kirk Orch. (VR: Pha Terrell)
3   A STAR FELL OUT OF HEAVEN   Hal Kemp Orch.
4   WHEN I'M WITH YOU   Hal Kemp Orch. (VR: Skinnay Ennis)
5   WHEN DID YOU LEAVE HEAVEN   Guy Lombardo Orch. (VR: Carmen Lombardo)

6   NO REGRETS   Tommy Dorsey Orch. (VR: Jack Leonard)
7   BYE, BYE, BABY   Fats Waller (VR: Fats Waller)
8   SING, BABY, SING   Ruby Newman Orch (VR: Barry McKinley)
9   ME AND THE MOON   Hal Kemp Orch.
10 A RENDEZVOUS WITH A DREAM   Johnny Green Orch.
11 KNOCK, KNOCK, WHO'S THERE?   Ted Weems Orch. (VR: Chorus)
12 UNTIL TODAY   Fletcher Henderson Orch.
13 EMPTY SADDLES   Bing Crosby
14 THESE FOOLISH THINGS   Benny Goodman Orch. (VR: Helen Ward)
15 THE WAY YOU LOOK TONIGHT   Fred Astaire

September 26, 1936
1   DID I REMEMBER   Shep Fields Orch. (VR: Charles Chester)
2   UNTIL THE REAL THING COMES ALONG   Andy Kirk Orch. (VR: Pha Terrell)
3   A STAR FELL OUT OF HEAVEN   Hal Kemp Orch.
4   BYE, BYE, BABY   Fats Waller (VR: Fats Waller)
5   WHEN DID YOU LEAVE HEAVEN   Guy Lombardo Orch. (VR: Carmen Lombardo)
6   WHEN I'M WITH YOU   Hal Kemp Orch. (VR: Skinnay Ennis)
7   SING, BABY, SING   Ruby Newman Orch (VR: Barry McKinley)
8   EMPTY SADDLES   Bing Crosby
9   A RENDEZVOUS WITH A DREAM   Johnny Green Orch.
10 I CAN'T ESCAPE FROM YOU   Bing Crosby with Jimmy Dorsey Orch.
11 UNTIL TODAY   Fletcher Henderson Orch.
12 THE WAY YOU LOOK TONIGHT   Fred Astaire
13 ME AND THE MOON   Hal Kemp Orch.
14 I'M AN OLD COWHAND   Bing Crosby with Jimmy Dorsey Orch.
15 NO REGRETS   Tommy Dorsey Orch. (VR: Jack Leonard)

October 3, 1936
1   DID I REMEMBER   Shep Fields Orch. (VR: Charles Chester)
2   UNTIL THE REAL THING COMES ALONG   Andy Kirk Orch. (VR: Pha Terrell)
3   WHEN DID YOU LEAVE HEAVEN   Guy Lombardo Orch. (VR: Carmen Lombardo)
4   A STAR FELL OUT OF HEAVEN   Hal Kemp Orch.
5   WHEN I'M WITH YOU   Hal Kemp Orch. (VR: Skinnay Ennis)
6   BYE, BYE, BABY   Fats Waller (VR: Fats Waller)
7   SING, BABY, SING   Ruby Newman Orch (VR: Barry McKinley)
8   ME AND THE MOON   Hal Kemp Orch.
9   THE WAY YOU LOOK TONIGHT   Fred Astaire
10 I CAN'T ESCAPE FROM YOU   Bing Crosby with Jimmy Dorsey Orch.
11 A RENDEZVOUS WITH A DREAM   Johnny Green Orch.
12 A FINE ROMANCE   Fred Astaire
13 NO REGRETS   Tommy Dorsey Orch. (VR: Jack Leonard)
14 I'M AN OLD COWHAND   Bing Crosby with Jimmy Dorsey Orch.
15 EMPTY SADDLES   Bing Crosby

October 10, 1936
1   WHEN DID YOU LEAVE HEAVEN   Guy Lombardo Orch. (VR: Carmen Lombardo)
2   UNTIL THE REAL THING COMES ALONG   Andy Kirk Orch. (VR: Pha Terrell)

3 A STAR FELL OUT OF HEAVEN   Hal Kemp Orch.

4 THE WAY YOU LOOK TONIGHT   Fred Astaire

5 DID I REMEMBER   Shep Fields Orch. (VR: Charles Chester)

6 SING, BABY, SING   Ruby Newman Orch (VR: Barry McKinley)

7 BYE, BYE, BABY   Fats Waller (VR: Fats Waller)

8 A FINE ROMANCE   Fred Astaire

9 WHEN I'M WITH YOU   Hal Kemp Orch. (VR: Skinnay Ennis)

10 WHO LOVES YOU   Teddy Wilson Orch. (VR: Billie Holiday)

11 ME AND THE MOON   Hal Kemp Orch.

12 I'M AN OLD COWHAND   Bing Crosby with Jimmy Dorsey Orch.

13 A RENDEZVOUS WITH A DREAM   Johnny Green Orch.

14 I CAN'T ESCAPE FROM YOU   Bing Crosby with Jimmy Dorsey Orch.

15 MICKEY MOUSE'S BIRTHDAY PARTY   Wayne King Orch.

October 17, 1936

1 WHEN DID YOU LEAVE HEAVEN   Guy Lombardo Orch. (VR: Carmen Lombardo)

2 THE WAY YOU LOOK TONIGHT   Fred Astaire

3 DID I REMEMBER   Shep Fields Orch. (VR: Charles Chester)

4 UNTIL THE REAL THING COMES ALONG   Andy Kirk Orch. (VR: Pha Terrell)

5 SING, BABY, SING   Ruby Newman Orch (VR: Barry McKinley)

6 I CAN'T ESCAPE FROM YOU   Bing Crosby with Jimmy Dorsey Orch.

7 BYE, BYE, BABY   Fats Waller (VR: Fats Waller)

8 A STAR FELL OUT OF HEAVEN   Hal Kemp Orch.

9 I'M AN OLD COWHAND   Bing Crosby with Jimmy Dorsey Orch.

10 ME AND THE MOON   Hal Kemp Orch.

11 WHEN A LADY MEETS A GENTLEMAN DOWN SOUTH   Benny Goodman Orch. (VR: Helen Ward)

12 A FINE ROMANCE   Fred Astaire

13 YOU TURNED THE TABLES ON ME   Benny Goodman Orch. (VR: Helen Ward)

14 WHEN I'M WITH YOU   Hal Kemp Orch. (VR: Skinnay Ennis)

15 UNTIL TODAY   Fletcher Henderson Orch.

October 24, 1936

1 THE WAY YOU LOOK TONIGHT   Fred Astaire

2 WHEN DID YOU LEAVE HEAVEN   Guy Lombardo Orch. (VR: Carmen Lombardo)

3 UNTIL THE REAL THING COMES ALONG   Andy Kirk Orch. (VR: Pha Terrell)

4 DID I REMEMBER   Shep Fields Orch. (VR: Charles Chester)

5 SING, BABY, SING   Ruby Newman Orch (VR: Barry McKinley)

6 ME AND THE MOON   Hal Kemp Orch.

7 A FINE ROMANCE   Fred Astaire

8 A STAR FELL OUT OF HEAVEN   Hal Kemp Orch.

9 I'LL SING YOU A THOUSAND LOVE SONGS   Eddy Duchin Orch. (VR: Jimmy Newell)

10 BYE, BYE, BABY   Fats Waller (VR: Fats Waller)

11 WHEN A LADY MEETS A GENTLEMAN DOWN SOUTH   Benny Goodman Orch. (VR: Helen Ward)

12 YOU TURNED THE TABLES ON ME   Benny Goodman Orch. (VR: Helen Ward)

13 CLOSE TO ME   Tommy Dorsey Orch. (VR: Jack Leonard)

14 I CAN'T ESCAPE FROM YOU   Bing Crosby with Jimmy Dorsey Orch.

15 SOUTH SEA ISLAND MAGIC   Bing Crosby

October 31, 1936

1 THE WAY YOU LOOK TONIGHT   Fred Astaire

2 WHEN DID YOU LEAVE HEAVEN   Guy Lombardo Orch. (VR: Carmen Lombardo)

3 A FINE ROMANCE   Fred Astaire

4 SING, BABY, SING   Ruby Newman Orch (VR: Barry McKinley)

5 UNTIL THE REAL THING COMES ALONG   Andy Kirk Orch. (VR: Pha Terrell)

6 DID I REMEMBER   Shep Fields Orch. (VR: Charles Chester)

7 A STAR FELL OUT OF HEAVEN   Hal Kemp Orch.

8 I'LL SING YOU A THOUSAND LOVE SONGS   Eddy Duchin Orch. (VR: Jimmy Newell)

9 BYE, BYE, BABY   Fats Waller (VR: Fats Waller)

10 WHO LOVES YOU   Teddy Wilson Orch. (VR: Billie Holiday)

11 ME AND THE MOON   Hal Kemp Orch.

12 YOU TURNED THE TABLES ON ME   Benny Goodman Orch. (VR: Helen Ward)

13 UNTIL TODAY   Fletcher Henderson Orch.

14 I CAN'T ESCAPE FROM YOU   Bing Crosby with Jimmy Dorsey Orch.

15 DREAM AWHILE   Eddy Duchin Orch. (VR: Lew Sherwood)

November 7, 1936

1 THE WAY YOU LOOK TONIGHT   Fred Astaire

2 WHEN DID YOU LEAVE HEAVEN   Guy Lombardo Orch. (VR: Carmen Lombardo)

3 A FINE ROMANCE   Fred Astaire

4 YOU TURNED THE TABLES ON ME   Benny Goodman Orch. (VR: Helen Ward)

5 I'LL SING YOU A THOUSAND LOVE SONGS   Eddy Duchin Orch. (VR: Jimmy Newell)

6 SING, BABY, SING   Ruby Newman Orch (VR: Barry McKinley)

7 WHO LOVES YOU   Teddy Wilson Orch. (VR: Billie Holiday)

8 DID YOU MEAN IT?   Kay Kyser Orch.

9 ME AND THE MOON   Hal Kemp Orch.

10 SOUTH SEA ISLAND MAGIC   Bing Crosby

11 DID I REMEMBER   Shep Fields Orch. (VR: Charles Chester)

12 UNTIL THE REAL THING COMES ALONG   Andy Kirk Orch. (VR: Pha Terrell)

13 I CAN'T ESCAPE FROM YOU   Bing Crosby with Jimmy Dorsey Orch.

14 ORGAN GRINDER'S SWING   Jimmy Lunceford Orch.

15 MIDNIGHT BLUE   Russ Morgan Orch.

November 14, 1936

1 THE WAY YOU LOOK TONIGHT   Fred Astaire

2 WHEN DID YOU LEAVE HEAVEN   Guy Lombardo Orch. (VR: Carmen Lombardo)

3 I'LL SING YOU A THOUSAND LOVE SONGS   Eddy Duchin Orch. (VR: Jimmy Newell)

4 A FINE ROMANCE   Fred Astaire

5 DID YOU MEAN IT?   Kay Kyser Orch.

6 SOUTH SEA ISLAND MAGIC   Bing Crosby

7 WHO LOVES YOU   Teddy Wilson Orch. (VR: Billie Holiday)

8 YOU TURNED THE TABLES ON ME   Benny Goodman Orch. (VR: Helen Ward)

9 DID I REMEMBER   Shep Fields Orch. (VR: Charles Chester)

10 ME AND THE MOON   Hal Kemp Orch.
11 MIDNIGHT BLUE   Russ Morgan Orch.
12 IN THE CHAPEL IN THE MOONLIGHT   Shep Fields Orch.
13 PENNIES FROM HEAVEN   Bing Crosby
14 SING, BABY, SING   Ruby Newman Orch (VR: Barry McKinley)
15 TO MARY WITH LOVE   Tempo King

November 21, 1936

1 THE WAY YOU LOOK TONIGHT   Fred Astaire
2 WHEN DID YOU LEAVE HEAVEN   Guy Lombardo Orch. (VR: Carmen Lombardo)
3 YOU TURNED THE TABLES ON ME   Benny Goodman Orch. (VR: Helen Ward)
4 ORGAN GRINDER'S SWING   Jimmy Lunceford Orch.
5 I'LL SING YOU A THOUSAND LOVE SONGS   Eddy Duchin Orch. (VR: Jimmy Newell)
6 A FINE ROMANCE   Fred Astaire
7 SOUTH SEA ISLAND MAGIC   Bing Crosby
8 IN THE CHAPEL IN THE MOONLIGHT   Shep Fields Orch.
9 WHO LOVES YOU   Teddy Wilson Orch. (VR: Billie Holiday)
10 HERE'S LOVE IN YOUR EYES   Benny Goodman Orch.
11 CLOSE TO ME   Tommy Dorsey Orch. (VR: Jack Leonard)
12 ME AND THE MOON   Hal Kemp Orch.
13 TO MARY WITH LOVE   Tempo King
14 DID I REMEMBER   Shep Fields Orch. (VR: Charles Chester)
15 I'M IN A DANCING MOOD   Tommy Dorsey Orch. (VR: Jack Leonard) *
   Note: * Another version by: Russ Morgan Orch.

November 28, 1936

1 THE WAY YOU LOOK TONIGHT   Fred Astaire
2 I'LL SING YOU A THOUSAND LOVE SONGS   Eddy Duchin Orch. (VR: Jimmy Newell)
3 IN THE CHAPEL IN THE MOONLIGHT   Shep Fields Orch.
4 WHEN DID YOU LEAVE HEAVEN   Guy Lombardo Orch. (VR: Carmen Lombardo)
5 YOU TURNED THE TABLES ON ME   Benny Goodman Orch. (VR: Helen Ward)
6 ORGAN GRINDER'S SWING   Jimmy Lunceford Orch.
7 IT'S DE-LOVELY   Eddy Duchin Orch. (VR: Jerry Cooper)

December 5, 1936

1 I'LL SING YOU A THOUSAND LOVE SONGS   Eddy Duchin Orch. (VR: Jimmy Newell)
2 IN THE CHAPEL IN THE MOONLIGHT   Shep Fields Orch.
3 YOU TURNED THE TABLES ON ME   Benny Goodman Orch. (VR: Helen Ward)
4 THE WAY YOU LOOK TONIGHT   Fred Astaire
5 DID YOU MEAN IT?   Kay Kyser Orch.
6 IT'S DE-LOVELY   Eddy Duchin Orch. (VR: Jerry Cooper)
7 SOUTH SEA ISLAND MAGIC   Bing Crosby

December 12, 1936

1 IN THE CHAPEL IN THE MOONLIGHT   Shep Fields Orch. *
2 I'LL SING YOU A THOUSAND LOVE SONGS   Eddy Duchin Orch. (VR: Jimmy Newell)
3 IT'S DE-LOVELY   Eddy Duchin Orch. (VR: Jerry Cooper)
4 I'VE GOT YOU UNDER MY SKIN   Ray Noble Orch. (VR: Al Bowlly)
5 YOU TURNED THE TABLES ON ME   Benny Goodman Orch. (VR: Helen Ward)
6 THE WAY YOU LOOK TONIGHT   Fred Astaire
7 PENNIES FROM HEAVEN   Bing Crosby

December 19, 1936

1 PENNIES FROM HEAVEN   Bing Crosby
2 IN THE CHAPEL IN THE MOONLIGHT   Shep Fields Orch.
3 I'LL SING YOU A THOUSAND LOVE SONGS   Eddy Duchin Orch. (VR: Jimmy Newell)
4 I'VE GOT YOU UNDER MY SKIN   Ray Noble Orch. (VR: Al Bowlly)
5 IT'S DE-LOVELY   Eddy Duchin Orch. (VR: Jerry Cooper)
6 THE WAY YOU LOOK TONIGHT   Fred Astaire
7 ORGAN GRINDER'S SWING   Jimmy Lunceford Orch.

December 26, 1936

1 IN THE CHAPEL IN THE MOONLIGHT   Shep Fields Orch.
2 IT'S DE-LOVELY   Eddy Duchin Orch. (VR: Jerry Cooper)
3 PENNIES FROM HEAVEN   Bing Crosby
4 I'VE GOT YOU UNDER MY SKIN   Ray Noble Orch. (VR: Al Bowlly)
5 WHEN MY DREAM BOAT COMES HOME   Guy Lombardo Orch. (VR: Carmen Lombardo)
6 I'M IN A DANCING MOOD   Tommy Dorsey Orch. (VR: Jack Leonard) *
7 I'LL SING YOU A THOUSAND LOVE SONGS   Eddy Duchin Orch. (VR: Jimmy Newell)
   Note: * Another version by: Russ Morgan Orch.

January 2, 1937

1 IN THE CHAPEL IN THE MOONLIGHT   Shep Fields Orch.
2 IT'S DE-LOVELY   Eddy Duchin Orch. (VR: Jerry Cooper)
3 I'VE GOT YOU UNDER MY SKIN   Ray Noble Orch. (VR: Al Bowlly)
4 PENNIES FROM HEAVEN   Bing Crosby
5 I'LL SING YOU A THOUSAND LOVE SONGS   Eddy Duchin Orch. (VR: Jimmy Newell)
6 I'M IN A DANCING MOOD   Tommy Dorsey Orch. (VR: Jack Leonard) *
7 THE NIGHT IS YOUNG AND YOU'RE SO BEAUTIFUL   Jan Garber Orch.
   Note: * Another version by: Russ Morgan Orch.

January 9, 1937

1 PENNIES FROM HEAVEN   Bing Crosby
2 IT'S DE-LOVELY   Eddy Duchin Orch. (VR: Jerry Cooper)
3 IN THE CHAPEL IN THE MOONLIGHT   Shep Fields Orch.
4 I'VE GOT YOU UNDER MY SKIN   Ray Noble Orch. (VR: Al Bowlly)
5 THE NIGHT IS YOUNG AND YOU'RE SO BEAUTIFUL   Jan Garber Orch.
6 I'M IN A DANCING MOOD   Tommy Dorsey Orch. (VR: Jack Leonard) *
7 EASY TO LOVE   Ray Noble Orch. (VR: Al Bowlly)
   Note: * Another version by: Russ Morgan Orch.

January 16, 1937

1 IT'S DE-LOVELY   Eddy Duchin Orch. (VR: Jerry Cooper)
2 PENNIES FROM HEAVEN   Bing Crosby
3 IN THE CHAPEL IN THE MOONLIGHT   Shep Fields Orch.
4 I'VE GOT YOU UNDER MY SKIN   Ray Noble Orch. (VR: Al Bowlly)
5 WITH PLENTY OF MONEY AND YOU   Henry Busse Orch. (VR: Bob Hannon)
6 I'M IN A DANCING MOOD   Tommy Dorsey Orch. (VR: Jack Leonard) *
7 THE NIGHT IS YOUNG AND YOU'RE SO BEAUTIFUL   Jan Garber Orch.
   Note: * Another version by: Russ Morgan Orch.

January 23, 1937
1 PENNIES FROM HEAVEN   Bing Crosby
2 GOODNIGHT, MY LOVE   Benny Goodman Orch. (VR: Ella Fitzgerald)
3 WHEN MY DREAM BOAT COMES HOME   Guy Lombardo Orch. (VR: Carmen Lombardo)
4 IT'S DE-LOVELY   Eddy Duchin Orch. (VR: Jerry Cooper)
5 WITH PLENTY OF MONEY AND YOU   Henry Busse Orch. (VR: Bob Hannon)
6 IN THE CHAPEL IN THE MOONLIGHT   Shep Fields Orch.
7 I'VE GOT YOU UNDER MY SKIN   Ray Noble Orch. (VR: Al Bowlly)

January 30, 1937
1 PENNIES FROM HEAVEN   Bing Crosby
2 IT'S DE-LOVELY   Eddy Duchin Orch. (VR: Jerry Cooper)
3 IN THE CHAPEL IN THE MOONLIGHT   Shep Fields Orch.
4 WITH PLENTY OF MONEY AND YOU   Henry Busse Orch. (VR: Bob Hannon)
5 WHEN MY DREAM BOAT COMES HOME   Guy Lombardo Orch. (VR: Carmen Lombardo)
6 GOODNIGHT, MY LOVE   Benny Goodman Orch. (VR: Ella Fitzgerald)
7 I'VE GOT YOU UNDER MY SKIN   Ray Noble Orch. (VR: Al Bowlly)

February 6, 1936
1 GOODNIGHT, MY LOVE   Benny Goodman Orch. (VR: Ella Fitzgerald)
2 PENNIES FROM HEAVEN   Bing Crosby
3 WITH PLENTY OF MONEY AND YOU   Henry Busse Orch. (VR: Bob Hannon)
4 IN THE CHAPEL IN THE MOONLIGHT   Shep Fields Orch.
5 THE NIGHT IS YOUNG AND YOU'RE SO BEAUTIFUL   Jan Garber Orch.
6 WHEN MY DREAM BOAT COMES HOME   Guy Lombardo Orch. (VR: Carmen Lombardo)
7 THERE'S SOMETHING IN THE AIR   Shep Fields Orch. (VR: Bob Goday)

February 13, 1937
1 GOODNIGHT, MY LOVE   Benny Goodman Orch. (VR: Ella Fitzgerald)
2 WITH PLENTY OF MONEY AND YOU   Henry Busse Orch. (VR: Bob Hannon)
3 PENNIES FROM HEAVEN   Bing Crosby
4 THE NIGHT IS YOUNG AND YOU'RE SO BEAUTIFUL   Jan Garber Orch.
5 WHEN MY DREAM BOAT COMES HOME   Guy Lombardo Orch. (VR: Carmen Lombardo)
6 THERE'S SOMETHING IN THE AIR   Shep Fields Orch. (VR: Bob Goday)
7 TRUST IN ME   Mildred Bailey

February 20, 1937
1 WITH PLENTY OF MONEY AND YOU   Henry Busse Orch. (VR: Bob Hannon)
2 GOODNIGHT, MY LOVE   Benny Goodman Orch. (VR: Ella Fitzgerald)
3 THIS YEAR'S KISSES   Benny Goodman Orch. (VR: Margaret Macrae) *
4 WHEN MY DREAM BOAT COMES HOME   Guy Lombardo Orch. (VR: Carmen Lombardo)
5 THERE'S SOMETHING IN THE AIR   Shep Fields Orch. (VR: Bob Goday)
6 IN THE CHAPEL IN THE MOONLIGHT   Shep Fields Orch.
7 PENNIES FROM HEAVEN   Bing Crosby
   Note: * Another version by: Hal Kemp Orch. (VR: Skinnay Ennis).

February 27, 1937
1 GOODNIGHT, MY LOVE   Benny Goodman Orch. (VR: Ella Fitzgerald)
2 TRUST IN ME   Mildred Bailey
3 WITH PLENTY OF MONEY AND YOU   Henry Busse Orch. (VR: Bob Hannon)
4 THE NIGHT IS YOUNG AND YOU'RE SO BEAUTIFUL   Jan Garber Orch.
5 THIS YEAR'S KISSES   Benny Goodman Orch. (VR: Margaret Macrae) *
6 WHEN MY DREAM BOAT COMES HOME   Guy Lombardo Orch. (VR: Carmen Lombardo)
7 PENNIES FROM HEAVEN   Bing Crosby
   Note: * Another version by: Hal Kemp Orch. (VR: Skinnay Ennis).

March 6, 1937
1 GOODNIGHT, MY LOVE   Benny Goodman Orch. (VR: Ella Fitzgerald)
2 THIS YEAR'S KISSES   Benny Goodman Orch. (VR: Margaret Macrae) *
3 WHEN MY DREAM BOAT COMES HOME   Guy Lombardo Orch. (VR: Carmen Lombardo)
4 BOO HOO   Guy Lombardo Orch. (VR: Carmen Lombardo)
5 LITTLE OLD LADY   Abe Lyman Orch. (VR: Sonny Schuyler)
6 GOODNIGHT, MY LOVE   Benny Goodman Orch. (VR: Ella Fitzgerald)
7 WHAT WILL I TELL MY HEART   Andy Kirk Orch. (VR: Pha Terrell)
   Note: * Another version by: Hal Kemp Orch. (VR: Skinnay Ennis).

March 13, 1937
1 WHEN MY DREAM BOAT COMES HOME   Guy Lombardo Orch. (VR: Carmen Lombardo)
2 GOODNIGHT, MY LOVE   Benny Goodman Orch. (VR: Ella Fitzgerald)
3 WHEN MY DREAM BOAT COMES HOME   Guy Lombardo Orch. (VR: Carmen Lombardo)
4 TRUST IN ME   Mildred Bailey
5 I'VE GOT MY LOVE TO KEEP ME WARM   Ray Noble Orch. (VR: Howard Phillips)
6 YOU'RE LAUGHING AT ME   Fats Waller (VR: Fats Waller)
7 SERENADE IN THE NIGHT   Mantovani

March 20, 1937
1 THIS YEAR'S KISSES   Benny Goodman Orch. (VR: Margaret Macrae) *
2 MOONLIGHT AND SHADOWS   Shep Fields Orch. (VR: Bob Goday)
3 WHEN MY DREAM BOAT COMES HOME   Guy Lombardo Orch. (VR: Carmen Lombardo)
4 BOO HOO   Guy Lombardo Orch. (VR: Carmen Lombardo)
5 LITTLE OLD LADY   Abe Lyman Orch. (VR: Sonny Schuyler)
6 GOODNIGHT, MY LOVE   Benny Goodman Orch. (VR: Ella Fitzgerald)
7 WHAT WILL I TELL MY HEART   Andy Kirk Orch. (VR: Pha Terrell)
   Note: * Another version by: Hal Kemp Orch. (VR: Skinnay Ennis).

March 27, 1937

1 THIS YEAR'S KISSES   Benny Goodman Orch. (VR: Margaret Macrae) *
2 BOO HOO   Guy Lombardo Orch. (VR: Carmen Lombardo)
3 WHEN MY DREAM BOAT COMES HOME   Guy Lombardo Orch. (VR: Carmen Lombardo)
4 I'VE GOT MY LOVE TO KEEP ME WARM   Ray Noble Orch. (VR: Howard Phillips)
5 WHAT WILL I TELL MY HEART   Andy Kirk Orch. (VR: Pha Terrell)
6 GOODNIGHT, MY LOVE   Benny Goodman Orch. (VR: Ella Fitzgerald)
7 MOONLIGHT AND SHADOWS   Shep Fields Orch. (VR: Bob Goday)
   Note: * Another version by: Hal Kemp Orch. (VR: Skinnay Ennis).

April 3, 1937

1 BOO HOO   Guy Lombardo Orch. (VR: Carmen Lombardo)
2 LITTLE OLD LADY   Abe Lyman Orch. (VR: Sonny Schuyler)
3 I'VE GOT MY LOVE TO KEEP ME WARM   Ray Noble Orch. (VR: Howard Phillips)
4 WHAT WILL I TELL MY HEART   Andy Kirk Orch. (VR: Pha Terrell)
5 WHEN THE POPPIES BLOOM AGAIN   Russ Morgan Orch. (VR: Mert Curtis)
6 MOONLIGHT AND SHADOWS   Shep Fields Orch. (VR: Bob Goday)
7 TRUST IN ME   Mildred Bailey

April 10, 1937

1 BOO HOO   Guy Lombardo Orch. (VR: Carmen Lombardo)
2 LITTLE OLD LADY   Abe Lyman Orch. (VR: Sonny Schuyler)
3 MOONLIGHT AND SHADOWS   Shep Fields Orch. (VR: Bob Goday)
4 TRUST IN ME   Mildred Bailey
5 THIS YEAR'S KISSES   Benny Goodman Orch. (VR: Margaret Macrae) *
6 I'VE GOT MY LOVE TO KEEP ME WARM   Ray Noble Orch. (VR: Howard Phillips)
7 WHAT WILL I TELL MY HEART   Andy Kirk Orch. (VR: Pha Terrell)
   Note: * Another version by: Hal Kemp Orch. (VR: Skinnay Ennis).

April 17, 1937

1 BOO HOO   Guy Lombardo Orch. (VR: Carmen Lombardo)
2 LITTLE OLD LADY   Abe Lyman Orch. (VR: Sonny Schuyler)
3 MOONLIGHT AND SHADOWS   Shep Fields Orch. (VR: Bob Goday)
4 I'VE GOT MY LOVE TO KEEP ME WARM   Ray Noble Orch. (VR: Howard Phillips)
5 WHAT WILL I TELL MY HEART   Andy Kirk Orch. (VR: Pha Terrell)
6 TOO MARVELOUS FOR WORDS   Bing Crosby with Jimmy Dorsey Orch.
7 THIS YEAR'S KISSES   Benny Goodman Orch. (VR: Margaret Macrae) *
8 WHERE ARE YOU   Mildred Bailey
9 SWEET IS THE WORD FOR YOU   Bing Crosby
10 TRUST IN ME   Mildred Bailey
   Note: * Another version by: Hal Kemp Orch. (VR: Skinnay Ennis).

April 24, 1937

1 BOO HOO   Guy Lombardo Orch. (VR: Carmen Lombardo)

2 LITTLE OLD LADY   Abe Lyman Orch. (VR: Sonny Schuyler)
3 TOO MARVELOUS FOR WORDS   Bing Crosby with Jimmy Dorsey Orch.
4 MOONLIGHT AND SHADOWS   Shep Fields Orch. (VR: Bob Goday)
5 WHAT WILL I TELL MY HEART   Andy Kirk Orch. (VR: Pha Terrell)
6 SEPTEMBER IN THE RAIN   Guy Lombardo Orch. (VR: Carmen Lombardo)
7 I'VE GOT MY LOVE TO KEEP ME WARM   Ray Noble Orch. (VR: Howard Phillips)
8 WHERE ARE YOU   Mildred Bailey
9 CARELESSLY   Teddy Wilson Orch. (VR: Billie Holiday)
10 THE LOVE BUG WILL BITE YOU   Jimmy Dorsey Orch. (VR: Ray McKinley)

May 1, 1937

1 BOO HOO   Guy Lombardo Orch. (VR: Carmen Lombardo)
2 LITTLE OLD LADY   Abe Lyman Orch. (VR: Sonny Schuyler)
3 TOO MARVELOUS FOR WORDS   Bing Crosby with Jimmy Dorsey Orch.
4 MOONLIGHT AND SHADOWS   Shep Fields Orch. (VR: Bob Goday)
5 CARELESSLY   Teddy Wilson Orch. (VR: Billie Holiday)
6 SEPTEMBER IN THE RAIN   Guy Lombardo Orch. (VR: Carmen Lombardo)
7 SWEET IS THE WORD FOR YOU   Bing Crosby
8 WHAT WILL I TELL MY HEART   Andy Kirk Orch. (VR: Pha Terrell)
9 THE LOVE BUG WILL BITE YOU   Jimmy Dorsey Orch. (VR: Ray McKinley)
10 NEVER IN A MILLION YEARS   Bing Crosby with Jimmy Dorsey Orch.

May 8, 1937

1 BOO HOO   Guy Lombardo Orch. (VR: Carmen Lombardo)
2 THE LOVE BUG WILL BITE YOU   Jimmy Dorsey Orch. (VR: Ray McKinley)
3 TOO MARVELOUS FOR WORDS   Bing Crosby with Jimmy Dorsey Orch.
4 SEPTEMBER IN THE RAIN   Guy Lombardo Orch. (VR: Carmen Lombardo)
5 MOONLIGHT AND SHADOWS   Shep Fields Orch. (VR: Bob Goday)
6 WHERE ARE YOU   Mildred Bailey
7 WHAT WILL I TELL MY HEART   Andy Kirk Orch. (VR: Pha Terrell)
8 LITTLE OLD LADY   Abe Lyman Orch. (VR: Sonny Schuyler)
9 CARELESSLY   Teddy Wilson Orch. (VR: Billie Holiday)
10 HOW COULD YOU   Anson Weeks Orch. (VR: Maggie Dee)

May 15, 1937

1 SEPTEMBER IN THE RAIN   Guy Lombardo Orch. (VR: Carmen Lombardo)
2 BOO HOO   Guy Lombardo Orch. (VR: Carmen Lombardo)
3 NEVER IN A MILLION YEARS   Bing Crosby with Jimmy Dorsey Orch.
4 CARELESSLY   Teddy Wilson Orch. (VR: Billie Holiday)
5 THERE'S A LULL IN MY LIFE   Teddy Wilson Orch. (VR: Billie Holiday)
6 TOO MARVELOUS FOR WORDS   Bing Crosby with Jimmy Dorsey Orch.
7 THE LOVE BUG WILL BITE YOU   Jimmy Dorsey Orch. (VR: Ray McKinley)
8 BLUE HAWAII   Bing Crosby
9 LITTLE OLD LADY   Abe Lyman Orch. (VR: Sonny Schuyler)

10   WHERE ARE YOU   Mildred Bailey

May 22, 1937
1   CARELESSLY   Teddy Wilson Orch. (VR: Billie Holiday)
2   SEPTEMBER IN THE RAIN   Guy Lombardo Orch. (VR: Carmen Lombardo)
3   THERE'S A LULL IN MY LIFE   Teddy Wilson Orch. (VR: Billie Holiday)
4   BOO HOO   Guy Lombardo Orch. (VR: Carmen Lombardo)
5   WHERE ARE YOU   Mildred Bailey
6   NEVER IN A MILLION YEARS   Bing Crosby with Jimmy Dorsey Orch.
7   THE LOVE BUG WILL BITE YOU   Jimmy Dorsey Orch. (VR: Ray McKinley)
8   TOO MARVELOUS FOR WORDS   Bing Crosby with Jimmy Dorsey Orch.
9   LITTLE OLD LADY   Abe Lyman Orch. (VR: Sonny Schuyler)
10   LET'S CALL THE WHOLE THING OFF   Fred Astaire

May 29, 1937
1   CARELESSLY   Teddy Wilson Orch. (VR: Billie Holiday)
2   NEVER IN A MILLION YEARS   Bing Crosby with Jimmy Dorsey Orch.
3   SEPTEMBER IN THE RAIN   Guy Lombardo Orch. (VR: Carmen Lombardo)
4   THE LOVE BUG WILL BITE YOU   Jimmy Dorsey Orch. (VR: Ray McKinley)
5   THERE'S A LULL IN MY LIFE   Teddy Wilson Orch. (VR: Billie Holiday)
6   WHERE ARE YOU   Mildred Bailey
7   LITTLE OLD LADY   Abe Lyman Orch. (VR: Sonny Schuyler)
8   SWEET LEILANI   Bing Crosby
9   BLUE HAWAII   Bing Crosby
10   BOO HOO   Guy Lombardo Orch. (VR: Carmen Lombardo)

June 5, 1937
1   SEPTEMBER IN THE RAIN   Guy Lombardo Orch. (VR: Carmen Lombardo)
2   CARELESSLY   Teddy Wilson Orch. (VR: Billie Holiday)
3   THERE'S A LULL IN MY LIFE   Teddy Wilson Orch. (VR: Billie Holiday)
4   NEVER IN A MILLION YEARS   Bing Crosby with Jimmy Dorsey Orch.
5   THE LOVE BUG WILL BITE YOU   Jimmy Dorsey Orch. (VR: Ray McKinley)
6   WHERE ARE YOU   Mildred Bailey
7   LET'S CALL THE WHOLE THING OFF   Fred Astaire
8   LITTLE OLD LADY   Abe Lyman Orch. (VR: Sonny Schuyler)
9   THEY CAN'T TAKE THAT AWAY FROM ME   Fred Astaire
10   SWEET LEILANI   Bing Crosby

June 12, 1937
1   SEPTEMBER IN THE RAIN   Guy Lombardo Orch. (VR: Carmen Lombardo)
2   NEVER IN A MILLION YEARS   Bing Crosby with Jimmy Dorsey Orch.
3   CARELESSLY   Teddy Wilson Orch. (VR: Billie Holiday)
4   THERE'S A LULL IN MY LIFE   Teddy Wilson Orch. (VR: Billie Holiday)
5   WHERE ARE YOU   Mildred Bailey
6   THEY CAN'T TAKE THAT AWAY FROM ME   Fred Astaire
7   IT LOOKS LIKE RAIN IN CHERRY BLOSSOM LANE   Guy Lombardo Orch. (VR: Carmen Lombardo)
8   THE LOVE BUG WILL BITE YOU   Jimmy Dorsey Orch. (VR: Ray McKinley)
9   SWEET LEILANI   Bing Crosby

10   BLUE HAWAII   Bing Crosby

June 19, 1937
1   SEPTEMBER IN THE RAIN   Guy Lombardo Orch. (VR: Carmen Lombardo)
2   CARELESSLY   Teddy Wilson Orch. (VR: Billie Holiday)
3   NEVER IN A MILLION YEARS   Bing Crosby with Jimmy Dorsey Orch.
4   IT LOOKS LIKE RAIN IN CHERRY BLOSSOM LANE   Guy Lombardo Orch. (VR: Carmen Lombardo)
5   THERE'S A LULL IN MY LIFE   Teddy Wilson Orch. (VR: Billie Holiday)
6   SWEET LEILANI   Bing Crosby
7   WHERE ARE YOU   Mildred Bailey
8   SAILBOAT IN THE MOONLIGHT   Guy Lombardo Orch. (VR: Carmen Lombardo)
9   THE LOVE BUG WILL BITE YOU   Jimmy Dorsey Orch. (VR: Ray McKinley)
10   BLUE HAWAII   Bing Crosby

June 26, 1937
1   SEPTEMBER IN THE RAIN   Guy Lombardo Orch. (VR: Carmen Lombardo)
2   IT LOOKS LIKE RAIN IN CHERRY BLOSSOM LANE   Guy Lombardo Orch. (VR: Carmen Lombardo)
3   THE MERRY-GO-ROUND BROKE DOWN   Russ Morgan Orch. (VR: Jimmy Lewis) *
4   NEVER IN A MILLION YEARS   Bing Crosby with Jimmy Dorsey Orch.
5   SWEET LEILANI   Bing Crosby
6   CARELESSLY   Teddy Wilson Orch. (VR: Billie Holiday)
7   WAS IT RAIN   Frances Langford
8   THEY CAN'T TAKE THAT AWAY FROM ME   Fred Astaire
9   SAILBOAT IN THE MOONLIGHT   Guy Lombardo Orch. (VR: Carmen Lombardo)
10   THERE'S A LULL IN MY LIFE   Teddy Wilson Orch. (VR: Billie Holiday)
  Note: * Another version by: Shep Fields Orch. (VR: Bod Goday).

July 3, 1937
1   IT LOOKS LIKE RAIN IN CHERRY BLOSSOM LANE   Guy Lombardo Orch. (VR: Carmen Lombardo)
2   SWEET LEILANI   Bing Crosby
3   THE MERRY-GO-ROUND BROKE DOWN   Russ Morgan Orch. (VR: Jimmy Lewis) *
4   SEPTEMBER IN THE RAIN   Guy Lombardo Orch. (VR: Carmen Lombardo)
5   THERE'S A LULL IN MY LIFE   Teddy Wilson Orch. (VR: Billie Holiday)
6   NEVER IN A MILLION YEARS   Bing Crosby with Jimmy Dorsey Orch.
7   SAILBOAT IN THE MOONLIGHT   Guy Lombardo Orch. (VR: Carmen Lombardo)
8   CARELESSLY   Teddy Wilson Orch. (VR: Billie Holiday)
9   THE YOU AND ME THAT USED TO BE   Dolly Dawn Orch. (VR: Dolly Dawn)
10   BLUE HAWAII   Bing Crosby
  Note: * Another version by: Shep Fields Orch. (VR: Bod Goday).

July 10, 1937
1   IT LOOKS LIKE RAIN IN CHERRY BLOSSOM LANE   Guy Lombardo Orch. (VR: Carmen Lombardo)
2   SAILBOAT IN THE MOONLIGHT   Guy Lombardo Orch. (VR: Carmen Lombardo)

3 SWEET LEILANI   Bing Crosby
4 THE MERRY-GO-ROUND BROKE DOWN   Russ Morgan Orch. (VR: Jimmy Lewis) *
5 WHERE OR WHEN   Hal Kemp Orch. (VR: Bob Allen)
6 SEPTEMBER IN THE RAIN   Guy Lombardo Orch. (VR: Carmen Lombardo)
7 NEVER IN A MILLION YEARS   Bing Crosby with Jimmy Dorsey Orch.
8 THEY CAN'T TAKE THAT AWAY FROM ME   Fred Astaire
9 THE YOU AND ME THAT USED TO BE   Dolly Dawn Orch. (VR: Dolly Dawn)
10 CARELESSLY   Teddy Wilson Orch. (VR: Billie Holiday)
   Note: * Another version by: Shep Fields Orch. (VR: Bod Goday).

July 17, 1937

1 IT LOOKS LIKE RAIN IN CHERRY BLOSSOM LANE   Guy Lombardo Orch. (VR: Carmen Lombardo)
2 THE MERRY-GO-ROUND BROKE DOWN   Russ Morgan Orch. (VR: Jimmy Lewis) *
3 SAILBOAT IN THE MOONLIGHT   Guy Lombardo Orch. (VR: Carmen Lombardo)
4 WHERE OR WHEN   Hal Kemp Orch. (VR: Bob Allen)
5 SEPTEMBER IN THE RAIN   Guy Lombardo Orch. (VR: Carmen Lombardo)
6 SWEET LEILANI   Bing Crosby
7 THE YOU AND ME THAT USED TO BE   Dolly Dawn Orch. (VR: Dolly Dawn)
8 THERE'S A LULL IN MY LIFE   Teddy Wilson Orch. (VR: Billie Holiday)
9 I KNOW NOW   Guy Lombardo Orch. (VR: Carmen Lombardo)
10 BLUE HAWAII   Bing Crosby
   Note: * Another version by: Shep Fields Orch. (VR: Bod Goday).

July 24, 1937

1 IT LOOKS LIKE RAIN IN CHERRY BLOSSOM LANE   Guy Lombardo Orch. (VR: Carmen Lombardo)
2 THE MERRY-GO-ROUND BROKE DOWN   Russ Morgan Orch. (VR: Jimmy Lewis) *
3 SAILBOAT IN THE MOONLIGHT   Guy Lombardo Orch. (VR: Carmen Lombardo)
4 WHERE OR WHEN   Hal Kemp Orch. (VR: Bob Allen)
5 GONE WITH THE WIND   Horace Heidt (VR: Larry Cotton)
6 THE YOU AND ME THAT USED TO BE   Dolly Dawn Orch. (VR: Dolly Dawn)
7 SWEET LEILANI   Bing Crosby
8 SEPTEMBER IN THE RAIN   Guy Lombardo Orch. (VR: Carmen Lombardo)
9 BLUE HAWAII   Bing Crosby
10 'CAUSE MY BABY SAYS IT'S SO   Kay Kyser Orch.
   Note: * Another version by: Shep Fields Orch. (VR: Bod Goday).

July 31, 1937

1 IT LOOKS LIKE RAIN IN CHERRY BLOSSOM LANE   Guy Lombardo Orch. (VR: Carmen Lombardo)
2 THE MERRY-GO-ROUND BROKE DOWN   Russ Morgan Orch. (VR: Jimmy Lewis) *
3 SAILBOAT IN THE MOONLIGHT   Guy Lombardo Orch. (VR: Carmen Lombardo)
4 WHERE OR WHEN   Hal Kemp Orch. (VR: Bob Allen)
5 GONE WITH THE WIND   Horace Heidt (VR: Larry Cotton)
6 SO RARE   Guy Lombardo Orch. (VR: Carmen Lombardo)
7 SWEET LEILANI   Bing Crosby

8 THE FIRST TIME I SAW YOU   Bunny Berigan Orch. (VR: Ford Leary)
9 TOMMOROW IS ANOTHER DAY   Ted Fio Rito Orch. (VR: Muzzy Macellino)
10 THE YOU AND ME THAT USED TO BE   Dolly Dawn Orch. (VR: Dolly Dawn)
   Note: * Another version by: Shep Fields Orch. (VR: Bod Goday)

August 7, 1937

1 SAILBOAT IN THE MOONLIGHT   Guy Lombardo Orch. (VR: Carmen Lombardo)
2 IT LOOKS LIKE RAIN IN CHERRY BLOSSOM LANE   Guy Lombardo Orch. (VR: Carmen Lombardo)
3 WHERE OR WHEN   Hal Kemp Orch. (VR: Bob Allen)
4 THE MERRY-GO-ROUND BROKE DOWN   Russ Morgan Orch. (VR: Jimmy Lewis) *
5 THE YOU AND ME THAT USED TO BE   Dolly Dawn Orch. (VR: Dolly Dawn)
6 SO RARE   Guy Lombardo Orch. (VR: Carmen Lombardo)
7 I KNOW NOW   Guy Lombardo Orch. (VR: Carmen Lombardo)
8 SWEET LEILANI   Bing Crosby
9 GONE WITH THE WIND   Horace Heidt (VR: Larry Cotton)
10 STOP, YOU'RE BREAKING MY HEART   Russ Morgan Orch. (VR: Russ Morgan & Dave Franklin)
   Note: * Another version by: Shep Fields Orch. (VR: Bod Goday).

August 14, 1937

1 IT LOOKS LIKE RAIN IN CHERRY BLOSSOM LANE   Guy Lombardo Orch. (VR: Carmen Lombardo)
2 WHERE OR WHEN   Hal Kemp Orch. (VR: Bob Allen)
3 THE MERRY-GO-ROUND BROKE DOWN   Russ Morgan Orch. (VR: Jimmy Lewis) *
4 I KNOW NOW   Guy Lombardo Orch. (VR: Carmen Lombardo)
5 SAILBOAT IN THE MOONLIGHT   Guy Lombardo Orch. (VR: Carmen Lombardo)
6 SATAN TAKES A HOLIDAY   Tommy Dorsey Orch.
7 WHISPERS IN THE DARK   Bob Crosby Orch. (VR: Kay Weber)
8 SWEET LEILANI   Bing Crosby
9 MY CABIN OF DREAMS   Tommy Dorsey Orch. (VR: Edythe Wright)
10 SO RARE   Guy Lombardo Orch. (VR: Carmen Lombardo)
   Note: * Another version by: Shep Fields Orch. (VR: Bod Goday).

August 21, 1937

1 SAILBOAT IN THE MOONLIGHT   Guy Lombardo Orch. (VR: Carmen Lombardo)
2 I KNOW NOW   Guy Lombardo Orch. (VR: Carmen Lombardo)
3 WHERE OR WHEN   Hal Kemp Orch. (VR: Bob Allen)
4 IT LOOKS LIKE RAIN IN CHERRY BLOSSOM LANE   Guy Lombardo Orch. (VR: Carmen Lombardo)
5 SO RARE   Guy Lombardo Orch. (VR: Carmen Lombardo)
6 THE MERRY-GO-ROUND BROKE DOWN   Russ Morgan Orch. (VR: Jimmy Lewis) *
7 MY CABIN OF DREAMS   Tommy Dorsey Orch. (VR: Edythe Wright)
8 THE FIRST TIME I SAW YOU   Bunny Berigan Orch. (VR: Ford Leary)
9 STARDUST ON THE MOON   Tommy Dorsey Orch. (VR: Edythe Wright)

10 WHISPERS IN THE DARK   Bob Crosby Orch. (VR: Kay Weber)
   Note: * Another version by: Shep Fields Orch. (VR: Bod Goday).

August 28, 1937
1 SAILBOAT IN THE MOONLIGHT   Guy Lombardo Orch. (VR: Carmen Lombardo)
2 SO RARE   Guy Lombardo Orch. (VR: Carmen Lombardo)
3 WHISPERS IN THE DARK   Bob Crosby Orch. (VR: Kay Weber)
4 IT LOOKS LIKE RAIN IN CHERRY BLOSSOM LANE   Guy Lombardo Orch. (VR: Carmen Lombardo)
5 MY CABIN OF DREAMS   Tommy Dorsey Orch. (VR: Edythe Wright)
6 I KNOW NOW   Guy Lombardo Orch. (VR: Carmen Lombardo)
7 WHERE OR WHEN   Hal Kemp Orch. (VR: Bob Allen)
8 THE FIRST TIME I SAW YOU   Bunny Berigan Orch. (VR: Ford Leary)
9 STARDUST ON THE MOON   Tommy Dorsey Orch. (VR: Edythe Wright)
10 THE MERRY-GO-ROUND BROKE DOWN   Russ Morgan Orch. (VR: Jimmy Lewis) *
   Note: * Another version by: Shep Fields Orch. (VR: Bod Goday).

September 4, 1937
1 WHISPERS IN THE DARK   Bob Crosby Orch. (VR: Kay Weber)
2 I KNOW NOW   Guy Lombardo Orch. (VR: Carmen Lombardo)
3 MY CABIN OF DREAMS   Tommy Dorsey Orch. (VR: Edythe Wright)
4 SO RARE   Guy Lombardo Orch. (VR: Carmen Lombardo)
5 THE FIRST TIME I SAW YOU   Bunny Berigan Orch. (VR: Ford Leary)
6 AFRAID TO DREAM   Benny Goodman Orch. (VR: Betty Van)
7 SAILBOAT IN THE MOONLIGHT   Guy Lombardo Orch. (VR: Carmen Lombardo)
8 IT LOOKS LIKE RAIN IN CHERRY BLOSSOM LANE   Guy Lombardo Orch. (VR: Carmen Lombardo)
9 HAVE YOU GOT ANY CASTLES, BABY   Tommy Dorsey Orch. (VR: Jack Leonard)
10 THAT OLD FEELING   Shep Fields Orch. (VR: Bob Goday)

September 11, 1937
1 SO RARE   Guy Lombardo Orch. (VR: Carmen Lombardo)
2 MY CABIN OF DREAMS   Tommy Dorsey Orch. (VR: Edythe Wright)
3 WHISPERS IN THE DARK   Bob Crosby Orch. (VR: Kay Weber)
4 THAT OLD FEELING   Shep Fields Orch. (VR: Bob Goday)
5 I KNOW NOW   Guy Lombardo Orch. (VR: Carmen Lombardo)
6 THE FIRST TIME I SAW YOU   Bunny Berigan Orch. (VR: Ford Leary)
7 SAILBOAT IN THE MOONLIGHT   Guy Lombardo Orch. (VR: Carmen Lombardo)
8 AFRAID TO DREAM   Benny Goodman Orch. (VR: Betty Van)
9 STARDUST ON THE MOON   Tommy Dorsey Orch. (VR: Edythe Wright)
10 YOURS AND MINE   Hudson-DeLange Orch. (VR: Nan Wynn)

September 18, 1937
1 WHISPERS IN THE DARK   Bob Crosby Orch. (VR: Kay Weber)
2 SO RARE   Guy Lombardo Orch. (VR: Carmen Lombardo)
3 MY CABIN OF DREAMS   Tommy Dorsey Orch. (VR: Edythe Wright)
4 I KNOW NOW   Guy Lombardo Orch. (VR: Carmen Lombardo)
5 THAT OLD FEELING   Shep Fields Orch. (VR: Bob Goday)
6 HARBOR LIGHTS   Claude Thornhill Orch. (VR: Jimmy Farrell)
7 SAILBOAT IN THE MOONLIGHT   Guy Lombardo Orch. (VR: Carmen Lombardo)
8 AFRAID TO DREAM   Benny Goodman Orch. (VR: Betty Van)
9 HAVE YOU GOT ANY CASTLES, BABY   Tommy Dorsey Orch. (VR: Jack Leonard)
10 YOURS AND MINE   Hudson-DeLange Orch. (VR: Nan Wynn)

September 25, 1937
1 WHISPERS IN THE DARK   Bob Crosby Orch. (VR: Kay Weber)
2 THAT OLD FEELING   Shep Fields Orch. (VR: Bob Goday)
3 SO RARE   Guy Lombardo Orch. (VR: Carmen Lombardo)
4 MY CABIN OF DREAMS   Tommy Dorsey Orch. (VR: Edythe Wright)
5 HAVE YOU GOT ANY CASTLES, BABY   Tommy Dorsey Orch. (VR: Jack Leonard)
6 AFRAID TO DREAM   Benny Goodman Orch. (VR: Betty Van)
7 REMEMBER ME   Bing Crosby
8 THE FIRST TIME I SAW YOU   Bunny Berigan Orch. (VR: Ford Leary)
9 THE MOON GOT IN MY EYES   Bing Crosby
10 HARBOR LIGHTS   Claude Thornhill Orch. (VR: Jimmy Farrell)

Frances Langford
Also released a version of ``Harbor Lights.''

41

October 2, 1937
1 WHISPERS IN THE DARK   Bob Crosby Orch. (VR: Kay Weber)
2 THAT OLD FEELING   Shep Fields Orch. (VR: Bob Goday)
3 MY CABIN OF DREAMS   Tommy Dorsey Orch. (VR: Edythe Wright)
4 HAVE YOU GOT ANY CASTLES, BABY   Tommy Dorsey Orch. (VR: Jack Leonard)
5 THE MOON GOT IN MY EYES   Bing Crosby
6 HARBOR LIGHTS   Claude Thornhill Orch. (VR: Jimmy Farrell)
7 AFRAID TO DREAM   Benny Goodman Orch. (VR: Betty Van)
8 SO RARE   Guy Lombardo Orch. (VR: Carmen Lombardo)
9 ROSES IN DECEMBER   Ozzie Nelson Orch. (VR: Harriet Hilliard)
10 REMEMBER ME   Bing Crosby

October 9, 1937
1 THAT OLD FEELING   Shep Fields Orch. (VR: Bob Goday)
2 HAVE YOU GOT ANY CASTLES, BABY   Tommy Dorsey Orch. (VR: Jack Leonard)
3 WHISPERS IN THE DARK   Bob Crosby Orch. (VR: Kay Weber)
4 REMEMBER ME   Bing Crosby
5 THE MOON GOT IN MY EYES   Bing Crosby
6 SO RARE   Guy Lombardo Orch. (VR: Carmen Lombardo)
7 MY CABIN OF DREAMS   Tommy Dorsey Orch. (VR: Edythe Wright)
8 HARBOR LIGHTS   Claude Thornhill Orch. (VR: Jimmy Farrell)
9 AFRAID TO DREAM   Benny Goodman Orch. (VR: Betty Van)
10 ROSES IN DECEMBER   Ozzie Nelson Orch. (VR: Harriet Hilliard)

October 16, 1937
1 THAT OLD FEELING   Shep Fields Orch. (VR: Bob Goday)
2 REMEMBER ME   Bing Crosby
3 THE MOON GOT IN MY EYES   Bing Crosby
4 MY CABIN OF DREAMS   Tommy Dorsey Orch. (VR: Edythe Wright)
5 WHISPERS IN THE DARK   Bob Crosby Orch. (VR: Kay Weber)
6 HARBOR LIGHTS   Claude Thornhill Orch. (VR: Jimmy Farrell)
7 HAVE YOU GOT ANY CASTLES, BABY   Tommy Dorsey Orch. (VR: Jack Leonard)
8 AFRAID TO DREAM   Benny Goodman Orch. (VR: Betty Van)
9 ONE ROSE   Bing Crosby
10 YOU CAN'T STOP ME FROM DREAMING   Teddy Wilson Orch.

October 23, 1937
1 THAT OLD FEELING   Shep Fields Orch. (VR: Bob Goday)
2 HAVE YOU GOT ANY CASTLES, BABY   Tommy Dorsey Orch. (VR: Jack Leonard)
3 WHISPERS IN THE DARK   Bob Crosby Orch. (VR: Kay Weber)
4 THE MOON GOT IN MY EYES   Bing Crosby
5 REMEMBER ME   Bing Crosby
6 ROSES IN DECEMBER   Ozzie Nelson Orch. (VR: Harriet Hilliard)
7 SO MANY MEMORIES   Russ Morgan Orch. (VR: Mert Curtis)

8 HARBOR LIGHTS   Claude Thornhill Orch. (VR: Jimmy Farrell)
9 BLOSSOMS ON BROADWAY   Dick Robertson Orch. (VR: Dick Robertson)
10 MY CABIN OF DREAMS   Tommy Dorsey Orch. (VR: Edythe Wright)

October 30, 1937
1 THAT OLD FEELING   Shep Fields Orch. (VR: Bob Goday) *
2 REMEMBER ME   Bing Crosby
3 ROSES IN DECEMBER   Ozzie Nelson Orch. (VR: Harriet Hilliard)
4 VIENI, VIENI   Rudy Vallee
5 HAVE YOU GOT ANY CASTLES, BABY   Tommy Dorsey Orch. (VR: Jack Leonard)
6 HARBOR LIGHTS   Claude Thornhill Orch. (VR: Jimmy Farrell)
7 THE MOON GOT IN MY EYES   Bing Crosby
8 YOU CAN'T STOP ME FROM DREAMING   Teddy Wilson Orch.
9 WHISPERS IN THE DARK   Bob Crosby Orch. (VR: Kay Weber)
10 BLOSSOMS ON BROADWAY   Dick Robertson Orch. (VR: Dick Robertson)

November 6, 1937
1 REMEMBER ME   Bing Crosby
2 THAT OLD FEELING   Shep Fields Orch. (VR: Bob Goday)
3 ROSES IN DECEMBER   Ozzie Nelson Orch. (VR: Harriet Hilliard)
4 YOU CAN'T STOP ME FROM DREAMING   Teddy Wilson Orch.
5 VIENI, VIENI   Rudy Vallee
6 THE MOON GOT IN MY EYES   Bing Crosby
7 ONE ROSE   Bing Crosby
8 HARBOR LIGHTS   Claude Thornhill Orch. (VR: Jimmy Farrell)
9 HAVE YOU GOT ANY CASTLES, BABY   Tommy Dorsey Orch. (VR: Jack Leonard)
10 YOU AND I KNOW   Glenn Miller Orch. (VR: Ray Eberle)

November 13, 1937
1 YOU CAN'T STOP ME FROM DREAMING   Teddy Wilson Orch.
2 REMEMBER ME   Bing Crosby
3 VIENI, VIENI   Rudy Vallee
4 THAT OLD FEELING   Shep Fields Orch. (VR: Bob Goday)
5 BLOSSOMS ON BROADWAY   Dick Robertson Orch. (VR: Dick Robertson)
6 MY CABIN OF DREAMS   Tommy Dorsey Orch. (VR: Edythe Wright)
7 HAVE YOU GOT ANY CASTLES, BABY   Tommy Dorsey Orch. (VR: Jack Leonard)
8 HARBOR LIGHTS   Claude Thornhill Orch. (VR: Jimmy Farrell)
9 FAREWELL, MY LOVE   Russ Morgan Orch. (VR: Mert Curtis)
10 IF IT'S THE LAST THING I DO   Tommy Dorsey Orch. (VR: Jack Leonard)

November 20, 1937
1 VIENI, VIENI   Rudy Vallee
2 YOU CAN'T STOP ME FROM DREAMING   Teddy Wilson Orch.
3 ONCE IN A WHILE   Tommy Dorsey Orch. (VR: Jack Leonard)

Shep Fields

``That Old Feeling'' hits #1 (Oct. 9), as will next spring's ``Thanks For The Memory'' from the film
``Vogues of '38'' (a tune which becomes Bob Hope's theme song).

4 REMEMBER ME   Bing Crosby
5 BLOSSOMS ON BROADWAY   Dick Robertson Orch. (VR: Dick Robertson)
6 I STILL LOVE TO KISS YOU GOODNIGHT   Bing Crosby
7 THAT OLD FEELING   Shep Fields Orch. (VR: Bob Goday)
8 IF IT'S THE LAST THING I DO   Tommy Dorsey Orch. (VR: Jack Leonard)
9 HARBOR LIGHTS   Claude Thornhill Orch. (VR: Jimmy Farrell)
10 ROSES IN DECEMBER   Ozzie Nelson Orch. (VR: Harriet Hilliard)

November 27, 1937
1 ONCE IN A WHILE   Tommy Dorsey Orch. (VR: Jack Leonard)
2 VIENI, VIENI   Rudy Vallee
3 YOU CAN'T STOP ME FROM DREAMING   Teddy Wilson Orch.
4 BLOSSOMS ON BROADWAY   Dick Robertson Orch. (VR: Dick Robertson)
5 IF IT'S THE LAST THING I DO   Tommy Dorsey Orch. (VR: Jack Leonard)
6 NICE WORK IF YOU CAN GET IT   Fred Astaire
7 ONE ROSE   Bing Crosby
8 ROSES IN DECEMBER   Ozzie Nelson Orch. (VR: Harriet Hilliard)
9 HARBOR LIGHTS   Claude Thornhill Orch. (VR: Jimmy Farrell)
10 REMEMBER ME   Bing Crosby

December 4, 1937
1 ONCE IN A WHILE   Tommy Dorsey Orch. (VR: Jack Leonard)
2 YOU CAN'T STOP ME FROM DREAMING   Teddy Wilson Orch.
3 VIENI, VIENI   Rudy Vallee
4 IF IT'S THE LAST THING I DO   Tommy Dorsey Orch. (VR: Jack Leonard)
5 BLOSSOMS ON BROADWAY   Dick Robertson Orch. (VR: Dick Robertson)
6 REMEMBER ME   Bing Crosby
7 NICE WORK IF YOU CAN GET IT   Fred Astaire
8 ROSES IN DECEMBER   Ozzie Nelson Orch. (VR: Harriet Hilliard)
9 EBB TIDE   Bunny Berigan Orch. (VR: Gail Reese)
10 ONE ROSE   Bing Crosby

December 11, 1937
1 ONCE IN A WHILE   Tommy Dorsey Orch. (VR: Jack Leonard)
2 YOU CAN'T STOP ME FROM DREAMING   Teddy Wilson Orch.
3 VIENI, VIENI   Rudy Vallee
4 IF IT'S THE LAST THING I DO   Tommy Dorsey Orch. (VR: Jack Leonard)
5 NICE WORK IF YOU CAN GET IT   Fred Astaire
6 FAREWELL, MY LOVE   Russ Morgan Orch. (VR: Mert Curtis)
7 THERE'S A GOLD MINE IN THE SKY   Bing Crosby
8 I STILL LOVE TO KISS YOU GOODNIGHT   Bing Crosby
9 BLOSSOMS ON BROADWAY   Dick Robertson Orch. (VR: Dick Robertson)
10 ONE ROSE   Bing Crosby

December 18, 1937
1 ONCE IN A WHILE   Tommy Dorsey Orch. (VR: Jack Leonard)

2 VIENI, VIENI   Rudy Vallee
3 BLOSSOMS ON BROADWAY   Dick Robertson Orch. (VR: Dick Robertson)
4 NICE WORK IF YOU CAN GET IT   Fred Astaire
5 IF IT'S THE LAST THING I DO   Tommy Dorsey Orch. (VR: Jack Leonard)
6 ROSALIE   Sammy Kaye Orch. (VR: Tommy Ryan)
7 FAREWELL, MY LOVE   Russ Morgan Orch. (VR: Mert Curtis)
8 THERE'S A GOLD MINE IN THE SKY   Bing Crosby
9 YOU CAN'T STOP ME FROM DREAMING   Teddy Wilson Orch.
10 EBB TIDE   Bunny Berigan Orch. (VR: Gail Reese)

December 25, 1937
1 ONCE IN A WHILE   Tommy Dorsey Orch. (VR: Jack Leonard)
2 ROSALIE   Sammy Kaye Orch. (VR: Tommy Ryan)
3 NICE WORK IF YOU CAN GET IT   Fred Astaire
4 YOU CAN'T STOP ME FROM DREAMING   Teddy Wilson Orch.
5 I STILL LOVE TO KISS YOU GOODNIGHT   Bing Crosby
6 VIENI, VIENI   Rudy Vallee
7 THERE'S A GOLD MINE IN THE SKY   Bing Crosby
8 BLOSSOMS ON BROADWAY   Dick Robertson Orch. (VR: Dick Robertson)
9 TRUE CONFESSION   Larry Clinton Orch. (VR: Bea Wain)
10 ONE ROSE   Bing Crosby

January 1, 1938
1 ONCE IN A WHILE   Tommy Dorsey Orch. (VR: Jack Leonard)
2 ROSALIE   Sammy Kaye Orch. (VR: Tommy Ryan)
3 NICE WORK IF YOU CAN GET IT   Fred Astaire
4 BOB WHITE   Benny Goodman Orch. (VR: Martha Tilton)
5 YOU'RE A SWEETHEART   Dollie Dawn
6 THERE'S A GOLD MINE IN THE SKY   Bing Crosby
7 TRUE CONFESSION   Larry Clinton Orch. (VR: Bea Wain)
8 VIENI, VIENI   Rudy Vallee
9 YOU CAN'T STOP ME FROM DREAMING   Teddy Wilson Orch.
10 IF IT'S THE LAST THING I DO   Tommy Dorsey Orch. (VR: Jack Leonard)

January 8, 1938
1 ONCE IN A WHILE   Tommy Dorsey Orch. (VR: Jack Leonard)
2 ROSALIE   Sammy Kaye Orch. (VR: Tommy Ryan)
3 YOU'RE A SWEETHEART   Dollie Dawn
4 TRUE CONFESSION   Larry Clinton Orch. (VR: Bea Wain)
5 THERE'S A GOLD MINE IN THE SKY   Bing Crosby
6 BEI MIR BIST DU SCHOEN   Andrews Sisters *
7 VIENI, VIENI   Rudy Vallee
8 BOB WHITE   Benny Goodman Orch. (VR: Martha Tilton)
9 I DOUBLE DARE YOU   Russ Morgan Orch. (VR: Bernice Parks)
10 YOU CAN'T STOP ME FROM DREAMING   Teddy Wilson Orch.
   Note: * Another version by: Guy Lombardo Orch. (VR: Carmen Lombardo).

January 15, 1938
1 ROSALIE   Sammy Kaye Orch. (VR: Tommy Ryan)
2 ONCE IN A WHILE   Tommy Dorsey Orch. (VR: Jack Leonard)
3 BEI MIR BIST DU SCHOEN   Andrews Sisters *

4   TRUE CONFESSION   Larry Clinton Orch. (VR: Bea Wain)
5   YOU'RE A SWEETHEART   Dollie Dawn
6   THERE'S A GOLD MINE IN THE SKY   Bing Crosby
7   NICE WORK IF YOU CAN GET IT   Fred Astaire
8   VIENI, VIENI   Rudy Vallee
9   BOB WHITE   Benny Goodman Orch. (VR: Martha Tilton)
10   I DOUBLE DARE YOU   Russ Morgan Orch. (VR: Bernice
     Parks)
     Note: * Another version by: Guy Lombardo Orch. (VR:
     Carmen Lombardo).

January 22, 1938
1   BEI MIR BIST DU SCHOEN   Andrews Sisters *
2   ROSALIE   Sammy Kaye Orch. (VR: Tommy Ryan)
3   TRUE CONFESSION   Larry Clinton Orch. (VR: Bea Wain)
4   YOU'RE A SWEETHEART   Dollie Dawn
5   ONCE IN A WHILE   Tommy Dorsey Orch. (VR: Jack
     Leonard)
6   DIPSY DOODLE   Tommy Dorsey Orch. (VR: Edythe
     Wright)
7   THERE'S A GOLD MINE IN THE SKY   Bing Crosby
8   I DOUBLE DARE YOU   Russ Morgan Orch. (VR: Bernice
     Parks)
9   SWEET SOMEONE   Horace Heidt Orch. (VR: Larry Cotton)
10   IN THE STILL OF THE NIGHT   Tommy Dorsey Orch. (VR:
     Jack Leonard)
     Note: * Another version by: Guy Lombardo Orch. (VR:
     Carmen Lombardo).

January 29, 1938
1   YOU'RE A SWEETHEART   Dollie Dawn
2   BEI MIR BIST DU SCHOEN   Andrews Sisters *
3   ROSALIE   Sammy Kaye Orch. (VR: Tommy Ryan)
4   TRUE CONFESSION   Larry Clinton Orch. (VR: Bea Wain)
5   ONCE IN A WHILE   Tommy Dorsey Orch. (VR: Jack
     Leonard)
6   I DOUBLE DARE YOU   Russ Morgan Orch. (VR: Bernice
     Parks)
7   DIPSY DOODLE   Tommy Dorsey Orch. (VR: Edythe
     Wright)
8   THERE'S A GOLD MINE IN THE SKY   Bing Crosby
9   NICE WORK IF YOU CAN GET IT   Fred Astaire
10   YOU TOOK THE WORDS RIGHT OUT OF MY HEART
     Benny Goodman Orch. (VR: Martha Tilton)
     Note: * Another version by: Guy Lombardo Orch. (VR:
     Carmen Lombardo).

February 5, 1938
1   ROSALIE   Sammy Kaye Orch. (VR: Tommy Ryan)
2   BEI MIR BIST DU SCHOEN   Andrews Sisters *
3   YOU'RE A SWEETHEART   Dollie Dawn
4   DIPSY DOODLE   Tommy Dorsey Orch. (VR: Edythe
     Wright)
5   I DOUBLE DARE YOU   Russ Morgan Orch. (VR: Bernice
     Parks)
6   TRUE CONFESSION   Larry Clinton Orch. (VR: Bea Wain)
7   THERE'S A GOLD MINE IN THE SKY   Bing Crosby
8   YOU TOOK THE WORDS RIGHT OUT OF MY HEART
     Benny Goodman Orch. (VR: Martha Tilton)
9   MAMA, THAT MOON IS HERE AGAIN   Shep Fields
10   WHISTLE WHILE YOU WORK   Shep Fields Orch. (VR: Bob
     Goday)
     Note: * Another version by: Guy Lombardo Orch. (VR:
     Carmen Lombardo).

February 12, 1938
1   BEI MIR BIST DU SCHOEN   Andrews Sisters *

2   YOU'RE A SWEETHEART   Dollie Dawn
3   I DOUBLE DARE YOU   Russ Morgan Orch. (VR: Bernice
     Parks)
4   DIPSY DOODLE   Tommy Dorsey Orch. (VR: Edythe
     Wright)
5   THANKS FOR THE MEMORY   Shep Fields Orch. (VR: Bob
     Goday) **
6   ROSALIE   Sammy Kaye Orch. (VR: Tommy Ryan)
7   WHISTLE WHILE YOU WORK   Shep Fields Orch. (VR: Bob
     Goday)
8   SWEET SOMEONE   Horace Heidt Orch. (VR: Larry Cotton)
9   THERE'S A GOLD MINE IN THE SKY   Bing Crosby
10   TRUE CONFESSION   Larry Clinton Orch. (VR: Bea Wain)
     Note: * Another version by: Guy Lombardo Orch. (VR:
     Carmen Lombardo).
     ** Became Bob Hope's theme song.

February 19, 1938
1   YOU'RE A SWEETHEART   Dollie Dawn
2   BEI MIR BIST DU SCHOEN   Andrews Sisters *
3   I DOUBLE DARE YOU   Russ Morgan Orch. (VR: Bernice
     Parks)
4   DIPSY DOODLE   Tommy Dorsey Orch. (VR: Edythe
     Wright)
5   TRUE CONFESSION   Larry Clinton Orch. (VR: Bea Wain)
6   THANKS FOR THE MEMORY   Shep Fields Orch. (VR: Bob
     Goday) **
7   ROSALIE   Sammy Kaye Orch. (VR: Tommy Ryan)
8   YOU TOOK THE WORDS RIGHT OUT OF MY HEART
     Benny Goodman Orch. (VR: Martha Tilton)
9   THERE'S A GOLD MINE IN THE SKY   Bing Crosby
10   WHISTLE WHILE YOU WORK   Shep Fields Orch. (VR: Bob
     Goday)
     Note: * Another version by: Guy Lombardo Orch. (VR:
     Carmen Lombardo).
     ** Became Bob Hope's theme song.

February 26, 1938
1   I DOUBLE DARE YOU   Russ Morgan Orch. (VR: Bernice
     Parks)
2   THANKS FOR THE MEMORY   Shep Fields Orch. (VR: Bob
     Goday) *
3   DIPSY DOODLE   Tommy Dorsey Orch. (VR: Edythe
     Wright)
4   YOU'RE A SWEETHEART   Dollie Dawn
5   BEI MIR BIST DU SCHOEN   Andrews Sisters **
6   ROSALIE   Sammy Kaye Orch. (VR: Tommy Ryan)
7   GOODNIGHT, ANGEL   Artie Shaw Orch. (VR: Nita Bradley)
8   THERE'S A GOLD MINE IN THE SKY   Bing Crosby
9   WHISTLE WHILE YOU WORK   Shep Fields Orch. (VR: Bob
     Goday)
10   I CAN DREAM, CAN'T I?   Tommy Dorsey Orch. (VR: Jack
     Leonard)
     Note: * Became Bob Hope's theme song.
     ** Another version by: Guy Lombardo Orch. (VR:
     Carmen Lombardo).

March 5, 1938
1   THANKS FOR THE MEMORY   Shep Fields Orch. (VR: Bob
     Goday) *
2   I DOUBLE DARE YOU   Russ Morgan Orch. (VR: Bernice
     Parks)
3   WHISTLE WHILE YOU WORK   Shep Fields Orch. (VR: Bob
     Goday)
4   YOU'RE A SWEETHEART   Dollie Dawn
5   SWEET AS A SONG   Horace Heidt Orch. (VR: Larry
     Cotton)

6 THERE'S A GOLD MINE IN THE SKY   Bing Crosby
7 DIPSY DOODLE   Tommy Dorsey Orch. (VR: Edythe Wright)
8 GOODNIGHT, ANGEL   Artie Shaw Orch. (VR: Nita Bradley)
9 BEI MIR BIST DU SCHOEN   Andrews Sisters **
10 ROSALIE   Sammy Kaye Orch. (VR: Tommy Ryan)
   Note: * Became Bob Hope's theme song.
          ** Another version by: Guy Lombardo Orch. (VR: Carmen Lombardo).

March 12, 1938
1 THANKS FOR THE MEMORY   Shep Fields Orch. (VR: Bob Goday) *
2 WHISTLE WHILE YOU WORK   Shep Fields Orch. (VR: Bob Goday)
3 I DOUBLE DARE YOU   Russ Morgan Orch. (VR: Bernice Parks)
4 I CAN DREAM, CAN'T I?   Tommy Dorsey Orch. (VR: Jack Leonard)
5 DIPSY DOODLE   Tommy Dorsey Orch. (VR: Edythe Wright)
6 YOU'RE A SWEETHEART   Dollie Dawn
7 SWEET AS A SONG   Horace Heidt Orch. (VR: Larry Cotton)
8 THERE'S A GOLD MINE IN THE SKY   Bing Crosby
9 I SEE YOUR FACE BEFORE ME   Guy Lombardo Orch. (VR: Carmen Lombardo)
10 ROSALIE   Sammy Kaye Orch. (VR: Tommy Ryan)
   Note: * Became Bob Hope's theme song.

March 19, 1938
1 THANKS FOR THE MEMORY   Shep Fields Orch. (VR: Bob Goday) *
2 WHISTLE WHILE YOU WORK   Shep Fields Orch. (VR: Bob Goday)
3 I DOUBLE DARE YOU   Russ Morgan Orch. (VR: Bernice Parks)
4 SWEET AS A SONG   Horace Heidt Orch. (VR: Larry Cotton)
5 DIPSY DOODLE   Tommy Dorsey Orch. (VR: Edythe Wright)
6 PLEASE BE KIND   Red Norvo Orch. (VR: Mildred Bailey)
7 TI PI TIN   Horace Heidt Orch. (VR: Lysbeth Hughes & Larry Cotton)
8 HEIGH HO   Horace Heidt Orch. (VR: King's Men & Glee Club) **
9 YOU'RE AN EDUCATION   Larry Clinton (VR: Bea Wain)
10 LET'S SAIL TO DREAMLAND   Guy Lombardo Orch. (VR: Carmen Lombardo)
   Note: * Became Bob Hope's theme song.
          ** From the movie "Snow White And The Seven Dwarfs."

March 26, 1938
1 TI PI TIN   Horace Heidt Orch. (VR: Lysbeth Hughes & Larry Cotton)
2 THANKS FOR THE MEMORY   Shep Fields Orch. (VR: Bob Goday) *
3 WHISTLE WHILE YOU WORK   Shep Fields Orch. (VR: Bob Goday)
4 GOODNIGHT, ANGEL   Artie Shaw Orch. (VR: Nita Bradley)
5 IT'S WONDERFUL   Benny Goodman Orch. (VR: Martha Tilton)
6 HEIGH HO   Horace Heidt Orch. (VR: King's Men & Glee Club) **
7 I DOUBLE DARE YOU   Russ Morgan Orch. (VR: Bernice Parks)

8 SWEET AS A SONG   Horace Heidt Orch. (VR: Larry Cotton)
9 HOW JA LIKE TO LOVE ME   Jimmy Dorsey Orch. (VR: Don Mattison)
10 DIPSY DOODLE   Tommy Dorsey Orch. (VR: Edythe Wright)
   Note: * Became Bob Hope's theme song.
          ** From the movie "Snow White And The Seven Dwarfs."

April 2, 1938
1 TI PI TIN   Horace Heidt Orch. (VR: Lysbeth Hughes & Larry Cotton)
2 THANKS FOR THE MEMORY   Shep Fields Orch. (VR: Bob Goday) *
3 WHISTLE WHILE YOU WORK   Shep Fields Orch. (VR: Bob Goday)
4 GOODNIGHT, ANGEL   Artie Shaw Orch. (VR: Nita Bradley)
5 THERE'S A GOLD MINE IN THE SKY   Bing Crosby
6 YOU'RE AN EDUCATION   Larry Clinton (VR: Bea Wain)
7 PLEASE BE KIND   Red Norvo Orch. (VR: Mildred Bailey)
8 IT'S WONDERFUL   Benny Goodman Orch. (VR: Martha Tilton)
9 LOVE WALKED IN   Sammy Kay Orch. (VR: Tommy Ryan)
10 HEIGH HO   Horace Heidt Orch. (VR: King's Men & Glee Club) **
   Note: * Became Bob Hope's theme song.
          ** From the movie "Snow White And The Seven Dwarfs."

April 9, 1938
1 TI PI TIN   Horace Heidt Orch. (VR: Lysbeth Hughes & Larry Cotton)
2 THANKS FOR THE MEMORY   Shep Fields Orch. (VR: Bob Goday) *
3 PLEASE BE KIND   Red Norvo Orch. (VR: Mildred Bailey)
4 HEIGH HO   Horace Heidt Orch. (VR: King's Men & Glee Club) **
5 WHISTLE WHILE YOU WORK   Shep Fields Orch. (VR: Bob Goday)
6 YOU'RE AN EDUCATION   Larry Clinton (VR: Bea Wain)
7 LOVE WALKED IN   Sammy Kay Orch. (VR: Tommy Ryan)
8 I CAN DREAM, CAN'T I?   Tommy Dorsey Orch. (VR: Jack Leonard)
9 GOODNIGHT, ANGEL   Artie Shaw Orch. (VR: Nita Bradley)
10 ALWAYS AND ALWAYS   Larry Clinton Orch. (VR: Bea Wain)
   Note: * Became Bob Hope's theme song.
          ** From the movie "Snow White And The Seven Dwarfs."

April 16, 1938
1 TI PI TIN   Horace Heidt Orch. (VR: Lysbeth Hughes & Larry Cotton)
2 PLEASE BE KIND   Red Norvo Orch. (VR: Mildred Bailey)
3 LOVE WALKED IN   Sammy Kay Orch. (VR: Tommy Ryan)
4 HEIGH HO   Horace Heidt Orch. (VR: King's Men & Glee Club) *
5 GOODNIGHT, ANGEL   Artie Shaw Orch. (VR: Nita Bradley)
6 YOU'RE AN EDUCATION   Larry Clinton (VR: Bea Wain)
7 THANKS FOR THE MEMORY   Shep Fields Orch. (VR: Bob Goday) **
8 I FALL IN LOVE WITH YOU EVERY DAY   Jimmy Dorsey Orch. (VR: Bob Eberly)
9 WHISTLE WHILE YOU WORK   Shep Fields Orch. (VR: Bob Goday)

10   I LOVE TO WHISTLE   Fats Waller Orch. (VR: Fats Waller)
    Note: * From the movie "Snow White And The Seven Dwarfs."
         ** Became Bob Hope's theme song.

April 23, 1938

1   TI PI TIN   Horace Heidt Orch. (VR: Lysbeth Hughes & Larry Cotton)
2   GOODNIGHT, ANGEL   Artie Shaw Orch. (VR: Nita Bradley)
3   PLEASE BE KIND   Red Norvo Orch. (VR: Mildred Bailey)
4   WHISTLE WHILE YOU WORK   Shep Fields Orch. (VR: Bob Goday)
5   ON THE SENTIMENTAL SIDE   Bing Crosby
6   HOW JA LIKE TO LOVE ME   Jimmy Dorsey Orch. (VR: Don Mattison)
7   LOVE WALKED IN   Sammy Kay Orch. (VR: Tommy Ryan)
8   HEIGH HO   Horace Heidt Orch. (VR: King's Men & Glee Club) *
9   AT A PERFUME COUNTER   Jimmy Dorsey Orch. (VR: Bob Eberly)
10   YOU'RE AN EDUCATION   Larry Clinton (VR: Bea Wain)
    Note: * From the movie "Snow White And The Seven Dwarfs."

April 30, 1938

1   TI PI TIN   Horace Heidt Orch. (VR: Lysbeth Hughes & Larry Cotton)
2   PLEASE BE KIND   Red Norvo Orch. (VR: Mildred Bailey)
3   LOVE WALKED IN   Sammy Kay Orch. (VR: Tommy Ryan)
4   HOW JA LIKE TO LOVE ME   Jimmy Dorsey Orch. (VR: Don Mattison)
5   DON'T BE THAT WAY   Benny Goodman Orch.
6   CRY, BABY, CRY   Larry Clinton Orch. (VR: Bea Wain)
7   HEIGH HO   Horace Heidt Orch. (VR: King's Men & Glee Club) *
8   I FALL IN LOVE WITH YOU EVERY DAY   Jimmy Dorsey Orch. (VR: Bob Eberly)
9   GOODNIGHT, ANGEL   Artie Shaw Orch. (VR: Nita Bradley)
10   SUNDAY IN THE PARK   Hudson-DeLange Orch. (VR: Mary McHugh)
    Note: * From the movie "Snow White And The Seven Dwarfs."

May 7, 1938

1   PLEASE BE KIND   Red Norvo Orch. (VR: Mildred Bailey)
2   TI PI TIN   Horace Heidt Orch. (VR: Lysbeth Hughes & Larry Cotton)
3   CRY, BABY, CRY   Larry Clinton Orch. (VR: Bea Wain)
4   HOW JA LIKE TO LOVE ME   Jimmy Dorsey Orch. (VR: Don Mattison)
5   YOU'RE AN EDUCATION   Larry Clinton (VR: Bea Wain)
6   HEIGH HO   Horace Heidt Orch. (VR: King's Men & Glee Club) *
7   LOVE WALKED IN   Sammy Kay Orch. (VR: Tommy Ryan)
8   YOU COULDN'T BE CUTER   Tommy Dorsey Orch. (VR: Edythe Wright)
9   ON THE SENTIMENTAL SIDE   Bing Crosby
10   DON'T BE THAT WAY   Benny Goodman Orch.
    Note: * From the movie "Snow White And The Seven Dwarfs."

May 14, 1938

1   LOVE WALKED IN   Sammy Kay Orch. (VR: Tommy Ryan)
2   PLEASE BE KIND   Red Norvo Orch. (VR: Mildred Bailey)
3   CRY, BABY, CRY   Larry Clinton Orch. (VR: Bea Wain)
4   DON'T BE THAT WAY   Benny Goodman Orch.
5   TI PI TIN   Horace Heidt Orch. (VR: Lysbeth Hughes & Larry Cotton)
6   HOW JA LIKE TO LOVE ME   Jimmy Dorsey Orch. (VR: Don Mattison)

7   YOU'RE AN EDUCATION   Larry Clinton (VR: Bea Wain)
8   I LOVE TO WHISTLE   Fats Waller Orch. (VR: Fats Waller)
9   GOODNIGHT, ANGEL   Artie Shaw Orch. (VR: Nita Bradley)
10   HEIGH HO   Horace Heidt Orch. (VR: King's Men & Glee Club) *
    Note: * From the movie "Snow White And The Seven Dwarfs."

May 21, 1938

1   LOVE WALKED IN   Sammy Kay Orch. (VR: Tommy Ryan)
2   PLEASE BE KIND   Red Norvo Orch. (VR: Mildred Bailey)
3   CRY, BABY, CRY   Larry Clinton Orch. (VR: Bea Wain)
4   DON'T BE THAT WAY   Benny Goodman Orch.
5   I LOVE TO WHISTLE   Fats Waller Orch. (VR: Fats Waller)
6   TI PI TIN   Horace Heidt Orch. (VR: Lysbeth Hughes & Larry Cotton)
7   ON THE SENTIMENTAL SIDE   Bing Crosby
8   YOU'RE AN EDUCATION   Larry Clinton (VR: Bea Wain)
9   YOU COULDN'T BE CUTER   Tommy Dorsey Orch. (VR: Edythe Wright)
10   HEIGH HO   Horace Heidt Orch. (VR: King's Men & Glee Club) *
    Note: * From the movie "Snow White And The Seven Dwarfs."

May 28, 1938

1   LOVE WALKED IN   Sammy Kay Orch. (VR: Tommy Ryan)
2   PLEASE BE KIND   Red Norvo Orch. (VR: Mildred Bailey)
3   DON'T BE THAT WAY   Benny Goodman Orch.
4   CRY, BABY, CRY   Larry Clinton Orch. (VR: Bea Wain)
5   TI PI TIN   Horace Heidt Orch. (VR: Lysbeth Hughes & Larry Cotton)
6   CATHEDRAL IN THE PINES   Shep Fields Orch. (VR: Jerry Steward)
7   HOW JA LIKE TO LOVE ME   Jimmy Dorsey Orch. (VR: Don Mattison)
8   ON THE SENTIMENTAL SIDE   Bing Crosby
9   HEIGH HO   Horace Heidt Orch. (VR: King's Men & Glee Club) *
10   I LET A SONG GO OUT OF MY HEART   Duke Ellington Orch. **
    Note: * From the movie "Snow White And The Seven Dwarfs."
         ** Another version by: Benny Goodman Orch. (VR: Martha Tilton).

June 4, 1938

1   LOVE WALKED IN   Sammy Kay Orch. (VR: Tommy Ryan)
2   DON'T BE THAT WAY   Benny Goodman Orch.
3   CRY, BABY, CRY   Larry Clinton Orch. (VR: Bea Wain)
4   PLEASE BE KIND   Red Norvo Orch. (VR: Mildred Bailey)
5   ON THE SENTIMENTAL SIDE   Bing Crosby
6   LOVELIGHT IN THE STARLIGHT   Horace Heidt Orch. (VR: Larry Cotton)
7   CATHEDRAL IN THE PINES   Shep Fields Orch. (VR: Jerry Steward)
8   TI PI TIN   Horace Heidt Orch. (VR: Lysbeth Hughes & Larry Cotton)
9   BEWILDERED   Tommy Dorsey Orch. (VR: Jack Leonard)
10   YOU LEAVE ME BREATHLESS   Tommy Dorsey Orch. (VR: Jack Leonard)

June 11, 1938

1   CRY, BABY, CRY   Larry Clinton Orch. (VR: Bea Wain)
2   SAYS MY HEART   Red Norvo Orch. (VR: Mildred Bailey)
3   LOVELIGHT IN THE STARLIGHT   Horace Heidt Orch. (VR: Larry Cotton)
4   LOVE WALKED IN   Sammy Kay Orch. (VR: Tommy Ryan)
5   YOU LEAVE ME BREATHLESS   Tommy Dorsey Orch. (VR: Jack Leonard)

6 PLEASE BE KIND   Red Norvo Orch. (VR: Mildred Bailey)
7 DON'T BE THAT WAY   Benny Goodman Orch.
8 LET ME WHISPER   Bing Crosby
9 CATHEDRAL IN THE PINES   Shep Fields Orch. (VR: Jerry Steward)
10 YOU COULDN'T BE CUTER   Tommy Dorsey Orch. (VR: Edythe Wright)

June 18, 1938

1 SAYS MY HEART   Red Norvo Orch. (VR: Mildred Bailey)
2 CRY, BABY, CRY   Larry Clinton Orch. (VR: Bea Wain)
3 YOU LEAVE ME BREATHLESS   Tommy Dorsey Orch. (VR: Jack Leonard)
4 LOVELIGHT IN THE STARLIGHT   Horace Heidt Orch. (VR: Larry Cotton)
5 CATHEDRAL IN THE PINES   Shep Fields Orch. (VR: Jerry Steward)
6 DON'T BE THAT WAY   Benny Goodman Orch.
7 LOVE WALKED IN   Sammy Kay Orch. (VR: Tommy Ryan)
8 I LET A SONG GO OUT OF MY HEART   Duke Ellington Orch. *
9 LET ME WHISPER   Bing Crosby
10 PLEASE BE KIND   Red Norvo Orch. (VR: Mildred Bailey)
   Note: * Another version by: Benny Goodman Orch. (VR: Martha Tilton).

June 25, 1938

1 SAYS MY HEART   Red Norvo Orch. (VR: Mildred Bailey)
2 I LET A SONG GO OUT OF MY HEART   Duke Ellington Orch. *
3 MUSIC, MAESTRO, PLEASE   Tommy Dorsey Orch. (VR: Edythe Wright)
4 YOU LEAVE ME BREATHLESS   Tommy Dorsey Orch. (VR: Jack Leonard)
5 LOVELIGHT IN THE STARLIGHT   Horace Heidt Orch. (VR: Larry Cotton)
6 CRY, BABY, CRY   Larry Clinton Orch. (VR: Bea Wain)
7 LOVE WALKED IN   Sammy Kay Orch. (VR: Tommy Ryan)
8 OH, MA, MA   Rudy Vallee
9 CATHEDRAL IN THE PINES   Shep Fields Orch. (VR: Jerry Steward)
10 DON'T BE THAT WAY   Benny Goodman Orch.
   Note: * Another version by: Benny Goodman Orch. (VR: Martha Tilton).

July 2, 1938

1 SAYS MY HEART   Red Norvo Orch. (VR: Mildred Bailey)
2 MUSIC, MAESTRO, PLEASE   Tommy Dorsey Orch. (VR: Edythe Wright)
3 I LET A SONG GO OUT OF MY HEART   Duke Ellington Orch. *
4 YOU LEAVE ME BREATHLESS   Tommy Dorsey Orch. (VR: Jack Leonard)
5 LOVELIGHT IN THE STARLIGHT   Horace Heidt Orch. (VR: Larry Cotton)
6 THIS TIME IT'S REAL   Horace Heidt Orch. (VR: Larry Cotton)
7 CATHEDRAL IN THE PINES   Shep Fields Orch. (VR: Jerry Steward)
8 OH, MA, MA   Rudy Vallee
9 LOVE WALKED IN   Sammy Kay Orch. (VR: Tommy Ryan)
10 MY MARGUERITA   Horace Heidt Orch. (VR: Larry Cotton, Bob McCoy & the Charioteers)
   Note: * Another version by: Benny Goodman Orch. (VR: Martha Tilton).

July 9, 1938

1 SAYS MY HEART   Red Norvo Orch. (VR: Mildred Bailey)
2 I LET A SONG GO OUT OF MY HEART   Duke Ellington Orch. *
3 MUSIC, MAESTRO, PLEASE   Tommy Dorsey Orch. (VR: Edythe Wright)
4 I MARRIED AN ANGEL   Larry Clinton Orch. (VR: Bea Wain)
5 YOU LEAVE ME BREATHLESS   Tommy Dorsey Orch. (VR: Jack Leonard)
6 FLAT FOOT FLOOGEY   Slim & Slam
7 DAY DREAMING   Rudy Vallee
8 OH, MA, MA   Rudy Vallee
9 I HADN'T ANYONE 'TIL YOU   Ray Noble Orch. (VR: Tony Martin)
10 CATHEDRAL IN THE PINES   Shep Fields Orch. (VR: Jerry Steward)
   Note: * Another version by: Benny Goodman Orch. (VR: Martha Tilton).

July 16, 1938

1 MUSIC, MAESTRO, PLEASE   Tommy Dorsey Orch. (VR: Edythe Wright)
2 SAYS MY HEART   Red Norvo Orch. (VR: Mildred Bailey)
3 I LET A SONG GO OUT OF MY HEART   Duke Ellington Orch. *
4 YOU LEAVE ME BREATHLESS   Tommy Dorsey Orch. (VR: Jack Leonard)
5 I HADN'T ANYONE 'TIL YOU   Ray Noble Orch. (VR: Tony Martin)
6 I MARRIED AN ANGEL   Larry Clinton Orch. (VR: Bea Wain)
7 LITTLE LADY MAKE BELIEVE   Guy Lombardo Orch. (VR: Carmen Lombardo)
8 FLAT FOOT FLOOGEY   Slim & Slam
9 CATHEDRAL IN THE PINES   Shep Fields Orch. (VR: Jerry Steward)
10 LOVELIGHT IN THE STARLIGHT   Horace Heidt Orch. (VR: Larry Cotton)
   Note: * Another version by: Benny Goodman Orch. (VR: Martha Tilton).

July 23, 1938

1 MUSIC, MAESTRO, PLEASE   Tommy Dorsey Orch. (VR: Edythe Wright)
2 SAYS MY HEART   Red Norvo Orch. (VR: Mildred Bailey)
3 I LET A SONG GO OUT OF MY HEART   Duke Ellington Orch. *
4 I HADN'T ANYONE 'TIL YOU   Ray Noble Orch. (VR: Tony Martin)
5 FLAT FOOT FLOOGEY   Slim & Slam
6 YOU LEAVE ME BREATHLESS   Tommy Dorsey Orch. (VR: Jack Leonard)
7 LOVELIGHT IN THE STARLIGHT   Horace Heidt Orch. (VR: Larry Cotton)
8 I MARRIED AN ANGEL   Larry Clinton Orch. (VR: Bea Wain)
9 WHEN THEY PLAYED THE POLKA   Sammy Kaye Orch. (VR: Glee Club)
10 THERE'S HONEY ON THE MOON TONIGHT   Vincent Lopez Orch. (VR: Johnny Morris)
   Note: * Another version by: Benny Goodman Orch. (VR: Martha Tilton).

July 30, 1938

1 I LET A SONG GO OUT OF MY HEART   Duke Ellington Orch. *
2 SAYS MY HEART   Red Norvo Orch. (VR: Mildred Bailey)
3 MUSIC, MAESTRO, PLEASE   Tommy Dorsey Orch. (VR: Edythe Wright)

4 I MARRIED AN ANGEL   Larry Clinton Orch. (VR: Bea Wain)
5 FLAT FOOT FLOOGEY   Slim & Slam
6 WHEN MOTHER NATURE SINGS HER LULLABY   Bing Crosby
7 WHERE IN THE WORLD   Hal Kemp Orch. (VR: Bob Allen)
8 THIS TIME IT'S REAL   Horace Heidt Orch. (VR: Larry Cotton)
9 I'M GONNA LOCK MY HEART   Billie Holiday
10 LITTLE LADY MAKE BELIEVE   Guy Lombardo Orch. (VR: Carmen Lombardo)
   Note: * Another version by: Benny Goodman Orch. (VR: Martha Tilton).

August 6, 1938
1 MUSIC, MAESTRO, PLEASE   Tommy Dorsey Orch. (VR: Edythe Wright)
2 I LET A SONG GO OUT OF MY HEART   Duke Ellington Orch. *
3 SAYS MY HEART   Red Norvo Orch. (VR: Mildred Bailey)
4 I MARRIED AN ANGEL   Larry Clinton Orch. (VR: Bea Wain)
5 I HADN'T ANYONE 'TIL YOU   Ray Noble Orch. (VR: Tony Martin)
6 WHEN MOTHER NATURE SINGS HER LULLABY   Bing Crosby
7 FLAT FOOT FLOOGEY   Slim & Slam
8 NOW IT CAN BE TOLD   Tommy Dorsey Orch. (VR: Jack Leonard)
9 A-TISKET, A-TASKET   Ella Fitzgerald with Chuck Webb Orch.
10 LITTLE LADY MAKE BELIEVE   Guy Lombardo Orch. (VR: Carmen Lombardo)
   Note: * Another version by: Benny Goodman Orch. (VR: Martha Tilton).

August 13, 1938
1 MUSIC, MAESTRO, PLEASE   Tommy Dorsey Orch. (VR: Edythe Wright)
2 A-TISKET, A-TASKET   Ella Fitzgerald with Chuck Webb Orch.
3 I LET A SONG GO OUT OF MY HEART   Duke Ellington Orch. *
4 WHEN MOTHER NATURE SINGS HER LULLABY   Bing Crosby
5 I HADN'T ANYONE 'TIL YOU   Ray Noble Orch. (VR: Tony Martin)
6 SAYS MY HEART   Red Norvo Orch. (VR: Mildred Bailey)
7 I'M GONNA LOCK MY HEART   Billie Holiday
8 FLAT FOOT FLOOGEY   Slim & Slam
9 NOW IT CAN BE TOLD   Tommy Dorsey Orch. (VR: Jack Leonard)
10 I MARRIED AN ANGEL   Larry Clinton Orch. (VR: Bea Wain)
   Note: * Another version by: Benny Goodman Orch. (VR: Martha Tilton).

August 20, 1938
1 A-TISKET, A-TASKET   Ella Fitzgerald with Chuck Webb Orch.
2 MUSIC, MAESTRO, PLEASE   Tommy Dorsey Orch. (VR: Edythe Wright)
3 I'M GONNA LOCK MY HEART   Billie Holiday
4 I LET A SONG GO OUT OF MY HEART   Duke Ellington Orch. *
5 I HADN'T ANYONE 'TIL YOU   Ray Noble Orch. (VR: Tony Martin)
6 NOW IT CAN BE TOLD   Tommy Dorsey Orch. (VR: Jack Leonard)
7 SAYS MY HEART   Red Norvo Orch. (VR: Mildred Bailey)

8 I MARRIED AN ANGEL   Larry Clinton Orch. (VR: Bea Wain)
9 WHERE IN THE WORLD   Hal Kemp Orch. (VR: Bob Allen)
10 YOU GO TO MY HEAD   Larry Clinton Orch. (VR: Bea Wain)
   Note: * Another version by: Benny Goodman Orch. (VR: Martha Tilton).

August 27, 1938
1 A-TISKET, A-TASKET   Ella Fitzgerald with Chuck Webb Orch.
2 MUSIC, MAESTRO, PLEASE   Tommy Dorsey Orch. (VR: Edythe Wright)
3 I'M GONNA LOCK MY HEART   Billie Holiday
4 NOW IT CAN BE TOLD   Tommy Dorsey Orch. (VR: Jack Leonard)
5 WHEN MOTHER NATURE SINGS HER LULLABY   Bing Crosby
6 I LET A SONG GO OUT OF MY HEART   Duke Ellington Orch. *
7 WHAT GOES ON HERE IN MY HEART   Benny Goodman Orch. (VR: Martha Tilton)
8 YOU GO TO MY HEAD   Larry Clinton Orch. (VR: Bea Wain)
9 SAYS MY HEART   Red Norvo Orch. (VR: Mildred Bailey)
10 I HADN'T ANYONE 'TIL YOU   Ray Noble Orch. (VR: Tony Martin)
   Note: * Another version by: Benny Goodman Orch. (VR: Martha Tilton).

September 3, 1938
1 A-TISKET, A-TASKET   Ella Fitzgerald with Chuck Webb Orch.
2 NOW IT CAN BE TOLD   Tommy Dorsey Orch. (VR: Jack Leonard)
3 YOU GO TO MY HEAD   Larry Clinton Orch. (VR: Bea Wain)
4 I'M GONNA LOCK MY HEART   Billie Holiday
5 MUSIC, MAESTRO, PLEASE   Tommy Dorsey Orch. (VR: Edythe Wright)
6 WHEN MOTHER NATURE SINGS HER LULLABY   Bing Crosby
7 I'VE GOT A POCKETFUL OF DREAMS   Bing Crosby *
8 STOP BEATING 'ROUND THE MULBERRY BUSH   Tommy Dorsey Orch. (VR: Edythe Wright & Skeets Herfurt)
9 WHAT GOES ON HERE IN MY HEART   Benny Goodman Orch. (VR: Martha Tilton)
10 SO HELP ME   Mildred Bailey
   Note: * Another version by: Russ Morgan Orch. (VR: Russ Morgan).

September 10, 1938
1 A-TISKET, A-TASKET   Ella Fitzgerald with Chuck Webb Orch.
2 I'M GONNA LOCK MY HEART   Billie Holiday
3 YOU GO TO MY HEAD   Larry Clinton Orch. (VR: Bea Wain)
4 NOW IT CAN BE TOLD   Tommy Dorsey Orch. (VR: Jack Leonard)
5 I'VE GOT A POCKETFUL OF DREAMS   Bing Crosby *
6 MUSIC, MAESTRO, PLEASE   Tommy Dorsey Orch. (VR: Edythe Wright)
7 WHEN MOTHER NATURE SINGS HER LULLABY   Bing Crosby
8 I'VE GOT A DATE WITH A DREAM   Benny Goodman Orch. (VR: Martha Tilton)
9 SO HELP ME   Mildred Bailey
10 ALEXANDER'S RAGTIME BAND   Bing Crosby & Connee Boswell
   Note: * Another version by: Russ Morgan Orch. (VR: Russ Morgan).

September 17, 1938
1   A-TISKET, A-TASKET   Ella Fitzgerald with Chuck Webb Orch.
2   YOU GO TO MY HEAD   Larry Clinton Orch. (VR: Bea Wain)
3   I'VE GOT A POCKETFUL OF DREAMS   Bing Crosby *
4   NOW IT CAN BE TOLD   Tommy Dorsey Orch. (VR: Jack Leonard)
5   I'M GONNA LOCK MY HEART   Billie Holiday
6   STOP BEATING 'ROUND THE MULBERRY BUSH   Tommy Dorsey Orch. (VR: Edythe Wright & Skeets Herfurt)
7   I'VE GOT A DATE WITH A DREAM   Benny Goodman Orch. (VR: Martha Tilton)
8   SO HELP ME   Mildred Bailey
9   ALEXANDER'S RAGTIME BAND   Bing Crosby & Connee Boswell
10 TULIE TULIP TIME   Horace Heidt Orch. (VR: Lysbeth Hughes & Larry Cotton)
    Note: * Another version by: Russ Morgan Orch. (VR: Russ Morgan).

September 24, 1938
1   A-TISKET, A-TASKET   Ella Fitzgerald with Chuck Webb Orch.
2   I'VE GOT A POCKETFUL OF DREAMS   Bing Crosby *
3   YOU GO TO MY HEAD   Larry Clinton Orch. (VR: Bea Wain)
4   STOP BEATING 'ROUND THE MULBERRY BUSH   Tommy Dorsey Orch. (VR: Edythe Wright & Skeets Herfurt)
5   SO HELP ME   Mildred Bailey
6   WHAT GOES ON HERE IN MY HEART   Benny Goodman Orch. (VR: Martha Tilton)
7   NOW IT CAN BE TOLD   Tommy Dorsey Orch. (VR: Jack Leonard)
8   ALEXANDER'S RAGTIME BAND   Bing Crosby & Connee Boswell
9   I'M GONNA LOCK MY HEART   Billie Holiday
10 BAMBINA   Jan Garber Orch. (VR: Lee Bennett)
    Note: * Another version by: Russ Morgan Orch. (VR: Russ Morgan).

October 1, 1938
1   I'VE GOT A POCKETFUL OF DREAMS   Bing Crosby *
2   A-TISKET, A-TASKET   Ella Fitzgerald with Chuck Webb Orch.
3   CHANGE PARTNERS   Fred Astaire **
4   SO HELP ME   Mildred Bailey
5   NOW IT CAN BE TOLD   Tommy Dorsey Orch. (VR: Jack Leonard)
6   STOP BEATING 'ROUND THE MULBERRY BUSH   Tommy Dorsey Orch. (VR: Edythe Wright & Skeets Herfurt)
7   I'VE GOT A DATE WITH A DREAM   Benny Goodman Orch. (VR: Martha Tilton)
8   WHAT GOES ON HERE IN MY HEART   Benny Goodman Orch. (VR: Martha Tilton)
9   YOU GO TO MY HEAD   Larry Clinton Orch. (VR: Bea Wain)
10 ALEXANDER'S RAGTIME BAND   Bing Crosby & Connee Boswell
    Note: * Another version by: Russ Morgan Orch. (VR: Russ Morgan).
    ** Another version by: Jimmy Dorsey Orch. (VR: Bob Eberly).

October 8, 1938
1   I'VE GOT A POCKETFUL OF DREAMS   Bing Crosby *
2   CHANGE PARTNERS   Fred Astaire **
3   LAMBETH WALK   Russ Morgan Orch. (VR: Jimmy Lewis)
4   STOP BEATING 'ROUND THE MULBERRY BUSH   Tommy Dorsey Orch. (VR: Edythe Wright & Skeets Herfurt)
5   SO HELP ME   Mildred Bailey
6   A-TISKET, A-TASKET   Ella Fitzgerald with Chuck Webb Orch.
7   WHAT GOES ON HERE IN MY HEART   Benny Goodman Orch. (VR: Martha Tilton)
8   AT LONG LAST LOVE   Ozzie Nelson Orch. (VR: Ozzie Nelson)
9   ALEXANDER'S RAGTIME BAND   Bing Crosby & Connee Boswell
10 SMALL FRY   Bing Crosby & Johnny Mercer
    Note: * Another version by: Russ Morgan Orch. (VR: Russ Morgan).
    ** Another version by: Jimmy Dorsey Orch. (VR: Bob Eberly).

October 15, 1938
1   CHANGE PARTNERS   Fred Astaire *
2   I'VE GOT A POCKETFUL OF DREAMS   Bing Crosby **
3   STOP BEATING 'ROUND THE MULBERRY BUSH   Tommy Dorsey Orch. (VR: Edythe Wright & Skeets Herfurt)
4   SO HELP ME   Mildred Bailey
5   LAMBETH WALK   Russ Morgan Orch. (VR: Jimmy Lewis)
6   I'VE GOT A DATE WITH A DREAM   Benny Goodman Orch. (VR: Martha Tilton)
7   A-TISKET, A-TASKET   Ella Fitzgerald with Chuck Webb Orch.
8   AT LONG LAST LOVE   Ozzie Nelson Orch. (VR: Ozzie Nelson)
9   ALEXANDER'S RAGTIME BAND   Bing Crosby & Connee Boswell
10 WHAT GOES ON HERE IN MY HEART   Benny Goodman Orch. (VR: Martha Tilton)
    Note: * Another version by: Jimmy Dorsey Orch. (VR: Bob Eberly).
    ** Another version by: Russ Morgan Orch. (VR: Russ Morgan).

October 22, 1938
1   I'VE GOT A POCKETFUL OF DREAMS   Bing Crosby *
2   STOP BEATING 'ROUND THE MULBERRY BUSH   Tommy Dorsey Orch. (VR: Edythe Wright & Skeets Herfurt)
3   ALEXANDER'S RAGTIME BAND   Bing Crosby & Connee Boswell
4   CHANGE PARTNERS   Fred Astaire **
5   SO HELP ME   Mildred Bailey
6   AT LONG LAST LOVE   Ozzie Nelson Orch. (VR: Ozzie Nelson)
7   WHILE A CIGARETTE WAS BURNING   Buddy Rogers Orch. (VR: Buddy Rogers)
8   SMALL FRY   Bing Crosby & Johnny Mercer
9   HEART AND SOUL   Larry Clinton Orch. (VR: Bea Wain)
10 MY REVERIE   Larry Clinton Orch. (VR: Bea Wain)
    Note: * Another version by: Russ Morgan Orch. (VR: Russ Morgan).
    ** Another version by: Jimmy Dorsey Orch. (VR: Bob Eberly).

October 29, 1938
1   I'VE GOT A POCKETFUL OF DREAMS   Bing Crosby *
2   CHANGE PARTNERS   Fred Astaire **
3   SO HELP ME   Mildred Bailey
4   STOP BEATING 'ROUND THE MULBERRY BUSH   Tommy Dorsey Orch. (VR: Edythe Wright & Skeets Herfurt)
5   MY OWN   Tommy Dorsey Orch. (VR: Edythe Wright)
6   HEART AND SOUL   Larry Clinton Orch. (VR: Bea Wain)
7   WHILE A CIGARETTE WAS BURNING   Buddy Rogers Orch. (VR: Buddy Rogers)

Ella Fitzgerald
Ella scores a #1 hit with ``A-Tisket A-Tasket'' (Aug. 20 through Sept. 24).

8 LAMBETH WALK   Russ Morgan Orch. (VR: Jimmy Lewis)
9 AT LONG LAST LOVE   Ozzie Nelson Orch. (VR: Ozzie Nelson)
10 ALEXANDER'S RAGTIME BAND   Bing Crosby & Connee Boswell
Note: * Another version by: Russ Morgan Orch. (VR: Russ Morgan).
    ** Another version by: Jimmy Dorsey Orch. (VR: Bob Eberly).

November 5, 1938
1 CHANGE PARTNERS   Fred Astaire *
2 I'VE GOT A POCKETFUL OF DREAMS   Bing Crosby **
3 LAMBETH WALK   Russ Morgan Orch. (VR: Jimmy Lewis)
4 AT LONG LAST LOVE   Ozzie Nelson Orch. (VR: Ozzie Nelson)
5 HEART AND SOUL   Larry Clinton Orch. (VR: Bea Wain)
6 WHILE A CIGARETTE WAS BURNING   Buddy Rogers Orch. (VR: Buddy Rogers)
7 SO HELP ME   Mildred Bailey
8 MY OWN   Tommy Dorsey Orch. (VR: Edythe Wright)
9 MY REVERIE   Larry Clinton Orch. (VR: Bea Wain)
10 STOP BEATING 'ROUND THE MULBERRY BUSH   Tommy Dorsey Orch. (VR: Edythe Wright & Skeets Herfurt)
Note: * Another version by: Jimmy Dorsey Orch. (VR: Bob Eberly).
    ** Another version by: Russ Morgan Orch. (VR: Russ Morgan).

November 12, 1938
1 MY REVERIE   Larry Clinton Orch. (VR: Bea Wain)
2 HEART AND SOUL   Larry Clinton Orch. (VR: Bea Wain)
3 I'VE GOT A POCKETFUL OF DREAMS   Bing Crosby *
4 CHANGE PARTNERS   Fred Astaire **
5 MY OWN   Tommy Dorsey Orch. (VR: Edythe Wright)
6 WHILE A CIGARETTE WAS BURNING   Buddy Rogers Orch. (VR: Buddy Rogers)
7 ALL ASHORE   Sammy Kaye Orch. (VR: Tommy Ryan)
8 AT LONG LAST LOVE   Ozzie Nelson Orch. (VR: Ozzie Nelson)
9 LAMBETH WALK   Russ Morgan Orch. (VR: Jimmy Lewis)
10 SO HELP ME   Mildred Bailey
Note: * Another version by: Russ Morgan Orch. (VR: Russ Morgan).
    ** Another version by: Jimmy Dorsey Orch. (VR: Bob Eberly).

November 19, 1938
1 MY REVERIE   Larry Clinton Orch. (VR: Bea Wain)
2 HEART AND SOUL   Larry Clinton Orch. (VR: Bea Wain)
3 CHANGE PARTNERS   Fred Astaire *
4 SUMMER SOUVENIRS   Larry Clinton Orch. (VR: Bea Wain)
5 ALL ASHORE   Sammy Kaye Orch. (VR: Tommy Ryan)
6 WHO BLEW OUT THE FLAME   Larry Clinton Orch. (VR: Bea Wain)
7 I'VE GOT A POCKETFUL OF DREAMS   Bing Crosby **
8 SO HELP ME   Mildred Bailey
9 DAY AFTER DAY   Richard Himber Orch. (VR: Stuart Allen)
10 MY OWN   Tommy Dorsey Orch. (VR: Edythe Wright)
Note: * Another version by: Jimmy Dorsey Orch. (VR: Bob Eberly).
    ** Another version by: Russ Morgan Orch. (VR: Russ Morgan).

November 26, 1938
1 MY REVERIE   Larry Clinton Orch. (VR: Bea Wain)
2 HEART AND SOUL   Larry Clinton Orch. (VR: Bea Wain)

3 WHILE A CIGARETTE WAS BURNING   Buddy Rogers Orch. (VR: Buddy Rogers)
4 I'VE GOT A POCKETFUL OF DREAMS   Bing Crosby *
5 ALL ASHORE   Sammy Kaye Orch. (VR: Tommy Ryan)
6 TWO SLEEPY PEOPLE   Fats Waller Orch. (VR: Fats Waller)
7 MY OWN   Tommy Dorsey Orch. (VR: Edythe Wright)
8 LAMBETH WALK   Russ Morgan Orch. (VR: Jimmy Lewis)
9 SUMMER SOUVENIRS   Larry Clinton Orch. (VR: Bea Wain)
10 CHANGE PARTNERS   Fred Astaire **
Note: * Another version by: Russ Morgan Orch. (VR: Russ Morgan).
    ** Another version by: Jimmy Dorsey Orch. (VR: Bob Eberly).

December 3, 1938
1 MY REVERIE   Larry Clinton Orch. (VR: Bea Wain)
2 HEART AND SOUL   Larry Clinton Orch. (VR: Bea Wain)
3 TWO SLEEPY PEOPLE   Fats Waller Orch. (VR: Fats Waller)
4 WHILE A CIGARETTE WAS BURNING   Buddy Rogers Orch. (VR: Buddy Rogers)
5 HAVE YOU FORGOTTEN SO SOON?   Red Norvo Orch. (VR: Mildred Bailey)
6 ALL ASHORE   Sammy Kaye Orch. (VR: Tommy Ryan)
7 DEEP IN A DREAM   Artie Shaw Orch. (VR: Helen Forrest)
8 SIXTY SECONDS GET TOGETHER   Mills Brothers
9 I'VE GOT A POCKETFUL OF DREAMS   Bing Crosby *
10 LAMBETH WALK   Russ Morgan Orch. (VR: Jimmy Lewis)
Note: * Another version by: Russ Morgan Orch. (VR: Russ Morgan).

December 10, 1938
1 MY REVERIE   Larry Clinton Orch. (VR: Bea Wain)
2 TWO SLEEPY PEOPLE   Fats Waller Orch. (VR: Fats Waller)
3 WHILE A CIGARETTE WAS BURNING   Buddy Rogers Orch. (VR: Buddy Rogers)
4 ALL ASHORE   Sammy Kaye Orch. (VR: Tommy Ryan)
5 DEEP IN A DREAM   Artie Shaw Orch. (VR: Helen Forrest)
6 HAVE YOU FORGOTTEN SO SOON?   Red Norvo Orch. (VR: Mildred Bailey)
7 HEART AND SOUL   Larry Clinton Orch. (VR: Bea Wain)
8 LAMBETH WALK   Russ Morgan Orch. (VR: Jimmy Lewis)
9 I'VE GOT A POCKETFUL OF DREAMS   Bing Crosby *
10 SIXTY SECONDS GET TOGETHER   Mills Brothers
Note: * Another version by: Russ Morgan Orch. (VR: Russ Morgan).

December 17, 1938
1 MY REVERIE   Larry Clinton Orch. (VR: Bea Wain)
2 TWO SLEEPY PEOPLE   Fats Waller Orch. (VR: Fats Waller)
3 YOU MUST HAVE BEEN A BEAUTIFUL BABY   Bing Crosby
4 ALL ASHORE   Sammy Kaye Orch. (VR: Tommy Ryan)
5 HAVE YOU FORGOTTEN SO SOON?   Red Norvo Orch. (VR: Mildred Bailey)
6 WHILE A CIGARETTE WAS BURNING   Buddy Rogers Orch. (VR: Buddy Rogers)
7 DEEP IN A DREAM   Artie Shaw Orch. (VR: Helen Forrest)
8 HEART AND SOUL   Larry Clinton Orch. (VR: Bea Wain)
9 MY OWN   Tommy Dorsey Orch. (VR: Edythe Wright)
10 SIXTY SECONDS GET TOGETHER   Mills Brothers

December 24, 1938
1 MY REVERIE   Larry Clinton Orch. (VR: Bea Wain)

Larry Clinton
``My Reverie'' stays in the #1 position for seven weeks (beginning Nov. 12).

2 YOU MUST HAVE BEEN A BEAUTIFUL BABY   Bing Crosby
3 DEEP IN A DREAM   Artie Shaw Orch. (VR: Helen Forrest)
4 ALL ASHORE   Sammy Kaye Orch. (VR: Tommy Ryan)
5 TWO SLEEPY PEOPLE   Fats Waller Orch. (VR: Fats Waller)
6 THIS CAN'T BE LOVE   Benny Goodman Orch. (VR: Martha Tilton)
7 JEEPERS CREEPERS   Al Donohue Orch. (VR: Paula Kelly)
8 NIGHT BEFORE CHRISTMAS   Eddy Duchin Orch. (VR: Stanley Worth)
9 WHAT HAVE YOU GOT THAT GETS ME   Benny Goodman Orch. (VR: Martha Tilton)
10 HEART AND SOUL   Larry Clinton Orch. (VR: Bea Wain)

December 31, 1938
1 YOU MUST HAVE BEEN A BEAUTIFUL BABY   Bing Crosby
2 MY REVERIE   Larry Clinton Orch. (VR: Bea Wain)
3 ALL ASHORE   Sammy Kaye Orch. (VR: Tommy Ryan)
4 TWO SLEEPY PEOPLE   Fats Waller Orch. (VR: Fats Waller)
5 NIGHT BEFORE CHRISTMAS   Eddy Duchin Orch. (VR: Stanley Worth)
6 I WON'T TELL A SOUL   Andy Kirk Orch. (VR: Pha Terrell)
7 THIS CAN'T BE LOVE   Benny Goodman Orch. (VR: Martha Tilton)
8 DEEP IN A DREAM   Artie Shaw Orch. (VR: Helen Forrest)
9 YOU GOT ME   Tommy Dorsey Orch. (VR: Edythe Wright)
10 WHAT HAVE YOU GOT THAT GETS ME   Benny Goodman Orch. (VR: Martha Tilton)

January 7, 1939
1 MY REVERIE   Larry Clinton Orch. (VR: Bea Wain)
2 DEEP IN A DREAM   Artie Shaw Orch. (VR: Helen Forrest)
3 TWO SLEEPY PEOPLE   Fats Waller Orch. (VR: Fats Waller)
4 YOU MUST HAVE BEEN A BEAUTIFUL BABY   Bing Crosby
5 ALL ASHORE   Sammy Kaye Orch. (VR: Tommy Ryan)
6 THEY SAY   Artie Shaw Orch. (VR: Helen Forrest)
7 THANKS FOR EVERYTHING   Artie Shaw Orch. (VR: Helen Forrest)
8 HAVE YOU FORGOTTEN SO SOON?   Red Norvo Orch. (VR: Mildred Bailey)
9 JEEPERS CREEPERS   Al Donohue Orch. (VR: Paula Kelly)
10 THIS CAN'T BE LOVE   Benny Goodman Orch. (VR: Martha Tilton)

January 14, 1939
1 YOU MUST HAVE BEEN A BEAUTIFUL BABY   Bing Crosby
2 TWO SLEEPY PEOPLE   Fats Waller Orch. (VR: Fats Waller)
3 MY REVERIE   Larry Clinton Orch. (VR: Bea Wain)
4 JEEPERS CREEPERS   Al Donohue Orch. (VR: Paula Kelly)
5 THIS CAN'T BE LOVE   Benny Goodman Orch. (VR: Martha Tilton)
6 DEEP IN A DREAM   Artie Shaw Orch. (VR: Helen Forrest)
7 I MUST SEE ANNIE TONIGHT   Guy Lombardo Orch. (VR: Carmen Lombardo, Larry Owen & Fred Henry)
8 UMBRELLA MAN   Kay Kyser Orch. (VR: Ginny Simms & Harry Babbitt)
9 THANKS FOR EVERYTHING   Artie Shaw Orch. (VR: Helen Forrest)
10 F.D.R. JONES   Ella Fitzgerald with Chuck Webb Orch.

January 21, 1939
1 JEEPERS CREEPERS   Al Donohue Orch. (VR: Paula Kelly)

2 MY REVERIE   Larry Clinton Orch. (VR: Bea Wain)
3 YOU MUST HAVE BEEN A BEAUTIFUL BABY   Bing Crosby
4 I MUST SEE ANNIE TONIGHT   Guy Lombardo Orch. (VR: Carmen Lombardo, Larry Owen & Fred Henry)
5 THIS CAN'T BE LOVE   Benny Goodman Orch. (VR: Martha Tilton)
6 UMBRELLA MAN   Kay Kyser Orch. (VR: Ginny Simms & Harry Babbitt)
7 DEEP IN A DREAM   Artie Shaw Orch. (VR: Helen Forrest)
8 TWO SLEEPY PEOPLE   Fats Waller Orch. (VR: Fats Waller)
9 F.D.R. JONES   Ella Fitzgerald with Chuck Webb Orch.
10 THANKS FOR EVERYTHING   Artie Shaw Orch. (VR: Helen Forrest)

January 28, 1939
1 YOU MUST HAVE BEEN A BEAUTIFUL BABY   Bing Crosby
2 JEEPERS CREEPERS   Al Donohue Orch. (VR: Paula Kelly)
3 DEEP IN A DREAM   Artie Shaw Orch. (VR: Helen Forrest)
4 THIS CAN'T BE LOVE   Benny Goodman Orch. (VR: Martha Tilton)
5 TWO SLEEPY PEOPLE   Fats Waller Orch. (VR: Fats Waller)
6 UMBRELLA MAN   Kay Kyser Orch. (VR: Ginny Simms & Harry Babbitt)
7 THANKS FOR EVERYTHING   Artie Shaw Orch. (VR: Helen Forrest)
8 MY REVERIE   Larry Clinton Orch. (VR: Bea Wain)
9 GET OUT OF TOWN   Eddy Duchin
10 THEY SAY   Artie Shaw Orch. (VR: Helen Forrest)

February 4, 1939
1 JEEPERS CREEPERS   Al Donohue Orch. (VR: Paula Kelly)
2 YOU MUST HAVE BEEN A BEAUTIFUL BABY   Bing Crosby
3 DEEP IN A DREAM   Artie Shaw Orch. (VR: Helen Forrest)
4 THANKS FOR EVERYTHING   Artie Shaw Orch. (VR: Helen Forrest)
5 THIS CAN'T BE LOVE   Benny Goodman Orch. (VR: Martha Tilton)
6 UMBRELLA MAN   Kay Kyser Orch. (VR: Ginny Simms & Harry Babbitt)
7 TWO SLEEPY PEOPLE   Fats Waller Orch. (VR: Fats Waller)
8 I HAVE EYES   Bing Crosby
9 THEY SAY   Artie Shaw Orch. (VR: Helen Forrest)
10 F.D.R. JONES   Ella Fitzgerald with Chuck Webb Orch.

February 11, 1939
1 JEEPERS CREEPERS   Al Donohue Orch. (VR: Paula Kelly)
2 THIS CAN'T BE LOVE   Benny Goodman Orch. (VR: Martha Tilton)
3 THANKS FOR EVERYTHING   Artie Shaw Orch. (VR: Helen Forrest)
4 UMBRELLA MAN   Kay Kyser Orch. (VR: Ginny Simms & Harry Babbitt)
5 THEY SAY   Artie Shaw Orch. (VR: Helen Forrest)
6 DEEP IN A DREAM   Artie Shaw Orch. (VR: Helen Forrest)
7 TWO SLEEPY PEOPLE   Fats Waller Orch. (VR: Fats Waller)
8 F.D.R. JONES   Ella Fitzgerald with Chuck Webb Orch.
9 GET OUT OF TOWN   Eddy Duchin
10 I HAVE EYES   Bing Crosby

February 18, 1939
1 JEEPERS CREEPERS   Al Donohue Orch. (VR: Paula Kelly)
2 THIS CAN'T BE LOVE   Benny Goodman Orch. (VR: Martha Tilton)

3 DEEP IN A DREAM   Artie Shaw Orch. (VR: Helen Forrest)
4 I HAVE EYES   Bing Crosby
5 THANKS FOR EVERYTHING   Artie Shaw Orch. (VR: Helen Forrest)
6 UMBRELLA MAN   Kay Kyser Orch. (VR: Ginny Simms & Harry Babbitt)
7 COULD BE   Johnny Messner Orch.
8 THEY SAY   Artie Shaw Orch. (VR: Helen Forrest)
9 HURRY HOME   Sammy Kay Orch. (VR: Charlie Wilson)
10 ANNABELLE   Lawrence Welk Orch.

February 25, 1939
1 JEEPERS CREEPERS   Al Donohue Orch. (VR: Paula Kelly)
2 DEEP PURPLE   Larry Clinton Orch. (VR: Bea Wain)
3 HURRY HOME   Sammy Kay Orch. (VR: Charlie Wilson)
4 COULD BE   Johnny Messner Orch.
5 UMBRELLA MAN   Kay Kyser Orch. (VR: Ginny Simms & Harry Babbitt)
6 THIS CAN'T BE LOVE   Benny Goodman Orch. (VR: Martha Tilton)
7 I PROMISE YOU   Kay Kyser Orch. (VR: Harry Babbitt)
8 PENNY SERENADE   Guy Lombardo Orch. (VR: Carmen Lombardo) *
9 DEEP IN A DREAM   Artie Shaw Orch. (VR: Helen Forrest)
10 ANNABELLE   Lawrence Welk Orch.
   Note: * Another version by: Sammy Kaye Orch. (VR: Jimmy Brown).

March 4, 1939
1 DEEP PURPLE   Larry Clinton Orch. (VR: Bea Wain)
2 UMBRELLA MAN   Kay Kyser Orch. (VR: Ginny Simms & Harry Babbitt)
3 PENNY SERENADE   Guy Lombardo Orch. (VR: Carmen Lombardo) *
4 JEEPERS CREEPERS   Al Donohue Orch. (VR: Paula Kelly)
5 I HAVE EYES   Bing Crosby
6 COULD BE   Johnny Messner Orch.
7 YOU'RE A SWEET LITTLE HEADACHE   Bing Crosby
8 I GET ALONG WITHOUT YOU VERY WELL   Red Norvo Orch. (VR: Terry Allen)
9 DEEP IN A DREAM   Artie Shaw Orch. (VR: Helen Forrest)
10 I CRIED FOR YOU   Glen Gray Orch. (VR: Kenny Sargent)
   Note: * Another version by: Sammy Kaye Orch. (VR: Jimmy Brown).

March 11, 1939
1 DEEP PURPLE   Larry Clinton Orch. (VR: Bea Wain)
2 PENNY SERENADE   Guy Lombardo Orch. (VR: Carmen Lombardo) *
3 YOU'RE A SWEET LITTLE HEADACHE   Bing Crosby
4 COULD BE   Johnny Messner Orch.
5 UMBRELLA MAN   Kay Kyser Orch. (VR: Ginny Simms & Harry Babbitt)
6 JEEPERS CREEPERS   Al Donohue Orch. (VR: Paula Kelly)
7 GOTTA GET SOME SHUTEYE   Kay Kyser Orch. (VR: Harry Babbitt)
8 I HAVE EYES   Bing Crosby
9 I GET ALONG WITHOUT YOU VERY WELL   Red Norvo Orch. (VR: Terry Allen)
10 THE MASQUERADE IS OVER   Jimmy Dorsey Orch. (VR: Bob Eberly)
   Note: * Another version by: Sammy Kaye Orch. (VR: Jimmy Brown)

March 18, 1939
1 DEEP PURPLE   Larry Clinton Orch. (VR: Bea Wain)

2 PENNY SERENADE   Guy Lombardo Orch. (VR: Carmen Lombardo) *
3 UMBRELLA MAN   Kay Kyser Orch. (VR: Ginny Simms & Harry Babbitt)
4 I HAVE EYES   Bing Crosby
5 COULD BE   Johnny Messner Orch.
6 THIS IS IT   Tommy Dorsey Orch. (VR: Jack Leonard)
7 GOTTA GET SOME SHUTEYE   Kay Kyser Orch. (VR: Harry Babbitt)
8 YOU'RE A SWEET LITTLE HEADACHE   Bing Crosby
9 HEAVEN CAN WAIT   Glen Gray Orch. (VR: Clyde Burke)
10 THE MASQUERADE IS OVER   Jimmy Dorsey Orch. (VR: Bob Eberly)
   Note: * Another version by: Sammy Kaye Orch. (VR: Jimmy Brown).

March 25, 1939
1 DEEP PURPLE   Larry Clinton Orch. (VR: Bea Wain)
2 PENNY SERENADE   Guy Lombardo Orch. (VR: Carmen Lombardo) *
3 COULD BE   Johnny Messner Orch.
4 HEAVEN CAN WAIT   Glen Gray Orch. (VR: Clyde Burke)
5 UMBRELLA MAN   Kay Kyser Orch. (VR: Ginny Simms & Harry Babbitt)
6 GOTTA GET SOME SHUTEYE   Kay Kyser Orch. (VR: Harry Babbitt)
7 GOOD FOR NOTHING   Fats Waller Orch. (VR: Fats Waller)
8 I GET ALONG WITHOUT YOU VERY WELL   Red Norvo Orch. (VR: Terry Allen)
9 I CRIED FOR YOU   Glen Gray Orch. (VR: Kenny Sargent)
10 THE MASQUERADE IS OVER   Jimmy Dorsey Orch. (VR: Bob Eberly)
   Note: * Another version by: Sammy Kaye Orch. (VR: Jimmy Brown).

April 1, 1939
1 DEEP PURPLE   Larry Clinton Orch. (VR: Bea Wain)
2 PENNY SERENADE   Guy Lombardo Orch. (VR: Carmen Lombardo) *
3 COULD BE   Johnny Messner Orch.
4 I GET ALONG WITHOUT YOU VERY WELL   Red Norvo Orch. (VR: Terry Allen)
5 HOLD TIGHT   Andrews Sisters
6 THE MASQUERADE IS OVER   Jimmy Dorsey Orch. (VR: Bob Eberly)
7 GOTTA GET SOME SHUTEYE   Kay Kyser Orch. (VR: Harry Babbitt)
8 LITTLE SIR ECHO   Guy Lombardo Orch. (VR: Carmen Lombardo)
9 HEAVEN CAN WAIT   Glen Gray Orch. (VR: Clyde Burke)
10 THIS IS IT   Tommy Dorsey Orch. (VR: Jack Leonard)
   Note: * Another version by: Sammy Kaye Orch. (VR: Jimmy Brown).

April 8, 1939
1 DEEP PURPLE   Larry Clinton Orch. (VR: Bea Wain)
2 PENNY SERENADE   Guy Lombardo Orch. (VR: Carmen Lombardo) *
3 I GET ALONG WITHOUT YOU VERY WELL   Red Norvo Orch. (VR: Terry Allen)
4 HEAVEN CAN WAIT   Glen Gray Orch. (VR: Clyde Burke)
5 THE MASQUERADE IS OVER   Jimmy Dorsey Orch. (VR: Bob Eberly)
6 LITTLE SIR ECHO   Guy Lombardo Orch. (VR: Carmen Lombardo)
7 HOLD TIGHT   Andrews Sisters
8 COULD BE   Johnny Messner Orch.

9　GOTTA GET SOME SHUTEYE　Kay Kyser Orch. (VR: Harry Babbitt)

10　THE MOON IS A SILVER DOLLAR　Lawrence Welk Orch. (VR: Walter Bloom)

　Note: * Another version by: Sammy Kaye Orch. (VR: Jimmy Brown).

April 15, 1939

1　DEEP PURPLE　Larry Clinton Orch. (VR: Bea Wain)
2　HEAVEN CAN WAIT　Glen Gray Orch. (VR: Clyde Burke)
3　PENNY SERENADE　Guy Lombardo Orch. (VR: Carmen Lombardo) *
4　HOLD TIGHT　Andrews Sisters
5　I GET ALONG WITHOUT YOU VERY WELL　Red Norvo Orch. (VR: Terry Allen)
6　LITTLE SIR ECHO　Guy Lombardo Orch. (VR: Carmen Lombardo)
7　THE MASQUERADE IS OVER　Jimmy Dorsey Orch. (VR: Bob Eberly)
8　LITTLE SKIPPER　Ozzie Nelson Orch. (VR: Ozzie Nelson)
9　OUR LOVE　Tommy Dorsey Orch. (VR: Jack Leonard)
10　I WANT MY SHARE OF LOVE　Larry Clinton Orch. (VR: Bea Wain)

　Note: * Another version by: Sammy Kaye Orch. (VR: Jimmy Brown).

April 22, 1939

1　HEAVEN CAN WAIT　Glen Gray Orch. (VR: Clyde Burke)
2　LITTLE SIR ECHO　Guy Lombardo Orch. (VR: Carmen Lombardo)
3　DEEP PURPLE　Larry Clinton Orch. (VR: Bea Wain)
4　OUR LOVE　Tommy Dorsey Orch. (VR: Jack Leonard)
5　PENNY SERENADE　Guy Lombardo Orch. (VR: Carmen Lombardo) *
6　LITTLE SKIPPER　Ozzie Nelson Orch. (VR: Ozzie Nelson)
7　THE MASQUERADE IS OVER　Jimmy Dorsey Orch. (VR: Bob Eberly)
8　I GET ALONG WITHOUT YOU VERY WELL　Red Norvo Orch. (VR: Terry Allen)
9　IT'S NEVER TOO LATE　Jan Garber Orch. (VR: Lee Bennett)
10　THE MOON IS A SILVER DOLLAR　Lawrence Welk Orch. (VR: Walter Bloom)

　Note: * Another version by: Sammy Kaye Orch. (VR: Jimmy Brown).

April 29, 1939

1　HEAVEN CAN WAIT　Glen Gray Orch. (VR: Clyde Burke)
2　DEEP PURPLE　Larry Clinton Orch. (VR: Bea Wain)
3　LITTLE SIR ECHO　Guy Lombardo Orch. (VR: Carmen Lombardo)
4　OUR LOVE　Tommy Dorsey Orch. (VR: Jack Leonard)
5　LITTLE SKIPPER　Ozzie Nelson Orch. (VR: Ozzie Nelson)
6　I CRIED FOR YOU　Glen Gray Orch. (VR: Kenny Sargent)
7　THE MASQUERADE IS OVER　Jimmy Dorsey Orch. (VR: Bob Eberly)
8　PENNY SERENADE　Guy Lombardo Orch. (VR: Carmen Lombardo) *
9　AND THE ANGELS SING　Benny Goodman Orch. (VR: Martha Tilton)
10　I'M BUILDING A SAILBOAT OF DREAMS　Dick Robertson Orch. (VR: Dick Robertson)

　Note: * Another version by: Sammy Kaye Orch. (VR: Jimmy Brown)

May 6, 1939

1　OUR LOVE　Tommy Dorsey Orch. (VR: Jack Leonard)

2　HEAVEN CAN WAIT　Glen Gray Orch. (VR: Clyde Burke)
3　LITTLE SIR ECHO　Guy Lombardo Orch. (VR: Carmen Lombardo)
4　AND THE ANGELS SING　Benny Goodman Orch. (VR: Martha Tilton)
5　DEEP PURPLE　Larry Clinton Orch. (VR: Bea Wain)
6　LITTLE SKIPPER　Ozzie Nelson Orch. (VR: Ozzie Nelson)
7　TEARS FROM MY INKWELL　Glen Gray Orch. (VR: Kenny Sargent)
8　THREE LITTLE FISHIES　Kay Kyser Orch. (VR: Ginny Simms, Ish Kabibble & Harry Babbitt)
9　THE MOON IS A SILVER DOLLAR　Lawrence Welk Orch. (VR: Walter Bloom)
10　DON'T WORRY 'BOUT ME　Hal Kemp Orch. (VR: Bob Allen)

May 13, 1939

1　OUR LOVE　Tommy Dorsey Orch. (VR: Jack Leonard)
2　AND THE ANGELS SING　Benny Goodman Orch. (VR: Martha Tilton)
3　HEAVEN CAN WAIT　Glen Gray Orch. (VR: Clyde Burke)
4　LITTLE SKIPPER　Ozzie Nelson Orch. (VR: Ozzie Nelson)
5　THREE LITTLE FISHIES　Kay Kyser Orch. (VR: Ginny Simms, Ish Kabibble & Harry Babbitt)
6　LITTLE SIR ECHO　Guy Lombardo Orch. (VR: Carmen Lombardo)
7　DEEP PURPLE　Larry Clinton Orch. (VR: Bea Wain)
8　I'M BUILDING A SAILBOAT OF DREAMS　Dick Robertson Orch. (VR: Dick Robertson)
9　THE MASQUERADE IS OVER　Jimmy Dorsey Orch. (VR: Bob Eberly)
10　PENNY SERENADE　Guy Lombardo Orch. (VR: Carmen Lombardo) *

　Note: * Another version by: Sammy Kaye Orch. (VR: Jimmy Brown).

May 20, 1939

1　AND THE ANGELS SING　Benny Goodman Orch. (VR: Martha Tilton)
2　THREE LITTLE FISHIES　Kay Kyser Orch. (VR: Ginny Simms, Ish Kabibble & Harry Babbitt)
3　OUR LOVE　Tommy Dorsey Orch. (VR: Jack Leonard)
4　HEAVEN CAN WAIT　Glen Gray Orch. (VR: Clyde Burke)
5　LITTLE SKIPPER　Ozzie Nelson Orch. (VR: Ozzie Nelson)
6　LITTLE SIR ECHO　Guy Lombardo Orch. (VR: Carmen Lombardo)
7　WISHING　Glenn Miller Orch. (VR: Ray Eberle)
8　DON'T WORRY 'BOUT ME　Hal Kemp Orch. (VR: Bob Allen)
9　THE LADY'S IN LOVE WITH YOU　Glenn Miller Orch. (VR: Tex Beneke)
10　I NEVER KNEW HEAVEN COULD SPEAK　Bob Crosby Orch. (VR: Marion Mann)

May 27, 1939

1　AND THE ANGELS SING　Benny Goodman Orch. (VR: Martha Tilton)
2　THREE LITTLE FISHIES　Kay Kyser Orch. (VR: Ginny Simms, Ish Kabibble & Harry Babbitt)
3　WISHING　Glenn Miller Orch. (VR: Ray Eberle)
4　OUR LOVE　Tommy Dorsey Orch. (VR: Jack Leonard)
5　HEAVEN CAN WAIT　Glen Gray Orch. (VR: Clyde Burke)
6　DON'T WORRY 'BOUT ME　Hal Kemp Orch. (VR: Bob Allen)
7　NEW MOON AND OLD SERENADE　Tommy Dorsey Orch. (VR: Jack Leonard)
8　LITTLE SIR ECHO　Guy Lombardo Orch. (VR: Carmen Lombardo)

9 I NEVER KNEW HEAVEN COULD SPEAK   Bob Crosby
Orch. (VR: Marion Mann)
10 LITTLE SKIPPER   Ozzie Nelson Orch. (VR: Ozzie Nelson)

June 3, 1939
1 AND THE ANGELS SING   Benny Goodman Orch. (VR:
Martha Tilton)
2 OUR LOVE   Tommy Dorsey Orch. (VR: Jack Leonard)
3 THREE LITTLE FISHIES   Kay Kyser Orch. (VR: Ginny
Simms, Ish Kabibble & Harry Babbitt)
4 WISHING   Glenn Miller Orch. (VR: Ray Eberle)
5 DON'T WORRY 'BOUT ME   Hal Kemp Orch. (VR: Bob
Allen)
6 I NEVER KNEW HEAVEN COULD SPEAK   Bob Crosby
Orch. (VR: Marion Mann)
7 THE LADY'S IN LOVE WITH YOU   Glenn Miller Orch. (VR:
Tex Beneke)
8 NEW MOON AND OLD SERENADE   Tommy Dorsey Orch.
(VR: Jack Leonard)
9 IF I DIDN'T CARE   Ink Spots
10 LITTLE SKIPPER   Ozzie Nelson Orch. (VR: Ozzie Nelson)

June 10, 1939
1 AND THE ANGELS SING   Benny Goodman Orch. (VR:
Martha Tilton)
2 WISHING   Glenn Miller Orch. (VR: Ray Eberle)
3 IF I DIDN'T CARE   Ink Spots
4 THE LADY'S IN LOVE WITH YOU   Glenn Miller Orch. (VR:
Tex Beneke)
5 THREE LITTLE FISHIES   Kay Kyser Orch. (VR: Ginny
Simms, Ish Kabibble & Harry Babbitt)
6 DON'T WORRY 'BOUT ME   Hal Kemp Orch. (VR: Al
Hibbler)
7 OUR LOVE   Tommy Dorsey Orch. (VR: Jack Leonard)
8 LITTLE SKIPPER   Ozzie Nelson Orch. (VR: Ozzie Nelson)
9 I NEVER KNEW HEAVEN COULD SPEAK   Bob Crosby
Orch. (VR: Marion Mann)
10 LITTLE SIR ECHO   Guy Lombardo Orch. (VR: Carmen
Lombardo)

June 17, 1939
1 WISHING   Glenn Miller Orch. (VR: Ray Eberle)
2 AND THE ANGELS SING   Benny Goodman Orch. (VR:
Martha Tilton)
3 THE LADY'S IN LOVE WITH YOU   Glenn Miller Orch. (VR:
Tex Beneke)
4 THREE LITTLE FISHIES   Kay Kyser Orch. (VR: Ginny
Simms, Ish Kabibble & Harry Babbitt)
5 DON'T WORRY 'BOUT ME   Hal Kemp Orch. (VR: Al
Hibbler)
6 I NEVER KNEW HEAVEN COULD SPEAK   Bob Crosby
Orch. (VR: Marion Mann)
7 IF I DIDN'T CARE   Ink Spots
8 NEW MOON AND OLD SERENADE   Tommy Dorsey Orch.
(VR: Jack Leonard)
9 OUR LOVE   Tommy Dorsey Orch. (VR: Jack Leonard)
10 STRANGE ENCHANTMENT   Dorothy Lamour

June 24, 1939
1 WISHING   Glenn Miller Orch. (VR: Ray Eberle)
2 AND THE ANGELS SING   Benny Goodman Orch. (VR:
Martha Tilton)
3 BEER BARREL POLKA   Will Glahe Musette
4 THREE LITTLE FISHIES   Kay Kyser Orch. (VR: Ginny
Simms, Ish Kabibble & Harry Babbitt)
5 NEW MOON AND OLD SERENADE   Tommy Dorsey Orch.
(VR: Jack Leonard)

6 THE LADY'S IN LOVE WITH YOU   Glenn Miller Orch. (VR:
Tex Beneke)
7 DON'T WORRY 'BOUT ME   Hal Kemp Orch. (VR: Al
Hibbler)
8 IF I DIDN'T CARE   Ink Spots
9 STRANGE ENCHANTMENT   Dorothy Lamour
10 STAIRWAY TO THE STARS   Glenn Miller Orch. (VR: Ray
Eberle)

July 1, 1939
1 WISHING   Glenn Miller Orch. (VR: Ray Eberle)
2 THE LADY'S IN LOVE WITH YOU   Glenn Miller Orch. (VR:
Tex Beneke)
3 AND THE ANGELS SING   Benny Goodman Orch. (VR:
Martha Tilton)
4 IF I DIDN'T CARE   Ink Spots
5 STAIRWAY TO THE STARS   Glenn Miller Orch. (VR: Ray
Eberle)
6 BEER BARREL POLKA   Will Glahe Musette
7 SUNRISE SERENADE   Glen Gray Orch.
8 DON'T WORRY 'BOUT ME   Hal Kemp Orch. (VR: Al
Hibbler)
9 WHITE SAILS   Ozzie Nelson Orch. (VR: Ozzie Nelson)
10 THREE LITTLE FISHIES   Kay Kyser Orch. (VR: Ginny
Simms, Ish Kabibble & Harry Babbitt)

July 8, 1939
1 WISHING   Glenn Miller Orch. (VR: Ray Eberle)
2 BEER BARREL POLKA   Will Glahe Musette
3 STAIRWAY TO THE STARS   Glenn Miller Orch. (VR: Ray
Eberle)
4 THE LADY'S IN LOVE WITH YOU   Glenn Miller Orch. (VR:
Tex Beneke)
5 AND THE ANGELS SING   Benny Goodman Orch. (VR:
Martha Tilton)
6 SUNRISE SERENADE   Glen Gray Orch.
7 WHITE SAILS   Ozzie Nelson Orch. (VR: Ozzie Nelson)
8 STRANGE ENCHANTMENT   Dorothy Lamour
9 IF I DIDN'T CARE   Ink Spots
10 DON'T WORRY 'BOUT ME   Hal Kemp Orch. (VR: Al
Hibbler)

July 15, 1939
1 STAIRWAY TO THE STARS   Glenn Miller Orch. (VR: Ray
Eberle)
2 BEER BARREL POLKA   Will Glahe Musette
3 WISHING   Glenn Miller Orch. (VR: Ray Eberle)
4 WHITE SAILS   Ozzie Nelson Orch. (VR: Ozzie Nelson)
5 MOON LOVE   Glenn Miller Orch. (VR: Ray Eberle)
6 AND THE ANGELS SING   Benny Goodman Orch. (VR:
Martha Tilton)
7 SUNRISE SERENADE   Glen Gray Orch.
8 STRANGE ENCHANTMENT   Dorothy Lamour
9 BLUE EVENING   Woody Herman Orch. (VR: Woody
Herman)
10 ALL I REMEMBER IS YOU   Tommy Dorsey Orch. (VR: Jack
Leonard)

July 22, 1939
1 STAIRWAY TO THE STARS   Glenn Miller Orch. (VR: Ray
Eberle)
2 WHITE SAILS   Ozzie Nelson Orch. (VR: Ozzie Nelson)
3 BEER BARREL POLKA   Will Glahe Musette
4 WISHING   Glenn Miller Orch. (VR: Ray Eberle)
5 MOON LOVE   Glenn Miller Orch. (VR: Ray Eberle)
6 SUNRISE SERENADE   Glen Gray Orch.

57

7 IN THE MIDDLE OF A DREAM   Tommy Dorsey Orch. (VR: Jack Leonard)
8 THE LADY'S IN LOVE WITH YOU   Glenn Miller Orch. (VR: Tex Beneke)
9 IF I DIDN'T CARE   Ink Spots
10 I POURED MY HEART INTO A SONG   Artie Shaw Orch. (VR: Tony Pastor)

July 29, 1939
1 STAIRWAY TO THE STARS   Glenn Miller Orch. (VR: Ray Eberle)
2 WHITE SAILS   Ozzie Nelson Orch. (VR: Ozzie Nelson)
3 MOON LOVE   Glenn Miller Orch. (VR: Ray Eberle)
4 SUNRISE SERENADE   Glen Gray Orch.
5 WISHING   Glenn Miller Orch. (VR: Ray Eberle)
6 BEER BARREL POLKA   Will Glahe Musette
7 IN THE MIDDLE OF A DREAM   Tommy Dorsey Orch. (VR: Jack Leonard)
8 I POURED MY HEART INTO A SONG   Artie Shaw Orch. (VR: Tony Pastor)
9 THIS IS NO DREAM   Tommy Dorsey Orch. (VR: Jack Leonard)
10 THE LADY'S IN LOVE WITH YOU   Glenn Miller Orch. (VR: Tex Beneke)

August 5, 1939
1 STAIRWAY TO THE STARS   Glenn Miller Orch. (VR: Ray Eberle)
2 SUNRISE SERENADE   Glen Gray Orch.
3 BEER BARREL POLKA   Will Glahe Musette
4 MOON LOVE   Glenn Miller Orch. (VR: Ray Eberle)
5 WHITE SAILS   Ozzie Nelson Orch. (VR: Ozzie Nelson)
6 I POURED MY HEART INTO A SONG   Artie Shaw Orch. (VR: Tony Pastor)
7 WISHING   Glenn Miller Orch. (VR: Ray Eberle)
8 THE LAMP IS LOW   Tommy Dorsey Orch. (VR: Jack Leonard)
9 THIS IS NO DREAM   Tommy Dorsey Orch. (VR: Jack Leonard)
10 TO YOU   Tommy Dorsey Orch. (VR: Jack Leonard)

August 12, 1939
1 MOON LOVE   Glenn Miller Orch. (VR: Ray Eberle)
2 STAIRWAY TO THE STARS   Glenn Miller Orch. (VR: Ray Eberle)
3 WHITE SAILS   Ozzie Nelson Orch. (VR: Ozzie Nelson)
4 I POURED MY HEART INTO A SONG   Artie Shaw Orch. (VR: Tony Pastor)
5 SUNRISE SERENADE   Glen Gray Orch.
6 THE LAMP IS LOW   Tommy Dorsey Orch. (VR: Jack Leonard)
7 WISHING   Glenn Miller Orch. (VR: Ray Eberle)
8 BEER BARREL POLKA   Will Glahe Musette
9 COMES LOVE   Artie Shaw Orch. (VR: Helen Forrest)
10 IN THE MIDDLE OF A DREAM   Tommy Dorsey Orch. (VR: Jack Leonard)

August 19, 1939
1 MOON LOVE   Glenn Miller Orch. (VR: Ray Eberle)
2 STAIRWAY TO THE STARS   Glenn Miller Orch. (VR: Ray Eberle)
3 WHITE SAILS   Ozzie Nelson Orch. (VR: Ozzie Nelson)
4 I POURED MY HEART INTO A SONG   Artie Shaw Orch. (VR: Tony Pastor)
5 BEER BARREL POLKA   Will Glahe Musette
6 SUNRISE SERENADE   Glen Gray Orch.

7 COMES LOVE   Artie Shaw Orch. (VR: Helen Forrest)
8 BLUE EVENING   Woody Herman Orch. (VR: Woody Herman)
9 WISHING   Glenn Miller Orch. (VR: Ray Eberle)
10 OVER THE RAINBOW   Glenn Miller Orch. (VR: Ray Eberle) *
Note: * Another version by: Judy Garland.

August 26, 1939
1 MOON LOVE   Glenn Miller Orch. (VR: Ray Eberle)
2 STAIRWAY TO THE STARS   Glenn Miller Orch. (VR: Ray Eberle)
3 BEER BARREL POLKA   Will Glahe Musette
4 I POURED MY HEART INTO A SONG   Artie Shaw Orch. (VR: Tony Pastor)
5 THE LAMP IS LOW   Tommy Dorsey Orch. (VR: Jack Leonard)
6 COMES LOVE   Artie Shaw Orch. (VR: Helen Forrest)
7 OVER THE RAINBOW   Glenn Miller Orch. (VR: Ray Eberle) *
8 SUNRISE SERENADE   Glen Gray Orch.
9 WHITE SAILS   Ozzie Nelson Orch. (VR: Ozzie Nelson)
10 MAN WITH THE MANDOLIN   Glenn Miller Orch. (VR: Marion Hutton)
Note: * Another version by: Judy Garland.

September 2, 1939
1 MOON LOVE   Glenn Miller Orch. (VR: Ray Eberle)
2 OVER THE RAINBOW   Glenn Miller Orch. (VR: Ray Eberle) *
3 THE LAMP IS LOW   Tommy Dorsey Orch. (VR: Jack Leonard)
4 COMES LOVE   Artie Shaw Orch. (VR: Helen Forrest)
5 I POURED MY HEART INTO A SONG   Artie Shaw Orch. (VR: Tony Pastor)
6 STAIRWAY TO THE STARS   Glenn Miller Orch. (VR: Ray Eberle)
7 SUNRISE SERENADE   Glen Gray Orch.
8 TO YOU   Tommy Dorsey Orch. (VR: Jack Leonard)
9 BEER BARREL POLKA   Will Glahe Musette
10 WHITE SAILS   Ozzie Nelson Orch. (VR: Ozzie Nelson)
Note: * Another version by: Judy Garland.

September 9, 1939
1 OVER THE RAINBOW   Glenn Miller Orch. (VR: Ray Eberle) *
2 MOON LOVE   Glenn Miller Orch. (VR: Ray Eberle)
3 TO YOU   Tommy Dorsey Orch. (VR: Jack Leonard)
4 THE LAMP IS LOW   Tommy Dorsey Orch. (VR: Jack Leonard)
5 I POURED MY HEART INTO A SONG   Artie Shaw Orch. (VR: Tony Pastor)
6 STAIRWAY TO THE STARS   Glenn Miller Orch. (VR: Ray Eberle)
7 OH, YOU CRAZY MOON   Tommy Dorsey Orch. (VR: Jack Leonard)
8 BEER BARREL POLKA   Will Glahe Musette
9 SUNRISE SERENADE   Glen Gray Orch.
10 COMES LOVE   Artie Shaw Orch. (VR: Helen Forrest)
Note: * Another version by: Judy Garland.

September 16, 1939
1 OVER THE RAINBOW   Glenn Miller Orch. (VR: Ray Eberle) *
2 MOON LOVE   Glenn Miller Orch. (VR: Ray Eberle)
3 CINDERELLA, STAY IN MY ARMS   Guy Lombardo Orch. (VR: Carmen Lombardo)

Judy Garland

Even though Glenn Miller had the #1 hit, Judy (pictured here with Sophie Tucker) turned "Over The Rainbow" into an American classic.

4   MAN WITH THE MANDOLIN   Glenn Miller Orch. (VR: Marion Hutton)
5   COMES LOVE   Artie Shaw Orch. (VR: Helen Forrest)
6   SUNRISE SERENADE   Glen Gray Orch.
7   THE LAMP IS LOW   Tommy Dorsey Orch. (VR: Jack Leonard)
8   I POURED MY HEART INTO A SONG   Artie Shaw Orch. (VR: Tony Pastor)
9   DAY IN, DAY OUT   Bob Crosby Orch. (VR: Helen Ward)
10 BEER BARREL POLKA   Will Glahe Musette
    Note: * Another version by: Judy Garland.

September 23, 1939
1   OVER THE RAINBOW   Glenn Miller Orch. (VR: Ray Eberle) *
2   OH, YOU CRAZY MOON   Tommy Dorsey Orch. (VR: Jack Leonard)
3   MOON LOVE   Glenn Miller Orch. (VR: Ray Eberle)
4   A MAN AND HIS DREAM   Bing Crosby
5   COMES LOVE   Artie Shaw Orch. (VR: Helen Forrest)
6   DAY IN, DAY OUT   Bob Crosby Orch. (VR: Helen Ward)
7   SUNRISE SERENADE   Glen Gray Orch.
8   THE LAMP IS LOW   Tommy Dorsey Orch. (VR: Jack Leonard)
9   MAN WITH THE MANDOLIN   Glenn Miller Orch. (VR: Marion Hutton)
10 GO FLY A KITE   Bing Crosby
    Note: * Another version by: Judy Garland.

September 30, 1939
1   OVER THE RAINBOW   Glenn Miller Orch. (VR: Ray Eberle) *
2   OH, YOU CRAZY MOON   Tommy Dorsey Orch. (VR: Jack Leonard)

3   MAN WITH THE MANDOLIN   Glenn Miller Orch. (VR: Marion Hutton)
4   DAY IN, DAY OUT   Bob Crosby Orch. (VR: Helen Ward)
5   TO YOU   Tommy Dorsey Orch. (VR: Jack Leonard)
6   BEER BARREL POLKA   Will Glahe Musette
7   SUNRISE SERENADE   Glen Gray Orch.
8   MOONLIGHT SERENADE   Glenn Miller Orch.
9   AN APPLE FOR THE TEACHER   Bing Crosby & Connee Boswell
10 THE LAMP IS LOW   Tommy Dorsey Orch. (VR: Jack Leonard)
    Note: * Another version by: Judy Garland.

October 7, 1939
1   OVER THE RAINBOW   Glenn Miller Orch. (VR: Ray Eberle) *
2   OH, YOU CRAZY MOON   Tommy Dorsey Orch. (VR: Jack Leonard)
3   MAN WITH THE MANDOLIN   Glenn Miller Orch. (VR: Marion Hutton)
4   DAY IN, DAY OUT   Bob Crosby Orch. (VR: Helen Ward)
5   A MAN AND HIS DREAM   Bing Crosby
6   CINDERELLA, STAY IN MY ARMS   Guy Lombardo Orch. (VR: Carmen Lombardo)
7   MELANCHOLY MOOD   Artie Shaw Orch. (VR: Helen Forrest)
8   SUNRISE SERENADE   Glen Gray Orch.
9   BEER BARREL POLKA   Will Glahe Musette
10 MOON LOVE   Glenn Miller Orch. (VR: Ray Eberle)
    Note: * Another version by: Judy Garland.

October 14, 1939
1   OVER THE RAINBOW   Glenn Miller Orch. (VR: Ray Eberle) *
2   DAY IN, DAY OUT   Bob Crosby Orch. (VR: Helen Ward)
3   A MAN AND HIS DREAM   Bing Crosby
4   MAN WITH THE MANDOLIN   Glenn Miller Orch. (VR: Marion Hutton)
5   OH, YOU CRAZY MOON   Tommy Dorsey Orch. (VR: Jack Leonard)
6   MOONLIGHT SERENADE   Glenn Miller Orch.
7   IN AN EIGHTEENTH CENTURY DRAWING ROOM   Guy Lombardo Orch.
8   WHAT'S NEW   Bing Crosby
9   MELANCHOLY MOOD   Artie Shaw Orch. (VR: Helen Forrest)
10 AN APPLE FOR THE TEACHER   Bing Crosby & Connee Boswell
    Note: * Another version by: Judy Garland.

October 21, 1939
1   DAY IN, DAY OUT   Bob Crosby Orch. (VR: Helen Ward)
2   MAN WITH THE MANDOLIN   Glenn Miller Orch. (VR: Marion Hutton)
3   OVER THE RAINBOW   Glenn Miller Orch. (VR: Ray Eberle) *
4   BLUE ORCHIDS   Glenn Miller Orch. (VR: Ray Eberle)
5   SOUTH OF THE BORDER   Shep Fields Orch. (VR: Hal Derwin) **
6   WHAT'S NEW   Bing Crosby
7   TO YOU   Tommy Dorsey Orch. (VR: Jack Leonard)
8   IT'S A HUNDRED TO ONE YOU'RE IN LOVE   Dick Jurgens Orch. (VR: Eddy Howard)
9   BEER BARREL POLKA   Will Glahe Musette
10 ARE YOU HAVING ANY FUN?   Tommy Dorsey Orch. (VR: Edythe Wright)
    Note: * Another version by: Judy Garland.
          ** Country hit by Gene Autry.

October 28, 1939

1. OVER THE RAINBOW   Glenn Miller Orch. (VR: Ray Eberle) *
2. SOUTH OF THE BORDER   Shep Fields Orch. (VR: Hal Derwin) **
3. DAY IN, DAY OUT   Bob Crosby Orch. (VR: Helen Ward)
4. MAN WITH THE MANDOLIN   Glenn Miller Orch. (VR: Marion Hutton)
5. BLUE ORCHIDS   Glenn Miller Orch. (VR: Ray Eberle)
6. MY PRAYER   Glenn Miller Orch. (VR: Ray Eberle)
7. WHAT'S NEW   Bing Crosby
8. LAST NIGHT   Glenn Miller Orch. (VR: Ray Eberle)
9. ARE YOU HAVING ANY FUN?   Tommy Dorsey Orch. (VR: Edythe Wright)
10. OH, YOU CRAZY MOON   Tommy Dorsey Orch. (VR: Jack Leonard)

Note: * Another version by: Judy Garland.
** Country hit by Gene Autry.

November 4, 1939

1. BLUE ORCHIDS   Glenn Miller Orch. (VR: Ray Eberle)
2. SOUTH OF THE BORDER   Shep Fields Orch. (VR: Hal Derwin) *
3. OVER THE RAINBOW   Glenn Miller Orch. (VR: Ray Eberle) **
4. WHAT'S NEW   Bing Crosby
5. MAN WITH THE MANDOLIN   Glenn Miller Orch. (VR: Marion Hutton)
6. ARE YOU HAVING ANY FUN?   Tommy Dorsey Orch. (VR: Edythe Wright)
7. MY PRAYER   Glenn Miller Orch. (VR: Ray Eberle)
8. LILACS IN THE RAIN   Bob Crosby Orch. (VR: Bob Crosby)
9. DAY IN, DAY OUT   Bob Crosby Orch. (VR: Helen Ward)
10. GOOD MORNING   Abe Lyman Orch. (VR: Rose Blane)

Note: * Country hit by Gene Autry.
** Another version by: Judy Garland.

November 11, 1939

1. SOUTH OF THE BORDER   Shep Fields Orch. (VR: Hal Derwin) *
2. WHAT'S NEW   Bing Crosby
3. BLUE ORCHIDS   Glenn Miller Orch. (VR: Ray Eberle)
4. MY PRAYER   Glenn Miller Orch. (VR: Ray Eberle)
5. LILACS IN THE RAIN   Bob Crosby Orch. (VR: Bob Crosby)
6. SCATTERBRAIN   Frankie Masters Orch. (VR: Frankie Masters)
7. MAN WITH THE MANDOLIN   Glenn Miller Orch. (VR: Marion Hutton)
8. DAY IN, DAY OUT   Bob Crosby Orch. (VR: Helen Ward)
9. ARE YOU HAVING ANY FUN?   Tommy Dorsey Orch. (VR: Edythe Wright)
10. OVER THE RAINBOW   Glenn Miller Orch. (VR: Ray Eberle) **

Note: * Country hit by Gene Autry.
** Another version by: Judy Garland.

November 18, 1939

1. SOUTH OF THE BORDER   Shep Fields Orch. (VR: Hal Derwin) *
2. SCATTERBRAIN   Frankie Masters Orch. (VR: Frankie Masters)
3. MY PRAYER   Glenn Miller Orch. (VR: Ray Eberle)
4. WHAT'S NEW   Bing Crosby
5. BLUE ORCHIDS   Glenn Miller Orch. (VR: Ray Eberle)
6. DAY IN, DAY OUT   Bob Crosby Orch. (VR: Helen Ward)
7. LAST NIGHT   Glenn Miller Orch. (VR: Ray Eberle)
8. ARE YOU HAVING ANY FUN?   Tommy Dorsey Orch. (VR: Edythe Wright)

9. OVER THE RAINBOW   Glenn Miller Orch. (VR: Ray Eberle) **
10. LILACS IN THE RAIN   Bob Crosby Orch. (VR: Bob Crosby)

Note: * Country hit by Gene Autry.
** Another version by: Judy Garland.

November 25, 1939

1. SOUTH OF THE BORDER   Shep Fields Orch. (VR: Hal Derwin) *
2. BLUE ORCHIDS   Glenn Miller Orch. (VR: Ray Eberle)
3. MY PRAYER   Glenn Miller Orch. (VR: Ray Eberle)
4. LILACS IN THE RAIN   Bob Crosby Orch. (VR: Bob Crosby)
5. SCATTERBRAIN   Frankie Masters Orch. (VR: Frankie Masters)
6. LAST NIGHT   Glenn Miller Orch. (VR: Ray Eberle)
7. WHAT'S NEW   Bing Crosby
8. I DIDN'T KNOW WHAT TIME IT WAS   Benny Goodman Orch. (VR: Louise Tobin)
9. OVER THE RAINBOW   Glenn Miller Orch. (VR: Ray Eberle) **
10. ARE YOU HAVING ANY FUN?   Tommy Dorsey Orch. (VR: Edythe Wright)

Note: * Country hit by Gene Autry.
** Another version by: Judy Garland.

December 2, 1939

1. SCATTERBRAIN   Frankie Masters Orch. (VR: Frankie Masters)
2. SOUTH OF THE BORDER   Shep Fields Orch. (VR: Hal Derwin) *
3. LILACS IN THE RAIN   Bob Crosby Orch. (VR: Bob Crosby)
4. MY PRAYER   Glenn Miller Orch. (VR: Ray Eberle)
5. LAST NIGHT   Glenn Miller Orch. (VR: Ray Eberle)
6. I DIDN'T KNOW WHAT TIME IT WAS   Benny Goodman Orch. (VR: Louise Tobin)
7. BLUE ORCHIDS   Glenn Miller Orch. (VR: Ray Eberle)
8. CAN I HELP IT?   Bob Crosby Orch. (VR: Bob Crosby)
9. ARE YOU HAVING ANY FUN?   Tommy Dorsey Orch. (VR: Edythe Wright)
10. EL RANCHO GRANDE   Bing Crosby

Note: * Country hit by Gene Autry.

December 9, 1939

1. SOUTH OF THE BORDER   Shep Fields Orch. (VR: Hal Derwin) *
2. SCATTERBRAIN   Frankie Masters Orch. (VR: Frankie Masters)
3. MY PRAYER   Glenn Miller Orch. (VR: Ray Eberle)
4. LILACS IN THE RAIN   Bob Crosby Orch. (VR: Bob Crosby)
5. BLUE ORCHIDS   Glenn Miller Orch. (VR: Ray Eberle)
6. I DIDN'T KNOW WHAT TIME IT WAS   Benny Goodman Orch. (VR: Louise Tobin)
7. EL RANCHO GRANDE   Bing Crosby
8. SPEAKING OF HEAVEN   Glenn Miller Orch. (VR: Ray Eberle)
9. OH, JOHNNY, OH   Orrin Tucker Orch. (VR: Bonnie Baker)
10. STOP, IT'S WONDERFUL   Orrin Tucker Orch. (VR: Bonnie Baker)

Note: * Country hit by Gene Autry.

December 16, 1939

1. SCATTERBRAIN   Frankie Masters Orch. (VR: Frankie Masters)
2. SOUTH OF THE BORDER   Shep Fields Orch. (VR: Hal Derwin) *
3. MY PRAYER   Glenn Miller Orch. (VR: Ray Eberle)

4   LILACS IN THE RAIN   Bob Crosby Orch. (VR: Bob Crosby)
5   LAST NIGHT   Glenn Miller Orch. (VR: Ray Eberle)
6   EL RANCHO GRANDE   Bing Crosby
7   OH, JOHNNY, OH   Orrin Tucker Orch. (VR: Bonnie Baker)
8   I DIDN'T KNOW WHAT TIME IT WAS   Benny Goodman Orch. (VR: Louise Tobin)
9   GOODY GOODBYE   Dolly Dawn Orch. (VR: Dolly Dawn)
10   BLUE ORCHIDS   Glenn Miller Orch. (VR: Ray Eberle)
    Note: * Country hit by Gene Autry.

December 23, 1939

1   SOUTH OF THE BORDER   Shep Fields Orch. (VR: Hal Derwin) *
2   SCATTERBRAIN   Frankie Masters Orch. (VR: Frankie Masters)
3   OH, JOHNNY, OH   Orrin Tucker Orch. (VR: Bonnie Baker)
4   LILACS IN THE RAIN   Bob Crosby Orch. (VR: Bob Crosby)
5   ALL THE THINGS YOU ARE   Tommy Dorsey Orch. (VR: Jack Leonard)
6   MY PRAYER   Glenn Miller Orch. (VR: Ray Eberle)
7   LAST NIGHT   Glenn Miller Orch. (VR: Ray Eberle)
8   I DIDN'T KNOW WHAT TIME IT WAS   Benny Goodman Orch. (VR: Louise Tobin)

9   CAN I HELP IT?   Bob Crosby Orch. (VR: Bob Crosby)
10   INDIAN SUMMER   Tommy Dorsey Orch. (VR: Jack Leonard)
    Note: * Country hit by Gene Autry.

December 30, 1939

1   SCATTERBRAIN   Frankie Masters Orch. (VR: Frankie Masters)
2   MY PRAYER   Glenn Miller Orch. (VR: Ray Eberle)
3   LILACS IN THE RAIN   Bob Crosby Orch. (VR: Bob Crosby)
4   OH, JOHNNY, OH   Orrin Tucker Orch. (VR: Bonnie Baker)
5   ALL THE THINGS YOU ARE   Tommy Dorsey Orch. (VR: Jack Leonard)
6   SOUTH OF THE BORDER   Shep Fields Orch. (VR: Hal Derwin) *
7   I DIDN'T KNOW WHAT TIME IT WAS   Benny Goodman Orch. (VR: Louise Tobin)
8   BLUE ORCHIDS   Glenn Miller Orch. (VR: Ray Eberle)
9   SPEAKING OF HEAVEN   Glenn Miller Orch. (VR: Ray Eberle)
10   GOODY GOODBYE   Dolly Dawn Orch. (VR: Dolly Dawn)
    Note: * Country hit by Gene Autry.

Glenn Miller
``Careless'' reaches #1 (Feb 3). Ironically, Miller's greatest hit—``In The Mood''—only made
it to #9 on the Hit Parade, although it was #1 on other charts.

The Forties

January 6, 1940
1   SCATTERBRAIN   Frankie Masters Orch. (VR: Frankie Masters)
2   ALL THE THINGS YOU ARE   Tommy Dorsey Orch. (VR: Jack Leonard)
3   MY PRAYER   Glenn Miller Orch. (VR: Ray Eberle)
4   FAITHFUL FOREVER   Glenn Miller Orch. (VR: Ray Eberle)
5   SOUTH OF THE BORDER   Shep Fields Orch. (VR: Hal Derwin) *
6   OH, JOHNNY, OH   Orrin Tucker Orch. (VR: Bonnie Baker)
7   STOP, IT'S WONDERFUL   Orrin Tucker Orch. (VR: Bonnie Baker)
8   I DIDN'T KNOW WHAT TIME IT WAS   Benny Goodman Orch. (VR: Louise Tobin)
9   LILACS IN THE RAIN   Bob Crosby Orch. (VR: Bob Crosby)
10   CARELESS   Glenn Miller Orch. (VR: Ray Eberle)
   Note: * Country hit by Gene Autry.

January 13, 1940
1   SCATTERBRAIN   Frankie Masters Orch. (VR: Frankie Masters)
2   OH, JOHNNY, OH   Orrin Tucker Orch. (VR: Bonnie Baker)
3   SOUTH OF THE BORDER   Shep Fields Orch. (VR: Hal Derwin) *
4   ALL THE THINGS YOU ARE   Tommy Dorsey Orch. (VR: Jack Leonard)
5   FAITHFUL FOREVER   Glenn Miller Orch. (VR: Ray Eberle)
6   CARELESS   Glenn Miller Orch. (VR: Ray Eberle)
7   AT THE BALALAIKA   Orrin Tucker Orch. (VR: Gil Mershon)
8   MY PRAYER   Glenn Miller Orch. (VR: Ray Eberle)
9   INDIAN SUMMER   Tommy Dorsey Orch. (VR: Jack Leonard)
10   LILACS IN THE RAIN   Bob Crosby Orch. (VR: Bob Crosby)
   Note: * Country hit by Gene Autry.

January 20, 1940
1   SCATTERBRAIN   Frankie Masters Orch. (VR: Frankie Masters)
2   ALL THE THINGS YOU ARE   Tommy Dorsey Orch. (VR: Jack Leonard)
3   CARELESS   Glenn Miller Orch. (VR: Ray Eberle)
4   OH, JOHNNY, OH   Orrin Tucker Orch. (VR: Bonnie Baker)
5   FAITHFUL FOREVER   Glenn Miller Orch. (VR: Ray Eberle)
6   SOUTH OF THE BORDER   Shep Fields Orch. (VR: Hal Derwin) *
7   AT THE BALALAIKA   Orrin Tucker Orch. (VR: Gil Mershon)
8   INDIAN SUMMER   Tommy Dorsey Orch. (VR: Jack Leonard)
9   MY PRAYER   Glenn Miller Orch. (VR: Ray Eberle)
10   STOP, IT'S WONDERFUL   Orrin Tucker Orch. (VR: Bonnie Baker)
   Note: * Country hit by Gene Autry.

January 27, 1940
1   ALL THE THINGS YOU ARE   Tommy Dorsey Orch. (VR: Jack Leonard)
2   CARELESS   Glenn Miller Orch. (VR: Ray Eberle)
3   SCATTERBRAIN   Frankie Masters Orch. (VR: Frankie Masters)
4   OH, JOHNNY, OH   Orrin Tucker Orch. (VR: Bonnie Baker)
5   INDIAN SUMMER   Tommy Dorsey Orch. (VR: Jack Leonard)
6   FAITHFUL FOREVER   Glenn Miller Orch. (VR: Ray Eberle)
7   SOUTH OF THE BORDER   Shep Fields Orch. (VR: Hal Derwin) *
8   AT THE BALALAIKA   Orrin Tucker Orch. (VR: Gil Mershon)
9   MY PRAYER   Glenn Miller Orch. (VR: Ray Eberle)
10   THIS CHANGING WORLD   Glenn Miller Orch. (VR: Ray Eberle)
   Note: * Country hit by Gene Autry.

February 3, 1940
1   CARELESS   Glenn Miller Orch. (VR: Ray Eberle)
2   ALL THE THINGS YOU ARE   Tommy Dorsey Orch. (VR: Jack Leonard)
3   INDIAN SUMMER   Tommy Dorsey Orch. (VR: Jack Leonard)
4   FAITHFUL FOREVER   Glenn Miller Orch. (VR: Ray Eberle)
5   OH, JOHNNY, OH   Orrin Tucker Orch. (VR: Bonnie Baker)
6   DARN THAT DREAM   Benny Goodman Orch. (VR: Mildred Bailey)
7   AT THE BALALAIKA   Orrin Tucker Orch. (VR: Gil Mershon)
8   THIS CHANGING WORLD   Glenn Miller Orch. (VR: Ray Eberle)
9   IN THE MOOD   Glenn Miller Orch.
10   SOUTH OF THE BORDER   Shep Fields Orch. (VR: Hal Derwin) *
   Note: * Country hit by Gene Autry.

February 10, 1940
1   ALL THE THINGS YOU ARE   Tommy Dorsey Orch. (VR: Jack Leonard)
2   CARELESS   Glenn Miller Orch. (VR: Ray Eberle)
3   INDIAN SUMMER   Tommy Dorsey Orch. (VR: Jack Leonard)
4   FAITHFUL FOREVER   Glenn Miller Orch. (VR: Ray Eberle)
5   LITTLE RED FOX   Kay Kyser Orch. (VR: Kay Kyser & Harry Babbitt)
6   OH, JOHNNY, OH   Orrin Tucker Orch. (VR: Bonnie Baker)
7   IN AN OLD DUTCH GARDEN   Dick Jurgens Orch. (VR: Eddy Howard)
8   SCATTERBRAIN   Frankie Masters Orch. (VR: Frankie Masters)
9   DO I LOVE YOU?   Leo Reisman Orch. (VR: Lee Sullivan)
10   TO YOU, SWEETHEART, ALOHA   Tommy Dorsey Orch. (VR: Jack Leonard)

February 17, 1940
1   CARELESS   Glenn Miller Orch. (VR: Ray Eberle)
2   INDIAN SUMMER   Tommy Dorsey Orch. (VR: Jack Leonard)
3   AT THE BALALAIKA   Orrin Tucker Orch. (VR: Gil Mershon)
4   ALL THE THINGS YOU ARE   Tommy Dorsey Orch. (VR: Jack Leonard)
5   FAITHFUL FOREVER   Glenn Miller Orch. (VR: Ray Eberle)
6   IN AN OLD DUTCH GARDEN   Dick Jurgens Orch. (VR: Eddy Howard)
7   DARN THAT DREAM   Benny Goodman Orch. (VR: Mildred Bailey)

8 IT'S A BLUE WORLD   Tony Martin
9 LITTLE RED FOX   Kay Kyser Orch. (VR: Kay Kyser & Harry Babbitt)
10 OH, JOHNNY, OH   Orrin Tucker Orch. (VR: Bonnie Baker)

February 24, 1940
1 INDIAN SUMMER   Tommy Dorsey Orch. (VR: Jack Leonard)
2 CARELESS   Glenn Miller Orch. (VR: Ray Eberle)
3 ALL THE THINGS YOU ARE   Tommy Dorsey Orch. (VR: Jack Leonard)
4 LITTLE RED FOX   Kay Kyser Orch. (VR: Kay Kyser & Harry Babbitt)
5 DARN THAT DREAM   Benny Goodman Orch. (VR: Mildred Bailey)
6 AT THE BALALAIKA   Orrin Tucker Orch. (VR: Gil Mershon)
7 IN AN OLD DUTCH GARDEN   Dick Jurgens Orch. (VR: Eddy Howard)
8 FAITHFUL FOREVER   Glenn Miller Orch. (VR: Ray Eberle)
9 GAUCHO SERENADE   Dick Todd
10 IT'S A BLUE WORLD   Tony Martin

March 2, 1940
1 CARELESS   Glenn Miller Orch. (VR: Ray Eberle)
2 INDIAN SUMMER   Tommy Dorsey Orch. (VR: Jack Leonard)
3 DARN THAT DREAM   Benny Goodman Orch. (VR: Mildred Bailey)
4 AT THE BALALAIKA   Orrin Tucker Orch. (VR: Gil Mershon)
5 IT'S A BLUE WORLD   Tony Martin
6 ALL THE THINGS YOU ARE   Tommy Dorsey Orch. (VR: Jack Leonard)
7 DO I LOVE YOU?   Leo Reisman Orch. (VR: Lee Sullivan)
8 IN AN OLD DUTCH GARDEN   Dick Jurgens Orch. (VR: Eddy Howard)
9 FAITHFUL FOREVER   Glenn Miller Orch. (VR: Ray Eberle)
10 I'VE GOT MY EYES ON YOU   Tommy Dorsey Orch. (VR: Alan DeWitt)

March 9, 1940
1 CARELESS   Glenn Miller Orch. (VR: Ray Eberle)
2 INDIAN SUMMER   Tommy Dorsey Orch. (VR: Jack Leonard)
3 IN AN OLD DUTCH GARDEN   Dick Jurgens Orch. (VR: Eddy Howard)
4 STARLIT HOUR   Glenn Miller Orch. (VR: Ray Eberle)
5 DARN THAT DREAM   Benny Goodman Orch. (VR: Mildred Bailey)
6 I'VE GOT MY EYES ON YOU   Tommy Dorsey Orch. (VR: Alan DeWitt)
7 AT THE BALALAIKA   Orrin Tucker Orch. (VR: Gil Mershon)
8 DO I LOVE YOU?   Leo Reisman Orch. (VR: Lee Sullivan)
9 WHEN YOU WISH UPON A STAR   Glenn Miller Orch. (VR: Ray Eberle) *
10 LEANIN' ON THE OLD TOP RAIL   Bob Crosby Orch. (VR: Bob Crosby)
   Note: * From Walt Disney's "Pinocchio."

March 16, 1940
1 DARN THAT DREAM   Benny Goodman Orch. (VR: Mildred Bailey)
2 IT'S A BLUE WORLD   Tony Martin
3 IN AN OLD DUTCH GARDEN   Dick Jurgens Orch. (VR: Eddy Howard)
4 INDIAN SUMMER   Tommy Dorsey Orch. (VR: Jack Leonard)

5 ON THE ISLE OF MAY   Connee Boswell
6 STARLIT HOUR   Glenn Miller Orch. (VR: Ray Eberle)
7 CARELESS   Glenn Miller Orch. (VR: Ray Eberle)
8 WHEN YOU WISH UPON A STAR   Glenn Miller Orch. (VR: Ray Eberle) *
9 AT THE BALALAIKA   Orrin Tucker Orch. (VR: Gil Mershon)
10 LEANIN' ON THE OLD TOP RAIL   Bob Crosby Orch. (VR: Bob Crosby)
   Note: * From Walt Disney's "Pinocchio."

March 23, 1940
1 CARELESS   Glenn Miller Orch. (VR: Ray Eberle)
2 IT'S A BLUE WORLD   Tony Martin
3 STARLIT HOUR   Glenn Miller Orch. (VR: Ray Eberle)
4 ON THE ISLE OF MAY   Connee Boswell
5 DARN THAT OLD DREAM   Benny Goodman Orch. (VR: Mildred Bailey)
6 IN AN OLD DUTCH GARDEN   Dick Jurgens Orch. (VR: Eddy Howard)
7 WHEN YOU WISH UPON A STAR   Glenn Miller Orch. (VR: Ray Eberle) *
8 INDIAN SUMMER   Tommy Dorsey Orch. (VR: Jack Leonard)
9 AT THE BALALAIKA   Orrin Tucker Orch. (VR: Gil Mershon)
10 DO I LOVE YOU?   Leo Reisman Orch. (VR: Lee Sullivan)
   Note: * From Walt Disney's "Pinocchio."

March 30, 1940
1 WHEN YOU WISH UPON A STAR   Glenn Miller Orch. (VR: Ray Eberle) *
2 IT'S A BLUE WORLD   Tony Martin
3 STARLIT HOUR   Glenn Miller Orch. (VR: Ray Eberle)
4 INDIAN SUMMER   Tommy Dorsey Orch. (VR: Jack Leonard)
5 ON THE ISLE OF MAY   Connee Boswell
6 IN AN OLD DUTCH GARDEN   Dick Jurgens Orch. (VR: Eddy Howard)
7 LEANIN' ON THE OLD TOP RAIL   Bob Crosby Orch. (VR: Bob Crosby)
8 CARELESS   Glenn Miller Orch. (VR: Ray Eberle)
9 I'VE GOT MY EYES ON YOU   Tommy Dorsey Orch. (VR: Alan DeWitt)
10 WITH THE WIND AND THE RAIN IN YOUR HAIR   Bob Crosby Orch. (VR: Marion Mann)
   Note: * From Walt Disney's "Pinocchio."

April 6, 1940
1 WHEN YOU WISH UPON A STAR   Glenn Miller Orch. (VR: Ray Eberle) *
2 STARLIT HOUR   Glenn Miller Orch. (VR: Ray Eberle)
3 WOODPECKER SONG   Glenn Miller Orch. (VR: Marion Hutton)
4 ON THE ISLE OF MAY   Connee Boswell
5 IN AN OLD DUTCH GARDEN   Dick Jurgens Orch. (VR: Eddy Howard)
6 IT'S A BLUE WORLD   Tony Martin
7 GAUCHO SERENADE   Dick Todd
8 WITH THE WIND AND THE RAIN IN YOUR HAIR   Bob Crosby Orch. (VR: Marion Mann)
9 INDIAN SUMMER   Tommy Dorsey Orch. (VR: Jack Leonard)
10 AT THE BALALAIKA   Orrin Tucker Orch. (VR: Gil Mershon)
   Note: * From Walt Disney's "Pinocchio."

April 13, 1940
1 WHEN YOU WISH UPON A STAR   Glenn Miller Orch. (VR: Ray Eberle) *
2 WOODPECKER SONG   Glenn Miller Orch. (VR: Marion Hutton)
3 ON THE ISLE OF MAY   Connee Boswell
4 IN AN OLD DUTCH GARDEN   Dick Jurgens Orch. (VR: Eddy Howard)
5 WITH THE WIND AND THE RAIN IN YOUR HAIR   Bob Crosby Orch. (VR: Marion Mann)
6 STARLIT HOUR   Glenn Miller Orch. (VR: Ray Eberle)
7 THE SINGING HILLS   Bing Crosby
8 LET THERE BE LOVE   Sammy Kaye Orch. (VR: Tommy Ryan)
9 ALICE BLUE GOWN   Frankie Masters Orch. (VR: Marion Francis)
10 IT'S A BLUE WORLD   Tony Martin
   Note: * From Walt Disney's "Pinocchio."

April 20, 1940
1 WHEN YOU WISH UPON A STAR   Glenn Miller Orch. (VR: Ray Eberle) *
2 WITH THE WIND AND THE RAIN IN YOUR HAIR   Bob Crosby Orch. (VR: Marion Mann)
3 ON THE ISLE OF MAY   Connee Boswell
4 WOODPECKER SONG   Glenn Miller Orch. (VR: Marion Hutton)
5 LET THERE BE LOVE   Sammy Kaye Orch. (VR: Tommy Ryan)
6 IN AN OLD DUTCH GARDEN   Dick Jurgens Orch. (VR: Eddy Howard)
7 HOW HIGH THE MOON   Benny Goodman Orch. (VR: Helen Forrest)
8 I'VE GOT MY EYES ON YOU   Tommy Dorsey Orch. (VR: Alan DeWitt)
9 THE SINGING HILLS   Bing Crosby
10 SO FAR SO GOOD   Bob Crosby Orch. (VR: Marion Mann)
   Note: * From Walt Disney's "Pinocchio."

April 27, 1940
1 WHEN YOU WISH UPON A STAR   Glenn Miller Orch. (VR: Ray Eberle) *
2 WOODPECKER SONG   Glenn Miller Orch. (VR: Marion Hutton)
3 WITH THE WIND AND THE RAIN IN YOUR HAIR   Bob Crosby Orch. (VR: Marion Mann)
4 THE SINGING HILLS   Bing Crosby
5 TOO ROMANTIC   Bing Crosby
6 ON THE ISLE OF MAY   Connee Boswell
7 HOW HIGH THE MOON   Benny Goodman Orch. (VR: Helen Forrest)
8 STARLIT HOUR   Glenn Miller Orch. (VR: Ray Eberle)
9 LET THERE BE LOVE   Sammy Kaye Orch. (VR: Tommy Ryan)
10 IT'S A BLUE WORLD   Tony Martin
   Note: * From Walt Disney's "Pinocchio."

May 4, 1940
1 WOODPECKER SONG   Glenn Miller Orch. (VR: Marion Hutton)
2 WHEN YOU WISH UPON A STAR   Glenn Miller Orch. (VR: Ray Eberle) *
3 WITH THE WIND AND THE RAIN IN YOUR HAIR   Bob Crosby Orch. (VR: Marion Mann)
4 THE SINGING HILLS   Bing Crosby
5 ON THE ISLE OF MAY   Connee Boswell
6 HOW HIGH THE MOON   Benny Goodman Orch. (VR: Helen Forrest)
7 TOO ROMANTIC   Bing Crosby
8 LET THERE BE LOVE   Sammy Kaye Orch. (VR: Tommy Ryan)
9 LITTLE CURLY HAIR IN A HIGHCHAIR   Fats Waller Orch. (VR: Fats Waller)
10 YOU, YOU DARLING   Kay Kyser Orch. (VR: Ginny Simms)
   Note: * From Walt Disney's "Pinocchio."

May 11, 1940
1 WOODPECKER SONG   Glenn Miller Orch. (VR: Marion Hutton)
2 WITH THE WIND AND THE RAIN IN YOUR HAIR   Bob Crosby Orch. (VR: Marion Mann)
3 WHEN YOU WISH UPON A STAR   Glenn Miller Orch. (VR: Ray Eberle) *
4 LET THERE BE LOVE   Sammy Kaye Orch. (VR: Tommy Ryan)
5 THE SINGING HILLS   Bing Crosby
6 SAY IT   Glenn Miller Orch. (VR: Ray Eberle)
7 ON THE ISLE OF MAY   Connee Boswell
8 APPLE BLOSSOMS AND CHAPEL BELLS   Orrin Tucker Orch. (VR: Orrin Tucker)
9 LOVER'S LULLABY   Glen Gray Orch. (VR: Kenny Sargent)
10 PLAYMATES   Kay Kyser Orch. (VR: Sully Mason)
   Note: * From Walt Disney's "Pinocchio."

May 18, 1940
1 WOODPECKER SONG   Glenn Miller Orch. (VR: Marion Hutton)
2 WITH THE WIND AND THE RAIN IN YOUR HAIR   Bob Crosby Orch. (VR: Marion Mann)
3 THE SINGING HILLS   Bing Crosby
4 IMAGINATION   Glenn Miller Orch. (VR: Ray Eberly)
5 WHEN YOU WISH UPON A STAR   Glenn Miller Orch. (VR: Ray Eberle) *
6 LET THERE BE LOVE   Sammy Kaye Orch. (VR: Tommy Ryan)
7 SHAKE DOWN THE STARS   Glenn Miller Orch. (VR: Ray Eberle)
8 LOVER'S LULLABY   Glen Gray Orch. (VR: Kenny Sargent)
9 SAY IT   Glenn Miller Orch. (VR: Ray Eberle)
10 TOO ROMANTIC   Bing Crosby
   Note: * From Walt Disney's "Pinocchio."

May 25, 1940
1 WOODPECKER SONG   Glenn Miller Orch. (VR: Marion Hutton)
2 IMAGINATION   Glenn Miller Orch. (VR: Ray Eberly)
3 WHEN YOU WISH UPON A STAR   Glenn Miller Orch. (VR: Ray Eberle) *
4 WITH THE WIND AND THE RAIN IN YOUR HAIR   Bob Crosby Orch. (VR: Marion Mann)
5 SAY IT   Glenn Miller Orch. (VR: Ray Eberle)
6 MAKE BELIEVE ISLAND   Mitchell Ayres Orch. (VR: Mary Ann Mercer)
7 LITTLE CURLY HAIR IN A HIGHCHAIR   Fats Waller Orch. (VR: Fats Waller)
8 THE SINGING HILLS   Bing Crosby
9 PLAYMATES   Kay Kyser Orch. (VR: Sully Mason)
10 I CAN'T LOVE YOU ANYMORE   Benny Goodman Orch. (VR: Helen Forrest)
   Note: * From Walt Disney's "Pinocchio."

June 1, 1940

1 WOODPECKER SONG   Glenn Miller Orch. (VR: Marion Hutton)
2 SAY IT   Glenn Miller Orch. (VR: Ray Eberle)
3 TOO ROMANTIC   Bing Crosby
4 IMAGINATION   Glenn Miller Orch. (VR: Ray Eberly)
5 PLAYMATES   Kay Kyser Orch. (VR: Sully Mason)
6 WHERE WAS I?   Charlie Barent Orch. (VR: Mary Ann McCall)
7 THE SINGING HILLS   Bing Crosby
8 WHEN YOU WISH UPON A STAR   Glenn Miller Orch. (VR: Ray Eberle) *
9 WITH THE WIND AND THE RAIN IN YOUR HAIR   Bob Crosby Orch. (VR: Marion Mann)
10 LITTLE CURLY HAIR IN A HIGHCHAIR   Fats Waller Orch. (VR: Fats Waller)

Note: * From Walt Disney's "Pinocchio."

June 8, 1940

1 WOODPECKER SONG   Glenn Miller Orch. (VR: Marion Hutton)
2 SAY IT   Glenn Miller Orch. (VR: Ray Eberle)
3 WHERE WAS I?   Charlie Barent Orch. (VR: Mary Ann McCall)
4 SHAKE DOWN THE STARS   Glenn Miller Orch. (VR: Ray Eberle)
5 IMAGINATION   Glenn Miller Orch. (VR: Ray Eberly)
6 WITH THE WIND AND THE RAIN IN YOUR HAIR   Bob Crosby Orch. (VR: Marion Mann)
7 PLAYMATES   Kay Kyser Orch. (VR: Sully Mason)
8 IT'S A WONDERFUL WORLD   Charlie Barent Orch. (VR: Mary Ann McCall)
9 TOO ROMANTIC   Bing Crosby
10 THE SINGING HILLS   Bing Crosby

June 15, 1940

1 WOODPECKER SONG   Glenn Miller Orch. (VR: Marion Hutton)
2 IMAGINATION   Glenn Miller Orch. (VR: Ray Eberly)
3 SAY IT   Glenn Miller Orch. (VR: Ray Eberle)
4 MAKE BELIEVE ISLAND   Mitchell Ayres Orch. (VR: Mary Ann Mercer)
5 SHAKE DOWN THE STARS   Glenn Miller Orch. (VR: Ray Eberle)
6 DEVIL MAY CARE   Glenn Miller Orch. (VR: Ray Eberle)
7 BLUE LOVEBIRD   Kay Kyser Orch. (VR: Ginny Simms)
8 WHERE WAS I?   Charlie Barent Orch. (VR: Mary Ann McCall)
9 PLAYMATES   Kay Kyser Orch. (VR: Sully Mason)
10 THE SINGING HILLS   Bing Crosby

June 22, 1940

1 IMAGINATION   Glenn Miller Orch. (VR: Ray Eberly)
2 MAKE BELIEVE ISLAND   Mitchell Ayres Orch. (VR: Mary Ann Mercer)
3 WHERE WAS I?   Charlie Barent Orch. (VR: Mary Ann McCall)
4 SAY IT   Glenn Miller Orch. (VR: Ray Eberle)
5 WOODPECKER SONG   Glenn Miller Orch. (VR: Marion Hutton)
6 PLAYMATES   Kay Kyser Orch. (VR: Sully Mason)
7 SIERRA SUE   Bing Crosby
8 THE BREEZE AND I   Jimmy Dorsey Orch. (VR: Bob Eberly)
9 BLUE LOVEBIRD   Kay Kyser Orch. (VR: Ginny Simms)
10 THE SINGING HILLS   Bing Crosby

June 29, 1940

1 MAKE BELIEVE ISLAND   Mitchell Ayres Orch. (VR: Mary Ann Mercer)
2 WHERE WAS I?   Charlie Barent Orch. (VR: Mary Ann McCall)
3 IMAGINATION   Glenn Miller Orch. (VR: Ray Eberly)
4 WOODPECKER SONG   Glenn Miller Orch. (VR: Marion Hutton)
5 FOOLS RUSH IN   Glenn Miller Orch. (VR: Ray Eberle)
6 I CAN'T LOVE YOU ANYMORE   Benny Goodman Orch. (VR: Helen Forrest)
7 PLAYMATES   Kay Kyser Orch. (VR: Sully Mason)
8 THE BREEZE AND I   Jimmy Dorsey Orch. (VR: Bob Eberly)
9 DEVIL MAY CARE   Glenn Miller Orch. (VR: Ray Eberle)
10 YOU'RE LONELY AND I'M LONELY   Tommy Dorsey Orch. (VR: Frank Sinatra)

July 6, 1940

1 IMAGINATION   Glenn Miller Orch. (VR: Ray Eberly)
2 WOODPECKER SONG   Glenn Miller Orch. (VR: Marion Hutton)
3 MAKE BELIEVE ISLAND   Mitchell Ayres Orch. (VR: Mary Ann Mercer)
4 WHERE WAS I?   Charlie Barent Orch. (VR: Mary Ann McCall)
5 PLAYMATES   Kay Kyser Orch. (VR: Sully Mason)
6 I CAN'T LOVE YOU ANYMORE   Benny Goodman Orch. (VR: Helen Forrest)
7 THE BREEZE AND I   Jimmy Dorsey Orch. (VR: Bob Eberly)
8 I'M STEPPIN' OUT WITH A MEMORY TONIGHT   Glenn Miller Orch. (VR: Ray Eberle)
9 YOU'RE LONELY AND I'M LONELY   Tommy Dorsey Orch. (VR: Frank Sinatra)
10 DEVIL MAY CARE   Glenn Miller Orch. (VR: Ray Eberle)

July 13, 1940

1 IMAGINATION   Glenn Miller Orch. (VR: Ray Eberly)
2 MAKE BELIEVE ISLAND   Mitchell Ayres Orch. (VR: Mary Ann Mercer)
3 WOODPECKER SONG   Glenn Miller Orch. (VR: Marion Hutton)
4 SIERRA SUE   Bing Crosby
5 THE BREEZE AND I   Jimmy Dorsey Orch. (VR: Bob Eberly)
6 BLUE LOVEBIRD   Kay Kyser Orch. (VR: Ginny Simms)
7 WHERE WAS I?   Charlie Barent Orch. (VR: Mary Ann McCall)
8 PLAYMATES   Kay Kyser Orch. (VR: Sully Mason)
9 I CAN'T LOVE YOU ANYMORE   Benny Goodman Orch. (VR: Helen Forrest)
10 DEVIL MAY CARE   Glenn Miller Orch. (VR: Ray Eberle)

July 20, 1940

1 FOOLS RUSH IN   Glenn Miller Orch. (VR: Ray Eberle)
2 THE BREEZE AND I   Jimmy Dorsey Orch. (VR: Bob Eberly)
3 MAKE BELIEVE ISLAND   Mitchell Ayres Orch. (VR: Mary Ann Mercer)
4 PLAYMATES   Kay Kyser Orch. (VR: Sully Mason)
5 WHERE WAS I?   Charlie Barent Orch. (VR: Mary Ann McCall)
6 WOODPECKER SONG   Glenn Miller Orch. (VR: Marion Hutton)
7 SIERRA SUE   Bing Crosby
8 IMAGINATION   Glenn Miller Orch. (VR: Ray Eberly)
9 I'LL NEVER SMILE AGAIN   Tommy Dorsey Orch. (VR: Frank Sinatra)
10 I'M STEPPIN' OUT WITH A MEMORY TONIGHT   Glenn Miller Orch. (VR: Ray Eberle)

Mitchell Ayers
Formerly with Little Jack Little's band, Mitch's solo effort ``Make Believe Island'' hits #1 (June 29).
He later became Perry Como's musical director.

July 27, 1940
1 MAKE BELIEVE ISLAND   Mitchell Ayres Orch. (VR: Mary Ann Mercer)
2 I'LL NEVER SMILE AGAIN   Tommy Dorsey Orch. (VR: Frank Sinatra)
3 SIERRA SUE   Bing Crosby
4 FOOLS RUSH IN   Glenn Miller Orch. (VR: Ray Eberle)
5 IMAGINATION   Glenn Miller Orch. (VR: Ray Eberly)
6 THE BREEZE AND I   Jimmy Dorsey Orch. (VR: Bob Eberly)
7 I CAN'T LOVE YOU ANYMORE   Benny Goodman Orch. (VR: Helen Forrest)
8 PLAYMATES   Kay Kyser Orch. (VR: Sully Mason)
9 WHERE WAS I?   Charlie Barent Orch. (VR: Mary Ann McCall)
10 I'M NOBODY'S BABY   Judy Garland

August 3, 1940
1 I'LL NEVER SMILE AGAIN   Tommy Dorsey Orch. (VR: Frank Sinatra)
2 THE BREEZE AND I   Jimmy Dorsey Orch. (VR: Bob Eberly)
3 SIERRA SUE   Bing Crosby
4 FOOLS RUSH IN   Glenn Miller Orch. (VR: Ray Eberle)
5 MAKE BELIEVE ISLAND   Mitchell Ayres Orch. (VR: Mary Ann Mercer)
6 PLAYMATES   Kay Kyser Orch. (VR: Sully Mason)
7 IMAGINATION   Glenn Miller Orch. (VR: Ray Eberly)
8 WHERE WAS I?   Charlie Barent Orch. (VR: Mary Ann McCall)
9 WHEN THE SWALLOWS COME BACK TO CAPISTRANO   Glenn Miller Orch. (VR: Ray Eberle)
10 I'M NOBODY'S BABY   Judy Garland

August 10, 1940
1 I'LL NEVER SMILE AGAIN   Tommy Dorsey Orch. (VR: Frank Sinatra)
2 FOOLS RUSH IN   Glenn Miller Orch. (VR: Ray Eberle)
3 THE BREEZE AND I   Jimmy Dorsey Orch. (VR: Bob Eberly)
4 SIERRA SUE   Bing Crosby
5 WHEN THE SWALLOWS COME BACK TO CAPISTRANO   Glenn Miller Orch. (VR: Ray Eberle)
6 MAKE BELIEVE ISLAND   Mitchell Ayres Orch. (VR: Mary Ann Mercer)
7 I'M NOBODY'S BABY   Judy Garland
8 IMAGINATION   Glenn Miller Orch. (VR: Ray Eberly)
9 ALL THIS AND HEAVEN, TOO   Jimmy Dorsey Orch. (VR: Bob Eberly)
10 YOU THINK OF EVERYTHING   Jimmy Dorsey Orch. (VR: Connie Haines)

August 17, 1940
1 SIERRA SUE   Bing Crosby
2 I'LL NEVER SMILE AGAIN   Tommy Dorsey Orch. (VR: Frank Sinatra)
3 FOOLS RUSH IN   Glenn Miller Orch. (VR: Ray Eberle)
4 THE BREEZE AND I   Jimmy Dorsey Orch. (VR: Bob Eberly)
5 WHEN THE SWALLOWS COME BACK TO CAPISTRANO   Glenn Miller Orch. (VR: Ray Eberle)
6 MAKE BELIEVE ISLAND   Mitchell Ayres Orch. (VR: Mary Ann Mercer)
7 SIX LESSONS FROM MADAME LA ZONGA   Jimmy Dorsey Orch. (VR: Helen O'Connell)
8 THE NEARNESS OF YOU   Glenn Miller Orch. (VR: Ray Eberle)
9 I'M NOBODY'S BABY   Judy Garland
10 ALL THIS AND HEAVEN, TOO   Jimmy Dorsey Orch. (VR: Bob Eberly)

August 24, 1940
1 I'LL NEVER SMILE AGAIN   Tommy Dorsey Orch. (VR: Frank Sinatra)
2 WHEN THE SWALLOWS COME BACK TO CAPISTRANO   Glenn Miller Orch. (VR: Ray Eberle)
3 I'M NOBODY'S BABY   Judy Garland
4 FOOLS RUSH IN   Glenn Miller Orch. (VR: Ray Eberle)
5 SIERRA SUE   Bing Crosby
6 BLUEBERRY HILL   Glenn Miller Orch. (VR: Ray Eberle) *
7 THE BREEZE AND I   Jimmy Dorsey Orch. (VR: Bob Eberly)
8 THE NEARNESS OF YOU   Glenn Miller Orch. (VR: Ray Eberle)
9 PRACTICE MAKES PERFECT   Bob Chester Orch. (VR: Al Stuart)
10 MAKE BELIEVE ISLAND   Mitchell Ayres Orch. (VR: Mary Ann Mercer)
   Note: * As popular as this song was for Glenn Miller (and later for Fats Domino), it never reached the #1 position.

August 31, 1940
1 I'LL NEVER SMILE AGAIN   Tommy Dorsey Orch. (VR: Frank Sinatra)
2 SIERRA SUE   Bing Crosby
3 FOOLS RUSH IN   Glenn Miller Orch. (VR: Ray Eberle)
4 I'M NOBODY'S BABY   Judy Garland
5 WHEN THE SWALLOWS COME BACK TO CAPISTRANO   Glenn Miller Orch. (VR: Ray Eberle)
6 ALL THIS AND HEAVEN, TOO   Jimmy Dorsey Orch. (VR: Bob Eberly)
7 BLUEBERRY HILL   Glenn Miller Orch. (VR: Ray Eberle) *
8 THE BREEZE AND I   Jimmy Dorsey Orch. (VR: Bob Eberly)
9 THE NEARNESS OF YOU   Glenn Miller Orch. (VR: Ray Eberle)
10 PRACTICE MAKES PERFECT   Bob Chester Orch. (VR: Al Stuart)
   Note: * As popular as this song was for Glenn Miller (and later for Fats Domino), it never reached the #1 position.

September 7, 1940
1 I'LL NEVER SMILE AGAIN   Tommy Dorsey Orch. (VR: Frank Sinatra)
2 WHEN THE SWALLOWS COME BACK TO CAPISTRANO   Glenn Miller Orch. (VR: Ray Eberle)
3 SIERRA SUE   Bing Crosby
4 BLUEBERRY HILL   Glenn Miller Orch. (VR: Ray Eberle)
5 FOOLS RUSH IN   Glenn Miller Orch. (VR: Ray Eberle)
6 I'M NOBODY'S BABY   Judy Garland
7 ALL THIS AND HEAVEN, TOO   Jimmy Dorsey Orch. (VR: Bob Eberly)
8 THE NEARNESS OF YOU   Glenn Miller Orch. (VR: Ray Eberle)
9 PRACTICE MAKES PERFECT   Bob Chester Orch. (VR: Al Stuart)
10 THE BREEZE AND I   Jimmy Dorsey Orch. (VR: Bob Eberly)
   Note: * As popular as this song was for Glenn Miller (and later for Fats Domino), it never reached the #1 position.

September 14, 1940
1 I'LL NEVER SMILE AGAIN   Tommy Dorsey Orch. (VR: Frank Sinatra)
2 I'M NOBODY'S BABY   Judy Garland
3 WHEN THE SWALLOWS COME BACK TO CAPISTRANO   Glenn Miller Orch. (VR: Ray Eberle)
4 ALL THIS AND HEAVEN, TOO   Jimmy Dorsey Orch. (VR: Bob Eberly)

Bob Chester
Chester's Detroit-based band lands its only #1 song with ``Practice Makes Perfect'' (Oct. 5).

5 BLUEBERRY HILL   Glenn Miller Orch. (VR: Ray Eberle) *
6 SIERRA SUE   Bing Crosby
7 THE NEARNESS OF YOU   Glenn Miller Orch. (VR: Ray Eberle)
8 PRACTICE MAKES PERFECT   Bob Chester Orch. (VR: Al Stuart)
9 MAYBE   Ink Spots
10 THE BREEZE AND I   Jimmy Dorsey Orch. (VR: Bob Eberly)
   Note: * As popular as this song was for Glenn Miller (and later for Fats Domino), it never reached the #1 position.

September 21, 1940
1 I'LL NEVER SMILE AGAIN   Tommy Dorsey Orch. (VR: Frank Sinatra)
2 BLUEBERRY HILL   Glenn Miller Orch. (VR: Ray Eberle) *
3 ALL THIS AND HEAVEN, TOO   Jimmy Dorsey Orch. (VR: Bob Eberly)
4 I'M NOBODY'S BABY   Judy Garland
5 WHEN THE SWALLOWS COME BACK TO CAPISTRANO   Glenn Miller Orch. (VR: Ray Eberle)
6 PRACTICE MAKES PERFECT   Bob Chester Orch. (VR: Al Stuart)
7 SIERRA SUE   Bing Crosby
8 TRADE WINDS   Bing Crosby
9 MAYBE   Ink Spots
10 SAME OLD STORY   Frankie Masters Orch. (VR: Frankie Masters)
   Note: * As popular as this song was for Glenn Miller (and later for Fats Domino), it never reached the #1 position.

September 28, 1940
1 MAYBE   Ink Spots
2 WHEN THE SWALLOWS COME BACK TO CAPISTRANO   Glenn Miller Orch. (VR: Ray Eberle)
3 I'LL NEVER SMILE AGAIN   Tommy Dorsey Orch. (VR: Frank Sinatra)
4 BLUEBERRY HILL   Glenn Miller Orch. (VR: Ray Eberle) *
5 PRACTICE MAKES PERFECT   Bob Chester Orch. (VR: Al Stuart)
6 TRADE WINDS   Bing Crosby
7 I'M NOBODY'S BABY   Judy Garland
8 SIERRA SUE   Bing Crosby
9 OUR LOVE AFFAIR   Tommy Dorsey Orch. (VR: Frank Sinatra)
10 SAME OLD STORY   Frankie Masters Orch. (VR: Frankie Masters)
   Note: * As popular as this song was for Glenn Miller (and later for Fats Domino), it never reached the #1 position.

October 5, 1940
1 PRACTICE MAKES PERFECT   Bob Chester Orch. (VR: Al Stuart)
2 I'LL NEVER SMILE AGAIN   Tommy Dorsey Orch. (VR: Frank Sinatra)
3 MAYBE   Ink Spots
4 BLUEBERRY HILL   Glenn Miller Orch. (VR: Ray Eberle) *
5 I'M NOBODY'S BABY   Judy Garland
6 WHEN THE SWALLOWS COME BACK TO CAPISTRANO   Glenn Miller Orch. (VR: Ray Eberle)
7 ONLY FOREVER   Bing Crosby
8 TRADE WINDS   Bing Crosby
9 AND SO DO I   Jimmy Dorsey Orch. (VR: Bob Eberly)
10 SIERRA SUE   Bing Crosby
   Note: * As popular as this song was for Glenn Miller (and later for Fats Domino), it never reached the #1 position.

October 12, 1940
1 MAYBE   Ink Spots
2 PRACTICE MAKES PERFECT   Bob Chester Orch. (VR: Al Stuart)
3 BLUEBERRY HILL   Glenn Miller Orch. (VR: Ray Eberle) *
4 I'LL NEVER SMILE AGAIN   Tommy Dorsey Orch. (VR: Frank Sinatra)
5 TRADE WINDS   Bing Crosby
6 ONLY FOREVER   Bing Crosby
7 CALL OF THE CANYON   Glenn Miller Orch. (VR: Ray Eberly)
8 WHEN THE SWALLOWS COME BACK TO CAPISTRANO   Glenn Miller Orch. (VR: Ray Eberle)
9 A MILLION DREAMS AGO   Dick Jurgens Orch. (VR: Harry Cool)
10 NOW I LAY ME DOWN TO DREAM   Bob Chester Orch. (VR: Dolores O'Neill)
   Note: * As popular as this song was for Glenn Miller (and later for Fats Domino), it never reached the #1 position.

October 19, 1940
1 MAYBE   Ink Spots
2 PRACTICE MAKES PERFECT   Bob Chester Orch. (VR: Al Stuart)
3 TRADE WINDS   Bing Crosby
4 BLUEBERRY HILL   Glenn Miller Orch. (VR: Ray Eberle) *
5 I'LL NEVER SMILE AGAIN   Tommy Dorsey Orch. (VR: Frank Sinatra)
6 ONLY FOREVER   Bing Crosby
7 WHEN THE SWALLOWS COME BACK TO CAPISTRANO   Glenn Miller Orch. (VR: Ray Eberle)
8 OUR LOVE AFFAIR   Tommy Dorsey Orch. (VR: Frank Sinatra)
9 FERRYBOAT SERENADE   Andrews Sisters **
10 THERE I GO   Vaughn Monroe Orch. (VR: Vaughn Monroe)
   Note: * As popular as this song was for Glenn Miller (and later for Fats Domino), it never reached the #1 position.
   ** Another version by: Kay Kyser Orch. (VR: Harry Babbitt).

October 26, 1940
1 PRACTICE MAKES PERFECT   Bob Chester Orch. (VR: Al Stuart)
2 TRADE WINDS   Bing Crosby
3 ONLY FOREVER   Bing Crosby
4 MAYBE   Ink Spots
5 OUR LOVE AFFAIR   Tommy Dorsey Orch. (VR: Frank Sinatra)
6 FERRYBOAT SERENADE   Andrews Sisters *
7 BLUEBERRY HILL   Glenn Miller Orch. (VR: Ray Eberle) **
8 I'LL NEVER SMILE AGAIN   Tommy Dorsey Orch. (VR: Frank Sinatra)
9 THERE I GO   Vaughn Monroe Orch. (VR: Vaughn Monroe)
10 WHEN THE SWALLOWS COME BACK TO CAPISTRANO   Glenn Miller Orch. (VR: Ray Eberle)
   Note: * Another version by: Kay Kyser Orch. (VR: Harry Babbitt).
   ** As popular as this song was for Glenn Miller (and later for Fats Domino), it never reached the #1 position.

November 2, 1940
1 ONLY FOREVER   Bing Crosby
2 PRACTICE MAKES PERFECT   Bob Chester Orch. (VR: Al Stuart)
3 MAYBE   Ink Spots
4 FERRYBOAT SERENADE   Andrews Sisters *

5 TRADE WINDS Bing Crosby
6 BLUEBERRY HILL Glenn Miller Orch. (VR: Ray Eberle) **
7 OUR LOVE AFFAIR Tommy Dorsey Orch. (VR: Frank Sinatra)
8 I'LL NEVER SMILE AGAIN Tommy Dorsey Orch. (VR: Frank Sinatra)
9 THERE I GO Vaughn Monroe Orch. (VR: Vaughn Monroe)
10 TWO DREAMS MET Mitchell Ayres Orch. (VR: Mary Ann Mercer)
  Note: * Another version by: Kay Kyser Orch. (VR: Harry Babbitt).
  ** As popular as this song was for Glenn Miller (and later for Fats Domino), it never reached the #1 position.

November 9, 1940
1 ONLY FOREVER Bing Crosby
2 FERRYBOAT SERENADE Andrews Sisters *
3 MAYBE Ink Spots
4 PRACTICE MAKES PERFECT Bob Chester Orch. (VR: Al Stuart)
5 TRADE WINDS Bing Crosby
6 BLUEBERRY HILL Glenn Miller Orch. (VR: Ray Eberle) **
7 THERE I GO Vaughn Monroe Orch. (VR: Vaughn Monroe)
8 OUR LOVE AFFAIR Tommy Dorsey Orch. (VR: Frank Sinatra)
9 LOOKING FOR YESTERDAY Woody Herman Orch. (VR: Woody Herman)
10 NOW I LAY ME DOWN TO DREAM Bob Chester Orch. (VR: Dolores O'Neill)
  Note: * Another version by: Kay Kyser Orch. (VR: Harry Babbitt).
  ** As popular as this song was for Glenn Miller (and later for Fats Domino), it never reached the #1 position.

November 16, 1940
1 ONLY FOREVER Bing Crosby
2 FERRYBOAT SERENADE Andrews Sisters *
3 MAYBE Ink Spots
4 PRACTICE MAKES PERFECT Bob Chester Orch. (VR: Al Stuart)
5 TRADE WINDS Bing Crosby
6 WE THREE Ink Spots
7 THERE I GO Vaughn Monroe Orch. (VR: Vaughn Monroe)
8 OUR LOVE AFFAIR Tommy Dorsey Orch. (VR: Frank Sinatra)
9 BLUEBERRY HILL Glenn Miller Orch. (VR: Ray Eberle) **
10 DREAM VALLEY Sammy Kaye Orch. (VR: Tommy Ryan)
  Note: * Another version by: Kay Kyser Orch. (VR: Harry Babbitt).
  ** As popular as this song was for Glenn Miller (and later for Fats Domino), it never reached the #1 position.

November 23, 1940
1 FERRYBOAT SERENADE Andrews Sisters *
2 TRADE WINDS Bing Crosby
3 ONLY FOREVER Bing Crosby
4 THERE I GO Vaughn Monroe Orch. (VR: Vaughn Monroe)
5 PRACTICE MAKES PERFECT Bob Chester Orch. (VR: Al Stuart)
6 WE THREE Ink Spots
7 MAYBE Ink Spots
8 OUR LOVE AFFAIR Tommy Dorsey Orch. (VR: Frank Sinatra)
9 DREAM VALLEY Sammy Kaye Orch. (VR: Tommy Ryan)
10 BLUEBERRY HILL Glenn Miller Orch. (VR: Ray Eberle) **
  Note: * Another version by: Kay Kyser Orch. (VR: Harry Babbitt).

** As popular as this song was for Glenn Miller (and later for Fats Domino), it never reached the #1 position.

November 30, 1940
1 TRADE WINDS Bing Crosby
2 FERRYBOAT SERENADE Andrews Sisters *
3 ONLY FOREVER Bing Crosby
4 THERE I GO Vaughn Monroe Orch. (VR: Vaughn Monroe)
5 WE THREE Ink Spots
6 OUR LOVE AFFAIR Tommy Dorsey Orch. (VR: Frank Sinatra)
7 MAYBE Ink Spots
8 PRACTICE MAKES PERFECT Bob Chester Orch. (VR: Al Stuart)
9 SO YOU'RE THE ONE Eddy Duchin Orch. (VR: June Robbins)
10 WHEN THE NIGHTINGALE SANG IN BERKELEY SQUARE Glenn Miller Orch. (VR: Ray Eberle)
  Note: * Another version by: Kay Kyser Orch. (VR: Harry Babbitt).

December 7, 1940
1 WE THREE Ink Spots
2 FERRYBOAT SERENADE Andrews Sisters *
3 THERE I GO Vaughn Monroe Orch. (VR: Vaughn Monroe)
4 ONLY FOREVER Bing Crosby
5 DOWN ARGENTINE WAY Bob Crosby Orch. (VR: Bonnie King)
6 TRADE WINDS Bing Crosby
7 WHEN THE NIGHTINGALE SANG IN BERKELEY SQUARE Glenn Miller Orch. (VR: Ray Eberle)
8 OUR LOVE AFFAIR Tommy Dorsey Orch. (VR: Frank Sinatra)
9 FRENESI Artie Shaw Orch.
10 MAYBE Ink Spots
  Note: * Another version by: Kay Kyser Orch. (VR: Harry Babbitt).

December 14, 1940
1 THERE I GO Vaughn Monroe Orch. (VR: Vaughn Monroe)
2 FERRYBOAT SERENADE Andrews Sisters *
3 WE THREE Ink Spots
4 ONLY FOREVER Bing Crosby
5 TRADE WINDS Bing Crosby
6 WHEN THE NIGHTINGALE SANG IN BERKELEY SQUARE Glenn Miller Orch. (VR: Ray Eberle)
7 DOWN ARGENTINE WAY Bob Crosby Orch. (VR: Bonnie King)
8 FRENESI Artie Shaw Orch.
9 I GIVE YOU MY WORD Eddy Duchin Orch. (VR: June Robbins)
10 SO YOU'RE THE ONE Eddy Duchin Orch. (VR: June Robbins)
  Note: * Another version by: Kay Kyser Orch. (VR: Harry Babbitt).

December 21, 1940
1 THERE I GO Vaughn Monroe Orch. (VR: Vaughn Monroe)
2 FERRYBOAT SERENADE Andrews Sisters *
3 WHEN THE NIGHTINGALE SANG IN BERKELEY SQUARE Glenn Miller Orch. (VR: Ray Eberle)
4 DOWN ARGENTINE WAY Bob Crosby Orch. (VR: Bonnie King)
5 WE THREE Ink Spots
6 ONLY FOREVER Bing Crosby
7 FRENESI Artie Shaw Orch.
8 TRADE WINDS Bing Crosby

9 SO YOU'RE THE ONE   Eddy Duchin Orch. (VR: June Robbins)
10 I GIVE YOU MY WORD   Eddy Duchin Orch. (VR: June Robbins)
   Note: * Another version by: Kay Kyser Orch. (VR: Harry Babbitt).

December 28, 1940
1 THERE I GO   Vaughn Monroe Orch. (VR: Vaughn Monroe)
2 FRENESI   Artie Shaw Orch.
3 WHEN THE NIGHTINGALE SANG IN BERKELEY SQUARE   Glenn Miller Orch. (VR: Ray Eberle)
4 WE THREE   Ink Spots
5 DOWN ARGENTINE WAY   Bob Crosby Orch. (VR: Bonnie King)
6 FERRYBOAT SERENADE   Andrews Sisters *
7 ONLY FOREVER   Bing Crosby
8 SO YOU'RE THE ONE   Eddy Duchin Orch. (VR: June Robbins)
9 TRADE WINDS   Bing Crosby
10 I GIVE YOU MY WORD   Eddy Duchin Orch. (VR: June Robbins)
   Note: * Another version by: Kay Kyser Orch. (VR: Harry Babbitt).

January 4, 1941
1 THERE I GO   Vaughn Monroe Orch. (VR: Vaughn Monroe)
2 FRENESI   Artie Shaw Orch.
3 I GIVE YOU MY WORD   Eddy Duchin Orch. (VR: June Robbins)
4 SO YOU'RE THE ONE   Eddy Duchin Orch. (VR: June Robbins)
5 I HEAR A RHAPSODY   Charlie Barnet Orch. (VR: Bob Carroll) *
6 PERFIDIA   Xavier Cugat
7 SAME OLD STORY   Frankie Masters Orch. (VR: Frankie Masters)
8 YOU WALK BY   Eddy Duchin Orch. (VR: Johnny Drake)
9 KEEP AN EYE ON YOUR HEART   Glenn Miller Orch. (VR: Marion Hutton)
10 PRACTICE MAKES PERFECT   Bob Chester Orch. (VR: Al Stuart)
   Note: * Another version by: Jimmy Dorsey Orch. (VR: Bob Eberly)

January 11, 1941
1 FRENESI   Artie Shaw Orch.
2 THERE I GO   Vaughn Monroe Orch. (VR: Vaughn Monroe)
3 I GIVE YOU MY WORD   Eddy Duchin Orch. (VR: June Robbins)
4 SO YOU'RE THE ONE   Eddy Duchin Orch. (VR: June Robbins)
5 I HEAR A RHAPSODY   Charlie Barnet Orch. (VR: Bob Carroll) *
6 YOU WALK BY   Eddy Duchin Orch. (VR: Johnny Drake)
7 PRACTICE MAKES PERFECT   Bob Chester Orch. (VR: Al Stuart)
8 PERFIDIA   Xavier Cugat
9 SAME OLD STORY   Frankie Masters Orch. (VR: Frankie Masters)
10 MAY I NEVER LOVE AGAIN   Bob Chester Orch. (VR: Dolores O'Neill)
   Note: * Another version by: Jimmy Dorsey Orch. (VR: Bob Eberly)

January 18, 1941
1 FRENESI   Artie Shaw Orch.

2 THERE I GO   Vaughn Monroe Orch. (VR: Vaughn Monroe)
3 I HEAR A RHAPSODY   Charlie Barnet Orch. (VR: Bob Carroll) *
4 I GIVE YOU MY WORD   Eddy Duchin Orch. (VR: June Robbins)
5 SO YOU'RE THE ONE   Eddy Duchin Orch. (VR: June Robbins)
6 YOU WALK BY   Eddy Duchin Orch. (VR: Johnny Drake)
7 SAME OLD STORY   Frankie Masters Orch. (VR: Frankie Masters)
8 MAY I NEVER LOVE AGAIN   Bob Chester Orch. (VR: Dolores O'Neill)
9 IT ALL COMES BACK TO ME NOW   Gene Krupa Orch. (VR: Howard Dulany)
10 PERFIDIA   Xavier Cugat
   Note: * Another version by: Jimmy Dorsey Orch. (VR: Bob Eberly)

January 25, 1941
1 FRENESI   Artie Shaw Orch.
2 I HEAR A RHAPSODY   Charlie Barnet Orch. (VR: Bob Carroll) *
3 THERE I GO   Vaughn Monroe Orch. (VR: Vaughn Monroe)
4 I GIVE YOU MY WORD   Eddy Duchin Orch. (VR: June Robbins)
5 SO YOU'RE THE ONE   Eddy Duchin Orch. (VR: June Robbins)
6 YOU WALK BY   Eddy Duchin Orch. (VR: Johnny Drake)
7 IT ALL COMES BACK TO ME NOW   Gene Krupa Orch. (VR: Howard Dulany)
8 THERE'LL BE SOME CHANGES MADE   Benny Goodman Orch. (VR: Louise Tobin)
9 MAY I NEVER LOVE AGAIN   Bob Chester Orch. (VR: Dolores O'Neill)
10 PERFIDIA   Xavier Cugat
   Note: * Another version by: Jimmy Dorsey Orch. (VR: Bob Eberly)

February 1, 1941
1 I HEAR A RHAPSODY   Charlie Barnet Orch. (VR: Bob Carroll) *
2 FRENESI   Artie Shaw Orch.
3 I GIVE YOU MY WORD   Eddy Duchin Orch. (VR: June Robbins)
4 THERE I GO   Vaughn Monroe Orch. (VR: Vaughn Monroe)
5 SO YOU'RE THE ONE   Eddy Duchin Orch. (VR: June Robbins)
6 YOU WALK BY   Eddy Duchin Orch. (VR: Johnny Drake)
7 PERFIDIA   Xavier Cugat
8 MAY I NEVER LOVE AGAIN   Bob Chester Orch. (VR: Dolores O'Neill)
9 THERE'LL BE SOME CHANGES MADE   Benny Goodman Orch. (VR: Louise Tobin)
10 HIGH ON A WINDY HILL   Jimmy Dorsey Orch. (VR: Bob Eberly)
   Note: * Another version by: Jimmy Dorsey Orch. (VR: Bob Eberly)

February 8, 1941
1 I HEAR A RHAPSODY   Charlie Barnet Orch. (VR: Bob Carroll) *
2 FRENESI   Artie Shaw Orch.
3 YOU WALK BY   Eddy Duchin Orch. (VR: Johnny Drake)
4 SO YOU'RE THE ONE   Eddy Duchin Orch. (VR: June Robbins)
5 I GIVE YOU MY WORD   Eddy Duchin Orch. (VR: June Robbins)

Artie Shaw
Shaw starts the new year with the #1 hit, ``Frenesi'' (Jan. 11).

6   THERE I GO   Vaughn Monroe Orch. (VR: Vaughn Monroe)
7   PERFIDIA   Xavier Cugat
8   HIGH ON A WINDY HILL   Jimmy Dorsey Orch. (VR: Bob Eberly)
9   IT ALL COMES BACK TO ME NOW   Gene Krupa Orch. (VR: Howard Dulany)
10   THERE'LL BE SOME CHANGES MADE   Benny Goodman Orch. (VR: Louise Tobin)
     Note: * Another version by: Jimmy Dorsey Orch. (VR: Bob Eberly)

February 15, 1941
1   I HEAR A RHAPSODY   Charlie Barnet Orch. (VR: Bob Carroll) *
2   FRENESI   Artie Shaw Orch.
3   YOU WALK BY   Eddy Duchin Orch. (VR: Johnny Drake)
4   I GIVE YOU MY WORD   Eddy Duchin Orch. (VR: June Robbins)
5   SO YOU'RE THE ONE   Eddy Duchin Orch. (VR: June Robbins)
6   IT ALL COMES BACK TO ME NOW   Gene Krupa Orch. (VR: Howard Dulany)
7   HIGH ON A WINDY HILL   Jimmy Dorsey Orch. (VR: Bob Eberly)
8   PERFIDIA   Xavier Cugat
9   THERE I GO   Vaughn Monroe Orch. (VR: Vaughn Monroe)
10   MAY I NEVER LOVE AGAIN   Bob Chester Orch. (VR: Dolores O'Neill)
     Note: * Another version by: Jimmy Dorsey Orch. (VR: Bob Eberly)

February 22, 1941
1   I HEAR A RHAPSODY   Charlie Barnet Orch. (VR: Bob Carroll) *
2   FRENESI   Artie Shaw Orch.
3   YOU WALK BY   Eddy Duchin Orch. (VR: Johnny Drake)
4   PERFIDIA   Xavier Cugat
5   SO YOU'RE THE ONE   Eddy Duchin Orch. (VR: June Robbins)
6   HIGH ON A WINDY HILL   Jimmy Dorsey Orch. (VR: Bob Eberly)
7   IT ALL COMES BACK TO ME NOW   Gene Krupa Orch. (VR: Howard Dulany)
8   I GIVE YOU MY WORD   Eddy Duchin Orch. (VR: June Robbins)
9   THERE'LL BE SOME CHANGES MADE   Benny Goodman Orch. (VR: Louise Tobin)
10   MAY I NEVER LOVE AGAIN   Bob Chester Orch. (VR: Dolores O'Neill)
     Note: * Another version by: Jimmy Dorsey Orch. (VR: Bob Eberly)

March 1, 1941
1   I HEAR A RHAPSODY   Charlie Barnet Orch. (VR: Bob Carroll) *
2   YOU WALK BY   Eddy Duchin Orch. (VR: Johnny Drake)
3   FRENESI   Artie Shaw Orch.
4   IT ALL COMES BACK TO ME NOW   Gene Krupa Orch. (VR: Howard Dulany)
5   HIGH ON A WINDY HILL   Jimmy Dorsey Orch. (VR: Bob Eberly)
6   PERFIDIA   Xavier Cugat
7   THERE'LL BE SOME CHANGES MADE   Benny Goodman Orch. (VR: Louise Tobin)
8   SO YOU'RE THE ONE   Eddy Duchin Orch. (VR: June Robbins)
9   I GIVE YOU MY WORD   Eddy Duchin Orch. (VR: June Robbins)

10   THERE I GO   Vaughn Monroe Orch. (VR: Vaughn Monroe)
     Note: * Another version by: Jimmy Dorsey Orch. (VR: Bob Eberly)

March 8, 1941
1   I HEAR A RHAPSODY   Charlie Barnet Orch. (VR: Bob Carroll) *
2   FRENESI   Artie Shaw Orch.
3   IT ALL COMES BACK TO ME NOW   Gene Krupa Orch. (VR: Howard Dulany)
4   YOU WALK BY   Eddy Duchin Orch. (VR: Johnny Drake)
5   HIGH ON A WINDY HILL   Jimmy Dorsey Orch. (VR: Bob Eberly)
6   PERFIDIA   Xavier Cugat
7   THERE'LL BE SOME CHANGES MADE   Benny Goodman Orch. (VR: Louise Tobin)
8   SO YOU'RE THE ONE   Eddy Duchin Orch. (VR: June Robbins)
9   I GIVE YOU MY WORD   Eddy Duchin Orch. (VR: June Robbins)
10   LET'S DREAM THIS ONE OUT   Frankie Masters Orch. (VR: Swingmasters)
     Note: * Another version by: Jimmy Dorsey Orch. (VR: Bob Eberly)

March 15, 1941
1   I HEAR A RHAPSODY   Charlie Barnet Orch. (VR: Bob Carroll) *
2   IT ALL COMES BACK TO ME NOW   Gene Krupa Orch. (VR: Howard Dulany)
3   YOU WALK BY   Eddy Duchin Orch. (VR: Johnny Drake)
4   HIGH ON A WINDY HILL   Jimmy Dorsey Orch. (VR: Bob Eberly)
5   PERFIDIA   Xavier Cugat
6   FRENESI   Artie Shaw Orch.
7   THERE'LL BE SOME CHANGES MADE   Benny Goodman Orch. (VR: Louise Tobin)
8   SO YOU'RE THE ONE   Eddy Duchin Orch. (VR: June Robbins)
9   AMAPOLA   Jimmy Dorsey Orch. (VR: Bob Eberly and Helen O'Connell)
10   GEORGIA ON MY MIND   Gene Krupa (VR: Anita O'Day)
     Note: * Another version by: Jimmy Dorsey Orch. (VR: Bob Eberly)

March 22, 1941
1   I HEAR A RHAPSODY   Charlie Barnet Orch. (VR: Bob Carroll) *
2   IT ALL COMES BACK TO ME NOW   Gene Krupa Orch. (VR: Howard Dulany)
3   YOU WALK BY   Eddy Duchin Orch. (VR: Johnny Drake)
4   THERE'LL BE SOME CHANGES MADE   Benny Goodman Orch. (VR: Louise Tobin)
5   HIGH ON A WINDY HILL   Jimmy Dorsey Orch. (VR: Bob Eberly)
6   FRENESI   Artie Shaw Orch.
7   PERFIDIA   Xavier Cugat
8   AMAPOLA   Jimmy Dorsey Orch. (VR: Bob Eberly and Helen O'Connell)
9   GEORGIA ON MY MIND   Gene Krupa (VR: Anita O'Day)
10   THE WISE OLD OWL   Al Donohue Orch. (VR: Dee Keating)
     Note: * Another version by: Jimmy Dorsey Orch. (VR: Bob Eberly)

March 29, 1941
1   I HEAR A RHAPSODY   Charlie Barnet Orch. (VR: Bob Carroll) *

2   IT ALL COMES BACK TO ME NOW   Gene Krupa Orch. (VR: Howard Dulany)
3   FRENESI   Artie Shaw Orch.
4   HIGH ON A WINDY HILL   Jimmy Dorsey Orch. (VR: Bob Eberly)
5   PERFIDIA   Xavier Cugat
6   YOU WALK BY   Eddy Duchin Orch. (VR: Johnny Drake)
7   THERE'LL BE SOME CHANGES MADE   Benny Goodman Orch. (VR: Louise Tobin)
8   THE WISE OLD OWL   Al Donohue Orch. (VR: Dee Keating)
9   OH, LOOK AT ME NOW   Tommy Dorsey Orch. (VR: Frank Sinatra, Connie Haines & Pied Pipers)
10 AMAPOLA   Jimmy Dorsey Orch. (VR: Bob Eberly and Helen O'Connell)
    Note: * Another version by: Jimmy Dorsey Orch. (VR: Bob Eberly)

April 5, 1941
1   AMAPOLA   Jimmy Dorsey Orch. (VR: Bob Eberly and Helen O'Connell)
2   IT ALL COMES BACK TO ME NOW   Gene Krupa Orch. (VR: Howard Dulany)
3   THERE'LL BE SOME CHANGES MADE   Benny Goodman Orch. (VR: Louise Tobin)
4   I HEAR A RHAPSODY   Charlie Barnet Orch. (VR: Bob Carroll) *
5   YOU WALK BY   Eddy Duchin Orch. (VR: Johnny Drake)
6   PERFIDIA   Xavier Cugat
7   HIGH ON A WINDY HILL   Jimmy Dorsey Orch. (VR: Bob Eberly)
8   THE WISE OLD OWL   Al Donohue Orch. (VR: Dee Keating)
9   WALKIN' BY THE RIVER   Una Mae Carlisle
10 FRENESI   Artie Shaw Orch.
    Note: * Another version by: Jimmy Dorsey Orch. (VR: Bob Eberly)

April 12, 1941
1   I HEAR A RHAPSODY   Charlie Barnet Orch. (VR: Bob Carroll) *
2   THERE'LL BE SOME CHANGES MADE   Benny Goodman Orch. (VR: Louise Tobin)
3   IT ALL COMES BACK TO ME NOW   Gene Krupa Orch. (VR: Howard Dulany)
4   AMAPOLA   Jimmy Dorsey Orch. (VR: Bob Eberly and Helen O'Connell)
5   YOU WALK BY   Eddy Duchin Orch. (VR: Johnny Drake)
6   THE WISE OLD OWL   Al Donohue Orch. (VR: Dee Keating)
7   HIGH ON A WINDY HILL   Jimmy Dorsey Orch. (VR: Bob Eberly)
8   FRENESI   Artie Shaw Orch.
9   PERFIDIA   Xavier Cugat
10 OH, LOOK AT ME NOW   Tommy Dorsey Orch. (VR: Frank Sinatra, Connie Haines & Pied Pipers)
    Note: * Another version by: Jimmy Dorsey Orch. (VR: Bob Eberly)

April 19, 1941
1   THE WISE OLD OWL   Al Donohue Orch. (VR: Dee Keating)
2   AMAPOLA   Jimmy Dorsey Orch. (VR: Bob Eberly and Helen O'Connell)
3   HIGH ON A WINDY HILL   Jimmy Dorsey Orch. (VR: Bob Eberly)
4   I HEAR A RHAPSODY   Charlie Barnet Orch. (VR: Bob Carroll) *
5   PERFIDIA   Xavier Cugat
6   YOU WALK BY   Eddy Duchin Orch. (VR: Johnny Drake)
7   THERE'LL BE SOME CHANGES MADE   Benny Goodman Orch. (VR: Louise Tobin)

8   OH, LOOK AT ME NOW   Tommy Dorsey Orch. (VR: Frank Sinatra, Connie Haines & Pied Pipers
9   GEORGIA ON MY MIND   Gene Krupa (VR: Anita O'Day)
10 IT ALL COMES BACK TO ME NOW   Gene Krupa Orch. (VR: Howard Dulany)
    Note: * Another version by: Jimmy Dorsey Orch. (VR: Bob Eberly)

April 26, 1941
1   AMAPOLA   Jimmy Dorsey Orch. (VR: Bob Eberly and Helen O'Connell)
2   THERE'LL BE SOME CHANGES MADE   Benny Goodman Orch. (VR: Louise Tobin)
3   WALKIN' BY THE RIVER   Una Mae Carlisle
4   IT ALL COMES BACK TO ME NOW   Gene Krupa Orch. (VR: Howard Dulany)
5   THE WISE OLD OWL   Al Donohue Orch. (VR: Dee Keating)
6   OH, LOOK AT ME NOW   Tommy Dorsey Orch. (VR: Frank Sinatra, Connie Haines & Pied Pipers)
7   HIGH ON A WINDY HILL   Jimmy Dorsey Orch. (VR: Bob Eberly)
8   NUMBER TEN LULLABYE LANE   Eddy Duchin Orch. (VR: June Robbins)
9   DO I WORRY   Tommy Dorsey Orch. (VR: Frank Sinatra & the Pied Pipers)
10 PERFIDIA   Xavier Cugat

May 3, 1941
1   AMAPOLA   Jimmy Dorsey Orch. (VR: Bob Eberly and Helen O'Connell)
2   THE WISE OLD OWL   Al Donohue Orch. (VR: Dee Keating)
3   THERE'LL BE SOME CHANGES MADE   Benny Goodman Orch. (VR: Louise Tobin)
4   WALKIN' BY THE RIVER   Una Mae Carlisle
5   DO I WORRY   Tommy Dorsey Orch. (VR: Frank Sinatra & the Pied Pipers)
6   OH, LOOK AT ME NOW   Tommy Dorsey Orch. (VR: Frank Sinatra, Connie Haines & Pied Pipers
7   MY SISTER AND I   Jimmy Dorsey Orch. (VR: Bob Eberly)
8   IT ALL COMES BACK TO ME NOW   Gene Krupa Orch. (VR: Howard Dulany)
9   GEORGIA ON MY MIND   Gene Krupa (VR: Anita O'Day)
10 MARIA ELENA   Jimmy Dorsey Orch. (VR: Bob Eberly)

May 10, 1941
1   AMAPOLA   Jimmy Dorsey Orch. (VR: Bob Eberly and Helen O'Connell)
2   THE WISE OLD OWL   Al Donohue Orch. (VR: Dee Keating)
3   MY SISTER AND I   Jimmy Dorsey Orch. (VR: Bob Eberly)
4   INTERMEZZO   Guy Lombardo Orch.
5   WALKIN' BY THE RIVER   Una Mae Carlisle
6   DO I WORRY   Tommy Dorsey Orch. (VR: Frank Sinatra & the Pied Pipers)
7   OH, LOOK AT ME NOW   Tommy Dorsey Orch. (VR: Frank Sinatra, Connie Haines & Pied Pipers
8   THERE'LL BE SOME CHANGES MADE   Benny Goodman Orch. (VR: Louise Tobin)   .
9   MARIA ELENA   Jimmy Dorsey Orch. (VR: Bob Eberly)
10 NUMBER TEN LULLABYE LANE   Eddy Duchin Orch. (VR: June Robbins)

May 17, 1941
1   AMAPOLA   Jimmy Dorsey Orch. (VR: Bob Eberly and Helen O'Connell)
2   MY SISTER AND I   Jimmy Dorsey Orch. (VR: Bob Eberly)
3   DO I WORRY   Tommy Dorsey Orch. (VR: Frank Sinatra & the Pied Pipers)

4 INTERMEZZO   Guy Lombardo Orch.
5 THE WISE OLD OWL   Al Donohue Orch. (VR: Dee Keating)
6 WALKIN' BY THE RIVER   Una Mae Carlisle
7 THE THINGS I LOVE   Jimmy Dorsey Orch. (VR: Bob Eberly)
8 MARIA ELENA   Jimmy Dorsey Orch. (VR: Bob Eberly)
9 G'BYE NOW   Horace Heidt (VR: Ronnie Kemper)
10 OH, LOOK AT ME NOW   Tommy Dorsey Orch. (VR: Frank Sinatra, Connie Haines & Pied Pipers)

May 24, 1941
1 AMAPOLA   Jimmy Dorsey Orch. (VR: Bob Eberly and Helen O'Connell)
2 MY SISTER AND I   Jimmy Dorsey Orch. (VR: Bob Eberly)
3 INTERMEZZO   Guy Lombardo Orch.
4 MARIA ELENA   Jimmy Dorsey Orch. (VR: Bob Eberly)
5 DO I WORRY   Tommy Dorsey Orch. (VR: Frank Sinatra & the Pied Pipers)
6 WALKIN' BY THE RIVER   Una Mae Carlisle
7 THE THINGS I LOVE   Jimmy Dorsey Orch. (VR: Bob Eberly)
8 NUMBER TEN LULLABYE LANE   Eddy Duchin Orch. (VR: June Robbins)
9 TWO HEARTS THAT PASS IN THE NIGHT   Sammy Kaye Orch. (VR: Arthur Wright)
10 THE WISE OLD OWL   Al Donohue Orch. (VR: Dee Keating)

May 31, 1941
1 MY SISTER AND I   Jimmy Dorsey Orch. (VR: Bob Eberly)
2 INTERMEZZO   Guy Lombardo Orch.
3 AMAPOLA   Jimmy Dorsey Orch. (VR: Bob Eberly and Helen O'Connell)
4 MARIA ELENA   Jimmy Dorsey Orch. (VR: Bob Eberly)
5 DO I WORRY   Tommy Dorsey Orch. (VR: Frank Sinatra & the Pied Pipers)
6 NUMBER TEN LULLABYE LANE   Eddy Duchin Orch. (VR: June Robbins)
7 THE THINGS I LOVE   Jimmy Dorsey Orch. (VR: Bob Eberly)
8 G'BYE NOW   Horace Heidt (VR: Ronnie Kemper)
9 WALKIN' BY THE RIVER   Una Mae Carlisle
10 OH, LOOK AT ME NOW   Tommy Dorsey Orch. (VR: Frank Sinatra, Connie Haines & Pied Pipers)

June 7, 1941
1 MY SISTER AND I   Jimmy Dorsey Orch. (VR: Bob Eberly)
2 INTERMEZZO   Guy Lombardo Orch.
3 MARIA ELENA   Jimmy Dorsey Orch. (VR: Bob Eberly)
4 AMAPOLA   Jimmy Dorsey Orch. (VR: Bob Eberly and Helen O'Connell)
5 DO I WORRY   Tommy Dorsey Orch. (VR: Frank Sinatra & the Pied Pipers)
6 THE THINGS I LOVE   Jimmy Dorsey Orch. (VR: Bob Eberly)
7 G'BYE NOW   Horace Heidt (VR: Ronnie Kemper)
8 WALKIN' BY THE RIVER   Una Mae Carlisle
9 TWO HEARTS THAT PASS IN THE NIGHT   Sammy Kaye Orch. (VR: Arthur Wright)
10 GEORGIA ON MY MIND   Gene Krupa (VR: Anita O'Day)

June 14, 1941
1 INTERMEZZO   Guy Lombardo Orch.
2 MARIA ELENA   Jimmy Dorsey Orch. (VR: Bob Eberly)
3 MY SISTER AND I   Jimmy Dorsey Orch. (VR: Bob Eberly)
4 THE THINGS I LOVE   Jimmy Dorsey Orch. (VR: Bob Eberly)

5 DO I WORRY   Tommy Dorsey Orch. (VR: Frank Sinatra & the Pied Pipers)
6 AMAPOLA   Jimmy Dorsey Orch. (VR: Bob Eberly and Helen O'Connell)
7 THE HUT SUT SONG   Freddy Martin Orch. (VR: Eddie Stone) *
8 JUST A LITTLE BIT SOUTH OF NORTH CAROLINA   Gene Krupa Orch. (VR: Anita O'Day)
9 WALKIN' BY THE RIVER   Una Mae Carlisle
10 TWO HEARTS THAT PASS IN THE NIGHT   Sammy Kaye Orch. (VR: Arthur Wright)
   Note: * Over the years, this song has been more closely associated with The Merry Macs, whose version peaked at #13.

June 21, 1941
1 MARIA ELENA   Jimmy Dorsey Orch. (VR: Bob Eberly)
2 INTERMEZZO   Guy Lombardo Orch.
3 MY SISTER AND I   Jimmy Dorsey Orch. (VR: Bob Eberly)
4 THE THINGS I LOVE   Jimmy Dorsey Orch. (VR: Bob Eberly)
5 THE HUT SUT SONG   Freddy Martin Orch. (VR: Eddie Stone) *
6 DO I WORRY   Tommy Dorsey Orch. (VR: Frank Sinatra & the Pied Pipers)
7 AMAPOLA   Jimmy Dorsey Orch. (VR: Bob Eberly and Helen O'Connell)
8 JUST A LITTLE BIT SOUTH OF NORTH CAROLINA   Gene Krupa Orch. (VR: Anita O'Day)
9 TWO HEARTS THAT PASS IN THE NIGHT   Sammy Kaye Orch. (VR: Arthur Wright)
10 DADDY   Sammy Kaye Orch. (VR: Choir)
   Note: * Over the years, this song has been more closely associated with The Merry Macs, whose version peaked at #13.

June 28, 1941
1 MARIA ELENA   Jimmy Dorsey Orch. (VR: Bob Eberly)
2 INTERMEZZO   Guy Lombardo Orch.
3 THE HUT SUT SONG   Freddy Martin Orch. (VR: Eddie Stone) *
4 THE THINGS I LOVE   Jimmy Dorsey Orch. (VR: Bob Eberly)
5 MY SISTER AND I   Jimmy Dorsey Orch. (VR: Bob Eberly)
6 DO I WORRY   Tommy Dorsey Orch. (VR: Frank Sinatra & the Pied Pipers)
7 AMAPOLA   Jimmy Dorsey Orch. (VR: Bob Eberly and Helen O'Connell)
8 DADDY   Sammy Kaye Orch. (VR: Choir)
9 JUST A LITTLE BIT SOUTH OF NORTH CAROLINA   Gene Krupa Orch. (VR: Anita O'Day)
10 G'BYE NOW   Horace Heidt (VR: Ronnie Kemper)
   Note: * Over the years, this song has been more closely associated with The Merry Macs, whose version peaked at #13.

July 5, 1941
1 THE HUT SUT SONG   Freddy Martin Orch. (VR: Eddie Stone) *
2 INTERMEZZO   Guy Lombardo Orch.
3 MARIA ELENA   Jimmy Dorsey Orch. (VR: Bob Eberly)
4 THE THINGS I LOVE   Jimmy Dorsey Orch. (VR: Bob Eberly)
5 MY SISTER AND I   Jimmy Dorsey Orch. (VR: Bob Eberly)
6 DADDY   Sammy Kaye Orch. (VR: Choir)
7 JUST A LITTLE BIT SOUTH OF NORTH CAROLINA   Gene Krupa Orch. (VR: Anita O'Day)

8 G'BYE NOW   Horace Heidt (VR: Ronnie Kemper)
9 DO I WORRY   Tommy Dorsey Orch. (VR: Frank Sinatra & the Pied Pipers)
10 AMAPOLA   Jimmy Dorsey Orch. (VR: Bob Eberly and Helen O'Connell)
   Note: * Over the years, this song has been more closely associated with The Merry Macs, whose version peaked at #13.

July 12, 1941
1 THE HUT SUT SONG   Freddy Martin Orch. (VR: Eddie Stone) *
2 MARIA ELENA   Jimmy Dorsey Orch. (VR: Bob Eberly)
3 INTERMEZZO   Guy Lombardo Orch.
4 THE THINGS I LOVE   Jimmy Dorsey Orch. (VR: Bob Eberly)
5 DADDY   Sammy Kaye Orch. (VR: Choir)
6 JUST A LITTLE BIT SOUTH OF NORTH CAROLINA   Gene Krupa Orch. (VR: Anita O'Day)
7 MY SISTER AND I   Jimmy Dorsey Orch. (VR: Bob Eberly)
8 DO I WORRY   Tommy Dorsey Orch. (VR: Frank Sinatra & the Pied Pipers)
9 AMAPOLA   Jimmy Dorsey Orch. (VR: Bob Eberly and Helen O'Connell)
10 GREEN EYES   Jimmy Dorsey Orch. (VR: Bob Eberly & Helen O'Connell)
   Note: * Over the years, this song has been more closely associated with The Merry Macs, whose version peaked at #13.

July 19, 1941
1 THE HUT SUT SONG   Freddy Martin Orch. (VR: Eddie Stone) *
2 INTERMEZZO   Guy Lombardo Orch.
3 MARIA ELENA   Jimmy Dorsey Orch. (VR: Bob Eberly)
4 THE THINGS I LOVE   Jimmy Dorsey Orch. (VR: Bob Eberly)
5 DADDY   Sammy Kaye Orch. (VR: Choir)
6 MY SISTER AND I   Jimmy Dorsey Orch. (VR: Bob Eberly)
7 GREEN EYES   Jimmy Dorsey Orch. (VR: Bob Eberly & Helen O'Connell)
8 JUST A LITTLE BIT SOUTH OF NORTH CAROLINA   Gene Krupa Orch. (VR: Anita O'Day)
9 DO I WORRY   Tommy Dorsey Orch. (VR: Frank Sinatra & the Pied Pipers)
10 AMAPOLA   Jimmy Dorsey Orch. (VR: Bob Eberly and Helen O'Connell)
   Note: * Over the years, this song has been more closely associated with The Merry Macs, whose version peaked at #13.

July 26, 1941
1 INTERMEZZO   Guy Lombardo Orch.
2 DADDY   Sammy Kaye Orch. (VR: Choir)
3 THE HUT SUT SONG   Freddy Martin Orch. (VR: Eddie Stone)
4 MARIA ELENA   Jimmy Dorsey Orch. (VR: Bob Eberly)
5 THE THINGS I LOVE   Jimmy Dorsey Orch. (VR: Bob Eberly)
6 GREEN EYES   Jimmy Dorsey Orch. (VR: Bob Eberly & Helen O'Connell)
7 JUST A LITTLE BIT SOUTH OF NORTH CAROLINA   Gene Krupa Orch. (VR: Anita O'Day)
8 MY SISTER AND I   Jimmy Dorsey Orch. (VR: Bob Eberly)
9 YOURS   Jimmy Dorsey Orch. (VR: Bob Eberly & Helen O'Connell)

10 DO I WORRY   Tommy Dorsey Orch. (VR: Frank Sinatra & the Pied Pipers)
   Note: * Over the years, this song has been more closely associated with The Merry Macs, whose version peaked at #13.

August 2, 1941
1 DADDY   Sammy Kaye Orch. (VR: Choir)
2 THE HUT SUT SONG   Freddy Martin Orch. (VR: Eddie Stone) *
3 MARIA ELENA   Jimmy Dorsey Orch. (VR: Bob Eberly)
4 INTERMEZZO   Guy Lombardo Orch.
5 THE THINGS I LOVE   Jimmy Dorsey Orch. (VR: Bob Eberly)
6 GREEN EYES   Jimmy Dorsey Orch. (VR: Bob Eberly & Helen O'Connell)
7 YOURS   Jimmy Dorsey Orch. (VR: Bob Eberly & Helen O'Connell)
8 JUST A LITTLE BIT SOUTH OF NORTH CAROLINA   Gene Krupa Orch. (VR: Anita O'Day)
9 'TIL REVEILLE   Kay Kyser Orch. (VR: Harry Babbitt & Ginny Sims)
10 MY SISTER AND I   Jimmy Dorsey Orch. (VR: Bob Eberly)
   Note: * Over the years, this song has been more closely associated with The Merry Macs, whose version peaked at #13.

August 9, 1941
1 DADDY   Sammy Kaye Orch. (VR: Choir)
2 MARIA ELENA   Jimmy Dorsey Orch. (VR: Bob Eberly)
3 THE THINGS I LOVE   Jimmy Dorsey Orch. (VR: Bob Eberly)
4 INTERMEZZO   Guy Lombardo Orch.
5 THE HUT SUT SONG   Freddy Martin Orch. (VR: Eddie Stone) *
6 GREEN EYES   Jimmy Dorsey Orch. (VR: Bob Eberly & Helen O'Connell)
7 YOURS   Jimmy Dorsey Orch. (VR: Bob Eberly & Helen O'Connell)
8 'TIL REVEILLE   Kay Kyser Orch. (VR: Harry Babbitt & Ginny Sims)
9 I WENT OUT OF MY WAY   Teddy Powell Orch. (VR: Ruth Gaylor)
10 JUST A LITTLE BIT SOUTH OF NORTH CAROLINA   Gene Krupa Orch. (VR: Anita O'Day)
   Note: * Over the years, this song has been more closely associated with The Merry Macs, whose version peaked at #13.

August 16, 1941
1 DADDY   Sammy Kaye Orch. (VR: Choir)
2 'TIL REVEILLE   Kay Kyser Orch. (VR: Harry Babbitt & Ginny Sims)
3 GREEN EYES   Jimmy Dorsey Orch. (VR: Bob Eberly & Helen O'Connell)
4 THE THINGS I LOVE   Jimmy Dorsey Orch. (VR: Bob Eberly)
5 THE HUT SUT SONG   Freddy Martin Orch. (VR: Eddie Stone) *
6 MARIA ELENA   Jimmy Dorsey Orch. (VR: Bob Eberly)
7 INTERMEZZO   Guy Lombardo Orch.
8 YOURS   Jimmy Dorsey Orch. (VR: Bob Eberly & Helen O'Connell)
9 YOU AND I   Glenn Miller Orch. (VR: Ray Eberle)
10 DO YOU CARE   Dinah Shore
   Note: * Over the years, this song has been more closely

associated with The Merry Macs, whose version peaked at #13.

August 23, 1941
1   DADDY   Sammy Kaye Orch. (VR: Choir)
2   MARIA ELENA   Jimmy Dorsey Orch. (VR: Bob Eberly)
3   GREEN EYES   Jimmy Dorsey Orch. (VR: Bob Eberly & Helen O'Connell)
4   THE THINGS I LOVE   Jimmy Dorsey Orch. (VR: Bob Eberly)
5   INTERMEZZO   Guy Lombardo Orch.
6   YOURS   Jimmy Dorsey Orch. (VR: Bob Eberly & Helen O'Connell)
7   YOU AND I   Glenn Miller Orch. (VR: Ray Eberle)
8   THE HUT SUT SONG   Freddy Martin Orch. (VR: Eddie Stone) *
9   'TIL REVEILLE   Kay Kyser Orch. (VR: Harry Babbitt & Ginny Sims)
10   DO YOU CARE   Dinah Shore
  Note: * Over the years, this song has been more closely associated with The Merry Macs, whose version peaked at #13.

August 30, 1941
1   DADDY   Sammy Kaye Orch. (VR: Choir)
2   MARIA ELENA   Jimmy Dorsey Orch. (VR: Bob Eberly)
3   'TIL REVEILLE   Kay Kyser Orch. (VR: Harry Babbitt & Ginny Sims)
4   INTERMEZZO   Guy Lombardo Orch.
5   GREEN EYES   Jimmy Dorsey Orch. (VR: Bob Eberly & Helen O'Connell)
6   THE THINGS I LOVE   Jimmy Dorsey Orch. (VR: Bob Eberly)
7   YOURS   Jimmy Dorsey Orch. (VR: Bob Eberly & Helen O'Connell)
8   I GUESS I'LL HAVE TO DREAM THE REST   Glenn Miller Orch. (VR: Ray Eberle & Modernaires)
9   YOU AND I   Glenn Miller Orch. (VR: Ray Eberle)
10   THE HUT SUT SONG   Freddy Martin Orch. (VR: Eddie Stone) *
  Note: * Over the years, this song has been more closely associated with The Merry Macs, whose version peaked at #13.

September 6, 1941
1   DADDY   Sammy Kaye Orch. (VR: Choir)
2   YOURS   Jimmy Dorsey Orch. (VR: Bob Eberly & Helen O'Connell)
3   'TIL REVEILLE   Kay Kyser Orch. (VR: Harry Babbitt & Ginny Sims)
4   GREEN EYES   Jimmy Dorsey Orch. (VR: Bob Eberly & Helen O'Connell)
5   YOU AND I   Glenn Miller Orch. (VR: Ray Eberle)
6   THE THINGS I LOVE   Jimmy Dorsey Orch. (VR: Bob Eberly)
7   MARIA ELENA   Jimmy Dorsey Orch. (VR: Bob Eberly)
8   I GUESS I'LL HAVE TO DREAM THE REST   Glenn Miller Orch. (VR: Ray Eberle & Modernaires)
9   INTERMEZZO   Guy Lombardo Orch.
10   TIME WAS   Jimmy Dorsey Orch. (VR: Bob Eberly & Helen O'Connell)

September 13, 1941
1   YOU AND I   Glenn Miller Orch. (VR: Ray Eberle)
2   'TIL REVEILLE   Kay Kyser Orch. (VR: Harry Babbitt & Ginny Sims)

3   GREEN EYES   Jimmy Dorsey Orch. (VR: Bob Eberly & Helen O'Connell)
4   YOURS   Jimmy Dorsey Orch. (VR: Bob Eberly & Helen O'Connell)
5   DADDY   Sammy Kaye Orch. (VR: Choir)
6   DO YOU CARE   Dinah Shore
7   MARIA ELENA   Jimmy Dorsey Orch. (VR: Bob Eberly)
8   INTERMEZZO   Guy Lombardo Orch.
9   THE THINGS I LOVE   Jimmy Dorsey Orch. (VR: Bob Eberly)
10   I GUESS I'LL HAVE TO DREAM THE REST   Glenn Miller Orch. (VR: Ray Eberle & Modernaires)

September 20, 1941
1   YOU AND I   Glenn Miller Orch. (VR: Ray Eberle)
2   YOURS   Jimmy Dorsey Orch. (VR: Bob Eberly & Helen O'Connell)
3   'TIL REVEILLE   Kay Kyser Orch. (VR: Harry Babbitt & Ginny Sims)
4   GREEN EYES   Jimmy Dorsey Orch. (VR: Bob Eberly & Helen O'Connell)
5   I GUESS I'LL HAVE TO DREAM THE REST   Glenn Miller Orch. (VR: Ray Eberle & Modernaires)
6   DO YOU CARE   Dinah Shore
7   DADDY   Sammy Kaye Orch. (VR: Choir)
8   MARIA ELENA   Jimmy Dorsey Orch. (VR: Bob Eberly)
9   TIME WAS   Jimmy Dorsey Orch. (VR: Bob Eberly & Helen O'Connell)
10   JIM   Jimmy Dorsey Orch. (VR: Bob Eberly & Helen O'Connell)

September 27, 1941
1   YOU AND I   Glenn Miller Orch. (VR: Ray Eberle)
2   YOURS   Jimmy Dorsey Orch. (VR: Bob Eberly & Helen O'Connell)
3   'TIL REVEILLE   Kay Kyser Orch. (VR: Harry Babbitt & Ginny Sims)
4   I GUESS I'LL HAVE TO DREAM THE REST   Glenn Miller Orch. (VR: Ray Eberle & Modernaires)
5   I DON'T WANT TO SET THE WORLD ON FIRE   Horace Heidt Orch. (VR: Larry Cotton, Donna Wood & the Don Juans) *
6   DO YOU CARE   Dinah Shore
7   DADDY   Sammy Kaye Orch. (VR: Choir)
8   TIME WAS   Jimmy Dorsey Orch. (VR: Bob Eberly & Helen O'Connell)
9   MARIA ELENA   Jimmy Dorsey Orch. (VR: Bob Eberly)
10   JIM   Jimmy Dorsey Orch. (VR: Bob Eberly & Helen O'Connell)
  Note: * Over the years, this song has been more closely associated with The Ink Spots, whose version reached #4.

October 4, 1941
1   YOU AND I   Glenn Miller Orch. (VR: Ray Eberle)
2   YOURS   Jimmy Dorsey Orch. (VR: Bob Eberly & Helen O'Connell)
3   I DON'T WANT TO SET THE WORLD ON FIRE   Horace Heidt Orch. (VR: Larry Cotton, Donna Wood & the Don Juans) *
4   'TIL REVEILLE   Kay Kyser Orch. (VR: Harry Babbitt & Ginny Sims)
5   DO YOU CARE   Dinah Shore
6   TIME WAS   Jimmy Dorsey Orch. (VR: Bob Eberly & Helen O'Connell)
7   JIM   Jimmy Dorsey Orch. (VR: Bob Eberly & Helen O'Connell)

8   I GUESS I'LL HAVE TO DREAM THE REST   Glenn Miller Orch. (VR: Ray Eberle & Modernaires)
9   INTERMEZZO   Guy Lombardo Orch.
10   YES, INDEED   Tommy Dorsey Orch. (VR: Jo Stafford & Sy Oliver)
   Note: * Over the years, this song has been more closely associated with The Ink Spots, whose version reached #4.

October 11, 1941
1   YOU AND I   Glenn Miller Orch. (VR: Ray Eberle)
2   I DON'T WANT TO SET THE WORLD ON FIRE   Horace Heidt Orch. (VR: Larry Cotton, Donna Wood & the Don Juans) *
3   'TIL REVEILLE   Kay Kyser Orch. (VR: Harry Babbitt & Ginny Sims)
4   JIM   Jimmy Dorsey Orch. (VR: Bob Eberly & Helen O'Connell)
5   I GUESS I'LL HAVE TO DREAM THE REST   Glenn Miller Orch. (VR: Ray Eberle & Modernaires)
6   YOURS   Jimmy Dorsey Orch. (VR: Bob Eberly & Helen O'Connell)
7   DO YOU CARE   Dinah Shore
8   TIME WAS   Jimmy Dorsey Orch. (VR: Bob Eberly & Helen O'Connell)
9   GREEN EYES   Jimmy Dorsey Orch. (VR: Bob Eberly & Helen O'Connell)
10   TONIGHT WE LOVE (TCHAIKOVSKY'S PIANO CONCERTO #1)   Freddy Martin Orch.
   Note: * Over the years, this song has been more closely associated with The Ink Spots, whose version reached #4.

October 18, 1941
1   I DON'T WANT TO SET THE WORLD ON FIRE   Horace Heidt Orch. (VR: Larry Cotton, Donna Wood & the Don Juans) *
2   YOU AND I   Glenn Miller Orch. (VR: Ray Eberle)
3   JIM   Jimmy Dorsey Orch. (VR: Bob Eberly & Helen O'Connell)
4   YOURS   Jimmy Dorsey Orch. (VR: Bob Eberly & Helen O'Connell)
5   'TIL REVEILLE   Kay Kyser Orch. (VR: Harry Babbitt & Ginny Sims)
6   DO YOU CARE   Dinah Shore
7   I GUESS I'LL HAVE TO DREAM THE REST   Glenn Miller Orch. (VR: Ray Eberle & Modernaires)
8   TIME WAS   Jimmy Dorsey Orch. (VR: Bob Eberly & Helen O'Connell)
9   TONIGHT WE LOVE (TCHAIKOVSKY'S PIANO CONCERTO #1)   Freddy Martin Orch.
10   GREEN EYES   Jimmy Dorsey Orch. (VR: Bob Eberly & Helen O'Connell)
   Note: * Over the years, this song has been more closely associated with The Ink Spots, whose version reached #4.

October 25, 1941
1   I DON'T WANT TO SET THE WORLD ON FIRE   Horace Heidt Orch. (VR: Larry Cotton, Donna Wood & the Don Juans) *
2   YOU AND I   Glenn Miller Orch. (VR: Ray Eberle)
3   JIM   Jimmy Dorsey Orch. (VR: Bob Eberly & Helen O'Connell)
4   TIME WAS   Jimmy Dorsey Orch. (VR: Bob Eberly & Helen O'Connell)
5   DO YOU CARE   Dinah Shore
6   YOURS   Jimmy Dorsey Orch. (VR: Bob Eberly & Helen O'Connell)

7   I GUESS I'LL HAVE TO DREAM THE REST   Glenn Miller Orch. (VR: Ray Eberle & Modernaires)
8   'TIL REVEILLE   Kay Kyser Orch. (VR: Harry Babbitt & Ginny Sims)
9   TONIGHT WE LOVE (TCHAIKOVSKY'S PIANO CONCERTO #1)   Freddy Martin Orch.
10   HI, NEIGHBOR   Orrin Tucker Orch. (VR: Bonnie Baker & O. Tucker)
   Note: * Over the years, this song has been more closely associated with The Ink Spots, whose version reached #4.

November 1, 1941
1   I DON'T WANT TO SET THE WORLD ON FIRE   Horace Heidt Orch. (VR: Larry Cotton, Donna Wood & the Don Juans) *
2   YOU AND I   Glenn Miller Orch. (VR: Ray Eberle)
3   JIM   Jimmy Dorsey Orch. (VR: Bob Eberly & Helen O'Connell)
4   I GUESS I'LL HAVE TO DREAM THE REST   Glenn Miller Orch. (VR: Ray Eberle & Modernaires)
5   DO YOU CARE   Dinah Shore
6   TONIGHT WE LOVE (TCHAIKOVSKY'S PIANO CONCERTO #1)   Freddy Martin Orch.
7   YOURS   Jimmy Dorsey Orch. (VR: Bob Eberly & Helen O'Connell)
8   TIME WAS   Jimmy Dorsey Orch. (VR: Bob Eberly & Helen O'Connell)
9   'TIL REVEILLE   Kay Kyser Orch. (VR: Harry Babbitt & Ginny Sims)
10   I SEE A MILLION PEOPLE   Cab Calloway Orch.
   Note: * Over the years, this song has been more closely associated with The Ink Spots, whose version reached #4.

November 8, 1941
1   I DON'T WANT TO SET THE WORLD ON FIRE   Horace Heidt Orch. (VR: Larry Cotton, Donna Wood & the Don Juans) *
2   TONIGHT WE LOVE (TCHAIKOVSKY'S PIANO CONCERTO #1)   Freddy Martin Orch.
3   JIM   Jimmy Dorsey Orch. (VR: Bob Eberly & Helen O'Connell)
4   YOU AND I   Glenn Miller Orch. (VR: Ray Eberle)
5   DO YOU CARE   Dinah Shore
6   I GUESS I'LL HAVE TO DREAM THE REST   Glenn Miller Orch. (VR: Ray Eberle & Modernaires)
7   SHEPHERD SERENADE   Bing Crosby
8   TIME WAS   Jimmy Dorsey Orch. (VR: Bob Eberly & Helen O'Connell)
9   YOURS   Jimmy Dorsey Orch. (VR: Bob Eberly & Helen O'Connell)
10   'TIL REVEILLE   Kay Kyser Orch. (VR: Harry Babbitt & Ginny Sims)
   Note: * Over the years, this song has been more closely associated with The Ink Spots, whose version reached #4.

November 15, 1941
1   TONIGHT WE LOVE (TCHAIKOVSKY'S PIANO CONCERTO #1)   Freddy Martin Orch.
2   I DON'T WANT TO SET THE WORLD ON FIRE   Horace Heidt Orch. (VR: Larry Cotton, Donna Wood & the Don Juans) *
3   YOU AND I   Glenn Miller Orch. (VR: Ray Eberle)
4   JIM   Jimmy Dorsey Orch. (VR: Bob Eberly & Helen O'Connell)
5   TIME WAS   Jimmy Dorsey Orch. (VR: Bob Eberly & Helen O'Connell)

6 SHEPHERD SERENADE   Bing Crosby

7 DO YOU CARE   Dinah Shore

8 YOURS   Jimmy Dorsey Orch. (VR: Bob Eberly & Helen O'Connell)

9 I GUESS I'LL HAVE TO DREAM THE REST   Glenn Miller Orch. (VR: Ray Eberle & Modernaires)

10 TWO IN LOVE   Tommy Dorsey Orch. (VR: Frank Sinatra)

Note: * Over the years, this song has been more closely associated with The Ink Spots, whose version reached #4.

November 22, 1941

1 TONIGHT WE LOVE (TCHAIKOVSKY'S PIANO CONCERTO #1)   Freddy Martin Orch.

2 I DON'T WANT TO SET THE WORLD ON FIRE   Horace Heidt Orch. (VR: Larry Cotton, Donna Wood & the Don Juans) *

3 JIM   Jimmy Dorsey Orch. (VR: Bob Eberly & Helen O'Connell)

4 SHEPHERD SERENADE   Bing Crosby

5 ELMER'S TUNE   Glenn Miller Orch. (VR: Ray Eberle)

6 DO YOU CARE   Dinah Shore

7 YOU AND I   Glenn Miller Orch. (VR: Ray Eberle)

8 CHATTANOOGA CHOO CHOO   Glenn Miller Orch. (VR: Tex Beneke & Modernaires with Paula Kelly)

9 I GUESS I'LL HAVE TO DREAM THE REST   Glenn Miller Orch. (VR: Ray Eberle & Modernaires)

10 THIS LOVE OF MINE   Tommy Dorsey Orch. (VR: Frank Sinatra)

Note: * Over the years, this song has been more closely associated with The Ink Spots, whose version reached #4.

November 29, 1941

1 TONIGHT WE LOVE (TCHAIKOVSKY'S PIANO CONCERTO #1)   Freddy Martin Orch.

2 SHEPHERD SERENADE   Bing Crosby

3 ELMER'S TUNE   Glenn Miller Orch. (VR: Ray Eberle)

4 I DON'T WANT TO SET THE WORLD ON FIRE   Horace Heidt Orch. (VR: Larry Cotton, Donna Wood & the Don Juans) *

5 YOU AND I   Glenn Miller Orch. (VR: Ray Eberle)

6 JIM   Jimmy Dorsey Orch. (VR: Bob Eberly & Helen O'Connell)

7 THIS LOVE OF MINE   Tommy Dorsey Orch. (VR: Frank Sinatra)

8 MADELEINE   Sammy Kaye Orch. (Allan Foster)

9 TWO IN LOVE   Tommy Dorsey Orch. (VR: Frank Sinatra)

10 THE BELLS OF SAN RAQUEL   Dick Jurgens Orch. (VR: Harry Cool)

Note: * Over the years, this song has been more closely associated with The Ink Spots, whose version reached #4.

December 6, 1941

1 TONIGHT WE LOVE (TCHAIKOVSKY'S PIANO CONCERTO #1)   Freddy Martin Orch.

2 ELMER'S TUNE   Glenn Miller Orch. (VR: Ray Eberle)

3 CHATTANOOGA CHOO CHOO   Glenn Miller Orch. (VR: Tex Beneke & Modernaires with Paula Kelly)

4 SHEPHERD SERENADE   Bing Crosby

5 I DON'T WANT TO SET THE WORLD ON FIRE   Horace Heidt Orch. (VR: Larry Cotton, Donna Wood & the Don Juans) *

6 THIS LOVE OF MINE   Tommy Dorsey Orch. (VR: Frank Sinatra)

7 YOU AND I   Glenn Miller Orch. (VR: Ray Eberle)

8 JIM   Jimmy Dorsey Orch. (VR: Bob Eberly & Helen O'Connell)

9 A SINNER KISSED AN ANGEL   Tommy Dorsey Orch. (VR: Frank Sinatra)

10 EV'RYTHING I LOVE   Glenn Miller Orch. (VR: Ray Eberle)

Note: * Over the years, this song has been more closely associated with The Ink Spots, whose version reached #4.

December 13, 1941

1 ELMER'S TUNE   Glenn Miller Orch. (VR: Ray Eberle)

2 SHEPHERD SERENADE   Bing Crosby

3 TONIGHT WE LOVE (TCHAIKOVSKY'S PIANO CONCERTO #1)   Freddy Martin Orch.

4 CHATTANOOGA CHOO CHOO   Glenn Miller Orch. (VR: Tex Beneke & Modernaires with Paula Kelly)

5 I DON'T WANT TO SET THE WORLD ON FIRE   Horace Heidt Orch. (VR: Larry Cotton, Donna Wood & the Don Juans) *

6 THIS LOVE OF MINE   Tommy Dorsey Orch. (VR: Frank Sinatra)

7 ORANGE BLOSSOM LANE   Glenn Miller Orch. (VR: Ray Eberle)

8 YOU AND I   Glenn Miller Orch. (VR: Ray Eberle)

9 THE WHITE CLIFFS OF DOVER   Kay Kyser Orch. (VR: Harry Babbitt)

10 JIM   Jimmy Dorsey Orch. (VR: Bob Eberly & Helen O'Connell)

Note: * Over the years, this song has been more closely associated with The Ink Spots, whose version reached #4.

December 20, 1941

1 CHATTANOOGA CHOO CHOO   Glenn Miller Orch. (VR: Tex Beneke & Modernaires with Paula Kelly)

2 ELMER'S TUNE   Glenn Miller Orch. (VR: Ray Eberle)

3 TONIGHT WE LOVE (TCHAIKOVSKY'S PIANO CONCERTO #1)   Freddy Martin Orch.

4 SHEPHERD SERENADE   Bing Crosby

5 THIS LOVE OF MINE   Tommy Dorsey Orch. (VR: Frank Sinatra)

6 I DON'T WANT TO SET THE WORLD ON FIRE   Horace Heidt Orch. (VR: Larry Cotton, Donna Wood & the Don Juans) *

7 MADELEINE   Sammy Kaye Orch. (Allan Foster)

8 YOU AND I   Glenn Miller Orch. (VR: Ray Eberle)

9 TWO IN LOVE   Tommy Dorsey Orch. (VR: Frank Sinatra)

10 JIM   Jimmy Dorsey Orch. (VR: Bob Eberly & Helen O'Connell)

Note: * Over the years, this song has been more closely associated with The Ink Spots, whose version reached #4.

December 27, 1941

1 ELMER'S TUNE   Glenn Miller Orch. (VR: Ray Eberle)

2 CHATTANOOGA CHOO CHOO   Glenn Miller Orch. (VR: Tex Beneke & Modernaires with Paula Kelly)

3 THE WHITE CLIFFS OF DOVER   Kay Kyser Orch. (VR: Harry Babbitt)

4 TONIGHT WE LOVE (TCHAIKOVSKY'S PIANO CONCERTO #1)   Freddy Martin Orch.

5 SHEPHERD SERENADE   Bing Crosby

6 THIS LOVE OF MINE   Tommy Dorsey Orch. (VR: Frank Sinatra)

7 THE BELLS OF SAN RAQUEL   Dick Jurgens Orch. (VR: Harry Cool)

8 I DON'T WANT TO SET THE WORLD ON FIRE   Horace Heidt Orch. (VR: Larry Cotton, Donna Wood & the Don Juans) *

9 THIS IS NO LAUGHING MATTER   Charlie Spivak Orch. (VR: Garry Stevens)

10   EV'RYTHING I LOVE   Glenn Miller Orch. (VR: Ray Eberle)
      Note: * Over the years, this song has been more closely
      associated with The Ink Spots, whose version reached #4.

January 3, 1942
1   CHATTANOOGA CHOO CHOO   Glenn Miller Orch. (VR:
     Tex Beneke & Modernaires with Paula Kelly)
2   THE WHITE CLIFFS OF DOVER   Kay Kyser Orch. (VR:
     Harry Babbitt)
3   ELMER'S TUNE   Glenn Miller Orch. (VR: Ray Eberle)
4   TONIGHT WE LOVE (TCHAIKOVSKY'S PIANO CONCERTO
     #1)   Freddy Martin Orch.
5   SHEPHERD SERENADE   Bing Crosby
6   THIS LOVE OF MINE   Tommy Dorsey Orch. (VR: Frank
     Sinatra)
7   EV'RYTHING I LOVE   Glenn Miller Orch. (VR: Ray Eberle)
8   I DON'T WANT TO SET THE WORLD ON FIRE   Horace
     Heidt Orch. (VR: Larry Cotton, Donna Wood & the Don
     Juans) *
9   THIS IS NO LAUGHING MATTER   Charlie Spivak Orch.
     (VR: Garry Stevens)
10   ROSE O'DAY   Freddy Martin Orch. (VR: Eddie Stone)
     Note: * Over the years, this song has been more closely
     associated with The Ink Spots, whose version reached #4.

January 10, 1942
1   THE WHITE CLIFFS OF DOVER   Kay Kyser Orch. (VR:
     Harry Babbitt)
2   ELMER'S TUNE   Glenn Miller Orch. (VR: Ray Eberle)
3   CHATTANOOGA CHOO CHOO   Glenn Miller Orch. (VR:
     Tex Beneke & Modernaires with Paula Kelly)
4   SHEPHERD SERENADE   Bing Crosby
5   TONIGHT WE LOVE (TCHAIKOVSKY'S PIANO CONCERTO
     #1)   Freddy Martin Orch.
6   MADELEINE   Sammy Kaye Orch. (Allan Foster)
7   THIS LOVE OF MINE   Tommy Dorsey Orch. (VR: Frank
     Sinatra)
8   HOW ABOUT YOU?   Tommy Dorsey Orch. (VR: Frank
     Sinatra)
9   EV'RYTHING I LOVE   Glenn Miller Orch. (VR: Ray Eberle)
10   THE SHRINE OF ST. CECELIA   Andrews Sisters

January 17, 1942
1   ELMER'S TUNE   Glenn Miller Orch. (VR: Ray Eberle)
2   THE WHITE CLIFFS OF DOVER   Kay Kyser Orch. (VR:
     Harry Babbitt)
3   CHATTANOOGA CHOO CHOO   Glenn Miller Orch. (VR:
     Tex Beneke & Modernaires with Paula Kelly)
4   THE BELLS OF SAN RAQUEL   Dick Jurgens Orch. (VR:
     Harry Cool)
5   THIS LOVE OF MINE   Tommy Dorsey Orch. (VR: Frank
     Sinatra)
6   TONIGHT WE LOVE (TCHAIKOVSKY'S PIANO CONCERTO
     #1)   Freddy Martin Orch.
7   SHEPHERD SERENADE   Bing Crosby
8   MADELEINE   Sammy Kaye Orch. (Allan Foster)
9   EV'RYTHING I LOVE   Glenn Miller Orch. (VR: Ray Eberle)
10   ROSE O'DAY   Freddy Martin Orch. (VR: Eddie Stone)

January 24, 1942
1   THE WHITE CLIFFS OF DOVER   Kay Kyser Orch. (VR:
     Harry Babbitt)
2   ELMER'S TUNE   Glenn Miller Orch. (VR: Ray Eberle)
3   CHATTANOOGA CHOO CHOO   Glenn Miller Orch. (VR:
     Tex Beneke & Modernaires with Paula Kelly)
4   THIS LOVE OF MINE   Tommy Dorsey Orch. (VR: Frank
     Sinatra)

5   ROSE O'DAY   Freddy Martin Orch. (VR: Eddie Stone)
6   EV'RYTHING I LOVE   Glenn Miller Orch. (VR: Ray Eberle)
7   THE SHRINE OF ST. CECELIA   Andrews Sisters
8   SHEPHERD SERENADE   Bing Crosby
9   I GOT IT BAD   Duke Ellington Orch. (VR: Ivie Anderson)
10   THIS IS NO LAUGHING MATTER   Charlie Spivak Orch.
     (VR: Garry Stevens)

January 31, 1942
1   THE WHITE CLIFFS OF DOVER   Kay Kyser Orch. (VR:
     Harry Babbitt)
2   ELMER'S TUNE   Glenn Miller Orch. (VR: Ray Eberle)
3   ROSE O'DAY   Freddy Martin Orch. (VR: Eddie Stone)
4   CHATTANOOGA CHOO CHOO   Glenn Miller Orch. (VR:
     Tex Beneke & Modernaires with Paula Kelly)
5   EV'RYTHING I LOVE   Glenn Miller Orch. (VR: Ray Eberle)
6   THIS LOVE OF MINE   Tommy Dorsey Orch. (VR: Frank
     Sinatra)
7   THE SHRINE OF ST. CECELIA   Andrews Sisters
8   BLUES IN THE NIGHT   Woody Herman Orch. (VR: Woody
     Herman)
9   SHEPHERD SERENADE   Bing Crosby
10   HUMPTY DUMPTY HEART   Glenn Miller Orch. (VR: Ray
     Eberle)

February 7, 1942
1   THE WHITE CLIFFS OF DOVER   Kay Kyser Orch. (VR:
     Harry Babbitt)
2   ROSE O'DAY   Freddy Martin Orch. (VR: Eddie Stone)
3   BLUES IN THE NIGHT   Woody Herman Orch. (VR: Woody
     Herman)
4   ELMER'S TUNE   Glenn Miller Orch. (VR: Ray Eberle)
5   EV'RYTHING I LOVE   Glenn Miller Orch. (VR: Ray Eberle)
6   CHATTANOOGA CHOO CHOO   Glenn Miller Orch. (VR:
     Tex Beneke & Modernaires with Paula Kelly)
7   THE SHRINE OF ST. CECELIA   Andrews Sisters
8   WE'RE THE COUPLE OF THE CASTLE   Glenn Miller Orch.
     (VR: Ray Eberle)
9   THIS LOVE OF MINE   Tommy Dorsey Orch. (VR: Frank
     Sinatra)
10   DEEP IN THE HEART OF TEXAS   Alvino Rey Orch. (VR: Bill
     Schallen & Skeets Herfurt)

February 14, 1942
1   THE WHITE CLIFFS OF DOVER   Kay Kyser Orch. (VR:
     Harry Babbitt)
2   BLUES IN THE NIGHT   Woody Herman Orch. (VR: Woody
     Herman)
3   ROSE O'DAY   Freddy Martin Orch. (VR: Eddie Stone)
4   EV'RYTHING I LOVE   Glenn Miller Orch. (VR: Ray Eberle)
5   THE SHRINE OF ST. CECELIA   Andrews Sisters
6   ELMER'S TUNE   Glenn Miller Orch. (VR: Ray Eberle)
7   THIS IS NO LAUGHING MATTER   Charlie Spivak Orch.
     (VR: Garry Stevens)
8   REMEMBER PEARL HARBOR   Sammy Kaye Orch. (VR:
     Choir)
9   CHATTANOOGA CHOO CHOO   Glenn Miller Orch. (VR:
     Tex Beneke & Modernaires with Paula Kelly)
10   THIS LOVE OF MINE   Tommy Dorsey Orch. (VR: Frank
     Sinatra)

February 21, 1942
1   BLUES IN THE NIGHT   Woody Herman Orch. (VR: Woody
     Herman)
2   THE WHITE CLIFFS OF DOVER   Kay Kyser Orch. (VR:
     Harry Babbitt)

3 ROSE O'DAY   Freddy Martin Orch. (VR: Eddie Stone)
4 EV'RYTHING I LOVE   Glenn Miller Orch. (VR: Ray Eberle)
5 I DON'T WANT TO WALK WITHOUT YOU   Harry James Orch. (VR: Helen Forrest)
6 THE SHRINE OF ST. CECELIA   Andrews Sisters
7 ELMER'S TUNE   Glenn Miller Orch. (VR: Ray Eberle)
8 CHATTANOOGA CHOO CHOO   Glenn Miller Orch. (VR: Tex Beneke & Modernaires with Paula Kelly)
9 DEEP IN THE HEART OF TEXAS   Alvino Rey Orch. (VR: Bill Schallen & Skeets Herfurt)
10 REMEMBER PEARL HARBOR   Sammy Kaye Orch. (VR: Choir)
  Note: * Another version by: Jimmy Dorsey Orch. (VR: Bob Eberly)

February 28, 1942
1 THE WHITE CLIFFS OF DOVER   Kay Kyser Orch. (VR: Harry Babbitt)
2 BLUES IN THE NIGHT   Woody Herman Orch. (VR: Woody Herman)
3 DEEP IN THE HEART OF TEXAS   Alvino Rey Orch. (VR: Bill Schallen & Skeets Herfurt)
4 ROSE O'DAY   Freddy Martin Orch. (VR: Eddie Stone)
5 THE SHRINE OF ST. CECELIA   Andrews Sisters
6 HOW ABOUT YOU?   Tommy Dorsey Orch. (VR: Frank Sinatra)
7 DAY DREAMING   Rudy Vallee
8 REMEMBER PEARL HARBOR   Sammy Kaye Orch. (VR: Choir)
9 EV'RYTHING I LOVE   Glenn Miller Orch. (VR: Ray Eberle)
10 ELMER'S TUNE   Glenn Miller Orch. (VR: Ray Eberle)

March 7, 1942
1 BLUES IN THE NIGHT   Woody Herman Orch. (VR: Woody Herman)
2 DEEP IN THE HEART OF TEXAS   Alvino Rey Orch. (VR: Bill Schallen & Skeets Herfurt)
3 I DON'T WANT TO WALK WITHOUT YOU   Harry James Orch. (VR: Helen Forrest)
4 THE WHITE CLIFFS OF DOVER   Kay Kyser Orch. (VR: Harry Babbitt)
5 ROSE O'DAY   Freddy Martin Orch. (VR: Eddie Stone)
6 HOW ABOUT YOU?   Tommy Dorsey Orch. (VR: Frank Sinatra)
7 THE SHRINE OF ST. CECELIA   Andrews Sisters
8 EV'RYTHING I LOVE   Glenn Miller Orch. (VR: Ray Eberle)
9 REMEMBER PEARL HARBOR   Sammy Kaye Orch. (VR: Choir)
10 SOMETIMES   Eddy Duchin Orch. (VR: June Robbins)

March 14, 1942
1 DEEP IN THE HEART OF TEXAS   Alvino Rey Orch. (VR: Bill Schallen & Skeets Herfurt)
2 BLUES IN THE NIGHT   Woody Herman Orch. (VR: Woody Herman)
3 I DON'T WANT TO WALK WITHOUT YOU   Harry James Orch. (VR: Helen Forrest)
4 THE WHITE CLIFFS OF DOVER   Kay Kyser Orch. (VR: Harry Babbitt)
5 HOW ABOUT YOU?   Tommy Dorsey Orch. (VR: Frank Sinatra)
6 ROSE O'DAY   Freddy Martin Orch. (VR: Eddie Stone)
7 THE SHRINE OF ST. CECELIA   Andrews Sisters
8 MISS YOU   Dinah Shore
9 MOONLIGHT COCKTAIL   Glenn Miller Orch. (VR: Ray Eberle)

10 HOW DO I KNOW IT'S REAL   Kay Kyser (VR: Dorothy Dunn)

March 21, 1942
1 DEEP IN THE HEART OF TEXAS   Alvino Rey Orch. (VR: Bill Schallen & Skeets Herfurt)
2 BLUES IN THE NIGHT   Woody Herman Orch. (VR: Woody Herman)
3 I DON'T WANT TO WALK WITHOUT YOU   Harry James Orch. (VR: Helen Forrest)
4 THE WHITE CLIFFS OF DOVER   Kay Kyser Orch. (VR: Harry Babbitt)
5 HOW ABOUT YOU?   Tommy Dorsey Orch. (VR: Frank Sinatra)
6 ROSE O'DAY   Freddy Martin Orch. (VR: Eddie Stone)
7 MOONLIGHT COCKTAIL   Glenn Miller Orch. (VR: Ray Eberle)
8 THE SHRINE OF ST. CECELIA   Andrews Sisters
9 SOMEBODY ELSE IS TAKING MY PLACE   Benny Goodman Orch. (VR: Peggy Lee)
10 MISS YOU   Dinah Shore

March 28, 1942
1 DEEP IN THE HEART OF TEXAS   Alvino Rey Orch. (VR: Bill Schallen & Skeets Herfurt)
2 I DON'T WANT TO WALK WITHOUT YOU   Harry James Orch. (VR: Helen Forrest)
3 ROSE O'DAY   Freddy Martin Orch. (VR: Eddie Stone)
4 BLUES IN THE NIGHT   Woody Herman Orch. (VR: Woody Herman)
5 MISS YOU   Dinah Shore
6 SOMEBODY ELSE IS TAKING MY PLACE   Benny Goodman Orch. (VR: Peggy Lee)
7 THE WHITE CLIFFS OF DOVER   Kay Kyser Orch. (VR: Harry Babbitt)
8 MOONLIGHT COCKTAIL   Glenn Miller Orch. (VR: Ray Eberle)
9 TANGERINE   Jimmy Dorsey Orch. (VR: Bob Eberly & Helen O'Connell)
10 SOMETIMES   Eddy Duchin Orch. (VR: June Robbins)

April 4, 1942
1 DEEP IN THE HEART OF TEXAS   Alvino Rey Orch. (VR: Bill Schallen & Skeets Herfurt)
2 I DON'T WANT TO WALK WITHOUT YOU   Harry James Orch. (VR: Helen Forrest)
3 SOMEBODY ELSE IS TAKING MY PLACE   Benny Goodman Orch. (VR: Peggy Lee)
4 MISS YOU   Dinah Shore
5 BLUES IN THE NIGHT   Woody Herman Orch. (VR: Woody Herman)
6 MOONLIGHT COCKTAIL   Glenn Miller Orch. (VR: Ray Eberle)
7 THE WHITE CLIFFS OF DOVER   Kay Kyser Orch. (VR: Harry Babbitt)
8 SHE'LL ALWAYS REMEMBER   Glenn Miller Orch. (VR: Ray Eberle)
9 TANGERINE   Jimmy Dorsey Orch. (VR: Bob Eberly & Helen O'Connell)
10 I REMEMBER YOU   Jimmy Dorsey Orch. (VR: Bob Eberly)

April 11, 1942
1 DEEP IN THE HEART OF TEXAS   Alvino Rey Orch. (VR: Bill Schallen & Skeets Herfurt)
2 I DON'T WANT TO WALK WITHOUT YOU   Harry James Orch. (VR: Helen Forrest)

3 SOMEBODY ELSE IS TAKING MY PLACE Benny Goodman Orch. (VR: Peggy Lee)
4 MISS YOU Dinah Shore
5 MOONLIGHT COCKTAIL Glenn Miller Orch. (VR: Ray Eberle)
6 BLUES IN THE NIGHT Woody Herman Orch. (VR: Woody Herman)
7 HOW ABOUT YOU? Tommy Dorsey Orch. (VR: Frank Sinatra)
8 ALWAYS IN MY HEART Glenn Miller Orch. (VR: Ray Eberle)
9 I REMEMBER YOU Jimmy Dorsey Orch. (VR: Bob Eberly)
10 THE WHITE CLIFFS OF DOVER Kay Kyser Orch. (VR: Harry Babbitt)

April 18, 1942
1 I DON'T WANT TO WALK WITHOUT YOU Harry James Orch. (VR: Helen Forrest)
2 DEEP IN THE HEART OF TEXAS Alvino Rey Orch. (VR: Bill Schallen & Skeets Herfurt)
3 SOMEBODY ELSE IS TAKING MY PLACE Benny Goodman Orch. (VR: Peggy Lee)
4 MOONLIGHT COCKTAIL Glenn Miller Orch. (VR: Ray Eberle)
5 TANGERINE Jimmy Dorsey Orch. (VR: Bob Eberly & Helen O'Connell)
6 SKYLARK Dinah Shore
7 BLUES IN THE NIGHT Woody Herman Orch. (VR: Woody Herman)
8 MISS YOU Dinah Shore
9 I'LL PRAY FOR YOU Andrews Sisters
10 ME AND MY MELINDA Kay Kyser Orch. (VR: Glee Club)

April 25, 1942
1 SOMEBODY ELSE IS TAKING MY PLACE Benny Goodman Orch. (VR: Peggy Lee)
2 TANGERINE Jimmy Dorsey Orch. (VR: Bob Eberly & Helen O'Connell)
3 I DON'T WANT TO WALK WITHOUT YOU Harry James Orch. (VR: Helen Forrest)
4 MOONLIGHT COCKTAIL Glenn Miller Orch. (VR: Ray Eberle)
5 SKYLARK Dinah Shore
6 DEEP IN THE HEART OF TEXAS Alvino Rey Orch. (VR: Bill Schallen & Skeets Herfurt)
7 DON'T SIT UNDER THE APPLE TREE Glenn Miller Orch. (VR: Marion Hutton, Tex Beneke & Modernaires) *
8 MISS YOU Dinah Shore
9 BLUES IN THE NIGHT Woody Herman Orch. (VR: Woody Herman)
10 HAPPY IN LOVE Dick Jurgens Orch.
Note: * Closely associated in later years with The Andrews Sisters.

May 2, 1942
1 SOMEBODY ELSE IS TAKING MY PLACE Benny Goodman Orch. (VR: Peggy Lee)
2 TANGERINE Jimmy Dorsey Orch. (VR: Bob Eberly & Helen O'Connell)
3 MISS YOU Dinah Shore
4 MOONLIGHT COCKTAIL Glenn Miller Orch. (VR: Ray Eberle)
5 I DON'T WANT TO WALK WITHOUT YOU Harry James Orch. (VR: Helen Forrest)
6 SKYLARK Dinah Shore
7 DEEP IN THE HEART OF TEXAS Alvino Rey Orch. (VR: Bill Schallen & Skeets Herfurt)

8 I REMEMBER YOU Jimmy Dorsey Orch. (VR: Bob Eberly)
9 FULL MOON Jimmy Dorsey Orch. (VR: Bob Eberly)
10 HAPPY IN LOVE Dick Jurgens Orch.

May 9, 1942
1 SOMEBODY ELSE IS TAKING MY PLACE Benny Goodman Orch. (VR: Peggy Lee)
2 SKYLARK Dinah Shore
3 TANGERINE Jimmy Dorsey Orch. (VR: Bob Eberly & Helen O'Connell)
4 ALWAYS IN MY HEART Glenn Miller Orch. (VR: Ray Eberle)
5 DON'T SIT UNDER THE APPLE TREE Glenn Miller Orch. (VR: Marion Hutton, Tex Beneke & Modernaires) *
6 I DON'T WANT TO WALK WITHOUT YOU Harry James Orch. (VR: Helen Forrest)
7 MOONLIGHT COCKTAIL Glenn Miller Orch. (VR: Ray Eberle)
8 MISS YOU Dinah Shore
9 JERSEY BOUNCE Benny Goodman Orch.
10 JOHNNY DOUGHBOY FOUND A ROSE IN IRELAND Kay Kyser Orch. (VR: Glee Club)
Note: * Closely associated in later years with The Andrews Sisters.

May 16, 1942
1 DON'T SIT UNDER THE APPLE TREE Glenn Miller Orch. (VR: Marion Hutton, Tex Beneke & Modernaires) *
2 TANGERINE Jimmy Dorsey Orch. (VR: Bob Eberly & Helen O'Connell)
3 SKYLARK Dinah Shore
4 SOMEBODY ELSE IS TAKING MY PLACE Benny Goodman Orch. (VR: Peggy Lee)
5 I DON'T WANT TO WALK WITHOUT YOU Harry James Orch. (VR: Helen Forrest)
6 MOONLIGHT COCKTAIL Glenn Miller Orch. (VR: Ray Eberle)
7 JERSEY BOUNCE Benny Goodman Orch.
8 SLEEPY LAGOON Harry James Orch.
9 MISS YOU Dinah Shore
10 ONE DOZEN ROSES Dick Jurgens Orch. (VR: Buddy Moreno) **
Note: * Closely associated in later years with The Andrews Sisters.
** Another version by: Harry James (VR: Jimmy Saunders).

May 23, 1942
1 DON'T SIT UNDER THE APPLE TREE Glenn Miller Orch. (VR: Marion Hutton, Tex Beneke & Modernaires) *
2 SOMEBODY ELSE IS TAKING MY PLACE Benny Goodman Orch. (VR: Peggy Lee)
3 TANGERINE Jimmy Dorsey Orch. (VR: Bob Eberly & Helen O'Connell)
4 SLEEPY LAGOON Harry James Orch.
5 SKYLARK Dinah Shore
6 MOONLIGHT COCKTAIL Glenn Miller Orch. (VR: Ray Eberle)
7 JOHNNY DOUGHBOY FOUND A ROSE IN IRELAND Kay Kyser Orch. (VR: Glee Club)
8 JERSEY BOUNCE Benny Goodman Orch.
9 MISS YOU Dinah Shore
10 SHE'LL ALWAYS REMEMBER Glenn Miller Orch. (VR: Ray Eberle)
Note: * Closely associated in later years with The Andrews Sisters.

** Another version by: Harry James (VR: Jimmy Saunders).

May 30, 1942
1 DON'T SIT UNDER THE APPLE TREE   Glenn Miller Orch. (VR: Marion Hutton, Tex Beneke & Modernaires) *
2 TANGERINE   Jimmy Dorsey Orch. (VR: Bob Eberly & Helen O'Connell)
3 SOMEBODY ELSE IS TAKING MY PLACE   Benny Goodman Orch. (VR: Peggy Lee)
4 SLEEPY LAGOON   Harry James Orch.
5 SKYLARK   Dinah Shore
6 ONE DOZEN ROSES   Dick Jurgens Orch. (VR: Buddy Moreno) **
7 JERSEY BOUNCE   Benny Goodman Orch.
8 JOHNNY DOUGHBOY FOUND A ROSE IN IRELAND   Kay Kyser Orch. (VR: Glee Club)
9 MOONLIGHT COCKTAIL   Glenn Miller Orch. (VR: Ray Eberle)
10 I'LL KEEP THE LOVELIGHT BURNING   Freddy Martin Orch. (VR: Stuart Wade)
   Note: * Closely associated in later years with The Andrews Sisters.
         ** Another version by: Harry James (VR: Jimmy Saunders).

June 6, 1942
1 DON'T SIT UNDER THE APPLE TREE   Glenn Miller Orch. (VR: Marion Hutton, Tex Beneke & Modernaires) *
2 SLEEPY LAGOON   Harry James Orch.
3 JOHNNY DOUGHBOY FOUND A ROSE IN IRELAND   Kay Kyser Orch. (VR: Glee Club)
4 SKYLARK   Dinah Shore
5 TANGERINE   Jimmy Dorsey Orch. (VR: Bob Eberly & Helen O'Connell)
6 JERSEY BOUNCE   Benny Goodman Orch.
7 ONE DOZEN ROSES   Dick Jurgens Orch. (VR: Buddy Moreno) **
8 SOMEBODY ELSE IS TAKING MY PLACE   Benny Goodman Orch. (VR: Peggy Lee)
9 THREE LITTLE SISTERS   Andrews Sisters
10 MOONLIGHT COCKTAIL   Glenn Miller Orch. (VR: Ray Eberle)
   Note: * Closely associated in later years with The Andrews Sisters.
         ** Another version by: Harry James (VR: Jimmy Saunders).

June 13, 1942
1 SLEEPY LAGOON   Harry James Orch.
2 DON'T SIT UNDER THE APPLE TREE   Glenn Miller Orch. (VR: Marion Hutton, Tex Beneke & Modernaires) *
3 JOHNNY DOUGHBOY FOUND A ROSE IN IRELAND   Kay Kyser Orch. (VR: Glee Club)
4 ONE DOZEN ROSES   Dick Jurgens Orch. (VR: Buddy Moreno) **
5 TANGERINE   Jimmy Dorsey Orch. (VR: Bob Eberly & Helen O'Connell)
6 SKYLARK   Dinah Shore
7 JERSEY BOUNCE   Benny Goodman Orch.
8 ALWAYS IN MY HEART   Glenn Miller Orch. (VR: Ray Eberle)
9 THREE LITTLE SISTERS   Andrews Sisters
10 WHO WOULDN'T LOVE YOU   Kay Kyser Orch. (VR: Trudy & Harry Babbitt)
   Note: * Closely associated in later years with The Andrews Sisters.

** Another version by: Harry James (VR: Jimmy Saunders).

June 20, 1942
1 DON'T SIT UNDER THE APPLE TREE   Glenn Miller Orch. (VR: Marion Hutton, Tex Beneke & Modernaires) *
2 JOHNNY DOUGHBOY FOUND A ROSE IN IRELAND   Kay Kyser Orch. (VR: Glee Club)
3 ONE DOZEN ROSES   Dick Jurgens Orch. (VR: Buddy Moreno) **
4 SKYLARK   Dinah Shore
5 JERSEY BOUNCE   Benny Goodman Orch.
6 THREE LITTLE SISTERS   Andrews Sisters
7 SLEEPY LAGOON   Harry James Orch.
8 TANGERINE   Jimmy Dorsey Orch. (VR: Bob Eberly & Helen O'Connell)
9 WHO WOULDN'T LOVE YOU   Kay Kyser Orch. (VR: Trudy & Harry Babbitt)
10 IDAHO   Alvino Rey Orch. (VR: Yvonne King)
   Note: * Closely associated in later years with The Andrews Sisters.
         ** Another version by: Harry James (VR: Jimmy Saunders).

June 27, 1942
1 SLEEPY LAGOON   Harry James Orch.
2 ONE DOZEN ROSES   Dick Jurgens Orch. (VR: Buddy Moreno) *
3 JOHNNY DOUGHBOY FOUND A ROSE IN IRELAND   Kay Kyser Orch. (VR: Glee Club)
4 JERSEY BOUNCE   Benny Goodman Orch.
5 DON'T SIT UNDER THE APPLE TREE   Glenn Miller Orch. (VR: Marion Hutton, Tex Beneke & Modernaires) **
6 TANGERINE   Jimmy Dorsey Orch. (VR: Bob Eberly & Helen O'Connell)
7 THREE LITTLE SISTERS   Andrews Sisters
8 WHO WOULDN'T LOVE YOU   Kay Kyser Orch. (VR: Trudy & Harry Babbitt)
9 SKYLARK   Dinah Shore
10 THIS IS WORTH FIGHTING FOR   Jimmy Dorsey Orch. (VR: Bob Eberly)
   Note: * Another version by: Harry James (VR: Jimmy Saunders).
         ** Closely associated in later years with The Andrews Sisters.

July 4, 1942
1 ONE DOZEN ROSES   Dick Jurgens Orch. (VR: Buddy Moreno) *
2 SLEEPY LAGOON   Harry James Orch.
3 JOHNNY DOUGHBOY FOUND A ROSE IN IRELAND   Kay Kyser Orch. (VR: Glee Club)
4 JERSEY BOUNCE   Benny Goodman Orch.
5 JINGLE, JANGLE, JINGLE   Kay Kyser Orch. (VR: Julie Conway & Harry Babbitt)
6 DON'T SIT UNDER THE APPLE TREE   Glenn Miller Orch. (VR: Marion Hutton, Tex Beneke & Modernaires) **
7 THREE LITTLE SISTERS   Andrews Sisters
8 HERE YOU ARE   Sammy Kaye Orch. (VR: Elaine Beatty)
9 WHO WOULDN'T LOVE YOU   Kay Kyser Orch. (VR: Trudy & Harry Babbitt)
10 SKYLARK   Dinah Shore
   Note: * Another version by: Harry James (VR: Jimmy Saunders).
         ** Closely associated in later years with The Andrews Sisters.

July 11, 1942
1   ONE DOZEN ROSES   Dick Jurgens Orch. (VR: Buddy Moreno) *
2   SLEEPY LAGOON   Harry James Orch.
3   JOHNNY DOUGHBOY FOUND A ROSE IN IRELAND   Kay Kyser Orch. (VR: Glee Club)
4   JINGLE, JANGLE, JINGLE   Kay Kyser Orch. (VR: Julie Conway & Harry Babbitt)
5   JERSEY BOUNCE   Benny Goodman Orch.
6   DON'T SIT UNDER THE APPLE TREE   Glenn Miller Orch. (VR: Marion Hutton, Tex Beneke & Modernaires) **
7   THREE LITTLE SISTERS   Andrews Sisters
8   WHO WOULDN'T LOVE YOU   Kay Kyser Orch. (VR: Trudy & Harry Babbitt)
9   I'LL KEEP THE LOVELIGHT BURNING   Freddy Martin Orch. (VR: Stuart Wade)
10   HERE YOU ARE   Sammy Kaye Orch. (VR: Elaine Beatty)
   Note: * Another version by: Harry James (VR: Jimmy Saunders).
      ** Closely associated in later years with The Andrews Sisters.

July 18, 1942
1   SLEEPY LAGOON   Harry James Orch.
2   ONE DOZEN ROSES   Dick Jurgens Orch. (VR: Buddy Moreno) *
3   JINGLE, JANGLE, JINGLE   Kay Kyser Orch. (VR: Julie Conway & Harry Babbitt)
4   JOHNNY DOUGHBOY FOUND A ROSE IN IRELAND   Kay Kyser Orch. (VR: Glee Club)
5   JERSEY BOUNCE   Benny Goodman Orch.
6   WHO WOULDN'T LOVE YOU   Kay Kyser Orch. (VR: Trudy & Harry Babbitt)
7   DON'T SIT UNDER THE APPLE TREE   Glenn Miller Orch. (VR: Marion Hutton, Tex Beneke & Modernaires) **
8   HE WEARS A PAIR OF SILVER WINGS   Kay Kyser Orch. (VR: Harry Babbitt)
9   THREE LITTLE SISTERS   Andrews Sisters
10   THIS IS WORTH FIGHTING FOR   Jimmy Dorsey Orch. (VR: Bob Eberly)
   Note: * Another version by: Harry James (VR: Jimmy Saunders).
      ** Closely associated in later years with The Andrews Sisters.

July 25, 1942
1   JINGLE, JANGLE, JINGLE   Kay Kyser Orch. (VR: Julie Conway & Harry Babbitt)
2   SLEEPY LAGOON   Harry James Orch.
3   WHO WOULDN'T LOVE YOU   Kay Kyser Orch. (VR: Trudy & Harry Babbitt)
4   ONE DOZEN ROSES   Dick Jurgens Orch. (VR: Buddy Moreno) *
5   JOHNNY DOUGHBOY FOUND A ROSE IN IRELAND   Kay Kyser Orch. (VR: Glee Club)
6   JERSEY BOUNCE   Benny Goodman Orch.
7   HE WEARS A PAIR OF SILVER WINGS   Kay Kyser Orch. (VR: Harry Babbitt)
8   THREE LITTLE SISTERS   Andrews Sisters
9   HERE YOU ARE   Sammy Kaye Orch. (VR: Elaine Beatty)
10   BE CAREFUL, IT'S MY HEART   Bing Crosby
   Note: * Another version by: Harry James (VR: Jimmy Saunders).

August 1, 1942
1   JINGLE, JANGLE, JINGLE   Kay Kyser Orch. (VR: Julie Conway & Harry Babbitt)

2   ONE DOZEN ROSES   Dick Jurgens Orch. (VR: Buddy Moreno) *
3   WHO WOULDN'T LOVE YOU   Kay Kyser Orch. (VR: Trudy & Harry Babbitt)
4   HE WEARS A PAIR OF SILVER WINGS   Kay Kyser Orch. (VR: Harry Babbitt)
5   JOHNNY DOUGHBOY FOUND A ROSE IN IRELAND   Kay Kyser Orch. (VR: Glee Club)
6   SLEEPY LAGOON   Harry James Orch.
7   IDAHO   Alvino Rey Orch. (VR: Yvonne King)
8   JERSEY BOUNCE   Benny Goodman Orch.
9   THREE LITTLE SISTERS   Andrews Sisters
10   ALWAYS IN MY HEART   Glenn Miller Orch. (VR: Ray Eberle)
   Note: * Another version by: Harry James (VR: Jimmy Saunders).

August 8, 1942
1   JINGLE, JANGLE, JINGLE   Kay Kyser Orch. (VR: Julie Conway & Harry Babbitt)
2   SLEEPY LAGOON   Harry James Orch.
3   HE WEARS A PAIR OF SILVER WINGS   Kay Kyser Orch. (VR: Harry Babbitt)
4   ONE DOZEN ROSES   Dick Jurgens Orch. (VR: Buddy Moreno) *
5   WHO WOULDN'T LOVE YOU   Kay Kyser Orch. (VR: Trudy & Harry Babbitt)
6   STAGE DOOR CANTEEN   Sammy Kaye Orch. (VR: Don Cornell)
7   JOHNNY DOUGHBOY FOUND A ROSE IN IRELAND   Kay Kyser Orch. (VR: Glee Club)
8   JERSEY BOUNCE   Benny Goodman Orch.
9   THIS IS WORTH FIGHTING FOR   Jimmy Dorsey Orch. (VR: Bob Eberly)
10   BE CAREFUL, IT'S MY HEART   Bing Crosby
   Note: * Another version by: Harry James (VR: Jimmy Saunders).

August 15, 1942
1   JINGLE, JANGLE, JINGLE   Kay Kyser Orch. (VR: Julie Conway & Harry Babbitt)
2   HE WEARS A PAIR OF SILVER WINGS   Kay Kyser Orch. (VR: Harry Babbitt)
3   ONE DOZEN ROSES   Dick Jurgens Orch. (VR: Buddy Moreno) *
4   WHO WOULDN'T LOVE YOU   Kay Kyser Orch. (VR: Trudy & Harry Babbitt)
5   STAGE DOOR CANTEEN   Sammy Kaye Orch. (VR: Don Cornell)
6   IDAHO   Alvino Rey Orch. (VR: Yvonne King)
7   SLEEPY LAGOON   Harry James Orch.
8   TAKE ME   Tommy Dorsey Orch. (VR: Frank Sinatra)
9   BE CAREFUL, IT'S MY HEART   Bing Crosby
10   JOHNNY DOUGHBOY FOUND A ROSE IN IRELAND   Kay Kyser Orch. (VR: Glee Club)
   Note: * Another version by: Harry James (VR: Jimmy Saunders).

August 22, 1942
1   JINGLE, JANGLE, JINGLE   Kay Kyser Orch. (VR: Julie Conway & Harry Babbitt)
2   HE WEARS A PAIR OF SILVER WINGS   Kay Kyser Orch. (VR: Harry Babbitt)
3   BE CAREFUL, IT'S MY HEART   Bing Crosby
4   IDAHO   Alvino Rey Orch. (VR: Yvonne King)
5   WHO WOULDN'T LOVE YOU   Kay Kyser Orch. (VR: Trudy & Harry Babbitt)

6 SLEEPY LAGOON   Harry James Orch.
7 STAGE DOOR CANTEEN   Sammy Kaye Orch. (VR: Don Cornell)
8 JOHNNY DOUGHBOY FOUND A ROSE IN IRELAND   Kay Kyser Orch. (VR: Glee Club)
9 MY DEVOTION   Charlie Spivak Orch. (VR: Garry Stevens)
10 ONE DOZEN ROSES   Dick Jurgens Orch. (VR: Buddy Moreno) *
Note: * Another version by: Harry James (VR: Jimmy Saunders).

August 29, 1942
1 HE WEARS A PAIR OF SILVER WINGS   Kay Kyser Orch. (VR: Harry Babbitt)
2 JINGLE, JANGLE, JINGLE   Kay Kyser Orch. (VR: Julie Conway & Harry Babbitt)
3 STAGE DOOR CANTEEN   Sammy Kaye Orch. (VR: Don Cornell)
4 BE CAREFUL, IT'S MY HEART   Bing Crosby
5 MY DEVOTION   Charlie Spivak Orch. (VR: Garry Stevens)
6 SLEEPY LAGOON   Harry James Orch.
7 WHO WOULDN'T LOVE YOU   Kay Kyser Orch. (VR: Trudy & Harry Babbitt)
8 TAKE ME   Tommy Dorsey Orch. (VR: Frank Sinatra)
9 IDAHO   Alvino Rey Orch. (VR: Yvonne King)
10 AT LAST   Glenn Miller Orch. (VR: Ray Eberle)

September 5, 1942
1 HE WEARS A PAIR OF SILVER WINGS   Kay Kyser Orch. (VR: Harry Babbitt)
2 STAGE DOOR CANTEEN   Sammy Kaye Orch. (VR: Don Cornell)
3 JINGLE, JANGLE, JINGLE   Kay Kyser Orch. (VR: Julie Conway & Harry Babbitt)
4 MY DEVOTION   Charlie Spivak Orch. (VR: Garry Stevens)
5 BE CAREFUL, IT'S MY HEART   Bing Crosby
6 IDAHO   Alvino Rey Orch. (VR: Yvonne King)
7 KALAMAZOO   Glenn Miller Orch. (VR: Tex Beneke & Modernaires)
8 SLEEPY LAGOON   Harry James Orch.
9 JOHNNY DOUGHBOY FOUND A ROSE IN IRELAND   Kay Kyser Orch. (VR: Glee Club)
10 WHO WOULDN'T LOVE YOU   Kay Kyser Orch. (VR: Trudy & Harry Babbitt)

September 12, 1942
1 HE WEARS A PAIR OF SILVER WINGS   Kay Kyser Orch. (VR: Harry Babbitt)
2 STAGE DOOR CANTEEN   Sammy Kaye Orch. (VR: Don Cornell)
3 JINGLE, JANGLE, JINGLE   Kay Kyser Orch. (VR: Julie Conway & Harry Babbitt)
4 MY DEVOTION   Charlie Spivak Orch. (VR: Garry Stevens)
5 BE CAREFUL, IT'S MY HEART   Bing Crosby
6 KALAMAZOO   Glenn Miller Orch. (VR: Tex Beneke & Modernaires)
7 IDAHO   Alvino Rey Orch. (VR: Yvonne King)
8 AT LAST   Glenn Miller Orch. (VR: Ray Eberle)
9 SLEEPY LAGOON   Harry James Orch.
10 TAKE ME   Tommy Dorsey Orch. (VR: Frank Sinatra)

September 19, 1942
1 HE WEARS A PAIR OF SILVER WINGS   Kay Kyser Orch. (VR: Harry Babbitt)
2 MY DEVOTION   Charlie Spivak Orch. (VR: Garry Stevens)
3 BE CAREFUL, IT'S MY HEART   Bing Crosby

4 STAGE DOOR CANTEEN   Sammy Kaye Orch. (VR: Don Cornell)
5 KALAMAZOO   Glenn Miller Orch. (VR: Tex Beneke & Modernaires)
6 IDAHO   Alvino Rey Orch. (VR: Yvonne King)
7 JINGLE, JANGLE, JINGLE   Kay Kyser Orch. (VR: Julie Conway & Harry Babbitt)
8 TAKE ME   Tommy Dorsey Orch. (VR: Frank Sinatra)
9 AT LAST   Glenn Miller Orch. (VR: Ray Eberle)
10 DEARLY BELOVED   Glenn Miller Orch. (VR: Skip Nelson)

September 26, 1942
1 MY DEVOTION   Charlie Spivak Orch. (VR: Garry Stevens)
2 KALAMAZOO   Glenn Miller Orch. (VR: Tex Beneke & Modernaires)
3 HE WEARS A PAIR OF SILVER WINGS   Kay Kyser Orch. (VR: Harry Babbitt)
4 STAGE DOOR CANTEEN   Sammy Kaye Orch. (VR: Don Cornell)
5 BE CAREFUL, IT'S MY HEART   Bing Crosby
6 SERENADE IN BLUE   Glenn Miller Orch. (VR: Ray Eberle & Modernaires)
7 JINGLE, JANGLE, JINGLE   Kay Kyser Orch. (VR: Julie Conway & Harry Babbitt)
8 TAKE ME   Tommy Dorsey Orch. (VR: Frank Sinatra)
9 IDAHO   Alvino Rey Orch. (VR: Yvonne King)
10 WONDER WHEN MY BABY'S COMING HOME   Sammy Kaye Orch. (VR: Nancy Norman)

October 3, 1942
1 MY DEVOTION   Charlie Spivak Orch. (VR: Garry Stevens)
2 KALAMAZOO   Glenn Miller Orch. (VR: Tex Beneke & Modernaires)
3 BE CAREFUL, IT'S MY HEART   Bing Crosby
4 HE WEARS A PAIR OF SILVER WINGS   Kay Kyser Orch. (VR: Harry Babbitt)
5 AT LAST   Glenn Miller Orch. (VR: Ray Eberle)
6 STAGE DOOR CANTEEN   Sammy Kaye Orch. (VR: Don Cornell)
7 TAKE ME   Tommy Dorsey Orch. (VR: Frank Sinatra)
8 JINGLE, JANGLE, JINGLE   Kay Kyser Orch. (VR: Julie Conway & Harry Babbitt)
9 MANHATTAN SERENADE   Tommy Dorsey Orch. (VR: Jo Stafford)
10 WONDER WHEN MY BABY'S COMING HOME   Sammy Kaye Orch. (VR: Nancy Norman)

October 10, 1942
1 KALAMAZOO   Glenn Miller Orch. (VR: Tex Beneke & Modernaires)
2 BE CAREFUL, IT'S MY HEART   Bing Crosby
3 MY DEVOTION   Charlie Spivak Orch. (VR: Garry Stevens)
4 STAGE DOOR CANTEEN   Sammy Kaye Orch. (VR: Don Cornell)
5 IDAHO   Alvino Rey Orch. (VR: Yvonne King)
6 HE WEARS A PAIR OF SILVER WINGS   Kay Kyser Orch. (VR: Harry Babbitt)
7 AT LAST   Glenn Miller Orch. (VR: Ray Eberle)
8 SERENADE IN BLUE   Glenn Miller Orch. (VR: Ray Eberle & Modernaires)
9 THERE WILL NEVER BE ANOTHER YOU   Sammy Kaye Orch. (VR: Nancy Norman)
10 HE'S MY GUY   Harry James Orch. (VR: Helen Forrest)

October 17, 1942
1 MY DEVOTION   Charlie Spivak Orch. (VR: Garry Stevens)

2 BE CAREFUL, IT'S MY HEART   Bing Crosby
3 KALAMAZOO   Glenn Miller Orch. (VR: Tex Beneke & Modernaires)
4 STAGE DOOR CANTEEN   Sammy Kaye Orch. (VR: Don Cornell)
5 MANHATTAN SERENADE   Tommy Dorsey Orch. (VR: Jo Stafford)
6 SERENADE IN BLUE   Glenn Miller Orch. (VR: Ray Eberle & Modernaires)
7 WHITE CHRISTMAS   Bing Crosby *
8 HE WEARS A PAIR OF SILVER WINGS   Kay Kyser Orch. (VR: Harry Babbitt)
9 HE'S MY GUY   Harry James Orch. (VR: Helen Forrest)
10 WHEN THE LIGHTS GO ON AGAIN   Vaughn Monroe Orch. (VR: Vaughn Monroe)
   Note: * The biggest-selling recod of all time.

October 24, 1942
1 MY DEVOTION   Charlie Spivak Orch. (VR: Garry Stevens)
2 WHITE CHRISTMAS   Bing Crosby *
3 KALAMAZOO   Glenn Miller Orch. (VR: Tex Beneke & Modernaires)
4 SERENADE IN BLUE   Glenn Miller Orch. (VR: Ray Eberle & Modernaires)
5 BE CAREFUL, IT'S MY HEART   Bing Crosby
6 DEARLY BELOVED   Glenn Miller Orch. (VR: Skip Nelson)
7 WONDER WHEN MY BABY'S COMING HOME   Sammy Kaye Orch. (VR: Nancy Norman)
8 STAGE DOOR CANTEEN   Sammy Kaye Orch. (VR: Don Cornell)
9 PRAISE THE LORD AND PASS THE AMMUNITION   Kay Kyser Orch. (VR: Glee Club)
10 AT LAST   Glenn Miller Orch. (VR: Ray Eberle)
   Note: * The biggest-selling record of all time.

October 31, 1942
1 WHITE CHRISTMAS   Bing Crosby *
2 PRAISE THE LORD AND PASS THE AMMUNITION   Kay Kyser Orch. (VR: Glee Club)
3 MY DEVOTION   Charlie Spivak Orch. (VR: Garry Stevens)
4 KALAMAZOO   Glenn Miller Orch. (VR: Tex Beneke & Modernaires)
5 WHEN THE LIGHTS GO ON AGAIN   Vaughn Monroe Orch. (VR: Vaughn Monroe)
6 BE CAREFUL, IT'S MY HEART   Bing Crosby
7 MANHATTAN SERENADE   Tommy Dorsey Orch. (VR: Jo Stafford)
8 SERENADE IN BLUE   Glenn Miller Orch. (VR: Ray Eberle & Modernaires)
9 AT LAST   Glenn Miller Orch. (VR: Ray Eberle)
10 HE WEARS A PAIR OF SILVER WINGS   Kay Kyser Orch. (VR: Harry Babbitt)
   Note: * The biggest-selling record of all time.

November 7, 1942
1 WHITE CHRISTMAS   Bing Crosby *
2 PRAISE THE LORD AND PASS THE AMMUNITION   Kay Kyser Orch. (VR: Glee Club)
3 MY DEVOTION   Charlie Spivak Orch. (VR: Garry Stevens)
4 KALAMAZOO   Glenn Miller Orch. (VR: Tex Beneke & Modernaires)
5 SERENADE IN BLUE   Glenn Miller Orch. (VR: Ray Eberle & Modernaires)
6 I CAME HERE TO TALK FOR JOE   Sammy Kaye Orch. (VR: Don Cornell)
7 DEARLY BELOVED   Glenn Miller Orch. (VR: Skip Nelson)

8 DAYBREAK   Tommy Dorsey Orch. (VR: Frank Sinatra)
9 MANHATTAN SERENADE   Tommy Dorsey Orch. (VR: Jo Stafford)
10 GOBS OF LOVE   King Sisters
   Note: * The biggest-selling record of all time.

November 14, 1942
1 WHITE CHRISTMAS   Bing Crosby *
2 PRAISE THE LORD AND PASS THE AMMUNITION   Kay Kyser Orch. (VR: Glee Club)
3 MY DEVOTION   Charlie Spivak Orch. (VR: Garry Stevens)
4 WHEN THE LIGHTS GO ON AGAIN   Vaughn Monroe Orch. (VR: Vaughn Monroe)
5 THERE WILL NEVER BE ANOTHER YOU   Sammy Kaye Orch. (VR: Nancy Norman)
6 KALAMAZOO   Glenn Miller Orch. (VR: Tex Beneke & Modernaires)
7 SERENADE IN BLUE   Glenn Miller Orch. (VR: Ray Eberle & Modernaires)
8 MANHATTAN SERENADE   Tommy Dorsey Orch. (VR: Jo Stafford)
9 BE CAREFUL, IT'S MY HEART   Bing Crosby
10 WHY DON'T YOU FALL IN LOVE WITH ME?   Dinah Shore **
   Note: * The biggest-selling record of all time.
      ** Another version by: Dick Jurgens Orch. (VR: Harry Cool)

November 21, 1942
1 WHITE CHRISTMAS   Bing Crosby *
2 PRAISE THE LORD AND PASS THE AMMUNITION   Kay Kyser Orch. (VR: Glee Club)
3 MANHATTAN SERENADE   Tommy Dorsey Orch. (VR: Jo Stafford)
4 WHEN THE LIGHTS GO ON AGAIN   Vaughn Monroe Orch. (VR: Vaughn Monroe)
5 DEARLY BELOVED   Glenn Miller Orch. (VR: Skip Nelson)
6 MISTER FIVE BY FIVE   Harry James Orch. (VR: Helen Forrest)
7 SERENADE IN BLUE   Glenn Miller Orch. (VR: Ray Eberle & Modernaires)
8 MY DEVOTION   Charlie Spivak Orch. (VR: Garry Stevens)
9 DAYBREAK   Tommy Dorsey Orch. (VR: Frank Sinatra)
10 THERE WILL NEVER BE ANOTHER YOU   Sammy Kaye Orch. (VR: Nancy Norman)
   Note: * The biggest-selling record of all time.

November 28, 1942
1 WHITE CHRISTMAS   Bing Crosby *
2 PRAISE THE LORD AND PASS THE AMMUNITION   Kay Kyser Orch. (VR: Glee Club)
3 DEARLY BELOVED   Glenn Miller Orch. (VR: Skip Nelson)
4 MISTER FIVE BY FIVE   Harry James Orch. (VR: Helen Forrest)
5 WHEN THE LIGHTS GO ON AGAIN   Vaughn Monroe Orch. (VR: Vaughn Monroe)
6 I CAME HERE TO TALK FOR JOE   Sammy Kaye Orch. (VR: Don Cornell)
7 MY DEVOTION   Charlie Spivak Orch. (VR: Garry Stevens)
8 MANHATTAN SERENADE   Tommy Dorsey Orch. (VR: Jo Stafford)
9 THERE WILL NEVER BE ANOTHER YOU   Sammy Kaye Orch. (VR: Nancy Norman)
10 SERENADE IN BLUE   Glenn Miller Orch. (VR: Ray Eberle & Modernaires)
   Note: * The biggest-selling record of all time.

Bing Crosby
Bing hits #1 with the best-selling record of all time, ``White Christmas.''
After a ten-week stay at the top, it was a Top 10 hit 38 more times during the Hit Parade era.

December 5, 1942

1. WHITE CHRISTMAS   Bing Crosby *
2. WHEN THE LIGHTS GO ON AGAIN   Vaughn Monroe Orch. (VR: Vaughn Monroe)
3. MISTER FIVE BY FIVE   Harry James Orch. (VR: Helen Forrest)
4. DEARLY BELOVED   Glenn Miller Orch. (VR: Skip Nelson)
5. MANHATTAN SERENADE   Tommy Dorsey Orch. (VR: Jo Stafford)
6. PRAISE THE LORD AND PASS THE AMMUNITION   Kay Kyser Orch. (VR: Glee Club)
7. DAYBREAK   Tommy Dorsey Orch. (VR: Frank Sinatra)
8. I'M GETTING TIRED SO I CAN SLEEP   Jimmy Dorsey Orch. (VR: Bob Eberly)
9. MY DEVOTION   Charlie Spivak Orch. (VR: Garry Stevens)
10. THERE ARE SUCH THINGS   Tommy Dorsey Orch. (VR: Frank Sinatra & Pied Pipers)
   Note: * The biggest-selling record of all time.

December 12, 1942

1. WHITE CHRISTMAS   Bing Crosby *
2. MISTER FIVE BY FIVE   Harry James Orch. (VR: Helen Forrest)
3. WHEN THE LIGHTS GO ON AGAIN   Vaughn Monroe Orch. (VR: Vaughn Monroe)
4. DEARLY BELOVED   Glenn Miller Orch. (VR: Skip Nelson)
5. PRAISE THE LORD AND PASS THE AMMUNITION   Kay Kyser Orch. (VR: Glee Club)
6. MANHATTAN SERENADE   Tommy Dorsey Orch. (VR: Jo Stafford)
7. WHY DON'T YOU FALL IN LOVE WITH ME?   Dinah Shore **
8. I HAD THE CRAZIEST DREAM   Harry James Orch. (VR: Helen Forrest)
9. DAYBREAK   Tommy Dorsey Orch. (VR: Frank Sinatra)
10. THERE ARE SUCH THINGS   Tommy Dorsey Orch. (VR: Frank Sinatra & Pied Pipers)
   Note: * The biggest-selling record of all time.
   ** Another version by: Dick Jurgens Orch. (VR: Harry Cool)

December 19, 1942

1. WHITE CHRISTMAS   Bing Crosby *
2. MISTER FIVE BY FIVE   Harry James Orch. (VR: Helen Forrest)
3. PRAISE THE LORD AND PASS THE AMMUNITION   Kay Kyser Orch. (VR: Glee Club)
4. THERE ARE SUCH THINGS   Tommy Dorsey Orch. (VR: Frank Sinatra & Pied Pipers)
5. WHEN THE LIGHTS GO ON AGAIN   Vaughn Monroe Orch. (VR: Vaughn Monroe)
6. DEARLY BELOVED   Glenn Miller Orch. (VR: Skip Nelson)
7. WHY DON'T YOU FALL IN LOVE WITH ME?   Dinah Shore**
8. I HAD THE CRAZIEST DREAM   Harry James Orch. (VR: Helen Forrest)
9. MANHATTAN SERENADE   Tommy Dorsey Orch. (VR: Jo Stafford)
10. THERE'S A STAR SPANGLED BANNER WAVING SOME-WHERE   Elton Britt
   Note: * The biggest-selling record of all time.
   ** Another version by: Dick Jurgens Orch. (VR: Harry Cool)

December 26, 1942

1. WHITE CHRISTMAS   Bing Crosby *
2. THERE ARE SUCH THINGS   Tommy Dorsey Orch. (VR: Frank Sinatra & Pied Pipers)

3. WHEN THE LIGHTS GO ON AGAIN   Vaughn Monroe Orch. (VR: Vaughn Monroe)
4. MISTER FIVE BY FIVE   Harry James Orch. (VR: Helen Forrest)
5. PRAISE THE LORD AND PASS THE AMMUNITION   Kay Kyser Orch. (VR: Glee Club)
6. WHY DON'T YOU FALL IN LOVE WITH ME? Dinah Shore**
7. DEARLY BELOVED   Glenn Miller Orch. (VR: Skip Nelson)
8. I HAD THE CRAZIEST DREAM   Harry James Orch. (VR: Helen Forrest)
9. MANHATTAN SERENADE   Tommy Dorsey Orch. (VR: Jo Stafford)
10. ROSE ANN OF CHARING CROSS   Peter Piper Orch. (VR: Black Pepper)
   Note: * The biggest-selling record of all time.
   ** Another version by: Dick Jurgens Orch. (VR: Harry Cool)

January 2, 1943

1. WHITE CHRISTMAS   Bing Crosby *
2. I HAD THE CRAZIEST DREAM   Harry James Orch. (VR: Helen Forrest)
3. THERE ARE SUCH THINGS   Tommy Dorsey Orch. (VR: Frank Sinatra & Pied Pipers)
4. MOONLIGHT BECOMES YOU   Bing Crosby
5. WHEN THE LIGHTS GO ON AGAIN   Vaughn Monroe Orch. (VR: Vaughn Monroe)
6. PRAISE THE LORD AND PASS THE AMMUNITION   Kay Kyser Orch. (VR: Glee Club)
7. DEARLY BELOVED   Glenn Miller Orch. (VR: Skip Nelson)
8. MISTER FIVE BY FIVE   Harry James Orch. (VR: Helen Forrest)
9. WHY DON'T YOU FALL IN LOVE WITH ME? Dinah Shore**
10. YOU'D BE SO NICE TO COME HOME TO   Dinah Shore
   Note: * The biggest-selling record of all time.
   ** Another version by: Dick Jurgens Orch. (VR: Harry Cool)

January 9, 1943

1. THERE ARE SUCH THINGS   Tommy Dorsey Orch. (VR: Frank Sinatra & Pied Pipers)
2. WHITE CHRISTMAS   Bing Crosby *
3. WHY DON'T YOU FALL IN LOVE WITH ME? Dinah Shore**
4. MOONLIGHT BECOMES YOU   Bing Crosby
5. WHEN THE LIGHTS GO ON AGAIN   Vaughn Monroe Orch. (VR: Vaughn Monroe)
6. I HAD THE CRAZIEST DREAM   Harry James Orch. (VR: Helen Forrest)
7. MISTER FIVE BY FIVE   Harry James Orch. (VR: Helen Forrest)
8. PRAISE THE LORD AND PASS THE AMMUNITION   Kay Kyser Orch. (VR: Glee Club)
9. DEARLY BELOVED   Glenn Miller Orch. (VR: Skip Nelson)
10. BRAZIL   Xavier Cugat Orch. (VR: Band)
   Note: * The biggest-selling record of all time.
   ** Another version by: Dick Jurgens Orch. (VR: Harry Cool)

January 16, 1943

1. THERE ARE SUCH THINGS   Tommy Dorsey Orch. (VR: Frank Sinatra & Pied Pipers)
2. I HAD THE CRAZIEST DREAM   Harry James Orch. (VR: Helen Forrest)
3. MOONLIGHT BECOMES YOU   Bing Crosby
4. MISTER FIVE BY FIVE   Harry James Orch. (VR: Helen Forrest)
5. WHEN THE LIGHTS GO ON AGAIN   Vaughn Monroe Orch. (VR: Vaughn Monroe)

6   WHY DON'T YOU FALL IN LOVE WITH ME?   Dinah Shore *
7   WHITE CHRISTMAS   Bing Crosby **
8   DEARLY BELOVED   Glenn Miller Orch. (VR: Skip Nelson)
9   BRAZIL   Xavier Cugat Orch. (VR: Band)
10 ROSE ANN OF CHARING CROSS   Peter Piper Orch. (VR: Black Pepper)
   Note: * Another version by: Dick Jurgens Orch. (VR: Harry Cool)
        ** The biggest-selling record of all time.

January 23, 1943
1   MOONLIGHT BECOMES YOU   Bing Crosby
2   THERE ARE SUCH THINGS   Tommy Dorsey Orch. (VR: Frank Sinatra & Pied Pipers)
3   I HAD THE CRAZIEST DREAM   Harry James Orch. (VR: Helen Forrest)
4   WHY DON'T YOU FALL IN LOVE WITH ME?   Dinah Shore *
5   WHEN THE LIGHTS GO ON AGAIN   Vaughn Monroe Orch. (VR: Vaughn Monroe)
6   YOU'D BE SO NICE TO COME HOME TO   Dinah Shore
7   MISTER FIVE BY FIVE   Harry James Orch. (VR: Helen Forrest)
8   WHITE CHRISTMAS   Bing Crosby **
9   DEARLY BELOVED   Glenn Miller Orch. (VR: Skip Nelson)
10 BRAZIL   Xavier Cugat Orch. (VR: Band)
   Note: * Another version by: Dick Jurgens Orch. (VR: Harry Cool)
        ** The biggest-selling record of all time.

January 30, 1943
1   THERE ARE SUCH THINGS   Tommy Dorsey Orch. (VR: Frank Sinatra & Pied Pipers)
2   I HAD THE CRAZIEST DREAM   Harry James Orch. (VR: Helen Forrest)
3   WHY DON'T YOU FALL IN LOVE WITH ME?   Dinah Shore *
4   WHEN THE LIGHTS GO ON AGAIN   Vaughn Monroe Orch. (VR: Vaughn Monroe)
5   MOONLIGHT BECOMES YOU   Bing Crosby
6   BRAZIL   Xavier Cugat Orch. (VR: Band)
7   YOU'D BE SO NICE TO COME HOME TO   Dinah Shore
8   MOONLIGHT MOOD   Glenn Miller Orch. (VR: Skip Nelson & Modernaires)
9   DEARLY BELOVED   Glenn Miller Orch. (VR: Skip Nelson)
10 ROSE ANN OF CHARING CROSS   Peter Piper Orch. (VR: Black Pepper)
   Note: * Another version by: Dick Jurgens Orch. (VR: Harry Cool)

February 6, 1943
1   MOONLIGHT BECOMES YOU   Bing Crosby
2   THERE ARE SUCH THINGS   Tommy Dorsey Orch. (VR: Frank Sinatra & Pied Pipers)
3   I HAD THE CRAZIEST DREAM   Harry James Orch. (VR: Helen Forrest)
4   WHY DON'T YOU FALL IN LOVE WITH ME?   Dinah Shore *
5   WHEN THE LIGHTS GO ON AGAIN   Vaughn Monroe Orch. (VR: Vaughn Monroe)
6   YOU'D BE SO NICE TO COME HOME TO   Dinah Shore
7   BRAZIL   Xavier Cugat Orch. (VR: Band)
8   MOONLIGHT MOOD   Glenn Miller Orch. (VR: Skip Nelson & Modernaires)
9   DEARLY BELOVED   Glenn Miller Orch. (VR: Skip Nelson)
10 I'M GETTING TIRED SO I CAN SLEEP   Jimmy Dorsey Orch. (VR: Bob Eberly)
   Note: * Another version by: Dick Jurgens Orch. (VR: Harry Cool)

February 13, 1943
1   THERE ARE SUCH THINGS   Tommy Dorsey Orch. (VR: Frank Sinatra & Pied Pipers)
2   I HAD THE CRAZIEST DREAM   Harry James Orch. (VR: Helen Forrest)
3   MOONLIGHT BECOMES YOU   Bing Crosby
4   YOU'D BE SO NICE TO COME HOME TO   Dinah Shore
5   WHY DON'T YOU FALL IN LOVE WITH ME?   Dinah Shore *
6   ROSE ANN OF CHARING CROSS   Peter Piper Orch. (VR: Black Pepper)
7   WHEN THE LIGHTS GO ON AGAIN   Vaughn Monroe Orch. (VR: Vaughn Monroe)
8   BRAZIL   Xavier Cugat Orch. (VR: Band)
9   MOONLIGHT MOOD   Glenn Miller Orch. (VR: Skip Nelson & Modernaires)
10 DEARLY BELOVED   Glenn Miller Orch. (VR: Skip Nelson)
   Note: * Another version by: Dick Jurgens Orch. (VR: Harry Cool)

February 20, 1943
1   THERE ARE SUCH THINGS   Tommy Dorsey Orch. (VR: Frank Sinatra & Pied Pipers)
2   BRAZIL   Xavier Cugat Orch. (VR: Band)
3   YOU'D BE SO NICE TO COME HOME TO   Dinah Shore
4   I'VE HEARD THAT SONG BEFORE   Harry James Orch. (VR: Helen Forrest)
5   WHY DON'T YOU FALL IN LOVE WITH ME?   Dinah Shore *
6   MOONLIGHT BECOMES YOU   Bing Crosby
7   I HAD THE CRAZIEST DREAM   Harry James Orch. (VR: Helen Forrest)
8   WHEN THE LIGHTS GO ON AGAIN   Vaughn Monroe Orch. (VR: Vaughn Monroe)
9   ROSE ANN OF CHARING CROSS   Peter Piper Orch. (VR: Black Pepper)
10 FOR ME AND MY GAL   Judy Garland & Gene Kelly
   Note: * Another version by: Dick Jurgens Orch. (VR: Harry Cool)

February 27, 1943
1   THERE ARE SUCH THINGS   Tommy Dorsey Orch. (VR: Frank Sinatra & Pied Pipers)
2   YOU'D BE SO NICE TO COME HOME TO   Dinah Shore
3   I'VE HEARD THAT SONG BEFORE   Harry James Orch. (VR: Helen Forrest)
4   MOONLIGHT BECOMES YOU   Bing Crosby
5   BRAZIL   Xavier Cugat Orch. (VR: Band)
6   MOONLIGHT MOOD   Glenn Miller Orch. (VR: Skip Nelson & Modernaires)
7   FOR ME AND MY GAL   Judy Garland & Gene Kelly
8   WHY DON'T YOU FALL IN LOVE WITH ME?   Dinah Shore *
9   I HAD THE CRAZIEST DREAM   Harry James Orch. (VR: Helen Forrest)
10 THAT OLD BLACK MAGIC   Glenn Miller Orch. (VR: Skip Nelson & Modernaires)
   Note: * Another version by: Dick Jurgens Orch. (VR: Harry Cool)

March 6, 1943
1   BRAZIL   Xavier Cugat Orch. (VR: Band)
2   I'VE HEARD THAT SONG BEFORE   Harry James Orch. (VR: Helen Forrest)
3   YOU'D BE SO NICE TO COME HOME TO   Dinah Shore
4   THERE ARE SUCH THINGS   Tommy Dorsey Orch. (VR: Frank Sinatra & Pied Pipers)
5   MOONLIGHT BECOMES YOU   Bing Crosby
6   I HAD THE CRAZIEST DREAM   Harry James Orch. (VR: Helen Forrest)

7   THAT OLD BLACK MAGIC   Glenn Miller Orch. (VR: Skip Nelson & Modernaires)
8   MOONLIGHT MOOD   Glenn Miller Orch. (VR: Skip Nelson & Modernaires)
9   WHY DON'T YOU FALL IN LOVE WITH ME?   Dinah Shore *
10   TAKING A CHANCE ON LOVE   Benny Goodman Orch. (VR: Helen Forrest)
    Note: * Another version by: Dick Jurgens Orch. (VR: Harry Cool)

March 13, 1943

1   BRAZIL   Xavier Cugat Orch. (VR: Band)
2   I'VE HEARD THAT SONG BEFORE   Harry James Orch. (VR: Helen Forrest)
3   YOU'D BE SO NICE TO COME HOME TO   Dinah Shore
4   THERE ARE SUCH THINGS   Tommy Dorsey Orch. (VR: Frank Sinatra & Pied Pipers)
5   THAT OLD BLACK MAGIC   Glenn Miller Orch. (VR: Skip Nelson & Modernaires)
6   MOONLIGHT BECOMES YOU   Bing Crosby
7   I HAD THE CRAZIEST DREAM   Harry James Orch. (VR: Helen Forrest)
8   TAKING A CHANCE ON LOVE   Benny Goodman Orch. (VR: Helen Forrest)
9   FOR ME AND MY GAL   Judy Garland & Gene Kelly
10   WHY DON'T YOU FALL IN LOVE WITH ME?   Dinah Shore *
    Note: * Another version by: Dick Jurgens Orch. (VR: Harry Cool)

March 20, 1943

1   I'VE HEARD THAT SONG BEFORE   Harry James Orch. (VR: Helen Forrest)
2   YOU'D BE SO NICE TO COME HOME TO   Dinah Shore
3   THAT OLD BLACK MAGIC   Glenn Miller Orch. (VR: Skip Nelson & Modernaires)
4   BRAZIL   Xavier Cugat Orch. (VR: Band)
5   THERE ARE SUCH THINGS   Tommy Dorsey Orch. (VR: Frank Sinatra & Pied Pipers)
6   AS TIME GOES BY   Rudy Vallee
7   MOONLIGHT BECOMES YOU   Bing Crosby
8   I HAD THE CRAZIEST DREAM   Harry James Orch. (VR: Helen Forrest)
9   IT CAN'T BE WRONG   Dick Haymes
10   FOR ME AND MY GAL   Judy Garland & Gene Kelly

March 27, 1943

1   I'VE HEARD THAT SONG BEFORE   Harry James Orch. (VR: Helen Forrest)
2   THAT OLD BLACK MAGIC   Glenn Miller Orch. (VR: Skip Nelson & Modernaires)
3   AS TIME GOES BY   Rudy Vallee
4   YOU'D BE SO NICE TO COME HOME TO   Dinah Shore
5   BRAZIL   Xavier Cugat Orch. (VR: Band)
6   THERE ARE SUCH THINGS   Tommy Dorsey Orch. (VR: Frank Sinatra & Pied Pipers)
7   DON'T GET AROUND MUCH ANY MORE   Ink Spots
8   MOONLIGHT BECOMES YOU   Bing Crosby
9   FOR ME AND MY GAL   Judy Garland & Gene Kelly
10   TAKING A CHANCE ON LOVE   Benny Goodman Orch. (VR: Helen Forrest)

April 3, 1943

1   I'VE HEARD THAT SONG BEFORE   Harry James Orch. (VR: Helen Forrest)
2   THAT OLD BLACK MAGIC   Glenn Miller Orch. (VR: Skip Nelson & Modernaires)

3   AS TIME GOES BY   Rudy Vallee
4   YOU'D BE SO NICE TO COME HOME TO   Dinah Shore
5   BRAZIL   Xavier Cugat Orch. (VR: Band)
6   TAKING A CHANCE ON LOVE   Benny Goodman Orch. (VR: Helen Forrest)
7   THERE ARE SUCH THINGS   Tommy Dorsey Orch. (VR: Frank Sinatra & Pied Pipers)
8   DON'T GET AROUND MUCH ANY MORE   Ink Spots
9   MOONLIGHT BECOMES YOU   Bing Crosby
10   FOR ME AND MY GAL   Judy Garland & Gene Kelly

April 10, 1943

1   BRAZIL   Xavier Cugat Orch. (VR: Band)
2   I'VE HEARD THAT SONG BEFORE   Harry James Orch. (VR: Helen Forrest)
3   THAT OLD BLACK MAGIC   Glenn Miller Orch. (VR: Skip Nelson & Modernaires)
4   AS TIME GOES BY   Rudy Vallee
5   YOU'D BE SO NICE TO COME HOME TO   Dinah Shore
6   DON'T GET AROUND MUCH ANYMORE   Ink Spots
7   TAKING A CHANCE ON LOVE   Benny Goodman Orch. (VR: Helen Forrest)
8   FOR ME AND MY GAL   Judy Garland & Gene Kelly
9   IT CAN'T BE WRONG   Dick Haymes
10   HARBOR OF DREAMBOATS   Song Spinners

April 17, 1943

1   I'VE HEARD THAT SONG BEFORE   Harry James Orch. (VR: Helen Forrest)
2   AS TIME GOES BY   Rudy Vallee
3   IT CAN'T BE WRONG   Dick Haymes
4   BRAZIL   Xavier Cugat Orch. (VR: Band)
5   YOU'D BE SO NICE TO COME HOME TO   Dinah Shore
6   I'VE HEARD THAT SONG BEFORE   Harry James Orch. (VR: Helen Forrest)
7   THAT OLD BLACK MAGIC   Glenn Miller Orch. (VR: Skip Nelson & Modernaires)
8   FOR ME AND MY GAL   Judy Garland & Gene Kelly
9   TAKING A CHANCE ON LOVE   Benny Goodman Orch. (VR: Helen Forrest)
10   LET'S GET LOST   Vaughn Monroe Orch. (VR: Vaughn Monroe)

April 24, 1943

1   AS TIME GOES BY   Rudy Vallee
2   THAT OLD BLACK MAGIC   Glenn Miller Orch. (VR: Skip Nelson & Modernaires)
3   DON'T GET AROUND MUCH ANY MORE   Ink Spots
4   I'VE HEARD THAT SONG BEFORE   Harry James Orch. (VR: Helen Forrest)
5   YOU'D BE SO NICE TO COME HOME TO   Dinah Shore
6   IT CAN'T BE WRONG   Dick Haymes
7   BRAZIL   Xavier Cugat Orch. (VR: Band)
8   WHAT'S THE GOOD WORD, MR. BLUEBIRD   Kay Kyser (VR: Harry Babbitt & Chorus)
9   DON'T CRY   Erskine Hawkins Orch. (VR: Jimmie Mitchelle)
10   TAKING A CHANCE ON LOVE   Benny Goodman Orch. (VR: Helen Forrest)

May 1, 1943

1   DON'T GET AROUND MUCH ANY MORE   Ink Spots
2   AS TIME GOES BY   Rudy Vallee
3   IT CAN'T BE WRONG   Dick Haymes
4   BRAZIL   Xavier Cugat Orch. (VR: Band)
5   YOU'D BE SO NICE TO COME HOME TO   Dinah Shore

6   I'VE HEARD THAT SONG BEFORE   Harry James Orch.
     (VR: Helen Forrest)
7   THAT OLD BLACK MAGIC   Glenn Miller Orch. (VR: Skip
     Nelson & Modernaires)
8   FOR ME AND MY GAL   Judy Garland & Gene Kelly
9   TAKING A CHANCE ON LOVE   Benny Goodman Orch.
     (VR: Helen Forrest)
10 LET'S GET LOST   Vaughn Monroe Orch. (VR: Vaughn
     Monroe)

May 8, 1943
1   AS TIME GOES BY   Rudy Vallee
2   DON'T GET AROUND MUCH ANY MORE   Ink Spots
3   THAT OLD BLACK MAGIC   Glenn Miller Orch. (VR: Skip
     Nelson & Modernaires)
4   I'VE HEARD THAT SONG BEFORE   Harry James Orch.
     (VR: Helen Forrest)
5   IT CAN'T BE WRONG   Dick Haymes
6   TAKING A CHANCE ON LOVE   Benny Goodman Orch.
     (VR: Helen Forrest)
7   BRAZIL   Xavier Cugat Orch. (VR: Band)
8   HARBOR OF DREAMBOATS   Song Spinners
9   YOU'LL NEVER KNOW   Dick Haymes
10 COMIN' IN ON A WING AND A PRAYER   Song Spinners

May 15, 1943
1   AS TIME GOES BY   Rudy Vallee
2   THAT OLD BLACK MAGIC   Glenn Miller Orch. (VR: Skip
     Nelson & Modernaires)
3   IT CAN'T BE WRONG   Dick Haymes
4   DON'T GET AROUND MUCH ANY MORE   Ink Spots
5   TAKING A CHANCE ON LOVE   Benny Goodman Orch.
     (VR: Helen Forrest)
6   I'VE HEARD THAT SONG BEFORE   Harry James Orch.
     (VR: Helen Forrest)
7   COMIN' IN ON A WING AND A PRAYER   Song Spinners
8   IT'S ALWAYS YOU   Tommy Dorsey Orch. (VR: Frank
     Sinatra)
9   YOU'LL NEVER KNOW   Dick Haymes
10 IN THE BLUE OF EVENING   Tommy Dorsey Orch. (VR:
     Frank Sinatra)

May 22, 1943
1   AS TIME GOES BY   Rudy Vallee
2   DON'T GET AROUND MUCH ANYMORE   Ink Spots
3   COMIN' IN ON A WING AND A PRAYER   Song Spinners
4   IT CAN'T BE WRONG   Dick Haymes
5   YOU'LL NEVER KNOW   Dick Haymes
6   LET'S GET LOST   Vaughn Monroe Orch. (VR: Vaughn
     Monroe)
7   THAT OLD BLACK MAGIC   Glenn Miller Orch. (VR: Skip
     Nelson & Modernaires)
8   I'VE HEARD THAT SONG BEFORE   Harry James Orch.
     (VR: Helen Forrest)
9   BRAZIL   Xavier Cugat Orch. (VR: Band)
10 TAKING A CHANCE ON LOVE   Benny Goodman Orch.
     (VR: Helen Forrest)

May 29, 1943
1   DON'T GET AROUND MUCH ANY MORE   Ink Spots
2   AS TIME GOES BY   Rudy Vallee
3   COMIN' IN ON A WING AND A PRAYER   Song Spinners
4   IT CAN'T BE WRONG   Dick Haymes
5   YOU'LL NEVER KNOW   Dick Haymes
6   THAT OLD BLACK MAGIC   Glenn Miller Orch. (VR: Skip
     Nelson & Modernaires)

Rudy Vallee
``As Time Goes By'' (from the movie ``Casablanca'')
was actually recorded in 1931.

Dick Haymes
One of the forties' best-loved singers peaks at #1
with ``You'll Never Know'' (July 3).

7   I'VE HEARD THAT SONG BEFORE   Harry James Orch.
    (VR: Helen Forrest)
8   LET'S GET LOST   Vaughn Monroe Orch. (VR: Vaughn
    Monroe)
9   TAKING A CHANCE ON LOVE   Benny Goodman Orch.
    (VR: Helen Forrest)
10 IN THE BLUE OF EVENING   Tommy Dorsey Orch. (VR:
    Frank Sinatra)

June 5, 1943
1   DON'T GET AROUND MUCH ANY MORE   Ink Spots
2   YOU'LL NEVER KNOW   Dick Haymes
3   COMIN' IN ON A WING AND A PRAYER   Song Spinners
4   IT CAN'T BE WRONG   Dick Haymes
5   LET'S GET LOST   Vaughn Monroe Orch. (VR: Vaughn
    Monroe)
6   AS TIME GOES BY   Rudy Vallee
7   TAKING A CHANCE ON LOVE   Benny Goodman Orch.
    (VR: Helen Forrest)
8   THAT OLD BLACK MAGIC   Glenn Miller Orch. (VR: Skip
    Nelson & Modernaires)
9   IN THE BLUE OF EVENING   Tommy Dorsey Orch. (VR:
    Frank Sinatra)
10 WHAT'S THE GOOD WORD, MR. BLUEBIRD   Kay Kyser
    (VR: Harry Babbitt & Chorus)

June 12, 1943
1   LET'S GET LOST   Vaughn Monroe Orch. (VR: Vaughn
    Monroe)
2   IN THE BLUE OF EVENING   Tommy Dorsey Orch. (VR:
    Frank Sinatra)
3   YOU'LL NEVER KNOW   Dick Haymes
4   DON'T GET AROUND MUCH ANY MORE   Ink Spots
5   AS TIME GOES BY   Rudy Vallee
6   IT CAN'T BE WRONG   Dick Haymes
7   IT'S ALWAYS YOU   Tommy Dorsey Orch. (VR: Frank
    Sinatra)
8   I NEVER MENTION YOUR NAME   Jack Leonard
9   YOU RHYME WITH EVERYTHING THAT'S BEAUTIFUL
    Alan Miller Orch.
10 TAKING A CHANCE ON LOVE   Benny Goodman Orch.
    (VR: Helen Forrest)

June 19, 1943
1   COMIN' IN ON A WING AND A PRAYER   Song Spinners
2   YOU'LL NEVER KNOW   Dick Haymes
3   LET'S GET LOST   Vaughn Monroe Orch. (VR: Vaughn
    Monroe)
4   AS TIME GOES BY   Rudy Vallee
5   IN THE BLUE OF EVENING   Tommy Dorsey Orch. (VR:
    Frank Sinatra)
6   DON'T GET AROUND MUCH ANY MORE   Ink Spots
7   IT'S ALWAYS YOU   Tommy Dorsey Orch. (VR: Frank
    Sinatra)
8   IT CAN'T BE WRONG   Dick Haymes
9   TAKING A CHANCE ON LOVE   Benny Goodman Orch.
    (VR: Helen Forrest)
10 PEOPLE WILL SAY WE'RE IN LOVE   Bing Crosby *
    Note: * Another version by: Frank Sinatra.

June 26, 1943
1   COMIN' IN ON A WING AND A PRAYER   Song Spinners
2   YOU'LL NEVER KNOW   Dick Haymes
3   AS TIME GOES BY   Rudy Vallee
4   LET'S GET LOST   Vaughn Monroe Orch. (VR: Vaughn
    Monroe)

5   IN THE BLUE OF THE EVENING   Tommy Dorsey Orch.
    (VR: Frank Sinatra)
6   DON'T GET AROUND MUCH ANY MORE   Ink Spots
7   TAKING A CHANCE ON LOVE   Benny Goodman Orch.
    (VR: Helen Forrest)
8   IT'S ALWAYS YOU   Tommy Dorsey Orch. (VR: Frank
    Sinatra)
9   IT CAN'T BE WRONG   Dick Haymes
10 JOHNNY ZERO   Song Spinners

July 3, 1943
1   YOU'LL NEVER KNOW   Dick Haymes
2   COMIN' IN ON A WING AND A PRAYER   Song Spinners
3   IT CAN'T BE WRONG   Dick Haymes
4   IN THE BLUE OF EVENING   Tommy Dorsey Orch. (VR:
    Frank Sinatra)
5   DON'T GET AROUND MUCH ANY MORE   Ink Spots
6   AS TIME GOES BY   Rudy Vallee
7   LET'S GET LOST   Vaughn Monroe Orch. (VR: Vaughn
    Monroe)
8   IT'S ALWAYS YOU   Tommy Dorsey Orch. (VR: Frank
    Sinatra)
9   JOHNNY ZERO   Song Spinners
10 YOU RHYME WITH EVERYTHING THAT'S BEAUTIFUL
    Alan Miller Orch.

July 10, 1943
1   YOU'LL NEVER KNOW   Dick Haymes
2   COMIN' IN ON A WING AND A PRAYER   Song Spinners
3   IN THE BLUE OF EVENING   Tommy Dorsey Orch. (VR:
    Frank Sinatra)
4   AS TIME GOES BY   Rudy Vallee
5   DON'T GET AROUND MUCH ANY MORE   Ink Spots
6   LET'S GET LOST   Vaughn Monroe Orch. (VR: Vaughn
    Monroe)
7   TAKING A CHANCE ON LOVE   Benny Goodman Orch.
    (VR: Helen Forrest)
8   ALL OR NOTHING AT ALL   Harry James Orch. (VR: Frank
    Sinatra)
9   JOHNNY ZERO   Song Spinners
10 IT CAN'T BE WRONG   Dick Haymes

July 17, 1943
1   COMIN' IN ON A WING AND A PRAYER   Song Spinners
2   YOU'LL NEVER KNOW   Dick Haymes
3   IN THE BLUE OF EVENING   Tommy Dorsey Orch. (VR:
    Frank Sinatra)
4   IT CAN'T BE WRONG   Dick Haymes
5   ALL OR NOTHING AT ALL   Harry James Orch. (VR: Frank
    Sinatra)
6   AS TIME GOES BY   Rudy Vallee
7   LET'S GET LOST   Vaughn Monroe Orch. (VR: Vaughn
    Monroe)
8   IN MY ARMS   Dick Haymes
9   JOHNNY ZERO   Song Spinners
10 PEOPLE WILL SAY WE'RE IN LOVE   Bing Crosby *
    Note: * Another version by: Frank Sinatra.

July 24, 1943
1   YOU'LL NEVER KNOW   Dick Haymes
2   IN THE BLUE OF THE EVENING   Tommy Dorsey Orch.
    (VR: Frank Sinatra)
3   COMIN' IN ON A WING AND A PRAYER   Song Spinners
4   IT CAN'T BE WRONG   Dick Haymes
5   LET'S GET LOST   Vaughn Monroe Orch. (VR: Vaughn
    Monroe)

6 PEOPLE WILL SAY WE'RE IN LOVE   Bing Crosby *
7 AS TIME GOES BY   Rudy Vallee
8 JOHNNY ZERO   Song Spinners
9 PUT YOUR ARMS AROUND ME, HONEY   Dick Kuhn (VR: Trio)
10 IT'S ALWAYS YOU   Tommy Dorsey Orch. (VR: Frank Sinatra)
   Note: * Another version by: Frank Sinatra.

July 31, 1943
1 YOU'LL NEVER KNOW   Dick Haymes
2 COMIN' IN ON A WING AND A PRAYER   Song Spinners
3 IN THE BLUE OF EVENING   Tommy Dorsey Orch. (VR: Frank Sinatra)
4 ALL OR NOTHING AT ALL   Harry James Orch. (VR: Frank Sinatra)
5 LET'S GET LOST   Vaughn Monroe Orch. (VR: Vaughn Monroe)
6 IN MY ARMS   Dick Haymes
7 AS TIME GOES BY   Rudy Vallee
8 PEOPLE WILL SAY WE'RE IN LOVE   Bing Crosby *
9 IT CAN'T BE WRONG   Dick Haymes
10 JOHNNY ZERO   Song Spinners
   Note: * Another version by: Frank Sinatra.

August 7, 1943
1 YOU'LL NEVER KNOW   Dick Haymes
2 IN THE BLUE OF EVENING   Tommy Dorsey Orch. (VR: Frank Sinatra)
3 ALL OR NOTHING AT ALL   Harry James Orch. (VR: Frank Sinatra)
4 COMIN' IN ON A WING AND A PRAYER   Song Spinners
5 PEOPLE WILL SAY WE'RE IN LOVE   Bing Crosby *
6 LET'S GET LOST   Vaughn Monroe Orch. (VR: Vaughn Monroe)
7 IT'S ALWAYS YOU   Tommy Dorsey Orch. (VR: Frank Sinatra)
8 IT CAN'T BE WRONG   Dick Haymes
9 AS TIME GOES BY   Rudy Vallee
10 IN MY ARMS   Dick Haymes
   Note: * Another version by: Frank Sinatra.

August 14, 1943
1 YOU'LL NEVER KNOW   Dick Haymes
2 IN THE BLUE OF EVENING   Tommy Dorsey Orch. (VR: Frank Sinatra)
3 PEOPLE WILL SAY WE'RE IN LOVE   Bing Crosby *
4 COMIN' IN ON A WING AND A PRAYER   Song Spinners
5 ALL OR NOTHING AT ALL   Harry James Orch. (VR: Frank Sinatra)
6 IT'S ALWAYS YOU   Tommy Dorsey Orch. (VR: Frank Sinatra)
7 SUNDAY, MONDAY, OR ALWAYS   Bing Crosby
8 IT CAN'T BE WRONG   Dick Haymes
9 I HEARD YOU CRIED LAST NIGHT   Harry James Orch. (VR: Helen Forrest)
   Note: * Another version by: Frank Sinatra.

August 21,1943
1 YOU'LL NEVER KNOW   Dick Haymes
2 IN THE BLUE OF EVENING   Tommy Dorsey Orch. (VR: Frank Sinatra)
3 ALL OR NOTHING AT ALL   Harry James Orch. (VR: Frank Sinatra)
4 PEOPLE WILL SAY WE'RE IN LOVE   Bing Crosby *
5 COMIN' IN ON A WING AND A PRAYER   Song Spinners
6 IN MY ARMS   Dick Haymes

7 IT'S ALWAYS YOU   Tommy Dorsey Orch. (VR: Frank Sinatra)
8 SUNDAY, MONDAY, OR ALWAYS   Bing Crosby
9 PUT YOUR ARMS AROUND ME, HONEY   Dick Kuhn (VR: Trio)
   Note: * Another version by: Frank Sinatra.

August 28, 1943
1 YOU'LL NEVER KNOW   Dick Haymes
2 IN THE BLUE OF EVENING   Tommy Dorsey Orch. (VR: Frank Sinatra)
3 SUNDAY, MONDAY, OR ALWAYS   Bing Crosby
4 ALL OR NOTHING AT ALL   Harry James Orch. (VR: Frank Sinatra)
5 IN MY ARMS   Dick Haymes
6 PEOPLE WILL SAY WE'RE IN LOVE   Bing Crosby *
7 PUT YOUR ARMS AROUND ME, HONEY   Dick Kuhn (VR: Trio)
8 COMIN' IN ON A WING AND A PRAYER   Song Spinners
9 I HEARD YOU CRIED LAST NIGHT   Harry James Orch. (VR: Helen Forrest)
   Note: * Another version by: Frank Sinatra.

September 4, 1943
1 YOU'LL NEVER KNOW   Dick Haymes
2 SUNDAY, MONDAY, OR ALWAYS   Bing Crosby
3 IN THE BLUE OF EVENING   Tommy Dorsey Orch. (VR: Frank Sinatra)
4 PEOPLE WILL SAY WE'RE IN LOVE   Bing Crosby *
5 ALL OR NOTHING AT ALL   Harry James Orch. (VR: Frank Sinatra)
6 I HEARD YOU CRIED LAST NIGHT   Harry James Orch. (VR: Helen Forrest)
7 IN MY ARMS   Dick Haymes
8 COMIN' IN ON A WING AND A PRAYER   Song Spinners
9 PUT YOUR ARMS AROUND ME, HONEY   Dick Kuhn (VR: Trio)
   Note: * Another version by: Frank Sinatra.

September 11, 1943
1 SUNDAY, MONDAY, OR ALWAYS   Bing Crosby
2 YOU'LL NEVER KNOW   Dick Haymes
3 ALL OR NOTHING AT ALL   Harry James Orch. (VR: Frank Sinatra)
4 IN THE BLUE OF EVENING   Tommy Dorsey Orch. (VR: Frank Sinatra)
5 PEOPLE WILL SAY WE'RE IN LOVE   Bing Crosby *
6 IN MY ARMS   Dick Haymes
7 PAPER DOLL   Mills Brothers
8 PUT YOUR ARMS AROUND ME, HONEY   Dick Kuhn (VR: Trio)
9 I HEARD YOU CRIED LAST NIGHT   Harry James Orch. (VR: Helen Forrest)
   Note: * Another version by: Frank Sinatra.

September 18, 1943
1 SUNDAY, MONDAY, OR ALWAYS   Bing Crosby
2 PEOPLE WILL SAY WE'RE IN LOVE   Bing Crosby *
3 ALL OR NOTHING AT ALL   Harry James Orch. (VR: Frank Sinatra)
4 I HEARD YOU CRIED LAST NIGHT   Harry James Orch. (VR: Helen Forrest)
5 IN THE BLUE OF EVENING   Tommy Dorsey Orch. (VR: Frank Sinatra)
6 YOU'LL NEVER KNOW   Dick Haymes
7 PUT YOUR ARMS AROUND ME, HONEY   Dick Kuhn (VR: Trio)

8   IN MY ARMS   Dick Haymes
9   PAPER DOLL   Mills Brothers
  Note: * Another version by: Frank Sinatra.

September 25, 1943
1   ALL OR NOTHING AT ALL   Harry James Orch. (VR: Frank Sinatra)
2   PAPER DOLL   Mills Brothers
3   PEOPLE WILL SAY WE'RE IN LOVE   Bing Crosby *
4   YOU'LL NEVER KNOW   Dick Haymes
5   SUNDAY, MONDAY, OR ALWAYS   Bing Crosby
6   IN THE BLUE OF EVENING   Tommy Dorsey Orch. (VR: Frank Sinatra)
7   I HEARD YOU CRIED LAST NIGHT   Harry James Orch. (VR: Helen Forrest)
8   PUT YOUR ARMS AROUND ME, HONEY   Dick Kuhn (VR: Trio)
9   HOW SWEET YOU ARE   Kay Armen
  Note: * Another version by: Frank Sinatra.

October 2, 1943
1   SUNDAY, MONDAY, OR ALWAYS   Bing Crosby
2   PEOPLE WILL SAY WE'RE IN LOVE   Bing Crosby *
3   I HEARD YOU CRIED LAST NIGHT   Harry James Orch. (VR: Helen Forrest)
4   PUT YOUR ARMS AROUND ME, HONEY   Dick Kuhn (VR: Trio)
5   YOU'LL NEVER KNOW   Dick Haymes
6   ALL OR NOTHING AT ALL   Harry James Orch. (VR: Frank Sinatra)
7   PAPER DOLL   Mills Brothers
8   IN MY ARMS   Dick Haymes
9   PISTOL PACKIN' MAMA   Al Dexter **
  Note: * Another version by: Frank Sinatra.
    ** Another version by Bing Crosby and The Andrews Sisters.

October 9, 1943
1   SUNDAY, MONDAY, OR ALWAYS   Bing Crosby
2   PEOPLE WILL SAY WE'RE IN LOVE   Bing Crosby *
3   I HEARD YOU CRIED LAST NIGHT   Harry James Orch. (VR: Helen Forrest)
4   PAPER DOLL   Mills Brothers
5   PISTOL PACKIN' MAMA   Al Dexter **
6   PUT YOUR ARMS AROUND ME, HONEY   Dick Kuhn (VR: Trio)
8   IF YOU PLEASE   Bing Crosby
9   IN MY ARMS   Dick Haymes
  Note: * Another version by: Frank Sinatra.
    ** Another version by Bing Crosby and The Andrews Sisters.

October 16, 1943
1   SUNDAY, MONDAY, OR ALWAYS   Bing Crosby
2   PEOPLE WILL SAY WE'RE IN LOVE   Bing Crosby *
3   PAPER DOLL   Mills Brothers
4   I HEARD YOU CRIED LAST NIGHT   Harry James Orch. (VR: Helen Forrest)
5   PISTOL PACKIN' MAMA   Al Dexter **
6   PUT YOUR ARMS AROUND ME, HONEY   Dick Kuhn (VR: Trio)
7   ALL OR NOTHING AT ALL   Harry James Orch. (VR: Frank Sinatra)
8   YOU'LL NEVER KNOW   Dick Haymes
9   THEY'RE EITHER TOO YOUNG OR TOO OLD   Jimmy Dorsey Orch. (VR: Kitty Kallen)
  Note: * Another version by: Frank Sinatra.

** Another version by Bing Crosby and The Andrews Sisters.

October 23, 1943
1   SUNDAY, MONDAY, OR ALWAYS   Bing Crosby
2   PEOPLE WILL SAY WE'RE IN LOVE   Bing Crosby *
3   PAPER DOLL   Mills Brothers
4   PISTOL PACKIN' MAMA   Al Dexter **
5   I HEARD YOU CRIED LAST NIGHT   Harry James Orch. (VR: Helen Forrest)
6   IF YOU PLEASE   Bing Crosby
7   THEY'RE EITHER TOO YOUNG OR TOO OLD   Jimmy Dorsey Orch. (VR: Kitty Kallen)
8   ALL OR NOTHING AT ALL   Harry James Orch. (VR: Frank Sinatra)
9   PUT YOUR ARMS AROUND ME, HONEY   Dick Kuhn (VR: Trio)
  Note: * Another version by: Frank Sinatra.
    ** Another version by Bing Crosby and The Andrews Sisters.

October 30, 1943
1   PEOPLE WILL SAY WE'RE IN LOVE   Bing Crosby *
2   PISTOL PACKIN' MAMA   Al Dexter **
3   SUNDAY, MONDAY, OR ALWAYS   Bing Crosby
4   PAPER DOLL   Mills Brothers
5   IF YOU PLEASE   Bing Crosby
6   PUT YOUR ARMS AROUND ME, HONEY   Dick Kuhn (VR: Trio)
7   THEY'RE EITHER TOO YOUNG OR TOO OLD   Jimmy Dorsey Orch. (VR: Kitty Kallen)
8   I HEARD YOU CRIED LAST NIGHT   Harry James Orch. (VR: Helen Forrest)
9   FOR THE FIRST TIME   Dick Haymes
  Note: * Another version by: Frank Sinatra.
    ** Another version by Bing Crosby and The Andrews Sisters.

November 6, 1943
1   PAPER DOLL   Mills Brothers
2   PEOPLE WILL SAY WE'RE IN LOVE   Bing Crosby *
3   PISTOL PACKIN' MAMA   Al Dexter **
4   SUNDAY, MONDAY, OR ALWAYS   Bing Crosby
5   THEY'RE EITHER TOO YOUNG OR TOO OLD   Jimmy Dorsey Orch. (VR: Kitty Kallen)
6   PUT YOUR ARMS AROUND ME, HONEY   Dick Kuhn (VR: Trio)
7   I HEARD YOU CRIED LAST NIGHT   Harry James Orch. (VR: Helen Forrest)
8   FOR THE FIRST TIME   Dick Haymes
9   IF YOU PLEASE   Bing Crosby
  Note: * Another version by: Frank Sinatra.
    ** Another version by Bing Crosby and The Andrews Sisters.

November 13, 1943
1   PAPER DOLL   Mills Brothers
2   PEOPLE WILL SAY WE'RE IN LOVE   Bing Crosby *
3   PISTOL PACKIN' MAMA   Al Dexter **
4   SUNDAY, MONDAY, OR ALWAYS   Bing Crosby
5   IF YOU PLEASE   Bing Crosby
6   THEY'RE EITHER TOO YOUNG OR TOO OLD   Jimmy Dorsey Orch. (VR: Kitty Kallen)
7   MY HEART TELLS ME   Glen Gray Orch. (VR: Eugenie Baird)
8   PUT YOUR ARMS AROUND ME, HONEY   Dick Kuhn (VR: Trio)

The Mills Brothers
Three of the four brothers peak at #1 with ``Paper Doll'' (Nov. 6).

9   HOW SWEET YOU ARE   Kay Armen
Note: * Another version by: Frank Sinatra.
       ** Another version by Bing Crosby and The Andrews Sisters.

November 20, 1943
1   PEOPLE WILL SAY WE'RE IN LOVE   Bing Crosby *
2   PAPER DOLL   Mills Brothers
3   THEY'RE EITHER TOO YOUNG OR TOO OLD   Jimmy Dorsey Orch. (VR: Kitty Kallen)
4   SUNDAY, MONDAY, OR ALWAYS   Bing Crosby
5   PISTOL PACKIN' MAMA   Al Dexter **
6   IF YOU PLEASE   Bing Crosby
7   MY HEART TELLS ME   Glen Gray Orch. (VR: Eugenie Baird)
8   PUT YOUR ARMS AROUND ME, HONEY   Dick Kuhn (VR: Trio)
9   OH, WHAT A BEAUTIFUL MORNIN'   Bing Crosby
Note: * Another version by: Frank Sinatra.
       ** Another version by Bing Crosby and The Andrews Sisters.

November 27, 1943
1   PAPER DOLL   Mills Brothers
2   THEY'RE EITHER TOO YOUNG OR TOO OLD   Jimmy Dorsey Orch. (VR: Kitty Kallen)
3   PISTOL PACKIN' MAMA   Al Dexter *
4   MY HEART TELLS ME   Glen Gray Orch. (VR: Eugenie Baird)
5   PEOPLE WILL SAY WE'RE IN LOVE   Bing Crosby **
6   SUNDAY, MONDAY, OR ALWAYS   Bing Crosby
7   OH, WHAT A BEAUTIFUL MORNIN'   Bing Crosby
8   LITTLE DID I KNOW   Glen Gray Orch. (VR: Phil Brito)
9   PUT YOUR ARMS AROUND ME, HONEY   Dick Kuhn (VR: Trio)
Note: * Another version by Bing Crosby and The Andrews Sisters.
       ** Another version by: Frank Sinatra.

December 4, 1943
1   PEOPLE WILL SAY WE'RE IN LOVE   Bing Crosby *
2   PAPER DOLL   Mills Brothers
3   MY HEART TELLS ME   Glen Gray Orch. (VR: Eugenie Baird)
4   PISTOL PACKIN' MAMA   Al Dexter **
5   HOW SWEET YOU ARE   Kay Armen
6   OH, WHAT A BEAUTIFUL MORNIN'   Bing Crosby
7   SUNDAY, MONDAY, OR ALWAYS   Bing Crosby
8   SHOO, SHOO, BABY   Andrews Sisters
9   FOR THE FIRST TIME   Dick Haymes
Note: * Another version by: Frank Sinatra.
       ** Another version by Bing Crosby and The Andrews Sisters.

December 11, 1943
1   MY HEART TELLS ME   Glen Gray Orch. (VR: Eugenie Baird)
2   THEY'RE EITHER TOO YOUNG OR TOO OLD   Jimmy Dorsey Orch. (VR: Kitty Kallen)
3   PEOPLE WILL SAY WE'RE IN LOVE   Bing Crosby *
4   PAPER DOLL   Mills Brothers
5   PISTOL PACKIN' MAMA   Al Dexter **
6   OH, WHAT A BEAUTIFUL MORNIN'   Bing Crosby
7   SHOO, SHOO, BABY   Andrews Sisters
8   SUNDAY, MONDAY, OR ALWAYS   Bing Crosby
9   FOR THE FIRST TIME   Dick Haymes

Note: * Another version by: Frank Sinatra.
       ** Another version by Bing Crosby and The Andrews Sisters.

December 18, 1943
1   MY HEART TELLS ME   Glen Gray Orch. (VR: Eugenie Baird)
2   OH, WHAT A BEAUTIFUL MORNIN'   Bing Crosby
3   PAPER DOLL   Mills Brothers
4   PEOPLE WILL SAY WE'RE IN LOVE   Bing Crosby *
5   PISTOL PACKIN' MAMA   Al Dexter **
6   THEY'RE EITHER TOO YOUNG OR TOO OLD   Jimmy Dorsey Orch. (VR: Kitty Kallen)
7   FOR THE FIRST TIME   Dick Haymes
8   SPEAK LOW   Guy Lombardo Orch. (VR: Billy Leach)
9   MY IDEAL   Jimmy' Dorsey Orch. (VR: Bob Eberly)
Note: * Another version by: Frank Sinatra.
       ** Another version by Bing Crosby and The Andrews Sisters.

December 25, 1943
1   MY HEART TELLS ME   Glen Gray Orch. (VR: Eugenie Baird)
2   PAPER DOLL   Mills Brothers
3   WHITE CHRISTMAS   Bing Crosby
4   OH, WHAT A BEAUTIFUL MORNIN'   Bing Crosby
5   PEOPLE WILL SAY WE'RE IN LOVE   Bing Crosby *
6   FOR THE FIRST TIME   Dick Haymes
7   THEY'RE EITHER TOO YOUNG OR TOO OLD   Jimmy Dorsey Orch. (VR: Kitty Kallen)
8   PISTOL PACKIN' MAMA   Al Dexter **
9   SHOO, SHOO, BABY   Andrews Sisters
Note: * Another version by: Frank Sinatra.
       ** Another version by Bing Crosby and The Andrews Sisters.

January 1, 1944
1   MY HEART TELLS ME   Glen Gray Orch. (VR: Eugenie Baird)
2   WHITE CHRISTMAS   Bing Crosby
3   I'LL BE HOME FOR CHRISTMAS   Bing Crosby
4   PAPER DOLL   Mills Brothers
5   SHOO, SHOO, BABY   Andrews Sisters
6   OH, WHAT A BEAUTIFUL MORNIN'   Bing Crosby
7   PEOPLE WILL SAY WE'RE IN LOVE   Bing Crosby *
8   FOR THE FIRST TIME   Dick Haymes
9   PISTOL PACKIN' MAMA   Al Dexter **
Note: * Another version by: Frank Sinatra.
       ** Another version by Bing Crosby and The Andrews Sisters.

January 8, 1944
1   MY HEART TELLS ME   Glen Gray Orch. (VR: Eugenie Baird)
2   PAPER DOLL   Mills Brothers
3   PEOPLE WILL SAY WE'RE IN LOVE   Bing Crosby *
4   SHOO, SHOO, BABY   Andrews Sisters
5   OH, WHAT A BEAUTIFUL MORNIN'   Bing Crosby
6   WHITE CHRISTMAS   Bing Crosby
7   I'LL BE HOME FOR CHRISTMAS   Bing Crosby
8   THEY'RE EITHER TOO YOUNG OR TOO OLD   Jimmy Dorsey Orch. (VR: Kitty Kallen)
9   NO LOVE, NO NOTHIN'   Ella Mae Morse
Note: * Another version by: Frank Sinatra.

January 15, 1944
1. MY HEART TELLS ME   Glen Gray Orch. (VR: Eugenie Baird)
2. SHOO, SHOO, BABY   Andrews Sisters
3. PAPER DOLL   Mills Brothers
4. PEOPLE WILL SAY WE'RE IN LOVE   Bing Crosby *
5. OH, WHAT A BEAUTIFUL MORNIN'   Bing Crosby
6. FOR THE FIRST TIME   Dick Haymes
7. SPEAK LOW   Guy Lombardo Orch. (VR: Billy Leach)
8. THEY'RE EITHER TOO YOUNG OR TOO OLD   Jimmy Dorsey Orch. (VR: Kitty Kallen)
9. STAR EYES   Jimmy Dorsey Orch. (VR: Bob Eberly & Kitty Kallen)
   Note: * Another version by: Frank Sinatra.

January 22, 1944
1. MY HEART TELLS ME   Glen Gray Orch. (VR: Eugenie Baird)
2. SHOO, SHOO, BABY   Andrews Sisters
3. MY IDEAL   Jimmy' Dorsey Orch. (VR: Bob Eberly)
4. PAPER DOLL   Mills Brothers
5. OH, WHAT A BEAUTIFUL MORNIN'   Bing Crosby
6. NO LOVE, NO NOTHIN'   Ella Mae Morse
7. FOR THE FIRST TIME   Dick Haymes
8. MY SHINING HOUR   Glen Gray Orch. (VR: Eugenie Baird)
9. PEOPLE WILL SAY WE'RE IN LOVE   Bing Crosby *
   Note: * Another version by: Frank Sinatra.

January 29, 1944
1. MY HEART TELLS ME   Glen Gray Orch. (VR: Eugenie Baird)
2. SHOO, SHOO, BABY   Andrews Sisters
3. PEOPLE WILL SAY WE'RE IN LOVE   Bing Crosby *
4. NO LOVE, NO NOTHIN'   Ella Mae Morse
5. OH, WHAT A BEAUTIFUL MORNIN'   Bing Crosby
6. PAPER DOLL   Mills Brothers
7. I COULDN'T SLEEP A WINK LAST NIGHT   Frank Sinatra
8. MY IDEAL   Jimmy' Dorsey Orch. (VR: Bob Eberly)
9. FOR THE FIRST TIME   Dick Haymes
   Note: * Another version by: Frank Sinatra.

February 5, 1944
1. MY HEART TELLS ME   Glen Gray Orch. (VR: Eugenie Baird)
2. SHOO, SHOO, BABY   Andrews Sisters
3. NO LOVE, NO NOTHIN'   Ella Mae Morse
4. BESAME MUCHO   Jimmy Dorsey Orch. (VR: Bob Eberly & Kitty Kallen)
5. MY IDEAL   Jimmy' Dorsey Orch. (VR: Bob Eberly)
6. PAPER DOLL   Mills Brothers
7. MAIRZY DOATS   Merry Macs
8. OH, WHAT A BEAUTIFUL MORNIN'   Bing Crosby
9. WHEN THEY ASK ABOUT YOU   Jimmy Dorsey Orch. (VR: Kitty Kallen)

February 12, 1944
1. SHOO, SHOO, BABY   Andrews Sisters
2. MY HEART TELLS ME   Glen Gray Orch. (VR: Eugenie Baird)
3. MAIRZY DOATS   Merry Macs
4. BESAME MUCHO   Jimmy Dorsey Orch. (VR: Bob Eberly & Kitty Kallen)
5. NO LOVE, NO NOTHIN'   Ella Mae Morse
6. MY IDEAL   Jimmy' Dorsey Orch. (VR: Bob Eberly)
7. STAR EYES   Jimmy Dorsey Orch. (VR: Bob Eberly & Kitty Kallen)
8. SPEAK LOW   Guy Lombardo Orch. (VR: Billy Leach)
9. PAPER DOLL   Mills Brothers

February 19, 1944
1. SHOO, SHOO, BABY   Andrews Sisters
2. MY HEART TELLS ME   Glen Gray Orch. (VR: Eugenie Baird)
3. BESAME MUCHO   Jimmy Dorsey Orch. (VR: Bob Eberly & Kitty Kallen)
4. MAIRZY DOATS   Merry Macs
5. NO LOVE, NO NOTHIN'   Ella Mae Morse
6. FOR THE FIRST TIME   Dick Haymes
7. I COULDN'T SLEEP A WINK LAST NIGHT   Frank Sinatra
8. A LOVELY WAY TO SPEND AN EVENING   Frank Sinatra
9. OH, WHAT A BEAUTIFUL MORNIN'   Bing Crosby

February 26, 1944
1. BESAME MUCHO   Jimmy Dorsey Orch. (VR: Bob Eberly & Kitty Kallen)
2. MY HEART TELLS ME   Glen Gray Orch. (VR: Eugenie Baird)
3. SHOO, SHOO, BABY   Andrews Sisters
4. MAIRZY DOATS   Merry Macs
5. NO LOVE, NO NOTHIN'   Ella Mae Morse
6. A LOVELY WAY TO SPEND AN EVENING   Frank Sinatra
7. I COULDN'T SLEEP A WINK LAST NIGHT   Frank Sinatra
8. MY IDEAL   Jimmy' Dorsey Orch. (VR: Bob Eberly)
9. MY SHINING HOUR   Glen Gray Orch. (VR: Eugenie Baird)

March 4, 1944
1. BESAME MUCHO   Jimmy Dorsey Orch. (VR: Bob Eberly & Kitty Kallen)
2. MAIRZY DOATS   Merry Macs
3. I COULDN'T SLEEP A WINK LAST NIGHT   Frank Sinatra
4. SHOO, SHOO, BABY   Andrews Sisters
5. MY HEART TELLS ME   Glen Gray Orch. (VR: Eugenie Baird)
6. NO LOVE, NO NOTHIN'   Ella Mae Morse
7. WHEN THEY ASK ABOUT YOU   Jimmy Dorsey Orch. (VR: Kitty Kallen)
8. POINCIANA   Bing Crosby
9. I LOVE YOU   Bing Crosby

March 11, 1944
1. MAIRZY DOATS   Merry Macs
2. BESAME MUCHO   Jimmy Dorsey Orch. (VR: Bob Eberly & Kitty Kallen)
3. NO LOVE, NO NOTHIN'   Ella Mae Morse
4. MY HEART TELLS ME   Glen Gray Orch. (VR: Eugenie Baird)
5. I COULDN'T SLEEP A WINK LAST NIGHT   Frank Sinatra
6. SHOO, SHOO, BABY   Andrews Sisters
7. I LOVE YOU   Bing Crosby
8. WHEN THEY ASK ABOUT YOU   Jimmy Dorsey Orch. (VR: Kitty Kallen)
9. IT'S LOVE, LOVE, LOVE   Guy Lombardo Orch. (VR: Skip Nelson)

March 18, 1944
1. I COULDN'T SLEEP A WINK LAST NIGHT   Frank Sinatra
2. MAIRZY DOATS   Merry Macs
3. BESAME MUCHO   Jimmy Dorsey Orch. (VR: Bob Eberly & Kitty Kallen)
4. WHEN THEY ASK ABOUT YOU   Jimmy Dorsey Orch. (VR: Kitty Kallen)

The Andrews Sisters
They're #1 again with ``Shoo, Shoo, Baby'' from the movie ``Three Cheers For The Boys'' (Feb. 12).

5 I LOVE YOU   Bing Crosby
6 A LOVELY WAY TO SPEND AN EVENING   Frank Sinatra
7 SHOO, SHOO, BABY   Andrews Sisters
8 NO LOVE, NO NOTHIN'   Ella Mae Morse
9 MY HEART TELLS ME   Glen Gray Orch. (VR: Eugenie Baird)

March 25, 1944
1 BESAME MUCHO   Jimmy Dorsey Orch. (VR: Bob Eberly & Kitty Kallen)
2 POINCIANA   Bing Crosby
3 MAIRZY DOATS   Merry Macs
4 WHEN THEY ASK ABOUT YOU   Jimmy Dorsey Orch. (VR: Kitty Kallen)
5 I COULDN'T SLEEP A WINK LAST NIGHT   Frank Sinatra
6 I LOVE YOU   Bing Crosby
7 A LOVELY WAY TO SPEND AN EVENING   Frank Sinatra
8 DON'T SWEETHEART ME   Lawrence Welk Orch. (VR: Wayne Marsh)
9 SHOO, SHOO, BABY   Andrews Sisters

April 1, 1944
1 IT'S LOVE, LOVE, LOVE   Guy Lombardo Orch. (VR: Skip Nelson)
2 I COULDN'T SLEEP A WINK LAST NIGHT   Frank Sinatra
3 BESAME MUCHO   Jimmy Dorsey Orch. (VR: Bob Eberly & Kitty Kallen)
4 POINCIANA   Bing Crosby
5 I LOVE YOU   Bing Crosby
6 MAIRZY DOATS   Merry Macs
7 A LOVELY WAY TO SPEND AN EVENING   Frank Sinatra
8 WHEN THEY ASK ABOUT YOU   Jimmy Dorsey Orch. (VR: Kitty Kallen)
9 SHOO, SHOO, BABY   Andrews Sisters

April 8, 1944
1 IT'S LOVE, LOVE, LOVE   Guy Lombardo Orch. (VR: Skip Nelson)
2 I LOVE YOU   Bing Crosby
3 BESAME MUCHO   Jimmy Dorsey Orch. (VR: Bob Eberly & Kitty Kallen)
4 POINCIANA   Bing Crosby
5 WHEN THEY ASK ABOUT YOU   Jimmy Dorsey Orch. (VR: Kitty Kallen)
6 MAIRZY DOATS   Merry Macs
7 I'LL GET BY   Harry James Orch. (VR: Dick Haymes)
8 I COULDN'T SLEEP A WINK LAST NIGHT   Frank Sinatra
9 LONG AGO AND FAR AWAY   Helen Forrest & Dick Haymes

April 15, 1944
1 I LOVE YOU   Bing Crosby
2 IT'S LOVE, LOVE, LOVE   Guy Lombardo Orch. (VR: Skip Nelson)
3 BESAME MUCHO   Jimmy Dorsey Orch. (VR: Bob Eberly & Kitty Kallen)
4 MAIRZY DOATS   Merry Macs
5 POINCIANA   Bing Crosby
6 DO NOTHIN' TIL YOU HEAR FROM ME   Woody Herman Orch. (VR: Woody Herman)
7 LONG AGO AND FAR AWAY   Helen Forrest & Dick Haymes
8 I COULDN'T SLEEP A WINK LAST NIGHT   Frank Sinatra
9 SAN FERNANDO VALLEY   Bing Crosby

April 22, 1944
1 IT'S LOVE, LOVE, LOVE   Guy Lombardo Orch. (VR: Skip Nelson)

2 I LOVE YOU   Bing Crosby
3 POINCIANA   Bing Crosby
4 WHEN THEY ASK ABOUT YOU   Jimmy Dorsey Orch. (VR: Kitty Kallen)
5 BESAME MUCHO   Jimmy Dorsey Orch. (VR: Bob Eberly & Kitty Kallen)
6 EASTER PARADE   Guy Lombardo
7 I'LL GET BY   Harry James Orch. (VR: Dick Haymes)
8 LONG AGO AND FAR AWAY   Helen Forrest & Dick Haymes
9 SAN FERNANDO VALLEY   Bing Crosby

April 29, 1944
1 I LOVE YOU   Bing Crosby
2 IT'S LOVE, LOVE, LOVE   Guy Lombardo Orch. (VR: Skip Nelson)
3 SAN FERNANDO VALLEY   Bing Crosby
4 LONG AGO AND FAR AWAY   Helen Forrest & Dick Haymes
5 I'LL GET BY   Harry James Orch. (VR: Dick Haymes)
6 WHEN THEY ASK ABOUT YOU   Jimmy Dorsey Orch. (VR: Kitty Kallen)
7 POINCIANA   Bing Crosby
8 GOODNIGHT, WHEREVER YOU ARE   Russ Morgan Orch. (VR: Russ Morgan)
9 BESAME MUCHO   Jimmy Dorsey Orch. (VR: Bob Eberly & Kitty Kallen)

May 6, 1944
1 I LOVE YOU   Bing Crosby
2 I'LL GET BY   Harry James Orch. (VR: Dick Haymes)
3 LONG AGO AND FAR AWAY   Helen Forrest & Dick Haymes
4 IT'S LOVE, LOVE, LOVE   Guy Lombardo Orch. (VR: Skip Nelson)
5 I'LL BE SEEING YOU   Bing Crosby *
6 WHEN THEY ASK ABOUT YOU   Jimmy Dorsey Orch. (VR: Kitty Kallen)
7 DON'T SWEETHEART ME   Lawrence Welk Orch. (VR: Wayne Marsh)
8 SAN FERNANDO VALLEY   Bing Crosby
9 POINCIANA   Bing Crosby
   Note: * Another version by: Tommy Dorsey Orch. (VR: Frank Sinatra)

May 13, 1944
1 LONG AGO AND FAR AWAY   Helen Forrest & Dick Haymes
2 I LOVE YOU   Bing Crosby
3 IT'S LOVE, LOVE, LOVE   Guy Lombardo Orch. (VR: Skip Nelson)
4 SAN FERNANDO VALLEY   Bing Crosby
5 I'LL GET BY   Harry James Orch. (VR: Dick Haymes)
6 POINCIANA   Bing Crosby
7 I'LL BE SEEING YOU   Bing Crosby *
8 BESAME MUCHO   Jimmy Dorsey Orch. (VR: Bob Eberly & Kitty Kallen)
9 GOODNIGHT, WHEREVER YOU ARE   Russ Morgan Orch. (VR: Russ Morgan)
   Note: * Another version by: Tommy Dorsey Orch. (VR: Frank Sinatra)

May 20, 1944
1 LONG AGO AND FAR AWAY   Helen Forrest & Dick Haymes
2 SAN FERNANDO VALLEY   Bing Crosby
3 I'LL GET BY   Harry James Orch. (VR: Dick Haymes)
4 IT'S LOVE, LOVE, LOVE   Guy Lombardo Orch. (VR: Skip Nelson)
5 I LOVE YOU   Bing Crosby
6 POINCIANA   Bing Crosby

7 I'LL BE SEEING YOU   Bing Crosby *
8 GOODNIGHT, WHEREVER YOU ARE   Russ Morgan Orch.
   (VR: Russ Morgan)
9 AMOR   Bing Crosby
   Note: * Another version by: Tommy Dorsey Orch. (VR: Frank
   Sinatra)

May 27, 1944
1 LONG AGO AND FAR AWAY   Helen Forrest & Dick Haymes
2 I'LL GET BY   Harry James Orch. (VR: Dick Haymes)
3 IT'S LOVE, LOVE, LOVE   Guy Lombardo Orch. (VR: Skip
   Nelson)
4 SAN FERNANDO VALLEY   Bing Crosby
5 I'LL BE SEEING YOU   Bing Crosby *
6 AMOR   Bing Crosby
7 I LOVE YOU   Bing Crosby
8 GOODNIGHT, WHEREVER YOU ARE   Russ Morgan Orch.
   (VR: Russ Morgan)
9 POINCIANA   Bing Crosby
   Note: * Another version by: Tommy Dorsey Orch. (VR: Frank
   Sinatra)

June 3, 1944
1 LONG AGO AND FAR AWAY   Helen Forrest & Dick Haymes
2 I'LL GET BY   Harry James Orch. (VR: Dick Haymes)
3 I'LL BE SEEING YOU   Bing Crosby *
4 SAN FERNANDO VALLEY   Bing Crosby
5 IT'S LOVE, LOVE, LOVE   Guy Lombardo Orch. (VR: Skip
   Nelson)
6 I LOVE YOU   Bing Crosby
7 AMOR   Bing Crosby
8 GOODNIGHT, WHEREVER YOU ARE   Russ Morgan Orch.
   (VR: Russ Morgan)
9 HOW BLUE THE NIGHT   Dick Haymes
   Note: * Another version by: Tommy Dorsey Orch. (VR: Frank
   Sinatra)

June 10, 1944
1 LONG AGO AND FAR AWAY   Helen Forrest & Dick Haymes
2 I'LL BE SEEING YOU   Bing Crosby *
3 I'LL GET BY   Harry James Orch. (VR: Dick Haymes)
4 SAN FERNANDO VALLEY   Bing Crosby
5 GOODNIGHT, WHEREVER YOU ARE   Russ Morgan Orch.
   (VR: Russ Morgan)
6 I LOVE YOU   Bing Crosby
7 AMOR   Bing Crosby
8 IT'S LOVE, LOVE, LOVE   Guy Lombardo Orch. (VR: Skip
   Nelson)
9 SWINGING ON A STAR   Bing Crosby **
   Note: * Another version by: Tommy Dorsey Orch. (VR: Frank
   Sinatra)
        ** The b-side song, "Going My Way," featured The
   Williams Brothers Quartet, including brother Andy, age 7.

June 17, 1944
1 LONG AGO AND FAR AWAY   Helen Forrest & Dick Haymes
2 I'LL BE SEEING YOU   Bing Crosby *
3 I'LL GET BY   Harry James Orch. (VR: Dick Haymes)
4 SAN FERNANDO VALLEY   Bing Crosby
5 AMOR   Bing Crosby
6 I LOVE YOU   Bing Crosby
7 IT'S LOVE, LOVE, LOVE   Guy Lombardo Orch. (VR: Skip
   Nelson)
8 GOODNIGHT, WHEREVER YOU ARE   Russ Morgan Orch.
   (VR: Russ Morgan)
9 SOMEDAY I'LL MEET YOU AGAIN   Ink Spots
   Note: * Another version by: Tommy Dorsey Orch. (VR: Frank
   Sinatra)

June 24, 1944
1 I'LL BE SEEING YOU   Bing Crosby *
2 I'LL GET BY   Harry James Orch. (VR: Dick Haymes)
3 LONG AGO AND FAR AWAY   Helen Forrest & Dick Haymes
4 GOODNIGHT, WHEREVER YOU ARE   Russ Morgan Orch.
   (VR: Russ Morgan)
5 SAN FERNANDO VALLEY   Bing Crosby
6 AMOR   Bing Crosby
7 SWINGING ON A STAR   Bing Crosby **
8 TIME WAITS FOR NO ONE   Helen Forrest
9 I LOVE YOU   Bing Crosby
   Note: * Another version by: Tommy Dorsey Orch. (VR: Frank
   Sinatra)
        ** The b-side song, "Going My Way," featured The
   Williams Brothers Quartet, including brother Andy, age 7.

July 1, 1944
1 I'LL BE SEEING YOU   Bing Crosby *
2 LONG AGO AND FAR AWAY   Helen Forrest & Dick Haymes
3 AMOR   Bing Crosby
4 SAN FERNANDO VALLEY   Bing Crosby
5 GOODNIGHT, WHEREVER YOU ARE   Russ Morgan Orch.
   (VR: Russ Morgan)
6 SWINGING ON A STAR   Bing Crosby **
7 I'LL GET BY   Harry James Orch. (VR: Dick Haymes)
8 TIME WAITS FOR NO ONE   Helen Forrest
9 I LOVE YOU   Bing Crosby
   Note: * Another version by: Tommy Dorsey Orch. (VR: Frank
   Sinatra)
        ** The b-side song, "Going My Way," featured The
   Williams Brothers Quartet, including brother Andy, age 7.

July 8, 1944
1 I'LL BE SEEING YOU   Bing Crosby *
2 AMOR   Bing Crosby
3 LONG AGO AND FAR AWAY   Helen Forrest & Dick Haymes
4 I'LL GET BY   Harry James Orch. (VR: Dick Haymes)
5 MILKMAN, KEEP THOSE BOTTLES QUIET   Ella Mae
   Morse
6 SAN FERNANDO VALLEY   Bing Crosby
7 GOODNIGHT, WHEREVER YOU ARE   Russ Morgan Orch.
   (VR: Russ Morgan)
8 TIME WAITS FOR NO ONE   Helen Forrest
9 SWINGING ON A STAR   Bing Crosby **
   Note: * Another version by: Tommy Dorsey Orch. (VR: Frank
   Sinatra)
        ** The b-side song, "Going My Way," featured The
   Williams Brothers Quartet, including brother Andy, age 7.

July 15, 1944
1 I'LL BE SEEING YOU   Bing Crosby *
2 LONG AGO AND FAR AWAY   Helen Forrest & Dick Haymes
3 AMOR   Bing Crosby
4 I'LL GET BY   Harry James Orch. (VR: Dick Haymes)
5 SWINGING ON A STAR   Bing Crosby **
6 MILKMAN, KEEP THOSE BOTTLES QUIET   Ella Mae
   Morse
7 TIME WAITS FOR NO ONE   Helen Forrest
8 SAN FERNANDO VALLEY   Bing Crosby
9 GOODNIGHT, WHEREVER YOU ARE   Russ Morgan Orch.
   (VR: Russ Morgan)
   Note: * Another version by: Tommy Dorsey Orch. (VR: Frank
   Sinatra)
        ** The b-side song, "Going My Way," featured The
   Williams Brothers Quartet, including brother Andy, age 7.

101

July 22, 1944

1 I'LL BE SEEING YOU   Bing Crosby *
2 SWINGING ON A STAR   Bing Crosby **
3 LONG AGO AND FAR AWAY   Helen Forrest & Dick Haymes
4 AMOR   Bing Crosby
5 I'LL GET BY   Harry James Orch. (VR: Dick Haymes)
6 GOODNIGHT, WHEREVER YOU ARE   Russ Morgan Orch.
   (VR: Russ Morgan)
7 SWEET LORRAINE   Bing Crosby
8 AND THEN YOU KISSED ME   Frank Sinatra
9 MILKMAN, KEEP THOSE BOTTLES QUIET   Ella Mae
   Morse
   Note: * Another version by: Tommy Dorsey Orch. (VR: Frank
   Sinatra)
      ** The b-side song, "Going My Way," featured The
   Williams Brothers Quartet, including brother Andy, age 7.

July 29, 1944

1 AMOR   Bing Crosby
2 I'LL BE SEEING YOU   Bing Crosby *
3 LONG AGO AND FAR AWAY   Helen Forrest & Dick Haymes
4 SWINGING ON A STAR   Bing Crosby **
5 I'LL GET BY   Harry James Orch. (VR: Dick Haymes)
6 TIME WAITS FOR NO ONE   Helen Forrest
7 GOODNIGHT, WHEREVER YOU ARE   Russ Morgan Orch.
   (VR: Russ Morgan)
8 MILKMAN, KEEP THOSE BOTTLES QUIET   Ella Mae
   Morse
9 IT COULD HAPPEN TO YOU   Jo Stafford
   Note: * Another version by: Tommy Dorsey Orch. (VR: Frank
   Sinatra)
      ** The b-side song, "Going My Way," featured The
   Williams Brothers Quartet, including brother Andy, age 7.

August 5, 1944

1 I'LL BE SEEING YOU   Bing Crosby *
2 AMOR   Bing Crosby
3 SWINGING ON A STAR   Bing Crosby **
4 TIME WAITS FOR NO ONE   Helen Forrest
5 LONG AGO AND FAR AWAY   Helen Forrest & Dick Haymes
6 I'LL GET BY   Harry James Orch. (VR: Dick Haymes)
7 MILKMAN, KEEP THOSE BOTTLES QUIET   Ella Mae
   Morse
8 IT COULD HAPPEN TO YOU   Jo Stafford
9 GOODNIGHT, WHEREVER YOU ARE   Russ Morgan Orch.
   (VR: Russ Morgan)
   Note: * Another version by: Tommy Dorsey Orch. (VR: Frank
   Sinatra)
      ** The b-side song, "Going My Way," featured The
   Williams Brothers Quartet, including brother Andy, age 7.

August 12, 1944

1 I'LL BE SEEING YOU   Bing Crosby *
2 AMOR   Bing Crosby
3 SWINGING ON A STAR   Bing Crosby **
4 I'LL GET BY   Harry James Orch. (VR: Dick Haymes)
5 LONG AGO AND FAR AWAY   Helen Forrest & Dick Haymes
6 I'LL WALK ALONE   Dinah Shore
7 MILKMAN, KEEP THOSE BOTTLES QUIET   Ella Mae
   Morse
8 TIME WAITS FOR NO ONE   Helen Forrest
9 IS YOU IS OR IS YOU AIN'T   Bing Crosby & Andrews
   Sisters
   Note: * Another version by: Tommy Dorsey Orch. (VR: Frank
   Sinatra)
      ** The b-side song, "Going My Way," featured The
   Williams Brothers Quartet, including brother Andy, age 7.

August 19, 1944

1 AMOR   Bing Crosby
2 SWINGING ON A STAR   Bing Crosby *
3 I'LL BE SEEING YOU   Bing Crosby **
4 TIME WAITS FOR NO ONE   Helen Forrest
5 I'LL GET BY   Harry James Orch. (VR: Dick Haymes)
6 LONG AGO AND FAR AWAY   Helen Forrest & Dick Haymes
7 I'LL WALK ALONE   Dinah Shore
8 IT COULD HAPPEN TO YOU   Jo Stafford
9 IS YOU IS OR IS YOU AIN'T   Bing Crosby & Andrews
   Sisters
   Note: * The b-side song, "Going My Way," featured The
   Williams Brothers Quartet, including brother Andy, age 7.
      ** Another version by: Tommy Dorsey Orch. (VR: Frank
   Sinatra)

August 26, 1944

1 I'LL BE SEEING YOU   Bing Crosby *
2 TIME WAITS FOR NO ONE   Helen Forrest
3 SWINGING ON A STAR   Bing Crosby **
4 AMOR   Bing Crosby
5 IT COULD HAPPEN TO YOU   Jo Stafford
6 IT HAD TO BE YOU   Helen Forrest & Dick Haymes
7 I'LL WALK ALONE   Dinah Shore
8 I'LL GET BY   Harry James Orch. (VR: Dick Haymes)
9 PRETTY KITTY BLUE EYES   Merry Macs
   Note: * Another version by: Tommy Dorsey Orch. (VR: Frank
   Sinatra)
      ** The b-side song, "Going My Way," featured The
   Williams Brothers Quartet, including brother Andy, age 7.

September 2, 1944

1 I'LL BE SEEING YOU   Bing Crosby *
2 SWINGING ON A STAR   Bing Crosby **
3 AMOR   Bing Crosby
4 TIME WAITS FOR NO ONE   Helen Forrest
5 IS YOU IS OR IS YOU AIN'T   Bing Crosby & Andrews
   Sisters
6 I'LL WALK ALONE   Dinah Shore
7 I'LL GET BY   Harry James Orch. (VR: Dick Haymes)
8 IT COULD HAPPEN TO YOU   Jo Stafford
9 IT HAD TO BE YOU   Helen Forrest & Dick Haymes
   Note: * Another version by: Tommy Dorsey Orch. (VR: Frank
   Sinatra)
      ** The b-side song, "Going My Way," featured The
   Williams Brothers Quartet, including brother Andy, age 7.

September 9, 1944

1 I'LL BE SEEING YOU   Bing Crosby *
2 SWINGING ON A STAR   Bing Crosby **
3 TIME WAITS FOR NO ONE   Helen Forrest
4 IS YOU IS OR IS YOU AIN'T   Bing Crosby & Andrews
   Sisters
5 AMOR   Bing Crosby
6 I'LL WALK ALONE   Dinah Shore
7 IT COULD HAPPEN TO YOU   Jo Stafford
8 FELLOW ON A FURLOUGH   Phil Hanna
9 IT HAD TO BE YOU   Helen Forrest & Dick Haymes
   Note: * Another version by: Tommy Dorsey Orch. (VR: Frank
   Sinatra)
      ** The b-side song, "Going My Way," featured The
   Williams Brothers Quartet, including brother Andy, age 7.

September 16, 1944

1 I'LL WALK ALONE   Dinah Shore
2 SWINGING ON A STAR   Bing Crosby *
3 TIME WAITS FOR NO ONE   Helen Forrest

4   IS YOU IS OR IS YOU AIN'T   Bing Crosby & Andrews Sisters
5   AMOR   Bing Crosby
6   I'LL BE SEEING YOU   Bing Crosby **
7   IT COULD HAPPEN TO YOU   Jo Stafford
8   I'LL GET BY   Harry James Orch. (VR: Dick Haymes)
9   IT HAD TO BE YOU   Helen Forrest & Dick Haymes
    Note: * The b-side song, "Going My Way," featured The Williams Brothers Quartet, including brother Andy, age 7.
    ** Another version by: Tommy Dorsey Orch. (VR: Frank Sinatra).

September 23, 1944
1   I'LL WALK ALONE   Dinah Shore
2   IS YOU IS OR IS YOU AIN'T   Bing Crosby & Andrews Sisters
3   I'LL BE SEEING YOU   Bing Crosby *
4   TIME WAITS FOR NO ONE   Helen Forrest
5   IT COULD HAPPEN TO YOU   Jo Stafford
6   SWINGING ON A STAR   Bing Crosby **
7   HOW MANY HEARTS HAVE YOU BROKEN   Three Suns
8   IT HAD TO BE YOU   Helen Forrest & Dick Haymes
9   AMOR   Bing Crosby
    Note: * Another version by: Tommy Dorsey Orch. (VR: Frank Sinatra)
    ** The b-side song, "Going My Way," featured The Williams Brothers Quartet, including brother Andy, age 7.

September 30, 1944
1   I'LL WALK ALONE   Dinah Shore
2   IS YOU IS OR IS YOU AIN'T   Bing Crosby & Andrews Sisters
3   IT HAD TO BE YOU   Helen Forrest & Dick Haymes
4   TIME WAITS FOR NO ONE   Helen Forrest
5   SWINGING ON A STAR   Bing Crosby *
6   IT COULD HAPPEN TO YOU   Jo Stafford
7   HOW MANY HEARTS HAVE YOU BROKEN   Three Suns
8   I'LL BE SEEING YOU   Bing Crosby **
9   TOGETHER   Helen Forrest & Dick Haymes
    Note: * The b-side song, "Going My Way," featured The Williams Brothers Quartet, including brother Andy, age 7.
    ** Another version by: Tommy Dorsey Orch. (VR: Frank Sinatra).

October 7, 1944
1   I'LL WALK ALONE   Dinah Shore
2   IS YOU IS OR IS YOU AIN'T   Bing Crosby & Andrews Sisters
3   TOGETHER   Helen Forrest & Dick Haymes
4   IT HAD TO BE YOU   Helen Forrest & Dick Haymes
5   SWINGING ON A STAR   Bing Crosby *
6   TIME WAITS FOR NO ONE   Helen Forrest
7   HOW MANY HEARTS HAVE YOU BROKEN   Three Suns
8   I'LL BE SEEING YOU   Bing Crosby **
9   LET ME LOVE YOU TONIGHT   Woody Herman Orch. (VR: Billie Rogers)
    Note: * The b-side song, "Going My Way," featured The Williams Brothers Quartet, including brother Andy, age 7.
    ** Another version by: Tommy Dorsey Orch. (VR: Frank Sinatra).

October 14, 1944
1   I'LL WALK ALONE   Dinah Shore
2   IS YOU IS OR IS YOU AIN'T   Bing Crosby & Andrews Sisters
3   IT HAD TO BE YOU   Helen Forrest & Dick Haymes
4   DANCE WITH THE DOLLY   Russ Morgan Orch. (VR: Al Jennings)

5   TIME WAITS FOR NO ONE   Helen Forrest
6   IT COULD HAPPEN TO YOU   Jo Stafford
7   HOW MANY HEARTS HAVE YOU BROKEN   Three Suns
8   SWINGING ON A STAR   Bing Crosby *
9   I'LL BE SEEING YOU   Bing Crosby **
    Note: * The b-side song, "Going My Way," featured The Williams Brothers Quartet, including brother Andy, age 7.
    ** Another version by: Tommy Dorsey Orch. (VR: Frank Sinatra).

October 21, 1944
1   I'LL WALK ALONE   Dinah Shore
2   DANCE WITH THE DOLLY   Russ Morgan Orch. (VR: Al Jennings)
3   HOW MANY HEARTS HAVE YOU BROKEN   Three Suns
4   IS YOU IS OR IS YOU AIN'T   Bing Crosby & Andrews Sisters
5   IT HAD TO BE YOU   Helen Forrest & Dick Haymes
6   IT COULD HAPPEN TO YOU   Jo Stafford
7   SWINGING ON A STAR   Bing Crosby *
8   ALWAYS   Gordon Jenkins Orch.
9   I'M MAKING BELIEVE   Ella Fitzgerald & the Ink Spots
    Note: * The b-side song, "Going My Way," featured The Williams Brothers Quartet, including brother Andy, age 7.

October 28, 1944
1   I'LL WALK ALONE   Dinah Shore
2   DANCE WITH THE DOLLY   Russ Morgan Orch. (VR: Al Jennings)
3   THE TROLLEY SONG   Pied Pipers *
4   IS YOU IS OR IS YOU AIN'T   Bing Crosby & Andrews Sisters
5   TOGETHER   Helen Forrest & Dick Haymes
6   HOW MANY HEARTS HAVE YOU BROKEN   Three Suns
7   IT HAD TO BE YOU   Helen Forrest & Dick Haymes
8   ALWAYS   Gordon Jenkins Orch.
9   LET ME LOVE YOU TONIGHT   Woody Herman Orch. (VR: Billie Rogers)
    Note: * Another version by: Judy Garland.

November 4, 1944
1   I'LL WALK ALONE   Dinah Shore
2   DANCE WITH THE DOLLY   Russ Morgan Orch. (VR: Al Jennings)
3   IS YOU IS OR IS YOU AIN'T   Bing Crosby & Andrews Sisters
4   TOGETHER   Helen Forrest & Dick Haymes
5   HOW MANY HEARTS HAVE YOU BROKEN   Three Suns
6   THE TROLLEY SONG   Pied Pipers *
7   IT HAD TO BE YOU   Helen Forrest & Dick Haymes
8   SWEET AND LOVELY   Bing Crosby
9   WHISPERING   Frank Froba Orch.
    Note: * Another version by: Judy Garland.

November 11, 1944
1   DANCE WITH THE DOLLY   Russ Morgan Orch. (VR: Al Jennings)
2   I'LL WALK ALONE   Dinah Shore
3   THE TROLLEY SONG   Pied Pipers *
4   ALWAYS   Gordon Jenkins Orch.
5   TOGETHER   Helen Forrest & Dick Haymes
6   HOW MANY HEARTS HAVE YOU BROKEN   Three Suns
7   IT HAD TO BE YOU   Helen Forrest & Dick Haymes
8   STRANGE MUSIC   James Melton
9   I'M MAKING BELIEVE   Ella Fitzgerald & the Ink Spots
    Note: * Another version by: Judy Garland.

November 18, 1944
1. THE TROLLEY SONG Pied Pipers *
2. I'LL WALK ALONE Dinah Shore
3. TOGETHER Helen Forrest & Dick Haymes
4. DANCE WITH THE DOLLY Russ Morgan Orch. (VR: Al Jennings)
5. ALWAYS Gordon Jenkins Orch.
6. I'M MAKING BELIEVE Ella Fitzgerald & the Ink Spots
7. HOW MANY HEARTS HAVE YOU BROKEN Three Suns
8. WHAT A DIFF'RENCE A DAY MADE Andy Russell
   Note: * Another version by: Judy Garland.

November 25, 1944
1. THE TROLLEY SONG Pied Pipers *
2. DANCE WITH THE DOLLY Russ Morgan Orch. (VR: Al Jennings)
3. I'LL WALK ALONE Dinah Shore
4. TOGETHER Helen Forrest & Dick Haymes
5. ALWAYS Gordon Jenkins Orch.
6. THE VERY THOUGHT OF YOU Vaughn Monroe Orch. (VR: Vaughn Monroe)
7. HOW MANY HEARTS HAVE YOU BROKEN Three Suns
8. I DON'T WANT TO LOVE YOU Phil Brito
   Note: * Another version by: Judy Garland.

December 2, 1944
1. THE TROLLEY SONG Pied Pipers *
2. DANCE WITH THE DOLLY Russ Morgan Orch. (VR: Al Jennings)
3. I'M MAKING BELIEVE Ella Fitzgerald & the Ink Spots
4. TOGETHER Helen Forrest & Dick Haymes
5. DON'T FENCE ME IN Bing Crosby & Andrews Sisters
6. I'LL WALK ALONE Dinah Shore
7. ALWAYS Gordon Jenkins Orch.
8. I'M CONFESSIN' Perry Como
9. THERE GOES THAT SONG AGAIN Russ Morgan Orch. (VR: Russ Morgan)
   Note: * Another version by: Judy Garland.

December 9, 1944
1. THE TROLLEY SONG Pied Pipers *
2. I'M MAKING BELIEVE Ella Fitzgerald & the Ink Spots
3. DON'T FENCE ME IN Bing Crosby & Andrews Sisters
4. I'LL WALK ALONE Dinah Shore
5. DANCE WITH THE DOLLY Russ Morgan Orch. (VR: Al Jennings)
6. ALWAYS Gordon Jenkins Orch.
7. TOGETHER Helen Forrest & Dick Haymes
8. I DREAM OF YOU Tommy Dorsey Orch. (VR: Freddy Stewart)
9. LET ME LOVE YOU TONIGHT Woody Herman Orch. (VR: Billie Rogers)
   Note: * Another version by: Judy Garland.

December 16, 1944
1. THE TROLLEY SONG Pied Pipers *
2. DON'T FENCE ME IN Bing Crosby & Andrews Sisters
3. WHITE CHRISTMAS Bing Crosby
4. I'M MAKING BELIEVE Ella Fitzgerald & the Ink Spots
5. TOGETHER Helen Forrest & Dick Haymes
6. I DREAM OF YOU Tommy Dorsey Orch. (VR: Freddy Stewart)
7. THERE GOES THAT SONG AGAIN Russ Morgan Orch. (VR: Russ Morgan)
8. DANCE WITH THE DOLLY Russ Morgan Orch. (VR: Al Jennings)
9. I'LL WALK ALONE Dinah Shore
   Note: * Another version by: Judy Garland.

December 23, 1944
1. DON'T FENCE ME IN Bing Crosby & Andrews Sisters
2. THE TROLLEY SONG Pied Pipers *
3. I'M MAKING BELIEVE Ella Fitzgerald & the Ink Spots
4. THERE GOES THAT SONG AGAIN Russ Morgan Orch. (VR: Russ Morgan)
5. DANCE WITH THE DOLLY Russ Morgan Orch. (VR: Al Jennings)
6. WHITE CHRISTMAS Bing Crosby
7. I DREAM OF YOU Tommy Dorsey Orch. (VR: Freddy Stewart)
8. TOGETHER Helen Forrest & Dick Haymes
9. I'LL WALK ALONE Dinah Shore
   Note: * Another version by: Judy Garland.

December 30, 1944
1. DON'T FENCE ME IN Bing Crosby & Andrews Sisters
2. THE TROLLEY SONG Pied Pipers *
3. THERE GOES THAT SONG AGAIN Russ Morgan Orch. (VR: Russ Morgan)
4. WHITE CHRISTMAS Bing Crosby
5. I'M MAKING BELIEVE Ella Fitzgerald & the Ink Spots
6. I DREAM OF YOU Tommy Dorsey Orch. (VR: Freddy Stewart)
7. DANCE WITH THE DOLLY Russ Morgan Orch. (VR: Al Jennings)
8. ALWAYS Gordon Jenkins Orch.
9. SANTA CLAUS IS COMING TO TOWN Bing Crosby & Andrews Sisters
   Note: * Another version by: Judy Garland.

January 6, 1945
1. DON'T FENCE ME IN Bing Crosby & Andrews Sisters
2. THERE GOES THAT SONG AGAIN Russ Morgan Orch. (VR: Russ Morgan)
3. I'M MAKING BELIEVE Ella Fitzgerald & the Ink Spots
4. I DREAM OF YOU Tommy Dorsey Orch. (VR: Freddy Stewart)
5. THE TROLLEY SONG Pied Pipers *
6. DANCE WITH THE DOLLY Russ Morgan Orch. (VR: Al Jennings)
7. TOGETHER Helen Forrest & Dick Haymes
8. I DON'T WANT TO LOVE YOU Phil Brito
9. SWEET DREAMS, SWEETHEART Ray Noble Orch. (VR: Larry Stewart)
   Note: * Another version by: Judy Garland.

January 13, 1945
1. DON'T FENCE ME IN Bing Crosby & Andrews Sisters
2. THERE GOES THAT SONG AGAIN Russ Morgan Orch. (VR: Russ Morgan)
3. THE TROLLEY SONG Pied Pipers *
4. I DREAM OF YOU Tommy Dorsey Orch. (VR: Freddy Stewart)
5. I'M MAKING BELIEVE Ella Fitzgerald & the Ink Spots
6. MORE AND MORE Tommy Dorsey Orch. (VR: Bonnie Lou Williams)
7. DANCE WITH THE DOLLY Russ Morgan Orch. (VR: Al Jennings)
8. I'M CONFESSIN' Perry Como
9. TOGETHER Helen Forrest & Dick Haymes
   Note: * Another version by: Judy Garland.

Judy Garland
Judy also scored with a Top 10 version of ``The Trolley Song'' (Dec. 2).

January 20, 1945
1 DON'T FENCE ME IN   Bing Crosby & Andrews Sisters
2 THERE GOES THAT SONG AGAIN   Russ Morgan Orch. (VR: Russ Morgan)
3 I'M MAKING BELIEVE   Ella Fitzgerald & the Ink Spots
4 I DREAM OF YOU   Tommy Dorsey Orch. (VR: Freddy Stewart)
5 THE TROLLEY SONG   Pied Pipers *
6 ACCENTUATE THE POSITIVE   Johnny Mercer **
7 I DIDN'T KNOW ABOUT YOU   Count Basie (VR: Thelma Carpenter)
8 DANCE WITH THE DOLLY   Russ Morgan Orch. (VR: Al Jennings)
9 ALWAYS   Gordon Jenkins Orch.
   Note: * Another version by: Judy Garland.
   ** Another version by: Bing Crosby & Andrews Sisters.

January 27, 1945
1 DON'T FENCE ME IN   Bing Crosby & Andrews Sisters
2 THERE GOES THAT SONG AGAIN   Russ Morgan Orch. (VR: Russ Morgan)
3 I DREAM OF YOU   Tommy Dorsey Orch. (VR: Freddy Stewart)
4 ACCENTUATE THE POSITIVE   Johnny Mercer *
5 I'M MAKING BELIEVE   Ella Fitzgerald & the Ink Spots
6 SWEET DREAMS, SWEETHEART   Ray Noble Orch. (VR: Larry Stewart)
7 THE TROLLEY SONG   Pied Pipers **
8 DON'T YOU KNOW I CARE   Duke Ellington Orch. (VR: Al Hibbler)
9 DON'T EVER CHANGE   Tommy Tucker Orch. (VR: Don Brown)
   Note: * Another version by: Bing Crosby & Andrews Sisters.
   ** Another version by: Judy Garland.

February 3, 1945
1 DON'T FENCE ME IN   Bing Crosby & Andrews Sisters
2 THERE GOES THAT SONG AGAIN   Russ Morgan Orch. (VR: Russ Morgan)
3 ACCENTUATE THE POSITIVE   Johnny Mercer *
4 I DREAM OF YOU   Tommy Dorsey Orch. (VR: Freddy Stewart)
5 I'M MAKING BELIEVE   Ella Fitzgerald & the Ink Spots
6 EVALINA   Bing Crosby
7 SWEET DREAMS, SWEETHEART   Ray Noble Orch. (VR: Larry Stewart)
8 SLEIGHRIDE IN JULY   Dinah Shore
9 MORE AND MORE   Tommy Dorsey Orch. (VR: Bonnie Lou Williams)
   Note: * Another version by: Bing Crosby & Andrews Sisters.

February 10, 1945
1 ACCENTUATE THE POSITIVE   Johnny Mercer *
2 DON'T FENCE ME IN   Bing Crosby & Andrews Sisters
3 THERE GOES THAT SONG AGAIN   Russ Morgan Orch. (VR: Russ Morgan)
4 I DREAM OF YOU   Tommy Dorsey Orch. (VR: Freddy Stewart)
5 MY DREAMS ARE GETTING BETTER ALL THE TIME   Les Brown Orch. (VR: Doris Day)
6 A LITTLE ON THE LONELY SIDE   Frankie Carle Orch. (VR: Paul Allen) **
7 I'M MAKING BELIEVE   Ella Fitzgerald & the Ink Spots
8 I'M CONFESSIN'   Perry Como
9 EV'RYTIME WE SAY GOODBYE   Benny Goodman Orch. (VR: Peggy Mann)
   Note: * Another version by: Bing Crosby & Andrews Sisters.

** Another version by: Guy Lombardo Orch. (VR: Jimmy Brown).

February 17, 1945
1 DON'T FENCE ME IN   Bing Crosby & Andrews Sisters
2 ACCENTUATE THE POSITIVE   Johnny Mercer *
3 I'M CONFESSIN'   Perry Como
4 THERE GOES THAT SONG AGAIN   Russ Morgan Orch. (VR: Russ Morgan)
5 SATURDAY NIGHT   Frank Sinatra
6 I DREAM OF YOU   Tommy Dorsey Orch. (VR: Freddy Stewart)
7 RUM AND COCA COLA   Andrews Sisters
8 A LITTLE ON THE LONELY SIDE   Frankie Carle Orch. (VR: Paul Allen) **
9 SWEET DREAMS, SWEETHEART   Ray Noble Orch. (VR: Larry Stewart)
   Note: * Another version by: Bing Crosby & Andrews Sisters.
   ** Another version by: Guy Lombardo Orch. (VR: Jimmy Brown).

February 24, 1945
1 ACCENTUATE THE POSITIVE   Johnny Mercer *
2 I DREAM OF YOU   Tommy Dorsey Orch. (VR: Freddy Stewart)
3 DON'T FENCE ME IN   Bing Crosby & Andrews Sisters
4 SATURDAY NIGHT   Frank Sinatra
5 A LITTLE ON THE LONELY SIDE   Frankie Carle Orch. (VR: Paul Allen) **
6 SWEET DREAMS, SWEETHEART   Ray Noble Orch. (VR: Larry Stewart)
7 RUM AND COCA COLA   Andrews Sisters
8 THERE GOES THAT SONG AGAIN   Russ Morgan Orch. (VR: Russ Morgan)
9 SLEIGHRIDE IN JULY   Dinah Shore
   Note: * Another version by: Bing Crosby & Andrews Sisters.
   ** Another version by: Guy Lombardo Orch. (VR: Jimmy Brown).

March 3, 1945
1 ACCENTUATE THE POSITIVE   Johnny Mercer *
2 I DREAM OF YOU   Tommy Dorsey Orch. (VR: Freddy Stewart)
3 A LITTLE ON THE LONELY SIDE   Frankie Carle Orch. (VR: Paul Allen) **
4 SATURDAY NIGHT   Frank Sinatra
5 MY DREAMS ARE GETTING BETTER ALL THE TIME   Les Brown Orch. (VR: Doris Day)
6 DON'T FENCE ME IN   Bing Crosby & Andrews Sisters
7 MORE AND MORE   Tommy Dorsey Orch. (VR: Bonnie Lou Williams)
8 SWEET DREAMS, SWEETHEART   Ray Noble Orch. (VR: Larry Stewart)
9 RUM AND COCA COLA   Andrews Sisters
   Note: * Another version by: Bing Crosby & Andrews Sisters.
   ** Another version by: Guy Lombardo Orch. (VR: Jimmy Brown).

March 10, 1945
1 ACCENTUATE THE POSITIVE   Johnny Mercer *
2 SATURDAY NIGHT   Frank Sinatra
3 MY DREAMS ARE GETTING BETTER ALL THE TIME   Les Brown Orch. (VR: Doris Day)
4 RUM AND COCA COLA   Andrews Sisters
5 DON'T FENCE ME IN   Bing Crosby & Andrews Sisters
6 SLEIGHRIDE IN JULY   Dinah Shore
7 SWEET DREAMS, SWEETHEART   Ray Noble Orch. (VR: Larry Stewart)

8   A LITTLE ON THE LONELY SIDE   Frankie Carle Orch. (VR: Paul Allen) **
9   I DREAM OF YOU   Pied Pipers
   Note: * Another version by: Bing Crosby & Andrews Sisters.
      ** Another version by: Guy Lombardo Orch. (VR: Jimmy Brown).

March 17, 1945
1   A LITTLE ON THE LONELY SIDE   Frankie Carle Orch. (VR: Paul Allen) *
2   SATURDAY NIGHT   Frank Sinatra
3   ACCENTUATE THE POSITIVE   Johnny Mercer **
4   MY DREAMS ARE GETTING BETTER ALL THE TIME   Pied Pipers
5   MORE AND MORE   Tommy Dorsey Orch. (VR: Bonnie Lou Williams)
6   RUM AND COCA COLA   Andrews Sisters
7   I'M BEGINNING TO SEE THE LIGHT   Harry James Orch. (VR: Kitty Kallen)
8   SWEET DREAMS, SWEETHEART   Pied Pipers
9   DON'T FENCE ME IN   Bing Crosby & Andrews Sisters
   Note: * Another version by: Bing Crosby & Andrews Sisters.
      ** Another version by: Guy Lombardo Orch. (VR: Jimmy Brown).

March 24, 1945
1   MY DREAMS ARE GETTING BETTER ALL THE TIME   Pied Pipers
2   A LITTLE ON THE LONELY SIDE   Frankie Carle Orch. (VR: Paul Allen) *
3   ACCENTUATE THE POSITIVE   Johnny Mercer **
4   SATURDAY NIGHT   Frank Sinatra
5   RUM AND COCA COLA   Andrews Sisters
6   SWEET DREAMS, SWEETHEART   Pied Pipers
7   I'M BEGINNING TO SEE THE LIGHT   Harry James Orch. (VR: Kitty Kallen)
8   TOO-RA LOO-RA LOO-RAL   Bing Crosby
9   AFTER AWHILE   Benny Goodman Orch.
   Note: * Another version by: Guy Lombardo Orch. (VR: Jimmy Brown).
      ** Another version by: Bing Crosby & Andrews Sisters.

March 31, 1945
1   I'M BEGINNING TO SEE THE LIGHT   Harry James Orch. (VR: Kitty Kallen)
2   A LITTLE ON THE LONELY SIDE   Frankie Carle Orch. (VR: Paul Allen) *
3   MY DREAMS ARE GETTING BETTER ALL THE TIME   Pied Pipers
4   SATURDAY NIGHT   Frank Sinatra
5   SWEET DREAMS, SWEETHEART   Pied Pipers
6   ACCENTUATE THE POSITIVE   Johnny Mercer **
7   CANDY   Johnny Mercer & Jo Stafford
8   RUM AND COCA COLA   Andrews Sisters
9   MORE AND MORE   Tommy Dorsey Orch. (VR: Bonnie Lou Williams)
   Note: * Another version by: Guy Lombardo Orch. (VR: Jimmy Brown).
      ** Another version by: Bing Crosby & Andrews Sisters.

April 7, 1945
1   MY DREAMS ARE GETTING BETTER ALL THE TIME   Pied Pipers
2   I'M BEGINNING TO SEE THE LIGHT   Harry James Orch. (VR: Kitty Kallen)
3   A LITTLE ON THE LONELY SIDE   Frankie Carle Orch. (VR: Paul Allen) *

4   CANDY   Johnny Mercer & Jo Stafford
5   SATURDAY NIGHT   Frank Sinatra
6   RUM AND COCA COLA   Andrews Sisters
7   SWEET DREAMS, SWEETHEART   Pied Pipers
8   LET'S TAKE THE LONG WAY HOME   Jo Stafford
9   ACCENTUATE THE POSITIVE   Johnny Mercer **
   Note: * Another version by: Guy Lombardo Orch. (VR: Jimmy Brown).
      ** Another version by: Bing Crosby & Andrews Sisters.

April 14, 1945
1   MY DREAMS ARE GETTING BETTER ALL THE TIME   Pied Pipers
2   I'M BEGINNING TO SEE THE LIGHT   Harry James Orch. (VR: Kitty Kallen)
3   CANDY   Johnny Mercer & Jo Stafford
4   A LITTLE ON THE LONELY SIDE   Frankie Carle Orch. (VR: Paul Allen) *
5   SATURDAY NIGHT   Frank Sinatra
6   MORE AND MORE   Tommy Dorsey Orch. (VR: Bonnie Lou Williams)
7   ALL OF MY LIFE   Sammy Kaye Orch. (VR: Billy Williams)**
8   RUM AND COCA COLA   Andrews Sisters
9   ACCENTUATE THE POSITIVE   Johnny Mercer @
   Note: * Another version by: Guy Lombardo Orch. (VR: Jimmy Brown).
      ** Three Suns.
      @ Another version by: Bing Crosby & Andrews Sisters.

April 21, 1945
1   CANDY   Johnny Mercer & Jo Stafford
2   I'M BEGINNING TO SEE THE LIGHT   Harry James Orch. (VR: Kitty Kallen)
3   MY DREAMS ARE GETTING BETTER ALL THE TIME   Pied Pipers
4   SATURDAY NIGHT   Frank Sinatra
5   JUST A PRAYER AWAY   Bing Crosby
6   LAURA   Woody Herman Orch.
7   A LITTLE ON THE LONELY SIDE   Frankie Carle Orch. (VR: Paul Allen) *
8   MORE AND MORE   Tommy Dorsey Orch. (VR: Bonnie Lou Williams)
9   I DIDN'T KNOW ABOUT YOU   Count Basie (VR: Thelma Carpenter)
   Note: * Another version by: Guy Lombardo Orch. (VR: Jimmy Brown).

April 28, 1945
1   CANDY   Johnny Mercer & Jo Stafford
2   I'M BEGINNING TO SEE THE LIGHT   Harry James Orch. (VR: Kitty Kallen)
3   MY DREAMS ARE GETTING BETTER ALL THE TIME   Pied Pipers
4   ALL OF MY LIFE   Sammy Kaye Orch. (VR: Billy Williams) *
5   JUST A PRAYER AWAY   Bing Crosby
6   A LITTLE ON THE LONELY SIDE   Frankie Carle Orch. (VR: Paul Allen) **
7   THE MORE I SEE YOU   Dick Haymes
8   LAURA   Woody Herman Orch.
9   THERE MUST BE A WAY   Charlie Spivak Orch. (VR: Jimmie Saunders)
   Note: * Another version by: Three Suns.
      ** Another version by: Guy Lombardo Orch. (VR: Jimmy Brown).

May 5, 1945
1   CANDY   Johnny Mercer & Jo Stafford

Jo Stafford
Her first big hit is ``Candy'' (Apr. 21).

2   I'M BEGINNING TO SEE THE LIGHT   Harry James Orch.
     (VR: Kitty Kallen)
3   MY DREAMS ARE GETTING BETTER ALL THE TIME   Pied
     Pipers
4   LAURA   Woody Herman Orch.
5   ALL OF MY LIFE   Sammy Kaye Orch. (VR: Billy Williams) *
6   JUST A PRAYER AWAY   Bing Crosby
7   DREAM   Pied Pipers
8   HE'S HOME FOR A LITTLE WHILE   Dinah Shore
9   A LITTLE ON THE LONELY SIDE   Frankie Carle Orch. (VR:
     Paul Allen) **
     Note: * Another version by: Three Suns.
          ** Another version by: Guy Lombardo Orch. (VR:
          Jimmy Brown).

May 12, 1945
1   CANDY   Johnny Mercer & Jo Stafford
2   LAURA   Woody Herman Orch.
3   DREAM   Pied Pipers
4   MY DREAMS ARE GETTING BETTER ALL THE TIME   Pied
     Pipers
5   ALL OF MY LIFE   Sammy Kaye Orch. (VR: Billy Williams) *
6   I'M BEGINNING TO SEE THE LIGHT   Harry James Orch.
     (VR: Kitty Kallen)
7   I SHOULD CARE   Frank Sinatra
8   JUST A PRAYER AWAY   Bing Crosby
9   SENTIMENTAL JOURNEY   Les Brown Orch. (VR: Doris
     Day)
     Note: * Another version by: Three Suns.

May 19, 1945
1   I'M BEGINNING TO SEE THE LIGHT   Harry James Orch.
     (VR: Kitty Kallen)
2   CANDY   Johnny Mercer & Jo Stafford
3   SENTIMENTAL JOURNEY   Les Brown Orch. (VR: Doris
     Day)
4   ALL OF MY LIFE   Sammy Kaye Orch. (VR: Billy Williams) *
5   JUST A PRAYER AWAY   Bing Crosby
6   MY DREAMS ARE GETTING BETTER ALL THE TIME   Pied
     Pipers
7   LAURA   Woody Herman Orch.
8   DREAM   Pied Pipers
9   I SHOULD CARE   Frank Sinatra
     Note: * Another version by: Three Suns.

May 26, 1945
1   DREAM   Pied Pipers
2   CANDY   Johnny Mercer & Jo Stafford
3   I'M BEGINNING TO SEE THE LIGHT   Harry James Orch.
     (VR: Kitty Kallen)
4   SENTIMENTAL JOURNEY   Les Brown Orch. (VR: Doris
     Day)
5   LAURA   Woody Herman Orch.
6   ALL OF MY LIFE   Sammy Kaye Orch. (VR: Billy Williams) *
7   JUST A PRAYER AWAY   Bing Crosby
8   I SHOULD CARE   Frank Sinatra
9   MY DREAMS ARE GETTING BETTER ALL THE TIME   Pied
     Pipers
     Note: * Another version by: Three Suns.

June 2, 1945
1   LAURA   Woody Herman Orch.
2   DREAM   Pied Pipers
3   SENTIMENTAL JOURNEY   Les Brown Orch. (VR: Doris
     Day)
4   ALL OF MY LIFE   Sammy Kaye Orch. (VR: Billy Williams) *
5   JUST A PRAYER AWAY   Bing Crosby
6   CANDY   Johnny Mercer & Jo Stafford
7   I SHOULD CARE   Frank Sinatra
8   MY DREAMS ARE GETTING BETTER ALL THE TIME
     Pied Pipers
9   A FRIEND OF YOURS   Tommy Dorsey (VR: Stuart Foster)
     Note: * Another version by: Three Suns.

June 9, 1945
1   SENTIMENTAL JOURNEY   Les Brown Orch. (VR: Doris
     Day)
2   LAURA   Woody Herman Orch.
3   DREAM   Pied Pipers
4   I SHOULD CARE   Frank Sinatra
5   CANDY   Johnny Mercer & Jo Stafford
6   ALL OF MY LIFE   Sammy Kaye Orch. (VR: Billy Williams) *
7   THERE, I'VE SAID IT AGAIN   Vaughn Monroe Orch. (VR:
     Vaughn Monroe)
8   THERE MUST BE A WAY   Charlie Spivak Orch. (VR:
     Jimmie Saunders)
9   THE MORE I SEE YOU   Dick Haymes
     Note: * Another version by: Three Suns.

Woody Herman
``Laura'' (from the film ``Laura'') is #1 (June 2).

June 16, 1945
1   SENTIMENTAL JOURNEY   Les Brown Orch. (VR: Doris Day)
2   DREAM   Pied Pipers
3   LAURA   Woody Herman Orch.
4   I SHOULD CARE   Frank Sinatra
5   CANDY   Johnny Mercer & Jo Stafford
6   YOU BELONG TO MY HEART   Bing Crosby
7   THERE, I'VE SAID IT AGAIN   Vaughn Monroe Orch. (VR: Vaughn Monroe)
8   BELL BOTTOM TROUSERS   Tony Pastor Orch. (VR: Tony Pastor)
9   THE MORE I SEE YOU   Dick Haymes

June 23, 1945
1   SENTIMENTAL JOURNEY   Les Brown Orch. (VR: Doris Day)
2   DREAM   Pied Pipers
3   LAURA   Woody Herman Orch.
4   THERE, I'VE SAID IT AGAIN   Vaughn Monroe Orch. (VR: Vaughn Monroe)
5   BELL BOTTOM TROUSERS   Tony Pastor Orch. (VR: Tony Pastor)
6   I WISH I KNEW   Dick Haymes
7   ALL OF MY LIFE   Sammy Kaye Orch. (VR: Billy Williams) *
8   THE MORE I SEE YOU   Dick Haymes
9   I SHOULD CARE   Frank Sinatra
    Note: * Another version by: Three Suns.

June 30, 1945
1   SENTIMENTAL JOURNEY   Les Brown Orch. (VR: Doris Day)
2   LAURA   Woody Herman Orch.
3   DREAM   Pied Pipers
4   ALL OF MY LIFE   Sammy Kaye Orch. (VR: Billy Williams) *
5   THERE, I'VE SAID IT AGAIN   Vaughn Monroe Orch. (VR: Vaughn Monroe)
6   BELL BOTTOM TROUSERS   Tony Pastor Orch. (VR: Tony Pastor)
7   THE MORE I SEE YOU   Dick Haymes
8   YOU BELONG TO MY HEART   Bing Crosby
9   EV'RY TIME   Freddy Martin Orch. (VR: Glenn Hughes)
    Note: * Another version by: Three Suns.

July 7, 1945
1   SENTIMENTAL JOURNEY   Les Brown Orch. (VR: Doris Day)
2   LAURA   Woody Herman Orch.
3   DREAM   Pied Pipers
4   YOU BELONG TO MY HEART   Bing Crosby
5   THE MORE I SEE YOU   Dick Haymes
6   BELL BOTTOM TROUSERS   Tony Pastor Orch. (VR: Tony Pastor)
7   THERE, I'VE SAID IT AGAIN   Vaughn Monroe Orch. (VR: Vaughn Monroe)
8   WHILE YOU'RE AWAY   Glen Gray Orch. (VR: Skip Nelson)
9   BAIA   Bing Crosby

July 14, 1945
1   DREAM   Pied Pipers
2   SENTIMENTAL JOURNEY   Les Brown Orch. (VR: Doris Day)
3   BELL BOTTOM TROUSERS   Tony Pastor Orch. (VR: Tony Pastor)
4   THERE, I'VE SAID IT AGAIN   Vaughn Monroe Orch. (VR: Vaughn Monroe)

5   THE MORE I SEE YOU   Dick Haymes
6   LAURA   Woody Herman Orch.
7   YOU CAME ALONG   Tommy Dorsey Orch. (VR: Stuart Foster)
8   OUT OF THIS WORLD   Jo Stafford
9   IF I LOVED YOU   Perry Como

July 21, 1945
1   DREAM   Pied Pipers
2   SENTIMENTAL JOURNEY   Les Brown Orch. (VR: Doris Day)
3   THE MORE I SEE YOU   Dick Haymes
4   BELL BOTTOM TROUSERS   Tony Pastor Orch. (VR: Tony Pastor)
5   GOTTA BE THIS OR THAT   Benny Goodman Orch. (VR: Benny Goodman)
6   YOU BELONG TO MY HEART   Bing Crosby
7   LAURA   Woody Herman Orch.
8   A FRIEND OF YOURS   Tommy Dorsey (VR: Stuart Foster)
9   CAN'T YOU READ BETWEEN THE LINES   Jimmy Dorsey Orch. (VR: Jean Cromwell)

July 28, 1945
1   THE MORE I SEE YOU   Dick Haymes
2   DREAM   Pied Pipers
3   SENTIMENTAL JOURNEY   Les Brown Orch. (VR: Doris Day)
4   I WISH I KNEW   Dick Haymes
5   THERE, I'VE SAID IT AGAIN   Vaughn Monroe Orch. (VR: Vaughn Monroe)
6   BELL BOTTOM TROUSERS   Tony Pastor Orch. (VR: Tony Pastor)
7   IF I LOVED YOU   Perry Como
8   THE WISH THAT I WISH TONIGHT   Russ Morgan Orch.
9   YOU BELONG TO MY HEART   Bing Crosby

August 4, 1945
1   DREAM   Pied Pipers
2   I WISH I KNEW   Dick Haymes
3   IF I LOVED YOU   Perry Como
4   THERE, I'VE SAID IT AGAIN   Vaughn Monroe Orch. (VR: Vaughn Monroe)
5   SENTIMENTAL JOURNEY   Les Brown Orch. (VR: Doris Day)
6   I DON'T CARE WHO KNOWS IT   Harry James Orch. (VR: Kitty Kallen)
7   THE MORE I SEE YOU   Dick Haymes
8   BELL BOTTOM TROUSERS   Tony Pastor Orch. (VR: Tony Pastor)
9   REMEMBER WHEN   Russ Morgan Orch. (VR: Marjorie Lee)

August 11, 1945
1   DREAM   Pied Pipers
2   THERE, I'VE SAID IT AGAIN   Vaughn Monroe Orch. (VR: Vaughn Monroe)
3   IF I LOVED YOU   Perry Como
4   THE MORE I SEE YOU   Dick Haymes
5   SENTIMENTAL JOURNEY   Les Brown Orch. (VR: Doris Day)
6   I DON'T CARE WHO KNOWS IT   Harry James Orch. (VR: Kitty Kallen)
7   YOU BELONG TO MY HEART   Bing Crosby
8   BELL BOTTOM TROUSERS   Tony Pastor Orch. (VR: Tony Pastor)
9   GOTTA BE THIS OR THAT   Benny Goodman Orch. (VR: Benny Goodman)

August 18, 1945
1 IF I LOVED YOU   Perry Como
2 I WISH I KNEW   Dick Haymes
3 TILL THE END OF TIME   Perry Como
4 GOTTA BE THIS OR THAT   Benny Goodman Orch. (VR: Benny Goodman)
5 ON THE ATCHISON, TOPEKA AND SANTA FE   Johnny Mercer
6 DREAM   Pied Pipers
7 CAN'T YOU READ BETWEEN THE LINES   Jimmy Dorsey Orch. (VR: Jean Cromwell)
8 THE MORE I SEE YOU   Dick Haymes
9 SENTIMENTAL JOURNEY   Les Brown Orch. (VR: Doris Day)

August 25, 1945
1 IF I LOVED YOU   Perry Como
2 TILL THE END OF TIME   Perry Como
3 ON THE ATCHISON, TOPEKA AND SANTA FE   Johnny Mercer
4 GOTTA BE THIS OR THAT   Benny Goodman Orch. (VR: Benny Goodman)
5 I WISH I KNEW   Dick Haymes
6 SENTIMENTAL JOURNEY   Les Brown Orch. (VR: Doris Day)
7 THE MORE I SEE YOU   Dick Haymes
8 DREAM   Pied Pipers
9 BELL BOTTOM TROUSERS   Tony Pastor Orch. (VR: Tony Pastor)

September 1, 1945
1 TILL THE END OF TIME   Perry Como
2 ON THE ATCHISON, TOPEKA AND SANTA FE   Johnny Mercer
3 GOTTA BE THIS OR THAT   Benny Goodman Orch. (VR: Benny Goodman)
4 THE MORE I SEE YOU   Dick Haymes
5 IF I LOVED YOU   Perry Como
6 I WISH I KNEW   Dick Haymes
7 DREAM   Pied Pipers
8 ALONG THE NAVAJO TRAIL   Bing Crosby & Andrews Sisters
9 THERE MUST BE A WAY   Charlie Spivak Orch. (VR: Jimmie Saunders)

September 8, 1945
1 TILL THE END OF TIME   Perry Como
2 IF I LOVED YOU   Perry Como
3 GOTTA BE THIS OR THAT   Benny Goodman Orch. (VR: Benny Goodman)
4 ON THE ATCHISON, TOPEKA AND SANTA FE   Johnny Mercer
5 I WISH I KNEW   Dick Haymes
6 DREAM   Pied Pipers
7 I'M GONNA LOVE THAT GUY   Benny Goodman Orch. (VR: Dottie Reid)
8 THERE'S NO YOU   Jo Stafford
9 THE MORE I SEE YOU   Dick Haymes

September 15, 1945
1 TILL THE END OF TIME   Perry Como
2 IF I LOVED YOU   Perry Como
3 ON THE ATCHISON, TOPEKA AND SANTA FE   Johnny Mercer
4 GOTTA BE THIS OR THAT   Benny Goodman Orch. (VR: Benny Goodman)
5 I WISH I KNEW   Dick Haymes
6 THE MORE I SEE YOU   Dick Haymes
7 I'M GONNA LOVE THAT GUY   Benny Goodman Orch. (VR: Dottie Reid)
8 BELL BOTTOM TROUSERS   Tony Pastor Orch. (VR: Tony Pastor)
9 I'D DO IT ALL OVER AGAIN   Hal McIntyre Orch. (VR: Frank Lester & Quartet)

September 22, 1945
1 IF I LOVED YOU   Perry Como
2 ON THE ATCHISON, TOPEKA AND SANTA FE   Johnny Mercer
3 TILL THE END OF TIME   Perry Como
4 GOTTA BE THIS OR THAT   Benny Goodman Orch. (VR: Benny Goodman)
5 I'M GONNA LOVE THAT GUY   Benny Goodman Orch. (VR: Dottie Reid)
6 I WISH I KNEW   Dick Haymes
7 I'LL BUY THAT DREAM   Pied Pipers
8 HOW DEEP IS THE OCEAN   Benny Goodman Orch. (VR: Peggy Lee)
9 BELL BOTTOM TROUSERS   Tony Pastor Orch. (VR: Tony Pastor)

September 29, 1945
1 TILL THE END OF TIME   Perry Como
2 ON THE ATCHISON, TOPEKA AND SANTA FE   Johnny Mercer
3 IF I LOVED YOU   Perry Como
4 I'M GONNA LOVE THAT GUY   Benny Goodman Orch. (VR: Dottie Reid)
5 I'LL BUY THAT DREAM   Pied Pipers
6 ALONG THE NAVAJO TRAIL   Bing Crosby & Andrews Sisters
7 I WISH I KNEW   Dick Haymes
8 GOTTA BE THIS OR THAT   Benny Goodman Orch. (VR: Benny Goodman)
9 THAT'S FOR ME   Dick Haymes

October 6, 1945
1 TILL THE END OF TIME   Perry Como
2 IF I LOVED YOU   Perry Como
3 I'M GONNA LOVE THAT GUY   Benny Goodman Orch. (VR: Dottie Reid)
4 GOTTA BE THIS OR THAT   Benny Goodman Orch. (VR: Benny Goodman)
5 I'LL BUY THAT DREAM   Pied Pipers
6 ON THE ATCHISON, TOPEKA AND SANTA FE   Johnny Mercer
7 AND THERE YOU ARE   Kate Smith
8 WAITIN' FOR THE TRAIN TO COME IN   Peggy Lee
9 I WISH I KNEW   Dick Haymes

October 13, 1945
1 TILL THE END OF TIME   Perry Como
2 IF I LOVED YOU   Perry Como
3 ALONG THE NAVAJO TRAIL   Bing Crosby & Andrews Sisters
4 ON THE ATCHISON, TOPEKA AND SANTA FE   Johnny Mercer
5 GOTTA BE THIS OR THAT   Benny Goodman Orch. (VR: Benny Goodman)
6 I'M GONNA LOVE THAT GUY   Benny Goodman Orch. (VR: Dottie Reid)
7 I'LL BUY THAT DREAM   Pied Pipers

Perry Como
Debuting on CBS radio in 1943 as a soloist, ``Till The End Of Time'' is Perry's first big hit (Sep. 1).

8 HOMESICK, THAT'S ALL   Frank Sinatra
9 THAT'S FOR ME   Dick Haymes

October 20, 1945
1 I'LL BUY THAT DREAM   Pied Pipers
2 TILL THE END OF TIME   Perry Como
3 ON THE ATCHISON, TOPEKA AND SANTA FE   Johnny Mercer
4 IF I LOVED YOU   Perry Como
5 I'M GONNA LOVE THAT GUY   Benny Goodman Orch. (VR: Dottie Reid)
6 ALONG THE NAVAJO TRAIL   Bing Crosby & Andrews Sisters
7 THAT'S FOR ME   Dick Haymes
8 HOW DEEP IS THE OCEAN   Benny Goodman Orch. (VR: Peggy Lee)
9 AUTUMN SERENADE   Harry James Orch.

October 27, 1945
1 I'LL BUY THAT DREAM   Pied Pipers
2 THAT'S FOR ME   Dick Haymes
3 ALONG THE NAVAJO TRAIL   Bing Crosby & Andrews Sisters
4 IF I LOVED YOU   Perry Como
5 TILL THE END OF TIME   Perry Como
6 ON THE ATCHISON, TOPEKA AND SANTA FE   Johnny Mercer
7 GOTTA BE THIS OR THAT   Benny Goodman Orch. (VR: Benny Goodman)
8 I CAN'T BEGIN TO TELL YOU   Bing Crosby with Carmen Cavallaro Orch.
9 I'M GONNA LOVE THAT GUY   Benny Goodman Orch. (VR: Dottie Reid)

November 3, 1945
1 TILL THE END OF TIME   Perry Como
2 I'LL BUY THAT DREAM   Pied Pipers
3 THAT'S FOR ME   Dick Haymes
4 I'M GONNA LOVE THAT GUY   Benny Goodman Orch. (VR: Dottie Reid)
5 IF I LOVED YOU   Perry Como
6 ON THE ATCHISON, TOPEKA AND SANTA FE   Johnny Mercer
7 ALONG THE NAVAJO TRAIL   Bing Crosby & Andrews Sisters
8 IT'S BEEN A LONG, LONG TIME   Harry James Orch. (VR: Kitty Kallen)
9 LOVE LETTERS   Dick Haymes

November 10, 1945
1 IT'S BEEN A LONG, LONG TIME   Harry James Orch. (VR: Kitty Kallen)
2 I'LL BUY THAT DREAM   Pied Pipers
3 ON THE ATCHISON, TOPEKA AND SANTA FE   Johnny Mercer
4 TILL THE END OF TIME   Perry Como
5 THAT'S FOR ME   Dick Haymes
6 ALONG THE NAVAJO TRAIL   Bing Crosby & Andrews Sisters
7 CHICKERY CHICK   Sammy Kaye Orch. (VR: Nancy Norman & Billy Williams)
8 IF I LOVED YOU   Perry Como
9 LOVE LETTERS   Dick Haymes

November 17, 1945
1 IT'S BEEN A LONG, LONG TIME   Harry James Orch. (VR: Kitty Kallen)

2 TILL THE END OF TIME   Perry Como
3 I'LL BUY THAT DREAM   Pied Pipers
4 THAT'S FOR ME   Dick Haymes
5 IF I LOVED YOU   Perry Como
6 WAITIN' FOR THE TRAIN TO COME IN   Peggy Lee
7 NO CAN DO   Guy Lombardo Orch. (VR: Don Rodney & Rose Marie Lombardo)
8 ON THE ATCHISON, TOPEKA AND SANTA FE   Johnny Mercer
9 ALONG THE NAVAJO TRAIL   Bing Crosby & Andrews Sisters

November 24, 1945
1 IT'S BEEN A LONG, LONG TIME   Harry James Orch. (VR: Kitty Kallen)
2 THAT'S FOR ME   Dick Haymes
3 I'LL BUY THAT DREAM   Pied Pipers
4 IT MIGHT AS WELL BE SPRING   Sammy Kaye Orch. (VR: Billy Williams)
5 TILL THE END OF TIME   Perry Como
6 ALONG THE NAVAJO TRAIL   Bing Crosby & Andrews Sisters
7 A STRANGER IN TOWN   Martha Tilton
8 WALKIN' WITH MY HONEY   Sammy Kaye Orch. (VR: Nancy Norman & Billy Williams)
9 CHICKERY CHICK   Sammy Kaye Orch. (VR: Nancy Norman & Billy Williams)

December 1, 1945
1 IT'S BEEN A LONG, LONG TIME   Harry James Orch. (VR: Kitty Kallen)
2 IT MIGHT AS WELL BE SPRING   Sammy Kaye Orch. (VR: Billy Williams)
3 I'LL BUY THAT DREAM   Pied Pipers
4 CHICKERY CHICK   Sammy Kaye Orch. (VR: Nancy Norman & Billy Williams)
5 TILL THE END OF TIME   Perry Como
6 THAT'S FOR ME   Dick Haymes
7 I CAN'T BEGIN TO TELL YOU   Bing Crosby with Carmen Cavallaro Orch.
8 IF I LOVED YOU   Perry Como
9 DID YOU EVER GET THAT FEELING IN THE MOONLIGHT   Perry Como

December 8, 1945
1 IT'S BEEN A LONG, LONG TIME   Harry James Orch. (VR: Kitty Kallen)
2 THAT'S FOR ME   Dick Haymes
3 IT MIGHT AS WELL BE SPRING   Sammy Kaye Orch. (VR: Billy Williams)
4 CHICKERY CHICK   Sammy Kaye Orch. (VR: Nancy Norman & Billy Williams)
5 I'LL BUY THAT DREAM   Pied Pipers
6 IT'S ONLY A PAPER MOON   Ella Fitzgerald
7 TILL THE END OF TIME   Perry Como
8 ALONG THE NAVAJO TRAIL   Bing Crosby & Andrews Sisters
9 I CAN'T BEGIN TO TELL YOU   Bing Crosby with Carmen Cavallaro Orch.

December 15, 1945
1 IT MIGHT AS WELL BE SPRING   Sammy Kaye Orch. (VR: Billy Williams)
2 IT'S BEEN A LONG, LONG TIME   Harry James Orch. (VR: Kitty Kallen)
3 I CAN'T BEGIN TO TELL YOU   Bing Crosby with Carmen Cavallaro Orch.

4 CHICKERY CHICK   Sammy Kaye Orch. (VR: Nancy Norman & Billy Williams)
5 SYMPHONY   Freddy Martin Orch. (VR: Clyde Rogers)
6 THAT'S FOR ME   Dick Haymes
7 I'LL BUY THAT DREAM   Pied Pipers
8 TILL THE END OF TIME   Perry Como
9 JUST A LITTLE FOND AFFECTION   Gene Krupa Orch. (VR: Buddy Stewart)

December 22, 1945
1 IT MIGHT AS WELL BE SPRING   Sammy Kaye Orch. (VR: Billy Williams)
2 I CAN'T BEGIN TO TELL YOU   Bing Crosby with Carmen Cavallaro Orch.
3 IT'S BEEN A LONG, LONG TIME   Harry James Orch. (VR: Kitty Kallen)
4 SYMPHONY   Freddy Martin Orch. (VR: Clyde Rogers)
5 CHICKERY CHICK   Sammy Kaye Orch. (VR: Nancy Norman & Billy Williams)
6 THAT'S FOR ME   Dick Haymes
7 WHITE CHRISTMAS   Bing Crosby
8 PUT THAT RING ON MY FINGER   Woody Herman Orch. (VR: Woody Herman)
9 TILL THE END OF TIME   Perry Como

December 29, 1945
1 IT MIGHT AS WELL BE SPRING   Sammy Kaye Orch. (VR: Billy Williams)
2 I CAN'T BEGIN TO TELL YOU   Bing Crosby with Carmen Cavallaro Orch.
3 SYMPHONY   Freddy Martin Orch. (VR: Clyde Rogers)
4 IT'S BEEN A LONG, LONG TIME   Harry James Orch. (VR: Kitty Kallen)
5 CHICKERY CHICK   Sammy Kaye Orch. (VR: Nancy Norman & Billy Williams)
6 WHITE CHRISTMAS   Bing Crosby
7 JUST A LITTLE FOND AFFECTION   Gene Krupa Orch. (VR: Buddy Stewart)
8 THAT'S FOR ME   Dick Haymes
9 WAITIN' FOR THE TRAIN TO COME IN   Peggy Lee

January 5, 1946
1 SYMPHONY   Freddy Martin Orch. (VR: Clyde Rogers)
2 I CAN'T BEGIN TO TELL YOU   Bing Crosby with Carmen Cavallaro Orch.
3 IT MIGHT AS WELL BE SPRING   Sammy Kaye Orch. (VR: Billy Williams)
4 IT'S BEEN A LONG, LONG TIME   Harry James Orch. (VR: Kitty Kallen)
5 JUST A LITTLE FOND AFFECTION   Gene Krupa Orch. (VR: Buddy Stewart)
6 THAT'S FOR ME   Dick Haymes
7 WAITIN' FOR THE TRAIN TO COME IN   Peggy Lee
8 CHICKERY CHICK   Sammy Kaye Orch. (VR: Nancy Norman & Billy Williams)
9 LET IT SNOW   Vaughn Monroe Orch. (VR: Vaughn Monroe)

January 12, 1946
1 I CAN'T BEGIN TO TELL YOU   Bing Crosby with Carmen Cavallaro Orch.
2 SYMPHONY   Freddy Martin Orch. (VR: Clyde Rogers)
3 IT MIGHT AS WELL BE SPRING   Sammy Kaye Orch. (VR: Billy Williams)
4 IT'S BEEN A LONG, LONG TIME   Harry James Orch. (VR: Kitty Kallen)
5 CHICKERY CHICK   Sammy Kaye Orch. (VR: Nancy Norman & Billy Williams)

6 THAT'S FOR ME   Dick Haymes
7 LET IT SNOW   Vaughn Monroe Orch. (VR: Vaughn Monroe)
8 JUST A LITTLE FOND AFFECTION   Gene Krupa Orch. (VR: Buddy Stewart)
9 WAITIN' FOR THE TRAIN TO COME IN   Peggy Lee

January 19, 1946
1 SYMPHONY   Freddy Martin Orch. (VR: Clyde Rogers)
2 IT MIGHT AS WELL BE SPRING   Sammy Kaye Orch. (VR: Billy Williams)
3 I CAN'T BEGIN TO TELL YOU   Bing Crosby with Carmen Cavallaro Orch.
4 LET IT SNOW   Vaughn Monroe Orch. (VR: Vaughn Monroe)
5 CHICKERY CHICK   Sammy Kaye Orch. (VR: Nancy Norman & Billy Williams)
6 IT'S BEEN A LONG, LONG TIME   Harry James Orch. (VR: Kitty Kallen)
7 COME TO BABY, DO   Les Brown Orch. (VR: Doris Day)
8 WAIT AND SEE   Judy Garland
9 JUST A LITTLE FOND AFFECTION   Gene Krupa Orch. (VR: Buddy Stewart)

January 26, 1946
1 SYMPHONY   Freddy Martin Orch. (VR: Clyde Rogers)
2 I CAN'T BEGIN TO TELL YOU   Bing Crosby with Carmen Cavallaro Orch.
3 LET IT SNOW   Vaughn Monroe Orch. (VR: Vaughn Monroe)
4 IT MIGHT AS WELL BE SPRING   Sammy Kaye Orch. (VR: Billy Williams)
5 AREN'T YOU GLAD YOU'RE YOU   Bing Crosby
6 I'M ALWAYS CHASING RAINBOWS   Harry James Orch. (VR: Buddy Di Vito)
7 IT'S BEEN A LONG, LONG TIME   Harry James Orch. (VR: Kitty Kallen)
8 JUST A LITTLE FOND AFFECTION   Gene Krupa Orch. (VR: Buddy Stewart)
9 CHICKERY CHICK   Sammy Kaye Orch. (VR: Nancy Norman & Billy Williams)

February 2, 1946
1 SYMPHONY   Freddy Martin Orch. (VR: Clyde Rogers)
2 IT MIGHT AS WELL BE SPRING   Sammy Kaye Orch. (VR: Billy Williams)
3 I CAN'T BEGIN TO TELL YOU   Bing Crosby with Carmen Cavallaro Orch.
4 LET IT SNOW   Vaughn Monroe Orch. (VR: Vaughn Monroe)
5 AREN'T YOU GLAD YOU'RE YOU   Bing Crosby
6 JUST A LITTLE FOND AFFECTION   Gene Krupa Orch. (VR: Buddy Stewart)
7 CHICKERY CHICK   Sammy Kaye Orch. (VR: Nancy Norman & Billy Williams)
8 IT'S BEEN A LONG, LONG TIME   Harry James Orch. (VR: Kitty Kallen)
9 I'M ALWAYS CHASING RAINBOWS   Harry James Orch. (VR: Buddy Di Vito)

February 9, 1946
1 SYMPHONY   Freddy Martin Orch. (VR: Clyde Rogers)
2 I CAN'T BEGIN TO TELL YOU   Bing Crosby with Carmen Cavallaro Orch.
3 LET IT SNOW   Vaughn Monroe Orch. (VR: Vaughn Monroe)
4 IT MIGHT AS WELL BE SPRING   Sammy Kaye Orch. (VR: Billy Williams)

5 AREN'T YOU GLAD YOU'RE YOU   Bing Crosby
6 DAY BY DAY   Frank Sinatra
7 JUST A LITTLE FOND AFFECTION   Gene Krupa Orch. (VR: Buddy Stewart)
8 CHICKERY CHICK   Sammy Kaye Orch. (VR: Nancy Norman & Billy Williams)
9 I'M ALWAYS CHASING RAINBOWS   Harry James Orch. (VR: Buddy Di Vito)

February 16, 1946
1 SYMPHONY   Freddy Martin Orch. (VR: Clyde Rogers)
2 I CAN'T BEGIN TO TELL YOU   Bing Crosby with Carmen Cavallaro Orch.
3 AREN'T YOU GLAD YOU'RE YOU   Bing Crosby
4 I'M ALWAYS CHASING RAINBOWS   Harry James Orch. (VR: Buddy Di Vito)
5 IT MIGHT AS WELL BE SPRING   Sammy Kaye Orch. (VR: Billy Williams)
6 LET IT SNOW   Vaughn Monroe Orch. (VR: Vaughn Monroe)
7 DAY BY DAY   Frank Sinatra
8 OH, WHAT IT SEEMED TO BE   Frankie Carle Orch. (VR: Marjorie Hughes)
9 SOME SUNDAY MORNING   Helen Forrest & Dick Haymes

February 23, 1946
1 LET IT SNOW   Vaughn Monroe Orch. (VR: Vaughn Monroe)
2 I CAN'T BEGIN TO TELL YOU   Bing Crosby with Carmen Cavallaro Orch.
3 SYMPHONY   Freddy Martin Orch. (VR: Clyde Rogers)
4 I'M ALWAYS CHASING RAINBOWS   Harry James Orch. (VR: Buddy Di Vito)
5 DOCTOR, LAWYER, INDIAN CHIEF   Betty Hutton
6 AREN'T YOU GLAD YOU'RE YOU   Bing Crosby
7 OH, WHAT IT SEEMED TO BE   Frankie Carle Orch. (VR: Marjorie Hughes)
8 DAY BY DAY   Frank Sinatra
9 IT MIGHT AS WELL BE SPRING   Sammy Kaye Orch. (VR: Billy Williams)

March 2, 1946
1 LET IT SNOW   Vaughn Monroe Orch. (VR: Vaughn Monroe)
2 SYMPHONY   Freddy Martin Orch. (VR: Clyde Rogers)
3 I CAN'T BEGIN TO TELL YOU   Bing Crosby with Carmen Cavallaro Orch.
4 I'M ALWAYS CHASING RAINBOWS   Harry James Orch. (VR: Buddy Di Vito)
5 OH, WHAT IT SEEMED TO BE   Frankie Carle Orch. (VR: Marjorie Hughes)
6 PERSONALITY   Johnny Mercer
7 DAY BY DAY   Frank Sinatra
8 DOCTOR, LAWYER, INDIAN CHIEF   Betty Hutton
9 AREN'T YOU GLAD YOU'RE YOU   Bing Crosby

March 9, 1946
1 SYMPHONY   Freddy Martin Orch. (VR: Clyde Rogers)
2 LET IT SNOW   Vaughn Monroe Orch. (VR: Vaughn Monroe)
3 OH, WHAT IT SEEMED TO BE   Frankie Carle Orch. (VR: Marjorie Hughes)
4 AREN'T YOU GLAD YOU'RE YOU   Bing Crosby
5 DAY BY DAY   Frank Sinatra
6 PERSONALITY   Johnny Mercer
7 I CAN'T BEGIN TO TELL YOU   Bing Crosby with Carmen Cavallaro Orch.

8 DOCTOR, LAWYER, INDIAN CHIEF   Betty Hutton
9 I'M ALWAYS CHASING RAINBOWS   Harry James Orch. (VR: Buddy Di Vito)

March 16, 1946
1 OH, WHAT IT SEEMED TO BE   Frankie Carle Orch. (VR: Marjorie Hughes)
2 SYMPHONY   Freddy Martin Orch. (VR: Clyde Rogers)
3 LET IT SNOW   Vaughn Monroe Orch. (VR: Vaughn Monroe)
4 I'M ALWAYS CHASING RAINBOWS   Harry James Orch. (VR: Buddy Di Vito)
5 DAY BY DAY   Frank Sinatra
6 PERSONALITY   Johnny Mercer
7 AREN'T YOU GLAD YOU'RE YOU   Bing Crosby
8 DOCTOR, LAWYER, INDIAN CHIEF   Betty Hutton
9 I CAN'T BEGIN TO TELL YOU   Bing Crosby with Carmen Cavallaro Orch.

March 23, 1946
1 OH, WHAT IT SEEMED TO BE   Frankie Carle Orch. (VR: Marjorie Hughes)
2 PERSONALITY   Johnny Mercer
3 DAY BY DAY   Frank Sinatra
4 LET IT SNOW   Vaughn Monroe Orch. (VR: Vaughn Monroe)
5 SYMPHONY   Freddy Martin Orch. (VR: Clyde Rogers)
6 I'M ALWAYS CHASING RAINBOWS   Harry James Orch. (VR: Buddy Di Vito)
7 DOCTOR, LAWYER, INDIAN CHIEF   Betty Hutton
8 AREN'T YOU GLAD YOU'RE YOU   Bing Crosby
9 SOME SUNDAY MORNING   Helen Forrest & Dick Haymes

March 30, 1946
1 OH, WHAT IT SEEMED TO BE   Frankie Carle Orch. (VR: Marjorie Hughes)
2 DAY BY DAY   Frank Sinatra
3 PERSONALITY   Johnny Mercer
4 DOCTOR, LAWYER, INDIAN CHIEF   Betty Hutton
5 YOU WON'T BE SATISFIED   Les Brown Orch. (VR: Doris Day)
6 SYMPHONY   Freddy Martin Orch. (VR: Clyde Rogers)
7 I'M ALWAYS CHASING RAINBOWS   Harry James Orch. (VR: Buddy Di Vito)
8 AREN'T YOU GLAD YOU'RE YOU   Bing Crosby
9 LET IT SNOW   Vaughn Monroe Orch. (VR: Vaughn Monroe)

April 6, 1946
1 OH, WHAT IT SEEMED TO BE   Frankie Carle Orch. (VR: Marjorie Hughes)
2 PERSONALITY   Johnny Mercer
3 YOU WON'T BE SATISFIED   Les Brown Orch. (VR: Doris Day)
4 DAY BY DAY   Frank Sinatra
5 DOCTOR, LAWYER, INDIAN CHIEF   Betty Hutton
6 SYMPHONY   Freddy Martin Orch. (VR: Clyde Rogers)
7 ONE-ZY, TWO-ZY   Phil Harris
8 I'M ALWAYS CHASING RAINBOWS   Harry James Orch. (VR: Buddy Di Vito)
9 ALL THROUGH THE DAY   Perry Como

April 13, 1946
1 OH, WHAT IT SEEMED TO BE   Frankie Carle Orch. (VR: Marjorie Hughes)
2 YOU WON'T BE SATISFIED   Les Brown Orch. (VR: Doris Day)

3 PERSONALITY   Johnny Mercer
4 DOCTOR, LAWYER, INDIAN CHIEF   Betty Hutton
5 DAY BY DAY   Frank Sinatra
6 I'M ALWAYS CHASING RAINBOWS   Harry James Orch.
   (VR: Buddy Di Vito)
7 ONE-ZY, TWO-ZY   Phil Harris
8 SYMPHONY   Freddy Martin Orch. (VR: Clyde Rogers)
9 ALL THROUGH THE DAY   Perry Como

April 20, 1946
1 OH, WHAT IT SEEMED TO BE   Frankie Carle Orch. (VR:
   Marjorie Hughes)
2 PERSONALITY   Johnny Mercer
3 DAY BY DAY   Frank Sinatra
4 YOU WON'T BE SATISFIED   Les Brown Orch. (VR: Doris
   Day)
5 SHOO FLY PIE   Stan Kenton Orch. (VR: June Christy)
6 DOCTOR, LAWYER, INDIAN CHIEF   Betty Hutton
7 ONE-ZY, TWO-ZY   Phil Harris
8 ALL THROUGH THE DAY   Perry Como
9 SYMPHONY   Freddy Martin Orch. (VR: Clyde Rogers)

April 27, 1946
1 OH, WHAT IT SEEMED TO BE   Frankie Carle Orch. (VR:
   Marjorie Hughes)
2 DAY BY DAY   Frank Sinatra
3 YOU WON'T BE SATISFIED   Les Brown Orch. (VR: Doris
   Day)
4 SHOO FLY PIE   Stan Kenton Orch. (VR: June Christy)
5 ALL THROUGH THE DAY   Perry Como
6 ONE-ZY, TWO-ZY   Phil Harris
7 SIOUX CITY SUE   Bing Crosby
8 PERSONALITY   Johnny Mercer
9 EASTER PARADE   Guy Lombardo

May 4, 1946
1 OH, WHAT IT SEEMED TO BE   Frankie Carle Orch. (VR:
   Marjorie Hughes)
2 ONE-ZY, TWO-ZY   Phil Harris
3 SHOO FLY PIE   Stan Kenton Orch. (VR: June Christy)
4 ALL THROUGH THE DAY   Perry Como
5 DAY BY DAY   Frank Sinatra
6 PERSONALITY   Johnny Mercer
7 YOU WON'T BE SATISFIED   Les Brown Orch. (VR: Doris
   Day)
8 LAUGHING ON THE OUTSIDE   Sammy Kaye Orch. (VR:
   Billy Williams) *
9 SIOUX CITY SUE   Bing Crosby
  Note: * Another version by: Dinah Shore.

May 11, 1946
1 ALL THROUGH THE DAY   Perry Como
2 LAUGHING ON THE OUTSIDE   Sammy Kaye Orch. (VR:
   Billy Williams) *
3 OH, WHAT IT SEEMED TO BE   Frankie Carle Orch. (VR:
   Marjorie Hughes)
4 SHOO FLY PIE   Stan Kenton Orch. (VR: June Christy)
5 YOU WON'T BE SATISFIED   Les Brown Orch. (VR: Doris
   Day)
6 SIOUX CITY SUE   Bing Crosby
7 PRISONER OF LOVE   Perry Como
8 SEEMS LIKE OLD TIMES   Guy Lombardo Orch. (VR: Don
   Rodney)
9 THE GYPSY   Ink Spots
  Note: * Another version by: Dinah Shore.

May 18, 1946
1 ALL THROUGH THE DAY   Perry Como
2 THE GYPSY   Ink Spots
3 SHOO FLY PIE   Stan Kenton Orch. (VR: June Christy)
4 LAUGHING ON THE OUTSIDE   Sammy Kaye Orch. (VR:
   Billy Williams) *
5 OH, WHAT IT SEEMED TO BE   Frankie Carle Orch. (VR:
   Marjorie Hughes)
6 SIOUX CITY SUE   Bing Crosby
7 YOU WON'T BE SATISFIED   Les Brown Orch. (VR: Doris
   Day)
8 PRISONER OF LOVE   Perry Como
9 IN LOVE IN VAIN   Helen Forrest & Dick Haymes
  Note: * Another version by: Dinah Shore.

May 25, 1946
1 LAUGHING ON THE OUTSIDE   Sammy Kaye Orch. (VR:
   Billy Williams) *
2 ALL THROUGH THE DAY   Perry Como
3 THE GYPSY   Ink Spots
4 OH, WHAT IT SEEMED TO BE   Frankie Carle Orch. (VR:
   Marjorie Hughes)
5 PRISONER OF LOVE   Perry Como
6 SHOO FLY PIE   Stan Kenton Orch. (VR: June Christy)
7 SIOUX CITY SUE   Bing Crosby
8 FULL MOON AND EMPTY ARMS   Frank Sinatra
9 THEY SAY IT'S WONDERFUL   Frank Sinatra
  Note: * Another version by: Dinah Shore.

June 1, 1946
1 THE GYPSY   Ink Spots
2 ALL THROUGH THE DAY   Perry Como
3 LAUGHING ON THE OUTSIDE   Sammy Kaye Orch. (VR:
   Billy Williams) *
4 SHOO FLY PIE   Stan Kenton Orch. (VR: June Christy)
5 PRISONER OF LOVE   Perry Como
6 SIOUX CITY SUE   Bing Crosby
7 THEY SAY IT'S WONDERFUL   Frank Sinatra
8 FULL MOON AND EMPTY ARMS   Frank Sinatra
9 OH, WHAT IT SEEMED TO BE   Frankie Carle Orch. (VR:
   Marjorie Hughes)
  Note: * Another version by: Dinah Shore.

June 8, 1946
1 THE GYPSY   Ink Spots
2 LAUGHING ON THE OUTSIDE   Sammy Kaye Orch. (VR:
   Billy Williams) *
3 THEY SAY IT'S WONDERFUL   Frank Sinatra
4 SIOUX CITY SUE   Bing Crosby
5 PRISONER OF LOVE   Perry Como
6 ALL THROUGH THE DAY   Perry Como
7 OH, WHAT IT SEEMED TO BE   Frankie Carle Orch. (VR:
   Marjorie Hughes)
8 FULL MOON AND EMPTY ARMS   Frank Sinatra
9 SHOO FLY PIE   Stan Kenton Orch. (VR: June Christy)
  Note: * Another version by: Dinah Shore.

June 15, 1946
1 THE GYPSY   Ink Spots
2 ALL THROUGH THE DAY   Perry Como
3 THEY SAY IT'S WONDERFUL   Frank Sinatra
4 LAUGHING ON THE OUTSIDE   Sammy Kaye Orch. (VR:
   Billy Williams) *
5 SIOUX CITY SUE   Bing Crosby
6 PRISONER OF LOVE   Perry Como
7 IN LOVE IN VAIN   Helen Forrest & Dick Haymes

The Ink Spots
``The Gypsy'' hits #1 (June 1).

8 COME RAIN OR COME SHINE   Margaret Whiting
9 I DON'T KNOW ENOUGH ABOUT YOU   Mills Brothers
Note: * Another version by: Dinah Shore.

June 22, 1946
1 THE GYPSY   Ink Spots
2 THEY SAY IT'S WONDERFUL   Frank Sinatra
3 ALL THROUGH THE DAY   Perry Como
4 LAUGHING ON THE OUTSIDE   Sammy Kaye Orch. (VR: Billy Williams) *
5 SIOUX CITY SUE   Bing Crosby
6 FULL MOON AND EMPTY ARMS   Frank Sinatra
7 IN LOVE IN VAIN   Helen Forrest & Dick Haymes
8 I DON'T KNOW ENOUGH ABOUT YOU   Mills Brothers
9 PRISONER OF LOVE   Perry Como
Note: * Another version by: Dinah Shore.

June 29, 1946
1 THE GYPSY   Ink Spots
2 THEY SAY IT'S WONDERFUL   Frank Sinatra
3 ALL THROUGH THE DAY   Perry Como
4 LAUGHING ON THE OUTSIDE   Sammy Kaye Orch. (VR: Billy Williams) *
5 SIOUX CITY SUE   Bing Crosby
6 PRISONER OF LOVE   Perry Como
7 I DON'T KNOW ENOUGH ABOUT YOU   Mills Brothers
8 FULL MOON AND EMPTY ARMS   Frank Sinatra
9 COME RAIN OR COME SHINE   Margaret Whiting
Note: * Another version by: Dinah Shore.

July 6, 1946
1 THEY SAY IT'S WONDERFUL   Frank Sinatra
2 THE GYPSY   Ink Spots
3 ALL THROUGH THE DAY   Perry Como
4 SIOUX CITY SUE   Bing Crosby
5 PRISONER OF LOVE   Perry Como

6 LAUGHING ON THE OUTSIDE   Sammy Kaye Orch. (VR: Billy Williams) *
7 I DON'T KNOW ENOUGH ABOUT YOU   Mills Brothers
8 IN LOVE IN VAIN   Helen Forrest & Dick Haymes
9 I GOT THE SUN IN THE MORNING   Les Brown Orch. (VR: Doris Day)
Note: * Another version by: Dinah Shore.

July 13, 1946
1 THEY SAY IT'S WONDERFUL   Frank Sinatra
2 THE GYPSY   Ink Spots
3 PRISONER OF LOVE   Perry Como
4 ALL THROUGH THE DAY   Perry Como
5 I DON'T KNOW ENOUGH ABOUT YOU   Mills Brothers
6 LAUGHING ON THE OUTSIDE   Sammy Kaye Orch. (VR: Billy Williams) *
7 IN LOVE IN VAIN   Helen Forrest & Dick Haymes
8 SIOUX CITY SUE   Bing Crosby
9 DOIN' WHAT COMES NATURALLY   Freddy Martin Orch. (VR: Glenn Hughes) **
Note: * Another version by: Dinah Shore.
          ** Another version by: Dinah Shore.

July 20, 1946
1 THE GYPSY   Ink Spots
2 THEY SAY IT'S WONDERFUL   Frank Sinatra
3 I DON'T KNOW ENOUGH ABOUT YOU   Mills Brothers
4 ALL THROUGH THE DAY   Perry Como
5 SIOUX CITY SUE   Bing Crosby
6 DOIN' WHAT COMES NATURALLY   Freddy Martin Orch. (VR: Glenn Hughes) *
7 IN LOVE IN VAIN   Helen Forrest & Dick Haymes
8 COME RAIN OR COME SHINE   Margaret Whiting
9 LAUGHING ON THE OUTSIDE   Sammy Kaye Orch. (VR: Billy Williams) **
Note: * Another version by: Dinah Shore.
          ** Another version by: Dinah Shore.

July 27, 1946
1 THEY SAY IT'S WONDERFUL   Frank Sinatra
2 THE GYPSY   Ink Spots
3 SURRENDER   Perry Como
4 I DON'T KNOW ENOUGH ABOUT YOU   Mills Brothers
5 DOIN' WHAT COMES NATURALLY   Freddy Martin Orch. (VR: Glenn Hughes) *
6 PRISONER OF LOVE   Perry Como
7 ALL THROUGH THE DAY   Perry Como
8 IN LOVE IN VAIN   Helen Forrest & Dick Haymes
9 SIOUX CITY SUE   Bing Crosby
Note: * Another version by: Dinah Shore.

August 3, 1946
1 THE GYPSY   Ink Spots
2 DOIN' WHAT COMES NATURALLY   Freddy Martin Orch. (VR: Glenn Hughes) *
3 THEY SAY IT'S WONDERFUL   Frank Sinatra
4 SURRENDER   Perry Como
5 I DON'T KNOW ENOUGH ABOUT YOU   Mills Brothers
6 ALL THROUGH THE DAY   Perry Como
7 TO EACH HIS OWN   Eddy Howard Orch. (VR: Eddy Howard)
8 PRISONER OF LOVE   Perry Como
9 I GOT THE SUN IN THE MORNING   Les Brown Orch. (VR: Doris Day)
Note: * Another version by: Dinah Shore.

August 10, 1946
1   THEY SAY IT'S WONDERFUL   Frank Sinatra
2   THE GYPSY   Ink Spots
3   SURRENDER   Perry Como
4   DOIN' WHAT COMES NATURALLY   Freddy Martin Orch.
    (VR: Glenn Hughes) *
5   TO EACH HIS OWN   Eddy Howard Orch. (VR: Eddy
    Howard)
6   I DON'T KNOW ENOUGH ABOUT YOU   Mills Brothers
7   PRISONER OF LOVE   Perry Como
8   I GOT THE SUN IN THE MORNING   Les Brown Orch. (VR:
    Doris Day)
9   IN LOVE IN VAIN   Helen Forrest & Dick Haymes
    Note: *   Another version by: Dinah Shore.

August 17, 1946
1   THE GYPSY   Ink Spots
2   THEY SAY IT'S WONDERFUL   Frank Sinatra
3   TO EACH HIS OWN   Eddy Howard Orch. (VR: Eddy
    Howard)
4   I DON'T KNOW ENOUGH ABOUT YOU   Mills Brothers
5   DOIN' WHAT COMES NATURALLY   Freddy Martin Orch.
    (VR: Glenn Hughes) *
6   SURRENDER   Perry Como
7   PRISONER OF LOVE   Perry Como
8   I GOT THE SUN IN THE MORNING   Les Brown Orch. (VR:
    Doris Day)
9   IN LOVE IN VAIN   Helen Forrest & Dick Haymes
    Note: *   Another version by: Dinah Shore.

August 24, 1946
1   TO EACH HIS OWN   Eddy Howard Orch. (VR: Eddy
    Howard)
2   SURRENDER   Perry Como
3   THEY SAY IT'S WONDERFUL   Frank Sinatra
4   I GOT THE SUN IN THE MORNING   Les Brown Orch. (VR:
    Doris Day)
5   THE GYPSY   Ink Spots
6   DOIN' WHAT COMES NATURALLY   Freddy Martin Orch.
    (VR: Glenn Hughes) *
7   IN LOVE IN VAIN   Helen Forrest & Dick Haymes
8   PRISONER OF LOVE   Perry Como
9   I DON'T KNOW ENOUGH ABOUT YOU   Mills Brothers
    Note: *   Another version by: Dinah Shore.

August 31,1946
1   TO EACH HIS OWN   Eddy Howard Orch. (VR: Eddy
    Howard)
2   SURRENDER   Perry Como
3   DOIN' WHAT COMES NATURALLY   Freddy Martin Orch.
    (VR: Glenn Hughes) *
4   THEY SAY IT'S WONDERFUL   Frank Sinatra
5   I DON'T KNOW ENOUGH ABOUT YOU   Mills Brothers
6   THE GYPSY   Ink Spots
7   I GOT THE SUN IN THE MORNING   Les Brown Orch. (VR:
    Doris Day)
8   SOUTH AMERICA, TAKE IT AWAY   Bing Crosby & Andrews
    Sisters
9   FIVE MINUTES MORE   Frank Sinatra **
    Note: *   Another version by: Dinah Shore.
         **   Another version by: Tex Beneke Orch. (VR: Tex
    Beneke).

September 7, 1946
1   TO EACH HIS OWN   Eddy Howard Orch. (VR: Eddy
    Howard)

2   THEY SAY IT'S WONDERFUL   Frank Sinatra
3   SURRENDER   Perry Como
4   SOUTH AMERICA, TAKE IT AWAY   Bing Crosby & Andrews
    Sisters
5   FIVE MINUTES MORE   Frank Sinatra *
6   I GOT THE SUN IN THE MORNING   Les Brown Orch. (VR:
    Doris Day)
7   THE GYPSY   Ink Spots
8   I DON'T KNOW WHY   Andrews Sisters
9   I DON'T KNOW ENOUGH ABOUT YOU   Mills Brothers
    Note: *   Another version by: Tex Beneke Orch. (VR: Tex
    Beneke).

September 14, 1946
1   TO EACH HIS OWN   Eddy Howard Orch. (VR: Eddy
    Howard)
2   FIVE MINUTES MORE   Frank Sinatra *
3   SURRENDER   Perry Como
4   THEY SAY IT'S WONDERFUL   Frank Sinatra
5   SOUTH AMERICA, TAKE IT AWAY   Bing Crosby &
    Andrews Sisters
6   THE GYPSY   Ink Spots
7   I GOT THE SUN IN THE MORNING   Les Brown Orch. (VR:
    Doris Day)
8   DOIN' WHAT COMES NATURALLY   Freddy Martin Orch.
    (VR: Glenn Hughes) **
9   I DON'T KNOW ENOUGH ABOUT YOU   Mills Brothers
    Note: *   Another version by: Tex Beneke Orch. (VR: Tex
    Beneke).
         **   Another version by: Dinah Shore.

September 21, 1946
1   TO EACH HIS OWN   Eddy Howard Orch. (VR: Eddy
    Howard)
2   FIVE MINUTES MORE   Frank Sinatra *
3   SURRENDER   Perry Como
4   THEY SAY IT'S WONDERFUL   Frank Sinatra
5   SOUTH AMERICA, TAKE IT AWAY   Bing Crosby & Andrews
    Sisters
6   DOIN' WHAT COMES NATURALLY   Freddy Martin Orch.
    (VR: Glenn Hughes) **

The Modernaires
The group rivaled the Eddy Howard hit
of ``To Each His Own'' with their own #3 version.

117

7 I GOT THE SUN IN THE MORNING   Les Brown Orch. (VR: Doris Day)
8 THE GYPSY   Ink Spots
9 I DON'T KNOW ENOUGH ABOUT YOU   Mills Brothers
Note: * Another version by: Tex Beneke Orch. (VR: Tex Beneke).
   ** Another version by: Dinah Shore.

September 28, 1946
1 TO EACH HIS OWN   Eddy Howard Orch. (VR: Eddy Howard)
2 FIVE MINUTES MORE   Frank Sinatra *
3 SOUTH AMERICA, TAKE IT AWAY   Bing Crosby & Andrews Sisters
4 SURRENDER   Perry Como
5 THEY SAY IT'S WONDERFUL   Frank Sinatra
6 I GOT THE SUN IN THE MORNING   Les Brown Orch. (VR: Doris Day)
7 DOIN' WHAT COMES NATURALLY   Freddy Martin Orch. (VR: Glenn Hughes) **
8 I DON'T KNOW ENOUGH ABOUT YOU   Mills Brothers
9 LINGER IN MY ARMS A LITTLE LONGER   Peggy Lee
Note: * Another version by: Tex Beneke Orch. (VR: Tex Beneke).
   ** Another version by: Dinah Shore.

October 5, 1946
1 TO EACH HIS OWN   Eddy Howard Orch. (VR: Eddy Howard)
2 FIVE MINUTES MORE   Frank Sinatra *
3 SOUTH AMERICA, TAKE IT AWAY   Bing Crosby & Andrews Sisters
4 SURRENDER   Perry Como
5 THEY SAY IT'S WONDERFUL   Frank Sinatra
6 DOIN' WHAT COMES NATURALLY   Freddy Martin Orch. (VR: Glenn Hughes) **
7 I GOT THE SUN IN THE MORNING   Les Brown Orch. (VR: Doris Day)
8 RUMORS ARE FLYING   Frankie Carle Orch. (VR: Marjorie Hughes)
9 LINGER IN MY ARMS A LITTLE LONGER   Peggy Lee
Note: * Another version by: Tex Beneke Orch. (VR: Tex Beneke).
   ** Another version by: Dinah Shore.

October 12, 1946
1 TO EACH HIS OWN   Eddy Howard Orch. (VR: Eddy Howard)
2 FIVE MINUTES MORE   Frank Sinatra *
3 SOUTH AMERICA, TAKE IT AWAY   Bing Crosby & Andrews Sisters
4 RUMORS ARE FLYING   Frankie Carle Orch. (VR: Marjorie Hughes)
5 SURRENDER   Perry Como
6 I GOT THE SUN IN THE MORNING   Les Brown Orch. (VR: Doris Day)
7 YOU KEEP COMING BACK LIKE A SONG   Dinah Shore
8 DOIN' WHAT COMES NATURALLY   Freddy Martin Orch. (VR: Glenn Hughes) **
9 THEY SAY IT'S WONDERFUL   Frank Sinatra
Note: * Another version by: Tex Beneke Orch. (VR: Tex Beneke).
   ** Another version by: Dinah Shore.

October 19, 1946
1 FIVE MINUTES MORE   Frank Sinatra *
2 TO EACH HIS OWN   Eddy Howard Orch. (VR: Eddy Howard)

3 SOUTH AMERICA, TAKE IT AWAY   Bing Crosby & Andrews Sisters
4 THEY SAY IT'S WONDERFUL   Frank Sinatra
5 DOIN' WHAT COMES NATURALLY   Freddy Martin Orch. (VR: Glenn Hughes) **
6 OLE BUTTERMILK SKY   Kay Kyser Orch. (VR: Mike Douglas & Campus Kids)
7 SURRENDER   Perry Como
8 RUMORS ARE FLYING   Frankie Carle Orch. (VR: Marjorie Hughes)
9 THIS IS ALWAYS   Harry James Orch. (VR: Buddy Di Vito)
Note: * Another version by: Tex Beneke Orch. (VR: Tex Beneke).
   ** Another version by: Dinah Shore.

October 26, 1946
1 FIVE MINUTES MORE   Frank Sinatra *
2 SOUTH AMERICA, TAKE IT AWAY   Bing Crosby & Andrews Sisters
3 RUMORS ARE FLYING   Frankie Carle Orch. (VR: Marjorie Hughes)
4 TO EACH HIS OWN   Eddy Howard Orch. (VR: Eddy Howard)
5 THIS IS ALWAYS   Harry James Orch. (VR: Buddy Di Vito)
6 SURRENDER   Perry Como
7 IF YOU WERE THE ONLY GIRL   Perry Como
8 OLE BUTTERMILK SKY   Kay Kyser Orch. (VR: Mike Douglas & Campus Kids)
9 YOU KEEP COMING BACK LIKE A SONG   Dinah Shore
Note: * Another version by: Dinah Shore.

November 2, 1946
1 FIVE MINUTES MORE   Frank Sinatra *
2 SOUTH AMERICA, TAKE IT AWAY   Bing Crosby & Andrews Sisters
3 YOU KEEP COMING BACK LIKE A SONG   Dinah Shore
4 OLE BUTTERMILK SKY   Kay Kyser Orch. (VR: Mike Douglas & Campus Kids)
5 RUMORS ARE FLYING   Frankie Carle Orch. (VR: Marjorie Hughes)
6 TO EACH HIS OWN   Eddy Howard Orch. (VR: Eddy Howard)
7 THIS IS ALWAYS   Harry James Orch. (VR: Buddy Di Vito)
8 LINGER IN MY ARMS A LITTLE LONGER   Peggy Lee
9 SURRENDER   Perry Como
Note: * Another version by: Dinah Shore.

November 9, 1946
1 RUMORS ARE FLYING   Frankie Carle Orch. (VR: Marjorie Hughes)
2 OLE BUTTERMILK SKY   Kay Kyser Orch. (VR: Mike Douglas & Campus Kids)
3 SOUTH AMERICA, TAKE IT AWAY   Bing Crosby & Andrews Sisters
4 THIS IS ALWAYS   Harry James Orch. (VR: Buddy Di Vito)
5 YOU KEEP COMING BACK LIKE A SONG   Dinah Shore
6 TO EACH HIS OWN   Eddy Howard Orch. (VR: Eddy Howard)
7 FIVE MINUTES MORE   Frank Sinatra *
8 THE WHOLE WORLD IS SINGING MY SONG   Les Brown Orch. (VR: Doris Day)
9 IF YOU WERE THE ONLY GIRL   Perry Como
Note: * Another version by: Tex Beneke Orch. (VR: Tex Beneke).

November 16, 1946
1 FIVE MINUTES MORE   Frank Sinatra *

Frank Sinatra
One of music's greatest, the forties idol hits #1
with ``Five Minutes More'' (Oct. 19).

2   RUMORS ARE FLYING   Frankie Carle Orch. (VR: Marjorie Hughes)
3   YOU KEEP COMING BACK LIKE A SONG   Dinah Shore
4   THIS IS ALWAYS   Harry James Orch. (VR: Buddy Di Vito)
5   SOUTH AMERICA, TAKE IT AWAY   Bing Crosby & Andrews Sisters
6   OLE BUTTERMILK SKY   Kay Kyser Orch. (VR: Mike Douglas & Campus Kids)
7   TO EACH HIS OWN   Eddy Howard Orch. (VR: Eddy Howard)
8   SOMEWHERE IN THE NIGHT   Dick Haymes
9   ZIP A DEE DOO DAH   Johnny Mercer **
10   THE COFFEE SONG   Frank Sinatra
    Note: * Another version by: Tex Beneke Orch. (VR: Tex Beneke).
        ** From Walt Disney's "Song Of The South."

November 23, 1946

1   RUMORS ARE FLYING   Frankie Carle Orch. (VR: Marjorie Hughes)
2   OLE BUTTERMILK SKY   Kay Kyser Orch. (VR: Mike Douglas & Campus Kids)
3   THE WHOLE WORLD IS SINGING MY SONG   Les Brown Orch. (VR: Doris Day)
4   FIVE MINUTES MORE   Frank Sinatra *
5   YOU KEEP COMING BACK LIKE A SONG   Dinah Shore
6   TO EACH HIS OWN   Eddy Howard Orch. (VR: Eddy Howard)
7   SOUTH AMERICA, TAKE IT AWAY   Bing Crosby & Andrews Sisters
8   THIS IS ALWAYS   Harry James Orch. (VR: Buddy Di Vito)
9   THE THINGS WE DID LAST SUMMER   Jo Stafford
10   ZIP A DEE DOO DAH   Johnny Mercer **
    Note: * Another version by: Tex Beneke Orch. (VR: Tex Beneke).
        ** From Walt Disney's "Song Of The South."

November 30, 1946

1   OLE BUTTERMILK SKY   Kay Kyser Orch. (VR: Mike Douglas & Campus Kids)
2   THE WHOLE WORLD IS SINGING MY SONG   Les Brown Orch. (VR: Doris Day)
3   FIVE MINUTES MORE   Frank Sinatra *
4   YOU KEEP COMING BACK LIKE A SONG   Dinah Shore
5   RUMORS ARE FLYING   Frankie Carle Orch. (VR: Marjorie Hughes)
6   THE OLD LAMPLIGHTER   Sammy Kaye Orch. (VR: Billy Williams)
7   THE THINGS WE DID LAST SUMMER   Jo Stafford
8   TO EACH HIS OWN   Eddy Howard Orch. (VR: Eddy Howard)
9   FOR YOU, FOR ME, FOREVERMORE   Judy Garland & Dick Haymes
10   SOUTH AMERICA, TAKE IT AWAY   Bing Crosby & Andrews Sisters
    Note: * Another version by: Tex Beneke Orch. (VR: Tex Beneke).

December 7, 1946

1   OLE BUTTERMILK SKY   Kay Kyser Orch. (VR: Mike Douglas & Campus Kids)
2   RUMORS ARE FLYING   Frankie Carle Orch. (VR: Marjorie Hughes)
3   THE OLD LAMPLIGHTER   Sammy Kaye Orch. (VR: Billy Williams)
4   THE WHOLE WORLD IS SINGING MY SONG   Les Brown Orch. (VR: Doris Day)

5 YOU KEEP COMING BACK LIKE A SONG   Dinah Shore
6 TO EACH HIS OWN   Eddy Howard Orch. (VR: Eddy Howard)
7 FIVE MINUTES MORE   Frank Sinatra *
8 THE THINGS WE DID LAST SUMMER   Jo Stafford
9 ZIP A DEE DOO DAH   Johnny Mercer **
10 THIS IS ALWAYS   Harry James Orch. (VR: Buddy Di Vito)
   Note: * Another version by: Tex Beneke Orch. (VR: Tex Beneke).
   ** From Walt Disney's "Song Of The South."

December 14, 1946

1 OLE BUTTERMILK SKY   Kay Kyser Orch. (VR: Mike Douglas & Campus Kids)
2 RUMORS ARE FLYING   Frankie Carle Orch. (VR: Marjorie Hughes)
3 THE THINGS WE DID LAST SUMMER   Jo Stafford
4 THE OLD LAMPLIGHTER   Sammy Kaye Orch. (VR: Billy Williams)
5 THE WHOLE WORLD IS SINGING MY SONG   Les Brown Orch. (VR: Doris Day)
6 FOR SENTIMENTAL REASONS   Nat King Cole
7 FIVE MINUTES MORE   Frank Sinatra *
8 FOR YOU, FOR ME, FOREVERMORE   Judy Garland & Dick Haymes
9 ZIP A DEE DOO DAH   Johnny Mercer **
10 TO EACH HIS OWN   Eddy Howard Orch. (VR: Eddy Howard)
   Note: * Another version by: Tex Beneke Orch. (VR: Tex Beneke).
   ** From Walt Disney's "Song Of The South."

December 21, 1946

1 OLE BUTTERMILK SKY   Kay Kyser Orch. (VR: Mike Douglas & Campus Kids)
2 THE WHOLE WORLD IS SINGING MY SONG   Les Brown Orch. (VR: Doris Day)
3 THE OLD LAMPLIGHTER   Sammy Kaye Orch. (VR: Billy Williams)
4 FOR SENTIMENTAL REASONS   Nat King Cole
5 RUMORS ARE FLYING   Frankie Carle Orch. (VR: Marjorie Hughes)
6 YOU KEEP COMING BACK LIKE A SONG   Dinah Shore
7 ZIP A DEE DOO DAH   Johnny Mercer *
8 A GAL IN CALICO   Johnny Mercer
9 THE THINGS WE DID LAST SUMMER   Jo Stafford
10 FOR YOU, FOR ME, FOREVERMORE   Judy Garland & Dick Haymes
   Note: * From Walt Disney's "Song Of The South."

December 28, 1946

1 OLE BUTTERMILK SKY   Kay Kyser Orch. (VR: Mike Douglas & Campus Kids)
2 THE OLD LAMPLIGHTER   Sammy Kaye Orch. (VR: Billy Williams)
3 FOR SENTIMENTAL REASONS   Nat King Cole
4 WHITE CHRISTMAS   Bing Crosby
5 THE THINGS WE DID LAST SUMMER   Jo Stafford
6 THE WHOLE WORLD IS SINGING MY SONG   Les Brown Orch. (VR: Doris Day)
7 A GAL IN CALICO   Johnny Mercer
8 RUMORS ARE FLYING   Frankie Carle Orch. (VR: Marjorie Hughes)
9 ZIP A DEE DOO DAH   Johnny Mercer *
10 YOU KEEP COMING BACK LIKE A SONG   Dinah Shore
   Note: * From Walt Disney's "Song Of The South."

January 4, 1947

1 OLE BUTTERMILK SKY   Kay Kyser Orch. (VR: Mike Douglas & Campus Kids)
2 THE OLD LAMPLIGHTER   Sammy Kaye Orch. (VR: Billy Williams)
3 FOR SENTIMENTAL REASONS   Nat King Cole
4 A GAL IN CALICO   Johnny Mercer
5 ZIP A DEE DOO DAH   Johnny Mercer *
6 THE WHOLE WORLD IS SINGING MY SONG   Les Brown Orch. (VR: Doris Day)
7 THE THINGS WE DID LAST SUMMER   Jo Stafford
8 WHITE CHRISTMAS   Bing Crosby
9 RUMORS ARE FLYING   Frankie Carle Orch. (VR: Marjorie Hughes)
10 THE CHRISTMAS SONG   Nat King Cole
   Note: * From Walt Disney's "Song Of The South."

January 11, 1947

1 FOR SENTIMENTAL REASONS   Nat King Cole
2 OLE BUTTERMILK SKY   Kay Kyser Orch. (VR: Mike Douglas & Campus Kids)
3 THE OLD LAMPLIGHTER   Sammy Kaye Orch. (VR: Billy Williams)
4 ZIP A DEE DOO DAH   Johnny Mercer *
5 A GAL IN CALICO   Johnny Mercer
6 THE THINGS WE DID LAST SUMMER   Jo Stafford
7 THE WHOLE WORLD IS SINGING MY SONG   Les Brown Orch. (VR: Doris Day)
8 RUMORS ARE FLYING   Frankie Carle Orch. (VR: Marjorie Hughes)
9 SOONER OR LATER   Sammy Kaye Orch. (VR: Betty Barclay)
10 YOU KEEP COMING BACK LIKE A SONG   Dinah Shore
   Note: * From Walt Disney's "Song Of The South."

January 18, 1947

1 FOR SENTIMENTAL REASONS   Nat King Cole
2 OLE BUTTERMILK SKY   Kay Kyser Orch. (VR: Mike Douglas & Campus Kids)
3 A GAL IN CALICO   Johnny Mercer
4 THE WHOLE WORLD IS SINGING MY SONG   Les Brown Orch. (VR: Doris Day)
5 ZIP A DEE DOO DAH   Johnny Mercer *
6 THE OLD LAMPLIGHTER   Sammy Kaye Orch. (VR: Billy Williams)
7 FOR YOU, FOR ME, FOREVERMORE   Judy Garland & Dick Haymes
8 THE THINGS WE DID LAST SUMMER   Jo Stafford
9 OH, BUT I DO   Margaret Whiting
10 I'LL CLOSE MY EYES   Andy Russell
   Note: * From Walt Disney's "Song Of The South."

January 25, 1947

1 FOR SENTIMENTAL REASONS   Nat King Cole
2 A GAL IN CALICO   Johnny Mercer
3 OLE BUTTERMILK SKY   Kay Kyser Orch. (VR: Mike Douglas & Campus Kids)
4 ZIP A DEE DOO DAH   Johnny Mercer *
5 THE OLD LAMPLIGHTER   Sammy Kaye Orch. (VR: Billy Williams)
6 OH, BUT I DO   Margaret Whiting
7 SOONER OR LATER   Sammy Kaye Orch. (VR: Betty Barclay)
8 THE WHOLE WORLD IS SINGING MY SONG   Les Brown Orch. (VR: Doris Day)
9 I'LL CLOSE MY EYES   Andy Russell
10 THE THINGS WE DID LAST SUMMER   Jo Stafford

Note: * From Walt Disney's "Song Of The South."

February 1, 1947
1. FOR SENTIMENTAL REASONS   Nat King Cole
2. A GAL IN CALICO   Johnny Mercer
3. ZIP A DEE DOO DAH   Johnny Mercer *
4. THE OLD LAMPLIGHTER   Sammy Kaye Orch. (VR: Billy Williams)
5. OH, BUT I DO   Margaret Whiting
6. OLE BUTTERMILK SKY   Kay Kyser Orch. (VR: Mike Douglas & Campus Kids)
7. SOONER OR LATER   Sammy Kaye Orch. (VR: Betty Barclay)
8. THE THINGS WE DID LAST SUMMER   Jo Stafford
9. THE WHOLE WORLD IS SINGING MY SONG   Les Brown Orch. (VR: Doris Day)
10. LIFE CAN BE BEAUTIFUL   Harry James Orch. (VR: Marian Morgan)
   Note: * From Walt Disney's "Song Of The South."

February 8, 1947
1. FOR SENTIMENTAL REASONS   Nat King Cole
2. A GAL IN CALICO   Johnny Mercer
3. ZIP A DEE DOO DAH   Johnny Mercer *
4. OH, BUT I DO   Margaret Whiting
5. THE OLD LAMPLIGHTER   Sammy Kaye Orch. (VR: Billy Williams)
6. OLE BUTTERMILK SKY   Kay Kyser Orch. (VR: Mike Douglas & Campus Kids)
7. SOONER OR LATER   Sammy Kaye Orch. (VR: Betty Barclay)
8. THE WHOLE WORLD IS SINGING MY SONG   Les Brown Orch. (VR: Doris Day)
9. GUILTY   Margaret Whiting
10. I'LL CLOSE MY EYES   Andy Russell
   Note: * From Walt Disney's "Song Of The South."

February 15, 1947
1. FOR SENTIMENTAL REASONS   Nat King Cole
2. A GAL IN CALICO   Johnny Mercer
3. OH, BUT I DO   Margaret Whiting
4. ZIP A DEE DOO DAH   Johnny Mercer *
5. THE ANNIVERSARY SONG   Dinah Shore
6. I'LL CLOSE MY EYES   Andy Russell
7. THE OLD LAMPLIGHTER   Sammy Kaye Orch. (VR: Billy Williams)
8. OLE BUTTERMILK SKY   Kay Kyser Orch. (VR: Mike Douglas & Campus Kids)
9. MANAGUA, NICARAGUA   Guy Lombardo Orch. (VR: Don Rodney) **
10. GUILTY   Margaret Whiting
   Note: * From Walt Disney's "Song Of The South."
   ** Another version by: Kay Kyser Orch. (VR: Harry Babbitt).

February 22, 1947
1. A GAL IN CALICO   Johnny Mercer
2. THE ANNIVERSARY SONG   Dinah Shore
3. OH, BUT I DO   Margaret Whiting
4. FOR SENTIMENTAL REASONS   Nat King Cole
5. I'LL CLOSE MY EYES   Andy Russell
6. THE OLD LAMPLIGHTER   Sammy Kaye Orch. (VR: Billy Williams)
7. ZIP A DEE DOO DAH   Johnny Mercer *
8. OLE BUTTERMILK SKY   Kay Kyser Orch. (VR: Mike Douglas & Campus Kids)
9. GUILTY   Margaret Whiting

10. YOU'LL ALWAYS BE THE ONE I LOVE   Frank Sinatra
   Note: * From Walt Disney's "Song Of The South."

March 1, 1947
1. FOR SENTIMENTAL REASONS   Nat King Cole
2. THE ANNIVERSARY SONG   Dinah Shore
3. OH, BUT I DO   Margaret Whiting
4. GUILTY   Margaret Whiting
5. A GAL IN CALICO   Johnny Mercer
6. ZIP A DEE DOO DAH   Johnny Mercer *
7. OPEN THE DOOR, RICHARD   Three Flames **
8. MANAGUA, NICARAGUA   Guy Lombardo Orch. (VR: Don Rodney) @
9. I'LL CLOSE MY EYES   Andy Russell
10. THE OLD LAMPLIGHTER   Sammy Kaye Orch. (VR: Billy Williams)
   Note: * From Walt Disney's "Song Of The South."
   ** Freddy Martin Orch. (VR: Stuart Wade)
   @ Count Basie Orch. (VR: Harry Edison & Bill Johnson)

March 8, 1947
1. THE ANNIVERSARY SONG   Dinah Shore
2. MANAGUA, NICARAGUA   Guy Lombardo Orch. (VR: Don Rodney) *
3. OH, BUT I DO   Margaret Whiting
4. A GAL IN CALICO   Johnny Mercer
5. FOR SENTIMENTAL REASONS   Nat King Cole
6. I'LL CLOSE MY EYES   Andy Russell
7. GUILTY   Margaret Whiting
8. ZIP A DEE DOO DAH   Johnny Mercer **
9. HOW ARE THINGS IN GLOCCA MORRA   Buddy Clark
10. THE OLD LAMPLIGHTER   Sammy Kaye Orch. (VR: Billy Williams)
   Note: * Freddy Martin Orch. (VR: Stuart Wade)
   ** From Walt Disney's "Song Of The South."

March 22, 1947
1. THE ANNIVERSARY SONG   Dinah Shore
2. MANAGUA, NICARAGUA   Guy Lombardo Orch. (VR: Don Rodney) *
3. HOW ARE THINGS IN GLOCCA MORRA   Buddy Clark
4. I'LL CLOSE MY EYES   Andy Russell
5. GUILTY   Margaret Whiting
6. FOR SENTIMENTAL REASONS   Nat King Cole
7. A GAL IN CALICO   Johnny Mercer
8. LINDA   Buddy Clark with Ray Noble Orch.
9. ZIP A DEE DOO DAH   Johnny Mercer **
10. OH, BUT I DO   Margaret Whiting
   Note: * Freddy Martin Orch. (VR: Stuart Wade)
   ** From Walt Disney's "Song Of The South."

March 29, 1947
1. THE ANNIVERSARY SONG   Dinah Shore
2. HOW ARE THINGS IN GLOCCA MORRA   Buddy Clark
3. MANAGUA, NICARAGUA   Guy Lombardo Orch. (VR: Don Rodney) *
4. HEARTACHES   Ted Weems Orch. (Whistling solo: Elmore Cannon)
5. FOR SENTIMENTAL REASONS   Nat King Cole
6. I'LL CLOSE MY EYES   Andy Russell
7. GUILTY   Margaret Whiting
8. LINDA   Buddy Clark with Ray Noble Orch.
9. IT'S A GOOD DAY   Peggy Lee
10. OH, BUT I DO   Margaret Whiting
   Note: * Freddy Martin Orch. (VR: Stuart Wade)

April 5, 1947
1. THE ANNIVERSARY SONG   Dinah Shore
2. HOW ARE THINGS IN GLOCCA MORRA   Buddy Clark
3. MANAGUA, NICARAGUA   Guy Lombardo Orch. (VR: Don Rodney) *
4. HEARTACHES   Ted Weems Orch. (Whistling solo: Elmore Cannon)
5. I'LL CLOSE MY EYES   Andy Russell
6. LINDA   Buddy Clark with Ray Noble Orch.
7. GUILTY   Margaret Whiting
8. FOR SENTIMENTAL REASONS   Nat King Cole
9. YOU CAN'T SEE THE SUN WHEN YOU'RE CRYING   Ink Spots
10. IT'S A GOOD DAY   Peggy Lee
   Note: * Freddy Martin Orch. (VR: Stuart Wade)

April 12, 1947
1. THE ANNIVERSARY SONG   Dinah Shore
2. HEARTACHES   Ted Weems Orch. (Whistling solo: Elmore Cannon)
3. HOW ARE THINGS IN GLOCCA MORRA   Buddy Clark
4. LINDA   Buddy Clark with Ray Noble Orch.
5. MANAGUA, NICARAGUA   Guy Lombardo Orch. (VR: Don Rodney) **
6. I'LL CLOSE MY EYES   Andy Russell
7. GUILTY   Margaret Whiting
8. EASTER PARADE   Guy Lombardo
9. APRIL SHOWERS   Guy Lombardo (VR: Don Rodney)
10. IT'S A GOOD DAY   Peggy Lee
   Note: * Freddy Martin Orch. (VR: Stuart Wade)

April 19, 1947
1. HEARTACHES   Ted Weems Orch. (Whistling solo: Elmore Cannon)
2. LINDA   Buddy Clark with Ray Noble Orch.
3. THE ANNIVERSARY SONG   Dinah Shore
4. HOW ARE THINGS IN GLOCCA MORRA   Buddy Clark
5. MANAGUA, NICARAGUA   Guy Lombardo Orch. (VR: Don Rodney) *
6. IT'S A GOOD DAY   Peggy Lee
7. I'LL CLOSE MY EYES   Andy Russell
8. GUILTY   Margaret Whiting
9. APRIL SHOWERS   Guy Lombardo (VR: Don Rodney)
10. ALEXANDER'S RAGTIME BAND   Bing Crosby & Al Jolson **
   Note: * Freddy Martin Orch. (VR: Stuart Wade)
   ** Original hit for Arthur Collins in 1911.

April 26, 1947
1. HEARTACHES   Ted Weems Orch. (Whistling solo: Elmore Cannon)
2. THE ANNIVERSARY SONG   Dinah Shore
3. LINDA   Buddy Clark with Ray Noble Orch.
4. M'AMSELLE   Art Lund
5. HOW ARE THINGS IN GLOCCA MORRA   Buddy Clark
6. MANAGUA, NICARAGUA   Guy Lombardo Orch. (VR: Don Rodney) *
7. IT'S A GOOD DAY   Peggy Lee
   Note: * Freddy Martin Orch. (VR: Stuart Wade)

May 3, 1947
1. LINDA   Buddy Clark with Ray Noble Orch.
2. THE ANNIVERSARY SONG   Dinah Shore
3. M'AMSELLE   Art Lund
4. MANAGUA, NICARAGUA   Guy Lombardo Orch. (VR: Don Rodney) *

5. HEARTACHES   Ted Weems Orch. (Whistling solo: Elmore Cannon)
6. HOW ARE THINGS IN GLOCCA MORRA   Buddy Clark
7. MY ADOBE HACIENDA   Eddy Howard (VR: Eddy Howard)
   Note: * Freddy Martin Orch. (VR: Stuart Wade)

May 10, 1947
1. LINDA   Buddy Clark with Ray Noble Orch.
2. HEARTACHES   Ted Weems Orch. (Whistling solo: Elmore Cannon)
3. THE ANNIVERSARY SONG   Dinah Shore
4. M'AMSELLE   Art Lund
5. MY ADOBE HACIENDA   Eddy Howard (VR: Eddy Howard)
6. APRIL SHOWERS   Guy Lombardo (VR: Don Rodney)
7. HOW ARE THINGS IN GLOCCA MORRA   Buddy Clark

May 17, 1947
1. M'AMSELLE   Art Lund
2. LINDA   Buddy Clark with Ray Noble Orch.
3. HEARTACHES   Ted Weems Orch. (Whistling solo: Elmore Cannon)
4. THE ANNIVERSARY SONG   Dinah Shore
5. MY ADOBE HACIENDA   Eddy Howard (VR: Eddy Howard)
6. HOW ARE THINGS IN GLOCCA MORRA   Buddy Clark
7. TIME AFTER TIME   Frank Sinatra

May 24, 1947
1. LINDA   Buddy Clark with Ray Noble Orch.
2. MY ADOBE HACIENDA   Eddy Howard (VR: Eddy Howard)
3. HEARTACHES   Ted Weems Orch. (Whistling solo: Elmore Cannon)
4. M'AMSELLE   Art Lund
5. APRIL SHOWERS   Guy Lombardo (VR: Don Rodney)
6. THE ANNIVERSARY SONG   Dinah Shore
7. TIME AFTER TIME   Frank Sinatra

May 31, 1947
1. M'AMSELLE   Art Lund
2. MY ADOBE HACIENDA   Eddy Howard (VR: Eddy Howard)
3. LINDA   Buddy Clark with Ray Noble Orch.
4. HEARTACHES   Ted Weems Orch. (Whistling solo: Elmore Cannon)
5. THE ANNIVERSARY SONG   Dinah Shore
6. TIME AFTER TIME   Frank Sinatra
7. PEG O' MY HEART   Harmonicats

June 7, 1947
1. M'AMSELLE   Art Lund
2. LINDA   Buddy Clark with Ray Noble Orch.
3. MY ADOBE HACIENDA   Eddy Howard (VR: Eddy Howard)
4. I WONDER, I WONDER, I WONDER   Eddy Howard Orch. (VR: Eddy Howard)
5. HEARTACHES   Ted Weems Orch. (Whistling solo: Elmore Cannon)
6. THE ANNIVERSARY SONG   Dinah Shore
7. TIME AFTER TIME   Frank Sinatra

June 14, 1947
1. LINDA   Buddy Clark with Ray Noble Orch.
2. MY ADOBE HACIENDA   Eddy Howard (VR: Eddy Howard)
3. M'AMSELLE   Art Lund
4. I WONDER, I WONDER, I WONDER   Eddy Howard Orch. (VR: Eddy Howard)
5. HEARTACHES   Ted Weems Orch. (Whistling solo: Elmore Cannon)
6. MIDNIGHT MASQUERADE   Monica Lewis

7 CHI-BABA, CHI-BABA   Perry Como

June 21, 1947
1 PEG O' MY HEART   Harmonicats
2 M'AMSELLE   Art Lund
3 LINDA   Buddy Clark with Ray Noble Orch.
4 I WONDER, I WONDER, I WONDER   Eddy Howard Orch.
   (VR: Eddy Howard)
5 CHI-BABA, CHI-BABA   Perry Como
6 MY ADOBE HACIENDA   Eddy Howard (VR: Eddy Howard)
7 HEARTACHES   Ted Weems Orch. (Whistling solo: Elmore Cannon)

June 28, 1947
1 I WONDER, I WONDER, I WONDER   Eddy Howard Orch.
   (VR: Eddy Howard)
2 PEG O' MY HEART   Harmonicats
3 M'AMSELLE   Art Lund
4 MY ADOBE HACIENDA   Eddy Howard (VR: Eddy Howard)
5 CHI-BABA, CHI-BABA   Perry Como
6 LINDA   Buddy Clark with Ray Noble Orch.
7 THAT'S MY DESIRE   Sammy Kaye Orch. (VR: Don Cornell)

July 5, 1947
1 PEG O' MY HEART   Harmonicats
2 I WONDER, I WONDER, I WONDER   Eddy Howard Orch.
   (VR: Eddy Howard)
3 M'AMSELLE   Art Lund
4 CHI-BABA, CHI-BABA   Perry Como
5 MY ADOBE HACIENDA   Eddy Howard (VR: Eddy Howard)
6 LINDA   Buddy Clark with Ray Noble Orch.
7 THAT'S MY DESIRE   Sammy Kaye Orch. (VR: Don Cornell)

July 12, 1947
1 PEG O' MY HEART   Harmonicats
2 I WONDER, I WONDER, I WONDER   Eddy Howard Orch.
   (VR: Eddy Howard)
3 CHI-BABA, CHI-BABA   Perry Como
4 THAT'S MY DESIRE   Sammy Kaye Orch. (VR: Don Cornell)
5 M'AMSELLE   Art Lund
6 ACROSS THE ALLEY FROM THE ALAMO   Mills Brothers
7 LINDA   Buddy Clark with Ray Noble Orch.

July 19, 1947
1 PEG O' MY HEART   Harmonicats
2 I WONDER, I WONDER, I WONDER   Eddy Howard Orch.
   (VR: Eddy Howard)
3 CHI-BABA, CHI-BABA   Perry Como
4 ACROSS THE ALLEY FROM THE ALAMO   Mills Brothers
5 THAT'S MY DESIRE   Sammy Kaye Orch. (VR: Don Cornell)
6 M'AMSELLE   Art Lund
7 LINDA   Buddy Clark with Ray Noble Orch.

July 26, 1947
1 PEG O' MY HEART   Harmonicats
2 I WONDER, I WONDER, I WONDER   Eddy Howard Orch.
   (VR: Eddy Howard)
3 CHI-BABA, CHI-BABA   Perry Como
4 ACROSS THE ALLEY FROM THE ALAMO   Mills Brothers
5 M'AMSELLE   Art Lund
6 THAT'S MY DESIRE   Sammy Kaye Orch. (VR: Don Cornell)
7 ALMOST LIKE BEING IN LOVE   Frank Sinatra

August 2, 1947
1 PEG O' MY HEART   Harmonicats
2 THAT'S MY DESIRE   Sammy Kaye Orch. (VR: Don Cornell)

3 I WONDER, I WONDER, I WONDER   Eddy Howard Orch.
   (VR: Eddy Howard)
4 ACROSS THE ALLEY FROM THE ALAMO   Mills Brothers
5 CHI-BABA, CHI-BABA   Perry Como
6 IVY   Jo Stafford
7 ASK ANYONE WHO KNOWS   Ink Spots

August 9, 1947
1 PEG O' MY HEART   Harmonicats
2 I WONDER, I WONDER, I WONDER   Eddy Howard Orch.
   (VR: Eddy Howard)
3 CHI-BABA, CHI-BABA   Perry Como
4 THAT'S MY DESIRE   Sammy Kaye Orch. (VR: Don Cornell)
5 ASK ANYONE WHO KNOWS   Ink Spots
6 ACROSS THE ALLEY FROM THE ALAMO   Mills Brothers
7 I WONDER WHO'S KISSING HER NOW   Perry Como

August 16, 1947
1 PEG O' MY HEART   Harmonicats
2 I WONDER, I WONDER, I WONDER   Eddy Howard Orch.
   (VR: Eddy Howard)
3 THAT'S MY DESIRE   Sammy Kaye Orch. (VR: Don Cornell)
4 ASK ANYONE WHO KNOWS   Ink Spots
5 CHI-BABA, CHI-BABA   Perry Como
6 ACROSS THE ALLEY FROM THE ALAMO   Mills Brothers
7 I WONDER WHO'S KISSING HER NOW   Perry Como

August 23, 1947
1 THAT'S MY DESIRE   Sammy Kaye Orch. (VR: Don Cornell)
2 PEG O' MY HEART   Harmonicats
3 I WONDER, I WONDER, I WONDER   Eddy Howard Orch.
   (VR: Eddy Howard)
4 CHI-BABA, CHI-BABA   Perry Como
5 ASK ANYONE WHO KNOWS   Ink Spots
6 TALLAHASSEE   Bing Crosby & Andrews Sisters
7 I WONDER WHO'S KISSING HER NOW   Perry Como

August 30, 1947
1 PEG O' MY HEART   Harmonicats
2 THAT'S MY DESIRE   Sammy Kaye Orch. (VR: Don Cornell)
3 I WONDER WHO'S KISSING HER NOW   Perry Como
4 ASK ANYONE WHO KNOWS   Ink Spots
5 TALLAHASSEE   Bing Crosby & Andrews Sisters
6 I WONDER, I WONDER, I WONDER   Eddy Howard Orch.
   (VR: Eddy Howard)
7 ALMOST LIKE BEING IN LOVE   Frank Sinatra

September 6, 1947
1 I WONDER WHO'S KISSING HER NOW   Perry Como
2 PEG O' MY HEART   Harmonicats
3 ASK ANYONE WHO KNOWS   Ink Spots
4 FEUDIN' AND FIGHTIN'   Dorothy Shay
5 THAT'S MY DESIRE   Sammy Kaye Orch. (VR: Don Cornell)
6 I WONDER, I WONDER, I WONDER   Eddy Howard Orch.
   (VR: Eddy Howard)
7 APPLE BLOSSOM WEDDING   Sammy Kaye Orch. (VR: Don Cornell)

September 13, 1947
1 THAT'S MY DESIRE   Sammy Kaye Orch. (VR: Don Cornell)
2 PEG O' MY HEART   Harmonicats
3 I WONDER WHO'S KISSING HER NOW   Perry Como
4 I WISH I DIDN'T LOVE YOU SO   Vaughn Monroe Orch.
   (VR: Vaughn Monroe)
5 FEUDIN' AND FIGHTIN'   Dorothy Shay
6 WHEN YOU WERE SWEET SIXTEEN   Perry Como

7 ASK ANYONE WHO KNOWS   Ink Spots

September 20, 1947
1 PEG O' MY HEART   Harmonicats
2 THAT'S MY DESIRE   Sammy Kaye Orch. (VR: Don Cornell)
3 I WONDER WHO'S KISSING HER NOW   Perry Como
4 FEUDIN' AND FIGHTIN'   Dorothy Shay
5 ASK ANYONE WHO KNOWS   Ink Spots
6 I WISH I DIDN'T LOVE YOU SO   Vaughn Monroe Orch. (VR: Vaughn Monroe)
7 ALMOST LIKE BEING IN LOVE   Frank Sinatra

September 27, 1947
1 FEUDIN' AND FIGHTIN'   Dorothy Shay
2 I WISH I DIDN'T LOVE YOU SO   Vaughn Monroe Orch. (VR: Vaughn Monroe)
3 I WONDER WHO'S KISSING HER NOW   Perry Como
4 PEG O' MY HEART   Harmonicats
5 THAT'S MY DESIRE   Sammy Kaye Orch. (VR: Don Cornell)
6 ASK ANYONE WHO KNOWS   Ink Spots
7 APPLE BLOSSOM WEDDING   Sammy Kaye Orch. (VR: Don Cornell)

October 4, 1947
1 I WISH I DIDN'T LOVE YOU SO   Vaughn Monroe Orch. (VR: Vaughn Monroe)
2 NEAR YOU   Francis Craig Orch. (VR: Bob Lamm)
3 FEUDIN' AND FIGHTIN'   Dorothy Shay
4 I WONDER WHO'S KISSING HER NOW   Perry Como
5 THAT'S MY DESIRE   Sammy Kaye Orch. (VR: Don Cornell)
6 THE LADY FROM 29 PALMS   Freddy Martin Orch. (VR: The Martin Men)
7 PEG O' MY HEART   Harmonicats

October 11, 1947
1 I WISH I DIDN'T LOVE YOU SO   Vaughn Monroe Orch. (VR: Vaughn Monroe)
2 FEUDIN' AND FIGHTIN'   Dorothy Shay
3 NEAR YOU   Francis Craig Orch. (VR: Bob Lamm)
4 PEG O' MY HEART   Harmonicats
5 YOU DO   Dinah Shore
6 ALMOST LIKE BEING IN LOVE   Frank Sinatra
7 I WONDER WHO'S KISSING HER NOW   Perry Como

October 18, 1947
1 NEAR YOU   Francis Craig Orch. (VR: Bob Lamm)
2 I WISH I DIDN'T LOVE YOU SO   Vaughn Monroe Orch. (VR: Vaughn Monroe)
3 FEUDIN' AND FIGHTIN'   Dorothy Shay
4 YOU DO   Dinah Shore
5 I WONDER WHO'S KISSING HER NOW   Perry Como
6 THE LADY FROM 29 PALMS   Freddy Martin Orch. (VR: The Martin Men)
7 PEG O' MY HEART   Harmonicats

October 25, 1947
1 NEAR YOU   Francis Craig Orch. (VR: Bob Lamm)
2 I WISH I DIDN'T LOVE YOU SO   Vaughn Monroe Orch. (VR: Vaughn Monroe)
3 I WONDER WHO'S KISSING HER NOW   Perry Como
4 YOU DO   Dinah Shore
5 FEUDIN' AND FIGHTIN'   Dorothy Shay
6 THE LADY FROM 29 PALMS   Freddy Martin Orch. (VR: The Martin Men)
7 PEG O' MY HEART   Harmonicats

November 1, 1947
1 NEAR YOU   Francis Craig Orch. (VR: Bob Lamm)
2 FEUDIN' AND FIGHTIN'   Dorothy Shay
3 I WISH I DIDN'T LOVE YOU SO   Vaughn Monroe Orch. (VR: Vaughn Monroe)
4 YOU DO   Dinah Shore
5 I WONDER WHO'S KISSING HER NOW   Perry Como
6 THE LADY FROM 29 PALMS   Freddy Martin Orch. (VR: The Martin Men)
7 WHEN YOU WERE SWEET SIXTEEN   Perry Como

November 8, 1947
1 NEAR YOU   Francis Craig Orch. (VR: Bob Lamm)
2 YOU DO   Dinah Shore
3 FEUDIN' AND FIGHTIN'   Dorothy Shay
4 I WISH I DIDN'T LOVE YOU SO   Vaughn Monroe Orch. (VR: Vaughn Monroe)
5 THE LADY FROM 29 PALMS   Freddy Martin Orch. (VR: The Martin Men)
6 AND MIMI   Art Lund *
7 APPLE BLOSSOM WEDDING   Sammy Kaye Orch. (VR: Don Cornell)
Note: * Another version by: Dick Haymes.

November 15, 1947
1 I WISH I DIDN'T LOVE YOU SO   Vaughn Monroe Orch. (VR: Vaughn Monroe)
2 NEAR YOU   Francis Craig Orch. (VR: Bob Lamm)
3 YOU DO   Dinah Shore
4 FEUDIN' AND FIGHTIN'   Dorothy Shay
5 AND MIMI   Art Lund *
6 APPLE BLOSSOM WEDDING   Sammy Kaye Orch. (VR: Don Cornell)
7 CIVILIZATION   Louis Prima Orch. (VR: Group)
Note: * Another version by: Dick Haymes.

November 22, 1947
1 YOU DO   Dinah Shore
2 I WISH I DIDN'T LOVE YOU SO   Vaughn Monroe Orch. (VR: Vaughn Monroe)
3 NEAR YOU   Francis Craig Orch. (VR: Bob Lamm)
4 FEUDIN' AND FIGHTIN'   Dorothy Shay
5 AND MIMI   Art Lund *
6 THE WHIFFINPOOF SONG   Bing Crosby
7 CIVILIZATION   Louis Prima Orch. (VR: Group)
Note: * Another version by: Dick Haymes.

November 29, 1947
1 NEAR YOU   Francis Craig Orch. (VR: Bob Lamm)
2 YOU DO   Dinah Shore
3 I WISH I DIDN'T LOVE YOU SO   Vaughn Monroe Orch. (VR: Vaughn Monroe)
4 AND MIMI   Art Lund *
5 HOW SOON   Jack Owens
6 CIVILIZATION   Louis Prima Orch. (VR: Group)
7 SO FAR   Perry Como
Note: * Another version by: Dick Haymes.

December 6, 1947
1 NEAR YOU   Francis Craig Orch. (VR: Bob Lamm)
2 YOU DO   Dinah Shore
3 AND MIMI   Art Lund *
4 CIVILIZATION   Louis Prima Orch. (VR: Group)
5 I WISH I DIDN'T LOVE YOU SO   Vaughn Monroe Orch. (VR: Vaughn Monroe)
6 HOW SOON   Jack Owens

7 BALLERINA   Vaughn Monroe Orch. (VR: Vaughn Monroe)
   Note: * Another version by: Dick Haymes.

December 13, 1947
1 CIVILIZATION   Louis Prima Orch. (VR: Group)
2 HOW SOON   Jack Owens
3 YOU DO   Dinah Shore
4 AND MIMI   Art Lund *
5 NEAR YOU   Francis Craig Orch. (VR: Bob Lamm)
6 BALLERINA   Vaughn Monroe Orch. (VR: Vaughn Monroe)
7 I WISH I DIDN'T LOVE YOU SO   Vaughn Monroe Orch.
   (VR: Vaughn Monroe)
   Note: * Another version by: Dick Haymes.

December 20, 1947
1 HOW SOON   Jack Owens
2 CIVILIZATION   Louis Prima Orch. (VR: Group)
3 AND MIMI   Art Lund *
4 BALLERINA   Vaughn Monroe Orch. (VR: Vaughn Monroe)
5 YOU DO   Dinah Shore
6 SERENADE OF THE BELLS   Sammy Kaye Orch. (VR: Don
   Cornell)
7 NEAR YOU   Francis Craig Orch. (VR: Bob Lamm)
   Note: * Another version by: Dick Haymes.

December 27, 1947
1 BALLERINA   Vaughn Monroe Orch. (VR: Vaughn Monroe)
2 HOW SOON   Jack Owens
3 NEAR YOU   Francis Craig Orch. (VR: Bob Lamm)
4 YOU DO   Dinah Shore
5 AND MIMI   Art Lund *
6 SERENADE OF THE BELLS   Sammy Kaye Orch. (VR: Don
   Cornell)
7 WHITE CHRISTMAS   Bing Crosby
   Note: * Another version by: Dick Haymes.

January 3, 1948
1 BALLERINA   Vaughn Monroe Orch. (VR: Vaughn Monroe)
2 HOW SOON   Jack Owens
3 NEAR YOU   Francis Craig Orch. (VR: Bob Lamm)
4 SERENADE OF THE BELLS   Sammy Kaye Orch. (VR: Don
   Cornell)
5 CIVILIZATION   Louis Prima Orch. (VR: Group)
6 WHITE CHRISTMAS   Bing Crosby
7 AND MIMI   Art Lund *
   Note: * Another version by: Dick Haymes.

January 10, 1948
1 BALLERINA   Vaughn Monroe Orch. (VR: Vaughn Monroe)
2 HOW SOON   Jack Owens
3 SERENADE OF THE BELLS   Sammy Kaye Orch. (VR: Don
   Cornell)
4 CIVILIZATION   Louis Prima Orch. (VR: Group)
5 NEAR YOU   Francis Craig Orch. (VR: Bob Lamm)
6 GOLDEN EARRINGS   Peggy Lee
7 I'LL DANCE AT YOUR WEDDING   Buddy Clark with Ray
   Noble Orch.

January 17, 1948
1 HOW SOON   Jack Owens
2 BALLERINA   Vaughn Monroe Orch. (VR: Vaughn Monroe)
3 SERENADE OF THE BELLS   Sammy Kaye Orch. (VR: Don
   Cornell)
4 I'LL DANCE AT YOUR WEDDING   Buddy Clark with Ray
   Noble Orch.
5 GOLDEN EARRINGS   Peggy Lee

6 CIVILIZATION   Louis Prima Orch. (VR: Group)
7 SO FAR   Perry Como

January 24, 1948
1 HOW SOON   Jack Owens
2 BALLERINA   Vaughn Monroe Orch. (VR: Vaughn Monroe)
3 SERENADE OF THE BELLS   Sammy Kaye Orch. (VR: Don
   Cornell)
4 I'LL DANCE AT YOUR WEDDING   Buddy Clark with Ray
   Noble Orch.
5 GOLDEN EARRINGS   Peggy Lee
6 CIVILIZATION   Louis Prima Orch. (VR: Group)
7 TOO FAT POLKA   Arthur Godfrey

January 31, 1948
1 GOLDEN EARRINGS   Peggy Lee
2 SERENADE OF THE BELLS   Sammy Kaye Orch. (VR: Don
   Cornell)
3 BALLERINA   Vaughn Monroe Orch. (VR: Vaughn Monroe)
4 HOW SOON   Jack Owens
5 I'LL DANCE AT YOUR WEDDING   Buddy Clark with Ray
   Noble Orch.
6 CIVILIZATION   Louis Prima Orch. (VR: Group)
7 I'M LOOKING OVER A FOUR LEAF CLOVER   Art Mooney
   Orch. (VR: Ensemble)

February 7, 1948
1 BALLERINA   Vaughn Monroe Orch. (VR: Vaughn Monroe)
2 HOW SOON   Jack Owens
3 GOLDEN EARRINGS   Peggy Lee
4 I'LL DANCE AT YOUR WEDDING   Buddy Clark with Ray
   Noble Orch.
5 NOW IS THE HOUR   Bing Crosby
6 I'M LOOKING OVER A FOUR LEAF CLOVER   Art Mooney
   Orch. (VR: Ensemble)
7 SERENADE OF THE BELLS   Sammy Kaye Orch. (VR: Don
   Cornell)

February 14, 1948
1 BALLERINA   Vaughn Monroe Orch. (VR: Vaughn Monroe)
2 I'LL DANCE AT YOUR WEDDING   Buddy Clark with Ray
   Noble Orch.
3 SERENADE OF THE BELLS   Sammy Kaye Orch. (VR: Don
   Cornell)
4 NOW IS THE HOUR   Bing Crosby
5 I'M LOOKING OVER A FOUR LEAF CLOVER   Art Mooney
   Orch. (VR: Ensemble)
6 BUT BEAUTIFUL   Frank Sinatra
7 HOW SOON   Jack Owens

February 21, 1948
1 I'M LOOKING OVER A FOUR LEAF CLOVER   Art Mooney
   Orch. (VR: Ensemble)
2 BALLERINA   Vaughn Monroe Orch. (VR: Vaughn Monroe)
3 NOW IS THE HOUR   Bing Crosby
4 GOLDEN EARRINGS   Peggy Lee
5 SERENADE OF THE BELLS   Sammy Kaye Orch. (VR: Don
   Cornell)
6 I'LL DANCE AT YOUR WEDDING   Buddy Clark with Ray
   Noble Orch.
7 THE BEST THINGS IN LIFE ARE FREE   Dinah Shore

February 28, 1948
1 NOW IS THE HOUR   Bing Crosby
2 I'M LOOKING OVER A FOUR LEAF CLOVER   Art Mooney
   Orch. (VR: Ensemble)

3 BALLERINA   Vaughn Monroe Orch. (VR: Vaughn Monroe)
4 SERENADE OF THE BELLS   Sammy Kaye Orch. (VR: Don Cornell)
5 BEG YOUR PARDON   Francis Craig
6 I'LL DANCE AT YOUR WEDDING   Buddy Clark with Ray Noble Orch.
7 GOLDEN EARRINGS   Peggy Lee

March 6, 1948
1 NOW IS THE HOUR   Bing Crosby
2 I'M LOOKING OVER A FOUR LEAF CLOVER   Art Mooney Orch. (VR: Ensemble)
3 BEG YOUR PARDON   Francis Craig
4 BALLERINA   Vaughn Monroe Orch. (VR: Vaughn Monroe)
5 GOLDEN EARRINGS   Peggy Lee
6 SERENADE OF THE BELLS   Sammy Kaye Orch. (VR: Don Cornell)
7 MANANA   Peggy Lee

March 13, 1948
1 NOW IS THE HOUR   Bing Crosby
2 I'M LOOKING OVER A FOUR LEAF CLOVER   Art Mooney Orch. (VR: Ensemble)
3 BEG YOUR PARDON   Francis Craig
4 MANANA   Peggy Lee
5 SERENADE OF THE BELLS   Sammy Kaye Orch. (VR: Don Cornell)
6 GOLDEN EARRINGS   Peggy Lee
7 BALLERINA   Vaughn Monroe Orch. (VR: Vaughn Monroe)

March 20, 1948
1 I'M LOOKING OVER A FOUR LEAF CLOVER   Art Mooney Orch. (VR: Ensemble)
2 NOW IS THE HOUR   Bing Crosby
3 MANANA   Peggy Lee
4 SERENADE OF THE BELLS   Sammy Kaye Orch. (VR: Don Cornell)
5 BUT BEAUTIFUL   Frank Sinatra
6 BALLERINA   Vaughn Monroe Orch. (VR: Vaughn Monroe)
7 BEG YOUR PARDON   Francis Craig

March 27, 1948
1 NOW IS THE HOUR   Bing Crosby
2 I'M LOOKING OVER A FOUR LEAF CLOVER   Art Mooney Orch. (VR: Ensemble)
3 BEG YOUR PARDON   Francis Craig
4 MANANA   Peggy Lee
5 BUT BEAUTIFUL   Frank Sinatra
6 SERENADE OF THE BELLS   Sammy Kaye Orch. (VR: Don Cornell)
7 BALLERINA   Vaughn Monroe Orch. (VR: Vaughn Monroe)
*Note: * Another version by: Dick Haymes.*

April 3, 1948
1 NOW IS THE HOUR   Bing Crosby
2 MANANA   Peggy Lee
3 I'M LOOKING OVER A FOUR LEAF CLOVER   Art Mooney Orch. (VR: Ensemble)
4 BEG YOUR PARDON   Francis Craig
5 BUT BEAUTIFUL   Frank Sinatra
6 SERENADE OF THE BELLS   Sammy Kaye Orch. (VR: Don Cornell)
7 EASTER PARADE   Guy Lombardo

April 10, 1948
1 MANANA   Peggy Lee

2 NOW IS THE HOUR   Bing Crosby
3 I'M LOOKING OVER A FOUR LEAF CLOVER   Art Mooney Orch. (VR: Ensemble)
4 BUT BEAUTIFUL   Frank Sinatra
5 BEG YOUR PARDON   Francis Craig
6 SABRE DANCE   Woody Herman Orch.
7 HAUNTED HEART   Perry Como

April 17, 1948
1 NOW IS THE HOUR   Bing Crosby
2 I'M LOOKING OVER A FOUR LEAF CLOVER   Art Mooney Orch. (VR: Ensemble)
3 BEG YOUR PARDON   Francis Craig
4 BUT BEAUTIFUL   Frank Sinatra
5 MANANA   Peggy Lee
6 BABY FACE   Art Mooney Orch. (VR: Ensemble)
7 DICKEY BIRD SONG   Freddy Martin Orch. (VR: Glenn Hughes)

April 24, 1948
1 NOW IS THE HOUR   Bing Crosby
2 MANANA   Peggy Lee
3 BUT BEAUTIFUL   Frank Sinatra
4 BABY FACE   Art Mooney Orch. (VR: Ensemble)
5 I'M LOOKING OVER A FOUR LEAF CLOVER   Art Mooney Orch. (VR: Ensemble)
6 BEG YOUR PARDON   Francis Craig
7 DICKEY BIRD SONG   Freddy Martin Orch. (VR: Glenn Hughes)

May 1, 1948
1 NOW IS THE HOUR   Bing Crosby
2 DICKEY BIRD SONG   Freddy Martin Orch. (VR: Glenn Hughes)
3 BEG YOUR PARDON   Francis Craig
4 I'M LOOKING OVER A FOUR LEAF CLOVER   Art Mooney Orch. (VR: Ensemble)
5 MANANA   Peggy Lee
6 BUT BEAUTIFUL   Frank Sinatra
7 LAROO, LAROO, LILLI BOLERO   Peggy Lee

May 8, 1948
1 NOW IS THE HOUR   Bing Crosby
2 MANANA   Peggy Lee
3 DICKEY BIRD SONG   Freddy Martin Orch. (VR: Glenn Hughes)
4 BABY FACE   Art Mooney Orch. (VR: Ensemble)
5 BUT BEAUTIFUL   Frank Sinatra
6 LAROO, LAROO, LILLI BOLERO   Peggy Lee
7 BEG YOUR PARDON   Francis Craig

May 15, 1948
1 NOW IS THE HOUR   Bing Crosby
2 BABY FACE   Art Mooney Orch. (VR: Ensemble)
3 DICKEY BIRD SONG   Freddy Martin Orch. (VR: Glenn Hughes)
4 TOOLIE OOLIE DOOLIE   Andrews Sisters
5 LAROO, LAROO, LILLI BOLERO   Peggy Lee
6 SABRE DANCE   Woody Herman Orch.
7 HAUNTED HEART   Perry Como

May 22, 1948
1 NATURE BOY   Nat King Cole
2 NOW IS THE HOUR   Bing Crosby
3 DICKEY BIRD SONG   Freddy Martin Orch. (VR: Glenn Hughes)

4   BABY FACE   Art Mooney Orch. (VR: Ensemble)
5   TOOLIE OOLIE DOOLIE   Andrews Sisters
6   LAROO, LAROO, LILLI BOLERO   Peggy Lee
7   HAUNTED HEART   Perry Como

May 29, 1948
1   NATURE BOY   Nat King Cole
2   NOW IS THE HOUR   Bing Crosby
3   BABY FACE   Art Mooney Orch. (VR: Ensemble)
4   TOOLIE OOLIE DOOLIE   Andrews Sisters
5   YOU CAN'T BE TRUE, DEAR   Ken Griffin Orch. (VR: Jerry Wayne)
6   HAUNTED HEART   Perry Como
7   LAROO, LAROO, LILLI BOLERO   Peggy Lee

June 5, 1948
1   NATURE BOY   Nat King Cole
2   YOU CAN'T BE TRUE, DEAR   Ken Griffin Orch. (VR: Jerry Wayne)
3   NOW IS THE HOUR   Bing Crosby
4   BABY FACE   Art Mooney Orch. (VR: Ensemble)
5   HAUNTED HEART   Perry Como
6   SABRE DANCE   Woody Herman Orch.
7   LAROO, LAROO, LILLI BOLERO   Peggy Lee

June 12, 1948
1   NATURE BOY   Nat King Cole
2   TOOLIE OOLIE DOOLIE   Andrews Sisters
3   BABY FACE   Art Mooney Orch. (VR: Ensemble)
4   YOU CAN'T BE TRUE, DEAR   Ken Griffin Orch. (VR: Jerry Wayne)
5   SABRE DANCE   Woody Herman Orch.
6   DICKEY BIRD SONG   Freddy Martin Orch. (VR: Glenn Hughes)
7   HAUNTED HEART   Perry Como

June 19, 1948
1   NATURE BOY   Nat King Cole
2   YOU CAN'T BE TRUE, DEAR   Ken Griffin Orch. (VR: Jerry Wayne)
3   BABY FACE   Art Mooney Orch. (VR: Ensemble)
4   TOOLIE OOLIE DOOLIE   Andrews Sisters
5   DICKEY BIRD SONG   Freddy Martin Orch. (VR: Glenn Hughes)
6   LITTLE WHITE LIES   Dick Haymes
7   HAUNTED HEART   Perry Como

June 26, 1948
1   NATURE BOY   Nat King Cole
2   TOOLIE OOLIE DOOLIE   Andrews Sisters
3   WOODY WOODPECKER SONG   Kay Kyser Orch. (VR: Gloria Wood & Campus Kids)
4   YOU CAN'T BE TRUE, DEAR   Ken Griffin Orch. (VR: Jerry Wayne)
5   MY HAPPINESS   Jon & Sandra Steele
6   LITTLE WHITE LIES   Dick Haymes
7   HAUNTED HEART   Perry Como

July 3, 1948
1   YOU CAN'T BE TRUE, DEAR   Ken Griffin Orch. (VR: Jerry Wayne)
2   NATURE BOY   Nat King Cole
3   WOODY WOODPECKER SONG   Kay Kyser Orch. (VR: Gloria Wood & Campus Kids)
4   HAUNTED HEART   Perry Como
5   LITTLE WHITE LIES   Dick Haymes

6   MY HAPPINESS   Jon & Sandra Steele
7   NOW IS THE HOUR   Bing Crosby

July 10, 1948
1   WOODY WOODPECKER SONG   Kay Kyser Orch. (VR: Gloria Wood & Campus Kids)
2   YOU CAN'T BE TRUE, DEAR   Ken Griffin Orch. (VR: Jerry Wayne)
3   MY HAPPINESS   Jon & Sandra Steele
4   LITTLE WHITE LIES   Dick Haymes
5   HAUNTED HEART   Perry Como
6   NATURE BOY   Nat King Cole
7   TOOLIE OOLIE DOOLIE   Andrews Sisters

July 17, 1948
1   YOU CAN'T BE TRUE, DEAR   Ken Griffin Orch. (VR: Jerry Wayne)
2   WOODY WOODPECKER SONG   Kay Kyser Orch. (VR: Gloria Wood & Campus Kids)
3   NATURE BOY   Nat King Cole
4   LITTLE WHITE LIES   Dick Haymes
5   TOOLIE OOLIE DOOLIE   Andrews Sisters
6   MY HAPPINESS   Jon & Sandra Steele
7   HAUNTED HEART   Perry Como

July 24, 1948
1   WOODY WOODPECKER SONG   Kay Kyser Orch. (VR: Gloria Wood & Campus Kids)
2   YOU CAN'T BE TRUE, DEAR   Ken Griffin Orch. (VR: Jerry Wayne)
3   MY HAPPINESS   Jon & Sandra Steele
4   IT'S MAGIC   Doris Day
5   TOOLIE OOLIE DOOLIE   Andrews Sisters
6   A TREE IN THE MEADOW   Margaret Whiting
7   NATURE BOY   Nat King Cole

July 31, 1948
1   YOU CAN'T BE TRUE, DEAR   Ken Griffin Orch. (VR: Jerry Wayne)
2   WOODY WOODPECKER SONG   Kay Kyser Orch. (VR: Gloria Wood & Campus Kids)
3   IT'S MAGIC   Doris Day
4   A TREE IN THE MEADOW   Margaret Whiting
5   MY HAPPINESS   Jon & Sandra Steele
6   LITTLE WHITE LIES   Dick Haymes
7   LOVE SOMEBODY   Doris Day & Buddy Clark

August 7, 1948
1   IT'S MAGIC   Doris Day
2   WOODY WOODPECKER SONG   Kay Kyser Orch. (VR: Gloria Wood & Campus Kids)
3   A TREE IN THE MEADOW   Margaret Whiting
4   MY HAPPINESS   Jon & Sandra Steele
5   LITTLE WHITE LIES   Dick Haymes
6   YOU CAN'T BE TRUE, DEAR   Ken Griffin Orch. (VR: Jerry Wayne)
7   YOU CALL EVERYBODY DARLIN'   Al Trace (VR: Bob Vincent)

August 14, 1948
1   IT'S MAGIC   Doris Day
2   A TREE IN THE MEADOW   Margaret Whiting
3   YOU CAN'T BE TRUE, DEAR   Ken Griffin Orch. (VR: Jerry Wayne)
4   MY HAPPINESS   Jon & Sandra Steele
5   LOVE SOMEBODY   Doris Day & Buddy Clark

Margaret Whiting

The daughter of Richard Whiting (``On The Good Ship Lollipop'')
scores her first solo #1 hit, ``A Tree In The Meadow.''

6 YOU CALL EVERYBODY DARLIN'   Al Trace (VR: Bob
   Vincent)
7 WOODY WOODPECKER SONG   Kay Kyser Orch. (VR:
   Gloria Wood & Campus Kids)

August 21, 1948
1 A TREE IN THE MEADOW   Margaret Whiting
2 MY HAPPINESS   Jon & Sandra Steele
3 IT'S MAGIC   Doris Day
4 YOU CALL EVERYBODY DARLIN'   Al Trace (VR: Bob
   Vincent)
5 LOVE SOMEBODY   Doris Day & Buddy Clark
6 YOU CAN'T BE TRUE, DEAR   Ken Griffin Orch. (VR: Jerry
   Wayne)
7 WOODY WOODPECKER SONG   Kay Kyser Orch. (VR:
   Gloria Wood & Campus Kids)

August 28, 1948
1 A TREE IN THE MEADOW   Margaret Whiting
2 YOU CALL EVERYBODY DARLIN'   Al Trace (VR: Bob
   Vincent)
3 IT'S MAGIC   Doris Day
4 MY HAPPINESS   Jon & Sandra Steele
5 LOVE SOMEBODY   Doris Day & Buddy Clark
6 MAYBE YOU'LL BE THERE   Gordon Jenkins Orch.
7 YOU CAN'T BE TRUE, DEAR   Ken Griffin Orch. (VR: Jerry
   Wayne)

September 4, 1948
1 A TREE IN THE MEADOW   Margaret Whiting
2 IT'S MAGIC   Doris Day
3 YOU CALL EVERYBODY DARLIN'   Al Trace (VR: Bob
   Vincent)
4 MY HAPPINESS   Jon & Sandra Steele
5 LOVE SOMEBODY   Doris Day & Buddy Clark
6 MAYBE YOU'LL BE THERE   Gordon Jenkins Orch.

7 YOU CAN'T BE TRUE, DEAR   Ken Griffin Orch. (VR: Jerry
   Wayne)

September 11, 1948
1 A TREE IN THE MEADOW   Margaret Whiting
2 IT'S MAGIC   Doris Day
3 YOU CALL EVERYBODY DARLIN'   Al Trace (VR: Bob
   Vincent)
4 MY HAPPINESS   Jon & Sandra Steele
5 LOVE SOMEBODY   Doris Day & Buddy Clark
6 IT ONLY HAPPENS WHEN I DANCE WITH YOU   Frank
   Sinatra
7 HAIR OF GOLD, EYES OF BLUE   Gordon MacRae

September 18, 1948
1 A TREE IN THE MEADOW   Margaret Whiting
2 IT'S MAGIC   Doris Day
3 YOU CALL EVERYBODY DARLIN'   Al Trace (VR: Bob
   Vincent)
4 BLUEBIRD OF HAPPINESS   Art Mooney Orch. (VR: Bud
   Brees & Galli Sister)
5 HAIR OF GOLD, EYES OF BLUE   Gordon MacRae
6 LOVE SOMEBODY   Doris Day & Buddy Clark
7 MY HAPPINESS   Jon & Sandra Steele

September 25, 1948
1 A TREE IN THE MEADOW   Margaret Whiting
2 IT'S MAGIC   Doris Day
3 YOU CALL EVERYBODY DARLIN'   Al Trace (VR: Bob
   Vincent)
4 MAYBE YOU'LL BE THERE   Gordon Jenkins Orch.
5 HAIR OF GOLD, EYES OF BLUE   Gordon MacRae
6 LOVE SOMEBODY   Doris Day & Buddy Clark
7 MY HAPPINESS   Jon & Sandra Steele

October 2, 1948
1 A TREE IN THE MEADOW   Margaret Whiting
2 YOU CALL EVERYBODY DARLIN'   Al Trace (VR: Bob
   Vincent)
3 IT'S MAGIC   Doris Day
4 HAIR OF GOLD, EYES OF BLUE   Gordon MacRae
5 MAYBE YOU'LL BE THERE   Gordon Jenkins Orch.
6 LOVE SOMEBODY   Doris Day & Buddy Clark
7 MY HAPPINESS   Jon & Sandra Steele

October 9, 1948
1 A TREE IN THE MEADOW   Margaret Whiting
2 YOU CALL EVERYBODY DARLIN'   Al Trace (VR: Bob
   Vincent)
3 IT'S MAGIC   Doris Day
4 MY HAPPINESS   Jon & Sandra Steele
5 MAYBE YOU'LL BE THERE   Gordon Jenkins Orch.
6 UNDERNEATH THE ARCHES   Andrews Sisters
7 HAIR OF GOLD, EYES OF BLUE   Gordon MacRae

October 16, 1948
1 A TREE IN THE MEADOW   Margaret Whiting
2 YOU CALL EVERYBODY DARLIN'   Al Trace (VR: Bob
   Vincent)
3 HAIR OF GOLD, EYES OF BLUE   Gordon MacRae
4 IT'S MAGIC   Doris Day
5 BLUEBIRD OF HAPPINESS   Art Mooney Orch. (VR: Bud
   Brees & Galli Sister)
6 MY HAPPINESS   Jon & Sandra Steele
7 LOVE SOMEBODY   Doris Day & Buddy Clark

October 23, 1948
1 YOU CALL EVERYBODY DARLIN'   Al Trace (VR: Bob Vincent)
2 A TREE IN THE MEADOW   Margaret Whiting
3 IT'S MAGIC   Doris Day
4 HAIR OF GOLD, EYES OF BLUE   Gordon MacRae
5 MAYBE YOU'LL BE THERE   Gordon Jenkins Orch.
6 BUTTONS AND BOWS   Dinah Shore *
7 EVERY DAY I LOVE YOU   Vaughn Monroe Orch. (VR: Vaughn Monroe)
   Note: * From the movie "Paleface."

October 30, 1948
1 A TREE IN THE MEADOW   Margaret Whiting
2 BUTTONS AND BOWS   Dinah Shore *
3 HAIR OF GOLD, EYES OF BLUE   Gordon MacRae
4 MAYBE YOU'LL BE THERE   Gordon Jenkins Orch.
5 YOU CALL EVERYBODY DARLIN'   Al Trace (VR: Bob Vincent)
6 UNDERNEATH THE ARCHES   Andrews Sisters
7 IT'S MAGIC   Doris Day
   Note: * From the movie "Paleface."

November 6, 1948
1 BUTTONS AND BOWS   Dinah Shore *
2 HAIR OF GOLD, EYES OF BLUE   Gordon MacRae
3 A TREE IN THE MEADOW   Margaret Whiting
4 IT'S MAGIC   Doris Day
5 MAYBE YOU'LL BE THERE   Gordon Jenkins Orch.
6 YOU WERE ONLY FOOLING   Kay Starr
7 TWELFTH STREET RAG   Pee Wee Hunt
   Note: * From the movie "Paleface."

November 13, 1948
1 BUTTONS AND BOWS   Dinah Shore *
2 ON A SLOW BOAT TO CHINA   Kay Kyser Orch. (VR: Harry Babbitt & Gloria Wood)
3 YOU CALL EVERYBODY DARLIN'   Al Trace (VR: Bob Vincent)
4 A TREE IN THE MEADOW   Margaret Whiting
5 YOU WERE ONLY FOOLING   Kay Starr
6 MAYBE YOU'LL BE THERE   Gordon Jenkins Orch.
7 HAIR OF GOLD, EYES OF BLUE   Gordon MacRae
   Note: * From the movie "Paleface."

November 20, 1948
1 BUTTONS AND BOWS   Dinah Shore *
2 ON A SLOW BOAT TO CHINA   Kay Kyser Orch. (VR: Harry Babbitt & Gloria Wood)
3 A TREE IN THE MEADOW   Margaret Whiting
4 YOU WERE ONLY FOOLING   Kay Starr
5 MAYBE YOU'LL BE THERE   Gordon Jenkins Orch.
6 YOU CALL EVERYBODY DARLIN'   Al Trace (VR: Bob Vincent)
7 HAIR OF GOLD, EYES OF BLUE   Gordon MacRae
8 UNDERNEATH THE ARCHES   Andrews Sisters
9 UNTIL   Tommy Dorsey Orch. (VR: Harry Prime)
10 EVERY DAY I LOVE YOU   Vaughn Monroe Orch. (VR: Vaughn Monroe)
   Note: * From the movie "Paleface."

November 27, 1948
1 BUTTONS AND BOWS   Dinah Shore *
2 ON A SLOW BOAT TO CHINA   Kay Kyser Orch. (VR: Harry Babbitt & Gloria Wood)
3 YOU WERE ONLY FOOLING   Kay Starr

4 UNTIL   Tommy Dorsey Orch. (VR: Harry Prime)
5 A TREE IN THE MEADOW   Margaret Whiting
6 HAIR OF GOLD, EYES OF BLUE   Gordon MacRae
7 MY DARLING, MY DARLING   Jo Stafford & Gordon MacRae
8 MAYBE YOU'LL BE THERE   Gordon Jenkins Orch.
9 YOU CALL EVERYBODY DARLIN'   Al Trace (VR: Bob Vincent)
10 CUANTA LA GUSTA   Andrews Sisters & Carmen Miranda
   Note: * From the movie "Paleface."

December 4, 1948
1 BUTTONS AND BOWS   Dinah Shore *
2 ON A SLOW BOAT TO CHINA   Kay Kyser Orch. (VR: Harry Babbitt & Gloria Wood)
3 MY DARLING, MY DARLING   Jo Stafford & Gordon MacRae
4 YOU WERE ONLY FOOLING   Kay Starr
5 UNTIL   Tommy Dorsey Orch. (VR: Harry Prime)
6 A TREE IN THE MEADOW   Margaret Whiting
7 MAYBE YOU'LL BE THERE   Gordon Jenkins Orch.
8 CUANTA LA GUSTA   Andrews Sisters & Carmen Miranda
9 HAIR OF GOLD, EYES OF BLUE   Gordon MacRae
10 MY HAPPINESS   Jon & Sandra Steele
   Note: * From the movie "Paleface."

December 11, 1948
1 BUTTONS AND BOWS   Dinah Shore *
2 ON A SLOW BOAT TO CHINA   Kay Kyser Orch. (VR: Harry Babbitt & Gloria Wood)
3 MY DARLING, MY DARLING   Jo Stafford & Gordon MacRae
4 YOU WERE ONLY FOOLING   Kay Starr
5 UNTIL   Tommy Dorsey Orch. (VR: Harry Prime)
6 HAIR OF GOLD, EYES OF BLUE   Gordon MacRae
7 CUANTA LA GUSTA   Andrews Sisters & Carmen Miranda
8 A LITTLE BIRD TOLD ME   Evelyn Knight

Dinah Shore
``Buttons & Bows''—Dinah's biggest hit—stays #1 for ten weeks.

9   A TREE IN THE MEADOW   Margaret Whiting
10   MAYBE YOU'LL BE THERE   Gordon Jenkins Orch.
     *Note: * From the movie "Paleface."*

December 18, 1948
1   BUTTONS AND BOWS   Dinah Shore *
2   MY DARLING, MY DARLING   Jo Stafford & Gordon
     MacRae
3   ON A SLOW BOAT TO CHINA   Kay Kyser Orch. (VR: Harry
     Babbitt & Gloria Wood)
4   YOU WERE ONLY FOOLING   Kay Starr
5   A LITTLE BIRD TOLD ME   Evelyn Knight
6   UNTIL   Tommy Dorsey Orch. (VR: Harry Prime)
7   CUANTA LA GUSTA   Andrews Sisters & Carmen Miranda
8   MAYBE YOU'LL BE THERE   Gordon Jenkins Orch.
9   FOR YOU   Glen Gray Orch. (VR: Kenny Sargent)
10   SAY SOMETHING SWEET TO YOUR SWEETHEART   Jo
     Stafford & Gordon MacRae
     *Note: * From the movie "Paleface."*

December 25, 1948
1   BUTTONS AND BOWS   Dinah Shore *
2   ON A SLOW BOAT TO CHINA   Kay Kyser Orch. (VR: Harry
     Babbitt & Gloria Wood)
3   MY DARLING, MY DARLING   Jo Stafford & Gordon
     MacRae
4   A LITTLE BIRD TOLD ME   Evelyn Knight
5   UNTIL   Tommy Dorsey Orch. (VR: Harry Prime)
6   LAVENDER BLUE   Sammy Kaye Orch. (VR: Three
     Kaydets)
7   YOU WERE ONLY FOOLING   Kay Starr
8   WHITE CHRISTMAS   Bing Crosby
9   CUANTA LA GUSTA   Andrews Sisters & Carmen Miranda
10   MAYBE YOU'LL BE THERE   Gordon Jenkins Orch.
     *Note: * From the movie "Paleface."*

January 1, 1949
1   BUTTONS AND BOWS   Dinah Shore *
2   MY DARLING, MY DARLING   Jo Stafford & Gordon
     MacRae
3   ON A SLOW BOAT TO CHINA   Kay Kyser Orch. (VR: Harry
     Babbitt & Gloria Wood)
4   A LITTLE BIRD TOLD ME   Evelyn Knight
5   WHITE CHRISTMAS   Bing Crosby
6   YOU WERE ONLY FOOLING   Kay Starr
7   LAVENDER BLUE   Sammy Kaye Orch. (VR: Three
     Kaydets)
8   UNTIL   Tommy Dorsey Orch. (VR: Harry Prime)
9   SANTA CLAUS IS COMING TO TOWN   Bing Crosby &
     Andrews Sisters
10   ALL I WANT FOR CHRISTMAS IS MY TWO FRONT TEETH
     Spike Jones Orch. (VR: George Rock)
     *Note: * From the movie "Paleface."*

January 8, 1949
1   ON A SLOW BOAT TO CHINA   Kay Kyser Orch. (VR: Harry
     Babbitt & Gloria Wood)
2   BUTTONS AND BOWS   Dinah Shore *
3   MY DARLING, MY DARLING   Jo Stafford & Gordon
     MacRae
4   A LITTLE BIRD TOLD ME   Evelyn Knight
5   YOU WERE ONLY FOOLING   Kay Starr
6   LAVENDER BLUE   Sammy Kaye Orch. (VR: Three
     Kaydets)
7   FAR AWAY PLACES   Margaret Whiting
8   CUANTA LA GUSTA   Andrews Sisters & Carmen Miranda

9   UNTIL   Tommy Dorsey Orch. (VR: Harry Prime)
10   MAYBE YOU'LL BE THERE   Gordon Jenkins Orch.
     *Note: * From the movie "Paleface."*

January 15, 1949
1   ON A SLOW BOAT TO CHINA   Kay Kyser Orch. (VR: Harry
     Babbitt & Gloria Wood)
2   BUTTONS AND BOWS   Dinah Shore *
3   MY DARLING, MY DARLING   Jo Stafford & Gordon
     MacRae
4   A LITTLE BIRD TOLD ME   Evelyn Knight
5   FAR AWAY PLACES   Margaret Whiting
6   LAVENDER BLUE   Sammy Kaye Orch. (VR: Three
     Kaydets)
7   CUANTA LA GUSTA   Andrews Sisters & Carmen Miranda
8   YOU WERE ONLY FOOLING   Kay Starr
9   UNTIL   Tommy Dorsey Orch. (VR: Harry Prime)
10   HERE I'LL STAY   Jo Stafford
     *Note: * From the movie "Paleface."*

January 22, 1949
1   BUTTONS AND BOWS   Dinah Shore *
2   A LITTLE BIRD TOLD ME   Evelyn Knight
3   ON A SLOW BOAT TO CHINA   Kay Kyser Orch. (VR: Harry
     Babbitt & Gloria Wood)
4   MY DARLING, MY DARLING   Jo Stafford & Gordon
     MacRae
5   LAVENDER BLUE   Sammy Kaye Orch. (VR: Three
     Kaydets)
6   YOU WERE ONLY FOOLING   Kay Starr
7   FAR AWAY PLACES   Margaret Whiting
8   UNTIL   Tommy Dorsey Orch. (VR: Harry Prime)
9   CUANTA LA GUSTA   Andrews Sisters & Carmen Miranda
10   GALWAY BAY   Bing Crosby
     *Note: * From the movie "Paleface."*

January 29, 1949
1   A LITTLE BIRD TOLD ME   Evelyn Knight
2   MY DARLING, MY DARLING   Jo Stafford & Gordon
     MacRae
3   BUTTONS AND BOWS   Dinah Shore *
4   FAR AWAY PLACES   Margaret Whiting
5   ON A SLOW BOAT TO CHINA   Kay Kyser Orch. (VR: Harry
     Babbitt & Gloria Wood)
6   GALWAY BAY   Bing Crosby
7   YOU WERE ONLY FOOLING   Kay Starr
8   LAVENDER BLUE   Sammy Kaye Orch. (VR: Three
     Kaydets)
9   POWDER YOUR FACE WITH SUNSHINE   Evelyn Knight
10   HERE I'LL STAY   Jo Stafford
     *Note: * From the movie "Paleface."*

February 5, 1949
1   A LITTLE BIRD TOLD ME   Evelyn Knight
2   FAR AWAY PLACES   Margaret Whiting
3   POWDER YOUR FACE WITH SUNSHINE   Evelyn Knight
4   ON A SLOW BOAT TO CHINA   Kay Kyser Orch. (VR: Harry
     Babbitt & Gloria Wood)
5   BUTTONS AND BOWS   Dinah Shore *
6   MY DARLING, MY DARLING   Jo Stafford & Gordon
     MacRae
7   LAVENDER BLUE   Sammy Kaye Orch. (VR: Three
     Kaydets)
8   GALWAY BAY   Bing Crosby
9   I'VE GOT MY LOVE TO KEEP ME WARM   Les Brown Orch.
10   SO IN LOVE   Patti Page
     *Note: * From the movie "Paleface."*

February 12, 1949
1 A LITTLE BIRD TOLD ME   Evelyn Knight
2 POWDER YOUR FACE WITH SUNSHINE   Evelyn Knight
3 FAR AWAY PLACES   Margaret Whiting
4 LAVENDER BLUE   Sammy Kaye Orch. (VR: Three Kaydets)
5 MY DARLING, MY DARLING   Jo Stafford & Gordon MacRae
6 GALWAY BAY   Bing Crosby
7 BUTTONS AND BOWS   Dinah Shore *
8 I'VE GOT MY LOVE TO KEEP ME WARM   Les Brown Orch.
9 SO IN LOVE   Patti Page
10 ON A SLOW BOAT TO CHINA   Kay Kyser Orch. (VR: Harry Babbitt & Gloria Wood)
   Note: * From the movie "Paleface."

February 19, 1949
1 POWDER YOUR FACE WITH SUNSHINE   Evelyn Knight
2 FAR AWAY PLACES   Margaret Whiting
3 A LITTLE BIRD TOLD ME   Evelyn Knight
4 LAVENDER BLUE   Sammy Kaye Orch. (VR: Three Kaydets)
5 MY DARLING, MY DARLING   Jo Stafford & Gordon MacRae
6 I'VE GOT MY LOVE TO KEEP ME WARM   Les Brown Orch.
7 ON A SLOW BOAT TO CHINA   Kay Kyser Orch. (VR: Harry Babbitt & Gloria Wood)
8 BUTTONS AND BOWS   Dinah Shore *
9 GALWAY BAY   Bing Crosby
10 HERE I'LL STAY   Jo Stafford
   Note: * From the movie "Paleface."

February 26, 1949
1 FAR AWAY PLACES   Margaret Whiting
2 POWDER YOUR FACE WITH SUNSHINE   Evelyn Knight
3 A LITTLE BIRD TOLD ME   Evelyn Knight
4 LAVENDER BLUE   Sammy Kaye Orch. (VR: Three Kaydets)
5 GALWAY BAY   Bing Crosby
6 I'VE GOT MY LOVE TO KEEP ME WARM   Les Brown Orch.
7 SO IN LOVE   Patti Page
8 CRUISING DOWN THE RIVER   Russ Morgan Orch. (VR: The Skyliners) *
9 ON A SLOW BOAT TO CHINA   Kay Kyser Orch. (VR: Harry Babbitt & Gloria Wood)
10 SUNFLOWER   Russ Morgan Orch. (VR: Skylarks)
   Note: * Another version by: Blue Barron Orch. (VR: Ensemble).

March 5, 1949
1 FAR AWAY PLACES   Margaret Whiting
2 POWDER YOUR FACE WITH SUNSHINE   Evelyn Knight
3 GALWAY BAY   Bing Crosby
4 A LITTLE BIRD TOLD ME   Evelyn Knight
5 I'VE GOT MY LOVE TO KEEP ME WARM   Les Brown Orch.
6 CRUISING DOWN THE RIVER   Russ Morgan Orch. (VR: The Skyliners) *
7 LAVENDER BLUE   Sammy Kaye Orch. (VR: Three Kaydets)
8 SO IN LOVE   Patti Page
9 SUNFLOWER   Russ Morgan Orch. (VR: Skylarks)
10 BUTTONS AND BOWS   Dinah Shore **
   Note: * Another version by: Blue Barron Orch. (VR: Ensemble).
   ** From the movie "Paleface."

March 12, 1949
1 FAR AWAY PLACES   Margaret Whiting
2 POWDER YOUR FACE WITH SUNSHINE   Evelyn Knight
3 I'VE GOT MY LOVE TO KEEP ME WARM   Les Brown Orch.
4 SO IN LOVE   Patti Page
5 LAVENDER BLUE   Sammy Kaye Orch. (VR: Three Kaydets)
6 CRUISING DOWN THE RIVER   Russ Morgan Orch. (VR: The Skyliners) *
7 RED ROSES FOR A BLUE LADY   Vaughn Monroe Orch. (VR: Vaughn Monroe)
8 SUNFLOWER   Russ Morgan Orch. (VR: Skylarks)
9 GALWAY BAY   Bing Crosby
10 A LITTLE BIRD TOLD ME   Evelyn Knight
   Note: * Another version by: Blue Barron Orch. (VR: Ensemble).

March 19, 1949
1 POWDER YOUR FACE WITH SUNSHINE   Evelyn Knight
2 CRUISING DOWN THE RIVER   Russ Morgan Orch. (VR: The Skyliners) *
3 SO IN LOVE   Patti Page
4 FAR AWAY PLACES   Margaret Whiting
5 A LITTLE BIRD TOLD ME   Evelyn Knight
6 RED ROSES FOR A BLUE LADY   Vaughn Monroe Orch. (VR: Vaughn Monroe)
7 I'VE GOT MY LOVE TO KEEP ME WARM   Les Brown Orch.
8 SUNFLOWER   Russ Morgan Orch. (VR: Skylarks)
9 GALWAY BAY   Bing Crosby
10 LAVENDER BLUE   Sammy Kaye Orch. (VR: Three Kaydets)
   Note: * Another version by: Blue Barron Orch. (VR: Ensemble).

March 26, 1949
1 CRUISING DOWN THE RIVER   Russ Morgan Orch. (VR: The Skyliners) *
2 GALWAY BAY   Bing Crosby
3 POWDER YOUR FACE WITH SUNSHINE   Evelyn Knight
4 FAR AWAY PLACES   Margaret Whiting
5 SO IN LOVE   Patti Page
6 RED ROSES FOR A BLUE LADY   Vaughn Monroe Orch. (VR: Vaughn Monroe)
7 SUNFLOWER   Russ Morgan Orch. (VR: Skylarks)
8 I'VE GOT MY LOVE TO KEEP ME WARM   Les Brown Orch.
9 LAVENDER BLUE   Sammy Kaye Orch. (VR: Three Kaydets)
10 A LITTLE BIRD TOLD ME   Evelyn Knight
   Note: * Another version by: Blue Barron Orch. (VR: Ensemble).

April 2, 1949
1 CRUISING DOWN THE RIVER   Russ Morgan Orch. (VR: The Skyliners) *
2 FAR AWAY PLACES   Margaret Whiting
3 RED ROSES FOR A BLUE LADY   Vaughn Monroe Orch. (VR: Vaughn Monroe)
4 SUNFLOWER   Russ Morgan Orch. (VR: Skylarks)
5 SO IN LOVE   Patti Page
6 POWDER YOUR FACE WITH SUNSHINE   Evelyn Knight
7 I'VE GOT MY LOVE TO KEEP ME WARM   Les Brown Orch.
8 GALWAY BAY   Bing Crosby
9 SOMEONE LIKE YOU   Doris Day
10 FOREVER AND EVER   Russ Morgan Orch. (VR: The Skylarks) **
   Note: * Another version by: Blue Barron Orch. (VR: Ensemble).

** Another version by: Perry Como.

April 9, 1949
1 CRUISING DOWN THE RIVER   Russ Morgan Orch. (VR: The Skyliners) *
2 SUNFLOWER   Russ Morgan Orch. (VR: Skylarks)
3 POWDER YOUR FACE WITH SUNSHINE   Evelyn Knight
4 FAR AWAY PLACES   Margaret Whiting
5 SO IN LOVE   Patti Page
6 I'VE GOT MY LOVE TO KEEP ME WARM   Les Brown Orch.
7 FOREVER AND EVER   Russ Morgan Orch. (VR: The Skylarks) **
8 GALWAY BAY   Bing Crosby
9 RED ROSES FOR A BLUE LADY   Vaughn Monroe Orch. (VR: Vaughn Monroe
10 SOMEONE LIKE YOU   Doris Day
   Note: * Another version by: Blue Barron Orch. (VR: Ensemble).
      ** Another version by: Perry Como.

April 16, 1949
1 CRUISING DOWN THE RIVER   Russ Morgan Orch. (VR: The Skyliners) *
2 RED ROSES FOR A BLUE LADY   Vaughn Monroe Orch. (VR: Vaughn Monroe
3 FAR AWAY PLACES   Margaret Whiting
4 SUNFLOWER   Russ Morgan Orch. (VR: Skylarks)
5 POWDER YOUR FACE WITH SUNSHINE   Evelyn Knight
6 FOREVER AND EVER   Russ Morgan Orch. (VR: The Skylarks) **
7 YOU WAS   Patti Page & Vic Damone
8 SOMEONE LIKE YOU   Doris Day
9 I'VE GOT MY LOVE TO KEEP ME WARM   Les Brown Orch.
10 SO IN LOVE   Patti Page
   Note: * Another version by: Blue Barron Orch. (VR: Ensemble).
      ** Another version by: Perry Como.

April 23, 1949
1 CRUISING DOWN THE RIVER   Russ Morgan Orch. (VR: The Skyliners) *
2 SUNFLOWER   Russ Morgan Orch. (VR: Skylarks)
3 FOREVER AND EVER   Russ Morgan Orch. (VR: The Skylarks) **
4 RED ROSES FOR A BLUE LADY   Vaughn Monroe Orch. (VR: Vaughn Monroe
5 SO IN LOVE   Patti Page
6 FAR AWAY PLACES   Margaret Whiting
7 POWDER YOUR FACE WITH SUNSHINE   Evelyn Knight
8 CARELESS HANDS   Mel Torme @
9 EASTER PARADE   Guy Lombardo
10 "A" YOU'RE ADORABLE   Perry Como
   Note: * Another version by: Blue Barron Orch. (VR: Ensemble).
      ** Another version by: Perry Como.
      @ Another version by: Sammy Kaye Orch. (VR: Don Cornell).

April 30, 1949
1 CRUISING DOWN THE RIVER   Russ Morgan Orch. (VR: The Skyliners) *
2 FOREVER AND EVER   Russ Morgan Orch. (VR: The Skylarks) **
3 RED ROSES FOR A BLUE LADY   Vaughn Monroe Orch. (VR: Vaughn Monroe
4 SUNFLOWER   Russ Morgan Orch. (VR: Skylarks)
5 AGAIN   Doris Day @

6 POWDER YOUR FACE WITH SUNSHINE   Evelyn Knight
7 CARELESS HANDS   Mel Torme @@
8 FAR AWAY PLACES   Margaret Whiting
9 "A" YOU'RE ADORABLE   Perry Como
10 SO IN LOVE   Patti Page
   Note: * Another version by: Blue Barron Orch. (VR: Ensemble).
      ** Another version by: Perry Como.
      @ Another version by: Gordon Jenkins.
      @@ Another version by: Sammy Kaye Orch. (VR: Don Cornell).

May 7, 1949
1 CRUISING DOWN THE RIVER   Russ Morgan Orch. (VR: The Skyliners) *
2 RED ROSES FOR A BLUE LADY   Vaughn Monroe Orch. (VR: Vaughn Monroe
3 "A" YOU'RE ADORABLE   Perry Como
4 AGAIN   Doris Day **
5 FOREVER AND EVER   Russ Morgan Orch. (VR: The Skylarks) @
6 CARELESS HANDS   Mel Torme @@
7 POWDER YOUR FACE WITH SUNSHINE   Evelyn Knight
8 SOMEONE LIKE YOU   Doris Day
9 SUNFLOWER   Russ Morgan Orch. (VR: Skylarks)
10 FAR AWAY PLACES   Margaret Whiting
   Note: * Another version by: Blue Barron Orch. (VR: Ensemble).
      ** Another version by: Gordon Jenkins.
      @ Another version by: Perry Como.
      @@ Another version by: Sammy Kaye Orch. (VR: Don Cornell).

May 14, 1949
1 CRUISING DOWN THE RIVER   Russ Morgan Orch. (VR: The Skyliners) *
2 AGAIN   Doris Day **
3 FOREVER AND EVER   Russ Morgan Orch. (VR: The Skylarks) @
4 "A" YOU'RE ADORABLE   Perry Como
5 CARELESS HANDS   Mel Torme @@
6 SUNFLOWER   Russ Morgan Orch. (VR: Skylarks)
7 FAR AWAY PLACES   Margaret Whiting
8 RED ROSES FOR A BLUE LADY   Vaughn Monroe Orch. (VR: Vaughn Monroe
9 A WONDERFUL GUY   Margaret Whiting
10 SOMEONE LIKE YOU   Doris Day
   Note: * Another version by: Blue Barron Orch. (VR: Ensemble).
      ** Another version by: Gordon Jenkins.
      @ Another version by: Perry Como.
      @@ Another version by: Sammy Kaye Orch. (VR: Don Cornell).

May 21, 1949
1 RIDERS IN THE SKY   Vaughn Monroe (VR: Vaughn Monroe)
2 AGAIN   Doris Day *
3 FOREVER AND EVER   Russ Morgan Orch. (VR: The Skylarks) **
4 CARELESS HANDS   Mel Torme @
5 "A" YOU'RE ADORABLE   Perry Como
6 SOME ENCHANTED EVENING   Perry Como
7 CRUISING DOWN THE RIVER   Russ Morgan Orch. (VR: The Skyliners) @@
8 SOMEONE LIKE YOU   Doris Day
9 SUNFLOWER   Russ Morgan Orch. (VR: Skylarks)

10   RED ROSES FOR A BLUE LADY   Vaughn Monroe Orch.
(VR: Vaughn Monroe
Note: * Another version by: Gordon Jenkins.
    ** Another version by: Perry Como.
    @ Another version by: Sammy Kaye Orch. (VR: Don
Cornell).
    @@ Another version by: Blue Barron Orch. (VR:
Ensemble).

May 28, 1949
1   AGAIN   Doris Day *
2   RIDERS IN THE SKY   Vaughn Monroe (VR: Vaughn
Monroe)
3   "A" YOU'RE ADORABLE   Perry Como
4   CRUISING DOWN THE RIVER   Russ Morgan Orch. (VR:
The Skyliners) **
5   FOREVER AND EVER   Russ Morgan Orch. (VR: The
Skylarks) @
6   SOME ENCHANTED EVENING   Perry Como
7   CARELESS HANDS   Mel Torme @@
8   KISS ME, SWEET   Sammy Kaye Orch. (VR: Don Cornell &
Laura Leslie)
9   BALI HA'I   Perry Como
10   RED ROSES FOR A BLUE LADY   Vaughn Monroe Orch.
(VR: Vaughn Monroe
Note: * Another version by: Gordon Jenkins.
    ** Another version by: Blue Barron Orch. (VR:
Ensemble).
    @ Another version by: Perry Como.
    @@ Another version by: Sammy Kaye Orch. (VR: Don
Cornell).

June 4, 1949
1   RIDERS IN THE SKY   Vaughn Monroe (VR: Vaughn
Monroe)
2   AGAIN   Doris Day *
3   SOME ENCHANTED EVENING   Perry Como
4   CARELESS HANDS   Mel Torme **
5   "A" YOU'RE ADORABLE   Perry Como
6   FOREVER AND EVER   Russ Morgan Orch. (VR: The
Skylarks) @
7   CRUISING DOWN THE RIVER   Russ Morgan Orch. (VR:
The Skyliners) @@
8   BALI HA'I   Perry Como
9   I DON'T SEE ME IN YOUR EYES ANYMORE   Gordon
Jenkins Orch. (VR: Stardusters)
10   FIVE FOOT TWO, EYES OF BLUE   Benny Strong
Note: * Another version by: Gordon Jenkins.
    ** Another version by: Sammy Kaye Orch. (VR: Don
Cornell).
    @ Another version by: Perry Como.
    @@ Another version by: Blue Barron Orch. (VR:
Ensemble).

June 11, 1949
1   RIDERS IN THE SKY   Vaughn Monroe (VR: Vaughn
Monroe)
2   SOME ENCHANTED EVENING   Perry Como
3   "A" YOU'RE ADORABLE   Perry Como
4   AGAIN   Doris Day *
5   FOREVER AND EVER   Russ Morgan Orch. (VR: The
Skylarks) **
6   CRUISING DOWN THE RIVER   Russ Morgan Orch. (VR:
The Skyliners) @
7   BALI HA'I   Perry Como
8   A WONDERFUL GUY   Margaret Whiting
9   I DON'T SEE ME IN YOUR EYES ANYMORE   Gordon
Jenkins Orch. (VR: Stardusters)

10   EVERYWHERE YOU GO   Guy Lombardo Orch. (VR: Don
Rodney)
Note: * Another version by: Gordon Jenkins.
    ** Another version by: Perry Como.
    @ Another version by: Blue Barron Orch. (VR:
Ensemble).

June 18, 1949
1   AGAIN   Doris Day *
2   RIDERS IN THE SKY   Vaughn Monroe (VR: Vaughn
Monroe)
3   SOME ENCHANTED EVENING   Perry Como
4   "A" YOU'RE ADORABLE   Perry Como
5   FOREVER AND EVER   Russ Morgan Orch. (VR: The
Skylarks) **
6   BALI HA'I   Perry Como
7   A WONDERFUL GUY   Margaret Whiting
8   CARELESS HANDS   Mel Torme @
9   HOW IT LIES, HOW IT LIES, HOW IT LIES   Connie Haines
10   CRUISING DOWN THE RIVER   Russ Morgan Orch. (VR:
The Skyliners) @@
Note: * Another version by: Gordon Jenkins.
    ** Another version by: Perry Como.
    @ Another version by: Sammy Kaye Orch. (VR: Don
Cornell).
    @@ Another version by: Blue Barron Orch. (VR:
Ensemble).

June 25, 1949
1   SOME ENCHANTED EVENING   Perry Como
2   RIDERS IN THE SKY   Vaughn Monroe (VR: Vaughn
Monroe)
3   BALI HA'I   Perry Como
4   AGAIN   Doris Day *
5   "A" YOU'RE ADORABLE   Perry Como
6   A WONDERFUL GUY   Margaret Whiting
7   FOREVER AND EVER   Russ Morgan Orch. (VR: The
Skylarks) **
8   I DON'T SEE ME IN YOUR EYES ANYMORE   Gordon
Jenkins Orch. (VR: Stardusters)
9   KISS ME, SWEET   Sammy Kaye Orch. (VR: Don Cornell &
Laura Leslie)
10   CRUISING DOWN THE RIVER   Russ Morgan Orch. (VR:
The Skyliners) @
Note: * Another version by: Gordon Jenkins.
    ** Another version by: Perry Como.
    @ Another version by: Blue Barron Orch. (VR:
Ensemble).

July 2, 1949
1   SOME ENCHANTED EVENING   Perry Como
2   RIDERS IN THE SKY   Vaughn Monroe (VR: Vaughn
Monroe)
3   BALI HA'I   Perry Como
4   AGAIN   Doris Day *
5   A WONDERFUL GUY   Margaret Whiting
6   I DON'T SEE ME IN YOUR EYES ANYMORE   Gordon
Jenkins Orch. (VR: Stardusters)
7   FOREVER AND EVER   Russ Morgan Orch. (VR: The
Skylarks) **
8   "A" YOU'RE ADORABLE   Perry Como
9   BABY, IT'S COLD OUTSIDE   Johnny Mercer & Margaret
Whiting @
10   CRUISING DOWN THE RIVER   Russ Morgan Orch. (VR:
The Skyliners) @@
Note: * Another version by: Gordon Jenkins.
    ** Another version by: Perry Como.
    @ Country hit for Homer And Jethro.

@@ Another version by: Blue Barron Orch. (VR: Ensemble).

July 9, 1949
1   SOME ENCHANTED EVENING   Perry Como
2   AGAIN   Doris Day *
3   BALI HA'I   Perry Como
4   RIDERS IN THE SKY   Vaughn Monroe (VR: Vaughn Monroe)
5   A WONDERFUL GUY   Margaret Whiting
6   FOREVER AND EVER   Russ Morgan Orch. (VR: The Skylarks) **
7   BABY, IT'S COLD OUTSIDE   Johnny Mercer & Margaret Whiting @
8   "A" YOU'RE ADORABLE   Perry Como
9   MY ONE AND ONLY HIGHLAND FLING   Dinah Shore & Buddy Clark
10 I DON'T SEE ME IN YOUR EYES ANYMORE   Gordon Jenkins Orch. (VR: Stardusters)
    Note: * Another version by: Gordon Jenkins.
    ** Another version by: Perry Como.
    @ Country hit for Homer And Jethro.

July 16, 1949
1   SOME ENCHANTED EVENING   Perry Como
2   BALI HA'I   Perry Como
3   AGAIN   Doris Day *
4   RIDERS IN THE SKY   Vaughn Monroe (VR: Vaughn Monroe)
5   FOREVER AND EVER   Russ Morgan Orch. (VR: The Skylarks) **
6   A WONDERFUL GUY   Margaret Whiting
7   BABY, IT'S COLD OUTSIDE   Johnny Mercer & Margaret Whiting @
8   "A" YOU'RE ADORABLE   Perry Como
9   I DON'T SEE ME IN YOUR EYES ANYMORE   Gordon Jenkins Orch. (VR: Stardusters)
10 JUST ONE WAY TO SAY 'I LOVE YOU'   Jo Stafford
    Note: * Another version by: Gordon Jenkins.
    ** Another version by: Perry Como.
    @ Country hit for Homer And Jethro.

July 23, 1949
1   SOME ENCHANTED EVENING   Perry Como
2   AGAIN   Doris Day *
3   BALI HA'I   Perry Como
4   A WONDERFUL GUY   Margaret Whiting
5   THERE'S 'YES, YES' IN YOUR EYES   Eddy Howard Orch. (VR: Eddy Howard)
6   RIDERS IN THE SKY   Vaughn Monroe (VR: Vaughn Monroe)
7   BABY, IT'S COLD OUTSIDE   Johnny Mercer & Margaret Whiting **
8   FOREVER AND EVER   Russ Morgan Orch. (VR: The Skylarks) @
9   I DON'T SEE ME IN YOUR EYES ANYMORE   Gordon Jenkins Orch. (VR: Stardusters)
10 JUST ONE WAY TO SAY 'I LOVE YOU'   Jo Stafford
    Note: * Another version by: Gordon Jenkins.
    ** Country hit for Homer And Jethro.
    @ Another version by: Perry Como.

July 30, 1949
1   SOME ENCHANTED EVENING   Perry Como
2   BALI HA'I   Perry Como
3   RIDERS IN THE SKY   Vaughn Monroe (VR: Vaughn Monroe)

4   AGAIN   Doris Day *
5   A WONDERFUL GUY   Margaret Whiting
6   FOREVER AND EVER   Russ Morgan Orch. (VR: The Skylarks) **
7   BABY, IT'S COLD OUTSIDE   Johnny Mercer & Margaret Whiting @
8   THERE'S 'YES, YES' IN YOUR EYES   Eddy Howard Orch. (VR: Eddy Howard)
9   LET'S TAKE AN OLD FASHIONED WALK   Perry Como
10 MAYBE IT'S BECAUSE   Dick Haymes
    Note: * Another version by: Gordon Jenkins.
    ** Another version by: Perry Como.
    @ Country hit for Homer And Jethro.

August 6, 1949
1   SOME ENCHANTED EVENING   Perry Como
2   AGAIN   Doris Day *
3   RIDERS IN THE SKY   Vaughn Monroe (VR: Vaughn Monroe)
4   BALI HA'I   Perry Como
5   FOUR WINDS AND THE SEVEN SEAS   Sammy Kaye Orch. (VR: Tony Alamo)
6   BABY, IT'S COLD OUTSIDE   Johnny Mercer & Margaret Whiting **
7   THERE'S 'YES, YES' IN YOUR EYES   Eddy Howard Orch. (VR: Eddy Howard)
8   FOREVER AND EVER   Russ Morgan Orch. (VR: The Skylarks) @
9   I DON'T SEE ME IN YOUR EYES ANYMORE   Gordon Jenkins Orch. (VR: Stardusters)
10 LOVER'S GOLD   Dinah Shore
    Note: * Another version by: Gordon Jenkins.
    ** Country hit for Homer And Jethro.
    @ Another version by: Perry Como.

August 13, 1949
1   SOME ENCHANTED EVENING   Perry Como
2   BALI HA'I   Perry Como
3   AGAIN   Doris Day *
4   BABY, IT'S COLD OUTSIDE   Johnny Mercer & Margaret Whiting **
5   JUST ONE WAY TO SAY 'I LOVE YOU'   Jo Stafford
6   THE HUCKLEBUCK   Tommy Dorsey Orch. (VR: Charlie Shavers)
7   FOREVER AND EVER   Russ Morgan Orch. (VR: The Skylarks) @
8   ROOM FULL OF ROSES   Sammy Kaye Orch. (VR: Don Cornell)
9   RIDERS IN THE SKY   Vaughn Monroe (VR: Vaughn Monroe)
10 THERE'S 'YES, YES' IN YOUR EYES   Eddy Howard Orch. (VR: Eddy Howard)
    Note: * Another version by: Gordon Jenkins.
    ** Country hit for Homer And Jethro.
    @ Another version by: Perry Como.

August 20, 1949
1   SOME ENCHANTED EVENING   Perry Como
2   ROOM FULL OF ROSES   Sammy Kaye Orch. (VR: Don Cornell)
3   BALI HA'I   Perry Como
4   YOU'RE BREAKING MY HEART   Vic Damone
5   THERE'S 'YES, YES' IN YOUR EYES   Eddy Howard Orch. (VR: Eddy Howard)
6   AGAIN   Doris Day *
7   JUST ONE WAY TO SAY 'I LOVE YOU'   Jo Stafford
8   FOREVER AND EVER   Russ Morgan Orch. (VR: The Skylarks) **

9 LET'S TAKE AN OLD FASHIONED WALK   Perry Como
10 AND IT STILL GOES   Vaughn Monroe Orch. (VR: Vaughn Monroe)
   Note: * Another version by: Gordon Jenkins.
          ** Another version by: Perry Como.

August 27, 1949
1 YOU'RE BREAKING MY HEART   Vic Damone
2 ROOM FULL OF ROSES   Sammy Kaye Orch. (VR: Don Cornell)
3 SOME ENCHANTED EVENING   Perry Como
4 LET'S TAKE AN OLD FASHIONED WALK   Perry Como
5 BALI HA'I   Perry Como
6 AGAIN   Doris Day *
7 JUST ONE WAY TO SAY 'I LOVE YOU'   Jo Stafford
8 THERE'S 'YES, YES' IN YOUR EYES   Eddy Howard Orch. (VR: Eddy Howard)
9 AND IT STILL GOES   Vaughn Monroe Orch. (VR: Vaughn Monroe)
10 IT'S A GREAT FEELING   Doris Day
   Note: * Another version by: Gordon Jenkins.

September 3, 1949
1 SOME ENCHANTED EVENING   Perry Como
2 ROOM FULL OF ROSES   Sammy Kaye Orch. (VR: Don Cornell)
3 YOU'RE BREAKING MY HEART   Vic Damone
4 JUST ONE WAY TO SAY 'I LOVE YOU'   Jo Stafford
5 LET'S TAKE AN OLD FASHIONED WALK   Perry Como
6 BALI HA'I   Perry Como
7 AGAIN   Doris Day *
8 FIDDLE DEE DEE   Sammy Kaye Orch. (VR: The Kaydets)
9 IT'S A GREAT FEELING   Doris Day
10 TWENTY FOUR HOURS OF SUNSHINE   Art Mooney Orch. (VR: Choir)
   Note: * Another version by: Gordon Jenkins.

September 10, 1949
1 ROOM FULL OF ROSES   Sammy Kaye Orch. (VR: Don Cornell)
2 YOU'RE BREAKING MY HEART   Vic Damone
3 MAYBE IT'S BECAUSE   Dick Haymes
4 SOME ENCHANTED EVENING   Perry Como
5 JUST ONE WAY TO SAY 'I LOVE YOU'   Jo Stafford
6 LET'S TAKE AN OLD FASHIONED WALK   Perry Como
7 THERE'S 'YES, YES' IN YOUR EYES   Eddy Howard Orch. (VR: Eddy Howard)
8 SOMEDAY   Vaughn Monroe (VR: Vaughn Monroe)
9 BALI HA'I   Perry Como
10 FIDDLE DEE DEE   Sammy Kaye Orch. (VR: The Kaydets)

September 17, 1949
1 YOU'RE BREAKING MY HEART   Vic Damone
2 LET'S TAKE AN OLD FASHIONED WALK   Perry Como
3 SOMEDAY   Vaughn Monroe (VR: Vaughn Monroe)
4 SOME ENCHANTED EVENING   Perry Como
5 ROOM FULL OF ROSES   Sammy Kaye Orch. (VR: Don Cornell)
6 BALI HA'I   Perry Como
7 MAYBE IT'S BECAUSE   Dick Haymes
8 JUST ONE WAY TO SAY 'I LOVE YOU'   Jo Stafford
9 FIDDLE DEE DEE   Sammy Kaye Orch. (VR: The Kaydets)
10 AGAIN   Doris Day *
   Note: * Another version by: Gordon Jenkins.

Vic Damone
``You're Breaking My Heart'' is Vic's first #1 hit (Aug. 27).

September 24, 1949
1 YOU'RE BREAKING MY HEART   Vic Damone
2 ROOM FULL OF ROSES   Sammy Kaye Orch. (VR: Don Cornell)
3 SOMEDAY   Vaughn Monroe (VR: Vaughn Monroe)
4 SOME ENCHANTED EVENING   Perry Como
5 MAYBE IT'S BECAUSE   Dick Haymes
6 THERE'S 'YES, YES' IN YOUR EYES   Eddy Howard Orch. (VR: Eddy Howard)
7 YOUNGER THAN SPRINGTIME   Gordon MacRae
8 JUST ONE WAY TO SAY 'I LOVE YOU'   Jo Stafford
9 TWENTY FOUR HOURS OF SUNSHINE   Art Mooney Orch. (VR: Choir)
10 FIDDLE DEE DEE   Sammy Kaye Orch. (VR: The Kaydets)

October 1, 1949
1 YOU'RE BREAKING MY HEART   Vic Damone
2 MAYBE IT'S BECAUSE   Dick Haymes
3 SOME ENCHANTED EVENING   Perry Como
4 ROOM FULL OF ROSES   Sammy Kaye Orch. (VR: Don Cornell)
5 SOMEDAY   Vaughn Monroe (VR: Vaughn Monroe)
6 THAT LUCKY OLD SUN   Frankie Laine
7 LET'S TAKE AN OLD FASHIONED WALK   Perry Como

October 8, 1949
1 ROOM FULL OF ROSES   Sammy Kaye Orch. (VR: Don Cornell)
2 THAT LUCKY OLD SUN   Frankie Laine
3 SOMEDAY   Vaughn Monroe (VR: Vaughn Monroe)
4 MAYBE IT'S BECAUSE   Dick Haymes
5 YOU'RE BREAKING MY HEART   Vic Damone
6 LET'S TAKE AN OLD FASHIONED WALK   Perry Como
7 SOME ENCHANTED EVENING   Perry Como

October 15, 1949
1 YOU'RE BREAKING MY HEART   Vic Damone
2 SOMEDAY   Vaughn Monroe (VR: Vaughn Monroe)
3 THAT LUCKY OLD SUN   Frankie Laine
4 MAYBE IT'S BECAUSE   Dick Haymes

5   ROOM FULL OF ROSES   Sammy Kaye Orch. (VR: Don Cornell)
6   TWENTY FOUR HOURS OF SUNSHINE   Art Mooney Orch. (VR: Choir)
7   JEALOUS HEART   Al Morgan

October 22, 1949
1   YOU'RE BREAKING MY HEART   Vic Damone
2   THAT LUCKY OLD SUN   Frankie Laine
3   SOMEDAY   Vaughn Monroe (VR: Vaughn Monroe)
4   DON'T CRY, JOE   Gordon Jenkins Orch. (VR: Betty Brewer)
5   ROOM FULL OF ROSES   Sammy Kaye Orch. (VR: Don Cornell)
6   MAYBE IT'S BECAUSE   Dick Haymes
7   LET'S TAKE AN OLD FASHIONED WALK   Perry Como

October 29, 1949
1   THAT LUCKY OLD SUN   Frankie Laine
2   YOU'RE BREAKING MY HEART   Vic Damone
3   ROOM FULL OF ROSES   Sammy Kaye Orch. (VR: Don Cornell)
4   DON'T CRY, JOE   Gordon Jenkins Orch. (VR: Betty Brewer)
5   SOMEDAY   Vaughn Monroe (VR: Vaughn Monroe)
6   I CAN DREAM, CAN'T I?   Tommy Dorsey Orch. (VR: Jack Leonard)
7   MAYBE IT'S BECAUSE   Dick Haymes

November 5, 1949
1   THAT LUCKY OLD SUN   Frankie Laine
2   YOU'RE BREAKING MY HEART   Vic Damone
3   DON'T CRY, JOE   Gordon Jenkins Orch. (VR: Betty Brewer)
4   I CAN DREAM, CAN'T I?   Tommy Dorsey Orch. (VR: Jack Leonard)
5   ROOM FULL OF ROSES   Sammy Kaye Orch. (VR: Don Cornell)
6   SOMEDAY   Vaughn Monroe (VR: Vaughn Monroe)
7   JEALOUS HEART   Al Morgan

November 12, 1949
1   THAT LUCKY OLD SUN   Frankie Laine
2   DON'T CRY, JOE   Gordon Jenkins Orch. (VR: Betty Brewer)
3   I CAN DREAM, CAN'T I?   Tommy Dorsey Orch. (VR: Jack Leonard)
4   YOU'RE BREAKING MY HEART   Vic Damone
5   A DREAMER'S HOLIDAY   Perry Como
6   SLIPPING AROUND   Margaret Whiting & Jimmy Wakely
7   ROOM FULL OF ROSES   Sammy Kaye Orch. (VR: Don Cornell)

November 19, 1949
1   DON'T CRY, JOE   Gordon Jenkins Orch. (VR: Betty Brewer)
2   THAT LUCKY OLD SUN   Frankie Laine
3   I CAN DREAM, CAN'T I?   Tommy Dorsey Orch. (VR: Jack Leonard)
4   A DREAMER'S HOLIDAY   Perry Como
5   MULE TRAIN   Frankie Laine *
6   SLIPPING AROUND   Margaret Whiting & Jimmy Wakely
7   SOMEDAY   Vaughn Monroe (VR: Vaughn Monroe)
   Note: * Country hit for Tennessee Ernie Ford.

November 26, 1949
1   DON'T CRY, JOE   Gordon Jenkins Orch. (VR: Betty Brewer)
2   I CAN DREAM, CAN'T I?   Tommy Dorsey Orch. (VR: Jack Leonard)
3   A DREAMER'S HOLIDAY   Perry Como

4   MULE TRAIN   Frankie Laine *
5   THAT LUCKY OLD SUN   Frankie Laine
6   SLIPPING AROUND   Margaret Whiting & Jimmy Wakely
7   YOU'RE BREAKING MY HEART   Vic Damone
   Note: * Country hit for Tennessee Ernie Ford.

December 3, 1949
1   DON'T CRY, JOE   Gordon Jenkins Orch. (VR: Betty Brewer)
2   THAT LUCKY OLD SUN   Frankie Laine
3   I CAN DREAM, CAN'T I?   Tommy Dorsey Orch. (VR: Jack Leonard)
4   A DREAMER'S HOLIDAY   Perry Como
5   MULE TRAIN   Frankie Laine *
6   YOU'RE BREAKING MY HEART   Vic Damone
7   SLIPPING AROUND   Margaret Whiting & Jimmy Wakely
   Note: * Country hit for Tennessee Ernie Ford.

December 10, 1949
1   MULE TRAIN   Frankie Laine *
2   I CAN DREAM, CAN'T I?   Tommy Dorsey Orch. (VR: Jack Leonard)
3   DON'T CRY, JOE   Gordon Jenkins Orch. (VR: Betty Brewer)
4   A DREAMER'S HOLIDAY   Perry Como
5   THAT LUCKY OLD SUN   Frankie Laine
6   SLIPPING AROUND   Margaret Whiting & Jimmy Wakely
7   DEAR HEARTS AND GENTLE PEOPLE   Bing Crosby **
   Note: * Country hit for Tennessee Ernie Ford.
      ** Another version by: Dinah Shore.

December 17, 1949
1   I CAN DREAM, CAN'T I?   Tommy Dorsey Orch. (VR: Jack Leonard)
2   DON'T CRY, JOE   Gordon Jenkins Orch. (VR: Betty Brewer)
3   A DREAMER'S HOLIDAY   Perry Como
4   MULE TRAIN   Frankie Laine *
5   DEAR HEARTS AND GENTLE PEOPLE   Bing Crosby **
6   THAT LUCKY OLD SUN   Frankie Laine
7   SLIPPING AROUND   Margaret Whiting & Jimmy Wakely
   Note: * Country hit for Tennessee Ernie Ford.
      ** Another version by: Dinah Shore.

December 24, 1949
1   I CAN DREAM, CAN'T I?   Tommy Dorsey Orch. (VR: Jack Leonard)
2   A DREAMER'S HOLIDAY   Perry Como
3   DEAR HEARTS AND GENTLE PEOPLE   Bing Crosby *
4   DON'T CRY, JOE   Gordon Jenkins Orch. (VR: Betty Brewer)
5   MULE TRAIN   Frankie Laine **
6   RUDOLPH, THE RED NOSED REINDEER   Gene Autry
7   SLIPPING AROUND   Margaret Whiting & Jimmy Wakely
   Note: * Another version by: Dinah Shore.
      ** Country hit for Tennessee Ernie Ford.

December 31, 1949
1   A DREAMER'S HOLIDAY   Perry Como
2   RUDOLPH, THE RED NOSED REINDEER   Gene Autry
3   DEAR HEARTS AND GENTLE PEOPLE   Bing Crosby *
4   MULE TRAIN   Frankie Laine **
5   I CAN DREAM, CAN'T I?   Tommy Dorsey Orch. (VR: Jack Leonard)
6   DON'T CRY, JOE   Gordon Jenkins Orch. (VR: Betty Brewer)
7   WHITE CHRISTMAS   Bing Crosby
   Note: * Another version by: Dinah Shore.
      ** Country hit for Tennessee Ernie Ford.

Big Band Trivia Quiz

1. His two-year stint as "Your Hit Parade" boy vocalist ended when he blew the words to "Don't Fence Me In," the last of his several on-the-air gaffes. His name was?

2. This Decca record sold a million copies several months before Glenn Miller's supposed first gold single, "Chattanooga Choo Choo." Name the recording that Decca executives had so much trouble counting.

3. Two arch rival universities, twelve miles apart, produced band leaders Jan Garber, Hal Kemp, and Kay Kyser on the one hand, and Johnny Long on the other. Name them.

4. None of Sammy Kaye's three #1 *Billboard* hits carried a singing song title. What were they?

5. Harriet Hilliard co-starred with this then unknown comedian on his first radio series. Name him.

6. Name the vocalist Helen Forrest replaced in Artie Shaw's band in the fall of 1941.

7. What was the earliest Big Band hit single, a record which eventually sold a million copies?

8. A very young female vocalist, not ready for the big time, sang on "Your Hit Parade" for four weeks in the fall of 1941 between the stints of Louise King and Joan Edwards. Can you name her?

9. Frank Sinatra replaced him on "Your Hit Parade," much as he had replaced Lanny Ross some three years earlier. Who is he?

10. Name the song which was announced, on the January 4, 1941 "Your Hit Parade" broadcast, using the wrong title.

11. What was Vog-horn (Vaughn) Monroe's first record hit (and a big one it was)?

12. What was the effect on "Your Hit Parade" of the ASCAP broadcast ban which took effect on January 1, 1941?

13. The biggest hit ever, according to "Your Hit Parade" records?

14. What do "Harbor Lights," "My Prayer," and "Blueberry Hill" have in common in Hit Parade history?

15. Name the vocalist who picked up her Navy V-12 Officer fiance on the campus at Chapel Hill, North Carolina, on September 1, 1945, and married him the next day.

16. Which university's prom committee booked Glenn Miller, Harry James, Benny Goodman, and Dick Jurgens in four campus ballrooms in the same building for Prom Night" in 1942?

17. Which bandleader was involved in numerous clashes and lawsuits with university prom committees over various contract violations—usually: fewer musicians than contracted, star vocalist not present, and leaving the bandstand early?

18. Which band was featured with Bob Hope in his first big film, "Big Broadcast of 1938"? (Thanks for the memories, Bob.)

19. Why was Bea Wain's version of "The Dipsy Doodle" (with Larry Clinton) not released by RCA?

20. The year 1949 saw his band become the number one big band in the country; one week that year, four of the top ten best-selling records were his. What's his name?

21. Which trombonist replaced Russ Morgan with the famous Scranton Sirenes?

22. When she came to listen to the big bands, circa 1930, the management of the Montmartre provided her with screens to preserve her privacy. Can you name her?

23. In 1928, Paul Whiteman was paying Bing Crosby $150 per week; Bix Beiderbecke, Jimmy Dorsey, and Frankie Trumbauer earned $200, and this future bandleader $350. He was?

24. Name the Chicago AFM Local 10 president who bellowed at Henry Busse, behind in payment to his musicians, "You goddam Kraut! You pay these guys or else—and you know what I mean!"

25. According to George Simon, Bunny Berigan died of it. What?

26. Name the contest award winner, Sammy Kaye's first female vocalist, who recorded "Here You Are" (from "My Gal Sal") with the band in 1942.

27. She sang briefly with Glenn Miller's band in 1939, dropped from view, then resurfaced years later as one of the top vocalist of the 1950s. Who was she?

28. She was, according to Irving Townsend, "deservedly the most popular band singer of her day who wasn't named Helen." Can you name her?

29. He shut down the U.S. recording industry from late 1942 to late 1944, defying President Roosevelt's mid-war appeal to his patriotism. Name him.

30. Piqued that Columbia beat them out in introducing long-playing records in 1948, how did RCA show its contempt for the record buying public?

31. Has either RCA or Columbia, in recent decades, passed up an opportunity to gouge the record-buying public?

32. Is RCA actually managing to put less music on many of its CD's than it did on its LP's?

33. Risque songs such as "She Had To Go And Lose It To An Astor" and "She Really Meant To Keep It 'Til She Got Married" were a specialty of which band?

34. Name the pianist on the Freddy Martin 1941 hit recording of Tchaikovsky's Piano Concerto #1.

35. Which big band continued to feature violins straight through the big band era as if the 1920's had never ended?

36. What was the effect of Tommy Dorsey's addition of violins to his band in 1942?

37. Who was the announcer, later a movie star, on Hal Kemp's Chesterfield broadcasts, 1936-37?

38. Who choked to death on cauliflower at Lawry's Restaurant in L.A. on June 3, 1963?

39. Which band recorded the hit version of the first "Your Hit Parade" #1 song, "Soon"?

40. Who was the female vocalist, later a movie and Broadway star, with Hal Kemp's band at the time of his death (December 1940)?

41. What was Peggy Lee's first big record hit?

42. He won football letters and a law degree at Rutger's, but couldn't make the glee club because they said he couldn't sing. Name him.

43. She recorded "Bewitched" in 1940 with Benny Goodman; neither her version nor the musical it is from flew at the time, but both are now recognized as gems. Name the vocalist and the Broadway musical.

44. What name is mentioned most often as the greatest big band arranger?

45. Name Guy Lombardo's much younger contralto sister, who sang briefly with the band in 1944.

46. Who said "Their Either Too Young Or Too Old" in the 1943 film "Hollywood Canteen."

47. Which big band leader was most commonly regarded as the biggest s.o.b.?

48. Which big band leader had the best reputation with regard to musicians' salaries and first-class travel?

49. What was the first Hit Parade song to have its lyrics banned from radio broadcasts?

50. With the benefit of over fifty years of hindsight, who are considered to have been the best male and female "Your Hit Parade" vocalists, 1935-38?

The Fifties

January 7, 1950
1 DEAR HEARTS AND GENTLE PEOPLE   Bing Crosby *
2 A DREAMER'S HOLIDAY   Perry Como
3 THE OLD MASTER PAINTER   Richard Hayes **
4 I CAN DREAM, CAN'T I?   Tommy Dorsey Orch. (VR: Jack Leonard)
5 DON'T CRY, JOE   Gordon Jenkins Orch. (VR: Betty Brewer)
6 RUDOLPH, THE RED NOSED REINDEER   Gene Autry
7 I'VE GOT A LOVELY BUNCH OF COCOANUTS   Freddy Martin Orch. (VR: Merv Griffin)
   Note: * Another version by: Dinah Shore.
      ** Another version by "Your Hit Parade" star, Snooky Lanson.

January 14, 1950
1 DEAR HEARTS AND GENTLE PEOPLE   Bing Crosby *
2 A DREAMER'S HOLIDAY   Perry Como
3 I CAN DREAM, CAN'T I?   Tommy Dorsey Orch. (VR: Jack Leonard)
4 I'VE GOT A LOVELY BUNCH OF COCOANUTS   Freddy Martin Orch. (VR: Merv Griffin)
5 THE OLD MASTER PAINTER   Richard Hayes **
6 SLIPPING AROUND   Margaret Whiting & Jimmy Wakely
7 DON'T CRY, JOE   Gordon Jenkins Orch. (VR: Betty Brewer)
   Note: * Another version by: Dinah Shore.
      ** Another version by "Your Hit Parade" star, Snooky Lanson.

January 21, 1950
1 DEAR HEARTS AND GENTLE PEOPLE   Bing Crosby *
2 THE OLD MASTER PAINTER   Richard Hayes **
3 I CAN DREAM, CAN'T I?   Tommy Dorsey Orch. (VR: Jack Leonard)
4 A DREAMER'S HOLIDAY   Perry Como
5 I'VE GOT A LOVELY BUNCH OF COCOANUTS   Freddy Martin Orch. (VR: Merv Griffin)
6 BIBBIDI BOBBIDI BOO   Jo Stafford & Gordon MacRae
7 SLIPPING AROUND   Margaret Whiting & Jimmy Wakely
   Note: * Another version by: Dinah Shore.
      ** Another version by "Your Hit Parade" star, Snooky Lanson.

January 28, 1950
1 DEAR HEARTS AND GENTLE PEOPLE   Bing Crosby *
2 THE OLD MASTER PAINTER   Richard Hayes **
3 A DREAMER'S HOLIDAY   Perry Como
4 I CAN DREAM, CAN'T I?   Tommy Dorsey Orch. (VR: Jack Leonard)
5 THERE'S NO TOMORROW   Tony Martin
6 I'VE GOT A LOVELY BUNCH OF COCOANUTS   Freddy Martin Orch. (VR: Merv Griffin)
7 BIBBIDI BOBBIDI BOO   Jo Stafford & Gordon MacRae
   Note: * Another version by: Dinah Shore.
      ** Another version by "Your Hit Parade" star, Snooky Lanson.

February 4, 1950
1 DEAR HEARTS AND GENTLE PEOPLE   Bing Crosby *
2 A DREAMER'S HOLIDAY   Perry Como
3 THE OLD MASTER PAINTER   Richard Hayes **
4 I CAN DREAM, CAN'T I?   Tommy Dorsey Orch. (VR: Jack Leonard)
5 THERE'S NO TOMORROW   Tony Martin
6 BIBBIDI BOBBIDI BOO   Jo Stafford & Gordon MacRae
7 JOHNSON RAG   Jack Teter Trio
   Note: * Another version by: Dinah Shore.
      ** Another version by "Your Hit Parade" star, Snooky Lanson.

February 11, 1950
1 DEAR HEARTS AND GENTLE PEOPLE   Bing Crosby *
2 THE OLD MASTER PAINTER   Richard Hayes **
3 THERE'S NO TOMORROW   Tony Martin
4 I CAN DREAM, CAN'T I?   Tommy Dorsey Orch. (VR: Jack Leonard)
5 BIBBIDI BOBBIDI BOO   Jo Stafford & Gordon MacRae
6 CHATTANOOGA SHOE SHINE BOY   Red Foley @
7 A DREAMER'S HOLIDAY   Perry Como
   Note: * Another version by: Dinah Shore.
      ** Another version by "Your Hit Parade" star, Snooky Lanson.
      @ Another version by: Bing Crosby.

February 18, 1950
1 DEAR HEARTS AND GENTLE PEOPLE   Bing Crosby *
2 THERE'S NO TOMORROW   Tony Martin
3 THE OLD MASTER PAINTER   Richard Hayes **
4 JOHNSON RAG   Jack Teter Trio
5 A DREAMER'S HOLIDAY   Perry Como
6 I CAN DREAM, CAN'T I?   Tommy Dorsey Orch. (VR: Jack Leonard)
7 CHATTANOOGA SHOE SHINE BOY   Red Foley @
   Note: * Another version by: Dinah Shore.
      ** Another version by "Your Hit Parade" star, Snooky Lanson.
      @ Another version by: Bing Crosby.

February 25, 1950
1 CHATTANOOGA SHOE SHINE BOY   Red Foley *
2 DEAR HEARTS AND GENTLE PEOPLE   Bing Crosby **
3 BIBBIDI BOBBIDI BOO   Jo Stafford & Gordon MacRae
4 THE OLD MASTER PAINTER   Richard Hayes @
5 I SAID MY PAJAMAS   Tony Martin & Fran Warren
6 RAG MOP   Ames Brothers
7 THERE'S NO TOMORROW   Tony Martin
   Note: * Another version by: Bing Crosby.
      ** Another version by: Dinah Shore.
      @ Another version by "Your Hit Parade" star, Snooky Lanson.

March 4, 1950
1 CHATTANOOGA SHOE SHINE BOY   Red Foley *
2 DEAR HEARTS AND GENTLE PEOPLE   Bing Crosby **
3 MUSIC, MUSIC, MUSIC   Teresa Brewer
4 I SAID MY PAJAMAS   Tony Martin & Fran Warren

139

Tony Martin

Martin's first Top 10 hit—``There's No Tomorrow''—charts in the early months of 1950.

5 BIBBIDI BOBBIDI BOO   Jo Stafford & Gordon MacRae
6 THERE'S NO TOMORROW   Tony Martin
7 RAG MOP   Ames Brothers
Note: * A #1 country hit for Red Foley.
    ** Another version by: Dinah Shore.

March 11, 1950

1 CHATTANOOGA SHOE SHINE BOY   Red Foley *
2 MUSIC, MUSIC, MUSIC   Teresa Brewer
3 I SAID MY PAJAMAS   Tony Martin & Fran Warren
4 RAG MOP   Ames Brothers
5 THERE'S NO TOMORROW   Tony Martin
6 DEAR HEARTS AND GENTLE PEOPLE   Bing Crosby **
7 ENJOY YOURSELF   Guy Lombardo Orch. (VR: Kenny
    Gardner)
Note: * Another version by: Bing Crosby.
    ** Another version by: Dinah Shore.

March 18, 1950

1 CHATTANOOGA SHOE SHINE BOY   Red Foley *
2 I SAID MY PAJAMAS   Tony Martin & Fran Warren
3 MUSIC, MUSIC, MUSIC   Teresa Brewer
4 DEAR HEARTS AND GENTLE PEOPLE   Bing Crosby **
5 DADDY'S LITTLE GIRL   Mills Brothers
6 RAG MOP   Ames Brothers
7 THERE'S NO TOMORROW   Tony Martin
Note: * Another version by: Bing Crosby.
    ** Another version by: Dinah Shore.

March 25, 1950

1 CHATTANOOGA SHOE SHINE BOY   Red Foley *
2 MUSIC, MUSIC, MUSIC   Teresa Brewer
3 THERE'S NO TOMORROW   Tony Martin
4 IF I KNEW YOU WERE COMIN' I'D'VE BAKED A CAKE
    Eileen Barton
5 I SAID MY PAJAMAS   Tony Martin & Fran Warren
6 RAG MOP   Ames Brothers
7 DEARIE   Guy Lombardo Orch. (VR: Kenny Gardner & Trio)
Note: * Another version by: Bing Crosby.

April 1, 1950

1 CHATTANOOGA SHOE SHINE BOY   Red Foley *
2 IF I KNEW YOU WERE COMIN' I'D'VE BAKED A CAKE
    Eileen Barton
3 DEARIE   Guy Lombardo Orch. (VR: Kenny Gardner & Trio)
4 MUSIC, MUSIC, MUSIC   Teresa Brewer
5 IT ISN'T FAIR   Sammy Kaye Orch. (VR: Don Cornell)
6 MY FOOLISH HEART   Gordon Jenkins Orch. (VR: Eileen
    Wilson)
7 ENJOY YOURSELF   Guy Lombardo Orch. (VR: Kenny
    Gardner)
Note: * Another version by: Bing Crosby.

April 8, 1950

1 IF I KNEW YOU WERE COMIN' I'D'VE BAKED A CAKE
    Eileen Barton
2 MUSIC, MUSIC, MUSIC   Teresa Brewer
3 CHATTANOOGA SHOE SHINE BOY   Red Foley *
4 MY FOOLISH HEART   Gordon Jenkins Orch. (VR: Eileen
    Wilson)
5 DEARIE   Guy Lombardo Orch. (VR: Kenny Gardner & Trio)
6 IT ISN'T FAIR   Sammy Kaye Orch. (VR: Don Cornell)
7 I SAID MY PAJAMAS   Tony Martin & Fran Warren
Note: * Another version by: Bing Crosby.

April 15, 1950

1 IF I KNEW YOU WERE COMIN' I'D'VE BAKED A CAKE
    Eileen Barton
2 PETER COTTONTAIL   Gene Autry *
3 DEARIE   Guy Lombardo Orch. (VR: Kenny Gardner & Trio)
4 MUSIC, MUSIC, MUSIC   Teresa Brewer
5 MY FOOLISH HEART   Gordon Jenkins Orch. (VR: Eileen
    Wilson)
6 IT ISN'T FAIR   Sammy Kaye Orch. (VR: Don Cornell)
7 DADDY'S LITTLE GIRL   Mills Brothers
Note: * Easter hit.

April 22, 1950

1 IF I KNEW YOU WERE COMIN' I'D'VE BAKED A CAKE
    Eileen Barton
2 MY FOOLISH HEART   Gordon Jenkins Orch. (VR: Eileen
    Wilson)
3 DEARIE   Guy Lombardo Orch. (VR: Kenny Gardner & Trio)
4 IT ISN'T FAIR   Sammy Kaye Orch. (VR: Don Cornell)
5 DADDY'S LITTLE GIRL   Mills Brothers
6 MUSIC, MUSIC, MUSIC   Teresa Brewer
7 CANDY AND CAKE   Mindy Carson

April 29, 1950

1 MY FOOLISH HEART   Gordon Jenkins Orch. (VR: Eileen
    Wilson)
2 THE THIRD MAN THEME   Alton Karas *
3 IT ISN'T FAIR   Sammy Kaye Orch. (VR: Don Cornell)
4 MUSIC, MUSIC, MUSIC   Teresa Brewer
5 IF I KNEW YOU WERE COMIN' I'D'VE BAKED A CAKE
    Eileen Barton
6 DEARIE   Guy Lombardo Orch. (VR: Kenny Gardner & Trio)
7 DADDY'S LITTLE GIRL   Mills Brothers
Note: * Another version by: Guy Lombardo Orch.

May 6, 1950

1 MY FOOLISH HEART   Gordon Jenkins Orch. (VR: Eileen
    Wilson)
2 IF I KNEW YOU WERE COMIN' I'D'VE BAKED A CAKE
    Eileen Barton
3 THE THIRD MAN THEME   Alton Karas *
4 DEARIE   Guy Lombardo Orch. (VR: Kenny Gardner & Trio)
5 IT ISN'T FAIR   Sammy Kaye Orch. (VR: Don Cornell)
6 MUSIC, MUSIC, MUSIC   Teresa Brewer
7 CANDY AND CAKE   Mindy Carson
Note: * Another version by: Guy Lombardo Orch.

May 13, 1950

1 MY FOOLISH HEART   Gordon Jenkins Orch. (VR: Eileen
    Wilson)
2 IT ISN'T FAIR   Sammy Kaye Orch. (VR: Don Cornell)
3 THE THIRD MAN THEME   Alton Karas *
4 IF I KNEW YOU WERE COMIN' I'D'VE BAKED A CAKE
    Eileen Barton
5 SENTIMENTAL ME   Ames Brothers
6 DEARIE   Guy Lombardo Orch. (VR: Kenny Gardner & Trio)
7 BEWITCHED   Bill Snyder Orch. **
Note: * Another version by: Guy Lombardo Orch.
    ** Another version by: Gordon Jenkins Orch. (VR:
    Mary Lou Williams).

May 20, 1950

1 MY FOOLISH HEART   Gordon Jenkins Orch. (VR: Eileen
    Wilson)
2 BEWITCHED   Bill Snyder Orch. *
3 IF I KNEW YOU WERE COMIN' I'D'VE BAKED A CAKE
    Eileen Barton

4 THE THIRD MAN THEME   Alton Karas **
5 DEARIE   Guy Lombardo Orch. (VR: Kenny Gardner & Trio)
6 IT ISN'T FAIR   Sammy Kaye Orch. (VR: Don Cornell)
7 HOOP-DEE-DOO   Perry Como
Note: * Another version by: Gordon Jenkins Orch. (VR: Mary Lou Williams).
** Another version by: Guy Lombardo Orch.

May 27, 1950
1 MY FOOLISH HEART   Gordon Jenkins Orch. (VR: Eileen Wilson)
2 BEWITCHED   Bill Snyder Orch. *
3 IF I KNEW YOU WERE COMIN' I'D'VE BAKED A CAKE   Eileen Barton
4 IT ISN'T FAIR   Sammy Kaye Orch. (VR: Don Cornell)
5 HOOP-DEE-DOO   Perry Como
6 THE THIRD MAN THEME   Alton Karas **
7 THE OLD PIANO ROLL BLUES   Hoagy Carmichael & Cass Daley
Note: * Another version by: Gordon Jenkins Orch. (VR: Mary Lou Williams).
** Another version by: Guy Lombardo Orch.

June 3, 1950
1 MY FOOLISH HEART   Gordon Jenkins Orch. (VR: Eileen Wilson)
2 BEWITCHED   Bill Snyder Orch. *
3 THE THIRD MAN THEME   Alton Karas **
4 IF I KNEW YOU WERE COMIN' I'D'VE BAKED A CAKE   Eileen Barton
5 THE OLD PIANO ROLL BLUES   Hoagy Carmichael & Cass Daley
6 SENTIMENTAL ME   Ames Brothers
7 IT ISN'T FAIR   Sammy Kaye Orch. (VR: Don Cornell)
Note: * Another version by: Gordon Jenkins Orch. (VR: Mary Lou Williams).
** Another version by: Guy Lombardo Orch.

June 10, 1950
1 MY FOOLISH HEART   Gordon Jenkins Orch. (VR: Eileen Wilson)
2 BEWITCHED   Bill Snyder Orch. *
3 THE THIRD MAN THEME   Alton Karas **
4 THE OLD PIANO ROLL BLUES   Hoagy Carmichael & Cass Daley
5 HOOP-DEE-DOO   Perry Como
6 SENTIMENTAL ME   Ames Brothers
7 IT ISN'T FAIR   Sammy Kaye Orch. (VR: Don Cornell)
Note: * Another version by: Gordon Jenkins Orch. (VR: Mary Lou Williams).
** Another version by: Guy Lombardo Orch.

June 17, 1950
1 MY FOOLISH HEART   Gordon Jenkins Orch. (VR: Eileen Wilson)
2 BEWITCHED   Bill Snyder Orch. *
3 THE THIRD MAN THEME   Alton Karas **
4 HOOP-DEE-DOO   Perry Como
5 THE OLD PIANO ROLL BLUES   Hoagy Carmichael & Cass Daley
6 SENTIMENTAL ME   Ames Brothers
7 IT ISN'T FAIR   Sammy Kaye Orch. (VR: Don Cornell)
Note: * Another version by: Gordon Jenkins Orch. (VR: Mary Lou Williams).
** Another version by: Guy Lombardo Orch.

June 24, 1950
1 BEWITCHED   Bill Snyder Orch. *
2 MY FOOLISH HEART   Gordon Jenkins Orch. (VR: Eileen Wilson)
3 SENTIMENTAL ME   Ames Brothers
4 HOOP-DEE-DOO   Perry Como
5 THE OLD PIANO ROLL BLUES   Hoagy Carmichael & Cass Daley
6 THE THIRD MAN THEME   Alton Karas **
7 I DON'T CARE IF THE SUN DON'T SHINE   Patti Page
Note: * Another version by: Gordon Jenkins Orch. (VR: Mary Lou Williams).
** Another version by: Guy Lombardo Orch.

July 1, 1950
1 BEWITCHED   Bill Snyder Orch. *
2 MY FOOLISH HEART   Gordon Jenkins Orch. (VR: Eileen Wilson)
3 HOOP-DEE-DOO   Perry Como
4 THE OLD PIANO ROLL BLUES   Hoagy Carmichael & Cass Daley
5 SENTIMENTAL ME   Ames Brothers
6 THE THIRD MAN THEME   Alton Karas **
7 I DON'T CARE IF THE SUN DON'T SHINE   Patti Page
Note: * Another version by: Gordon Jenkins Orch. (VR: Mary Lou Williams).
** Another version by: Guy Lombardo Orch.

July 8, 1950
1 MY FOOLISH HEART   Gordon Jenkins Orch. (VR: Eileen Wilson)
2 BEWITCHED   Bill Snyder Orch. *
3 I WANNA BE LOVED   Andrews Sisters
4 THE THIRD MAN THEME   Alton Karas **
5 HOOP-DEE-DOO   Perry Como
6 I DON'T CARE IF THE SUN DON'T SHINE   Patti Page
7 COUNT EVERY STAR   Ray Anthony Orch. (VR: Dick Noel)
Note: * Another version by: Gordon Jenkins Orch. (VR: Mary Lou Williams).
** Another version by: Guy Lombardo Orch.

July 15, 1950
1 BEWITCHED   Bill Snyder Orch. *
2 I WANNA BE LOVED   Andrews Sisters
3 MY FOOLISH HEART   Gordon Jenkins Orch. (VR: Eileen Wilson)
4 HOOP-DEE-DOO   Perry Como
5 THE THIRD MAN THEME   Alton Karas **
6 COUNT EVERY STAR   Ray Anthony Orch. (VR: Dick Noel)
7 MONA LISA   Nat King Cole
Note: * Another version by: Gordon Jenkins Orch. (VR: Mary Lou Williams).
** Another version by: Guy Lombardo Orch.

July 22, 1950
1 BEWITCHED   Bill Snyder Orch. *
2 MONA LISA   Nat King Cole
3 I WANNA BE LOVED   Andrews Sisters
4 HOOP-DEE-DOO   Perry Como
5 THE THIRD MAN THEME   Alton Karas **
6 I DON'T CARE IF THE SUN DON'T SHINE   Patti Page
7 MY FOOLISH HEART   Gordon Jenkins Orch. (VR: Eileen Wilson)
Note: * Another version by: Gordon Jenkins Orch. (VR: Mary Lou Williams).
** Another version by: Guy Lombardo Orch.

The Nat King Cole Trio
In early '47, Nat's first #1 hit—``For Sentimental
Reason's''—topped the Hit Parade for six weeks.

Nat "King" Cole
Velvet-voiced Nat Cole hits #1 with his classic rendition of ``Mona Lisa'' (Aug. 12).

The Weavers
L - R: Pete Seeger, Lee Hays,
Ronnie Gilbert and Fred Hellerman
have a huge hit with
``Goodnight Irene'' (Sep. 30).

Gene Autry
Autry scored with several other big-time hits,
but his holiday classics—``Rudolph The
Red-Nosed Reindeer'' (Dec. 23),
``Frosty The Snowman'' and
``Petter Cottontail'' will endure forever.

July 29, 1950
1 MONA LISA   Nat King Cole
2 BEWITCHED   Bill Snyder Orch. *
3 MY FOOLISH HEART   Gordon Jenkins Orch. (VR: Eileen Wilson)
4 I WANNA BE LOVED   Andrews Sisters
5 THE THIRD MAN THEME   Alton Karas **
6 COUNT EVERY STAR   Ray Anthony Orch. (VR: Dick Noel)
7 I DON'T CARE IF THE SUN DON'T SHINE   Patti Page
  Note: * Another version by: Gordon Jenkins Orch. (VR: Mary Lou Williams).
     ** Another version by: Guy Lombardo Orch.

August 5, 1950
1 BEWITCHED   Bill Snyder Orch. *
2 MONA LISA   Nat King Cole
3 COUNT EVERY STAR   Ray Anthony Orch. (VR: Dick Noel)
4 I WANNA BE LOVED   Andrews Sisters
5 HOOP-DEE-DOO   Perry Como
6 SAM'S SONG   Bing & Gary Crosby
7 TZENA, TZENA, TZENA   The Weavers with Gordon Jenkins Orch.
  Note: * Another version by: Gordon Jenkins Orch. (VR: Mary Lou Williams).

August 12, 1950
1 MONA LISA   Nat King Cole
2 I WANNA BE LOVED   Andrews Sisters
3 BEWITCHED   Bill Snyder Orch. *
4 COUNT EVERY STAR   Ray Anthony Orch. (VR: Dick Noel)
5 SAM'S SONG   Bing & Gary Crosby
6 THE THIRD MAN THEME   Alton Karas **
7 HOOP-DEE-DOO   Perry Como
  Note: * Another version by: Gordon Jenkins Orch. (VR: Mary Lou Williams).
     ** Another version by: Guy Lombardo Orch.

August 19, 1950
1 MONA LISA   Nat King Cole
2 SAM'S SONG   Bing & Gary Crosby
3 I WANNA BE LOVED   Andrews Sisters
4 BEWITCHED   Bill Snyder Orch. *
5 PLAY A SIMPLE MELODY   Bing Crosby
6 COUNT EVERY STAR   Ray Anthony Orch. (VR: Dick Noel)
7 GOODNIGHT IRENE   The Weavers
  Note: * Another version by: Gordon Jenkins Orch. (VR: Mary Lou Williams).

August 26, 1950
1 MONA LISA   Nat King Cole
2 PLAY A SIMPLE MELODY   Bing Crosby
3 SAM'S SONG   Bing & Gary Crosby
4 GOODNIGHT IRENE   The Weavers
5 COUNT EVERY STAR   Ray Anthony Orch. (VR: Dick Noel)
6 BEWITCHED   Bill Snyder Orch. *
7 I WANNA BE LOVED   Andrews Sisters
  Note: * Another version by: Gordon Jenkins Orch. (VR: Mary Lou Williams).

September 2, 1950
1 MONA LISA   Nat King Cole
2 PLAY A SIMPLE MELODY   Bing Crosby
3 GOODNIGHT IRENE   The Weavers
4 SAM'S SONG   Bing & Gary Crosby
5 TZENA, TZENA, TZENA   The Weavers with Gordon Jenkins Orch.
6 LA VIE EN ROSE   Tony Martin
7 I WANNA BE LOVED   Andrews Sisters

September 9, 1950
1 MONA LISA   Nat King Cole
2 GOODNIGHT IRENE   The Weavers
3 PLAY A SIMPLE MELODY   Bing Crosby
4 LA VIE EN ROSE   Tony Martin
5 SAM'S SONG   Bing & Gary Crosby
6 ALL MY LOVE   Patti Page
7 I DON'T CARE IF THE SUN DON'T SHINE   Patti Page

September 16, 1950
1 MONA LISA   Nat King Cole
2 GOODNIGHT IRENE   The Weavers
3 PLAY A SIMPLE MELODY   Bing Crosby
4 SAM'S SONG   Bing & Gary Crosby
5 TZENA, TZENA, TZENA   The Weavers with Gordon Jenkins Orch.
6 ALL MY LOVE   Patti Page
7 LA VIE EN ROSE   Tony Martin

September 23, 1950
1 MONA LISA   Nat King Cole
2 GOODNIGHT IRENE   The Weavers
3 PLAY A SIMPLE MELODY   Bing Crosby
4 SAM'S SONG   Bing & Gary Crosby
5 ALL MY LOVE   Patti Page
6 LA VIE EN ROSE   Tony Martin
7 SOMETIME   The Mariners

September 30, 1950
1 GOODNIGHT IRENE   The Weavers
2 LA VIE EN ROSE   Tony Martin
3 ALL MY LOVE   Patti Page
4 MONA LISA   Nat King Cole
5 PLAY A SIMPLE MELODY   Bing Crosby
6 SAM'S SONG   Bing & Gary Crosby
7 CAN ANYONE EXPLAIN   Ames Brothers *
  Note: * Another version by: Ray Anthony Orch. (VR: Ronnie Deauville & the Skyliners).

October 7, 1950
1 LA VIE EN ROSE   Tony Martin
2 GOODNIGHT IRENE   The Weavers
3 MONA LISA   Nat King Cole
4 SAM'S SONG   Bing & Gary Crosby
5 ALL MY LOVE   Patti Page
6 PLAY A SIMPLE MELODY   Bing Crosby
7 BONAPARTE'S RETREAT   Kay Starr

October 14, 1950
1 GOODNIGHT IRENE   The Weavers
2 ALL MY LOVE   Patti Page
3 LA VIE EN ROSE   Tony Martin
4 MONA LISA   Nat King Cole
5 CAN ANYONE EXPLAIN   Ames Brothers *
6 PLAY A SIMPLE MELODY   Bing Crosby
7 SAM'S SONG   Bing & Gary Crosby
  Note: * Another version by: Ray Anthony Orch. (VR: Ronnie Deauville & the Skyliners).

October 21, 1950
1 GOODNIGHT IRENE   The Weavers
2 MONA LISA   Nat King Cole
3 ALL MY LOVE   Patti Page

Decades later, Patti's beauty, like her music, has survived the test of time.

Patti Page
Patti has back-to-back #1 hits with ``All My Love'' (Oct. 28, 1950) and ``Tennessee Waltz'' (Jan. 6, 1951).

The Patti Page Story

In 1970, Patti Page sold her 60-millionth record. Was it "Gentle On My Mind" or "Little Green Apples"—both hits for Patti that year? Or was it "Tennessee Waltz," which topped the seven million mark in sales in the seventies and continues to sell years after its initial release?

It matters not. What does count is the durability of Patti Page to survive where others have not in that most perilous of all fields—the recording industry. In that world, Patti is the all-time, best-selling female vocalist of the Hit Parade era, and her recording of "Tennessee Waltz" is one of the biggest-selling single records ever recorded by a female singer. In truth, today, as she was in the fifties, Patti Page is. . . "The Singing Rage."

In Claremore, Oklahoma, Patti, then Clara Ann Fowler, was the second youngest of eleven children. The Fowlers eked out an existence of the fifty dollars a month Patti's father earned as a railroad section foreman. Some of Patti's earliest recollections are of walking to school barefoot (the only pair of shoes she owned were earmarked for Sunday dress only), and of visiting her mother in the cotton fields where she worked to supplement the family income.

Patti dreamed of a better life; she started out with plans to become a commercial artist, and was near realizing this ambition when she was awarded a scholarship in art at Tulsa University. However, the prospect of four years of study didn't seem as promising as an actual job, so when a position in the art department of a local radio station was offered to her, Patti took it.

Her career in art was short-lived. Shortly after she began the job, an emergency call went out at the station for a singer to replace the regular vocalist of a fifteen-minute musical show sponsored by the Page Milk Company. Patti—who had sung in the church choir with her seven sisters, and who had done some professional singing around Tulsa—applied for and got the job. She also assumed the name of her sponsor, Page.

One day, Jack Rael, a professional musician with Jimmy Joy's band, visited Tulsa. While resting in his hotel room, he heard Patti singing on the radio; convinced that the voice he heard had star potential, he sought her out.

Thus began one of the most successful artist/manager relationships in history. Rael, still Patti's manager, launched her to fame and fortune, but not without paying some dues. Many months and many more small clubs and venues came and went before Rael arranged an audition for Patti with Don McNeil, perennial host of ABC's "Breakfast Club." McNeil quickly echoed Rael's enthusiasm. A series of appearances on his program soon led Patti to a show of her own on CBS.

Mercury Records signed Patti to a recording contract without much fanfare (the news was greeted with a yawn from the industry). Patti's first twelve records merely fostered more yawns, but the thirteenth (lucky thirteen, in this case) changed everything. A crazy, mixed up, nutty, inventive fluke of a recording, it totally revolutionized the industry.

In the late forties, Patti and Jack were recording in Chicago at Universal Studios. Bill Putnam was the engineer. Rael had found a song called "Confess," but Mercury cut the backing down to only a trio—the George Barnes Trio. When the basic recording was completed, it sounded like it "needed something" to make it different.

Rael suggested to Putnam that Patti sing answers to the song lyric by "overdubbing," which Putnam initially felt couldn't be done. Patti suggested they try it anyway. (Remember...tape was not yet invented; even wire recording was not available. They had only acetate discs—it meant cutting in Patti's voice over a disc already cut.) Patti and Jack convinced Putnam to see what he could do, and "overdubbing" was invented.

The recording was Patti's first hit (the idea of one person singing with herself was probably more exciting to listeners than the song itself), but it was only the beginning. Mitch Miller, then an oboist who managed Mercury's New York office, was soon visited by Jack Rael. What about a four-part harmony with Patti singing all voices, Rael asked. Miller felt "it could not be done."

Patti and Rael did the first eight bars of the song "With My Eyes Wide Open I'm Dreaming," rehearsing in the basement of a club in Milwaukee, Wisconsin, and then fixing the four-part harmony on disc. Mercury could not believe the results, and pleaded with Patti to finish the record. Four-part harmony by one singer was born, and the record was Patti's first truly big hit—the first of thirteen million-selling records.

The success of Patti's multiple-voice recordings was responsible for an October 1950 booking at New York's Copacabana, a nightclub appearance which led indirectly to the release of one of the greatest hits of all time.

It was pre-Christmas, and Mercury executives decided their singing rage should cut a Christmas novelty which they felt would sell millions. The song, "Boogie Woogie Santa Claus," was not one of Patti's more inspired efforts. Nevertheless, Mercury put on an all-out push to promote the record until audiences at the Copa convinced them otherwise. When Patti sang "Boogie Woogie Santa Claus," people would yell out: "Sing the other side!"

The other side—the "B" or throwaway side in record circles—just happened to be a little ditty called "Tennessee Waltz." It rapidly became the most successful recording since Bing Crosby's "White Christmas." At one point, it was reported that copies were selling at twenty dollars a copy on the black market in—of all places—Shanghai, Red China.

Hit after hit followed "Tennessee Waltz." Among them were "All My Love," "Mockingbird Hill," "Would I Love You, Love You, Love You," "Mr. And Mississippi," "Detour," "I Went To Your Wedding" (which sold a million records within two months of release), and "Doggie In The Window" (which barked its way to a three-million sales mark).

"The Singing Rage" sang on into the fifties, racking up such million-record successes as "Changing Partners," "Left Right Out Of Your Heart," "Cross Over The Bridge," "Allegheny Moon," and "Old Cape Cod." In 1963, Patti signed an exclusive contract with Columbia Records. Her albums for the label—"Say Wonderful Things," "Hush, Hush, Sweet Charlotte," and "Gentle On My Mind"—were all successes. (The success of "Sweet Charlotte" had a lot to do with Patti's appearance on the 1965 Oscar broadcast. The tune didn't win the coveted statue, but it did earn Patti another Top Ten hit, both for the single and for the album.)

With all Patti's successes, it was only natural that television would welcome her. Beginning with a twice-a-week fifteen-minute song session on CBS-TV, she was then signed for an every-other week appearance on NBC-TV's "Scott Music Hall." Later, Patti began filming her own twice-weekly television program, "The Oldsmobile Patti Page Show." When CBS decided to try and attract the tremendous phonograph record audience to a weekly show called "The Big Record," they quite naturally signed Patti Page, the big name in the record industry, to host the show.

During the 1958-59 season, Patti starred in an informal but fast-paced musical variety program called "The Patti Page Show," which was aired on an unprecedented 234 stations by the ABC television network. In succeeding years, she headlined a syndicated TV special called "Something Special," co-hosted a "Country Music Awards Show," and guested on a Dick Clark anniversary show and an ABC 25th anniversary show.

Patti moved to Plantation Records, where her first single for the label—"No Aces"—reached into the thirties on country music charts everywhere, and ended up as the title song for her first Plantation album. Her second single from the album—"On The Inside"—also did well on the country charts.

Divorced, Patti, who settled in Rancho Santa Fe, California, with her two children, Kathleen Patricia and Daniel Benjamin, was never forgotten by native Oklahomans. Claremore's Second Street was renamed "Patti Page Boulevard" in her honor, and she was made an honorary cadet of the Oklahoma Military Academy.

"I love to sing and entertain people," she's stated. "People were put on earth for a purpose. I think that's why I'm here. And, if I'm able to make people happy...well, I won't argue with that."

4 LA VIE EN ROSE   Tony Martin
5 SAM'S SONG   Bing & Gary Crosby
6 HARBOR LIGHTS   Sammy Kaye Orch. (VR: Tony Alamo)
7 PLAY A SIMPLE MELODY   Bing Crosby

October 28, 1950
1 ALL MY LOVE   Patti Page
2 HARBOR LIGHTS   Sammy Kaye Orch. (VR: Tony Alamo)
3 LA VIE EN ROSE   Tony Martin
4 GOODNIGHT IRENE   The Weavers
5 MONA LISA   Nat King Cole
6 THINKING OF YOU   Don Cherry
7 PLAY A SIMPLE MELODY   Bing Crosby

November 4, 1950
1 GOODNIGHT IRENE   The Weavers
2 ALL MY LOVE   Patti Page
3 HARBOR LIGHTS   Sammy Kaye Orch. (VR: Tony Alamo)
4 LA VIE EN ROSE   Tony Martin
5 THINKING OF YOU   Don Cherry
6 MONA LISA   Nat King Cole
7 NEVERTHELESS   Jack Denny

November 11, 1950
1 ALL MY LOVE   Patti Page
2 GOODNIGHT IRENE   The Weavers
3 THINKING OF YOU   Don Cherry
4 HARBOR LIGHTS   Sammy Kaye Orch. (VR: Tony Alamo)
5 NEVERTHELESS   Jack Denny
6 LA VIE EN ROSE   Tony Martin
7 ORANGE COLORED SKY   Nat King Cole with Stan Kenton
   Orch.

November 18, 1950
1 HARBOR LIGHTS   Sammy Kaye Orch. (VR: Tony Alamo)
2 GOODNIGHT IRENE   The Weavers
3 THINKING OF YOU   Don Cherry
4 ALL MY LOVE   Patti Page
5 LA VIE EN ROSE   Tony Martin
6 A BUSHEL AND A PECK   Perry Como & Betty Hutton
7 NEVERTHELESS   Jack Denny

November 25, 1950
1 HARBOR LIGHTS   Sammy Kaye Orch. (VR: Tony Alamo)
2 NEVERTHELESS   Jack Denny
3 ALL MY LOVE   Patti Page
4 THINKING OF YOU   Don Cherry
5 A BUSHEL AND A PECK   Perry Como & Betty Hutton
6 GOODNIGHT IRENE   The Weavers
7 LA VIE EN ROSE   Tony Martin

December 2, 1950
1 ALL MY LOVE   Patti Page
2 THINKING OF YOU   Don Cherry
3 A BUSHEL AND A PECK   Perry Como & Betty Hutton
4 NEVERTHELESS   Jack Denny
5 HARBOR LIGHTS   Sammy Kaye Orch. (VR: Tony Alamo)
6 LA VIE EN ROSE   Tony Martin
7 RUDOLPH, THE RED NOSED REINDEER   Gene Autry

December 9, 1950
1 NEVERTHELESS   Jack Denny
2 A BUSHEL AND A PECK   Perry Como & Betty Hutton
3 ALL MY LOVE   Patti Page
4 HARBOR LIGHTS   Sammy Kaye Orch. (VR: Tony Alamo)
5 THE THING   Phil Harris (VR: Phil Harris)

6 THINKING OF YOU   Don Cherry
7 RUDOLPH, THE RED NOSED REINDEER   Gene Autry

December 16, 1950
1 A BUSHEL AND A PECK   Perry Como & Betty Hutton
2 RUDOLPH, THE RED NOSED REINDEER   Gene Autry
3 HARBOR LIGHTS   Sammy Kaye Orch. (VR: Tony Alamo)
4 ALL MY LOVE   Patti Page
5 NEVERTHELESS   Jack Denny
6 THE THING   Phil Harris (VR: Phil Harris)
7 TENNESSEE WALTZ   Patti Page

December 23, 1950
1 RUDOLPH, THE RED NOSED REINDEER   Gene Autry
2 A BUSHEL AND A PECK   Perry Como & Betty Hutton
3 TENNESSEE WALTZ   Patti Page
4 THE THING   Phil Harris (VR: Phil Harris)
5 HARBOR LIGHTS   Sammy Kaye Orch. (VR: Tony Alamo)
6 NEVERTHELESS   Jack Denny
7 IT'S A MARSHMELLOW WORLD   Bing Crosby

December 30, 1950
1 RUDOLPH, THE RED NOSED REINDEER   Gene Autry
2 FROSTY THE SNOWMAN   Gene Autry
3 THE THING   Phil Harris (VR: Phil Harris)
4 TENNESSEE WALTZ   Patti Page
5 A BUSHEL AND A PECK   Perry Como & Betty Hutton
6 WHITE CHRISTMAS   Bing Crosby
7 HARBOR LIGHTS   Sammy Kaye Orch. (VR: Tony Alamo)

January 6, 1951
1 TENNESSEE WALTZ   Patti Page
2 A BUSHEL AND A PECK   Perry Como & Betty Hutton
3 NEVERTHELESS   Jack Denny
4 THE THING   Phil Harris (VR: Phil Harris)
5 ALL MY LOVE   Patti Page
6 IT'S A MARSHMELLOW WORLD   Bing Crosby
7 HARBOR LIGHTS   Sammy Kaye Orch. (VR: Tony Alamo)

January 13, 1951
1 TENNESSEE WALTZ   Patti Page
2 THE THING   Phil Harris (VR: Phil Harris)
3 HARBOR LIGHTS   Sammy Kaye Orch. (VR: Tony Alamo)
4 A BUSHEL AND A PECK   Perry Como & Betty Hutton
5 NEVERTHELESS   Jack Denny
6 MY HEART CRIES FOR YOU   Guy Mitchell
7 ALL MY LOVE   Patti Page

January 20, 1951
1 TENNESSEE WALTZ   Patti Page
2 THE THING   Phil Harris (VR: Phil Harris)
3 A BUSHEL AND A PECK   Perry Como & Betty Hutton
4 NEVERTHELESS   Jack Denny
5 MY HEART CRIES FOR YOU   Guy Mitchell
6 HARBOR LIGHTS   Sammy Kaye Orch. (VR: Tony Alamo)
7 IT'S A MARSHMELLOW WORLD   Bing Crosby

January 27, 1951
1 MY HEART CRIES FOR YOU   Guy Mitchell
2 TENNESSEE WALTZ   Patti Page
3 A BUSHEL AND A PECK   Perry Como & Betty Hutton
4 NEVERTHELESS   Jack Denny
5 YOU'RE JUST IN LOVE   Perry Como
6 BE MY LOVE   Mario Lanza
7 HARBOR LIGHTS   Sammy Kaye Orch. (VR: Tony Alamo)

February 3, 1951
1. TENNESSEE WALTZ   Patti Page
2. MY HEART CRIES FOR YOU   Guy Mitchell
3. IF   Perry Como
4. BE MY LOVE   Mario Lanza
5. A BUSHEL AND A PECK   Perry Como & Betty Hutton
6. HARBOR LIGHTS   Sammy Kaye Orch. (VR: Tony Alamo)
7. YOU'RE JUST IN LOVE   Perry Como

February 10, 1951
1. MY HEART CRIES FOR YOU   Guy Mitchell
2. TENNESSEE WALTZ   Patti Page
3. IF   Perry Como
4. YOU'RE JUST IN LOVE   Perry Como
5. BE MY LOVE   Mario Lanza
6. HARBOR LIGHTS   Sammy Kaye Orch. (VR: Tony Alamo)
7. A BUSHEL AND A PECK   Perry Como & Betty Hutton

February 17, 1951
1. TENNESSEE WALTZ   Patti Page
2. MY HEART CRIES FOR YOU   Guy Mitchell
3. IF   Perry Como
4. BE MY LOVE   Mario Lanza
5. YOU'RE JUST IN LOVE   Perry Como
6. A BUSHEL AND A PECK   Perry Como & Betty Hutton
7. HARBOR LIGHTS   Sammy Kaye Orch. (VR: Tony Alamo)

February 24, 1951
1. IF   Perry Como
2. MY HEART CRIES FOR YOU   Guy Mitchell
3. BE MY LOVE   Mario Lanza
4. TENNESSEE WALTZ   Patti Page
5. YOU'RE JUST IN LOVE   Perry Como
6. A BUSHEL AND A PECK   Perry Como & Betty Hutton
7. A PENNY A KISS   Dinah Shore

March 3, 1951
1. IF   Perry Como
2. MY HEART CRIES FOR YOU   Guy Mitchell
3. TENNESSEE WALTZ   Patti Page
4. BE MY LOVE   Mario Lanza
5. YOU'RE JUST IN LOVE   Perry Como
6. A PENNY A KISS   Dinah Shore
7. ZING, ZING, ZOOM, ZOOM   Perry Como

March 10, 1051
1. IF   Perry Como
2. TENNESSEE WALTZ   Patti Page
3. BE MY LOVE   Mario Lanza
4. YOU'RE JUST IN LOVE   Perry Como
5. MY HEART CRIES FOR YOU   Guy Mitchell
6. ABA DABA HONEYMOON   Debbie Reynolds & Carleton Carpenter
7. A PENNY A KISS   Dinah Shore

March 17, 1951
1. IF   Perry Como
2. BE MY LOVE   Mario Lanza
3. YOU'RE JUST IN LOVE   Perry Como
4. MY HEART CRIES FOR YOU   Guy Mitchell
5. ABA DABA HONEYMOON   Debbie Reynolds & Carleton Carpenter
6. TENNESSEE WALTZ   Patti Page
7. WOULD I LOVE YOU   Patti Page

March 24, 1951
1. IF   Perry Como
2. BE MY LOVE   Mario Lanza
3. MY HEART CRIES FOR YOU   Guy Mitchell
4. MOCKING BIRD HILL   Les Paul & Mary Ford *
5. YOU'RE JUST IN LOVE   Perry Como
6. TENNESSEE WALTZ   Patti Page
7. ABA DABA HONEYMOON   Debbie Reynolds & Carleton Carpenter
   Note: * Another version by: Patti Page.

March 31, 1951
1. IF   Perry Como
2. ABA DABA HONEYMOON   Debbie Reynolds & Carleton Carpenter
3. MOCKING BIRD HILL   Les Paul & Mary Ford *
4. BE MY LOVE   Mario Lanza
5. WOULD I LOVE YOU   Patti Page
6. MY HEART CRIES FOR YOU   Guy Mitchell
7. YOU'RE JUST IN LOVE   Perry Como
   Note: * Another version by: Patti Page.

April 7, 1951
1. IF   Perry Como
2. BE MY LOVE   Mario Lanza
3. ABA DABA HONEYMOON   Debbie Reynolds & Carleton Carpenter
4. MOCKING BIRD HILL   Les Paul & Mary Ford *
5. WOULD I LOVE YOU   Patti Page
6. YOU'RE JUST IN LOVE   Perry Como
7. MY HEART CRIES FOR YOU   Guy Mitchell
   Note: * Another version by: Patti Page.

April 14, 1951
1. MOCKING BIRD HILL   Les Paul & Mary Ford *
2. IF   Perry Como
3. WOULD I LOVE YOU   Patti Page
4. ABA DABA HONEYMOON   Debbie Reynolds & Carleton Carpenter
5. BE MY LOVE   Mario Lanza
6. SPARROW IN THE TREETOP   Bing Crosby & Andrews Sisters
7. YOU'RE JUST IN LOVE   Perry Como
   Note: * Another version by: Patti Page.

April 21, 1951
1. IF   Perry Como
2. MOCKING BIRD HILL   Les Paul & Mary Ford *
3. BE MY LOVE   Mario Lanza
4. WOULD I LOVE YOU   Patti Page
5. ABA DABA HONEYMOON   Debbie Reynolds & Carleton Carpenter
6. SPARROW IN THE TREETOP   Bing Crosby & Andrews Sisters
7. YOU'RE JUST IN LOVE   Perry Como
   Note: * Another version by: Patti Page.

April 28, 1951
1. MOCKING BIRD HILL   Les Paul & Mary Ford *
2. IF   Perry Como
3. BE MY LOVE   Mario Lanza
4. ABA DABA HONEYMOON   Debbie Reynolds & Carleton Carpenter
5. WOULD I LOVE YOU   Patti Page
6. BEAUTIFUL BROWN EYES   Rosemary Clooney
7. SPARROW IN THE TREETOP   Bing Crosby & Andrews Sisters

Note: * Another version by: Patti Page.

May 5, 1951
1   IF   Perry Como
2   MOCKING BIRD HILL   Les Paul & Mary Ford *
3   WOULD I LOVE YOU   Patti Page
4   ABA DABA HONEYMOON   Debbie Reynolds & Carleton Carpenter
5   BE MY LOVE   Mario Lanza
6   ON TOP OF OLD SMOKY   The Weavers (VR: Terry Gilkyson)
7   SPARROW IN THE TREETOP   Bing Crosby & Andrews Sisters
   Note: * Another version by: Patti Page.

May 12, 1951
1   IF   Perry Como
2   MOCKING BIRD HILL   Les Paul & Mary Ford *
3   ON TOP OF OLD SMOKY   The Weavers (VR: Terry Gilkyson)
4   SPARROW IN THE TREETOP   Bing Crosby & Andrews Sisters
5   WOULD I LOVE YOU   Patti Page
6   BE MY LOVE   Mario Lanza
7   HOW HIGH THE MOON   Les Paul & Mary Ford
   Note: * Another version by: Patti Page.

May 19, 1951
1   MOCKING BIRD HILL   Les Paul & Mary Ford *
2   BE MY LOVE   Mario Lanza
3   TOO YOUNG   Nat King Cole **
4   ON TOP OF OLD SMOKY   The Weavers (VR: Terry Gilkyson)
5   WOULD I LOVE YOU   Patti Page
6   IF   Perry Como
7   HOW HIGH THE MOON   Les Paul & Mary Ford
   Note: * Another version by: Patti Page.
         ** 12 weeks at #1, a record not bested until 1992.

May 26, 1951
1   ON TOP OF OLD SMOKY   The Weavers (VR: Terry Gilkyson)
2   TOO YOUNG   Nat King Cole *
3   MOCKING BIRD HILL   Les Paul & Mary Ford **
4   WOULD I LOVE YOU   Patti Page
5   HOW HIGH THE MOON   Les Paul & Mary Ford
6   BE MY LOVE   Mario Lanza
7   IF   Perry Como
   Note: * 12 weeks at #1, a record not bested until 1992.
         ** Another version by: Patti Page.

June 2, 1951
1   TOO YOUNG   Nat King Cole *
2   ON TOP OF OLD SMOKY   The Weavers (VR: Terry Gilkyson)
3   MOCKING BIRD HILL   Les Paul & Mary Ford **
4   HOW HIGH THE MOON   Les Paul & Mary Ford
5   BE MY LOVE   Mario Lanza
6   IF   Perry Como
7   I APOLOGIZE   Billy Eckstine
   Note: * 12 weeks at #1, a record not bested until 1992.
         ** Another version by: Patti Page.

June 9, 1951
1   ON TOP OF OLD SMOKY   The Weavers (VR: Terry Gilkyson)

2   TOO YOUNG   Nat King Cole *
3   MOCKING BIRD HILL   Les Paul & Mary Ford **
4   THE LOVELIEST NIGHT OF THE YEAR   Mario Lanza
5   HOW HIGH THE MOON   Les Paul & Mary Ford
6   WOULD I LOVE YOU   Patti Page
7   MISTER AND MISSISSIPPI   Patti Page
   Note: * 12 weeks at #1, a record not bested until 1992.
         ** Another version by: Patti Page.

June 16, 1951
1   TOO YOUNG   Nat King Cole *
2   ON TOP OF OLD SMOKY   The Weavers (VR: Terry Gilkyson)
3   HOW HIGH THE MOON   Les Paul & Mary Ford
4   MOCKING BIRD HILL   Les Paul & Mary Ford **
5   THE LOVELIEST NIGHT OF THE YEAR   Mario Lanza
6   MISTER AND MISSISSIPPI   Patti Page
7   SYNCOPATED CLOCK   Leroy Anderson Orch.
   Note: * 12 weeks at #1, a record not bested until 1992.
         ** Another version by: Patti Page.

June 23, 1951
1   TOO YOUNG   Nat King Cole *
2   ON TOP OF OLD SMOKY   The Weavers (VR: Terry Gilkyson)
3   HOW HIGH THE MOON   Les Paul & Mary Ford
4   MISTER AND MISSISSIPPI   Patti Page
5   THE LOVELIEST NIGHT OF THE YEAR   Mario Lanza
6   MY TRULY, TRULY FAIR   Guy Mitchell
7   MOCKING BIRD HILL   Les Paul & Mary Ford **
   Note: * 12 weeks at #1, a record not bested until 1992.
         ** Another version by: Patti Page.

June 30, 1951
1   TOO YOUNG   Nat King Cole *
2   MISTER AND MISSISSIPPI   Patti Page
3   HOW HIGH THE MOON   Les Paul & Mary Ford
4   THE LOVELIEST NIGHT OF THE YEAR   Mario Lanza
5   MOCKING BIRD HILL   Les Paul & Mary Ford **
6   ON TOP OF OLD SMOKY   The Weavers (VR: Terry Gilkyson)
7   MY TRULY, TRULY FAIR   Guy Mitchell
   Note: * 12 weeks at #1, a record not bested until 1992.
         ** Another version by: Patti Page.

July 7, 1951
1   TOO YOUNG   Nat King Cole *
2   MISTER AND MISSISSIPPI   Patti Page
3   ON TOP OF OLD SMOKY   The Weavers (VR: Terry Gilkyson)
4   HOW HIGH THE MOON   Les Paul & Mary Ford
5   THE LOVELIEST NIGHT OF THE YEAR   Mario Lanza
6   MY TRULY, TRULY FAIR   Guy Mitchell
7   MOCKING BIRD HILL   Les Paul & Mary Ford **
   Note: * 12 weeks at #1, a record not bested until 1992.
         ** Another version by: Patti Page.

July 14, 1951
1   TOO YOUNG   Nat King Cole*
2   MISTER AND MISSISSIPPI   Patti Page
3   THE LOVELIEST NIGHT OF THE YEAR   Mario Lanza
4   MY TRULY, TRULY FAIR   Guy Mitchell
5   HOW HIGH THE MOON   Les Paul & Mary Ford
6   ON TOP OF OLD SMOKY   The Weavers (VR: Terry Gilkyson)
7   MOCKING BIRD HILL   Les Paul & Mary Ford **
   Note: * 12 weeks at #1, a record not bested until 1992.

** Another version by: Patti Page.

July 21, 1951
1   TOO YOUNG   Nat King Cole *
2   MISTER AND MISSISSIPPI   Patti Page
3   THE LOVELIEST NIGHT OF THE YEAR   Mario Lanza
4   MY TRULY, TRULY FAIR   Guy Mitchell
5   BECAUSE OF YOU   Tony Bennett
6   MOCKING BIRD HILL   Les Paul & Mary Ford **
7   ON TOP OF OLD SMOKY   The Weavers (VR: Terry Gilkyson)
    Note: * 12 weeks at #1, a record not bested until 1992.
    ** Another version by: Patti Page.

July 28, 1951
1   TOO YOUNG   Nat King Cole *
2   MY TRULY, TRULY FAIR   Guy Mitchell
3   MISTER AND MISSISSIPPI   Patti Page
4   THE LOVELIEST NIGHT OF THE YEAR   Mario Lanza
5   SHANGHAI   Doris Day
6   BECAUSE OF YOU   Tony Bennett
7   ON TOP OF OLD SMOKY   The Weavers (VR: Terry Gilkyson)
    Note: * 12 weeks at #1, a record not bested until 1992.

August 4, 1951
1   TOO YOUNG   Nat King Cole *
2   MISTER AND MISSISSIPPI   Patti Page
3   BECAUSE OF YOU   Tony Bennett
4   SHANGHAI   Doris Day
5   THE LOVELIEST NIGHT OF THE YEAR   Mario Lanza
6   COME ON-A MY HOUSE   Rosemary Clooney
7   MY TRULY, TRULY FAIR   Guy Mitchell
    Note: * 12 weeks at #1, a record not bested until 1992.

August 11, 1951
1   TOO YOUNG   Nat King Cole *
2   COME ON-A MY HOUSE   Rosemary Clooney
3   MY TRULY, TRULY FAIR   Guy Mitchell
4   SHANGHAI   Doris Day
5   BECAUSE OF YOU   Tony Bennett
6   SWEET VIOLETS   Dinah Shore
7   THE LOVELIEST NIGHT OF THE YEAR   Mario Lanza
    Note: * 12 weeks at #1, a record not bested until 1992.

August 18, 1951
1   TOO YOUNG   Nat King Cole *
2   BECAUSE OF YOU   Tony Bennett
3   MY TRULY, TRULY FAIR   Guy Mitchell
4   SHANGHAI   Doris Day
5   COME ON-A MY HOUSE   Rosemary Clooney
6   MORNING SIDE OF THE MOUNTAIN   Paul Weston Orch. (VR: Norman Luboff Choir)
7   THE LOVELIEST NIGHT OF THE YEAR   Mario Lanza
    Note: * 12 weeks at #1, a record not bested until 1992.

August 25, 1951
1   TOO YOUNG   Nat King Cole *
2   BECAUSE OF YOU   Tony Bennett
3   COME ON-A MY HOUSE   Rosemary Clooney
4   SHANGHAI   Doris Day
5   THE LOVELIEST NIGHT OF THE YEAR   Mario Lanza
6   MY TRULY, TRULY FAIR   Guy Mitchell
7   SWEET VIOLETS   Dinah Shore
    Note: * 12 weeks at #1, a record not bested until 1992.

September 1, 1951
1   BECAUSE OF YOU   Tony Bennett
2   COME ON-A MY HOUSE   Rosemary Clooney
3   SHANGHAI   Doris Day
4   TOO YOUNG   Nat King Cole *
5   THE LOVELIEST NIGHT OF THE YEAR   Mario Lanza
6   MORNING SIDE OF THE MOUNTAIN   Paul Weston Orch. (VR: Norman Luboff Choir)
7   SWEET VIOLETS   Dinah Shore
    Note: * 12 weeks at #1, a record not bested until 1992.

September 8, 1951
1   BECAUSE OF YOU   Tony Bennett
2   TOO YOUNG   Nat King Cole *
3   COME ON-A MY HOUSE   Rosemary Clooney
4   SHANGHAI   Doris Day
5   THE LOVELIEST NIGHT OF THE YEAR   Mario Lanza
6   I GET IDEAS   Tony Martin
7   SWEET VIOLETS   Dinah Shore
    Note: * 12 weeks at #1, a record not bested until 1992.

September 15, 1951
1   BECAUSE OF YOU   Tony Bennett
2   TOO YOUNG   Nat King Cole *
3   THE LOVELIEST NIGHT OF THE YEAR   Mario Lanza
4   SHANGHAI   Doris Day
5   COME ON-A MY HOUSE   Rosemary Clooney
6   I GET IDEAS   Tony Martin
7   SWEET VIOLETS   Dinah Shore
    Note: * 12 weeks at #1, a record not bested until 1992.

September 20, 1951
1   BECAUSE OF YOU   Tony Bennett
2   TOO YOUNG   Nat King Cole *
3   I GET IDEAS   Tony Martin
4   COME ON-A MY HOUSE   Rosemary Clooney
5   SHANGHAI   Doris Day
6   THE LOVELIEST NIGHT OF THE YEAR   Mario Lanza
7   SWEET VIOLETS   Dinah Shore
    Note: * 12 weeks at #1, a record not bested until 1992.

September 27, 1951
1   BECAUSE OF YOU   Tony Bennett
2   THE LOVELIEST NIGHT OF THE YEAR   Mario Lanza
3   SHANGHAI   Doris Day
4   TOO YOUNG   Nat King Cole *
5   I GET IDEAS   Tony Martin
6   COLD, COLD HEART   Tony Bennett **
7   IN THE COOL, COOL, COOL OF THE EVENING   Bing Crosby & Jane Wyman
    Note: * 12 weeks at #1, a record not bested until 1992.
    ** Country hit written and recorded by Hank Williams.

October 4, 1951
1   BECAUSE OF YOU   Tony Bennett
2   I GET IDEAS   Tony Martin
3   COME ON-A MY HOUSE   Rosemary Clooney
4   TOO YOUNG   Nat King Cole *
5   SHANGHAI   Doris Day
6   THE LOVELIEST NIGHT OF THE YEAR   Mario Lanza
7   COLD, COLD HEART   Tony Bennett **
    Note: * 12 weeks at #1, a record not bested until 1992.
    ** Country hit written and recorded by Hank Williams.

October 11, 1951
1   BECAUSE OF YOU   Tony Bennett

2 I GET IDEAS Tony Martin
3 COLD, COLD HEART Tony Bennett *
4 SHANGHAI Doris Day
5 COME ON-A MY HOUSE Rosemary Clooney
6 THE LOVELIEST NIGHT OF THE YEAR Mario Lanza
7 IN THE COOL, COOL, COOL OF THE EVENING Bing
    Crosby & Jane Wyman
Note: * Country hit written and recorded by Hank Williams.

October 18, 1951

1 BECAUSE OF YOU Tony Bennett
2 I GET IDEAS Tony Martin
3 COLD, COLD HEART Tony Bennett *
4 SHANGHAI Doris Day
5 TOO YOUNG Nat King Cole **
6 THE LOVELIEST NIGHT OF THE YEAR Mario Lanza
7 THE WORLD IS WAITING FOR THE SUNRISE Les Paul &
    Mary Ford
Note: * Country hit written and recorded by Hank Williams.
    ** 12 weeks at #1, a record not bested until 1992.

October 25, 1951

1 BECAUSE OF YOU Tony Bennett
2 COLD, COLD HEART Tony Bennett *
3 I GET IDEAS Tony Martin
4 SIN (IT'S NO) Eddy Howard Orch. (VR: Eddy Howard)
5 SHANGHAI Doris Day
6 THE LOVELIEST NIGHT OF THE YEAR Mario Lanza
7 THE WORLD IS WAITING FOR THE SUNRISE Les Paul &
    Mary Ford
Note: * Country hit written and recorded by Hank Williams.

November 1, 1951

1 BECAUSE OF YOU Tony Bennett
2 I GET IDEAS Tony Martin
3 DOWN YONDER Del Wood
4 SIN (IT'S NO) Eddy Howard Orch. (VR: Eddy Howard)
5 COLD, COLD HEART Tony Bennett *
6 THE LOVELIEST NIGHT OF THE YEAR Mario Lanza
7 IN THE COOL, COOL, COOL OF THE EVENING Bing
    Crosby & Jane Wyman
Note: * Country hit written and recorded by Hank Williams.

November 8, 1951

1 BECAUSE OF YOU Tony Bennett
2 SIN (IT'S NO) Eddy Howard Orch. (VR: Eddy Howard)
3 AND SO TO SLEEP AGAIN Patti Page
4 I GET IDEAS Tony Martin
5 COLD, COLD HEART Tony Bennett *
6 DOWN YONDER Del Wood
7 THE LOVELIEST NIGHT OF THE YEAR Mario Lanza
Note: * Country hit written and recorded by Hank Williams.

November 15, 1951

1 SIN (IT'S NO) Eddy Howard Orch. (VR: Eddy Howard)
2 COLD, COLD HEART Tony Bennett *
3 BECAUSE OF YOU Tony Bennett
4 DOWN YONDER Del Wood
5 I GET IDEAS Tony Martin
6 AND SO TO SLEEP AGAIN Patti Page
7 UNDECIDED Ames Brothers
Note: * Country hit written and recorded by Hank Williams.

November 22, 1951

1 SIN (IT'S NO) Eddy Howard Orch. (VR: Eddy Howard)
2 BECAUSE OF YOU Tony Bennett

Tony Bennett

Tony's ``Because Of You'' stays #1 for eleven weeks.

3 DOWN YONDER Del Wood
4 COLD, COLD HEART Tony Bennett *
5 AND SO TO SLEEP AGAIN Patti Page
6 UNDECIDED Ames Brothers
7 I GET IDEAS Tony Martin
Note: * Country hit written and recorded by Hank Williams.

Novmeber 29, 1951

1 SIN (IT'S NO) Eddy Howard Orch. (VR: Eddy Howard)
2 BECAUSE OF YOU Tony Bennett
3 DOWN YONDER Del Wood
4 COLD, COLD HEART Tony Bennett *
5 I GET IDEAS Tony Martin
6 UNDECIDED Ames Brothers
7 AND SO TO SLEEP AGAIN Patti Page
Note: * Country hit written and recorded by Hank Williams.

December 6, 1951

1 SIN (IT'S NO) Eddy Howard Orch. (VR: Eddy Howard)
2 BECAUSE OF YOU Tony Bennett
3 DOWN YONDER Del Wood
4 UNDECIDED Ames Brothers
5 AND SO TO SLEEP AGAIN Patti Page
6 COLD, COLD HEART Tony Bennett *
7 I GET IDEAS Tony Martin
Note: * Country hit written and recorded by Hank Williams.

December 13, 1951

1 SIN (IT'S NO) Eddy Howard Orch. (VR: Eddy Howard)
2 BECAUSE OF YOU Tony Bennett
3 DOWN YONDER Del Wood

4 UNDECIDED   Ames Brothers
5 AND SO TO SLEEP AGAIN   Patti Page
6 I GET IDEAS   Tony Martin
7 SLOWPOKE   Pee Wee King

December 20, 1951
1 SIN (IT'S NO)   Eddy Howard Orch. (VR: Eddy Howard)
2 SLOWPOKE   Pee Wee King
3 DOWN YONDER   Del Wood
4 UNDECIDED   Ames Brothers
5 DOMINO   Tony Martin
6 RUDOLPH, THE RED NOSED REINDEER   Gene Autry
7 BECAUSE OF YOU   Tony Bennett

December 27, 1951
1 SLOWPOKE   Pee Wee King
2 UNDECIDED   Ames Brothers
3 DOWN YONDER   Del Wood
4 RUDOLPH, THE RED NOSED REINDEER   Gene Autry
5 DOMINO   Tony Martin
6 SIN (IT'S NO)   Eddy Howard Orch. (VR: Eddy Howard)
7 WHITE CHRISTMAS   Bing Crosby

January 3, 1952
1 SLOWPOKE   Pee Wee King
2 SIN (IT'S NO)   Eddy Howard Orch. (VR: Eddy Howard)
3 DOWN YONDER   Del Wood
4 SHRIMP BOATS   Jo Stafford
5 UNDECIDED   Ames Brothers
6 RUDOLPH, THE RED NOSED REINDEER   Gene Autry

Johnnie Ray
Tammy Faye Bakker had nothing on this soulful singer of ``Cry''
(#1 on Feb. 21) and ``Little White Cloud That Cried.''

7 DOMINO   Tony Martin

January 10, 1952
1 SIN (IT'S NO)   Eddy Howard Orch. (VR: Eddy Howard)
2 SLOWPOKE   Pee Wee King
3 DOWN YONDER   Del Wood
4 UNDECIDED   Ames Brothers
5 SHRIMP BOATS   Jo Stafford
6 CHARMAINE   Paul Weston Orch. (VR: Norman Luboff Choir)
7 DOMINO   Tony Martin

January 17, 1952
1 SLOWPOKE   Pee Wee King
2 DOWN YONDER   Del Wood
3 SIN (IT'S NO)   Eddy Howard Orch. (VR: Eddy Howard)
4 UNDECIDED   Ames Brothers
5 CHARMAINE   Paul Weston Orch. (VR: Norman Luboff Choir)
6 DOMINO   Tony Martin
7 SHRIMP BOATS   Jo Stafford

January 24, 1952
1 SLOWPOKE   Pee Wee King
2 SIN (IT'S NO)   Eddy Howard Orch. (VR: Eddy Howard)
3 SHRIMP BOATS   Jo Stafford
4 DOWN YONDER   Del Wood
5 UNDECIDED   Ames Brothers
6 ANYTIME   Eddie Fisher
7 CRY   Johnnie Ray

January 31, 1952
1 CRY   Johnnie Ray
2 SLOWPOKE   Pee Wee King
3 DOWN YONDER   Del Wood
4 SIN (IT'S NO)   Eddy Howard Orch. (VR: Eddy Howard)
5 ANYTIME   Eddie Fisher
6 SHRIMP BOATS   Jo Stafford
7 UNDECIDED   Ames Brothers

February 7, 1952
1 SLOWPOKE   Pee Wee King
2 CRY   Johnnie Ray
3 SHRIMP BOATS   Jo Stafford
4 SIN (IT'S NO)   Eddy Howard Orch. (VR: Eddy Howard)
5 THE LITTLE WHITE CLOUD THAT CRIED   Johnnie Ray
6 UNDECIDED   Ames Brothers
7 TELL ME WHY   Four Aces

February 14, 1952
1 SLOWPOKE   Pee Wee King
2 CRY   Johnnie Ray
3 ANYTIME   Eddie Fisher
4 SHRIMP BOATS   Jo Stafford
5 TELL ME WHY   Four Aces
6 THE LITTLE WHITE CLOUD THAT CRIED   Johnnie Ray
7 SIN (IT'S NO)   Eddy Howard Orch. (VR: Eddy Howard)

February 21, 1952
1 CRY   Johnnie Ray
2 SLOWPOKE   Pee Wee King
3 ANYTIME   Eddie Fisher
4 TELL ME WHY   Four Aces
5 THE LITTLE WHITE CLOUD THAT CRIED   Johnnie Ray
6 SHRIMP BOATS   Jo Stafford
7 PLEASE, MR. SUN   Johnnie Ray

February 28, 1952
1 CRY   Johnnie Ray
2 SLOWPOKE   Pee Wee King
3 ANYTIME   Eddie Fisher
4 THE LITTLE WHITE CLOUD THAT CRIED   Johnnie Ray
5 TELL ME WHY   Four Aces
6 PLEASE, MR. SUN   Johnnie Ray
7 SHRIMP BOATS   Jo Stafford

March 6, 1952
1 CRY   Johnnie Ray
2 TELL ME WHY   Four Aces
3 PLEASE, MR. SUN   Johnnie Ray
4 SLOWPOKE   Pee Wee King
5 ANYTIME   Eddie Fisher
6 THE LITTLE WHITE CLOUD THAT CRIED   Johnnie Ray
7 SHRIMP BOATS   Jo Stafford

March 13, 1952
1 SLOWPOKE   Pee Wee King
2 TELL ME WHY   Four Aces
3 PLEASE, MR. SUN   Johnnie Ray
4 CRY   Johnnie Ray
5 ANYTIME   Eddie Fisher
6 WHEEL OF FORTUNE   Kay Starr
7 THE LITTLE WHITE CLOUD THAT CRIED   Johnnie Ray

March 20, 1952
1 CRY   Johnnie Ray
2 WHEEL OF FORTUNE   Kay Starr
3 ANYTIME   Eddie Fisher
4 TELL ME WHY   Four Aces
5 PLEASE, MR. SUN   Johnnie Ray
6 SLOWPOKE   Pee Wee King
7 THE LITTLE WHITE CLOUD THAT CRIED   Johnnie Ray

March 27, 1952
1 WHEEL OF FORTUNE   Kay Starr
2 ANYTIME   Eddie Fisher
3 PLEASE, MR. SUN   Johnnie Ray
4 TELL ME WHY   Four Aces
5 CRY   Johnnie Ray
6 SLOWPOKE   Pee Wee King
7 BE MY LIFE'S COMPANION   Mills Brothers

April 3, 1952
1 WHEEL OF FORTUNE   Kay Starr
2 ANYTIME   Eddie Fisher
3 PLEASE, MR. SUN   Johnnie Ray
4 CRY   Johnnie Ray
5 TELL ME WHY   Four Aces
6 BE MY LIFE'S COMPANION   Mills Brothers
7 BLUE TANGO   Leroy Anderson Orch.

April 10, 1952
1 WHEEL OF FORTUNE   Kay Starr
2 PLEASE, MR. SUN   Johnnie Ray
3 CRY   Johnnie Ray
4 ANYTIME   Eddie Fisher
5 BLUE TANGO   Leroy Anderson Orch.
6 TELL ME WHY   Four Aces
7 BE MY LIFE'S COMPANION   Mills Brothers

April 17, 1952
1 WHEEL OF FORTUNE   Kay Starr
2 ANYTIME   Eddie Fisher

3 PLEASE, MR. SUN   Johnnie Ray
4 BLUE TANGO   Leroy Anderson Orch.
5 BLACKSMITH BLUES   Ella Mae Morse
6 CRY   Johnnie Ray
7 BE MY LIFE'S COMPANION   Mills Brothers

April 24, 1952
1 WHEEL OF FORTUNE   Kay Starr
2 ANYTIME   Eddie Fisher
3 CRY   Johnnie Ray
4 BLACKSMITH BLUES   Ella Mae Morse
5 BLUE TANGO   Leroy Anderson Orch.
6 PLEASE, MR. SUN   Johnnie Ray
7 BE MY LIFE'S COMPANION   Mills Brothers

May 1, 1952
1 WHEEL OF FORTUNE   Kay Starr
2 ANYTIME   Eddie Fisher
3 BLUE TANGO   Leroy Anderson Orch.
4 A GUY IS A GUY   Doris Day
5 PLEASE, MR. SUN   Johnnie Ray
6 BLACKSMITH BLUES   Ella Mae Morse
7 BE ANYTHING   Eddy Howard Orch. (VR: Eddy Howard)

May 8, 1952
1 BLUE TANGO   Leroy Anderson Orch.
2 BLACKSMITH BLUES   Ella Mae Morse
3 ANYTIME   Eddie Fisher
4 WHEEL OF FORTUNE   Kay Starr
5 A GUY IS A GUY   Doris Day
6 PLEASE, MR. SUN   Johnnie Ray
7 BE ANYTHING   Eddy Howard Orch. (VR: Eddy Howard)

May 15, 1952
1 BLUE TANGO   Leroy Anderson Orch.
2 ANYTIME   Eddie Fisher
3 BLACKSMITH BLUES   Ella Mae Morse
4 A GUY IS A GUY   Doris Day
5 KISS OF FIRE   Georgia Gibbs
6 BE ANYTHING   Eddy Howard Orch. (VR: Eddy Howard)
7 WHEEL OF FORTUNE   Kay Starr

May 22, 1952
1 KISS OF FIRE   Georgia Gibbs
2 BLUE TANGO   Leroy Anderson Orch.
3 BE ANYTHING   Eddy Howard Orch. (VR: Eddy Howard)
4 BLACKSMITH BLUES   Ella Mae Morse
5 A GUY IS A GUY   Doris Day
6 ANYTIME   Eddie Fisher
7 FORGIVE ME   Eddie Fisher

May 29, 1952
1 KISS OF FIRE   Georgia Gibbs
2 A GUY IS A GUY   Doris Day
3 BE ANYTHING   Eddy Howard Orch. (VR: Eddy Howard)
4 BLUE TANGO   Leroy Anderson Orch.
5 I'M YOURS   Eddie Fisher *
6 BLACKSMITH BLUES   Ella Mae Morse
7 FORGIVE ME   Eddie Fisher
Note: * Another version by: Don Cornell.

June 5, 1952
1 KISS OF FIRE   Georgia Gibbs
2 BLUE TANGO   Leroy Anderson Orch.
3 BE ANYTHING   Eddy Howard Orch. (VR: Eddy Howard)
4 A GUY IS A GUY   Doris Day

5 BLACKSMITH BLUES   Ella Mae Morse
6 I WALK ALONE   Don Cornell
7 I'M YOURS   Eddie Fisher *
Note: * Another version by: Don Cornell.

June 12, 1952
1 KISS OF FIRE   Georgia Gibbs
2 BLUE TANGO   Leroy Anderson Orch.
3 BE ANYTHING   Eddy Howard Orch. (VR: Eddy Howard)
4 I'M YOURS   Eddie Fisher *
5 A GUY IS A GUY   Doris Day
6 FORGIVE ME   Eddie Fisher
7 BLACKSMITH BLUES   Ella Mae Morse
Note: * Another version by: Don Cornell.

June 19, 1952
1 KISS OF FIRE   Georgia Gibbs
2 I'M YOURS   Eddie Fisher *
3 BE ANYTHING   Eddy Howard Orch. (VR: Eddy Howard)
4 HERE IN MY HEART   Al Martino
5 BLUE TANGO   Leroy Anderson Orch.
6 A GUY IS A GUY   Doris Day
7 I WALK ALONE   Don Cornell
Note: * Another version by: Don Cornell.

June 26, 1952
1 KISS OF FIRE   Georgia Gibbs
2 BE ANYTHING   Eddy Howard Orch. (VR: Eddy Howard)
3 I'M YOURS   Eddie Fisher *
4 BLUE TANGO   Leroy Anderson Orch.
5 HERE IN MY HEART   Al Martino
6 I WALK ALONE   Don Cornell
7 DELICADO   Percy Faith Orch.
Note: * Another version by: Don Cornell.

July 3, 1952
1 I'M YOURS   Eddie Fisher *
2 KISS OF FIRE   Georgia Gibbs
3 DELICADO   Percy Faith Orch.
4 BE ANYTHING   Eddy Howard Orch. (VR: Eddy Howard)
5 BLUE TANGO   Leroy Anderson Orch.
6 I WALK ALONE   Don Cornell
7 HERE IN MY HEART   Al Martino
Note: * Another version by: Don Cornell.

July 10, 1952
1 KISS OF FIRE   Georgia Gibbs
2 BLUE TANGO   Leroy Anderson Orch.
3 DELICADO   Percy Faith Orch.
4 I'M YOURS   Eddie Fisher *
5 WALKIN' MY BABY BACK HOME   Johnnie Ray
6 HERE IN MY HEART   Al Martino
7 BE ANYTHING   Eddy Howard Orch. (VR: Eddy Howard)
Note: * Another version by: Don Cornell.

July 17, 1952
1 I'M YOURS   Eddie Fisher *
2 HERE IN MY HEART   Al Martino
3 DELICADO   Percy Faith Orch.
4 WALKIN' MY BABY BACK HOME   Johnnie Ray
5 BLUE TANGO   Leroy Anderson Orch.
6 KISS OF FIRE   Georgia Gibbs
7 AUF WIEDERSEHN, SWEETHEART   Vera Lynn
Note: * Another version by: Don Cornell.

Georgia Gibbs
Georgia's ``Kiss Of Fire'' spent six weeks at #1 in May and June.

Jo Stafford
A member of The Pied Pipers in the forties, Jo Stafford scores her biggest hit with ``You Belong To Me'' (Sep. 19).

July 24, 1952
1 WALKIN' MY BABY BACK HOME   Johnnie Ray
2 AUF WIEDERSEHN, SWEETHEART   Vera Lynn
3 KISS OF FIRE   Georgia Gibbs
4 BLUE TANGO   Leroy Anderson Orch.
5 DELICADO   Percy Faith Orch.
6 I'M YOURS   Eddie Fisher *
7 HERE IN MY HEART   Al Martino
   Note: * Another version by: Don Cornell.

July 31, 1952
1 I'M YOURS   Eddie Fisher *
2 DELICADO   Percy Faith Orch.
3 AUF WIEDERSEHN, SWEETHEART   Vera Lynn
4 WALKIN' MY BABY BACK HOME   Johnnie Ray
5 BLUE TANGO   Leroy Anderson Orch.
6 MAYBE   Perry Como & Eddie Fisher
7 KISS OF FIRE   Georgia Gibbs
   Note: * Another version by: Don Cornell.

August 7, 1952
1 WALKIN' MY BABY BACK HOME   Johnnie Ray
2 AUF WIEDERSEHN, SWEETHEART   Vera Lynn
3 I'M YOURS   Eddie Fisher *
4 DELICADO   Percy Faith Orch.
5 HALF AS MUCH   Rosemary Clooney
6 KISS OF FIRE   Georgia Gibbs
7 BLUE TANGO   Leroy Anderson Orch.
   Note: * Another version by: Don Cornell.

August 14, 1952
1 WALKIN' MY BABY BACK HOME   Johnnie Ray
2 AUF WIEDERSEHN, SWEETHEART   Vera Lynn
3 DELICADO   Percy Faith Orch.
4 BLUE TANGO   Leroy Anderson Orch.
5 HALF AS MUCH   Rosemary Clooney
6 I'M YOURS   Eddie Fisher *
7 SOMEWHERE ALONG THE WAY   Nat King Cole
   Note: * Another version by: Don Cornell.

August 21, 1952
1 AUF WIEDERSEHN, SWEETHEART   Vera Lynn
2 WALKIN' MY BABY BACK HOME   Johnnie Ray
3 KISS OF FIRE   Georgia Gibbs
4 WISH YOU WERE HERE   Eddie Fisher
5 HALF AS MUCH   Rosemary Clooney
6 I'M YOURS   Eddie Fisher *
7 DELICADO   Percy Faith Orch.
   Note: * Another version by: Don Cornell.

August 29, 1952
1 AUF WIEDERSEHN, SWEETHEART   Vera Lynn
2 WALKIN' MY BABY BACK HOME   Johnnie Ray
3 HALF AS MUCH   Rosemary Clooney
4 WISH YOU WERE HERE   Eddie Fisher
5 BLUE TANGO   Leroy Anderson Orch.
6 SOMEWHERE ALONG THE WAY   Nat King Cole
7 HERE IN MY HEART   Al Martino

September 5, 1952
1 AUF WIEDERSEHN, SWEETHEART   Vera Lynn
2 WALKIN' MY BABY BACK HOME   Johnnie Ray
3 HALF AS MUCH   Rosemary Clooney
4 WISH YOU WERE HERE   Eddie Fisher
5 SOMEWHERE ALONG THE WAY   Nat King Cole
6 BLUE TANGO   Leroy Anderson Orch.

7 HERE IN MY HEART   Al Martino

September 12, 1952
1 WISH YOU WERE HERE   Eddie Fisher
2 AUF WIEDERSEHN, SWEETHEART   Vera Lynn
3 HALF AS MUCH   Rosemary Clooney
4 WALKIN' MY BABY BACK HOME   Johnnie Ray
5 YOU BELONG TO ME   Jo Stafford
6 SOMEWHERE ALONG THE WAY   Nat King Cole
7 I'M YOURS   Eddie Fisher *
   Note: * Another version by: Don Cornell.

September 19, 1952
1 YOU BELONG TO ME   Jo Stafford
2 WISH YOU WERE HERE   Eddie Fisher
3 AUF WIEDERSEHN, SWEETHEART   Vera Lynn
4 HALF AS MUCH   Rosemary Clooney
5 WALKIN' MY BABY BACK HOME   Johnnie Ray
6 SOMEWHERE ALONG THE WAY   Nat King Cole
7 I'M YOURS   Eddie Fisher *
   Note: * Another version by: Don Cornell.

September 26, 1952
1 YOU BELONG TO ME   Jo Stafford
2 WISH YOU WERE HERE   Eddie Fisher
3 HALF AS MUCH   Rosemary Clooney
4 AUF WIEDERSEHN, SWEETHEART   Vera Lynn
5 WALKIN' MY BABY BACK HOME   Johnnie Ray
6 SOMEWHERE ALONG THE WAY   Nat King Cole
7 JAMBALAYA   Jo Stafford *
   Note: * Country hit by Hank Williams.

October 3, 1952
1 YOU BELONG TO ME   Jo Stafford
2 WISH YOU WERE HERE   Eddie Fisher
3 AUF WIEDERSEHN, SWEETHEART   Vera Lynn
4 I WENT TO YOUR WEDDING   Patti Page
5 HALF AS MUCH   Rosemary Clooney
6 SOMEWHERE ALONG THE WAY   Nat King Cole
7 JAMBALAYA   Jo Stafford *
   Note: * Country hit by Hank Williams.

October 10, 1952
1 YOU BELONG TO ME   Jo Stafford
2 WISH YOU WERE HERE   Eddie Fisher
3 JAMBALAYA   Jo Stafford *
4 I WENT TO YOUR WEDDING   Patti Page
5 HALF AS MUCH   Rosemary Clooney
6 AUF WIEDERSEHN, SWEETHEART   Vera Lynn
7 SOMEWHERE ALONG THE WAY   Nat King Cole
   Note: * Country hit by Hank Williams.

October 17, 1952
1 WISH YOU WERE HERE   Eddie Fisher
2 YOU BELONG TO ME   Jo Stafford
3 I WENT TO YOUR WEDDING   Patti Page
4 JAMBALAYA   Jo Stafford *
5 HALF AS MUCH   Rosemary Clooney
6 AUF WIEDERSEHN, SWEETHEART   Vera Lynn
7 SOMEWHERE ALONG THE WAY   Nat King Cole
   Note: * Country hit by Hank Williams.

October 24, 1952
1 YOU BELONG TO ME   Jo Stafford
2 WISH YOU WERE HERE   Eddie Fisher

Joni James
Joni celebrated Christmas 1952 with a #1 chart-topper, ``Why Don't You Believe Me.''

3 I WENT TO YOUR WEDDING   Patti Page
4 JAMBALAYA   Jo Stafford *
5 HALF AS MUCH   Rosemary Clooney
6 SOMEWHERE ALONG THE WAY   Nat King Cole
7 AUF WIEDERSEHN, SWEETHEART   Vera Lynn
   Note: * Country hit by Hank Williams.

October 31, 1952
1 WISH YOU WERE HERE   Eddie Fisher
2 YOU BELONG TO ME   Jo Stafford
3 JAMBALAYA   Jo Stafford *
4 I WENT TO YOUR WEDDING   Patti Page
5 HALF AS MUCH   Rosemary Clooney
6 SOMEWHERE ALONG THE WAY   Nat King Cole
7 AUF WIEDERSEHN, SWEETHEART   Vera Lynn
   Note: * Country hit by Hank Williams.

November 7, 1952
1 YOU BELONG TO ME   Jo Stafford
2 WISH YOU WERE HERE   Eddie Fisher
3 JAMBALAYA   Jo Stafford *
4 BECAUSE YOU'RE MINE   Mario Lanza
5 I WENT TO YOUR WEDDING   Patti Page
6 SOMEWHERE ALONG THE WAY   Nat King Cole
7 GLOW WORM   Mills Brothers
   Note: * Country hit by Hank Williams.

November 14, 1952
1 YOU BELONG TO ME   Jo Stafford
2 JAMBALAYA   Jo Stafford *
3 WISH YOU WERE HERE   Eddie Fisher
4 I WENT TO YOUR WEDDING   Patti Page
5 GLOW WORM   Mills Brothers
6 BECAUSE YOU'RE MINE   Mario Lanza
7 LADY OF SPAIN   Eddie Fisher
   Note: * Country hit by Hank Williams.

November 21, 1952
1 YOU BELONG TO ME   Jo Stafford
2 GLOW WORM   Mills Brothers
3 BECAUSE YOU'RE MINE   Mario Lanza
4 I WENT TO YOUR WEDDING   Patti Page
5 JAMBALAYA   Jo Stafford *
6 WISH YOU WERE HERE   Eddie Fisher
7 LADY OF SPAIN   Eddie Fisher
   Note: * Country hit by Hank Williams.

November 28, 1952
1 YOU BELONG TO ME   Jo Stafford
2 JAMBALAYA   Jo Stafford *
3 BECAUSE YOU'RE MINE   Mario Lanza
4 GLOW WORM   Mills Brothers
5 I WENT TO YOUR WEDDING   Patti Page
6 WISH YOU WERE HERE   Eddie Fisher
7 LADY OF SPAIN   Eddie Fisher
   Note: * Country hit by Hank Williams.

December 5, 1952
1 GLOW WORM   Mills Brothers
2 BECAUSE YOU'RE MINE   Mario Lanza
3 JAMBALAYA   Jo Stafford *
4 YOU BELONG TO ME   Jo Stafford
5 I WENT TO YOUR WEDDING   Patti Page
6 WISH YOU WERE HERE   Eddie Fisher
7 LADY OF SPAIN   Eddie Fisher
   Note: * Country hit by Hank Williams.

December 12, 1952
1 GLOW WORM   Mills Brothers
2 YOU BELONG TO ME   Jo Stafford
3 BECAUSE YOU'RE MINE   Mario Lanza
4 WHY DON'T YOU BELIEVE ME   Joni James
5 JAMBALAYA   Jo Stafford *
6 I WENT TO YOUR WEDDING   Patti Page
7 WHITE CHRISTMAS   Bing Crosby
   Note: * Country hit by Hank Williams.

December 19, 1952
1 WHY DON'T YOU BELIEVE ME   Joni James
2 BECAUSE YOU'RE MINE   Mario Lanza
3 GLOW WORM   Mills Brothers
4 I WENT TO YOUR WEDDING   Patti Page
5 YOU BELONG TO ME   Jo Stafford
6 JAMBALAYA   Jo Stafford *
7 DON'T LET THE STARS GET IN YOUR EYES   Perry Como
   Note: * Country hit by Hank Williams.

December 26, 1952
1 WHY DON'T YOU BELIEVE ME   Joni James
2 BECAUSE YOU'RE MINE   Mario Lanza
3 DON'T LET THE STARS GET IN YOUR EYES   Perry Como
4 YOU BELONG TO ME   Jo Stafford
5 GLOW WORM   Mills Brothers
6 RUDOLPH, THE RED NOSED REINDEER   Gene Autry
7 JAMBALAYA   Jo Stafford *
   Note: * Country hit by Hank Williams.

January 3, 1953
1 I SAW MOMMY KISSING SANTA CLAUS   Jimmy Boyd
2 WHY DON'T YOU BELIEVE ME   Joni James
3 DON'T LET THE STARS GET IN YOUR EYES   Perry Como
4 GLOW WORM   Mills Brothers
5 YOU BELONG TO ME   Jo Stafford
6 BECAUSE YOU'RE MINE   Mario Lanza
7 WHITE CHRISTMAS   Bing Crosby

January 10, 1953
1 WHY DON'T YOU BELIEVE ME   Joni James
2 DON'T LET THE STARS GET IN YOUR EYES   Perry Como
3 GLOW WORM   Mills Brothers
4 BECAUSE YOU'RE MINE   Mario Lanza
5 KEEP IT A SECRET   Jo Stafford
6 YOU BELONG TO ME   Jo Stafford
7 LADY OF SPAIN   Eddie Fisher

January 17, 1953
1 DON'T LET THE STARS GET IN YOUR EYES   Perry Como
2 WHY DON'T YOU BELIEVE ME   Joni James
3 KEEP IT A SECRET   Jo Stafford
4 GLOW WORM   Mills Brothers
5 BECAUSE YOU'RE MINE   Mario Lanza
6 LADY OF SPAIN   Eddie Fisher
7 OUTSIDE OF HEAVEN   Eddie Fisher

January 24, 1953
1 WHY DON'T YOU BELIEVE ME   Joni James
2 DON'T LET THE STARS GET IN YOUR EYES   Perry Como
3 GLOW WORM   Mills Brothers
4 KEEP IT A SECRET   Jo Stafford
5 LADY OF SPAIN   Eddie Fisher
6 TILL I WALTZ AGAIN WITH YOU   Teresa Brewer
7 YOU BELONG TO ME   Jo Stafford

January 31, 1953
1 WHY DON'T YOU BELIEVE ME   Joni James
2 DON'T LET THE STARS GET IN YOUR EYES   Perry Como
3 KEEP IT A SECRET   Jo Stafford
4 BECAUSE YOU'RE MINE   Mario Lanza
5 TILL I WALTZ AGAIN WITH YOU   Teresa Brewer
6 LADY OF SPAIN   Eddie Fisher
7 GLOW WORM   Mills Brothers

February 7, 1953
1 DON'T LET THE STARS GET IN YOUR EYES   Perry Como
2 KEEP IT A SECRET   Jo Stafford
3 WHY DON'T YOU BELIEVE ME   Joni James
4 TILL I WALTZ AGAIN WITH YOU   Teresa Brewer
5 BECAUSE YOU'RE MINE   Mario Lanza
6 GLOW WORM   Mills Brothers
7 LADY OF SPAIN   Eddie Fisher

February 14, 1953
1 DON'T LET THE STARS GET IN YOUR EYES   Perry Como
2 TILL I WALTZ AGAIN WITH YOU   Teresa Brewer
3 KEEP IT A SECRET   Jo Stafford
4 WHY DON'T YOU BELIEVE ME   Joni James
5 BECAUSE YOU'RE MINE   Mario Lanza
6 GLOW WORM   Mills Brothers
7 OH HAPPY DAY   Don Howard

February 21, 1953
1 DON'T LET THE STARS GET IN YOUR EYES   Perry Como
2 TILL I WALTZ AGAIN WITH YOU   Teresa Brewer
3 WHY DON'T YOU BELIEVE ME   Joni James
4 KEEP IT A SECRET   Jo Stafford
5 GLOW WORM   Mills Brothers
6 OH HAPPY DAY   Don Howard
7 TELL ME YOU'RE MINE   The Gaylords

February 28, 1953
1 TILL I WALTZ AGAIN WITH YOU   Teresa Brewer
2 DON'T LET THE STARS GET IN YOUR EYES   Perry Como
3 KEEP IT A SECRET   Jo Stafford
4 WHY DON'T YOU BELIEVE ME   Joni James
5 OH HAPPY DAY   Don Howard
6 TELL ME YOU'RE MINE   The Gaylords
7 HOLD ME, THRILL ME, KISS ME   Karen Chandler

March 7, 1953
1 DON'T LET THE STARS GET IN YOUR EYES   Perry Como
2 TILL I WALTZ AGAIN WITH YOU   Teresa Brewer
3 KEEP IT A SECRET   Jo Stafford
4 WHY DON'T YOU BELIEVE ME   Joni James
5 OH HAPPY DAY   Don Howard
6 HOLD ME, THRILL ME, KISS ME   Karen Chandler
7 TELL ME YOU'RE MINE   The Gaylords

March 14, 1953
1 TILL I WALTZ AGAIN WITH YOU   Teresa Brewer
2 DON'T LET THE STARS GET IN YOUR EYES   Perry Como
3 WHY DON'T YOU BELIEVE ME   Joni James
4 KEEP IT A SECRET   Jo Stafford
5 SIDE BY SIDE   Kay Starr
6 DOGGIE IN THE WINDOW   Patti Page
7 OH HAPPY DAY   Don Howard

March 21, 1953
1 TILL I WALTZ AGAIN WITH YOU   Teresa Brewer

2 DON'T LET THE STARS GET IN YOUR EYES   Perry Como
3 DOGGIE IN THE WINDOW   Patti Page
4 PRETEND   Nat King Cole
5 SIDE BY SIDE   Kay Starr
6 HOLD ME, THRILL ME, KISS ME   Karen Chandler
7 KEEP IT A SECRET   Jo Stafford

March 28, 1953
1 TILL I WALTZ AGAIN WITH YOU   Teresa Brewer
2 DON'T LET THE STARS GET IN YOUR EYES   Perry Como
3 PRETEND   Nat King Cole
4 DOGGIE IN THE WINDOW   Patti Page
5 KEEP IT A SECRET   Jo Stafford
6 SIDE BY SIDE   Kay Starr
7 YOUR CHEATIN' HEART   Joni James *
   Note: * Country hit by Hank Williams.

April 4, 1953
1 PRETEND   Nat King Cole
2 TILL I WALTZ AGAIN WITH YOU   Teresa Brewer
3 DOGGIE IN THE WINDOW   Patti Page
4 DON'T LET THE STARS GET IN YOUR EYES   Perry Como
5 SIDE BY SIDE   Kay Starr
6 YOUR CHEATIN' HEART   Joni James *
7 I BELIEVE   Frankie Laine
   Note: * Country hit by Hank Williams.

April 11, 1953
1 I BELIEVE   Frankie Laine
2 DOGGIE IN THE WINDOW   Patti Page
3 TILL I WALTZ AGAIN WITH YOU   Teresa Brewer
4 PRETEND   Nat King Cole
5 YOUR CHEATIN' HEART   Joni James *
6 SIDE BY SIDE   Kay Starr
7 DON'T LET THE STARS GET IN YOUR EYES   Perry Como
   Note: * Country hit by Hank Williams.

April 18, 1953
1 DOGGIE IN THE WINDOW   Patti Page
2 PRETEND   Nat King Cole
3 I BELIEVE   Frankie Laine
4 TILL I WALTZ AGAIN WITH YOU   Teresa Brewer
5 YOUR CHEATIN' HEART   Joni James *
6 DON'T LET THE STARS GET IN YOUR EYES   Perry Como
7 SIDE BY SIDE   Kay Starr
   Note: * Country hit by Hank Williams.

April 25, 1953
1 PRETEND   Nat King Cole
2 TILL I WALTZ AGAIN WITH YOU   Teresa Brewer
3 I BELIEVE   Frankie Laine
4 DOGGIE IN THE WINDOW   Patti Page
5 YOUR CHEATIN' HEART   Joni James *
6 DON'T LET THE STARS GET IN YOUR EYES   Perry Como
7 SIDE BY SIDE   Kay Starr
   Note: * Country hit by Hank Williams.

May 2, 1953
1 I BELIEVE   Frankie Laine
2 PRETEND   Nat King Cole
3 DOGGIE IN THE WINDOW   Patti Page
4 TILL I WALTZ AGAIN WITH YOU   Teresa Brewer
5 YOUR CHEATIN' HEART   Joni James *
6 SONG FROM MOULIN ROUGE   Percy Faith Orch.
7 APRIL IN PORTUGAL   Les Baxter Orch.
   Note: * Country hit by Hank Williams.

Teresa Brewer
Teresa hits #1 with ``Til I Waltz Again With You'' (Feb. 28).

May 9, 1953
1   PRETEND   Nat King Cole
2   SONG FROM MOULIN ROUGE   Percy Faith Orch.
3   DOGGIE IN THE WINDOW   Patti Page
4   YOUR CHEATIN' HEART   Joni James *
5   I BELIEVE   Frankie Laine
6   APRIL IN PORTUGAL   Les Baxter Orch.
7   SIDE BY SIDE   Kay Starr
    Note: * Country hit by Hank Williams.

May 16, 1953
1   I BELIEVE   Frankie Laine
2   APRIL IN PORTUGAL   Les Baxter Orch.
3   SONG FROM MOULIN ROUGE   Percy Faith Orch.
4   PRETEND   Nat King Cole
5   YOUR CHEATIN' HEART   Joni James *
6   DOGGIE IN THE WINDOW   Patti Page
7   RUBY   Richard Hayman
    Note: * Country hit by Hank Williams.

May 23, 1953
1   SONG FROM MOULIN ROUGE   Percy Faith Orch.
2   I BELIEVE   Frankie Laine
3   PRETEND   Nat King Cole
4   YOUR CHEATIN' HEART   Joni James *
5   APRIL IN PORTUGAL   Les Baxter Orch.
6   DOGGIE IN THE WINDOW   Patti Page
7   SIDE BY SIDE   Kay Starr
    Note: * Country hit by Hank Williams.

May 30, 1953
1   SONG FROM MOULIN ROUGE   Percy Faith Orch.
2   I BELIEVE   Frankie Laine
3   APRIL IN PORTUGAL   Les Baxter Orch.
4   DOGGIE IN THE WINDOW   Patti Page
5   RUBY   Richard Hayman
6   YOUR CHEATIN' HEART   Joni James *
7   PRETEND   Nat King Cole
    Note: * Country hit by Hank Williams.

June 6, 1953
1   SONG FROM MOULIN ROUGE   Percy Faith Orch.
2   APRIL IN PORTUGAL   Les Baxter Orch.
3   PRETEND   Nat King Cole
4   I BELIEVE   Frankie Laine
5   RUBY   Richard Hayman
6   YOUR CHEATIN' HEART   Joni James *
7   SAY YOU'RE MINE AGAIN   Perry Como
    Note: * Country hit by Hank Williams.

June 13, 1953
1   APRIL IN PORTUGAL   Les Baxter Orch.
2   SONG FROM MOULIN ROUGE   Percy Faith Orch.
3   I BELIEVE   Frankie Laine
4   RUBY   Richard Hayman
5   I'M WALKING BEHIND YOU   Eddie Fisher
6   SAY YOU'RE MINE AGAIN   Perry Como
7   PRETEND   Nat King Cole

June 20, 1953
1   SONG FROM MOULIN ROUGE   Percy Faith Orch.

Frankie Laine
After two big late-forties hits—````That Lucky Old Sun'' and
``Mule Train''—Frankie is back on top with ``I Believe.''

2 RUBY   Richard Hayman
3 I BELIEVE   Frankie Laine
4 APRIL IN PORTUGAL   Les Baxter Orch.
5 I'M WALKING BEHIND YOU   Eddie Fisher
6 PRETEND   Nat King Cole
7 YOUR CHEATIN' HEART   Joni James *
   Note: * Country hit by Hank Williams.

June 27, 1953
1 SONG FROM MOULIN ROUGE   Percy Faith Orch.
2 APRIL IN PORTUGAL   Les Baxter Orch.
3 I BELIEVE   Frankie Laine
4 I'M WALKING BEHIND YOU   Eddie Fisher
5 RUBY   Richard Hayman
6 SAY YOU'RE MINE AGAIN   Perry Como
7 YOUR CHEATIN' HEART   Joni James *
   Note: * Country hit by Hank Williams.

July 4, 1953
1 SONG FROM MOULIN ROUGE   Percy Faith Orch.
2 RUBY   Richard Hayman
3 APRIL IN PORTUGAL   Les Baxter Orch.
4 I BELIEVE   Frankie Laine
5 I'M WALKING BEHIND YOU   Eddie Fisher
6 SAY YOU'RE MINE AGAIN   Perry Como
7 NO OTHER LOVE   Perry Como

July 11, 1953
1 SONG FROM MOULIN ROUGE   Percy Faith Orch.
2 RUBY   Richard Hayman
3 APRIL IN PORTUGAL   Les Baxter Orch.
4 I BELIEVE   Frankie Laine
5 I'M WALKING BEHIND YOU   Eddie Fisher
6 NO OTHER LOVE   Perry Como
7 SAY YOU'RE MINE AGAIN   Perry Como

July 18, 1953
1 APRIL IN PORTUGAL   Les Baxter Orch.
2 SONG FROM MOULIN ROUGE   Percy Faith Orch.
3 I'M WALKING BEHIND YOU   Eddie Fisher
4 I BELIEVE   Frankie Laine
5 NO OTHER LOVE   Perry Como
6 RUBY   Richard Hayman
7 YOUR CHEATIN' HEART   Joni James *
   Note: * Country hit by Hank Williams.

July 25, 1953
1 SONG FROM MOULIN ROUGE   Percy Faith Orch.
2 APRIL IN PORTUGAL   Les Baxter Orch.
3 I'M WALKING BEHIND YOU   Eddie Fisher
4 NO OTHER LOVE   Perry Como
5 RUBY   Richard Hayman
6 I BELIEVE   Frankie Laine
7 VAYA CON DIOS   Les Paul & Mary Ford

August 1, 1953
1 I'M WALKING BEHIND YOU   Eddie Fisher
2 NO OTHER LOVE   Perry Como
3 RUBY   Richard Hayman
4 SONG FROM MOULIN ROUGE   Percy Faith Orch.
5 VAYA CON DIOS   Les Paul & Mary Ford
6 APRIL IN PORTUGAL   Les Baxter Orch.
7 I BELIEVE   Frankie Laine

August 8, 1953
1 NO OTHER LOVE   Perry Como

2 I'M WALKING BEHIND YOU   Eddie Fisher
3 I BELIEVE   Frankie Laine
4 VAYA CON DIOS   Les Paul & Mary Ford
5 APRIL IN PORTUGAL   Les Baxter Orch.
6 P.S. I LOVE YOU   Hilltoppers
7 SONG FROM MOULIN ROUGE   Percy Faith Orch.

August 15, 1953
1 NO OTHER LOVE   Perry Como
2 SONG FROM MOULIN ROUGE   Percy Faith Orch.
3 I'M WALKING BEHIND YOU   Eddie Fisher
4 VAYA CON DIOS   Les Paul & Mary Ford
5 RUBY   Richard Hayman
6 APRIL IN PORTUGAL   Les Baxter Orch.
7 P.S. I LOVE YOU   Hilltoppers

August 22, 1953
1 I'M WALKING BEHIND YOU   Eddie Fisher
2 NO OTHER LOVE   Perry Como
3 SONG FROM MOULIN ROUGE   Percy Faith Orch.
4 VAYA CON DIOS   Les Paul & Mary Ford
5 P.S. I LOVE YOU   Hilltoppers
6 YOU, YOU, YOU   Ames Brothers
7 I BELIEVE   Frankie Laine

August 29, 1953
1 I'M WALKING BEHIND YOU   Eddie Fisher
2 NO OTHER LOVE   Perry Como
3 VAYA CON DIOS   Les Paul & Mary Ford
4 P.S. I LOVE YOU   Hilltoppers
5 OH   Pee Wee Hunt
6 CRYING IN THE CHAPEL   June Valli
7 YOU, YOU, YOU   Ames Brothers

September 5, 1953
1 VAYA CON DIOS   Les Paul & Mary Ford
2 NO OTHER LOVE   Perry Como
3 SONG FROM MOULIN ROUGE   Percy Faith Orch.
4 YOU, YOU, YOU   Ames Brothers
5 P.S. I LOVE YOU   Hilltoppers
6 OH   Pee Wee Hunt
7 I'M WALKING BEHIND YOU   Eddie Fisher

September 12, 1953
1 VAYA CON DIOS   Les Paul & Mary Ford
2 NO OTHER LOVE   Perry Como
3 YOU, YOU, YOU   Ames Brothers
4 OH   Pee Wee Hunt
5 CRYING IN THE CHAPEL   June Valli
6 SONG FROM MOULIN ROUGE   Percy Faith Orch.
7 P.S. I LOVE YOU   Hilltoppers

September 19, 1953
1 YOU, YOU, YOU   Ames Brothers
2 VAYA CON DIOS   Les Paul & Mary Ford
3 CRYING IN THE CHAPEL   June Valli
4 NO OTHER LOVE   Perry Como
5 OH   Pee Wee Hunt
6 P.S. I LOVE YOU   Hilltoppers
7 I'M WALKING BEHIND YOU   Eddie Fisher

September 26, 1953
1 NO OTHER LOVE   Perry Como
2 VAYA CON DIOS   Les Paul & Mary Ford
3 CRYING IN THE CHAPEL   June Valli

4   YOU, YOU, YOU   Ames Brothers
5   I'M WALKING BEHIND YOU   Eddie Fisher
6   OH   Pee Wee Hunt
7   P.S. I LOVE YOU   Hilltoppers

October 3, 1953
1   YOU, YOU, YOU   Ames Brothers
2   NO OTHER LOVE   Perry Como
3   VAYA CON DIOS   Les Paul & Mary Ford
4   OH   Pee Wee Hunt
5   CRYING IN THE CHAPEL   June Valli
6   P.S. I LOVE YOU   Hilltoppers
7   I'M WALKING BEHIND YOU   Eddie Fisher

October 10, 1953
1   VAYA CON DIOS   Les Paul & Mary Ford
2   YOU, YOU, YOU   Ames Brothers
3   NO OTHER LOVE   Perry Como
4   CRYING IN THE CHAPEL   June Valli
5   OH   Pee Wee Hunt
6   P.S. I LOVE YOU   Hilltoppers
7   DRAGNET   Ray Anthony Orch.

October 17, 1953
1   VAYA CON DIOS   Les Paul & Mary Ford
2   YOU, YOU, YOU   Ames Brothers
3   CRYING IN THE CHAPEL   June Valli
4   OH   Pee Wee Hunt
5   NO OTHER LOVE   Perry Como
6   EBB TIDE   Frank Chacksfield Orch.
7   MANY TIMES   Eddie Fisher

October 24, 1953
1   YOU, YOU, YOU   Ames Brothers
2   NO OTHER LOVE   Perry Como
3   OH   Pee Wee Hunt
4   VAYA CON DIOS   Les Paul & Mary Ford
5   CRYING IN THE CHAPEL   June Valli
6   EBB TIDE   Frank Chacksfield Orch.
7   DRAGNET   Ray Anthony Orch.

October 31, 1953
1   VAYA CON DIOS   Les Paul & Mary Ford
2   YOU, YOU, YOU   Ames Brothers
3   EBB TIDE   Frank Chacksfield Orch.
4   CRYING IN THE CHAPEL   June Valli
5   MANY TIMES   Eddie Fisher
6   OH   Pee Wee Hunt
7   I'M WALKING BEHIND YOU   Eddie Fisher

November 7, 1953
1   EBB TIDE   Frank Chacksfield Orch.
2   YOU, YOU, YOU   Ames Brothers
3   VAYA CON DIOS   Les Paul & Mary Ford
4   MANY TIMES   Eddie Fisher
5   CRYING IN THE CHAPEL   June Valli
6   OH   Pee Wee Hunt
7   I LOVE PARIS   Les Baxter Orch.

November 14, 1953
1   EBB TIDE   Frank Chacksfield Orch.
2   RAGS TO RICHES   Tony Bennett
3   MANY TIMES   Eddie Fisher
4   VAYA CON DIOS   Les Paul & Mary Ford
5   YOU, YOU, YOU   Ames Brothers
6   CRYING IN THE CHAPEL   June Valli

7   C'EST MAGNIFIQUE   Gordon MacRae

November 21, 1953
1   EBB TIDE   Frank Chacksfield Orch.
2   VAYA CON DIOS   Les Paul & Mary Ford
3   MANY TIMES   Eddie Fisher
4   YOU, YOU, YOU   Ames Brothers
5   NO OTHER LOVE   Perry Como
6   OH   Pee Wee Hunt
7   I SEE THE MOON   The Mariners

November 28, 1953
1   YOU, YOU, YOU   Ames Brothers
2   EBB TIDE   Frank Chacksfield Orch.
3   VAYA CON DIOS   Les Paul & Mary Ford
4   MANY TIMES   Eddie Fisher
5   RAGS TO RICHES   Tony Bennett
6   RICOCHET   Teresa Brewer
7   OH   Pee Wee Hunt

December 5, 1953
1   RAGS TO RICHES   Tony Bennett
2   EBB TIDE   Frank Chacksfield Orch.
3   MANY TIMES   Eddie Fisher
4   YOU, YOU, YOU   Ames Brothers
5   RICOCHET   Teresa Brewer
6   VAYA CON DIOS   Les Paul & Mary Ford
7   YOU ALONE   Perry Como

December 12, 1953
1   RAGS TO RICHES   Tony Bennett
2   YOU, YOU, YOU   Ames Brothers
3   EBB TIDE   Frank Chacksfield Orch.
4   RICOCHET   Teresa Brewer
5   STRANGER IN PARADISE   Tony Bennett
6   VAYA CON DIOS   Les Paul & Mary Ford
7   MANY TIMES   Eddie Fisher

December 19, 1953
1   EBB TIDE   Frank Chacksfield Orch.
2   RAGS TO RICHES   Tony Bennett
3   THAT'S AMORE   Dean Martin
4   CHANGING PARTNERS   Patti Page
5   EH, CUMPARI   Julius La Rosa
6   MANY TIMES   Eddie Fisher
7   VAYA CON DIOS   Les Paul & Mary Ford

December 26, 1953
1   RICOCHET   Teresa Brewer
2   EBB TIDE   Frank Chacksfield Orch.
3   YOU, YOU, YOU   Ames Brothers
4   RAGS TO RICHES   Tony Bennett
5   THAT'S AMORE   Dean Martin
6   STRANGER IN PARADISE   Tony Bennett
7   VAYA CON DIOS   Les Paul & Mary Ford

January 2, 1954
1   EBB TIDE   Frank Chacksfield Orch.
2   STRANGER IN PARADISE   Tony Bennett
3   THAT'S AMORE   Dean Martin
4   RICOCHET   Teresa Brewer
5   YOU, YOU, YOU   Ames Brothers
6   OFF SHORE   Lee Diamond
7   WHITE CHRISTMAS   Bing Crosby

Doris Day

Doris Day had two of the fifties' best-remembered songs: ``Secret Love'' (#1 on Feb. 27)
and ``Que Sera Sera (Whatever Will Be Will Be).''

January 9, 1954
1. STRANGER IN PARADISE Tony Bennett
2. THAT'S AMORE Dean Martin
3. HEART OF MY HEART Don Cornell, Alan Hale & Johnny Desmond
4. RAGS TO RICHES Tony Bennett
5. RICOCHET Teresa Brewer
6. OH, MY PAPA Eddie Fisher
7. YOU, YOU, YOU Ames Brothers

January 16, 1954
1. STRANGER IN PARADISE Tony Bennett
2. THAT'S AMORE Dean Martin
3. OH, MY PAPA Eddie Fisher
4. CHANGING PARTNERS Patti Page
5. RICOCHET Teresa Brewer
6. EBB TIDE Frank Chacksfield Orch.
7. HEART OF MY HEART Don Cornell, Alan Dale & Johnny Desmond

January 23, 1954
1. STRANGER IN PARADISE Tony Bennett
2. THAT'S AMORE Dean Martin
3. OH, MY PAPA Eddie Fisher
4. CHANGING PARTNERS Patti Page
5. RAGS TO RICHES Tony Bennett
6. HEART OF MY HEART Don Cornell, Alan Dale & Johnny Desmond
7. SECRET LOVE Doris Day

January 30, 1954
1. STRANGER IN PARADISE Tony Bennett
2. OH, MY PAPA Eddie Fisher
3. THAT'S AMORE Dean Martin
4. CHANGING PARTNERS Patti Page
5. SECRET LOVE Doris Day
6. RAGS TO RICHES Tony Bennett
7. EBB TIDE Frank Chacksfield Orch.

February 6, 1954
1. STRANGER IN PARADISE Tony Bennett
2. OH, MY PAPA Eddie Fisher
3. CHANGING PARTNERS Patti Page
4. THAT'S AMORE Dean Martin
5. SECRET LOVE Doris Day
6. HEART OF MY HEART Don Cornell, Alan Dale & Johnny Desmond
7. RICOCHET Teresa Brewer

February 13, 1954
1. SECRET LOVE Doris Day
2. STRANGER IN PARADISE Tony Bennett
3. OH, MY PAPA Eddie Fisher
4. THAT'S AMORE Dean Martin
5. CHANGING PARTNERS Patti Page
6. HEART OF MY HEART Don Cornell, Alan Dale & Johnny Desmond
7. RICOCHET Teresa Brewer

February 20, 1954
1. STRANGER IN PARADISE Tony Bennett
2. SECRET LOVE Doris Day
3. OH, MY PAPA Eddie Fisher
4. THAT'S AMORE Dean Martin
5. HEART OF MY HEART Don Cornell, Alan Dale & Johnny Desmond
6. CHANGING PARTNERS Patti Page
7. RICOCHET Teresa Brewer

February 27, 1954
1. SECRET LOVE Doris Day
2. STRANGER IN PARADISE Tony Bennett
3. THAT'S AMORE Dean Martin
4. CHANGING PARTNERS Patti Page
5. OH, MY PAPA Eddie Fisher
6. HEART OF MY HEART Don Cornell, Alan Dale & Johnny Desmond
7. WOMAN Jose Ferrer & Rosemary Clooney

March 6, 1954
1. SECRET LOVE Doris Day
2. STRANGER IN PARADISE Tony Bennett
3. OH, MY PAPA Eddie Fisher
4. MAKE LOVE TO ME Jo Stafford
5. HEART OF MY HEART Don Cornell, Alan Dale & Johnny Desmond
6. THAT'S AMORE Dean Martin
7. YOUNG AT HEART Frank Sinatra

March 13, 1954
1. SECRET LOVE Doris Day
2. OH, MY PAPA Eddie Fisher
3. STRANGER IN PARADISE Tony Bennett
4. MAKE LOVE TO ME Jo Stafford
5. YOUNG AT HEART Frank Sinatra
6. CHANGING PARTNERS Patti Page
7. HEART OF MY HEART Don Cornell, Alan Dale & Johnny Desmond

March 20, 1954
1. SECRET LOVE Doris Day
2. MAKE LOVE TO ME Jo Stafford
3. YOUNG AT HEART Frank Sinatra
4. WANTED Perry Como
5. OH, MY PAPA Eddie Fisher
6. STRANGER IN PARADISE Tony Bennett
7. I GET SO LONELY Four Knights

March 27, 1954
1. SECRET LOVE Doris Day
2. YOUNG AT HEART Frank Sinatra
3. MAKE LOVE TO ME Jo Stafford
4. WANTED Perry Como
5. I GET SO LONELY Four Knights
6. STRANGER IN PARADISE Tony Bennett
7. OH, MY PAPA Eddie Fisher

April 3, 1954
1. SECRET LOVE Doris Day
2. WANTED Perry Como
3. YOUNG AT HEART Frank Sinatra
4. CROSS OVER THE BRIDGE Patti Page
5. I GET SO LONELY Four Knights
6. MAKE LOVE TO ME Jo Stafford
7. STRANGER IN PARADISE Tony Bennett

April 10, 1954
1. WANTED Perry Como
2. SECRET LOVE Doris Day
3. MAKE LOVE TO ME Jo Stafford
4. YOUNG AT HEART Frank Sinatra

5 I GET SO LONELY   Four Knights
6 CROSS OVER THE BRIDGE   Patti Page
7 STRANGER IN PARADISE   Tony Bennett

April 17, 1954
1 YOUNG AT HEART   Frank Sinatra
2 MAKE LOVE TO ME   Jo Stafford
3 WANTED   Perry Como
4 SECRET LOVE   Doris Day
5 I GET SO LONELY   Four Knights
6 CROSS OVER THE BRIDGE   Patti Page
7 ANSWER ME, MY LOVE   Nat King Cole

April 24, 1954
1 YOUNG AT HEART   Frank Sinatra
2 WANTED   Perry Como
3 EASTER PARADE   Guy Lombardo
4 MAKE LOVE TO ME   Jo Stafford
5 SECRET LOVE   Doris Day
6 CROSS OVER THE BRIDGE   Patti Page
7 I GET SO LONELY   Four Knights

May 1, 1954
1 WANTED   Perry Como
2 YOUNG AT HEART   Frank Sinatra
3 MAKE LOVE TO ME   Jo Stafford
4 CROSS OVER THE BRIDGE   Patti Page
5 I GET SO LONELY   Four Knights
6 SECRET LOVE   Doris Day
7 ANSWER ME, MY LOVE   Nat King Cole

May 8, 1954
1 WANTED   Perry Como
2 YOUNG AT HEART   Frank Sinatra
3 CROSS OVER THE BRIDGE   Patti Page
4 MAKE LOVE TO ME   Jo Stafford
5 I GET SO LONELY   Four Knights
6 ANSWER ME, MY LOVE   Nat King Cole
7 SECRET LOVE   Doris Day

May 15, 1954
1 WANTED   Perry Como
2 YOUNG AT HEART   Frank Sinatra
3 MAKE LOVE TO ME   Jo Stafford
4 I GET SO LONELY   Four Knights
5 CROSS OVER THE BRIDGE   Patti Page
6 ANSWER ME, MY LOVE   Nat King Cole
7 HERE   Tony Martin

May 22, 1954
1 WANTED   Perry Como
2 YOUNG AT HEART   Frank Sinatra
3 MAKE LOVE TO ME   Jo Stafford
4 I GET SO LONELY   Four Knights
5 ANSWER ME, MY LOVE   Nat King Cole
6 HERE   Tony Martin
7 CROSS OVER THE BRIDGE   Patti Page

May 29, 1954
1 WANTED   Perry Como
2 ANSWER ME, MY LOVE   Nat King Cole
3 YOUNG AT HEART   Frank Sinatra
4 LITTLE THINGS MEAN A LOT   Kitty Kallen
5 CROSS OVER THE BRIDGE   Patti Page
6 I GET SO LONELY   Four Knights

7 MAKE LOVE TO ME   Jo Stafford

June 5, 1954
1 WANTED   Perry Como
2 THREE COINS IN THE FOUNTAIN   Four Aces
3 YOUNG AT HEART   Frank Sinatra
4 LITTLE THINGS MEAN A LOT   Kitty Kallen
5 I GET SO LONELY   Four Knights
6 HAPPY WANDERER   Frankie Weir
7 ANSWER ME, MY LOVE   Nat King Cole

June 12, 1954
1 LITTLE THINGS MEAN A LOT   Kitty Kallen
2 THREE COINS IN THE FOUNTAIN   Four Aces
3 WANTED   Perry Como
4 HAPPY WANDERER   Frankie Weir
5 I GET SO LONELY   Four Knights
6 HERNANDO'S HIDEAWAY   Archie Bleyer
7 YOUNG AT HEART   Frank Sinatra

June 19, 1954
1 THREE COINS IN THE FOUNTAIN   Four Aces
2 LITTLE THINGS MEAN A LOT   Kitty Kallen
3 WANTED   Perry Como
4 HERNANDO'S HIDEAWAY   Archie Bleyer
5 YOUNG AT HEART   Frank Sinatra
6 MAKE LOVE TO ME   Jo Stafford
7 ANSWER ME, MY LOVE   Nat King Cole

June 26, 1954
1 LITTLE THINGS MEAN A LOT   Kitty Kallen
2 THREE COINS IN THE FOUNTAIN   Four Aces
3 HERNANDO'S HIDEAWAY   Archie Bleyer
4 HAPPY WANDERER   Frankie Weir
5 WANTED   Perry Como
6 YOUNG AT HEART   Frank Sinatra
7 I GET SO LONELY   Four Knights

July 3, 1954
1 THREE COINS IN THE FOUNTAIN   Four Aces
2 LITTLE THINGS MEAN A LOT   Kitty Kallen
3 HERNANDO'S HIDEAWAY   Archie Bleyer
4 HAPPY WANDERER   Frankie Weir
5 ANSWER ME, MY LOVE   Nat King Cole
6 WANTED   Perry Como
7 IF YOU LOVE ME   Kay Starr

July 10, 1954
1 LITTLE THINGS MEAN A LOT   Kitty Kallen
2 HERNANDO'S HIDEAWAY   Archie Bleyer
3 THREE COINS IN THE FOUNTAIN   Four Aces
4 HAPPY WANDERER   Frankie Weir
5 IF YOU LOVE ME   Kay Starr
6 WANTED   Perry Como
7 YOUNG AT HEART   Frank Sinatra

July 17, 1954
1 THREE COINS IN THE FOUNTAIN   Four Aces
2 LITTLE THINGS MEAN A LOT   Kitty Kallen
3 HERNANDO'S HIDEAWAY   Archie Bleyer
4 HAPPY WANDERER   Frankie Weir
5 IF YOU LOVE ME   Kay Starr
6 THE LITTLE SHOEMAKER   Gaylords
7 I UNDERSTAND JUST HOW YOU FEEL   Four Tunes

The Four Aces

The Four Aces followed up their #1 smash
``Three Coins In The Fountain'' (Aug. 7)—from the movie of
the same name—with their equally successful
``Love Is A Many-Splendored Thing'' (Nov. 1955).

July 24, 1954
1. LITTLE THINGS MEAN A LOT   Kitty Kallen
2. HERNANDO'S HIDEAWAY   Archie Bleyer
3. THREE COINS IN THE FOUNTAIN   Four Aces
4. IF YOU LOVE ME   Kay Starr
5. HAPPY WANDERER   Frankie Weir
6. THE LITTLE SHOEMAKER   Gaylords
7. I UNDERSTAND JUST HOW YOU FEEL   Four Tunes

July 31, 1954
1. LITTLE THINGS MEAN A LOT   Kitty Kallen
2. HERNANDO'S HIDEAWAY   Archie Bleyer
3. THREE COINS IN THE FOUNTAIN   Four Aces
4. THE LITTLE SHOEMAKER   Gaylords
5. HAPPY WANDERER   Frankie Weir
6. HEY THERE   Rosemary Clooney
7. SH-BOOM   Crew Cuts

August 7, 1954
1. THREE COINS IN THE FOUNTAIN   Four Aces
2. HERNANDO'S HIDEAWAY   Archie Bleyer
3. LITTLE THINGS MEAN A LOT   Kitty Kallen
4. THE LITTLE SHOEMAKER   Gaylords
5. HEY THERE   Rosemary Clooney
6. SH-BOOM   Crew Cuts
7. I UNDERSTAND JUST HOW YOU FEEL   Four Tunes

August 14, 1954
1. HERNANDO'S HIDEAWAY   Archie Bleyer
2. HEY THERE   Rosemary Clooney
3. THE LITTLE SHOEMAKER   Gaylords
4. LITTLE THINGS MEAN A LOT   Kitty Kallen
5. THREE COINS IN THE FOUNTAIN   Four Aces
6. THE HIGH AND THE MIGHTY   Les Baxter Orch.
7. SH-BOOM   Crew Cuts

August 21, 1954
1. LITTLE THINGS MEAN A LOT   Kitty Kallen
2. HEY THERE   Rosemary Clooney
3. SH-BOOM   Crew Cuts
4. THE LITTLE SHOEMAKER   Gaylords
5. THE HIGH AND THE MIGHTY   Les Baxter Orch.
6. HERNANDO'S HIDEAWAY   Archie Bleyer
7. THREE COINS IN THE FOUNTAIN   Four Aces

August 28, 1954
1. HEY THERE   Rosemary Clooney
2. THE HIGH AND THE MIGHTY   Les Baxter Orch.
3. SH-BOOM   Crew Cuts
4. THE LITTLE SHOEMAKER   Gaylords
5. HERNANDO'S HIDEAWAY   Archie Bleyer
6. LITTLE THINGS MEAN A LOT   Kitty Kallen
7. THREE COINS IN THE FOUNTAIN   Four Aces

September 4, 1954
1. HEY THERE   Rosemary Clooney
2. THE HIGH AND THE MIGHTY   Les Baxter Orch.
3. THE LITTLE SHOEMAKER   Gaylords
4. SH-BOOM   Crew Cuts
5. IN THE CHAPEL IN THE MOONLIGHT   Kitty Kallen
6. LITTLE THINGS MEAN A LOT   Kitty Kallen
7. HERNANDO'S HIDEAWAY   Archie Bleyer

September 11, 1954
1. HEY THERE   Rosemary Clooney

167

The Crew Cuts

``Sh-Boom'' is considered by many to be a seminal fifties
song—a forerunner of many changes to come in music.

2 THE HIGH AND THE MIGHTY   Les Baxter Orch.
3 THE LITTLE SHOEMAKER   Gaylords
4 SH-BOOM   Crew Cuts
5 IN THE CHAPEL IN THE MOONLIGHT   Kitty Kallen
6 LITTLE THINGS MEAN A LOT   Kitty Kallen
7 HERNANDO'S HIDEAWAY   Archie Bleyer

September 18, 1954
1 HEY THERE   Rosemary Clooney
2 THE HIGH AND THE MIGHTY   Les Baxter Orch.
3 THE LITTLE SHOEMAKER   Gaylords
4 SH-BOOM   Crew Cuts
5 IN THE CHAPEL IN THE MOONLIGHT   Kitty Kallen
6 LITTLE THINGS MEAN A LOT   Kitty Kallen
7 THIS OLE HOUSE   Rosemary Clooney *
Note: * Country hit by Stuart Hamblen.

September 25, 1954
1 HEY THERE   Rosemary Clooney
2 THE HIGH AND THE MIGHTY   Les Baxter Orch.
3 SH-BOOM   Crew Cuts
4 THE LITTLE SHOEMAKER   Gaylords
5 IF I GIVE MY HEART TO YOU   Doris Day
6 SKOKIAAN   Ralph Marterie Orch.
7 THEY WERE DOIN' THE MAMBO   Vaughn Monroe Orch.
   (VR: Vaughn Monroe)

October 2, 1954
1 HEY THERE   Rosemary Clooney
2 THE HIGH AND THE MIGHTY   Les Baxter Orch.
3 IF I GIVE MY HEART TO YOU   Doris Day
4 THE LITTLE SHOEMAKER   Gaylords
5 SH-BOOM   Crew Cuts
6 SKOKIAAN   Ralph Marterie Orch.
7 THIS OLE HOUSE   Rosemary Clooney *
Note: * Country hit by Stuart Hamblen.

October 9, 1954
1 HEY THERE   Rosemary Clooney
2 IF I GIVE MY HEART TO YOU   Doris Day
3 THE HIGH AND THE MIGHTY   Les Baxter Orch.
4 SKOKIAAN   Ralph Marterie Orch.
5 THIS OLE HOUSE   Rosemary Clooney *
6 SH-BOOM   Crew Cuts
7 I NEED YOU NOW   Eddie Fisher
Note: * Country hit by Stuart Hamblen.

October 16, 1954
1 HEY THERE   Rosemary Clooney
2 IF I GIVE MY HEART TO YOU   Doris Day
3 THE HIGH AND THE MIGHTY   Les Baxter Orch.
4 I NEED YOU NOW   Eddie Fisher
5 SKOKIAAN   Ralph Marterie Orch.
6 THIS OLE HOUSE   Rosemary Clooney *
7 SH-BOOM   Crew Cuts
Note: * Country hit by Stuart Hamblen.

October 23, 1954
1 HEY THERE   Rosemary Clooney
2 THIS OLE HOUSE   Rosemary Clooney *
3 I NEED YOU NOW   Eddie Fisher
4 IF I GIVE MY HEART TO YOU   Doris Day
5 SKOKIAAN   Ralph Marterie Orch.
6 THE HIGH AND THE MIGHTY   Les Baxter Orch.
7 PAPA LOVES MAMBO   Perry Como
Note: * Country hit by Stuart Hamblen.

Rosemary Clooney
``Hey There''—another #1 hit for Rosie (Aug. 28).

October 30, 1954
1 I NEED YOU NOW   Eddie Fisher
2 HEY THERE   Rosemary Clooney
3 IF I GIVE MY HEART TO YOU   Doris Day
4 PAPA LOVES MAMBO   Perry Como
5 THIS OLE HOUSE   Rosemary Clooney *
6 THE HIGH AND THE MIGHTY   Les Baxter Orch.
7 COUNT YOUR BLESSINGS   Eddie Fisher
   Note: * Country hit by Stuart Hamblen.

November 6, 1954
1 IF I GIVE MY HEART TO YOU   Doris Day
2 I NEED YOU NOW   Eddie Fisher
3 THIS OLE HOUSE   Rosemary Clooney *
4 HOLD MY HAND   Don Cornell
5 HEY THERE   Rosemary Clooney
6 PAPA LOVES MAMBO   Perry Como
7 SKOKIAAN   Ralph Marterie Orch.
   Note: * Country hit by Stuart Hamblen.

November 13, 1954
1 HEY THERE   Rosemary Clooney
2 I NEED YOU NOW   Eddie Fisher
3 IF I GIVE MY HEART TO YOU   Doris Day
4 PAPA LOVES MAMBO   Perry Como
5 COUNT YOUR BLESSINGS   Eddie Fisher
6 THIS OLE HOUSE   Rosemary Clooney *
7 MISTER SANDMAN   The Chordettes
   Note: * Country hit by Stuart Hamblen.

November 20, 1954
1 IF I GIVE MY HEART TO YOU   Doris Day
2 HEY THERE   Rosemary Clooney
3 PAPA LOVES MAMBO   Perry Como
4 THIS OLE HOUSE   Rosemary Clooney *
5 COUNT YOUR BLESSINGS   Eddie Fisher
6 MISTER SANDMAN   The Chordettes
7 I NEED YOU NOW   Eddie Fisher
   Note: * Country hit by Stuart Hamblen.

November 27, 1954
1 MISTER SANDMAN   The Chordettes
2 PAPA LOVES MAMBO   Perry Como
3 I NEED YOU NOW   Eddie Fisher
4 IF I GIVE MY HEART TO YOU   Doris Day
5 COUNT YOUR BLESSINGS   Eddie Fisher
6 THIS OLE HOUSE   Rosemary Clooney *
7 TEACH ME TONIGHT   Jo Stafford
   Note: * Country hit by Stuart Hamblen.

December 4, 1954
1 MISTER SANDMAN   The Chordettes
2 COUNT YOUR BLESSINGS   Eddie Fisher
3 IF I GIVE MY HEART TO YOU   Doris Day
4 THIS OLE HOUSE   Rosemary Clooney *
5 TEACH ME TONIGHT   Jo Stafford
6 PAPA LOVES MAMBO   Perry Como
7 I NEED YOU NOW   Eddie Fisher
   Note: * Country hit by Stuart Hamblen.

December 11, 1954
1 TEACH ME TONIGHT   Jo Stafford
2 MISTER SANDMAN   The Chordettes
3 COUNT YOUR BLESSINGS   Eddie Fisher
4 PAPA LOVES MAMBO   Perry Como
5 IF I GIVE MY HEART TO YOU   Doris Day
6 LET ME GO, LOVER   Peggy Lee
7 THE NAUGHTY LADY OF SHADY LANE   Ames Brothers

December 18, 1954
1 MISTER SANDMAN   The Chordettes
2 TEACH ME TONIGHT   Jo Stafford
3 LET ME GO, LOVER   Peggy Lee
4 COUNT YOUR BLESSINGS   Eddie Fisher
5 PAPA LOVES MAMBO   Perry Como
6 THE NAUGHTY LADY OF SHADY LANE   Ames Brothers
7 I NEED YOU NOW   Eddie Fisher

December 25, 1954
1 MISTER SANDMAN   The Chordettes
2 LET ME GO, LOVER   Peggy Lee
3 COUNT YOUR BLESSINGS   Eddie Fisher
4 THE NAUGHTY LADY OF SHADY LANE   Ames Brothers
5 I NEED YOU NOW   Eddie Fisher
6 TEACH ME TONIGHT   Jo Stafford
7 WHITE CHRISTMAS   Bing Crosby

January 1, 1955
1 MISTER SANDMAN   The Chordettes
2 LET ME GO, LOVER   Peggy Lee
3 COUNT YOUR BLESSINGS   Eddie Fisher
4 THE NAUGHTY LADY OF SHADY LANE   Ames Brothers
5 WHITE CHRISTMAS   Bing Crosby
6 TEACH ME TONIGHT   Jo Stafford
7 I NEED YOU NOW   Eddie Fisher

January 8, 1955
1 LET ME GO, LOVER   Peggy Lee
2 MISTER SANDMAN   The Chordettes
3 TEACH ME TONIGHT   Jo Stafford
4 COUNT YOUR BLESSINGS   Eddie Fisher
5 THE NAUGHTY LADY OF SHADY LANE   Ames Brothers
6 PAPA LOVES MAMBO   Perry Como
7 I NEED YOU NOW   Eddie Fisher

January 15, 1955
1 MISTER SANDMAN   The Chordettes
2 THE NAUGHTY LADY OF SHADY LANE   Ames Brothers
3 LET ME GO, LOVER   Peggy Lee
4 TEACH ME TONIGHT   Jo Stafford
5 COUNT YOUR BLESSINGS   Eddie Fisher
6 MELODY OF LOVE   Billy Vaughn Orch.
7 MAKE YOURSELF COMFORTABLE   Sarah Vaughn

January 22, 1955
1 MISTER SANDMAN   The Chordettes
2 LET ME GO, LOVER   Peggy Lee
3 TEACH ME TONIGHT   Jo Stafford
4 THE NAUGHTY LADY OF SHADY LANE   Ames Brothers
5 MELODY OF LOVE   Billy Vaughn Orch.
6 HEARTS OF STONE   Fontane Sisters
7 COUNT YOUR BLESSINGS   Eddie Fisher

January 29, 1955
1 LET ME GO, LOVER   Peggy Lee
2 MISTER SANDMAN   The Chordettes
3 MELODY OF LOVE   Billy Vaughn Orch.
4 THE NAUGHTY LADY OF SHADY LANE   Ames Brothers
5 HEARTS OF STONE   Fontane Sisters
6 TEACH ME TONIGHT   Jo Stafford
7 COUNT YOUR BLESSINGS   Eddie Fisher

February 5, 1955
1 MELODY OF LOVE   Billy Vaughn Orch.
2 LET ME GO, LOVER   Peggy Lee
3 MISTER SANDMAN   The Chordettes
4 THE NAUGHTY LADY OF SHADY LANE   Ames Brothers
5 MAKE YOURSELF COMFORTABLE   Sarah Vaughn
6 HEARTS OF STONE   Fontane Sisters
7 THAT'S ALL I WANT FROM YOU   Jaye P. Morgan

February 12, 1955
1 MISTER SANDMAN   The Chordettes
2 MELODY OF LOVE   Billy Vaughn Orch.
3 LET ME GO, LOVER   Peggy Lee
4 SINCERELY   McGuire Sisters
5 THE NAUGHTY LADY OF SHADY LANE   Ames Brothers
6 HEARTS OF STONE   Fontane Sisters
7 THAT'S ALL I WANT FROM YOU   Jaye P. Morgan

February 19, 1955
1 MELODY OF LOVE   Billy Vaughn Orch.
2 HEARTS OF STONE   Fontane Sisters
3 MISTER SANDMAN   The Chordettes
4 LET ME GO, LOVER   Peggy Lee
5 SINCERELY   McGuire Sisters
6 TWEEDLE DEE   Georgia Gibbs
7 THAT'S ALL I WANT FROM YOU   Jaye P. Morgan

February 26, 1955
1 MELODY OF LOVE   Billy Vaughn Orch.
2 HEARTS OF STONE   Fontane Sisters
3 THAT'S ALL I WANT FROM YOU   Jaye P. Morgan
4 MISTER SANDMAN   The Chordettes
5 KO KO MO   Perry Como *
6 SINCERELY   McGuire Sisters
7 TWEEDLE DEE   Georgia Gibbs
   Note: * Another version by: The Crew Cuts.

March 5, 1955
1 MELODY OF LOVE   Billy Vaughn Orch.
2 SINCERELY   McGuire Sisters
3 TWEEDLE DEE   Georgia Gibbs
4 HEARTS OF STONE   Fontane Sisters
5 THAT'S ALL I WANT FROM YOU   Jaye P. Morgan
6 MISTER SANDMAN   The Chordettes
7 KO KO MO   Perry Como *
   Note: * Another version by: The Crew Cuts.

March 12, 1955
1 MELODY OF LOVE   Billy Vaughn Orch.
2 KO KO MO   Perry Como *
3 SINCERELY   McGuire Sisters
4 TWEEDLE DEE   Georgia Gibbs
5 HEARTS OF STONE   Fontane Sisters
6 THAT'S ALL I WANT FROM YOU   Jaye P. Morgan
7 OPEN UP YOUR HEART   Bing Crosby
   Note: * Another version by: The Crew Cuts.

March 19, 1955
1 TWEEDLE DEE   Georgia Gibbs
2 MELODY OF LOVE   Billy Vaughn Orch.
3 THE BALLAD OF DAVY CROCKETT   Bill Hayes *
4 SINCERELY   McGuire Sisters
5 KO KO MO   Perry Como **
6 THAT'S ALL I WANT FROM YOU   Jaye P. Morgan
7 MISTER SANDMAN   The Chordettes
   Note: * Cover versions by Fess Parker, Tennessee Ernie
   Ford, Burl Ives, Mac Wiseman.
      ** Another version by: The Crew Cuts.

March 26, 1955
1 MELODY OF LOVE   Billy Vaughn Orch.
2 SINCERELY   McGuire Sisters
3 THE BALLAD OF DAVY CROCKETT   Bill Hayes *
4 TWEEDLE DEE   Georgia Gibbs
5 HOW IMPORTANT CAN IT BE   Joni James
6 KO KO MO   Perry Como **
7 THAT'S ALL I WANT FROM YOU   Jaye P. Morgan
   Note: * Cover versions by Fess Parker, Tennessee Ernie
   Ford, Burl Ives, Mac Wiseman.
      ** Another version by: The Crew Cuts.

April 2, 1955
1 THE BALLAD OF DAVY CROCKETT   Bill Hayes *
2 TWEEDLE DEE   Georgia Gibbs
3 MELODY OF LOVE   Billy Vaughn Orch.
4 HOW IMPORTANT CAN IT BE   Joni James
5 SINCERELY   McGuire Sisters
6 KO KO MO   Perry Como **
7 THAT'S ALL I WANT FROM YOU   Jaye P. Morgan
   Note: * Cover versions by Fess Parker, Tennessee Ernie
   Ford, Burl Ives, Mac Wiseman.
      ** Another version by: The Crew Cuts.

April 9, 1955
1 THE BALLAD OF DAVY CROCKETT   Bill Hayes *
2 TWEEDLE DEE   Georgia Gibbs
3 MELODY OF LOVE   Billy Vaughn Orch.
4 SINCERELY   McGuire Sisters
5 KO KO MO   Perry Como **
6 HOW IMPORTANT CAN IT BE   Joni James
7 THAT'S ALL I WANT FROM YOU   Jaye P. Morgan
   Note: * Cover versions by Fess Parker, Tennessee Ernie
   Ford, Burl Ives, Mac Wiseman.
      ** Another version by: The Crew Cuts.

April 16, 1955
1 THE BALLAD OF DAVY CROCKETT   Bill Hayes *
2 MELODY OF LOVE   Billy Vaughn Orch.
3 EASTER PARADE   Guy Lombardo
4 TWEEDLE DEE   Georgia Gibbs
5 HOW IMPORTANT CAN IT BE   Joni James
6 SINCERELY   McGuire Sisters
7 CHERRY PINK AND APPLE BLOSSOM WHITE   Perez
   Prado
   Note: * Cover versions by Fess Parker, Tennessee Ernie
   Ford, Burl Ives, Mac Wiseman.

April 23, 1955
1 THE BALLAD OF DAVY CROCKETT   Bill Hayes *
2 MELODY OF LOVE   Billy Vaughn Orch.
3 CHERRY PINK AND APPLE BLOSSOM WHITE   Perez
   Prado
4 TWEEDLE DEE   Georgia Gibbs
5 SINCERELY   McGuire Sisters
6 DANCE WITH ME, HENRY   Georgia Gibbs
7 HOW IMPORTANT CAN IT BE   Joni James
   Note: * Cover versions by Fess Parker, Tennessee Ernie
   Ford, Burl Ives, Mac Wiseman.

April 30, 1955
1 THE BALLAD OF DAVY CROCKETT   Bill Hayes *
2 CHERRY PINK AND APPLE BLOSSOM WHITE   Perez
   Prado

3 MELODY OF LOVE   Billy Vaughn Orch.
4 TWEEDLE DEE   Georgia Gibbs
5 UNCHAINED MELODY   Les Baxter Orch. **
6 HOW IMPORTANT CAN IT BE   Joni James
7 DANCE WITH ME, HENRY   Georgia Gibbs
   Note: * Cover versions by Fess Parker, Tennessee Ernie
       Ford, Burl Ives, Mac Wiseman,
          ** Another version by: Al Hibbler.

May 7, 1955
1 THE BALLAD OF DAVY CROCKETT   Bill Hayes *
2 UNCHAINED MELODY   Les Baxter Orch. **
3 CHERRY PINK AND APPLE BLOSSOM WHITE   Perez
   Prado
4 DANCE WITH ME, HENRY   Georgia Gibbs
5 TWEEDLE DEE   Georgia Gibbs
6 MELODY OF LOVE   Billy Vaughn Orch.
7 HOW IMPORTANT CAN IT BE   Joni James
   Note: * Cover versions by Fess Parker, Tennessee Ernie
       Ford, Burl Ives, Mac Wiseman,
          ** Another version by: Al Hibbler.

May 14, 1955
1 THE BALLAD OF DAVY CROCKETT   Bill Hayes *
2 CHERRY PINK AND APPLE BLOSSOM WHITE   Perez
   Prado
3 UNCHAINED MELODY   Les Baxter Orch. **
4 TWEEDLE DEE   Georgia Gibbs
5 MELODY OF LOVE   Billy Vaughn Orch.
6 DANCE WITH ME, HENRY   Georgia Gibbs
7 WHATEVER LOLA WANTS   Gwen Verdon
   Note: * Cover versions by Fess Parker, Tennessee Ernie
       Ford, Burl Ives, Mac Wiseman,
          ** Another version by: Al Hibbler.

May 21, 1955
1 THE BALLAD OF DAVY CROCKETT   Bill Hayes *
2 UNCHAINED MELODY   Les Baxter Orch. **
3 CHERRY PINK AND APPLE BLOSSOM WHITE   Perez
   Prado
4 DANCE WITH ME, HENRY   Georgia Gibbs
5 MELODY OF LOVE   Billy Vaughn Orch.
6 TWEEDLE DEE   Georgia Gibbs
7 WHATEVER LOLA WANTS   Gwen Verdon
   Note: * Cover versions by Fess Parker, Tennessee Ernie
       Ford, Burl Ives, Mac Wiseman,
          ** Another version by: Al Hibbler.

May 28, 1955
1 THE BALLAD OF DAVY CROCKETT   Bill Hayes *
2 CHERRY PINK AND APPLE BLOSSOM WHITE   Perez
   Prado
3 UNCHAINED MELODY   Les Baxter Orch. **
4 DANCE WITH ME, HENRY   Georgia Gibbs
5 WHATEVER LOLA WANTS   Gwen Verdon
6 TWEEDLE DEE   Georgia Gibbs
7 MELODY OF LOVE   Billy Vaughn Orch.
   Note: * Cover versions by Fess Parker, Tennessee Ernie
       Ford, Burl Ives, Mac Wiseman,
          ** Another version by: Al Hibbler.

June 4, 1955
1 UNCHAINED MELODY   Les Baxter Orch. *
2 THE BALLAD OF DAVY CROCKETT   Bill Hayes
3 CHERRY PINK AND APPLE BLOSSOM WHITE   Perez
   Prado
4 WHATEVER LOLA WANTS   Gwen Verdon

5 DANCE WITH ME, HENRY   Georgia Gibbs
6 HEART   Eddie Fisher
7 HONEY BABE   Art Mooney Orch.
   Note: * Another version by: Al Hibbler.

June 11, 1955
1 UNCHAINED MELODY   Les Baxter Orch. *
2 CHERRY PINK AND APPLE BLOSSOM WHITE   Perez
   Prado
3 THE BALLAD OF DAVY CROCKETT   Bill Hayes
4 DANCE WITH ME, HENRY   Georgia Gibbs
5 WHATEVER LOLA WANTS   Gwen Verdon
6 HEART   Eddie Fisher
7 LEARNIN' THE BLUES   Frank Sinatra
   Note: * Another version by: Al Hibbler.

June 18, 1955
1 UNCHAINED MELODY   Les Baxter Orch. *
2 CHERRY PINK AND APPLE BLOSSOM WHITE   Perez
   Prado
3 THE BALLAD OF DAVY CROCKETT   Bill Hayes
4 SOMETHING'S GOTTA GIVE   McGuire Sisters
5 WHATEVER LOLA WANTS   Gwen Verdon
6 HONEY BABE   Art Mooney Orch.
7 HEART   Eddie Fisher
   Note: * Another version by: Al Hibbler.

June 25, 1955
1 CHERRY PINK AND APPLE BLOSSOM WHITE   Perez
   Prado
2 UNCHAINED MELODY   Les Baxter Orch. *
3 HEART   Eddie Fisher
4 LEARNIN' THE BLUES   Frank Sinatra
5 SOMETHING'S GOTTA GIVE   McGuire Sisters
6 WHATEVER LOLA WANTS   Gwen Verdon
7 DANCE WITH ME, HENRY   Georgia Gibbs
   Note: * Another version by: Al Hibbler.

July 2, 1955
1 UNCHAINED MELODY   Les Baxter Orch. *
2 CHERRY PINK AND APPLE BLOSSOM WHITE   Perez
   Prado
3 THE BALLAD OF DAVY CROCKETT   Bill Hayes
4 LEARNIN' THE BLUES   Frank Sinatra
5 SOMETHING'S GOTTA GIVE   McGuire Sisters
6 HEART   Eddie Fisher
7 HONEY BABE   Art Mooney Orch.
   Note: * Another version by: Al Hibbler.

July 9, 1955
1 UNCHAINED MELODY   Les Baxter Orch. *
2 CHERRY PINK AND APPLE BLOSSOM WHITE   Perez
   Prado
3 LEARNIN' THE BLUES   Frank Sinatra
4 SOMETHING'S GOTTA GIVE   McGuire Sisters
5 ROCK AROUND THE CLOCK   Bill Haley & Comets **
6 HEART   Eddie Fisher
7 A BLOSSOM FELL   Nat King Cole
   Note: * Another version by: Al Hibbler.
       ** Generally regarded as the catalyst that launched a
       new age in music: Rock & Roll.

July 16, 1955
1 UNCHAINED MELODY   Les Baxter Orch. *
2 CHERRY PINK AND APPLE BLOSSOM WHITE   Perez
   Prado
3 SOMETHING'S GOTTA GIVE   McGuire Sisters

4   LEARNIN' THE BLUES   Frank Sinatra
5   A BLOSSOM FELL   Nat King Cole
6   ROCK AROUND THE CLOCK   Bill Haley & Comets **
7   HONEY BABE   Art Mooney Orch.
   Note: * Another version by: Al Hibbler.
        ** Generally regarded as the catalyst that launched a
        new age in music: Rock & Roll.

July 23, 1955
1   SOMETHING'S GOTTA GIVE   McGuire Sisters
2   UNCHAINED MELODY   Les Baxter Orch. *
3   CHERRY PINK AND APPLE BLOSSOM WHITE   Perez
       Prado
4   ROCK AROUND THE CLOCK   Bill Haley & Comets **
5   LEARNIN' THE BLUES   Frank Sinatra
6   A BLOSSOM FELL   Nat King Cole
7   HEART   Eddie Fisher
   Note: * Another version by: Al Hibbler.
        ** Generally regarded as the catalyst that launched a
        new age in music: Rock & Roll.

July 30, 1955
1   UNCHAINED MELODY   Les Baxter Orch. *
2   ROCK AROUND THE CLOCK   Bill Haley & Comets **
3   LEARNIN' THE BLUES   Frank Sinatra
4   SOMETHING'S GOTTA GIVE   McGuire Sisters
5   HARD TO GET   Gisele MacKenzie
6   CHERRY PINK AND APPLE BLOSSOM WHITE   Perez
       Prado
7   SWEET AND GENTLE   Alan Dale
   Note: * Another version by: Al Hibbler.
        ** Generally regarded as the catalyst that launched a
        new age in music: Rock & Roll.

August 6, 1955
1   LEARNIN' THE BLUES   Frank Sinatra
2   ROCK AROUND THE CLOCK   Bill Haley & Comets *
3   HARD TO GET   Gisele MacKenzie
4   UNCHAINED MELODY   Les Baxter Orch. **
5   SWEET AND GENTLE   Alan Dale
6   SOMETHING'S GOTTA GIVE   McGuire Sisters
7   CHERRY PINK AND APPLE BLOSSOM WHITE   Perez
       Prado
   Note: * Generally regarded as the catalyst that launched a
        new age in music: Rock & Roll.
        ** Another version by: Al Hibbler.

August 13, 1955
1   ROCK AROUND THE CLOCK   Bill Haley & Comets *
2   LEARNIN' THE BLUES   Frank Sinatra
3   UNCHAINED MELODY   Les Baxter Orch. **
4   HARD TO GET   Gisele MacKenzie
5   SOMETHING'S GOTTA GIVE   McGuire Sisters
6   YELLOW ROSE OF TEXAS   Mitch Miller
7   SWEET AND GENTLE   Alan Dale
   Note: * Generally regarded as the catalyst that launched a
        new age in music: Rock & Roll.
        ** Another version by: Al Hibbler.

August 20, 1955
1   ROCK AROUND THE CLOCK   Bill Haley & Comets *
2   LEARNIN' THE BLUES   Frank Sinatra
3   YELLOW ROSE OF TEXAS   Mitch Miller
4   HARD TO GET   Gisele MacKenzie
5   SOMETHING'S GOTTA GIVE   McGuire Sisters
6   UNCHAINED MELODY   Les Baxter Orch. **
7   A BLOSSOM FELL   Nat King Cole

   Note: * Generally regarded as the catalyst that launched a
        new age in music: Rock & Roll.
        ** Another version by: Al Hibbler.

August 27, 1955
1   YELLOW ROSE OF TEXAS   Mitch Miller
2   ROCK AROUND THE CLOCK   Bill Haley & Comets *
3   AIN'T THAT A SHAME   Fats Domino
4   A BLOSSOM FELL   Nat King Cole
5   HARD TO GET   Gisele MacKenzie
6   HUMMINGBIRD   Les Paul & Mary Ford
7   WAKE THE TOWN AND TELL THE PEOPLE   Les Baxter
       Orch.
   Note: * Generally regarded as the catalyst that launched a
        new age in music: Rock & Roll.

September 3, 1955
1   YELLOW ROSE OF TEXAS   Mitch Miller
2   ROCK AROUND THE CLOCK   Bill Haley & Comets *
3   AIN'T THAT A SHAME   Fats Domino
4   HARD TO GET   Gisele MacKenzie
5   LOVE IS A MANY-SPLENDORED THING   Four Aces
6   LEARNIN' THE BLUES   Frank Sinatra
7   SEVENTEEN   Fontane Sisters
   Note: * Generally regarded as the catalyst that launched a
        new age in music: Rock & Roll.

September 10, 1955
1   YELLOW ROSE OF TEXAS   Mitch Miller
2   HARD TO GET   Gisele MacKenzie
3   SEVENTEEN   Fontane Sisters
4   AIN'T THAT A SHAME   Fats Domino
5   LEARNIN' THE BLUES   Frank Sinatra
6   LOVE IS A MANY-SPLENDORED THING   Four Aces
7   ROCK AROUND THE CLOCK   Bill Haley & Comets *
   Note: * Generally regarded as the catalyst that launched a
        new age in music: Rock & Roll.

September 17, 1955
1   YELLOW ROSE OF TEXAS   Mitch Miller
2   LOVE IS A MANY-SPLENDORED THING   Four Aces
3   WAKE THE TOWN AND TELL THE PEOPLE   Les Baxter
       Orch.
4   AIN'T THAT A SHAME   Fats Domino
5   AUTUMN LEAVES   Roger Williams Orch.
6   SEVENTEEN   Fontane Sisters
7   ROCK AROUND THE CLOCK   Bill Haley & Comets *
   Note: * Generally regarded as the catalyst that launched a
        new age in music: Rock & Roll.

September 24, 1955
1   YELLOW ROSE OF TEXAS   Mitch Miller
2   AIN'T THAT A SHAME   Fats Domino
3   LOVE IS A MANY-SPLENDORED THING   Four Aces
4   AUTUMN LEAVES   Roger Williams Orch.
5   WAKE THE TOWN AND TELL THE PEOPLE   Les Baxter
       Orch.
6   HARD TO GET   Gisele MacKenzie
7   SEVENTEEN   Fontane Sisters

October 1, 1955
1   YELLOW ROSE OF TEXAS   Mitch Miller
2   AUTUMN LEAVES   Roger Williams Orch.
3   LOVE IS A MANY-SPLENDORED THING   Four Aces
4   WAKE THE TOWN AND TELL THE PEOPLE   Les Baxter
       Orch.

Bill Haley & The Comets

"Rock Around The Clock" hits #1 (Aug. 13)—the song that started the whole world rockin'.

5 SEVENTEEN   Fontane Sisters
6 THE LONGEST WALK   Jaye P. Morgan
7 ROCK AROUND THE CLOCK   Bill Haley & Comets *
  Note: * Generally regarded as the catalyst that launched a
    new age in music: Rock & Roll.

October 8, 1955
1 YELLOW ROSE OF TEXAS   Mitch Miller
2 LOVE IS A MANY-SPLENDORED THING   Four Aces
3 AUTUMN LEAVES   Roger Williams Orch.
4 SEVENTEEN   Fontane Sisters
5 WAKE THE TOWN AND TELL THE PEOPLE   Les Baxter
    Orch.
6 THE BIBLE TELLS ME SO   Don Cornell
7 AIN'T THAT A SHAME   Fats Domino

October 15, 1955
1 YELLOW ROSE OF TEXAS   Mitch Miller
2 LOVE IS A MANY-SPLENDORED THING   Four Aces
3 AUTUMN LEAVES   Roger Williams Orch.
4 THE LONGEST WALK   Jaye P. Morgan
5 TINA MARIE   Perry Como
6 WAKE THE TOWN AND TELL THE PEOPLE   Les Baxter
    Orch.
7 SEVENTEEN   Fontane Sisters

October 22, 1955
1 YELLOW ROSE OF TEXAS   Mitch Miller
2 LOVE IS A MANY-SPLENDORED THING   Four Aces
3 AUTUMN LEAVES   Roger Williams Orch.
4 WAKE THE TOWN AND TELL THE PEOPLE   Les Baxter
    Orch.
5 THE BIBLE TELLS ME SO   Don Cornell
6 THE LONGEST WALK   Jaye P. Morgan
7 SEVENTEEN   Fontane Sisters

October 29, 1955
1 AUTUMN LEAVES   Roger Williams Orch.
2 LOVE IS A MANY-SPLENDORED THING   Four Aces
3 YELLOW ROSE OF TEXAS   Mitch Miller
4 SUDDENLY, THERE'S A VALLEY   Gogi Grant
5 SEVENTEEN   Fontane Sisters
6 THE BIBLE TELLS ME SO   Don Cornell
7 MOMENTS TO REMEMBER   Four Lads

November 5, 1955
1 LOVE IS A MANY-SPLENDORED THING   Four Aces
2 AUTUMN LEAVES   Roger Williams Orch.
3 YELLOW ROSE OF TEXAS   Mitch Miller
4 MOMENTS TO REMEMBER   Four Lads
5 SUDDENLY, THERE'S A VALLEY   Gogi Grant
6 SEVENTEEN   Fontane Sisters
7 HE   McGuire Sisters

November 12, 1955
1 AUTUMN LEAVES   Roger Williams Orch.
2 LOVE IS A MANY-SPLENDORED THING   Four Aces
3 YELLOW ROSE OF TEXAS   Mitch Miller
4 SUDDENLY, THERE'S A VALLEY   Gogi Grant
5 MOMENTS TO REMEMBER   Four Lads
6 LOVE AND MARRIAGE   Frank Sinatra *
7 THE SHIFTING, WHISPERING SANDS   Billy Vaughn Orch.
  Note: * Regained popularity in the late eighties as the theme
    for the Fox Network comedy "Married...With Children."

Mitch Miller
Bandleader Mitch Miller's biggest hit, ``Yellow Rose Of Texas,''
was adapted from a Civil War-era campfire song.

November 19, 1955
1 LOVE IS A MANY-SPLENDORED THING   Four Aces
2 AUTUMN LEAVES   Roger Williams Orch.
3 HE   McGuire Sisters
4 SUDDENLY, THERE'S A VALLEY   Gogi Grant
5 MOMENTS TO REMEMBER   Four Lads
6 SIXTEEN TONS   Tennessee Ernie Ford
7 LOVE AND MARRIAGE   Frank Sinatra *
  Note: * Regained popularity in the late eighties as the theme
    for the Fox Network comedy "Married...With Children."

November 26, 1955
1 AUTUMN LEAVES   Roger Williams Orch.
2 LOVE IS A MANY-SPLENDORED THING   Four Aces
3 LOVE AND MARRIAGE   Frank Sinatra *
4 SIXTEEN TONS   Tennessee Ernie Ford
5 MOMENTS TO REMEMBER   Four Lads
6 SUDDENLY, THERE'S A VALLEY   Gogi Grant
7 HE   McGuire Sisters
  Note: * Regained popularity in the late eighties as the theme
    for the Fox Network comedy "Married...With Children."

December 3, 1955
1 SIXTEEN TONS   Tennessee Ernie Ford
2 AUTUMN LEAVES   Roger Williams Orch.
3 LOVE IS A MANY-SPLENDORED THING   Four Aces
4 MOMENTS TO REMEMBER   Four Lads
5 HE   McGuire Sisters
6 LOVE AND MARRIAGE   Frank Sinatra *
7 ONLY YOU   The Platters

Note: * Regained popularity in the late eighties as the theme for the Fox Network comedy "Married...With Children."

December 10, 1955
1   SIXTEEN TONS   Tennessee Ernie Ford
2   AUTUMN LEAVES   Roger Williams Orch.
3   LOVE IS A MANY-SPLENDORED THING   Four Aces
4   LOVE AND MARRIAGE   Frank Sinatra *
5   I HEAR YOU KNOCKING   Gale Storm
6   HE   McGuire Sisters
7   MOMENTS TO REMEMBER   Four Lads
Note: * Regained popularity in the late eighties as the theme for the Fox Network comedy "Married...With Children."

December 17, 1955
1   SIXTEEN TONS   Tennessee Ernie Ford
2   AUTUMN LEAVES   Roger Williams Orch.
3   LOVE AND MARRIAGE   Frank Sinatra *
4   MOMENTS TO REMEMBER   Four Lads
5   LOVE IS A MANY-SPLENDORED THING   Four Aces
6   HE   McGuire Sisters
7   ONLY YOU   The Platters
Note: * Regained popularity in the late eighties as the theme for the Fox Network comedy "Married...With Children."

December 24, 1955
1   SIXTEEN TONS   Tennessee Ernie Ford
2   AUTUMN LEAVES   Roger Williams Orch.
3   MEMORIES ARE MADE OF THIS   Dean Martin

Tennessee Ernie Ford
While ``Sixteen Tons'' was Ernie's biggest hit, he is best known for his religious albums.

4   LOVE AND MARRIAGE   Frank Sinatra *
5   LOVE IS A MANY-SPLENDORED THING   Four Aces
6   HE   McGuire Sisters
7   MOMENTS TO REMEMBER   Four Lads
Note: * Regained popularity in the late eighties as the theme for the Fox Network comedy "Married...With Children."

December 31, 1955
1   SIXTEEN TONS   Tennessee Ernie Ford
2   MEMORIES ARE MADE OF THIS   Dean Martin
3   AUTUMN LEAVES   Roger Williams Orch.
4   HE   McGuire Sisters
5   MOMENTS TO REMEMBER   Four Lads
6   WHITE CHRISTMAS   Bing Crosby
7   LOVE AND MARRIAGE   Frank Sinatra *
Note: * Regained popularity in the late eighties as the theme for the Fox Network comedy "Married...With Children."

January 7, 1956
1   SIXTEEN TONS   Tennessee Ernie Ford
2   MEMORIES ARE MADE OF THIS   Dean Martin
3   LOVE AND MARRIAGE   Frank Sinatra *
4   AUTUMN LEAVES   Roger Williams Orch.
5   MOMENTS TO REMEMBER   Four Lads
6   HE   McGuire Sisters
7   IT'S ALMOST TOMORROW   Dream Weavers **
Note: * Regained popularity in the late eighties as the theme for the Fox Network comedy "Married...With Children."
   ** Another version by "Your Hit Parade" star, Snooky Lanson.

January 14, 1956
1   SIXTEEN TONS   Tennessee Ernie Ford
2   MEMORIES ARE MADE OF THIS   Dean Martin
3   MOMENTS TO REMEMBER   Four Lads
4   LOVE AND MARRIAGE   Frank Sinatra *
5   A WOMAN IN LOVE   Frankie Laine
6   IT'S ALMOST TOMORROW   Dream Weavers **
7   AUTUMN LEAVES   Roger Williams Orch.
Note: * Regained popularity in the late eighties as the theme for the Fox Network comedy "Married...With Children."
   ** Another version by "Your Hit Parade" star, Snooky Lanson.

January 21, 1956
1   MEMORIES ARE MADE OF THIS   Dean Martin
2   SIXTEEN TONS   Tennessee Ernie Ford
3   HE   McGuire Sisters
4   AUTUMN LEAVES   Roger Williams Orch.
5   LOVE AND MARRIAGE   Frank Sinatra *
6   LISBON ANTIGUA   Nelson Riddle Orch.
7   MOMENTS TO REMEMBER   Four Lads
Note: * Regained popularity in the late eighties as the theme for the Fox Network comedy "Married...With Children."

January 28, 1955
1   MEMORIES ARE MADE OF THIS   Dean Martin
2   SIXTEEN TONS   Tennessee Ernie Ford
3   IT'S ALMOST TOMORROW   Dream Weavers *
4   ROCK AND ROLL WALTZ   Kay Starr
5   THE GREAT PRETENDER   The Platters
6   LISBON ANTIGUA   Nelson Riddle Orch.
7   AUTUMN LEAVES   Roger Williams Orch.
Note: * Another version by "Your Hit Parade" star, Snooky Lanson.

February 4, 1956
1   MEMORIES ARE MADE OF THIS   Dean Martin
2   SIXTEEN TONS   Tennessee Ernie Ford
3   LISBON ANTIGUA   Nelson Riddle Orch.
4   THE ROCK AND ROLL WALTZ   Kay Starr
5   THE GREAT PRETENDER   The Platters
6   LOVE AND MARRIAGE   Frank Sinatra *
7   BAND OF GOLD   Don Cherry
    Note: * Regained popularity in the late eighties as the theme
       for the Fox Network comedy "Married...With Children."

February 11, 1956
1   MEMORIES ARE MADE OF THIS   Dean Martin
2   ROCK AND ROLL WALTZ   Kay Starr
3   SIXTEEN TONS   Tennessee Ernie Ford
4   LISBON ANTIGUA   Nelson Riddle Orch.
5   THE GREAT PRETENDER   The Platters
6   BAND OF GOLD   Don Cherry
7   HE   McGuire Sisters

February 18, 1956
1   THE ROCK AND ROLL WALTZ   Kay Starr
2   LISBON ANTIGUA   Nelson Riddle Orch.
3   THE GREAT PRETENDER   The Platters
4   MEMORIES ARE MADE OF THIS   Dean Martin
5   SIXTEEN TONS   Tennessee Ernie Ford
6   IT'S ALMOST TOMORROW   Dream Weavers
7   DUNGAREE DOLL   Eddie Fisher

February 25, 1956
1   LISBON ANTIGUA   Nelson Riddle Orch.
2   THE ROCK AND ROLL WALTZ   Kay Starr
3   MEMORIES ARE MADE OF THIS   Dean Martin
4   THE GREAT PRETENDER   The Platters
5   BAND OF GOLD   Don Cherry
6   MORITAT   Dick Hyman *
7   SIXTEEN TONS   Tennessee Ernie Ford
    Note: * Also known as "Mack The Knife."

March 3, 1956
1   THE ROCK AND ROLL WALTZ   Kay Starr
2   LISBON ANTIGUA   Nelson Riddle Orch.
3   THE GREAT PRETENDER   The Platters
4   NO, NOT MUCH   Four Lads
5   MEMORIES ARE MADE OF THIS   Dean Martin
6   MORITAT   Dick Hyman *
7   BAND OF GOLD   Don Cherry
    Note: * Also known as "Mack The Knife."

March 10, 1956
1   LISBON ANTIGUA   Nelson Riddle Orch.
2   ROCK AND ROLL WALTZ   Kay Starr
3   NO, NOT MUCH   Four Lads
4   POOR PEOPLE OF PARIS   Les Baxter Orch.
5   MORITAT   Dick Hyman *
6   MEMORIES ARE MADE OF THIS   Dean Martin
7   THE GREAT PRETENDER   The Platters
    Note: * Also known as "Mack The Knife."

March 17, 1956
1   LISBON ANTIGUA   Nelson Riddle Orch.
2   THE ROCK AND ROLL WALTZ   Kay Starr
3   NO, NOT MUCH   Four Lads
4   THE GREAT PRETENDER   The Platters
5   POOR PEOPLE OF PARIS   Les Baxter Orch.

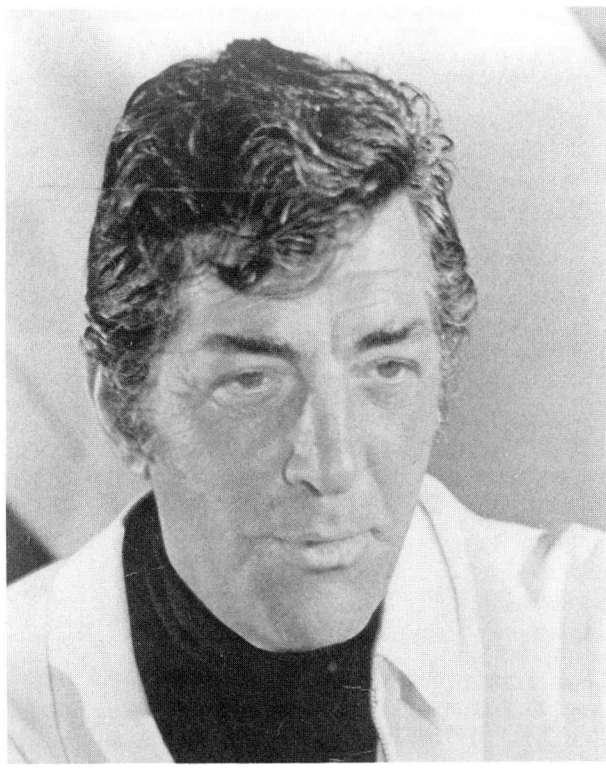

Dean Martin
Dino's first #1 hit is ``Memories Are Made Of This'' (Jan. 21).

Kay Starr
Kay's ``Rock And Roll Waltz'' peaks at #1 (Feb. 18).

6 MORITAT   Dick Hyman *
7 BAND OF GOLD   Don Cherry
   *Note: * Also known as "Mack The Knife."*

March 24, 1956
1 THE ROCK AND ROLL WALTZ   Kay Starr
2 POOR PEOPLE OF PARIS   Les Baxter Orch.
3 LISBON ANTIGUA   Nelson Riddle Orch.
4 MORITAT   Dick Hyman *
5 NO, NOT MUCH   Four Lads
6 THE GREAT PRETENDER   The Platters
7 MEMORIES ARE MADE OF THIS   Dean Martin
   *Note: * Also known as "Mack The Knife."*

March 31, 1956
1 LISBON ANTIGUA   Nelson Riddle Orch.
2 THE ROCK AND ROLL WALTZ   Kay Starr
3 NO, NOT MUCH   Four Lads
4 POOR PEOPLE OF PARIS   Les Baxter Orch.
5 MORITAT   Dick Hyman *
6 HOT DIGGITY   Perry Como
7 THE GREAT PRETENDER   The Platters
   *Note: * Also known as "Mack The Knife."*

April 7, 1956
1 POOR PEOPLE OF PARIS   Les Baxter Orch.
2 NO, NOT MUCH   Four Lads
3 EASTER PARADE   Guy Lombardo
4 LISBON ANTIGUA   Nelson Riddle Orch.
5 MORITAT   Dick Hyman *
6 THE ROCK AND ROLL WALTZ   Kay Starr
7 THE GREAT PRETENDER   The Platters
   *Note: * Also known as "Mack The Knife."*

April 14, 1956
1 POOR PEOPLE OF PARIS   Les Baxter Orch.
2 LISBON ANTIGUA   Nelson Riddle Orch.
3 MORITAT   Dick Hyman *
4 HOT DIGGITY   Perry Como
5 NO, NOT MUCH   Four Lads
6 THE ROCK AND ROLL WALTZ   Kay Starr
7 BLUE SUEDE SHOES   Carl Perkins
   *Note: * Also known as "Mack The Knife."*

April 21, 1956
1 POOR PEOPLE OF PARIS   Les Baxter Orch.
2 LISBON ANTIGUA   Nelson Riddle Orch.
3 NO, NOT MUCH   Four Lads
4 HOT DIGGITY   Perry Como
5 WHY DO FOOLS FALL IN LOVE   The Teenagers (Frankie Lymon)
6 THE ROCK AND ROLL WALTZ   Kay Starr
7 BLUE SUEDE SHOES   Carl Perkins

April 28, 1956
1 POOR PEOPLE OF PARIS   Les Baxter Orch.
2 HOT DIGGITY   Perry Como
3 BLUE SUEDE SHOES   Carl Perkins
4 MR. WONDERFUL   Olga James
5 HEARTBREAK HOTEL   Elvis Presley
6 LISBON ANTIGUA   Nelson Riddle Orch.
7 THE ROCK AND ROLL WALTZ   Kay Starr

May 5, 1956
1 POOR PEOPLE OF PARIS   Les Baxter Orch.

2 BLUE SUEDE SHOES   Carl Perkins
3 HOT DIGGITY   Perry Como
4 MOONGLOW (THEME FROM "PICNIC")   Morris Stoloff Orch.
5 LISBON ANTIGUA   Nelson Riddle Orch.
6 HEARTBREAK HOTEL   Elvis Presley
7 MORITAT   Dick Hyman

May 12, 1956
1 POOR PEOPLE OF PARIS   Les Baxter Orch.
2 BLUE SUEDE SHOES   Carl Perkins
3 HOT DIGGITY   Perry Como
4 HEARTBREAK HOTEL   Elvis Presley
5 MOONGLOW (THEME FROM "PICNIC")   Morris Stoloff Orch.
6 PICNIC   McGuire Sisters
7 IVORY TOWER   Cathy Carr

May 19, 1956
1 HEARTBREAK HOTEL   Elvis Presley
2 MOONGLOW (THEME FROM "PICNIC")   Morris Stoloff Orch.
3 HOT DIGGITY   Perry Como
4 POOR PEOPLE OF PARIS   Les Baxter Orch.
5 BLUE SUEDE SHOES   Carl Perkins
6 PICNIC   McGuire Sisters
7 IVORY TOWER   Cathy Carr

May 26, 1956
1 HEARTBREAK HOTEL   Elvis Presley
2 MOONGLOW (THEME FROM "PICNIC")   Morris Stoloff Orch.
3 HOT DIGGITY   Perry Como
4 POOR PEOPLE OF PARIS   Les Baxter Orch.
5 IVORY TOWER   Cathy Carr
6 PICNIC   McGuire Sisters
7 BLUE SUEDE SHOES   Carl Perkins

June 2, 1956
1 MOONGLOW (THEME FROM "PICNIC")   Morris Stoloff Orch.
2 PICNIC   McGuire Sisters
3 HOT DIGGITY   Perry Como
4 STANDING ON THE CORNER   Four Lads
5 HEARTBREAK HOTEL   Elvis Presley
6 ON THE STREET WHERE YOU LIVE   Vic Damone
7 IVORY TOWER   Cathy Carr

June 9, 1956
1 PICNIC   McGuire Sisters
2 STANDING ON THE CORNER   Four Lads
3 MOONGLOW (THEME FROM "PICNIC")   Morris Stoloff Orch.
4 IVORY TOWER   Cathy Carr
5 WAYWARD WIND   Gogi Grant
6 HOT DIGGITY   Perry Como
7 HEARTBREAK HOTEL   Elvis Presley

June 16, 1956
1 MOONGLOW (THEME FROM "PICNIC")   Morris Stoloff Orch.
2 PICNIC   McGuire Sisters
3 THE WAYWARD WIND   Gogi Grant
4 STANDING ON THE CORNER   Four Lads
5 IVORY TOWER   Cathy Carr
6 ON THE STREET WHERE YOU LIVE   Vic Damone

.IN PERSON I
ELVIS PRESLEY
WITH HOST OF OTHER COUNTRY MUSIC FAVORITES

COUNTY HALL AUDITORIUM   CHARLESTON, S.C.
SUNDAY, MARCH 18, 1956
Ticket good 3:30 p.m. show only — Doors open 2:00 p.m.

SPECIAL RESERVED SECTION

Est. Price	$1.50
Fed. Tax	.15
State Tax	.15
TOTAL	$1.80

SHOW RAIN OR SHINE   NO REFUNDS

N° 123

ELVIS PRESLEY
Sensational new RCA-Victor
Star - In Person

My parents bought this $1.80 ticket to Elvis' March 18, 1956,
concert in Charleston, SC, but ended up not going . —**B.E.**

Elvis Presley
The greatest rock-and-roll singer of all time hits #1 with ``Heartbreak Hotel'' (May 19).
Elvis had over 150 hit recordings in his career, which ended with his untimely death on August 16, 1977.

7   HEARTBREAK HOTEL   Elvis Presley

June 23, 1956
1   PICNIC   McGuire Sisters
2   MOONGLOW (THEME FROM "PICNIC")   Morris Stoloff Orch.
3   THE WAYWARD WIND   Gogi Grant
4   STANDING ON THE CORNER   Four Lads
5   ON THE STREET WHERE YOU LIVE   Vic Damone
6   IVORY TOWER   Cathy Carr
7   I COULD HAVE DANCED ALL NIGHT   Sylvia Syms

June 30, 1956
1   MOONGLOW (THEME FROM "PICNIC")   Morris Stoloff Orch.
2   PICNIC   McGuire Sisters
3   THE WAYWARD WIND   Gogi Grant
4   ON THE STREET WHERE YOU LIVE   Vic Damone
5   STANDING ON THE CORNER   Four Lads
6   IVORY TOWER   Cathy Carr
7   I COULD HAVE DANCED ALL NIGHT   Sylvia Syms

July 7, 1956
1   PICNIC   McGuire Sisters
2   MOONGLOW (THEME FROM "PICNIC")   Morris Stoloff Orch.
3   STANDING ON THE CORNER   Four Lads
4   ON THE STREET WHERE YOU LIVE   Vic Damone
5   THE WAYWARD WIND   Gogi Grant
6   I ALMOST LOST MY MIND   Pat Boone
7   IVORY TOWER   Cathy Carr

July 14, 1956
1   THE WAYWARD WIND   Gogi Grant
2   PICNIC   McGuire Sisters
3   MOONGLOW (THEME FROM "PICNIC")   Morris Stoloff Orch.
4   ON THE STREET WHERE YOU LIVE   Vic Damone
5   STANDING ON THE CORNER   Four Lads
6   I COULD HAVE DANCED ALL NIGHT   Sylvia Syms
7   I ALMOST LOST MY MIND   Pat Boone

July 21, 1956
1   THE WAYWARD WIND   Gogi Grant
2   ON THE STREET WHERE YOU LIVE   Vic Damone
3   PICNIC   McGuire Sisters
4   MOONGLOW (THEME FROM "PICNIC")   Morris Stoloff Orch.
5   ALLEGHENY MOON   Patti Page
6   STANDING ON THE CORNER   Four Lads
7   I COULD HAVE DANCED ALL NIGHT   Sylvia Syms

July 28, 1956
1   THE WAYWARD WIND   Gogi Grant
2   ON THE STREET WHERE YOU LIVE   Vic Damone
3   ALLEGHENY MOON   Patti Page
4   MOONGLOW (THEME FROM "PICNIC")   Morris Stoloff Orch.
5   I ALMOST LOST MY MIND   Pat Boone
6   PICNIC   McGuire Sisters
7   STANDING ON THE CORNER   Four Lads

August 4, 1956
1   ON THE STREET WHERE YOU LIVE   Vic Damone
2   THE WAYWARD WIND   Gogi Grant

3   MOONGLOW (THEME FROM "PICNIC")   Morris Stoloff Orch.
4   WHATEVER WILL BE, WILL BE   Doris Day
5   ALLEGHENY MOON   Patti Page
6   MY PRAYER   The Platters
7   PICNIC   McGuire Sisters

August 11, 1956
1   WHATEVER WILL BE, WILL BE   Doris Day
2   ALLEGHENY MOON   Patti Page
3   THE WAYWARD WIND   Gogi Grant
4   ON THE STREET WHERE YOU LIVE   Vic Damone
5   MY PRAYER   The Platters
6   I ALMOST LOST MY MIND   Pat Boone
7   CANADIAN SUNSET   Hugo Winderhalter Orch.

August 18, 1956
1   MY PRAYER   The Platters
2   WHATEVER WILL BE, WILL BE   Doris Day
3   THE WAYWARD WIND   Gogi Grant
4   ALLEGHENY MOON   Patti Page
5   ON THE STREET WHERE YOU LIVE   Vic Damone
6   CANADIAN SUNSET   Hugo Winderhalter Orch.
7   I ALMOST LOST MY MIND   Pat Boone

August 25, 1956
1   WHATEVER WILL BE, WILL BE   Doris Day
2   ALLEGHENY MOON   Patti Page
3   MY PRAYER   The Platters
4   THE WAYWARD WIND   Gogi Grant
5   I ALMOST LOST MY MIND   Pat Boone
6   CANADIAN SUNSET   Hugo Winderhalter Orch.
7   ON THE STREET WHERE YOU LIVE   Vic Damone

September 1, 1956
1   CANADIAN SUNSET   Hugo Winderhalter Orch.
2   ALLEGHENY MOON   Patti Page
3   MY PRAYER   The Platters
4   WHATEVER WILL BE, WILL BE   Doris Day
5   ON THE STREET WHERE YOU LIVE   Vic Damone
6   HOUND DOG   Elvis Presley *
7   THE WAYWARD WIND   Gogi Grant
   Note: * Both "Hound Dog" and "Don't Be Cruel'"peaked at #1 on other national charts for 11 weeks.

September 8, 1956
1   WHATEVER WILL BE, WILL BE   Doris Day
2   MY PRAYER   The Platters
3   CANADIAN SUNSET   Hugo Winderhalter Orch.
4   ALLEGHENY MOON   Patti Page
5   HOUND DOG   Elvis Presley *
6   ON THE STREET WHERE YOU LIVE   Vic Damone
7   DON'T BE CRUEL   Elvis Presley
   Note: * Both "Hound Dog" and "Don't Be Cruel" peaked at #1 on other national charts for 11 weeks.

September 15, 1956
1   CANADIAN SUNSET   Hugo Winderhalter Orch.
2   MY PRAYER   The Platters
3   WHATEVER WILL BE, WILL BE   Doris Day
4   HOUND DOG   Elvis Presley *
5   DON'T BE CRUEL   Elvis Presley
6   ALLEGHENY MOON   Patti Page
7   ON THE STREET WHERE YOU LIVE   Vic Damone
   Note: * Both "Hound Dog" and "Don't Be Cruel" peaked at #1 on other national charts for 11 weeks.

The rare LP cover of ``The Wayward Wind.''

Gogi Grant

``The Wayward Wind'' not only hit #1 in 1956 (July 14), but peaked at #50 in the same month four years later.

September 22, 1956
1 WHATEVER WILL BE, WILL BE   Doris Day
2 CANADIAN SUNSET   Hugo Winderhalter Orch.
3 MY PRAYER   The Platters
4 ALLEGHENY MOON   Patti Page
5 TONIGHT YOU BELONG TO ME   Patience & Prudence
6 DON'T BE CRUEL   Elvis Presley
7 HOUND DOG   Elvis Presley *
Note: * Both "Hound Dog" and "Don't Be Cruel" peaked at #1 on other national charts for 11 weeks.

September 29, 1956
1 CANADIAN SUNSET   Hugo Winderhalter Orch.
2 WHATEVER WILL BE, WILL BE   Doris Day
3 ALLEGHENY MOON   Patti Page
4 MY PRAYER   The Platters
5 HOUND DOG   Elvis Presley *
6 DON'T BE CRUEL   Elvis Presley
7 TONIGHT YOU BELONG TO ME   Patience & Prudence
Note: * Both "Hound Dog" and "Don't Be Cruel" peaked at #1 on other national charts for 11 weeks.

October 6, 1956
1 CANADIAN SUNSET   Hugo Winderhalter Orch.
2 DON'T BE CRUEL   Elvis Presley
3 WHATEVER WILL BE, WILL BE   Doris Day
4 ALLEGHENY MOON   Patti Page
5 MY PRAYER   The Platters
6 HOUND DOG   Elvis Presley *
7 TONIGHT YOU BELONG TO ME   Patience & Prudence
Note: * Both "Hound Dog" and "Don't Be Cruel" peaked at #1 on other national charts for 11 weeks.

October 13, 1956
1 CANADIAN SUNSET   Hugo Winderhalter Orch.
2 DON'T BE CRUEL   Elvis Presley
3 TONIGHT YOU BELONG TO ME   Patience & Prudence
4 ALLEGHENY MOON   Patti Page
5 WHATEVER WILL BE, WILL BE   Doris Day
6 JUST WALKIN' IN THE RAIN   Johnnie Ray
7 TRUE LOVE   Bing Crosby & Grace Kelly *
Note: * The same Grace Kelly who left her music and film career to become Princess Grace of Monaco.

October 20, 1956
1 CANADIAN SUNSET   Hugo Winderhalter Orch.
2 TONIGHT YOU BELONG TO ME   Patience & Prudence
3 MY PRAYER   The Platters
4 DON'T BE CRUEL   Elvis Presley
5 JUST WALKIN' IN THE RAIN   Johnnie Ray
6 ALLEGHENY MOON   Patti Page
7 WHATEVER WILL BE, WILL BE   Doris Day

October 27, 1956
1 CANADIAN SUNSET   Hugo Winderhalter Orch.
2 TONIGHT YOU BELONG TO ME   Patience & Prudence
3 TRUE LOVE   Bing Crosby & Grace Kelly *
4 DON'T BE CRUEL   Elvis Presley
5 LOVE ME TENDER   Elvis Presley
6 WHATEVER WILL BE, WILL BE   Doris Day
7 JUST WALKIN' IN THE RAIN   Johnnie Ray
Note: * The same Grace Kelly who left her music and film career to become Princess Grace of Monaco.

November 3, 1956
1 LOVE ME TENDER   Elvis Presley

2 CANADIAN SUNSET   Hugo Winderhalter Orch.
3 TRUE LOVE   Bing Crosby & Grace Kelly *
4 GREEN DOOR   Jim Lowe
5 FRIENDLY PERSUASION   Pat Boone
6 DON'T BE CRUEL   Elvis Presley
7 JUST WALKIN' IN THE RAIN   Johnnie Ray
Note: * The same Grace Kelly who left her music and film career to become Princess Grace of Monaco.

November 10, 1956
1 JUST WALKIN' IN THE RAIN   Johnnie Ray
2 CANADIAN SUNSET   Hugo Winderhalter Orch.
3 TRUE LOVE   Bing Crosby & Grace Kelly *
4 LOVE ME TENDER   Elvis Presley
5 FRIENDLY PERSUASION   Pat Boone
6 GREEN DOOR   Jim Lowe
7 BLUEBERRY HILL   Fats Domino
Note: * The same Grace Kelly who left her music and film career to become Princess Grace of Monaco.

November 17, 1956
1 LOVE ME TENDER   Elvis Presley
2 TRUE LOVE   Bing Crosby & Grace Kelly *
3 JUST WALKIN' IN THE RAIN   Johnnie Ray
4 CANADIAN SUNSET   Hugo Winderhalter Orch.
5 BLUEBERRY HILL   Fats Domino
6 GREEN DOOR   Jim Lowe
7 FRIENDLY PERSUASION   Pat Boone
Note: * The same Grace Kelly who left her music and film career to become Princess Grace of Monaco.

November 24, 1956
1 LOVE ME TENDER   Elvis Presley
2 TRUE LOVE   Bing Crosby & Grace Kelly *
3 SINGING THE BLUES   Guy Mitchell
4 BLUEBERRY HILL   Fats Domino
5 CINDY, OH CINDY   Eddie Fisher
6 GREEN DOOR   Jim Lowe
7 JUST WALKIN' IN THE RAIN   Johnnie Ray
Note: * The same Grace Kelly who left her music and film career to become Princess Grace of Monaco.

December 1, 1956
1 LOVE ME TENDER   Elvis Presley
2 TRUE LOVE   Bing Crosby & Grace Kelly *
3 GREEN DOOR   Jim Lowe
4 JUST WALKIN' IN THE RAIN   Johnnie Ray
5 SINGING THE BLUES   Guy Mitchell
6 FRIENDLY PERSUASION   Pat Boone
7 BLUEBERRY HILL   Fats Domino
Note: * The same Grace Kelly who left her music and film career to become Princess Grace of Monaco.

December 8, 1956
1 LOVE ME TENDER   Elvis Presley
2 SINGING THE BLUES   Guy Mitchell
3 GREEN DOOR   Jim Lowe
4 TRUE LOVE   Bing Crosby & Grace Kelly *
5 JUST WALKIN' IN THE RAIN   Johnnie Ray
6 CINDY, OH CINDY   Eddie Fisher
7 FRIENDLY PERSUASION   Pat Boone
Note: * The same Grace Kelly who left her music and film career to become Princess Grace of Monaco.

December 15, 1956
1 SINGING THE BLUES   Guy Mitchell

Fats Domino

``Blueberry Hill'' was first a hit for Glenn Miller, but The Fat Man's version is best remembered.
Fats never had a #1 hit—``Blueberry Hill'' only got to #4 on the Hit Parade, but fared two positions higher on the *Billboard* charts.

2 LOVE ME TENDER   Elvis Presley
3 TRUE LOVE   Bing Crosby & Grace Kelly *
4 JUST WALKIN' IN THE RAIN   Johnnie Ray
5 GREEN DOOR   Jim Lowe
6 BLUEBERRY HILL   Fats Domino
7 HEY, JEALOUS LOVER   Frank Sinatra
Note: * The same Grace Kelly who left her music and film career to become Princess Grace of Monaco.

December 22, 1956
1 SINGING THE BLUES   Guy Mitchell
2 LOVE ME TENDER   Elvis Presley
3 GREEN DOOR   Jim Lowe
4 TRUE LOVE   Bing Crosby & Grace Kelly *
5 BLUEBERRY HILL   Fats Domino
6 CINDY, OH CINDY   Eddie Fisher
7 JUST WALKIN' IN THE RAIN   Johnnie Ray
Note: * The same Grace Kelly who left her music and film career to become Princess Grace of Monaco.

December 29, 1956
1 SINGING THE BLUES   Guy Mitchell
2 LOVE ME TENDER   Elvis Presley
3 GREEN DOOR   Jim Lowe
4 BLUEBERRY HILL   Fats Domino
5 TRUE LOVE   Bing Crosby & Grace Kelly *
6 JUST WALKIN' IN THE RAIN   Johnnie Ray
7 CINDY, OH CINDY   Eddie Fisher
Note: * The same Grace Kelly who left her music and film career to become Princess Grace of Monaco.

January 5, 1957
1 SINGING THE BLUES   Guy Mitchell
2 LOVE ME TENDER   Elvis Presley
3 TRUE LOVE   Bing Crosby & Grace Kelly *
4 GREEN DOOR   Jim Lowe
5 JUST WALKIN' IN THE RAIN   Johnnie Ray
6 BLUEBERRY HILL   Fats Domino
7 CINDY, OH CINDY   Eddie Fisher
Note: * The same Grace Kelly who left her music and film career to become Princess Grace of Monaco.

January 12, 1957
1 SINGING THE BLUES   Guy Mitchell
2 LOVE ME TENDER   Elvis Presley
3 GREEN DOOR   Jim Lowe
4 TRUE LOVE   Bing Crosby & Grace Kelly *
5 JUST WALKIN' IN THE RAIN   Johnnie Ray
6 BLUEBERRY HILL   Fats Domino
7 HEY, JEALOUS LOVER   Frank Sinatra
Note: * The same Grace Kelly who left her music and film career to become Princess Grace of Monaco.

January 19, 1957
1 SINGING THE BLUES   Guy Mitchell
2 THE BANANA BOAT SONG   Harry Belafonte
3 LOVE ME TENDER   Elvis Presley
4 GREEN DOOR   Jim Lowe
5 BLUEBERRY HILL   Fats Domino
6 YOUNG LOVE   Sonny James *
7 TRUE LOVE   Bing Crosby & Grace Kelly **
Note: * Another version by: Tab Hunter.
     ** The same Grace Kelly who left her music and film career to become Princess Grace of Monaco.

January 26, 1957
1 SINGING THE BLUES   Guy Mitchell
2 THE BANANA BOAT SONG   Harry Belafonte
3 YOUNG LOVE   Sonny James *
4 DON'T FORBID ME   Pat Boone
5 TRUE LOVE   Bing Crosby & Grace Kelly **
6 JUST WALKIN' IN THE RAIN   Johnnie Ray
7 LOVE ME TENDER   Elvis Presley
Note: * Another version by: Tab Hunter.
     ** The same Grace Kelly who left her music and film career to become Princess Grace of Monaco.

February 2, 1957
1 THE BANANA BOAT SONG   Harry Belafonte
2 SINGING THE BLUES   Guy Mitchell
3 YOUNG LOVE   Sonny James *
4 TRUE LOVE   Bing Crosby & Grace Kelly **
5 DON'T FORBID ME   Pat Boone
6 BLUEBERRY HILL   Fats Domino
7 LOVE ME TENDER   Elvis Presley
Note: * Another version by: Tab Hunter.
     ** The same Grace Kelly who left her music and film career to become Princess Grace of Monaco.

February 9, 1957
1 YOUNG LOVE   Sonny James *
2 THE BANANA BOAT SONG   Harry Belafonte
3 SINGING THE BLUES   Guy Mitchell
4 DON'T FORBID ME   Pat Boone
5 MOONLIGHT GAMBLER   Frankie Laine
6 BLUEBERRY HILL   Fats Domino
7 TRUE LOVE   Bing Crosby & Grace Kelly **
Note: * Another version by: Tab Hunter.
     ** The same Grace Kelly who left her music and film career to become Princess Grace of Monaco.

February 16, 1957
1 YOUNG LOVE   Sonny James *
2 DON'T FORBID ME   Pat Boone
3 THE BANANA BOAT SONG   Harry Belafonte
4 SINGING THE BLUES   Guy Mitchell
5 MOONLIGHT GAMBLER   Frankie Laine
6 MARIANNE   The Hilltoppers
7 TOO MUCH   Elvis Presley
Note: * Another version by: Tab Hunter.

February 23, 1957
1 YOUNG LOVE   Sonny James *
2 DON'T FORBID ME   Pat Boone
3 THE BANANA BOAT SONG   Harry Belafonte
4 MARIANNE   The Hilltoppers
5 MOONLIGHT GAMBLER   Frankie Laine
6 TOO MUCH   Elvis Presley
7 SINGING THE BLUES   Guy Mitchell
Note: * Another version by: Tab Hunter.

March 2, 1957
1 YOUNG LOVE   Sonny James *
2 MARIANNE   The Hilltoppers
3 DON'T FORBID ME   Pat Boone
4 TOO MUCH   Elvis Presley
5 THE BANANA BOAT SONG   Harry Belafonte
6 SINGING THE BLUES   Guy Mitchell
7 DAY-O   Harry Belafonte
Note: * Another version by: Tab Hunter.

March 9, 1957
1 YOUNG LOVE   Sonny James *
2 MARIANNE   The Hilltoppers
3 DON'T FORBID ME   Pat Boone
4 THE BANANA BOAT SONG   Harry Belafonte
5 TOO MUCH   Elvis Presley
6 DAY-O   Harry Belafonte
7 BUTTERFLY   Andy Williams **
   Note: * Another version by: Tab Hunter.
          ** Another version by: Charlie Gracie.

March 16, 1957
1 MARIANNE   The Hilltoppers
2 YOUNG LOVE   Sonny James *
3 BUTTERFLY   Andy Williams **
4 DON'T FORBID ME   Pat Boone
5 THE BANANA BOAT SONG   Harry Belafonte
6 ROUND AND ROUND   Perry Como
7 TOO MUCH   Elvis Presley
   Note: * Another version by: Tab Hunter.
          ** Another version by: Charlie Gracie.

March 23, 1957
1 MARIANNE   The Hilltoppers
2 YOUNG LOVE   Sonny James *
3 BUTTERFLY   Andy Williams **
4 ROUND AND ROUND   Perry Como
5 PARTY DOLL   Buddy Knox
6 DON'T FORBID ME   Pat Boone
7 THE BANANA BOAT SONG   Harry Belafonte
   Note: * Another version by: Tab Hunter.
          ** Another version by: Charlie Gracie.

March 30, 1957
1 MARIANNE   The Hilltoppers
2 BUTTERFLY   Andy Williams *
3 YOUNG LOVE   Sonny James **
4 ROUND AND ROUND   Perry Como
5 PARTY DOLL   Buddy Knox
6 THE BANANA BOAT SONG   Harry Belafonte
7 TEENAGE CRUSH   Tommy Sands
   Note: * Another version by: Charlie Gracie.
          ** Another version by: Tab Hunter.

April 6, 1957
1 ROUND AND ROUND   Perry Como
2 BUTTERFLY   Andy Williams *
3 MARIANNE   The Hilltoppers
4 PARTY DOLL   Buddy Knox
5 YOUNG LOVE   Sonny James **
6 I'M WALKIN'   Fats Domino
7 LITTLE DARLIN'   The Diamonds
   Note: * Another version by: Charlie Gracie.
          ** Another version by: Tab Hunter.

April 13, 1957
1 ROUND AND ROUND   Perry Como
2 PARTY DOLL   Buddy Knox
3 MARIANNE   The Hilltoppers
4 BUTTERFLY   Andy Williams *
5 YOUNG LOVE   Sonny James **
6 ALL SHOOK UP   Elvis Presley
7 LITTLE DARLIN'   The Diamonds
   Note: * Another version by: Charlie Gracie.
          ** Another version by: Tab Hunter.

Charlie Gracie
Gracie's ``Butterfly'' was #2 Hit Parade (#1 *Billboard*).

Pat Boone
Country legend Red Foley's son-in-law scores his biggest
hit—``Love Letters In The Sand''—on June 8.

April 20, 1957
1 ROUND AND ROUND   Perry Como
2 BUTTERFLY   Andy Williams
3 ALL SHOOK UP   Elvis Presley
4 LITTLE DARLIN'   The Diamonds
5 PARTY DOLL   Buddy Knox
6 MARIANNE   The Hilltoppers
7 I'M WALKIN'   Fats Domino
   Note: * Another version by: Charlie Gracie.

April 27, 1957
1 ROUND AND ROUND   Perry Como
2 ALL SHOOK UP   Elvis Presley
3 EASTER PARADE   Guy Lombardo
4 BUTTERFLY   Andy Williams *
5 PARTY DOLL   Buddy Knox
6 LITTLE DARLIN'   The Diamonds
7 I'M WALKIN'   Fats Domino
   Note: * Another version by: Charlie Gracie.

May 4, 1957
1 ROUND AND ROUND   Perry Como
2 ALL SHOOK UP   Elvis Presley
3 LITTLE DARLIN'   The Diamonds
4 BUTTERFLY   Andy Williams *
5 PARTY DOLL   Buddy Knox
6 WHY, BABY, WHY   Pat Boone
7 GONE   Ferlin Huskey
   Note: * Another version by: Charlie Gracie.

May 11, 1957
1 ALL SHOOK UP   Elvis Presley
2 ROUND AND ROUND   Perry Como
3 LITTLE DARLIN'   The Diamonds
4 I'M WALKIN'   Fats Domino
5 PARTY DOLL   Buddy Knox
6 GONE   Ferlin Huskey
7 BUTTERFLY   Andy Williams *
   Note: * Another version by: Charlie Gracie.

May 18, 1957
1 ALL SHOOK UP   Elvis Presley
2 ROUND AND ROUND   Perry Como
3 LITTLE DARLIN'   The Diamonds
4 DARK MOON   Gale Storm
5 PARTY DOLL   Buddy Knox
6 GONE   Ferlin Huskey
7 I'M WALKIN'   Fats Domino

May 25, 1957
1 LITTLE DARLIN'   The Diamonds
2 ALL SHOOK UP   Elvis Presley
3 ROUND AND ROUND   Perry Como
4 DARK MOON   Gale Storm
5 GONE   Ferlin Huskey
6 SO RARE   Jimmy Dorsey Orch.
7 I'M WALKIN'   Fats Domino

June 1, 1957
1 ALL SHOOK UP   Elvis Presley
2 DARK MOON   Gale Storm
3 LITTLE DARLIN'   The Diamonds
4 SO RARE   Jimmy Dorsey Orch.
5 LOVE LETTERS IN THE SAND   Pat Boone
6 ROUND AND ROUND   Perry Como
7 A WHITE SPORT COAT   Marty Robbins

June 8, 1957
1 LOVE LETTERS IN THE SAND   Pat Boone
2 DARK MOON   Gale Storm
3 ALL SHOOK UP   Elvis Presley
4 LITTLE DARLIN'   The Diamonds
5 SO RARE   Jimmy Dorsey Orch.
6 SCHOOL DAYS   Chuck Berry
7 A WHITE SPORT COAT   Marty Robbins

June 15, 1957
1 LOVE LETTERS IN THE SAND   Pat Boone
2 SO RARE   Jimmy Dorsey Orch.
3 DARK MOON   Gale Storm
4 ALL SHOOK UP   Elvis Presley
5 A WHITE SPORT COAT   Marty Robbins
6 LITTLE DARLIN'   The Diamonds
7 SCHOOL DAYS   Chuck Berry

June 22, 1957
1 LOVE LETTERS IN THE SAND   Pat Boone
2 SO RARE   Jimmy Dorsey Orch.
3 ALL SHOOK UP   Elvis Presley
4 DARK MOON   Gale Storm
5 A WHITE SPORT COAT   Marty Robbins
6 LITTLE DARLIN'   The Diamonds
7 FOUR WALLS   Jim Reeves

June 29, 1957
1 LOVE LETTERS IN THE SAND   Pat Boone
2 SO RARE   Jimmy Dorsey Orch.
3 BYE BYE LOVE   Everly Brothers
4 DARK MOON   Gale Storm
5 A WHITE SPORT COAT   Marty Robbins
6 AROUND THE WORLD   Mantovani
7 OLD CAPE COD   Patti Page

July 6, 1957
1 LOVE LETTERS IN THE SAND   Pat Boone
2 SO RARE   Jimmy Dorsey Orch.
3 BYE BYE LOVE   Everly Brothers
4 DARK MOON   Gale Storm
5 AROUND THE WORLD   Mantovani
6 A WHITE SPORT COAT   Marty Robbins
7 OLD CAPE COD   Patti Page

July 13, 1957
1 LOVE LETTERS IN THE SAND   Pat Boone
2 SO RARE   Jimmy Dorsey Orch.
3 BYE BYE LOVE   Everly Brothers
4 AROUND THE WORLD   Mantovani
5 OLD CAPE COD   Patti Page
6 DARK MOON   Gale Storm
7 I'M GONNA SIT RIGHT DOWN AND WRITE MYSELF A
   LETTER   Billy Williams

July 20, 1957
1 LOVE LETTERS IN THE SAND   Pat Boone
2 SO RARE   Jimmy Dorsey Orch.
3 BYE BYE LOVE   Everly Brothers
4 AROUND THE WORLD   Mantovani
5 I'M GONNA SIT RIGHT DOWN AND WRITE MYSELF A
   LETTER   Billy Williams
6 OLD CAPE COD   Patti Page
7 IT'S NOT FOR ME TO SAY   Johnny Mathis

July 27, 1957
1. LOVE LETTERS IN THE SAND   Pat Boone
2. AROUND THE WORLD   Mantovani
3. I'M GONNA SIT RIGHT DOWN AND WRITE MYSELF A LETTER   Billy Williams
4. SO RARE   Jimmy Dorsey Orch.
5. OLD CAPE COD   Patti Page
6. BYE BYE LOVE   Everly Brothers
7. TEDDY BEAR   Elvis Presley

August 3, 1957
1. LOVE LETTERS IN THE SAND   Pat Boone
2. AROUND THE WORLD   Mantovani
3. I'M GONNA SIT RIGHT DOWN AND WRITE MYSELF A LETTER   Billy Williams
4. TEDDY BEAR   Elvis Presley
5. OLD CAPE COD   Patti Page
6. SO RARE   Jimmy Dorsey Orch.
7. BYE BYE LOVE   Everly Brothers

August 10, 1957
1. LOVE LETTERS IN THE SAND   Pat Boone
2. AROUND THE WORLD   Mantovani
3. I'M GONNA SIT RIGHT DOWN AND WRITE MYSELF A LETTER   Billy Williams
4. BYE BYE LOVE   Everly Brothers
5. OLD CAPE COD   Patti Page
6. WHITE SILVER SANDS   Dave Gardner *
7. TAMMY   Debbie Reynolds
   Note: * Don Rondo

August 17, 1957
1. AROUND THE WORLD   Mantovani
2. TAMMY   Debbie Reynolds
3. LOVE LETTERS IN THE SAND   Pat Boone
4. I'M GONNA SIT RIGHT DOWN AND WRITE MYSELF A LETTER   Billy Williams
5. IT'S NOT FOR ME TO SAY   Johnny Mathis
6. TEDDY BEAR   Elvis Presley
7. BYE BYE LOVE   Everly Brothers

August 24, 1957
1. TAMMY   Debbie Reynolds
2. AROUND THE WORLD   Mantovani
3. I'M GONNA SIT RIGHT DOWN AND WRITE MYSELF A LETTER   Billy Williams
4. WHITE SILVER SANDS   Dave Gardner *
5. LOVE LETTERS IN THE SAND   Pat Boone
6. IT'S NOT FOR ME TO SAY   Johnny Mathis
7. BYE BYE LOVE   Everly Brothers
   Note: * Don Rondo

August 31, 1957
1. TAMMY   Debbie Reynolds
2. AROUND THE WORLD   Mantovani
3. I'M GONNA SIT RIGHT DOWN AND WRITE MYSELF A LETTER   Billy Williams
4. FASCINATION   Jane Morgan
5. TEDDY BEAR   Elvis Presley
6. LOVE LETTERS IN THE SAND   Pat Boone
7. IT'S NOT FOR ME TO SAY   Johnny Mathis

September 7, 1957
1. TAMMY   Debbie Reynolds
2. AROUND THE WORLD   Mantovani
3. I'M GONNA SIT RIGHT DOWN AND WRITE MYSELF A LETTER   Billy Williams
4. FASCINATION   Jane Morgan
5. DIANA   Paul Anka
6. RAINBOW   Russ Hamilton
7. IN THE MIDDLE OF AN ISLAND   Tony Bennett

September 14, 1957
1. TAMMY   Debbie Reynolds
2. AROUND THE WORLD   Mantovani
3. DIANA   Paul Anka
4. FASCINATION   Jane Morgan
5. HONEYCOMB   Jimmie Rodgers
6. I'M GONNA SIT RIGHT DOWN AND WRITE MYSELF A LETTER   Billy Williams
7. IN THE MIDDLE OF AN ISLAND   Tony Bennett

September 21, 1957
1. TAMMY   Debbie Reynolds
2. FASCINATION   Jane Morgan
3. DIANA   Paul Anka
4. AROUND THE WORLD   Mantovani
5. HONEYCOMB   Jimmie Rodgers
6. IN THE MIDDLE OF AN ISLAND   Tony Bennett
7. THAT'LL BE THE DAY   Buddy Holly & The Crickets

September 28, 1957
1. TAMMY   Debbie Reynolds
2. FASCINATION   Jane Morgan
3. DIANA   Paul Anka

Debbie Reynolds
Debbie skyrockets to #1 with ``Tammy'' (Aug. 24), from the film ``Tammy & The Bachelor.''

Paul Anka
Anka is fifteen years old when ``Diana'' enters the Top 10.

4 THAT'LL BE THE DAY   Buddy Holly & The Crickets
5 AROUND THE WORLD   Mantovani
6 HONEYCOMB   Jimmie Rodgers
7 IN THE MIDDLE OF AN ISLAND   Tony Bennett

October 5, 1957
1 TAMMY   Debbie Reynolds
2 FASCINATION   Jane Morgan
3 HONEYCOMB   Jimmie Rodgers
4 DIANA   Paul Anka
5 THAT'LL BE THE DAY   Buddy Holly & The Crickets
6 AROUND THE WORLD   Mantovani
7 IN THE MIDDLE OF AN ISLAND   Tony Bennett

October 12, 1957
1 TAMMY   Debbie Reynolds
2 FASCINATION   Jane Morgan
3 CHANCES ARE   Johnny Mathis
4 HONEYCOMB   Jimmie Rodgers
5 WAKE UP LITTLE SUSIE   Everly Brothers
6 DIANA   Paul Anka
7 AROUND THE WORLD   Mantovani

October 19, 1957
1 TAMMY   Debbie Reynolds
2 HONEYCOMB   Jimmie Rodgers
3 FASCINATION   Jane Morgan
4 CHANCES ARE   Johnny Mathis
5 WAKE UP LITTLE SUSIE   Everly Brothers
6 IN THE MIDDLE OF AN ISLAND   Tony Bennett
7 DIANA   Paul Anka

October 26, 1957
1 TAMMY   Debbie Reynolds
2 FASCINATION   Jane Morgan
3 HONEYCOMB   Jimmie Rodgers
4 CHANCES ARE   Johnny Mathis
5 WAKE UP LITTLE SUSIE   Everly Brothers
6 AROUND THE WORLD   Mantovani
7 JAILHOUSE ROCK   Elvis Presley

November 2, 1957
1 FASCINATION   Jane Morgan
2 CHANCES ARE   Johnny Mathis
3 WAKE UP LITTLE SUSIE   Everly Brothers
4 TAMMY   Debbie Reynolds
5 JAILHOUSE ROCK   Elvis Presley
6 MELODIE D'AMOUR   Ames Brothers
7 HONEYCOMB   Jimmie Rodgers

November 9, 1957
1 CHANCES ARE   Johnny Mathis
2 HONEYCOMB   Jimmie Rodgers
3 FASCINATION   Jane Morgan
4 WAKE UP LITTLE SUSIE   Everly Brothers
5 JAILHOUSE ROCK   Elvis Presley
6 TAMMY   Debbie Reynolds
7 SILHOUETTES   The Rays

November 16, 1957
1 CHANCES ARE   Johnny Mathis
2 WAKE UP LITTLE SUSIE   Everly Brothers
3 JAILHOUSE ROCK   Elvis Presley
4 FASCINATION   Jane Morgan

Jimmie Rodgers
Jimmie's``Honeycomb'' peaked at #2 (Oct. 19).

5 MELODIE D'AMOUR Ames Brothers
6 HONEYCOMB Jimmie Rodgers
7 SILHOUETTES The Rays

November 23, 1957
1 CHANCES ARE Johnny Mathis
2 APRIL LOVE Pat Boone
3 MELODIE D'AMOUR Ames Brothers
4 YOU SEND ME Sam Cooke
5 FASCINATION Jane Morgan
6 WAKE UP LITTLE SUSIE Everly Brothers
7 JAILHOUSE ROCK Elvis Presley

November 30, 1957
1 APRIL LOVE Pat Boone
2 FASCINATION Jane Morgan
3 JAILHOUSE ROCK Elvis Presley
4 ALL THE WAY Frank Sinatra
5 SILHOUETTES The Rays
6 YOU SEND ME Sam Cooke
7 CHANCES ARE Johnny Mathis

December 7, 1957
1 APRIL LOVE Pat Boone
2 YOU SEND ME Sam Cooke
3 CHANCES ARE Johnny Mathis
4 ALL THE WAY Frank Sinatra
5 SILHOUETTES The Rays
6 JAILHOUSE ROCK Elvis Presley
7 MELODIE D'AMOUR Ames Brothers

December 14, 1957
1 ALL THE WAY Frank Sinatra
2 APRIL LOVE Pat Boone
3 YOU SEND ME Sam Cooke
4 RAUNCHY Bill Justis
5 CHANCES ARE Johnny Mathis
6 KISSES SWEETER THAN WINE Jimmie Rodgers
7 SILHOUETTES The Rays

December 21, 1957
1 APRIL LOVE Pat Boone
2 ALL THE WAY Frank Sinatra
3 YOU SEND ME Sam Cooke
4 RAUNCHY Bill Justis
5 SILHOUETTES The Rays
6 JAILHOUSE ROCK Elvis Presley
7 CHANCES ARE Johnny Mathis

December 28, 1957
1 APRIL LOVE Pat Boone
2 ALL THE WAY Frank Sinatra
3 RAUNCHY Bill Justis
4 YOU SEND ME Sam Cooke
5 KISSES SWEETER THAN WINE Jimmie Rodgers
6 PEGGY SUE Buddy Holly
7 SILHOUETTES The Rays

January 4, 1958
1 APRIL LOVE Pat Boone
2 ALL THE WAY Frank Sinatra
3 RAUNCHY Bill Justis
4 AT THE HOP Danny & the Juniors
5 PEGGY SUE Buddy Holly

Johnny Mathis
Johnny's ``Chances Are'' hits #1 (Nov. 9).

6 YOU SEND ME Sam Cooke
7 KISSES SWEETER THAN WINE Jimmie Rodgers

January 11, 1958
1 APRIL LOVE Pat Boone
2 ALL THE WAY Frank Sinatra
3 AT THE HOP Danny & the Juniors
4 RAUNCHY Bill Justis
5 YOU SEND ME Sam Cooke
6 PEGGY SUE Buddy Holly
7 KISSES SWEETER THAN WINE Jimmie Rodgers

January 18, 1958
1 APRIL LOVE Pat Boone
2 ALL THE WAY Frank Sinatra
3 AT THE HOP Danny & the Juniors
4 RAUNCHY Bill Justis
5 PEGGY SUE Buddy Holly
6 KISSES SWEETER THAN WINE Jimmie Rodgers
7 LIECHTENSTEINER POLKA Will Glahe Musette

January 25, 1958
1 AT THE HOP Danny & the Juniors
2 ALL THE WAY Frank Sinatra
3 APRIL LOVE Pat Boone
4 PEGGY SUE Buddy Holly
5 SUGARTIME McGuire Sisters
6 RAUNCHY Bill Justis
7 GET A JOB The Silhouettes

February 1, 1958
1 AT THE HOP   Danny & the Juniors
2 ALL THE WAY   Frank Sinatra
3 APRIL LOVE   Pat Boone
4 PEGGY SUE   Buddy Holly
5 RAUNCHY   Bill Justis
6 GET A JOB   The Silhouettes
7 SAIL ALONG, SILVERY MOON   Billy Vaughn

February 8, 1958
1 AT THE HOP   Danny & the Juniors
2 SUGARTIME   McGuire Sisters
3 SAIL ALONG, SILVERY MOON   Billy Vaughn
4 GET A JOB   The Silhouettes
5 THE STROLL   The Diamonds
6 APRIL LOVE   Pat Boone
7 ALL THE WAY   Frank Sinatra

February 15, 1958
1 CATCH A FALLING STAR   Perry Como
2 SAIL ALONG, SILVERY MOON   Billy Vaughn
3 SUGARTIME   McGuire Sisters
4 AT THE HOP   Danny & the Juniors
5 GET A JOB   The Silhouettes
6 WITCHCRAFT   Frank Sinatra
7 THE STROLL   The Diamonds

February 22, 1958
1 SUGARTIME   McGuire Sisters
2 AT THE HOP   Danny & the Juniors

Perry Como
Perry's ``Catch A Falling Star'' is #1 (Feb. 15).

3 SAIL ALONG, SILVERY MOON   Billy Vaughn
4 CATCH A FALLING STAR   Perry Como
5 GET A JOB   The Silhouettes

March 1, 1958
1 CATCH A FALLING STAR   Perry Como
2 SUGARTIME   McGuire Sisters
3 SAIL ALONG, SILVERY MOON   Billy Vaughn
4 WITCHCRAFT   Frank Sinatra
5 GET A JOB   The Silhouettes

March 8, 1958
1 CATCH A FALLING STAR   Perry Como
2 GET A JOB   The Silhouettes
3 SAIL ALONG, SILVERY MOON   Billy Vaughn
4 SUGARTIME   McGuire Sisters
5 TEQUILA   The Champs

March 15, 1958
1 SUGARTIME   McGuire Sisters
2 CATCH A FALLING STAR   Perry Como
3 SAIL ALONG, SILVERY MOON   Billy Vaughn
4 TEQUILA   The Champs
5 WHO'S SORRY NOW   Connie Francis

March 22, 1958
1 CATCH A FALLING STAR   Perry Como
2 TEQUILA   The Champs
3 SUGARTIME   McGuire Sisters
4 SAIL ALONG, SILVERY MOON   Billy Vaughn
5 IT'S TOO SOON TO KNOW   Pat Boone

March 29, 1958
1 TEQUILA   The Champs
2 CATCH A FALLING STAR   Perry Como
3 WHO'S SORRY NOW   Connie Francis
4 SUGARTIME   McGuire Sisters
5 26 MILES   Four Preps

April 5, 1958
1 TEQUILA   The Champs
2 CATCH A FALLING STAR   Perry Como
3 LOLLIPOP   The Chordettes
4 ARE YOU SINCERE   Andy Williams
5 WHO'S SORRY NOW   Connie Francis

April 12, 1958
1 TEQUILA   The Champs
2 EASTER PARADE   Guy Lombardo
3 WHO'S SORRY NOW   Connie Francis
4 LOLLIPOP   The Chordettes
5 HE'S GOT THE WHOLE WORLD IN HIS HANDS   Laurie London

April 19, 1958
1 HE'S GOT THE WHOLE WORLD IN HIS HANDS   Laurie London
2 TEQUILA   The Champs
3 WHO'S SORRY NOW   Connie Francis
4 LOLLIPOP   The Chordettes
5 CATCH A FALLING STAR   Perry Como

April 26, 1958
1 HE'S GOT THE WHOLE WORLD IN HIS HANDS   Laurie London

Danny & The Juniors
Danny is only sixteen when ``At The Hop'' tops the Hit Parade (Jan. 25).

2   TEQUILA   The Champs
3   WITCH DOCTOR   David Seville
4   TWILIGHT TIME   Platters
5   WHO'S SORRY NOW   Connie Francis

May 3, 1958
1   HE'S GOT THE WHOLE WORLD IN HIS HANDS   Laurie
    London
2   WITCH DOCTOR   David Seville
3   TWILIGHT TIME   Platters
4   CHANSON D'AMOUR   Art & Dotty Todd
5   ALL I HAVE TO DO IS DREAM   Everly Brothers

May 10, 1958
1   TWILIGHT TIME   Platters
2   HE'S GOT THE WHOLE WORLD IN HIS HANDS   Laurie
    London
3   WITCH DOCTOR   David Seville
4   ALL I HAVE TO DO IS DREAM   Everly Brothers
5   RETURN TO ME   Dean Martin

May 17, 1958
1   CHANSON D'AMOUR   Art & Dotty Todd
2   TWILIGHT TIME   Platters
3   ALL I HAVE TO DO IS DREAM   Everly Brothers
4   WITCH DOCTOR   David Seville
5   HE'S GOT THE WHOLE WORLD IN HIS HANDS   Laurie
    London

May 24, 1958
1   ALL I HAVE TO DO IS DREAM   Everly Brothers
2   CHANSON D'AMOUR   Art & Dotty Todd
3   WITCH DOCTOR   David Seville
4   RETURN TO ME   Dean Martin
5   TWILIGHT TIME   Platters

May 31, 1958
1   ALL I HAVE TO DO IS DREAM   Everly Brothers
2   TWILIGHT TIME   Platters
3   RETURN TO ME   Dean Martin
4   WITCH DOCTOR   David Seville
5   CHANSON D'AMOUR   Art & Dotty Todd

June 7, 1958
1   ALL I HAVE TO DO IS DREAM   Everly Brothers
2   RETURN TO ME   Dean Martin
3   WITCH DOCTOR   David Seville
4   PURPLE PEOPLE EATER   Sheb Wooley
5   CHANSON D'AMOUR   Art & Dotty Todd

Editor's Note: This was the final broadcast featuring the
    original Hit Parade cast members, who were all "retired"
    as of June 29, 1958. The new cast and format lasted less
    than a year (final show aired April 1959).

``So Long For Awhile,
That's All The Songs For Awhile.
So Long To Your Hit Parade
And The Tunes You Picked To Be Played.
So Long....''

``Tune In Again Next Week When 'Your Hit Parade'
Will Bring You The Top 7 Tunes Of The Week.
This Is Your Announcer Andre Baruch.
Be Happy, Go Lucky.''

American Top Ten Hits 1958-1994

The Everly Brothers

Shown here two decades later, the #1 duo of the Rock Era has another chart-topper with ``All I Have To Do Is Dream.''
(Peaking June 13 on the *Billboard* charts, the song had reached the same position on the Hit Parade a month earlier).

June 7, 1958

1   TWILIGHT TIME   Platters
2   BIG MAN   Four Preps
3   SECRETLY   Jimmie Rodgers
4   HE'S GOT THE WHOLE WORLD IN HIS HANDS   Laurie London
5   SUGAR MOON   Pat Boone
6   WEAR MY RING AROUND YOUR NECK   Elvis Presley
7   KEWPIE DOLL   Perry Como
8   LOOKING BACK   Nat King Cole
9   ALL I HAVE TO DO IS DREAM   Everly Brothers
10   WITCH DOCTOR   David Seville

June 13, 1958

1   ALL I HAVE TO DO IS DREAM   Everly Brothers
2   PURPLE PEOPLE EATER   Sheb Wooley
3   WITCH DOCTOR   David Seville
4   TWILIGHT TIME   Platters
5   CHANSON D'AMOUR   Art & Dotty Todd
6   RETURN TO ME   Dean Martin
7   BIG MAN   Four Preps
8   SECRETLY   Jimmie Rodgers
9   HE'S GOT THE WHOLE WORLD IN HIS HANDS   Laurie London
10   SUGAR MOON   Pat Boone

June 20, 1958

1   PURPLE PEOPLE EATER   Sheb Wooley
2   ALL I HAVE TO DO IS DREAM   Everly Brothers
3   RETURN TO ME   Dean Martin
4   SECRETLY   Jimmie Rodgers
5   WITCH DOCTOR   David Seville
6   TWILIGHT TIME   Platters
7   SUGAR MOON   Pat Boone
8   CHANSON D'AMOUR   Art & Dotty Todd
9   BIG MAN   Four Preps
10   HE'S GOT THE WHOLE WORLD IN HIS HANDS   Laurie London

June 27, 1958

1   PURPLE PEOPLE EATER   Sheb Wooley
2   ALL I HAVE TO DO IS DREAM   Everly Brothers
3   RETURN TO ME   Dean Martin
4   SECRETLY   Jimmie Rodgers
5   WITCH DOCTOR   David Seville
6   BIG MAN   Four Preps
7   SUGAR MOON   Pat Boone
8   TWILIGHT TIME   Platters
9   YAKETY YAK   Coasters
10   CHANSON D'AMOUR   Art & Dotty Todd

July 4, 1958

1   PURPLE PEOPLE EATER   Sheb Wooley
2   ALL I HAVE TO DO IS DREAM   Everly Brothers
3   SECRETLY   Jimmie Rodgers
4   RETURN TO ME   Dean Martin
5   YAKETY YAK   Coasters
6   BIG MAN   Four Preps
7   WITCH DOCTOR   David Seville
8   SUGAR MOON   Pat Boone
9   ENDLESS SLEEP   Jody Reynolds
10   TWILIGHT TIME   Platters

July 11, 1958

1   PURPLE PEOPLE EATER   Sheb Wooley
2   ALL I HAVE TO DO IS DREAM   Everly Brothers

3   YAKETY YAK   Coasters
4   SECRETLY   Jimmie Rodgers
5   RETURN TO ME   Dean Martin
6   HARD HEADED WOMAN   Elvis Presley
7   SUGAR MOON   Pat Boone
8   TWILIGHT TIME   Platters
9   ENDLESS SLEEP   Jody Reynolds
10   PATRICIA   Perez Prado

July 18, 1958

1   PURPLE PEOPLE EATER   Sheb Wooley
2   YAKETY YAK   Coasters
3   HARD HEADED WOMAN   Elvis Presley
4   SECRETLY   Jimmie Rodgers
5   ALL I HAVE TO DO IS DREAM   Everly Brothers
6   PATRICIA   Perez Prado
7   SPLISH SPLASH   Bobby Darin
8   POOR LITTLE FOOL   Ricky Nelson
9   RETURN TO ME   Dean Martin
10   PADRE   Toni Arden

July 25, 1958

1   HARD HEADED WOMAN   Elvis Presley
2   YAKETY YAK   Coasters
3   PURPLE PEOPLE EATER   Sheb Wooley
4   PATRICIA   Perez Prado
5   SPLISH SPLASH   Bobby Darin
6   POOR LITTLE FOOL   Ricky Nelson
7   WHEN   Kalin Twins
8   SECRETLY   Jimmie Rodgers
9   IF DREAMS COME TRUE   Pat Boone
10   ALL I HAVE TO DO IS DREAM   Everly Brothers

August 1, 1958

1   PATRICIA   Perez Prado
2   HARD HEADED WOMAN   Elvis Presley
3   POOR LITTLE FOOL   Ricky Nelson
4   YAKETY YAK   Coasters
5   SPLISH SPLASH   Bobby Darin
6   PURPLE PEOPLE EATER   Sheb Wooley
7   WHEN   Kalin Twins
8   SECRETLY   Jimmie Rodgers
9   LEFT RIGHT OUT OF YOUR HEART   Patti Page
10   REBEL-ROUSER   Duane Eddy

August 8, 1958

1   POOR LITTLE FOOL   Ricky Nelson
2   PATRICIA   Perez Prado
3   YAKETY YAK   Coasters
4   SPLISH SPLASH   Bobby Darin
5   WHEN   Kalin Twins
6   REBEL-ROUSER   Duane Eddy
7   VOLARE (NEL BLU DIPINTO DI BLU)   Domenico Modugno
8   LITTLE STAR   Elegants
9   HARD HEADED WOMAN   Elvis Presley
10   SECRETLY   Jimmie Rodgers

August 15, 1958

1   PATRICIA   Perez Prado
2   POOR LITTLE FOOL   Ricky Nelson
3   VOLARE (NEL BLU DIPINTO DI BLU)   Domenico Modugno
4   SPLISH SPLASH   Bobby Darin
5   WHEN   Kalin Twins
6   LITTLE STAR   Elegants
7   REBEL-ROUSER   Duane Eddy
8   HARD HEADED WOMAN   Elvis Presley

Peggy Lee
``Fever`` briefly entered the lower end of the Top 10 in August 1958.

9   YAKETY YAK   Coasters
10   MY TRUE LOVE   Jack Scott

August 22, 1958

1   VOLARE (NEL BLU DIPINTO DI BLU)   Domenico Modugno
2   PATRICIA   Perez Prado
3   JUST A DREAM   Jimmy Clanton
4   POOR LITTLE FOOL   Ricky Nelson
5   LITTLE STAR   Elegants
6   MY TRUE LOVE   Jack Scott
7   BIRD DOG   Everly Brothers
8   REBEL-ROUSER   Duane Eddy
9   FEVER   Peggy Lee
10   WHEN   Kalin Twins

August 29, 1958

1   VOLARE (NEL BLU DIPINTO DI BLU)   Domenico Modugno
2   LITTLE STAR   Elegants
3   PATRICIA   Perez Prado
4   POOR LITTLE FOOL   Ricky Nelson
5   JUST A DREAM   Jimmy Clanton
6   BIRD DOG   Everly Brothers
7   MY TRUE LOVE   Jack Scott
8   REBEL-ROUSER   Duane Eddy
9   WHEN   Kalin Twins
10   FEVER   Peggy Lee

September 5, 1958

1   VOLARE (NEL BLU DIPINTO DI BLU)   Domenico Modugno
2   LITTLE STAR   Elegants
3   PATRICIA   Perez Prado
4   POOR LITTLE FOOL   Ricky Nelson
5   JUST A DREAM   Jimmy Clanton
6   BIRD DOG   Everly Brothers
7   MY TRUE LOVE   Jack Scott
8   EVERYBODY LOVES A LOVER   Doris Day
9   BORN TOO LATE   Poni-Tales
10   WHEN   Kalin Twins

September 12, 1958

1   VOLARE (NEL BLU DIPINTO DI BLU)   Domenico Modugno
2   LITTLE STAR   Elegants
3   BIRD DOG   Everly Brothers
4   JUST A DREAM   Jimmy Clanton
5   PATRICIA   Perez Prado
6   POOR LITTLE FOOL   Ricky Nelson
7   MY TRUE LOVE   Jack Scott
8   BORN TOO LATE   Poni-Tales
9   IT'S ALL IN THE GAME   Tommy Edwards
10   DEVOTED TO YOU   Everly Brothers

September 19, 1958

1   VOLARE (NEL BLU DIPINTO DI BLU)   Domenico Modugno
2   BIRD DOG   Everly Brothers
3   LITTLE STAR   Elegants
4   IT'S ALL IN THE GAME   Tommy Edwards
5   JUST A DREAM   Jimmy Clanton
6   PATRICIA   Perez Prado
7   ROCKIN' ROBIN   Bobby Day
8   BORN TOO LATE   Poni-Tales
9   MY TRUE LOVE   Jack Scott
10   POOR LITTLE FOOL   Ricky Nelson

September 26, 1958

1   VOLARE (NEL BLU DIPINTO DI BLU)   Domenico Modugno
2   BIRD DOG   Everly Brothers

3   IT'S ALL IN THE GAME   Tommy Edwards
4   LITTLE STAR   Elegants
5   ROCKIN' ROBIN   Bobby Day
6   PATRICIA   Perez Prado
7   JUST A DREAM   Jimmy Clanton
8   TEARS ON MY PILLOW   Little Anthony & The Imperials
9   BORN TOO LATE   Poni-Tales
10   NEAR YOU   Roger Williams

October 3, 1958

1   VOLARE (NEL BLU DIPINTO DI BLU)   Domenico Modugno
2   IT'S ALL IN THE GAME   Tommy Edwards
3   BIRD DOG   Everly Brothers
4   LITTLE STAR   Elegants
5   ROCKIN' ROBIN   Bobby Day
6   PATRICIA   Perez Prado
7   TEARS ON MY PILLOW   Little Anthony & The Imperials
8   SUSIE DARLIN'   Robin Luke
9   NEAR YOU   Roger Williams
10   JUST A DREAM   Jimmy Clanton

October 10, 1958

1   IT'S ALL IN THE GAME   Tommy Edwards
2   VOLARE (NEL BLU DIPINTO DI BLU)   Domenico Modugno
3   BIRD DOG   Everly Brothers
4   ROCKIN' ROBIN   Bobby Day
5   LITTLE STAR   Elegants
6   TEARS ON MY PILLOW   Little Anthony & The Imperials
7   SUSIE DARLIN'   Robin Luke
8   PATRICIA   Perez Prado
9   NEAR YOU   Roger Williams
10   TEA FOR TWO [CHA-CHA]   Tommy Dorsey

October 17, 1958

1   IT'S ALL IN THE GAME   Tommy Edwards
2   VOLARE (NEL BLU DIPINTO DI BLU)   Domenico Modugno
3   BIRD DOG   Everly Brothers
4   ROCKIN' ROBIN   Bobby Day
5   TEARS ON MY PILLOW   Little Anthony & The Imperials
6   SUSIE DARLIN'   Robin Luke
7   LITTLE STAR   Elegants
8   NEAR YOU   Roger Williams
9   TEA FOR TWO [CHA-CHA]   Tommy Dorsey
10   PATRICIA   Perez Prado

October 24, 1958

1   IT'S ALL IN THE GAME   Tommy Edwards
2   ROCKIN' ROBIN   Bobby Day
3   VOLARE (NEL BLU DIPINTO DI BLU)   Domenico Modugno
4   BIRD DOG   Everly Brothers
5   TOPSY II   Cozy Cole
6   IT'S ONLY MAKE BELIEVE   Conway Twitty
7   TEARS ON MY PILLOW   Little Anthony & The Imperials
8   TOM DOOLEY   Kingston Trio
9   TEA FOR TWO [CHA-CHA]   Tommy Dorsey
10   CHANTILLY LACE   Big Bopper

October 31, 1958

1   IT'S ALL IN THE GAME   Tommy Edwards
2   IT'S ONLY MAKE BELIEVE   Conway Twitty
3   TOPSY II   Cozy Cole
4   TOM DOOLEY   Kingston Trio
5   ROCKIN' ROBIN   Bobby Day
6   TEA FOR TWO [CHA-CHA]   Tommy Dorsey
7   BIRD DOG   Everly Brothers
8   TEARS ON MY PILLOW   Little Anthony & The Imperials

Tommy Edwards
The only song written by a vice president of the United States (Charles Dawes in 1912),
Tommy's rendition of ``It's All In The Game'' becomes a huge #1 hit (Oct. 10 - Nov. 14).

9   VOLARE (NEL BLU DIPINTO DI BLU)   Domenico Modugno
10   CHANTILLY LACE   Big Bopper

November 7, 1958
1   IT'S ALL IN THE GAME   Tommy Edwards
2   IT'S ONLY MAKE BELIEVE   Conway Twitty
3   TOM DOOLEY   Kingston Trio
4   TOPSY II   Cozy Cole
5   ROCKIN' ROBIN   Bobby Day
6   TEA FOR TWO [CHA-CHA]   Tommy Dorsey
7   CHANTILLY LACE   Big Bopper
8   THE END   Earl Grand
9   TEARS ON MY PILLOW   Little Anthony & The Imperials
10   BIRD DOG   Everly Brothers

November 14, 1958
1   IT'S ALL IN THE GAME   Tommy Edwards
2   IT'S ONLY MAKE BELIEVE   Conway Twitty
3   TOM DOOLEY   Kingston Trio
4   TOPSY II   Cozy Cole
5   TO KNOW HIM IS TO LOVE HIM   Teddy Bears
6   THE END   Earl Grand
7   TEA FOR TWO [CHA-CHA]   Tommy Dorsey
8   CHANTILLY LACE   Big Bopper
9   ROCKIN' ROBIN   Bobby Day
10   THE DAY THE RAINS CAME   Jane Morgan

November 21, 1958
1   TOM DOOLEY   Kingston Trio
2   IT'S ONLY MAKE BELIEVE   Conway Twitty
3   IT'S ALL IN THE GAME   Tommy Edwards
4   TOPSY II   Cozy Cole
5   TO KNOW HIM IS TO LOVE HIM   Teddy Bears
6   THE END   Earl Grand
7   CHANTILLY LACE   Big Bopper
8   LONESOME TOWN   Ricky Nelson
9   BEEP BEEP   Playmates
10   TEA FOR TWO [CHA-CHA]   Tommy Dorsey

November 28, 1958
1   TOM DOOLEY   Kingston Trio
2   TO KNOW HIM IS TO LOVE HIM   Teddy Bears
3   IT'S ONLY MAKE BELIEVE   Conway Twitty
4   TOPSY II   Cozy Cole
5   IT'S ALL IN THE GAME   Tommy Edwards
6   BEEP BEEP   Playmates
7   LONESOME TOWN   Ricky Nelson
8   I GOT STUNG   Elvis Presley
9   ONE NIGHT   Elvis Presley
10   THE END   Earl Grand

December 5, 1958
1   TOM DOOLEY   Kingston Trio
2   TO KNOW HIM IS TO LOVE HIM   Teddy Bears
3   IT'S ONLY MAKE BELIEVE   Conway Twitty
4   TOPSY II   Cozy Cole
5   LONESOME TOWN   Ricky Nelson
6   BEEP BEEP   Playmates
7   IT'S ALL IN THE GAME   Tommy Edwards
8   ONE NIGHT   Elvis Presley
9   I GOT STUNG   Elvis Presley
10   PROBLEMS   Everly Brothers

December 12, 1958
1   TOM DOOLEY   Kingston Trio
2   TO KNOW HIM IS TO LOVE HIM   Teddy Bears

3   IT'S ONLY MAKE BELIEVE   Conway Twitty
4   LONESOME TOWN   Ricky Nelson
5   ONE NIGHT   Elvis Presley
6   BEEP BEEP   Playmates
7   PROBLEMS   Everly Brothers
8   I GOT STUNG   Elvis Presley
9   TOPSY II   Cozy Cole
10   IT'S ALL IN THE GAME   Tommy Edwards

December 19, 1958
1   TOM DOOLEY   Kingston Trio
2   TO KNOW HIM IS TO LOVE HIM   Teddy Bears
3   ONE NIGHT   Elvis Presley
4   PROBLEMS   Everly Brothers
5   IT'S ONLY MAKE BELIEVE   Conway Twitty
6   LONESOME TOWN   Ricky Nelson
7   BEEP BEEP   Playmates
8   I GOT STUNG   Elvis Presley
9   SMOKE GETS IN YOUR EYES   Platters
10   CHIPMUNK SONG   Chipmunks

December 26, 1958
1   TO KNOW HIM IS TO LOVE HIM   Teddy Bears
2   CHIPMUNK SONG   Chipmunks
3   TOM DOOLEY   Kingston Trio
4   SMOKE GETS IN YOUR EYES   Platters
5   ONE NIGHT   Elvis Presley
6   LONESOME TOWN   Ricky Nelson
7   PROBLEMS   Everly Brothers
8   BEEP BEEP   Playmates
9   IT'S ONLY MAKE BELIEVE   Conway Twitty
10   I GOT STUNG   Elvis Presley

January 3, 1959
1   CHIPMUNK SONG   Chipmunks
2   SMOKE GETS IN YOUR EYES   Platters
3   TO KNOW HIM IS TO LOVE HIM   Teddy Bears
4   TOM DOOLEY   Kingston Trio
5   ONE NIGHT   Elvis Presley
6   LONESOME TOWN   Ricky Nelson
7   PROBLEMS   Everly Brothers
8   BEEP BEEP   Playmates
9   IT'S ONLY MAKE BELIEVE   Conway Twitty
10   WHOLE LOTTA LOVING   Fats Domino

January 10, 1959
1   CHIPMUNK SONG   Chipmunks
2   SMOKE GETS IN YOUR EYES   Platters
3   TO KNOW HIM IS TO LOVE HIM   Teddy Bears
4   TOM DOOLEY   Kingston Trio
5   ONE NIGHT   Elvis Presley
6   LONESOME TOWN   Ricky Nelson
7   PROBLEMS   Everly Brothers
8   MY HAPPINESS   Connie Francis
9   BEEP BEEP   Playmates
10   A LOVER'S QUESTION   Clyde McPhatter

January 17, 1959
1   CHIPMUNK SONG   Chipmunks
2   SMOKE GETS IN YOUR EYES   Platters
3   MY HAPPINESS   Connie Francis
4   TO KNOW HIM IS TO LOVE HIM   Teddy Bears
5   TOM DOOLEY   Kingston Trio
6   LONESOME TOWN   Ricky Nelson
7   ONE NIGHT   Elvis Presley
8   GOTTA TRAVEL ON   Billy Grammar

9 WHOLE LOTTA LOVING Fats Domino
10 PROBLEMS Everly Brothers

January 24, 1959
1 SMOKE GETS IN YOUR EYES Platters
2 CHIPMUNK SONG Chipmunks
3 MY HAPPINESS Connie Francis
4 16 CANDLES Crests
5 DONNA Ritchie Valens
6 TO KNOW HIM IS TO LOVE HIM Teddy Bears
7 GOTTA TRAVEL ON Billy Grammar
8 A LOVER'S QUESTION Clyde McPhatter
9 TOM DOOLEY Kingston Trio
10 WHOLE LOTTA LOVING Fats Domino

January 31, 1959
1 SMOKE GETS IN YOUR EYES Platters
2 DONNA Ritchie Valens
3 MY HAPPINESS Connie Francis
4 16 CANDLES Crests
5 STAGGER LEE Lloyd Price
6 CHIPMUNK SONG Chipmunks
7 GOTTA TRAVEL ON Billy Grammar
8 A LOVER'S QUESTION Clyde McPhatter
9 LONESOME TOWN Ricky Nelson
10 LONELY TEARDROPS Jackie Wilson

February 7, 1959
1 SMOKE GETS IN YOUR EYES Platters
2 DONNA Ritchie Valens

Jackie Wilson
''Lonely Teardrops'' enters the Top 10.
(Jackie had 54 hits for Brunswick from 1957-1972.
He died January 21, 1984.)

3 16 CANDLES Crests
4 MY HAPPINESS Connie Francis
5 STAGGER LEE Lloyd Price
6 ALL AMERICAN BOY Bill Parsons (Bobby Bare)
7 GOTTA TRAVEL ON Billy Grammar
8 LONELY TEARDROPS Jackie Wilson
9 THE CHILDREN'S MARCHING SONG Mitch Miller
10 A LOVER'S QUESTION Clyde McPhatter

February 14, 1959
1 SMOKE GETS IN YOUR EYES Platters
2 16 CANDLES Crests
3 STAGGER LEE Lloyd Price
4 DONNA Ritchie Valens
5 MY HAPPINESS Connie Francis
6 ALL AMERICAN BOY Bill Parsons (Bobby Bare)
7 GOTTA TRAVEL ON Billy Grammar
8 THE CHILDREN'S MARCHING SONG Mitch Miller
9 LONELY TEARDROPS Jackie Wilson
10 GOODBYE BABY Jack Scott

February 21, 1959
1 STAGGER LEE Lloyd Price
2 SMOKE GETS IN YOUR EYES Platters
3 16 CANDLES Crests
4 DONNA Ritchie Valens
5 THE CHILDREN'S MARCHING SONG Mitch Miller
6 MY HAPPINESS Connie Francis
7 ALL AMERICAN BOY Bill Parsons (Bobby Bare)
8 HAWAIIAN WEDDING SONG Andy Williams
9 GOTTA TRAVEL ON Billy Grammar
10 LONELY TEARDROPS Jackie Wilson

February 28, 1959
1 STAGGER LEE Lloyd Price
2 DONNA Ritchie Valens
3 16 CANDLES Crests
4 THE CHILDREN'S MARCHING SONG Mitch Miller
5 SMOKE GETS IN YOUR EYES Platters
6 MY HAPPINESS Connie Francis
7 ALL AMERICAN BOY Bill Parsons (Bobby Bare)
8 PETITE FLEUR Chris Barber's Jazz Band
9 HAWAIIAN WEDDING SONG Andy Williams
10 TALL PAUL Annette

March 7, 1959
1 STAGGER LEE Lloyd Price
2 DONNA Ritchie Valens
3 CHARLIE BROWN Coasters
4 16 CANDLES Crests
5 PETITE FLEUR Chris Barber's Jazz Band
6 THE CHILDREN'S MARCHING SONG Mitch Miller
7 HAWAIIAN WEDDING SONG Andy Williams
8 MY HAPPINESS Connie Francis
9 SMOKE GETS IN YOUR EYES Platters
10 I CRIED A TEAR LaVern Baker

March 14, 1959
1 VENUS Frankie Avalon
2 STAGGER LEE Lloyd Price
3 DONNA Ritchie Valens
4 CHARLIE BROWN Coasters
5 ALVIN'S HARMONICA Chipmunks
6 PETITE FLEUR Chris Barber's Jazz Band
7 THE CHILDREN'S MARCHING SONG Mitch Miller
8 HAWAIIAN WEDDING SONG Andy Williams

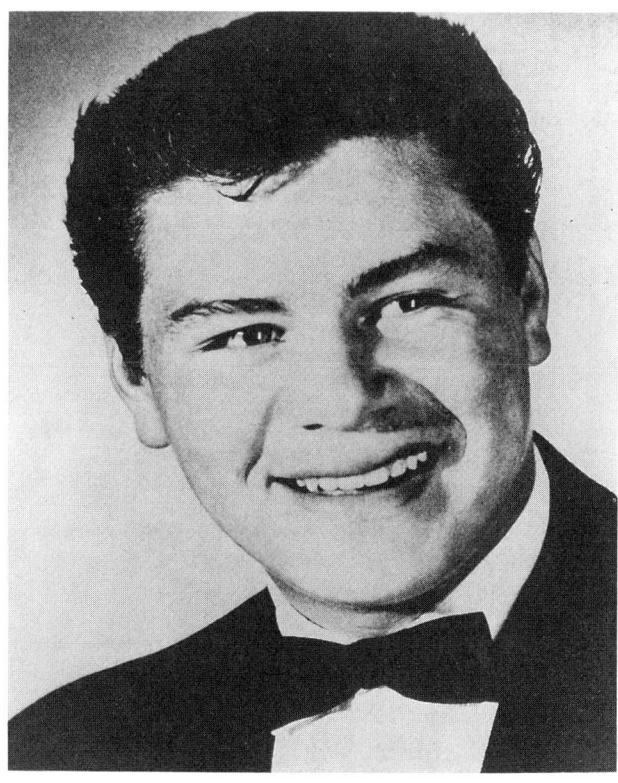

Ritchie Valens

The first Hispanic rock-and-roll singer was killed in a plane crash with Buddy Holly just as ``Donna'' peaked on the charts.

9   I'VE HAD IT   Bell Notes
10   16 CANDLES   Crests

March 21, 1959
1   VENUS   Frankie Avalon
2   CHARLIE BROWN   Coasters
3   ALVIN'S HARMONICA   Chipmunks
4   STAGGER LEE   Lloyd Price
5   DONNA   Ritchie Valens
6   IT'S JUST A MATTER OF TIME   Brook Benton
7   I'VE HAD IT   Bell Notes
8   HAWAIIAN WEDDING SONG   Andy Williams
9   THE CHILDREN'S MARCHING SONG   Mitch Miller
10   PETITE FLEUR   Chris Barber's Jazz Band

March 28, 1959
1   VENUS   Frankie Avalon
2   CHARLIE BROWN   Coasters
3   ALVIN'S HARMONICA   Chipmunks
4   IT'S JUST A MATTER OF TIME   Brook Benton
5   TRAGEDY   Thomas Wayne
6   COME SOFTLY TO ME   Fleetwoods
7   STAGGER LEE   Lloyd Price
8   DONNA   Ritchie Valens
9   I'VE HAD IT   Bell Notes
10   HAWAIIAN WEDDING SONG   Andy Williams

April 4, 1959
1   VENUS   Frankie Avalon
2   CHARLIE BROWN   Coasters
3   COME SOFTLY TO ME   Fleetwoods
4   IT'S JUST A MATTER OF TIME   Brook Benton

5   ALVIN'S HARMONICA   Chipmunks
6   TRAGEDY   Thomas Wayne
7   NEVER BE ANYONE ELSE BUT YOU   Ricky Nelson
8   PINK SHOE LACES   Dodie Stevens
9   I'VE HAD IT   Bell Notes
10   HAWAIIAN WEDDING SONG   Andy Williams

April 11, 1959
1   VENUS   Frankie Avalon
2   COME SOFTLY TO ME   Fleetwoods
3   CHARLIE BROWN   Coasters
4   IT'S JUST A MATTER OF TIME   Brook Benton
5   PINK SHOE LACES   Dodie Stevens
6   NEVER BE ANYONE ELSE BUT YOU   Ricky Nelson
7   TRAGEDY   Thomas Wayne
8   ALVIN'S HARMONICA   Chipmunks
9   IT'S LATE   Ricky Nelson
10   HAWAIIAN WEDDING SONG   Andy Williams

April 18, 1959
1   COME SOFTLY TO ME   Fleetwoods
2   VENUS   Frankie Avalon
3   PINK SHOE LACES   Dodie Stevens
4   NEVER BE ANYONE ELSE BUT YOU   Ricky Nelson
5   IT'S JUST A MATTER OF TIME   Brook Benton
6   CHARLIE BROWN   Coasters
7   TRAGEDY   Thomas Wayne
8   I NEED YOUR LOVE TONIGHT   Elvis Presley
9   GUITAR BOOGIE SHUFFLE   Virtues
10   A FOOL SUCH AS I   Elvis Presley

April 25, 1959
1   COME SOFTLY TO ME   Fleetwoods
2   VENUS   Frankie Avalon
3   PINK SHOE LACES   Dodie Stevens
4   I NEED YOUR LOVE TONIGHT   Elvis Presley
5   NEVER BE ANYONE ELSE BUT YOU   Ricky Nelson
6   GUITAR BOOGIE SHUFFLE   Virtues
7   IT'S JUST A MATTER OF TIME   Brook Benton
8   A FOOL SUCH AS I   Elvis Presley
9   IT'S LATE   Ricky Nelson
10   TRAGEDY   Thomas Wayne

May 2, 1959
1   COME SOFTLY TO ME   Fleetwoods
2   VENUS   Frankie Avalon
3   PINK SHOE LACES   Dodie Stevens
4   A FOOL SUCH AS I   Elvis Presley
5   GUITAR BOOGIE SHUFFLE   Virtues
6   I NEED YOUR LOVE TONIGHT   Elvis Presley
7   HAPPY ORGAN   Dave "Baby" Cortez
8   TELL HIM NO   Travis & Bob
9   SORRY (I RAN ALL THE WAY HOME)   Impalas
10   NEVER BE ANYONE ELSE BUT YOU   Ricky Nelson

May 9, 1959
1   COME SOFTLY TO ME   Fleetwoods
2   PINK SHOE LACES   Dodie Stevens
3   GUITAR BOOGIE SHUFFLE   Virtues
4   HAPPY ORGAN   Dave "Baby" Cortez
5   SORRY (I RAN ALL THE WAY HOME)   Impalas
6   VENUS   Frankie Avalon
7   A FOOL SUCH AS I   Elvis Presley
8   I NEED YOUR LOVE TONIGHT   Elvis Presley
9   TELL HIM NO   Travis & Bob
10   TURN ME LOOSE   Fabian

Dodie Stevens

One day short of her thirteenth birthday, Dodie Stevens enters the Top 10 with "Pink Shoe Laces."

May 16, 1959
1. COME SOFTLY TO ME   Fleetwoods
2. HAPPY ORGAN   Dave "Baby" Cortez
3. PINK SHOE LACES   Dodie Stevens
4. GUITAR BOOGIE SHUFFLE   Virtues
5. SORRY (I RAN ALL THE WAY HOME)   Impalas
6. KOOKIE, KOOKIE (LEND ME YOUR COMB)   Ed Byrnes & Connie Stevens
7. KANSAS CITY   Wilbert Harrison
8. A FOOL SUCH AS I   Elvis Presley
9. TURN ME LOOSE   Fabian
10. TEENAGER IN LOVE   Dion & The Belmonts

May 23, 1959
1. KANSAS CITY   Wilbert Harrison
2. HAPPY ORGAN   Dave "Baby" Cortez
3. KOOKIE, KOOKIE (LEND ME YOUR COMB)   Ed Byrnes & Connie Stevens
4. TEENAGER IN LOVE   Dion & The Belmonts
5. SORRY (I RAN ALL THE WAY HOME)   Impalas
6. DREAM LOVER   Bobby Darin
7. PINK SHOE LACES   Dodie Stevens
8. COME SOFTLY TO ME   Fleetwoods
9. GUITAR BOOGIE SHUFFLE   Virtues
10. QUIET VILLAGE   Martin Denny

May 30, 1959
1. KANSAS CITY   Wilbert Harrison
2. HAPPY ORGAN   Dave "Baby" Cortez

3. THE BATTLE OF NEW ORLEANS   Johnny Horton
4. DREAM LOVER   Bobby Darin
5. TEENAGER IN LOVE   Dion & The Belmonts
6. QUIET VILLAGE   Martin Denny
7. KOOKIE, KOOKIE (LEND ME YOUR COMB)   Ed Byrnes & Connie Stevens
8. SORRY (I RAN ALL THE WAY HOME)   Impalas
9. PERSONALITY   Lloyd Price
10. GUITAR BOOGIE SHUFFLE   Virtues

June 6, 1959
1. THE BATTLE OF NEW ORLEANS   Johnny Horton
2. KANSAS CITY   Wilbert Harrison
3. DREAM LOVER   Bobby Darin
4. QUIET VILLAGE   Martin Denny
5. PERSONALITY   Lloyd Price
6. HAPPY ORGAN   Dave "Baby" Cortez
7. TEENAGER IN LOVE   Dion & The Belmonts
8. KOOKIE, KOOKIE (LEND ME YOUR COMB)   Ed Byrnes & Connie Stevens
9. SORRY (I RAN ALL THE WAY HOME)   Impalas
10. ONLY YOU   Franck Pourcel's French Fiddles

June 13, 1959
1. THE BATTLE OF NEW ORLEANS   Johnny Horton
2. QUIET VILLAGE   Martin Denny
3. KANSAS CITY   Wilbert Harrison
4. DREAM LOVER   Bobby Darin
5. PERSONALITY   Lloyd Price
6. TEENAGER IN LOVE   Dion & The Belmonts
7. HAPPY ORGAN   Dave "Baby" Cortez
8. KOOKIE, KOOKIE (LEND ME YOUR COMB)   Ed Byrnes & Connie Stevens
9. SORRY (I RAN ALL THE WAY HOME)   Impalas
10. ONLY YOU   Franck Pourcel's French Fiddles

June 20, 1959
1. THE BATTLE OF NEW ORLEANS   Johnny Horton
2. PERSONALITY   Lloyd Price
3. QUIET VILLAGE   Martin Denny
4. DREAM LOVER   Bobby Darin
5. KANSAS CITY   Wilbert Harrison
6. TEENAGER IN LOVE   Dion & The Belmonts
7. TALLAHASSEE LASSIE   Freddy Cannon
8. HAPPY ORGAN   Dave "Baby" Cortez
9. LONELY BOY   Paul Anka
10. KOOKIE, KOOKIE (LEND ME YOUR COMB)   Ed Byrnes & Connie Stevens

June 27, 1959
1. THE BATTLE OF NEW ORLEANS   Johnny Horton
2. PERSONALITY   Lloyd Price
3. DREAM LOVER   Bobby Darin
4. KANSAS CITY   Wilbert Harrison
5. QUIET VILLAGE   Martin Denny
6. LONELY BOY   Paul Anka
7. TALLAHASSEE LASSIE   Freddy Cannon
8. TEENAGER IN LOVE   Dion & The Belmonts
9. ALONG CAME JONES   Coasters
10. LIPSTICK ON YOUR COLLAR   Connie Francis

July 4, 1959
1. THE BATTLE OF NEW ORLEANS   Johnny Horton
2. PERSONALITY   Lloyd Price
3. LONELY BOY   Paul Anka
4. DREAM LOVER   Bobby Darin

5 QUIET VILLAGE   Martin Denny
6 KANSAS CITY   Wilbert Harrison
7 TALLAHASSEE LASSIE   Freddy Cannon
8 LIPSTICK ON YOUR COLLAR   Connie Francis
9 TEENAGER IN LOVE   Dion & The Belmonts
10 ALONG CAME JONES   Coasters

July 11, 1959
1 THE BATTLE OF NEW ORLEANS   Johnny Horton
2 PERSONALITY   Lloyd Price
3 LONELY BOY   Paul Anka
4 DREAM LOVER   Bobby Darin
5 LIPSTICK ON YOUR COLLAR   Connie Francis
6 TALLAHASSEE LASSIE   Freddy Cannon
7 WATERLOO   Stonewall Jackson
8 QUIET VILLAGE   Martin Denny
9 KANSAS CITY   Wilbert Harrison
10 FRANKIE   Connie Francis

July 18, 1959
1 THE BATTLE OF NEW ORLEANS   Johnny Horton
2 LONELY BOY   Paul Anka
3 PERSONALITY   Lloyd Price
4 WATERLOO   Stonewall Jackson
5 LIPSTICK ON YOUR COLLAR   Connie Francis
6 DREAM LOVER   Bobby Darin
7 TIGER   Fabian
8 TALLAHASSEE LASSIE   Freddy Cannon
9 MY HEART IS AN OPEN BOOK   Carl Dobkins, Jr.
10 QUIET VILLAGE   Martin Denny

July 25, 1959
1 THE BATTLE OF NEW ORLEANS   Johnny Horton
2 LONELY BOY   Paul Anka
3 PERSONALITY   Lloyd Price
4 WATERLOO   Stonewall Jackson
5 TIGER   Fabian
6 LIPSTICK ON YOUR COLLAR   Connie Francis
7 MY HEART IS AN OPEN BOOK   Carl Dobkins, Jr.
8 DREAM LOVER   Bobby Darin
9 TALLAHASSEE LASSIE   Freddy Cannon
10 A BIG HUNK O' LOVE   Elvis Presley

August 1, 1959
1 THE BATTLE OF NEW ORLEANS   Johnny Horton
2 LONELY BOY   Paul Anka
3 WATERLOO   Stonewall Jackson
4 TIGER   Fabian
5 PERSONALITY   Lloyd Price
6 LIPSTICK ON YOUR COLLAR   Connie Francis
7 MY HEART IS AN OPEN BOOK   Carl Dobkins, Jr.
8 A BIG HUNK O' LOVE   Elvis Presley
9 THERE GOES MY BABY   Drifters
10 FORTY MILES OF BAD ROAD   Duane Eddy

August 8, 1959
1 THE BATTLE OF NEW ORLEANS   Johnny Horton
2 LONELY BOY   Paul Anka
3 MY HEART IS AN OPEN BOOK   Carl Dobkins, Jr.
4 A BIG HUNK O' LOVE   Elvis Presley
5 WATERLOO   Stonewall Jackson
6 TIGER   Fabian
7 THERE GOES MY BABY   Drifters
8 LIPSTICK ON YOUR COLLAR   Connie Francis
9 FORTY MILES OF BAD ROAD   Duane Eddy
10 PERSONALITY   Lloyd Price

August 15, 1959
1 LONELY BOY   Paul Anka
2 THE BATTLE OF NEW ORLEANS   Johnny Horton
3 A BIG HUNK O' LOVE   Elvis Presley
4 MY HEART IS AN OPEN BOOK   Carl Dobkins, Jr.
5 THERE GOES MY BABY   Drifters
6 TIGER   Fabian
7 WATERLOO   Stonewall Jackson
8 LAVENDER BLUE   Sammy Turner
9 SEA OF LOVE   Phil Phillips with The Twilights
10 FORTY MILES OF BAD ROAD   Duane Eddy

August 22, 1959
1 A BIG HUNK O' LOVE   Elvis Presley
2 THERE GOES MY BABY   Drifters
3 MY HEART IS AN OPEN BOOK   Carl Dobkins, Jr.
4 LONELY BOY   Paul Anka
5 THE BATTLE OF NEW ORLEANS   Johnny Horton
6 WHAT'D I SAY   Ray Charles
7 THE THREE BELLS   Browns
8 LAVENDER BLUE   Sammy Turner
9 WHAT A DIFF'RENCE A DAY MAKES   Dinah Washington
10 WATERLOO   Stonewall Jackson

August 29, 1959
1 THE THREE BELLS   Browns
2 SEA OF LOVE   Phil Phillips with The Twilights
3 MY HEART IS AN OPEN BOOK   Carl Dobkins, Jr.
4 A BIG HUNK O' LOVE   Elvis Presley
5 THERE GOES MY BABY   Drifters

Fabian
Fabian hits the charts with ``Tiger.'' He is the first teen idol with
no singing or acting background to enter the Top 10.

6 LAVENDER BLUE Sammy Turner
7 WHAT'D I SAY Ray Charles
8 SLEEP WALK Santo & Johnny
9 LONELY BOY Paul Anka
10 THE BATTLE OF NEW ORLEANS Johnny Horton

September 5, 1959
1 THE THREE BELLS Browns
2 SEA OF LOVE Phil Phillips with The Twilights
3 SLEEP WALK Santo & Johnny
4 LAVENDER BLUE Sammy Turner
5 I'M GONNA GET MARRIED Lloyd Price
6 THERE GOES MY BABY Drifters
7 A BIG HUNK O' LOVE Elvis Presley
8 WHAT'D I SAY Ray Charles
9 MY HEART IS AN OPEN BOOK Carl Dobkins, Jr.
10 RED RIVER ROCK Johnny & The Hurricanes

September 12, 1959
1 THE THREE BELLS Browns
2 SLEEP WALK Santo & Johnny
3 SEA OF LOVE Phil Phillips with The Twilights
4 I'M GONNA GET MARRIED Lloyd Price
5 BROKEN-HEARTED MELODY Sarah Vaughn
6 RED RIVER ROCK Johnny & The Hurricanes
7 LAVENDER BLUE Sammy Turner
8 (TILL) I KISSED YOU Everly Brothers
9 WHAT'D I SAY Ray Charles
10 THERE GOES MY BABY Drifters

September 19, 1959
1 THE THREE BELLS Browns
2 SLEEP WALK Santo & Johnny
3 SEA OF LOVE Phil Phillips with The Twilights
4 I'M GONNA GET MARRIED Lloyd Price
5 (TILL) I KISSED YOU Everly Brothers
6 BROKEN-HEARTED MELODY Sarah Vaughn
7 RED RIVER ROCK Johnny & The Hurricanes
8 I WANT TO WALK YOU HOME Fats Domino
9 MACK THE KNIFE Bobby Darin
10 LAVENDER BLUE Sammy Turner

September 26, 1959
1 THE THREE BELLS Browns
2 SLEEP WALK Santo & Johnny
3 I'M GONNA GET MARRIED Lloyd Price
4 SEA OF LOVE Phil Phillips with The Twilights
5 (TILL) I KISSED YOU Everly Brothers
6 MACK THE KNIFE Bobby Darin
7 RED RIVER ROCK Johnny & The Hurricanes
8 BROKEN-HEARTED MELODY Sarah Vaughn
9 I WANT TO WALK YOU HOME Fats Domino
10 PUT YOUR HEAD ON MY SHOULDER Paul Anka

October 3, 1959
1 THE THREE BELLS Browns
2 SLEEP WALK Santo & Johnny
3 MACK THE KNIFE Bobby Darin
4 I'M GONNA GET MARRIED Lloyd Price
5 (TILL) I KISSED YOU Everly Brothers
6 SEA OF LOVE Phil Phillips with The Twilights
7 RED RIVER ROCK Johnny & The Hurricanes
8 PUT YOUR HEAD ON MY SHOULDER Paul Anka
9 BROKEN-HEARTED MELODY Sarah Vaughn
10 TEEN BEAT Sandy Nelson

October 10, 1959
1 MACK THE KNIFE Bobby Darin
2 THE THREE BELLS Browns
3 SLEEP WALK Santo & Johnny
4 (TILL) I KISSED YOU Everly Brothers
5 PUT YOUR HEAD ON MY SHOULDER Paul Anka
6 I'M GONNA GET MARRIED Lloyd Price
7 RED RIVER ROCK Johnny & The Hurricanes
8 MR. BLUE Fleetwoods
9 SEA OF LOVE Phil Phillips with The Twilights
10 TEEN BEAT Sandy Nelson

October 17, 1959
1 MACK THE KNIFE Bobby Darin
2 THE THREE BELLS Browns
3 SLEEP WALK Santo & Johnny
4 PUT YOUR HEAD ON MY SHOULDER Paul Anka
5 MR. BLUE Fleetwoods
6 (TILL) I KISSED YOU Everly Brothers
7 TEEN BEAT Sandy Nelson
8 I'M GONNA GET MARRIED Lloyd Price
9 RED RIVER ROCK Johnny & The Hurricanes
10 POISON IVY Coasters

October 24, 1959
1 MACK THE KNIFE Bobby Darin
2 PUT YOUR HEAD ON MY SHOULDER Paul Anka
3 MR. BLUE Fleetwoods
4 TEEN BEAT Sandy Nelson
5 THE THREE BELLS Browns
6 SLEEP WALK Santo & Johnny
7 (TILL) I KISSED YOU Everly Brothers
8 POISON IVY Coasters
9 LONELY STREET Andy Williams
10 JUST ASK YOUR HEART Frankie Avalon

October 31, 1959
1 MACK THE KNIFE Bobby Darin
2 MR. BLUE Fleetwoods
3 PUT YOUR HEAD ON MY SHOULDER Paul Anka
4 TEEN BEAT Sandy Nelson
5 DON'T YOU KNOW Della Reese
6 LONELY STREET Andy Williams
7 PRIMROSE LANE Jerry Wallace
8 DECK OF CARDS Wink Martindale
9 JUST ASK YOUR HEART Frankie Avalon
10 (TILL) I KISSED YOU Everly Brothers

November 7, 1959
1 MACK THE KNIFE Bobby Darin
2 MR. BLUE Fleetwoods
3 PUT YOUR HEAD ON MY SHOULDER Paul Anka
4 DON'T YOU KNOW Della Reese
5 TEEN BEAT Sandy Nelson
6 DECK OF CARDS Wink Martindale
7 LONELY STREET Andy Williams
8 PRIMROSE LANE Jerry Wallace
9 (TILL) I KISSED YOU Everly Brothers
10 JUST ASK YOUR HEART Frankie Avalon

November 14, 1959
1 MACK THE KNIFE Bobby Darin
2 MR. BLUE Fleetwoods
3 PUT YOUR HEAD ON MY SHOULDER Paul Anka
4 DON'T YOU KNOW Della Reese
5 DECK OF CARDS Wink Martindale

6 LONELY STREET Andy Williams
7 PRIMROSE LANE Jerry Wallace
8 TEEN BEAT Sandy Nelson
9 POISON IVY Coasters
10 SEVEN LITTLE GIRLS SITTING IN THE BACK SEAT Paul Evans

November 21, 1959
1 MACK THE KNIFE Bobby Darin
2 MR. BLUE Fleetwoods
3 DON'T YOU KNOW Della Reese
4 PUT YOUR HEAD ON MY SHOULDER Paul Anka
5 LONELY STREET Andy Williams
6 PRIMROSE LANE Jerry Wallace
7 DECK OF CARDS Wink Martindale
8 TEEN BEAT Sandy Nelson
9 HEARTACHES BY THE NUMBER Guy Mitchell
10 SO MANY WAYS Brook Benton

November 28, 1959
1 MACK THE KNIFE Bobby Darin
2 MR. BLUE Fleetwoods
3 DON'T YOU KNOW Della Reese
4 PUT YOUR HEAD ON MY SHOULDER Paul Anka
5 HEARTACHES BY THE NUMBER Guy Mitchell
6 DECK OF CARDS Wink Martindale
7 PRIMROSE LANE Jerry Wallace
8 LONELY STREET Andy Williams
9 SO MANY WAYS Brook Benton
10 IN THE MOOD Ernie Fields

December 5, 1959
1 MACK THE KNIFE Bobby Darin
2 MR. BLUE Fleetwoods
3 DON'T YOU KNOW Della Reese
4 HEARTACHES BY THE NUMBER Guy Mitchell
5 PUT YOUR HEAD ON MY SHOULDER Paul Anka
6 MISTY Johnny Mathis
7 SO MANY WAYS Brook Benton
8 IN THE MOOD Ernie Fields

9 PRIMROSE LANE Jerry Wallace
10 SEVEN LITTLE GIRLS SITTING IN THE BACK SEAT Paul Evans

December 12, 1959
1 MACK THE KNIFE Bobby Darin
2 MR. BLUE Fleetwoods
3 HEARTACHES BY THE NUMBER Guy Mitchell
4 DON'T YOU KNOW Della Reese
5 IN THE MOOD Ernie Fields
6 WE GOT LOVE Bobby Rydell
7 PUT YOUR HEAD ON MY SHOULDER Paul Anka
8 SO MANY WAYS Brook Benton
9 MISTY Johnny Mathis
10 OH CAROL Neil Sedaka

December 19, 1959
1 HEARTACHES BY THE NUMBER Guy Mitchell
2 MACK THE KNIFE Bobby Darin
3 MR. BLUE Fleetwoods
4 DON'T YOU KNOW Della Reese
5 IN THE MOOD Ernie Fields
6 WHY Frankie Avalon
7 WE GOT LOVE Bobby Rydell
8 SO MANY WAYS Brook Benton
9 MISTY Johnny Mathis
10 EL PASO Marty Robbins

December 26, 1959
1 MACK THE KNIFE Bobby Darin
2 HEARTACHES BY THE NUMBER Guy Mitchell
3 WHY Frankie Avalon
4 EL PASO Marty Robbins
5 MR. BLUE Fleetwoods
6 THE BIG HURT Miss Toni Fisher
7 WAY DOWN YONDER IN NEW ORLEANS Freddy Cannon
8 IT'S TIME TO CRY Paul Anka
9 DON'T YOU KNOW Della Reese
10 WE GOT LOVE Bobby Rydell

Frankie Avalon
Frankie starts the sixties off with its first #1 hit, ``Why,'' first recorded at X Records when he was eleven years old.

The Sixties

January 1, 1960
1. WHY   Frankie Avalon
2. HEARTACHES BY THE NUMBER   Guy Mitchell
3. MACK THE KNIFE   Bobby Darin
4. EL PASO   Marty Robbins
5. THE BIG HURT   Miss Toni Fisher
6. WAY DOWN YONDER IN NEW ORLEANS   Freddy Cannon
7. IT'S TIME TO CRY   Paul Anka
8. AMONG MY SOUVENIRS   Connie Francis
9. MR. BLUE   Fleetwoods
10. PRETTY BLUE EYES   Steve Lawrence

January 8, 1960
1. WHY   Frankie Avalon
2. EL PASO   Marty Robbins
3. HEARTACHES BY THE NUMBER   Guy Mitchell
4. THE BIG HURT   Miss Toni Fisher
5. RUNNING BEAR   Johnny Preston
6. WAY DOWN YONDER IN NEW ORLEANS   Freddy Cannon
7. MACK THE KNIFE   Bobby Darin
8. IT'S TIME TO CRY   Paul Anka
9. AMONG MY SOUVENIRS   Connie Francis
10. UH! OH! (PART II)   Nutty Squirrels

January 15, 1960
1. WHY   Frankie Avalon
2. EL PASO   Marty Robbins
3. RUNNING BEAR   Johnny Preston
4. WAY DOWN YONDER IN NEW ORLEANS   Freddy Cannon
5. THE BIG HURT   Miss Toni Fisher
6. IT'S TIME TO CRY   Paul Anka
7. HEARTACHES BY THE NUMBER   Guy Mitchell
8. MACK THE KNIFE   Bobby Darin
9. AMONG MY SOUVENIRS   Connie Francis
10. PRETTY BLUE EYES   Steve Lawrence

January 22, 1960
1. WHY   Frankie Avalon
2. EL PASO   Marty Robbins
3. RUNNING BEAR   Johnny Preston
4. THE BIG HURT   Miss Toni Fisher
5. WAY DOWN YONDER IN NEW ORLEANS   Freddy Cannon
6. AMONG MY SOUVENIRS   Connie Francis
7. IT'S TIME TO CRY   Paul Anka
8. HEARTACHES BY THE NUMBER   Guy Mitchell
9. GO, JIMMY, GO   Jimmy Clanton
10. TEEN ANGEL   Mark Dinning

January 29, 1960
1. RUNNING BEAR   Johnny Preston
2. EL PASO   Marty Robbins
3. WHY   Frankie Avalon
4. TEEN ANGEL   Mark Dinning
5. WAY DOWN YONDER IN NEW ORLEANS   Freddy Cannon
6. THE BIG HURT   Miss Toni Fisher
7. THE VILLAGE OF ST. BERNADETTE   Andy Williams
8. PRETTY BLUE EYES   Steve Lawrence
9. GO, JIMMY, GO   Jimmy Clanton
10. AMONG MY SOUVENIRS   Connie Francis

February 5, 1960
1. RUNNING BEAR   Johnny Preston
2. EL PASO   Marty Robbins
3. TEEN ANGEL   Mark Dinning
4. WHY   Frankie Avalon
5. GO, JIMMY, GO   Jimmy Clanton
6. WHERE OR WHEN   Dion & The Belmonts
7. WAY DOWN YONDER IN NEW ORLEANS   Freddy Cannon
8. THE BIG HURT   Miss Toni Fisher
9. THE VILLAGE OF ST. BERNADETTE   Andy Williams
10. PRETTY BLUE EYES   Steve Lawrence

February 12, 1960
1. RUNNING BEAR   Johnny Preston
2. TEEN ANGEL   Mark Dinning
3. EL PASO   Marty Robbins
4. WHY   Frankie Avalon
5. WHERE OR WHEN   Dion & The Belmonts
6. GO, JIMMY, GO   Jimmy Clanton
7. HANDY MAN   Jimmy Jones
8. YOU GOT WHAT IT TAKES   Marv Johnson
9. PRETTY BLUE EYES   Steve Lawrence
10. LONELY BLUE BOY   Conway Twitty

February 19, 1960
1. TEEN ANGEL   Mark Dinning
2. RUNNING BEAR   Johnny Preston
3. EL PASO   Marty Robbins
4. THEME FROM "A SUMMER PLACE"   Percy Faith
5. HANDY MAN   Jimmy Jones
6. WHERE OR WHEN   Dion & The Belmonts
7. HE'LL HAVE TO GO   Jim Reeves
8. WHY   Frankie Avalon
9. WHAT IN THE WORLD'S COME OVER YOU   Jack Scott
10. LONELY BLUE BOY   Conway Twitty

February 26, 1960
1. TEEN ANGEL   Mark Dinning
2. RUNNING BEAR   Johnny Preston
3. THEME FROM "A SUMMER PLACE"   Percy Faith
4. HANDY MAN   Jimmy Jones
5. HE'LL HAVE TO GO   Jim Reeves
6. WHAT IN THE WORLD'S COME OVER YOU   Jack Scott
7. WHERE OR WHEN   Dion & The Belmonts
8. LET IT BE ME   Everly Brothers
9. EL PASO   Marty Robbins
10. BEYOND THE SEA   Bobby Darin

March 4, 1960
1. THEME FROM "A SUMMER PLACE"   Percy Faith
2. TEEN ANGEL   Mark Dinning
3. HANDY MAN   Jimmy Jones
4. HE'LL HAVE TO GO   Jim Reeves
5. RUNNING BEAR   Johnny Preston
6. WHAT IN THE WORLD'S COME OVER YOU   Jack Scott
7. BEYOND THE SEA   Bobby Darin
8. WHERE OR WHEN   Dion & The Belmonts
9. LET IT BE ME   Everly Brothers
10. WILD ONE   Bobby Rydell

Mark Dinning
Dinning sent rock's first ``tragedy'' song to #1 (Feb. 19).
(Mark himself died March 22, 1986.)

March 11, 1960
1   THEME FROM "A SUMMER PLACE"   Percy Faith
2   HE'LL HAVE TO GO   Jim Reeves
3   TEEN ANGEL   Mark Dinning
4   HANDY MAN   Jimmy Jones
5   WHAT IN THE WORLD'S COME OVER YOU   Jack Scott
6   WILD ONE   Bobby Rydell
7   RUNNING BEAR   Johnny Preston
8   BEYOND THE SEA   Bobby Darin
9   LET IT BE ME   Everly Brothers
10 BABY   Brook Benton & Dinah Washington

March 18, 1960
1   THEME FROM "A SUMMER PLACE"   Percy Faith
2   HE'LL HAVE TO GO   Jim Reeves
3   WILD ONE   Bobby Rydell
4   HANDY MAN   Jimmy Jones
5   TEEN ANGEL   Mark Dinning
6   WHAT IN THE WORLD'S COME OVER YOU   Jack Scott
7   BEYOND THE SEA   Bobby Darin
8   BABY   Brook Benton & Dinah Washington
9   RUNNING BEAR   Johnny Preston
10 LET IT BE ME   Everly Brothers

March 25, 1960
1   THEME FROM "A SUMMER PLACE"   Percy Faith
2   HE'LL HAVE TO GO   Jim Reeves
3   WILD ONE   Bobby Rydell
4   HANDY MAN   Jimmy Jones
5   WHAT IN THE WORLD'S COME OVER YOU   Jack Scott
6   PUPPY LOVE   Paul Anka
7   TEEN ANGEL   Mark Dinning

8   BEYOND THE SEA   Bobby Darin
9   BABY   Brook Benton & Dinah Washington
10 SWEET NOTHIN'S   Brenda Lee

April 1, 1960
1   THEME FROM "A SUMMER PLACE"   Percy Faith
2   HE'LL HAVE TO GO   Jim Reeves
3   WILD ONE   Bobby Rydell
4   PUPPY LOVE   Paul Anka
5   SWEET NOTHIN'S   Brenda Lee
6   HANDY MAN   Jimmy Jones
7   BABY   Brook Benton & Dinah Washington
8   BEYOND THE SEA   Bobby Darin
9   HARBOR LIGHTS   The Platters
10 MAMA   Connie Francis

April 8, 1960
1   THEME FROM "A SUMMER PLACE"   Percy Faith
2   HE'LL HAVE TO GO   Jim Reeves
3   WILD ONE   Bobby Rydell
4   PUPPY LOVE   Paul Anka
5   SWEET NOTHIN'S   Brenda Lee
6   HANDY MAN   Jimmy Jones
7   SINK THE BISMARCK   Johnny Horton
8   HARBOR LIGHTS   The Platters
9   MAMA   Connie Francis
10 BABY   Brook Benton & Dinah Washington

April 15, 1960
1   THEME FROM "A SUMMER PLACE"   Percy Faith
2   HE'LL HAVE TO GO   Jim Reeves
3   WILD ONE   Bobby Rydell

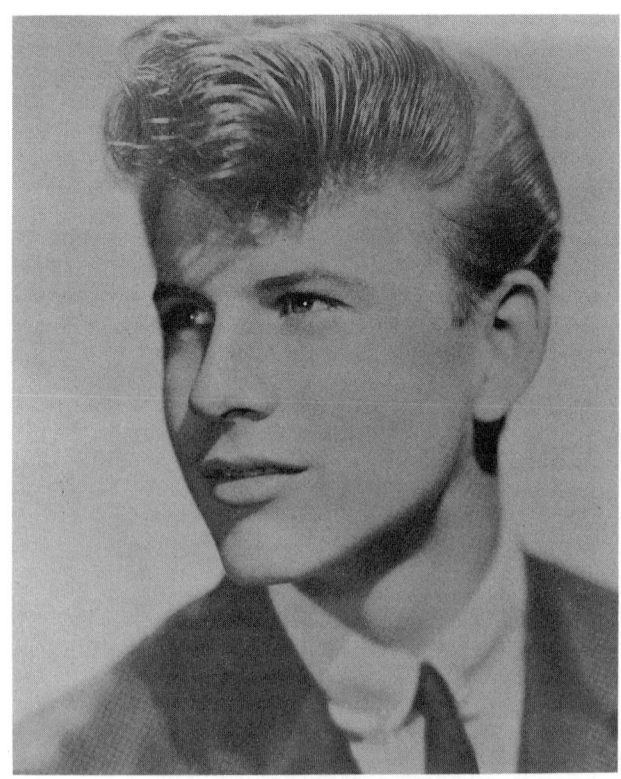

Bobby Rydell
``Wild One,'' Bobby's biggest record, peaked at #3.

4   PUPPY LOVE   Paul Anka
5   SWEET NOTHIN'S   Brenda Lee
6   SINK THE BISMARCK   Johnny Horton
7   MAMA   Connie Francis
8   GREENFIELDS   Brothers Four
9   I LOVE THE WAY YOU LOVE   Marv Johnson
10 HANDY MAN   Jimmy Jones

April 22, 1960
1   THEME FROM "A SUMMER PLACE"   Percy Faith
2   HE'LL HAVE TO GO   Jim Reeves
3   WILD ONE   Bobby Rydell
4   GREENFIELDS   Brothers Four
5   SWEET NOTHIN'S   Brenda Lee
6   PUPPY LOVE   Paul Anka
7   SINK THE BISMARCK   Johnny Horton
8   STUCK ON YOU   Elvis Presley
9   MAMA   Connie Francis
10 FOOTSTEPS   Steve Lawrence

April 29, 1960
1   STUCK ON YOU   Elvis Presley
2   THEME FROM "A SUMMER PLACE"   Percy Faith
3   GREENFIELDS   Brothers Four
4   HE'LL HAVE TO GO   Jim Reeves
5   SINK THE BISMARCK   Johnny Horton
6   SIXTEEN REASONS   Connie Stevens
7   SWEET NOTHIN'S   Brenda Lee
8   PUPPY LOVE   Paul Anka
9   WILD ONE   Bobby Rydell
10 NIGHT   Jackie Wilson

May 6, 1960
1   STUCK ON YOU   Elvis Presley
2   GREENFIELDS   Brothers Four
3   THEME FROM "A SUMMER PLACE"   Percy Faith
4   SIXTEEN REASONS   Connie Stevens
5   HE'LL HAVE TO GO   Jim Reeves
6   SINK THE BISMARCK   Johnny Horton
7   NIGHT   Jackie Wilson
8   THE OLD LAMPLIGHTER   Browns
9   SWEET NOTHIN'S   Brenda Lee
10 WHITE SILVER SANDS   Bill Black's Combo

May 13, 1960
1   STUCK ON YOU   Elvis Presley
2   GREENFIELDS   Brothers Four
3   SIXTEEN REASONS   Connie Stevens
4   THEME FROM "A SUMMER PLACE"   Percy Faith
5   NIGHT   Jackie Wilson
6   THE OLD LAMPLIGHTER   Browns
7   CATHY'S CLOWN   Everly Brothers
8   SINK THE BISMARCK   Johnny Horton
9   LET THE LITTLE GIRL DANCE   Billy Bland
10 WHITE SILVER SANDS   Bill Black's Combo

May 20, 1960
1   STUCK ON YOU   Elvis Presley
2   CATHY'S CLOWN   Everly Brothers
3   GREENFIELDS   Brothers Four
4   SIXTEEN REASONS   Connie Stevens
5   NIGHT   Jackie Wilson
6   SINK THE BISMARCK   Johnny Horton
7   THE OLD LAMPLIGHTER   Browns
8   GOOD TIMIN'   Jimmy Jones
9   LET THE LITTLE GIRL DANCE   Billy Bland
10 CRADLE OF LOVE   Johnny Preston

May 27, 1960
1   CATHY'S CLOWN   Everly Brothers
2   STUCK ON YOU   Elvis Presley
3   GREENFIELDS   Brothers Four
4   SIXTEEN REASONS   Connie Stevens
5   SINK THE BISMARCK   Johnny Horton
6   GOOD TIMIN'   Jimmy Jones
7   NIGHT   Jackie Wilson
8   HE'LL HAVE TO STAY   Jeanne Black
9   LOVE YOU SO   Ron Holden
10 THE OLD LAMPLIGHTER   Browns

June 3, 1960
1   CATHY'S CLOWN   Everly Brothers
2   STUCK ON YOU   Elvis Presley
3   GREENFIELDS   Brothers Four
4   GOOD TIMIN'   Jimmy Jones
5   SIXTEEN REASONS   Connie Stevens
6   NIGHT   Jackie Wilson
7   HE'LL HAVE TO STAY   Jeanne Black
8   PAPER ROSES   Anita Bryant
9   SINK THE BISMARCK   Johnny Horton
10 BURNING BRIDGES   Jack Scott

June 10, 1960
1   CATHY'S CLOWN   Everly Brothers
2   STUCK ON YOU   Elvis Presley
3   GOOD TIMIN'   Jimmy Jones
4   HE'LL HAVE TO STAY   Jeanne Black
5   BURNING BRIDGES   Jack Scott
6   GREENFIELDS   Brothers Four
7   SIXTEEN REASONS   Connie Stevens
8   NIGHT   Jackie Wilson
9   PAPER ROSES   Anita Bryant
10 LOVE YOU SO   Ron Holden

June 17, 1960
1   CATHY'S CLOWN   Everly Brothers
2   STUCK ON YOU   Elvis Presley
3   GOOD TIMIN'   Jimmy Jones
4   EVERYBODY'S SOMEBODY'S FOOL   Connie Francis
5   BURNING BRIDGES   Jack Scott
6   PAPER ROSES   Anita Bryant
7   ALLEY-OOP   Hollywood Argyles
8   LOVE YOU SO   Ron Holden
9   HE'LL HAVE TO STAY   Jeanne Black
10 GREENFIELDS   Brothers Four

June 24, 1960
1   CATHY'S CLOWN   Everly Brothers
2   ALLEY-OOP   Hollywood Argyles
3   EVERYBODY'S SOMEBODY'S FOOL   Connie Francis
4   PAPER ROSES   Anita Bryant
5   GOOD TIMIN'   Jimmy Jones
6   BURNING BRIDGES   Jack Scott
7   STUCK ON YOU   Elvis Presley
8   HE'LL HAVE TO STAY   Jeanne Black
9   BECAUSE THEY'RE YOUNG   Duane Eddy
10 SWINGIN' SCHOOL   Bobby Rydell

July 1, 1960
1   CATHY'S CLOWN   Everly Brothers
2   ALLEY-OOP   Hollywood Argyles
3   EVERYBODY'S SOMEBODY'S FOOL   Connie Francis
4   PAPER ROSES   Anita Bryant
5   BECAUSE THEY'RE YOUNG   Duane Eddy

  6   BURNING BRIDGES   Jack Scott
  7   GOOD TIMIN'   Jimmy Jones
  8   A ROCKIN' GOOD WAY (TO MESS AROUND AND FALL IN
       LOVE)   Brook Benton & Dinah Washington
  9   STUCK ON YOU   Elvis Presley
10   I'M SORRY   Brenda Lee

July 8, 1960
  1   ALLEY-OOP   Hollywood Argyles
  2   CATHY'S CLOWN   Everly Brothers
  3   EVERYBODY'S SOMEBODY'S FOOL   Connie Francis
  4   BECAUSE THEY'RE YOUNG   Duane Eddy
  5   I'M SORRY   Brenda Lee
  6   PAPER ROSES   Anita Bryant
  7   MULE SKINNER BLUES   Fendermen
  8   BURNING BRIDGES   Jack Scott
  9   A ROCKIN' GOOD WAY (TO MESS AROUND AND FALL IN
       LOVE)   Brook Benton & Dinah Washington
10   THAT'S ALL YOU GOTTA DO   Brenda Lee

July 15, 1960
  1   ALLEY-OOP   Hollywood Argyles
  2   I'M SORRY   Brenda Lee
  3   EVERYBODY'S SOMEBODY'S FOOL   Connie Francis
  4   BECAUSE THEY'RE YOUNG   Duane Eddy
  5   MULE SKINNER BLUES   Fendermen
  6   CATHY'S CLOWN   Everly Brothers
  7   PAPER ROSES   Anita Bryant
  8   ONLY THE LONELY   Roy Orbison
  9   THAT'S ALL YOU GOTTA DO   Brenda Lee
10   BURNING BRIDGES   Jack Scott

July 22, 1960
  1   ALLEY-OOP   Hollywood Argyles
  2   I'M SORRY   Brenda Lee
  3   EVERYBODY'S SOMEBODY'S FOOL   Connie Francis
  4   BECAUSE THEY'RE YOUNG   Duane Eddy
  5   ONLY THE LONELY   Roy Orbison
  6   MULE SKINNER BLUES   Fendermen
  7   TELL LAURA I LOVE HER   Ray Peterson
  8   THAT'S ALL YOU GOTTA DO   Brenda Lee
  9   LOOK FOR A STAR   Garry Miles
10   CATHY'S CLOWN   Everly Brothers

July 29, 1960
  1   ALLEY-OOP   Hollywood Argyles
  2   I'M SORRY   Brenda Lee
  3   EVERYBODY'S SOMEBODY'S FOOL   Connie Francis
  4   ONLY THE LONELY   Roy Orbison
  5   BECAUSE THEY'RE YOUNG   Duane Eddy
  6   ITSY BITSY TEENIE WEENIE YELLOW POLKA DOT BIKINI
       Brian Hyland
  7   MULE SKINNER BLUES   Fendermen
  8   IMAGE OF A GIRL   Safaris
  9   LOOK FOR A STAR   Garry Miles
10   PLEASE HELP ME I'M FALLING   Hank Locklin

August 5, 1960
  1   ITSY BITSY TEENIE WEENIE YELLOW POLKA DOT BIKINI
       Brian Hyland
  2   I'M SORRY   Brenda Lee
  3   ALLEY-OOP   Hollywood Argyles
  4   ONLY THE LONELY   Roy Orbison
  5   IT'S NOW OR NEVER   Elvis Presley
  6   LOOK FOR A STAR   Garry Miles
  7   PLEASE HELP ME I'M FALLING   Hank Locklin
  8   MULE SKINNER BLUES   Fendermen

Brian Hyland
Brian, age 17, spends four weeks at #1 with
"Itsy Bitsy Teenie Weenie Yellow Polka Dot Bikini."

  9   IMAGE OF A GIRL   Safaris
10   TELL LAURA I LOVE HER   Ray Peterson

August 12, 1960
  1   ITSY BITSY TEENIE WEENIE YELLOW POLKA DOT BIKINI
       Brian Hyland
  2   I'M SORRY   Brenda Lee
  3   IT'S NOW OR NEVER   Elvis Presley
  4   ONLY THE LONELY   Roy Orbison
  5   ALLEY-OOP   Hollywood Argyles
  6   BECAUSE THEY'RE YOUNG   Duane Eddy
  7   PLEASE HELP ME I'M FALLING   Hank Locklin
  8   LOOK FOR A STAR   Garry Miles
  9   MULE SKINNER BLUES   Fendermen
10   TELL LAURA I LOVE HER   Ray Peterson

August 19, 1960
  1   ITSY BITSY TEENIE WEENIE YELLOW POLKA DOT BIKINI
       Brian Hyland
  2   IT'S NOW OR NEVER   Elvis Presley
  3   I'M SORRY   Brenda Lee
  4   ONLY THE LONELY   Roy Orbison
  5   ALLEY-OOP   Hollywood Argyles
  6   LOOK FOR A STAR   Garry Miles
  7   WALK DON'T RUN   Ventures
  8   TELL LAURA I LOVE HER   Ray Peterson
  9   IMAGE OF A GIRL   Safaris
10   PLEASE HELP ME I'M FALLING   Hank Locklin

August 26, 1960
  1   ITSY BITSY TEENIE WEENIE YELLOW POLKA DOT BIKINI
       Brian Hyland

2   IT'S NOW OR NEVER   Elvis Presley
3   I'M SORRY   Brenda Lee
4   TWIST   Chubby Checker *
5   WALK DON'T RUN   Ventures
6   ONLY THE LONELY   Roy Orbison
7   LOOK FOR A STAR   Garry Miles
8   VOLARE (NEL BLU DIPINTO DI BLU)   Bobby Rydell
9   PLEASE HELP ME I'M FALLING   Hank Locklin
10 FINGER POPPIN' TIME   Hank Ballard
   Note: * The only single to go to #1 twice, first in 1960 and
   again in January 1962.

September 2, 1960
1   IT'S NOW OR NEVER   Elvis Presley
2   ITSY BITSY TEENIE WEENIE YELLOW POLKA DOT BIKINI
    Brian Hyland
3   TWIST   Chubby Checker *
4   WALK DON'T RUN   Ventures
5   I'M SORRY   Brenda Lee
6   VOLARE (NEL BLU DIPINTO DI BLU)   Bobby Rydell
7   ONLY THE LONELY   Roy Orbison
8   MISSION BELLS   Donnie Brooks
9   FINGER POPPIN' TIME   Hank Ballard
10 LOOK FOR A STAR   Garry Miles
   Note: * The only single to go to #1 twice, first in 1960 and
   again in January 1962.

September 9, 1960
1   IT'S NOW OR NEVER   Elvis Presley
2   TWIST   Chubby Checker *
3   WALK DON'T RUN   Ventures
4   ITSY BITSY TEENIE WEENIE YELLOW POLKA DOT BIKINI
    Brian Hyland
5   VOLARE (NEL BLU DIPINTO DI BLU)   Bobby Rydell
6   I'M SORRY   Brenda Lee
7   THEME FROM "THE APARTMENT"   Ferrante & Teicher
8   MISSION BELLS   Donnie Brooks
9   FINGER POPPIN' TIME   Hank Ballard
10 ONLY THE LONELY   Roy Orbison
   Note: * The only single to go to #1 twice, first in 1960 and
   again in January 1962.

September 16, 1960
1   TWIST   Chubby Checker *
2   IT'S NOW OR NEVER   Elvis Presley
3   MY HEART HAS A MIND OF ITS OWN   Connie Francis
4   WALK DON'T RUN   Ventures
5   ITSY BITSY TEENIE WEENIE YELLOW POLKA DOT BIKINI
    Brian Hyland
6   VOLARE (NEL BLU DIPINTO DI BLU)   Bobby Rydell
7   THEME FROM "THE APARTMENT"   Ferrante & Teicher
8   MR. CUSTER   Larry Verne
9   CHAIN GANG   Sam Cooke
10 A MILLION TO ONE   Jimmy Charles
   Note: * The only single to go to #1 twice, first in 1960 and
   again in January 1962.

September 23, 1960
1   TWIST   Chubby Checker *
2   IT'S NOW OR NEVER   Elvis Presley
3   WALK DON'T RUN   Ventures
4   MY HEART HAS A MIND OF ITS OWN   Connie Francis
5   MR. CUSTER   Larry Verne
6   THEME FROM "THE APARTMENT"   Ferrante & Teicher
7   VOLARE (NEL BLU DIPINTO DI BLU)   Bobby Rydell
8   CHAIN GANG   Sam Cooke
9   A MILLION TO ONE   Jimmy Charles

10 YOGI   Ivy Three
   Note: * The only single to go to #1 twice, first in 1960 and
   again in January 1962.

September 30, 1960
1   TWIST   Chubby Checker *
2   IT'S NOW OR NEVER   Elvis Presley
3   MY HEART HAS A MIND OF ITS OWN   Connie Francis
4   MR. CUSTER   Larry Verne
5   CHAIN GANG   Sam Cooke
6   A MILLION TO ONE   Jimmy Charles
7   WALK DON'T RUN   Ventures
8   THEME FROM "THE APARTMENT"   Ferrante & Teicher
9   KIDDIO   Brook Benton
10 VOLARE (NEL BLU DIPINTO DI BLU)   Bobby Rydell
   Note: * The only single to go to #1 twice, first in 1960 and
   again in January 1962.

October 7, 1960
1   MY HEART HAS A MIND OF ITS OWN   Connie Francis
2   MR. CUSTER   Larry Verne
3   IT'S NOW OR NEVER   Elvis Presley
4   CHAIN GANG   Sam Cooke
5   TWIST   Chubby Checker *
6   THEME FROM "THE APARTMENT"   Ferrante & Teicher
7   A MILLION TO ONE   Jimmy Charles
8   WALK DON'T RUN   Ventures
9   SO SAD (TO WATCH A GOOD LOVE GO BAD)   Everly
    Brothers
10 SAVE THE LAST DANCE FOR ME   Drifters
   Note: * The only single to go to #1 twice, first in 1960 and
   again in January 1962.

Chubby Checker
Chubby's ``The Twist'' is the only record to hit #1 twice in
separate years, excluding only ``White Christmas.''

October 14, 1960
1 MR. CUSTER   Larry Verne
2 MY HEART HAS A MIND OF ITS OWN   Connie Francis
3 CHAIN GANG   Sam Cooke
4 TWIST   Chubby Checker *
5 IT'S NOW OR NEVER   Elvis Presley
6 SAVE THE LAST DANCE FOR ME   Drifters
7 A MILLION TO ONE   Jimmy Charles
8 THEME FROM "THE APARTMENT"   Ferrante & Teicher
9 WALK DON'T RUN   Ventures
10 SO SAD (TO WATCH A GOOD LOVE GO BAD)   Everly Brothers
   Note: * The only single to go to #1 twice, first in 1960 and again in January 1962.

October 21, 1960
1 MY HEART HAS A MIND OF ITS OWN   Connie Francis
2 TWIST   Chubby Checker *
3 SAVE THE LAST DANCE FOR ME   Drifters
4 CHAIN GANG   Sam Cooke
5 MR. CUSTER   Larry Verne
6 DEVIL OR ANGEL   Bobby Vee
7 IT'S NOW OR NEVER   Elvis Presley
8 I WANT TO BE WANTED   Brenda Lee
9 A MILLION TO ONE   Jimmy Charles
10 THEME FROM "THE APARTMENT"   Ferrante & Teicher
   Note: * The only single to go to #1 twice, first in 1960 and again in January 1962.

October 28, 1960
1 TWIST   Chubby Checker *
2 I WANT TO BE WANTED   Brenda Lee
3 SAVE THE LAST DANCE FOR ME   Drifters
4 MY HEART HAS A MIND OF ITS OWN   Connie Francis
5 CHAIN GANG   Sam Cooke
6 THEME FROM "THE APARTMENT"   Ferrante & Teicher
7 MR. CUSTER   Larry Verne
8 DEVIL OR ANGEL   Bobby Vee
9 IT'S NOW OR NEVER   Elvis Presley
10 SO SAD (TO WATCH A GOOD LOVE GO BAD)   Everly Brothers
   Note: * The only single to go to #1 twice, first in 1960 and again in January 1962.

November 4, 1960
1 SAVE THE LAST DANCE FOR ME   Drifters
2 I WANT TO BE WANTED   Brenda Lee
3 MY HEART HAS A MIND OF ITS OWN   Connie Francis
4 TWIST   Chubby Checker *
5 THEME FROM "THE APARTMENT"   Ferrante & Teicher
6 CHAIN GANG   Sam Cooke
7 POETRY IN MOTION   Johnny Tillotson
8 LET'S THINK ABOUT LIVIN'   Bob Luman
9 MR. CUSTER   Larry Verne
10 DEVIL OR ANGEL   Bobby Vee
   Note: * The only single to go to #1 twice, first in 1960 and again in January 1962.

November 11, 1960
1 SAVE THE LAST DANCE FOR ME   Drifters
2 I WANT TO BE WANTED   Brenda Lee
3 POETRY IN MOTION   Johnny Tillotson
4 GEORGIA ON MY MIND   Ray Charles
5 MY HEART HAS A MIND OF ITS OWN   Connie Francis
6 THEME FROM "THE APARTMENT"   Ferrante & Teicher
7 YOU TALK TOO MUCH   Joe Jones
8 CHAIN GANG   Sam Cooke
9 STAY   Maurice Williams
10 DEVIL OR ANGEL   Bobby Vee

November 18, 1960
1 I WANT TO BE WANTED   Brenda Lee
2 SAVE THE LAST DANCE FOR ME   Drifters
3 GEORGIA ON MY MIND   Ray Charles
4 POETRY IN MOTION   Johnny Tillotson
5 YOU TALK TOO MUCH   Joe Jones
6 STAY   Maurice Williams
7 NEW ORLEANS   U.S. Bonds
8 LAST DATE   Floyd Cramer
9 LET'S GO, LET'S GO, LET'S GO   Hank Ballard
10 THEME FROM "THE APARTMENT"   Ferrante & Teicher

November 25, 1960
1 LAST DATE   Floyd Cramer
2 STAY   Maurice Williams
3 POETRY IN MOTION   Johnny Tillotson
4 SAVE THE LAST DANCE FOR ME   Drifters
5 NEW ORLEANS   U.S. Bonds
6 I WANT TO BE WANTED   Brenda Lee
7 GEORGIA ON MY MIND   Ray Charles
8 THOUSAND STARS   Kathy Young & The Innocents
9 ARE YOU LONESOME TONIGHT?   Ferrante & Teicher
10 LET'S GO, LET'S GO, LET'S GO   Hank Ballard

December 2, 1960
1 LAST DATE   Floyd Cramer
2 ARE YOU LONESOME TONIGHT?   Ferrante & Teicher
3 STAY   Maurice Williams
4 POETRY IN MOTION   Johnny Tillotson
5 THOUSAND STARS   Kathy Young & The Innocents
6 NORTH TO ALASKA   Johnny Horton
7 NEW ORLEANS   U.S. Bonds
8 SAVE THE LAST DANCE FOR ME   Drifters
9 ALONE AT LAST   Jackie Wilson
10 GEORGIA ON MY MIND   Ray Charles

December 9, 1960
1 LAST DATE   Floyd Cramer
2 ARE YOU LONESOME TONIGHT?   Ferrante & Teicher
3 POETRY IN MOTION   Johnny Tillotson
4 THOUSAND STARS   Kathy Young & The Innocents
5 STAY   Maurice Williams
6 NEW ORLEANS   U.S. Bonds
7 NORTH TO ALASKA   Johnny Horton
8 WONDERLAND BY NIGHT   Bert Kaempfert
9 HE WILL BREAK YOUR HEART   Jerry Butler
10 SAVE THE LAST DANCE FOR ME   Drifters

December 16, 1960
1 LAST DATE   Floyd Cramer
2 ARE YOU LONESOME TONIGHT?   Ferrante & Teicher
3 WONDERLAND BY NIGHT   Bert Kaempfert
4 THOUSAND STARS   Kathy Young & The Innocents
5 EXODUS   Ferrante & Teicher
6 SAILOR (YOUR HOME IS IN THE SEA)   Lolita
7 POETRY IN MOTION   Johnny Tillotson
8 NORTH TO ALASKA   Johnny Horton
9 NEW ORLEANS   U.S. Bonds
10 HE WILL BREAK YOUR HEART   Jerry Butler

December 23, 1960
1 ARE YOU LONESOME TONIGHT?   Ferrante & Teicher

2   WONDERLAND BY NIGHT   Bert Kaempfert
3   LAST DATE   Floyd Cramer
4   NORTH TO ALASKA   Johnny Horton
5   EXODUS   Ferrante & Teicher
6   THOUSAND STARS   Kathy Young & The Innocents
7   SAILOR (YOUR HOME IS IN THE SEA)   Lolita
8   MANY TEARS AGO   Connie Francis
9   POETRY IN MOTION   Johnny Tillotson
10 HE WILL BREAK YOUR HEART   Jerry Butler

December 30, 1960
1   WONDERLAND BY NIGHT   Bert Kaempfert
2   ARE YOU LONESOME TONIGHT?   Ferrante & Teicher
3   LAST DATE   Floyd Cramer
4   EXODUS   Ferrante & Teicher
5   THOUSAND STARS   Kathy Young & The Innocents
6   NORTH TO ALASKA   Johnny Horton
7   SAILOR (YOUR HOME IS IN THE SEA)   Lolita
8   MANY TEARS AGO   Connie Francis
9   YOU'RE SIXTEEN   Johnny Burnette
10 HE WILL BREAK YOUR HEART   Jerry Butler

January 5, 1961
1   WONDERLAND BY NIGHT   Bert Kaempfert
2   ARE YOU LONESOME TONIGHT?   Ferrante & Teicher
3   LAST DATE   Floyd Cramer
4   EXODUS   Ferrante & Teicher
5   THOUSAND STARS   Kathy Young & The Innocents
6   NORTH TO ALASKA   Johnny Horton
7   MANY TEARS AGO   Connie Francis
8   YOU'RE SIXTEEN   Johnny Burnette
9   SAILOR (YOUR HOME IS IN THE SEA)   Lolita
10 ANGEL BABY   Rosie & The Originals

January 13, 1961
1   WONDERLAND BY NIGHT   Bert Kaempfert
2   ARE YOU LONESOME TONIGHT?   Ferrante & Teicher
3   EXODUS   Ferrante & Teicher
4   LAST DATE   Floyd Cramer
5   THOUSAND STARS   Kathy Young & The Innocents
6   NORTH TO ALASKA   Johnny Horton
7   (WILL YOU LOVE ME) TOMORROW   Shirelles
8   MANY TEARS AGO   Connie Francis
9   YOU'RE SIXTEEN   Johnny Burnette
10 CALCUTTA   Lawrence Welk

January 20, 1961
1   WONDERLAND BY NIGHT   Bert Kaempfert
2   EXODUS   Ferrante & Teicher
3   ARE YOU LONESOME TONIGHT?   Ferrante & Teicher
4   CALCUTTA   Lawrence Welk
5   LAST DATE   Floyd Cramer
6   NORTH TO ALASKA   Johnny Horton
7   (WILL YOU LOVE ME) TOMORROW   Shirelles
8   ANGEL BABY   Rosie & The Originals
9   THOUSAND STARS   Kathy Young & The Innocents
10 RUBBER BALL   Bobby Vee

January 27, 1961
1   WONDERLAND BY NIGHT   Bert Kaempfert
2   EXODUS   Ferrante & Teicher
3   CALCUTTA   Lawrence Welk
4   ARE YOU LONESOME TONIGHT?   Ferrante & Teicher
5   (WILL YOU LOVE ME) TOMORROW   Shirelles
6   LAST DATE   Floyd Cramer
7   ANGEL BABY   Rosie & The Originals

8   SHOP AROUND   Miracles
9   RUBBER BALL   Bobby Vee
10 CALENDAR GIRL   Neil Sedaka

February 3, 1961
1   EXODUS   Ferrante & Teicher
2   CALCUTTA   Lawrence Welk
3   (WILL YOU LOVE ME) TOMORROW   Shirelles
4   WONDERLAND BY NIGHT   Bert Kaempfert
5   ARE YOU LONESOME TONIGHT?   Ferrante & Teicher
6   ANGEL BABY   Rosie & The Originals
7   SHOP AROUND   Miracles
8   CALENDAR GIRL   Neil Sedaka
9   RUBBER BALL   Bobby Vee
10 LAST DATE   Floyd Cramer

February 10, 1961
1   EXODUS   Ferrante & Teicher
2   CALCUTTA   Lawrence Welk
3   WONDERLAND BY NIGHT   Bert Kaempfert
4   (WILL YOU LOVE ME) TOMORROW   Shirelles
5   SHOP AROUND   Miracles
6   CALENDAR GIRL   Neil Sedaka
7   ANGEL BABY   Rosie & The Originals
8   ARE YOU LONESOME TONIGHT?   Ferrante & Teicher
9   RUBBER BALL   Bobby Vee
10 EMOTIONS   Brenda Lee

February 17, 1961
1   CALCUTTA   Lawrence Welk
2   EXODUS   Ferrante & Teicher
3   (WILL YOU LOVE ME) TOMORROW   Shirelles
4   WONDERLAND BY NIGHT   Bert Kaempfert
5   CALENDAR GIRL   Neil Sedaka
6   SHOP AROUND   Miracles
7   ANGEL BABY   Rosie & The Originals
8   ARE YOU LONESOME TONIGHT?   Ferrante & Teicher
9   EMOTIONS   Brenda Lee
10 THERE'S A MOON OUT TONIGHT   Capris

February 24, 1961
1   CALCUTTA   Lawrence Welk
2   EXODUS   Ferrante & Teicher
3   (WILL YOU LOVE ME) TOMORROW   Shirelles
4   SHOP AROUND   Miracles
5   CALENDAR GIRL   Neil Sedaka
6   THERE'S A MOON OUT TONIGHT   Capris
7   PONY TIME   Chubby Checker
8   WONDERLAND BY NIGHT   Bert Kaempfert
9   EMOTIONS   Brenda Lee
10 WHEELS   String-A-Longs

March 3, 1961
1   CALCUTTA   Lawrence Welk
2   EXODUS   Ferrante & Teicher
3   PONY TIME   Chubby Checker
4   WHEELS   String-A-Longs
5   (WILL YOU LOVE ME) TOMORROW   Shirelles
6   THERE'S A MOON OUT TONIGHT   Capris
7   DON'T WORRY   Marty Robbins
8   SHOP AROUND   Miracles
9   WHERE THE BOYS ARE   Connie Francis
10 DEDICATED TO THE ONE I LOVE   Shirelles

March 10, 1961
1   CALCUTTA   Lawrence Welk

213

Lawrence Welk
Reason to smile: even in the Rock Era, Larry scores big with ``Calcutta'' (#1, Feb. 17 through Mar. 24).

2 PONY TIME   Chubby Checker
3 EXODUS   Ferrante & Teicher
4 WHEELS   String-A-Longs
5 WHERE THE BOYS ARE   Connie Francis
6 THERE'S A MOON OUT TONIGHT   Capris
7 SURRENDER   Elvis Presley
8 DON'T WORRY   Marty Robbins
9 BABY SITTIN' BOOGIE   Buzz Clifford
10 DEDICATED TO THE ONE I LOVE   Shirelles

March 17, 1961
1 CALCUTTA   Lawrence Welk
2 WHEELS   String-A-Longs
3 PONY TIME   Chubby Checker
4 SURRENDER   Elvis Presley
5 WHERE THE BOYS ARE   Connie Francis
6 EXODUS   Ferrante & Teicher
7 DON'T WORRY   Marty Robbins
8 BABY SITTIN' BOOGIE   Buzz Clifford
9 DEDICATED TO THE ONE I LOVE   Shirelles
10 EBONY EYES   Everly Brothers

March 24, 1961
1 CALCUTTA   Lawrence Welk
2 SURRENDER   Elvis Presley
3 WHEELS   String-A-Longs
4 PONY TIME   Chubby Checker
5 WHERE THE BOYS ARE   Connie Francis
6 APACHE   Jorgen Ingmann
7 EXODUS   Ferrante & Teicher
8 DON'T WORRY   Marty Robbins
9 EBONY EYES   Everly Brothers
10 DEDICATED TO THE ONE I LOVE   Shirelles

March 31, 1961
1 SURRENDER   Elvis Presley
2 PONY TIME   Chubby Checker
3 APACHE   Jorgen Ingmann
4 WHEELS   String-A-Longs
5 CALCUTTA   Lawrence Welk
6 WHERE THE BOYS ARE   Connie Francis
7 DEDICATED TO THE ONE I LOVE   Shirelles
8 BLUE MOON   Marcels
9 DON'T WORRY   Marty Robbins
10 EBONY EYES   Everly Brothers

April 7, 1961
1 BLUE MOON   Marcels
2 APACHE   Jorgen Ingmann
3 SURRENDER   Elvis Presley
4 PONY TIME   Chubby Checker
5 WHEELS   String-A-Longs
6 DON'T WORRY   Marty Robbins
7 DEDICATED TO THE ONE I LOVE   Shirelles
8 WHERE THE BOYS ARE   Connie Francis
9 ASIA MINOR   Kokomo
10 THINK TWICE   Brook Benton

April 14, 1961
1 BLUE MOON   Marcels
2 APACHE   Jorgen Ingmann
3 DEDICATED TO THE ONE I LOVE   Shirelles
4 SURRENDER   Elvis Presley
5 PONY TIME   Chubby Checker
6 RUNAWAY   Del Shannon
7 DON'T WORRY   Marty Robbins

8 ON THE REBOUND   Floyd Cramer
9 WHEELS   String-A-Longs
10 ASIA MINOR   Kokomo

April 21, 1961
1 BLUE MOON   Marcels
2 APACHE   Jorgen Ingmann
3 RUNAWAY   Del Shannon
4 ON THE REBOUND   Floyd Cramer
5 MOTHER-IN-LAW   Ernie K-Doe
6 ASIA MINOR   Kokomo
7 SURRENDER   Elvis Presley
8 DEDICATED TO THE ONE I LOVE   Shirelles
9 BUT I DO   Clarence "Frogman" Henry
10 WHEELS   String-A-Longs

April 28, 1961
1 BLUE MOON   Marcels
2 RUNAWAY   Del Shannon
3 MOTHER-IN-LAW   Ernie K-Doe
4 ON THE REBOUND   Floyd Cramer
5 BUT I DO   Clarence "Frogman" Henry
6 I'VE TOLD EVERY LITTLE STAR   Linda Scott
7 APACHE   Jorgen Ingmann
8 ONE HUNDRED POUNDS OF CLAY   Gene McDaniels
9 ASIA MINOR   Kokomo
10 SURRENDER   Elvis Presley

May 5, 1961
1 RUNAWAY   Del Shannon
2 BLUE MOON   Marcels
3 MOTHER-IN-LAW   Ernie K-Doe
4 I'VE TOLD EVERY LITTLE STAR   Linda Scott
5 BUT I DO   Clarence "Frogman" Henry
6 ON THE REBOUND   Floyd Cramer
7 ONE HUNDRED POUNDS OF CLAY   Gene McDaniels
8 TAKE GOOD CARE OF HER   Adam Wade
9 ONE MINT JULIP   Ray Charles
10 APACHE   Jorgen Ingmann

May 12, 1961
1 RUNAWAY   Del Shannon
2 MOTHER-IN-LAW   Ernie K-Doe
3 BLUE MOON   Marcels
4 ONE HUNDRED POUNDS OF CLAY   Gene McDaniels
5 ON THE REBOUND   Floyd Cramer
6 I'VE TOLD EVERY LITTLE STAR   Linda Scott
7 YOU CAN DEPEND ON ME   Brenda Lee
8 TAKE GOOD CARE OF HER   Adam Wade
9 BUT I DO   Clarence "Frogman" Henry
10 PORTRAIT OF MY LOVE   Steve Lawrence

May 19, 1961
1 RUNAWAY   Del Shannon
2 MOTHER-IN-LAW   Ernie K-Doe
3 ONE HUNDRED POUNDS OF CLAY   Gene McDaniels
4 BLUE MOON   Marcels
5 I'VE TOLD EVERY LITTLE STAR   Linda Scott
6 YOU CAN DEPEND ON ME   Brenda Lee
7 DADDY'S HOME   Shep & The Limeliters
8 PORTRAIT OF MY LOVE   Steve Lawrence
9 ON THE REBOUND   Floyd Cramer
10 TRAVELIN' MAN   Ricky Nelson

May 26, 1961
1 MOTHER-IN-LAW   Ernie K-Doe

215

Del Shannon

The #1 hit ``Runaway'' (May 5-19) was reprised as
the theme song of TV's ``Crime Story,'' 1986-88.

2 RUNAWAY Del Shannon
3 ONE HUNDRED POUNDS OF CLAY Gene McDaniels
4 DADDY'S HOME Shep & The Limeliters
5 RUNNING SCARED Roy Orbison
6 BLUE MOON Marcels
7 TRAVELIN' MAN Ricky Nelson
8 I'VE TOLD EVERY LITTLE STAR Linda Scott
9 MAMA SAID Shirelles
10 PORTRAIT OF MY LOVE Steve Lawrence

June 2, 1961
1 MOTHER-IN-LAW Ernie K-Doe
2 RUNAWAY Del Shannon
3 TRAVELIN' MAN Ricky Nelson
4 DADDY'S HOME Shep & The Limeliters
5 RUNNING SCARED Roy Orbison
6 ONE HUNDRED POUNDS OF CLAY Gene McDaniels
7 BREAKIN' IN A BRAND NEW BROKEN HEART Connie Francis
8 MAMA SAID Shirelles
9 I FEEL SO BAD Elvis Presley
10 BLUE MOON Marcels

June 9, 1961
1 TRAVELIN' MAN Ricky Nelson
2 RUNNING SCARED Roy Orbison
3 DADDY'S HOME Shep & The Limeliters
4 RUNAWAY Del Shannon
5 ONE HUNDRED POUNDS OF CLAY Gene McDaniels
6 MOTHER-IN-LAW Ernie K-Doe
7 STAND BY ME Ben E. King

8 WRITING ON THE WALL Adam Wade
9 MAMA SAID Shirelles
10 BREAKIN' IN A BRAND NEW BROKEN HEART Connie Francis

June 16, 1961
1 TRAVELIN' MAN Ricky Nelson
2 RUNNING SCARED Roy Orbison
3 MOODY RIVER Pat Boone
4 WRITING ON THE WALL Adam Wade
5 STAND BY ME Ben E. King
6 EVERY BEAT OF MY HEART Pips
7 RAINDROPS Dee Clark
8 ONE HUNDRED POUNDS OF CLAY Gene McDaniels
9 DADDY'S HOME Shep & The Limeliters
10 QUARTER TO THREE Gary U.S. Bonds

June 23, 1961
1 TRAVELIN' MAN Ricky Nelson
2 MOODY RIVER Pat Boone
3 STAND BY ME Ben E. King
4 WRITING ON THE WALL Adam Wade
5 RAINDROPS Dee Clark
6 QUARTER TO THREE Gary U.S. Bonds
7 EVERY BEAT OF MY HEART Pips
8 TOSSIN' AND TURNIN' Bobby Lewis
9 YELLOW BIRD Arthur Lyman
10 BOLL WEEVIL SONG Brook Benton

June 30, 1961
1 MOODY RIVER Pat Boone
2 QUARTER TO THREE Gary U.S. Bonds

Gary "U.S." Bonds

``Quarter To Three'' hits #1 (July 7).

3 RAINDROPS Dee Clark
4 TRAVELIN' MAN Ricky Nelson
5 WRITING ON THE WALL Adam Wade
6 TOSSIN' AND TURNIN' Bobby Lewis
7 EVERY BEAT OF MY HEART Pips
8 BOLL WEEVIL SONG Brook Benton
9 THOSE OLDIES BUT GOODIES (REMIND ME OF YOU)
    Little Caesar & The Romans
10 YELLOW BIRD Arthur Lyman

July 7, 1961
1 QUARTER TO THREE Gary U.S. Bonds
2 TOSSIN' AND TURNIN' Bobby Lewis
3 BOLL WEEVIL SONG Brook Benton
4 MOODY RIVER Pat Boone
5 WRITING ON THE WALL Adam Wade
6 EVERY BEAT OF MY HEART Pips
7 RAINDROPS Dee Clark
8 TRAVELIN' MAN Ricky Nelson
9 YELLOW BIRD Arthur Lyman
10 NEVER ON SUNDAY Chordettes

July 14, 1961
1 TOSSIN' AND TURNIN' Bobby Lewis
2 BOLL WEEVIL SONG Brook Benton
3 QUARTER TO THREE Gary U.S. Bonds
4 EVERY BEAT OF MY HEART Pips
5 WRITING ON THE WALL Adam Wade
6 NEVER ON SUNDAY Chordettes
7 MOODY RIVER Pat Boone
8 RAINDROPS Dee Clark
9 YELLOW BIRD Arthur Lyman
10 SAN ANTONIO ROSE Floyd Cramer

July 21, 1961
1 BOLL WEEVIL SONG Brook Benton
2 TOSSIN' AND TURNIN' Bobby Lewis
3 QUARTER TO THREE Gary U.S. Bonds
4 NEVER ON SUNDAY Chordettes
5 EVERY BEAT OF MY HEART Pips
6 YELLOW BIRD Arthur Lyman
7 SAN ANTONIO ROSE Floyd Cramer
8 RAINDROPS Dee Clark
9 MOODY RIVER Pat Boone
10 HATS OFF TO LARRY Del Shannon

July 28, 1961
1 TOSSIN' AND TURNIN' Bobby Lewis
2 BOLL WEEVIL SONG Brook Benton
3 NEVER ON SUNDAY Chordettes
4 QUARTER TO THREE Gary U.S. Bonds
5 YELLOW BIRD Arthur Lyman
6 EVERY BEAT OF MY HEART Pips
7 SAN ANTONIO ROSE Floyd Cramer
8 RAINDROPS Dee Clark
9 MOODY RIVER Pat Boone
10 HATS OFF TO LARRY Del Shannon

August 4, 1961
1 TOSSIN' AND TURNIN' Bobby Lewis
2 BOLL WEEVIL SONG Brook Benton
3 NEVER ON SUNDAY Chordettes
4 DUM DUM Brenda Lee
5 YELLOW BIRD Arthur Lyman
6 I LIKE IT LIKE THAT Chris Kenner
7 SAN ANTONIO ROSE Floyd Cramer
8 HATS OFF TO LARRY Del Shannon
9 QUARTER TO THREE Gary U.S. Bonds
10 LAST NIGHT Mar-Keys

August 11, 1961
1 TOSSIN' AND TURNIN' Bobby Lewis
2 NEVER ON SUNDAY Chordettes
3 DUM DUM Brenda Lee
4 I LIKE IT LIKE THAT Chris Kenner
5 LAST NIGHT Mar-Keys
6 TOGETHER Connie Francis
7 BOLL WEEVIL SONG Brook Benton
8 HATS OFF TO LARRY Del Shannon
9 WOODEN HEART Joe Dowell
10 MICHAEL Highwaymen

August 18, 1961
1 TOSSIN' AND TURNIN' Bobby Lewis
2 DUM DUM Brenda Lee
3 NEVER ON SUNDAY Chordettes
4 I LIKE IT LIKE THAT Chris Kenner
5 LAST NIGHT Mar-Keys
6 WOODEN HEART Joe Dowell
7 MICHAEL Highwaymen
8 TOGETHER Connie Francis
9 PRETTY LITTLE ANGEL EYES Curtis Lee
10 LET'S TWIST AGAIN Chubby Checker

August 25, 1961
1 WOODEN HEART Joe Dowell
2 MICHAEL Highwaymen
3 TOSSIN' AND TURNIN' Bobby Lewis
4 DUM DUM Brenda Lee
5 NEVER ON SUNDAY Chordettes
6 I LIKE IT LIKE THAT Chris Kenner
7 LAST NIGHT Mar-Keys
8 PRETTY LITTLE ANGEL EYES Curtis Lee
9 YOU DON'T KNOW WHAT YOU'VE GOT (UNTIL YOU LOSE
    IT) Ral Donner
10 TOGETHER Connie Francis

September 1, 1961
1 WOODEN HEART Joe Dowell
2 MICHAEL Highwaymen
3 TOSSIN' AND TURNIN' Bobby Lewis
4 LAST NIGHT Mar-Keys
5 YOU DON'T KNOW WHAT YOU'VE GOT (UNTIL YOU LOSE
    IT) Ral Donner
6 AS IF I DIDN'T KNOW Adam Wade
7 I LIKE IT LIKE THAT Chris Kenner
8 DUM DUM Brenda Lee
9 PRETTY LITTLE ANGEL EYES Curtis Lee
10 SCHOOL IS OUT Gary U.S. Bonds

September 8, 1961
1 MICHAEL Highwaymen
2 TOSSIN' AND TURNIN' Bobby Lewis
3 WOODEN HEART Joe Dowell
4 YOU DON'T KNOW WHAT YOU'VE GOT (UNTIL YOU LOSE
    IT) Ral Donner
5 AS IF I DIDN'T KNOW Adam Wade
6 MY TRUE LOVE Jack Scott
7 SCHOOL IS OUT Gary U.S. Bonds
8 I FALL TO PIECES Patsy Cline
9 DOES THE CHEWING GUM LOSE ITS FLAVOR Lonnie
    Donegan
10 WITHOUT YOU Johnny Tillotson

217

September 15, 1961
1 MICHAEL   Highwaymen
2 MY TRUE STORY   Jive Five
3 HURT   Timi Yuro
4 TAKE GOOD CARE OF MY BABY   Bobby Vee
5 WOODEN HEART   Joe Dowell
6 TOSSIN' AND TURNIN'   Bobby Lewis
7 DOES THE CHEWING GUM LOSE ITS FLAVOR   Lonnie Donegan
8 YOU DON'T KNOW WHAT YOU'VE GOT (UNTIL YOU LOSE IT)   Ral Donner
9 WITHOUT YOU   Johnny Tillotson
10 WHEN WE GET MARRIED   Dreamlovers

September 22, 1961
1 MICHAEL   Highwaymen
2 TAKE GOOD CARE OF MY BABY   Bobby Vee
3 MY TRUE STORY   Jive Five
4 (MARIE'S THE NAME) HIS LATEST FLAME   Elvis Presley
5 WOODEN HEART   Joe Dowell
6 DOES THE CHEWING GUM LOSE ITS FLAVOR   Lonnie Donegan
7 WITHOUT YOU   Johnny Tillotson
8 CRYING   Roy Orbison
9 TOSSIN' AND TURNIN'   Bobby Lewis
10 WHEN WE GET MARRIED   Dreamlovers

September 29, 1961
1 TAKE GOOD CARE OF MY BABY   Bobby Vee
2 MICHAEL   Highwaymen
3 THE MOUNTAIN'S HIGH   Dick & Deedee
4 DOES THE CHEWING GUM LOSE ITS FLAVOR   Lonnie Donegan
5 CRYING   Roy Orbison
6 LITTLE SISTER   Elvis Presley
7 WHO PUT THE BOMP (IN THE BOMP, BOMP, BOMP)   Barry Mann
8 WITHOUT YOU   Johnny Tillotson
9 MY TRUE STORY   Jive Five
10 (MARIE'S THE NAME) HIS LATEST FLAME   Elvis Presley

October 6, 1961
1 TAKE GOOD CARE OF MY BABY   Bobby Vee
2 THE MOUNTAIN'S HIGH   Dick & Deedee
3 CRYING   Roy Orbison
4 LITTLE SISTER   Elvis Presley
5 MICHAEL   Highwaymen
6 MEXICO   Bob Moore
7 HIT THE ROAD JACK   Ray Charles
8 YOU MUST HAVE BEEN A BEAUTIFUL BABY   Bobby Darin
9 DOES THE CHEWING GUM LOSE ITS FLAVOR   Lonnie Donegan
10 WHO PUT THE BOMP (IN THE BOMP, BOMP, BOMP)   Barry Mann

October 13, 1961
1 TAKE GOOD CARE OF MY BABY   Bobby Vee
2 CRYING   Roy Orbison
3 HIT THE ROAD JACK   Ray Charles
4 THE MOUNTAIN'S HIGH   Dick & Deedee
5 LITTLE SISTER   Elvis Presley
6 BRISTOL STOMP   Dovells
7 YOU MUST HAVE BEEN A BEAUTIFUL BABY   Bobby Darin
8 RUNAROUND SUE   Dion
9 MICHAEL   Highwaymen
10 LET'S GET TOGETHER   Connie Francis

October 20, 1961
1 HIT THE ROAD JACK   Ray Charles
2 RUNAROUND SUE   Dion
3 BRISTOL STOMP   Dovells
4 YOU MUST HAVE BEEN A BEAUTIFUL BABY   Bobby Darin
5 CRYING   Roy Orbison
6 TAKE GOOD CARE OF MY BABY   Bobby Vee
7 SAD MOVIES (MAKE ME CRY)   Sue Thompson
8 MEXICO   Bob Moore
9 BIG BAD JOHN   Jimmy Dean
10 THE MOUNTAIN'S HIGH   Dick & Dee Dee

October 27, 1961
1 RUNAROUND SUE   Dion
2 BRISTOL STOMP   Dovells
3 HIT THE ROAD JACK   Ray Charles
4 BIG BAD JOHN   Jimmy Dean
5 SAD MOVIES (MAKE ME CRY)   Sue Thompson
6 CRYING   Roy Orbison
7 THIS TIME   Troy Shondell
8 LET'S GET TOGETHER   Connie Francis
9 MEXICO   Bob Moore
10 I LOVE HOW YOU LOVE ME   Paris Sisters

November 3, 1961
1 RUNAROUND SUE   Dion
2 BRISTOL STOMP   Dovells
3 HIT THE ROAD JACK   Ray Charles
4 BIG BAD JOHN   Jimmy Dean
5 SAD MOVIES (MAKE ME CRY)   Sue Thompson
6 I LOVE HOW YOU LOVE ME   Paris Sisters
7 LET'S GET TOGETHER   Connie Francis
8 YA YA   Lee Dorsey
9 MEXICO   Bob Moore
10 THIS TIME   Troy Shondell

November 10, 1961
1 BIG BAD JOHN   Jimmy Dean
2 RUNAROUND SUE   Dion
3 BRISTOL STOMP   Dovells
4 HIT THE ROAD JACK   Ray Charles
5 SAD MOVIES (MAKE ME CRY)   Sue Thompson
6 FOOL #1   Brenda Lee
7 LET'S GET TOGETHER   Connie Francis
8 THIS TIME   Troy Shondell
9 THE FLY   Chubby Checker
10 I LOVE HOW YOU LOVE ME   Paris Sisters

November 17, 1961
1 BIG BAD JOHN   Jimmy Dean
2 RUNAROUND SUE   Dion
3 BRISTOL STOMP   Dovells
4 FOOL #1   Brenda Lee
5 HIT THE ROAD JACK   Ray Charles
6 THIS TIME   Troy Shondell
7 SAD MOVIES (MAKE ME CRY)   Sue Thompson
8 TOWER OF STRENGTH   Gene McDaniels
9 THE FLY   Chubby Checker
10 YOU'RE THE REASON   Bobby Edwards

November 24, 1961
1 BIG BAD JOHN   Jimmy Dean
2 RUNAROUND SUE   Dion
3 FOOL #1   Brenda Lee
4 GOODBYE CRUEL WORLD   James Darren
5 BRISTOL STOMP   Dovells

Jimmy Dean

``Big Bad John'' was one of several hits Jimmy had
before becoming ``The Sausage King.''

6   THIS TIME   Troy Shondell
7   HIT THE ROAD JACK   Ray Charles
8   YOU'RE THE REASON   Bobby Edwards
9   PLEASE MR. POSTMAN   Marvelettes
10   TOWER OF STRENGTH   Gene McDaniels

December 1, 1961
1   BIG BAD JOHN   Jimmy Dean
2   RUNAROUND SUE   Dion
3   PLEASE MR. POSTMAN   Marvelettes
4   GOODBYE CRUEL WORLD   James Darren
5   FOOL #1   Brenda Lee
6   BRISTOL STOMP   Dovells
7   THIS TIME   Troy Shondell
8   MOON RIVER   Jerry Butler
9   HEARTACHES   Marcels
10   CRAZY   Patsy Cline

December 8, 1961
1   BIG BAD JOHN   Jimmy Dean
2   PLEASE MR. POSTMAN   Marvelettes
3   GOODBYE CRUEL WORLD   James Darren
4   RUNAROUND SUE   Dion
5   MOON RIVER   Jerry Butler
6   FOOL #1   Brenda Lee
7   WALK ON BY   Leroy Van Dyke
8   TWIST   Chubby Checker *
9   CRAZY   Patsy Cline
10   TOWER OF STRENGTH   Gene McDaniels
      Note: * The only single to go to #1 twice, first in 1960 and
         again in January 1962.

December 15, 1961
1   PLEASE MR. POSTMAN   Marvelettes
2   BIG BAD JOHN   Jimmy Dean
3   GOODBYE CRUEL WORLD   James Darren
4   MOON RIVER   Jerry Butler
5   WALK ON BY   Leroy Van Dyke
6   TWIST   Chubby Checker *
7   THE LION SLEEPS TONIGHT   Tokens
8   RUN TO HIM   Bobby Vee
9   TONIGHT   Ferrante & Teicher
10   LET THERE BE DRUMS   Sandy Nelson
      Note: * The only single to go to #1 twice, first in 1960 and
         again in January 1962.

December 22, 1961
1   PLEASE MR. POSTMAN   Marvelettes
2   THE LION SLEEPS TONIGHT   Tokens
3   MOON RIVER   Jerry Butler
4   TWIST   Chubby Checker *
5   RUN TO HIM   Bobby Vee
6   WALK ON BY   Leroy Van Dyke
7   GOODBYE CRUEL WORLD   James Darren
8   BIG BAD JOHN   Jimmy Dean
9   LET THERE BE DRUMS   Sandy Nelson
10   TONIGHT   Ferrante & Teicher
      Note: * The only single to go to #1 twice, first in 1960 and
         again in January 1962.

December 29, 1961
1   THE LION SLEEPS TONIGHT   Tokens
2   MOON RIVER   Jerry Butler
3   TWIST   Chubby Checker *
4   RUN TO HIM   Bobby Vee
5   GOODBYE CRUEL WORLD   James Darren
6   WALK ON BY   Leroy Van Dyke
7   PLEASE MR. POSTMAN   Marvelettes
8   PEPPERMINT TWIST   Chubby Checker
9   LET THERE BE DRUMS   Sandy Nelson
10   HAPPY BIRTHDAY SWEET SIXTEEN   Neil Sedaka
      Note: * The only single to go to #1 twice, first in 1960 and
         again in January 1962.

January 5, 1962
1   THE LION SLEEPS TONIGHT   Tokens
2   TWIST   Chubby Checker *
3   RUN TO HIM   Bobby Vee
4   MOON RIVER   Jerry Butler
5   PEPPERMINT TWIST   Chubby Checker
6   CAN'T HELP FALLING IN LOVE   Elvis Presley
7   GOODBYE CRUEL WORLD   James Darren
8   HAPPY BIRTHDAY SWEET SIXTEEN   Neil Sedaka
9   WALK ON BY   Leroy Van Dyke
10   WHEN I FALL IN LOVE   Lettermen
      Note: * The only single to go to #1 twice, first in 1960 and
         again in January 1962.

January 12, 1962
1   TWIST   Chubby Checker *
2   THE LION SLEEPS TONIGHT   Tokens
3   PEPPERMINT TWIST   Chubby Checker
4   CAN'T HELP FALLING IN LOVE   Elvis Presley
5   RUN TO HIM   Bobby Vee
6   HAPPY BIRTHDAY SWEET SIXTEEN   Neil Sedaka
7   GOODBYE CRUEL WORLD   James Darren
8   WALK ON BY   Leroy Van Dyke
9   I KNOW   Barbara George

The Tokens
``The Lion Sleeps Tonight'' is based on a South African folk song, ``Wemoweh.''
Long before The Tokens hit #1 (Dec. 29, 1961), the Weavers had a hit version in 1952.

10 WHEN THE BOY IN YOUR ARMS (IS THE BOY IN YOUR HEART)   Connie Francis
   Note: * The only single to go to #1 twice, first in 1960 and again in January 1962.

January 19, 1962
1 TWIST   Chubby Checker *
2 PEPPERMINT TWIST   Chubby Checker
3 THE LION SLEEPS TONIGHT   Tokens
4 CAN'T HELP FALLING IN LOVE   Elvis Presley
5 HAPPY BIRTHDAY SWEET SIXTEEN   Neil Sedaka
6 RUN TO HIM   Bobby Vee
7 WALK ON BY   Leroy Van Dyke
8 I KNOW   Barbara George
9 WHEN I FALL IN LOVE   Lettermen
10 WHEN THE BOY IN YOUR ARMS (IS THE BOY IN YOUR HEART)   Connie Francis
   Note: * The only single to go to #1 twice, first in 1960 and again in January 1962.

January 26, 1962
1 PEPPERMINT TWIST   Chubby Checker
2 TWIST   Chubby Checker *
3 CAN'T HELP FALLING IN LOVE   Elvis Presley
4 I KNOW   Barbara George
5 THE LION SLEEPS TONIGHT   Tokens
6 NORMAN   Sue Thompson
7 HAPPY BIRTHDAY SWEET SIXTEEN   Neil Sedaka
8 WHEN I FALL IN LOVE   Lettermen
9 WALK ON BY   Leroy Van Dyke
10 RUN TO HIM   Bobby Vee
   Note: * The only single to go to #1 twice, first in 1960 and again in January 1962.

February 2, 1962
1 PEPPERMINT TWIST   Joey Dee & The Starliters
2 TWIST   Chubby Checker *
3 CAN'T HELP FALLING IN LOVE   Elvis Presley
4 NORMAN   Sue Thompson
5 I KNOW   Barbara George
6 THE WANDERER   Dion
7 BABY IT'S YOU   Shirelles
8 THE LION SLEEPS TONIGHT   Tokens
9 DUKE OF EARL   Gene Chandler
10 HAPPY BIRTHDAY SWEET SIXTEEN   Neil Sedaka
   Note: * The only single to go to #1 twice, first in 1960 and again in January 1962.

February 9, 1962
1 PEPPERMINT TWIST   Joey Dee & The Starliters
2 TWIST   Chubby Checker *
3 CAN'T HELP FALLING IN LOVE   Elvis Presley
4 DUKE OF EARL   Gene Chandler
5 I KNOW   Barbara George
6 NORMAN   Sue Thompson
7 THE WANDERER   Dion
8 A LITTLE BITTY TEAR   Burl Ives
9 BABY IT'S YOU   Shirelles
10 THE LION SLEEPS TONIGHT   Tokens
   Note: * The only single to go to #1 twice, first in 1960 and again in January 1962.

February 16, 1962
1 PEPPERMINT TWIST   Joey Dee & The Starliters
2 TWIST   Chubby Checker *
3 DUKE OF EARL   Gene Chandler

4 NORMAN   Sue Thompson
5 THE WANDERER   Dion
6 I KNOW   Barbara George
7 CAN'T HELP FALLING IN LOVE   Elvis Presley
8 A LITTLE BITTY TEAR   Burl Ives
9 DEAR LADY TWIST   Gary U.S. Bonds
10 BREAK IT TO ME GENTLY   Brenda Lee
   Note: * The only single to go to #1 twice, first in 1960 and again in January 1962.

February 23, 1962
1 DUKE OF EARL   Gene Chandler
2 TWIST   Chubby Checker *
3 THE WANDERER   Dion
4 NORMAN   Sue Thompson
5 PEPPERMINT TWIST   Joey Dee & The Starliters
6 A LITTLE BITTY TEAR   Burl Ives
7 HEY! BABY   Bruce Channel
8 DEAR LADY TWIST   Gary U.S. Bonds
9 BREAK IT TO ME GENTLY   Brenda Lee
10 CRYING IN THE RAIN   Everly Brothers
   Note: * The only single to go to #1 twice, first in 1960 and again in January 1962.

March 2, 1962
1 DUKE OF EARL   Gene Chandler
2 TWIST   Chubby Checker *
3 THE WANDERER   Dion
4 HEY! BABY   Bruce Channel
5 NORMAN   Sue Thompson
6 PEPPERMINT TWIST   Joey Dee & The Starliters
7 BREAK IT TO ME GENTLY   Brenda Lee
8 CRYING IN THE RAIN   Everly Brothers
9 DEAR LADY TWIST   Gary U.S. Bonds
10 MIDNIGHT IN MOSCOW   Kenny Ball
   Note: * The only single to go to #1 twice, first in 1960 and again in January 1962.

March 9, 1962
1 DUKE OF EARL   Gene Chandler
2 HEY! BABY   Bruce Channel
3 MIDNIGHT IN MOSCOW   Kenny Ball
4 LET ME IN   Sensations
5 DON'T BREAK THE HEART THAT LOVES YOU   Connie Francis
6 TWIST   Chubby Checker *
7 CRYING IN THE RAIN   Everly Brothers
8 BREAK IT TO ME GENTLY   Brenda Lee
9 HER ROYAL MAJESTY   James Darren
10 DEAR LADY TWIST   Gary U.S. Bonds
   Note: * The only single to go to #1 twice, first in 1960 and again in January 1962.

March 16, 1962
1 HEY! BABY   Bruce Channel
2 DUKE OF EARL   Gene Chandler
3 MIDNIGHT IN MOSCOW   Kenny Ball
4 LET ME IN   Sensations
5 DON'T BREAK THE HEART THAT LOVES YOU   Connie Francis
6 HER ROYAL MAJESTY   James Darren
7 CRYING IN THE RAIN   Everly Brothers
8 WHAT'S YOUR NAME?   Don & Juan
9 BREAK IT TO ME GENTLY   Brenda Lee
10 PERCOLATOR (TWIST)   Billy Joe & The Checkmates

March 23, 1962
1 HEY! BABY   Bruce Channel
2 DON'T BREAK THE HEART THAT LOVES YOU   Connie Francis
3 MIDNIGHT IN MOSCOW   Kenny Ball
4 LET ME IN   Sensations
5 DUKE OF EARL   Gene Chandler
6 HER ROYAL MAJESTY   James Darren
7 WHAT'S YOUR NAME?   Don & Juan
8 TWISTING THE NIGHT AWAY   Sam Cooke
9 DREAM BABY   Roy Orbison
10 CRYING IN THE RAIN   Everly Brothers

March 30, 1962
1 DON'T BREAK THE HEART THAT LOVES YOU   Connie Francis
2 HEY! BABY   Bruce Channel
3 MIDNIGHT IN MOSCOW   Kenny Ball
4 JOHNNY ANGEL   Shelley Fabares
5 DREAM BABY   Roy Orbison
6 SLOW TWISTIN'   Chubby Checker
7 WHAT'S YOUR NAME?   Don & Juan
8 LET ME IN   Sensations
9 TWISTING THE NIGHT AWAY   Sam Cooke
10 GOOD LUCK CHARM   Elvis Presley

April 6, 1962
1 JOHNNY ANGEL   Shelley Fabares
2 DON'T BREAK THE HEART THAT LOVES YOU   Connie Francis
3 GOOD LUCK CHARM   Elvis Presley

Connie Francis
The top female vocalist of the Rock Era hits #1
with ``Don't Break The Heart That Loves You'' (Mar. 30).

4 HEY! BABY   Bruce Channel
5 MIDNIGHT IN MOSCOW   Kenny Ball
6 SLOW TWISTIN'   Chubby Checker
7 DREAM BABY   Roy Orbison
8 YOUNG WORLD   Rick Nelson
9 WHAT'S YOUR NAME?   Don & Juan
10 LET ME IN   Sensations

April 13, 1962
1 JOHNNY ANGEL   Shelley Fabares
2 GOOD LUCK CHARM   Elvis Presley
3 SLOW TWISTIN'   Chubby Checker
4 MASHED POTATOE TIME   Dee Dee Sharp
5 MIDNIGHT IN MOSCOW   Kenny Ball
6 YOUNG WORLD   Rick Nelson
7 LOVE LETTERS   Ketty Lester
8 DON'T BREAK THE HEART THAT LOVES YOU   Connie Francis
9 HEY! BABY   Bruce Channel
10 LOVER PLEASE   Clyde McPhatter

April 20, 1962
1 GOOD LUCK CHARM   Elvis Presley
2 JOHNNY ANGEL   Shelley Fabares
3 MASHED POTATOE TIME   Dee Dee Sharp
4 SLOW TWISTIN'   Chubby Checker
5 YOUNG WORLD   Rick Nelson
6 SOLDIER BOY   Shirelles
7 LOVE LETTERS   Ketty Lester
8 LOVER PLEASE   Clyde McPhatter
9 SHOUT   Joey Dee & The Starliters
10 MIDNIGHT IN MOSCOW   Kenny Ball

April 27, 1962
1 GOOD LUCK CHARM   Elvis Presley
2 JOHNNY ANGEL   Shelley Fabares
3 MASHED POTATOE TIME   Dee Dee Sharp
4 SLOW TWISTIN'   Chubby Checker
5 SOLDIER BOY   Shirelles
6 YOUNG WORLD   Rick Nelson
7 STRANGER ON THE SHORE   Mr. Acker Bilk
8 SHOUT   Joey Dee & The Starliters
9 LOVE LETTERS   Ketty Lester
10 LOVER PLEASE   Clyde McPhatter

May 4, 1962
1 SOLDIER BOY   Shirelles
2 JOHNNY ANGEL   Shelley Fabares
3 MASHED POTATOE TIME   Dee Dee Sharp
4 GOOD LUCK CHARM   Elvis Presley
5 STRANGER ON THE SHORE   Mr. Acker Bilk
6 SLOW TWISTIN'   Chubby Checker
7 SHOUT   Joey Dee & The Starliters
8 LOVER PLEASE   Clyde McPhatter
9 YOUNG WORLD   Rick Nelson
10 P.T. 109   Jimmy Dean

May 11, 1962
1 SOLDIER BOY   Shirelles
2 MASHED POTATOE TIME   Dee Dee Sharp
3 STRANGER ON THE SHORE   Mr. Acker Bilk
4 JOHNNY ANGEL   Shelley Fabares
5 GOOD LUCK CHARM   Elvis Presley
6 SHE CRIED   Jay & The Americans
7 SHOUT   Joey Dee & The Starliters
8 SLOW TWISTIN'   Chubby Checker

9   OLD RIVERS   Walter Brennan
10 TWIST TWIST SENORA   Gary U.S. Bonds

May 18, 1962
1   SOLDIER BOY   Shirelles
2   STRANGER ON THE SHORE   Mr. Acker Bilk
3   MASHED POTATOE TIME   Dee Dee Sharp
4   JOHNNY ANGEL   Shelley Fabares
5   SHE CRIED   Jay & The Americans
6   SHOUT SHOUT! (KNOCK YOURSELF OUT)   Ernie
     Maresca
7   GOOD LUCK CHARM   Elvis Presley
8   OLD RIVERS   Walter Brennan
9   P.T. 109   Jimmy Dean
10 EVERYBODY LOVES ME BUT YOU   Brenda Lee

May 25, 1962
1   STRANGER ON THE SHORE   Mr. Acker Bilk
2   SOLDIER BOY   Shirelles
3   MASHED POTATOE TIME   Dee Dee Sharp
4   OLD RIVERS   Walter Brennan
5   P.T. 109   Jimmy Dean
6   JOHNNY ANGEL   Shelley Fabares
7   I CAN'T STOP LOVING YOU   Ray Charles
8   EVERYBODY LOVES ME BUT YOU   Brenda Lee
9   SHE CRIED   Jay & The Americans
10 SHOUT SHOUT! (KNOCK YOURSELF OUT)   Ernie
     Maresca

June 1, 1962
1   I CAN'T STOP LOVING YOU   Ray Charles
2   STRANGER ON THE SHORE   Mr. Acker Bilk
3   SOLDIER BOY   Shirelles
4   MASHED POTATOE TIME   Dee Dee Sharp
5   LOVERS WHO WANDER   Dion
6   OLD RIVERS   Walter Brennan
7   SHOUT SHOUT! (KNOCK YOURSELF OUT)   Ernie
     Maresca
8   EVERYBODY LOVES ME BUT YOU   Brenda Lee
9   ONE WHO REALLY LOVES YOU   Mary Wells
10 CONSCIENCE   James Darren

June 8, 1962
1   I CAN'T STOP LOVING YOU   Ray Charles
2   STRANGER ON THE SHORE   Mr. Acker Bilk
3   SOLDIER BOY   Shirelles
4   LOVERS WHO WANDER   Dion
5   (MAN WHO SHOT) LIBERTY VALANCE   Gene Pitney
6   IT KEEPS RIGHT ON A-HURTIN'   Johnny Tillotson
7   ONE WHO REALLY LOVES YOU   Mary Wells
8   MASHED POTATOE TIME   Dee Dee Sharp
9   SECOND HAND LOVE   Connie Francis
10 CONSCIENCE   James Darren

June 15, 1962
1   I CAN'T STOP LOVING YOU   Ray Charles
2   STRANGER ON THE SHORE   Mr. Acker Bilk
3   IT KEEPS RIGHT ON A-HURTIN'   Johnny Tillotson
4   (MAN WHO SHOT) LIBERTY VALANCE   Gene Pitney
5   LOVERS WHO WANDER   Dion
6   PALISADES PARK   Freddy Cannon
7   SECOND HAND LOVE   Connie Francis
8   ONE WHO REALLY LOVES YOU   Mary Wells
9   SOLDIER BOY   Shirelles
10 PLAYBOY   Marvelettes

Don & Juan
``What's Your Name'' enjoyed a brief but memorable
five-week stay in the Top 10 (March-April).

June 22, 1962
1   I CAN'T STOP LOVING YOU   Ray Charles
2   THE STRIPPER   David Rose
3   PALISADES PARK   Freddy Cannon
4   STRANGER ON THE SHORE   Mr. Acker Bilk
5   IT KEEPS RIGHT ON A-HURTIN'   Johnny Tillotson
6   (MAN WHO SHOT) LIBERTY VALANCE   Gene Pitney
7   PLAYBOY   Marvelettes
8   CINDY'S BIRTHDAY   Johnny Crawford
9   AL DI LA   Emilio Pericoli
10 THAT'S OLD FASHIONED (THAT'S THE WAY LOVE
     SHOULD BE)   Everly Brothers

June 29, 1962
1   I CAN'T STOP LOVING YOU   Ray Charles
2   THE STRIPPER   David Rose
3   PALISADES PARK   Freddy Cannon
4   IT KEEPS RIGHT ON A-HURTIN'   Johnny Tillotson
5   STRANGER ON THE SHORE   Mr. Acker Bilk
6   ROSES ARE RED (MY LOVE)   Bobby Vinton
7   (MAN WHO SHOT) LIBERTY VALANCE   Gene Pitney
8   AL DI LA   Emilio Pericoli
9   PLAYBOY   Marvelettes
10 GRAVY   Dee Dee Sharp

July 6, 1962
1   THE STRIPPER   David Rose
2   I CAN'T STOP LOVING YOU   Ray Charles
3   ROSES ARE RED (MY LOVE)   Bobby Vinton
4   PALISADES PARK   Freddy Cannon
5   AL DI LA   Emilio Pericoli

6 IT KEEPS RIGHT ON A-HURTIN' Johnny Tillotson
7 WOLVERTON MOUNTAIN Claude King
8 SNAP YOUR FINGERS Joe Henderson
9 JOHNNY GET ANGRY Joanie Sommers
10 PLAYBOY Marvelettes

July 13, 1962

1 THE STRIPPER David Rose
2 ROSES ARE RED (MY LOVE) Bobby Vinton
3 I CAN'T STOP LOVING YOU Ray Charles
4 WAH-WATUSI Orlons
5 SEALED WITH A KISS Brian Hyland
6 PALISADES PARK Freddy Cannon
7 WOLVERTON MOUNTAIN Claude King
8 IT KEEPS RIGHT ON A-HURTIN' Johnny Tillotson
9 AL DI LA Emilio Pericoli
10 GRAVY Dee Dee Sharp

July 20, 1962

1 ROSES ARE RED (MY LOVE) Bobby Vinton
2 I CAN'T STOP LOVING YOU Ray Charles
3 WAH-WATUSI Orlons
4 THE STRIPPER David Rose
5 SEALED WITH A KISS Brian Hyland
6 WOLVERTON MOUNTAIN Claude King
7 PALISADES PARK Freddy Cannon
8 JOHNNY GET ANGRY Joanie Sommers
9 SPEEDY GONZALES Pat Boone
10 AL DI LA Emilio Pericoli

July 27, 1962

1 ROSES ARE RED (MY LOVE) Bobby Vinton
2 WAH-WATUSI Orlons
3 I CAN'T STOP LOVING YOU Ray Charles
4 SEALED WITH A KISS Brian Hyland
5 THE STRIPPER David Rose
6 SPEEDY GONZALES Pat Boone
7 WOLVERTON MOUNTAIN Claude King
8 BREAKING UP IS HARD TO DO Neil Sedaka
9 JOHNNY GET ANGRY Joanie Sommers
10 AHAB THE ARAB Ray Stevens

August 4, 1962

1 ROSES ARE RED (MY LOVE) Bobby Vinton
2 BREAKING UP IS HARD TO DO Neil Sedaka
3 SEALED WITH A KISS Brian Hyland
4 I CAN'T STOP LOVING YOU Ray Charles
5 WAH-WATUSI Orlons
6 AHAB THE ARAB Ray Stevens
7 SPEEDY GONZALES Pat Boone
8 THE STRIPPER David Rose
9 LOCO-MOTION Little Eva
10 WOLVERTON MOUNTAIN Claude King

August 11, 1962

1 BREAKING UP IS HARD TO DO Neil Sedaka
2 ROSES ARE RED (MY LOVE) Bobby Vinton
3 WAH-WATUSI Orlons
4 LOCO-MOTION Little Eva
5 SEALED WITH A KISS Brian Hyland
6 AHAB THE ARAB Ray Stevens
7 SPEEDY GONZALES Pat Boone
8 YOU'LL LOSE A GOOD THING Barbara Lynn
9 THE STRIPPER David Rose
10 I CAN'T STOP LOVING YOU Ray Charles

August 18, 1962

1 BREAKING UP IS HARD TO DO Neil Sedaka
2 ROSES ARE RED (MY LOVE) Bobby Vinton
3 LOCO-MOTION Little Eva
4 WAH-WATUSI Orlons
5 YOU DON'T KNOW ME Ray Charles
6 THINGS Bobby Darin
7 AHAB THE ARAB Ray Stevens
8 SPEEDY GONZALES Pat Boone
9 SEALED WITH A KISS Brian Hyland
10 LITTLE DIANE Dion

August 25, 1962

1 LOCO-MOTION Little Eva
2 BREAKING UP IS HARD TO DO Neil Sedaka
3 ROSES ARE RED (MY LOVE) Bobby Vinton
4 THINGS Bobby Darin
5 YOU DON'T KNOW ME Ray Charles
6 SHEILA Tommy Roe
7 PARTY LIGHTS Claudine Clark
8 AHAB THE ARAB Ray Stevens
9 SHE'S NOT YOU Elvis Presley
10 LITTLE DIANE Dion

September 1, 1962

1 LOCO-MOTION Little Eva
2 SHEILA Tommy Roe
3 BREAKING UP IS HARD TO DO Neil Sedaka
4 YOU DON'T KNOW ME Ray Charles
5 PARTY LIGHTS Claudine Clark
6 ROSES ARE RED (MY LOVE) Bobby Vinton
7 SHE'S NOT YOU Elvis Presley
8 THINGS Bobby Darin
9 VACATION Connie Francis
10 LITTLE DIANE Dion

September 8, 1962

1 SHEILA Tommy Roe
2 LOCO-MOTION Little Eva
3 YOU DON'T KNOW ME Ray Charles
4 BREAKING UP IS HARD TO DO Neil Sedaka
5 RAMBLIN' ROSE Nat King Cole
6 SHE'S NOT YOU Elvis Presley
7 PARTY LIGHTS Claudine Clark
8 THINGS Bobby Darin
9 ROSES ARE RED (MY LOVE) Bobby Vinton
10 VACATION Connie Francis

September 15, 1962

1 SHERRY Four Seasons
2 SHEILA Tommy Roe
3 LOCO-MOTION Little Eva
4 RAMBLIN' ROSE Nat King Cole
5 SHE'S NOT YOU Elvis Presley
6 GREEN ONIONS Booker T & The MG's
7 TEEN AGE IDOL Rick Nelson
8 YOU DON'T KNOW ME Ray Charles
9 BREAKING UP IS HARD TO DO Neil Sedaka
10 PATCHES Dickey Lee

September 22, 1962

1 SHERRY Four Seasons
2 SHEILA Tommy Roe
3 RAMBLIN' ROSE Nat King Cole
4 GREEN ONIONS Booker T & The MG's
5 TEEN AGE IDOL Rick Nelson

Ray Charles
Ray took country singer Don Gibson's hit to #1 Pop (June 1).

Bobby Vinton
``Roses Are Red (My Love)'' hits #1 (July 20).

Jo-Ann Campbell
Jo-Ann peaked at #40 with her answer song to
Claude King's Top 10 ``Wolverton Mountain'' (July-Aug.).

Little Eva
The #1 ``Loco-Motion'' was a Goffin-King penned smash
recorded by their babysitter (Aug. 25).

Frankie Valli & The Four Seasons
The #1 hit ``Sherry'' (Sep. 15) showcased this group's inimitable falsetto style.

The Crystals
Though credited to The Crystals, the vocals for the #1 ``He's A Rebel'' (Nov. 3) were done by The Blossoms.
(The Crystals themselves did score with hits like ``Then He Kissed Me'' and ``Da Doo Ron Ron,'' however.)

6 LET'S DANCE   Chris Montez
7 PATCHES   Dickey Lee
8 SHE'S NOT YOU   Elvis Presley
9 YOU BELONG TO ME   Duprees
10 LOCO-MOTION   Little Eva

September 29, 1962

1 SHERRY   Four Seasons
2 RAMBLIN' ROSE   Nat King Cole
3 GREEN ONIONS   Booker T & The MG's
4 MONSTER MASH   Bobby "Boris" Pickett
5 SHEILA   Tommy Roe
6 LET'S DANCE   Chris Montez
7 PATCHES   Dickey Lee
8 ALLEY CAT   Bent Fabric
9 YOU BELONG TO ME   Duprees
10 TEEN AGE IDOL   Rick Nelson

October 6, 1962

1 SHERRY   Four Seasons
2 MONSTER MASH   Bobby "Boris" Pickett
3 RAMBLIN' ROSE   Nat King Cole
4 GREEN ONIONS   Booker T & The MG's
5 LET'S DANCE   Chris Montez
6 PATCHES   Dickey Lee
7 SHEILA   Tommy Roe
8 ALLEY CAT   Bent Fabric
9 VENUS IN BLUE JEANS   Jimmy Clanton
10 I REMEMBER YOU   Frank Ifield

October 13, 1962

1 SHERRY   Four Seasons
2 MONSTER MASH   Bobby "Boris" Pickett
3 RAMBLIN' ROSE   Nat King Cole
4 LET'S DANCE   Chris Montez
5 GREEN ONIONS   Booker T & The MG's
6 I REMEMBER YOU   Frank Ifield
7 PATCHES   Dickey Lee
8 DO YOU LOVE ME   Contours
9 ALLEY CAT   Bent Fabric
10 HE'S A REBEL   Crystals

October 20, 1962

1 SHERRY   Four Seasons
2 MONSTER MASH   Bobby "Boris" Pickett
3 DO YOU LOVE ME   Contours
4 HE'S A REBEL   Crystals
5 RAMBLIN' ROSE   Nat King Cole
6 I REMEMBER YOU   Frank Ifield
7 GREEN ONIONS   Booker T & The MG's
8 PATCHES   Dickey Lee
9 ONLY LOVE CAN BREAK A HEART   Gene Pitney
10 LET'S DANCE   Chris Montez

October 27, 1962

1 MONSTER MASH   Bobby "Boris" Pickett
2 SHERRY   Four Seasons
3 DO YOU LOVE ME   Contours
4 HE'S A REBEL   Crystals
5 ONLY LOVE CAN BREAK A HEART   Gene Pitney
6 ALL ALONE AM I   Brenda Lee
7 RAMBLIN' ROSE   Nat King Cole
8 I REMEMBER YOU   Frank Ifield
9 PATCHES   Dickey Lee
10 GREEN ONIONS   Booker T & The MG's

November 3, 1962

1 HE'S A REBEL   Crystals
2 ONLY LOVE CAN BREAK A HEART   Gene Pitney
3 DO YOU LOVE ME   Contours
4 MONSTER MASH   Bobby "Boris" Pickett
5 ALL ALONE AM I   Brenda Lee
6 SHERRY   Four Seasons
7 BIG GIRLS DON'T CRY   Four Seasons
8 LIMBO ROCK   Chubby Checker
9 NEXT DOOR TO AN ANGEL   Neil Sedaka
10 PATCHES   Dickey Lee

November 10, 1962

1 HE'S A REBEL   Crystals
2 BIG GIRLS DON'T CRY   Four Seasons
3 ALL ALONE AM I   Brenda Lee
4 ONLY LOVE CAN BREAK A HEART   Gene Pitney
5 RETURN TO SENDER   Elvis Presley
6 NEXT DOOR TO AN ANGEL   Neil Sedaka
7 MONSTER MASH   Bobby "Boris" Pickett
8 DO YOU LOVE ME   Contours
9 GINA   Johnny Mathis
10 POP EYE (THE HITCHHIKER)   Huey Smith

November 17, 1962

1 BIG GIRLS DON'T CRY   Four Seasons
2 RETURN TO SENDER   Elvis Presley
3 HE'S A REBEL   Crystals
4 ALL ALONE AM I   Brenda Lee
5 NEXT DOOR TO AN ANGEL   Neil Sedaka
6 BOBBY'S GIRL   Marcie Blane
7 GINA   Johnny Mathis
8 ONLY LOVE CAN BREAK A HEART   Gene Pitney
9 THE CHA-CHA-CHA   Bobby Rydell
10 LIMBO ROCK   Chubby Checker

November 24, 1962

1 BIG GIRLS DON'T CRY   Four Seasons
2 RETURN TO SENDER   Elvis Presley
3 ALL ALONE AM I   Brenda Lee
4 HE'S A REBEL   Crystals
5 BOBBY'S GIRL   Marcie Blane
6 NEXT DOOR TO AN ANGEL   Neil Sedaka
7 LIMBO ROCK   Chubby Checker
8 GINA   Johnny Mathis
9 DON'T HANG UP   Orlons
10 RIDE!   Dee Dee Sharp

December 1, 1962

1 BIG GIRLS DON'T CRY   Four Seasons
2 RETURN TO SENDER   Elvis Presley
3 BOBBY'S GIRL   Marcie Blane
4 LIMBO ROCK   Chubby Checker
5 ALL ALONE AM I   Brenda Lee
6 HE'S A REBEL   Crystals
7 DON'T HANG UP   Orlons
8 LONELY BULL   Herb Alpert
9 RIDE!   Dee Dee Sharp
10 GINA   Johnny Mathis

December 8, 1962

1 BIG GIRLS DON'T CRY   Four Seasons
2 RETURN TO SENDER   Elvis Presley
3 BOBBY'S GIRL   Marcie Blane
4 DON'T HANG UP   Orlons
5 LIMBO ROCK   Chubby Checker

6   RIDE!   Dee Dee Sharp
7   TELSTAR   Tornadoes
8   LONELY BULL   Herb Alpert
9   ALL ALONE AM I   Brenda Lee
10 HE'S A REBEL   Crystals

December 15, 1962
1   BIG GIRLS DON'T CRY   Four Seasons
2   RETURN TO SENDER   Elvis Presley
3   BOBBY'S GIRL   Marcie Blane
4   TELSTAR   Tornadoes
5   LIMBO ROCK   Chubby Checker
6   DON'T HANG UP   Orlons
7   RIDE!   Dee Dee Sharp
8   LONELY BULL   Herb Alpert
9   RELEASE ME   Esther Phillips
10 YOU ARE MY SUNSHINE   Ray Charles

December 22, 1962
1   TELSTAR   Tornadoes
2   LIMBO ROCK   Chubby Checker
3   RETURN TO SENDER   Elvis Presley
4   BIG GIRLS DON'T CRY   Four Seasons
5   BOBBY'S GIRL   Marcie Blane
6   DON'T HANG UP   Orlons
7   GO AWAY LITTLE GIRL   Steve Lawrence
8   LONELY BULL   Herb Alpert
9   RELEASE ME   Esther Phillips
10 YOU ARE MY SUNSHINE   Ray Charles

December 29, 1962
1   TELSTAR   Tornadoes
2   LIMBO ROCK   Chubby Checker
3   BOBBY'S GIRL   Marcie Blane
4   BIG GIRLS DON'T CRY   Four Seasons
5   RETURN TO SENDER   Elvis Presley
6   GO AWAY LITTLE GIRL   Steve Lawrence
7   YOU ARE MY SUNSHINE   Ray Charles
8   RELEASE ME   Esther Phillips
9   LONELY BULL   Herb Alpert
10 ZIP A DEE DOO DAH   Bob B. Sox & The Blue Jeans

January 5, 1963
1   TELSTAR   Tornadoes
2   GO AWAY LITTLE GIRL   Steve Lawrence
3   LIMBO ROCK   Chubby Checker
4   BOBBY'S GIRL   Marcie Blane
5   BIG GIRLS DON'T CRY   Four Seasons
6   RETURN TO SENDER   Elvis Presley
7   HOTEL HAPPINESS   Brook Benton
8   PIPENO THE ITALIAN MOUSE   Lou Monte
9   ZIP A DEE DOO DAH   Bob B. Sox & The Blue Jeans
10 YOU ARE MY SUNSHINE   Ray Charles

January 12, 1963
1   GO AWAY LITTLE GIRL   Steve Lawrence
2   TELSTAR   Tornadoes
3   LIMBO ROCK   Chubby Checker
4   HOTEL HAPPINESS   Brook Benton
5   PIPENO THE ITALIAN MOUSE   Lou Monte
6   TELL HIM   Exciters
7   BIG GIRLS DON'T CRY   Four Seasons
8   ZIP A DEE DOO DAH   Bob B. Sox & The Blue Jeans
9   BOBBY'S GIRL   Marcie Blane
10 NIGHT HAS A THOUSAND EYES   Bobby Vee

January 19, 1963
1   GO AWAY LITTLE GIRL   Steve Lawrence
2   TELSTAR   Tornadoes
3   HOTEL HAPPINESS   Brook Benton
4   LIMBO ROCK   Chubby Checker
5   TELL HIM   Exciters
6   NIGHT HAS A THOUSAND EYES   Bobby Vee
7   TWO LOVERS   Mary Wells
8   PIPENO THE ITALIAN MOUSE   Lou Monte
9   MY DAD   Paul Petersen
10 WALK RIGHT IN   Rooftop Singers

January 26, 1963
1   WALK RIGHT IN   Rooftop Singers
2   HEY PAULA   Paul & Paula
3   GO AWAY LITTLE GIRL   Steve Lawrence
4   TELSTAR   Tornadoes
5   TELL HIM   Exciters
6   NIGHT HAS A THOUSAND EYES   Bobby Vee
7   TWO LOVERS   Mary Wells
8   MY DAD   Paul Petersen
9   LIMBO ROCK   Chubby Checker
10 MY COLORING BOOK   Kitty Kallen

February 2, 1963
1   WALK RIGHT IN   Rooftop Singers
2   HEY PAULA   Paul & Paula
3   NIGHT HAS A THOUSAND EYES   Bobby Vee
4   GO AWAY LITTLE GIRL   Steve Lawrence
5   MY COLORING BOOK   Kitty Kallen
6   LOOP DE LOOP   Johnny Thunder
7   UP ON THE ROOF   Drifters
8   IT'S UP TO YOU   Rick Nelson
9   TELL HIM   Exciters
10 MY DAD   Paul Petersen

February 9, 1963
1   HEY PAULA   Paul & Paula
2   WALK RIGHT IN   Rooftop Singers
3   NIGHT HAS A THOUSAND EYES   Bobby Vee
4   LOOP DE LOOP   Johnny Thunder
5   UP ON THE ROOF   Drifters
6   WALK LIKE A MAN   Four Seasons
7   RUBY BABY   Dion
8   YOU'VE REALLY GOT A HOLD ON ME   Miracles
9   MY COLORING BOOK   Kitty Kallen
10 RHYTHM OF THE RAIN   Cascades

February 16, 1963
1   HEY PAULA   Paul & Paula
2   WALK RIGHT IN   Rooftop Singers
3   WALK LIKE A MAN   Four Seasons
4   RUBY BABY   Dion
5   RHYTHM OF THE RAIN   Cascades
6   NIGHT HAS A THOUSAND EYES   Bobby Vee
7   FROM A JACK TO A KING   Ned Miller
8   YOU'VE REALLY GOT A HOLD ON ME   Miracles
9   LOOP DE LOOP   Johnny Thunder
10 UP ON THE ROOF   Drifters

February 23, 1963
1   HEY PAULA   Paul & Paula
2   RUBY BABY   Dion
3   WALK LIKE A MAN   Four Seasons
4   WALK RIGHT IN   Rooftop Singers
5   RHYTHM OF THE RAIN   Cascades

6 FROM A JACK TO A KING   Ned Miller
7 YOU'RE THE REASON I'M LIVING   Bobby Darin
8 NIGHT HAS A THOUSAND EYES   Bobby Vee
9 YOU'VE REALLY GOT A HOLD ON ME   Miracles
10 HE'S SURE THE BOY I LOVE   Crystals

March 2, 1963
1 WALK LIKE A MAN   Four Seasons
2 RUBY BABY   Dion
3 HEY PAULA   Paul & Paula
4 RHYTHM OF THE RAIN   Cascades
5 WALK RIGHT IN   Rooftop Singers
6 YOU'RE THE REASON I'M LIVING   Bobby Darin
7 BLAME IT ON THE BOSSA NOVA   Eydie Gorme
8 FROM A JACK TO A KING   Ned Miller
9 WILD WEEKEND   Rebels
10 OUR DAY WILL COME   Ruby & The Romantics

March 9, 1963
1 WALK LIKE A MAN   Four Seasons
2 RUBY BABY   Dion
3 HEY PAULA   Paul & Paula
4 RHYTHM OF THE RAIN   Cascades
5 YOU'RE THE REASON I'M LIVING   Bobby Darin
6 OUR DAY WILL COME   Ruby & The Romantics
7 WALK RIGHT IN   Rooftop Singers
8 END OF THE WORLD   Skeeter Davis
9 WILD WEEKEND   Rebels
10 BLAME IT ON THE BOSSA NOVA   Eydie Gorme

March 16, 1963
1 WALK LIKE A MAN   Four Seasons
2 OUR DAY WILL COME   Ruby & The Romantics
3 YOU'RE THE REASON I'M LIVING   Bobby Darin
4 END OF THE WORLD   Skeeter Davis
5 RHYTHM OF THE RAIN   Cascades
6 RUBY BABY   Dion
7 HEY PAULA   Paul & Paula
8 BLAME IT ON THE BOSSA NOVA   Eydie Gorme
9 HE'S SO FINE   Chiffons
10 WHAT WILL MARY SAY   Johnny Mathis

March 23, 1963
1 OUR DAY WILL COME   Ruby & The Romantics
2 END OF THE WORLD   Skeeter Davis
3 HE'S SO FINE   Chiffons
4 YOU'RE THE REASON I'M LIVING   Bobby Darin
5 RHYTHM OF THE RAIN   Cascades
6 WALK LIKE A MAN   Four Seasons
7 SOUTH STREET   Orlons
8 BLAME IT ON THE BOSSA NOVA   Eydie Gorme
9 RUBY BABY   Dion
10 WHAT WILL MARY SAY   Johnny Mathis

March 30, 1963
1 HE'S SO FINE   Chiffons
2 OUR DAY WILL COME   Ruby & The Romantics
3 END OF THE WORLD   Skeeter Davis
4 SOUTH STREET   Orlons
5 RHYTHM OF THE RAIN   Cascades
6 YOU'RE THE REASON I'M LIVING   Bobby Darin
7 BABY WORKOUT   Jackie Wilson
8 OUR WINTER LOVE   Bill Pursell
9 IN DREAMS   Roy Orbison
10 BLAME IT ON THE BOSSA NOVA   Eydie Gorme

April 5, 1963
1 HE'S SO FINE   Chiffons
2 OUR DAY WILL COME   Ruby & The Romantics
3 END OF THE WORLD   Skeeter Davis
4 SOUTH STREET   Orlons
5 CAN'T GET USED TO LOSING YOU   Andy Williams
6 BABY WORKOUT   Jackie Wilson
7 RHYTHM OF THE RAIN   Cascades
8 YOU'RE THE REASON I'M LIVING   Bobby Darin
9 IN DREAMS   Roy Orbison
10 YOUNG LOVERS   Paul & Paula

April 13, 1963
1 HE'S SO FINE   Chiffons
2 CAN'T GET USED TO LOSING YOU   Andy Williams
3 SOUTH STREET   Orlons
4 END OF THE WORLD   Skeeter Davis
5 I WILL FOLLOW HIM   Little Peggy March
6 BABY WORKOUT   Jackie Wilson
7 OUR DAY WILL COME   Ruby & The Romantics
8 PUFF (THE MAGIC DRAGON)   Peter, Paul & Mary
9 YOUNG LOVERS   Paul & Paula
10 IN DREAMS   Roy Orbison

April 20, 1963
1 HE'S SO FINE   Chiffons
2 CAN'T GET USED TO LOSING YOU   Andy Williams
3 I WILL FOLLOW HIM   Little Peggy March
4 PUFF (THE MAGIC DRAGON)   Peter, Paul & Mary
5 BABY WORKOUT   Jackie Wilson
6 SOUTH STREET   Orlons
7 YOUNG LOVERS   Paul & Paula
8 END OF THE WORLD   Skeeter Davis
9 PIPELINE   Chantays
10 DON'T SAY NOTHING BAD ABOUT MY BABY   Cookies

April 27, 1963
1 I WILL FOLLOW HIM   Little Peggy March
2 CAN'T GET USED TO LOSING YOU   Andy Williams
3 HE'S SO FINE   Chiffons
4 PUFF (THE MAGIC DRAGON)   Peter, Paul & Mary
5 BABY WORKOUT   Jackie Wilson
6 PIPELINE   Chantays
7 DON'T SAY NOTHING BAD ABOUT MY BABY   Cookies
8 YOUNG LOVERS   Paul & Paula
9 ON BROADWAY   Drifters
10 SOUTH STREET   Orlons

May 4, 1963
1 I WILL FOLLOW HIM   Little Peggy March
2 CAN'T GET USED TO LOSING YOU   Andy Williams
3 PUFF (THE MAGIC DRAGON)   Peter, Paul & Mary
4 PIPELINE   Chantays
5 HE'S SO FINE   Chiffons
6 IF YOU WANT TO BE HAPPY   Jimmy Soul
7 SURFIN' U.S.A.   Beach Boys
8 DON'T SAY NOTHING BAD ABOUT MY BABY   Cookies
9 BABY WORKOUT   Jackie Wilson
10 WATERMELON MAN   Mongo Santamaria

May 11, 1963
1 I WILL FOLLOW HIM   Little Peggy March
2 PUFF (THE MAGIC DRAGON)   Peter, Paul & Mary
3 PIPELINE   Chantays
4 IF YOU WANT TO BE HAPPY   Jimmy Soul
5 CAN'T GET USED TO LOSING YOU   Andy Williams

The Beach Boys
Though it didn't reach #1, ``Surfin' U.S.A.'' epitomized the ``California Sound.''

6 HE'S SO FINE   Chiffons
7 FOOLISH LITTLE GIRL   Shirelles
8 REVEREND MR. BLACK   Kingston Trio
9 SURFIN' U.S.A.   Beach Boys
10 BABY WORKOUT   Jackie Wilson

May 18, 1963
1 I WILL FOLLOW HIM   Little Peggy March
2 IF YOU WANT TO BE HAPPY   Jimmy Soul
3 PUFF (THE MAGIC DRAGON)   Peter, Paul & Mary
4 PIPELINE   Chantays
5 SURFIN' U.S.A.   Beach Boys
6 FOOLISH LITTLE GIRL   Shirelles
7 CAN'T GET USED TO LOSING YOU   Andy Williams
8 LOSING YOU   Brenda Lee
9 REVEREND MR. BLACK   Kingston Trio
10 HOT PASTRAMI   Dartells

May 25, 1963
1 IF YOU WANT TO BE HAPPY   Jimmy Soul
2 I WILL FOLLOW HIM   Little Peggy March
3 SURFIN' U.S.A.   Beach Boys
4 I LOVE YOU BECAUSE   Al Martino
5 FOOLISH LITTLE GIRL   Shirelles
6 LOSING YOU   Brenda Lee
7 HOT PASTRAMI   Dartells
8 TWO FACES HAVE I   Lou Christie
9 IT'S MY PARTY   Lesley Gore
10 TAKE THESE CHAINS FROM MY HEART   Ray Charles

June 1, 1963
1 IT'S MY PARTY   Lesley Gore
2 IF YOU WANT TO BE HAPPY   Jimmy Soul
3 I LOVE YOU BECAUSE   Al Martino
4 DA DOO RON RON   Crystals
5 SURFIN' U.S.A.   Beach Boys
6 YOU CAN'T SIT DOWN   Dovells
7 TWO FACES HAVE I   Lou Christie
8 HOT PASTRAMI   Dartells
9 I WILL FOLLOW HIM   Little Peggy March
10 LOSING YOU   Brenda Lee

June 8, 1963
1 IT'S MY PARTY   Lesley Gore
2 SUKIYAKI   Kyu Sakamoto
3 DA DOO RON RON   Crystals
4 I LOVE YOU BECAUSE   Al Martino
5 IF YOU WANT TO BE HAPPY   Jimmy Soul
6 YOU CAN'T SIT DOWN   Dovells
7 TWO FACES HAVE I   Lou Christie
8 STILL   Bill Anderson
9 SURFIN' U.S.A.   Beach Boys
10 THOSE LAZY-HAZY-CRAZY DAYS OF SUMMER   Nat King Cole

June 15, 1963
1 IT'S MY PARTY   Lesley Gore
2 SUKIYAKI   Kyu Sakamoto
3 YOU CAN'T SIT DOWN   Dovells
4 DA DOO RON RON   Crystals
5 I LOVE YOU BECAUSE   Al Martino
6 BLUE ON BLUE   Bobby Vinton
7 STILL   Bill Anderson
8 THOSE LAZY-HAZY-CRAZY DAYS OF SUMMER   Nat King Cole
9 TWO FACES HAVE I   Lou Christie

10 HELLO STRANGER   Barbara Lewis

June 22, 1963
1 SUKIYAKI   Kyu Sakamoto
2 IT'S MY PARTY   Lesley Gore
3 HELLO STRANGER   Barbara Lewis
4 YOU CAN'T SIT DOWN   Dovells
5 DA DOO RON RON   Crystals
6 BLUE ON BLUE   Bobby Vinton
7 I LOVE YOU BECAUSE   Al Martino
8 STILL   Bill Anderson
9 THOSE LAZY-HAZY-CRAZY DAYS OF SUMMER   Nat King Cole
10 18 YELLOW ROSES   Bobby Darin

June 29, 1963
1 SUKIYAKI   Kyu Sakamoto
2 IT'S MY PARTY   Lesley Gore
3 HELLO STRANGER   Barbara Lewis
4 BLUE ON BLUE   Bobby Vinton
5 YOU CAN'T SIT DOWN   Dovells
6 EASIER SAID THAN DONE   Essex
7 THOSE LAZY-HAZY-CRAZY DAYS OF SUMMER   Nat King Cole
8 DA DOO RON RON   Crystals
9 ONE FINE DAY   Chiffons
10 MEMPHIS   Lonnie Mack

July 6, 1963
1 SUKIYAKI   Kyu Sakamoto
2 EASIER SAID THAN DONE   Essex
3 BLUE ON BLUE   Bobby Vinton
4 IT'S MY PARTY   Lesley Gore
5 HELLO STRANGER   Barbara Lewis
6 ONE FINE DAY   Chiffons
7 SURF CITY   Jan & Dean
8 MEMPHIS   Lonnie Mack
9 TIE ME KANGAROO DOWN SPORT   Rolf Harris
10 SO MUCH IN LOVE   Tymes

July 13, 1963
1 EASIER SAID THAN DONE   Essex
2 SURF CITY   Jan & Dean
3 TIE ME KANGAROO DOWN SPORT   Rolf Harris
4 SUKIYAKI   Kyu Sakamoto
5 SO MUCH IN LOVE   Tymes
6 ONE FINE DAY   Chiffons
7 BLUE ON BLUE   Bobby Vinton
8 MEMPHIS   Lonnie Mack
9 IT'S MY PARTY   Lesley Gore
10 HELLO STRANGER   Barbara Lewis

July 20, 1963
1 EASIER SAID THAN DONE   Essex
2 SURF CITY   Jan & Dean
3 TIE ME KANGAROO DOWN SPORT   Rolf Harris
4 SO MUCH IN LOVE   Tymes
5 MEMPHIS   Lonnie Mack
6 SUKIYAKI   Kyu Sakamoto
7 WIPE OUT   Surfaris
8 FINGERTIPS (PART II)   Stevie Wonder
9 ONE FINE DAY   Chiffons
10 BLUE ON BLUE   Bobby Vinton

July 27, 1963
1 SURF CITY   Jan & Dean

2   EASIER SAID THAN DONE   Essex
3   SO MUCH IN LOVE   Tymes
4   FINGERTIPS (PART II)   Stevie Wonder
5   TIE ME KANGAROO DOWN SPORT   Rolf Harris
6   WIPE OUT   Surfaris
7   MEMPHIS   Lonnie Mack
8   (YOU'RE THE) DEVIL IN DISGUISE   Elvis Presley
9   BLOWING IN THE WIND   Peter, Paul & Mary
10 JUST ONE LOOK   Doris Troy

August 3, 1963

1   FINGERTIPS (PART II)   Stevie Wonder
2   SO MUCH IN LOVE   Tymes
3   SURF CITY   Jan & Dean
4   EASIER SAID THAN DONE   Essex
5   (YOU'RE THE) DEVIL IN DISGUISE   Elvis Presley
6   WIPE OUT   Surfaris
7   BLOWING IN THE WIND   Peter, Paul & Mary
8   TIE ME KANGAROO DOWN SPORT   Rolf Harris
9   JUDY'S TURN TO CRY   Lesley Gore
10 MEMPHIS   Lonnie Mack

August 10, 1963

1   FINGERTIPS (PART II)   Stevie Wonder
2   WIPE OUT   Surfaris
3   BLOWING IN THE WIND   Peter, Paul & Mary
4   (YOU'RE THE) DEVIL IN DISGUISE   Elvis Presley
5   SO MUCH IN LOVE   Tymes
6   SURF CITY   Jan & Dean
7   EASIER SAID THAN DONE   Essex
8   JUDY'S TURN TO CRY   Lesley Gore
9   CANDY GIRL   Four Seasons
10 TIE ME KANGAROO DOWN SPORT   Rolf Harris

August 17, 1963

1   FINGERTIPS (PART II)   Stevie Wonder
2   BLOWING IN THE WIND   Peter, Paul & Mary
3   (YOU'RE THE) DEVIL IN DISGUISE   Elvis Presley
4   WIPE OUT   Surfaris
5   CANDY GIRL   Four Seasons
6   JUDY'S TURN TO CRY   Lesley Gore
7   SO MUCH IN LOVE   Tymes
8   HELLO MUDDAH, HELLO FADDUH   Allan Sherman
9   MORE   Kai Winding
10 EASIER SAID THAN DONE   Essex

August 24, 1963

1   FINGERTIPS (PART II)   Stevie Wonder
2   HELLO MUDDAH, HELLO FADDUH   Allan Sherman
3   CANDY GIRL   Four Seasons
4   BLOWING IN THE WIND   Peter, Paul & Mary
5   MY BOYFRIEND'S BACK   Angels
6   JUDY'S TURN TO CRY   Lesley Gore
7   WIPE OUT   Surfaris
8   (YOU'RE THE) DEVIL IN DISGUISE   Elvis Presley
9   MORE   Kai Winding
10 IF I HAD A HAMMER   Trini Lopez

August 31, 1963

1   FINGERTIPS (PART II)   Stevie Wonder
2   HELLO MUDDAH, HELLO FADDUH   Allan Sherman
3   MY BOYFRIEND'S BACK   Angels
4   BLOWING IN THE WIND   Peter, Paul & Mary
5   CANDY GIRL   Four Seasons
6   IF I HAD A HAMMER   Trini Lopez
7   JUDY'S TURN TO CRY   Lesley Gore

8   MOCKINGBIRD   Inez Foxx
9   MORE   Kai Winding
10 WIPE OUT   Surfaris

September 7, 1963

1   MY BOYFRIEND'S BACK   Angels
2   HELLO MUDDAH, HELLO FADDUH   Allan Sherman
3   IF I HAD A HAMMER   Trini Lopez
4   BLUE VELVET   Bobby Vinton
5   CANDY GIRL   Four Seasons
6   BLOWING IN THE WIND   Peter, Paul & Mary
7   FINGERTIPS (PART II)   Stevie Wonder
8   MOCKINGBIRD   Inez Foxx
9   MORE   Kai Winding
10 HEAT WAVE   Martha & The Vandellas

September 14, 1963

1   MY BOYFRIEND'S BACK   Angels
2   BLUE VELVET   Bobby Vinton
3   IF I HAD A HAMMER   Trini Lopez
4   HELLO MUDDAH, HELLO FADDUH   Allan Sherman
5   HEAT WAVE   Martha & The Vandellas
6   SURFER GIRL   Beach Boys
7   THEN HE KISSED ME   Crystals
8   MORE   Kai Winding
9   THE MONKEY TIME   Major Lance
10 MOCKINGBIRD   Inez Foxx

September 21, 1963

1   BLUE VELVET   Bobby Vinton
2   MY BOYFRIEND'S BACK   Angels
3   IF I HAD A HAMMER   Trini Lopez
4   HEAT WAVE   Martha & The Vandellas
5   THEN HE KISSED ME   Crystals
6   SURFER GIRL   Beach Boys
7   SALLY, GO 'ROUND THE ROSES   Jaynetts
8   MORE   Kai Winding
9   HELLO MUDDAH, HELLO FADDUH   Allan Sherman
10 MICKEY'S MONKEY   Miracles

September 28, 1963

1   BLUE VELVET   Bobby Vinton
2   MY BOYFRIEND'S BACK   Angels
3   SALLY, GO 'ROUND THE ROSES   Jaynetts
4   HEAT WAVE   Martha & The Vandellas
5   BE MY BABY   Ronettes
6   THEN HE KISSED ME   Crystals
7   IF I HAD A HAMMER   Trini Lopez
8   SURFER GIRL   Beach Boys
9   WONDERFUL! WONDERFUL!   Tymes
10 MICKEY'S MONKEY   Miracles

October 5, 1963

1   BLUE VELVET   Bobby Vinton
2   SALLY, GO 'ROUND THE ROSES   Jaynetts
3   BE MY BABY   Ronettes
4   MY BOYFRIEND'S BACK   Angels
5   CRY BABY   Garnet Mimms & The Enchanters
6   HEAT WAVE   Martha & The Vandellas
7   SUGAR SHACK   Jimmy Gilmer & The Fireballs
8   THEN HE KISSED ME   Crystals
9   WONDERFUL! WONDERFUL!   Tymes
10 MICKEY'S MONKEY   Miracles

October 12, 1963

1   BLUE VELVET   Bobby Vinton

2 BE MY BABY   Ronettes
3 SUGAR SHACK   Jimmy Gilmer & The Fireballs
4 CRY BABY   Garnet Mimms & The Enchanters
5 SALLY, GO 'ROUND THE ROSES   Jaynetts
6 MY BOYFRIEND'S BACK   Angels
7 BUSTED   Ray Charles
8 HEAT WAVE   Martha & The Vandellas
9 THEN HE KISSED ME   Crystals
10 MEAN WOMAN BLUES   Roy Orbison

October 19, 1963
1 SUGAR SHACK   Jimmy Gilmer & The Fireballs
2 BE MY BABY   Ronettes
3 BLUE VELVET   Bobby Vinton
4 CRY BABY   Garnet Mimms & The Enchanters
5 SALLY, GO 'ROUND THE ROSES   Jaynetts
6 BUSTED   Ray Charles
7 MEAN WOMAN BLUES   Roy Orbison
8 DONNA THE PRIMA DONNA   Dion
9 MY BOYFRIEND'S BACK   Angels
10 DEEP PURPLE   Nino Tempo & April Stevens

October 26, 1963
1 SUGAR SHACK   Jimmy Gilmer & The Fireballs
2 BE MY BABY   Ronettes
3 BLUE VELVET   Bobby Vinton
4 DEEP PURPLE   Nino Tempo & April Stevens
5 BUSTED   Ray Charles
6 DONNA THE PRIMA DONNA   Dion
7 MEAN WOMAN BLUES   Roy Orbison
8 WASHINGTON SQUARE   Village Stompers
9 CRY BABY   Garnet Mimms & The Enchanters
10 DON'T THINK TWICE IT'S ALL RIGHT   Impressions

November 2, 1963
1 SUGAR SHACK   Jimmy Gilmer & The Fireballs
2 DEEP PURPLE   Nino Tempo & April Stevens
3 WASHINGTON SQUARE   Village Stompers
4 MEAN WOMAN BLUES   Roy Orbison
5 BUSTED   Ray Charles
6 DONNA THE PRIMA DONNA   Dion
7 BE MY BABY   Ronettes
8 I CAN'T STAY MAD AT YOU   Skeeter Davis
9 IT'S ALL RIGHT   Impressions
10 MARIE ELENA   Los Indios Tabajaros

November 9, 1963
1 SUGAR SHACK   Jimmy Gilmer & The Fireballs
2 DEEP PURPLE   Nino Tempo & April Stevens
3 WASHINGTON SQUARE   Village Stompers
4 MEAN WOMAN BLUES   Roy Orbison
5 IT'S ALL RIGHT   Impressions
6 MARIE ELENA   Los Indios Tabajaros
7 I'M LEAVING IT UP TO YOU   Dale & Grace
8 BUSTED   Ray Charles
9 I CAN'T STAY MAD AT YOU   Skeeter Davis
10 DONNA THE PRIMA DONNA   Dion

November 16, 1963
1 SUGAR SHACK   Jimmy Gilmer & The Fireballs
2 DEEP PURPLE   Nino Tempo & April Stevens
3 WASHINGTON SQUARE   Village Stompers
4 I'M LEAVING IT UP TO YOU   Dale & Grace
5 IT'S ALL RIGHT   Impressions
6 MARIE ELENA   Los Indios Tabajaros
7 SHE'S A FOOL   Lesley Gore

8 BOSSA NOVA BABY   Elvis Presley
9 MEAN WOMAN BLUES   Roy Orbison
10 EVERYBODY   Tommy Roe

November 23, 1963
1 I'M LEAVING IT UP TO YOU   Dale & Grace
2 WASHINGTON SQUARE   Village Stompers
3 DEEP PURPLE   Nino Tempo & April Stevens
4 SUGAR SHACK   Jimmy Gilmer & The Fireballs
5 IT'S ALL RIGHT   Impressions
6 SHE'S A FOOL   Lesley Gore
7 EVERYBODY   Tommy Roe
8 BOSSA NOVA BABY   Elvis Presley
9 DOMINIQUE   Singing Nun
10 MARIE ELENA   Los Indios Tabajaros

November 30, 1963
1 I'M LEAVING IT UP TO YOU   Dale & Grace
2 DOMINIQUE   Singing Nun
3 WASHINGTON SQUARE   Village Stompers
4 SUGAR SHACK   Jimmy Gilmer & The Fireballs
5 IT'S ALL RIGHT   Impressions
6 SHE'S A FOOL   Lesley Gore
7 EVERYBODY   Tommy Roe
8 DEEP PURPLE   Nino Tempo & April Stevens
9 (DOWN AT) PAPA JOE'S   Dixiebelles
10 WALKING THE DOG   Rufus Thomas

December 7, 1963
1 DOMINIQUE   Singing Nun
2 I'M LEAVING IT UP TO YOU   Dale & Grace
3 EVERYBODY   Tommy Roe
4 LOUIE LOUIE   Kingsmen
5 SHE'S A FOOL   Lesley Gore
6 SUGAR SHACK   Jimmy Gilmer & The Fireballs
7 YOU DON'T HAVE TO BE A BABY TO CRY   Caravells
8 BE TRUE TO YOUR SCHOOL   Beach Boys
9 WASHINGTON SQUARE   Village Stompers
10 WALKING THE DOG   Rufus Thomas

December 14, 1963
1 DOMINIQUE   Singing Nun
2 LOUIE LOUIE   Kingsmen
3 EVERYBODY   Tommy Roe
4 I'M LEAVING IT UP TO YOU   Dale & Grace
5 YOU DON'T HAVE TO BE A BABY TO CRY   Caravells
6 SINCE I FELL FOR YOU   Lenny Welch
7 BE TRUE TO YOUR SCHOOL   Beach Boys
8 DRIP DROP   Dion
9 THERE I'VE SAID IT AGAIN   Bobby Vinton
10 WALKING THE DOG   Rufus Thomas

December 21, 1963
1 DOMINIQUE   Singing Nun
2 LOUIE LOUIE   Kingsmen
3 YOU DON'T HAVE TO BE A BABY TO CRY   Caravells
4 THERE I'VE SAID IT AGAIN   Bobby Vinton
5 SINCE I FELL FOR YOU   Lenny Welch
6 BE TRUE TO YOUR SCHOOL   Beach Boys
7 DRIP DROP   Dion
8 I'M LEAVING IT UP TO YOU   Dale & Grace
9 EVERYBODY   Tommy Roe
10 POPSICLES AND ICICLES   Murmaids

December 28, 1963
1 DOMINIQUE   Singing Nun

233

2   THERE I'VE SAID IT AGAIN   Bobby Vinton
3   LOUIE LOUIE   Kingsmen
4   SINCE I FELL FOR YOU   Lenny Welch
5   YOU DON'T HAVE TO BE A BABY TO CRY   Caravells
6   DRIP DROP   Dion
7   FORGET HIM   Bobby Rydell
8   POPSICLES AND ICICLES   Murmaids
9   TALK BACK TREMBLING LIPS   Johnny Tillotson
10   BE TRUE TO YOUR SCHOOL   Beach Boys

January 4, 1964
1   THERE I'VE SAID IT AGAIN   Bobby Vinton
2   LOUIE LOUIE   Kingsmen
3   DOMINIQUE   Singing Nun
4   SINCE I FELL FOR YOU   Lenny Welch
5   FORGET HIM   Bobby Rydell
6   POPSICLES AND ICICLES   Murmaids
7   TALK BACK TREMBLING LIPS   Johnny Tillotson
8   QUICKSAND   Martha & The Vandellas
9   NITTY GRITTY   Shirley Ellis
10   MIDNIGHT MARY   Joey Powers

January 11, 1964
1   THERE I'VE SAID IT AGAIN   Bobby Vinton
2   LOUIE LOUIE   Kingsmen
3   POPSICLES AND ICICLES   Murmaids
4   DOMINIQUE   Singing Nun
5   FORGET HIM   Bobby Rydell
6   SINCE I FELL FOR YOU   Lenny Welch
7   SURFIN' BIRD   Trashmen
8   NITTY GRITTY   Shirley Ellis
9   TALK BACK TREMBLING LIPS   Johnny Tillotson
10   MIDNIGHT MARY   Joey Powers

January 18, 1964
1   THERE I'VE SAID IT AGAIN   Bobby Vinton
2   LOUIE LOUIE   Kingsmen
3   POPSICLES AND ICICLES   Murmaids
4   FORGET HIM   Bobby Rydell
5   SURFIN' BIRD   Trashmen
6   DOMINIQUE   Singing Nun
7   HEY LITTLE COBRA   Rip Chords
8   NITTY GRITTY   Shirley Ellis
9   OUT OF LIMITS   Marketts
10   DRAG CITY   Jan & Dean

January 25, 1964
1   THERE I'VE SAID IT AGAIN   Bobby Vinton
2   LOUIE LOUIE   Kingsmen
3   I WANT TO HOLD YOUR HAND   Beatles *
4   SURFIN' BIRD   Trashmen
5   POPSICLES AND ICICLES   Murmaids
6   OUT OF LIMITS   Marketts
7   HEY LITTLE COBRA   Rip Chords
8   FORGET HIM   Bobby Rydell
9   UM, UM, UM, UM, UM, UM   Major Lance
10   DRAG CITY   Jan & Dean
   Note: * The unofficial beginning of "modern rock."

February 1, 1964
1   I WANT TO HOLD YOUR HAND   Beatles *
2   YOU DON'T OWN ME   Lesley Gore
3   OUT OF LIMITS   Marketts
4   SURFIN' BIRD   Trashmen
5   HEY LITTLE COBRA   Rip Chords
6   LOUIE LOUIE   Kingsmen

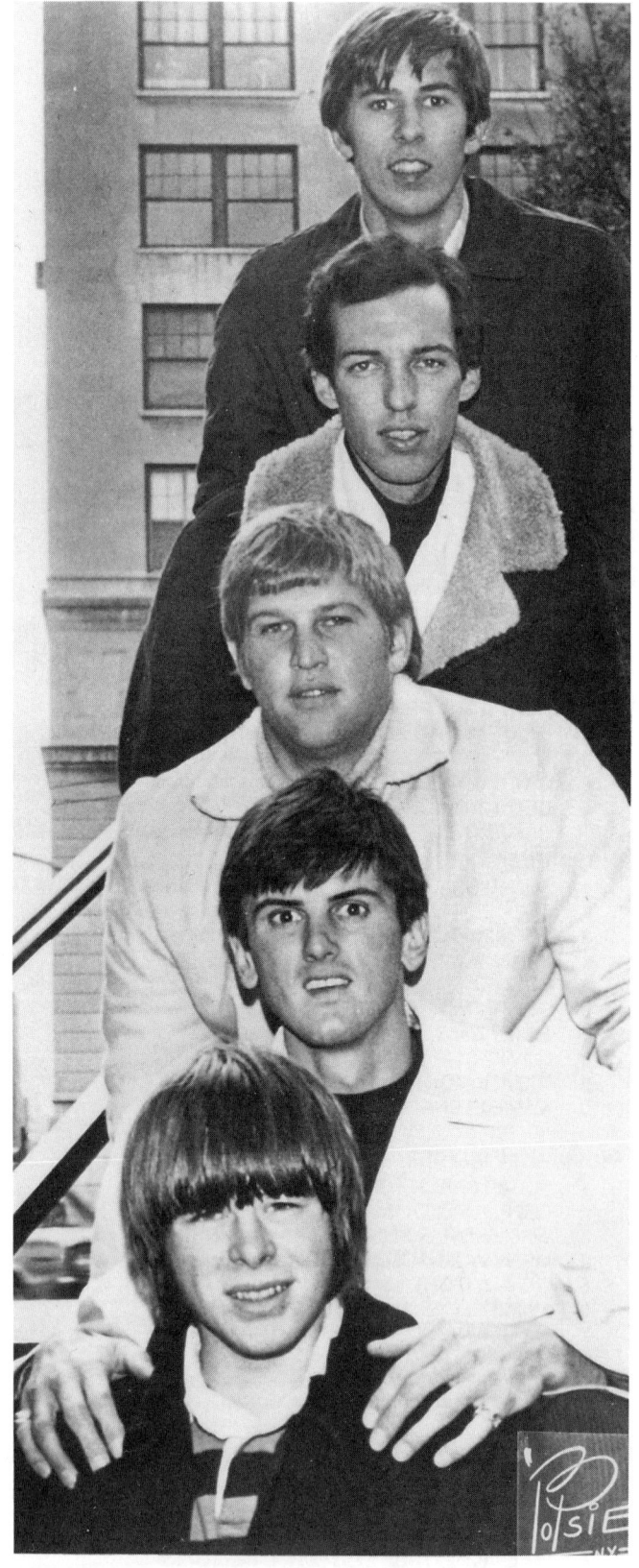

The Kingsmen
A nearly unintelligible lyric kept ``Louie, Louie''
in the #2 slot for a total of six weeks (Dec. '63-Jan. '64).

7   THERE I'VE SAID IT AGAIN   Bobby Vinton
8   UM, UM, UM, UM, UM, UM   Major Lance
9   ANYONE WHO HAD A HEART   Dionne Warwick
10 FOR YOU   Ricky Nelson
    Note: * The unofficial beginning of "modern rock."

February 8, 1964
1   I WANT TO HOLD YOUR HAND   Beatles *
2   YOU DON'T OWN ME   Lesley Gore
3   OUT OF LIMITS   Marketts
4   HEY LITTLE COBRA   Rip Chords
5   UM, UM, UM, UM, UM, UM   Major Lance
6   SURFIN' BIRD   Trashmen
7   THERE I'VE SAID IT AGAIN   Bobby Vinton
8   FOR YOU   Ricky Nelson
9   ANYONE WHO HAD A HEART   Dionne Warwick
10 SHE LOVES YOU   Beatles
    Note: * The unofficial beginning of "modern rock."

February 15, 1964
1   I WANT TO HOLD YOUR HAND   Beatles *
2   YOU DON'T OWN ME   Lesley Gore
3   SHE LOVES YOU   Beatles
4   HEY LITTLE COBRA   Rip Chords
5   UM, UM, UM, UM, UM, UM   Major Lance
6   FOR YOU   Ricky Nelson
7   OUT OF LIMITS   Marketts
8   ANYONE WHO HAD A HEART   Dionne Warwick
9   JAVA   Al Hirt
10 WHAT KIND OF FOOL   The Tams
    Note: * The unofficial beginning of "modern rock."

February 22, 1964
1   I WANT TO HOLD YOUR HAND   Beatles *
2   SHE LOVES YOU   Beatles
3   DAWN (GO AWAY)   Four Seasons
4   YOU DON'T OWN ME   Lesley Gore
5   JAVA   Al Hirt
6   UM, UM, UM, UM, UM, UM   Major Lance
7   HEY LITTLE COBRA   Rip Chords
8   CALIFORNIA SUN   Rivieras
9   WHAT KIND OF FOOL   The Tams
10 NAVY BLUE   Diane Renay
    Note: * The unofficial beginning of "modern rock."

February 29, 1964
1   I WANT TO HOLD YOUR HAND   Beatles *
2   SHE LOVES YOU   Beatles
3   DAWN (GO AWAY)   Four Seasons
4   JAVA   Al Hirt
5   CALIFORNIA SUN   Rivieras
6   PLEASE PLEASE ME   Beatles
7   YOU DON'T OWN ME   Lesley Gore
8   NAVY BLUE   Diane Renay
9   STOP AND THINK IT OVER   Dale & Grace
10 UM, UM, UM, UM, UM, UM   Major Lance
    Note: * The unofficial beginning of "modern rock."

March 7, 1964
1   I WANT TO HOLD YOUR HAND   Beatles *
2   SHE LOVES YOU   Beatles
3   DAWN (GO AWAY)   Four Seasons
4   PLEASE PLEASE ME   Beatles
5   JAVA   Al Hirt

The Beatles
The #1 group of all time score their first #1 hit, ``I Want To Hold Your Hand'' (Feb. 1).

6   CALIFORNIA SUN   Rivieras
7   NAVY BLUE   Diane Renay
8   STOP AND THINK IT OVER   Dale & Grace
9   FUN FUN FUN   Beach Boys
10 SEE THE FUNNY LITTLE CLOWN   Bobby Goldsboro
Note: * The unofficial beginning of "modern rock."

March 14, 1964

1   I WANT TO HOLD YOUR HAND   Beatles *
2   SHE LOVES YOU   Beatles
3   PLEASE PLEASE ME   Beatles
4   DAWN (GO AWAY)   Four Seasons
5   JAVA   Al Hirt
6   NAVY BLUE   Diane Renay
7   FUN FUN FUN   Beach Boys
8   CALIFORNIA SUN   Rivieras
9   SEE THE FUNNY LITTLE CLOWN   Bobby Goldsboro
10 I LOVE YOU MORE AND MORE EVERY DAY   Al Martino
Note: * The unofficial beginning of "modern rock."

March 21, 1964

1   SHE LOVES YOU   Beatles
2   I WANT TO HOLD YOUR HAND   Beatles *
3   PLEASE PLEASE ME   Beatles
4   DAWN (GO AWAY)   Four Seasons
5   FUN FUN FUN   Beach Boys
6   NAVY BLUE   Diane Renay
7   TWIST AND SHOUT   Beatles
8   JAVA   Al Hirt
9   I LOVE YOU MORE AND MORE EVERY DAY   Al Martino
10 HELLO DOLLY   Louis Armstrong
Note: * The unofficial beginning of "modern rock."

March 28, 1964

1   SHE LOVES YOU   Beatles
2   I WANT TO HOLD YOUR HAND   Beatles *
3   TWIST AND SHOUT   Beatles
4   PLEASE PLEASE ME   Beatles
5   DAWN (GO AWAY)   Four Seasons
6   FUN FUN FUN   Beach Boys
7   SUSPICION   Terry Stafford
8   HELLO DOLLY   Louis Armstrong
9   MY HEART BELONGS TO ONLY YOU   Barbra Streisand
10 GLAD ALL OVER   Dave Clark Five
Note: * The unofficial beginning of "modern rock."

April 4, 1964

1   CAN'T BUY ME LOVE   Beatles
2   TWIST AND SHOUT   Beatles
3   SHE LOVES YOU   Beatles
4   I WANT TO HOLD YOUR HAND   Beatles *
5   PLEASE PLEASE ME   Beatles
6   SUSPICION   Terry Stafford
7   HELLO DOLLY   Louis Armstrong
8   SHOOP SHOOP SONG   Betty Everette
9   MY HEART BELONGS TO ONLY YOU   Barbra Streisand
10 GLAD ALL OVER   Dave Clark Five
Note: * The unofficial beginning of "modern rock."

April 11, 1964

1   CAN'T BUY ME LOVE   Beatles
2   TWIST AND SHOUT   Beatles
3   SUSPICION   Terry Stafford
4   SHE LOVES YOU   Beatles
5   HELLO DOLLY   Louis Armstrong
6   SHOOP SHOOP SONG   Betty Everette
7   I WANT TO HOLD YOUR HAND   Beatles *

5 (OF) 10

8   GLAD ALL OVER   Dave Clark Five
9   PLEASE PLEASE ME   Beatles
10 DON'T LET THE RAIN COME DOWN   Serendipity Singers
Note: * The unofficial beginning of "modern rock."

April 18, 1964

1   CAN'T BUY ME LOVE   Beatles
2   TWIST AND SHOUT   Beatles
3   SUSPICION   Terry Stafford
4   HELLO DOLLY   Louis Armstrong
5   DO YOU WANT TO KNOW A SECRET   Beatles
6   SHOOP SHOOP SONG   Betty Everette
7   GLAD ALL OVER   Dave Clark Five
8   SHE LOVES YOU   Beatles
9   DON'T LET THE RAIN COME DOWN   Serendipity Singers
10 DEAD MAN'S CURVE   Jan & Dean

April 25, 1964

1   CAN'T BUY ME LOVE   Beatles
2   TWIST AND SHOUT   Beatles
3   DO YOU WANT TO KNOW A SECRET   Beatles
4   HELLO DOLLY   Louis Armstrong
5   SUSPICION   Terry Stafford
6   GLAD ALL OVER   Dave Clark Five
7   BITS AND PIECES   Dave Clark Five
8   DON'T LET THE RAIN COME DOWN   Serendipity Singers
9   MY GUY   Mary Wells
10 DEAD MAN'S CURVE   Jan & Dean

May 2, 1964

1   CAN'T BUY ME LOVE   Beatles

Louis Armstrong
The oldest #1 hitmaker of the Rock Era,
``Satchmo'' goes all the way with ``Hello Dolly'' (May 9).

2 HELLO DOLLY   Louis Armstrong
3 DO YOU WANT TO KNOW A SECRET   Beatles
4 BITS AND PIECES   Dave Clark Five
5 MY GUY   Mary Wells
6 DON'T LET THE RAIN COME DOWN   Serendipity Singers
7 TWIST AND SHOUT   Beatles
8 SUSPICION   Terry Stafford
9 DEAD MAN'S CURVE   Jan & Dean
10 RONNIE   Four Seasons

May 9, 1964
1 HELLO DOLLY   Louis Armstrong
2 DO YOU WANT TO KNOW A SECRET   Beatles
3 MY GUY   Mary Wells
4 BITS AND PIECES   Dave Clark Five
5 CAN'T BUY ME LOVE   Beatles
6 DON'T LET THE RAIN COME DOWN   Serendipity Singers
7 RONNIE   Four Seasons
8 DEAD MAN'S CURVE   Jan & Dean
9 SUSPICION   Terry Stafford
10 WHITE ON WHITE   Danny Williams

May 16, 1964
1 MY GUY   Mary Wells
2 HELLO DOLLY   Louis Armstrong
3 LOVE ME DO   Beatles
4 BITS AND PIECES   Dave Clark Five
5 DO YOU WANT TO KNOW A SECRET   Beatles
6 RONNIE   Four Seasons
7 DON'T LET THE RAIN COME DOWN   Serendipity Singers
8 DEAD MAN'S CURVE   Jan & Dean
9 WHITE ON WHITE   Danny Williams
10 IT'S OVER   Roy Orbison

May 23, 1964
1 MY GUY   Mary Wells
2 LOVE ME DO   Beatles
3 HELLO DOLLY   Louis Armstrong
4 CHAPEL OF LOVE   Dixie Cups
5 LOVE ME WITH ALL YOUR HEART   Ray Charles Singers
6 BITS AND PIECES   Dave Clark Five
7 (JUST LIKE) ROMEO AND JULIET   Reflections
8 RONNIE   Four Seasons
9 IT'S OVER   Roy Orbison
10 A WORLD WITHOUT LOVE   Peter & Gordon

May 30, 1964
1 LOVE ME DO   Beatles
2 CHAPEL OF LOVE   Dixie Cups
3 MY GUY   Mary Wells
4 LOVE ME WITH ALL YOUR HEART   Ray Charles Singers
5 HELLO DOLLY   Louis Armstrong
6 (JUST LIKE) ROMEO AND JULIET   Reflections
7 A WORLD WITHOUT LOVE   Peter & Gordon
8 LITTLE CHILDREN   Billy J. Kramer with The Dakotas
9 IT'S OVER   Roy Orbison
10 WALK ON BY   Leroy Van Dyke

June 6, 1964
1 CHAPEL OF LOVE   Dixie Cups
2 LOVE ME DO   Beatles
3 MY GUY   Mary Wells
4 LOVE ME WITH ALL YOUR HEART   Ray Charles Singers
5 HELLO DOLLY   Louis Armstrong
6 A WORLD WITHOUT LOVE   Peter & Gordon
7 WALK ON BY   Leroy Van Dyke

8 LITTLE CHILDREN   Billy J. Kramer with The Dakotas
9 (JUST LIKE) ROMEO AND JULIET   Reflections
10 P.S. I LOVE YOU   Beatles

June 13, 1964
1 CHAPEL OF LOVE   Dixie Cups
2 A WORLD WITHOUT LOVE   Peter & Gordon
3 LOVE ME WITH ALL YOUR HEART   Ray Charles Singers
4 LOVE ME DO   Beatles
5 MY GUY   Mary Wells
6 WALK ON BY   Leroy Van Dyke
7 LITTLE CHILDREN   Billy J. Kramer with The Dakotas
8 HELLO DOLLY   Louis Armstrong
9 PEOPLE   Barbra Streisand
10 I GET AROUND   Beach Boys

June 20, 1964
1 CHAPEL OF LOVE   Dixie Cups
2 A WORLD WITHOUT LOVE   Peter & Gordon
3 I GET AROUND   Beach Boys
4 LOVE ME WITH ALL YOUR HEART   Ray Charles Singers
5 MY BOY LOLLIPOP   Millie Small
6 WALK ON BY   Leroy Van Dyke
7 LOVE ME DO   Beatles
8 PEOPLE   Barbra Streisand
9 DON'T LET THE SUN CATCH YOU CRYING   Gerry & The Pacemakers
10 DIANE   Bachelors

June 27, 1964
1 A WORLD WITHOUT LOVE   Peter & Gordon
2 I GET AROUND   Beach Boys
3 CHAPEL OF LOVE   Dixie Cups
4 MY BOY LOLLIPOP   Millie Small
5 PEOPLE   Barbra Streisand
6 MEMPHIS   Johnny Rivers
7 DON'T LET THE SUN CATCH YOU CRYING   Gerry & The Pacemakers
8 LOVE ME WITH ALL YOUR HEART   Ray Charles Singers
9 BAD TO ME   Billy J. Kramer with The Dakotas
10 WALK ON BY   Dionne Warwick

July 4, 1964
1 I GET AROUND   Beach Boys
2 MY BOY LOLLIPOP   Millie Small
3 MEMPHIS   Johnny Rivers
4 DON'T LET THE SUN CATCH YOU CRYING   Gerry & The Pacemakers
5 PEOPLE   Barbra Streisand
6 A WORLD WITHOUT LOVE   Peter & Gordon
7 CHAPEL OF LOVE   Dixie Cups
8 RAG DOLL   Four Seasons
9 BAD TO ME   Billy J. Kramer with The Dakotas
10 CAN'T YOU SEE THAT SHE'S MINE   Dave Clark Five

July 11, 1964
1 I GET AROUND   Beach Boys
2 MEMPHIS   Johnny Rivers
3 RAG DOLL   Four Seasons
4 DON'T LET THE SUN CATCH YOU CRYING   Gerry & The Pacemakers
5 CAN'T YOU SEE THAT SHE'S MINE   Dave Clark Five
6 MY BOY LOLLIPOP   Millie Small
7 PEOPLE   Barbra Streisand
8 A WORLD WITHOUT LOVE   Peter & Gordon
9 THE GIRL FROM IPANEMA   Stan Getz & Astrud Gilberto
10 NO PARTICULAR PLACE TO GO   Chuck Berry

July 18, 1964
1 RAG DOLL   Four Seasons
2 MEMPHIS   Johnny Rivers
3 I GET AROUND   Beach Boys
4 CAN'T YOU SEE THAT SHE'S MINE   Dave Clark Five
5 THE GIRL FROM IPANEMA   Stan Getz & Astrud Gilberto
6 THE LITTLE OLD LADY (FROM PASADENA)   Jan & Dean
7 DON'T LET THE SUN CATCH YOU CRYING   Gerry & The Pacemakers
8 DANG ME   Roger Miller
9 MY BOY LOLLIPOP   Millie Small
10 KEEP ON PUSHING   Impressions

July 25, 1964
1 RAG DOLL   Four Seasons
2 A HARD DAY'S NIGHT   Beatles
3 I GET AROUND   Beach Boys
4 MEMPHIS   Johnny Rivers
5 THE GIRL FROM IPANEMA   Stan Getz & Astrud Gilberto
6 THE LITTLE OLD LADY (FROM PASADENA)   Jan & Dean
7 CAN'T YOU SEE THAT SHE'S MINE   Dave Clark Five
8 DANG ME   Roger Miller
9 WISHIN' AND HOPIN'   Dusty Springfield
10 KEEP ON PUSHING   Impressions

August 1, 1964
1 A HARD DAY'S NIGHT   Beatles
2 RAG DOLL   Four Seasons
3 THE LITTLE OLD LADY (FROM PASADENA)   Jan & Dean
4 EVERYBODY LOVES SOMEBODY   Dean Martin
5 WHERE DID OUR LOVE GO   Supremes
6 WISHIN' AND HOPIN'   Dusty Springfield
7 DANG ME   Roger Miller
8 I GET AROUND   Beach Boys
9 MEMPHIS   Johnny Rivers
10 THE GIRL FROM IPANEMA   Stan Getz & Astrud Gilberto

August 8, 1964
1 A HARD DAY'S NIGHT   Beatles
2 EVERYBODY LOVES SOMEBODY   Dean Martin
3 WHERE DID OUR LOVE GO   Supremes
4 THE LITTLE OLD LADY (FROM PASADENA)   Jan & Dean
5 RAG DOLL   Four Seasons
6 WISHIN' AND HOPIN'   Dusty Springfield
7 UNDER THE BOARDWALK   Drifters
8 DANG ME   Roger Miller
9 I WANNA LOVE HIM SO BAD   Jelly Beans
10 I GET AROUND   Beach Boys

August 15, 1964
1 EVERYBODY LOVES SOMEBODY   Dean Martin
2 WHERE DID OUR LOVE GO   Supremes
3 A HARD DAY'S NIGHT   Beatles
4 RAG DOLL   Four Seasons
5 UNDER THE BOARDWALK   Drifters
6 WISHIN' AND HOPIN'   Dusty Springfield
7 THE LITTLE OLD LADY (FROM PASADENA)   Jan & Dean
8 C'MON AND SWIM   Bobby Freeman
9 I WANNA LOVE HIM SO BAD   Jelly Beans
10 THE HOUSE OF THE RISING SUN   Animals

August 22, 1964
1 WHERE DID OUR LOVE GO   Supremes
2 EVERYBODY LOVES SOMEBODY   Dean Martin
3 A HARD DAY'S NIGHT   Beatles
4 UNDER THE BOARDWALK   Drifters
5 THE HOUSE OF THE RISING SUN   Animals
6 C'MON AND SWIM   Bobby Freeman
7 BECAUSE   Dave Clark Five
8 WALK - DON'T RUN '64   Ventures
9 WISHIN' AND HOPIN'   Dusty Springfield
10 HOW DO YOU DO IT   Gerry & The Pacemakers

August 29, 1964
1 WHERE DID OUR LOVE GO   Supremes
2 THE HOUSE OF THE RISING SUN   Animals
3 EVERYBODY LOVES SOMEBODY   Dean Martin
4 A HARD DAY'S NIGHT   Beatles
5 C'MON AND SWIM   Bobby Freeman
6 UNDER THE BOARDWALK   Drifters
7 BECAUSE   Dave Clark Five
8 UNDER THE BOARDWALK   Drifters
9 BREAD AND BUTTER   Newbeats
10 HOW DO YOU DO IT   Gerry & The Pacemakers

September 5, 1964
1 THE HOUSE OF THE RISING SUN   Animals
2 WHERE DID OUR LOVE GO   Supremes
3 EVERYBODY LOVES SOMEBODY   Dean Martin
4 BECAUSE   Dave Clark Five
5 C'MON AND SWIM   Bobby Freeman
6 BREAD AND BUTTER   Newbeats
7 UNDER THE BOARDWALK   Drifters
8 A HARD DAY'S NIGHT   Beatles
9 HOW DO YOU DO IT   Gerry & The Pacemakers
10 G.T.O.   Ronny & The Daytonas

September 12, 1964
1 THE HOUSE OF THE RISING SUN   Animals
2 WHERE DID OUR LOVE GO   Supremes
3 BECAUSE   Dave Clark Five
4 EVERYBODY LOVES SOMEBODY   Dean Martin
5 BREAD AND BUTTER   Newbeats
6 C'MON AND SWIM   Bobby Freeman
7 G.T.O.   Ronny & The Daytonas
8 A HARD DAY'S NIGHT   Beatles
9 REMEMBER (WALKIN' IN THE SAND)   Shangri-Las
10 OH, PRETTY WOMAN   Roy Orbison

September 19, 1964
1 THE HOUSE OF THE RISING SUN   Animals
2 BREAD AND BUTTER   Newbeats
3 WHERE DID OUR LOVE GO   Supremes
4 OH, PRETTY WOMAN   Roy Orbison
5 G.T.O.   Ronny & The Daytonas
6 EVERYBODY LOVES SOMEBODY   Dean Martin
7 REMEMBER (WALKIN' IN THE SAND)   Shangri-Las
8 BECAUSE   Dave Clark Five
9 DO WAH DIDDY DIDDY   Manfred Mann
10 DANCING IN THE STREET   Martha & The Vandellas

September 26, 1964
1 OH, PRETTY WOMAN   Roy Orbison
2 BREAD AND BUTTER   Newbeats
3 THE HOUSE OF THE RISING SUN   Animals
4 G.T.O.   Ronny & The Daytonas
5 REMEMBER (WALKIN' IN THE SAND)   Shangri-Las
6 DO WAH DIDDY DIDDY   Manfred Mann
7 WHERE DID OUR LOVE GO   Supremes
8 DANCING IN THE STREET   Martha & The Vandellas
9 IT HURTS TO BE IN LOVE   Gene Pitney
10 SAVE IT FOR ME   Four Seasons

Roy Orbison

Roy—without shades!— is #1 with "Pretty Woman" (Sep. 26).

October 3, 1964

1 OH, PRETTY WOMAN   Roy Orbison
2 DO WAH DIDDY DIDDY   Manfred Mann
3 BREAD AND BUTTER   Newbeats
4 DANCING IN THE STREET   Martha & The Vandellas
5 REMEMBER (WALKIN' IN THE SAND)   Shangri-Las
6 G.T.O.   Ronny & The Daytonas
7 IT HURTS TO BE IN LOVE   Gene Pitney
8 THE HOUSE OF THE RISING SUN   Animals
9 WE'LL SING IN THE SUNSHINE   Gale Garnett
10 SAVE IT FOR ME   Four Seasons

October 10, 1964

1 OH, PRETTY WOMAN   Roy Orbison
2 DO WAH DIDDY DIDDY   Manfred Mann
3 DANCING IN THE STREET   Martha & The Vandellas
4 BREAD AND BUTTER   Newbeats
5 REMEMBER (WALKIN' IN THE SAND)   Shangri-Las
6 WE'LL SING IN THE SUNSHINE   Gale Garnett
7 IT HURTS TO BE IN LOVE   Gene Pitney
8 G.T.O.   Ronny & The Daytonas
9 LAST KISS   J. Frank Wilson
10 A SUMMER SONG   Chad & Jeremy

October 17, 1964

1 DO WAH DIDDY DIDDY   Manfred Mann
2 DANCING IN THE STREET   Martha & The Vandellas
3 OH, PRETTY WOMAN   Roy Orbison
4 WE'LL SING IN THE SUNSHINE   Gale Garnett
5 LAST KISS   J. Frank Wilson
6 REMEMBER (WALKIN' IN THE SAND)   Shangri-Las
7 A SUMMER SONG   Chad & Jeremy
8 IT HURTS TO BE IN LOVE   Gene Pitney

9 WHEN I GROW UP TO BE A MAN   Beach Boys
10 LET IT BE ME   Everly Brothers

October 24, 1964

1 DO WAH DIDDY DIDDY   Manfred Mann
2 DANCING IN THE STREET   Martha & The Vandellas
3 LAST KISS   J. Frank Wilson
4 WE'LL SING IN THE SUNSHINE   Gale Garnett
5 OH, PRETTY WOMAN   Roy Orbison
6 BABY LOVE   Supremes
7 A SUMMER SONG   Chad & Jeremy
8 LET IT BE ME   Everly Brothers
9 WHEN I GROW UP TO BE A MAN   Beach Boys
10 HAVE I THE RIGHT   The Honeycombs

October 31, 1964

1 BABY LOVE   Supremes
2 DO WAH DIDDY DIDDY   Manfred Mann
3 LAST KISS   J. Frank Wilson
4 WE'LL SING IN THE SUNSHINE   Gale Garnett
5 DANCING IN THE STREET   Martha & The Vandellas
6 LET IT BE ME   Everly Brothers
7 HAVE I THE RIGHT   The Honeycombs
8 OH, PRETTY WOMAN   Roy Orbison
9 LITTLE HONDA   Hondells
10 CHUG-A-LUG   Roger Miller

November 7, 1964

1 BABY LOVE   Supremes
2 LAST KISS   J. Frank Wilson
3 DO WAH DIDDY DIDDY   Manfred Mann
4 LEADER OF THE PACK   Shangri-Las
5 LET IT BE ME   Everly Brothers
6 HAVE I THE RIGHT   The Honeycombs
7 COME A LITTLE BIT CLOSER   Jay & The Americans
8 THE DOOR IS STILL OPEN TO MY HEART   Dean Martin
9 CHUG-A-LUG   Roger Miller
10 WE'LL SING IN THE SUNSHINE   Gale Garnett

November 14, 1964

1 BABY LOVE   Supremes
2 LEADER OF THE PACK   Shangri-Las
3 LAST KISS   J. Frank Wilson
4 COME A LITTLE BIT CLOSER   Jay & The Americans
5 HAVE I THE RIGHT   The Honeycombs
6 THE DOOR IS STILL OPEN TO MY HEART   Dean Martin
7 DO WAH DIDDY DIDDY   Manfred Mann
8 LET IT BE ME   Everly Brothers
9 SHE'S NOT THERE   Zombies
10 RINGO   Lorne Greene

November 21, 1964

1 BABY LOVE   Supremes
2 LEADER OF THE PACK   Shangri-Las
3 COME A LITTLE BIT CLOSER   Jay & The Americans
4 LAST KISS   J. Frank Wilson
5 SHE'S NOT THERE   Zombies
6 RINGO   Lorne Greene
7 HAVE I THE RIGHT   The Honeycombs
8 YOU REALLY GOT ME   Kinks
9 THE DOOR IS STILL OPEN TO MY HEART   Dean Martin
10 TIME IS ON MY SIDE   Rolling Stones *
   Note: * The first Top Ten hit by The Rolling Stones.

November 28, 1964

1 LEADER OF THE PACK   Shangri-Las

Lorne Greene
The star of TV's ``Bonanza'' is #1 with ``Ringo'' (Dec. 5, '64).

Petula Clark
``Downtown'' takes Petula uptown—to #1 (Jan. 23, '65).

The Righteous Brothers
``You've Lost That Lovin' Feeling'' is a righteous #1 hit (Feb. 6).

The Temptations
The all-time #1 r&b group hits #1 with ``My Girl'' (Mar. 6).

2 BABY LOVE Supremes
3 COME A LITTLE BIT CLOSER Jay & The Americans
4 SHE'S NOT THERE Zombies
5 RINGO Lorne Greene
6 MR. LONELY Bobby Vinton
7 YOU REALLY GOT ME Kinks
8 TIME IS ON MY SIDE Rolling Stones *
9 LAST KISS J. Frank Wilson
10 MOUNTAIN OF LOVE Johnny Rivers
Note: * The first Top Ten hit by The Rolling Stones.

December 5, 1964
1 RINGO Lorne Greene
2 MR. LONELY Bobby Vinton
3 LEADER OF THE PACK Shangri-Las
4 SHE'S NOT THERE Zombies
5 BABY LOVE Supremes
6 TIME IS ON MY SIDE Rolling Stones *
7 YOU REALLY GOT ME Kinks
8 COME SEE ABOUT ME Supremes
9 MOUNTAIN OF LOVE Johnny Rivers
10 I'M GONNA BE STRONG Gene Pitney
Note: * The first Top Ten hit by The Rolling Stones.

December 12, 1964
1 MR. LONELY Bobby Vinton
2 SHE'S NOT THERE Zombies
3 RINGO Lorne Greene
4 COME SEE ABOUT ME Supremes
5 I FEEL FINE Beatles
6 TIME IS ON MY SIDE Rolling Stones *
7 YOU REALLY GOT ME Kinks
8 BABY LOVE Supremes
9 I'M GONNA BE STRONG Gene Pitney
10 DANCE DANCE DANCE Beach Boys
Note: * The first Top Ten hit by The Rolling Stones.

December 19, 1964
1 COME SEE ABOUT ME Supremes
2 I FEEL FINE Beatles
3 MR. LONELY Bobby Vinton
4 SHE'S NOT THERE Zombies
5 RINGO Lorne Greene
6 TIME IS ON MY SIDE Rolling Stones *
7 GOING OUT OF MY HEAD Little Anthony & The Imperials
8 DANCE DANCE DANCE Beach Boys
9 I'M GONNA BE STRONG Gene Pitney
10 YOU REALLY GOT ME Kinks
Note: * The first Top Ten hit by The Rolling Stones.

December 26, 1964
1 I FEEL FINE Beatles
2 COME SEE ABOUT ME Supremes
3 MR. LONELY Bobby Vinton
4 SHE'S A WOMAN Beatles
5 SHE'S NOT THERE Zombies
6 GOING OUT OF MY HEAD Little Anthony & The Imperials
7 RINGO Lorne Greene
8 DANCE DANCE DANCE Beach Boys
9 THE JERK Larks
10 TIME IS ON MY SIDE Rolling Stones *
Note: * The first Top Ten hit by The Rolling Stones.

January 2, 1965
1 I FEEL FINE Beatles
2 COME SEE ABOUT ME Supremes
3 MR. LONELY Bobby Vinton
4 SHE'S A WOMAN Beatles
5 LOVE POTION #9 Searchers
6 GOING OUT OF MY HEAD Little Anthony & The Imperials
7 SHE'S NOT THERE Zombies
8 AMEN Impressions
9 THE JERK Larks
10 THE WEDDING Julie Rogers

January 9, 1965
1 I FEEL FINE Beatles
2 COME SEE ABOUT ME Supremes
3 MR. LONELY Bobby Vinton
4 LOVE POTION #9 Searchers
5 DOWNTOWN Petula Clark
6 GOING OUT OF MY HEAD Little Anthony & The Imperials
7 AMEN Impressions
8 THE JERK Larks
9 YOU'VE LOST THAT LOVIN' FEELING Righteous Brothers
10 THE WEDDING Julie Rogers

January 16, 1965
1 COME SEE ABOUT ME Supremes
2 I FEEL FINE Beatles
3 LOVE POTION #9 Searchers
4 DOWNTOWN Petula Clark
5 YOU'VE LOST THAT LOVIN' FEELING Righteous Brothers
6 MR. LONELY Bobby Vinton
7 THE JERK Larks
8 GOING OUT OF MY HEAD Little Anthony & The Imperials
9 HOW SWEET IT IS (TO BE LOVED BY YOU) Marvin Gaye
10 KEEP SEARCHIN' Del Shannon

January 23, 1965
1 DOWNTOWN Petula Clark
2 YOU'VE LOST THAT LOVIN' FEELING Righteous Brothers
3 LOVE POTION #9 Searchers
4 I FEEL FINE Beatles
5 COME SEE ABOUT ME Supremes
6 NAME GAME Shirley Ellis
7 MR. LONELY Bobby Vinton
8 THE JERK Larks
9 HOW SWEET IT IS (TO BE LOVED BY YOU) Marvin Gaye
10 KEEP SEARCHIN' Del Shannon

January 30, 1965
1 DOWNTOWN Petula Clark
2 YOU'VE LOST THAT LOVIN' FEELING Righteous Brothers
3 NAME GAME Shirley Ellis
4 LOVE POTION #9 Searchers
5 HOLD WHAT YOU'VE GOT Joe Tex
6 HOW SWEET IT IS (TO BE LOVED BY YOU) Marvin Gaye
7 THIS DIAMOND RING Gary Lewis & The Playboys
8 COME SEE ABOUT ME Supremes
9 KEEP SEARCHIN' Del Shannon
10 ALL DAY AND ALL OF THE NIGHT Kinks

February 6, 1965
1 YOU'VE LOST THAT LOVIN' FEELING Righteous Brothers
2 DOWNTOWN Petula Clark
3 NAME GAME Shirley Ellis
4 THIS DIAMOND RING Gary Lewis & The Playboys
5 HOLD WHAT YOU'VE GOT Joe Tex
6 LOVE POTION #9 Searchers
7 ALL DAY AND ALL OF THE NIGHT Kinks
8 MY GIRL Temptations
9 HOW SWEET IT IS (TO BE LOVED BY YOU) Marvin Gaye
10 SHAKE Sam Cooke

February 13, 1965
1 YOU'VE LOST THAT LOVIN' FEELING Righteous Brothers
2 DOWNTOWN Petula Clark
3 THIS DIAMOND RING Gary Lewis & The Playboys
4 NAME GAME Shirley Ellis
5 MY GIRL Temptations
6 HOLD WHAT YOU'VE GOT Joe Tex
7 ALL DAY AND ALL OF THE NIGHT Kinks
8 SHAKE Sam Cooke
9 THE JOLLY GREEN GIANT Kingsmen
10 I GO TO PIECES Peter & Gordon

February 20, 1965
1 THIS DIAMOND RING Gary Lewis & The Playboys
2 YOU'VE LOST THAT LOVIN' FEELING Righteous Brothers
3 DOWNTOWN Petula Clark
4 MY GIRL Temptations
5 NAME GAME Shirley Ellis
6 THE JOLLY GREEN GIANT Kingsmen
7 ALL DAY AND ALL OF THE NIGHT Kinks
8 SHAKE Sam Cooke
9 I GO TO PIECES Peter & Gordon
10 THE BOY FROM NEW YORK CITY Ad Libs

February 27, 1965
1 THIS DIAMOND RING Gary Lewis & The Playboys
2 YOU'VE LOST THAT LOVIN' FEELING Righteous Brothers
3 MY GIRL Temptations
4 DOWNTOWN Petula Clark
5 THE JOLLY GREEN GIANT Kingsmen
6 TELL HER NO Zombies
7 SHAKE Sam Cooke
8 THE BOY FROM NEW YORK CITY Ad Libs
9 I GO TO PIECES Peter & Gordon
10 KING OF THE ROAD Roger Miller

March 6, 1965
1 MY GIRL Temptations
2 THIS DIAMOND RING Gary Lewis & The Playboys
3 YOU'VE LOST THAT LOVIN' FEELING Righteous Brothers
4 THE JOLLY GREEN GIANT Kingsmen
5 EIGHT DAYS A WEEK Beatles
6 TELL HER NO Zombies
7 KING OF THE ROAD Roger Miller
8 THE BIRDS AND THE BEES Jewel Akens
9 FERRY CROSS THE MERSEY Gerry & The Pacemakers
10 DOWNTOWN Petula Clark

March 13, 1965
1 EIGHT DAYS A WEEK Beatles
2 MY GIRL Temptations
3 STOP! IN THE NAME OF LOVE Supremes
4 THIS DIAMOND RING Gary Lewis & The Playboys
5 THE BIRDS AND THE BEES Jewel Akens
6 KING OF THE ROAD Roger Miller
7 FERRY CROSS THE MERSEY Gerry & The Pacemakers
8 CAN'T YOU HEAR MY HEARTBEAT Herman's Hermits
9 THE JOLLY GREEN GIANT Kingsmen
10 HURT SO BAD Little Anthony & The Imperials

March 20, 1965
1 EIGHT DAYS A WEEK Beatles
2 STOP! IN THE NAME OF LOVE Supremes
3 THE BIRDS AND THE BEES Jewel Akens
4 KING OF THE ROAD Roger Miller
5 CAN'T YOU HEAR MY HEARTBEAT Herman's Hermits
6 FERRY CROSS THE MERSEY Gerry & The Pacemakers
7 MY GIRL Temptations
8 THIS DIAMOND RING Gary Lewis & The Playboys
9 GOLDFINGER Shirley Bassey
10 SHOTGUN Jr. Walker & The All Stars

March 27, 1965
1 STOP! IN THE NAME OF LOVE Supremes
2 CAN'T YOU HEAR MY HEARTBEAT Herman's Hermits
3 THE BIRDS AND THE BEES Jewel Akens
4 EIGHT DAYS A WEEK Beatles
5 KING OF THE ROAD Roger Miller
6 FERRY CROSS THE MERSEY Gerry & The Pacemakers
7 SHOTGUN Jr. Walker & The All Stars
8 GOLDFINGER Shirley Bassey
9 MY GIRL Temptations
10 THIS DIAMOND RING Gary Lewis & The Playboys

April 3, 1965
1 STOP! IN THE NAME OF LOVE Supremes
2 CAN'T YOU HEAR MY HEARTBEAT Herman's Hermits
3 I'M TELLING YOU NOW Freddie & The Dreamers
4 SHOTGUN Jr. Walker & The All Stars
5 THE BIRDS AND THE BEES Jewel Akens
6 KING OF THE ROAD Roger Miller
7 EIGHT DAYS A WEEK Beatles
8 GOLDFINGER Shirley Bassey
9 NOWHERE TO RUN Martha & The Vandellas
10 RED ROSES FOR A BLUE LADY Vic Dana

April 10, 1965
1 I'M TELLING YOU NOW Freddie & The Dreamers
2 STOP! IN THE NAME OF LOVE Supremes
3 CAN'T YOU HEAR MY HEARTBEAT Herman's Hermits
4 SHOTGUN Jr. Walker & The All Stars
5 THE BIRDS AND THE BEES Jewel Akens
6 KING OF THE ROAD Roger Miller
7 GAME OF LOVE Wayne Fontana & The Mindbenders
8 NOWHERE TO RUN Martha & The Vandellas
9 I KNOW A PLACE Petula Clark
10 RED ROSES FOR A BLUE LADY Vic Dana

April 17, 1965
1 I'M TELLING YOU NOW Freddie & The Dreamers
2 STOP! IN THE NAME OF LOVE Supremes
3 GAME OF LOVE Wayne Fontana & The Mindbenders
4 I KNOW A PLACE Petula Clark
5 SHOTGUN Jr. Walker & The All Stars
6 CAN'T YOU HEAR MY HEARTBEAT Herman's Hermits
7 TIRED OF WAITING FOR YOU Kinks
8 NOWHERE TO RUN Martha & The Vandellas
9 THE CLAPPING SONG Shirley Ellis
10 GO NOW Moody Blues

April 24, 1965
1 GAME OF LOVE Wayne Fontana & The Mindbenders
2 MRS. BROWN YOU'VE GOT A LOVELY DAUGHTER
     Herman's Hermits
3 I'M TELLING YOU NOW Freddie & The Dreamers
4 I KNOW A PLACE Petula Clark
5 STOP! IN THE NAME OF LOVE Supremes
6 TIRED OF WAITING FOR YOU Kinks
7 I'LL NEVER FIND ANOTHER YOU The Seekers
8 THE CLAPPING SONG Shirley Ellis
9 SHOTGUN Jr. Walker & The All Stars
10 SILHOUETTES Herman's Hermits

May 1, 1965
1   MRS. BROWN YOU'VE GOT A LOVELY DAUGHTER
    Herman's Hermits
2   GAME OF LOVE   Wayne Fontana & The Mindbenders
3   I KNOW A PLACE   Petula Clark
4   I'M TELLING YOU NOW   Freddie & The Dreamers
5   I'LL NEVER FIND ANOTHER YOU   The Seekers
6   TIRED OF WAITING FOR YOU   Kinks
7   COUNT ME IN   Gary Lewis & The Playboys
8   SILHOUETTES   Herman's Hermits
9   THE LAST TIME   Rolling Stones
10 STOP! IN THE NAME OF LOVE   Supremes

May 8, 1965
1   MRS. BROWN YOU'VE GOT A LOVELY DAUGHTER
    Herman's Hermits
2   COUNT ME IN   Gary Lewis & The Playboys
3   TICKET TO RIDE   Beatles
4   GAME OF LOVE   Wayne Fontana & The Mindbenders
5   I'LL NEVER FIND ANOTHER YOU   The Seekers
6   I KNOW A PLACE   Petula Clark
7   SILHOUETTES   Herman's Hermits
8   I'M TELLING YOU NOW   Freddie & The Dreamers
9   THE LAST TIME   Rolling Stones
10 CAST YOUR FATE TO THE WIND   Sounds Orchestral

May 15, 1965
1   MRS. BROWN YOU'VE GOT A LOVELY DAUGHTER
    Herman's Hermits
2   COUNT ME IN   Gary Lewis & The Playboys
3   TICKET TO RIDE   Beatles
4   I'LL NEVER FIND ANOTHER YOU   The Seekers
5   SILHOUETTES   Herman's Hermits
6   HELP ME RHONDA   Beach Boys
7   I KNOW A PLACE   Petula Clark
8   I'LL BE DOGGONE   Marvin Gaye
9   JUST ONCE IN MY LIFE   Righteous Brothers
10 WOOLY BULLY   Sam The Sham & The Pharoahs

May 22, 1965
1   TICKET TO RIDE   Beatles
2   MRS. BROWN YOU'VE GOT A LOVELY DAUGHTER
    Herman's Hermits
3   COUNT ME IN   Gary Lewis & The Playboys
4   HELP ME RHONDA   Beach Boys
5   I'LL NEVER FIND ANOTHER YOU   The Seekers
6   BACK IN MY ARMS AGAIN   Supremes
7   SILHOUETTES   Herman's Hermits
8   WOOLY BULLY   Sam The Sham & The Pharoahs
9   JUST ONCE IN MY LIFE   Righteous Brothers
10 CRYING IN THE CHAPEL   Elvis Presley

May 29, 1965
1   HELP ME RHONDA   Beach Boys
2   TICKET TO RIDE   Beatles
3   BACK IN MY ARMS AGAIN   Supremes
4   MRS. BROWN YOU'VE GOT A LOVELY DAUGHTER
    Herman's Hermits
5   WOOLY BULLY   Sam The Sham & The Pharoahs
6   CRYING IN THE CHAPEL   Elvis Presley
7   COUNT ME IN   Gary Lewis & The Playboys
8   I'LL NEVER FIND ANOTHER YOU   The Seekers
9   JUST A LITTLE   Beau Brummels
10 IT'S NOT UNUSUAL   Tom Jones

June 5, 1965
1   HELP ME RHONDA   Beach Boys
2   WOOLY BULLY   Sam The Sham & The Pharoahs
3   BACK IN MY ARMS AGAIN   Supremes
4   CRYING IN THE CHAPEL   Elvis Presley
5   TICKET TO RIDE   Beatles
6   MRS. BROWN YOU'VE GOT A LOVELY DAUGHTER
    Herman's Hermits
7   I CAN'T HELP MYSELF   Four Tops
8   JUST A LITTLE   Beau Brummels
9   ENGINE ENGINE #9   Roger Miller
10 IT'S NOT UNUSUAL   Tom Jones

June 12, 1965
1   BACK IN MY ARMS AGAIN   Supremes
2   WOOLY BULLY   Sam The Sham & The Pharoahs
3   CRYING IN THE CHAPEL   Elvis Presley
4   I CAN'T HELP MYSELF   Four Tops
5   HELP ME RHONDA   Beach Boys
6   MR. TAMBOURINE MAN   Byrds
7   ENGINE ENGINE #9   Roger Miller
8   WONDERFUL WORLD   Herman's Hermits
9   TICKET TO RIDE   Beatles
10 JUST A LITTLE   Beau Brummels

June 19, 1965
1   I CAN'T HELP MYSELF   Four Tops
2   MR. TAMBOURINE MAN   Byrds
3   WOOLY BULLY   Sam The Sham & The Pharoahs
4   CRYING IN THE CHAPEL   Elvis Presley
5   BACK IN MY ARMS AGAIN   Supremes
6   WONDERFUL WORLD   Herman's Hermits
7   HELP ME RHONDA   Beach Boys
8   ENGINE ENGINE #9   Roger Miller
9   FOR YOUR LOVE   Yardbirds
10 HUSH HUSH SWEET CHARLOTTE   Patti Page *
    Note: * The last Top Ten song by the number 1 female
    vocalist of the Hit Parade era.

June 26, 1965
1   MR. TAMBOURINE MAN   Byrds
2   I CAN'T HELP MYSELF   Four Tops
3   WOOLY BULLY   Sam The Sham & The Pharoahs
4   SATISFACTION   Rolling Stones
5   WONDERFUL WORLD   Herman's Hermits
6   CRYING IN THE CHAPEL   Elvis Presley
7   FOR YOUR LOVE   Yardbirds
8   HUSH HUSH SWEET CHARLOTTE   Patti Page *
9   HELP ME RHONDA   Beach Boys
10 SEVENTH SON   Johnny Rivers
    Note: * The last Top Ten song by the number 1 female
    vocalist of the Hit Parade era.

July 3, 1965
1   I CAN'T HELP MYSELF   Four Tops
2   SATISFACTION   Rolling Stones
3   MR. TAMBOURINE MAN   Byrds
4   WOOLY BULLY   Sam The Sham & The Pharoahs
5   WONDERFUL WORLD   Herman's Hermits
6   FOR YOUR LOVE   Yardbirds
7   SEVENTH SON   Johnny Rivers
8   CRYING IN THE CHAPEL   Elvis Presley
9   YES, I'M READY   Barbara Mason
10 WHAT THE WORLD NEEDS NOW IS LOVE   Jackie
    DeShannon

The Four Tops
Another Motown success story help themselves to the #1 position with ``I Can't Help Myself'' (June 19).

July 10, 1965
1. SATISFACTION   Rolling Stones
2. I CAN'T HELP MYSELF   Four Tops
3. MR. TAMBOURINE MAN   Byrds
4. WONDERFUL WORLD   Herman's Hermits
5. WOOLY BULLY   Sam The Sham & The Pharoahs
6. YES, I'M READY   Barbara Mason
7. SEVENTH SON   Johnny Rivers
8. CARA, MIA   Jay & The Americans
9. YOU TURN ME ON   Ian Whitcomb
10. WHAT THE WORLD NEEDS NOW IS LOVE   Jackie DeShannon

July 17, 1965
1. SATISFACTION   Rolling Stones
2. I CAN'T HELP MYSELF   Four Tops
3. HENRY VIII   Herman's Hermits
4. MR. TAMBOURINE MAN   Byrds
5. CARA, MIA   Jay & The Americans
6. YES, I'M READY   Barbara Mason
7. SEVENTH SON   Johnny Rivers
8. YOU TURN ME ON   Ian Whitcomb
9. WHAT THE WORLD NEEDS NOW IS LOVE   Jackie DeShannon
10. WHAT'S NEW PUSSYCAT   Tom Jones

July 24, 1965
1. SATISFACTION   Rolling Stones
2. HENRY VIII   Herman's Hermits
3. I CAN'T HELP MYSELF   Four Tops
4. WHAT'S NEW PUSSYCAT   Tom Jones
5. CARA, MIA   Jay & The Americans
6. YES, I'M READY   Barbara Mason
7. WHAT THE WORLD NEEDS NOW IS LOVE   Jackie DeShannon
8. SEVENTH SON   Johnny Rivers
9. MR. TAMBOURINE MAN   Byrds
10. YOU TURN ME ON   Ian Whitcomb

July 31, 1965
1. SATISFACTION   Rolling Stones
2. HENRY VIII   Herman's Hermits
3. WHAT'S NEW PUSSYCAT   Tom Jones
4. CARA, MIA   Jay & The Americans
5. YES, I'M READY   Barbara Mason
6. I CAN'T HELP MYSELF   Four Tops
7. WHAT THE WORLD NEEDS NOW IS LOVE   Jackie DeShannon
8. SAVE YOUR HEART FOR ME   Gary Lewis & The Playboys
9. I LIKE IT LIKE THAT   Dave Clark Five
10. SEVENTH SON   Johnny Rivers

August 7, 1965
1. HENRY VIII   Herman's Hermits
2. SATISFACTION   Rolling Stones
3. WHAT'S NEW PUSSYCAT   Tom Jones
4. SAVE YOUR HEART FOR ME   Gary Lewis & The Playboys
5. I GOT YOU BABE   Sonny & Cher
6. YES, I'M READY   Barbara Mason
7. I LIKE IT LIKE THAT   Dave Clark Five
8. CARA, MIA   Jay & The Americans
9. I CAN'T HELP MYSELF   Four Tops
10. DON'T JUST STAND THERE   Patty Duke

August 14, 1965
1. I GOT YOU BABE   Sonny & Cher
2. SATISFACTION   Rolling Stones
3. SAVE YOUR HEART FOR ME   Gary Lewis & The Playboys
4. HENRY VIII   Herman's Hermits
5. WHAT'S NEW PUSSYCAT   Tom Jones
6. UNCHAINED MELODY   Righteous Brothers
7. IT'S THE SAME OLD SONG   Four Tops
8. DON'T JUST STAND THERE   Patty Duke
9. CALIFORNIA GIRLS   Beach Boys
10. DOWN IN THE BOONDOCKS   Billy Joe Royal

August 21, 1965
1. I GOT YOU BABE   Sonny & Cher
2. SAVE YOUR HEART FOR ME   Gary Lewis & The Playboys
3. HELP   Beatles
4. CALIFORNIA GIRLS   Beach Boys
5. UNCHAINED MELODY   Righteous Brothers
6. SATISFACTION   Rolling Stones
7. IT'S THE SAME OLD SONG   Four Tops
8. DON'T JUST STAND THERE   Patty Duke
9. HENRY VIII   Herman's Hermits
10. DOWN IN THE BOONDOCKS   Billy Joe Royal

August 28, 1965
1. I GOT YOU BABE   Sonny & Cher
2. HELP   Beatles
3. CALIFORNIA GIRLS   Beach Boys
4. UNCHAINED MELODY   Righteous Brothers
5. IT'S THE SAME OLD SONG   Four Tops
6. LIKE A ROLLING STONE   Bob Dylan
7. SAVE YOUR HEART FOR ME   Gary Lewis & The Playboys
8. HOLD ME, THRILL ME, KISS ME   Mel Carter
9. DOWN IN THE BOONDOCKS   Billy Joe Royal
10. PAPA'S GOT A BRAND NEW BAG   James Brown

September 4, 1965
1. HELP   Beatles
2. LIKE A ROLLING STONE   Bob Dylan
3. CALIFORNIA GIRLS   Beach Boys
4. UNCHAINED MELODY   Righteous Brothers
5. IT'S THE SAME OLD SONG   Four Tops
6. I GOT YOU BABE   Sonny & Cher
7. YOU WERE ON MY MIND   We Five
8. PAPA'S GOT A BRAND NEW BAG   James Brown
9. EVE OF DESTRUCTION   Barry McGuire
10. HOLD ME, THRILL ME, KISS ME   Mel Carter

September 11, 1965
1. HELP   Beatles
2. LIKE A ROLLING STONE   Bob Dylan
3. EVE OF DESTRUCTION   Barry McGuire
4. YOU WERE ON MY MIND   We Five
5. CALIFORNIA GIRLS   Beach Boys
6. UNCHAINED MELODY   Righteous Brothers
7. I GOT YOU BABE   Sonny & Cher
8. PAPA'S GOT A BRAND NEW BAG   James Brown
9. IT AIN'T ME BABE   Sonny & Cher
10. THE "IN" CROWD   Ramsey Lewis Trio

September 18, 1965
1. HELP   Beatles
2. EVE OF DESTRUCTION   Barry McGuire
3. LIKE A ROLLING STONE   Bob Dylan
4. YOU WERE ON MY MIND   We Five
5. CATCH US IF YOU CAN   Dave Clark Five
6. THE "IN" CROWD   Ramsey Lewis Trio
7. HANG ON SLOOPY   The McCoys

Sonny & Cher
A future Lori Davis hair-care spokesperson and a future Palm Springs mayor have a #1 hit: ``I Got You Babe'' (Aug. 14).

The Supremes
Florence, Mary and Diana are riding high with the #1 ``I Hear A Symphony'' (Nov. 20).

8   IT AIN'T ME BABE   Sonny & Cher
9   I GOT YOU BABE   Sonny & Cher
10   HEART FULL OF SOUL   Yardbirds

September 25, 1965
1   EVE OF DESTRUCTION   Barry McGuire
2   HANG ON SLOOPY   The McCoys
3   YOU WERE ON MY MIND   We Five
4   CATCH US IF YOU CAN   Dave Clark Five
5   HELP   Beatles
6   THE "IN" CROWD   Ramsey Lewis Trio
7   LIKE A ROLLING STONE   Bob Dylan
8   IT AIN'T ME BABE   Sonny & Cher
9   HEART FULL OF SOUL   Yardbirds
10   LAUGH AT ME   Sonny

October 2, 1965
1   HANG ON SLOOPY   The McCoys
2   EVE OF DESTRUCTION   Barry McGuire
3   YESTERDAY   Beatles
4   CATCH US IF YOU CAN   Dave Clark Five
5   YOU WERE ON MY MIND   We Five
6   THE "IN" CROWD   Ramsey Lewis Trio
7   TREAT HER RIGHT   Roy Head
8   YOU'VE GOT YOUR TROUBLES   Fortunes
9   BABY DON'T GO   Sonny & Cher
10   LAUGH AT ME   Sonny

October 9, 1965
1   YESTERDAY   Beatles
2   HANG ON SLOOPY   The McCoys
3   TREAT HER RIGHT   Roy Head
4   EVE OF DESTRUCTION   Barry McGuire
5   THE "IN" CROWD   Ramsey Lewis Trio
6   CATCH US IF YOU CAN   Dave Clark Five
7   YOU'VE GOT YOUR TROUBLES   Fortunes
8   BABY DON'T GO   Sonny & Cher
9   YOU WERE ON MY MIND   We Five
10   DO YOU BELIEVE IN MAGIC   Lovin' Spoonful

October 16, 1965
1   YESTERDAY   Beatles
2   TREAT HER RIGHT   Roy Head
3   HANG ON SLOOPY   The McCoys
4   LOVER'S CONCERTO   Toys
5   KEEP ON DANCING   Gentrys
6   THE "IN" CROWD   Ramsey Lewis Trio
7   JUST A LITTLE BIT BETTER   Herman's Hermits
8   BABY DON'T GO   Sonny & Cher
9   DO YOU BELIEVE IN MAGIC   Lovin' Spoonful
10   EVE OF DESTRUCTION   Barry McGuire

October 23, 1965
1   YESTERDAY   Beatles
2   TREAT HER RIGHT   Roy Head
3   LOVER'S CONCERTO   Toys
4   GET OFF OF MY CLOUD   Rolling Stones
5   KEEP ON DANCING   Gentrys
6   HANG ON SLOOPY   The McCoys
7   JUST A LITTLE BIT BETTER   Herman's Hermits
8   EVERYBODY LOVES A CLOWN   Gary Lewis & The
        Playboys
9   POSITIVELY 4TH STREET   Bob Dylan
10   YOU'RE THE ONE   Vogues

October 30, 1965
1   YESTERDAY   Beatles
2   LOVER'S CONCERTO   Toys
3   GET OFF OF MY CLOUD   Rolling Stones
4   KEEP ON DANCING   Gentrys
5   EVERYBODY LOVES A CLOWN   Gary Lewis & The
        Playboys
6   TREAT HER RIGHT   Roy Head
7   YOU'RE THE ONE   Vogues
8   POSITIVELY 4TH STREET   Bob Dylan
9   HANG ON SLOOPY   The McCoys
10   1-2-3   Len Barry

November 6, 1965
1   GET OFF OF MY CLOUD   Rolling Stones
2   LOVER'S CONCERTO   Toys
3   YESTERDAY   Beatles
4   EVERYBODY LOVES A CLOWN   Gary Lewis & The
        Playboys
5   KEEP ON DANCING   Gentrys
6   YOU'RE THE ONE   Vogues
7   POSITIVELY 4TH STREET   Bob Dylan
8   1-2-3   Len Barry
9   RESCUE ME   Fontella Bass
10   TASTE OF HONEY   Herb Alpert

November 13, 1965
1   GET OFF OF MY CLOUD   Rolling Stones
2   LOVER'S CONCERTO   Toys
3   1-2-3   Len Barry
4   YOU'RE THE ONE   Vogues
5   I HEAR A SYMPHONY   Supremes
6   RESCUE ME   Fontella Bass
7   EVERYBODY LOVES A CLOWN   Gary Lewis & The
        Playboys
8   LET'S HANG ON   Four Seasons
9   TASTE OF HONEY   Herb Alpert
10   AIN'T THAT PECULIAR   Marvin Gaye

November 20, 1965
1   I HEAR A SYMPHONY   Supremes
2   1-2-3   Len Barry
3   GET OFF OF MY CLOUD   Rolling Stones
4   RESCUE ME   Fontella Bass
5   LET'S HANG ON   Four Seasons
6   TURN! TURN! TURN!   Byrds
7   LOVER'S CONCERTO   Toys
8   AIN'T THAT PECULIAR   Marvin Gaye
9   TASTE OF HONEY   Herb Alpert
10   YOU'RE THE ONE   Vogues

November 27, 1965
1   I HEAR A SYMPHONY   Supremes
2   TURN! TURN! TURN!   Byrds
3   1-2-3   Len Barry
4   LET'S HANG ON   Four Seasons
5   GET OFF OF MY CLOUD   Rolling Stones
6   RESCUE ME   Fontella Bass
7   TASTE OF HONEY   Herb Alpert
8   AIN'T THAT PECULIAR   Marvin Gaye
9   I GOT YOU (I FEEL GOOD)   James Brown
10   YOU'VE GOT TO HIDE YOUR LOVE AWAY   Silkie

December 4, 1965
1   TURN! TURN! TURN!   Byrds
2   I HEAR A SYMPHONY   Supremes

247

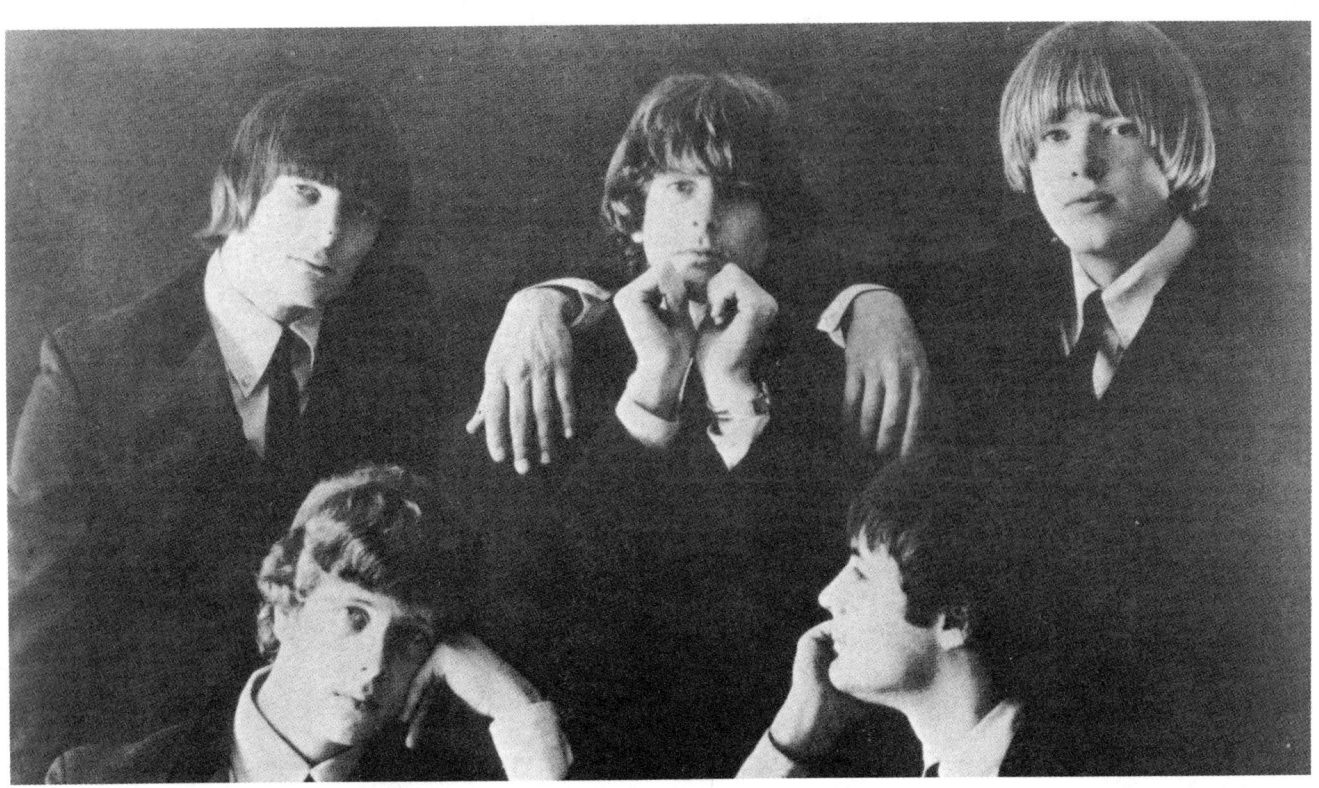

The Byrds
The God of the Bible provides a #1 hit to The Byrds of the field—``Turn! Turn! Turn!'' (Dec. 4, 1965).

Simon & Garfunkel
The #1 ``Sounds Of Silence'' echo mighty loud from the top of the hill (Jan. 1, 1966).

3 1-2-3 Len Barry
4 LET'S HANG ON Four Seasons
5 I GOT YOU (I FEEL GOOD) James Brown
6 RESCUE ME Fontella Bass
7 TASTE OF HONEY Herb Alpert
8 AIN'T THAT PECULIAR Marvin Gaye
9 I CAN NEVER GO HOME ANY MORE Shangri-Las
10 OVER AND OVER Dave Clark Five

December 11, 1965

1 TURN! TURN! TURN! Byrds
2 I HEAR A SYMPHONY Supremes
3 LET'S HANG ON Four Seasons
4 I GOT YOU (I FEEL GOOD) James Brown
5 OVER AND OVER Dave Clark Five
6 I CAN NEVER GO HOME ANY MORE Shangri-Las
7 1-2-3 Len Barry
8 TASTE OF HONEY Herb Alpert
9 RESCUE ME Fontella Bass
10 I WILL Dean Martin

December 18, 1965

1 TURN! TURN! TURN! Byrds
2 OVER AND OVER Dave Clark Five
3 I GOT YOU (I FEEL GOOD) James Brown
4 LET'S HANG ON Four Seasons
5 I HEAR A SYMPHONY Supremes
6 I CAN NEVER GO HOME ANY MORE Shangri-Las
7 MAKE THE WORLD GO AWAY Eddy Arnold
8 ENGLAND SWINGS Roger Miller
9 FEVER The McCoys
10 I WILL Dean Martin

December 25, 1965

1 OVER AND OVER Dave Clark Five
2 TURN! TURN! TURN! Byrds
3 I GOT YOU (I FEEL GOOD) James Brown
4 LET'S HANG ON Four Seasons
5 SOUNDS OF SILENCE Simon & Garfunkel
6 MAKE THE WORLD GO AWAY Eddy Arnold
7 FEVER The McCoys
8 ENGLAND SWINGS Roger Miller
9 EBB TIDE Righteous Brothers
10 I CAN NEVER GO HOME ANY MORE Shangri-Las

January 1, 1966

1 SOUNDS OF SILENCE Simon & Garfunkel
2 WE CAN WORK IT OUT Beatles
3 I GOT YOU (I FEEL GOOD) James Brown
4 TURN! TURN! TURN! Byrds
5 OVER AND OVER Dave Clark Five
6 LET'S HANG ON Four Seasons
7 FEVER The McCoys
8 EBB TIDE Righteous Brothers
9 ENGLAND SWINGS Roger Miller
10 MAKE THE WORLD GO AWAY Eddy Arnold

January 8, 1966

1 WE CAN WORK IT OUT Beatles
2 SOUNDS OF SILENCE Simon & Garfunkel
3 SHE'S JUST MY STYLE Gary Lewis & The Playboys
4 FLOWERS ON THE WALL Statler Brothers
5 EBB TIDE Righteous Brothers
6 OVER AND OVER Dave Clark Five
7 I GOT YOU (I FEEL GOOD) James Brown
8 FIVE O'CLOCK WORLD The Vogues

9 TURN! TURN! TURN! Byrds
10 DAY TRIPPER Beatles

January 15, 1966

1 WE CAN WORK IT OUT Beatles
2 SOUNDS OF SILENCE Simon & Garfunkel
3 SHE'S JUST MY STYLE Gary Lewis & The Playboys
4 FIVE O'CLOCK WORLD The Vogues
5 EBB TIDE Righteous Brothers
6 DAY TRIPPER Beatles
7 FLOWERS ON THE WALL Statler Brothers
8 MEN IN MY LITTLE GIRL'S LIFE Mike Douglas
9 AS TEARS GO BY Rolling Stones
10 NO MATTER WHAT SHAPE (YOUR STOMACH'S IN) T-Bones *
   Note: * From an Alka Seltzer jingle.

January 22, 1966

1 SOUNDS OF SILENCE Simon & Garfunkel
2 WE CAN WORK IT OUT Beatles
3 SHE'S JUST MY STYLE Gary Lewis & The Playboys
4 FIVE O'CLOCK WORLD The Vogues
5 DAY TRIPPER Beatles
6 NO MATTER WHAT SHAPE (YOUR STOMACH'S IN) T-Bones *
7 MEN IN MY LITTLE GIRL'S LIFE Mike Douglas
8 A MUST TO AVOID Herman's Hermits
9 AS TEARS GO BY Rolling Stones
10 YOU DIDN'T HAVE TO BE SO NICE Lovin' Spoonful
   Note: * From an Alka Seltzer jingle.

January 29, 1966

1 WE CAN WORK IT OUT Beatles
2 BARBARA ANN Beach Boys
3 SHE'S JUST MY STYLE Gary Lewis & The Playboys
4 NO MATTER WHAT SHAPE (YOUR STOMACH'S IN) T-Bones *
5 FIVE O'CLOCK WORLD The Vogues
6 AS TEARS GO BY Rolling Stones
7 MEN IN MY LITTLE GIRL'S LIFE Mike Douglas
8 A MUST TO AVOID Herman's Hermits
9 MY LOVE Petula Clark
10 JENNY TAKE A RIDE Mitch Ryder & The Detroit Wheels
   Note: * From an Alka Seltzer jingle.

February 5, 1966

1 MY LOVE Petula Clark
2 BARBARA ANN Beach Boys
3 NO MATTER WHAT SHAPE (YOUR STOMACH'S IN) T-Bones *
4 WE CAN WORK IT OUT Beatles
5 LIGHTNIN' STRIKES Lou Christie
6 MEN IN MY LITTLE GIRL'S LIFE Mike Douglas
7 SHE'S JUST MY STYLE Gary Lewis & The Playboys
8 FIVE O'CLOCK WORLD The Vogues
9 A MUST TO AVOID Herman's Hermits
10 CRYING TIME Ray Charles
   Note: * From an Alka Seltzer jingle.

February 12, 1966

1 MY LOVE Petula Clark
2 LIGHTNIN' STRIKES Lou Christie
3 UP TIGHT Stevie Wonder
4 BARBARA ANN Beach Boys
5 WE CAN WORK IT OUT Beatles
6 NO MATTER WHAT SHAPE (YOUR STOMACH'S IN) T-Bones *

7 CRYING TIME   Ray Charles
8 MY WORLD IS EMPTY WITHOUT YOU   Supremes
9 FIVE O'CLOCK WORLD   The Vogues
10 DON'T MESS WITH BILL   Marvelettes
   Note: * From an Alka Seltzer jingle.

February 19, 1966
1 LIGHTNIN' STRIKES   Lou Christie
2 THESE BOOTS ARE MADE FOR WALKIN'   Nancy Sinatra
3 UP TIGHT   Stevie Wonder
4 MY LOVE   Petula Clark
5 MY WORLD IS EMPTY WITHOUT YOU   Supremes
6 CRYING TIME   Ray Charles
7 BARBARA ANN   Beach Boys
8 DON'T MESS WITH BILL   Marvelettes
9 NO MATTER WHAT SHAPE (YOUR STOMACH'S IN)   T-Bones *
10 THE BALLAD OF THE GREEN BERETS   SSgt. Barry Sadler
   Note: * From an Alka Seltzer jingle.

February 26, 1966
1 THESE BOOTS ARE MADE FOR WALKIN'   Nancy Sinatra
2 LIGHTNIN' STRIKES   Lou Christie
3 THE BALLAD OF THE GREEN BERETS   SSgt. Barry Sadler
4 UP TIGHT   Stevie Wonder
5 MY WORLD IS EMPTY WITHOUT YOU   Supremes
6 MY LOVE   Petula Clark
7 DON'T MESS WITH BILL   Marvelettes
8 CALIFORNIA DREAMING   Mamas & Papas
9 ELUSIVE BUTTERFLY   Bob Lind
10 WORKING MY WAY BACK TO YOU   Four Seasons

March 5, 1966
1 THE BALLAD OF THE GREEN BERETS   SSgt. Barry Sadler
2 THESE BOOTS ARE MADE FOR WALKIN'   Nancy Sinatra
3 LIGHTNIN' STRIKES   Lou Christie
4 LISTEN PEOPLE   Herman's Hermits
5 CALIFORNIA DREAMING   Mamas & Papas
6 ELUSIVE BUTTERFLY   Bob Lind
7 MY LOVE   Petula Clark
8 UP TIGHT   Stevie Wonder
9 WORKING MY WAY BACK TO YOU   Four Seasons
10 MY WORLD IS EMPTY WITHOUT YOU   Supremes

March 12, 1966
1 THE BALLAD OF THE GREEN BERETS   SSgt. Barry Sadler
2 THESE BOOTS ARE MADE FOR WALKIN'   Nancy Sinatra
3 LISTEN PEOPLE   Herman's Hermits
4 CALIFORNIA DREAMING   Mamas & Papas
5 ELUSIVE BUTTERFLY   Bob Lind
6 19TH NERVOUS BREAKDOWN   Rolling Stones
7 NOWHERE MAN   Beatles
8 LIGHTNIN' STRIKES   Lou Christie
9 I FOUGHT THE LAW   Bobby Fuller Four
10 HOMEWARD BOUND   Simon & Garfunkel

March 19, 1966
1 THE BALLAD OF THE GREEN BERETS   SSgt. Barry Sadler
2 19TH NERVOUS BREAKDOWN   Rolling Stones
3 THESE BOOTS ARE MADE FOR WALKIN'   Nancy Sinatra
4 NOWHERE MAN   Beatles
5 ELUSIVE BUTTERFLY   Bob Lind
6 LISTEN PEOPLE   Herman's Hermits
7 CALIFORNIA DREAMING   Mamas & Papas
8 HOMEWARD BOUND   Simon & Garfunkel
9 I FOUGHT THE LAW   Bobby Fuller Four
10 DAYDREAM   Lovin' Spoonful

March 26, 1966
1 THE BALLAD OF THE GREEN BERETS   SSgt. Barry Sadler
2 19TH NERVOUS BREAKDOWN   Rolling Stones
3 NOWHERE MAN   Beatles
4 THESE BOOTS ARE MADE FOR WALKIN'   Nancy Sinatra
5 HOMEWARD BOUND   Simon & Garfunkel
6 DAYDREAM   Lovin' Spoonful
7 CALIFORNIA DREAMING   Mamas & Papas
8 (YOU'RE MY) SOUL AND INSPIRATION   Righteous Brothers
9 ELUSIVE BUTTERFLY   Bob Lind
10 LISTEN PEOPLE   Herman's Hermits

April 2, 1966
1 THE BALLAD OF THE GREEN BERETS   SSgt. Barry Sadler
2 19TH NERVOUS BREAKDOWN   Rolling Stones
3 (YOU'RE MY) SOUL AND INSPIRATION   Righteous Brothers
4 DAYDREAM   Lovin' Spoonful
5 HOMEWARD BOUND   Simon & Garfunkel
6 NOWHERE MAN   Beatles
7 CALIFORNIA DREAMING   Mamas & Papas
8 THESE BOOTS ARE MADE FOR WALKIN'   Nancy Sinatra
9 BANG BANG   Cher
10 SURE GONNA MISS HER   Gary Lewis & The Playboys

April 9, 1966
1 (YOU'RE MY) SOUL AND INSPIRATION   Righteous Brothers
2 DAYDREAM   Lovin' Spoonful
3 19TH NERVOUS BREAKDOWN   Rolling Stones
4 BANG BANG   Cher
5 THE BALLAD OF THE GREEN BERETS   SSgt. Barry Sadler
6 NOWHERE MAN   Beatles
7 SECRET AGENT MAN   Johnny Rivers
8 I'M SO LONESOME I COULD CRY   B. J. Thomas
9 SURE GONNA MISS HER   Gary Lewis & The Playboys
10 CALIFORNIA DREAMING   Mamas & Papas

April 16, 1966
1 (YOU'RE MY) SOUL AND INSPIRATION   Righteous Brothers
2 DAYDREAM   Lovin' Spoonful
3 BANG BANG   Cher
4 SECRET AGENT MAN   Johnny Rivers
5 TIME WON'T LET ME   Outsiders
6 19TH NERVOUS BREAKDOWN   Rolling Stones
7 THE BALLAD OF THE GREEN BERETS   SSgt. Barry Sadler
8 I'M SO LONESOME I COULD CRY   B. J. Thomas
9 GOOD LOVIN'   Young Rascals
10 KICKS   Paul Revere & The Raiders

April 23, 1966
1 (YOU'RE MY) SOUL AND INSPIRATION   Righteous Brothers
2 BANG BANG   Cher
3 SECRET AGENT MAN   Johnny Rivers
4 DAYDREAM   Lovin' Spoonful
5 TIME WON'T LET ME   Outsiders
6 GOOD LOVIN'   Young Rascals
7 KICKS   Paul Revere & The Raiders
8 SLOOP JOHN B.   Beach Boys
9 I'M SO LONESOME I COULD CRY   B. J. Thomas
10 MONDAY MONDAY   Mamas & Papas

April 30, 1966
1 GOOD LOVIN' Young Rascals
2 (YOU'RE MY) SOUL AND INSPIRATION Righteous Brothers
3 MONDAY MONDAY Mamas & Papas
4 SLOOP JOHN B. Beach Boys
5 SECRET AGENT MAN Johnny Rivers
6 KICKS Paul Revere & The Raiders
7 TIME WON'T LET ME Outsiders
8 BANG BANG Cher
9 DAYDREAM Lovin' Spoonful
10 LEANING ON THE LAMP POST Herman's Hermits

May 7, 1966
1 MONDAY MONDAY Mamas & Papas
2 GOOD LOVIN' Young Rascals
3 SLOOP JOHN B. Beach Boys
4 (YOU'RE MY) SOUL AND INSPIRATION Righteous Brothers
5 KICKS Paul Revere & The Raiders
6 SECRET AGENT MAN Johnny Rivers
7 RAINY DAY WOMEN #12 & 35 Bob Dylan
8 BANG BANG Cher
9 LEANING ON THE LAMP POST Herman's Hermits
10 GLORIA Shadows Of Night

May 14, 1966
1 MONDAY MONDAY Mamas & Papas
2 GOOD LOVIN' Young Rascals
3 RAINY DAY WOMEN #12 & 35 Bob Dylan
4 KICKS Paul Revere & The Raiders
5 SLOOP JOHN B. Beach Boys
6 (YOU'RE MY) SOUL AND INSPIRATION Righteous Brothers
7 HOW DOES THAT GRAB YOU DARLIN' Nancy Sinatra
8 MESSAGE TO MICHAEL Dionne Warwick
9 WHEN A MAN LOVES A WOMAN Percy Sledge
10 GLORIA Shadows Of Night

May 21, 1966
1 MONDAY MONDAY Mamas & Papas
2 RAINY DAY WOMEN #12 & 35 Bob Dylan
3 GOOD LOVIN' Young Rascals
4 WHEN A MAN LOVES A WOMAN Percy Sledge
5 A GROOVY KIND OF LOVE Mindbenders
6 KICKS Paul Revere & The Raiders
7 HOW DOES THAT GRAB YOU DARLIN' Nancy Sinatra
8 MESSAGE TO MICHAEL Dionne Warwick
9 SLOOP JOHN B. Beach Boys
10 LOVE IS LIKE AN ITCHING IN MY HEART Supremes

May 28, 1966
1 WHEN A MAN LOVES A WOMAN Percy Sledge
2 A GROOVY KIND OF LOVE Mindbenders
3 MONDAY MONDAY Mamas & Papas
4 PAINT IT BLACK Rolling Stones
5 RAINY DAY WOMEN #12 & 35 Bob Dylan
6 I AM A ROCK Simon & Garfunkel
7 DID YOU EVER HAVE TO MAKE UP YOUR MIND? Lovin' Spoonful
8 GOOD LOVIN' Young Rascals
9 LOVE IS LIKE AN ITCHING IN MY HEART Supremes
10 IT'S A MAN'S MAN'S MAN'S WORLD James Brown

June 4, 1966
1 WHEN A MAN LOVES A WOMAN Percy Sledge

2 A GROOVY KIND OF LOVE Mindbenders
3 PAINT IT BLACK Rolling Stones
4 DID YOU EVER HAVE TO MAKE UP YOUR MIND? Lovin' Spoonful
5 I AM A ROCK Simon & Garfunkel
6 MONDAY MONDAY Mamas & Papas
7 RAINY DAY WOMEN #12 & 35 Bob Dylan
8 IT'S A MAN'S MAN'S MAN'S WORLD James Brown
9 GREEN GRASS Gary Lewis & The Playboys
10 STRANGERS IN THE NIGHT Frank Sinatra

June 11, 1966
1 PAINT IT BLACK Rolling Stones
2 DID YOU EVER HAVE TO MAKE UP YOUR MIND? Lovin' Spoonful
3 I AM A ROCK Simon & Garfunkel
4 WHEN A MAN LOVES A WOMAN Percy Sledge
5 A GROOVY KIND OF LOVE Mindbenders
6 STRANGERS IN THE NIGHT Frank Sinatra
7 MONDAY MONDAY Mamas & Papas
8 IT'S A MAN'S MAN'S MAN'S WORLD James Brown
9 GREEN GRASS Gary Lewis & The Playboys
10 BAREFOOTIN' Robert Parker

June 18, 1966
1 PAINT IT BLACK Rolling Stones
2 DID YOU EVER HAVE TO MAKE UP YOUR MIND? Lovin' Spoonful
3 I AM A ROCK Simon & Garfunkel
4 WHEN A MAN LOVES A WOMAN Percy Sledge
5 STRANGERS IN THE NIGHT Frank Sinatra
6 A GROOVY KIND OF LOVE Mindbenders
7 BAREFOOTIN' Robert Parker
8 GREEN GRASS Gary Lewis & The Playboys
9 COOL JERK Capitols
10 RED RUBBER BALL Cyrkle

June 25, 1966
1 PAPERBACK WRITER Beatles
2 STRANGERS IN THE NIGHT Frank Sinatra
3 PAINT IT BLACK Rolling Stones
4 DID YOU EVER HAVE TO MAKE UP YOUR MIND? Lovin' Spoonful
5 I AM A ROCK Simon & Garfunkel
6 RED RUBBER BALL Cyrkle
7 BAREFOOTIN' Robert Parker
8 COOL JERK Capitols
9 YOU DON'T HAVE TO SAY YOU LOVE ME Dusty Springfield
10 SWEET TALKIN' GUY Chiffons

July 2, 1966
1 STRANGERS IN THE NIGHT Frank Sinatra
2 PAPERBACK WRITER Beatles
3 RED RUBBER BALL Cyrkle
4 PAINT IT BLACK Rolling Stones
5 YOU DON'T HAVE TO SAY YOU LOVE ME Dusty Springfield
6 HANKY PANKY Tommy James & The Shondells
7 COOL JERK Capitols
8 I AM A ROCK Simon & Garfunkel
9 DID YOU EVER HAVE TO MAKE UP YOUR MIND? Lovin' Spoonful
10 BAREFOOTIN' Robert Parker

July 9, 1966
1. PAPERBACK WRITER   Beatles
2. RED RUBBER BALL   Cyrkle
3. STRANGERS IN THE NIGHT   Frank Sinatra
4. HANKY PANKY   Tommy James & The Shondells
5. YOU DON'T HAVE TO SAY YOU LOVE ME   Dusty Springfield
6. WILD THING   Troggs
7. COOL JERK   Capitols
8. LITTLE GIRL   Syndicate Of Sound
9. PAINT IT BLACK   Rolling Stones
10. ALONG COMES MARY   Association

July 16, 1966
1. HANKY PANKY   Tommy James & The Shondells
2. WILD THING   Troggs
3. RED RUBBER BALL   Cyrkle
4. YOU DON'T HAVE TO SAY YOU LOVE ME   Dusty Springfield
5. PAPERBACK WRITER   Beatles
6. STRANGERS IN THE NIGHT   Frank Sinatra
7. ALONG COMES MARY   Association
8. LITTLE GIRL   Syndicate Of Sound
9. LIL' RED RIDING HOOD   Sam The Sham & The Pharoahs
10. HUNGRY   Paul Revere & The Raiders

July 23, 1966
1. HANKY PANKY   Tommy James & The Shondells
2. WILD THING   Troggs
3. LIL' RED RIDING HOOD   Sam The Sham & The Pharoahs
4. PIED PIPER   Crispian St. Peters
5. YOU DON'T HAVE TO SAY YOU LOVE ME   Dusty Springfield
6. PAPERBACK WRITER   Beatles
7. HUNGRY   Paul Revere & The Raiders
8. RED RUBBER BALL   Cyrkle
9. I SAW HER AGAIN   Mamas & Papas
10. SWEET PEA   Tommy Roe

July 30, 1966
1. WILD THING   Troggs
2. HANKY PANKY   Tommy James & The Shondells
3. LIL' RED RIDING HOOD   Sam The Sham & The Pharoahs
4. PIED PIPER   Crispian St. Peters
5. I SAW HER AGAIN   Mamas & Papas
6. HUNGRY   Paul Revere & The Raiders
7. SUMMER IN THE CITY   Lovin' Spoonful
8. SWEET PEA   Tommy Roe
9. MOTHER'S LITTLE HELPER   Rolling Stones
10. SOMEWHERE MY LOVE   Ray Conniff

August 6, 1966
1. WILD THING   Troggs
2. LIL' RED RIDING HOOD   Sam The Sham & The Pharoahs
3. SUMMER IN THE CITY   Lovin' Spoonful
4. PIED PIPER   Crispian St. Peters
5. THEY'RE COMING TO TAKE ME AWAY HA-HAA   Napoleon XIV
6. I SAW HER AGAIN   Mamas & Papas
7. HANKY PANKY   Tommy James & The Shondells
8. SWEET PEA   Tommy Roe
9. MOTHER'S LITTLE HELPER   Rolling Stones
10. SOMEWHERE MY LOVE   Ray Conniff

August 11, 1966
1. SUMMER IN THE CITY   Lovin' Spoonful

2. LIL' RED RIDING HOOD   Sam The Sham & The Pharoahs
3. THEY'RE COMING TO TAKE ME AWAY HA-HAA   Napoleon XIV
4. WILD THING   Troggs
5. PIED PIPER   Crispian St. Peters
6. I SAW HER AGAIN   Mamas & Papas
7. SUNNY   Bobby Hebb
8. MOTHER'S LITTLE HELPER   Rolling Stones
9. SOMEWHERE MY LOVE   Ray Conniff
10. SWEET PEA   Tommy Roe

August 20, 1966
1. SUMMER IN THE CITY   Lovin' Spoonful
2. SUNNY   Bobby Hebb
3. LIL' RED RIDING HOOD   Sam The Sham & The Pharoahs
4. WILD THING   Troggs
5. THEY'RE COMING TO TAKE ME AWAY HA-HAA   Napoleon XIV
6. SEE YOU IN SEPTEMBER   Happenings
7. PIED PIPER   Crispian St. Peters
8. MOTHER'S LITTLE HELPER   Rolling Stones
9. I COULDN'T LIVE WITHOUT YOUR LOVE   Petula Clark
10. SUNSHINE SUPERMAN   Donovan

August 27, 1966
1. SUMMER IN THE CITY   Lovin' Spoonful
2. SUNNY   Bobby Hebb
3. SEE YOU IN SEPTEMBER   Happenings
4. LIL' RED RIDING HOOD   Sam The Sham & The Pharoahs
5. SUNSHINE SUPERMAN   Donovan
6. WILD THING   Troggs
7. YOU CAN'T HURRY LOVE   Supremes
8. YELLOW SUBMARINE   Beatles
9. I COULDN'T LIVE WITHOUT YOUR LOVE   Petula Clark
10. SUMMERTIME   Billy Stewart

September 3, 1966
1. SUNSHINE SUPERMAN   Donovan
2. SUMMER IN THE CITY   Lovin' Spoonful
3. SEE YOU IN SEPTEMBER   Happenings
4. YOU CAN'T HURRY LOVE   Supremes
5. YELLOW SUBMARINE   Beatles
6. SUNNY   Bobby Hebb
7. LAND OF 1,000 DANCES   Wilson Pickett
8. WORKING IN THE COAL MINE   Lee Dorsey
9. BLOWING IN THE WIND   Peter, Paul & Mary
10. SUMMERTIME   Billy Stewart

September 10, 1966
1. YOU CAN'T HURRY LOVE   Supremes
2. SUNSHINE SUPERMAN   Donovan
3. YELLOW SUBMARINE   Beatles
4. SEE YOU IN SEPTEMBER   Happenings
5. SUMMER IN THE CITY   Lovin' Spoonful
6. LAND OF 1,000 DANCES   Wilson Pickett
7. SUNNY   Bobby Hebb
8. WORKING IN THE COAL MINE   Lee Dorsey
9. BUS STOP   Hollies
10. GUANTANAMERA   Sandpipers

September 17, 1966
1. YOU CAN'T HURRY LOVE   Supremes
2. YELLOW SUBMARINE   Beatles
3. SUNSHINE SUPERMAN   Donovan
4. CHERISH   Association
5. BUS STOP   Hollies

6 SEE YOU IN SEPTEMBER Happenings
7 LAND OF 1,000 DANCES Wilson Pickett
8 WOULDN'T IT BE NICE Beach Boys
9 GUANTANAMERA Sandpipers
10 SUNNY Bobby Hebb

September 24, 1966
1 CHERISH Association
2 YOU CAN'T HURRY LOVE Supremes
3 SUNSHINE SUPERMAN Donovan
4 YELLOW SUBMARINE Beatles
5 BUS STOP Hollies
6 BEAUTY IS ONLY SKIN DEEP Temptations
7 BLACK IS BLACK Los Bravos
8 96 TEARS ? & The Mysterians
9 WOULDN'T IT BE NICE Beach Boys
10 REACH OUT I'LL BE THERE Four Tops

October 1, 1966
1 CHERISH Association
2 YOU CAN'T HURRY LOVE Supremes
3 BEAUTY IS ONLY SKIN DEEP Temptations
4 BLACK IS BLACK Los Bravos
5 BUS STOP Hollies
6 96 TEARS ? & The Mysterians
7 REACH OUT I'LL BE THERE Four Tops
8 YELLOW SUBMARINE Beatles
9 SUNSHINE SUPERMAN Donovan
10 CHERRY CHERRY Neil Diamond

October 8, 1966
1 CHERISH Association
2 REACH OUT I'LL BE THERE Four Tops
3 96 TEARS ? & The Mysterians
4 BLACK IS BLACK Los Bravos
5 BEAUTY IS ONLY SKIN DEEP Temptations
6 LAST TRAIN TO CLARKSVILLE Monkees
7 CHERRY CHERRY Neil Diamond
8 YOU CAN'T HURRY LOVE Supremes
9 PSYCHOTIC REACTION Count Five
10 I'VE GOT YOU UNDER MY SKIN Four Seasons

October 15, 1966
1 REACH OUT I'LL BE THERE Four Tops
2 CHERISH Association
3 96 TEARS ? & The Mysterians
4 LAST TRAIN TO CLARKSVILLE Monkees
5 PSYCHOTIC REACTION Count Five
6 CHERRY CHERRY Neil Diamond
7 WALK AWAY RENEE Left Banke
8 WHAT BECOMES OF THE BROKEN HEARTED Jimmy Ruffin
9 I'VE GOT YOU UNDER MY SKIN Four Seasons
10 YOU CAN'T HURRY LOVE Supremes

October 22, 1966
1 REACH OUT I'LL BE THERE Four Tops
2 96 TEARS ? & The Mysterians
3 LAST TRAIN TO CLARKSVILLE Monkees
4 CHERISH Association
5 PSYCHOTIC REACTION Count Five
6 WALK AWAY RENEE Left Banke
7 POOR SIDE OF TOWN Johnny Rivers
8 WHAT BECOMES OF THE BROKEN HEARTED Jimmy Ruffin
9 DANDY Herman's Hermits
10 C. C. RIDER Animals

October 29, 1966
1 96 TEARS ? & The Mysterians
2 LAST TRAIN TO CLARKSVILLE Monkees
3 REACH OUT I'LL BE THERE Four Tops
4 POOR SIDE OF TOWN Johnny Rivers
5 WALK AWAY RENEE Left Banke
6 DANDY Herman's Hermits
7 WHAT BECOMES OF THE BROKEN HEARTED Jimmy Ruffin
8 HOORAY FOR HAZEL Tommy Roe
9 HAVE YOU SEEN YOUR MOTHER, BABY, STANDING IN THE SHADOW Rolling Stones
10 C. C. RIDER Animals

November 5, 1966
1 LAST TRAIN TO CLARKSVILLE Monkees
2 96 TEARS ? & The Mysterians
3 POOR SIDE OF TOWN Johnny Rivers
4 REACH OUT I'LL BE THERE Four Tops
5 DANDY Herman's Hermits
6 HOORAY FOR HAZEL Tommy Roe
7 WHAT BECOMES OF THE BROKEN HEARTED Jimmy Ruffin
8 IF I WERE A CARPENTER Bobby Darin
9 HAVE YOU SEEN YOUR MOTHER, BABY, STANDING IN THE SHADOW Rolling Stones
10 WALK AWAY RENEE Left Banke

November 12, 1966
1 POOR SIDE OF TOWN Johnny Rivers
2 LAST TRAIN TO CLARKSVILLE Monkees
3 96 TEARS ? & The Mysterians
4 GOOD VIBRATIONS Beach Boys
5 DANDY Herman's Hermits
6 WINCHESTER CATHEDRAL New Vaudeville Band
7 YOU KEEP ME HANGIN' ON Supremes
8 IF I WERE A CARPENTER Bobby Darin
9 DEVIL WITH A BLUE DRESS ON & GOOD GOLLY MISS MOLLY Mitch Ryder & The Detroit Wheels
10 I'M YOUR PUPPET James & Bobby Purify

November 19, 1966
1 YOU KEEP ME HANGIN' ON Supremes
2 GOOD VIBRATIONS Beach Boys
3 WINCHESTER CATHEDRAL New Vaudeville Band
4 LAST TRAIN TO CLARKSVILLE Monkees
5 POOR SIDE OF TOWN Johnny Rivers
6 DEVIL WITH A BLUE DRESS ON & GOOD GOLLY MISS MOLLY Mitch Ryder & The Detroit Wheels
7 I'M YOUR PUPPET James & Bobby Purify
8 96 TEARS ? & The Mysterians
9 IF I WERE A CARPENTER Bobby Darin
10 RAIN ON THE ROOF Lovin' Spoonful

November 26, 1966
1 YOU KEEP ME HANGIN' ON Supremes
2 GOOD VIBRATIONS Beach Boys
3 WINCHESTER CATHEDRAL New Vaudeville Band
4 DEVIL WITH A BLUE DRESS ON & GOOD GOLLY MISS MOLLY Mitch Ryder & The Detroit Wheels
5 POOR SIDE OF TOWN Johnny Rivers
6 I'M YOUR PUPPET James & Bobby Purify
7 LAST TRAIN TO CLARKSVILLE Monkees
8 LADY GODIVA Peter & Gordon
9 MELLOW YELLOW Donovan
10 BORN FREE Roger Williams

December 3, 1966
1 WINCHESTER CATHEDRAL   New Vaudeville Band
2 GOOD VIBRATIONS   Beach Boys
3 YOU KEEP ME HANGIN' ON   Supremes
4 DEVIL WITH A BLUE DRESS ON & GOOD GOLLY MISS MOLLY   Mitch Ryder & The Detroit Wheels
5 MELLOW YELLOW   Donovan
6 MELLOW YELLOW   Donovan
7 LADY GODIVA   Peter & Gordon
8 BORN FREE   Roger Williams
9 POOR SIDE OF TOWN   Johnny Rivers
10 STOP STOP STOP   Hollies

December 10, 1966
1 GOOD VIBRATIONS   Beach Boys
2 MELLOW YELLOW   Donovan
3 WINCHESTER CATHEDRAL   New Vaudeville Band
4 DEVIL WITH A BLUE DRESS ON & GOOD GOLLY MISS MOLLY   Mitch Ryder & The Detroit Wheels
5 YOU KEEP ME HANGIN' ON   Supremes
6 LADY GODIVA   Peter & Gordon
7 STOP STOP STOP   Hollies
8 BORN FREE   Roger Williams
9 I'M READY FOR LOVE   Martha & The Vandellas
10 THAT'S LIFE   Frank Sinatra

December 17, 1966
1 WINCHESTER CATHEDRAL   New Vaudeville Band
2 MELLOW YELLOW   Donovan
3 GOOD VIBRATIONS   Beach Boys
4 DEVIL WITH A BLUE DRESS ON & GOOD GOLLY MISS MOLLY   Mitch Ryder & The Detroit Wheels
5 YOU KEEP ME HANGIN' ON   Supremes
6 THAT'S LIFE   Frank Sinatra
7 BORN FREE   Roger Williams
8 I'M A BELIEVER   Monkees
9 SUGAR TOWN   Nancy Sinatra
10 A PLACE IN THE SUN   Stevie Wonder

December 24, 1966
1 WINCHESTER CATHEDRAL   New Vaudeville Band
2 MELLOW YELLOW   Donovan
3 I'M A BELIEVER   Monkees
4 THAT'S LIFE   Frank Sinatra
5 DEVIL WITH A BLUE DRESS ON & GOOD GOLLY MISS MOLLY   Mitch Ryder & The Detroit Wheels
6 SUGAR TOWN   Nancy Sinatra
7 SNOOPY VS. THE RED BARON   Royal Guardsmen
8 GOOD VIBRATIONS   Beach Boys
9 A PLACE IN THE SUN   Stevie Wonder
10 (I KNOW) I'M LOSING YOU   Temptations

December 31, 1966
1 I'M A BELIEVER   Monkees
2 SNOOPY VS. THE RED BARON   Royal Guardsmen
3 WINCHESTER CATHEDRAL   New Vaudeville Band
4 THAT'S LIFE   Frank Sinatra
5 SUGAR TOWN   Nancy Sinatra
6 MELLOW YELLOW   Donovan
7 TELL IT LIKE IT IS   Aaron Neville
8 (I KNOW) I'M LOSING YOU   Temptations
9 A PLACE IN THE SUN   Stevie Wonder
10 GOOD THING   Paul Revere & The Raiders

January 7, 1967
1 I'M A BELIEVER   Monkees

2 SNOOPY VS. THE RED BARON   Royal Guardsmen
3 TELL IT LIKE IT IS   Aaron Neville
4 WINCHESTER CATHEDRAL   New Vaudeville Band
5 SUGAR TOWN   Nancy Sinatra
6 THAT'S LIFE   Frank Sinatra
7 GOOD THING   Paul Revere & The Raiders
8 WORDS OF LOVE   Mamas & Papas
9 STANDING IN THE SHADOWS OF LOVE   Four Tops
10 MELLOW YELLOW   Donovan

January 14, 1967
1 I'M A BELIEVER   Monkees
2 SNOOPY VS. THE RED BARON   Royal Guardsmen
3 TELL IT LIKE IT IS   Aaron Neville
4 GOOD THING   Paul Revere & The Raiders
5 SUGAR TOWN   Nancy Sinatra
6 WORDS OF LOVE   Mamas & Papas
7 STANDING IN THE SHADOWS OF LOVE   Four Tops
8 WINCHESTER CATHEDRAL   New Vaudeville Band
9 THAT'S LIFE   Frank Sinatra
10 GEORGY GIRL   Seekers

January 21, 1967
1 I'M A BELIEVER   Monkees
2 SNOOPY VS. THE RED BARON   Royal Guardsmen
3 TELL IT LIKE IT IS   Aaron Neville
4 GOOD THING   Paul Revere & The Raiders
5 WORDS OF LOVE   Mamas & Papas
6 STANDING IN THE SHADOWS OF LOVE   Four Tops
7 GEORGY GIRL   Seekers
8 SUGAR TOWN   Nancy Sinatra
9 NASHVILLE CATS   Lovin' Spoonful
10 TELL IT TO THE RAIN   Four Seasons

January 28, 1967
1 I'M A BELIEVER   Monkees
2 TELL IT LIKE IT IS   Aaron Neville
3 SNOOPY VS. THE RED BARON   Royal Guardsmen
4 GEORGY GIRL   Seekers
5 WORDS OF LOVE   Mamas & Papas
6 STANDING IN THE SHADOWS OF LOVE   Four Tops
7 GOOD THING   Paul Revere & The Raiders
8 NASHVILLE CATS   Lovin' Spoonful
9 KIND OF A DRAG   Buckinghams
10 (WE AIN'T GOT) NOTHIN' YET   Blues Magoos

February 4, 1967
1 I'M A BELIEVER   Monkees
2 GEORGY GIRL   Seekers
3 SNOOPY VS. THE RED BARON   Royal Guardsmen
4 TELL IT LIKE IT IS   Aaron Neville
5 KIND OF A DRAG   Buckinghams
6 WORDS OF LOVE   Mamas & Papas
7 (WE AIN'T GOT) NOTHIN' YET   Blues Magoos
8 98.6   Keith
9 GOOD THING   Paul Revere & The Raiders
10 STANDING IN THE SHADOWS OF LOVE   Four Tops

February 11, 1967
1 I'M A BELIEVER   Monkees
2 GEORGY GIRL   Seekers
3 KIND OF A DRAG   Buckinghams
4 RUBY TUESDAY   Rolling Stones
5 (WE AIN'T GOT) NOTHIN' YET   Blues Magoos
6 TELL IT LIKE IT IS   Aaron Neville
7 98.6   Keith
8 SNOOPY VS. THE RED BARON   Royal Guardsmen

The Monkees
What a way to celebrate the New Year—``I'm A Believer'' is #1 for seven weeks (Dec.31, 1966-Feb. 11, 1967).

9 LOVE IS HERE AND NOW YOU'RE GONE Supremes
10 THE BEAT GOES ON Sonny & Cher

February 18, 1967
1 KIND OF A DRAG Buckinghams
2 I'M A BELIEVER Monkees
3 RUBY TUESDAY Rolling Stones
4 GEORGY GIRL Seekers
5 (WE AIN'T GOT) NOTHIN' YET Blues Magoos
6 LOVE IS HERE AND NOW YOU'RE GONE Supremes
7 98.6 Keith
8 TELL IT LIKE IT IS Aaron Neville
9 THE BEAT GOES ON Sonny & Cher
10 GIMME SOME LOVIN' Spencer Davis Group

February 25, 1967
1 KIND OF A DRAG Buckinghams
2 LOVE IS HERE AND NOW YOU'RE GONE Supremes
3 RUBY TUESDAY Rolling Stones
4 I'M A BELIEVER Monkees
5 GEORGY GIRL Seekers
6 THE BEAT GOES ON Sonny & Cher
7 GIMME SOME LOVIN' Spencer Davis Group
8 THEN YOU CAN TELL ME GOODBYE Casinos
9 (WE AIN'T GOT) NOTHIN' YET Blues Magoos
10 BABY, I NEED YOUR LOVING Johnny Rivers

March 4, 1967
1 RUBY TUESDAY Rolling Stones
2 LOVE IS HERE AND NOW YOU'RE GONE Supremes
3 KIND OF A DRAG Buckinghams
4 BABY, I NEED YOUR LOVING Johnny Rivers

5 GEORGY GIRL Seekers
6 THE BEAT GOES ON Sonny & Cher
7 GIMME SOME LOVIN' Spencer Davis Group
8 THEN YOU CAN TELL ME GOODBYE Casinos
9 SOCK IT TO ME - BABY Mitch Ryder & The Detroit Wheels
10 I'M A BELIEVER Monkees

March 11, 1967
1 LOVE IS HERE AND NOW YOU'RE GONE Supremes
2 RUBY TUESDAY Rolling Stones
3 BABY, I NEED YOUR LOVING Johnny Rivers
4 KIND OF A DRAG Buckinghams
5 PENNY LANE Beatles
6 THEN YOU CAN TELL ME GOODBYE Casinos
7 SOCK IT TO ME - BABY Mitch Ryder & The Detroit Wheels
8 HAPPY TOGETHER Turtles
9 MY CUP RUNNETH OVER Ed Ames
10 DEDICATED TO THE ONE I LOVE Mamas & Papas

March 18, 1967
1 PENNY LANE Beatles
2 HAPPY TOGETHER Turtles
3 BABY, I NEED YOUR LOVING Johnny Rivers
4 LOVE IS HERE AND NOW YOU'RE GONE Supremes
5 RUBY TUESDAY Rolling Stones
6 DEDICATED TO THE ONE I LOVE Mamas & Papas
7 SOCK IT TO ME - BABY Mitch Ryder & The Detroit Wheels
8 THERE'S A KIND OF HUSH (ALL OVER THE WORLD) Herman's Hermits
9 MY CUP RUNNETH OVER Ed Ames
10 THEN YOU CAN TELL ME GOODBYE Casinos

255

March 25, 1967
1 HAPPY TOGETHER   Turtles
2 DEDICATED TO THE ONE I LOVE   Mamas & Papas
3 PENNY LANE   Beatles
4 THERE'S A KIND OF HUSH (ALL OVER THE WORLD)
     Herman's Hermits
5 BABY, I NEED YOUR LOVING   Johnny Rivers
6 SOCK IT TO ME - BABY   Mitch Ryder & The Detroit Wheels
7 FOR WHAT IT'S WORTH   Buffalo Springfield
8 MY CUP RUNNETH OVER   Ed Ames
9 LOVE IS HERE AND NOW YOU'RE GONE   Supremes
10 RUBY TUESDAY   Rolling Stones

April 1, 1967
1 HAPPY TOGETHER   Turtles
2 DEDICATED TO THE ONE I LOVE   Mamas & Papas
3 PENNY LANE   Beatles
4 THERE'S A KIND OF HUSH (ALL OVER THE WORLD)
     Herman's Hermits
5 BERNADETTE   Four Tops
6 THIS IS MY SONG   Petula Clark
7 FOR WHAT IT'S WORTH   Buffalo Springfield
8 STRAWBERRY FIELDS FOREVER   Beatles
9 SOMETHIN' STUPID   Nancy & Frank Sinatra
10 WESTERN UNION   Five Americans

April 8, 1967
1 HAPPY TOGETHER   Turtles
2 DEDICATED TO THE ONE I LOVE   Mamas & Papas
3 SOMETHIN' STUPID   Nancy & Frank Sinatra
4 BERNADETTE   Four Tops
5 THIS IS MY SONG   Petula Clark
6 PENNY LANE   Beatles
7 WESTERN UNION   Five Americans
8 I THINK WE'RE ALONE NOW   Tommy James & The
     Shondells
9 A LITTLE BIT YOU, A LITTLE BIT ME   Monkees
10 THERE'S A KIND OF HUSH (ALL OVER THE WORLD)
     Herman's Hermits

April 15, 1967
1 SOMETHIN' STUPID   Nancy & Frank Sinatra
2 HAPPY TOGETHER   Turtles
3 THIS IS MY SONG   Petula Clark
4 BERNADETTE   Four Tops
5 A LITTLE BIT YOU, A LITTLE BIT ME   Monkees
6 WESTERN UNION   Five Americans
7 I THINK WE'RE ALONE NOW   Tommy James & The
     Shondells
8 DEDICATED TO THE ONE I LOVE   Mamas & Papas
9 I NEVER LOVED A MAN THE WAY I LOVE YOU   Aretha
     Franklin
10 JIMMY MACK   Martha & The Vandellas

April 22, 1967
1 SOMETHIN' STUPID   Nancy & Frank Sinatra
2 HAPPY TOGETHER   Turtles
3 A LITTLE BIT YOU, A LITTLE BIT ME   Monkees
4 I THINK WE'RE ALONE NOW   Tommy James & The
     Shondells
5 WESTERN UNION   Five Americans
6 THIS IS MY SONG   Petula Clark
7 SWEET SOUL MUSIC   Arthur Conley
8 BERNADETTE   Four Tops
9 I NEVER LOVED A MAN THE WAY I LOVE YOU   Aretha
     Franklin

10 JIMMY MACK   Martha & The Vandellas

April 29, 1967
1 SOMETHIN' STUPID   Nancy & Frank Sinatra
2 A LITTLE BIT YOU, A LITTLE BIT ME   Monkees
3 HAPPY TOGETHER   Turtles
4 SWEET SOUL MUSIC   Arthur Conley
5 I THINK WE'RE ALONE NOW   Tommy James & The
     Shondells
6 WESTERN UNION   Five Americans
7 THIS IS MY SONG   Petula Clark
8 THE HAPPENING   Supremes
9 BERNADETTE   Four Tops
10 JIMMY MACK   Martha & The Vandellas

May 6, 1967
1 SOMETHIN' STUPID   Nancy & Frank Sinatra
2 THE HAPPENING   Supremes
3 SWEET SOUL MUSIC   Arthur Conley
4 A LITTLE BIT YOU, A LITTLE BIT ME   Monkees
5 HAPPY TOGETHER   Turtles
6 I THINK WE'RE ALONE NOW   Tommy James & The
     Shondells
7 DON'T YOU CARE   Buckinghams
8 CLOSE YOUR EYES   Peaches & Herb
9 YOU GOT WHAT IT TAKES   Dave Clark Five
10 JIMMY MACK   Martha & The Vandellas

May 13, 1967
1 THE HAPPENING   Supremes
2 SWEET SOUL MUSIC   Arthur Conley
3 SOMETHIN' STUPID   Nancy & Frank Sinatra
4 GROOVIN'   Young Rascals
5 A LITTLE BIT YOU, A LITTLE BIT ME   Monkees
6 DON'T YOU CARE   Buckinghams
7 YOU GOT WHAT IT TAKES   Dave Clark Five
8 CLOSE YOUR EYES   Peaches & Herb
9 I GOT RHYTHM   Happenings
10 I THINK WE'RE ALONE NOW   Tommy James & The
     Shondells

May 20, 1967
1 GROOVIN'   Young Rascals
2 THE HAPPENING   Supremes
3 SWEET SOUL MUSIC   Arthur Conley
4 SOMETHIN' STUPID   Nancy & Frank Sinatra
5 RESPECT   Aretha Franklin
6 I GOT RHYTHM   Happenings
7 RELEASE ME   Englebert Humperdinck
8 CLOSE YOUR EYES   Peaches & Herb
9 DON'T YOU CARE   Buckinghams
10 YOU GOT WHAT IT TAKES   Dave Clark Five

May 27, 1967
1 GROOVIN'   Young Rascals
2 RESPECT   Aretha Franklin
3 I GOT RHYTHM   Happenings
4 RELEASE ME   Englebert Humperdinck
5 THE HAPPENING   Supremes
6 SWEET SOUL MUSIC   Arthur Conley
7 HIM OR ME, WHAT'S IT TO BE?   Paul Revere & The
     Raiders
8 CREEQUE ALLEY   Mamas & Papas
9 SOMETHIN' STUPID   Nancy & Frank Sinatra
10 GIRL, YOU'LL BE A WOMAN SOON   Neil Diamond

June 3, 1967
1. RESPECT   Aretha Franklin
2. GROOVIN'   Young Rascals
3. I GOT RHYTHM   Happenings
4. RELEASE ME   Englebert Humperdinck
5. CREEQUE ALLEY   Mamas & Papas
6. HIM OR ME, WHAT'S IT TO BE?   Paul Revere & The Raiders
7. THE HAPPENING   Supremes
8. SWEET SOUL MUSIC   Arthur Conley
9. SOMEBODY TO LOVE   Jefferson Airplane
10. ALL I NEED IS YOU   Temptations

June 10, 1967
1. RESPECT   Aretha Franklin
2. GROOVIN'   Young Rascals
3. I GOT RHYTHM   Happenings
4. RELEASE ME   Englebert Humperdinck
5. HIM OR ME, WHAT'S IT TO BE?   Paul Revere & The Raiders
6. SOMEBODY TO LOVE   Jefferson Airplane
7. SHE'D RATHER BE WITH ME   Turtles
8. LITTLE BIT O' SOUL   Music Explosion
9. ALL I NEED IS YOU   Temptations
10. CREEQUE ALLEY   Mamas & Papas

June 17, 1967
1. GROOVIN'   Young Rascals
2. RESPECT   Aretha Franklin
3. SHE'D RATHER BE WITH ME   Turtles
4. RELEASE ME   Englebert Humperdinck
5. SOMEBODY TO LOVE   Jefferson Airplane
6. LITTLE BIT O' SOUL   Music Explosion
7. WINDY   Association
8. ALL I NEED IS YOU   Temptations
9. I GOT RHYTHM   Happenings
10. MIRAGE   Tommy James & The Shondells

June 24, 1967
1. GROOVIN'   Young Rascals
2. RESPECT   Aretha Franklin
3. SHE'D RATHER BE WITH ME   Turtles
4. WINDY   Association
5. LITTLE BIT O' SOUL   Music Explosion
6. SAN FRANCISCO (WEAR SOME FLOWERS IN YOUR HAIR)   Scott McKenzie
7. SOMEBODY TO LOVE   Jefferson Airplane
8. CAN'T TAKE MY EYES OFF YOU   Frankie Valli
9. SUNDAY WILL NEVER BE THE SAME   Spanky & Our Gang
10. LET'S LIVE FOR TODAY   Grass Roots

July 1, 1967
1. WINDY   Association
2. GROOVIN'   Young Rascals
3. LITTLE BIT O' SOUL   Music Explosion
4. SAN FRANCISCO (WEAR SOME FLOWERS IN YOUR HAIR)   Scott McKenzie
5. SHE'D RATHER BE WITH ME   Turtles
6. RESPECT   Aretha Franklin
7. CAN'T TAKE MY EYES OFF YOU   Frankie Valli
8. LET'S LIVE FOR TODAY   Grass Roots
9. COME ON DOWN TO MY BOAT   Every Mother's Son
10. DON'T SLEEP IN THE SUBWAY   Petula Clark

July 8, 1967
1. WINDY   Association

2. LITTLE BIT O' SOUL   Music Explosion
3. CAN'T TAKE MY EYES OFF YOU   Frankie Valli
4. SAN FRANCISCO (WEAR SOME FLOWERS IN YOUR HAIR)   Scott McKenzie
5. DON'T SLEEP IN THE SUBWAY   Petula Clark
6. COME ON DOWN TO MY BOAT   Every Mother's Son
7. UP UP AND AWAY   5th Dimension
8. LET'S LIVE FOR TODAY   Grass Roots
9. GROOVIN'   Young Rascals
10. TRACKS OF MY TEARS   Johnny Rivers

July 15, 1967
1. WINDY   Association
2. LITTLE BIT O' SOUL   Music Explosion
3. CAN'T TAKE MY EYES OFF YOU   Frankie Valli
4. SAN FRANCISCO (WEAR SOME FLOWERS IN YOUR HAIR)   Scott McKenzie
5. DON'T SLEEP IN THE SUBWAY   Petula Clark
6. COME ON DOWN TO MY BOAT   Every Mother's Son
7. UP UP AND AWAY   5th Dimension
8. LIGHT MY FIRE   Doors
9. C'MON MARIANNE   Four Seasons
10. A WHITER SHADE OF PALE   Procol Harum

July 22, 1967
1. WINDY   Association
2. CAN'T TAKE MY EYES OFF YOU   Frankie Valli
3. LIGHT MY FIRE   Doors
4. SAN FRANCISCO (WEAR SOME FLOWERS IN YOUR HAIR)   Scott McKenzie
5. LITTLE BIT O' SOUL   Music Explosion
6. I WAS MADE TO LOVE HER   Stevie Wonder

Aretha Franklin
The Queen of Soul gets ``Respect'' (June 3).

7   UP UP AND AWAY   5th Dimension
8   A WHITER SHADE OF PALE   Procol Harum
9   C'MON MARIANNE   Four Seasons
10 COME ON DOWN TO MY BOAT   Every Mother's Son

July 29, 1967
1   LIGHT MY FIRE   Doors
2   I WAS MADE TO LOVE HER   Stevie Wonder
3   WINDY   Association
4   CAN'T TAKE MY EYES OFF YOU   Frankie Valli
5   A WHITER SHADE OF PALE   Procol Harum
6   LITTLE BIT O' SOUL   Music Explosion
7   MERCY, MERCY, MERCY   Buckinghams
8   WHITE RABBIT   Jefferson Airplane
9   UP UP AND AWAY   5th Dimension
10 C'MON MARIANNE   Four Seasons

August 5, 1967
1   LIGHT MY FIRE   Doors
2   I WAS MADE TO LOVE HER   Stevie Wonder
3   ALL YOU NEED IS LOVE   Beatles
4   WINDY   Association
5   A WHITER SHADE OF PALE   Procol Harum
6   CAN'T TAKE MY EYES OFF YOU   Frankie Valli
7   MERCY, MERCY, MERCY   Buckinghams
8   WHITE RABBIT   Jefferson Airplane
9   PLEASANT VALLEY SUNDAY   Monkees
10 LITTLE BIT O' SOUL   Music Explosion

August 12, 1967
1   LIGHT MY FIRE   Doors
2   ALL YOU NEED IS LOVE   Beatles
3   I WAS MADE TO LOVE HER   Stevie Wonder
4   PLEASANT VALLEY SUNDAY   Monkees
5   MERCY, MERCY, MERCY   Buckinghams
6   CAN'T TAKE MY EYES OFF YOU   Frankie Valli
7   A WHITER SHADE OF PALE   Procol Harum
8   WINDY   Association
9   CARRIE ANN   Hollies
10 A GIRL LIKE YOU   Young Rascals

August 19, 1967
1   ALL YOU NEED IS LOVE   Beatles
2   LIGHT MY FIRE   Doors
3   PLEASANT VALLEY SUNDAY   Monkees
4   I WAS MADE TO LOVE HER   Stevie Wonder
5   BABY I LOVE YOU   Andy Kim
6   MERCY, MERCY, MERCY   Buckinghams
7   ODE TO BILLIE JOE   Bobbie Gentry
8   COLD SWEAT   James Brown
9   A WHITER SHADE OF PALE   Procol Harum
10 A GIRL LIKE YOU   Young Rascals

August 26, 1967
1   ODE TO BILLIE JOE   Bobbie Gentry
2   ALL YOU NEED IS LOVE   Beatles
3   PLEASANT VALLEY SUNDAY   Monkees
4   LIGHT MY FIRE   Doors
5   BABY I LOVE YOU   Andy Kim
6   I WAS MADE TO LOVE HER   Stevie Wonder
7   COLD SWEAT   James Brown
8   REFLECTIONS   Supremes
9   YOU'RE MY EVERYTHING   Temptations
10 A WHITER SHADE OF PALE   Procol Harum

James Brown
The Godfather of Soul broke into a ``Cold Sweat''
(and into the Top 10) in August 1967.

Bobbie Gentry
Bobbie penned her own #1 hit, ``Ode To Billy Joe'' (Aug. 26).

September 2, 1967

1 ODE TO BILLIE JOE   Bobbie Gentry
2 ALL YOU NEED IS LOVE   Beatles
3 REFLECTIONS   Supremes
4 LIGHT MY FIRE   Doors
5 BABY I LOVE YOU   Andy Kim
6 COME BACK WHEN YOU GROW UP   Bobby Vee
7 APPLES PEACHES PUMPKIN PIE   Jay & The Techniques
8 PLEASANT VALLEY SUNDAY   Monkees
9 YOU'RE MY EVERYTHING   Temptations
10 I WAS MADE TO LOVE HER   Stevie Wonder

September 9, 1967

1 ODE TO BILLIE JOE   Bobbie Gentry
2 REFLECTIONS   Supremes
3 COME BACK WHEN YOU GROW UP   Bobby Vee
4 BABY I LOVE YOU   Andy Kim
5 THE LETTER   Box Tops
6 ALL YOU NEED IS LOVE   Beatles
7 YOU'RE MY EVERYTHING   Temptations
8 LIGHT MY FIRE   Doors
9 APPLES PEACHES PUMPKIN PIE   Jay & The Techniques
10 SAN FRANCISCAN NIGHTS   Eric Burdon & The Animals

September 16, 1967

1 ODE TO BILLIE JOE   Bobbie Gentry
2 REFLECTIONS   Supremes
3 COME BACK WHEN YOU GROW UP   Bobby Vee
4 THE LETTER   Box Tops
5 BABY I LOVE YOU   Andy Kim
6 YOU'RE MY EVERYTHING   Temptations
7 APPLES PEACHES PUMPKIN PIE   Jay & The Techniques
8 ALL YOU NEED IS LOVE   Beatles
9 SAN FRANCISCAN NIGHTS   Eric Burdon & The Animals
10 FUNKY BROADWAY   Wilson Pickett

September 23, 1967

1 THE LETTER   Box Tops
2 ODE TO BILLIE JOE   Bobbie Gentry
3 COME BACK WHEN YOU GROW UP   Bobby Vee
4 REFLECTIONS   Supremes
5 NEVER MY LOVE   Association
6 APPLES PEACHES PUMPKIN PIE   Jay & The Techniques
7 HIGHER AND HIGHER   Jackie Wilson
8 YOU'RE MY EVERYTHING   Temptations
9 I DIG ROCK AND ROLL MUSIC   Peter, Paul & Mary
10 FUNKY BROADWAY   Wilson Pickett

September 30, 1967

1 THE LETTER   Box Tops
2 ODE TO BILLIE JOE   Bobbie Gentry
3 NEVER MY LOVE   Association
4 COME BACK WHEN YOU GROW UP   Bobby Vee
5 REFLECTIONS   Supremes
6 APPLES PEACHES PUMPKIN PIE   Jay & The Techniques
7 HIGHER AND HIGHER   Jackie Wilson
8 FUNKY BROADWAY   Wilson Pickett
9 I DIG ROCK AND ROLL MUSIC   Peter, Paul & Mary
10 BROWN EYED GIRL   Van Morrison

October 7, 1967

1 THE LETTER   Box Tops
2 NEVER MY LOVE   Association
3 ODE TO BILLIE JOE   Bobbie Gentry
4 COME BACK WHEN YOU GROW UP   Bobby Vee
5 LITTLE OLE MAN (UPTIGHT - EVERYTHING'S ALRIGHT)
     Bill Cosby
6 HIGHER AND HIGHER   Jackie Wilson
7 REFLECTIONS   Supremes
8 APPLES PEACHES PUMPKIN PIE   Jay & The Techniques
9 HOW CAN I BE SURE   Rascals
10 GIMME LITTLE SIGN   Brenton Wood

October 14, 1967

1 THE LETTER   Box Tops
2 NEVER MY LOVE   Association
3 TO SIR WITH LOVE   Lulu
4 LITTLE OLE MAN (UPTIGHT - EVERYTHING'S ALRIGHT)
     Bill Cosby
5 ODE TO BILLIE JOE   Bobbie Gentry
6 HIGHER AND HIGHER   Jackie Wilson
7 COME BACK WHEN YOU GROW UP   Bobby Vee
8 HOW CAN I BE SURE   Rascals
9 GIMME LITTLE SIGN   Brenton Wood
10 SOUL MAN   Sam & Dave

October 21, 1967

1 TO SIR WITH LOVE   Lulu
2 THE LETTER   Box Tops
3 NEVER MY LOVE   Association
4 HOW CAN I BE SURE   Rascals
5 EXPRESSWAY TO YOUR HEART   Soul Survivors
6 IT MUST BE HIM   Vicki Carr
7 SOUL MAN   Sam & Dave
8 LITTLE OLE MAN (UPTIGHT - EVERYTHING'S ALRIGHT)
     Bill Cosby
9 GIMME LITTLE SIGN   Brenton Wood
10 YOUR PRECIOUS LOVE   Marvin Gaye & Tammi Terrell

October 28, 1967

1 TO SIR WITH LOVE   Lulu
2 THE LETTER   Box Tops
3 NEVER MY LOVE   Association
4 HOW CAN I BE SURE   Rascals
5 EXPRESSWAY TO YOUR HEART   Soul Survivors
6 IT MUST BE HIM   Vicki Carr
7 SOUL MAN   Sam & Dave
8 YOUR PRECIOUS LOVE   Marvin Gaye & Tammi Terrell
9 A NATURAL WOMAN   Aretha Franklin
10 INCENSE AND PEPPERMINT   Strawberry Alarm Clock

November 4, 1967

1 TO SIR WITH LOVE   Lulu
2 SOUL MAN   Sam & Dave
3 IT MUST BE HIM   Vicki Carr
4 EXPRESSWAY TO YOUR HEART   Soul Survivors
5 YOUR PRECIOUS LOVE   Marvin Gaye & Tammi Terrell
6 NEVER MY LOVE   Association
7 INCENSE AND PEPPERMINT   Strawberry Alarm Clock
8 A NATURAL WOMAN   Aretha Franklin
9 THE RAIN, THE PARK AND OTHER THINGS   Cowsills
10 PLEASE LOVE ME FOREVER   Bobby Vinton

November 11, 1967

1 TO SIR WITH LOVE   Lulu
2 SOUL MAN   Sam & Dave
3 IT MUST BE HIM   Vicki Carr
4 INCENSE AND PEPPERMINT   Strawberry Alarm Clock
5 YOUR PRECIOUS LOVE   Marvin Gaye & Tammi Terrell
6 THE RAIN, THE PARK AND OTHER THINGS   Cowsills
7 PLEASE LOVE ME FOREVER   Bobby Vinton
8 A NATURAL WOMAN   Aretha Franklin
9 EXPRESSWAY TO YOUR HEART   Soul Survivors
10 NEVER MY LOVE   Association

November 18, 1967
1. TO SIR WITH LOVE   Lulu
2. SOUL MAN   Sam & Dave
3. INCENSE AND PEPPERMINT   Strawberry Alarm Clock
4. THE RAIN, THE PARK AND OTHER THINGS   Cowsills
5. IT MUST BE HIM   Vicki Carr
6. PLEASE LOVE ME FOREVER   Bobby Vinton
7. YOUR PRECIOUS LOVE   Marvin Gaye & Tammi Terrell
8. I SAY A LITTLE PRAYER   Dionne Warwick
9. EXPRESSWAY TO YOUR HEART   Soul Survivors
10. I CAN SEE FOR MILES   Who

November 25, 1967
1. INCENSE AND PEPPERMINT   Strawberry Alarm Clock
2. TO SIR WITH LOVE   Lulu
3. THE RAIN, THE PARK AND OTHER THINGS   Cowsills
4. SOUL MAN   Sam & Dave
5. DAYDREAM BELIEVER   Monkees
6. PLEASE LOVE ME FOREVER   Bobby Vinton
7. I SAY A LITTLE PRAYER   Dionne Warwick
8. IT MUST BE HIM   Vicki Carr
9. I CAN SEE FOR MILES   Who
10. EXPRESSWAY TO YOUR HEART   Soul Survivors

December 2, 1967
1. DAYDREAM BELIEVER   Monkees
2. THE RAIN, THE PARK AND OTHER THINGS   Cowsills
3. INCENSE AND PEPPERMINT   Strawberry Alarm Clock
4. TO SIR WITH LOVE   Lulu
5. I SAY A LITTLE PRAYER   Dionne Warwick
6. PLEASE LOVE ME FOREVER   Bobby Vinton
7. SOUL MAN   Sam & Dave
8. I HEARD IT THROUGH THE GRAPEVINE   Gladys Knight & The Pips
9. I CAN SEE FOR MILES   Who
10. AN OPEN LETTER TO MY TEENAGE SON   Victor Lundberg

December 9, 1967
1. DAYDREAM BELIEVER   Monkees
2. THE RAIN, THE PARK AND OTHER THINGS   Cowsills
3. INCENSE AND PEPPERMINT   Strawberry Alarm Clock
4. I SAY A LITTLE PRAYER   Dionne Warwick
5. I HEARD IT THROUGH THE GRAPEVINE   Gladys Knight & The Pips
6. TO SIR WITH LOVE   Lulu
7. I SECOND THAT EMOTION   Miracles
8. HELLO GOODBYE   Beatles
9. IN AND OUT OF LOVE   Supremes
10. AN OPEN LETTER TO MY TEENAGE SON   Victor Lundberg

December 16, 1967
1. DAYDREAM BELIEVER   Monkees
2. I HEARD IT THROUGH THE GRAPEVINE   Gladys Knight & The Pips
3. HELLO GOODBYE   Beatles
4. I SECOND THAT EMOTION   Miracles
5. THE RAIN, THE PARK AND OTHER THINGS   Cowsills
6. INCENSE AND PEPPERMINT   Strawberry Alarm Clock
7. I SAY A LITTLE PRAYER   Dionne Warwick
8. BOOGALOO DOWN BROADWAY   Fantastic Johnny C
9. IN AND OUT OF LOVE   Supremes
10. YOU BETTER SIT DOWN KIDS   Cher

December 23, 1967
1. DAYDREAM BELIEVER   Monkees
2. I HEARD IT THROUGH THE GRAPEVINE   Gladys Knight & The Pips
3. HELLO GOODBYE   Beatles
4. I SECOND THAT EMOTION   Miracles
5. WOMAN, WOMAN   Gary Puckett & The Union Gap
6. THE RAIN, THE PARK AND OTHER THINGS   Cowsills
7. BOOGALOO DOWN BROADWAY   Fantastic Johnny C
8. INCENSE AND PEPPERMINT   Strawberry Alarm Clock
9. YOU BETTER SIT DOWN KIDS   Cher
10. I SAY A LITTLE PRAYER   Dionne Warwick

December 30, 1967
1. HELLO GOODBYE   Beatles
2. I HEARD IT THROUGH THE GRAPEVINE   Gladys Knight & The Pips
3. DAYDREAM BELIEVER   Monkees
4. I SECOND THAT EMOTION   Miracles
5. WOMAN, WOMAN   Gary Puckett & The Union Gap
6. JUDY IN DISGUISE   John Fred & The Playboy Band
7. CHAIN OF FOOLS   Aretha Franklin
8. BEND ME, SHAPE ME   American Breed
9. BOOGALOO DOWN BROADWAY   Fantastic Johnny C
10. SKINNY LEGS AND ALL   Joe Tex

January 6, 1968
1. HELLO GOODBYE   Beatles
2. DAYDREAM BELIEVER   Monkees
3. JUDY IN DISGUISE   John Fred & The Playboy Band
4. I HEARD IT THROUGH THE GRAPEVINE   Gladys Knight & The Pips
5. WOMAN, WOMAN   Gary Puckett & The Union Gap
6. I SECOND THAT EMOTION   Miracles
7. CHAIN OF FOOLS   Aretha Franklin
8. BEND ME, SHAPE ME   American Breed
9. BOOGALOO DOWN BROADWAY   Fantastic Johnny C
10. SKINNY LEGS AND ALL   Joe Tex

January 13, 1968
1. HELLO GOODBYE   Beatles
2. JUDY IN DISGUISE   John Fred & The Playboy Band
3. DAYDREAM BELIEVER   Monkees
4. WOMAN, WOMAN   Gary Puckett & The Union Gap
5. I HEARD IT THROUGH THE GRAPEVINE   Gladys Knight & The Pips
6. CHAIN OF FOOLS   Aretha Franklin
7. BEND ME, SHAPE ME   American Breed
8. I SECOND THAT EMOTION   Miracles
9. GREEN TAMBOURINE   Lemon Pipers
10. SKINNY LEGS AND ALL   Joe Tex

January 20, 1968
1. JUDY IN DISGUISE   John Fred & The Playboy Band
2. CHAIN OF FOOLS   Aretha Franklin
3. HELLO GOODBYE   Beatles
4. WOMAN, WOMAN   Gary Puckett & The Union Gap
5. GREEN TAMBOURINE   Lemon Pipers
6. DAYDREAM BELIEVER   Monkees
7. BEND ME, SHAPE ME   American Breed
8. I SECOND THAT EMOTION   Miracles
9. I HEARD IT THROUGH THE GRAPEVINE   Gladys Knight & The Pips
10. IF I COULD BUILD MY WHOLE WORLD AROUND YOU   Marvin Gaye & Tammi Terrell

January 27, 1968

1. JUDY IN DISGUISE   John Fred & The Playboy Band
2. CHAIN OF FOOLS   Aretha Franklin
3. GREEN TAMBOURINE   Lemon Pipers
4. WOMAN, WOMAN   Gary Puckett & The Union Gap
5. BEND ME, SHAPE ME   American Breed
6. HELLO GOODBYE   Beatles
7. SPOOKY   Classics IV
8. DAYDREAM BELIEVER   Monkees
9. I HEARD IT THROUGH THE GRAPEVINE   Gladys Knight & The Pips
10. IF I COULD BUILD MY WHOLE WORLD AROUND YOU   Marvin Gaye & Tammi Terrell

February 3, 1968

1. GREEN TAMBOURINE   Lemon Pipers
2. JUDY IN DISGUISE   John Fred & The Playboy Band
3. CHAIN OF FOOLS   Aretha Franklin
4. SPOOKY   Classics IV
5. BEND ME, SHAPE ME   American Breed
6. WOMAN, WOMAN   Gary Puckett & The Union Gap
7. LOVE IS BLUE   Paul Mauriat
8. NOBODY BUT ME   Human Beinz
9. GOING OUT OF MY HEAD/CAN'T TAKE MY EYES OFF YOU   Lettermen
10. I WONDER WHAT SHE'S DOING TONIGHT   Tommy Boyce & Bobby Hart

February 10, 1968

1. LOVE IS BLUE   Paul Mauriat
2. GREEN TAMBOURINE   Lemon Pipers
3. SPOOKY   Classics IV
4. JUDY IN DISGUISE   John Fred & The Playboy Band
5. CHAIN OF FOOLS   Aretha Franklin
6. I WISH IT WOULD RAIN   Temptations
7. GOING OUT OF MY HEAD/CAN'T TAKE MY EYES OFF YOU   Lettermen
8. NOBODY BUT ME   Human Beinz
9. WOMAN, WOMAN   Gary Puckett & The Union Gap
10. BEND ME, SHAPE ME   American Breed

February 17, 1968

1. LOVE IS BLUE   Paul Mauriat
2. GREEN TAMBOURINE   Lemon Pipers
3. SPOOKY   Classics IV
4. I WISH IT WOULD RAIN   Temptations
5. (THEME FROM) "VALLEY OF THE DOLLS"   Dionne Warwick
6. (SITTIN' ON) THE DOCK OF THE BAY   Otis Redding
7. GOING OUT OF MY HEAD/CAN'T TAKE MY EYES OFF YOU   Lettermen
8. NOBODY BUT ME   Human Beinz
9. JUDY IN DISGUISE   John Fred & The Playboy Band
10. I WONDER WHAT SHE'S DOING TONIGHT   Tommy Boyce & Bobby Hart

February 24, 1968

1. LOVE IS BLUE   Paul Mauriat
2. (THEME FROM) "VALLEY OF THE DOLLS"   Dionne Warwick
3. SPOOKY   Classics IV
4. I WISH IT WOULD RAIN   Temptations
5. (SITTIN' ON) THE DOCK OF THE BAY   Otis Redding
6. SIMON SAYS   1910 Fruitgum Co.
7. GREEN TAMBOURINE   Lemon Pipers
8. I WONDER WHAT SHE'S DOING TONIGHT   Tommy Boyce & Bobby Hart

9. GOING OUT OF MY HEAD/CAN'T TAKE MY EYES OFF YOU   Lettermen
10. NOBODY BUT ME   Human Beinz

March 2, 1968

1. LOVE IS BLUE   Paul Mauriat
2. (THEME FROM) "VALLEY OF THE DOLLS"   Dionne Warwick
3. (SITTIN' ON) THE DOCK OF THE BAY   Otis Redding
4. I WISH IT WOULD RAIN   Temptations
5. SIMON SAYS   1910 Fruitgum Co.
6. SPOOKY   Classics IV
7. JUST DROPPED IN (TO SEE WHAT CONDITION MY CONDITION WAS IN)   First Edition
8. I WONDER WHAT SHE'S DOING TONIGHT   Tommy Boyce & Bobby Hart
9. BOTTLE OF WINE   Fireballs
10. EVERYTHING THAT TOUCHES YOU   Association

March 9, 1968

1. LOVE IS BLUE   Paul Mauriat
2. (THEME FROM) "VALLEY OF THE DOLLS"   Dionne Warwick
3. (SITTIN' ON) THE DOCK OF THE BAY   Otis Redding
4. SIMON SAYS   1910 Fruitgum Co.
5. I WISH IT WOULD RAIN   Temptations
6. JUST DROPPED IN (TO SEE WHAT CONDITION MY CONDITION WAS IN)   First Edition
7. I WONDER WHAT SHE'S DOING TONIGHT   Tommy Boyce & Bobby Hart
8. BOTTLE OF WINE   Fireballs
9. LA LA MEANS I LOVE YOU   Delfonics
10. VALLERI   Monkees

March 16, 1968

1. (SITTIN' ON) THE DOCK OF THE BAY   Otis Redding
2. (THEME FROM) "VALLEY OF THE DOLLS"   Dionne Warwick
3. LOVE IS BLUE   Paul Mauriat
4. SIMON SAYS   1910 Fruitgum Co.
5. JUST DROPPED IN (TO SEE WHAT CONDITION MY CONDITION WAS IN)   First Edition
6. I WISH IT WOULD RAIN   Temptations
7. LA LA MEANS I LOVE YOU   Delfonics
8. VALLERI   Monkees
9. (SWEET SWEET BABY) SINCE YOU'VE BEEN GONE   Aretha Franklin
10. I THANK YOU   Sam & Dave

March 23, 1968

1. (SITTIN' ON) THE DOCK OF THE BAY   Otis Redding
2. LOVE IS BLUE   Paul Mauriat
3. (THEME FROM) "VALLEY OF THE DOLLS"   Dionne Warwick
4. SIMON SAYS   1910 Fruitgum Co.
5. JUST DROPPED IN (TO SEE WHAT CONDITION MY CONDITION WAS IN)   First Edition
6. LA LA MEANS I LOVE YOU   Delfonics
7. VALLERI   Monkees
8. (SWEET SWEET BABY) SINCE YOU'VE BEEN GONE   Aretha Franklin
9. I THANK YOU   Sam & Dave
10. THE BALLAD OF BONNIE AND CLYDE   Georgie Fame

March 30, 1968

1. (SITTIN' ON) THE DOCK OF THE BAY   Otis Redding

261

2 LOVE IS BLUE   Paul Mauriat
3 VALLERI   Monkees
4 SIMON SAYS   1910 Fruitgum Co.
5 (SWEET SWEET BABY) SINCE YOU'VE BEEN GONE
    Aretha Franklin
6 LA LA MEANS I LOVE YOU   Delfonics
7 YOUNG GIRL   Gary Puckett & The Union Gap
8 THE BALLAD OF BONNIE AND CLYDE   Georgie Fame
9 LADY MADONNA   Beatles
10 (THEME FROM) "VALLEY OF THE DOLLS"   Dionne
    Warwick

April 6, 1968
1 (SITTIN' ON) THE DOCK OF THE BAY   Otis Redding
2 YOUNG GIRL   Gary Puckett & The Union Gap
3 VALLERI   Monkees
4 LA LA MEANS I LOVE YOU   Delfonics
5 (SWEET SWEET BABY) SINCE YOU'VE BEEN GONE
    Aretha Franklin
6 CRY LIKE A BABY   Box Tops
7 LADY MADONNA   Beatles
8 THE BALLAD OF BONNIE AND CLYDE   Georgie Fame
9 LOVE IS BLUE   Paul Mauriat
10 HONEY   Bobby Goldsboro

April 13, 1968
1 HONEY   Bobby Goldsboro
2 YOUNG GIRL   Gary Puckett & The Union Gap
3 CRY LIKE A BABY   Box Tops
4 LADY MADONNA   Beatles
5 (SWEET SWEET BABY) SINCE YOU'VE BEEN GONE
    Aretha Franklin
6 (SITTIN' ON) THE DOCK OF THE BAY   Otis Redding
7 DANCE TO THE MUSIC   Sly & The Family Stone
8 THE BALLAD OF BONNIE AND CLYDE   Georgie Fame
9 I GOT THE FEELIN'   James Brown
10 MIGHTY QUINN (QUINN THE ESKIMO)   Manfred Mann

April 20, 1968
1 HONEY   Bobby Goldsboro
2 YOUNG GIRL   Gary Puckett & The Union Gap
3 CRY LIKE A BABY   Box Tops
4 LADY MADONNA   Beatles
5 (SWEET SWEET BABY) SINCE YOU'VE BEEN GONE
    Aretha Franklin
6 (SITTIN' ON) THE DOCK OF THE BAY   Otis Redding
7 THE BALLAD OF BONNIE AND CLYDE   Georgie Fame
8 DANCE TO THE MUSIC   Sly & The Family Stone
9 I GOT THE FEELIN'   James Brown
10 MIGHTY QUINN (QUINN THE ESKIMO)   Manfred Mann

April 27, 1968
1 HONEY   Bobby Goldsboro
2 CRY LIKE A BABY   Box Tops
3 YOUNG GIRL   Gary Puckett & The Union Gap
4 LADY MADONNA   Beatles
5 (SWEET SWEET BABY) SINCE YOU'VE BEEN GONE
    Aretha Franklin
6 I GOT THE FEELIN'   James Brown
7 (SITTIN' ON) THE DOCK OF THE BAY   Otis Redding
8 DANCE TO THE MUSIC   Sly & The Family Stone
9 TIGHTEN UP   Archie Bell & The Drells
10 THE BALLAD OF BONNIE AND CLYDE   Georgie Fame

May 4, 1968
1 HONEY   Bobby Goldsboro

Bobby Goldsboro
``Honey'' hangs on to #1 for five weeks in April and May.

2 CRY LIKE A BABY   Box Tops
3 YOUNG GIRL   Gary Puckett & The Union Gap
4 LADY MADONNA   Beatles
5 TIGHTEN UP   Archie Bell & The Drells
6 I GOT THE FEELIN'   James Brown
7 COWBOYS TO GIRLS   Intruders
8 THE GOOD, THE BAD AND THE UGLY   Hugo Montenegro
9 BEAUTIFUL MORNING   Rascals
10 THE UNICORN   Irish Rovers

May 11, 1968
1 HONEY   Bobby Goldsboro
2 TIGHTEN UP   Archie Bell & The Drells
3 YOUNG GIRL   Gary Puckett & The Union Gap
4 THE GOOD, THE BAD AND THE UGLY   Hugo Montenegro
5 CRY LIKE A BABY   Box Tops
6 BEAUTIFUL MORNING   Rascals
7 COWBOYS TO GIRLS   Intruders
8 THE UNICORN   Irish Rovers
9 MRS. ROBINSON   Simon & Garfunkel
10 LADY MADONNA   Beatles

May 18, 1968
1 TIGHTEN UP   Archie Bell & The Drells
2 MRS. ROBINSON   Simon & Garfunkel
3 HONEY   Bobby Goldsboro
4 THE GOOD, THE BAD AND THE UGLY   Hugo Montenegro
5 BEAUTIFUL MORNING   Rascals
6 COWBOYS TO GIRLS   Intruders
7 LOVE IS ALL AROUND   Troggs
8 THE UNICORN   Irish Rovers
9 YOUNG GIRL   Gary Puckett & The Union Gap

10 DO YOU KNOW THE WAY TO SAN JOSE? Dionne Warwick

May 25, 1968
1 TIGHTEN UP Archie Bell & The Drells
2 MRS. ROBINSON Simon & Garfunkel
3 BEAUTIFUL MORNING Rascals
4 THE GOOD, THE BAD AND THE UGLY Hugo Montenegro
5 HONEY Bobby Goldsboro
6 COWBOYS TO GIRLS Intruders
7 THE UNICORN Irish Rovers
8 AIN'T NOTHING LIKE THE REAL THING Marvin Gaye & Tammi Terrell
9 SHOO-BE-DOO-BE-DOO-DA-DAY Stevie Wonder
10 DO YOU KNOW THE WAY TO SAN JOSE? Dionne Warwick

June 1, 1968
1 MRS. ROBINSON Simon & Garfunkel
2 THE GOOD, THE BAD AND THE UGLY Hugo Montenegro
3 BEAUTIFUL MORNING Rascals
4 TIGHTEN UP Archie Bell & The Drells
5 HONEY Bobby Goldsboro
6 YUMMY YUMMY YUMMY Ohio Express
7 MONY MONY Tommy James & The Shondells
8 AIN'T NOTHING LIKE THE REAL THING Marvin Gaye & Tammi Terrell
9 COWBOYS TO GIRLS Intruders
10 DO YOU KNOW THE WAY TO SAN JOSE? Dionne Warwick

June 8, 1968
1 MRS. ROBINSON Simon & Garfunkel
2 TIGHTEN UP Archie Bell & The Drells
3 THIS GUY'S IN LOVE WITH YOU Herb Alpert
4 THE GOOD, THE BAD AND THE UGLY Hugo Montenegro
5 MONY MONY Tommy James & The Shondells
6 YUMMY YUMMY YUMMY Ohio Express
7 MACARTHUR PARK Richard Harris
8 BEAUTIFUL MORNING Rascals
9 THINK Aretha Franklin
10 HONEY Bobby Goldsboro

June 15, 1968
1 MRS. ROBINSON Simon & Garfunkel
2 THIS GUY'S IN LOVE WITH YOU Herb Alpert
3 MONY MONY Tommy James & The Shondells
4 YUMMY YUMMY YUMMY Ohio Express
5 MACARTHUR PARK Richard Harris
6 TIGHTEN UP Archie Bell & The Drells
7 THINK Aretha Franklin
8 BEAUTIFUL MORNING Rascals
9 THE GOOD, THE BAD AND THE UGLY Hugo Montenegro
10 LOOK OF LOVE Sergio Mendes & Brasil '66

June 22, 1968
1 THIS GUY'S IN LOVE WITH YOU Herb Alpert
2 MACARTHUR PARK Richard Harris
3 MRS. ROBINSON Simon & Garfunkel
4 YUMMY YUMMY YUMMY Ohio Express
5 LOOK OF LOVE Sergio Mendes & Brasil '66
6 MONY MONY Tommy James & The Shondells
7 THINK Aretha Franklin
8 ANGEL OF THE MORNING Merrilee Rush
9 TIGHTEN UP Archie Bell & The Drells
10 REACH OUT OF THE DARKNESS Friend And Lover

June 29, 1968
1 THIS GUY'S IN LOVE WITH YOU Herb Alpert
2 THE HORSE Cliff Nobles & Co.
3 MACARTHUR PARK Richard Harris
4 YUMMY YUMMY YUMMY Ohio Express
5 LOOK OF LOVE Sergio Mendes & Brasil '66
6 MONY MONY Tommy James & The Shondells
7 ANGEL OF THE MORNING Merrilee Rush
8 THINK Aretha Franklin
9 HERE COMES THE JUDGE Shorty Long
10 REACH OUT OF THE DARKNESS Friend And Lover

July 6, 1968
1 THIS GUY'S IN LOVE WITH YOU Herb Alpert
2 THE HORSE Cliff Nobles & Co.
3 JUMPIN' JACK FLASH Rolling Stones
4 LOOK OF LOVE Sergio Mendes & Brasil '66
5 GRAZING IN THE GRASS Hugh Masekela
6 LADY WILLPOWER Gary Puckett & The Union Gap
7 ANGEL OF THE MORNING Merrilee Rush
8 HERE COMES THE JUDGE Shorty Long
9 MACARTHUR PARK Richard Harris
10 REACH OUT OF THE DARKNESS Friend And Lover

July 13, 1968
1 THIS GUY'S IN LOVE WITH YOU Herb Alpert
2 THE HORSE Cliff Nobles & Co.
3 JUMPIN' JACK FLASH Rolling Stones
4 LADY WILLPOWER Gary Puckett & The Union Gap
5 GRAZING IN THE GRASS Hugh Masekela
6 LOOK OF LOVE Sergio Mendes & Brasil '66
7 ANGEL OF THE MORNING Merrilee Rush
8 STONED SOUL PICNIC 5th Dimension
9 HERE COMES THE JUDGE Shorty Long
10 INDIAN LAKE Cowsills

July 20, 1968
1 GRAZING IN THE GRASS Hugh Masekela
2 LADY WILLPOWER Gary Puckett & The Union Gap
3 JUMPIN' JACK FLASH Rolling Stones
4 THIS GUY'S IN LOVE WITH YOU Herb Alpert
5 THE HORSE Cliff Nobles & Co.
6 STONED SOUL PICNIC 5th Dimension
7 HURDY GURDY MAN Donovan
8 CLASSICAL GAS Mason Williams
9 HELLO I LOVE YOU Doors
10 INDIAN LAKE Cowsills

July 27, 1968
1 GRAZING IN THE GRASS Hugh Masekela
2 LADY WILLPOWER Gary Puckett & The Union Gap
3 STONED SOUL PICNIC 5th Dimension
4 JUMPIN' JACK FLASH Rolling Stones
5 THE HORSE Cliff Nobles & Co.
6 HURDY GURDY MAN Donovan
7 THIS GUY'S IN LOVE WITH YOU Herb Alpert
8 CLASSICAL GAS Mason Williams
9 HELLO I LOVE YOU Doors
10 INDIAN LAKE Cowsills

August 3, 1968
1 HELLO I LOVE YOU Doors
2 CLASSICAL GAS Mason Williams
3 STONED SOUL PICNIC 5th Dimension
4 GRAZING IN THE GRASS Hugh Masekela
5 HURDY GURDY MAN Donovan

The Doors
Fronted by rock legend Jim Morrison, The Doors are #1 with ``Hello I Love You'' for two weeks in August.

6 JUMPIN' JACK FLASH Rolling Stones
7 LADY WILLPOWER Gary Puckett & The Union Gap
8 THE HORSE Cliff Nobles & Co.
9 TURN AROUND LOOK AT ME Vogues
10 SUNSHINE OF YOUR LOVE Cream

August 10, 1968
1 HELLO I LOVE YOU Doors
2 CLASSICAL GAS Mason Williams
3 STONED SOUL PICNIC 5th Dimension
4 GRAZING IN THE GRASS Hugh Masekela
5 PEOPLE GOT TO BE FREE Rascals
6 HURDY GURDY MAN Donovan
7 LADY WILLPOWER Gary Puckett & The Union Gap
8 TURN AROUND LOOK AT ME Vogues
9 SUNSHINE OF YOUR LOVE Cream
10 JUMPIN' JACK FLASH Rolling Stones

August 17, 1968
1 PEOPLE GOT TO BE FREE Rascals
2 HELLO I LOVE YOU Doors
3 CLASSICAL GAS Mason Williams
4 BORN TO BE WILD Steppenwolf
5 LIGHT MY FIRE Jose Feliciano
6 STONED SOUL PICNIC 5th Dimension
7 TURN AROUND LOOK AT ME Vogues
8 SUNSHINE OF YOUR LOVE Cream
9 GRAZING IN THE GRASS Hugh Masekela
10 HURDY GURDY MAN Donovan

August 24, 1968
1 PEOPLE GOT TO BE FREE Rascals

2 BORN TO BE WILD Steppenwolf
3 HELLO I LOVE YOU Doors
4 LIGHT MY FIRE Jose Feliciano
5 CLASSICAL GAS Mason Williams
6 SUNSHINE OF YOUR LOVE Cream
7 TURN AROUND LOOK AT ME Vogues
8 STONED SOUL PICNIC 5th Dimension
9 I CAN'T STOP DANCING Archie Bell & The Drells
10 STAY IN MY CORNER Dells

August 31, 1968
1 PEOPLE GOT TO BE FREE Rascals
2 BORN TO BE WILD Steppenwolf
3 LIGHT MY FIRE Jose Feliciano
4 HELLO I LOVE YOU Doors
5 SUNSHINE OF YOUR LOVE Cream
6 YOU KEEP ME (HANGIN' ON) Joe Simon
7 HARPER VALLEY P.T.A. Jeannie C. Riley
8 YOU'RE ALL I NEED TO GET BY Marvin Gaye & Tammi Terrell
9 I CAN'T STOP DANCING Archie Bell & The Drells
10 STAY IN MY CORNER Dells

September 7, 1968
1 PEOPLE GOT TO BE FREE Rascals
2 BORN TO BE WILD Steppenwolf
3 LIGHT MY FIRE Jose Feliciano
4 HARPER VALLEY P.T.A. Jeannie C. Riley
5 HELLO I LOVE YOU Doors
6 THE HOUSE THAT JACK BUILT Aretha Franklin
7 1, 2, 3, RED LIGHT 1910 Fruitgum Co.
8 YOU'RE ALL I NEED TO GET BY Marvin Gaye & Tammi Terrell

9   I CAN'T STOP DANCING   Archie Bell & The Drells
10   STAY IN MY CORNER   Dells

September 14, 1968
1   PEOPLE GOT TO BE FREE   Rascals
2   HARPER VALLEY P.T.A.   Jeannie C. Riley
3   LIGHT MY FIRE   Jose Feliciano
4   BORN TO BE WILD   Steppenwolf
5   1, 2, 3, RED LIGHT   1910 Fruitgum Co.
6   THE HOUSE THAT JACK BUILT   Aretha Franklin
7   YOU'RE ALL I NEED TO GET BY   Marvin Gaye & Tammi Terrell
8   HUSH   Deep Purple
9   HELLO I LOVE YOU   Doors
10   HEY JUDE   Beatles

September 21, 1968
1   HARPER VALLEY P.T.A.   Jeannie C. Riley
2   PEOPLE GOT TO BE FREE   Rascals
3   HEY JUDE   Beatles
4   HUSH   Deep Purple
5   1, 2, 3, RED LIGHT   1910 Fruitgum Co.
6   LIGHT MY FIRE   Crazy World of Arthur Brown
7   BORN TO BE WILD   Steppenwolf
8   THE FOOL ON THE HILL   Beatles
9   I'VE GOTTA GET A MESSAGE TO YOU   Bee Gees
10   THE HOUSE THAT JACK BUILT   Aretha Franklin

September 28, 1968
1   HEY JUDE   Beatles
2   HARPER VALLEY P.T.A.   Jeannie C. Riley
3   PEOPLE GOT TO BE FREE   Rascals
4   HUSH   Deep Purple
5   FIRE   Crazy World of Arthur Brown
6   THE FOOL ON THE HILL   Beatles
7   1, 2, 3, RED LIGHT   1910 Fruitgum Co.
8   I'VE GOTTA GET A MESSAGE TO YOU   Bee Gees
9   GIRL WATCHER   O'Kaysions
10   SLIP AWAY   Clarence Carter

October 5, 1968
1   HEY JUDE   Beatles
2   HARPER VALLEY P.T.A.   Jeannie C. Riley
3   FIRE   Crazy World of Arthur Brown
4   LITTLE GREEN APPLES   O. C. Smith
5   GIRL WATCHER   O'Kaysions
6   SLIP AWAY   Clarence Carter
7   PEOPLE GOT TO BE FREE   Rascals
8   I'VE GOTTA GET A MESSAGE TO YOU   Bee Gees
9   1, 2, 3, RED LIGHT   1910 Fruitgum Co.
10   I SAY A LITTLE PRAYER   Dionne Warwick

October 12, 1968
1   HEY JUDE   Beatles
2   HARPER VALLEY P.T.A.   Jeannie C. Riley
3   FIRE   Crazy World of Arthur Brown
4   LITTLE GREEN APPLES   O. C. Smith
5   GIRL WATCHER   O'Kaysions
6   MIDNIGHT CONFESSIONS   Grass Roots
7   MY SPECIAL ANGEL   Vogues
8   I'VE GOTTA GET A MESSAGE TO YOU   Bee Gees
9   OVER YOU   Gary Puckett & The Union Gap
10   SLIP AWAY   Clarence Carter

October 19, 1968
1   HEY JUDE   Beatles

2   FIRE   Crazy World of Arthur Brown
3   LITTLE GREEN APPLES   O. C. Smith
4   HARPER VALLEY P.T.A.   Jeannie C. Riley
5   GIRL WATCHER   O'Kaysions
6   MIDNIGHT CONFESSIONS   Grass Roots
7   MY SPECIAL ANGEL   Vogues
8   I'VE GOTTA GET A MESSAGE TO YOU   Bee Gees
9   OVER YOU   Gary Puckett & The Union Gap
10   SAY IT LOUD (I'M BLACK AND I'M PROUD)   James Brown

October 26, 1968
1   HEY JUDE   Beatles
2   LITTLE GREEN APPLES   O. C. Smith
3   FIRE   Crazy World of Arthur Brown
4   THOSE WERE THE DAYS   Mary Hopkin
5   GIRL WATCHER   O'Kaysions
6   MIDNIGHT CONFESSIONS   Grass Roots
7   OVER YOU   Gary Puckett & The Union Gap
8   HARPER VALLEY P.T.A.   Jeannie C. Riley
9   ELENORE   Turtles
10   I'VE GOTTA GET A MESSAGE TO YOU   Bee Gees

November 2, 1968
1   HEY JUDE   Beatles
2   THOSE WERE THE DAYS   Mary Hopkin
3   LITTLE GREEN APPLES   O. C. Smith
4   FIRE   Crazy World of Arthur Brown
5   MIDNIGHT CONFESSIONS   Grass Roots
6   ELENORE   Turtles
7   OVER YOU   Gary Puckett & The Union Gap
8   HOLD ME TIGHT   Johnny Nash
9   LOVE CHILD   Supremes
10   WHITE ROOM   Cream

November 9, 1968
1   HEY JUDE   Beatles
2   THOSE WERE THE DAYS   Mary Hopkin
3   LOVE CHILD   Supremes
4   LITTLE GREEN APPLES   O. C. Smith
5   HOLD ME TIGHT   Johnny Nash
6   WHITE ROOM   Cream
7   MAGIC CARPET RIDE   Steppenwolf
8   ELENORE   Turtles
9   FIRE   Crazy World of Arthur Brown
10   MIDNIGHT CONFESSIONS   Grass Roots

November 16, 1968
1   HEY JUDE   Beatles
2   THOSE WERE THE DAYS   Mary Hopkin
3   LOVE CHILD   Supremes
4   MAGIC CARPET RIDE   Steppenwolf
5   HOLD ME TIGHT   Johnny Nash
6   WHITE ROOM   Cream
7   LITTLE GREEN APPLES   O. C. Smith
8   WHO'S MAKING LOVE   Johnnie Taylor
9   ABRAHAM, MARTIN AND JOHN   Dion
10   ELENORE   Turtles

November 23, 1968
1   HEY JUDE   Beatles
2   LOVE CHILD   Supremes
3   THOSE WERE THE DAYS   Mary Hopkin
4   MAGIC CARPET RIDE   Steppenwolf
5   ABRAHAM, MARTIN AND JOHN   Dion
6   WHITE ROOM   Cream
7   HOLD ME TIGHT   Johnny Nash

8 WHO'S MAKING LOVE   Johnnie Taylor
9 LITTLE GREEN APPLES   O. C. Smith
10 WICHITA LINEMAN   Glen Campbell

November 30, 1968
1 LOVE CHILD   Supremes
2 HEY JUDE   Beatles
3 MAGIC CARPET RIDE   Steppenwolf
4 THOSE WERE THE DAYS   Mary Hopkin
5 ABRAHAM, MARTIN AND JOHN   Dion
6 WHO'S MAKING LOVE   Johnnie Taylor
7 FOR ONCE IN MY LIFE   Stevie Wonder
8 WICHITA LINEMAN   Glen Campbell
9 HOLD ME TIGHT   Johnny Nash
10 WHITE ROOM   Cream

December 7, 1968
1 LOVE CHILD   Supremes
2 HEY JUDE   Beatles
3 FOR ONCE IN MY LIFE   Stevie Wonder
4 I HEARD IT THROUGH THE GRAPEVINE   Marvin Gaye
5 WHO'S MAKING LOVE   Johnnie Taylor
6 MAGIC CARPET RIDE   Steppenwolf
7 ABRAHAM, MARTIN AND JOHN   Dion
8 WICHITA LINEMAN   Glen Campbell
9 STORMY   Classics IV
10 THOSE WERE THE DAYS   Mary Hopkin

December 14, 1968
1 I HEARD IT THROUGH THE GRAPEVINE   Marvin Gaye
2 LOVE CHILD   Supremes
3 FOR ONCE IN MY LIFE   Stevie Wonder
4 ABRAHAM, MARTIN AND JOHN   Dion
5 WHO'S MAKING LOVE   Johnnie Taylor
6 HEY JUDE   Beatles
7 WICHITA LINEMAN   Glen Campbell
8 STORMY   Classics IV
9 I LOVE HOW YOU LOVE ME   Bobby Vinton
10 MAGIC CARPET RIDE   Steppenwolf

December 21, 1968
1 I HEARD IT THROUGH THE GRAPEVINE   Marvin Gaye
2 LOVE CHILD   Supremes
3 FOR ONCE IN MY LIFE   Stevie Wonder
4 ABRAHAM, MARTIN AND JOHN   Dion
5 WICHITA LINEMAN   Glen Campbell
6 STORMY   Classics IV
7 WHO'S MAKING LOVE   Johnnie Taylor
8 BOTH SIDES NOW   Judy Collins
9 I LOVE HOW YOU LOVE ME   Bobby Vinton
10 MAGIC CARPET RIDE   Steppenwolf

December 28, 1968
1 I HEARD IT THROUGH THE GRAPEVINE   Marvin Gaye
2 FOR ONCE IN MY LIFE   Stevie Wonder
3 LOVE CHILD   Supremes
4 WICHITA LINEMAN   Glen Campbell
5 STORMY   Classics IV
6 ABRAHAM, MARTIN AND JOHN   Dion
7 I'M GONNA MAKE YOU LOVE ME   Supremes & Temptations
8 WHO'S MAKING LOVE   Johnnie Taylor
9 I LOVE HOW YOU LOVE ME   Bobby Vinton
10 CLOUD NINE   Temptations

January 4, 1969
1 I HEARD IT THROUGH THE GRAPEVINE   Marvin Gaye
2 FOR ONCE IN MY LIFE   Stevie Wonder
3 I'M GONNA MAKE YOU LOVE ME   Supremes & Temptations
4 SOULFUL STRUT   Young-Holt Unlimited
5 WICHITA LINEMAN   Glen Campbell
6 CLOUD NINE   Temptations
7 LOVE CHILD   Supremes
8 STORMY   Classics IV
9 WHO'S MAKING LOVE   Johnnie Taylor
10 HOOKED ON A FEELING   B. J. Thomas

January 11, 1969
1 I HEARD IT THROUGH THE GRAPEVINE   Marvin Gaye
2 I'M GONNA MAKE YOU LOVE ME   Supremes & Temptations
3 WICHITA LINEMAN   Glen Campbell
4 SOULFUL STRUT   Young-Holt Unlimited
5 HOOKED ON A FEELING   B. J. Thomas
6 CLOUD NINE   Temptations
7 FOR ONCE IN MY LIFE   Stevie Wonder
8 CRIMSON AND CLOVER   Tommy James & The Shondells
9 LOVE CHILD   Supremes
10 I LOVE HOW YOU LOVE ME   Bobby Vinton

January 18, 1969
1 I HEARD IT THROUGH THE GRAPEVINE   Marvin Gaye
2 I'M GONNA MAKE YOU LOVE ME   Supremes & Temptations
3 SOULFUL STRUT   Young-Holt Unlimited
4 CRIMSON AND CLOVER   Tommy James & The Shondells
5 HOOKED ON A FEELING   B. J. Thomas
6 WICHITA LINEMAN   Glen Campbell
7 FOR ONCE IN MY LIFE   Stevie Wonder
8 TOUCH ME   Doors
9 WORST THAT COULD HAPPEN   Brooklyn Bridge
10 SON OF A PREACHER MAN   Dusty Springfield

January 25, 1969
1 I HEARD IT THROUGH THE GRAPEVINE   Marvin Gaye
2 CRIMSON AND CLOVER   Tommy James & The Shondells
3 I'M GONNA MAKE YOU LOVE ME   Supremes & Temptations
4 SOULFUL STRUT   Young-Holt Unlimited
5 EVERYDAY PEOPLE   Sly & The Family Stone
6 HOOKED ON A FEELING   B. J. Thomas
7 TOUCH ME   Doors
8 WORST THAT COULD HAPPEN   Brooklyn Bridge
9 I STARTED A JOKE   Bee Gees
10 SON OF A PREACHER MAN   Dusty Springfield

February 1, 1969
1 CRIMSON AND CLOVER   Tommy James & The Shondells
2 EVERYDAY PEOPLE   Sly & The Family Stone
3 WORST THAT COULD HAPPEN   Brooklyn Bridge
4 TOUCH ME   Doors
5 I HEARD IT THROUGH THE GRAPEVINE   Marvin Gaye
6 I'M GONNA MAKE YOU LOVE ME   Supremes & Temptations
7 I STARTED A JOKE   Bee Gees
8 HOOKED ON A FEELING   B. J. Thomas
9 SOULFUL STRUT   Young-Holt Unlimited
10 BUILD ME UP BUTTERCUP   Foundations

February 8, 1969
1. CRIMSON AND CLOVER   Tommy James & The Shondells
2. EVERYDAY PEOPLE   Sly & The Family Stone
3. WORST THAT COULD HAPPEN   Brooklyn Bridge
4. TOUCH ME   Doors
5. BUILD ME UP BUTTERCUP   Foundations
6. I STARTED A JOKE   Bee Gees
7. I HEARD IT THROUGH THE GRAPEVINE   Marvin Gaye
8. I'M GONNA MAKE YOU LOVE ME   Supremes & Temptations
9. HANG 'EM HIGH   Hugo Montenegro
10. CAN I CHANGE MY MIND   Tyrone Davis

February 15, 1969
1. EVERYDAY PEOPLE   Sly & The Family Stone
2. CRIMSON AND CLOVER   Tommy James & The Shondells
3. TOUCH ME   Doors
4. BUILD ME UP BUTTERCUP   Foundations
5. WORST THAT COULD HAPPEN   Brooklyn Bridge
6. CAN I CHANGE MY MIND   Tyrone Davis
7. YOU SHOWED ME   Turtles
8. I HEARD IT THROUGH THE GRAPEVINE   Marvin Gaye
9. HANG 'EM HIGH   Hugo Montenegro
10. I'M GONNA MAKE YOU LOVE ME   Supremes & Temptations

February 22, 1969
1. EVERYDAY PEOPLE   Sly & The Family Stone
2. CRIMSON AND CLOVER   Tommy James & The Shondells
3. BUILD ME UP BUTTERCUP   Foundations
4. TOUCH ME   Doors

Tommy Roe
Tommy reaches dizzying heights for four weeks
in March and April with the #1 ''Dizzy.''

5. CAN I CHANGE MY MIND   Tyrone Davis
6. WORST THAT COULD HAPPEN   Brooklyn Bridge
7. YOU SHOWED ME   Turtles
8. THIS MAGIC MOMENT   Jay & The Americans
9. PROUD MARY   Ike & Tina Turner
10. INDIAN GIVER   1910 Fruitgum Co.

March 1, 1969
1. EVERYDAY PEOPLE   Sly & The Family Stone
2. CRIMSON AND CLOVER   Tommy James & The Shondells
3. BUILD ME UP BUTTERCUP   Foundations
4. TOUCH ME   Doors
5. PROUD MARY   Ike & Tina Turner
6. YOU SHOWED ME   Turtles
7. THIS MAGIC MOMENT   Jay & The Americans
8. BABY BABY DON'T CRY   Miracles
9. WORST THAT COULD HAPPEN   Brooklyn Bridge
10. DIZZY   Tommy Roe

March 8, 1969
1. EVERYDAY PEOPLE   Sly & The Family Stone
2. PROUD MARY   Ike & Tina Turner
3. BUILD ME UP BUTTERCUP   Foundations
4. DIZZY   Tommy Roe
5. CRIMSON AND CLOVER   Tommy James & The Shondells
6. THIS MAGIC MOMENT   Jay & The Americans
7. THIS GIRL'S IN LOVE WITH YOU   Dionne Warwick
8. BABY BABY DON'T CRY   Miracles
9. TOUCH ME   Doors
10. INDIAN GIVER   1910 Fruitgum Co.

March 15, 1969
1. DIZZY   Tommy Roe
2. PROUD MARY   Ike & Tina Turner
3. EVERYDAY PEOPLE   Sly & The Family Stone
4. BUILD ME UP BUTTERCUP   Foundations
5. TRACES   Classics IV
6. CRIMSON AND CLOVER   Tommy James & The Shondells
7. THIS GIRL'S IN LOVE WITH YOU   Dionne Warwick
8. INDIAN GIVER   1910 Fruitgum Co.
9. TIME OF THE SEASON   Zombies
10. THIS MAGIC MOMENT   Jay & The Americans

March 22, 1969
1. DIZZY   Tommy Roe
2. PROUD MARY   Ike & Tina Turner
3. TRACES   Classics IV
4. BUILD ME UP BUTTERCUP   Foundations
5. INDIAN GIVER   1910 Fruitgum Co.
6. TIME OF THE SEASON   Zombies
7. THIS GIRL'S IN LOVE WITH YOU   Dionne Warwick
8. EVERYDAY PEOPLE   Sly & The Family Stone
9. CRIMSON AND CLOVER   Tommy James & The Shondells
10. RUN AWAY CHILD RUNNING WILD   Temptations

March 29, 1969
1. DIZZY   Tommy Roe
2. TRACES   Classics IV
3. TIME OF THE SEASON   Zombies
4. AQUARIUS/LET THE SUNSHINE IN   5th Dimension
5. PROUD MARY   Ike & Tina Turner
6. RUN AWAY CHILD RUNNING WILD   Temptations
7. INDIAN GIVER   1910 Fruitgum Co.
8. GALVESTON   Glen Campbell
9. MY WHOLE WORLD ENDED (THE MOMENT YOU LEFT ME)   David Ruffin
10. ONLY THE STRONG SURVIVE   Jerry Butler

April 5, 1969
1 DIZZY   Tommy Roe
2 AQUARIUS/LET THE SUNSHINE IN   5th Dimension
3 TIME OF THE SEASON   Zombies
4 YOU'VE MADE ME SO VERY HAPPY   Blood, Sweat & Tears
5 GALVESTON   Glen Campbell
6 RUN AWAY CHILD RUNNING WILD   Temptations
7 ONLY THE STRONG SURVIVE   Jerry Butler
8 TRACES   Classics IV
9 MY WHOLE WORLD ENDED (THE MOMENT YOU LEFT ME)   David Ruffin
10 PROUD MARY   Ike & Tina Turner

April 12, 1969
1 AQUARIUS/LET THE SUNSHINE IN   5th Dimension
2 YOU'VE MADE ME SO VERY HAPPY   Blood, Sweat & Tears
3 DIZZY   Tommy Roe
4 GALVESTON   Glen Campbell
5 TIME OF THE SEASON   Zombies
6 ONLY THE STRONG SURVIVE   Jerry Butler
7 IT'S YOUR THING   Isley Brothers
8 HAIR   Cowsills
9 RUN AWAY CHILD RUNNING WILD   Temptations
10 TWENTY-FIVE MILES   Edwin Starr

April 19, 1969
1 AQUARIUS/LET THE SUNSHINE IN   5th Dimension
2 YOU'VE MADE ME SO VERY HAPPY   Blood, Sweat & Tears
3 IT'S YOUR THING   Isley Brothers
4 ONLY THE STRONG SURVIVE   Jerry Butler
5 DIZZY   Tommy Roe
6 GALVESTON   Glen Campbell
7 HAIR   Cowsills
8 TWENTY-FIVE MILES   Edwin Starr
9 TIME OF THE SEASON   Zombies
10 ROCK ME   Steppenwolf

April 26, 1969
1 AQUARIUS/LET THE SUNSHINE IN   5th Dimension
2 YOU'VE MADE ME SO VERY HAPPY   Blood, Sweat & Tears
3 IT'S YOUR THING   Isley Brothers
4 HAIR   Cowsills
5 ONLY THE STRONG SURVIVE   Jerry Butler
6 TWENTY-FIVE MILES   Edwin Starr
7 GALVESTON   Glen Campbell
8 TIME IS TIGHT   Booker T & The MG's
9 DIZZY   Tommy Roe
10 SWEET CHERRY WINE   Tommy James & The Shondells

May 3, 1969
1 AQUARIUS/LET THE SUNSHINE IN   5th Dimension
2 IT'S YOUR THING   Isley Brothers
3 HAIR   Cowsills
4 YOU'VE MADE ME SO VERY HAPPY   Blood, Sweat & Tears
5 ONLY THE STRONG SURVIVE   Jerry Butler
6 TIME IS TIGHT   Booker T & The MG's
7 SWEET CHERRY WINE   Tommy James & The Shondells
8 HAWAII FIVE-O   Ventures
9 THE BOXER   Simon & Garfunkel
10 GALVESTON   Glen Campbell

May 10, 1969
1 AQUARIUS/LET THE SUNSHINE IN   5th Dimension
2 HAIR   Cowsills
3 IT'S YOUR THING   Isley Brothers
4 HAWAII FIVE-O   Ventures
5 YOU'VE MADE ME SO VERY HAPPY   Blood, Sweat & Tears
6 TIME IS TIGHT   Booker T & The MG's
7 SWEET CHERRY WINE   Tommy James & The Shondells
8 THE BOXER   Simon & Garfunkel
9 ATLANTIS   Donovan
10 GET BACK   Beatles

May 17, 1969
1 AQUARIUS/LET THE SUNSHINE IN   5th Dimension
2 HAIR   Cowsills
3 GET BACK   Beatles
4 IT'S YOUR THING   Isley Brothers
5 LOVE (CAN MAKE YOU HAPPY)   Mercy
6 HAWAII FIVE-O   Ventures
7 THE BOXER   Simon & Garfunkel
8 ATLANTIS   Donovan
9 GITARZAN   Ray Stevens
10 THESE EYES   Guess Who

May 24, 1969
1 GET BACK   Beatles
2 AQUARIUS/LET THE SUNSHINE IN   5th Dimension
3 LOVE (CAN MAKE YOU HAPPY)   Mercy
4 HAIR   Cowsills
5 OH HAPPY DAY   Edwin Hawkins' Singers
6 IT'S YOUR THING   Isley Brothers
7 ATLANTIS   Donovan
8 THE BOXER   Simon & Garfunkel
9 GITARZAN   Ray Stevens
10 THESE EYES   Guess Who

May 31, 1969
1 GET BACK   Beatles
2 LOVE (CAN MAKE YOU HAPPY)   Mercy
3 AQUARIUS/LET THE SUNSHINE IN   5th Dimension
4 OH HAPPY DAY   Edwin Hawkins' Singers
5 HAIR   Cowsills
6 THESE EYES   Guess Who
7 ATLANTIS   Donovan
8 GITARZAN   Ray Stevens
9 IN THE GHETTO   Elvis Presley
10 GRAZIN' IN THE GRASS   Hugh Masekela

June 7, 1969
1 GET BACK   Beatles
2 LOVE (CAN MAKE YOU HAPPY)   Mercy
3 HAIR   Cowsills
4 OH HAPPY DAY   Edwin Hawkins' Singers
5 BAD MOON RISING   Creedence Clearwater Revival
6 IN THE GHETTO   Elvis Presley
7 AQUARIUS/LET THE SUNSHINE IN   5th Dimension
8 LOVE THEME FROM "ROMEO AND JULIET"   Henry Mancini
9 THESE EYES   Guess Who
10 TOO BUSY THINKING ABOUT MY BABY   Marvin Gaye

June 14, 1969
1 GET BACK   Beatles
2 LOVE THEME FROM "ROMEO AND JULIET"   Henry Mancini

3 IN THE GHETTO Elvis Presley
4 BAD MOON RISING Creedence Clearwater Revival
5 LOVE (CAN MAKE YOU HAPPY) Mercy
6 GRAZIN' IN THE GRASS Hugh Masekela
7 OH HAPPY DAY Edwin Hawkins' Singers
8 TOO BUSY THINKING ABOUT MY BABY Marvin Gaye
9 THESE EYES Guess Who
10 ONE Three Dog Night

June 21, 1969
1 GET BACK Beatles
2 LOVE THEME FROM "ROMEO AND JULIET" Henry Mancini
3 BAD MOON RISING Creedence Clearwater Revival
4 IN THE GHETTO Elvis Presley
5 TOO BUSY THINKING ABOUT MY BABY Marvin Gaye
6 ONE Three Dog Night
7 LOVE (CAN MAKE YOU HAPPY) Mercy
8 GRAZIN' IN THE GRASS Hugh Masekela
9 GOOD MORNING STARSHINE Oliver
10 SPINNING WHEEL Blood, Sweat & Tears

June 28, 1969
1 LOVE THEME FROM "ROMEO AND JULIET" Henry Mancini
2 BAD MOON RISING Creedence Clearwater Revival
3 GET BACK Beatles
4 TOO BUSY THINKING ABOUT MY BABY Marvin Gaye
5 ONE Three Dog Night
6 SPINNING WHEEL Blood, Sweat & Tears
7 IN THE GHETTO Elvis Presley
8 GOOD MORNING STARSHINE Oliver
9 THE ISRAELITES Desmond Dekker & The Aces
10 GRAZIN' IN THE GRASS Hugh Masekela

July 5, 1969
1 LOVE THEME FROM "ROMEO AND JULIET" Henry Mancini
2 SPINNING WHEEL Blood, Sweat & Tears
3 BAD MOON RISING Creedence Clearwater Revival
4 GOOD MORNING STARSHINE Oliver
5 ONE Three Dog Night
6 GET BACK Beatles
7 CRYSTAL BLUE PERSUASION Tommy James & The Shondells
8 IN THE YEAR 2525 Zager & Evans
9 COLOR HIM FATHER Winstons
10 TOO BUSY THINKING ABOUT MY BABY Marvin Gaye

July 12, 1969
1 IN THE YEAR 2525 Zager & Evans
2 SPINNING WHEEL Blood, Sweat & Tears
3 GOOD MORNING STARSHINE Oliver
4 LOVE THEME FROM "ROMEO AND JULIET" Henry Mancini
5 ONE Three Dog Night
6 CRYSTAL BLUE PERSUASION Tommy James & The Shondells
7 BAD MOON RISING Creedence Clearwater Revival
8 THE BALLAD OF JOHN AND YOKO Beatles
9 COLOR HIM FATHER Winstons
10 WHAT DOES IT TAKE (TO WIN YOUR LOVE)? Jr. Walker & The All Stars

July 19, 1969
1 IN THE YEAR 2525 Zager & Evans

2 SPINNING WHEEL Blood, Sweat & Tears
3 GOOD MORNING STARSHINE Oliver
4 CRYSTAL BLUE PERSUASION Tommy James & The Shondells
5 WHAT DOES IT TAKE (TO WIN YOUR LOVE)? Jr. Walker & The All Stars
6 ONE Three Dog Night
7 COLOR HIM FATHER Winstons
8 THE BALLAD OF JOHN AND YOKO Beatles
9 MY CHERIE AMOUR Stevie Wonder
10 LOVE THEME FROM "ROMEO AND JULIET" Henry Mancini

July 26, 1969
1 IN THE YEAR 2525 Zager & Evans
2 CRYSTAL BLUE PERSUASION Tommy James & The Shondells
3 SPINNING WHEEL Blood, Sweat & Tears
4 MY CHERIE AMOUR Stevie Wonder
5 WHAT DOES IT TAKE (TO WIN YOUR LOVE)? Jr. Walker & The All Stars
6 GOOD MORNING STARSHINE Oliver
7 ONE Three Dog Night
8 THE BALLAD OF JOHN AND YOKO Beatles
9 BABY I LOVE YOU Andy Kim
10 LOVE THEME FROM "ROMEO AND JULIET" Henry Mancini

August 2, 1969
1 IN THE YEAR 2525 Zager & Evans
2 CRYSTAL BLUE PERSUASION Tommy James & The Shondells
3 SPINNING WHEEL Blood, Sweat & Tears
4 MY CHERIE AMOUR Stevie Wonder
5 WHAT DOES IT TAKE (TO WIN YOUR LOVE)? Jr. Walker & The All Stars
6 RUBY DON'T TAKE YOUR LOVE TO TOWN Kenny Rogers & The First Edition
7 SWEET CAROLINE (GOOD TIMES NEVER SEEMED SO GOOD) Neil Diamond
8 HONKY TONK WOMAN Rolling Stones
9 BABY I LOVE YOU Andy Kim
10 THE BALLAD OF JOHN AND YOKO Beatles

August 9, 1969
1 IN THE YEAR 2525 Zager & Evans
2 CRYSTAL BLUE PERSUASION Tommy James & The Shondells
3 HONKY TONK WOMAN Rolling Stones
4 WHAT DOES IT TAKE (TO WIN YOUR LOVE)? Jr. Walker & The All Stars
5 SWEET CAROLINE (GOOD TIMES NEVER SEEMED SO GOOD) Neil Diamond
6 RUBY DON'T TAKE YOUR LOVE TO TOWN Kenny Rogers & The First Edition
7 A BOY NAMED SUE Johnny Cash
8 MY CHERIE AMOUR Stevie Wonder
9 PUT A LITTLE LOVE IN YOUR HEART Jackie DeShannon
10 BABY I LOVE YOU Andy Kim

August 16, 1969
1 IN THE YEAR 2525 Zager & Evans
2 HONKY TONK WOMAN Rolling Stones
3 CRYSTAL BLUE PERSUASION Tommy James & The Shondells
4 SWEET CAROLINE (GOOD TIMES NEVER SEEMED SO GOOD) Neil Diamond

5 A BOY NAMED SUE   Johnny Cash
6 PUT A LITTLE LOVE IN YOUR HEART   Jackie DeShannon
7 RUBY DON'T TAKE YOUR LOVE TO TOWN   Kenny Rogers
   & The First Edition
8 MY CHERIE AMOUR   Stevie Wonder
9 WHAT DOES IT TAKE (TO WIN YOUR LOVE)?   Jr. Walker
   & The All Stars
10 BABY I LOVE YOU   Andy Kim

August 23, 1969
1 HONKY TONK WOMAN   Rolling Stones
2 A BOY NAMED SUE   Johnny Cash
3 CRYSTAL BLUE PERSUASION   Tommy James & The
   Shondells
4 SWEET CAROLINE (GOOD TIMES NEVER SEEMED SO
   GOOD)   Neil Diamond
5 IN THE YEAR 2525   Zager & Evans
6 PUT A LITTLE LOVE IN YOUR HEART   Jackie DeShannon
7 GREEN RIVER   Creedence Clearwater Revival
8 POLK SALAD ANNIE   Tony Joe White
9 GET TOGETHER   Youngbloods
10 LAUGHING   Guess Who

August 30, 1969
1 HONKY TONK WOMAN   Rolling Stones
2 A BOY NAMED SUE   Johnny Cash
3 SUGAR SUGAR   Archies
4 PUT A LITTLE LOVE IN YOUR HEART   Jackie DeShannon
5 SWEET CAROLINE (GOOD TIMES NEVER SEEMED SO
   GOOD)   Neil Diamond
6 GET TOGETHER   Youngbloods
7 GREEN RIVER   Creedence Clearwater Revival
8 IN THE YEAR 2525   Zager & Evans
9 LAY LADY LAY   Bob Dylan
10 CRYSTAL BLUE PERSUASION   Tommy James & The
   Shondells

September 6, 1969
1 HONKY TONK WOMAN   Rolling Stones
2 A BOY NAMED SUE   Johnny Cash
3 SUGAR SUGAR   Archies
4 GREEN RIVER   Creedence Clearwater Revival
5 GET TOGETHER   Youngbloods
6 PUT A LITTLE LOVE IN YOUR HEART   Jackie DeShannon
7 LAY LADY LAY   Bob Dylan
8 EASY TO BE HARD   Three Dog Night
9 SWEET CAROLINE (GOOD TIMES NEVER SEEMED SO
   GOOD)   Neil Diamond
10 I'LL NEVER FALL IN LOVE AGAIN   Dionne Warwick

September 13, 1969
1 HONKY TONK WOMAN   Rolling Stones
2 SUGAR SUGAR   Archies
3 A BOY NAMED SUE   Johnny Cash
4 GREEN RIVER   Creedence Clearwater Revival
5 GET TOGETHER   Youngbloods
6 I'LL NEVER FALL IN LOVE AGAIN   Dionne Warwick
7 LAY LADY LAY   Bob Dylan
8 EASY TO BE HARD   Three Dog Night
9 PUT A LITTLE LOVE IN YOUR HEART   Jackie DeShannon
10 I CAN'T GET NEXT TO YOU   Temptations

September 20, 1969
1 SUGAR SUGAR   Archies
2 HONKY TONK WOMAN   Rolling Stones
3 GREEN RIVER   Creedence Clearwater Revival

4 A BOY NAMED SUE   Johnny Cash
5 EASY TO BE HARD   Three Dog Night
6 I'LL NEVER FALL IN LOVE AGAIN   Dionne Warwick
7 GET TOGETHER   Youngbloods
8 JEAN   Oliver
9 LITTLE WOMAN   Bobby Sherman
10 I CAN'T GET NEXT TO YOU   Temptations

September 27, 1969
1 SUGAR SUGAR   Archies
2 GREEN RIVER   Creedence Clearwater Revival
3 HONKY TONK WOMAN   Rolling Stones
4 EASY TO BE HARD   Three Dog Night
5 LITTLE WOMAN   Bobby Sherman
6 I CAN'T GET NEXT TO YOU   Temptations
7 JEAN   Oliver
8 I'LL NEVER FALL IN LOVE AGAIN   Dionne Warwick
9 HOT FUN IN THE SUMMERTIME   Mungo Jerry
10 OH, WHAT A NIGHT!   Dells

October 4, 1969
1 SUGAR SUGAR   Archies
2 JEAN   Oliver
3 LITTLE WOMAN   Bobby Sherman
4 EASY TO BE HARD   Three Dog Night
5 I CAN'T GET NEXT TO YOU   Temptations
6 HONKY TONK WOMAN   Rolling Stones
7 GREEN RIVER   Creedence Clearwater Revival
8 EVERYBODY'S TALKIN'   Nilsson
9 HOT FUN IN THE SUMMERTIME   Mungo Jerry
10 OH, WHAT A NIGHT!   Dells

October 3, 1969
1 SUGAR SUGAR   Archies
2 JEAN   Oliver
3 LITTLE WOMAN   Bobby Sherman
4 I CAN'T GET NEXT TO YOU   Temptations
5 HOT FUN IN THE SUMMERTIME   Mungo Jerry
6 EVERYBODY'S TALKIN'   Nilsson
7 EASY TO BE HARD   Three Dog Night
8 HONKY TONK WOMAN   Rolling Stones
9 THIS GIRL IS A WOMAN NOW   Gary Puckett & The Union
   Gap
10 GREEN RIVER   Creedence Clearwater Revival

October 18, 1969
1 I CAN'T GET NEXT TO YOU   Temptations
2 HOT FUN IN THE SUMMERTIME   Mungo Jerry
3 SUGAR SUGAR   Archies
4 JEAN   Oliver
5 LITTLE WOMAN   Bobby Sherman
6 SUSPICIOUS MINDS   Elvis Presley
7 THAT'S THE WAY LOVE IS   Marvin Gaye
8 WEDDING BELL BLUES   5th Dimension
9 EASY TO BE HARD   Three Dog Night
10 TRACY   Cuff Links

October 25, 1969
1 I CAN'T GET NEXT TO YOU   Temptations
2 HOT FUN IN THE SUMMERTIME   Mungo Jerry
3 SUGAR SUGAR   Archies
4 JEAN   Oliver
5 SUSPICIOUS MINDS   Elvis Presley
6 LITTLE WOMAN   Bobby Sherman
7 WEDDING BELL BLUES   5th Dimension
8 BABY IT'S YOU   Smith

Peter, Paul & Mary
A turbulent decade ends with this trio ''Leaving On A Jet Plane'' (Dec. 20). Was that an opinion?

9   TRACY   Cuff Links
10   I'M GONNA MAKE YOU MINE   Lou Christie

November 1, 1969
1   SUSPICIOUS MINDS   Elvis Presley
2   WEDDING BELL BLUES   5th Dimension
3   SUGAR SUGAR   Archies
4   I CAN'T GET NEXT TO YOU   Temptations
5   BABY IT'S YOU   Smith
6   HOT FUN IN THE SUMMERTIME   Mungo Jerry
7   LITTLE WOMAN   Bobby Sherman
8   JEAN   Oliver
9   TRACY   Cuff Links
10   COME TOGETHER   Beatles

November 8, 1969
1   WEDDING BELL BLUES   5th Dimension
2   SUSPICIOUS MINDS   Elvis Presley
3   COME TOGETHER   Beatles
4   I CAN'T GET NEXT TO YOU   Temptations
5   BABY IT'S YOU   Smith
6   SUGAR SUGAR   Archies
7   HOT FUN IN THE SUMMERTIME   Mungo Jerry
8   AND WHEN I DIE   Blood, Sweat & Tears
9   SOMETHING   Beatles
10   SMILE A LITTLE SMILE FOR ME   Flying Machine

November 15, 1969
1   WEDDING BELL BLUES   5th Dimension
2   COME TOGETHER   Beatles
3   SOMETHING   Beatles
4   AND WHEN I DIE   Blood, Sweat & Tears

5   BABY IT'S YOU   Smith
6   I CAN'T GET NEXT TO YOU   Temptations
7   SUSPICIOUS MINDS   Elvis Presley
8   SMILE A LITTLE SMILE FOR ME   Flying Machine
9   SUGAR SUGAR   Archies
10   TAKE A LETTER MARIA   R. B. Greaves

November 22, 1969
1   WEDDING BELL BLUES   5th Dimension
2   TAKE A LETTER MARIA   R. B. Greaves
3   SOMETHING   Beatles
4   AND WHEN I DIE   Blood, Sweat & Tears
5   SMILE A LITTLE SMILE FOR ME   Flying Machine
6   NA NA HEY HEY KISS HIM GOODBYE   Steam
7   COME TOGETHER   Beatles
8   YESTER-ME, YESTER-YOU, YESTERDAY   Stevie Wonder
9   SUSPICIOUS MINDS   Elvis Presley
10   I CAN'T GET NEXT TO YOU   Temptations

November 29, 1969
1   COME TOGETHER/SOMETHING   Beatles
2   AND WHEN I DIE   Blood, Sweat & Tears
3   WEDDING BELL BLUES   5th Dimension
4   TAKE A LETTER MARIA   R. B. Greaves
5   NA NA HEY HEY KISS HIM GOODBYE   Steam
6   SMILE A LITTLE SMILE FOR ME   Flying Machine
7   LEAVING ON A JET PLANE   Peter, Paul & Mary
8   YESTER-ME, YESTER-YOU, YESTERDAY   Stevie Wonder
9   DOWN ON THE CORNER/FORTUNATE SON   Creedence
      Clearwater Revival
10   ELI'S COMING   Three Dog Night

December 6, 1969
1   NA NA HEY HEY KISS HIM GOODBYE   Steam
2   LEAVING ON A JET PLANE   Peter, Paul & Mary
3   COME TOGETHER/SOMETHING   Beatles
4   TAKE A LETTER MARIA   R. B. Greaves
5   DOWN ON THE CORNER/FORTUNATE SON   Creedence
      Clearwater Revival
6   AND WHEN I DIE   Blood, Sweat & Tears
7   WEDDING BELL BLUES   5th Dimension
8   YESTER-ME, YESTER-YOU, YESTERDAY   Stevie Wonder
9   SOMEDAY WE'LL BE TOGETHER   Supremes
10 ELI'S COMING   Three Dog Night

December 13, 1969
1   NA NA HEY HEY KISS HIM GOODBYE   Steam
2   LEAVING ON A JET PLANE   Peter, Paul & Mary
3   SOMEDAY WE'LL BE TOGETHER   Supremes
4   COME TOGETHER/SOMETHING   Beatles
5   DOWN ON THE CORNER/FORTUNATE SON   Creedence
      Clearwater Revival
6   TAKE A LETTER MARIA   R. B. Greaves
7   YESTER-ME, YESTER-YOU, YESTERDAY   Stevie Wonder
8   AND WHEN I DIE   Blood, Sweat & Tears
9   RAINDROPS KEEP FALLIN' ON MY HEAD   B. J. Thomas
10 ELI'S COMING   Three Dog Night

December 20, 1969
1   LEAVING ON A JET PLANE   Peter, Paul & Mary
2   SOMEDAY WE'LL BE TOGETHER   Supremes
3   DOWN ON THE CORNER/FORTUNATE SON   Creedence
      Clearwater Revival
4   NA NA HEY HEY KISS HIM GOODBYE   Steam
5   RAINDROPS KEEP FALLIN' ON MY HEAD   B. J. Thomas
6   COME TOGETHER/SOMETHING   Beatles
7   YESTER-ME, YESTER-YOU, YESTERDAY   Stevie Wonder
8   TAKE A LETTER MARIA   R. B. Greaves
9   HOLLY HOLY   Neil Diamond
10 AND WHEN I DIE   Blood, Sweat & Tears

December 27, 1969
1   SOMEDAY WE'LL BE TOGETHER   Supremes
2   LEAVING ON A JET PLANE   Peter, Paul & Mary
3   RAINDROPS KEEP FALLIN' ON MY HEAD   B. J. Thomas
4   DOWN ON THE CORNER/FORTUNATE SON   Creedence
      Clearwater Revival
5   NA NA HEY HEY KISS HIM GOODBYE   Steam
6   HOLLY HOLY   Neil Diamond
7   COME TOGETHER/SOMETHING   Beatles
8   I WANT YOU BACK   Jackson 5
9   WHOLE LOTTA LOVE   Led Zeppelin
10 TAKE A LETTER MARIA   R. B. Greaves

Miscellaneous Trivia Quiz #1

1. What country superstar once played in Buddy Holly's band?
2. What do opera star Edith Piaf and the country music group The Browns have in common?
3. What was Perry Como's profession before he took up singing?
4. Ray Price had a huge country hit with "Heartaches By The Number," and it became the second country hit "covered" by this pop artist. Who is he?
5. What country music legend sang the Indian chant on Johnny Preston's "Running Bear"?
6. Who once referred to themselves as "The Foreverly Brothers"?
7. The #1 version of "Alley Oop" by The Hollywood Argyles was actually recorded by someone else. Who was it?
8. Who played drums on The Marvelettes hit "Please Mr. Postman"?
9. Name the most famous blues singer in the world.
10. Name the back-up vocalists and the guitarist on the Shelley Fabares hit "Johnny Angel."
11. This blind singer's cover version of a 1958 Don Gibson country hit became an instant smash #1 hit. Can you name the singer and the song?
12. She wrote and sang backup on the hit song "Locomotion," recorded by Little Eva (her daughter's baby-sitter). Who is she?
13. In 1979, a mother/daughter team that went on to become country music superstars in the eighties were performing under the name Hillbilly Women. Name the team.
14. Another of Motown's star attractions sang backing vocals on the Stevie Wonder songs "You Haven't Done Nothin" and "All I Do" Who?
15. In the early seventies, a group called Wild Country was appearing at The Bowery in Myrtle Beach, South Carolina. Name the supergroup they were to become.
16. In 1936, "Wabash Cannon Ball" became a hit for this "original" country artist. Who is he?
17. Name the rock group that emerged from one originally called The Sex Gang Children.
18. Solo artist David Lee Roth, formerly lead singer with the group Van Halen, has a favorite singer—who is that singer?
19. Andreas Cornelius van Kuijk, who was born in Holland and apparently emigrated illegally to the U.S., became the most famous rock manager in the world. What does he call himself now?
20. A gospel group called The Soul Stirrers was the source from which this talented black star sprang. Who was he?
21. The Champs (of "Tequila" fame) got their name from a famous horse. Name the horse.
22. Marion Slaughter had a million-selling, country-flavored hit in 1924. What was Marion's stage name, and what was the name of the song?
23. Who once performed under the pseudonym The Harlem Footwarmers?
24. Can you name Capitol Records' first #1 record of the Rock era?
25. What singer's real name is Dino Crocetti?
26. Sun Records' Sam Phillips sold Elvis Presley's recording contract to RCA for what amount?
27. Gogi Grant's only #1 song was recorded in fifteen minutes of studio time. Name the song.
28. "Hound Dog" was originally a #1 r&b hit for what female singer?
29. What rock music legend was once the lead singer for a group called The Teen Kings?
30. Sam Cooke's manager turned the song down, and threw the studio tape in the garbage. Lou Chudd, head of Imperial Records, retrieved the demo and passed the song along to a young TV actor turned singer, who turned it into his second #1 hit. Name the singer and the song.
31. Who sang back-up for Dion on "Runaround Sue" and "The Wanderer"?
32. Seth Ward, who once had a #1 hit about a man named "John," now sells sausages. What was his stage name? J D
33. The Variations changed their name to The Four Lovers, then decided to change it again,

adopting the name of a New Jersey bowling alley chain. Can you name the chain and the group?

34. The Crystals did not actually sing on their #1 song, "He's A Rebel." What group stood in for them?

35. In 1976, George Harrison was sued and paid damages for plagiarism because his hit "My Sweet Lord" sounded too much like another song. Name the song.

36. A line uttered by Clark Gable in one of his movies inspired songwriters Bob Crewe and Bob Gaudio to write a second #1 single for The Four Seasons. What was the song?

37. In 1963, composer Quincy Jones had his first #1 chart success with a seventeen-year-old girl from Tenafly, New Jersey. Who is she?

38. The singing group called The Essex were all members of what other organization?

39. Jan and Dean's song "Linda" was originally written in 1944 about a real little girl named Linda. Do you know her full name?

40. Name the country music artist who first translated Kyo Sakamoto's Japanese-language hit "Sukiyaki" into English.

41. After Bill Haley's "Rock Around The Clock," what is the title of the song most experts regard as the second most influential in effecting a change of direction in rock music history?

42. A very old folk song called "The Eighth Of January" was re-written by Jimmy Driftwood in 1955. Under its new title, it became the #1 song of 1959. Name the song and the artists who recorded it.

43. Can you name Loretta Lynn's first hit single?

44. Who cracked the whip on Frankie Laine's "Mule Train"?

45. Name the answer record to Kitty Wells' "It Wasn't God Who Made Honky Tonk Angels"?

46. Name the female vocalist—now a country and pop crossover superstar—who sang back-up on the Bill Philips hit "Put It Off Until Tomorrow."

47. Colleen Carroll was a singer on Red Foley's Ozark Jubilee who recorded briefly for Capitol Records. Name her famous son.

48. Who began his career as the lead singer for a group called The Tassles?

49. Whose was the mystery background voice on Warner Mack's "Roc A Chicka," an appearance which probably caused the song to be banned from radio airplay?

50. Name the artist who recorded the first song about growing marijuana.

51. Who recorded the first version of "May The Bird Of Paradise Fly Up Your Nose," which Columbia Records then "stole" for Little Jimmy Dickens?

52. What was the most repetitious song ever recorded (excluding "Surfin' Bird" and "Hey Jude"—yes, there were 148 nah-nah-nah's, but also other lyrics as well)?

53. Who played fiddle on some early King-label bluegrass cuts?

54. Who recorded under the name Donny Young?

55. Who recorded under the name Billy Bryan?

56. Who recorded a song under the name Randy Ray?

57. Name the group who performed as The Rainbows for a one-night stand.

58. What song mentions three musical categories in its title?

59. Name the rock singer responsible for forming The Cream, Blind Faith, and Derek & The Dominoes.

60. The fourth member of The Quarrymen adlibed his ability to play. Who was he?

The Seventies

January 3, 1970
1. RAINDROPS KEEP FALLIN' ON MY HEAD   B. J. Thomas
2. LEAVING ON A JET PLANE   Peter, Paul & Mary
3. SOMEDAY WE'LL BE TOGETHER   Supremes
4. DOWN ON THE CORNER/FORTUNATE SON   Creedence Clearwater Revival
5. NA NA HEY HEY KISS HIM GOODBYE   Steam
6. WHOLE LOTTA LOVE   Led Zeppelin
7. I WANT YOU BACK   Jackson 5
8. VENUS   Shocking Blue
9. HOLLY HOLY   Neil Diamond
10. LA LA LA (IF I HAD YOU)   Bobby Sherman

January 10, 1970
1. RAINDROPS KEEP FALLIN' ON MY HEAD   B. J. Thomas
2. SOMEDAY WE'LL BE TOGETHER   Supremes
3. LEAVING ON A JET PLANE   Peter, Paul & Mary
4. I WANT YOU BACK   Jackson 5
5. WHOLE LOTTA LOVE   Led Zeppelin
6. VENUS   Shocking Blue
7. DOWN ON THE CORNER/FORTUNATE SON   Creedence Clearwater Revival
8. NA NA HEY HEY KISS HIM GOODBYE   Steam
9. LA LA LA (IF I HAD YOU)   Bobby Sherman
10. JAM UP JELLY TIGHT   Tommy Roe

January 17, 1970
1. RAINDROPS KEEP FALLIN' ON MY HEAD   B. J. Thomas
2. VENUS   Shocking Blue
3. I WANT YOU BACK   Jackson 5
4. SOMEDAY WE'LL BE TOGETHER   Supremes
5. WHOLE LOTTA LOVE   Led Zeppelin
6. LEAVING ON A JET PLANE   Peter, Paul & Mary
7. DON'T CRY DADDY/RUBBERNECKIN'   Elvis Presley
8. JAM UP JELLY TIGHT   Tommy Roe
9. DOWN ON THE CORNER/FORTUNATE SON   Creedence Clearwater Revival
10. MIDNIGHT COWBOY   Ferrante & Teicher

January 24, 1970
1. RAINDROPS KEEP FALLIN' ON MY HEAD   B. J. Thomas
2. VENUS   Shocking Blue
3. I WANT YOU BACK   Jackson 5
4. SOMEDAY WE'LL BE TOGETHER   Supremes
5. WHOLE LOTTA LOVE   Led Zeppelin
6. LEAVING ON A JET PLANE   Peter, Paul & Mary
7. DON'T CRY DADDY/RUBBERNECKIN'   Elvis Presley
8. WITHOUT LOVE (THERE IS NOTHING)   Tom Jones
9. JAM UP JELLY TIGHT   Tommy Roe
10. I'LL NEVER FALL IN LOVE AGAIN   Dionne Warwick

January 31, 1970
1. I WANT YOU BACK   Jackson 5
2. VENUS   Shocking Blue
3. RAINDROPS KEEP FALLIN' ON MY HEAD   B. J. Thomas
4. WHOLE LOTTA LOVE   Led Zeppelin
5. WITHOUT LOVE (THERE IS NOTHING)   Tom Jones
6. DON'T CRY DADDY/RUBBERNECKIN'   Elvis Presley
7. I'LL NEVER FALL IN LOVE AGAIN   Dionne Warwick

8. THANK YOU/EVERYBODY IS A STAR   Sly & The Family Stone
9. SOMEDAY WE'LL BE TOGETHER   Supremes
10. LEAVING ON A JET PLANE   Peter, Paul & Mary

February 7, 1970
1. VENUS   Shocking Blue
2. I WANT YOU BACK   Jackson 5
3. RAINDROPS KEEP FALLIN' ON MY HEAD   B. J. Thomas
4. THANK YOU/EVERYBODY IS A STAR   Sly & The Family Stone
5. WITHOUT LOVE (THERE IS NOTHING)   Tom Jones
6. I'LL NEVER FALL IN LOVE AGAIN   Dionne Warwick
7. HEY THERE LONELY GIRL   Eddie Holman
8. WHOLE LOTTA LOVE   Led Zeppelin
9. NO TIME   Guess Who
10. JINGLE JANGLE   Archies

February 14, 1970
1. THANK YOU/EVERYBODY IS A STAR   Sly & The Family Stone
2. I WANT YOU BACK   Jackson 5
3. RAINDROPS KEEP FALLIN' ON MY HEAD   B. J. Thomas
4. VENUS   Shocking Blue
5. HEY THERE LONELY GIRL   Eddie Holman
6. NO TIME   Guess Who
7. I'LL NEVER FALL IN LOVE AGAIN   Dionne Warwick
8. PSYCHEDELIC SHACK   Temptations
9. TRAVELIN' BAND/WHO'LL STOP THE RAIN   Creedence Clearwater Revival
10. ARIZONA   Mark Lindsay

February 21, 1970
1. THANK YOU/EVERYBODY IS A STAR   Sly & The Family Stone
2. HEY THERE LONELY GIRL   Eddie Holman
3. BRIDGE OVER TROUBLED WATER   Simon & Garfunkel
4. I WANT YOU BACK   Jackson 5
5. TRAVELIN' BAND/WHO'LL STOP THE RAIN   Creedence Clearwater Revival
6. NO TIME   Guess Who
7. RAINDROPS KEEP FALLIN' ON MY HEAD   B. J. Thomas
8. PSYCHEDELIC SHACK   Temptations
9. VENUS   Shocking Blue
10. RAINY NIGHT IN GEORGIA   Brook Benton

February 28, 1970
1. BRIDGE OVER TROUBLED WATER   Simon & Garfunkel
2. THANK YOU/EVERYBODY IS A STAR   Sly & The Family Stone
3. TRAVELIN' BAND/WHO'LL STOP THE RAIN   Creedence Clearwater Revival
4. HEY THERE LONELY GIRL   Eddie Holman
5. NO TIME   Guess Who
6. MA BELLE AMIE   Tee Set
7. PSYCHEDELIC SHACK   Temptations
8. RAINDROPS KEEP FALLIN' ON MY HEAD   B. J. Thomas
9. RAINY NIGHT IN GEORGIA   Brook Benton
10. VENUS   Shocking Blue

March 7, 1970
1 BRIDGE OVER TROUBLED WATER   Simon & Garfunkel
2 TRAVELIN' BAND/WHO'LL STOP THE RAIN   Creedence Clearwater Revival
3 THANK YOU/EVERYBODY IS A STAR   Sly & The Family Stone
4 RAINY NIGHT IN GEORGIA   Brook Benton
5 HEY THERE LONELY GIRL   Eddie Holman
6 MA BELLE AMIE   Tee Set
7 THE RAPPER   Jaggerz
8 GIVE ME JUST A LITTLE MORE TIME   Chairman of the Board
9 RAINDROPS KEEP FALLIN' ON MY HEAD   B. J. Thomas
10 HE AIN'T HEAVY, HE'S MY BROTHER   Hollies

March 14, 1970
1 BRIDGE OVER TROUBLED WATER   Simon & Garfunkel
2 TRAVELIN' BAND/WHO'LL STOP THE RAIN   Creedence Clearwater Revival
3 THE RAPPER   Jaggerz
4 RAINY NIGHT IN GEORGIA   Brook Benton
5 MA BELLE AMIE   Tee Set
6 GIVE ME JUST A LITTLE MORE TIME   Chairman of the Board
7 THANK YOU/EVERYBODY IS A STAR   Sly & The Family Stone
8 HEY THERE LONELY GIRL   Eddie Holman
9 HE AIN'T HEAVY, HE'S MY BROTHER   Hollies
10 EVIL WAYS   Santana

March 21, 1970
1 BRIDGE OVER TROUBLED WATER   Simon & Garfunkel
2 THE RAPPER   Jaggerz
3 GIVE ME JUST A LITTLE MORE TIME   Chairman of the Board
4 INSTANT KARMA   John Lennon
5 RAINY NIGHT IN GEORGIA   Brook Benton
6 LET IT BE   Beatles
7 HE AIN'T HEAVY, HE'S MY BROTHER   Hollies
8 LOVE GROWS (WHERE MY ROSEMARY GOES)   Edison Lighthouse
9 EVIL WAYS   Santana
10 DIDN'T I?   Delfonics

March 28, 1970
1 BRIDGE OVER TROUBLED WATER   Simon & Garfunkel
2 LET IT BE   Beatles
3 INSTANT KARMA   John Lennon
4 THE RAPPER   Jaggerz
5 LOVE GROWS (WHERE MY ROSEMARY GOES)   Edison Lighthouse
6 ABC   Jacksons
7 HE AIN'T HEAVY, HE'S MY BROTHER   Hollies
8 SPIRIT IN THE SKY   Norman Greenbaum
9 GIVE ME JUST A LITTLE MORE TIME   Chairman of the Board
10 COME AND GET IT   Badfinger

April 4, 1970
1 BRIDGE OVER TROUBLED WATER   Simon & Garfunkel
2 LET IT BE   Beatles
3 INSTANT KARMA   John Lennon
4 ABC   Jacksons
5 LOVE GROWS (WHERE MY ROSEMARY GOES)   Edison Lighthouse
6 SPIRIT IN THE SKY   Norman Greenbaum
7 HOUSE OF THE RISING SUN   Frijid Pink
8 THE RAPPER   Jaggerz
9 COME AND GET IT   Badfinger
10 EASY COME, EASY GO   Bobby Sherman

April 11, 1970
1 LET IT BE   Beatles
2 ABC   Jacksons
3 INSTANT KARMA   John Lennon
4 SPIRIT IN THE SKY   Norman Greenbaum
5 BRIDGE OVER TROUBLED WATER   Simon & Garfunkel
6 LOVE GROWS (WHERE MY ROSEMARY GOES)   Edison Lighthouse
7 HOUSE OF THE RISING SUN   Frijid Pink
8 COME AND GET IT   Badfinger
9 EASY COME, EASY GO   Bobby Sherman
10 THE RAPPER   Jaggerz

April 18, 1970
1 LET IT BE   Beatles
2 ABC   Jacksons
3 SPIRIT IN THE SKY   Norman Greenbaum
4 INSTANT KARMA   John Lennon
5 LOVE GROWS (WHERE MY ROSEMARY GOES)   Edison Lighthouse
6 BRIDGE OVER TROUBLED WATER   Simon & Garfunkel
7 COME AND GET IT   Badfinger
8 AMERICAN WOMAN/NO SUGAR TONIGHT   Guess Who
9 LOVE OR LET ME BE LONELY   Friends of Distinction
10 UP THE LADDER TO THE ROOF   Supremes

April 25, 1970
1 ABC   Jacksons
2 LET IT BE   Beatles
3 SPIRIT IN THE SKY   Norman Greenbaum
4 INSTANT KARMA   John Lennon
5 AMERICAN WOMAN/NO SUGAR TONIGHT   Guess Who
6 LOVE GROWS (WHERE MY ROSEMARY GOES)   Edison Lighthouse
7 COME AND GET IT   Badfinger
8 LOVE OR LET ME BE LONELY   Friends of Distinction
9 BRIDGE OVER TROUBLED WATER   Simon & Garfunkel
10 TURN BACK THE HANDS OF TIME   Tyrone Davis

May 2, 1970
1 ABC   Jacksons
2 LET IT BE   Beatles
3 SPIRIT IN THE SKY   Norman Greenbaum
4 AMERICAN WOMAN/NO SUGAR TONIGHT   Guess Who
5 INSTANT KARMA   John Lennon
6 LOVE OR LET ME BE LONELY   Friends of Distinction
7 LOVE GROWS (WHERE MY ROSEMARY GOES)   Edison Lighthouse
8 COME AND GET IT   Badfinger
9 VEHICLE   Ides Of March
10 TURN BACK THE HANDS OF TIME   Tyrone Davis

May 9, 1970
1 AMERICAN WOMAN/NO SUGAR TONIGHT   Guess Who
2 ABC   Jacksons
3 LET IT BE   Beatles
4 VEHICLE   Ides Of March
5 SPIRIT IN THE SKY   Norman Greenbaum
6 LOVE OR LET ME BE LONELY   Friends of Distinction
7 EVERYTHING IS BEAUTIFUL   Ray Stevens
8 INSTANT KARMA   John Lennon

276

9   TURN BACK THE HANDS OF TIME   Tyrone Davis
10 REFLECTIONS OF MY LIFE   Marmalade

May 16, 1970
1   AMERICAN WOMAN/NO SUGAR TONIGHT   Guess Who
2   ABC   Jacksons
3   VEHICLE   Ides Of March
4   LET IT BE   Beatles
5   CECILIA   Simon & Garfunkel
6   SPIRIT IN THE SKY   Norman Greenbaum
7   EVERYTHING IS BEAUTIFUL   Ray Stevens
8   TURN BACK THE HANDS OF TIME   Tyrone Davis
9   UP AROUND THE BEND   Creedence Clearwater Revival
10 REFLECTIONS OF MY LIFE   Marmalade

May 23, 1970
1   AMERICAN WOMAN/NO SUGAR TONIGHT   Guess Who
2   VEHICLE   Ides Of March
3   TURN BACK THE HANDS OF TIME   Tyrone Davis
4   EVERYTHING IS BEAUTIFUL   Ray Stevens
5   CECILIA   Simon & Garfunkel
6   LET IT BE   Beatles
7   LOVE ON A TWO WAY STREET   Moments
8   UP AROUND THE BEND   Creedence Clearwater Revival
9   ABC   Jacksons
10 REFLECTIONS OF MY LIFE   Marmalade

May 30, 1970
1   EVERYTHING IS BEAUTIFUL   Ray Stevens
2   AMERICAN WOMAN/NO SUGAR TONIGHT   Guess Who
3   LOVE ON A TWO WAY STREET   Moments
4   CECILIA   Simon & Garfunkel
5   UP AROUND THE BEND   Creedence Clearwater Revival
6   WHICH WAY YOU GOING BILLY   Poppy Family
7   THE LETTER   Box Tops
8   TURN BACK THE HANDS OF TIME   Tyrone Davis
9   VEHICLE   Ides Of March
10 LET IT BE   Beatles

June 6, 1970
1   EVERYTHING IS BEAUTIFUL   Ray Stevens
2   WHICH WAY YOU GOING BILLY   Poppy Family
3   LOVE ON A TWO WAY STREET   Moments
4   UP AROUND THE BEND   Creedence Clearwater Revival
5   CECILIA   Simon & Garfunkel
6   GET READY   Rare Earth
7   THE LETTER   Box Tops
8   AMERICAN WOMAN/NO SUGAR TONIGHT   Guess Who
9   MAKE ME SMILE   Chicago
10 THE LONG AND WINDING ROAD   Beatles

June 13, 1970
1   THE LONG AND WINDING ROAD   Beatles
2   WHICH WAY YOU GOING BILLY   Poppy Family
3   EVERYTHING IS BEAUTIFUL   Ray Stevens
4   GET READY   Rare Earth
5   LOVE ON A TWO WAY STREET   Moments
6   CECILIA   Simon & Garfunkel
7   THE LETTER   Box Tops
8   UP AROUND THE BEND   Creedence Clearwater Revival
9   MAKE ME SMILE   Chicago
10 LOVE YOU SAVE   Jackson 5

June 20, 1970
1   THE LONG AND WINDING ROAD   Beatles
2   LOVE YOU SAVE   Jackson 5
3   WHICH WAY YOU GOING BILLY   Poppy Family
4   GET READY   Rare Earth
5   MAMA TOLD ME (NOT TO COME)   Three Dog Night
6   BALL OF CONFUSION   Temptations
7   LOVE ON A TWO WAY STREET   Moments
8   THE LETTER   Box Tops
9   HITCHIN' A RIDE   Vanity Fare
10 LAY DOWN (CANDLES IN THE RAIN)   Melanie

June 27, 1970
1   LOVE YOU SAVE   Jackson 5
2   MAMA TOLD ME (NOT TO COME)   Three Dog Night
3   BALL OF CONFUSION   Temptations
4   THE LONG AND WINDING ROAD   Beatles
5   HITCHIN' A RIDE   Vanity Fare
6   RIDE CAPTAIN RIDE   Blue Image
7   GET READY   Rare Earth
8   LAY DOWN (CANDLES IN THE RAIN)   Melanie
9   THE WONDER OF YOU   Elvis Presley
10 WHICH WAY YOU GOING BILLY   Poppy Family

July 4, 1970
1   LOVE YOU SAVE   Jackson 5
2   MAMA TOLD ME (NOT TO COME)   Three Dog Night
3   BALL OF CONFUSION   Temptations
4   THE LONG AND WINDING ROAD   Beatles
5   HITCHIN' A RIDE   Vanity Fare
6   RIDE CAPTAIN RIDE   Blue Image
7   BAND OF GOLD   Freda Payne
8   LAY DOWN (CANDLES IN THE RAIN)   Melanie
9   THE WONDER OF YOU   Elvis Presley
10 GET READY   Rare Earth

July 11, 1970
1   MAMA TOLD ME (NOT TO COME)   Three Dog Night
2   LOVE YOU SAVE   Jackson 5
3   BALL OF CONFUSION   Temptations
4   RIDE CAPTAIN RIDE   Blue Image
5   BAND OF GOLD   Freda Payne
6   LAY DOWN (CANDLES IN THE RAIN)   Melanie
7   (THEY LONG TO BE) CLOSE TO YOU   Carpenters
8   THE LONG AND WINDING ROAD   Beatles
9   THE WONDER OF YOU   Elvis Presley
10 HITCHIN' A RIDE   Vanity Fare

July 18, 1970
1   MAMA TOLD ME (NOT TO COME)   Three Dog Night
2   LOVE YOU SAVE   Jackson 5
3   (THEY LONG TO BE) CLOSE TO YOU   Carpenters
4   BAND OF GOLD   Freda Payne
5   BALL OF CONFUSION   Temptations
6   RIDE CAPTAIN RIDE   Blue Image
7   LAY DOWN (CANDLES IN THE RAIN)   Melanie
8   O-O-H CHILD   Five Stairsteps
9   GIMME DAT DING   Pipkins
10 MAKE IT WITH YOU   Bread

July 25, 1970
1   CLOSE TO YOU   Carpenters
2   MAMA TOLD ME (NOT TO COME)   Three Dog Night
3   BAND OF GOLD   Freda Payne
4   LOVE YOU SAVE   Jackson 5
5   MAKE IT WITH YOU   Bread
6   BALL OF CONFUSION   Temptations
7   RIDE CAPTAIN RIDE   Blue Image
8   O-O-H CHILD   Five Stairsteps

9 SIGNED, SEALED, DELIVERED, I'M YOURS Stevie Wonder
10 LAY DOWN (CANDLES IN THE RAIN) Melanie

August 1, 1970
1 CLOSE TO YOU Carpenters
2 MAKE IT WITH YOU Bread
3 MAMA TOLD ME (NOT TO COME) Three Dog Night
4 BAND OF GOLD Freda Payne
5 SIGNED, SEALED, DELIVERED, I'M YOURS Stevie Wonder
6 LOVE YOU SAVE Jackson 5
7 SPILL THE WINE Eric Burdon & War
8 BALL OF CONFUSION Temptations
9 TIGHTER TIGHTER Alive & Kicking
10 O-O-H CHILD Five Stairsteps

August 8, 1970
1 CLOSE TO YOU Carpenters
2 MAKE IT WITH YOU Bread
3 SIGNED, SEALED, DELIVERED, I'M YOURS Stevie Wonder
4 SPILL THE WINE Eric Burdon & War
5 BAND OF GOLD Freda Payne
6 MAMA TOLD ME (NOT TO COME) Three Dog Night
7 TIGHTER TIGHTER Alive & Kicking
8 LOVE YOU SAVE Jackson 5
9 BALL OF CONFUSION Temptations
10 O-O-H CHILD Five Stairsteps

August 15, 1970
1 CLOSE TO YOU Carpenters
2 MAKE IT WITH YOU Bread
3 SIGNED, SEALED, DELIVERED, I'M YOURS Stevie Wonder
4 SPILL THE WINE Eric Burdon & War
5 IN THE SUMMERTIME Mungo Jerry
6 WAR Edwin Starr
7 BAND OF GOLD Freda Payne
8 MAMA TOLD ME (NOT TO COME) Three Dog Night
9 TIGHTER TIGHTER Alive & Kicking
10 BALL OF CONFUSION Temptations

August 22, 1970
1 MAKE IT WITH YOU Bread
2 CLOSE TO YOU Carpenters
3 SPILL THE WINE Eric Burdon & War
4 WAR Edwin Starr
5 IN THE SUMMERTIME Mungo Jerry
6 SIGNED, SEALED, DELIVERED, I'M YOURS Stevie Wonder
7 PATCHES Clarence Carter
8 BAND OF GOLD Freda Payne
9 I JUST CAN'T HELP BELIEVING B. J. Thomas
10 TIGHTER TIGHTER Alive & Kicking

August 29,1970
1 WAR Edwin Starr
2 MAKE IT WITH YOU Bread
3 CLOSE TO YOU Carpenters
4 IN THE SUMMERTIME Mungo Jerry
5 SPILL THE WINE Eric Burdon & War
6 SIGNED, SEALED, DELIVERED, I'M YOURS Stevie Wonder
7 PATCHES Clarence Carter
8 WHY CAN'T I TOUCH YOU Ronnie Dyson

9 AIN'T NO MOUNTAIN HIGH ENOUGH Diana Ross
10 25 OR 6 TO 4 Chicago

September 5, 1970
1 WAR Edwin Starr
2 AIN'T NO MOUNTAIN HIGH ENOUGH Diana Ross
3 MAKE IT WITH YOU Bread
4 IN THE SUMMERTIME Mungo Jerry
5 CLOSE TO YOU Carpenters
6 25 OR 6 TO 4 Chicago
7 PATCHES Clarence Carter
8 WHY CAN'T I TOUCH YOU Ronnie Dyson
9 SPILL THE WINE Eric Burdon & War
10 LOOKING OUT MY BACK DOOR/LONG AS I CAN SEE THE LIGHT Creedence Clearwater Revival

September 12, 1970
1 WAR Edwin Starr
2 AIN'T NO MOUNTAIN HIGH ENOUGH Diana Ross
3 IN THE SUMMERTIME Mungo Jerry
4 25 OR 6 TO 4 Chicago
5 LOOKING OUT MY BACK DOOR/LONG AS I CAN SEE THE LIGHT Creedence Clearwater Revival
6 PATCHES Clarence Carter
7 JULIE, DO YOU LOVE ME Bobby Sherman
8 CLOSE TO YOU Carpenters
9 MAKE IT WITH YOU Bread
10 SPILL THE WINE Eric Burdon & War

September 19, 1970
1 AIN'T NO MOUNTAIN HIGH ENOUGH Diana Ross
2 WAR Edwin Starr
3 LOOKING OUT MY BACK DOOR/LONG AS I CAN SEE THE LIGHT Creedence Clearwater Revival
4 PATCHES Clarence Carter
5 JULIE, DO YOU LOVE ME Bobby Sherman
6 25 OR 6 TO 4 Chicago
7 IN THE SUMMERTIME Mungo Jerry
8 CLOSE TO YOU Carpenters
9 CANDIDA Dawn
10 MAKE IT WITH YOU Bread

September 26, 1970
1 AIN'T NO MOUNTAIN HIGH ENOUGH Diana Ross
2 WAR Edwin Starr
3 LOOKING OUT MY BACK DOOR/LONG AS I CAN SEE THE LIGHT Creedence Clearwater Revival
4 PATCHES Clarence Carter
5 JULIE, DO YOU LOVE ME Bobby Sherman
6 CRACKLIN' ROSE Neil Diamond
7 CANDIDA Dawn
8 SNOWBIRD Anne Murray
9 (I KNOW) I'M LOSING YOU Temptations
10 25 OR 6 TO 4 Chicago

October 3, 1970
1 AIN'T NO MOUNTAIN HIGH ENOUGH Diana Ross
2 LOOKING OUT MY BACK DOOR/LONG AS I CAN SEE THE LIGHT Creedence Clearwater Revival
3 CANDIDA Dawn
4 CRACKLIN' ROSE Neil Diamond
5 JULIE, DO YOU LOVE ME Bobby Sherman
6 I'LL BE THERE Jackson 5
7 (I KNOW) I'M LOSING YOU Temptations
8 SNOWBIRD Anne Murray
9 WAR Edwin Starr
10 ALL RIGHT NOW Free

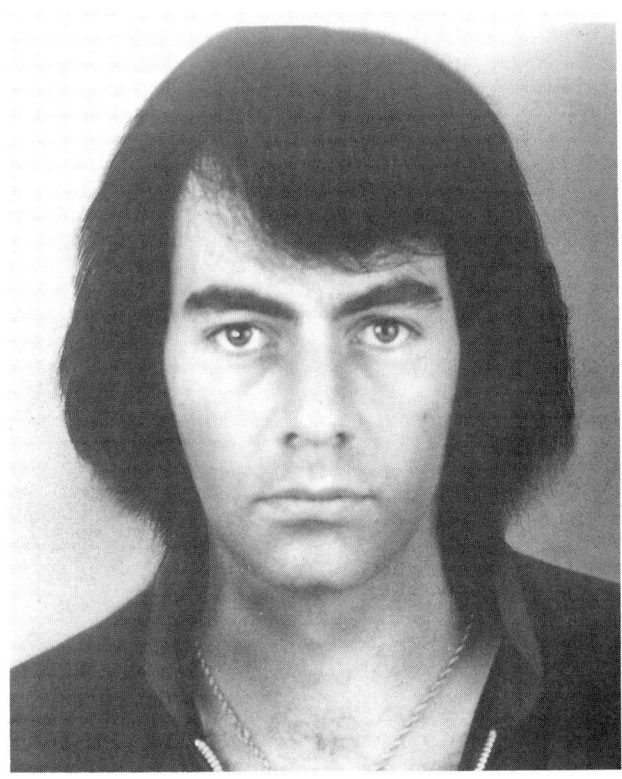

Neil Diamond
Neil's ''Cracklin' Rose'' hits #1 (Oct. 10).

October 10, 1970
1. CRACKLIN' ROSE   Neil Diamond
2. I'LL BE THERE   Jackson 5
3. CANDIDA   Dawn
4. AIN'T NO MOUNTAIN HIGH ENOUGH   Diana Ross
5. ALL RIGHT NOW   Free
6. JULIE, DO YOU LOVE ME   Bobby Sherman
7. LOOKING OUT MY BACK DOOR/LONG AS I CAN SEE THE LIGHT   Creedence Clearwater Revival
8. GREEN EYED LADY   Sugarloaf
9. WE'VE ONLY JUST BEGUN   Carpenters
10. (I KNOW) I'M LOSING YOU   Temptations

October 17, 1970
1. I'LL BE THERE   Jackson 5
2. CRACKLIN' ROSE   Neil Diamond
3. GREEN EYED LADY   Sugarloaf
4. ALL RIGHT NOW   Free
5. WE'VE ONLY JUST BEGUN   Carpenters
6. CANDIDA   Dawn
7. AIN'T NO MOUNTAIN HIGH ENOUGH   Diana Ross
8. LOOKING OUT MY BACK DOOR/LONG AS I CAN SEE THE LIGHT   Creedence Clearwater Revival
9. JULIE, DO YOU LOVE ME   Bobby Sherman
10. FIRE AND RAIN   James Taylor

October 24, 1970
1. I'LL BE THERE   Jackson 5
2. CRACKLIN' ROSE   Neil Diamond
3. GREEN EYED LADY   Sugarloaf
4. WE'VE ONLY JUST BEGUN   Carpenters
5. ALL RIGHT NOW   Free
6. FIRE AND RAIN   James Taylor
7. CANDIDA   Dawn
8. INDIANA WANTS ME   R. Dean Taylor
9. LOLA   Kinks
10. AIN'T NO MOUNTAIN HIGH ENOUGH   Diana Ross

October 31, 1970
1. I'LL BE THERE   Jackson 5
2. WE'VE ONLY JUST BEGUN   Carpenters
3. FIRE AND RAIN   James Taylor
4. CRACKLIN' ROSE   Neil Diamond
5. GREEN EYED LADY   Sugarloaf
6. ALL RIGHT NOW   Free
7. INDIANA WANTS ME   R. Dean Taylor
8. CANDIDA   Dawn
9. LOLA   Kinks
10. IT'S ONLY MAKE BELIEVE   Glen Campbell

November 7, 1970
1. I'LL BE THERE   Jackson 5
2. WE'VE ONLY JUST BEGUN   Carpenters
3. FIRE AND RAIN   James Taylor
4. GREEN EYED LADY   Sugarloaf
5. INDIANA WANTS ME   R. Dean Taylor
6. ALL RIGHT NOW   Free
7. I THINK I LOVE YOU   Partridge Family
8. CRACKLIN' ROSE   Neil Diamond
9. CANDIDA   Dawn
10. LOLA   Kinks

November 14, 1970
1. I'LL BE THERE   Jackson 5
2. WE'VE ONLY JUST BEGUN   Carpenters
3. FIRE AND RAIN   James Taylor
4. I THINK I LOVE YOU   Partridge Family
5. INDIANA WANTS ME   R. Dean Taylor
6. GREEN EYED LADY   Sugarloaf
7. THE TEARS OF A CLOWN   Miracles
8. SOMEBODY'S BEEN SLEEPING   100 Proof Aged In Soul
9. GYPSY WOMAN   Brian Hyland
10. IT DON'T MATTER TO ME   Bread

November 21, 1970
1. I THINK I LOVE YOU   Partridge Family
2. WE'VE ONLY JUST BEGUN   Carpenters
3. I'LL BE THERE   Jackson 5
4. THE TEARS OF A CLOWN   Miracles
5. FIRE AND RAIN   James Taylor
6. INDIANA WANTS ME   R. Dean Taylor
7. GREEN EYED LADY   Sugarloaf
8. SOMEBODY'S BEEN SLEEPING   100 Proof Aged In Soul
9. GYPSY WOMAN   Brian Hyland
10. MONTEGO BAY   Bobbly Bloom

November 29, 1970
1. I THINK I LOVE YOU   Partridge Family
2. THE TEARS OF A CLOWN   Miracles
3. I'LL BE THERE   Jackson 5
4. WE'VE ONLY JUST BEGUN   Carpenters
5. FIRE AND RAIN   James Taylor
6. GYPSY WOMAN   Brian Hyland
7. INDIANA WANTS ME   R. Dean Taylor
8. MONTEGO BAY   Bobbly Bloom
9. HEAVEN HELP US ALL   Stevie Wonder
10. GREEN EYED LADY   Sugarloaf

December 5, 1970
1. I THINK I LOVE YOU   Partridge Family
2. THE TEARS OF A CLOWN   Miracles
3. GYPSY WOMAN   Brian Hyland
4. I'LL BE THERE   Jackson 5
5. WE'VE ONLY JUST BEGUN   Carpenters
6. FIRE AND RAIN   James Taylor
7. ONE LESS BELL TO ANSWER   5th Dimension
8. NO MATTER WHAT   Badfinger
9. HEAVEN HELP US ALL   Stevie Wonder
10. SHARE THE LAND   Guess Who

December 12, 1970
1. THE TEARS OF A CLOWN   Miracles
2. I THINK I LOVE YOU   Partridge Family
3. GYPSY WOMAN   Brian Hyland
4. ONE LESS BELL TO ANSWER   5th Dimension
5. I'LL BE THERE   Jackson 5
6. MY SWEET LORD/ISN'T IT A PITY   George Harrison
7. BLACK MAGIC WOMAN   Santana
8. NO MATTER WHAT   Badfinger
9. DOES ANYBODY REALLY KNOW WHAT TIME IT IS
     Chicago
10. SHARE THE LAND   Guess Who

December 19, 1970
1. THE TEARS OF A CLOWN   Miracles
2. MY SWEET LORD/ISN'T IT A PITY   George Harrison
3. ONE LESS BELL TO ANSWER   5th Dimension
4. I THINK I LOVE YOU   Partridge Family
5. BLACK MAGIC WOMAN   Santana
6. KNOCK THREE TIMES   Dawn
7. STONED LOVE   Supremes
8. DOES ANYBODY REALLY KNOW WHAT TIME IT IS
     Chicago
9. GYPSY WOMAN   Brian Hyland
10. NO MATTER WHAT   Badfinger

December 26, 1970
1. MY SWEET LORD/ISN'T IT A PITY   George Harrison
2. ONE LESS BELL TO ANSWER   5th Dimension
3. THE TEARS OF A CLOWN   Miracles
4. KNOCK THREE TIMES   Dawn
5. BLACK MAGIC WOMAN   Santana
6. I THINK I LOVE YOU   Partridge Family
7. STONED LOVE   Supremes
8. DOES ANYBODY REALLY KNOW WHAT TIME IT IS
     Chicago
9. GYPSY WOMAN   Brian Hyland
10. NO MATTER WHAT   Badfinger

January 2, 1971
1. MY SWEET LORD/ISN'T IT A PITY   George Harrison
2. ONE LESS BELL TO ANSWER   5th Dimension
3. KNOCK THREE TIMES   Dawn
4. THE TEARS OF A CLOWN   Miracles
5. BLACK MAGIC WOMAN   Santana
6. I THINK I LOVE YOU   Partridge Family
7. DOES ANYBODY REALLY KNOW WHAT TIME IT IS
     Chicago
8. STONED LOVE   Supremes
9. DOMINO   Van Morrison
10. GYPSY WOMAN   Brian Hyland

January 9, 1971
1. MY SWEET LORD/ISN'T IT A PITY   George Harrison

George Harrison
George was the first ex-Beatle to top the charts (Dec. 26, '70).

2. KNOCK THREE TIMES   Dawn
3. ONE LESS BELL TO ANSWER   5th Dimension
4. BLACK MAGIC WOMAN   Santana
5. I THINK I LOVE YOU   Partridge Family
6. THE TEARS OF A CLOWN   Miracles
7. DOES ANYBODY REALLY KNOW WHAT TIME IT IS
     Chicago
8. STONED LOVE   Supremes
9. LONELY DAYS   Bee Gees
10. STONEY END   Barbra Streisand

January 16, 1971
1. MY SWEET LORD/ISN'T IT A PITY?   George Harrison
2. KNOCK THREE TIMES   Dawn
3. ONE LESS BELL TO ANSWER   5th Dimension
4. BLACK MAGIC WOMAN   Santana
5. I THINK I LOVE YOU   Partridge Family
6. LONELY DAYS   Bee Gees
7. GROOVE ME   King Floyd
8. STONED LOVE   Supremes
9. STONEY END   Barbra Streisand
10. THE TEARS OF A CLOWN   Miracles

January 23, 1971
1. KNOCK THREE TIMES   Dawn
2. MY SWEET LORD/ISN'T IT A PITY   George Harrison
3. ONE LESS BELL TO ANSWER   5th Dimension
4. LONELY DAYS   Bee Gees
5. BLACK MAGIC WOMAN   Santana
6. STONEY END   Barbra Streisand
7. GROOVE ME   King Floyd
8. YOUR SONG   Elton John
9. ROSE GARDEN   Lynn Anderson

280

10 IT'S IMPOSSIBLE   Perry Como

January 30, 1971
1 KNOCK THREE TIMES   Dawn
2 MY SWEET LORD/ISN'T IT A PITY   George Harrison
3 LONELY DAYS   Bee Gees
4 ONE LESS BELL TO ANSWER   5th Dimension
5 ROSE GARDEN   Lynn Anderson
6 GROOVE ME   King Floyd
7 I HEAR YOU KNOCKING   Dave Edmunds
8 YOUR SONG   Elton John
9 ONE BAD APPLE   Osmonds
10 STONEY END   Barbra Streisand

February 6, 1971
1 KNOCK THREE TIMES   Dawn
2 ONE BAD APPLE   Osmonds
3 MY SWEET LORD/ISN'T IT A PITY   George Harrison
4 LONELY DAYS   Bee Gees
5 ROSE GARDEN   Lynn Anderson
6 I HEAR YOU KNOCKING   Dave Edmunds
7 GROOVE ME   King Floyd
8 YOUR SONG   Elton John
9 ONE LESS BELL TO ANSWER   5th Dimension
10 IF I WERE YOUR WOMAN   Gladys Knight & The Pips

February 13, 1971
1 ONE BAD APPLE   Osmonds
2 KNOCK THREE TIMES   Dawn
3 ROSE GARDEN   Lynn Anderson
4 I HEAR YOU KNOCKING   Dave Edmunds
5 LONELY DAYS   Bee Gees
6 MY SWEET LORD/ISN'T IT A PITY   George Harrison
7 GROOVE ME   King Floyd
8 YOUR SONG   Elton John
9 IF I WERE YOUR WOMAN   Gladys Knight & The Pips
10 MAMA'S PEARL   Jackson 5

February 20, 1971
1 ONE BAD APPLE   Osmonds
2 KNOCK THREE TIMES   Dawn
3 ROSE GARDEN   Lynn Anderson
4 I HEAR YOU KNOCKING   Dave Edmunds
5 IF YOU COULD READ MY MIND   Gordon Lightfoot
6 MAMA'S PEARL   Jackson 5
7 GROOVE ME   King Floyd
8 SWEET MARY   Wadsworth Mansion
9 MR. BOJANGLES   Nitty Gritty Dirt Band
10 LONELY DAYS   Bee Gees

February 27, 1971
1 ONE BAD APPLE   Osmonds
2 MAMA'S PEARL   Jackson 5
3 KNOCK THREE TIMES   Dawn
4 ROSE GARDEN   Lynn Anderson
5 IF YOU COULD READ MY MIND   Gordon Lightfoot
6 I HEAR YOU KNOCKING   Dave Edmunds
7 SWEET MARY   Wadsworth Mansion
8 AMOS MOSES   Jerry Reed
9 MR. BOJANGLES   Nitty Gritty Dirt Band
10 ME AND BOBBY MCGEE   Janis Joplin

March 6, 1971
1 ONE BAD APPLE   Osmonds
2 MAMA'S PEARL   Jackson 5
3 ME AND BOBBY MCGEE   Janis Joplin

4 JUST MY IMAGINATION   Temptations
5 IF YOU COULD READ MY MIND   Gordon Lightfoot
6 SHE'S A LADY   Tom Jones
7 FOR ALL WE KNOW   Carpenters
8 AMOS MOSES   Jerry Reed
9 MR. BOJANGLES   Nitty Gritty Dirt Band
10 SWEET MARY   Wadsworth Mansion

March 13, 1971
1 ONE BAD APPLE   Osmonds
2 ME AND BOBBY MCGEE   Janis Joplin
3 FOR ALL WE KNOW   Carpenters
4 JUST MY IMAGINATION   Temptations
5 SHE'S A LADY   Tom Jones
6 MAMA'S PEARL   Jackson 5
7 PROUD MARY   Ike & Tina Turner
8 HAVE YOU EVER SEEN THE RAIN/HEY TONIGHT
   Creedence Clearwater Revival
9 DOESN'T SOMEBODY WANT TO BE WANTED?   Partridge
   Family
10 IF YOU COULD READ MY MIND   Gordon Lightfoot

March 20, 1971
1 ME AND BOBBY MCGEE   Janis Joplin
2 SHE'S A LADY   Tom Jones
3 JUST MY IMAGINATION   Temptations
4 ONE BAD APPLE   Osmonds
5 FOR ALL WE KNOW   Carpenters
6 PROUD MARY   Ike & Tina Turner
7 DOESN'T SOMEBODY WANT TO BE WANTED?   Partridge
   Family
8 WHAT'S GOING ON?   Marvin Gaye

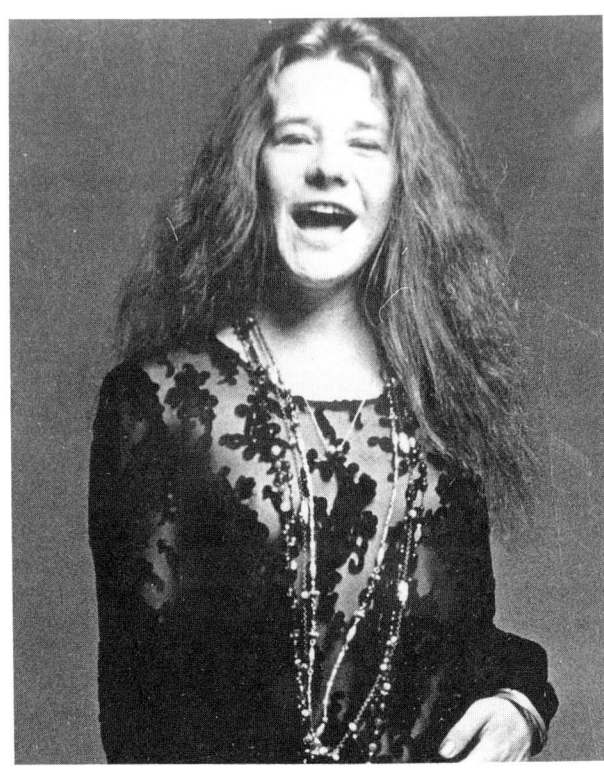

Janis Joplin
Janis peaks at #1 with a Kris Kristofferson song (Mar. 20).
(Tragically, Janis died October 4, 1970.)

281

9 HELP ME MAKE IT THROUGH THE NIGHT   Sammi Smith
10 IF YOU COULD READ MY MIND   Gordon Lightfoot

March 27, 1971

1 ME AND BOBBY MCGEE   Janis Joplin
2 JUST MY IMAGINATION   Temptations
3 SHE'S A LADY   Tom Jones
4 PROUD MARY   Ike & Tina Turner
5 FOR ALL WE KNOW   Carpenters
6 DOESN'T SOMEBODY WANT TO BE WANTED?   Partridge
   Family
7 WHAT'S GOING ON?   Marvin Gaye
8 HELP ME MAKE IT THROUGH THE NIGHT   Sammi Smith
9 ONE BAD APPLE   Osmonds
10 WHAT IS LIFE   George Harrison

April 3, 1971

1 JUST MY IMAGINATION   Temptations
2 ME AND BOBBY MCGEE   Janis Joplin
3 FOR ALL WE KNOW   Carpenters
4 SHE'S A LADY   Tom Jones
5 WHAT'S GOING ON?   Marvin Gaye
6 PROUD MARY   Ike & Tina Turner
7 DOESN'T SOMEBODY WANT TO BE WANTED?   Partridge
   Family
8 HELP ME MAKE IT THROUGH THE NIGHT   Sammi Smith
9 LOVE STORY (WHERE DO I BEGIN)   Andy Williams
10 ANOTHER DAY/OH WOMAN OH WHY   Paul McCartney

April 10, 1971

1 JUST MY IMAGINATION   Temptations
2 WHAT'S GOING ON?   Marvin Gaye
3 JOY TO THE WORLD   Three Dog Night
4 SHE'S A LADY   Tom Jones
5 FOR ALL WE KNOW   Carpenters
6 ME AND BOBBY MCGEE   Janis Joplin
7 DOESN'T SOMEBODY WANT TO BE WANTED?   Partridge
   Family
8 ANOTHER DAY/OH WOMAN OH WHY   Paul McCartney
9 PROUD MARY   Ike & Tina Turner
10 ONE TOKE OVER THE LINE   Brewer & Shipley

April 17, 1971

1 JOY TO THE WORLD   Three Dog Night
2 WHAT'S GOING ON?   Marvin Gaye
3 JUST MY IMAGINATION   Temptations
4 SHE'S A LADY   Tom Jones
5 ANOTHER DAY/OH WOMAN OH WHY   Paul McCartney
6 PUT YOUR HAND IN THE HAND   Ocean
7 ME AND BOBBY MCGEE   Janis Joplin
8 DOESN'T SOMEBODY WANT TO BE WANTED?   Partridge
   Family
9 FOR ALL WE KNOW   Carpenters
10 ONE TOKE OVER THE LINE   Brewer & Shipley

April 24, 1971

1 JOY TO THE WORLD   Three Dog Night
2 WHAT'S GOING ON?   Marvin Gaye
3 PUT YOUR HAND IN THE HAND   Ocean
4 NEVER CAN SAY GOODBYE   Jackson 5
5 ANOTHER DAY/OH WOMAN OH WHY   Paul McCartney
6 I AM...I SAID   Neil Diamond
7 JUST MY IMAGINATION   Temptations
8 IF   Bread
9 SHE'S A LADY   Tom Jones
10 STAY AWHILE   Bells

Tom Jones

``She's A Lady'' is a Top 10 hit for Tom in March and April.

May 1, 1971

1 JOY TO THE WORLD   Three Dog Night
2 PUT YOUR HAND IN THE HAND   Ocean
3 NEVER CAN SAY GOODBYE   Jackson 5
4 WHAT'S GOING ON?   Marvin Gaye
5 I AM...I SAID   Neil Diamond
6 IF   Bread
7 STAY AWHILE   Bells
8 ANOTHER DAY/OH WOMAN OH WHY   Paul McCartney
9 JUST MY IMAGINATION   Temptations
10 CHICK-A-BOOM   Daddy Dewdrop

May 8, 1971

1 JOY TO THE WORLD   Three Dog Night
2 PUT YOUR HAND IN THE HAND   Ocean
3 NEVER CAN SAY GOODBYE   Jackson 5
4 I AM...I SAID   Neil Diamond
5 IF   Bread
6 WHAT'S GOING ON?   Marvin Gaye
7 STAY AWHILE   Bells
8 BRIDGE OVER TROUBLED WATER   Simon & Garfunkel
9 CHICK-A-BOOM   Daddy Dewdrop
10 ME AND YOU AND A DOG NAMED BOO   Lobo

May 15, 1971

1 JOY TO THE WORLD   Three Dog Night
2 NEVER CAN SAY GOODBYE   Jackson 5
3 PUT YOUR HAND IN THE HAND   Ocean
4 IF   Bread
5 ME AND YOU AND A DOG NAMED BOO   Lobo
6 BROWN SUGAR   Rolling Stones
7 BRIDGE OVER TROUBLED WATER   Simon & Garfunkel

8 STAY AWHILE   Bells
9 I AM...I SAID   Neil Diamond
10 CHICK-A-BOOM   Daddy Dewdrop

May 22, 1971
1 JOY TO THE WORLD   Three Dog Night
2 NEVER CAN SAY GOODBYE   Jackson 5
3 BROWN SUGAR   Rolling Stones
4 PUT YOUR HAND IN THE HAND   Ocean
5 ME AND YOU AND A DOG NAMED BOO   Lobo
6 WANT ADS   Honey Cone
7 BRIDGE OVER TROUBLED WATER   Simon & Garfunkel
8 IT DON'T COME EASY   Ringo Starr
9 IF   Bread
10 CHICK-A-BOOM   Daddy Dewdrop

May 29, 1971
1 BROWN SUGAR   Rolling Stones
2 JOY TO THE WORLD   Three Dog Night
3 NEVER CAN SAY GOODBYE   Jackson 5
4 WANT ADS   Honey Cone
5 IT DON'T COME EASY   Ringo Starr
6 PUT YOUR HAND IN THE HAND   Ocean
7 BRIDGE OVER TROUBLED WATER   Simon & Garfunkel
8 SWEET AND INNOCENT   Donny Osmond
9 ME AND YOU AND A DOG NAMED BOO   Lobo
10 CHICK-A-BOOM   Daddy Dewdrop

June 5, 1971
1 BROWN SUGAR   Rolling Stones
2 JOY TO THE WORLD   Three Dog Night
3 WANT ADS   Honey Cone
4 IT DON'T COME EASY   Ringo Starr
5 RAINY DAYS AND MONDAYS   Carpenters
6 BRIDGE OVER TROUBLED WATER   Simon & Garfunkel
7 SWEET AND INNOCENT   Donny Osmond
8 NEVER CAN SAY GOODBYE   Jackson 5
9 IT'S TOO LATE   Carole King
10 ME AND YOU AND A DOG NAMED BOO   Lobo

June 12, 1971
1 WANT ADS   Honey Cone
2 BROWN SUGAR   Rolling Stones
3 RAINY DAYS AND MONDAYS   Carpenters
4 IT DON'T COME EASY   Ringo Starr
5 JOY TO THE WORLD   Three Dog Night
6 IT'S TOO LATE   Carole King
7 SWEET AND INNOCENT   Donny Osmond
8 TREAT HER LIKE A LADY   Cornelius Brothers & Sister Rose
9 I'LL MEET YOU HALFWAY   Partridge Family
10 BRIDGE OVER TROUBLED WATER   Simon & Garfunkel

June 19, 1971
1 IT'S TOO LATE   Carole King
2 RAINY DAYS AND MONDAYS   Carpenters
3 WANT ADS   Honey Cone
4 BROWN SUGAR   Rolling Stones
5 IT DON'T COME EASY   Ringo Starr
6 TREAT HER LIKE A LADY   Cornelius Brothers & Sister Rose
7 INDIAN RESERVATION   Raiders
8 JOY TO THE WORLD   Three Dog Night
9 I'LL MEET YOU HALFWAY   Partridge Family
10 SWEET AND INNOCENT   Donny Osmond

June 26, 1971
1 IT'S TOO LATE   Carole King
2 RAINY DAYS AND MONDAYS   Carpenters
3 WANT ADS   Honey Cone
4 INDIAN RESERVATION   Raiders
5 TREAT HER LIKE A LADY   Cornelius Brothers & Sister Rose
6 BROWN SUGAR   Rolling Stones
7 IT DON'T COME EASY   Ringo Starr
8 DON'T PULL YOUR LOVE   Hamilton, Joe Frank & Reynolds
9 WHEN YOU'RE HOT YOU'RE HOT   Jerry Reed
10 SWEET AND INNOCENT   Donny Osmond

July 3, 1971
1 IT'S TOO LATE   Carole King
2 INDIAN RESERVATION   Raiders
3 TREAT HER LIKE A LADY   Cornelius Brothers & Sister Rose
4 RAINY DAYS AND MONDAYS   Carpenters
5 DON'T PULL YOUR LOVE   Hamilton, Joe Frank & Reynolds
6 WANT ADS   Honey Cone
7 BROWN SUGAR   Rolling Stones
8 YOU'VE GOT A FRIEND   James Taylor
9 WHEN YOU'RE HOT YOU'RE HOT   Jerry Reed
10 IT DON'T COME EASY   Ringo Starr

July 10, 1971
1 IT'S TOO LATE   Carole King
2 INDIAN RESERVATION   Raiders
3 TREAT HER LIKE A LADY   Cornelius Brothers & Sister Rose
4 RAINY DAYS AND MONDAYS   Carpenters
5 DON'T PULL YOUR LOVE   Hamilton, Joe Frank & Reynolds
6 YOU'VE GOT A FRIEND   James Taylor
7 MR. BIG STUFF   Jean Knight
8 WANT ADS   Honey Cone
9 WHEN YOU'RE HOT YOU'RE HOT   Jerry Reed
10 THAT'S THE WAY I'VE ALWAYS HEARD IT SHOULD BE   Carly Simon

July 17, 1971
1 IT'S TOO LATE   Carole King
2 INDIAN RESERVATION   Raiders
3 YOU'VE GOT A FRIEND   James Taylor
4 DON'T PULL YOUR LOVE   Hamilton, Joe Frank & Reynolds
5 TREAT HER LIKE A LADY   Cornelius Brothers & Sister Rose
6 MR. BIG STUFF   Jean Knight
7 RAINY DAYS AND MONDAYS   Carpenters
8 DRAGGIN' THE LINE   Tommy James
9 HOW CAN YOU MEND A BROKEN HEART?   Bee Gees
10 THAT'S THE WAY I'VE ALWAYS HEARD IT SHOULD BE   Carly Simon

July 24, 1971
1 INDIAN RESERVATION   Raiders
2 IT'S TOO LATE   Carole King
3 YOU'VE GOT A FRIEND   James Taylor
4 DON'T PULL YOUR LOVE   Hamilton, Joe Frank & Reynolds
5 MR. BIG STUFF   Jean Knight
6 TREAT HER LIKE A LADY   Cornelius Brothers & Sister Rose

7   DRAGGIN' THE LINE   Tommy James
8   HOW CAN YOU MEND A BROKEN HEART?   Bee Gees
9   TAKE ME HOME COUNTRY ROADS   John Denver
10 SOONER OR LATER   Grass Roots

July 31, 1971
1   YOU'VE GOT A FRIEND   James Taylor
2   INDIAN RESERVATION   Raiders
3   IT'S TOO LATE   Carole King
4   MR. BIG STUFF   Jean Knight
5   DRAGGIN' THE LINE   Tommy James
6   HOW CAN YOU MEND A BROKEN HEART?   Bee Gees
7   DON'T PULL YOUR LOVE   Hamilton, Joe Frank & Reynolds
8   TAKE ME HOME COUNTRY ROADS   John Denver
9   SOONER OR LATER   Grass Roots
10 WHAT THE WORLD NEEDS NOW/ABRAHAM, MARTIN AND JOHN   Tom Clay

August 7, 1971
1   HOW CAN YOU MEND A BROKEN HEART?   Bee Gees
2   INDIAN RESERVATION   Raiders
3   YOU'VE GOT A FRIEND   James Taylor
4   MR. BIG STUFF   Jean Knight
5   DRAGGIN' THE LINE   Tommy James
6   TAKE ME HOME COUNTRY ROADS   John Denver
7   IT'S TOO LATE   Carole King
8   BEGINNINGS/COLOR MY WORLD   Chicago
9   WHAT THE WORLD NEEDS NOW/ABRAHAM, MARTIN AND JOHN   Tom Clay
10 MERCY MERCY   Marvin Gaye

August 14, 1971
1   HOW CAN YOU MEND A BROKEN HEART?   Bee Gees
2   MR. BIG STUFF   Jean Knight
3   TAKE ME HOME COUNTRY ROADS   John Denver
4   DRAGGIN' THE LINE   Tommy James
5   YOU'VE GOT A FRIEND   James Taylor
6   INDIAN RESERVATION   Raiders
7   BEGINNINGS/COLOR MY WORLD   Chicago
8   WHAT THE WORLD NEEDS NOW/ABRAHAM, MARTIN AND JOHN   Tom Clay
9   MERCY MERCY   Marvin Gaye
10 SIGNS   Five Man Electrical Band

August 21, 1971
1   HOW CAN YOU MEND A BROKEN HEART?   Bee Gees
2   MR. BIG STUFF   Jean Knight
3   TAKE ME HOME COUNTRY ROADS   John Denver
4   MERCY MERCY   Marvin Gaye
5   YOU'VE GOT A FRIEND   James Taylor
6   SWEET HITCH-HIKER   Creedence Clearwater Revival
7   BEGINNINGS/COLOR MY WORLD   Chicago
8   SIGNS   Five Man Electrical Band
9   DRAGGIN' THE LINE   Tommy James
10 LIAR   Three Dog Night

August 28, 1971
1   HOW CAN YOU MEND A BROKEN HEART?   Bee Gees
2   TAKE ME HOME COUNTRY ROADS   John Denver
3   SIGNS   Five Man Electrical Band
4   MERCY MERCY   Marvin Gaye
5   MR. BIG STUFF   Jean Knight
6   SWEET HITCH-HIKER   Creedence Clearwater Revival
7   LIAR   Three Dog Night
8   SMILING FACES SOMETIMES   Undisputed Truth
9   SPANISH HARLEM   Aretha Franklin
10 GO AWAY LITTLE GIRL   Donny Osmond

September 4, 1971
1   UNCLE ALBERT   Paul & Linda McCartney
2   HOW CAN YOU MEND A BROKEN HEART   Bee Gees
3   SMILING FACES SOMETIMES   Undisputed Truth
4   SPANISH HARLEM   Aretha Franklin
5   GO AWAY LITTLE GIRL   Donny Osmond
6   AIN'T NO SUNSHINE   Jonathan Edwards
7   TAKE ME HOME COUNTRY ROADS   John Denver
8   SIGNS   Five Man Electrical Band
9   LIAR   Three Dog Night
10 I JUST WANT TO CELEBRATE   Rare Earth

September 11, 1971
1   GO AWAY LITTLE GIRL   Donny Osmond
2   SPANISH HARLEM   Aretha Franklin
3   SMILING FACES SOMETIMES   Undisputed Truth
4   AIN'T NO SUNSHINE   Jonathan Edwards
5   UNCLE ALBERT   Paul & Linda McCartney
6   HOW CAN YOU MEND A BROKEN HEART?   Bee Gees
7   I JUST WANT TO CELEBRATE   Rare Earth
8   TAKE ME HOME COUNTRY ROADS   John Denver
9   SIGNS   Five Man Electrical Band
10 MAGGIE MAY   Rod Stewart

September 18, 1971
1   GO AWAY LITTLE GIRL   Donny Osmond
2   SPANISH HARLEM   Aretha Franklin
3   AIN'T NO SUNSHINE   Jonathan Edwards
4   MAGGIE MAY   Rod Stewart
5   UNCLE ALBERT   Paul & Linda McCartney
6   SMILING FACES SOMETIMES   Undisputed Truth
7   I JUST WANT TO CELEBRATE   Rare Earth
8   NIGHT THEY DROVE OLD DIXIE DOWN   Joan Baez
9   HOW CAN YOU MEND A BROKEN HEART   Bee Gees
10 WHATCHA SEE IS WHATCHA GET   Dramatics

September 25, 1971
1   GO AWAY LITTLE GIRL   Donny Osmond
2   MAGGIE MAY   Rod Stewart
3   AIN'T NO SUNSHINE   Jonathan Edwards
4   NIGHT THEY DROVE OLD DIXIE DOWN   Joan Baez
5   SPANISH HARLEM   Aretha Franklin
6   UNCLE ALBERT   Paul & Linda McCartney
7   SMILING FACES SOMETIMES   Undisputed Truth
8   SUPERSTAR   Carpenters
9   WHATCHA SEE IS WHATCHA GET   Dramatics
10 I JUST WANT TO CELEBRATE   Rare Earth

October 2, 1971
1   MAGGIE MAY   Rod Stewart
2   GO AWAY LITTLE GIRL   Donny Osmond
3   NIGHT THEY DROVE OLD DIXIE DOWN   Joan Baez
4   SUPERSTAR   Carpenters
5   AIN'T NO SUNSHINE   Jonathan Edwards
6   UNCLE ALBERT   Paul & Linda McCartney
7   SPANISH HARLEM   Aretha Franklin
8   SMILING FACES SOMETIMES   Undisputed Truth
9   YO-YO   Osmonds
10 DO YOU KNOW WHAT I MEAN   Lee Michaels

October 9, 1971
1   MAGGIE MAY   Rod Stewart
2   GO AWAY LITTLE GIRL   Donny Osmond

3   SUPERSTAR   Carpenters
4   NIGHT THEY DROVE OLD DIXIE DOWN   Joan Baez
5   YO-YO   Osmonds
6   DO YOU KNOW WHAT I MEAN   Lee Michaels
7   UNCLE ALBERT   Paul & Linda McCartney
8   AIN'T NO SUNSHINE   Jonathan Edwards
9   IF YOU REALLY LOVE ME   Stevie Wonder
10   SWEET CITY WOMAN   Stampeders

October 16, 1971
1   MAGGIE MAY   Rod Stewart
2   SUPERSTAR   Carpenters
3   YO-YO   Osmonds
4   NIGHT THEY DROVE OLD DIXIE DOWN   Joan Baez
5   GO AWAY LITTLE GIRL   Donny Osmond
6   DO YOU KNOW WHAT I MEAN   Lee Michaels
7   UNCLE ALBERT   Paul & Linda McCartney
8   IF YOU REALLY LOVE ME   Stevie Wonder
9   SWEET CITY WOMAN   Stampeders
10   GYPSIES, TRAMPS AND THIEVES   Cher

October 23, 1971
1   MAGGIE MAY   Rod Stewart
2   SUPERSTAR   Carpenters
3   YO-YO   Osmonds
4   GYPSIES, TRAMPS AND THIEVES   Cher
5   NIGHT THEY DROVE OLD DIXIE DOWN   Joan Baez
6   DO YOU KNOW WHAT I MEAN   Lee Michaels
7   GO AWAY LITTLE GIRL   Donny Osmond
8   SWEET CITY WOMAN   Stampeders
9   THEME FROM "SHAFT"   Isaac Hayes
10   IF YOU REALLY LOVE ME   Stevie Wonder

October 30, 1971
1   MAGGIE MAY   Rod Stewart
2   GYPSIES, TRAMPS AND THIEVES   Cher
3   YO-YO   Osmonds
4   SUPERSTAR   Carpenters
5   THEME FROM "SHAFT"   Isaac Hayes
6   IMAGINE   John Lennon
7   DO YOU KNOW WHAT I MEAN   Lee Michaels
8   NIGHT THEY DROVE OLD DIXIE DOWN   Joan Baez
9   PEACE TRAIN   Cat Stevens
10   I'VE FOUND SOMEONE OF MY OWN   Free Movement

November 6, 1971
1   GYPSIES, TRAMPS AND THIEVES   Cher
2   THEME FROM "SHAFT"   Isaac Hayes
3   MAGGIE MAY   Rod Stewart
4   IMAGINE   John Lennon
5   YO-YO   Osmonds
6   SUPERSTAR   Carpenters
7   PEACE TRAIN   Cat Stevens
8   I'VE FOUND SOMEONE OF MY OWN   Free Movement
9   INNER CITY BLUES   Marvin Gaye
10   NIGHT THEY DROVE OLD DIXIE DOWN   Joan Baez

November 13, 1971
1   GYPSIES, TRAMPS AND THIEVES   Cher
2   THEME FROM "SHAFT"   Isaac Hayes
3   IMAGINE   John Lennon
4   MAGGIE MAY   Rod Stewart
5   I'VE FOUND SOMEONE OF MY OWN   Free Movement
6   YO-YO   Osmonds
7   PEACE TRAIN   Cat Stevens
8   HAVE YOU SEEN HER?   Chi-lites

Cher
``Gypsies, Tramps And Thieves'' peaks at #1 (Nov. 6).

9   INNER CITY BLUES   Marvin Gaye
10   SUPERSTAR   Carpenters

November 20, 1971
1   THEME FROM "SHAFT"   Isaac Hayes
2   GYPSIES, TRAMPS AND THIEVES   Cher
3   IMAGINE   John Lennon
4   BABY I'M-A WANT YOU   Bread
5   HAVE YOU SEEN HER?   Chi-lites
6   MAGGIE MAY   Rod Stewart
7   PEACE TRAIN   Cat Stevens
8   FAMILY AFFAIR   Sly & The Family Stone
9   GOT TO BE THERE   Michael Jackson
10   YO-YO   Osmonds

November 27, 1971
1   THEME FROM "SHAFT"   Isaac Hayes
2   GYPSIES, TRAMPS AND THIEVES   Cher
3   BABY, I'M-A WANT YOU   Bread
4   HAVE YOU SEEN HER?   Chi-lites
5   FAMILY AFFAIR   Sly & The Family Stone
6   IMAGINE   John Lennon
7   GOT TO BE THERE   Michael Jackson
8   PEACE TRAIN   Cat Stevens
9   ROCK STEADY   Aretha Franklin
10   THE DESIDERATA   Les Crane

December 4, 1971
1   FAMILY AFFAIR   Sly & The Family Stone
2   THEME FROM "SHAFT"   Isaac Hayes
3   BABY I'M-A WANT YOU   Bread
4   HAVE YOU SEEN HER?   Chi-lites

Don McLean
The classic ``American Pie'' stays number one for a month, beginning Jan. 15, 1971.

5   GYPSIES, TRAMPS AND THIEVES   Cher
6   GOT TO BE THERE   Michael Jackson
7   THE DESIDERATA   Les Crane
8   AN OLD FASHIONED LOVE SONG   Three Dog Night
9   ROCK STEADY   Aretha Franklin
10   IMAGINE   John Lennon

December 11, 1971
1   FAMILY AFFAIR   Sly & The Family Stone
2   THEME FROM "SHAFT"   Isaac Hayes
3   HAVE YOU SEEN HER?   Chi-lites
4   GOT TO BE THERE   Michael Jackson
5   AN OLD FASHIONED LOVE SONG   Three Dog Night
6   BABY I'M-A WANT YOU   Bread
7   GYPSIES, TRAMPS AND THIEVES   Cher
8   ALL I EVER NEED IS YOU   Sonny & Cher
9   BRAND NEW KEY   Melanie
10   THE DESIDERATA   Les Crane

December 18, 1971
1   FAMILY AFFAIR   Sly & The Family Stone
2   BRAND NEW KEY   Melanie
3   HAVE YOU SEEN HER?   Chi-lites
4   AN OLD FASHIONED LOVE SONG   Three Dog Night
5   GOT TO BE THERE   Michael Jackson
6   THEME FROM "SHAFT"   Isaac Hayes
7   BABY I'M-A WANT YOU   Bread
8   ALL I EVER NEED IS YOU   Sonny & Cher
9   AMERICAN PIE   Don McLean
10   CHERISH   David Cassidy

December 25, 1971
1   BRAND NEW KEY   Melanie
2   FAMILY AFFAIR   Sly & The Family Stone
3   AMERICAN PIE   Don McLean
4   AN OLD FASHIONED LOVE SONG   Three Dog Night
5   GOT TO BE THERE   Michael Jackson
6   HAVE YOU SEEN HER?   Chi-lites
7   ALL I EVER NEED IS YOU   Sonny & Cher
8   SCORPIO   Dennis Coffey
9   CHERISH   David Cassidy
10   HEY GIRL/I KNEW YOU WHEN   Donny Osmond

January 1, 1972
1   BRAND NEW KEY   Melanie
2   AMERICAN PIE   Don McLean
3   FAMILY AFFAIR   Sly & The Family Stone
4   AN OLD FASHIONED LOVE SONG   Three Dog Night
5   GOT TO BE THERE   Michael Jackson
6   HAVE YOU SEEN HER?   Chi-lites
7   SCORPIO   Dennis Coffey
8   SUNSHINE   Jonathan Edwards
9   CHERISH   David Cassidy
10   HEY GIRL/I KNEW YOU WHEN   Donny Osmond

January 8, 1972
1   BRAND NEW KEY   Melanie
2   AMERICAN PIE   Don McLean
3   FAMILY AFFAIR   Sly & The Family Stone
4   LET'S STAY TOGETHER   Al Green
5   GOT TO BE THERE   Michael Jackson
6   SCORPIO   Dennis Coffey
7   SUNSHINE   Jonathan Edwards
8   I'D LIKE TO TEACH THE WORLD TO SING   New Seekers
9   CHERISH   David Cassidy
10   HEY GIRL/I KNEW YOU WHEN   Donny Osmond

January 15, 1972
1   AMERICAN PIE   Don McLean
2   BRAND NEW KEY   Melanie
3   LET'S STAY TOGETHER   Al Green
4   SUNSHINE   Jonathan Edwards
5   FAMILY AFFAIR   Sly & The Family Stone
6   SCORPIO   Dennis Coffey
7   I'D LIKE TO TEACH THE WORLD TO SING   New Seekers
8   GOT TO BE THERE   Michael Jackson
9   HEY GIRL/I KNEW YOU WHEN   Donny Osmond
10   CLEAN UP WOMAN   Betty Wright

January 22, 1972
1   AMERICAN PIE   Don McLean
2   BRAND NEW KEY   Melanie
3   LET'S STAY TOGETHER   Al Green
4   SUNSHINE   Jonathan Edwards
5   DAY AFTER DAY   Badfinger
6   SCORPIO   Dennis Coffey
7   I'D LIKE TO TEACH THE WORLD TO SING   New Seekers
8   CLEAN UP WOMAN   Betty Wright
9   YOU ARE EVERYTHING   Stylistics
10   SUGAR DADDY   Jackson 5

January 29, 1972
1   AMERICAN PIE   Don McLean
2   BRAND NEW KEY   Melanie
3   LET'S STAY TOGETHER   Al Green
4   SUNSHINE   Jonathan Edwards
5   DAY AFTER DAY   Badfinger
6   CLEAN UP WOMAN   Betty Wright
7   SCORPIO   Dennis Coffey
8   NEVER BEEN TO SPAIN   Three Dog Night
9   YOU ARE EVERYTHING   Stylistics
10   SUGAR DADDY   Jackson 5

February 5, 1972
1   AMERICAN PIE   Don McLean
2   LET'S STAY TOGETHER   Al Green
3   BRAND NEW KEY   Melanie
4   DAY AFTER DAY   Badfinger
5   WITHOUT YOU   Nilsson
6   NEVER BEEN TO SPAIN   Three Dog Night
7   SUNSHINE   Jonathan Edwards
8   PRECIOUS AND FEW   Climax
9   HURTING EACH OTHER   Carpenters
10   JOY   Apollo 100 featuring Tom Parker

February 12, 1972
1   LET'S STAY TOGETHER   Al Green
2   AMERICAN PIE   Don McLean
3   WITHOUT YOU   Nilsson
4   PRECIOUS AND FEW   Climax
5   NEVER BEEN TO SPAIN   Three Dog Night
6   HURTING EACH OTHER   Carpenters
7   DOWN BY THE LAZY RIVER   Osmonds
8   JOY   Apollo 100 featuring Tom Parker
9   BRAND NEW KEY   Melanie
10   DAY AFTER DAY   Badfinger

February 19, 1972
1   WITHOUT YOU   Nilsson
2   LET'S STAY TOGETHER   Al Green
3   HURTING EACH OTHER   Carpenters
4   PRECIOUS AND FEW   Climax
5   NEVER BEEN TO SPAIN   Three Dog Night

6 DOWN BY THE LAZY RIVER Osmonds
7 AMERICAN PIE Don McLean
8 JOY Apollo 100 featuring Tom Parker
9 LION SLEEPS TONIGHT Robert John
10 EVERYTHING I OWN Bread

February 26, 1972
1 WITHOUT YOU Nilsson
2 HURTING EACH OTHER Carpenters
3 PRECIOUS AND FEW Climax
4 LET'S STAY TOGETHER Al Green
5 DOWN BY THE LAZY RIVER Osmonds
6 JOY Apollo 100 featuring Tom Parker
7 LION SLEEPS TONIGHT Robert John
8 EVERYTHING I OWN Bread
9 AMERICAN PIE Don McLean
10 SWEET SEASONS Carole King

March 4, 1972
1 WITHOUT YOU Nilsson
2 HURTING EACH OTHER Carpenters
3 PRECIOUS AND FEW Climax
4 DOWN BY THE LAZY RIVER Osmonds
5 EVERYTHING I OWN Bread
6 LION SLEEPS TONIGHT Robert John
7 HEART OF GOLD Neil Young
8 LET'S STAY TOGETHER Al Green
9 SWEET SEASONS Carole King
10 BANG A GONG T. Rex

March 11, 1972
1 WITHOUT YOU Nilsson
2 HEART OF GOLD Neil Young
3 LION SLEEPS TONIGHT Robert John
4 DOWN BY THE LAZY RIVER Osmonds
5 EVERYTHING I OWN Bread
6 PRECIOUS AND FEW Climax
7 A HORSE WITH NO NAME America
8 HURTING EACH OTHER Carpenters
9 WAY OF LOVE Cher
10 BANG A GONG T. Rex

March 18, 1972
1 HEART OF GOLD Neil Young
2 A HORSE WITH NO NAME America
3 LION SLEEPS TONIGHT Robert John
4 WITHOUT YOU Nilsson
5 EVERYTHING I OWN Bread
6 MOTHER AND CHILD REUNION Paul Simon
7 PRECIOUS AND FEW Climax
8 WAY OF LOVE Cher
9 PUPPY LOVE Donny Osmond
10 DOWN BY THE LAZY RIVER Osmonds

March 25, 1972
1 A HORSE WITH NO NAME America
2 HEART OF GOLD Neil Young
3 LION SLEEPS TONIGHT Robert John
4 PUPPY LOVE Donny Osmond
5 MOTHER AND CHILD REUNION Paul Simon
6 WITHOUT YOU Nilsson
7 WAY OF LOVE Cher
8 JUNGLE FEVER Chakachas
9 EVERYTHING I OWN Bread
10 I GOTCHA Joe Tex

April 1, 1972
1 A HORSE WITH NO NAME America
2 HEART OF GOLD Neil Young
3 PUPPY LOVE Donny Osmond
4 MOTHER AND CHILD REUNION Paul Simon
5 LION SLEEPS TONIGHT Robert John
6 I GOTCHA Joe Tex
7 WITHOUT YOU Nilsson
8 JUNGLE FEVER Chakachas
9 ROCKIN' ROBIN Michael Jackson
10 THE FIRST TIME EVER I SAW YOUR FACE Roberta Flack

April 8, 1972
1 A HORSE WITH NO NAME America
2 HEART OF GOLD Neil Young
3 THE FIRST TIME EVER I SAW YOUR FACE Roberta Flack
4 I GOTCHA Joe Tex
5 ROCKIN' ROBIN Michael Jackson
6 PUPPY LOVE Donny Osmond
7 MOTHER AND CHILD REUNION Paul Simon
8 JUNGLE FEVER Chakachas
9 IN THE RAIN Dramatics
10 LION SLEEPS TONIGHT Tokens

April 15, 1972
1 THE FIRST TIME EVER I SAW YOUR FACE Roberta Flack
2 A HORSE WITH NO NAME America
3 I GOTCHA Joe Tex
4 ROCKIN' ROBIN Michael Jackson
5 HEART OF GOLD Neil Young
6 IN THE RAIN Dramatics
7 PUPPY LOVE Donny Osmond
8 BETCHA BY GOLLY WOW Stylistics
9 DAY DREAMING Aretha Franklin
10 A COWBOY'S WORK IS NEVER DONE Sonny & Cher

April 22, 1972
1 THE FIRST TIME EVER I SAW YOUR FACE Roberta Flack
2 ROCKIN' ROBIN Michael Jackson
3 I GOTCHA Joe Tex
4 A HORSE WITH NO NAME America
5 IN THE RAIN Dramatics
6 BETCHA BY GOLLY WOW Stylistics
7 DAY DREAMING Aretha Franklin
8 HEART OF GOLD Neil Young
9 A COWBOY'S WORK IS NEVER DONE Sonny & Cher
10 DOCTOR MY EYE Jackson Browne

April 29, 1972
1 THE FIRST TIME EVER I SAW YOUR FACE Roberta Flack
2 ROCKIN' ROBIN Michael Jackson
3 I GOTCHA Joe Tex
4 BETCHA BY GOLLY WOW Stylistics
5 A HORSE WITH NO NAME America
6 DAY DREAMING Aretha Franklin
7 IN THE RAIN Dramatics
8 A COWBOY'S WORK IS NEVER DONE Sonny & Cher
9 DOCTOR MY EYE Jackson Browne
10 LOOK WHAT YOU DONE FOR ME Al Green

May 6, 1972
1 THE FIRST TIME EVER I SAW YOUR FACE Roberta Flack
2 I GOTCHA Joe Tex
3 BETCHA BY GOLLY WOW Stylistics
4 ROCKIN' ROBIN Michael Jackson
5 DAY DREAMING Aretha Franklin

6   A HORSE WITH NO NAME   America
7   I'LL TAKE YOU THERE   Staple Singers
8   DOCTOR MY EYE   Jackson Browne
9   LOOK WHAT YOU DONE FOR ME   Al Green
10 BACK OFF BOOGALOO   Ringo Starr

May 13, 1972
1   THE FIRST TIME EVER I SAW YOUR FACE   Roberta Flack
2   I GOTCHA   Joe Tex
3   OH GIRL   Chi-lites
4   I'LL TAKE YOU THERE   Staple Singers
5   ROCKIN' ROBIN   Michael Jackson
6   BETCHA BY GOLLY WOW   Stylistics
7   LOOK WHAT YOU DONE FOR ME   Al Green
8   DAY DREAMING   Aretha Franklin
9   BACK OFF BOOGALOO   Ringo Starr
10 A HORSE WITH NO NAME   America

May 20, 19172
1   THE FIRST TIME EVER I SAW YOUR FACE   Roberta Flack
2   OH GIRL   Chi-lites
3   I'LL TAKE YOU THERE   Staple Singers
4   I GOTCHA   Joe Tex
5   LOOK WHAT YOU DONE FOR ME   Al Green
6   ROCKIN' ROBIN   Michael Jackson
7   BETCHA BY GOLLY WOW   Stylistics
8   TUMBLING DICE   Rolling Stones
9   BACK OFF BOOGALOO   Ringo Starr
10 MORNING HAS BROKEN   Cat Stevens

May 27, 1972
1   OH GIRL   Chi-lites
2   I'LL TAKE YOU THERE   Staple Singers
3   THE FIRST TIME EVER I SAW YOUR FACE   Roberta Flack
4   LOOK WHAT YOU DONE FOR ME   Al Green
5   THE CANDY MAN   Sammy Davis, Jr.
6   MORNING HAS BROKEN   Cat Stevens
7   TUMBLING DICE   Rolling Stones
8   I GOTCHA   Joe Tex
9   SYLVIA'S MOTHER   Dr. Hook
10 HOT ROD LINCOLN   Commander Cody

June 4, 1972
1   I'LL TAKE YOU THERE   Staple Singers
2   OH GIRL   Chi-lites
3   THE FIRST TIME EVER I SAW YOUR FACE   Roberta Flack
4   THE CANDY MAN   Sammy Davis, Jr.
5   SYLVIA'S MOTHER   Dr. Hook
6   MORNING HAS BROKEN   Cat Stevens
7   TUMBLING DICE   Rolling Stones
8   NICE TO BE WITH YOU   Gallery
9   HOT ROD LINCOLN   Commander Cody
10 LOOK WHAT YOU DONE FOR ME   Al Green

June 11, 1972
1   THE CANDY MAN   Sammy Davis, Jr.
2   I'LL TAKE YOU THERE   Staple Singers
3   SONG SUNG BLUE   Neil Diamond
4   OH GIRL   Chi-lites
5   SYLVIA'S MOTHER   Dr. Hook
6   NICE TO BE WITH YOU   Gallery
7   THE FIRST TIME EVER I SAW YOUR FACE   Roberta Flack
8   MORNING HAS BROKEN   Cat Stevens
9   OUTA-SPACE   Billy Preston
10 LAST NIGHT I DIDN'T GET TO SLEEP AT ALL   5th
     Dimension

Sammy Davis Jr.
Sammy's #1 hit ''Candy Man'' (June 11) came from the movie ''Willie Wonka And The Chocolate Factory.''

June 17, 1972
1   THE CANDY MAN   Sammy Davis, Jr.
2   I'LL TAKE YOU THERE   Staple Singers
3   SONG SUNG BLUE   Neil Diamond
4   OH GIRL   Chi-lites
5   NICE TO BE WITH YOU   Gallery
6   OUTA-SPACE   Billy Preston
7   TROGLODYTE (CAVEMAN)   Jimmy Castor Bunch
8   LAST NIGHT I DIDN'T GET TO SLEEP AT ALL   5th
     Dimension
9   SYLVIA'S MOTHER   Dr. Hook
10 LEAN ON ME   Bill Withers

June 24, 1972
1   THE CANDY MAN   Sammy Davis, Jr.
2   SONG SUNG BLUE   Neil Diamond
3   OUTA-SPACE   Billy Preston
4   NICE TO BE WITH YOU   Gallery
5   I'LL TAKE YOU THERE   Staple Singers
6   TROGLODYTE (CAVEMAN)   Jimmy Castor Bunch
7   LEAN ON ME   Bill Withers
8   LAST NIGHT I DIDN'T GET TO SLEEP AT ALL   5th
     Dimension
9   OH GIRL   Chi-lites
10 TOO LATE TO TURN BACK NOW   Cornelius Brothers &
     Sister Rose

July 1, 1972
1   SONG SUNG BLUE   Neil Diamond
2   THE CANDY MAN   Sammy Davis, Jr.
3   OUTA-SPACE   Billy Preston
4   LEAN ON ME   Bill Withers

5 TOO LATE TO TURN BACK NOW   Cornelius Brothers & Sister Rose
6 TROGLODYTE (CAVEMAN)   Jimmy Castor Bunch
7 NICE TO BE WITH YOU   Gallery
8 ROCKET MAN   Elton John
9 I NEED YOU   America
10 DADDY, DON'T YOU WALK SO FAST   Wayne Newton

July 8, 1972
1 LEAN ON ME   Bill Withers
2 OUTA-SPACE   Billy Preston
3 SONG SUNG BLUE   Neil Diamond
4 TOO LATE TO TURN BACK NOW   Cornelius Brothers & Sister Rose
5 THE CANDY MAN   Sammy Davis, Jr.
6 TROGLODYTE (CAVEMAN)   Jimmy Castor Bunch
7 ROCKET MAN   Elton John
8 DADDY, DON'T YOU WALK SO FAST   Wayne Newton
9 I NEED YOU   America
10 IF LOVING YOU IS WRONG I DON'T WANT TO BE RIGHT   Luther Ingram

July 15, 1972
1 LEAN ON ME   Bill Withers
2 TOO LATE TO TURN BACK NOW   Cornelius Brothers & Sister Rose
3 OUTA-SPACE   Billy Preston
4 SONG SUNG BLUE   Neil Diamond
5 BRANDY (YOU'RE A FINE GIRL)   Looking Glass
6 ROCKET MAN   Elton John
7 DADDY, DON'T YOU WALK SO FAST   Wayne Newton
8 ALONE AGAIN (NATURALLY)   Gilbert O'Sullivan
9 IF LOVING YOU IS WRONG I DON'T WANT TO BE RIGHT   Luther Ingram
10 WHERE IS THE LOVE   Roberta Flack & Donny Hathaway

July 22, 1972
1 LEAN ON ME   Bill Withers
2 TOO LATE TO TURN BACK NOW   Cornelius Brothers & Sister Rose
3 ALONE AGAIN (NATURALLY)   Gilbert O'Sullivan
4 BRANDY (YOU'RE A FINE GIRL)   Looking Glass
5 IF LOVING YOU IS WRONG I DON'T WANT TO BE RIGHT   Luther Ingram
6 DADDY, DON'T YOU WALK SO FAST   Wayne Newton
7 WHERE IS THE LOVE   Roberta Flack & Donny Hathaway
8 HOW DO YOU DO   Mouth & McNeal
9 ROCKET MAN   Elton John
10 SCHOOL'S OUT   Alice Cooper

July 29, 1972
1 ALONE AGAIN (NATURALLY)   Gilbert O'Sullivan
2 BRANDY (YOU'RE A FINE GIRL)   Looking Glass
3 TOO LATE TO TURN BACK NOW   Cornelius Brothers & Sister Rose
4 IF LOVING YOU IS WRONG I DON'T WANT TO BE RIGHT   Luther Ingram
5 DADDY, DON'T YOU WALK SO FAST   Wayne Newton
6 WHERE IS THE LOVE   Roberta Flack & Donny Hathaway
7 SCHOOL'S OUT   Alice Cooper
8 HOW DO YOU DO   Mouth & McNeal
9 LEAN ON ME   Bill Withers
10 LONG COOL WOMAN (IN A BLACK DRESS)   Hollies

August 5, 1972
1 ALONE AGAIN (NATURALLY)   Gilbert O'Sullivan

2 BRANDY (YOU'RE A FINE GIRL)   Looking Glass
3 IF LOVING YOU IS WRONG I DON'T WANT TO BE RIGHT   Luther Ingram
4 DADDY, DON'T YOU WALK SO FAST   Wayne Newton
5 TOO LATE TO TURN BACK NOW   Cornelius Brothers & Sister Rose
6 WHERE IS THE LOVE   Roberta Flack & Donny Hathaway
7 SCHOOL'S OUT   Alice Cooper
8 HOW DO YOU DO   Mouth & McNeal
9 LONG COOL WOMAN (IN A BLACK DRESS)   Hollies
10 LAYLA   Derek & The Dominos

August 12, 1972
1 ALONE AGAIN (NATURALLY)   Gilbert O'Sullivan
2 BRANDY (YOU'RE A FINE GIRL)   Looking Glass
3 IF LOVING YOU IS WRONG I DON'T WANT TO BE RIGHT   Luther Ingram
4 DADDY, DON'T YOU WALK SO FAST   Wayne Newton
5 WHERE IS THE LOVE   Roberta Flack & Donny Hathaway
6 LONG COOL WOMAN (IN A BLACK DRESS)   Hollies
7 I'M STILL IN LOVE WITH YOU   Al Green
8 TOO LATE TO TURN BACK NOW   Cornelius Brothers & Sister Rose
9 HOW DO YOU DO   Mouth & McNeal
10 SCHOOL'S OUT   Alice Cooper

August 19, 1972
1 ALONE AGAIN (NATURALLY)   Gilbert O'Sullivan
2 BRANDY (YOU'RE A FINE GIRL)   Looking Glass
3 LONG COOL WOMAN (IN A BLACK DRESS)   Hollies
4 IF LOVING YOU IS WRONG I DON'T WANT TO BE RIGHT   Luther Ingram
5 I'M STILL IN LOVE WITH YOU   Al Green
6 WHERE IS THE LOVE   Roberta Flack & Donny Hathaway
7 DADDY, DON'T YOU WALK SO FAST   Wayne Newton
8 HOLD YOUR HEAD UP   Argent
9 COCONUT   Nilsson
10 GOODBYE TO LOVE   Carpenters

August 26, 1972
1 BRANDY (YOU'RE A FINE GIRL)   Looking Glass
2 ALONE   Gilbert O'Sullivan
3 LONG COOL WOMAN (IN A BLACK DRESS)   Hollies
4 I'M STILL IN LOVE WITH YOU   Al Green
5 HOLD YOUR HEAD UP   Argent
6 IF LOVING YOU IS WRONG, I DON'T WANT TO BE RIGHT   Luther Ingram
7 GOODBYE TO LOVE   Carpenters
8 COCONUT   Nilsson
9 YOU DON'T MESS AROUND WITH JIM   Jim Croce
10 BABY DON'T GET HOOKED ON ME   Mac Davis

September 2, 1972
1 ALONE   Gilbert O'Sullivan
2 LONG COOL WOMAN (IN A BLACK DRESS)   Hollies
3 I'M STILL IN LOVE WITH YOU   Al Green
4 BRANDY (YOU'RE A FINE GIRL)   Looking Glass
5 HOLD YOUR HEAD UP   Argent
6 BABY DON'T GET HOOKED ON ME   Mac Davis
7 GOODBYE TO LOVE   Carpenters
8 YOU DON'T MESS AROUND WITH JIM   Jim Croce
9 ROCK AND ROLL   Gary Glitter
10 BACK STABBERS   O'Jays

September 9, 1972
1 ALONE AGAIN (NATURALLY)   Gilbert O'Sullivan

2 LONG COOL WOMAN (IN A BLACK DRESS)   Hollies
3 I'M STILL IN LOVE WITH YOU   Al Green
4 BABY DON'T GET HOOKED ON ME   Mac Davis
5 BRANDY (YOU'RE A FINE GIRL)   Looking Glass
6 BACK STABBERS   O'Jays
7 ROCK AND ROLL   Gary Glitter
8 YOU DON'T MESS AROUND WITH JIM   Jim Croce
9 BLACK AND WHITE   Three Dog Night
10 SATURDAY IN THE PARK   Chicago

September 16, 1972
1 BLACK AND WHITE   Three Dog Night
2 BABY DON'T GET HOOKED ON ME   Mac Davis
3 ALONE AGAIN (NATURALLY)   Gilbert O'Sullivan
4 SATURDAY IN THE PARK   Chicago
5 BACK STABBERS   O'Jays
6 LONG COOL WOMAN (IN A BLACK DRESS)   Hollies
7 ROCK AND ROLL   Gary Glitter
8 BRANDY (YOU'RE A FINE GIRL)   Looking Glass
9 HONKY CAT   Elton John
10 I'M STILL IN LOVE WITH YOU   Al Green

September 23, 1972
1 BABY DON'T GET HOOKED ON ME   Mac Davis
2 BLACK AND WHITE   Three Dog Night
3 SATURDAY IN THE PARK   Chicago
4 BACK STABBERS   O'Jays
5 ALONE AGAIN (NATURALLY)   Gilbert O'Sullivan
6 BEN   Michael Jackson
7 EVERYBODY PLAYS THE FOOL   Main Ingredient
8 HONKY CAT   Elton John
9 GO ALL THE WAY   Raspberries
10 ROCK AND ROLL   Gary Glitter

Mac Davis
Mac's "Baby Don't Get Hooked On Me" hooks #1 (Sep. 23).

September 30, 1972
1 BABY DON'T GET HOOKED ON ME   Mac Davis
2 BLACK AND WHITE   Three Dog Night
3 SATURDAY IN THE PARK   Chicago
4 BACK STABBERS   O'Jays
5 BEN   Michael Jackson
6 EVERYBODY PLAYS THE FOOL   Main Ingredient
7 GO ALL THE WAY   Raspberries
8 USE ME   Bill Withers
9 BURNING LOVE   Elvis Presley
10 POP CORN   Hot Butter

October 7, 1972
1 BABY DON'T GET HOOKED ON ME   Mac Davis
2 BEN   Michael Jackson
3 BACK STABBERS   O'Jays
4 EVERYBODY PLAYS THE FOOL   Main Ingredient
5 GO ALL THE WAY   Raspberries
6 USE ME   Bill Withers
7 BURNING LOVE   Elvis Presley
8 BLACK AND WHITE   Three Dog Night
9 MY DING-A-LING   Chuck Berry
10 POP CORN   Hot Butter

October 14, 1972
1 BEN   Michael Jackson
2 USE ME   Bill Withers
3 EVERYBODY PLAYS THE FOOL   Main Ingredient
4 BURNING LOVE   Elvis Presley
5 GO ALL THE WAY   Raspberries
6 BABY DON'T GET HOOKED ON ME   Mac Davis
7 MY DING-A-LING   Chuck Berry
8 NIGHTS IN WHITE SATIN   Moody Blues
9 BACK STABBERS   O'Jays
10 POP CORN   Hot Butter

October 21, 1972
1 MY DING-A-LING   Chuck Berry
2 USE ME   Bill Withers
3 BURNING LOVE   Elvis Presley
4 EVERYBODY PLAYS THE FOOL   Main Ingredient
5 NIGHTS IN WHITE SATIN   Moody Blues
6 BEN   Michael Jackson
7 BABY DON'T GET HOOKED ON ME   Mac Davis
8 GARDEN PARTY   Rick Nelson
9 POP CORN   Hot Butter
10 GO ALL THE WAY   Raspberries

October 28, 1972
1 MY DING-A-LING   Chuck Berry
2 BURNING LOVE   Elvis Presley
3 NIGHTS IN WHITE SATIN   Moody Blues
4 USE ME   Bill Withers
5 I CAN SEE CLEARLY NOW   Johnny Nash
6 FREDDIE'S DEAD (SUPERFLY)   Curtis Mayfield
7 GARDEN PARTY   Rick Nelson
8 BEN   Michael Jackson
9 EVERYBODY PLAYS THE FOOL   Main Ingredient
10 GOOD TIME CHARLIE'S GOT THE BLUES   Danny O'Keefe

November 4, 1972
1 I CAN SEE CLEARLY NOW   Johnny Nash
2 NIGHTS IN WHITE SATIN   Moody Blues
3 MY DING-A-LING   Chuck Berry
4 FREDDIE'S DEAD (SUPERFLY)   Curtis Mayfield

5 BURNING LOVE Elvis Presley
6 GARDEN PARTY Rick Nelson
7 I'LL BE AROUND Spinners
8 I'D LOVE YOU TO WANT ME Lobo
9 GOOD TIME CHARLIE'S GOT THE BLUES Danny O'Keefe
10 BEN Michael Jackson

November 11, 1972
1 I CAN SEE CLEARLY NOW Johnny Nash
2 NIGHTS IN WHITE SATIN Moody Blues
3 I'D LOVE YOU TO WANT ME Lobo
4 FREDDIE'S DEAD (SUPERFLY) Curtis Mayfield
5 I'LL BE AROUND Spinners
6 GARDEN PARTY Rick Nelson
7 MY DING-A-LING Chuck Berry
8 I AM WOMAN Helen Reddy
9 CONVENTION '72 Delegates
10 WITCHY WOMAN Eagles

November 18, 1972
1 I CAN SEE CLEARLY NOW Johnny Nash
2 I'D LOVE YOU TO WANT ME Lobo
3 I'LL BE AROUND Spinners
4 I AM WOMAN Helen Reddy
5 NIGHTS IN WHITE SATIN Moody Blues
6 PAPA WAS A ROLLING STONE Temptations
7 FREDDIE'S DEAD (SUPERFLY) Curtis Mayfield
8 CONVENTION '72 Delegates
9 WITCHY WOMAN Eagles
10 SUMMER BREEZE Seals & Crofts

November 25, 1972
1 I CAN SEE CLEARLY NOW Johnny Nash
2 I'D LOVE YOU TO WANT ME Lobo
3 I'LL BE AROUND Spinners
4 I AM WOMAN Helen Reddy
5 PAPA WAS A ROLLING STONE Temptations
6 SUMMER BREEZE Seals & Crofts
7 IF YOU DON'T KNOW ME BY NOW Harold Melvin & The
   Blue Notes
8 YOU OUGHT TO BE WITH ME Al Green
9 NIGHTS IN WHITE SATIN Moody Blues
10 IF I COULD REACH YOU 5th Dimension

December 2, 1972
1 PAPA WAS A ROLLING STONE Temptations
2 I AM WOMAN Helen Reddy
3 I CAN SEE CLEARLY NOW Johnny Nash
4 I'D LOVE YOU TO WANT ME Lobo
5 IF YOU DON'T KNOW ME BY NOW Harold Melvin & The
   Blue Notes
6 SUMMER BREEZE Seals & Crofts
7 YOU OUGHT TO BE WITH ME Al Green
8 IT NEVER RAINS IN SOUTHERN CALIFORNIA Albert
   Hammond
9 I'LL BE AROUND Spinners
10 VENTURA HIGHWAY America

December 9, 1972
1 I AM WOMAN Helen Reddy
2 PAPA WAS A ROLLING STONE Temptations
3 IF YOU DON'T KNOW ME BY NOW Harold Melvin & The
   Blue Notes
4 I CAN SEE CLEARLY NOW Johnny Nash
5 YOU OUGHT TO BE WITH ME Al Green
6 ME AND MRS. JONES Billy Paul

7 IT NEVER RAINS IN SOUTHERN CALIFORNIA Albert
   Hammond
8 VENTURA HIGHWAY America
9 CLAIR Gilbert O'Sullivan
10 I'M STONE IN LOVE WITH YOU Stylistics

December 16, 1972
1 ME AND MRS. JONES Billy Paul
2 I AM WOMAN Helen Reddy
3 IF YOU DON'T KNOW ME BY NOW Harold Melvin & The
   Blue Notes
4 YOU OUGHT TO BE WITH ME Al Green
5 IT NEVER RAINS IN SOUTHERN CALIFORNIA Albert
   Hammond
6 PAPA WAS A ROLLING STONE Temptations
7 CLAIR Gilbert O'Sullivan
8 VENTURA HIGHWAY America
9 I CAN SEE CLEARLY NOW Johnny Nash
10 I'M STONE IN LOVE WITH YOU Stylistics

December 23, 1972
1 ME AND MRS. JONES Billy Paul
2 I AM WOMAN Helen Reddy
3 YOU OUGHT TO BE WITH ME Al Green
4 CLAIR Gilbert O'Sullivan
5 IT NEVER RAINS IN SOUTHERN CALIFORNIA Albert
   Hammond
6 IF YOU DON'T KNOW ME BY NOW Harold Melvin & The
   Blue Notes
7 FUNNY FACE Donna Fargo
8 PAPA WAS A ROLLING STONE Temptations
9 YOU'RE SO VAIN Carly Simon
10 ROCKIN' PNEUMONIA AND THE BOOGIE WOOGIE FLU
   Johnny Rivers

December 30, 1972
1 ME AND MRS. JONES Billy Paul
2 CLAIR Gilbert O'Sullivan
3 YOU OUGHT TO BE WITH ME Al Green
4 YOU'RE SO VAIN Carly Simon
5 IT NEVER RAINS IN SOUTHERN CALIFORNIA Albert
   Hammond
6 FUNNY FACE Donna Fargo
7 I AM WOMAN Helen Reddy
8 ROCKIN' PNEUMONIA AND THE BOOGIE WOOGIE FLU
   Johnny Rivers
9 SUPERFLY Curtis Mayfield
10 YOUR MAMA DON'T DANCE Loggins & Messina

January 6, 1973
1 YOU'RE SO VAIN Carly Simon
2 CLAIR Gilbert O'Sullivan
3 ME AND MRS. JONES Billy Paul
4 SUPERSTITION Stevie Wonder
5 FUNNY FACE Donna Fargo
6 IT NEVER RAINS IN SOUTHERN CALIFORNIA Albert
   Hammond
7 ROCKIN' PNEUMONIA AND THE BOOGIE WOOGIE FLU
   Johnny Rivers
8 YOUR MAMA DON'T DANCE Loggins & Messina
9 SUPERFLY Curtis Mayfield
10 YOU OUGHT TO BE WITH ME Al Green

January 13, 1973
1 YOU'RE SO VAIN Carly Simon
2 SUPERSTITION Stevie Wonder

3   FUNNY FACE   Donna Fargo
4   CLAIR   Gilbert O'Sullivan
5   ME AND MRS. JONES   Billy Paul
6   YOUR MAMA DON'T DANCE   Loggins & Messina
7   ROCKIN' PNEUMONIA AND THE BOOGIE WOOGIE FLU
      Johnny Rivers
8   SUPERFLY   Curtis Mayfield
9   CROCODILE ROCK   Elton John
10 KEEPER OF THE CASTLE   Four Tops

January 20, 1973
1   YOU'RE SO VAIN   Carly Simon
2   SUPERSTITION   Stevie Wonder
3   ME AND MRS. JONES   Billy Paul
4   CROCODILE ROCK   Elton John
5   YOUR MAMA DON'T DANCE   Loggins & Messina
6   ROCKIN' PNEUMONIA AND THE BOOGIE WOOGIE FLU
      Johnny Rivers
7   CLAIR   Gilbert O'Sullivan
8   SUPERFLY   Curtis Mayfield
9   WHY CAN'T WE LIVE TOGETHER   Timmy Thomas
10 OH, BABE, WHAT WOULD YOU SAY   Hurricane Smith

January 27, 1973
1   SUPERSTITION   Stevie Wonder
2   CROCODILE ROCK   Elton John
3   YOU'RE SO VAIN   Carly Simon
4   YOUR MAMA DON'T DANCE   Loggins & Messina
5   WHY CAN'T WE LIVE TOGETHER   Timmy Thomas
6   ME AND MRS. JONES   Billy Paul
7   OH, BABE, WHAT WOULD YOU SAY   Hurricane Smith
8   TROUBLE MAN   Marvin Gaye
9   ROCKIN' PNEUMONIA AND THE BOOGIE WOOGIE FLU
      Johnny Rivers
10 THE WORLD IS A GHETTO   War

February 10, 1973
1   CROCODILE ROCK   Elton John
2   YOU'RE SO VAIN   Carly Simon
3   WHY CAN'T WE LIVE TOGETHER   Timmy Thomas
4   OH, BABE, WHAT WOULD YOU SAY   Hurricane Smith
5   SUPERSTITION   Stevie Wonder
6   DO IT AGAIN   Steely Dan
7   THE WORLD IS A GHETTO   War
8   TROUBLE MAN   Marvin Gaye
9   DON'T EXPECT ME TO BE YOUR FRIEND   Lobo
10 COULD IT BE I'M FALLING IN LOVE   Spinners

February 17, 1973
1   CROCODILE ROCK   Elton John
2   YOU'RE SO VAIN   Carly Simon
3   OH, BABE, WHAT WOULD YOU SAY   Hurricane Smith
4   DUELING BANJOS   Eric Weissberg & Steve Mandell
5   KILLING ME SOFTLY WITH HIS SONG   Roberta Flack
6   DO IT AGAIN   Steely Dan
7   COULD IT BE I'M FALLING IN LOVE   Spinners
8   DON'T EXPECT ME TO BE YOUR FRIEND   Lobo
9   WHY CAN'T WE LIVE TOGETHER   Timmy Thomas
10 ROCKY MOUNTAIN HIGH   John Denver

February 24, 1973
1   KILLING ME SOFTLY WITH HIS SONG   Roberta Flack
2   DUELING BANJOS   Eric Weissberg & Steve Mandell
3   CROCODILE ROCK   Elton John
4   YOU'RE SO VAIN   Carly Simon
5   COULD IT BE I'M FALLING IN LOVE   Spinners

6   DO IT AGAIN   Steely Dan
7   LAST SONG   Edward Bear
8   DON'T EXPECT ME TO BE YOUR FRIEND   Lobo
9   LOVE TRAIN   O'Jays
10 ROCKY MOUNTAIN HIGH   John Denver

March 3, 1973
1   KILLING ME SOFTLY WITH HIS SONG   Roberta Flack
2   DUELING BANJOS   Eric Weissberg & Steve Mandell
3   LAST SONG   Edward Bear
4   COULD IT BE I'M FALLING IN LOVE   Spinners
5   CROCODILE ROCK   Elton John
6   YOU'RE SO VAIN   Carly Simon
7   LOVE TRAIN   O'Jays
8   ALSO SPRACH ZARATHUSTRA (2001)   Deodato
9   ROCKY MOUNTAIN HIGH   John Denver
10 DON'T EXPECT ME TO BE YOUR FRIEND   Lobo

March 10, 1973
1   KILLING ME SOFTLY WITH HIS SONG   Roberta Flack
2   DUELING BANJOS   Eric Weissberg & Steve Mandell
3   LAST SONG   Edward Bear
4   COULD IT BE I'M FALLING IN LOVE   Spinners
5   LOVE TRAIN   O'Jays
6   ALSO SPRACH ZARATHUSTRA (2001)   Deodato
7   CROCODILE ROCK   Elton John
8   THE COVER OF THE ROLLING STONE   Dr. Hook
9   ROCKY MOUNTAIN HIGH   John Denver
10 DADDY'S HOME   Jermaine Jackson

March 17, 1973
1   KILLING ME SOFTLY WITH HIS SONG   Roberta Flack
2   DUELING BANJOS   Eric Weissberg & Steve Mandell
3   LOVE TRAIN   O'Jays
4   ALSO SPRACH ZARATHUSTRA (2001)   Deodato
5   LAST SONG   Edward Bear
6   THE COVER OF THE ROLLING STONE   Dr. Hook
7   COULD IT BE I'M FALLING IN LOVE   Spinners
8   NEITHER ONE OF US (WANTS TO BE THE FIRST TO SAY
      GOODBYE)   Gladys Knight & The Pips
9   DADDY'S HOME   Jermaine Jackson
10 DANNY'S SONG   Anne Murray

March 24, 1973
1   LOVE TRAIN   O'Jays
2   KILLING ME SOFTLY WITH HIS SONG   Roberta Flack
3   ALSO SPRACH ZARATHUSTRA (2001)   Deodato
4   NEITHER ONE OF US (WANTS TO BE THE FIRST TO SAY
      GOODBYE)   Gladys Knight & The Pips
5   LAST SONG   Edward Bear
6   THE COVER OF THE ROLLING STONE   Dr. Hook
7   DUELING BANJOS   Eric Weissberg & Steve Mandell
8   DANNY'S SONG   Anne Murray
9   BREAK UP TO MAKE UP   Stylistics
10 AIN'T NO WOMAN LIKE THE ONE I'VE GOT   Four Tops

March 31, 1973
1   KILLING ME SOFTLY WITH HIS SONG   Roberta Flack
2   ALSO SPRACH ZARATHUSTRA (2001)   Deodato
3   NEITHER ONE OF US (WANTS TO BE THE FIRST TO SAY
      GOODBYE)   Gladys Knight & The Pips
4   LOVE TRAIN   O'Jays
5   AIN'T NO WOMAN LIKE THE ONE I'VE GOT   Four Tops
6   BREAK UP TO MAKE UP   Stylistics
7   LAST SONG   Edward Bear
8   DANNY'S SONG   Anne Murray

Vicki Lawrence
Carol Burnett's pal went on to star in ``Mama's Family.''

9   SING   Carpenters
10   NIGHT THE LIGHTS WENT OUT IN GEORGIA   Vicki Lawrence

April 7, 1973
1   NIGHT THE LIGHTS WENT OUT IN GEORGIA   Vicki Lawrence
2   NEITHER ONE OF US (WANTS TO BE THE FIRST TO SAY GOODBYE)   Gladys Knight & The Pips
3   KILLING ME SOFTLY WITH HIS SONG   Roberta Flack
4   AIN'T NO WOMAN LIKE THE ONE I'VE GOT   Four Tops
5   BREAK UP TO MAKE UP   Stylistics
6   TIE A YELLOW RIBBON ROUND THE OLD OAK TREE   Dawn
7   SING   Carpenters
8   DANNY'S SONG   Anne Murray
9   ALSO SPRACH ZARATHUSTRA (2001)   Deodato
10   THE CISCO KID   War

April 14, 1973
1   NIGHT THE LIGHTS WENT OUT IN GEORGIA   Vicki Lawrence
2   NEITHER ONE OF US (WANTS TO BE THE FIRST TO SAY GOODBYE)   Gladys Knight & The Pips
3   TIE A YELLOW RIBBON ROUND THE OLD OAK TREE   Dawn
4   AIN'T NO WOMAN LIKE THE ONE I'VE GOT   Four Tops
5   SING   Carpenters
6   THE CISCO KID   War
7   DANNY'S SONG   Anne Murray
8   BREAK UP TO MAKE UP   Stylistics
9   KILLING ME SOFTLY WITH HIS SONG   Roberta Flack
10   CALL ME (COME BACK HOME)   Al Green

April 21, 1973
1   TIE A YELLOW RIBBON ROUND THE OLD OAK TREE   Dawn
2   NIGHT THE LIGHTS WENT OUT IN GEORGIA   Vicki Lawrence
3   SING   Carpenters
4   THE CISCO KID   War
5   AIN'T NO WOMAN LIKE THE ONE I'VE GOT   Four Tops
6   NEITHER ONE OF US (WANTS TO BE THE FIRST TO SAY GOODBYE)   Gladys Knight & The Pips
7   LITTLE WILLY   Sweet
8   MASTERPIECE   Temptations
9   DANNY'S SONG   Anne Murray
10   TWELFTH OF NEVER   Donny Osmond

April 28, 1973
1   TIE A YELLOW RIBBON ROUND THE OLD OAK TREE   Dawn
2   THE CISCO KID   War
3   SING   Carpenters
4   NIGHT THE LIGHTS WENT OUT IN GEORGIA   Vicki Lawrence
5   LITTLE WILLY   Sweet
6   YOU ARE THE SUNSHINE OF MY LIFE   Stevie Wonder
7   MASTERPIECE   Temptations
8   TWELFTH OF NEVER   Donny Osmond
9   STUCK IN THE MIDDLE WITH YOU   Stealers Wheel
10   AIN'T NO WOMAN LIKE THE ONE I'VE GOT   Four Tops

May 5, 1973
1   TIE A YELLOW RIBBON ROUND THE OLD OAK TREE   Dawn
2   THE CISCO KID   War
3   LITTLE WILLY   Sweet
4   YOU ARE THE SUNSHINE OF MY LIFE   Stevie Wonder
5   NIGHT THE LIGHTS WENT OUT IN GEORGIA   Vicki Lawrence
6   DRIFT AWAY   Dobie Gray
7   STUCK IN THE MIDDLE WITH YOU   Stealers Wheel
8   TWELFTH OF NEVER   Donny Osmond
9   SING   Carpenters
10   FRANKENSTEIN   Edgar Winter

May 12, 1973
1   TIE A YELLOW RIBBON ROUND THE OLD OAK TREE   Dawn
2   YOU ARE THE SUNSHINE OF MY LIFE   Stevie Wonder
3   LITTLE WILLY   Sweet
4   THE CISCO KID   War
5   DRIFT AWAY   Dobie Gray
6   STUCK IN THE MIDDLE WITH YOU   Stealers Wheel
7   FRANKENSTEIN   Edgar Winter
8   NIGHT THE LIGHTS WENT OUT IN GEORGIA   Vicki Lawrence
9   DANIEL   Elton John
10   TWELFTH OF NEVER   Donny Osmond

May 19, 1973
1   YOU ARE THE SUNSHINE OF MY LIFE   Stevie Wonder
2   TIE A YELLOW RIBBON ROUND THE OLD OAK TREE   Dawn
3   LITTLE WILLY   Sweet
4   FRANKENSTEIN   Edgar Winter
5   DANIEL   Elton John
6   MY LOVE   Paul McCartney
7   DRIFT AWAY   Dobie Gray

Tony Orlando & Dawn

''Tie A Yellow Ribbon''—#1 on April 21—also became a national anthem and raised American spirits during a troubled time.

8 STUCK IN THE MIDDLE WITH YOU   Stealers Wheel
9 PILLOW TALK   Sylvia
10 WILDFLOWER   Skylark

May 26, 1973
1 FRANKENSTEIN   Edgar Winter
2 MY LOVE   Paul McCartney
3 DANIEL   Elton John
4 TIE A YELLOW RIBBON ROUND THE OLD OAK TREE
  Dawn
5 YOU ARE THE SUNSHINE OF MY LIFE   Stevie Wonder
6 PILLOW TALK   Sylvia
7 LITTLE WILLY   Sweet
8 DRIFT AWAY   Dobie Gray
9 WILDFLOWER   Skylark
10 HOCUS POCUS   Focus

June 2, 1973
1 MY LOVE   Paul McCartney
2 DANIEL   Elton John
3 FRANKENSTEIN   Edgar Winter
4 PILLOW TALK   Sylvia
5 TIE A YELLOW RIBBON ROUND THE OLD OAK TREE
  Dawn
6 YOU ARE THE SUNSHINE OF MY LIFE   Stevie Wonder
7 I'M GONNA LOVE YOU JUST A LITTLE BIT MORE BABY
  Barry White
8 LITTLE WILLY   Sweet
9 HOCUS POCUS   Focus
10 PLAYGROUND IN MY MIND   Clint Holmes

June 9, 1973
1 MY LOVE   Paul McCartney

2 FRANKENSTEIN   Edgar Winter
3 PILLOW TALK   Sylvia
4 DANIEL   Elton John
5 PLAYGROUND IN MY MIND   Clint Holmes
6 I'M GONNA LOVE YOU JUST A LITTLE BIT MORE BABY
  Barry White
7 TIE A YELLOW RIBBON ROUND THE OLD OAK TREE
  Dawn
8 YOU ARE THE SUNSHINE OF MY LIFE   Stevie Wonder
9 HOCUS POCUS   Focus
10 LONG TRAIN RUNNIN'   Doobie Brothers

June 16, 1973
1 MY LOVE   Paul McCartney
2 PLAYGROUND IN MY MIND   Clint Holmes
3 PILLOW TALK   Sylvia
4 I'M GONNA LOVE YOU JUST A LITTLE BIT MORE BABY
  Barry White
5 DANIEL   Elton John
6 FRANKENSTEIN   Edgar Winter
7 WILL IT GO ROUND IN CIRCLES   Billy Preston
8 GIVE ME LOVE (GIVE ME PEACE ON EARTH)   George
  Harrison
9 KODACHROME   Paul Simon
10 TIE A YELLOW RIBBON ROUND THE OLD OAK TREE
  Dawn

June 23, 1973
1 MY LOVE   Paul McCartney
2 PLAYGROUND IN MY MIND   Clint Holmes
3 I'M GONNA LOVE YOU JUST A LITTLE BIT MORE BABY
  Barry White
4 WILL IT GO ROUND IN CIRCLES   Billy Preston

5 GIVE ME LOVE (GIVE ME PEACE ON EARTH) George Harrison
6 PILLOW TALK Sylvia
7 KODACHROME Paul Simon
8 DANIEL Elton John
9 LONG TRAIN RUNNIN' Doobie Brothers
10 RIGHT PLACE, WRONG TIME Dr. John

June 30, 1973

1 GIVE ME LOVE (GIVE ME PEACE ON EARTH) George Harrison
2 MY LOVE Paul McCartney
3 WILL IT GO ROUND IN CIRCLES Billy Preston
4 I'M GONNA LOVE YOU JUST A LITTLE BIT MORE BABY Barry White
5 KODACHROME Paul Simon
6 PILLOW TALK Sylvia
7 PLAYGROUND IN MY MIND Clint Holmes
8 LONG TRAIN RUNNIN' Doobie Brothers
9 RIGHT PLACE, WRONG TIME Dr. John
10 SHAMBALA Three Dog Night

July 7, 1973

1 WILL IT GO ROUND IN CIRCLES Billy Preston
2 KODACHROME Paul Simon
3 MY LOVE Paul McCartney
4 GIVE ME LOVE (GIVE ME PEACE ON EARTH) George Harrison
5 BAD, BAD LEROY BROWN Jim Croce
6 PLAYGROUND IN MY MIND Clint Holmes
7 SHAMBALA Three Dog Night
8 YESTERDAY ONCE MORE Carpenters
9 RIGHT PLACE, WRONG TIME Dr. John
10 I'M GONNA LOVE YOU JUST A LITTLE BIT MORE BABY Barry White

July 14, 1973

1 WILL IT GO ROUND IN CIRCLES Billy Preston
2 KODACHROME Paul Simon
3 BAD, BAD LEROY BROWN Jim Croce
4 SHAMBALA Three Dog Night
5 GIVE ME LOVE (GIVE ME PEACE ON EARTH) George Harrison
6 YESTERDAY ONCE MORE Carpenters
7 PLAYGROUND IN MY MIND Clint Holmes
8 SMOKE ON THE WATER Deep Purple
9 MY LOVE Paul McCartney
10 RIGHT PLACE, WRONG TIME Dr. John

July 21, 1973

1 BAD, BAD LEROY BROWN Jim Croce
2 WILL IT GO ROUND IN CIRCLES Billy Preston
3 YESTERDAY ONCE MORE Carpenters
4 SHAMBALA Three Dog Night
5 KODACHROME Paul Simon
6 GIVE ME LOVE (GIVE ME PEACE ON EARTH) George Harrison
7 SMOKE ON THE WATER Deep Purple
8 BOOGIE WOOGIE BUGLE BOY Bette Midler
9 PLAYGROUND IN MY MIND Clint Holmes
10 NATURAL HIGH Blood Stone

July 28, 1973

1 BAD, BAD LEROY BROWN Jim Croce
2 YESTERDAY ONCE MORE Carpenters
3 SHAMBALA Three Dog Night

4 SMOKE ON THE WATER Deep Purple
5 WILL IT GO ROUND IN CIRCLES Billy Preston
6 DIAMOND GIRL Seals & Crofts
7 KODACHROME Paul Simon
8 BOOGIE WOOGIE BUGLE BOY Bette Midler
9 MORNING AFTER Maureen McGovern
10 GIVE ME LOVE (GIVE ME PEACE ON EARTH) George Harrison

August 4, 1973

1 MORNING AFTER Maureen McGovern
2 BAD, BAD LEROY BROWN Jim Croce
3 LIVE AND LET DIE Wings
4 SMOKE ON THE WATER Deep Purple
5 YESTERDAY ONCE MORE Carpenters
6 DIAMOND GIRL Seals & Crofts
7 TOUCH ME IN THE MORNING Diana Ross
8 BROTHER LOUIE Stories
9 WILL IT GO ROUND IN CIRCLES Billy Preston
10 SHAMBALA Three Dog Night

August 11, 1973

1 MORNING AFTER Maureen McGovern
2 LIVE AND LET DIE Wings
3 BROTHER LOUIE Stories
4 TOUCH ME IN THE MORNING Diana Ross
5 BAD, BAD LEROY BROWN Jim Croce
6 SMOKE ON THE WATER Deep Purple
7 LET'S GET IT ON Marvin Gaye
8 YESTERDAY ONCE MORE Carpenters
9 UNEASY RIDER Charlie Daniels
10 MONSTER MASH Bobby "Boris" Pickett

August 18, 1973

1 TOUCH ME IN THE MORNING Diana Ross
2 LIVE AND LET DIE Wings
3 BROTHER LOUIE Stories
4 MORNING AFTER Maureen McGovern
5 LET'S GET IT ON Marvin Gaye
6 BAD, BAD LEROY BROWN Jim Croce
7 GET DOWN Gilbert O'Sullivan
8 DELTA DAWN Helen Reddy
9 UNEASY RIDER Charlie Daniels
10 FEELIN' STRONGER EVERY DAY Chicago

August 25, 1973

1 BROTHER LOUIE Stories
2 LIVE AND LET DIE Wings
3 TOUCH ME IN THE MORNING Diana Ross
4 LET'S GET IT ON Marvin Gaye
5 MORNING AFTER Maureen McGovern
6 DELTA DAWN Helen Reddy
7 GET DOWN Gilbert O'Sullivan
8 SAY, HAS ANYBODY SEEN MY SWEET GYPSY ROSE Dawn *
9 UNEASY RIDER Charlie Daniels
10 BAD, BAD LEROY BROWN Jim Croce
*Note: * Later Tony Orlando & Dawn.*

September 1, 1973

1 BROTHER LOUIE Stories
2 LET'S GET IT ON Marvin Gaye
3 DELTA DAWN Helen Reddy
4 TOUCH ME IN THE MORNING Diana Ross
5 LIVE AND LET DIE Wings
6 SAY, HAS ANYBODY SEEN MY SWEET GYPSY ROSE? Dawn *

7   MORNING AFTER   Maureen McGovern
8   GET DOWN   Gilbert O'Sullivan
9   LOVES ME LIKE A ROCK   Paul Simon
10 FEELIN' STRONGER EVERY DAY   Chicago
    Note: * Later Tony Orlando & Dawn.

September 8, 1973
1   LET'S GET IT ON   Marvin Gaye
2   BROTHER LOUIE   Stories
3   DELTA DAWN   Helen Reddy
4   SAY, HAS ANYBODY SEEN MY SWEET GYPSY ROSE?
    Dawn *
5   TOUCH ME IN THE MORNING   Diana Ross
6   LOVES ME LIKE A ROCK   Paul Simon
7   LIVE AND LET DIE   Wings
8   WE'RE AN AMERICAN BAND   Grand Funk
9   GYPSY MAN   War
10 HERE I AM (COME AND TAKE ME)   Al Green
    Note: * Later Tony Orlando & Dawn.

September 15, 1973
1   DELTA DAWN   Helen Reddy
2   LET'S GET IT ON   Marvin Gaye
3   SAY, HAS ANYBODY SEEN MY SWEET GYPSY ROSE?
    Dawn *
4   LOVES ME LIKE A ROCK   Paul Simon
5   WE'RE AN AMERICAN BAND   Grand Funk
6   BROTHER LOUIE   Stories
7   TOUCH ME IN THE MORNING   Diana Ross
8   GYPSY MAN   War
9   LIVE AND LET DIE   Wings
10 HERE I AM (COME AND TAKE ME)   Al Green
    Note: * Later Tony Orlando & Dawn.

September 22, 1973
1   LET'S GET IT ON   Marvin Gaye
2   WE'RE AN AMERICAN BAND   Grand Funk
3   DELTA DAWN   Helen Reddy
4   LOVE ME LIKE A ROCK   Paul Simon
5   MORNING AFTER   Maureen McGovern
6   BROTHER LOUIE   Stories
7   HALF-BREED   Cher
8   HIGHER GROUND   Stevie Wonder
9   TOUCH ME IN THE MORNING   Diana Ross
10 THAT LADY   Isley Brothers

September 29, 1973
1   WE'RE AN AMERICAN BAND   Grand Funk
2   LET'S GET IT ON   Marvin Gaye
3   HALF-BREED   Cher
4   LOVE ME LIKE A ROCK   Paul Simon
5   DELTA DAWN   Helen Reddy
6   HIGHER GROUND   Stevie Wonder
7   MORNING AFTER   Maureen McGovern
8   THAT LADY   Isley Brothers
9   MY MARIA   B. W. Stevenson
10 RAMBLIN' MAN   Allman Brothers Band

October 6, 1973
1   HALF-BREED   Cher
2   LOVE ME LIKE A ROCK   Paul Simon
3   LET'S GET IT ON   Marvin Gaye
4   WE'RE AN AMERICAN BAND   Grand Funk
5   HIGHER GROUND   Stevie Wonder
6   THAT LADY   Isley Brothers
7   RAMBLIN' MAN   Allman Brothers Band

8   ANGIE   Rolling Stones
9   DELTA DAWN   Helen Reddy
10 KEEP ON TRUCKIN'   Eddie Kendricks

October 13, 1973
1   HALF-BREED   Cher
2   RAMBLIN' MAN   Allman Brothers Band
3   LET'S GET IT ON   Marvin Gaye
4   HIGHER GROUND   Stevie Wonder
5   ANGIE   Rolling Stones
6   THAT LADY   Isley Brothers
7   LOVES ME LIKE A ROCK   Paul Simon
8   MIDNIGHT TRAIN TO GEORGIA   Gladys Knight & The Pips
9   KEEP ON TRUCKIN'   Eddie Kendricks
10 WE'RE AN AMERICAN BAND   Grand Funk

October 20, 1973
1   ANGIE   Rolling Stones
2   HALF-BREED   Cher
3   RAMBLIN' MAN   Allman Brothers Band
4   LET'S GET IT ON   Marvin Gaye
5   MIDNIGHT TRAIN TO GEORGIA   Gladys Knight & The Pips
6   THAT LADY   Isley Brothers
7   KEEP ON TRUCKIN'   Eddie Kendricks
8   HIGHER GROUND   Stevie Wonder
9   HEARTBEAT IT'S A LOVEBEAT   DeFranco Family
10 PAPER ROSES   Marie Osmond

October 27, 1973
1   MIDNIGHT TRAIN TO GEORGIA   Gladys Knight & The Pips
2   ANGIE   Rolling Stones
3   HALF-BREED   Cher
4   RAMBLIN' MAN   Allman Brothers Band
5   KEEP ON TRUCKIN'   Eddie Kendricks
6   LET'S GET IT ON   Marvin Gaye
7   PAPER ROSES   Marie Osmond
8   HEARTBEAT IT'S A LOVEBEAT   DeFranco Family
9   THAT LADY   Isley Brothers
10 HIGHER GROUND   Stevie Wonder

November 3, 1973
1   MIDNIGHT TRAIN TO GEORGIA   Gladys Knight & The Pips
2   ANGIE   Rolling Stones
3   KEEP ON TRUCKIN'   Eddie Kendricks
4   HALF-BREED   Cher
5   PAPER ROSES   Marie Osmond
6   HEARTBEAT IT'S A LOVEBEAT   DeFranco Family
7   RAMBLIN' MAN   Allman Brothers Band
8   LET'S GET IT ON   Marvin Gaye
9   SPACE RACE   Billy Preston
10 ALL I KNOW   Art Garfunkel

November 10, 1973
1   KEEP ON TRUCKIN'   Eddie Kendricks
2   MIDNIGHT TRAIN TO GEORGIA   Gladys Knight & The Pips
3   ANGIE   Rolling Stones
4   HEARTBEAT IT'S A LOVEBEAT   DeFranco Family
5   PAPER ROSES   Marie Osmond
6   PHOTOGRAPH   Ringo Starr
7   SPACE RACE   Billy Preston
8   HALF-BREED   Cher
9   ALL I KNOW   Art Garfunkel
10 TOP OF THE WORLD   Carpenters

November 17, 1973
1   KEEP ON TRUCKIN'   Eddie Kendricks

2   MIDNIGHT TRAIN TO GEORGIA   Gladys Knight & The Pips
3   HEARTBEAT IT'S A LOVEBEAT   DeFranco Family
4   PHOTOGRAPH   Ringo Starr
5   SPACE RACE   Billy Preston
6   PAPER ROSES   Marie Osmond
7   TOP OF THE WORLD   Carpenters
8   ANGIE   Rolling Stones
9   JUST YOU 'N ME   Chicago
10   I GOT A NAME   Jim Croce

November 24, 1973

1   PHOTOGRAPH   Ringo Starr
2   KEEP ON TRUCKIN'   Eddie Kendricks
3   TOP OF THE WORLD   Carpenters
4   SPACE RACE   Billy Preston
5   HEARTBEAT IT'S A LOVEBEAT   DeFranco Family
6   MIDNIGHT TRAIN TO GEORGIA   Gladys Knight & The Pips
7   JUST YOU 'N ME   Chicago
8   PAPER ROSES   Marie Osmond
9   GOODBYE YELLOW BRICK ROAD   Elton John
10   THE LOVE I LOST PART 1   Harold Melvin & The Bluenotes

December 1, 1973

1   TOP OF THE WORLD   Carpenters
2   PHOTOGRAPH   Ringo Starr
3   GOODBYE YELLOW BRICK ROAD   Elton John
4   SPACE RACE   Billy Preston
5   KEEP ON TRUCKIN'   Eddie Kendricks
6   JUST YOU 'N ME   Chicago
7   MIDNIGHT TRAIN TO GEORGIA   Gladys Knight & The Pips
8   THE LOVE I LOST PART 1   Harold Melvin & The Bluenotes
9   HEARTBEAT IT'S A LOVEBEAT   DeFranco Family
10   MOST BEAUTIFUL GIRL   Charlie Rich

Charlie Rich
``Most Beautiful Girl'' was #1 for two weeks in December 1973.

December 8, 1973

1   TOP OF THE WORLD   Carpenters
2   GOODBYE YELLOW BRICK ROAD   Elton John
3   MOST BEAUTIFUL GIRL   Charlie Rich
4   JUST YOU 'N ME   Chicago
5   PHOTOGRAPH   Ringo Starr
6   SPACE RACE   Billy Preston
7   THE LOVE I LOST PART 1   Harold Melvin & The Bluenotes
8   HELLO IT'S ME   Todd Rundgren
9   KEEP ON TRUCKIN'   Eddie Kendricks
10   LEAVE ME ALONE   Helen Reddy

December 16, 1973

1   MOST BEAUTIFUL GIRL   Charlie Rich
2   GOODBYE YELLOW BRICK ROAD   Elton John
3   TOP OF THE WORLD   Carpenters
4   JUST YOU 'N ME   Chicago
5   TIME IN A BOTTLE   Jim Croce
6   HELLO IT'S ME   Todd Rundgren
7   LEAVE ME ALONE   Helen Reddy
8   PHOTOGRAPH   Ringo Starr
9   THE JOKER   Steve Miller Band
10   IF YOU'RE READY COME GO WITH ME   Staple Singers

December 22, 1973

1   MOST BEAUTIFUL GIRL   Charlie Rich
2   GOODBYE YELLOW BRICK ROAD   Elton John
3   TIME IN A BOTTLE   Jim Croce
4   LEAVE ME ALONE   Helen Reddy
5   HELLO IT'S ME   Todd Rundgren
6   THE JOKER   Steve Miller Band
7   TOP OF THE WORLD   Carpenters
8   JUST YOU 'N ME   Chicago
9   IF YOU'RE READY COME GO WITH ME   Staple Singers
10   NEVER, NEVER GONNA GIVE YOU UP   Barry White

December 29, 1973

1   TIME IN A BOTTLE   Jim Croce
2   MOST BEAUTIFUL GIRL   Charlie Rich
3   LEAVE ME ALONE   Helen Reddy
4   THE JOKER   Steve Miller Band
5   GOODBYE YELLOW BRICK ROAD   Elton John
6   HELLO IT'S ME   Todd Rundgren
7   TOP OF THE WORLD   Carpenters
8   SHOW AND TELL   Al Wilson
9   SMOKIN' IN THE BOY'S ROOM   Brownsville Station
10   NEVER, NEVER GONNA GIVE YOU UP   Barry White

January 5, 1974

1   TIME IN A BOTTLE   Jim Croce
2   THE JOKER   Steve Miller Band
3   LEAVE ME ALONE   Helen Reddy
4   MOST BEAUTIFUL GIRL   Charlie Rich
5   SHOW AND TELL   Al Wilson
6   SMOKIN' IN THE BOY'S ROOM   Brownsville Station
7   GOODBYE YELLOW BRICK ROAD   Elton John
8   NEVER, NEVER GONNA GIVE YOU UP   Barry White
9   LIVING FOR THE CITY   Stevie Wonder
10   I'VE GOT TO USE MY IMAGINATION   Gladys Knight & The Pips

January 12, 1974

1   THE JOKER   Steve Miller Band
2   TIME IN A BOTTLE   Jim Croce
3   SHOW AND TELL   Al Wilson
4   SMOKIN' IN THE BOY'S ROOM   Brownsville Station

5   I'VE GOT TO USE MY IMAGINATION   Gladys Knight & The Pips
6   YOU'RE SIXTEEN   Ringo Starr
7   NEVER, NEVER GONNA GIVE YOU UP   Barry White
8   LIVING FOR THE CITY   Stevie Wonder
9   LET ME BE THERE   Olivia Newton-John
10 HELEN WHEELS   Wings

January 19, 1974
1   SHOW AND TELL   Al Wilson
2   THE JOKER   Steve Miller Band
3   SMOKIN' IN THE BOY'S ROOM   Brownsville Station
4   I'VE GOT TO USE MY IMAGINATION   Gladys Knight & The Pips
5   YOU'RE SIXTEEN   Ringo Starr
6   TIME IN A BOTTLE   Jim Croce
7   WAY WE WERE   Barbra Streisand
8   LIVING FOR THE CITY   Stevie Wonder
9   LET ME BE THERE   Olivia Newton-John
10 LOVE'S THEME   Love Unlimited Orchestra

January 26, 1974
1   YOU'RE SIXTEEN   Ringo Starr
2   SHOW AND TELL   Al Wilson
3   WAY WE WERE   Barbra Streisand
4   I'VE GOT TO USE MY IMAGINATION   Gladys Knight & The Pips
5   THE JOKER   Steve Miller Band
6   LOVE'S THEME   Love Unlimited Orchestra
7   SMOKIN' IN THE BOY'S ROOM   Brownsville Station
8   LET ME BE THERE   Olivia Newton-John
9   TIME IN A BOTTLE   Jim Croce
10 AMERICANS   Gordon Sinclair

February 2, 1974
1   LOVE'S THEME   Love Unlimited Orchestra
2   YOU'RE SIXTEEN   Ringo Starr
3   WAY WE WERE   Barbra Streisand
4   SHOW AND TELL   Al Wilson
5   AMERICANS   Gordon Sinclair
6   I'VE GOT TO USE MY IMAGINATION   Gladys Knight & The Pips
7   LET ME BE THERE   Olivia Newton-John
8   UNTIL YOU COME BACK TO ME (THAT'S WHAT I'M GONNA DO)   Aretha Franklin
9   THE JOKER   Steve Miller Band
10 SPIDERS AND SNAKES   Jim Stafford

February 9, 1974
1   LOVE'S THEME   Love Unlimited Orchestra
2   WAY WE WERE   Barbra Streisand
3   YOU'RE SIXTEEN   Ringo Starr
4   AMERICANS   Gordon Sinclair
5   UNTIL YOU COME BACK TO ME (THAT'S WHAT I'M GONNA DO)   Aretha Franklin
6   LET ME BE THERE   Olivia Newton-John
7   SPIDERS AND SNAKES   Jim Stafford
8   SHOW AND TELL   Al Wilson
9   I'VE GOT TO USE MY IMAGINATION   Gladys Knight & The Pips
10 JUNGLE BOOGIE   Kool & The Gang

February 16, 1974
1   WAY WE WERE   Barbra Streisand
2   LOVE'S THEME   Love Unlimited Orchestra
3   YOU'RE SIXTEEN   Ringo Starr

4   UNTIL YOU COME BACK TO ME (THAT'S WHAT I'M GONNA DO)   Aretha Franklin
5   SPIDERS AND SNAKES   Jim Stafford
6   AMERICANS   Gordon Sinclair
7   LET ME BE THERE   Olivia Newton-John
8   JUNGLE BOOGIE   Kool & The Gang
9   BOOGIE DOWN   Eddie Kendricks
10 ROCK ON   David Essex

February 23, 1974
1   WAY WE WERE   Barbra Streisand
2   SEASONS IN THE SUN   Terry Jacks
3   UNTIL YOU COME BACK TO ME (THAT'S WHAT I'M GONNA DO)   Aretha Franklin
4   SPIDERS AND SNAKES   Jim Stafford
5   LOVE'S THEME   Love Unlimited Orchestra
6   JUNGLE BOOGIE   Kool & The Gang
7   BOOGIE DOWN   Eddie Kendricks
8   ROCK ON   David Essex
9   YOU'RE SIXTEEN   Ringo Starr
10 LET ME BE THERE   Olivia Newton-John

March 2, 1974
1   SEASONS IN THE SUN   Terry Jacks
2   WAY WE WERE   Barbra Streisand
3   SPIDERS AND SNAKES   Jim Stafford
4   BOOGIE DOWN   Eddie Kendricks
5   JUNGLE BOOGIE   Kool & The Gang
6   ROCK ON   David Essex
7   UNTIL YOU COME BACK TO ME (THAT'S WHAT I'M GONNA DO)   Aretha Franklin
8   LOVE'S THEME   Love Unlimited Orchestra
9   DARK LADY   Styx
10 PUT YOUR HANDS TOGETHER   O'Jays

March 9, 1974
1   SEASONS IN THE SUN   Terry Jacks
2   BOOGIE DOWN   Eddie Kendricks
3   WAY WE WERE   Barbra Streisand
4   JUNGLE BOOGIE   Kool & The Gang
5   ROCK ON   David Essex
6   DARK LADY   Styx
7   SPIDERS AND SNAKES   Jim Stafford
8   MOCKINGBIRD   Carly Simon & James Taylor
9   UNTIL YOU COME BACK TO ME (THAT'S WHAT I'M GONNA DO)   Aretha Franklin
10 SUNSHINE ON MY SHOULDER   John Denver

March 16, 1974
1   SEASONS IN THE SUN   Terry Jacks
2   BOOGIE DOWN   Eddie Kendricks
3   DARK LADY   Styx
4   SUNSHINE ON MY SHOULDER   John Denver
5   WAY WE WERE   Barbra Streisand
6   MOCKINGBIRD   Carly Simon & James Taylor
7   JUNGLE BOOGIE   Kool & The Gang
8   ROCK ON   David Essex
9   SPIDERS AND SNAKES   Jim Stafford
10 JET   Paul McCartney

March 23, 1974
1   DARK LADY   Styx
2   SEASONS IN THE SUN   Terry Jacks
3   SUNSHINE ON MY SHOULDER   John Denver
4   BOOGIE DOWN   Eddie Kendricks
5   MOCKINGBIRD   Carly Simon & James Taylor

6   BENNIE AND THE JETS   Elton John
7   HOOKED ON A FEELING   B. J. Thomas
8   JET   Paul McCartney
9   ERES TU (TOUCH THE WIND)   Mocedades
10   JUNGLE BOOGIE   Kool & The Gang

March 30, 1974
1   SUNSHINE ON MY SHOULDER   John Denver
2   HOOKED ON A FEELING   B. J. Thomas
3   SEASONS IN THE SUN   Terry Jacks
4   BENNIE AND THE JETS   Elton John
5   DARK LADY   Styx
6   MOCKINGBIRD   Carly Simon & James Taylor
7   JET   Paul McCartney
8   COME AND GET YOUR LOVE   Redbone
9   ERES TU (TOUCH THE WIND)   Mocedades
10   LORD'S PRAYER   Sister Janet Mead

April 6, 1974
1   HOOKED ON A FEELING   B. J. Thomas
2   BENNIE AND THE JETS   Elton John
3   SUNSHINE ON MY SHOULDER   John Denver
4   SEASONS IN THE SUN   Terry Jacks
5   LORD'S PRAYER   Sister Janet Mead
6   COME AND GET YOUR LOVE   Redbone
7   DARK LADY   Styx
8   TSOP (THE SOUND OF PHILADELPHIA)   MFSB featuring
     The Three Degrees
9   MOCKINGBIRD   Carly Simon & James Taylor
10   BEST THING THAT EVER HAPPENED TO ME   Gladys
     Knight & The Pips

April 13, 1974
1   BENNIE AND THE JETS   Elton John
2   HOOKED ON A FEELING   B. J. Thomas
3   TSOP (THE SOUND OF PHILADELPHIA)   MFSB featuring
     The Three Degrees
4   LORD'S PRAYER   Sister Janet Mead
5   COME AND GET YOUR LOVE   Redbone
6   SUNSHINE ON MY SHOULDER   John Denver
7   BEST THING THAT EVER HAPPENED TO ME   Gladys
     Knight & The Pips
8   SEASONS IN THE SUN   Terry Jacks
9   OH MY MY   Ringo Starr
10   MOCKINGBIRD   Carly Simon & James Taylor

April 20, 1974
1   TSOP (THE SOUND OF PHILADELPHIA)   MFSB featuring
     The Three Degrees
2   BENNIE AND THE JETS   Elton John
3   HOOKED ON A FEELING   B. J. Thomas
4   BEST THING THAT EVER HAPPENED TO ME   Gladys
     Knight & The Pips
5   COME AND GET YOUR LOVE   Redbone
6   OH MY MY   Ringo Starr
7   SUNSHINE ON MY SHOULDER   John Denver
8   THE LOCO-MOTION   Grand Funk
9   LORD'S PRAYER   Sister Janet Mead
10   I'LL HAVE TO SAY I LOVE YOU IN A SONG   Jim Croce

April 27, 1974
1   TSOP (THE SOUND OF PHILADELPHIA)   MFSB featuring
     The Three Degrees
2   BENNIE AND THE JETS   Elton John
3   BEST THING THAT EVER HAPPENED TO ME   Gladys
     Knight & The Pips

4   THE LOCO-MOTION   Grand Funk
5   OH MY MY   Ringo Starr
6   HOOKED ON A FEELING   B. J. Thomas
7   COME AND GET YOUR LOVE   Redbone
8   DANCING MACHINE   Jackson 5
9   I'LL HAVE TO SAY I LOVE YOU IN A SONG   Jim Croce
10   LOOKIN' FOR A LOVE   Bobby Womack

May 4, 1974
1   THE LOCO-MOTION   Grand Funk
2   TSOP (THE SOUND OF PHILADELPHIA)   MFSB featuring
     The Three Degrees
3   BENNIE AND THE JETS   Elton John
4   BEST THING THAT EVER HAPPENED TO ME   Gladys
     Knight & The Pips
5   DANCING MACHINE   Jackson 5
6   THE STREAK   Ray Stevens
7   HOOKED ON A FEELING   B. J. Thomas
8   TUBULAR BELLS   Mike Oldfield
9   THE SHOW MUST GO ON   Three Dog Night
10   JUST DON'T WANT TO BE LONELY   Main Ingredient

May 11, 1974
1   THE LOCO-MOTION   Grand Funk
2   THE STREAK   Ray Stevens
3   DANCING MACHINE   Jackson 5
4   THE ENTERTAINER   Marvin Hamlisch
5   BENNIE AND THE JETS   Elton John
6   THE SHOW MUST GO ON   Three Dog Night
7   TUBULAR BELLS   Mike Oldfield
8   TSOP (THE SOUND OF PHILADELPHIA)   MFSB featuring
     The Three Degrees

Ray Stevens
The King of Novelty, Ray cashed in on a new national
fad—streaking—with a #1 hit (May 18).

9   I'VE BEEN SEARCHING SO LONG   Chicago
10   MIDNIGHT AT THE OASIS   Maria Muldaur

May 18, 1974
1   THE STREAK   Ray Stevens
2   DANCING MACHINE   Jackson 5
3   THE ENTERTAINER   Marvin Hamlisch
4   THE LOCO-MOTION   Grand Funk
5   THE SHOW MUST GO ON   Three Dog Night
6   BENNIE AND THE JETS   Elton John
7   BAND ON THE RUN   Paul McCartney
8   MIDNIGHT AT THE OASIS   Maria Muldaur
9   I'VE BEEN SEARCHING SO LONG   Chicago
10   YOU MAKE ME FEEL BRAND NEW   Stylistics

May 25, 1974
1   THE STREAK   Ray Stevens
2   DANCING MACHINE   Jackson 5
3   THE ENTERTAINER   Marvin Hamlisch
4   THE SHOW MUST GO ON   Three Dog Night
5   BAND ON THE RUN   Paul McCartney
6   YOU MAKE ME FEEL BRAND NEW   Stylistics
7   MIDNIGHT AT THE OASIS   Maria Muldaur
8   THE LOCO-MOTION   Grand Funk
9   I'VE BEEN SEARCHING SO LONG   Chicago
10   HELP ME   Joni Mitchell

June 1, 1974
1   THE STREAK   Ray Stevens
2   BAND ON THE RUN   Paul McCartney
3   DANCING MACHINE   Jackson 5
4   YOU MAKE ME FEEL BRAND NEW   Stylistics
5   THE ENTERTAINER   Marvin Hamlisch
6   MIDNIGHT AT THE OASIS   Maria Muldaur
7   SUNDOWN   Gordon Lightfoot
8   HELP ME   Joni Mitchell
9   BILLY, DON'T BE A HERO   Bo Donaldson & The
     Heywoods
10   OH VERY YOUNG   Cat Stevens

June 8, 1974
1   BAND ON THE RUN   Paul McCartney
2   THE STREAK   Ray Stevens
3   YOU MAKE ME FEEL BRAND NEW   Stylistics
4   DANCING MACHINE   Jackson 5
5   SUNDOWN   Gordon Lightfoot
6   BILLY, DON'T BE A HERO   Bo Donaldson & The
     Heywoods
7   HELP ME   Joni Mitchell
8   THE ENTERTAINER   Marvin Hamlisch
9   MIDNIGHT AT THE OASIS   Maria Muldaur
10   FOR THE LOVE OF MONEY   O'Jays

June 15, 1974
1   BILLY, DON'T BE A HERO   Bo Donaldson & The
     Heywoods
2   YOU MAKE ME FEEL BRAND NEW   Stylistics
3   SUNDOWN   Gordon Lightfoot
4   THE STREAK   Ray Stevens
5   BAND ON THE RUN   Paul McCartney
6   DANCING MACHINE   Jackson 5
7   BE THANKFUL FOR WHAT YOU'VE GOT   William
     DeVaughn
8   THE ENTERTAINER   Marvin Hamlisch
9   FOR THE LOVE OF MONEY   O'Jays
10   MIDNIGHT AT THE OASIS   Maria Muldaur

June 22, 1974
1   BILLY, DON'T BE A HERO   Bo Donaldson & The
     Heywoods
2   YOU MAKE ME FEEL BRAND NEW   Stylistics
3   SUNDOWN   Gordon Lightfoot
4   THE STREAK   Ray Stevens
5   BE THANKFUL FOR WHAT YOU'VE GOT   William
     DeVaughn
6   BAND ON THE RUN   Paul McCartney
7   IF YOU LOVE ME (LET ME KNOW)   Olivia Newton-John
8   DANCING MACHINE   Jackson 5
9   HOLLYWOOD SWINGING   Kool & The Gang
10   THE ENTERTAINER   Marvin Hamlisch

June 29, 1974
1   SUNDOWN   Gordon Lightfoot
2   BILLY, DON'T BE A HERO   Bo Donaldson & The
     Heywoods
3   YOU MAKE ME FEEL BRAND NEW   Stylistics
4   BE THANKFUL FOR WHAT YOU'VE GOT   William
     DeVaughn
5   IF YOU LOVE ME (LET ME KNOW)   Olivia Newton-John
6   ROCK THE BOAT   Hues Corporation
7   HOLLYWOOD SWINGING   Kool & The Gang
8   BAND ON THE RUN   Paul McCartney
9   ROCK YOUR BABY   George McCrae
10   ANNIE'S SONG   John Denver

July 6, 1974
1   ROCK THE BOAT   Hues Corporation
2   SUNDOWN   Gordon Lightfoot
3   BILLY, DON'T BE A HERO   Bo Donaldson & The
     Heywoods
4   ROCK YOUR BABY   George McCrae
5   IF YOU LOVE ME (LET ME KNOW)   Olivia Newton-John
6   HOLLYWOOD SWINGING   Kool & The Gang
7   YOU MAKE ME FEEL BRAND NEW   Stylistics
8   ANNIE'S SONG   John Denver
9   YOU WON'T SEE ME   Anne Murray
10   ON AND ON   Gladys Knight & The Pips

July 13, 1974
1   ROCK YOUR BABY   George McCrae
2   ANNIE'S SONG   John Denver
3   ROCK THE BOAT   Hues Corporation
4   SUNDOWN   Gordon Lightfoot
5   ON AND ON   Gladys Knight & The Pips
6   DON'T LET THE SUN GO DOWN ON ME   Elton John
7   BILLY, DON'T BE A HERO   Bo Donaldson & The
     Heywoods
8   YOU WON'T SEE ME   Anne Murray
9   THE AIR THAT I BREATHE   Hollies
10   ROCK AND ROLL HEAVEN   Righteous Brothers

July 20, 1974
1   ROCK YOUR BABY   George McCrae
2   ANNIE'S SONG   John Denver
3   ROCK AND ROLL HEAVEN   Righteous Brothers
4   DON'T LET THE SUN GO DOWN ON ME   Elton John
5   ON AND ON   Gladys Knight & The Pips
6   ROCK THE BOAT   Hues Corporation
7   RIKKI, DON'T LOSE THAT NUMBER   Steely Dan
8   YOU WON'T SEE ME   Anne Murray
9   THE AIR THAT I BREATHE   Hollies
10   IF YOU LOVE ME (LET ME KNOW)   Olivia Newton-John

July 27, 1974
1 ANNIE'S SONG   John Denver
2 DON'T LET THE SUN GO DOWN ON ME   Elton John
3 ROCK AND ROLL HEAVEN   Righteous Brothers
4 ROCK YOUR BABY   George McCrae
5 RIKKI, DON'T LOSE THAT NUMBER   Steely Dan
6 FEEL LIKE MAKIN' LOVE   Roberta Flack
7 THE AIR THAT I BREATHE   Hollies
8 ROCK THE BOAT   Hues Corporation
9 PLEASE COME TO BOSTON   Dave Loggins
10 CALL ON ME   Chicago

August 3, 1974
1 ANNIE'S SONG   John Denver
2 DON'T LET THE SUN GO DOWN ON ME   Elton John
3 FEEL LIKE MAKIN' LOVE   Roberta Flack
4 RIKKI, DON'T LOSE THAT NUMBER   Steely Dan
5 NIGHT CHICAGO DIED   Paper Lace
6 THE AIR THAT I BREATHE   Hollies
7 ROCK AND ROLL HEAVEN   Righteous Brothers
8 PLEASE COME TO BOSTON   Dave Loggins
9 CALL ON ME   Chicago
10 SIDESHOW   Blue Magic

August 10, 1974
1 FEEL LIKE MAKIN' LOVE   Roberta Flack
2 NIGHT CHICAGO DIED   Paper Lace
3 ANNIE'S SONG   John Denver
4 DON'T LET THE SUN GO DOWN ON ME   Elton John
5 PLEASE COME TO BOSTON   Dave Loggins
6 CALL ON ME   Chicago
7 WATERLOO   Abba
8 SIDESHOW   Blue Magic
9 WILDWOOD WEED   Jim Stafford
10 TELL ME SOMETHING GOOD   Rufus

August 17, 1974
1 NIGHT CHICAGO DIED   Paper Lace
2 FEEL LIKE MAKIN' LOVE   Roberta Flack
3 (YOU'RE) HAVING MY BABY   Paul Anka
4 TELL ME SOMETHING GOOD   Rufus
5 PLEASE COME TO BOSTON   Dave Loggins
6 CALL ON ME   Chicago
7 WATERLOO   Abba
8 WILDWOOD WEED   Jim Stafford
9 I'M LEAVING IT UP TO YOU   Donny & Marie Osmond
10 SIDESHOW   Blue Magic

August 24, 1974
1 (YOU'RE) HAVING MY BABY   Paul Anka
2 NIGHT CHICAGO DIED   Paper Lace
3 TELL ME SOMETHING GOOD   Rufus
4 FEEL LIKE MAKIN' LOVE   Roberta Flack
5 I SHOT THE SHERIFF   Eric Clapton
6 WATERLOO   Abba
7 WILDWOOD WEED   Jim Stafford
8 I'M LEAVING IT UP TO YOU   Donny & Marie Osmond
9 ROCK ME GENTLY   Andy Kim
10 KEEP ON SMILIN'   Wet Willie

August 31, 1974
1 (YOU'RE) HAVING MY BABY   Paul Anka
2 I SHOT THE SHERIFF   Eric Clapton
3 TELL ME SOMETHING GOOD   Rufus
4 NIGHT CHICAGO DIED   Paper Lace
5 FEEL LIKE MAKIN' LOVE   Roberta Flack
6 I'M LEAVING IT UP TO YOU   Donny & Marie Osmond
7 WILDWOOD WEED   Jim Stafford
8 ROCK ME GENTLY   Andy Kim
9 CAN'T GET ENOUGH OF YOUR LOVE BABE   Barry White
10 YOU AND ME AGAINST THE WORLD   Helen Reddy

September 7, 1974
1 (YOU'RE) HAVING MY BABY   Paul Anka
2 I SHOT THE SHERIFF   Eric Clapton
3 TELL ME SOMETHING GOOD   Rufus
4 ROCK ME GENTLY   Andy Kim
5 I'M LEAVING IT UP TO YOU   Donny & Marie Osmond
6 I CAN'T GET ENOUGH OF YOUR LOVE BABE   Barry White
7 NOTHING FROM NOTHING   Billy Preston
8 NIGHT CHICAGO DIED   Paper Lace
9 YOU AND ME AGAINST THE WORLD   Helen Reddy
10 THEN CAME YOU   Dionne Warwick & The Spinners

September 14, 1974
1 I SHOT THE SHERIFF   Eric Clapton
2 (YOU'RE) HAVING MY BABY   Paul Anka
3 ROCK ME GENTLY   Andy Kim
4 I'M LEAVING IT UP TO YOU   Donny & Marie Osmond
5 CAN'T GET ENOUGH OF YOUR LOVE BABE   Barry White
6 NOTHING FROM NOTHING   Billy Preston
7 TELL ME SOMETHING GOOD   Rufus
8 THEN CAME YOU   Dionne Warwick & The Spinners
9 YOU AND ME AGAINST THE WORLD   Helen Reddy
10 CLAP FOR THE WOLFMAN   Guess Who

September 21, 1974
1 CAN'T GET ENOUGH OF YOUR LOVE BABE   Barry White
2 ROCK ME GENTLY   Andy Kim
3 I HONESTLY LOVE YOU   Olivia Newton-John
4 NOTHING FROM NOTHING   Billy Preston
5 I SHOT THE SHERIFF   Eric Clapton
6 THEN CAME YOU   Dionne Warwick & The Spinners
7 (YOU'RE) HAVING MY BABY   Paul Anka
8 CLAP FOR THE WOLFMAN   Guess Who
9 YOU HAVEN'T DONE NOTHIN'   Stevie Wonder
10 HANG ON IN THERE BABY   Johnny Bristol

September 28, 1974
1 ROCK ME GENTLY   Andy Kim
2 I HONESTLY LOVE YOU   Olivia Newton-John
3 NOTHING FROM NOTHING   Billy Preston
4 THEN CAME YOU   Dionne Warwick & The Spinners
5 BEACH BABY   First Class
6 YOU HAVEN'T DONE NOTHIN'   Stevie Wonder
7 CLAP FOR THE WOLFMAN   Guess Who
8 ANOTHER SATURDAY NIGHT   Cat Stevens
9 HANG ON IN THERE BABY   Johnny Bristol
10 SWEET HOME ALABAMA   Lynyrd Skynyrd

October 5, 1974
1 I HONESTLY LOVE YOU   Olivia Newton-John
2 NOTHING FROM NOTHING   Billy Preston
3 THEN CAME YOU   Dionne Warwick & The Spinners
4 BEACH BABY   First Class
5 YOU HAVEN'T DONE NOTHIN'   Stevie Wonder
6 CLAP FOR THE WOLFMAN   Guess Who
7 ANOTHER SATURDAY NIGHT   Cat Stevens
8 HANG ON IN THERE BABY   Johnny Bristol
9 SWEET HOME ALABAMA   Lynyrd Skynyrd
10 EARACHE MY EYE   Cheech & Chong

Donnie & Marie Osmond
Reason to smile: a Top 10 hit with ``I'm Leaving It Up To You'' (Aug.-Sep.).

Lynyrd Skynyrd
Southern Rock at its finest. Formed in Jacksonville, the group was named for their high school gym teacher.
(Ronnie Van Zant, Steve Gaines and Cassie Gaines were killed in a plane crash, October 20, 1977.)

October 12, 1974

1 I HONESTLY LOVE YOU Olivia Newton-John
2 NOTHING FROM NOTHING Billy Preston
3 THEN CAME YOU Dionne Warwick & The Spinners
4 BEACH BABY First Class
5 YOU HAVEN'T DONE NOTHIN' Stevie Wonder
6 ANOTHER SATURDAY NIGHT Cat Stevens
7 THE BITCH IS BACK Elton John
8 NEVER MY LOVE Blue Swede
9 EARACHE MY EYE Cheech & Chong
10 CAN'T GET ENOUGH Bad Company

October 19, 1974

1 NOTHING FROM NOTHING Billy Preston
2 THEN CAME YOU Dionne Warwick & The Spinners
3 YOU HAVEN'T DONE NOTHIN' Stevie Wonder
4 I HONESTLY LOVE YOU Olivia Newton-John
5 JAZZMAN Carole King
6 THE BITCH IS BACK Elton John
7 NEVER MY LOVE Blue Swede
8 CAN'T GET ENOUGH Bad Company
9 STEPPIN' OUT (GONNA BOOGIE TONIGHT) Dawn
10 LOVE ME FOR A REASON Osmonds

October 26, 1974

1 THEN CAME YOU Dionne Warwick & The Spinners
2 YOU HAVEN'T DONE NOTHIN' Stevie Wonder
3 YOU AIN'T SEEN NOTHING YET Bachman-Turner Overdrive
4 JAZZMAN Carole King
5 THE BITCH IS BACK Elton John
6 CAN'T GET ENOUGH Bad Company
7 STEPPIN' OUT (GONNA BOOGIE TONIGHT) Dawn
8 SWEET HOME ALABAMA Lynyrd Skynyrd
9 STOP AND SMELL THE ROSES Mac Davis
10 LOVE ME FOR A REASON Osmonds

November 2, 1974

1 YOU HAVEN'T DONE NOTHIN' Stevie Wonder
2 YOU AIN'T SEEN NOTHING YET Bachman-Turner Overdrive
3 JAZZMAN Carole King
4 THE BITCH IS BACK Elton John
5 CAN'T GET ENOUGH Bad Company
6 WHATEVER GETS YOU THRU THE NIGHT John Lennon
7 STEPPIN' OUT (GONNA BOOGIE TONIGHT) Dawn
8 SWEET HOME ALABAMA Lynyrd Skynyrd
9 STOP AND SMELL THE ROSES Mac Davis
10 TIN MAN America

November 9, 1974

1 YOU AIN'T SEEN NOTHING YET Bachman-Turner Overdrive
2 JAZZMAN Carole King
3 WHATEVER GETS YOU THRU THE NIGHT John Lennon
4 TIN MAN America
5 BACK HOME AGAIN John Denver
6 MY MELODY OF LOVE Bobby Vinton
7 DO IT ('TIL YOU'RE SATISFIED) B. T. Express
8 THE BITCH IS BACK Elton John
9 LIFE IS A ROCK (BUT THE RADIO ROLLED ME) Reunion
10 CAREFREE HIGHWAY Gordon Lightfoot

November 16, 1974

1 WHATEVER GETS YOU THRU THE NIGHT John Lennon
2 DO IT ('TIL YOU'RE SATISFIED) B. T. Express
3 MY MELODY OF LOVE Bobby Vinton
4 TIN MAN America
5 BACK HOME AGAIN John Denver
6 I CAN HELP Billy Swan
7 LONGFELLOW SERENADE Neil Diamond
8 LIFE IS A ROCK (BUT THE RADIO ROLLED ME) Reunion
9 EVERLASTING LOVE Carl Carlton
10 CAREFREE HIGHWAY Gordon Lightfoot

November 23, 1974

1 I CAN HELP Billy Swan
2 DO IT ('TIL YOU'RE SATISFIED) B. T. Express
3 MY MELODY OF LOVE Bobby Vinton
4 TIN MAN America
5 LONGFELLOW SERENADE Neil Diamond
6 EVERLASTING LOVE Carl Carlton
7 KUNG FU FIGHTING Carl Douglas
8 WHEN WILL I SEE YOU AGAIN Three Degrees
9 BACK HOME AGAIN John Denver
10 CAT'S IN THE CRADLE Harry Chapin

November 30, 1974

1 I CAN HELP Billy Swan
2 KUNG FU FIGHTING Carl Douglas
3 WHEN WILL I SEE YOU AGAIN Three Degrees
4 DO IT ('TIL YOU'RE SATISFIED) B. T. Express
5 LONGFELLOW SERENADE Neil Diamond
6 EVERLASTING LOVE Carl Carlton
7 MY MELODY OF LOVE Bobby Vinton
8 YOU AIN'T SEEN NOTHING YET Bachman-Turner Overdrive
9 CAT'S IN THE CRADLE Harry Chapin
10 ANGIE BABY Helen Reddy

December 7, 1974

1 KUNG FU FIGHTING Carl Douglas
2 I CAN HELP Billy Swan
3 WHEN WILL I SEE YOU AGAIN Three Degrees
4 DO IT ('TIL YOU'RE SATISFIED) B. T. Express
5 CAT'S IN THE CRADLE Harry Chapin
6 ANGIE BABY Helen Reddy
7 MY MELODY OF LOVE Bobby Vinton
8 YOU AIN'T SEEN NOTHING YET Bachman-Turner Overdrive
9 SHA-LA-LA (MAKE ME HAPPY) Al Green
10 YOU'RE THE FIRST, THE LAST, MY EVERYTHING Barry White

December 14, 1974

1 KUNG FU FIGHTING Carl Douglas
2 WHEN WILL I SEE YOU AGAIN Three Degrees
3 I CAN HELP Billy Swan
4 CAT'S IN THE CRADLE Harry Chapin
5 ANGIE BABY Helen Reddy
6 DO IT ('TIL YOU'RE SATISFIED) B. T. Express
7 YOU'RE THE FIRST, THE LAST, MY EVERYTHING Barry White
8 SHA-LA-LA (MAKE ME HAPPY) Al Green
9 LUCY IN THE SKY WITH DIAMONDS Elton John
10 JUNIOR'S FARM/SALLY G Paul McCartney

December 21, 1974

1 CAT'S IN THE CRADLE Harry Chapin
2 KUNG FU FIGHTING Carl Douglas
3 ANGIE BABY Helen Reddy
4 WHEN WILL I SEE YOU AGAIN Three Degrees

5 YOU'RE THE FIRST, THE LAST, MY EVERYTHING   Barry White
6 LUCY IN THE SKY WITH DIAMONDS   Elton John
7 SHA-LA-LA (MAKE ME HAPPY)   Al Green
8 JUNIOR'S FARM/SALLY G   Paul McCartney
9 I CAN HELP   Billy Swan
10 DO IT ('TIL YOU'RE SATISFIED)   B. T. Express

December 28, 1974
1 ANGIE BABY   Helen Reddy
2 LUCY IN THE SKY WITH DIAMONDS   Elton John
3 YOU'RE THE FIRST, THE LAST, MY EVERYTHING   Barry White
4 KUNG FU FIGHTING   Carl Douglas
5 CAT'S IN THE CRADLE   Harry Chapin
6 JUNIOR'S FARM/SALLY G   Paul McCartney
7 WHEN WILL I SEE YOU AGAIN   Three Degrees
8 LAUGHTER IN THE RAIN   Neil Sedaka
9 ONLY YOU   Ringo Starr
10 BOOGIE ON REGGAE WOMAN   Stevie Wonder

January 4, 1975
1 LUCY IN THE SKY WITH DIAMONDS   Elton John
2 YOU'RE THE FIRST, THE LAST, MY EVERYTHING   Barry White
3 KUNG FU FIGHTING   Carl Douglas
4 JUNIOR'S FARM/SALLY G   Paul McCartney
5 LAUGHTER IN THE RAIN   Neil Sedaka
6 ANGIE BABY   Helen Reddy
7 ONLY YOU   Ringo Starr
8 BOOGIE ON REGGAE WOMAN   Stevie Wonder
9 PLEASE MR. POSTMAN   Carpenters
10 MANDY   Barry Manilow

January 11, 1975
1 LUCY IN THE SKY WITH DIAMONDS   Elton John
2 YOU'RE THE FIRST, THE LAST, MY EVERYTHING   Barry White
3 JUNIOR'S FARM/SALLY G   Paul McCartney
4 LAUGHTER IN THE RAIN   Neil Sedaka
5 MANDY   Barry Manilow
6 ONLY YOU   Ringo Starr
7 BOOGIE ON REGGAE WOMAN   Stevie Wonder
8 PLEASE MR. POSTMAN   Carpenters
9 KUNG FU FIGHTING   Carl Douglas
10 ONE MAN WOMAN/ONE WOMAN MAN   Paul Anka & Odia Coates

January 18, 1975
1 MANDY   Barry Manilow
2 PLEASE MR. POSTMAN   Carpenters
3 LAUGHTER IN THE RAIN   Neil Sedaka
4 YOU'RE THE FIRST, THE LAST, MY EVERYTHING   Barry White
5 LUCY IN THE SKY WITH DIAMONDS   Elton John
6 BOOGIE ON REGGAE WOMAN   Stevie Wonder
7 JUNIOR'S FARM/SALLY G   Paul McCartney
8 ONE MAN WOMAN/ONE WOMAN MAN   Paul Anka & Odia Coates
9 MORNING SIDE OF THE MOUNTAIN   Donny & Marie Osmond
10 NEVER CAN SAY GOODBYE   Jackson 5

January 26, 1975
1 PLEASE MR. POSTMAN   Carpenters
2 LAUGHTER IN THE RAIN   Neil Sedaka

Barry Manilow
A top composer becomes #1 singer with ``Mandy'' (Jan. 18).

Neil Sedaka
Neil's ``Laughter In The Rain'' peaks at #1 (Feb. 1).

3 MANDY   Barry Manilow
4 FIRE   Ohio Players
5 BOOGIE ON REGGAE WOMAN   Stevie Wonder
6 YOU'RE NO GOOD   Linda Ronstadt
7 ONE MAN WOMAN/ONE WOMAN MAN   Paul Anka & Odia Coates
8 MORNING SIDE OF THE MOUNTAIN   Donny & Marie Osmond
9 NEVER CAN SAY GOODBYE   Jackson 5
10 PICK UP THE PIECES   Average White Band

February 1, 1975

1 LAUGHTER IN THE RAIN   Neil Sedaka
2 FIRE   Ohio Players
3 BOOGIE ON REGGAE WOMAN   Stevie Wonder
4 YOU'RE NO GOOD   Linda Ronstadt
5 PICK UP THE PIECES   Average White Band
6 PLEASE MR. POSTMAN   Carpenters
7 MANDY   Barry Manilow
8 MORNING SIDE OF THE MOUNTAIN   Donny & Marie Osmond
9 BEST OF MY LOVE   Eagles
10 SOME KIND OF WONDERFUL   Grand Funk

February 8, 1975

1 FIRE   Ohio Players
2 YOU'RE NO GOOD   Linda Ronstadt
3 BOOGIE ON REGGAE WOMAN   Stevie Wonder
4 PICK UP THE PIECES   Average White Band
5 BEST OF MY LOVE   Eagles
6 SOME KIND OF WONDERFUL   Grand Funk
7 BLACK WATER   Doobie Brothers
8 LAUGHTER IN THE RAIN   Neil Sedaka
9 LONELY PEOPLE   America
10 GET DANCIN'   Disco Tex & The Sex-O-Lettes

February 15, 1975

1 YOU'RE NO GOOD   Linda Ronstadt
2 PICK UP THE PIECES   Average White Band
3 BEST OF MY LOVE   Eagles
4 SOME KIND OF WONDERFUL   Grand Funk
5 BLACK WATER   Doobie Brothers
6 FIRE   Ohio Players
7 LONELY PEOPLE   America
8 BOOGIE ON REGGAE WOMAN   Stevie Wonder
9 MY EYES ADORED YOU   Frankie Valli
10 #9 DREAM   John Lennon

February 22, 1975

1 PICK UP THE PIECES   Average White Band
2 BEST OF MY LOVE   Eagles
3 SOME KIND OF WONDERFUL   Grand Funk
4 BLACK WATER   Doobie Brothers
5 HAVE YOU NEVER BEEN MELLOW   Olivia Newton-John
6 LONELY PEOPLE   America
7 MY EYES ADORED YOU   Frankie Valli
8 YOU'RE NO GOOD   Linda Ronstadt
9 #9 DREAM   John Lennon
10 NIGHTINGALE   Carole King

March 1, 1975

1 BEST OF MY LOVE   Eagles
2 HAVE YOU NEVER BEEN MELLOW   Olivia Newton-John
3 BLACK WATER   Doobie Brothers
4 MY EYES ADORED YOU   Frankie Valli
5 SOME KIND OF WONDERFUL   Grand Funk

6 LONELY PEOPLE   America
7 PICK UP THE PIECES   Average White Band
8 LADY MARMALADE   LaBelle
9 NIGHTINGALE   Carole King
10 LADY   Styx

March 8, 1975

1 HAVE YOU NEVER BEEN MELLOW   Olivia Newton-John
2 BLACK WATER   Doobie Brothers
3 MY EYES ADORED YOU   Frankie Valli
4 LADY MARMALADE   LaBelle
5 LONELY PEOPLE   America
6 LADY   Styx
7 BEST OF MY LOVE   Eagles
8 LOVIN' YOU   Minnie Riperton
9 PICK UP THE PIECES   Average White Band
10 CAN'T GET IT OUT OF MY HEAD   Electric Light Orchestra

March 15, 1975

1 BLACK WATER   Doobie Brothers
2 MY EYES ADORED YOU   Frankie Valli
3 LADY MARMALADE   LaBelle
4 HAVE YOU NEVER BEEN MELLOW   Olivia Newton-John
5 LOVIN' YOU   Minnie Riperton
6 LADY   Styx
7 LONELY PEOPLE   America
8 EXPRESS   B. T. Express
9 CAN'T GET IT OUT OF MY HEAD   Electric Light Orchestra
10 DON'T CALL US, WE'LL CALL YOU   Sugarloaf

March 22, 1975

1 MY EYES ADORED YOU   Frankie Valli
2 LADY MARMALADE   LaBelle
3 LOVIN' YOU   Minnie Riperton
4 BLACK WATER   Doobie Brothers
5 HAVE YOU NEVER BEEN MELLOW   Olivia Newton-John
6 EXPRESS   B. T. Express
7 YOU ARE SO BEAUTIFUL   Joe Cocker
8 POETRY MAN   Phoebe Snow
9 NO NO SONG   Ringo Starr
10 DON'T CALL US, WE'LL CALL YOU   Sugarloaf

March 29, 1975

2 LADY MARMALADE   LaBelle
2 LOVIN' YOU   Minnie Riperton
3 PHILADELPHIA FREEDOM   Elton John
4 EXPRESS   B. T. Express
5 YOU ARE SO BEAUTIFUL   Joe Cocker
6 NO NO SONG   Ringo Starr
7 POETRY MAN   Phoebe Snow
8 MY EYES ADORED YOU   Frankie Valli
9 DON'T CALL US, WE'LL CALL YOU   Sugarloaf
10 HAVE YOU NEVER BEEN MELLOW   Olivia Newton-John

April 5, 1975

1 LOVIN' YOU   Minnie Riperton
2 PHILADELPHIA FREEDOM   Elton John
3 NO NO SONG   Ringo Starr
4 EXPRESS   B. T. Express
5 YOU ARE SO BEAUTIFUL   Joe Cocker
6 POETRY MAN   Phoebe Snow
7 LADY MARMALADE   LaBelle
8 HEY WON'T YOU PLAY ANOTHER SOMEBODY DONE SOMEBODY WRONG SONG   B. J. Thomas
9 HAVE YOU NEVER BEEN MELLOW   Olivia Newton-John
10 MY EYES ADORED YOU   Frankie Valli

April 12, 1975

1 PHILADELPHIA FREEDOM   Elton John
2 LOVIN' YOU   Minnie Riperton
3 NO NO SONG   Ringo Starr
4 EXPRESS   B. T. Express
5 POETRY MAN   Phoebe Snow
6 HEY WON'T YOU PLAY ANOTHER SOMEBODY DONE
     SOMEBODY WRONG SONG   B. J. Thomas
7 LADY MARMALADE   LaBelle
8 CHEVY VAN   Sammy Johns
9 WHAT AM I GONNA DO WITH YOU   Barry White
10 ONCE YOU GET STARTED   Rufus featuring Chaka Khan

April 19, 1975

1 PHILADELPHIA FREEDOM   Elton John
2 HEY WON'T YOU PLAY ANOTHER SOMEBODY DONE
     SOMEBODY WRONG SONG   B. J. Thomas
3 LOVIN' YOU   Minnie Riperton
4 NO NO SONG   Ringo Starr
5 HE DON'T LOVE YOU LIKE I LOVE YOU   Dawn
6 SUPERNATURAL THING   Ben E. King
7 CHEVY VAN   Sammy Johns
8 WHAT AM I GONNA DO WITH YOU   Barry White
9 EMMA   Hot Chocolate
10 BEFORE THE NEXT TEARDROP FALLS   Freddy Fender

April 26, 1975

1 HEY WON'T YOU PLAY ANOTHER SOMEBODY DONE
     SOMEBODY WRONG SONG   B. J. Thomas
2 PHILADELPHIA FREEDOM   Elton John
3 HE DON'T LOVE YOU LIKE I LOVE YOU   Dawn
4 LOVIN' YOU   Minnie Riperton
5 SUPERNATURAL THING   Ben E. King
6 CHEVY VAN   Sammy Johns
7 BEFORE THE NEXT TEARDROP FALLS   Freddy Fender
8 EMMA   Hot Chocolate
9 WHAT AM I GONNA DO WITH YOU   Barry White
10 WALKING IN RHYTHM   Blackbyrds

May 3, 1975

1 HE DON'T LOVE YOU LIKE I LOVE YOU   Dawn
2 HEY WON'T YOU PLAY ANOTHER SOMEBODY DONE
     SOMEBODY WRONG SONG   B. J. Thomas
3 BEFORE THE NEXT TEARDROP FALLS   Freddy Fender
4 PHILADELPHIA FREEDOM   Elton John
5 CHEVY VAN   Sammy Johns
6 JACKIE BLUE   Ozark Mountain Daredevils
7 SHINING STAR   Earth, Wind & Fire
8 WALKING IN RHYTHM   Blackbyrds
9 LONG TALL GLASSES (I CAN DANCE)   Leo Sayer
10 ONLY YESTERDAY   Carpenters

May 10, 1975

1 HE DON'T LOVE YOU LIKE I LOVE YOU   Dawn
2 BEFORE THE NEXT TEARDROP FALLS   Freddy Fender
3 HEY WON'T YOU PLAY ANOTHER SOMEBODY DONE
     SOMEBODY WRONG SONG   B. J. Thomas
4 JACKIE BLUE   Ozark Mountain Daredevils
5 SHINING STAR   Earth, Wind & Fire
6 WALKING IN RHYTHM   Blackbyrds
7 PHILADELPHIA FREEDOM   Elton John
8 ONLY YESTERDAY   Carpenters
9 LONG TALL GLASSES (I CAN DANCE)   Leo Sayer
10 I DON'T LIKE TO SLEEP ALONE   Paul Anka

May 17, 1975

1 HE DON'T LOVE YOU LIKE I LOVE YOU   Dawn
2 BEFORE THE NEXT TEARDROP FALLS   Freddy Fender
3 JACKIE BLUE   Ozark Mountain Daredevils
4 SHINING STAR   Earth, Wind & Fire
5 ONLY YESTERDAY   Carpenters
6 WALKING IN RHYTHM   Blackbyrds
7 THANK GOD I'M A COUNTRY BOY   John Denver
8 HOW LONG   Ace
9 I DON'T LIKE TO SLEEP ALONE   Paul Anka
10 HEY WON'T YOU PLAY ANOTHER SOMEBODY DONE
     SOMEBODY WRONG SONG   B. J. Thomas

May 24, 1975

1 SHINING STAR   Earth, Wind & Fire
2 BEFORE THE NEXT TEARDROP FALLS   Freddy Fender
3 JACKIE BLUE   Ozark Mountain Daredevils
4 ONLY YESTERDAY   Carpenters
5 THANK GOD I'M A COUNTRY BOY   John Denver
6 HOW LONG   Ace
7 HE DON'T LOVE YOU LIKE I LOVE YOU   Dawn
8 I DON'T LIKE TO SLEEP ALONE   Paul Anka
9 BAD TIME   Grand Funk
10 OLD DAYS   Chicago

May 31, 1975

1 BEFORE THE NEXT TEARDROP FALLS   Freddy Fender
2 THANK GOD I'M A COUNTRY BOY   John Denver
3 HOW LONG   Ace
4 ONLY YESTERDAY   Carpenters
5 SISTER GOLDEN HAIR   America
6 BAD TIME   Grand Funk
7 OLD DAYS   Chicago
8 SHINING STAR   Earth, Wind & Fire
9 I DON'T LIKE TO SLEEP ALONE   Paul Anka
10 WHEN WILL I BE LOVED   Linda Ronstadt

June 7, 1975

1 THANK GOD I'M A COUNTRY BOY   John Denver
2 SISTER GOLDEN HAIR   America
3 HOW LONG   Ace
4 BAD TIME   Grand Funk
5 OLD DAYS   Chicago
6 WHEN WILL I BE LOVED   Linda Ronstadt
7 BEFORE THE NEXT TEARDROP FALLS   Freddy Fender
8 I'M NOT LISA   Jessi Colter
9 LOVE WON'T LET ME WAIT   Major Harris
10 PHILADELPHIA FREEDOM   Elton John

June 14, 1975

1 SISTER GOLDEN HAIR   America
2 LOVE WILL KEEP US TOGETHER   Captain & Tennille
3 WHEN WILL I BE LOVED   Linda Ronstadt
4 BAD TIME   Grand Funk
5 OLD DAYS   Chicago
6 I'M NOT LISA   Jessi Colter
7 LOVE WON'T LET ME WAIT   Major Harris
8 THANK GOD I'M A COUNTRY BOY   John Denver
9 PHILADELPHIA FREEDOM   Elton John
10 GET DOWN, GET DOWN (GET ON THE FLOOR)   Joe
     Simon

June 21, 1975

1 LOVE WILL KEEP US TOGETHER   Captain & Tennille
2 WHEN WILL I BE LOVED   Linda Ronstadt
3 WILDFIRE   Michael Martin Murphy

Captain & Tennille
The Captain and the daughter of forties band leader Frank Tennille have a #1 hit with ``Love Will Keep Us Together'' (Jul. 5).

4 I'M NOT LISA   Jessi Colter
5 LOVE WON'T LET ME WAIT   Major Harris
6 SISTER GOLDEN HAIR   America
7 THE HUSTLE   Van McCoy
8 GET DOWN, GET DOWN (GET ON THE FLOOR)   Joe Simon
9 LISTEN TO WHAT THE MAN SAID   Wings
10 CUT THE CAKE   Average White Band

June 28, 1975
1 LOVE WILL KEEP US TOGETHER   Captain & Tennille
2 WHEN WILL I BE LOVED   Linda Ronstadt
3 WILDFIRE   Michael Martin Murphy
4 I'M NOT LISA   Jessi Colter
5 LOVE WON'T LET ME WAIT   Major Harris
6 THE HUSTLE   Van McCoy
7 LISTEN TO WHAT THE MAN SAID   Wings
8 GET DOWN, GET DOWN (GET ON THE FLOOR)   Joe Simon
9 MAGIC   Pilot
10 CUT THE CAKE   Average White Band

July 5, 1975
1 LOVE WILL KEEP US TOGETHER   Captain & Tennille
2 THE HUSTLE   Van McCoy
3 LISTEN TO WHAT THE MAN SAID   Wings
4 WILDFIRE   Michael Martin Murphy
5 LOVE WON'T LET ME WAIT   Major Harris
6 MAGIC   Pilot
7 I'M NOT LISA   Jessi Colter
8 WHEN WILL I BE LOVED   Linda Ronstadt
9 ONE OF THESE NIGHTS   Eagles
10 PLEASE MR. PLEASE   Olivia Newton-John

July 12, 1975
1 LOVE WILL KEEP US TOGETHER   Captain & Tennille
2 THE HUSTLE   Van McCoy
3 LISTEN TO WHAT THE MAN SAID   Wings
4 WILDFIRE   Michael Martin Murphy
5 MAGIC   Pilot
6 PLEASE MR. PLEASE   Olivia Newton-John
7 ONE OF THESE NIGHTS   Eagles
8 SWEARIN' TO GOD   Frankie Valli
9 WHEN WILL I BE LOVED   Linda Ronstadt
10 I'M NOT LISA   Jessi Colter

July 19, 1975
1 LISTEN TO WHAT THE MAN SAID   Wings
2 THE HUSTLE   Van McCoy
3 I'M NOT IN LOVE   10 CC
4 ONE OF THESE NIGHTS   Eagles
5 PLEASE MR. PLEASE   Olivia Newton-John
6 MAGIC   Pilot
7 SWEARIN' TO GOD   Frankie Valli
8 LOVE WILL KEEP US TOGETHER   Captain & Tennille
9 JIVE TALKIN'   Bee Gees
10 ROCKIN' CHAIR   Gwen McCrae

July 16, 1975
1 THE HUSTLE   Van McCoy
2 I'M NOT IN LOVE   10 CC
3 ONE OF THESE NIGHTS   Eagles
4 PLEASE MR. PLEASE   Olivia Newton-John
5 LISTEN TO WHAT THE MAN SAID   Wings
6 SWEARIN' TO GOD   Frankie Valli
7 JIVE TALKIN'   Bee Gees

8 SOMEONE SAVED MY LIFE TONIGHT   Elton John
9 MIDNIGHT BLUE   Melissa Manchester
10 ROCKIN' CHAIR   Gwen McCrae

August 2, 1975
1 ONE OF THESE NIGHTS   Eagles
2 I'M NOT IN LOVE   10 CC
3 JIVE TALKIN'   Bee Gees
4 PLEASE MR. PLEASE   Olivia Newton-John
5 THE HUSTLE   Van McCoy
6 SOMEONE SAVED MY LIFE TONIGHT   Elton John
7 MIDNIGHT BLUE   Melissa Manchester
8 LISTEN TO WHAT THE MAN SAID   Wings
9 ROCKIN' CHAIR   Gwen McCrae
10 DYNOMITE   Bazuka

August 9, 1975
1 JIVE TALKIN'   Bee Gees
2 I'M NOT IN LOVE   10 CC
3 PLEASE MR. PLEASE   Olivia Newton-John
4 ONE OF THESE NIGHTS   Eagles
5 SOMEONE SAVED MY LIFE TONIGHT   Elton John
6 MIDNIGHT BLUE   Melissa Manchester
7 RHINESTONE COWBOY   Glen Campbell
8 WHY CAN'T WE BE FRIENDS?   War
9 HOW SWEET IT IS TO BE LOVED BY YOU   James Taylor
10 ROCKFORD FILES   Mike Post

August 16, 1975
1 JIVE TALKIN'   Bee Gees
2 ONE OF THESE NIGHTS   Eagles
3 PLEASE MR. PLEASE   Olivia Newton-John
4 SOMEONE SAVED MY LIFE TONIGHT   Elton John
5 FALLIN' IN LOVE   Hamilton, Joe Frank & Reynolds
6 RHINESTONE COWBOY   Glen Campbell
7 WHY CAN'T WE BE FRIENDS?   War
8 HOW SWEET IT IS TO BE LOVED BY YOU   James Taylor
9 MIDNIGHT BLUE   Melissa Manchester
10 ROCKFORD FILES   Mike Post

August 23, 1975
1 FALLIN' IN LOVE   Hamilton, Joe Frank & Reynolds
2 ONE OF THESE NIGHTS   Eagles
3 GET DOWN TONIGHT   K. C. & The Sunshine Band
4 JIVE TALKIN'   Bee Gees
5 RHINESTONE COWBOY   Glen Campbell
6 WHY CAN'T WE BE FRIENDS?   War
7 HOW SWEET IT IS TO BE LOVED BY YOU   James Taylor
8 SOMEONE SAVED MY LIFE TONIGHT   Elton John
9 AT SEVENTEEN   Janis Ian
10 PLEASE MR. PLEASE   Olivia Newton-John

August 30, 1975
1 GET DOWN TONIGHT   K. C. & The Sunshine Band
2 FALLIN' IN LOVE   Hamilton, Joe Frank & Reynolds
3 RHINESTONE COWBOY   Glen Campbell
4 ONE OF THESE NIGHTS   Eagles
5 HOW SWEET IT IS TO BE LOVED BY YOU   James Taylor
6 JIVE TALKIN'   Bee Gees
7 AT SEVENTEEN   Janis Ian
8 SOMEONE SAVED MY LIFE TONIGHT   Elton John
9 WHY CAN'T WE BE FRIENDS?   War
10 FIGHT THE POWER   Isley Brothers

September 6, 1975
1 RHINESTONE COWBOY   Glen Campbell

309

Glen Campbell

``Rhinestone Cowboy'' is a #1 hit for Glen (Sep. 6).

John Denver

John wasn't sorry when ``I'm Sorry'' peaked at #1 (Sep. 27).

2	FALLIN' IN LOVE Hamilton, Joe Frank & Reynolds
3	GET DOWN TONIGHT K. C. & The Sunshine Band
4	AT SEVENTEEN Janis Ian
5	HOW SWEET IT IS TO BE LOVED BY YOU James Taylor
6	JIVE TALKIN' Bee Gees
7	FAME David Bowie
8	FIGHT THE POWER Isley Brothers
9	COULD IT BE MAGIC Pilot
10	ONE OF THESE NIGHTS Eagles

September 13, 1975

1	RHINESTONE COWBOY Glen Campbell
2	FALLIN' IN LOVE Hamilton, Joe Frank & Reynolds
3	AT SEVENTEEN Janis Ian
4	GET DOWN TONIGHT K. C. & The Sunshine Band
5	FAME David Bowie
6	FIGHT THE POWER Isley Brothers
7	COULD IT BE MAGIC Pilot
8	I'M SORRY John Denver
9	RUN JOEY RUN David Geddes
10	WASTED DAYS AND WASTED NIGHTS Freddy Fender

September 20, 1975

1	FAME David Bowie
2	RHINESTONE COWBOY Glen Campbell
3	AT SEVENTEEN Janis Ian
4	I'M SORRY John Denver
5	FIGHT THE POWER Isley Brothers
6	COULD IT BE MAGIC Pilot
7	RUN JOEY RUN David Geddes
8	FALLIN' IN LOVE Hamilton, Joe Frank & Reynolds
9	WASTED DAYS AND WASTED NIGHTS Freddy Fender
10	FEEL LIKE MAKIN' LOVE Bad Company

September 27, 1975

1	I'M SORRY John Denver
2	FAME David Bowie
3	RHINESTONE COWBOY Glen Campbell
4	FIGHT THE POWER Isley Brothers
5	RUN JOEY RUN David Geddes
6	COULD IT BE MAGIC Pilot
7	AT SEVENTEEN Janis Ian
8	WASTED DAYS AND WASTED NIGHTS Freddy Fender
9	BALLROOM BLITZ Sweet
10	FEEL LIKE MAKIN' LOVE Bad Company

October 4, 1975

1	FAME David Bowie
2	I'M SORRY John Denver
3	RHINESTONE COWBOY Glen Campbell
4	RUN JOEY RUN David Geddes
5	MR. JAWS Dickie Goodman
6	BAD BLOOD Neil Sedaka
7	BALLROOM BLITZ Sweet
8	DANCE WITH ME Orleans
9	AIN'T NO WAY TO TREAT A LADY Styx
10	ROCKY Austin Roberts

October 11, 1975

1	BAD BLOOD Neil Sedaka
2	I'M SORRY John Denver
3	FAME David Bowie
4	MR. JAWS Dickie Goodman
5	MIRACLES Jefferson Starship
6	BALLROOM BLITZ Sweet
7	DANCE WITH ME Orleans

  8   AIN'T NO WAY TO TREAT A LADY   Styx
  9   ROCKY   Austin Roberts
10   LYIN' EYES   Eagles

October 18, 1975
  1   BAD BLOOD   Neil Sedaka
  2   I'M SORRY   John Denver
  3   MIRACLES   Jefferson Starship
  4   LYIN' EYES   Eagles
  5   BALLROOM BLITZ   Sweet
  6   DANCE WITH ME   Orleans
  7   FEELINGS   Morris Alpert
  8   AIN'T NO WAY TO TREAT A LADY   Styx
  9   GAMES PEOPLE PLAY   Joe South
10   WHO LOVES YOU   Four Seasons

October 25, 1975
  1   BAD BLOOD   Neil Sedaka
  2   I'M SORRY   John Denver
  3   MIRACLES   Jefferson Starship
  4   LYIN' EYES   Eagles
  5   GAMES PEOPLE PLAY   Joe South
  6   FEELINGS   Morris Alpert
  7   WHO LOVES YOU   Four Seasons
  8   ISLAND GIRL   Elton John
  9   BALLROOM BLITZ   Sweet
10   IT ONLY TAKES A MINUTE   Tavares

November 11, 1975
  1   ISLAND GIRL   Elton John
  2   CALYPSO/I'M SORRY   John Denver
  3   MIRACLES   Jefferson Starship
  4   LYIN' EYES   Eagles
  5   GAMES PEOPLE PLAY   Joe South
  6   WHO LOVES YOU   Four Seasons
  7   FEELINGS   Morris Alpert
  8   BAD BLOOD   Neil Sedaka
  9   HEAT WAVE/LOVE IS A ROSE   Linda Ronstadt
10   THIS WILL BE   Natalie Cole

November 8, 1975
  1   ISLAND GIRL   Elton John
  2   LYIN' EYES   Eagles
  3   CALYPSO/I'M SORRY   John Denver
  4   WHO LOVES YOU   Four Seasons
  5   MIRACLES   Jefferson Starship
  6   HEAT WAVE/LOVE IS A ROSE   Linda Ronstadt
  7   GAMES PEOPLE PLAY   Joe South
  8   THIS WILL BE   Natalie Cole
  9   FEELINGS   Morris Alpert
10   THE WAY I WANT TO TOUCH YOU   Captain & Tennille

November 15, 1975
  1   ISLAND GIRL   Elton John
  2   LYIN' EYES   Eagles
  3   WHO LOVES YOU   Four Seasons
  4   MIRACLES   Jefferson Starship
  5   HEAT WAVE/LOVE IS A ROSE   Linda Ronstadt
  6   THAT'S THE WAY (I LIKE IT)   K. C. & The Sunshine Band
  7   THIS WILL BE   Natalie Cole
  8   FEELINGS   Morris Alpert
  9   THE WAY I WANT TO TOUCH YOU   Captain & Tennille
10   LOW RIDER   War

November 22, 1975
  1   THAT'S THE WAY (I LIKE IT)   K. C. & The Sunshine Band

  2   FLY, ROBIN, FLY   Silver Convention
  3   WHO LOVES YOU   Four Seasons
  4   ISLAND GIRL   Elton John
  5   THE WAY I WANT TO TOUCH YOU   Captain & Tennille
  6   THIS WILL BE   Natalie Cole
  7   FEELINGS   Morris Alpert
  8   LOW RIDER   War
  9   SKY HIGH   Jigsaw
10   LET'S DO IT AGAIN   Staple Singers

November 29, 1975
  1   FLY, ROBIN, FLY   Silver Convention
  2   THAT'S THE WAY (I LIKE IT)   K. C. & The Sunshine Band
  3   ISLAND GIRL   Elton John
  4   THE WAY I WANT TO TOUCH YOU   Captain & Tennille
  5   LET'S DO IT AGAIN   Staple Singers
  6   SKY HIGH   Jigsaw
  7   LOW RIDER   War
  8   THIS WILL BE   Natalie Cole
  9   NIGHTS ON BROADWAY   Bee Gees
10   WHO LOVES YOU   Four Seasons

December 6, 1975
  1   FLY, ROBIN, FLY   Silver Convention
  2   THAT'S THE WAY (I LIKE IT)   K. C. & The Sunshine Band
  3   SKY HIGH   Jigsaw
  4   LET'S DO IT AGAIN   Staple Singers
  5   THE WAY I WANT TO TOUCH YOU   Captain & Tennille
  6   ISLAND GIRL   Elton John
  7   LOW RIDER   War
  8   NIGHTS ON BROADWAY   Bee Gees
  9   SATURDAY NIGHT   Bay City Rollers
10   MY LITTLE TOWN   Simon & Garfunkel

December 13, 1975
  1   FLY, ROBIN, FLY   Silver Convention
  2   LET'S DO IT AGAIN   Staple Singers
  3   SKY HIGH   Jigsaw
  4   THAT'S THE WAY (I LIKE IT)   K. C. & The Sunshine Band
  5   SATURDAY NIGHT   Bay City Rollers
  6   LOVE ROLLERCOASTER   Ohio Players
  7   NIGHTS ON BROADWAY   Bee Gees
  8   THEME FROM "MAHOGANY" (DO YOU KNOW WHERE YOU'RE GOING TO)   Diana Ross
  9   MY LITTLE TOWN   Simon & Garfunkel
10   FOX ON THE RUN   Sweet

December 20, 1975
  1   THAT'S THE WAY (I LIKE IT)   K. C. & The Sunshine Band
  2   LET'S DO IT AGAIN   Staple Singers
  3   FLY, ROBIN, FLY   Silver Convention
  4   SATURDAY NIGHT   Bay City Rollers
  5   LOVE ROLLERCOASTER   Ohio Players
  6   THEME FROM "MAHOGANY" (DO YOU KNOW WHERE YOU'RE GOING TO)   Diana Ross
  7   SKY HIGH   Jigsaw
  8   I WRITE THE SONGS   Barry Manilow
  9   FOX ON THE RUN   Sweet
10   NIGHTS ON BROADWAY   Bee Gees

December 27, 1975
  1   LET'S DO IT AGAIN   Staple Singers
  2   SATURDAY NIGHT   Bay City Rollers
  3   THAT'S THE WAY (I LIKE IT)   K. C. & The Sunshine Band
  4   LOVE ROLLERCOASTER   Ohio Players
  5   THEME FROM "MAHOGANY" (DO YOU KNOW WHERE YOU'RE GOING TO)   Diana Ross

6 I WRITE THE SONGS   Barry Manilow
7 CONVOY   C. W. McCall
8 FOX ON THE RUN   Sweet
9 FLY, ROBIN, FLY   Silver Convention
10 I LOVE MUSIC   O'Jays

January 3, 1976
1 SATURDAY NIGHT   Bay City Rollers
2 I WRITE THE SONGS   Barry Manilow
3 THEME FROM "MAHOGANY" (DO YOU KNOW WHERE YOU'RE GOING TO)   Diana Ross
4 LOVE ROLLERCOASTER   Ohio Players
5 LET'S DO IT AGAIN   Staple Singers
6 CONVOY   C. W. McCall
7 FOX ON THE RUN   Sweet
8 THAT'S THE WAY (I LIKE IT)   K. C. & The Sunshine Band
9 I LOVE MUSIC   O'Jays
10 FLY, ROBIN, FLY   Silver Convention

January 10, 1976
1 CONVOY   C. W. McCall *
2 I WRITE THE SONGS   Barry Manilow
3 THEME FROM "MAHOGANY" (DO YOU KNOW WHERE YOU'RE GOING TO)   Diana Ross
4 LOVE ROLLERCOASTER   Ohio Players
5 SATURDAY NIGHT   Bay City Rollers
6 FOX ON THE RUN   Sweet
7 I LOVE MUSIC   O'Jays
8 THAT'S THE WAY (I LIKE IT)   K. C. & The Sunshine Band
9 LOVE TO LOVE YOU BABY   Donna Summer
10 TIME OF YOUR LIFE   Paul Anka
  Note: * The CB (citizen's band) radio craze sweeps the nation.

January 17, 1976
1 I WRITE THE SONGS   Barry Manilow
2 THEME FROM "MAHOGANY" (DO YOU KNOW WHERE YOU'RE GOING TO)   Diana Ross
3 CONVOY   C. W. McCall *
4 LOVE ROLLERCOASTER   Ohio Players
5 FOX ON THE RUN   Sweet
6 I LOVE MUSIC   O'Jays
7 LOVE TO LOVE YOU BABY   Donna Summer
8 YOU SEXY THING   Hot Chocolate
9 TIME OF YOUR LIFE   Paul Anka
10 WALK AWAY FROM LOVE   David Ruffin
  Note: * The CB (citizen's band) radio craze sweeps the nation.

January 24, 1976
1 THEME FROM "MAHOGANY" (DO YOU KNOW WHERE YOU'RE GOING TO)   Diana Ross
2 I WRITE THE SONGS   Barry Manilow
3 LOVE ROLLERCOASTER   Ohio Players
4 LOVE TO LOVE YOU BABY   Donna Summer
5 I LOVE MUSIC   O'Jays
6 YOU SEXY THING   Hot Chocolate
7 CONVOY   C. W. McCall *
8 TIME OF YOUR LIFE   Paul Anka
9 WALK AWAY FROM LOVE   David Ruffin
10 SING A SONG   Earth, Wind & Fire
  Note: * The CB (citizen's band) radio craze sweeps the nation.

January 31, 1976
1 LOVE ROLLERCOASTER   Ohio Players

2 I WRITE THE SONGS   Barry Manilow
3 LOVE TO LOVE YOU BABY   Donna Summer
4 YOU SEXY THING   Hot Chocolate
5 I LOVE MUSIC   O'Jays
6 CONVOY   C. W. McCall *
7 SING A SONG   Earth, Wind & Fire
8 TIME OF YOUR LIFE   Paul Anka
9 WALK AWAY FROM LOVE   David Ruffin
10 50 WAYS TO LEAVE YOUR LOVER   Paul Simon
  Note: * The CB (citizen's band) radio craze sweeps the nation.

February 7, 1976
1 50 WAYS TO LEAVE YOUR LOVER   Paul Simon
2 LOVE TO LOVE YOU BABY   Donna Summer
3 YOU SEXY THING   Hot Chocolate
4 I WRITE THE SONGS   Barry Manilow
5 SING A SONG   Earth, Wind & Fire
6 LOVE ROLLERCOASTER   Ohio Players
7 TIME OF YOUR LIFE   Paul Anka
8 THEME FROM "S.W.A.T."   Rhythm Heritage
9 CONVOY   C. W. McCall *
10 BREAKING UP IS HARD TO DO   Neil Sedaka
  Note: * The CB (citizen's band) radio craze sweeps the nation.

February 14, 1976
1 50 WAYS TO LEAVE YOUR LOVER   Paul Simon
2 LOVE TO LOVE YOU BABY   Donna Summer
3 YOU SEXY THING   Hot Chocolate
4 THEME FROM "S.W.A.T."   Rhythm Heritage
5 SING A SONG   Earth, Wind & Fire

Paul Simon

Solo Simon's ``50 Ways To Leave Your Lover''
was #1 for three weeks in February.

6   I WRITE THE SONGS   Barry Manilow
7   LOVE ROLLERCOASTER   Ohio Players
8   LOVE MACHINE   Miracles
9   BREAKING UP IS HARD TO DO   Neil Sedaka
10   EVIL WOMAN   Electric Light Orchestra

February 21, 1976
1   50 WAYS TO LEAVE YOUR LOVER   Paul Simon
2   THEME FROM "S.W.A.T."   Rhythm Heritage
3   YOU SEXY THING   Hot Chocolate
4   LOVE TO LOVE YOU BABY   Donna Summer
5   LOVE MACHINE   Miracles
6   I WRITE THE SONGS   Barry Manilow
7   ALL BY MYSELF   Eric Carmen
8   BREAKING UP IS HARD TO DO   Neil Sedaka
9   TAKE IT TO THE LIMIT   Eagles
10   EVIL WOMAN   Electric Light Orchestra

February 28, 1976
1   THEME FROM "S.W.A.T."   Rhythm Heritage
2   50 WAYS TO LEAVE YOUR LOVER   Paul Simon
3   LOVE MACHINE   Miracles
4   ALL BY MYSELF   Eric Carmen
5   DECEMBER 1963 (OH WHAT A NIGHT)   Four Seasons
6   YOU SEXY THING   Hot Chocolate
7   TAKE IT TO THE LIMIT   Eagles
8   DREAM WEAVER   Gary Wright
9   LONELY NIGHT (ANGEL FACE)   Captain & Tennille
10   LOVE HURTS   Nazareth

March 6, 1976
1   LOVE MACHINE   Miracles
2   ALL BY MYSELF   Eric Carmen
3   DECEMBER 1963 (OH WHAT A NIGHT)   Four Seasons
4   THEME FROM "S.W.A.T."   Rhythm Heritage
5   TAKE IT TO THE LIMIT   Eagles
6   DREAM WEAVER   Gary Wright
7   LONELY NIGHT   Captain & Tennille
8   50 WAYS TO LEAVE YOUR LOVER   Paul Simon
9   LOVE HURTS   Nazareth
10   YOU SEXY THING   Hot Chocolate

March 13, 1976
1   DECEMBER 1963 (OH WHAT A NIGHT)   Four Seasons
2   ALL BY MYSELF   Eric Carmen
3   LOVE MACHINE   Miracles
4   TAKE IT TO THE LIMIT   Eagles
5   DREAM WEAVER   Gary Wright
6   LONELY NIGHT   Captain & Tennille
7   THEME FROM "S.W.A.T."   Rhythm Heritage
8   LOVE HURTS   Nazareth
9   SWEET THING   Rufus featuring Chaka Khan
10   JUNK FOOD JUNKIE   Keep On Smilin'

March 20, 1976
1   DECEMBER 1963 (OH WHAT A NIGHT)   Four Seasons
2   ALL BY MYSELF   Eric Carmen
3   DREAM WEAVER   Gary Wright
4   TAKE IT TO THE LIMIT   Eagles
5   LONELY NIGHT   Captain & Tennille
6   LOVE MACHINE   Miracles
7   SWEET THING   Rufus featuring Chaka Khan
8   DREAM ON   Aerosmith
9   JUNK FOOD JUNKIE   Keep On Smilin'
10   DISCO LADY   Styx

March 27, 1976
1   DECEMBER 1963 (OH WHAT A NIGHT)   Four Seasons
2   DREAM WEAVER   Gary Wright
3   LONELY NIGHT   Captain & Tennille
4   ALL BY MYSELF   Eric Carmen
5   DISCO LADY   Styx
6   SWEET THING   Rufus featuring Chaka Khan
7   DREAM ON   Aerosmith
8   LET YOUR LOVE FLOW   Bellamy Brothers
9   RIGHT BACK WHERE WE STARTED FROM   Maxine Nightingale
10   MONEY HONEY   Bay City Rollers

April 3, 1976
1   DISCO LADY   Styx
2   DREAM WEAVER   Gary Wright
3   LONELY NIGHT   Captain & Tennille
4   LET YOUR LOVE FLOW   Bellamy Brothers
5   SWEET THING   Rufus featuring Chaka Khan
6   RIGHT BACK WHERE WE STARTED FROM   Maxine Nightingale
7   DREAM ON   Aerosmith
8   DECEMBER 1963 (OH WHAT A NIGHT)   Four Seasons
9   MONEY HONEY   Bay City Rollers
10   GOLDEN YEARS   David Bowie

April 10, 1976
1   DISCO LADY   Styx
2   DREAM WEAVER   Gary Wright
3   LONELY NIGHT   Captain & Tennille
4   LET YOUR LOVE FLOW   Bellamy Brothers
5   RIGHT BACK WHERE WE STARTED FROM   Maxine Nightingale
6   DREAM ON   Aerosmith
7   BOOGIE FEVER   Sylvers
8   ONLY SIXTEEN   Dr. Hook
9   SWEET LOVE   Commodores
10   GOLDEN YEARS   David Bowie

April 17, 1976
1   DISCO LADY   Styx
2   LET YOUR LOVE FLOW   Bellamy Brothers
3   RIGHT BACK WHERE WE STARTED FROM   Maxine Nightingale
4   LONELY NIGHT   Captain & Tennille
5   BOOGIE FEVER   Sylvers
6   ONLY SIXTEEN   Dr. Hook
7   SWEET LOVE   Commodores
8   DREAM WEAVER   Gary Wright
9   SHOW ME THE WAY   Peter Frampton
10   BOHEMIAN RHAPSODY   Queen

April 24, 1976
1   DISCO LADY   Styx
2   LET YOUR LOVE FLOW   Bellamy Brothers
3   RIGHT BACK WHERE WE STARTED FROM   Maxine Nightingale
4   BOOGIE FEVER   Sylvers
5   SWEET LOVE   Commodores
6   ONLY SIXTEEN   Dr. Hook
7   WELCOME BACK   John Sebastian
8   SHOW ME THE WAY   Peter Frampton
9   BOHEMIAN RHAPSODY   Queen
10   FOOLED AROUND AND FELL IN LOVE   Elvin Bishop

The Bellamy Brothers

"Let Your Love Flow" peaked at #1 (May 1).

May 1, 1976

1. LET YOUR LOVE FLOW   Bellamy Brothers
2. RIGHT BACK WHERE WE STARTED FROM   Maxine Nightingale
3. BOOGIE FEVER   Sylvers
4. WELCOME BACK   John Sebastian
5. SWEET LOVE   Commodores
6. DISCO LADY   Styx
7. SHOW ME THE WAY   Peter Frampton
8. FOOLED AROUND AND FELL IN LOVE   Elvin Bishop
9. BOHEMIAN RHAPSODY   Queen
10. LOVE HANGOVER   Diana Ross

May 8, 1976

1. WELCOME BACK   John Sebastian
2. RIGHT BACK WHERE WE STARTED FROM   Maxine Nightingale
3. BOOGIE FEVER   Sylvers
4. FOOLED AROUND AND FELL IN LOVE   Elvin Bishop
5. SILLY LOVE SONGS   Wings
6. SHOW ME THE WAY   Peter Frampton
7. LOVE HANGOVER   Diana Ross
8. GET UP AND BOOGIE   Silver Convention
9. LET YOUR LOVE FLOW   Bellamy Brothers
10. DISCO LADY   Styx

May 15, 1976

1. BOOGIE FEVER   Sylvers
2. WELCOME BACK   John Sebastian
3. SILLY LOVE SONGS   Wings
4. FOOLED AROUND AND FELL IN LOVE   Elvin Bishop
5. LOVE HANGOVER   Diana Ross
6. SHOW ME THE WAY   Peter Frampton
7. GET UP AND BOOGIE   Silver Convention
8. RIGHT BACK WHERE WE STARTED FROM   Maxine Nightingale
9. HAPPY DAYS   Pratt & McClain
10. SHANNON   Henry Gross

May 22, 1976

1. SILLY LOVE SONGS   Wings
2. LOVE HANGOVER   Diana Ross
3. FOOLED AROUND AND FELL IN LOVE   Elvin Bishop
4. BOOGIE FEVER   Sylvers
5. GET UP AND BOOGIE   Silver Convention
6. WELCOME BACK   John Sebastian
7. HAPPY DAYS   Pratt & McClain
8. MISTY BLUE   Dorothy Moore
9. SHANNON   Henry Gross
10. TRYIN' TO GET THAT FEELING AGAIN   Barry Manilow

May 29, 1976

1. LOVE HANGOVER   Diana Ross
2. SILLY LOVE SONGS   Wings
3. FOOLED AROUND AND FELL IN LOVE   Elvin Bishop
4. GET UP AND BOOGIE   Silver Convention
5. MISTY BLUE   Dorothy Moore
6. HAPPY DAYS   Pratt & McClain
7. WELCOME BACK   John Sebastian
8. SHANNON   Henry Gross
9. SARA SMILE   Daryl Hall & John Oates
10. TRYIN' TO GET THAT FEELING AGAIN   Barry Manilow

June 5, 1976

1. LOVE HANGOVER   Diana Ross
2. SILLY LOVE SONGS   Wings
3. GET UP AND BOOGIE   Silver Convention
4. MISTY BLUE   Dorothy Moore
5. HAPPY DAYS   Pratt & McClain
6. SHANNON   Henry Gross
7. WELCOME BACK   John Sebastian
8. SARA SMILE   Daryl Hall & John Oates
9. SHOP AROUND   Captain & Tennille
10. FOOL TO CRY   Rolling Stones

June 12, 1976

1. SILLY LOVE SONGS   Wings
2. GET UP AND BOOGIE   Silver Convention
3. MISTY BLUE   Dorothy Moore
4. LOVE HANGOVER   Diana Ross
5. HAPPY DAYS   Pratt & McClain
6. SHANNON   Henry Gross
7. SARA SMILE   Daryl Hall & John Oates
8. SHOP AROUND   Captain & Tennille
9. MORE, MORE, MORE (PART 1)   Andrea True Connection
10. FOOL TO CRY   Rolling Stones

June 19, 1976

1. SILLY LOVE SONGS   Wings
2. GET UP AND BOOGIE   Silver Convention
3. MISTY BLUE   Dorothy Moore
4. LOVE HANGOVER   Diana Ross
5. SARA SMILE   Daryl Hall & John Oates
6. SHANNON   Henry Gross
7. SHOP AROUND   Captain & Tennille
8. MORE, MORE, MORE (PART 1)   Andrea True Connection
9. AFTERNOON DELIGHT   Starland Vocal Band
10. I'LL BE GOOD TO YOU   Brothers Johnson

Top of column (above May 22, 1976):

6. SHOW ME THE WAY   Peter Frampton
7. GET UP AND BOOGIE   Silver Convention
8. RIGHT BACK WHERE WE STARTED FROM   Maxine Nightingale
9. HAPPY DAYS   Pratt & McClain
10. SHANNON   Henry Gross

June 26, 1976
1 SILLY LOVE SONGS   Wings
2 GET UP AND BOOGIE   Silver Convention
3 MISTY BLUE   Dorothy Moore
4 SARA SMILE   Daryl Hall & John Oates
5 SHOP AROUND   Captain & Tennille
6 MORE, MORE, MORE (PART 1)   Andrea True Connection
7 AFTERNOON DELIGHT   Starland Vocal Band
8 LOVE HANGOVER   Diana Ross
9 I'LL BE GOOD TO YOU   Brothers Johnson
10 KISS AND SAY GOODBYE   Manhattans

July 3, 1976
1 SILLY LOVE SONGS   Wings
2 AFTERNOON DELIGHT   Starland Vocal Band
3 MISTY BLUE   Dorothy Moore
4 SARA SMILE   Daryl Hall & John Oates
5 SHOP AROUND   Captain & Tennille
6 MORE, MORE, MORE (PART 1)   Andrea True Connection
7 GET UP AND BOOGIE   Silver Convention
8 I'LL BE GOOD TO YOU   Brothers Johnson
9 KISS AND SAY GOODBYE   Manhattans
10 LOVE IS ALIVE   Gary Wright

July 10, 1976
1 AFTERNOON DELIGHT   Starland Vocal Band
2 KISS AND SAY GOODBYE   Manhattans
3 I'LL BE GOOD TO YOU   Brothers Johnson
4 SHOP AROUND   Captain & Tennille
5 MORE, MORE, MORE (PART 1)   Andrea True Connection
6 SILLY LOVE SONGS   Wings
7 MISTY BLUE   Dorothy Moore
8 LOVE IS ALIVE   Gary Wright
9 SARA SMILE   Daryl Hall & John Oates
10 GOT TO GET YOU INTO MY LIFE   Beatles

July 17, 1976
1 AFTERNOON DELIGHT   Starland Vocal Band
2 KISS AND SAY GOODBYE   Manhattans
3 I'LL BE GOOD TO YOU   Brothers Johnson
4 MORE, MORE, MORE (PART 1)   Andrea True Connection
5 MOONLIGHT FEELS RIGHT   Starbuck
6 LOVE IS ALIVE   Gary Wright
7 SHOP AROUND   Captain & Tennille
8 GOT TO GET YOU INTO MY LIFE   Beatles
9 SILLY LOVE SONGS   Wings
10 ROCK AND ROLL MUSIC   Beach Boys

July 24, 1976
1 KISS AND SAY GOODBYE   Manhattans
2 AFTERNOON DELIGHT   Starland Vocal Band
3 I'LL BE GOOD TO YOU   Brothers Johnson
4 MOONLIGHT FEELS RIGHT   Starbuck
5 LOVE IS ALIVE   Gary Wright
6 GET CLOSER   Seals & Crofts
7 GOT TO GET YOU INTO MY LIFE   Beatles
8 DON'T GO BREAKING MY HEART   Elton John & Kiki Dee
9 ROCK AND ROLL MUSIC   Beach Boys
10 LET HER IN   John Travolta

July 31, 1976
1 KISS AND SAY GOODBYE   Manhattans
2 LOVE IS ALIVE   Gary Wright
3 MOONLIGHT FEELS RIGHT   Starbuck
4 AFTERNOON DELIGHT   Starland Vocal Band
5 DON'T GO BREAKING MY HEART   Elton John & Kiki Dee

6 GET CLOSER   Seals & Crofts
7 GOT TO GET YOU INTO MY LIFE   Beatles
8 ROCK AND ROLL MUSIC   Beach Boys
9 I'LL BE GOOD TO YOU   Brothers Johnson
10 LET EM IN   Wings

August 7, 1976
1 DON'T GO BREAKING MY HEART   Elton John & Kiki Dee
2 LOVE IS ALIVE   Gary Wright
3 MOONLIGHT FEELS RIGHT   Starbuck
4 LET EM IN   Wings
5 YOU SHOULD BE DANCING   Bee Gees
6 ROCK AND ROLL MUSIC   Beach Boys
7 GOT TO GET YOU INTO MY LIFE   Beatles
8 KISS AND SAY GOODBYE   Manhattans
9 YOU'LL NEVER FIND ANOTHER LOVE LIKE MINE   Lou Rawls
10 AFTERNOON DELIGHT   Starland Vocal Band

August 14, 1976
1 DON'T GO BREAKING MY HEART   Elton John & Kiki Dee
2 YOU SHOULD BE DANCING   Bee Gees
3 LET EM IN   Wings
4 YOU'LL NEVER FIND ANOTHER LOVE LIKE MINE   Lou Rawls
5 ROCK AND ROLL MUSIC   Beach Boys
6 LOVE IS ALIVE   Gary Wright
7 I'D REALLY LOVE TO SEE YOU TONIGHT   England Dan & John Ford Coley
8 (SHAKE SHAKE SHAKE) SHAKE YOUR BOOTY   K. C. & The Sunshine Band
9 KISS AND SAY GOODBYE   Manhattans
10 TURN THE BEAT AROUND   Vicki Sue Robinson

August 21, 1976
1 DON'T GO BREAKING MY HEART   Elton John & Kiki Dee
2 YOU SHOULD BE DANCING   Bee Gees
3 LET EM IN   Wings
4 YOU'LL NEVER FIND ANOTHER LOVE LIKE MINE   Lou Rawls
5 I'D REALLY LOVE TO SEE YOU TONIGHT   England Dan & John Ford Coley
6 (SHAKE SHAKE SHAKE) SHAKE YOUR BOOTY   K. C. & The Sunshine Band
7 ROCK AND ROLL MUSIC   Beach Boys
8 KISS AND SAY GOODBYE   Manhattans
9 GET CLOSER   Seals & Crofts
10 TURN THE BEAT AROUND   Vicki Sue Robinson

August 28, 1976
1 DON'T GO BREAKING MY HEART   Elton John & Kiki Dee
2 YOU SHOULD BE DANCING   Bee Gees
3 LET EM IN   Wings
4 YOU'LL NEVER FIND ANOTHER LOVE LIKE MINE   Lou Rawls
5 I'D REALLY LOVE TO SEE YOU TONIGHT   England Dan & John Ford Coley
6 (SHAKE SHAKE SHAKE) SHAKE YOUR BOOTY   K. C. & The Sunshine Band
7 PLAY THAT FUNKY MUSIC   Wild Cherry
8 A FIFTH OF BEETHOVEN   Walter Murphy
9 GET CLOSER   Seals & Crofts
10 THIS MASQUERADE   George Benson

September 4, 1976
1 YOU SHOULD BE DANCING   Bee Gees

315

2 YOU'LL NEVER FIND ANOTHER LOVE LIKE MINE   Lou Rawls
3 LET EM IN   Wings
4 I'D REALLY LOVE TO SEE YOU TONIGHT   England Dan & John Ford Coley
5 (SHAKE SHAKE SHAKE) SHAKE YOUR BOOTY   K. C. & The Sunshine Band
6 PLAY THAT FUNKY MUSIC   Wild Cherry
7 A FIFTH OF BEETHOVEN   Walter Murphy
8 DON'T GO BREAKING MY HEART   Elton John & Kiki Dee
9 LOWDOWN   Boz Scaggs
10 THIS MASQUERADE   George Benson

September 11, 1976

1 (SHAKE SHAKE SHAKE) SHAKE YOUR BOOTY   K. C. & The Sunshine Band
2 YOU'LL NEVER FIND ANOTHER LOVE LIKE MINE   Lou Rawls
3 PLAY THAT FUNKY MUSIC   Wild Cherry
4 I'D REALLY LOVE TO SEE YOU TONIGHT   England Dan & John Ford Coley
5 A FIFTH OF BEETHOVEN   Walter Murphy
6 YOU SHOULD BE DANCING   Bee Gees
7 LOWDOWN   Boz Scaggs
8 LET EM IN   Wings
9 DON'T GO BREAKING MY HEART   Elton John & Kiki Dee
10 SUMMER   War

September 18, 1976

1 PLAY THAT FUNKY MUSIC   Wild Cherry
2 (SHAKE SHAKE SHAKE) SHAKE YOUR BOOTY   K. C. & The Sunshine Band
3 I'D REALLY LOVE TO SEE YOU TONIGHT   England Dan & John Ford Coley
4 A FIFTH OF BEETHOVEN   Walter Murphy
5 YOU'LL NEVER FIND ANOTHER LOVE LIKE MINE   Lou Rawls
6 LOWDOWN   Boz Scaggs
7 DEVIL WOMAN   Cliff Richard
8 SUMMER   War
9 IF YOU LEAVE ME NOW   Chicago
10 YOU SHOULD BE DANCING   Bee Gees

September 25, 1976

1 PLAY THAT FUNKY MUSIC   Wild Cherry
2 I'D REALLY LOVE TO SEE YOU TONIGHT   England Dan & John Ford Coley
3 A FIFTH OF BEETHOVEN   Walter Murphy
4 (SHAKE SHAKE SHAKE) SHAKE YOUR BOOTY   K. C. & The Sunshine Band
5 LOWDOWN   Boz Scaggs
6 DEVIL WOMAN   Cliff Richard
7 SUMMER   War
8 IF YOU LEAVE ME NOW   Chicago
9 DISCO DUCK PART 1   Rick Dees
10 YOU'LL NEVER FIND ANOTHER LOVE LIKE MINE   Lou Rawls

October 2, 1976

1 PLAY THAT FUNKY MUSIC   Wild Cherry
2 I'D REALLY LOVE TO SEE YOU TONIGHT   England Dan & John Ford Coley
3 A FIFTH OF BEETHOVEN   Walter Murphy
4 DISCO DUCK PART 1   Rick Dees
5 LOWDOWN   Boz Scaggs
6 DEVIL WOMAN   Cliff Richard
7 SUMMER   War

8 IF YOU LEAVE ME NOW   Chicago
9 (SHAKE SHAKE SHAKE) SHAKE YOUR BOOTY   K. C. & The Sunshine Band
10 STILL THE ONE   Orleans

October 9, 1976

1 A FIFTH OF BEETHOVEN   Walter Murphy
2 PLAY THAT FUNKY MUSIC   Wild Cherry
3 LOWDOWN   Boz Scaggs
4 DISCO DUCK PART 1   Rick Dees
5 IF YOU LEAVE ME NOW   Chicago
6 DEVIL WOMAN   Cliff Richard
7 STILL THE ONE   Orleans
8 I'D REALLY LOVE TO SEE YOU TONIGHT   England Dan & John Ford Coley
9 (SHAKE SHAKE SHAKE) SHAKE YOUR BOOTY   K. C. & The Sunshine Band
10 SHE'S GONE   Daryl Hall & John Oates

October 16, 1976

1 DISCO DUCK PART 1   Rick Dees
2 A FIFTH OF BEETHOVEN   Walter Murphy
3 LOWDOWN   Boz Scaggs
4 IF YOU LEAVE ME NOW   Chicago
5 PLAY THAT FUNKY MUSIC   Wild Cherry
6 STILL THE ONE   Orleans
7 DEVIL WOMAN   Cliff Richard
8 (SHAKE SHAKE SHAKE) SHAKE YOUR BOOTY   K. C. & The Sunshine Band
9 SHE'S GONE   Daryl Hall & John Oates
10 I'D REALLY LOVE TO SEE YOU TONIGHT   England Dan & John Ford Coley

October 23, 1976

1 IF YOU LEAVE ME NOW   Chicago
2 DISCO DUCK PART 1   Rick Dees
3 A FIFTH OF BEETHOVEN   Walter Murphy
4 LOWDOWN   Boz Scaggs
5 STILL THE ONE   Orleans
6 PLAY THAT FUNKY MUSIC   Wild Cherry
7 (SHAKE SHAKE SHAKE) SHAKE YOUR BOOTY   K. C. & The Sunshine Band
8 SHE'S GONE   Daryl Hall & John Oates
9 LOVE SO RIGHT   Bee Gees
10 ROCK 'N ME   Steve Miller Band

October 30, 1976

1 IF YOU LEAVE ME NOW   Chicago
2 DISCO DUCK PART 1   Rick Dees
3 ROCK 'N ME   Steve Miller Band
4 THE WRECK OF THE EDMUND FITZGERALD   Gordon Lightfoot
5 A FIFTH OF BEETHOVEN   Walter Murphy
6 LOVE SO RIGHT   Bee Gees
7 SHE'S GONE   Daryl Hall & John Oates
8 PLAY THAT FUNKY MUSIC   Wild Cherry
9 MUSKRAT LOVE   Captain & Tennille
10 MAGIC MAN   Heart

November 6, 1976

1 ROCK 'N ME   Steve Miller Band
2 DISCO DUCK PART 1   Rick Dees
3 THE WRECK OF THE EDMUND FITZGERALD   Gordon Lightfoot
4 IF YOU LEAVE ME NOW   Chicago
5 LOVE SO RIGHT   Bee Gees
6 MUSKRAT LOVE   Captain & Tennille

7 SHE'S GONE Daryl Hall & John Oates
8 TONIGHT'S THE NIGHT (GONNA BE ALRIGHT) Rod Stewart
9 MAGIC MAN Heart
10 JUST TO BE CLOSE TO YOU Commodores

November 13, 1976
1 TONIGHT'S THE NIGHT (GONNA BE ALRIGHT) Rod Stewart
2 DISCO DUCK PART 1 Rick Dees
3 THE WRECK OF THE EDMUND FITZGERALD Gordon Lightfoot
4 LOVE SO RIGHT Bee Gees
5 MUSKRAT LOVE Captain & Tennille
6 ROCK 'N ME Steve Miller Band
7 IF YOU LEAVE ME NOW Chicago
8 JUST TO BE CLOSE TO YOU Commodores
9 THE RUBBERBAND MAN Spinners
10 DO YOU FEEL LIKE WE DO Peter Frampton

November 20, 1976
1 TONIGHT'S THE NIGHT (GONNA BE ALRIGHT) Rod Stewart
2 THE WRECK OF THE EDMUND FITZGERALD Gordon Lightfoot
3 LOVE SO RIGHT Bee Gees
4 MUSKRAT LOVE Captain & Tennille
5 DISCO DUCK PART 1 Rick Dees
6 THE RUBBERBAND MAN Spinners
7 ROCK 'N ME Steve Miller Band
8 JUST TO BE CLOSE TO YOU Commodores
9 BETH Kiss
10 DO YOU FEEL LIKE WE DO Peter Frampton

Rod Stewart
''Tonight's The Night'' stayed #1 for more than a month.

November 27, 1976
1 TONIGHT'S THE NIGHT (GONNA BE ALRIGHT) Rod Stewart
2 THE WRECK OF THE EDMUND FITZGERALD Gordon Lightfoot
3 LOVE SO RIGHT Bee Gees
4 MUSKRAT LOVE Captain & Tennille
5 THE RUBBERBAND MAN Spinners
6 DISCO DUCK PART 1 Rick Dees
7 JUST TO BE CLOSE TO YOU Commodores
8 BETH Kiss
9 MORE THAN A FEELING Boston
10 NADIA'S THEME (THE YOUNG AND THE RESTLESS) Barry DeVorzon & Perry Botkin, Jr.

December 4, 1976
1 TONIGHT'S THE NIGHT (GONNA BE ALRIGHT) Rod Stewart
2 THE RUBBERBAND MAN Spinners
3 LOVE SO RIGHT Bee Gees
4 MUSKRAT LOVE Captain & Tennille
5 THE WRECK OF THE EDMUND FITZGERALD Gordon Lightfoot
6 YOU DON'T HAVE TO BE A STAR (TO BE IN MY SHOW) Marilyn McCoo & Billy Davis, Jr.
7 BETH Kiss
8 MORE THAN A FEELING Boston
9 NADIA'S THEME (THE YOUNG AND THE RESTLESS) Barry DeVorzon & Perry Botkin, Jr.
10 YOU ARE THE WOMAN Firefall

December 11, 1976
1 TONIGHT'S THE NIGHT (GONNA BE ALRIGHT) Rod Stewart
2 THE RUBBERBAND MAN Spinners
3 LOVE SO RIGHT Bee Gees
4 MUSKRAT LOVE Captain & Tennille
5 YOU DON'T HAVE TO BE A STAR (TO BE IN MY SHOW) Marilyn McCoo & Billy Davis, Jr.
6 YOU MAKE ME FEEL LIKE DANCING Leo Sayer
7 MORE THAN A FEELING Boston
8 NADIA'S THEME (THE YOUNG AND THE RESTLESS) Barry DeVorzon & Perry Botkin, Jr.
9 YOU ARE THE WOMAN Firefall
10 NIGHTS ARE FOREVER WITHOUT YOU England Dan & John Ford Coley

December 18, 1976
1 TONIGHT'S THE NIGHT (GONNA BE ALRIGHT) Rod Stewart
2 THE RUBBERBAND MAN Spinners
3 YOU DON'T HAVE TO BE A STAR (TO BE IN MY SHOW) Marilyn McCoo & Billy Davis, Jr.
4 MUSKRAT LOVE Captain & Tennille
5 YOU MAKE ME FEEL LIKE DANCING Leo Sayer
6 MORE THAN A FEELING Boston
7 SORRY SEEMS TO BE THE HARDEST WORD Elton John
8 NADIA'S THEME (THE YOUNG AND THE RESTLESS) Barry DeVorzon & Perry Botkin, Jr.
9 YOU ARE THE WOMAN Firefall
10 NIGHTS ARE FOREVER WITHOUT YOU England Dan & John Ford Coley

December 25, 1976
1 TONIGHT'S THE NIGHT (GONNA BE ALRIGHT) Rod Stewart

2 YOU DON'T HAVE TO BE A STAR (TO BE IN MY SHOW)
   Marilyn McCoo & Billy Davis, Jr.
3 THE RUBBERBAND MAN   Spinners
4 YOU MAKE ME FEEL LIKE DANCING   Leo Sayer
5 MORE THAN A FEELING   Boston
6 SORRY SEEMS TO BE THE HARDEST WORD   Elton John
7 I WISH   Stevie Wonder
8 DAZZ   Brick
9 CAR WASH   Rose Royce
10 AFTER THE LOVING   Englebert Humperdinck

January 1, 1977

NO SURVEY

January 8, 1977

1 YOU DON'T HAVE TO BE A STAR (TO BE IN MY SHOW)
   Marilyn McCoo & Billy Davis, Jr.
2 YOU MAKE ME FEEL LIKE DANCING   Leo Sayer
3 TONIGHT'S THE NIGHT (GONNA BE ALRIGHT)   Rod
   Stewart
4 I WISH   Stevie Wonder
5 CAR WASH   Rose Royce
6 SORRY SEEMS TO BE THE HARDEST WORD   Elton John
7 DAZZ   Brick
8 THE RUBBERBAND MAN   Spinners
9 AFTER THE LOVING   Englebert Humperdinck
10 STAND TALL   Burton Cummings

January 15, 1977

1 YOU MAKE ME FEEL LIKE DANCING   Leo Sayer
2 I WISH   Stevie Wonder
3 CAR WASH   Rose Royce
4 YOU DON'T HAVE TO BE A STAR (TO BE IN MY SHOW)
   Marilyn McCoo & Billy Davis, Jr.
5 DAZZ   Brick
6 TONIGHT'S THE NIGHT (GONNA BE ALRIGHT)   Rod
   Stewart
7 SORRY SEEMS TO BE THE HARDEST WORD   Elton John
8 HOT LINE   Sylvers
9 LOVE THEME FROM "A STAR IS BORN"   Barbra Streisand
10 STAND TALL   Burton Cummings

January 22, 1977

1 I WISH   Stevie Wonder
2 CAR WASH   Rose Royce
3 YOU MAKE ME FEEL LIKE DANCING   Leo Sayer
4 DAZZ   Brick
5 YOU DON'T HAVE TO BE A STAR (TO BE IN MY SHOW)
   Marilyn McCoo & Billy Davis, Jr.
6 HOT LINE   Sylvers
7 NEW KID IN TOWN   Eagles
8 AFTER THE LOVING   Englebert Humperdinck
9 BLINDED BY THE LIGHT   Manfred Mann's Earth Band
10 TORN BETWEEN TWO LOVERS   Mary MacGregor

January 29, 1977

1 CAR WASH   Rose Royce
2 I WISH   Stevie Wonder
3 DAZZ   Brick
4 YOU MAKE ME FEEL LIKE DANCING   Leo Sayer
5 HOT LINE   Sylvers
6 NEW KID IN TOWN   Eagles
7 TORN BETWEEN TWO LOVERS   Mary MacGregor
8 BLINDED BY THE LIGHT   Manfred Mann's Earth Band
9 LOVE THEME FROM "A STAR IS BORN"   Barbra Streisand
10 WALK THIS WAY   Aerosmith

February 5, 1977

1 TORN BETWEEN TWO LOVERS   Mary MacGregor
2 CAR WASH   Rose Royce
3 DAZZ   Brick
4 NEW KID IN TOWN   Eagles
5 HOT LINE   Sylvers
6 BLINDED BY THE LIGHT   Manfred Mann's Earth Band
7 LOVE THEME FROM "A STAR IS BORN"   Barbra Streisand
8 I WISH   Stevie Wonder
9 ENJOY YOURSELF   The Jacksons
10 WALK THIS WAY   Aerosmith

February 12, 1977

1 TORN BETWEEN TWO LOVERS   Mary MacGregor
2 NEW KID IN TOWN   Eagles
3 BLINDED BY THE LIGHT   Manfred Mann's Earth Band
4 CAR WASH   Rose Royce
5 LOVE THEME FROM "A STAR IS BORN"   Barbra Streisand
6 DAZZ   Brick
7 ENJOY YOURSELF   The Jacksons
8 I WISH   Stevie Wonder
9 I LIKE DREAMIN'   Kenny Nolan
10 LOST WITHOUT YOUR LOVE   Bread

February 19, 1977

1 BLINDED BY THE LIGHT   Manfred Mann's Earth Band
2 NEW KID IN TOWN   Eagles
3 TORN BETWEEN TWO LOVERS   Mary MacGregor
4 LOVE THEME FROM "A STAR IS BORN"   Barbra Streisand
5 I LIKE DREAMIN'   Kenny Nolan
6 ENJOY YOURSELF   The Jacksons
7 CAR WASH   Rose Royce
8 FLY LIKE AN EAGLE   Steve Miller
9 LOST WITHOUT YOUR LOVE   Bread
10 NIGHT MOVES   Bob Seger

February 26, 1977

1 NEW KID IN TOWN   Eagles
2 LOVE THEME FROM "A STAR IS BORN"   Barbra Streisand
3 BLINDED BY THE LIGHT   Manfred Mann's Earth Band
4 FLY LIKE AN EAGLE   Steve Miller
5 I LIKE DREAMIN'   Kenny Nolan
6 ENJOY YOURSELF   The Jacksons
7 TORN BETWEEN TWO LOVERS   Mary MacGregor
8 NIGHT MOVES   Bob Seger
9 DANCING QUEEN   Abba
10 WEEKEND IN NEW ENGLAND   Barry Manilow

March 5, 1977

1 LOVE THEME FROM "A STAR IS BORN"   Barbra Streisand
2 NEW KID IN TOWN   Eagles
3 FLY LIKE AN EAGLE   Steve Miller
4 I LIKE DREAMIN'   Kenny Nolan
5 BLINDED BY THE LIGHT   Manfred Mann's Earth Band
6 NIGHT MOVES   Bob Seger
7 DANCING QUEEN   Abba
8 YEAR OF THE CAT   Al Stewart
9 TORN BETWEEN TWO LOVERS   Mary MacGregor
10 WEEKEND IN NEW ENGLAND   Barry Manilow

March 12, 1977

1 LOVE THEME FROM "A STAR IS BORN"   Barbra Streisand
2 FLY LIKE AN EAGLE   Steve Miller
3 I LIKE DREAMIN'   Kenny Nolan
4 NIGHT MOVES   Bob Seger
5 BLINDED BY THE LIGHT   Manfred Mann's Earth Band

6   DANCING QUEEN   Abba
7   TORN BETWEEN TWO LOVERS   Mary MacGregor
8   YEAR OF THE CAT   Al Stewart
9   RICH GIRL   Daryl Hall & John Oates
10   GO YOUR OWN WAY   Fleetwood Mac

March 19, 1977
1   LOVE THEME FROM "A STAR IS BORN"   Barbra Streisand
2   FLY LIKE AN EAGLE   Steve Miller
3   RICH GIRL   Daryl Hall & John Oates
4   NIGHT MOVES   Bob Seger
5   DANCING QUEEN   Abba
6   I LIKE DREAMIN'   Kenny Nolan
7   TORN BETWEEN TWO LOVERS   Mary MacGregor
8   DON'T GIVE UP ON US   David Soul
9   DON'T LEAVE ME THIS WAY   Thelma Houston
10   GO YOUR OWN WAY   Fleetwood Mac

March 26, 1977
1   RICH GIRL   Daryl Hall & John Oates
2   LOVE THEME FROM "A STAR IS BORN"   Barbra Streisand
3   DANCING QUEEN   Abba
4   DON'T GIVE UP ON US   David Soul
5   DON'T LEAVE ME THIS WAY   Thelma Houston
6   FLY LIKE AN EAGLE   Steve Miller
7   NIGHT MOVES   Bob Seger
8   THE THINGS WE DO FOR LOVE   10 CC
9   I LIKE DREAMIN'   Kenny Nolan
10   TORN BETWEEN TWO LOVERS   Mary MacGregor

April 2, 1977
1   RICH GIRL   Daryl Hall & John Oates
2   DANCING QUEEN   Abba
3   DON'T GIVE UP ON US   David Soul
4   DON'T LEAVE ME THIS WAY   Thelma Houston
5   LOVE THEME FROM "A STAR IS BORN"   Barbra Streisand
6   SOUTHERN NIGHTS   Glen Campbell
7   THE THINGS WE DO FOR LOVE   10 CC
8   HOTEL CALIFORNIA   Eagles
9   I'VE GOT LOVE ON MY MIND   Natalie Cole
10   MAYBE I'M AMAZED   Wings

April 9, 1977
1   DANCING QUEEN   Abba
2   DON'T GIVE UP ON US   David Soul
3   DON'T LEAVE ME THIS WAY   Thelma Houston
4   RICH GIRL   Daryl Hall & John Oates
5   SOUTHERN NIGHTS   Glen Campbell
6   THE THINGS WE DO FOR LOVE   10 CC
7   HOTEL CALIFORNIA   Eagles
8   I'VE GOT LOVE ON MY MIND   Natalie Cole
9   LOVE THEME FROM "A STAR IS BORN"   Barbra Streisand
10   SO IN TO YOU   Atlanta Rhythm Section

April 16, 1977
1   DON'T GIVE UP ON US   David Soul
2   DON'T LEAVE ME THIS WAY   Thelma Houston
3   SOUTHERN NIGHTS   Glen Campbell
4   HOTEL CALIFORNIA   Eagles
5   THE THINGS WE DO FOR LOVE   10 CC
6   DANCING QUEEN   Abba
7   I'VE GOT LOVE ON MY MIND   Natalie Cole
8   LOVE THEME FROM "A STAR IS BORN"   Barbra Streisand
9   SO IN TO YOU   Atlanta Rhythm Section
10   RICH GIRL   Daryl Hall & John Oates

April 23, 1977
1   DON'T LEAVE ME THIS WAY   Thelma Houston
2   SOUTHERN NIGHTS   Glen Campbell
3   HOTEL CALIFORNIA   Eagles
4   DON'T GIVE UP ON US   David Soul
5   THE THINGS WE DO FOR LOVE   10 CC
6   I'VE GOT LOVE ON MY MIND   Natalie Cole
7   LOVE THEME FROM "A STAR IS BORN"   Barbra Streisand
8   SO IN TO YOU   Atlanta Rhythm Section
9   WHEN I NEED YOU   Leo Sayer
10   RIGHT TIME OF THE NIGHT   Jennifer Warnes

April 30, 1977
1   SOUTHERN NIGHTS   Glen Campbell
2   HOTEL CALIFORNIA   Eagles
3   DON'T LEAVE ME THIS WAY   Thelma Houston
4   WHEN I NEED YOU   Leo Sayer
5   I'VE GOT LOVE ON MY MIND   Natalie Cole
6   DON'T GIVE UP ON US   David Soul
7   SO IN TO YOU   Atlanta Rhythm Section
8   RIGHT TIME OF THE NIGHT   Jennifer Warnes
9   SIR DUKE   Stevie Wonder
10   TRYING TO LOVE TWO   William Bell

May 7, 1977
1   HOTEL CALIFORNIA   Eagles
2   WHEN I NEED YOU   Leo Sayer
3   SOUTHERN NIGHTS   Glen Campbell
4   SIR DUKE   Stevie Wonder
5   DON'T LEAVE ME THIS WAY   Thelma Houston
6   RIGHT TIME OF THE NIGHT   Jennifer Warnes
7   SO IN TO YOU   Atlanta Rhythm Section
8   I'VE GOT LOVE ON MY MIND   Natalie Cole
9   COULDN'T GET IT RIGHT   Climax Blues Band
10   I WANNA GET NEXT TO YOU   Rose Royce

May 14, 1977
1   WHEN I NEED YOU   Leo Sayer
2   SIR DUKE   Stevie Wonder
3   HOTEL CALIFORNIA   Eagles
4   SOUTHERN NIGHTS   Glen Campbell
5   COULDN'T GET IT RIGHT   Climax Blues Band
6   RIGHT TIME OF THE NIGHT   Jennifer Warnes
7   SO IN TO YOU   Atlanta Rhythm Section
8   I'M YOUR BOOGIE MAN   K. C. & The Sunshine Band
9   GOT TO GIVE IT UP   Marvin Gaye
10   I WANNA GET NEXT TO YOU   Rose Royce

May 21, 1977
1   SIR DUKE   Stevie Wonder
2   WHEN I NEED YOU   Leo Sayer
3   COULDN'T GET IT RIGHT   Climax Blues Band
4   I'M YOUR BOOGIE MAN   K. C. & The Sunshine Band
5   GOT TO GIVE IT UP   Marvin Gaye
6   DREAMS   Fleetwood Mac
7   GONNA FLY NOW (THEME FROM "ROCKY")   Bill Conti
8   HOTEL CALIFORNIA   Eagles
9   SOUTHERN NIGHTS   Glen Campbell
10   LUCILLE   Kenny Rogers

May 28, 1977
1   SIR DUKE   Stevie Wonder
2   WHEN I NEED YOU   Leo Sayer
3   I'M YOUR BOOGIE MAN   K. C. & The Sunshine Band
4   DREAMS   Fleetwood Mac
5   GOT TO GIVE IT UP   Marvin Gaye

6 GONNA FLY NOW (THEME FROM "ROCKY") Bill Conti
7 COULDN'T GET IT RIGHT Climax Blues Band
8 LUCILLE Kenny Rogers
9 LONELY BOY Andrew Gold
10 FEELS LIKE THE FIRST TIME Foreigner

June 4, 1977
1 SIR DUKE Stevie Wonder
2 I'M YOUR BOOGIE MAN K. C. & The Sunshine Band
3 DREAMS Fleetwood Mac
4 GOT TO GIVE IT UP Marvin Gaye
5 GONNA FLY NOW (THEME FROM "ROCKY") Bill Conti
6 COULDN'T GET IT RIGHT Climax Blues Band
7 LUCILLE Kenny Rogers
8 LONELY BOY Andrew Gold
9 FEELS LIKE THE FIRST TIME Foreigner
10 WHEN I NEED YOU Leo Sayer

June 11, 1977
1 I'M YOUR BOOGIE MAN K. C. & The Sunshine Band
2 DREAMS Fleetwood Mac
3 GOT TO GIVE IT UP Marvin Gaye
4 GONNA FLY NOW (THEME FROM "ROCKY") Bill Conti
5 FEELS LIKE THE FIRST TIME Foreigner
6 LUCILLE Kenny Rogers
7 LONELY BOY Andrew Gold
8 UNDERCOVER ANGEL Alan O'Day
9 SIR DUKE Stevie Wonder
10 COULDN'T GET IT RIGHT Climax Blues Band

June 18, 1977
1 DREAMS Fleetwood Mac
2 GOT TO GIVE IT UP Marvin Gaye
3 GONNA FLY NOW (THEME FROM "ROCKY") Bill Conti
4 FEELS LIKE THE FIRST TIME Foreigner
5 LUCILLE Kenny Rogers
6 UNDERCOVER ANGEL Alan O'Day
7 LONELY BOY Andrew Gold
8 I'M YOUR BOOGIE MAN K. C. & The Sunshine Band
9 SIR DUKE Stevie Wonder
10 ANGEL IN YOUR ARMS Hot

June 25, 1977
1 GOT TO GIVE IT UP Marvin Gaye
2 GONNA FLY NOW (THEME FROM "ROCKY") Bill Conti
3 UNDERCOVER ANGEL Alan O'Day
4 FEELS LIKE THE FIRST TIME Foreigner
5 LUCILLE Kenny Rogers
6 DREAMS Fleetwood Mac
7 LONELY BOY Andrew Gold
8 DA DOO RON RON Shaun Cassidy
9 ANGEL IN YOUR ARMS Hot
10 JET AIRLINER Steve Miller Band

July 2, 1977
1 GONNA FLY NOW (THEME FROM "ROCKY") Bill Conti
2 UNDERCOVER ANGEL Alan O'Day
3 GOT TO GIVE IT UP Marvin Gaye
4 DA DOO RON RON Shaun Cassidy
5 LOOKS LIKE WE MADE IT Barry Manilow
6 DREAMS Fleetwood Mac
7 I JUST WANT TO BE YOUR EVERYTHING Andy Gibb
8 ANGEL IN YOUR ARMS Hot
9 JET AIRLINER Steve Miller Band
10 MARGARITAVILLE Jimmy Buffett

Shaun Cassidy
The co-star of TV's "Hardy Boys" hits #1 with
a remake of The Crystals "Da Doo Ron Ron" (July 16).

Andy Gibb
Andy's "I Just Want To Be Your Everything" hit #1 on July 30.

July 9, 1977

1 UNDERCOVER ANGEL   Alan O'Day
2 DA DOO RON RON   Shaun Cassidy
3 LOOKS LIKE WE MADE IT   Barry Manilow
4 GONNA FLY NOW (THEME FROM "ROCKY")   Bill Conti
5 I JUST WANT TO BE YOUR EVERYTHING   Andy Gibb
6 GOT TO GIVE IT UP   Marvin Gaye
7 ANGEL IN YOUR ARMS   Hot
8 JET AIRLINER   Steve Miller Band
9 MARGARITAVILLE   Jimmy Buffett
10 MY HEART BELONGS TO ME   Barbra Streisand

July 16, 1977

1 DA DOO RON RON   Shaun Cassidy
2 LOOKS LIKE WE MADE IT   Barry Manilow
3 UNDERCOVER ANGEL   Alan O'Day
4 I JUST WANT TO BE YOUR EVERYTHING   Andy Gibb
5 I'M IN YOU   Peter Frampton
6 ANGEL IN YOUR ARMS   Hot
7 MY HEART BELONGS TO ME   Barbra Streisand
8 JET AIRLINER   Steve Miller Band
9 MARGARITAVILLE   Jimmy Buffett
10 DO YOU WANNA MAKE LOVE   Peter McCann

July 23, 1977

1 LOOKS LIKE WE MADE IT   Barry Manilow
2 I JUST WANT TO BE YOUR EVERYTHING   Andy Gibb
3 DA DOO RON RON   Shaun Cassidy
4 I'M IN YOU   Peter Frampton
5 MY HEART BELONGS TO ME   Barbra Streisand
6 ANGEL IN YOUR ARMS   Hot
7 UNDERCOVER ANGEL   Alan O'Day
8 MARGARITAVILLE   Jimmy Buffett
9 DO YOU WANNA MAKE LOVE   Peter McCann
10 BEST OF MY LOVE   Eagles

July 30, 1977

1 I JUST WANT TO BE YOUR EVERYTHING   Andy Gibb
2 I'M IN YOU   Peter Frampton
3 LOOKS LIKE WE MADE IT   Barry Manilow
4 MY HEART BELONGS TO ME   Barbra Streisand
5 DA DOO RON RON   Shaun Cassidy
6 BEST OF MY LOVE   Eagles
7 DO YOU WANNA MAKE LOVE   Peter McCann
8 MARGARITAVILLE   Jimmy Buffett
9 HIGHER AND HIGHER   Rita Coolidge
10 WHATCHA GONNA DO   Pablo Cruise

August 6, 1977

1 I JUST WANT TO BE YOUR EVERYTHING   Andy Gibb
2 I'M IN YOU   Peter Frampton
3 BEST OF MY LOVE   Eagles
4 MY HEART BELONGS TO ME   Barbra Streisand
5 DO YOU WANNA MAKE LOVE   Peter McCann
6 DA DOO RON RON   Shaun Cassidy
7 HIGHER AND HIGHER   Rita Coolidge
8 EASY   Commodores
9 WHATCHA GONNA DO   Pablo Cruise
10 YOU AND ME   Alice Cooper

August 13, 1977

1 I JUST WANT TO BE YOUR EVERYTHING   Andy Gibb
2 I'M IN YOU   Peter Frampton
3 BEST OF MY LOVE   Eagles
4 HIGHER AND HIGHER   Rita Coolidge
5 DO YOU WANNA MAKE LOVE   Peter McCann
6 MY HEART BELONGS TO ME   Barbra Streisand
7 EASY   Commodores
8 WHATCHA GONNA DO   Pablo Cruise
9 YOU AND ME   Alice Cooper
10 YOU MADE ME BELIEVE IN MAGIC   Bay City Rollers

August 20, 1977

1 BEST OF MY LOVE   Eagles
2 I JUST WANT TO BE YOUR EVERYTHING   Andy Gibb
3 HIGHER AND HIGHER   Rita Coolidge
4 I'M IN YOU   Peter Frampton
5 EASY   Commodores
6 WHATCHA GONNA DO   Pablo Cruise
7 DO YOU WANNA MAKE LOVE   Peter McCann
8 JUST A SONG BEFORE I GO   Crosby, Stills & Nash
9 YOU AND ME   Alice Cooper
10 YOU MADE ME BELIEVE IN MAGIC   Bay City Rollers

August 27, 1977

1 BEST OF MY LOVE   Eagles
2 I JUST WANT TO BE YOUR EVERYTHING   Andy Gibb
3 HIGHER AND HIGHER   Rita Coolidge
4 EASY   Commodores
5 HANDY MAN   Jimmy Jones
6 WHATCHA GONNA DO   Pablo Cruise
7 JUST A SONG BEFORE I GO   Crosby, Stills & Nash
8 FLOAT ON   Floaters
9 DON'T STOP   Fleetwood Mac
10 STRAWBERRY LETTER #23   Brothers Johnson

September 3, 1977

1 BEST OF MY LOVE   Eagles
2 I JUST WANT TO BE YOUR EVERYTHING   Andy Gibb
3 HIGHER AND HIGHER   Rita Coolidge
4 EASY   Commodores
5 HANDY MAN   Jimmy Jones
6 FLOAT ON   Floaters
7 JUST A SONG BEFORE I GO   Crosby, Stills & Nash
8 DON'T STOP   Fleetwood Mac
9 STRAWBERRY LETTER #23   Brothers Johnson
10 TELEPHONE LINE   Electric Light Orchestra

September 10, 1977

1 BEST OF MY LOVE   Eagles
2 HIGHER AND HIGHER   Rita Coolidge
3 I JUST WANT TO BE YOUR EVERYTHING   Andy Gibb
4 HANDY MAN   Jimmy Jones
5 FLOAT ON   Floaters
6 DON'T STOP   Fleetwood Mac
7 EASY   Commodores
8 STRAWBERRY LETTER #23   Brothers Johnson
9 TELEPHONE LINE   Electric Light Orchestra
10 SMOKE FROM A DISTANT FIRE   Sanford/Townsend

September 17, 1977

1 I JUST WANT TO BE YOUR EVERYTHING   Andy Gibb
2 FLOAT ON   Floaters
3 BEST OF MY LOVE   Eagles
4 HANDY MAN   Jimmy Jones
5 DON'T STOP   Fleetwood Mac
6 KEEP IT COMIN' LOVE   K. C. & The Sunshine Band
7 STRAWBERRY LETTER #23   Brothers Johnson
8 TELEPHONE LINE   Electric Light Orchestra
9 SMOKE FROM A DISTANT FIRE   Sanford/Townsend
10 THEME FROM "STAR WARS"   Meco

Debbie Boone
Beginning October 16, Debbie stayed #1 for ten weeks with ``You Light Up My Life'' (from the movie of the same name).

September 24, 1977

1 BEST OF MY LOVE   Eagles
2 FLOAT ON   Floaters
3 DON'T STOP   Fleetwood Mac
4 KEEP IT COMIN' LOVE   K. C. & The Sunshine Band
5 STRAWBERRY LETTER #23   Brothers Johnson
6 I JUST WANT TO BE YOUR EVERYTHING   Andy Gibb
7 TELEPHONE LINE   Electric Light Orchestra
8 THEME FROM "STAR WARS"   Meco
9 THAT'S ROCK 'N' ROLL   Shaun Cassidy
10 COLD AS ICE   Foreigner

October 1, 1977

1 THEME FROM "STAR WARS"   Meco
2 KEEP IT COMIN' LOVE   K. C. & The Sunshine Band
3 DON'T STOP   Fleetwood Mac
4 BEST OF MY LOVE   Eagles
5 STRAWBERRY LETTER #23   Brothers Johnson
6 NOBODY DOES IT BETTER   Carly Simon
7 TELEPHONE LINE   Electric Light Orchestra
8 THAT'S ROCK 'N' ROLL   Shaun Cassidy
9 COLD AS ICE   Foreigner
10 I JUST WANT TO BE YOUR EVERYTHING   Andy Gibb

October 8, 1977

1 THEME FROM "STAR WARS"   Meco
2 KEEP IT COMIN' LOVE   K. C. & The Sunshine Band
3 YOU LIGHT UP MY LIFE   Debby Boone
4 NOBODY DOES IT BETTER   Carly Simon
5 THAT'S ROCK 'N' ROLL   Shaun Cassidy
6 BEST OF MY LOVE   Eagles
7 BOOGIE NIGHTS   Heatwave
8 COLD AS ICE   Foreigner
9 BRICK HOUSE   Commodores
10 I JUST WANT TO BE YOUR EVERYTHING   Andy Gibb

October 15, 1977

1 YOU LIGHT UP MY LIFE   Debby Boone
2 KEEP IT COMIN' LOVE   K. C. & The Sunshine Band
3 NOBODY DOES IT BETTER   Carly Simon
4 THAT'S ROCK 'N' ROLL   Shaun Cassidy
5 THEME FROM "STAR WARS"   Meco
6 BOOGIE NIGHTS   Heatwave
7 COLD AS ICE   Foreigner
8 BRICK HOUSE   Commodores
9 I FEEL LOVE   Donna Summer
10 I JUST WANT TO BE YOUR EVERYTHING   Andy Gibb

October 22, 1977

1 YOU LIGHT UP MY LIFE   Debby Boone
2 NOBODY DOES IT BETTER   Carly Simon
3 THAT'S ROCK 'N' ROLL   Shaun Cassidy
4 KEEP IT COMIN' LOVE   K. C. & The Sunshine Band
5 BOOGIE NIGHTS   Heatwave
6 COLD AS ICE   Foreigner
7 BRICK HOUSE   Commodores
8 I FEEL LOVE   Donna Summer
9 THEME FROM "STAR WARS"   Meco
10 SWAYIN' TO THE MUSIC   Johnny Rivers

October 29, 1977

1 YOU LIGHT UP MY LIFE   Debby Boone
2 NOBODY DOES IT BETTER   Carly Simon
3 THAT'S ROCK 'N' ROLL   Shaun Cassidy
4 BOOGIE NIGHTS   Heatwave
5 KEEP IT COMIN' LOVE   K. C. & The Sunshine Band
6 BRICK HOUSE   Commodores
7 I FEEL LOVE   Donna Summer
8 IT'S ECSTASY WHEN YOU LAY DOWN NEXT TO ME   Barry White
9 THEME FROM "STAR WARS"   Meco
10 DON'T IT MAKE MY BROWN EYES BLUE   Crystal Gayle

November 5, 1977

1 YOU LIGHT UP MY LIFE   Debby Boone
2 NOBODY DOES IT BETTER   Carly Simon
3 BOOGIE NIGHTS   Heatwave
4 THAT'S ROCK 'N' ROLL   Shaun Cassidy
5 BRICK HOUSE   Commodores
6 IT'S ECSTASY WHEN YOU LAY DOWN NEXT TO ME   Barry White
7 I FEEL LOVE   Donna Summer
8 DON'T IT MAKE MY BROWN EYES BLUE   Crystal Gayle
9 BABY, WHAT A BIG SURPRISE   Chicago
10 HEAVEN ON THE 7TH FLOOR   Paul Nichols

November 12, 1977

1 YOU LIGHT UP MY LIFE   Debby Boone
2 BOOGIE NIGHTS   Heatwave
3 NOBODY DOES IT BETTER   Carly Simon
4 IT'S ECSTASY WHEN YOU LAY DOWN NEXT TO ME   Barry White
5 DON'T IT MAKE MY BROWN EYES BLUE   Crystal Gayle
6 I FEEL LOVE   Donna Summer
7 BABY, WHAT A BIG SURPRISE   Chicago
8 HEAVEN ON THE 7TH FLOOR   Paul Nichols
9 HOW DEEP IS YOUR LOVE   Bee Gees
10 WE'RE ALL ALONE   Rita Coolidge

November 19, 1977

1 YOU LIGHT UP MY LIFE   Debby Boone
2 BOOGIE NIGHTS   Heatwave
3 DON'T IT MAKE MY BROWN EYES BLUE   Crystal Gayle
4 IT'S ECSTASY WHEN YOU LAY DOWN NEXT TO ME   Barry White
5 BABY, WHAT A BIG SURPRISE   Chicago
6 HOW DEEP IS YOUR LOVE   Bee Gees
7 HEAVEN ON THE 7TH FLOOR   Paul Nichols
8 WE'RE ALL ALONE   Rita Coolidge
9 BLUE BAYOU   Linda Ronstadt
10 NOBODY DOES IT BETTER   Carly Simon

November 26, 1977

1 YOU LIGHT UP MY LIFE   Debby Boone
2 DON'T IT MAKE MY BROWN EYES BLUE   Crystal Gayle
3 HOW DEEP IS YOUR LOVE   Bee Gees
4 BOOGIE NIGHTS   Heatwave
5 BABY, WHAT A BIG SURPRISE   Chicago
6 HEAVEN ON THE 7TH FLOOR   Paul Nichols
7 WE'RE ALL ALONE   Rita Coolidge
8 BLUE BAYOU   Linda Ronstadt
9 IT'S ECSTASY WHEN YOU LAY DOWN NEXT TO ME   Barry White
10 IT'S SO EASY   Commodores

December 3, 1977

1 YOU LIGHT UP MY LIFE   Debby Boone
2 DON'T IT MAKE MY BROWN EYES BLUE   Crystal Gayle
3 HOW DEEP IS YOUR LOVE   Bee Gees
4 BABY, WHAT A BIG SURPRISE   Chicago
5 BLUE BAYOU   Linda Ronstadt
6 HEAVEN ON THE 7TH FLOOR   Paul Nichols

7 WE'RE ALL ALONE   Rita Coolidge
8 BOOGIE NIGHTS   Heatwave
9 IT'S SO EASY   Commodores
10 BACK IN LOVE AGAIN   LTD

December 10, 1977
1 YOU LIGHT UP MY LIFE   Debby Boone
2 DON'T IT MAKE MY BROWN EYES BLUE   Crystal Gayle
3 HOW DEEP IS YOUR LOVE   Bee Gees
4 BLUE BAYOU   Linda Ronstadt
5 IT'S SO EASY   Commodores
6 HEAVEN ON THE 7TH FLOOR   Paul Nichols
7 WE'RE ALL ALONE   Rita Coolidge
8 BACK IN LOVE AGAIN   LTD
9 BABY, WHAT A BIG SURPRISE   Chicago
10 YOU MAKE LOVING FUN   Fleetwood Mac

December 17, 1977
1 YOU LIGHT UP MY LIFE   Debby Boone
2 HOW DEEP IS YOUR LOVE   Bee Gees
3 BLUE BAYOU   Linda Ronstadt
4 DON'T IT MAKE MY BROWN EYES BLUE   Crystal Gayle
5 IT'S SO EASY   Commodores
6 BACK IN LOVE AGAIN   LTD
7 WE'RE ALL ALONE   Rita Coolidge
8 BABY COME BACK   Player
9 YOU MAKE LOVING FUN   Fleetwood Mac
10 HERE YOU COME AGAIN   Dolly Parton

December 24, 1977
1 HOW DEEP IS YOUR LOVE   Bee Gees
2 YOU LIGHT UP MY LIFE   Debby Boone
3 BLUE BAYOU   Linda Ronstadt
4 BACK IN LOVE AGAIN   LTD
5 IT'S SO EASY   Commodores
6 BABY COME BACK   Player
7 DON'T IT MAKE MY BROWN EYES BLUE   Crystal Gayle
8 HERE YOU COME AGAIN   Dolly Parton
9 SENTIMENTAL LADY   Bob Welch
10 SLIP SLIDIN' AWAY   Paul Simon

December 31, 1977
1 NO SURVEY

January 7, 1978
1 HOW DEEP IS YOUR LOVE   Bee Gees
2 BABY COME BACK   Player
3 BLUE BAYOU   Linda Ronstadt
4 BACK IN LOVE AGAIN   LTD
5 HERE YOU COME AGAIN   Dolly Parton
6 YOU LIGHT UP MY LIFE   Debby Boone
7 SLIP SLIDIN' AWAY   Paul Simon
8 SENTIMENTAL LADY   Bob Welch
9 YOU'RE IN MY HEART (THE FINAL ACCLAIM)   Rod
   Stewart
10 HEY DEANIE   Shaun Cassidy

January 14, 1978
1 BABY COME BACK   Player
2 HOW DEEP IS YOUR LOVE   Bee Gees
3 HERE YOU COME AGAIN   Dolly Parton
4 YOU'RE IN MY HEART (THE FINAL ACCLAIM)   Rod
   Stewart
5 BACK IN LOVE AGAIN   LTD
6 SLIP SLIDIN' AWAY   Paul Simon
7 HEY DEANIE   Shaun Cassidy

Crystal Gayle
Crystal's #2 hit (Nov. 26) was probably kept from
the #1 slot by a persistent Debbie Boone favorite.

Eric Clapton
His Top 10 hit ``Lay Down Sally'' also peaked at #26 Country.

8 SENTIMENTAL LADY   Bob Welch
9 COME SAIL AWAY   Styx
10 WE ARE THE CHAMPIONS   Queen

January 21, 1978
1 BABY COME BACK   Player
2 HOW DEEP IS YOUR LOVE   Bee Gees
3 HERE YOU COME AGAIN   Dolly Parton
4 YOU'RE IN MY HEART (THE FINAL ACCLAIM)   Rod Stewart
5 SHORT PEOPLE   Randy Newman
6 SLIP SLIDIN' AWAY   Paul Simon
7 HEY DEANIE   Shaun Cassidy
8 WE ARE THE CHAMPIONS   Queen
9 COME SAIL AWAY   Styx
10 STAYIN' ALIVE   Bee Gees

January 27, 1978
1 BABY COME BACK   Player
2 SHORT PEOPLE   Randy Newman
3 STAYIN' ALIVE   Bee Gees
4 YOU'RE IN MY HEART (THE FINAL ACCLAIM)   Rod Stewart
5 SLIP SLIDIN' AWAY   Paul Simon
6 WE ARE THE CHAMPIONS   Queen
7 HOW DEEP IS YOUR LOVE   Bee Gees
8 COME SAIL AWAY   Styx
9 JUST THE WAY YOU ARE   Billy Joel
10 (LOVE IS) THICKER THAN WATER   Andy Gibb

February 4, 1978
1 STAYIN' ALIVE   Bee Gees
2 SHORT PEOPLE   Randy Newman
3 BABY COME BACK   Player
4 WE ARE THE CHAMPIONS   Queen
5 (LOVE IS) THICKER THAN WATER   Andy Gibb
6 JUST THE WAY YOU ARE   Billy Joel
7 HOW DEEP IS YOUR LOVE   Bee Gees
8 SOMETIMES WHEN WE TOUCH   Dan Hill
9 YOU'RE IN MY HEART (THE FINAL ACCLAIM)   Rod Stewart
10 EMOTION   Samantha Sang

February 11, 1978
1 STAYIN' ALIVE   Bee Gees
2 SHORT PEOPLE   Randy Newman
3 (LOVE IS) THICKER THAN WATER   Andy Gibb
4 WE ARE THE CHAMPIONS   Queen
5 JUST THE WAY YOU ARE   Billy Joel
6 SOMETIMES WHEN WE TOUCH   Dan Hill
7 BABY COME BACK   Player
8 EMOTION   Samantha Sang
9 DANCE, DANCE, DANCE   Chic
10 HOW DEEP IS YOUR LOVE   Bee Gees

February 18, 1978
1 STAYIN' ALIVE   Bee Gees
2 (LOVE IS) THICKER THAN WATER   Andy Gibb
3 JUST THE WAY YOU ARE   Billy Joel
4 WE ARE THE CHAMPIONS   Queen
5 SOMETIMES WHEN WE TOUCH   Dan Hill
6 EMOTION   Samantha Sang
7 DANCE, DANCE, DANCE   Chic
8 SHORT PEOPLE   Randy Newman
9 BABY COME BACK   Player
10 HOW DEEP IS YOUR LOVE   Bee Gees

February 25, 1978
1 STAYIN' ALIVE   Bee Gees *
2 (LOVE IS) THICKER THAN WATER   Andy Gibb
3 JUST THE WAY YOU ARE   Billy Joel
4 SOMETIMES WHEN WE TOUCH   Dan Hill
5 EMOTION   Samantha Sang
6 DANCE, DANCE, DANCE   Chic
7 WE ARE THE CHAMPIONS   Queen
8 NIGHT FEVER   Bee Gees
9 LAY DOWN SALLY   Eric Clapton
10 HOW DEEP IS YOUR LOVE   Bee Gees
   Note: * The Bee Gees have three songs in the Top Ten, not counting brother Andy Gibb's solo top ten hit.

March 4, 1978
1 (LOVE IS) THICKER THAN WATER   Andy Gibb
2 STAYIN' ALIVE   Bee Gees *
3 SOMETIMES WHEN WE TOUCH   Dan Hill
4 EMOTION   Samantha Sang
5 NIGHT FEVER   Bee Gees
6 DANCE, DANCE, DANCE   Chic
7 LAY DOWN SALLY   Eric Clapton
8 JUST THE WAY YOU ARE   Billy Joel
9 I GO CRAZY   Paul Davis
10 HOW DEEP IS YOUR LOVE   Bee Gees
   Note: * The Bee Gees have three songs in the Top Ten, not counting brother Andy Gibb's solo top ten hit.

March 11, 1978
1 (LOVE IS) THICKER THAN WATER   Andy Gibb
2 NIGHT FEVER   Bee Gees
3 SOMETIMES WHEN WE TOUCH   Dan Hill
4 EMOTION   Samantha Sang
5 LAY DOWN SALLY   Eric Clapton
6 STAYIN' ALIVE   Bee Gees
7 DANCE, DANCE, DANCE   Chic
8 I GO CRAZY   Paul Davis
9 JUST THE WAY YOU ARE   Billy Joel
10 CAN'T SMILE WITHOUT YOU   Barry Manilow

March 18, 1978
1 NIGHT FEVER   Bee Gees
2 STAYIN' ALIVE   Bee Gees
3 EMOTION   Samantha Sang
4 LAY DOWN SALLY   Eric Clapton
5 (LOVE IS) THICKER THAN WATER   Andy Gibb
6 CAN'T SMILE WITHOUT YOU   Barry Manilow
7 I GO CRAZY   Paul Davis
8 SOMETIMES WHEN WE TOUCH   Dan Hill
9 DANCE, DANCE, DANCE   Chic
10 JUST THE WAY YOU ARE   Billy Joel

March 25, 1978
1 NIGHT FEVER   Bee Gees
2 STAYIN' ALIVE   Bee Gees
3 EMOTION   Samantha Sang
4 LAY DOWN SALLY   Eric Clapton
5 CAN'T SMILE WITHOUT YOU   Barry Manilow
6 (LOVE IS) THICKER THAN WATER   Andy Gibb
7 I GO CRAZY   Paul Davis
8 SOMETIMES WHEN WE TOUCH   Dan Hill
9 IF I CAN'T HAVE YOU   Yvonne Elliman
10 THUNDER ISLAND   Jay Ferguson

April 1, 1978
1 NIGHT FEVER   Bee Gees

2   STAYIN' ALIVE   Bee Gees
3   LAY DOWN SALLY   Eric Clapton
4   CAN'T SMILE WITHOUT YOU   Barry Manilow
5   EMOTION   Samantha Sang
6   IF I CAN'T HAVE YOU   Yvonne Elliman
7   I GO CRAZY   Paul Davis
8   (LOVE IS) THICKER THAN WATER   Andy Gibb
9   THUNDER ISLAND   Jay Ferguson
10 DUST IN THE WIND   Kansas

April 8, 1978
1   NIGHT FEVER   Bee Gees
2   STAYIN' ALIVE   Bee Gees
3   LAY DOWN SALLY   Eric Clapton
4   CAN'T SMILE WITHOUT YOU   Barry Manilow
5   IF I CAN'T HAVE YOU   Yvonne Elliman
6   EMOTION   Samantha Sang
7   DUST IN THE WIND   Kansas
8   (LOVE IS) THICKER THAN WATER   Andy Gibb
9   THUNDER ISLAND   Jay Ferguson
10 JACK AND JILL   Raydio

April 15, 1978
1   NIGHT FEVER   Bee Gees
2   STAYIN' ALIVE   Bee Gees
3   LAY DOWN SALLY   Eric Clapton
4   CAN'T SMILE WITHOUT YOU   Barry Manilow
5   IF I CAN'T HAVE YOU   Yvonne Elliman
6   DUST IN THE WIND   Kansas
7   THE CLOSER I GET TO YOU   Roberta Flack & Donny Hathaway
8   JACK AND JILL   Raydio
9   WE'LL NEVER HAVE TO SAY GOODBYE AGAIN   England Dan & John Ford Coley
10 OUR LOVE   Natalie Cole

April 22, 1978
1   NIGHT FEVER   Bee Gees
2   IF I CAN'T HAVE YOU   Yvonne Elliman
3   CAN'T SMILE WITHOUT YOU   Barry Manilow
4   LAY DOWN SALLY   Eric Clapton
5   THE CLOSER I GET TO YOU   Roberta Flack & Donny Hathaway
6   DUST IN THE WIND   Kansas
7   WITH A LITTLE LUCK   Wings
8   JACK AND JILL   Raydio
9   WE'LL NEVER HAVE TO SAY GOODBYE AGAIN   England Dan & John Ford Coley
10 OUR LOVE   Natalie Cole

April 29, 1978
1   NIGHT FEVER   Bee Gees
2   IF I CAN'T HAVE YOU   Yvonne Elliman
3   CAN'T SMILE WITHOUT YOU   Barry Manilow
4   THE CLOSER I GET TO YOU   Roberta Flack & Donny Hathaway
5   WITH A LITTLE LUCK   Wings
6   LAY DOWN SALLY   Eric Clapton
7   DUST IN THE WIND   Kansas
8   JACK AND JILL   Raydio
9   YOU'RE THE ONE THAT I WANT   Olivia Newton-John & John Travolta
10 TOO MUCH, TOO LITTLE, TOO LATE   Johnny Mathis & Deniece Williams

May 6, 1978
1   NIGHT FEVER   Bee Gees
2   IF I CAN'T HAVE YOU   Yvonne Elliman
3   CAN'T SMILE WITHOUT YOU   Barry Manilow
4   THE CLOSER I GET TO YOU   Roberta Flack & Donny Hathaway
5   WITH A LITTLE LUCK   Wings
6   TOO MUCH, TOO LITTLE, TOO LATE   Johnny Mathis & Deniece Williams
7   YOU'RE THE ONE THAT I WANT   Olivia Newton-John & John Travolta
8   LAY DOWN SALLY   Eric Clapton
9   DUST IN THE WIND   Kansas
10 COUNT ON ME   Jefferson Starship

May 13, 1978
1   IF I CAN'T HAVE YOU   Yvonne Elliman
2   THE CLOSER I GET TO YOU   Roberta Flack & Donny Hathaway
3   WITH A LITTLE LUCK   Wings
4   TOO MUCH, TOO LITTLE, TOO LATE   Johnny Mathis & Deniece Williams
5   NIGHT FEVER   Bee Gees
6   YOU'RE THE ONE THAT I WANT   Olivia Newton-John & John Travolta
7   CAN'T SMILE WITHOUT YOU   Barry Manilow
8   COUNT ON ME   Jefferson Starship
9   DUST IN THE WIND   Kansas
10 IMAGINARY LOVER   Atlanta Rhythm Section

May 20, 1978
1   WITH A LITTLE LUCK   Wings
2   THE CLOSER I GET TO YOU   Roberta Flack & Donny Hathaway
3   TOO MUCH, TOO LITTLE, TOO LATE   Johnny Mathis & Deniece Williams
4   YOU'RE THE ONE THAT I WANT   Olivia Newton-John & John Travolta
5   IF I CAN'T HAVE YOU   Yvonne Elliman
6   SHADOW DANCING   Andy Gibb
7   FEELS SO GOOD   Chuck Mangione
8   COUNT ON ME   Jefferson Starship
9   IMAGINARY LOVER   Atlanta Rhythm Section
10 NIGHT FEVER   Bee Gees

May 27, 1978
1   WITH A LITTLE LUCK   Wings
2   TOO MUCH, TOO LITTLE, TOO LATE   Johnny Mathis & Deniece Williams
3   YOU'RE THE ONE THAT I WANT   Olivia Newton-John & John Travolta
4   SHADOW DANCING   Andy Gibb
5   THE CLOSER I GET TO YOU   Roberta Flack & Donny Hathaway
6   FEELS SO GOOD   Chuck Mangione
7   IF I CAN'T HAVE YOU   Yvonne Elliman
8   IMAGINARY LOVER   Atlanta Rhythm Section
9   COUNT ON ME   Jefferson Starship
10 ON BROADWAY   George Benson

June 3, 1978
1   TOO MUCH, TOO LITTLE, TOO LATE   Johnny Mathis & Deniece Williams
2   YOU'RE THE ONE THAT I WANT   Olivia Newton-John & John Travolta
3   SHADOW DANCING   Andy Gibb

4   WITH A LITTLE LUCK   Wings
5   FEELS SO GOOD   Chuck Mangione
6   THE CLOSER I GET TO YOU   Roberta Flack & Donny Hathaway
7   IMAGINARY LOVER   Atlanta Rhythm Section
8   ON BROADWAY   George Benson
9   TAKE A CHANCE ON ME   Abba
10 THIS TIME I'M IN IT FOR LOVE   Player

June 10, 1978
1   YOU'RE THE ONE THAT I WANT   Olivia Newton-John & John Travolta
2   SHADOW DANCING   Andy Gibb
3   TOO MUCH, TOO LITTLE, TOO LATE   Johnny Mathis & Deniece Williams
4   FEELS SO GOOD   Chuck Mangione
5   BAKER STREET   Gerry Rafferty
6   IT'S A HEARTACHE   Bonnie Tyler
7   ON BROADWAY   George Benson
8   TAKE A CHANCE ON ME   Abba
9   WITH A LITTLE LUCK   Wings
10 THIS TIME I'M IN IT FOR LOVE   Player

June 17, 1978
1   SHADOW DANCING   Andy Gibb
2   YOU'RE THE ONE THAT I WANT   Olivia Newton-John & John Travolta
3   BAKER STREET   Gerry Rafferty
4   IT'S A HEARTACHE   Bonnie Tyler
5   TOO MUCH, TOO LITTLE, TOO LATE   Johnny Mathis & Deniece Williams
6   TAKE A CHANCE ON ME   Abba
7   FEELS SO GOOD   Chuck Mangione
8   ON BROADWAY   George Benson
9   YOU BELONG TO ME   Carly Simon
10 LOVE IS LIKE OXYGEN   Sweet

June 24, 1978
1   SHADOW DANCING   Andy Gibb
2   BAKER STREET   Gerry Rafferty
3   IT'S A HEARTACHE   Bonnie Tyler
4   YOU'RE THE ONE THAT I WANT   Olivia Newton-John & John Travolta
5   TAKE A CHANCE ON ME   Abba
6   YOU BELONG TO ME   Carly Simon
7   USE TA BE MY GIRL   O'Jays
8   LOVE IS LIKE OXYGEN   Sweet
9   STILL THE SAME   Bob Seger
10 DANCE WITH ME   Orleans

July 1, 1978
1   SHADOW DANCING   Andy Gibb
2   BAKER STREET   Gerry Rafferty
3   IT'S A HEARTACHE   Bonnie Tyler
4   TAKE A CHANCE ON ME   Abba
5   USE TA BE MY GIRL   O'Jays
6   YOU BELONG TO ME   Carly Simon
7   STILL THE SAME   Bob Seger
8   LOVE IS LIKE OXYGEN   Sweet
9   DANCE WITH ME   Orleans
10 THE GROOVE LINE   Heatwave

July 8, 1978
1   SHADOW DANCING   Andy Gibb
2   BAKER STREET   Gerry Rafferty
3   TAKE A CHANCE ON ME   Abba
4   USE TA BE MY GIRL   O'Jays
5   STILL THE SAME   Bob Seger
6   IT'S A HEARTACHE   Bonnie Tyler
7   MISS YOU   Rolling Stones
8   DANCE WITH ME   Orleans
9   THE GROOVE LINE   Heatwave
10 YOU BELONG TO ME   Carly Simon

July 15, 1978
1   SHADOW DANCING   Andy Gibb
2   BAKER STREET   Gerry Rafferty
3   TAKE A CHANCE ON ME   Abba
4   USE TA BE MY GIRL   O'Jays
5   STILL THE SAME   Bob Seger
6   MISS YOU   Rolling Stones
7   THE GROOVE LINE   Heatwave
8   DANCE WITH ME   Orleans
9   IT'S A HEARTACHE   Bonnie Tyler
10 LAST DANCE   Donna Summer

July 22, 1978
1   SHADOW DANCING   Andy Gibb
2   BAKER STREET   Gerry Rafferty
3   MISS YOU   Rolling Stones
4   STILL THE SAME   Bob Seger
5   LAST DANCE   Donna Summer
6   GREASE   Frankie Valli
7   THE GROOVE LINE   Heatwave
8   USE TA BE MY GIRL   O'Jays
9   TAKE A CHANCE ON ME   Abba
10 THREE TIMES A LADY   Commodores

July 29, 1978
1   SHADOW DANCING   Andy Gibb
2   BAKER STREET   Gerry Rafferty
3   MISS YOU   Rolling Stones
4   LAST DANCE   Donna Summer
5   GREASE   Frankie Valli
6   THREE TIMES A LADY   Commodores
7   STILL THE SAME   Bob Seger
8   USE TA BE MY GIRL   O'Jays
9   THE GROOVE LINE   Heatwave
10 LOVE WILL FIND A WAY   Pablo Cruise

August 5, 1978
1   MISS YOU   Rolling Stones
2   THREE TIMES A LADY   Commodores
3   GREASE   Frankie Valli
4   LAST DANCE   Donna Summer
5   SHADOW DANCING   Andy Gibb
6   BAKER STREET   Gerry Rafferty
7   USE TA BE MY GIRL   O'Jays
8   HOT BLOODED   Foreigner
9   LOVE WILL FIND A WAY   Pablo Cruise
10 STILL THE SAME   Bob Seger

August 12, 1978
1   THREE TIMES A LADY   Commodores
2   GREASE   Frankie Valli
3   LAST DANCE   Donna Summer
4   MISS YOU   Rolling Stones
5   HOT BLOODED   Foreigner
6   BOOGIE OOGIE OOGIE   A Taste of Honey
7   LOVE WILL FIND A WAY   Pablo Cruise
8   COPACABANA   Barry Manilow
9   MAGNET AND STEEL   Walter Egan
10 AN EVERLASTING LOVE   Andy Gibb

August 19, 1978
1   THREE TIMES A LADY   Commodores
2   GREASE   Frankie Valli
3   LAST DANCE   Donna Summer
4   MISS YOU   Rolling Stones
5   HOT BLOODED   Foreigner
6   BOOGIE OOGIE OOGIE   A Taste of Honey
7   LOVE WILL FIND A WAY   Pablo Cruise
8   COPACABANA   Barry Manilow
9   MAGNET AND STEEL   Walter Egan
10 AN EVERLASTING LOVE   Andy Gibb

August 26, 1978
1   GREASE   Frankie Valli
2   THREE TIMES A LADY   Commodores
3   MISS YOU   Rolling Stones
4   BOOGIE OOGIE OOGIE   A Taste of Honey
5   HOT BLOODED   Foreigner
6   LOVE WILL FIND A WAY   Pablo Cruise
7   HOPELESSLY DEVOTED TO YOU   Olivia Newton-John
8   MAGNET AND STEEL   Walter Egan
9   AN EVERLASTING LOVE   Andy Gibb
10 LAST DANCE   Donna Summer

September 2, 1978
1   GREASE   Frankie Valli
2   THREE TIMES A LADY   Commodores
3   BOOGIE OOGIE OOGIE   A Taste of Honey
4   HOT BLOODED   Foreigner
5   HOPELESSLY DEVOTED TO YOU   Olivia Newton-John
6   MISS YOU   Rolling Stones
7   KISS YOU ALL OVER   Exile
8   AN EVERLASTING LOVE   Andy Gibb
9   MAGNET AND STEEL   Walter Egan
10 SHAME   Evelyn "Champagne" King

September 9, 1978
1   BOOGIE OOGIE OOGIE   A Taste of Honey
2   THREE TIMES A LADY   Commodores
3   HOT BLOODED   Foreigner
4   HOPELESSLY DEVOTED TO YOU   Olivia Newton-John
5   KISS YOU ALL OVER   Exile
6   GREASE   Frankie Valli
7   AN EVERLASTING LOVE   Andy Gibb
8   SUMMER NIGHTS   Olivia Newton-John & John Travolta
9   SHAME   Evelyn "Champagne" King
10 GOT TO GET YOU INTO MY LIFE   Earth, Wind & Fire

September 16, 1978
1   BOOGIE OOGIE OOGIE   A Taste of Honey
2   THREE TIMES A LADY   Commodores
3   HOT BLOODED   Foreigner
4   HOPELESSLY DEVOTED TO YOU   Olivia Newton-John
5   KISS YOU ALL OVER   Exile
6   AN EVERLASTING LOVE   Andy Gibb
7   SUMMER NIGHTS   Olivia Newton-John & John Travolta
8   DON'T LOOK BACK   Boston
9   GOT TO GET YOU INTO MY LIFE   Earth, Wind & Fire
10 SHAME   Evelyn "Champagne" King

September 23, 1978
1   BOOGIE OOGIE OOGIE   A Taste of Honey
2   KISS YOU ALL OVER   Exile
3   HOPELESSLY DEVOTED TO YOU   Olivia Newton-John
4   THREE TIMES A LADY   Commodores
5   AN EVERLASTING LOVE   Andy Gibb
6   SUMMER NIGHTS   Olivia Newton-John & John Travolta
7   DON'T LOOK BACK   Boston
8   HOT BLOODED   Foreigner
9   HOT CHILD IN THE CITY   Nick Gilder
10 REMINISCING   Little River Band

September 30, 1978
1   KISS YOU ALL OVER   Exile
2   BOOGIE OOGIE OOGIE   A Taste of Honey
3   HOPELESSLY DEVOTED TO YOU   Olivia Newton-John
4   THREE TIMES A LADY   Commodores
5   SUMMER NIGHTS   Olivia Newton-John & John Travolta
6   DON'T LOOK BACK   Boston
7   HOT CHILD IN THE CITY   Nick Gilder
8   REMINISCING   Little River Band
9   LOVE IS IN THE AIR   John Paul Young
10 AN EVERLASTING LOVE   Andy Gibb

October 7, 1978
1   KISS YOU ALL OVER   Exile
2   BOOGIE OOGIE OOGIE   A Taste of Honey
3   HOT CHILD IN THE CITY   Nick Gilder
4   DON'T LOOK BACK   Boston
5   SUMMER NIGHTS   Olivia Newton-John & John Travolta
6   REMINISCING   Little River Band
7   HOPELESSLY DEVOTED TO YOU   Olivia Newton-John
8   LOVE IS IN THE AIR   John Paul Young
9   YOU NEEDED ME   Anne Murray
10 WHENEVER I CALL YOU "FRIEND"   Kenny Loggins

October 14, 1978
1   KISS YOU ALL OVER   Exile
2   HOT CHILD IN THE CITY   Nick Gilder
3   BOOGIE OOGIE OOGIE   A Taste of Honey
4   DON'T LOOK BACK   Boston
5   REMINISCING   Little River Band
6   YOU NEEDED ME   Anne Murray
7   LOVE IS IN THE AIR   John Paul Young
8   WHENEVER I CALL YOU "FRIEND"   Kenny Loggins
9   SUMMER NIGHTS   Olivia Newton-John & John Travolta
10 HOPELESSLY DEVOTED TO YOU   Olivia Newton-John

October 21, 1978
1   KISS YOU ALL OVER   Exile
2   HOT CHILD IN THE CITY   Nick Gilder
3   BOOGIE OOGIE OOGIE   A Taste of Honey
4   REMINISCING   Little River Band
5   YOU NEEDED ME   Anne Murray
6   WHENEVER I CALL YOU "FRIEND"   Kenny Loggins
7   LOVE IS IN THE AIR   John Paul Young
8   MACARTHUR PARK   Donna Summer
9   DON'T LOOK BACK   Boston
10 SUMMER NIGHTS   Olivia Newton-John & John Travolta

October 28, 1978
1   HOT CHILD IN THE CITY   Nick Gilder
2   YOU NEEDED ME   Anne Murray
3   REMINISCING   Little River Band
4   MACARTHUR PARK   Donna Summer
5   WHENEVER I CALL YOU "FRIEND"   Kenny Loggins
6   KISS YOU ALL OVER   Exile
7   DOUBLE VISION   Foreigner
8   LOVE IS IN THE AIR   John Paul Young
9   HOW MUCH I FEEL   Ambrosia
10 BOOGIE OOGIE OOGIE   A Taste of Honey

Donna Summer
``MacArthur Park'' became another #1 hit for ``The Disco Queen'' (Nov. 11).

November 4, 1978
1 YOU NEEDED ME   Anne Murray
2 MACARTHUR PARK   Donna Summer
3 REMINISCING   Little River Band
4 DOUBLE VISION   Foreigner
5 WHENEVER I CALL YOU "FRIEND"   Kenny Loggins
6 HOT CHILD IN THE CITY   Nick Gilder
7 KISS YOU ALL OVER   Exile
8 HOW MUCH I FEEL   Ambrosia
9 BEAST OF BURDEN   Rolling Stones
10 GET OFF   Foxy

November 11, 1978
1 MACARTHUR PARK   Donna Summer
2 YOU NEEDED ME   Anne Murray
3 DOUBLE VISION   Foreigner
4 HOW MUCH I FEEL   Ambrosia
5 HOT CHILD IN THE CITY   Nick Gilder
6 KISS YOU ALL OVER   Exile
7 WHENEVER I CALL YOU "FRIEND"   Kenny Loggins
8 BEAST OF BURDEN   Rolling Stones
9 GET OFF   Foxy
10 I JUST WANNA STOP   Gino Vannelli

November 18, 1978
1 MACARTHUR PARK   Donna Summer
2 DOUBLE VISION   Foreigner
3 HOW MUCH I FEEL   Ambrosia
4 YOU NEEDED ME   Anne Murray
5 YOU DON'T BRING ME FLOWERS   Barbra Streisand & Neil Diamond
6 HOT CHILD IN THE CITY   Nick Gilder
7 KISS YOU ALL OVER   Exile
8 I JUST WANNA STOP   Gino Vannelli
9 WHENEVER I CALL YOU "FRIEND"   Kenny Loggins
10 YOU NEVER DONE IT LIKE THAT   Captain & Tennille

November 25, 1978
1 MACARTHUR PARK   Donna Summer
2 DOUBLE VISION   Foreigner
3 HOW MUCH I FEEL   Ambrosia
4 YOU DON'T BRING ME FLOWERS   Barbra Streisand & Neil Diamond
5 YOU NEEDED ME   Anne Murray
6 LE FREAK   Chic
7 I JUST WANNA STOP   Gino Vannelli
8 I LOVE THE NIGHT LIFE   Alicia Bridges
9 TIME PASSAGES   Al Stewart
10 YOU NEVER DONE IT LIKE THAT   Captain & Tennille

December 2, 1978
1 YOU DON'T BRING ME FLOWERS   Barbra Streisand & Neil Diamond
2 MACARTHUR PARK   Donna Summer
3 HOW MUCH I FEEL   Ambrosia
4 LE FREAK   Chic
5 I JUST WANNA STOP   Gino Vannelli
6 DOUBLE VISION   Foreigner
7 I LOVE THE NIGHT LIFE   Alicia Bridges
8 TIME PASSAGES   Al Stewart
9 MY LIFE   Billy Joel
10 SHARING THE NIGHT TOGETHER   Dr. Hook

December 9, 1978
1 LE FREAK   Chic
2 MACARTHUR PARK   Donna Summer

3 YOU DON'T BRING ME FLOWERS   Barbra Streisand & Neil Diamond
4 I JUST WANNA STOP   Gino Vannelli
5 HOW MUCH I FEEL   Ambrosia
6 I LOVE THE NIGHT LIFE   Alicia Bridges
7 TIME PASSAGES   Al Stewart
8 MY LIFE   Billy Joel
9 SHARING THE NIGHT TOGETHER   Dr. Hook
10 MACARTHUR PARK   Donna Summer

December 16, 1978
1 YOU DON'T BRING ME FLOWERS   Barbra Streisand & Neil Diamond
2 LE FREAK   Chic
3 TOO MUCH HEAVEN   Bee Gees
4 I JUST WANNA STOP   Gino Vannelli
5 MY LIFE   Billy Joel
6 I LOVE THE NIGHT LIFE   Alicia Bridges
7 TIME PASSAGES   Al Stewart
8 SHARING THE NIGHT TOGETHER   Dr. Hook
9 (OUR LOVE) DON'T THROW IT ALL AWAY   Andy Gibb
10 MACARTHUR PARK   Donna Summer

December 23, 1978
1 LE FREAK   Chic
2 TOO MUCH HEAVEN   Bee Gees
3 YOU DON'T BRING ME FLOWERS   Barbra Streisand & Neil Diamond
4 MY LIFE   Billy Joel
5 I LOVE THE NIGHT LIFE   Alicia Bridges
6 I JUST WANNA STOP   Gino Vannelli
7 SHARING THE NIGHT TOGETHER   Dr. Hook
8 Y.M.C.A.   Village People
9 (OUR LOVE) DON'T THROW IT ALL AWAY   Andy Gibb
10 HOLD THE LINE   Toto

December 30, 1978
NO SURVEY

January 6, 1979
1 TOO MUCH HEAVEN   Bee Gees
2 LE FREAK   Chic
3 MY LIFE   Billy Joel
4 YOU DON'T BRING ME FLOWERS   Barbra Streisand & Neil Diamond
5 I LOVE THE NIGHT LIFE   Alicia Bridges
6 SHARING THE NIGHT TOGETHER   Dr. Hook
7 Y.M.C.A.   Village People
8 HOLD THE LINE   Toto
9 (OUR LOVE) DON'T THROW IT ALL AWAY   Andy Gibb
10 OOH BABY BABY   Linda Ronstadt

January 13, 1979
1 TOO MUCH HEAVEN   Bee Gees
2 LE FREAK   Chic
3 MY LIFE   Billy Joel
4 YOU DON'T BRING ME FLOWERS   Barbra Streisand & Neil Diamond
5 HOLD THE LINE   Toto
6 SHARING THE NIGHT TOGETHER   Dr. Hook
7 Y.M.C.A.   Village People
8 OOH BABY BABY   Linda Ronstadt
9 (OUR LOVE) DON'T THROW IT ALL AWAY   Andy Gibb
10 PROMISES   Eric Clapton

January 20, 1979
1 LE FREAK   Chic
2 TOO MUCH HEAVEN   Bee Gees
3 MY LIFE   Billy Joel
4 Y.M.C.A.   Village People
5 HOLD THE LINE   Toto
6 YOU DON'T BRING ME FLOWERS   Barbra Streisand & Neil Diamond
7 OOH BABY BABY   Linda Ronstadt
8 A LITTLE MORE LOVE   Olivia Newton-John
9 PROMISES   Eric Clapton
10 DO YOU THINK I'M SEXY   Rod Stewart

January 27, 1979
1 LE FREAK   Chic
2 TOO MUCH HEAVEN   Bee Gees
3 Y.M.C.A.   Village People
4 DO YOU THINK I'M SEXY   Rod Stewart
5 MY LIFE   Billy Joel
6 A LITTLE MORE LOVE   Olivia Newton-John
7 OOH BABY BABY   Linda Ronstadt
8 HOLD THE LINE   Toto
9 EVERY 1'S A WINNER   Hot Chocolate
10 SEPTEMBER   Earth, Wind & Fire

February 3, 1979
1 LE FREAK   Chic
2 Y.M.C.A.   Village People
3 DO YOU THINK I'M SEXY   Rod Stewart
4 A LITTLE MORE LOVE   Olivia Newton-John
5 TOO MUCH HEAVEN   Bee Gees
6 MY LIFE   Billy Joel
7 EVERY 1'S A WINNER   Hot Chocolate
8 FIRE   Pointer Sisters
9 SEPTEMBER   Earth, Wind & Fire
10 I WILL SURVIVE   Gloria Gaynor

February 10, 1979
1 DO YOU THINK I'M SEXY   Rod Stewart
2 Y.M.C.A.   Village People
3 LE FREAK   Chic
4 A LITTLE MORE LOVE   Olivia Newton-John
5 FIRE   Pointer Sisters
6 EVERY 1'S A WINNER   Hot Chocolate
7 I WILL SURVIVE   Gloria Gaynor
8 SEPTEMBER   Earth, Wind & Fire
9 TOO MUCH HEAVEN   Bee Gees
10 LOTTA LOVE   Nicolette Larson

February 17, 1979
1 DO YOU THINK I'M SEXY   Rod Stewart
2 Y.M.C.A.   Village People
3 A LITTLE MORE LOVE   Olivia Newton-John
4 FIRE   Pointer Sisters
5 I WILL SURVIVE   Gloria Gaynor
6 EVERY 1'S A WINNER   Hot Chocolate
7 LE FREAK   Chic
8 LOTTA LOVE   Nicolette Larson
9 SOMEWHERE IN THE NIGHT   Barry Manilow
10 I WAS MADE FOR DANCING   Leif Garrett

February 24, 1979
1 DO YOU THINK I'M SEXY   Rod Stewart
2 FIRE   Pointer Sisters
3 A LITTLE MORE LOVE   Olivia Newton-John
4 I WILL SURVIVE   Gloria Gaynor
5 Y.M.C.A.   Village People
6 TRAGEDY   Bee Gees
7 LE FREAK   Chic
8 LOTTA LOVE   Nicolette Larson
9 SOMEWHERE IN THE NIGHT   Barry Manilow
10 I WAS MADE FOR DANCING   Leif Garrett

March 3, 1979
1 DO YOU THINK I'M SEXY   Rod Stewart
2 FIRE   Pointer Sisters
3 I WILL SURVIVE   Gloria Gaynor
4 TRAGEDY   Bee Gees
5 A LITTLE MORE LOVE   Olivia Newton-John
6 HEAVEN KNOWS   Donna Summer
7 LE FREAK   Chic
8 Y.M.C.A.   Village People
9 LOTTA LOVE   Nicolette Larson
10 WHAT A FOOL BELIEVES   Doobie Brothers

March 10, 1979
1 I WILL SURVIVE   Gloria Gaynor
2 DO YOU THINK I'M SEXY   Rod Stewart
3 TRAGEDY   Bee Gees
4 FIRE   Pointer Sisters
5 HEAVEN KNOWS   Donna Summer
6 A LITTLE MORE LOVE   Olivia Newton-John
7 SHAKE YOUR GROOVE THING   Peaches & Herb
8 WHAT A FOOL BELIEVES   Doobie Brothers
9 Y.M.C.A.   Village People
10 SULTANS OF SWING   Dire Straits

March 17, 1979
1 I WILL SURVIVE   Gloria Gaynor
2 TRAGEDY   Bee Gees
3 DO YOU THINK I'M SEXY   Rod Stewart
4 HEAVEN KNOWS   Donna Summer
5 SHAKE YOUR GROOVE THING   Peaches & Herb
6 WHAT A FOOL BELIEVES   Doobie Brothers
7 FIRE   Pointer Sisters
8 SULTANS OF SWING   Dire Straits
9 A LITTLE MORE LOVE   Olivia Newton-John
10 WHAT YOU WON'T DO FOR LOVE   Bobby Caldwell

March 24, 1979
1 TRAGEDY   Bee Gees
2 I WILL SURVIVE   Gloria Gaynor
3 WHAT A FOOL BELIEVES   Doobie Brothers
4 HEAVEN KNOWS   Donna Summer
5 SHAKE YOUR GROOVE THING   Peaches & Herb
6 DO YOU THINK I'M SEXY   Rod Stewart
7 SULTANS OF SWING   Dire Straits
8 FIRE   Pointer Sisters
9 WHAT YOU WON'T DO FOR LOVE   Bobby Caldwell
10 A LITTLE MORE LOVE   Olivia Newton-John

March 31, 1979
1 TRAGEDY   Bee Gees
2 I WILL SURVIVE   Gloria Gaynor
3 WHAT A FOOL BELIEVES   Doobie Brothers
4 HEAVEN KNOWS   Donna Summer
5 SHAKE YOUR GROOVE THING   Peaches & Herb
6 SULTANS OF SWING   Dire Straits
7 DO YOU THINK I'M SEXY   Rod Stewart
8 KNOCK ON WOOD   Amii Stewart
9 WHAT YOU WON'T DO FOR LOVE   Bobby Caldwell
10 DON'T CRY OUT LOUD   Melissa Manchester

Village People
``In The Navy'' was a solid Top 10 hit for the first openly gay group to top the charts.

Peaches & Herb
This duo stayed ``Reunited'' at the #1 position for the entire month of May.

April 7, 1979

1   I WILL SURVIVE   Gloria Gaynor
2   WHAT A FOOL BELIEVES   Doobie Brothers
3   TRAGEDY   Bee Gees
4   SULTANS OF SWING   Dire Straits
5   SHAKE YOUR GROOVE THING   Peaches & Herb
6   MUSIC BOX DANCER   Frank Mills
7   KNOCK ON WOOD   Amii Stewart
8   DO YOU THINK I'M SEXY   Rod Stewart
9   HEART OF GLASS   Blondie
10 LADY   Little River Band

April 14, 1979

1   WHAT A FOOL BELIEVES   Doobie Brothers
2   I WILL SURVIVE   Gloria Gaynor
3   KNOCK ON WOOD   Amii Stewart
4   SULTANS OF SWING   Dire Straits
5   MUSIC BOX DANCER   Frank Mills
6   TRAGEDY   Bee Gees
7   REUNITED   Peaches & Herb
8   HEART OF GLASS   Blondie
9   STUMBLIN' IN   Suzi Quatro & Chris Norman
10 LADY   Little River Band

April 21, 1979

1   KNOCK ON WOOD   Amii Stewart
2   I WILL SURVIVE   Gloria Gaynor
3   HEART OF GLASS   Blondie
4   MUSIC BOX DANCER   Frank Mills
5   WHAT A FOOL BELIEVES   Doobie Brothers
6   REUNITED   Peaches & Herb
7   STUMBLIN' IN   Suzi Quatro & Chris Norman
8   TRAGEDY   Bee Gees
9   I WANT YOUR LOVE   Chic
10 SULTANS OF SWING   Dire Straits

April 28, 1979

1   HEART OF GLASS   Blondie
2   REUNITED   Peaches & Herb
3   KNOCK ON WOOD   Amii Stewart
4   MUSIC BOX DANCER   Frank Mills
5   I WILL SURVIVE   Gloria Gaynor
6   STUMBLIN' IN   Suzi Quatro & Chris Norman
7   WHAT A FOOL BELIEVES   Doobie Brothers
8   I WANT YOUR LOVE   Chic
9   GOODNIGHT TONIGHT   Wings
10 IN THE NAVY   Village People

May 5, 1979

1   REUNITED   Peaches & Herb
2   HEART OF GLASS   Blondie
3   MUSIC BOX DANCER   Frank Mills
4   KNOCK ON WOOD   Amii Stewart
5   STUMBLIN' IN   Suzi Quatro & Chris Norman
6   IN THE NAVY   Village People
7   I WANT YOUR LOVE   Chic
8   GOODNIGHT TONIGHT   Wings
9   TAKE ME HOME   Phil Collins
10 HE'S THE GREATEST DANCER   Sister Sledge

May 12, 1979

1   REUNITED   Peaches & Herb
2   HEART OF GLASS   Blondie
3   HOT STUFF   Donna Summer
4   STUMBLIN' IN   Suzi Quatro & Chris Norman
5   IN THE NAVY   Village People

6   GOODNIGHT TONIGHT   Wings
7   I WANT YOUR LOVE   Chic
8   TAKE ME HOME   Phil Collins
9   HE'S THE GREATEST DANCER   Sister Sledge
10 SHAKE YOUR BODY (DOWN TO THE GROUND)
     Jacksons

May 19, 1979

1   REUNITED   Peaches & Herb
2   HOT STUFF   Donna Summer
3   IN THE NAVY   Village People
4   STUMBLIN' IN   Suzi Quatro & Chris Norman
5   GOODNIGHT TONIGHT   Wings
6   LOVE YOU INSIDE OUT   Bee Gees
7   SHAKE YOUR BODY (DOWN TO THE GROUND)
     Jacksons
8   TAKE ME HOME   Phil Collins
9   HE'S THE GREATEST DANCER   Sister Sledge
10 HEART OF GLASS   Blondie

May 26, 1979

1   REUNITED   Peaches & Herb
2   HOT STUFF   Donna Summer
3   IN THE NAVY   Village People
4   LOVE YOU INSIDE OUT   Bee Gees
5   GOODNIGHT TONIGHT   Wings
6   WE ARE FAMILY   Sister Sledge
7   SHAKE YOUR BODY (DOWN TO THE GROUND)
     Jacksons
8   JUST WHEN I NEEDED YOU MOST   Randy Vanwarmer
9   STUMBLIN' IN   Suzi Quatro & Chris Norman
10 LOVE IS THE ANSWER   England Dan & John Ford Coley

June 2, 1979

1   HOT STUFF   Donna Summer
2   REUNITED   Peaches & Herb
3   LOVE YOU INSIDE OUT   Bee Gees
4   WE ARE FAMILY   Sister Sledge
5   GOODNIGHT TONIGHT   Wings
6   JUST WHEN I NEEDED YOU MOST   Randy Vanwarmer
7   SHAKE YOUR BODY (DOWN TO THE GROUND)
     Jacksons
8   IN THE NAVY   Village People
9   THE LOGICAL SONG   Supertramp
10 LOVE IS THE ANSWER   England Dan & John Ford Coley

June 9, 1979

1   LOVE YOU INSIDE OUT   Bee Gees
2   HOT STUFF   Donna Summer
3   WE ARE FAMILY   Sister Sledge
4   REUNITED   Peaches & Herb
5   JUST WHEN I NEEDED YOU MOST   Randy Vanwarmer
6   RING MY BELL   Anita Ward
7   THE LOGICAL SONG   Supertramp
8   CHUCK E.'S IN LOVE   Rickie Lee Jones
9   SHAKE YOUR BODY (DOWN TO THE GROUND)
     Jacksons
10 SHE BELIEVES IN ME   Kenny Rogers

June 16, 1979

1   HOT STUFF   Donna Summer
2   WE ARE FAMILY   Sister Sledge
3   RING MY BELL   Anita Ward
4   JUST WHEN I NEEDED YOU MOST   Randy Vanwarmer
5   LOVE YOU INSIDE OUT   Bee Gees
6   THE LOGICAL SONG   Supertramp

7   CHUCK E.'S IN LOVE   Rickie Lee Jones
8   SHE BELIEVES IN ME   Kenny Rogers
9   REUNITED   Peaches & Herb
10 BOOGIE WONDERLAND   Earth, Wind & Fire with The Emotions

June 23, 1979

1   HOT STUFF   Donna Summer
2   WE ARE FAMILY   Sister Sledge
3   RING MY BELL   Anita Ward
4   JUST WHEN I NEEDED YOU MOST   Randy Vanwarmer
5   BAD GIRLS   Donna Summer
6   THE LOGICAL SONG   Supertramp
7   CHUCK E.'S IN LOVE   Rickie Lee Jones
8   SHE BELIEVES IN ME   Kenny Rogers
9   BOOGIE WONDERLAND   Earth, Wind & Fire with The Emotions
10 YOU TAKE MY BREATH AWAY   Rex Smith

June 30, 1979

1   RING MY BELL   Anita Ward
2   HOT STUFF   Donna Summer
3   BAD GIRLS   Donna Summer
4   WE ARE FAMILY   Sister Sledge
5   CHUCK E.'S IN LOVE   Rickie Lee Jones
6   THE LOGICAL SONG   Supertramp
7   SHE BELIEVES IN ME   Kenny Rogers
8   BOOGIE WONDERLAND   Earth, Wind & Fire with The Emotions
9   JUST WHEN I NEEDED YOU MOST   Randy Vanwarmer
10 YOU TAKE MY BREATH AWAY   Rex Smith

July 7, 1979

1   RING MY BELL   Anita Ward
2   BAD GIRLS   Donna Summer
3   HOT STUFF   Donna Summer
4   CHUCK E.'S IN LOVE   Rickie Lee Jones
5   SHE BELIEVES IN ME   Kenny Rogers
6   THE LOGICAL SONG   Supertramp
7   BOOGIE WONDERLAND   Earth, Wind & Fire with The Emotions
8   WE ARE FAMILY   Sister Sledge
9   MAKIN' IT   David Naughton
10 I WANT YOU TO WANT ME   Cheap Trick

July 14, 1979

1   BAD GIRLS   Donna Summer
2   RING MY BELL   Anita Ward
3   HOT STUFF   Donna Summer
4   CHUCK E.'S IN LOVE   Rickie Lee Jones
5   SHE BELIEVES IN ME   Kenny Rogers
6   BOOGIE WONDERLAND   Earth, Wind & Fire with The Emotions
7   MAKIN' IT   David Naughton
8   I WANT YOU TO WANT ME   Cheap Trick
9   SHINE A LITTLE LOVE   Electric Light Orchestra
10 BAD GIRLS   Donna Summer

July 21, 1979

1   BAD GIRLS   Donna Summer
2   RING MY BELL   Anita Ward
3   HOT STUFF   Donna Summer
4   GOOD TIMES   Chic
5   MAKIN' IT   David Naughton
6   BOOGIE WONDERLAND   Earth, Wind & Fire with The Emotions

7   I WANT YOU TO WANT ME   Cheap Trick
8   SHINE A LITTLE LOVE   Electric Light Orchestra
9   GOLD   John Stewart
10 SHE BELIEVES IN ME   Kenny Rogers

July 28, 1979

1   BAD GIRLS   Donna Summer
2   RING MY BELL   Anita Ward
3   GOOD TIMES   Chic
4   HOT STUFF   Donna Summer
5   MAKIN' IT   David Naughton
6   GOLD   John Stewart
7   I WANT YOU TO WANT ME   Cheap Trick
8   SHINE A LITTLE LOVE   Electric Light Orchestra
9   WHEN YOU'RE IN LOVE WITH A BEAUTIFUL WOMAN   Dr. Hook
10 MAIN EVENT   Barbra Streisand

August 4, 1979

1   BAD GIRLS   Donna Summer
2   GOOD TIMES   Chic
3   RING MY BELL   Anita Ward
4   MAIN EVENT   Barbra Streisand
5   GOLD   John Stewart
6   MY SHARONA   Knack
7   MAKIN' IT   David Naughton
8   WHEN YOU'RE IN LOVE WITH A BEAUTIFUL WOMAN   Dr. Hook
9   HOT STUFF   Donna Summer
10 I WANT YOU TO WANT ME   Cheap Trick

August 11, 1979

1   BAD GIRLS   Donna Summer
2   GOOD TIMES   Chic
3   MAIN EVENT   Barbra Streisand
4   MY SHARONA   Knack
5   GOLD   John Stewart
6   WHEN YOU'RE IN LOVE WITH A BEAUTIFUL WOMAN   Dr. Hook
7   RING MY BELL   Anita Ward
8   MAKIN' IT   David Naughton
9   HOT STUFF   Donna Summer
10 YOU CAN'T CHANGE THAT   Ray Parker, Jr. & Raydio

August 18, 1979

1   GOOD TIMES   Chic
2   MY SHARONA   Knack
3   MAIN EVENT   Barbra Streisand
4   BAD GIRLS   Donna Summer
5   AFTER THE LOVE HAS GONE   Earth, Wind & Fire
6   WHEN YOU'RE IN LOVE WITH A BEAUTIFUL WOMAN   Dr. Hook
7   RING MY BELL   Anita Ward
8   THE DEVIL WENT DOWN TO GEORGIA   Charlie Daniels Band
9   YOU CAN'T CHANGE THAT   Ray Parker, Jr. & Raydio
10 MAMA CAN'T BUY YOU LOVE   Elton John

August 25, 1979

1   MY SHARONA   Knack
2   GOOD TIMES   Chic
3   MAIN EVENT   Barbra Streisand
4   AFTER THE LOVE HAS GONE   Earth, Wind & Fire
5   BAD GIRLS   Donna Summer
6   DON'T BRING ME DOWN   Electric Light Orchestra
7   THE DEVIL WENT DOWN TO GEORGIA   Charlie Daniels Band

Charlie Daniels

It was't the Devil that changed the lyric ``son of a bitch'' to ``son of a gun'' in Charlie's Top 10 hit (Aug.-Sep.).

8   LEAD ME ON   Maxine Nightingale
9   MAMA CAN'T BUY YOU LOVE   Elton John
10   SAD EYES   Robert John

September 1, 1979
1   MY SHARONA   Knack
2   GOOD TIMES   Chic
3   MAIN EVENT   Barbra Streisand
4   AFTER THE LOVE HAS GONE   Earth, Wind & Fire
5   DON'T BRING ME DOWN   Electric Light Orchestra
6   THE DEVIL WENT DOWN TO GEORGIA   Charlie Daniels Band
7   LEAD ME ON   Maxine Nightingale
8   SAD EYES   Robert John
9   MAMA CAN'T BUY YOU LOVE   Elton John
10   I'LL NEVER LOVE THIS WAY AGAIN   Dionne Warwick

September 8, 1979
1   MY SHARONA   Knack
2   GOOD TIMES   Chic
3   AFTER THE LOVE HAS GONE   Earth, Wind & Fire
4   DON'T BRING ME DOWN   Electric Light Orchestra
5   THE DEVIL WENT DOWN TO GEORGIA   Charlie Daniels Band
6   LEAD ME ON   Maxine Nightingale
7   SAD EYES   Robert John
8   MAIN EVENT   Barbra Streisand
9   I'LL NEVER LOVE THIS WAY AGAIN   Dionne Warwick
10   LONESOME LOSER   Little River Band

September 15, 1979
1   MY SHARONA   Knack
2   AFTER THE LOVE HAS GONE   Earth, Wind & Fire
3   THE DEVIL WENT DOWN TO GEORGIA   Charlie Daniels Band
4   DON'T BRING ME DOWN   Electric Light Orchestra
5   LEAD ME ON   Maxine Nightingale
6   SAD EYES   Robert John
7   LONESOME LOSER   Little River Band
8   I'LL NEVER LOVE THIS WAY AGAIN   Dionne Warwick
9   GOOD TIMES   Chic
10   SAIL ON   Commodores

September 22, 1979
1   MY SHARONA   Knack
2   AFTER THE LOVE HAS GONE   Earth, Wind & Fire
3   THE DEVIL WENT DOWN TO GEORGIA   Charlie Daniels Band
4   RISE   Herb Alpert
5   LEAD ME ON   Maxine Nightingale
6   SAD EYES   Robert John
7   LONESOME LOSER   Little River Band
8   I'LL NEVER LOVE THIS WAY AGAIN   Dionne Warwick
9   SAIL ON   Commodores
10   DON'T BRING ME DOWN   Electric Light Orchestra

September 29, 1979
1   MY SHARONA   Knack
2   SAD EYES   Robert John
3   RISE   Herb Alpert
4   DON'T STOP 'TIL YOU GET ENOUGH   Michael Jackson
5   AFTER THE LOVE HAS GONE   Earth, Wind & Fire
6   LONESOME LOSER   Little River Band
7   I'LL NEVER LOVE THIS WAY AGAIN   Dionne Warwick
8   SAIL ON   Commodores
9   THE DEVIL WENT DOWN TO GEORGIA   Charlie Daniels Band
10   DON'T BRING ME DOWN   Electric Light Orchestra

October 6, 1979
1   SAD EYES   Robert John
2   DON'T STOP 'TIL YOU GET ENOUGH   Michael Jackson
3   RISE   Herb Alpert
4   MY SHARONA   Knack
5   SAIL ON   Commodores
6   LONESOME LOSER   Little River Band
7   I'LL NEVER LOVE THIS WAY AGAIN   Dionne Warwick
8   POP MUZIK   M
9   AFTER THE LOVE HAS GONE   Earth, Wind & Fire
10   DIM ALL THE LIGHTS   Donna Summer

October 13, 1979
1   DON'T STOP 'TIL YOU GET ENOUGH   Michael Jackson
2   RISE   Herb Alpert
3   SAD EYES   Robert John
4   SAIL ON   Commodores
5   MY SHARONA   Knack
6   I'LL NEVER LOVE THIS WAY AGAIN   Dionne Warwick
7   POP MUZIK   M
8   DIM ALL THE LIGHTS   Donna Summer
9   LONESOME LOSER   Little River Band
10   AFTER THE LOVE HAS GONE   Earth, Wind & Fire

October 20, 1979
1   RISE   Herb Alpert
2   DON'T STOP 'TIL YOU GET ENOUGH   Michael Jackson

3   POP MUZIK   M
4   SAIL ON   Commodores
5   I'LL NEVER LOVE THIS WAY AGAIN   Dionne Warwick
6   DIM ALL THE LIGHTS   Donna Summer
7   SAD EYES   Robert John
8   MY SHARONA   Knack
9   HEARTACHE TONIGHT   Eagles
10 STILL   Commodores

October 27, 1979
1   RISE   Herb Alpert
2   POP MUZIK   M
3   DON'T STOP 'TIL YOU GET ENOUGH   Michael Jackson
4   DIM ALL THE LIGHTS   Donna Summer
5   I'LL NEVER LOVE THIS WAY AGAIN   Dionne Warwick
6   SAIL ON   Commodores
7   HEARTACHE TONIGHT   Eagles
8   STILL   Commodores
9   TUSK   Fleetwood Mac
10 YOU DECORATED MY LIFE   Kenny Rogers

November 3, 1979
1   POP MUZIK   M
2   HEARTACHE TONIGHT   Eagles
3   DIM ALL THE LIGHTS   Donna Summer
4   RISE   Herb Alpert
5   STILL   Commodores
6   DON'T STOP 'TIL YOU GET ENOUGH   Michael Jackson
7   BABE   Styx
8   TUSK   Fleetwood Mac
9   YOU DECORATED MY LIFE   Kenny Rogers
10 NO MORE TEARS (ENOUGH IS ENOUGH)   Barbra
    Streisand & Donna Summer

November 10, 1979
1   HEARTACHE TONIGHT   Eagles
2   DIM ALL THE LIGHTS   Donna Summer
3   STILL   Commodores
4   RISE   Herb Alpert
5   POP MUZIK   M
6   BABE   Styx
7   NO MORE TEARS (ENOUGH IS ENOUGH)   Barbra
    Streisand & Donna Summer
8   TUSK   Fleetwood Mac
9   YOU DECORATED MY LIFE   Kenny Rogers
10 PLEASE DON'T GO   K. C. & The Sunshine Band

November 17, 1979
1   STILL   Commodores
2   DIM ALL THE LIGHTS   Donna Summer
3   NO MORE TEARS (ENOUGH IS ENOUGH)   Barbra
    Streisand & Donna Summer
4   BABE   Styx
5   HEARTACHE TONIGHT   Eagles
6   RISE   Herb Alpert
7   YOU DECORATED MY LIFE   Kenny Rogers
8   TUSK   Fleetwood Mac
9   PLEASE DON'T GO   K. C. & The Sunshine Band
10 POP MUZIK   M

November 24, 1979
1   NO MORE TEARS (ENOUGH IS ENOUGH)   Barbra
    Streisand & Donna Summer
2   BABE   Styx

3   STILL   Commodores
4   DIM ALL THE LIGHTS   Donna Summer
5   HEARTACHE TONIGHT   Eagles
6   PLEASE DON'T GO   K. C. & The Sunshine Band
7   YOU DECORATED MY LIFE   Kenny Rogers
8   SEND ONE YOUR LOVE   Stevie Wonder
9   TUSK   Fleetwood Mac
10 POP MUZIK   M

December 1, 1979
1   NO MORE TEARS (ENOUGH IS ENOUGH)   Barbra
    Streisand & Donna Summer
2   BABE   Styx
3   STILL   Commodores
4   PLEASE DON'T GO   K. C. & The Sunshine Band
5   HEARTACHE TONIGHT   Eagles
6   ESCAPE   Rupert Holmes
7   SEND ONE YOUR LOVE   Stevie Wonder
8   DIM ALL THE LIGHTS   Donna Summer
9   SHIPS   Barry Manilow
10 POP MUZIK   M

December 8, 1979
1   BABE   Styx
2   NO MORE TEARS (ENOUGH IS ENOUGH)   Barbra
    Streisand & Donna Summer
3   STILL   Commodores
4   PLEASE DON'T GO   K. C. & The Sunshine Band
5   ESCAPE   Rupert Holmes
6   SEND ONE YOUR LOVE   Stevie Wonder
7   HEARTACHE TONIGHT   Eagles
8   YOU'RE ONLY LONELY   J. D. Souther
9   SHIPS   Barry Manilow
10 DO THAT TO ME ONE MORE TIME   Captain & Tennille

December 15, 1979
1   BABE   Styx
2   STILL   Commodores
3   PLEASE DON'T GO   K. C. & The Sunshine Band
4   ESCAPE   Rupert Holmes
5   SEND ONE YOUR LOVE   Stevie Wonder
6   NO MORE TEARS (ENOUGH IS ENOUGH)   Barbra
    Streisand & Donna Summer
7   YOU'RE ONLY LONELY   J. D. Souther
8   DO THAT TO ME ONE MORE TIME   Captain & Tennille
9   HEARTACHE TONIGHT   Eagles
10 TAKE THE LONG WAY HOME   Supertramp

December 22, 1979
1   ESCAPE   Rupert Holmes
2   PLEASE DON'T GO   K. C. & The Sunshine Band
3   BABE   Styx
4   SEND ONE YOUR LOVE   Stevie Wonder
5   STILL   Commodores
6   DO THAT TO ME ONE MORE TIME   Captain & Tennille
7   YOU'RE ONLY LONELY   J. D. Souther
8   NO MORE TEARS (ENOUGH IS ENOUGH)   Barbra
    Streisand & Donna Summer
9   LADIES NIGHT   Kool & The Gang
10 TAKE THE LONG WAY HOME   Supertramp

December 29, 1979
NO SURVEY

The Eighties

January 5, 1980
1. PLEASE DON'T GO   K. C. & The Sunshine Band
2. ESCAPE   Rupert Holmes
3. ROCK WITH YOU   Michael Jackson
4. SEND ONE YOUR LOVE   Stevie Wonder
5. DO THAT TO ME ONE MORE TIME   Captain & Tennille
6. BABE   Styx
7. STILL   Commodores
8. COWARD OF THE COUNTY   Kenny Rogers
9. LADIES NIGHT   Kool & The Gang
10. WE DON'T TALK ANYMORE   Cliff Richard

January 12, 1980
1. ESCAPE   Rupert Holmes
2. ROCK WITH YOU   Michael Jackson
3. DO THAT TO ME ONE MORE TIME   Captain & Tennille
4. SEND ONE YOUR LOVE   Stevie Wonder
5. PLEASE DON'T GO   K. C. & The Sunshine Band
6. STILL   Commodores
7. COWARD OF THE COUNTY   Kenny Rogers
8. LADIES NIGHT   Kool & The Gang
9. WE DON'T TALK ANYMORE   Cliff Richard
10. BABE   Styx

January 19, 1980
1. ROCK WITH YOU   Michael Jackson
2. DO THAT TO ME ONE MORE TIME   Captain & Tennille
3. ESCAPE   Rupert Holmes
4. COWARD OF THE COUNTY   Kenny Rogers
5. SEND ONE YOUR LOVE   Stevie Wonder
6. CRUISIN'   Smokey Robinson
7. WE DON'T TALK ANYMORE   Cliff Richard
8. LADIES NIGHT   Kool & The Gang
9. PLEASE DON'T GO   K. C. & The Sunshine Band
10. COOL CHANGE   Little River Band

January 26, 1980
1. ROCK WITH YOU   Michael Jackson
2. DO THAT TO ME ONE MORE TIME   Captain & Tennille
3. COWARD OF THE COUNTY   Kenny Rogers
4. ESCAPE   Rupert Holmes
5. CRUISIN'   Smokey Robinson
6. SEND ONE YOUR LOVE   Stevie Wonder
7. WE DON'T TALK ANYMORE   Cliff Richard
8. CRAZY LITTLE THING CALLED LOVE   Queen
9. THE LONG RUN   Eagles
10. SARA   Fleetwood Mac

February 2, 1980
1. ROCK WITH YOU   Michael Jackson *
2. DO THAT TO ME ONE MORE TIME   Captain & Tennille
3. COWARD OF THE COUNTY   Kenny Rogers
4. CRUISIN'   Smokey Robinson
5. CRAZY LITTLE THING CALLED LOVE   Queen
6. ESCAPE   Rupert Holmes
7. SARA   Fleetwood Mac
8. THE LONG RUN   Eagles
9. YES, I'M READY   Barbara Mason
10. DON'T DO ME LIKE THAT   Tom Petty

February 9, 1980
1. ROCK WITH YOU   Michael Jackson
2. DO THAT TO ME ONE MORE TIME   Captain & Tennille
3. COWARD OF THE COUNTY   Kenny Rogers
4. CRUISIN'   Smokey Robinson
5. CRAZY LITTLE THING CALLED LOVE   Queen
6. YES, I'M READY   Barbara Mason
7. SARA   Fleetwood Mac
8. THE LONG RUN   Eagles
9. LONGER   Dan Fogelberg
10. DON'T DO ME LIKE THAT   Tom Petty

February 16, 1980
1. DO THAT TO ME ONE MORE TIME   Captain & Tennille
2. CRAZY LITTLE THING CALLED LOVE   Queen
3. COWARD OF THE COUNTY   Kenny Rogers
4. CRUISIN'   Smokey Robinson
5. ROCK WITH YOU   Michael Jackson
6. YES, I'M READY   Barbara Mason
7. SARA   Fleetwood Mac
8. LONGER   Dan Fogelberg
9. ON THE RADIO   Donna Summer
10. DESIRE   Andy Gibb

February 23, 1980
1. CRAZY LITTLE THING CALLED LOVE   Queen
2. DO THAT TO ME ONE MORE TIME   Captain & Tennille
3. YES, I'M READY   Barbara Mason
4. CRUISIN'   Smokey Robinson
5. ROCK WITH YOU   Michael Jackson
6. LONGER   Dan Fogelberg
7. ON THE RADIO   Donna Summer
8. DESIRE   Andy Gibb
9. COWARD OF THE COUNTY   Kenny Rogers
10. SARA   Fleetwood Mac

March 1, 1980
1. CRAZY LITTLE THING CALLED LOVE   Queen
2. YES, I'M READY   Barbara Mason
3. DO THAT TO ME ONE MORE TIME   Captain & Tennille
4. LONGER   Dan Fogelberg
5. DESIRE   Andy Gibb
6. ON THE RADIO   Donna Summer
7. CRUISIN'   Smokey Robinson
8. ROCK WITH YOU   Michael Jackson
9. WORKING MY WAY BACK TO YOU   Spinners
10. ANOTHER BRICK IN THE WALL   Pink Floyd

March 8, 1980
1. CRAZY LITTLE THING CALLED LOVE   Queen
2. YES, I'M READY   Barbara Mason
3. LONGER   Dan Fogelberg
4. DESIRE   Andy Gibb
5. ON THE RADIO   Donna Summer
6. ANOTHER BRICK IN THE WALL   Pink Floyd
7. DO THAT TO ME ONE MORE TIME   Captain & Tennille
8. WORKING MY WAY BACK TO YOU   Spinners
9. HIM   Rupert Holmes
10. THE SECOND TIME AROUND   Shalamar

Pink Floyd
``Another Brick In The Wall'' is a #1 hit for this persistent band of Englishmen (Mar. 22).

March 15, 1980
1   CRAZY LITTLE THING CALLED LOVE   Queen
2   LONGER   Dan Fogelberg
3   ANOTHER BRICK IN THE WALL   Pink Floyd
4   DESIRE   Andy Gibb
5   ON THE RADIO   Donna Summer
6   WORKING MY WAY BACK TO YOU   Spinners
7   YES, I'M READY   Barbara Mason
8   HIM   Rupert Holmes
9   THE SECOND TIME AROUND   Shalamar
10   TOO HOT   Kool & The Gang

March 22, 1980
1   ANOTHER BRICK IN THE WALL   Pink Floyd
2   LONGER   Dan Fogelberg
3   CRAZY LITTLE THING CALLED LOVE   Queen
4   DESIRE   Andy Gibb
5   WORKING MY WAY BACK TO YOU   Spinners
6   ON THE RADIO   Donna Summer
7   HIM   Rupert Holmes
8   THE SECOND TIME AROUND   Shalamar
9   TOO HOT   Kool & The Gang
10   HOW DO I MAKE YOU   Linda Ronstadt

March 29, 1980
1   ANOTHER BRICK IN THE WALL   Pink Floyd
2   WORKING MY WAY BACK TO YOU   Spinners
3   CRAZY LITTLE THING CALLED LOVE   Queen
4   DESIRE   Andy Gibb
5   CALL ME   Blondie
6   HIM   Rupert Holmes
7   TOO HOT   Kool & The Gang

8   THE SECOND TIME AROUND   Shalamar
9   RIDE LIKE THE WIND   Christopher Cross
10   HOW DO I MAKE YOU   Linda Ronstadt

April 5, 1980
1   ANOTHER BRICK IN THE WALL   Pink Floyd
2   WORKING MY WAY BACK TO YOU   Spinners
3   CALL ME   Blondie
4   CRAZY LITTLE THING CALLED LOVE   Queen
5   TOO HOT   Kool & The Gang
6   HIM   Rupert Holmes
7   RIDE LIKE THE WIND   Christopher Cross
8   SPECIAL LADY   Ray, Goodman & Brown
9   DESIRE   Andy Gibb
10   HOW DO I MAKE YOU   Linda Ronstadt

April 12, 1980
1   ANOTHER BRICK IN THE WALL   Pink Floyd
2   CALL ME   Blondie
3   WORKING MY WAY BACK TO YOU   Spinners
4   RIDE LIKE THE WIND   Christopher Cross
5   TOO HOT   Kool & The Gang
6   SPECIAL LADY   Ray, Goodman & Brown
7   WITH YOU I'M BORN AGAIN   Billy Preston & Syreeta
8   CRAZY LITTLE THING CALLED LOVE   Queen
9   I CAN'T TELL YOU WHY   Eagles
10   OFF THE WALL   Michael Jackson

April 19, 1980
1   CALL ME   Blondie
2   ANOTHER BRICK IN THE WALL   Pink Floyd
3   RIDE LIKE THE WIND   Christopher Cross

4 WITH YOU I'M BORN AGAIN   Billy Preston & Syreeta
5 SPECIAL LADY   Ray, Goodman & Brown
6 LOST IN LOVE   Air Supply
7 FIRE LAKE   Bob Seger
8 I CAN'T TELL YOU WHY   Eagles
9 WORKING MY WAY BACK TO YOU   Spinners
10 OFF THE WALL   Michael Jackson

April 26, 1980
1 CALL ME   Blondie
2 RIDE LIKE THE WIND   Christopher Cross
3 ANOTHER BRICK IN THE WALL   Pink Floyd
4 WITH YOU I'M BORN AGAIN   Billy Preston & Syreeta
5 SPECIAL LADY   Ray, Goodman & Brown
6 LOST IN LOVE   Air Supply
7 FIRE LAKE   Bob Seger
8 I CAN'T TELL YOU WHY   Eagles
9 YOU MAY BE RIGHT   Billy Joel
10 SEXY EYES   Dr. Hook

May 3, 1980
1 CALL ME   Blondie
2 RIDE LIKE THE WIND   Christopher Cross
3 LOST IN LOVE   Air Supply
4 WITH YOU I'M BORN AGAIN   Billy Preston & Syreeta
5 ANOTHER BRICK IN THE WALL   Pink Floyd
6 FIRE LAKE   Bob Seger
7 YOU MAY BE RIGHT   Billy Joel
8 I CAN'T TELL YOU WHY   Eagles
9 SEXY EYES   Dr. Hook
10 HOLD ON TO MY LOVE   Jimmy Ruffin

May 10, 1980
1 CALL ME   Blondie
2 RIDE LIKE THE WIND   Christopher Cross
3 LOST IN LOVE   Air Supply
4 WITH YOU I'M BORN AGAIN   Billy Preston & Syreeta
5 ANOTHER BRICK IN THE WALL   Pink Floyd
6 FIRE LAKE   Bob Seger
7 YOU MAY BE RIGHT   Billy Joel
8 SEXY EYES   Dr. Hook
9 DON'T FALL IN LOVE WITH A DREAMER   Kenny Rogers & Kim Carnes
10 HOLD ON TO MY LOVE   Jimmy Ruffin

May 17, 1980
1 CALL ME   Blondie
2 RIDE LIKE THE WIND   Christopher Cross
3 LOST IN LOVE   Air Supply
4 FUNKYTOWN   Lipps, Inc.
5 WITH YOU I'M BORN AGAIN   Billy Preston & Syreeta
6 SEXY EYES   Dr. Hook
7 YOU MAY BE RIGHT   Billy Joel
8 DON'T FALL IN LOVE WITH A DREAMER   Kenny Rogers & Kim Carnes
9 ANOTHER BRICK IN THE WALL   Pink Floyd
10 BIGGEST PART OF ME   Ambrosia

May 24, 1980
1 CALL ME   Blondie
2 FUNKYTOWN   Lipps, Inc.
3 LOST IN LOVE   Air Supply
4 DON'T FALL IN LOVE WITH A DREAMER   Kenny Rogers & Kim Carnes
5 SEXY EYES   Dr. Hook
6 BIGGEST PART OF ME   Ambrosia
7 STOMP!   Commodores

Deborah Harry
Blondie's ``Call Me'' spends six weeks at #1 (Apr. 19)

8 HURT SO BAD   Linda Ronstadt
9 RIDE LIKE THE WIND   Christopher Cross
10 CARS   Gary Numan

May 31, 1980
1 FUNKYTOWN   Lipps, Inc.
2 CALL ME   Blondie
3 COMING UP   Paul McCartney
4 DON'T FALL IN LOVE WITH A DREAMER   Kenny Rogers & Kim Carnes
5 SEXY EYES   Dr. Hook
6 BIGGEST PART OF ME   Ambrosia
7 STOMP!   Commodores
8 HURT SO BAD   Linda Ronstadt
9 AGAINST THE WIND   Bob Seger
10 CARS   Gary Numan

June 7, 1980
1 FUNKYTOWN   Lipps, Inc.
2 COMING UP   Paul McCartney
3 BIGGEST PART OF ME   Ambrosia
4 DON'T FALL IN LOVE WITH A DREAMER   Kenny Rogers & Kim Carnes
5 CALL ME   Blondie
6 THE ROSE   Bette Midler
7 AGAINST THE WIND   Bob Seger
8 HURT SO BAD   Linda Ronstadt
9 CARS   Gary Numan
10 LITTLE JEANNIE   Elton John

June 14, 1980
1 FUNKYTOWN   Lipps, Inc.

2 COMING UP   Paul McCartney
3 BIGGEST PART OF ME   Ambrosia
4 THE ROSE   Bette Midler
5 AGAINST THE WIND   Bob Seger
6 CALL ME   Blondie
7 IT'S STILL ROCK AND ROLL TO ME   Billy Joel
8 LITTLE JEANNIE   Elton John
9 CARS   Gary Numan
10 STEAL AWAY   Robbie Dupree

June 21, 1980
1 FUNKYTOWN   Lipps, Inc.
2 COMING UP   Paul McCartney
3 BIGGEST PART OF ME   Ambrosia
4 THE ROSE   Bette Midler
5 AGAINST THE WIND   Bob Seger
6 IT'S STILL ROCK AND ROLL TO ME   Billy Joel
7 LITTLE JEANNIE   Elton John
8 STEAL AWAY   Robbie Dupree
9 CARS   Gary Numan
10 SHE'S OUT OF MY LIFE   Michael Jackson

June 28, 1980
1 COMING UP   Paul McCartney
2 FUNKYTOWN   Lipps, Inc.
3 THE ROSE   Bette Midler
4 IT'S STILL ROCK AND ROLL TO ME   Billy Joel
5 AGAINST THE WIND   Bob Seger
6 LITTLE JEANNIE   Elton John
7 STEAL AWAY   Robbie Dupree
8 BIGGEST PART OF ME   Ambrosia
9 CUPID/I'VE LOVED YOU FOR A LONG TIME   Spinners
10 SHE'S OUT OF MY LIFE   Michael Jackson

July 5, 1980
1 COMING UP   Paul McCartney
2 FUNKYTOWN   Lipps, Inc.
3 THE ROSE   Bette Midler
4 IT'S STILL ROCK AND ROLL TO ME   Billy Joel
5 LITTLE JEANNIE   Elton John
6 AGAINST THE WIND   Bob Seger
7 STEAL AWAY   Robbie Dupree
8 CUPID/I'VE LOVED YOU FOR A LONG TIME   Spinners
9 BIGGEST PART OF ME   Ambrosia
10 LET'S GET SERIOUS   Jermaine Jackson

July 12, 1980
1 COMING UP   Paul McCartney
2 IT'S STILL ROCK AND ROLL TO ME   Billy Joel
3 THE ROSE   Bette Midler
4 LITTLE JEANNIE   Elton John
5 CUPID/I'VE LOVED YOU FOR A LONG TIME   Spinners
6 STEAL AWAY   Robbie Dupree
7 FUNKYTOWN   Lipps, Inc.
8 MAGIC   Olivia Newton-John
9 LET'S GET SERIOUS   Jermaine Jackson
10 LET ME LOVE YOU TONIGHT   Pure Prairie League

July 19, 1980
1 IT'S STILL ROCK AND ROLL TO ME   Billy Joel
2 COMING UP   Paul McCartney
3 LITTLE JEANNIE   Elton John
4 CUPID/I'VE LOVED YOU FOR A LONG TIME   Spinners
5 SHINING STAR   Manhattans
6 STEAL AWAY   Robbie Dupree
7 MAGIC   Olivia Newton-John

8 THE ROSE   Bette Midler
9 LET'S GET SERIOUS   Jermaine Jackson
10 LET ME LOVE YOU TONIGHT   Pure Prairie League

July 26, 1980
1 IT'S STILL ROCK AND ROLL TO ME   Billy Joel
2 MAGIC   Olivia Newton-John
3 LITTLE JEANNIE   Elton John
4 CUPID/I'VE LOVED YOU FOR A LONG TIME   Spinners
5 SHINING STAR   Manhattans
6 COMING UP   Paul McCartney
7 STEAL AWAY   Robbie Dupree
8 TIRED OF TOEIN' THE LINE   Rocky Burnette
9 TAKE YOUR TIME (DO IT RIGHT)   S.O.S. Band
10 THE ROSE   Bette Midler

August 2, 1980
1 MAGIC   Olivia Newton-John
2 IT'S STILL ROCK AND ROLL TO ME   Billy Joel
3 LITTLE JEANNIE   Elton John
4 CUPID/I'VE LOVED YOU FOR A LONG TIME   Spinners
5 SHINING STAR   Manhattans
6 TAKE YOUR TIME (DO IT RIGHT)   S.O.S. Band
7 COMING UP   Paul McCartney
8 TIRED OF TOEIN' THE LINE   Rocky Burnette
9 EMOTIONAL RESCUE   Rolling Stones
10 SAILING   Christopher Cross

August 9, 1980
1 MAGIC   Olivia Newton-John
2 IT'S STILL ROCK AND ROLL TO ME   Billy Joel
3 LITTLE JEANNIE   Elton John
4 TAKE YOUR TIME (DO IT RIGHT)   S.O.S. Band
5 SAILING   Christopher Cross
6 SHINING STAR   Manhattans
7 EMOTIONAL RESCUE   Rolling Stones
8 CUPID/I'VE LOVED YOU FOR A LONG TIME   Spinners
9 COMING UP   Paul McCartney
10 UPSIDE DOWN   Diana Ross

August 16, 1980
1 MAGIC   Olivia Newton-John
2 SAILING   Christopher Cross
3 TAKE YOUR TIME (DO IT RIGHT)   S.O.S. Band
4 EMOTIONAL RESCUE   Rolling Stones
5 UPSIDE DOWN   Diana Ross
6 IT'S STILL ROCK AND ROLL TO ME   Billy Joel
7 SHINING STAR   Manhattans
8 LITTLE JEANNIE   Elton John
9 LET MY LOVE OPEN THE DOOR   Pete Townshend
10 MORE LOVE   Kim Carnes

August 23, 1980
1 MAGIC   Olivia Newton-John
2 SAILING   Christopher Cross
3 TAKE YOUR TIME (DO IT RIGHT)   S.O.S. Band
4 EMOTIONAL RESCUE   Rolling Stones
5 UPSIDE DOWN   Diana Ross
6 IT'S STILL ROCK AND ROLL TO ME   Billy Joel
7 FAME   Irene Cara
8 ALL OUT OF LOVE   Air Supply
9 LET ME OPEN THE DOOR   Pete Townshend
10 MORE LOVE   Kim Carnes

August 30, 1980
1 SAILING   Christopher Cross

2 UPSIDE DOWN Diana Ross
3 MAGIC Olivia Newton-John
4 EMOTIONAL RESCUE Rolling Stones
5 TAKE YOUR TIME (DO IT RIGHT) S.O.S. Band
6 FAME Irene Cara
7 ALL OUT OF LOVE Air Supply
8 GIVE ME THE NIGHT George Benson
9 LET ME OPEN THE DOOR Pete Townshend
10 MORE LOVE Kim Carnes

September 6, 1980
1 UPSIDE DOWN Diana Ross
2 SAILING Christopher Cross
3 EMOTIONAL RESCUE Rolling Stones
4 ALL OUT OF LOVE Air Supply
5 FAME Irene Cara
6 MAGIC Olivia Newton-John
7 GIVE ME THE NIGHT George Benson
8 TAKE YOUR TIME (DO IT RIGHT) S.O.S. Band
9 LATE IN THE EVENING Paul Simon
10 LOOKING FOR LOVE Johnny Lee

September 13, 1980
1 UPSIDE DOWN Diana Ross
2 ALL OUT OF LOVE Air Supply
3 EMOTIONAL RESCUE Rolling Stones
4 FAME Irene Cara
5 SAILING Christopher Cross
6 GIVE ME THE NIGHT George Benson
7 LATE IN THE EVENING Paul Simon
8 LOOKING FOR LOVE Johnny Lee
9 ANOTHER ONE BITES THE DUST Queen
10 DRIVIN' MY LIFE AWAY Eddie Rabbitt

September 20, 1980
1 UPSIDE DOWN Diana Ross
2 ALL OUT OF LOVE Air Supply
3 ANOTHER ONE BITES THE DUST Queen
4 FAME Irene Cara
5 LOOKING FOR LOVE Johnny Lee
6 GIVE ME THE NIGHT George Benson
7 LATE IN THE EVENING Paul Simon
8 DRIVIN' MY LIFE AWAY Eddie Rabbitt
9 ONE IN A MILLION YOU Larry Graham
10 EMOTIONAL RESCUE Rolling Stones

September 27, 1980
1 UPSIDE DOWN Diana Ross
2 ALL OUT OF LOVE Air Supply
3 ANOTHER ONE BITES THE DUST Queen
4 GIVE ME THE NIGHT George Benson
5 LOOKING FOR LOVE Johnny Lee
6 LATE IN THE EVENING Paul Simon
7 DRIVIN' MY LIFE AWAY Eddie Rabbitt
8 FAME Irene Cara
9 ONE IN A MILLION YOU Larry Graham
10 I'M ALRIGHT Kenny Loggins

October 4, 1980
1 ANOTHER ONE BITES THE DUST Queen
2 ALL OUT OF LOVE Air Supply
3 UPSIDE DOWN Diana Ross
4 GIVE ME THE NIGHT George Benson
5 DRIVIN' MY LIFE AWAY Eddie Rabbitt
6 LATE IN THE EVENING Paul Simon
7 WOMAN IN LOVE Barbra Streisand

8 I'M ALRIGHT Kenny Loggins
9 LOOKING FOR LOVE Johnny Lee
10 XANADU Olivia Newton-John & Electric Light Orchestra

October 11, 1980
1 ANOTHER ONE BITES THE DUST Queen
2 WOMAN IN LOVE Barbra Streisand
3 UPSIDE DOWN Diana Ross
4 ALL OUT OF LOVE Air Supply
5 DRIVIN' MY LIFE AWAY Eddie Rabbitt
6 LATE IN THE EVENING Paul Simon
7 I'M ALRIGHT Kenny Loggins
8 XANADU Olivia Newton-John & Electric Light Orchestra
9 REAL LOVE Doobie Brothers
10 GIVE ME THE NIGHT George Benson

October 18, 1980
1 ANOTHER ONE BITES THE DUST Queen
2 WOMAN IN LOVE Barbra Streisand
3 UPSIDE DOWN Diana Ross
4 ALL OUT OF LOVE Air Supply
5 HE'S SO SHY Pointer Sisters
6 REAL LOVE Doobie Brothers
7 I'M ALRIGHT Kenny Loggins
8 XANADU Olivia Newton-John & Electric Light Orchestra
9 DRIVIN' MY LIFE AWAY Eddie Rabbitt
10 LATE IN THE EVENING Paul Simon

October 25, 1980
1 WOMAN IN LOVE Barbra Streisand
2 ANOTHER ONE BITES THE DUST Queen
3 HE'S SO SHY Pointer Sisters
4 UPSIDE DOWN Diana Ross
5 REAL LOVE Doobie Brothers
6 LADY Kenny Rogers
7 THE WANDERER Donna Summer
8 ALL OUT OF LOVE Air Supply
9 I'M ALRIGHT Kenny Loggins
10 NEVER KNEW LOVE LIKE THIS BEFORE Stephanie Mills

November 1, 1980
1 WOMAN IN LOVE Barbra Streisand
2 ANOTHER ONE BITES THE DUST Queen
3 HE'S SO SHY Pointer Sisters
4 LADY Kenny Rogers
5 REAL LOVE Doobie Brothers
6 THE WANDERER Donna Summer
7 UPSIDE DOWN Diana Ross
8 NEVER KNEW LOVE LIKE THIS BEFORE Stephanie Mills
9 I'M COMING OUT Diana Ross
10 MASTER BLASTER (JAMMIN') Stevie Wonder

November 8, 1980
1 WOMAN IN LOVE Barbra Streisand
2 LADY Kenny Rogers
3 HE'S SO SHY Pointer Sisters
4 ANOTHER ONE BITES THE DUST Queen
5 THE WANDERER Donna Summer
6 I'M COMING OUT Diana Ross
7 NEVER KNEW LOVE LIKE THIS BEFORE Stephanie Mills
8 MASTER BLASTER (JAMMIN') Stevie Wonder
9 REAL LOVE Doobie Brothers
10 UPSIDE DOWN Diana Ross

November 15, 1980
1 LADY Kenny Rogers

Kenny Rogers
``Lady'' starts six weeks at #1 for Kenny (Nov. 15).

2 WOMAN IN LOVE   Barbra Streisand
3 THE WANDERER   Donna Summer
4 ANOTHER ONE BITES THE DUST   Queen
5 I'M COMING OUT   Diana Ross
6 NEVER KNEW LOVE LIKE THIS BEFORE   Stephanie Mills
7 MASTER BLASTER (JAMMIN')   Stevie Wonder
8 HE'S SO SHY   Pointer Sisters
9 MORE THAN I CAN SAY   Leo Sayer
10 STARTING OVER   John Lennon

November 22, 1980
1 LADY   Kenny Rogers
2 WOMAN IN LOVE   Barbra Streisand
3 THE WANDERER   Donna Summer
4 ANOTHER ONE BITES THE DUST   Queen
5 I'M COMING OUT   Diana Ross
6 NEVER KNEW LOVE LIKE THIS BEFORE   Stephanie Mills
7 MASTER BLASTER (JAMMIN')   Stevie Wonder
8 MORE THAN I CAN SAY   Leo Sayer
9 STARTING OVER   John Lennon
10 DREAMING   Cliff Richard

November 29, 1980
1 LADY   Kenny Rogers
2 WOMAN IN LOVE   Barbra Streisand
3 THE WANDERER   Donna Summer
4 ANOTHER ONE BITES THE DUST   Queen
5 I'M COMING OUT   Diana Ross
6 MORE THAN I CAN SAY   Leo Sayer
7 MASTER BLASTER (JAMMIN')   Stevie Wonder
8 STARTING OVER   John Lennon
9 LOVE ON THE ROCKS   Neil Diamond

10 DREAMING   Cliff Richard

December 6, 1980
1 LADY   Kenny Rogers
2 MORE THAN I CAN SAY   Leo Sayer
3 ANOTHER ONE BITES THE DUST   Queen
4 WOMAN IN LOVE   Barbra Streisand
5 MASTER BLASTER (JAMMIN')   Stevie Wonder
6 STARTING OVER   John Lennon
7 LOVE ON THE ROCKS   Neil Diamond
8 HUNGRY HEART   Bruce Springsteen
9 I'M COMING OUT   Diana Ross
10 DREAMING   Cliff Richard

December 13, 1980
1 LADY   Kenny Rogers
2 MORE THAN I CAN SAY   Leo Sayer
3 ANOTHER ONE BITES THE DUST   Queen
4 STARTING OVER   John Lennon
5 MASTER BLASTER (JAMMIN')   Stevie Wonder
6 LOVE ON THE ROCKS   Neil Diamond
7 HUNGRY HEART   Bruce Springsteen
8 WOMAN IN LOVE   Barbra Streisand
9 GUILTY   Barbra Streisand & Barry Gibb
10 HIT ME WITH YOUR BEST SHOT   Pat Benatar

December 20, 1980
1 LADY   Kenny Rogers
2 MORE THAN I CAN SAY   Leo Sayer
3 STARTING OVER   John Lennon
4 LOVE ON THE ROCKS   Neil Diamond
5 MASTER BLASTER (JAMMIN')   Stevie Wonder
6 HUNGRY HEART   Bruce Springsteen
7 ANOTHER ONE BITES THE DUST   Queen
8 GUILTY   Barbra Streisand & Barry Gibb
9 HIT ME WITH YOUR BEST SHOT   Pat Benatar
10 EVERY WOMAN IN THE WORLD   Air Supply

December 27, 1980
1 STARTING OVER   John Lennon
2 MORE THAN I CAN SAY   Leo Sayer
3 LOVE ON THE ROCKS   Neil Diamond
4 LADY   Kenny Rogers
5 HUNGRY HEART   Bruce Springsteen
6 EVERY WOMAN IN THE WORLD   Air Supply
7 GUILTY   Barbra Streisand & Barry Gibb
8 THE TIDE IS HIGH   Blondie
9 HIT ME WITH YOUR BEST SHOT   Pat Benatar
10 TELL IT LIKE IT IS   Aaron Neville

January 3, 1981
NO SURVEY

January 10, 1981
1 STARTING OVER   John Lennon
2 LOVE ON THE ROCKS   Neil Diamond
3 GUILTY   Barbra Streisand & Barry Gibb
4 THE TIDE IS HIGH   Blondie
5 HUNGRY HEART   Bruce Springsteen
6 EVERY WOMAN IN THE WORLD   Air Supply
7 PASSION   Rod Stewart
8 TELL IT LIKE IT IS   Aaron Neville
9 LADY   Kenny Rogers
10 MORE THAN I CAN SAY   Leo Sayer

January 17, 1981
1 STARTING OVER   John Lennon
2 LOVE ON THE ROCKS   Neil Diamond
3 GUILTY   Barbra Streisand & Barry Gibb
4 THE TIDE IS HIGH   Blondie
5 HUNGRY HEART   Bruce Springsteen
6 EVERY WOMAN IN THE WORLD   Air Supply
7 PASSION   Rod Stewart
8 TELL IT LIKE IT IS   Aaron Neville
9 LADY   Kenny Rogers
10 DE DO DO DO, DE DA DA DA   Police

January 24, 1981
1 STARTING OVER   John Lennon
2 LOVE ON THE ROCKS   Neil Diamond
3 THE TIDE IS HIGH   Blondie
4 GUILTY   Barbra Streisand & Barry Gibb
5 HUNGRY HEART   Bruce Springsteen
6 EVERY WOMAN IN THE WORLD   Air Supply
7 PASSION   Rod Stewart
8 I LOVE A RAINY NIGHT   Eddie Rabbitt
9 IT'S MY TURN   Diana Ross
10 DE DO DO DO, DE DA DA DA   Police

January 31, 1981
1 THE TIDE IS HIGH   Blondie
2 STARTING OVER   John Lennon
3 CELEBRATION   Kool & The Gang
4 I LOVE A RAINY NIGHT   Eddie Rabbitt
5 EVERY WOMAN IN THE WORLD   Air Supply
6 PASSION   Rod Stewart
7 LOVE ON THE ROCKS   Neil Diamond
8 9 TO 5   Dolly Parton
9 IT'S MY TURN   Diana Ross
10 I MADE IT THROUGH THE RAIN   Barry Manilow

February 7, 1981
1 CELEBRATION   Kool & The Gang
2 THE TIDE IS HIGH   Blondie
3 I LOVE A RAINY NIGHT   Eddie Rabbitt
4 9 TO 5   Dolly Parton
5 PASSION   Rod Stewart
6 STARTING OVER   John Lennon
7 EVERY WOMAN IN THE WORLD   Air Supply
8 WOMAN   John Lennon
9 IT'S MY TURN   Diana Ross
10 GIVING IT UP FOR YOUR LOVE   Delbert McClinton

February 14, 1981
1 CELEBRATION   Kool & The Gang
2 9 TO 5   Dolly Parton
3 I LOVE A RAINY NIGHT   Eddie Rabbitt
4 THE TIDE IS HIGH   Blondie
5 PASSION   Rod Stewart
6 WOMAN   John Lennon
7 STARTING OVER   John Lennon
8 KEEP ON LOVING YOU   REO Speedwagon
9 GIVING IT UP FOR YOUR LOVE   Delbert McClinton
10 HEY NINETEEN   Steely Dan

February 21, 1981
1 9 TO 5   Dolly Parton
2 I LOVE A RAINY NIGHT   Eddie Rabbitt
3 CELEBRATION   Kool & The Gang
4 WOMAN   John Lennon
5 THE TIDE IS HIGH   Blondie

6 KEEP ON LOVING YOU   REO Speedwagon
7 THE BEST OF TIMES   Styx
8 GIVING IT UP FOR YOUR LOVE   Delbert McClinton
9 SAME OLDE LANG SYNE   Dan Fogelberg
10 HEY NINETEEN   Steely Dan

February 28, 1981
1 I LOVE A RAINY NIGHT   Eddie Rabbitt
2 9 TO 5   Dolly Parton
3 WOMAN   John Lennon
4 CELEBRATION   Kool & The Gang
5 KEEP ON LOVING YOU   REO Speedwagon
6 THE BEST OF TIMES   Styx
7 THE TIDE IS HIGH   Blondie
8 GIVING IT UP FOR YOUR LOVE   Delbert McClinton
9 SAME OLDE LANG SYNE   Dan Fogelberg
10 THE WINNER TAKES IT ALL   Abba

March 7, 1981
1 I LOVE A RAINY NIGHT   Eddie Rabbitt
2 9 TO 5   Dolly Parton
3 WOMAN   John Lennon
4 KEEP ON LOVING YOU   REO Speedwagon
5 THE BEST OF TIMES   Styx
6 CELEBRATION   Kool & The Gang
7 CRYING   Don McLean
8 GIVING IT UP FOR YOUR LOVE   Delbert McClinton
9 THE WINNER TAKES IT ALL   Abba
10 HELLO AGAIN   Neil Diamond

March 14, 1981
1 9 TO 5   Dolly Parton

Dolly Parton
Dolly's ``9 To 5'' labors yield a #1 song and hit movie (Feb. 21).

2 KEEP ON LOVING YOU   REO Speedwagon
3 WOMAN   John Lennon
4 THE BEST OF TIMES   Styx
5 I LOVE A RAINY NIGHT   Eddie Rabbitt
6 CRYING   Don McLean
7 RAPTURE   Blondie
8 THE WINNER TAKES IT ALL   Abba
9 HELLO AGAIN   Neil Diamond
10 CELEBRATION   Kool & The Gang

March 21, 1981
1 KEEP ON LOVING YOU   REO Speedwagon
2 WOMAN   John Lennon
3 THE BEST OF TIMES   Styx
4 9 TO 5   Dolly Parton
5 I LOVE A RAINY NIGHT   Eddie Rabbitt
6 CRYING   Don McLean
7 RAPTURE   Blondie
8 THE WINNER TAKES IT ALL   Abba
9 HELLO AGAIN   Neil Diamond
10 CELEBRATION   Kool & The Gang

March 28, 1981
1 RAPTURE   Blondie
2 WOMAN   John Lennon
3 THE BEST OF TIMES   Styx
4 KEEP ON LOVING YOU   REO Speedwagon
5 CRYING   Don McLean
6 HELLO AGAIN   Neil Diamond
7 9 TO 5   Dolly Parton
8 JUST THE TWO OF US   Grover Washington & Bill Withers
9 KISS ON MY LIST   Daryl Hall & John Oates
10 WHAT KIND OF FOOL   Barbra Streisand & Barry Gibb

April 4, 1981
1 RAPTURE   Blondie
2 WOMAN   John Lennon
3 THE BEST OF TIMES   Styx
4 KISS ON MY LIST   Daryl Hall & John Oates
5 CRYING   Don McLean
6 HELLO AGAIN   Neil Diamond
7 JUST THE TWO OF US   Grover Washington & Bill Withers
8 KEEP ON LOVING YOU   REO Speedwagon
9 WHILE YOU SEE A CHANCE   Steve Winwood
10 WHAT KIND OF FOOL   Barbra Streisand & Barry Gibb

April 11, 1981
1 KISS ON MY LIST   Daryl Hall & John Oates
2 RAPTURE   Blondie
3 THE BEST OF TIMES   Styx
4 WOMAN   John Lennon
5 JUST THE TWO OF US   Grover Washington & Bill Withers
6 MORNING TRAIN (NINE TO FIVE)   Sheena Easton
7 CRYING   Don McLean
8 WHILE YOU SEE A CHANCE   Steve Winwood
9 KEEP ON LOVING YOU   REO Speedwagon
10 DON'T STAND SO CLOSE TO ME   Police

April 18, 1981
1 KISS ON MY LIST   Daryl Hall & John Oates
2 RAPTURE   Blondie
3 MORNING TRAIN (NINE TO FIVE)   Sheena Easton
4 JUST THE TWO OF US   Grover Washington & Bill Withers
5 WOMAN   John Lennon
6 ANGEL OF THE MORNING   Juice Newton
7 WHILE YOU SEE A CHANCE   Steve Winwood

8 BEING WITH YOU   Smokey Robinson
9 THE BEST OF TIMES   Styx
10 DON'T STAND SO CLOSE TO ME   Police

April 25, 1981
1 KISS ON MY LIST   Daryl Hall & John Oates
2 MORNING TRAIN (NINE TO FIVE)   Sheena Easton
3 BEING WITH YOU   Smokey Robinson
4 JUST THE TWO OF US   Grover Washington & Bill Withers
5 ANGEL OF THE MORNING   Juice Newton
6 RAPTURE   Blondie
7 WHILE YOU SEE A CHANCE   Steve Winwood
8 WOMAN   John Lennon
9 THE BEST OF TIMES   Styx
10 DON'T STAND SO CLOSE TO ME   Police

May 2, 1981
1 MORNING TRAIN (NINE TO FIVE)   Sheena Easton
2 JUST THE TWO OF US   Grover Washington & Bill Withers
3 BEING WITH YOU   Smokey Robinson
4 ANGEL OF THE MORNING   Juice Newton
5 KISS ON MY LIST   Daryl Hall & John Oates
6 RAPTURE   Blondie
7 BETTE DAVIS EYES   Kim Carnes
8 WHILE YOU SEE A CHANCE   Steve Winwood
9 LIVING INSIDE MYSELF   Gino Vannelli
10 I CAN'T STAND IT   Eric Clapton

May 9, 1981
1 MORNING TRAIN (NINE TO FIVE)   Sheena Easton
2 JUST THE TWO OF US   Grover Washington & Bill Withers
3 BEING WITH YOU   Smokey Robinson
4 ANGEL OF THE MORNING   Juice Newton
5 BETTE DAVIS EYES   Kim Carnes
6 KISS ON MY LIST   Daryl Hall & John Oates
7 TAKE IT ON THE RUN   REO Speedwagon
8 LIVING INSIDE MYSELF   Gino Vannelli
9 SUKIYAKI   A Taste of Honey
10 I CAN'T STAND IT   Eric Clapton

May 16, 1981
1 BETTE DAVIS EYES   Kim Carnes
2 JUST THE TWO OF US   Grover Washington & Bill Withers
3 BEING WITH YOU   Smokey Robinson
4 ANGEL OF THE MORNING   Juice Newton
5 MORNING TRAIN (NINE TO FIVE)   Sheena Easton
6 TAKE IT ON THE RUN   REO Speedwagon
7 LIVING INSIDE MYSELF   Gino Vannelli
8 SUKIYAKI   A Taste of Honey
9 KISS ON MY LIST   Daryl Hall & John Oates
10 TOO MUCH TIME ON MY HANDS   Styx

May 23, 1981
1 BETTE DAVIS EYES   Kim Carnes
2 BEING WITH YOU   Smokey Robinson
3 JUST THE TWO OF US   Grover Washington & Bill Withers
4 ANGEL OF THE MORNING   Juice Newton
5 MEDLEY; STARS ON 45   Stars on 45
6 TAKE IT ON THE RUN   REO Speedwagon
7 LIVING INSIDE MYSELF   Gino Vannelli
8 SUKIYAKI   A Taste of Honey
9 TOO MUCH TIME ON MY HANDS   Styx
10 WATCHING THE WHEELS   John Lennon

May 30, 1981
1 BETTE DAVIS EYES   Kim Carnes

Bette Davis and those eyes.

Kim Carnes

Kim's raspy-voiced homage to one of Hollywood's greatest spent over a month at #1 beginning May 16.

2 BEING WITH YOU   Smokey Robinson
3 MEDLEY; STARS ON 45   Stars on 45
4 SUKIYAKI   A Taste of Honey
5 TAKE IT ON THE RUN   REO Speedwagon
6 LIVING INSIDE MYSELF   Gino Vannelli
7 JUST THE TWO OF US   Grover Washington & Bill Withers
8 WOMAN NEEDS LOVE (JUST LIKE YOU DO)   Ray Parker, Jr. & Raydio
9 TOO MUCH TIME ON MY HANDS   Styx
10 WATCHING THE WHEELS   John Lennon

June 6, 1981
1 BETTE DAVIS EYES   Kim Carnes
2 BEING WITH YOU   Smokey Robinson
3 MEDLEY; STARS ON 45   Stars on 45
4 SUKIYAKI   A Taste of Honey
5 TAKE IT ON THE RUN   REO Speedwagon
6 LIVING INSIDE MYSELF   Gino Vannelli
7 WOMAN NEEDS LOVE (JUST LIKE YOU DO)   Ray Parker, Jr. & Raydio
8 JUST THE TWO OF US   Grover Washington & Bill Withers
9 AMERICA   Neil Diamond
10 SWEETHEART   Franke & The Knockouts

June 13, 1981
1 BETTE DAVIS EYES   Kim Carnes
2 MEDLEY; STARS ON 45   Stars on 45
3 SUKIYAKI   A Taste of Honey
4 BEING WITH YOU   Smokey Robinson
5 WOMAN NEEDS LOVE (JUST LIKE YOU DO)   Ray Parker, Jr. & Raydio
6 LIVING INSIDE MYSELF   Gino Vannelli
7 ALL THOSE YEARS AGO   George Harrison
8 AMERICA   Neil Diamond
9 TAKE IT ON THE RUN   REO Speedwagon
10 SWEETHEART   Franke & The Knockouts

June 20, 1981
1 MEDLEY; STARS ON 45   Stars on 45
2 BETTE DAVIS EYES   Kim Carnes
3 SUKIYAKI   A Taste of Honey
4 WOMAN NEEDS LOVE (JUST LIKE YOU DO)   Ray Parker, Jr. & Raydio
5 ALL THOSE YEARS AGO   George Harrison
6 BEING WITH YOU   Smokey Robinson
7 THE ONE THAT YOU LOVE   Air Supply
8 AMERICA   Neil Diamond
9 YOU MAKE MY DREAMS   Daryl Hall & John Oates
10 JESSIE'S GIRL   Rick Springfield

June 27, 1981
1 BETTE DAVIS EYES   Kim Carnes
2 MEDLEY; STARS ON 45   Stars on 45
3 SUKIYAKI   A Taste of Honey
4 WOMAN NEEDS LOVE (JUST LIKE YOU DO)   Ray Parker, Jr. & Raydio
5 ALL THOSE YEARS AGO   George Harrison
6 THE ONE THAT YOU LOVE   Air Supply
7 YOU MAKE MY DREAMS   Daryl Hall & John Oates
8 AMERICA   Neil Diamond
9 JESSIE'S GIRL   Rick Springfield
10 ELVIRA   Oak Ridge Boys *
    Note: * First country single to ever be certified by the R.I.A.A. as Platinum: 1 million units sold.

July 4, 1981
1 BETTE DAVIS EYES   Kim Carnes

2 ALL THOSE YEARS AGO   George Harrison
3 THE ONE THAT YOU LOVE   Air Supply
4 JESSIE'S GIRL   Rick Springfield
5 YOU MAKE MY DREAMS   Daryl Hall & John Oates
6 ELVIRA   Oak Ridge Boys *
7 MEDLEY; STARS ON 45   Stars on 45
8 WOMAN NEEDS LOVE (JUST LIKE YOU DO)   Ray Parker, Jr. & Raydio
9 THEME FROM "GREATEST AMERICAN HERO" (BELIEVE IT OR NOT)   Joey Scarbury
10 I DON'T NEED YOU   Kenny Rogers
    Note: * First country single to ever be certified by the R.I.A.A. as Platinum: 1 million units sold.

July 11, 1981
1 BETTE DAVIS EYES   Kim Carnes
2 ALL THOSE YEARS AGO   George Harrison
3 THE ONE THAT YOU LOVE   Air Supply
4 JESSIE'S GIRL   Rick Springfield
5 YOU MAKE MY DREAMS   Daryl Hall & John Oates
6 ELVIRA   Oak Ridge Boys *
7 MEDLEY; STARS ON 45   Stars on 45
8 THEME FROM "GREATEST AMERICAN HERO" (BELIEVE IT OR NOT)   Joey Scarbury
9 I DON'T NEED YOU   Kenny Rogers
10 SLOW HAND   Pointer Sisters
    Note: * First country single to ever be certified by the R.I.A.A. as Platinum: 1 million units sold.

July 18, 1981
1 BETTE DAVIS EYES   Kim Carnes
2 ALL THOSE YEARS AGO   George Harrison
3 THE ONE THAT YOU LOVE   Air Supply
4 JESSIE'S GIRL   Rick Springfield
5 YOU MAKE MY DREAMS   Daryl Hall & John Oates
6 ELVIRA   Oak Ridge Boys *
7 THEME FROM "GREATEST AMERICAN HERO" (BELIEVE IT OR NOT)   Joey Scarbury
8 I DON'T NEED YOU   Kenny Rogers
9 SLOW HAND   Pointer Sisters
10 BOY FROM NEW YORK CITY   Manhattan Transfer
    Note: * First country single to ever be certified by the R.I.A.A. as Platinum: 1 million units sold.

July 25, 1981
1 THE ONE THAT YOU LOVE   Air Supply
2 BETTE DAVIS EYES   Kim Carnes
3 JESSIE'S GIRL   Rick Springfield
4 THEME FROM "GREATEST AMERICAN HERO" (BELIEVE IT OR NOT)   Joey Scarbury
5 ELVIRA   Oak Ridge Boys *
6 I DON'T NEED YOU   Kenny Rogers
7 SLOW HAND   Pointer Sisters
8 YOU MAKE MY DREAMS   Daryl Hall & John Oates
9 BOY FROM NEW YORK CITY   Manhattan Transfer
10 HEARTS   Marty Balin
    Note: * First country single to ever be certified by the R.I.A.A. as Platinum: 1 million units sold.

August 1, 1981
1 JESSIE'S GIRL   Rick Springfield
2 THE ONE THAT YOU LOVE   Air Supply
3 THEME FROM "GREATEST AMERICAN HERO" (BELIEVE IT OR NOT)   Joey Scarbury
4 I DON'T NEED YOU   Kenny Rogers
5 ELVIRA   Oak Ridge Boys *
6 SLOW HAND   Pointer Sisters

7 BETTE DAVIS EYES   Kim Carnes
8 BOY FROM NEW YORK CITY   Manhattan Transfer
9 HEARTS   Marty Balin
10 QUEEN OF HEARTS   Juice Newton
   Note: * First country single to ever be certified by the R.I.A.A. as Platinum: 1 million units sold.

August 8, 1981
1 JESSIE'S GIRL   Rick Springfield
2 ENDLESS LOVE   Diana Ross & Lionel Richie
3 THEME FROM "GREATEST AMERICAN HERO" (BELIEVE IT OR NOT)   Joey Scarbury
4 I DON'T NEED YOU   Kenny Rogers
5 ELVIRA   Oak Ridge Boys *
6 SLOW HAND   Pointer Sisters
7 BOY FROM NEW YORK CITY   Manhattan Transfer
8 HEARTS   Marty Balin
9 QUEEN OF HEARTS   Juice Newton
10 THE ONE THAT YOU LOVE   Air Supply
   Note: * First country single to ever be certified by the R.I.A.A. as Platinum: 1 million units sold.

August 15, 1981
1 ENDLESS LOVE   Diana Ross & Lionel Richie
2 THEME FROM "GREATEST AMERICAN HERO" (BELIEVE IT OR NOT)   Joey Scarbury
3 I DON'T NEED YOU   Kenny Rogers
4 JESSIE'S GIRL   Rick Springfield
5 ELVIRA   Oak Ridge Boys *
6 SLOW HAND   Pointer Sisters
7 BOY FROM NEW YORK CITY   Manhattan Transfer
8 HEARTS   Marty Balin

Juice Newton
``Queen of Hearts'' is a two-month Top 10 smash (Aug. 1-Oct. 13).

9 QUEEN OF HEARTS   Juice Newton
10 THERE'S NO GETTING OVER YOU   Ronnie Milsap
   Note: * First country single to ever be certified by the R.I.A.A. as Platinum: 1 million units sold.

August 22, 1981
1 ENDLESS LOVE   Diana Ross & Lionel Richie
2 THEME FROM "GREATEST AMERICAN HERO" (BELIEVE IT OR NOT)   Joey Scarbury
3 I DON'T NEED YOU   Kenny Rogers
4 SLOW HAND   Pointer Sisters
5 JESSIE'S GIRL   Rick Springfield
6 STOP DRAGGIN' MY HEART AROUND   Stevie Nicks & Tom Petty
7 BOY FROM NEW YORK CITY   Manhattan Transfer
8 QUEEN OF HEARTS   Juice Newton
9 THERE'S NO GETTING OVER YOU   Ronnie Milsap
10 LADY YOU BRING ME UP   Commodores

August 29, 1981
1 ENDLESS LOVE   Diana Ross & Lionel Richie
2 SLOW HAND   Pointer Sisters
3 THEME FROM "GREATEST AMERICAN HERO" (BELIEVE IT OR NOT)   Joey Scarbury
4 STOP DRAGGIN' MY HEART AROUND   Stevie Nicks & Tom Petty
5 JESSIE'S GIRL   Rick Springfield
6 QUEEN OF HEARTS   Juice Newton
7 THERE'S NO GETTING OVER YOU   Ronnie Milsap
8 URGENT   Foreigner
9 LADY YOU BRING ME UP   Commodores
10 WHO'S CRYING NOW   Journey

September 5, 1981
1 ENDLESS LOVE   Diana Ross & Lionel Richie
2 SLOW HAND   Pointer Sisters
3 STOP DRAGGIN' MY HEART AROUND   Stevie Nicks & Tom Petty
4 URGENT   Foreigner
5 THERE'S NO GETTING OVER YOU   Ronnie Milsap
6 QUEEN OF HEARTS   Juice Newton
7 WHO'S CRYING NOW   Journey
8 LADY YOU BRING ME UP   Commodores
9 JESSIE'S GIRL   Rick Springfield
10 THEME FROM "GREATEST AMERICAN HERO" (BELIEVE IT OR NOT)   Joey Scarbury

September 12, 1981
1 ENDLESS LOVE   Diana Ross & Lionel Richie
2 SLOW HAND   Pointer Sisters
3 STOP DRAGGIN' MY HEART AROUND   Stevie Nicks & Tom Petty
4 URGENT   Foreigner
5 THERE'S NO GETTING OVER YOU   Ronnie Milsap
6 QUEEN OF HEARTS   Juice Newton
7 WHO'S CRYING NOW   Journey
8 LADY YOU BRING ME UP   Commodores
9 ARTHUR'S THEME   Christopher Cross
10 STEP BY STEP   Eddie Rabbitt

September 19, 1981
1 ENDLESS LOVE   Diana Ross & Lionel Richie
2 QUEEN OF HEARTS   Juice Newton
3 STOP DRAGGIN' MY HEART AROUND   Stevie Nicks & Tom Petty
4 URGENT   Foreigner
5 THERE'S NO GETTING OVER YOU   Ronnie Milsap

6 WHO'S CRYING NOW Journey
7 ARTHUR'S THEME Christopher Cross
8 LADY YOU BRING ME UP Commodores
9 STEP BY STEP Eddie Rabbitt
10 SLOW HAND Pointer Sisters

September 26, 1981
1 ENDLESS LOVE Diana Ross & Lionel Richie
2 QUEEN OF HEARTS Juice Newton
3 STOP DRAGGIN' MY HEART AROUND Stevie Nicks & Tom Petty
4 URGENT Foreigner
5 THERE'S NO GETTING OVER YOU Ronnie Milsap
6 WHO'S CRYING NOW Journey
7 ARTHUR'S THEME Christopher Cross
8 STEP BY STEP Eddie Rabbitt
9 LADY YOU BRING ME UP Commodores
10 START ME UP Rolling Stones

October 3, 1981
1 ENDLESS LOVE Diana Ross & Lionel Richie
2 ARTHUR'S THEME Christopher Cross
3 STOP DRAGGIN' MY HEART AROUND Stevie Nicks & Tom Petty
4 WHO'S CRYING NOW Journey
5 THERE'S NO GETTING OVER YOU Ronnie Milsap
6 QUEEN OF HEARTS Juice Newton
7 STEP BY STEP Eddie Rabbitt
8 URGENT Foreigner
9 START ME UP Rolling Stones
10 HOLD ON TIGHT Electric Light Orchestra

Christopher Cross
``Arthur's Theme'' rode the success of a
popular movie to three weeks at #1 (Oct. 17).

October 10, 1981
1 ENDLESS LOVE Diana Ross & Lionel Richie
2 ARTHUR'S THEME Christopher Cross
3 STOP DRAGGIN' MY HEART AROUND Stevie Nicks & Tom Petty
4 WHO'S CRYING NOW Journey
5 FOR YOUR EYES ONLY Sheena Easton
6 STEP BY STEP Eddie Rabbitt
7 START ME UP Rolling Stones
8 PRIVATE EYES Daryl Hall & John Oates
9 URGENT Foreigner
10 HOLD ON TIGHT Electric Light Orchestra

October 17, 1981
1 ARTHUR'S THEME Christopher Cross
2 ENDLESS LOVE Diana Ross & Lionel Richie
3 START ME UP Rolling Stones
4 FOR YOUR EYES ONLY Sheena Easton
5 STEP BY STEP Eddie Rabbitt
6 PRIVATE EYES Daryl Hall & John Oates
7 STOP DRAGGIN' MY HEART AROUND Stevie Nicks & Tom Petty
8 WHO'S CRYING NOW Journey
9 HARD TO SAY Dan Fogelberg
10 THE NIGHT OWL Little River Band

October 24, 1981
1 ARTHUR'S THEME Christopher Cross
2 ENDLESS LOVE Diana Ross & Lionel Richie
3 START ME UP Rolling Stones
4 FOR YOUR EYES ONLY Sheena Easton
5 STEP BY STEP Eddie Rabbitt
6 PRIVATE EYES Daryl Hall & John Oates
7 STOP DRAGGIN' MY HEART AROUND Stevie Nicks & Tom Petty
8 HARD TO SAY Dan Fogelberg
9 THE NIGHT OWL Little River Band
10 I'VE DONE EVERYTHING FOR YOU Rick Springfield

October 31, 1981
1 ARTHUR'S THEME Christopher Cross
2 START ME UP Rolling Stones
3 PRIVATE EYES Daryl Hall & John Oates
4 FOR YOUR EYES ONLY Sheena Easton
5 ENDLESS LOVE Diana Ross & Lionel Richie
6 TRYING TO LIVE MY LIFE WITHOUT YOU Bob Seger
7 HARD TO SAY Dan Fogelberg
8 THE NIGHT OWL Little River Band
9 I'VE DONE EVERYTHING FOR YOU Rick Springfield
10 STEP BY STEP Eddie Rabbitt

November 7, 1981
1 PRIVATE EYES Daryl Hall & John Oates
2 START ME UP Rolling Stones
3 ARTHUR'S THEME Christopher Cross
4 FOR YOUR EYES ONLY Sheena Easton
5 TRYING TO LIVE MY LIFE WITHOUT YOU Bob Seger
6 THE NIGHT OWL Little River Band
7 HARD TO SAY Dan Fogelberg
8 I'VE DONE EVERYTHING FOR YOU Rick Springfield
9 HERE I AM Air Supply
10 WAITING FOR A GIRL LIKE YOU Foreigner

November 14, 1981
1 PRIVATE EYES Daryl Hall & John Oates
2 START ME UP Rolling Stones

Olivia Newton-John

``Physical'' remains #1 for a solid ten-week stay for this lovely and talented Aussie export (Nov. 21, 1981-Jan. 23, 1982).

3   PHYSICAL   Olivia Newton-John
4   WAITING FOR A GIRL LIKE YOU   Foreigner
5   TRYING TO LIVE MY LIFE WITHOUT YOU   Bob Seger
6   THE NIGHT OWL   Little River Band
7   HERE I AM   Air Supply
8   I'VE DONE EVERYTHING FOR YOU   Rick Springfield
9   ARTHUR'S THEME   Christopher Cross
10   THEME FROM "HILL STREET BLUES"   Mike Post

November 21, 1981
1   PHYSICAL   Olivia Newton-John
2   PRIVATE EYES   Daryl Hall & John Oates
3   WAITING FOR A GIRL LIKE YOU   Foreigner
4   START ME UP   Rolling Stones
5   HERE I AM   Air Supply
6   TRYING TO LIVE MY LIFE WITHOUT YOU   Bob Seger
7   THE NIGHT OWL   Little River Band
8   EVERY LITTLE THING SHE DOES IS MAGIC   Police
9   ARTHUR'S THEME   Christopher Cross
10   THEME FROM "HILL STREET BLUES"   Mike Post

November 28, 1981
1   PHYSICAL   Olivia Newton-John
2   WAITING FOR A GIRL LIKE YOU   Foreigner
3   PRIVATE EYES   Daryl Hall & John Oates
4   EVERY LITTLE THING SHE DOES IS MAGIC   Poiice
5   HERE I AM   Air Supply
6   OH NO   Commodores
7   START ME UP   Rolling Stones
8   TRYING TO LIVE MY LIFE WITHOUT YOU   Bob Seger
9   ARTHUR'S THEME   Christopher Cross
10   WHY DO FOOLS FALL IN LOVE   Diana Ross

December 5, 1981
1   PHYSICAL   Olivia Newton-John
2   WAITING FOR A GIRL LIKE YOU   Foreigner
3   EVERY LITTLE THING SHE DOES IS MAGIC   Police
4   OH NO   Commodores
5   HERE I AM   Air Supply
6   PRIVATE EYES   Daryl Hall & John Oates
7   LET'S GROOVE   Earth, Wind & Fire
8   YOUNG TURKS   Rod Stewart
9   WHY DO FOOLS FALL IN LOVE   Diana Ross
10   START ME UP   Rolling Stones

December 12, 1981
1   PHYSICAL   Olivia Newton-John
2   WAITING FOR A GIRL LIKE YOU   Foreigner
3   EVERY LITTLE THING SHE DOES IS MAGIC   Police
4   OH NO   Commodores
5   LET'S GROOVE   Earth, Wind & Fire
6   YOUNG TURKS   Rod Stewart
7   HERE I AM   Air Supply
8   WHY DO FOOLS FALL IN LOVE   Diana Ross
9   HARDEN MY HEART   Quarterflash
10   DON'T STOP BELIEVING   Journey

December 19, 1981
1   PHYSICAL   Olivia Newton-John
2   WAITING FOR A GIRL LIKE YOU   Foreigner
3   LET'S GROOVE   Earth, Wind & Fire
4   OH NO   Commodores
5   YOUNG TURKS   Rod Stewart
6   I CAN'T GO FOR THAT   Daryl Hall & John Oates
7   WHY DO FOOLS FALL IN LOVE   Diana Ross

<table>
<tr><td>8</td><td>HARDEN MY HEART</td><td>Quarterflash</td></tr>
<tr><td>9</td><td>DON'T STOP BELIEVING</td><td>Journey</td></tr>
<tr><td>10</td><td>LEATHER AND LACE</td><td>Stevie Nicks with Don Henley</td></tr>
</table>

December 26, 1981
1. PHYSICAL   Olivia Newton-John
2. WAITING FOR A GIRL LIKE YOU   Foreigner
3. LET'S GROOVE   Earth, Wind & Fire
4. I CAN'T GO FOR THAT   Daryl Hall & John Oates
5. YOUNG TURKS   Rod Stewart
6. HARDEN MY HEART   Quarterflash
7. WHY DO FOOLS FALL IN LOVE   Diana Ross
8. LEATHER AND LACE   Stevie Nicks with Don Henley
9. DON'T STOP BELIEVING   Journey
10. TROUBLE   Lindsey Buckingham

January 2, 1982
NO SURVEY

January 9, 1982
1. PHYSICAL   Olivia Newton-John
2. WAITING FOR A GIRL LIKE YOU   Foreigner
3. LET'S GROOVE   Earth, Wind & Fire
4. I CAN'T GO FOR THAT   Daryl Hall & John Oates
5. YOUNG TURKS   Rod Stewart
6. HARDEN MY HEART   Quarterflash
7. LEATHER AND LACE   Stevie Nicks with Don Henley
8. CENTERFOLD   J. Geils Band
9. TURN YOUR LOVE AROUND   George Benson
10. TROUBLE   Lindsey Buckingham

January 16, 1982
1. PHYSICAL   Olivia Newton-John
2. WAITING FOR A GIRL LIKE YOU   Foreigner
3. LET'S GROOVE   Earth, Wind & Fire
4. I CAN'T GO FOR THAT   Daryl Hall & John Oates
5. CENTERFOLD   J. Geils Band
6. HARDEN MY HEART   Quarterflash
7. LEATHER AND LACE   Stevie Nicks with Don Henley
8. TURN YOUR LOVE AROUND   George Benson
9. TROUBLE   Lindsey Buckingham
10. THE SWEETEST THING (I'VE EVER KNOWN)   Juice Newton

January 23, 1982
1. PHYSICAL   Olivia Newton-John
2. WAITING FOR A GIRL LIKE YOU   Foreigner
3. CENTERFOLD   J. Geils Band
4. I CAN'T GO FOR THAT   Daryl Hall & John Oates
5. HARDEN MY HEART   Quarterflash
6. LEATHER AND LACE   Stevie Nicks with Don Henley
7. TURN YOUR LOVE AROUND   George Benson
8. LET'S GROOVE   Earth, Wind & Fire
9. TROUBLE   Lindsey Buckingham
10. THE SWEETEST THING (I'VE EVER KNOWN)   Juice Newton

January 30, 1982
1. I CAN'T GO FOR THAT   Daryl Hall & John Oates
2. WAITING FOR A GIRL LIKE YOU   Foreigner
3. CENTERFOLD   J. Geils Band
4. PHYSICAL   Olivia Newton-John
5. HARDEN MY HEART   Quarterflash
6. LEATHER AND LACE   Stevie Nicks with Don Henley
7. TURN YOUR LOVE AROUND   George Benson
8. LET'S GROOVE   Earth, Wind & Fire

9. THE SWEETEST THING (I'VE EVER KNOWN)   Juice Newton
10. HOOKED ON CLASSICS   Royal Philharmonic Orchestra

February 6, 1982
1. CENTERFOLD   J. Geils Band
2. I CAN'T GO FOR THAT   Daryl Hall & John Oates
3. WAITING FOR A GIRL LIKE YOU   Foreigner
4. HARDEN MY HEART   Quarterflash
5. TURN YOUR LOVE AROUND   George Benson
6. LEATHER AND LACE   Stevie Nicks with Don Henley
7. PHYSICAL   Olivia Newton-John
8. THE SWEETEST THING (I'VE EVER KNOWN)   Juice Newton
9. SHAKE IT UP   Cars
10. HOOKED ON CLASSICS   Royal Philharmonic Orchestra

February 13, 1982
1. CENTERFOLD   J. Geils Band
2. I CAN'T GO FOR THAT   Daryl Hall & John Oates
3. HARDEN MY HEART   Quarterflash
4. OPEN ARMS   Journey
5. TURN YOUR LOVE AROUND   George Benson
6. SHAKE IT UP   Cars
7. THE SWEETEST THING (I'VE EVER KNOWN)   Juice Newton
8. PHYSICAL   Olivia Newton-John
9. WAITING FOR A GIRL LIKE YOU   Foreigner
10. SWEET DREAMS   Air Supply

March 6, 1982
1. CENTERFOLD   J. Geils Band
2. OPEN ARMS   Journey
3. I LOVE ROCK 'N ROLL   Joan Jett & The Blackhearts
4. SHAKE IT UP   Cars
5. THAT GIRL   Stevie Wonder
6. SWEET DREAMS   Air Supply
7. I CAN'T GO FOR THAT   Daryl Hall & John Oates
8. MIRROR MIRROR   Diana Ross
9. LEADER OF THE BAND   Dan Fogelberg
10. TAKE IT EASY ON ME   Little River Band

March 13, 1982
1. CENTERFOLD   J. Geils Band
2. OPEN ARMS   Journey
3. I LOVE ROCK 'N ROLL   Joan Jett & The Blackhearts
4. SHAKE IT UP   Cars
5. THAT GIRL   Stevie Wonder
6. SWEET DREAMS   Air Supply
7. WE GOT THE BEAT   Go-Go's
8. MIRROR MIRROR   Diana Ross
9. LEADER OF THE BAND   Dan Fogelberg
10. TAKE IT EASY ON ME   Little River Band

March 20, 1982
1. I LOVE ROCK 'N ROLL   Joan Jett & The Blackhearts
2. OPEN ARMS   Journey
3. CENTERFOLD   J. Geils Band
4. THAT GIRL   Stevie Wonder
5. SWEET DREAMS   Air Supply
6. WE GOT THE BEAT   Go-Go's
7. MAKE A MOVE ON ME   Olivia Newton-John
8. MIRROR MIRROR   Diana Ross
9. SHAKE IT UP   Cars
10. PAC-MAN FEVER   Buckner & Garcia

Joan Jett
Ex-Runaway guitarist and rock lover jets to #1 (Mar. 20-May 1).

March 27, 1982
1 I LOVE ROCK 'N ROLL   Joan Jett & The Blackhearts
2 OPEN ARMS   Journey
3 WE GOT THE BEAT   Go-Go's
4 THAT GIRL   Stevie Wonder
5 SWEET DREAMS   Air Supply
6 MAKE A MOVE ON ME   Olivia Newton-John
7 CENTERFOLD   J. Geils Band
8 CHARIOTS OF FIRE   Vangelis
9 PAC-MAN FEVER   Buckner & Garcia
10 FREEZE FRAME   J. Geils Band

April 3, 1982
1 I LOVE ROCK 'N ROLL   Joan Jett & The Blackhearts
2 OPEN ARMS   Journey
3 WE GOT THE BEAT   Go-Go's
4 THAT GIRL   Stevie Wonder
5 MAKE A MOVE ON ME   Olivia Newton-John
6 CHARIOTS OF FIRE   Vangelis
7 FREEZE FRAME   J. Geils Band
8 DON'T TALK TO STRANGERS   Rick Springfield
9 PAC-MAN FEVER   Buckner & Garcia
10 KEY LARGO   Bertie Higgins

April 10, 1982
1 I LOVE ROCK 'N ROLL   Joan Jett & The Blackhearts
2 WE GOT THE BEAT   Go-Go's
3 CHARIOTS OF FIRE   Vangelis
4 FREEZE FRAME   J. Geils Band
5 MAKE A MOVE ON ME   Olivia Newton-John
6 DON'T TALK TO STRANGERS   Rick Springfield
7 OPEN ARMS   Journey
8 THAT GIRL   Stevie Wonder
9 KEY LARGO   Bertie Higgins
10 DO YOU BELIEVE IN LOVE   Huey Lewis & The News

April 17, 1982
1 I LOVE ROCK 'N ROLL   Joan Jett & The Blackhearts
2 WE GOT THE BEAT   Go-Go's
3 CHARIOTS OF FIRE   Vangelis
4 FREEZE FRAME   J. Geils Band
5 MAKE A MOVE ON ME   Olivia Newton-John
6 DON'T TALK TO STRANGERS   Rick Springfield
7 DO YOU BELIEVE IN LOVE   Huey Lewis & The News
8 KEY LARGO   Bertie Higgins
9 OPEN ARMS   Journey
10 THAT GIRL   Stevie Wonder

April 24, 1982
1 I LOVE ROCK 'N ROLL   Joan Jett & The Blackhearts
2 WE GOT THE BEAT   Go-Go's
3 CHARIOTS OF FIRE   Vangelis
4 FREEZE FRAME   J. Geils Band
5 DON'T TALK TO STRANGERS   Rick Springfield
6 EBONY AND IVORY   Paul McCartney & Stevie Wonder
7 DO YOU BELIEVE IN LOVE   Huey Lewis & The News
8 KEY LARGO   Bertie Higgins
9 65 LOVE AFFAIR   Paul Davis
10 867-5309 JENNY   Tommy Tutone

May 1, 1982
1 I LOVE ROCK 'N ROLL   Joan Jett & The Blackhearts
2 CHARIOTS OF FIRE   Vangelis
3 EBONY AND IVORY   Paul McCartney & Stevie Wonder
4 FREEZE FRAME   J. Geils Band
5 DON'T TALK TO STRANGERS   Rick Springfield
6 WE GOT THE BEAT   Go-Go's
7 DO YOU BELIEVE IN LOVE   Huey Lewis & The News
8 867-5309 JENNY   Tommy Tutone
9 65 LOVE AFFAIR   Paul Davis
10 I'VE NEVER BEEN TO ME   Charlene

May 8, 1982
1 CHARIOTS OF FIRE   Vangelis
2 EBONY AND IVORY   Paul McCartney & Stevie Wonder
3 I LOVE ROCK 'N ROLL   Joan Jett & The Blackhearts
4 DON'T TALK TO STRANGERS   Rick Springfield
5 FREEZE FRAME   J. Geils Band
6 867-5309 JENNY   Tommy Tutone
7 WE GOT THE BEAT   Go-Go's
8 65 LOVE AFFAIR   Paul Davis
9 I'VE NEVER BEEN TO ME   Charlene
10 DID IT IN A MINUTE   Daryl Hall & John Oates

May 15, 1982
1 EBONY AND IVORY   Paul McCartney & Stevie Wonder
2 CHARIOTS OF FIRE   Vangelis
3 DON'T TALK TO STRANGERS   Rick Springfield
4 I LOVE ROCK 'N ROLL   Joan Jett & The Blackhearts
5 867-5309 JENNY   Tommy Tutone
6 I'VE NEVER BEEN TO ME   Charlene
7 65 LOVE AFFAIR   Paul Davis
8 FREEZE FRAME   J. Geils Band
9 OTHER WOMAN   Ray Parker, Jr.
10 DID IT IN A MINUTE   Daryl Hall & John Oates

May 22, 1982
1 EBONY AND IVORY   Paul McCartney & Stevie Wonder

2   DON'T TALK TO STRANGERS   Rick Springfield
3   I'VE NEVER BEEN TO ME   Charlene
4   867-5309 JENNY   Tommy Tutone
5   OTHER WOMAN   Ray Parker, Jr.
6   65 LOVE AFFAIR   Paul Davis
7   CHARIOTS OF FIRE   Vangelis
8   DON'T YOU WANT ME   Human League
9   DID IT IN A MINUTE   Daryl Hall & John Oates
10   GET DOWN ON IT   Kool & The Gang

May 29, 1982
1   EBONY AND IVORY   Paul McCartney & Stevie Wonder
2   DON'T TALK TO STRANGERS   Rick Springfield
3   I'VE NEVER BEEN TO ME   Charlene
4   867-5309 JENNY   Tommy Tutone
5   OTHER WOMAN   Ray Parker, Jr.
6   65 LOVE AFFAIR   Paul Davis
7   DON'T YOU WANT ME   Human League
8   ALWAYS ON MY MIND   Willie Nelson
9   DID IT IN A MINUTE   Daryl Hall & John Oates
10   GET DOWN ON IT   Kool & The Gang

June 5, 1982
1   EBONY AND IVORY   Paul McCartney & Stevie Wonder
2   DON'T TALK TO STRANGERS   Rick Springfield
3   I'VE NEVER BEEN TO ME   Charlene
4   867-5309 JENNY   Tommy Tutone
5   OTHER WOMAN   Ray Parker, Jr.
6   DON'T YOU WANT ME   Human League
7   ALWAYS ON MY MIND   Willie Nelson
8   HEAT OF THE MOMENT   Asia
9   65 LOVE AFFAIR   Paul Davis
10   ROSANNA   Toto

June 12, 1982
1   EBONY AND IVORY   Paul McCartney & Stevie Wonder
2   DON'T TALK TO STRANGERS   Rick Springfield
3   DON'T YOU WANT ME   Human League
4   OTHER WOMAN   Ray Parker, Jr.
5   ALWAYS ON MY MIND   Willie Nelson
6   HEAT OF THE MOMENT   Asia
7   ROSANNA   Toto
8   CRIMSON AND CLOVER   Joan Jett
9   867-5309 JENNY   Tommy Tutone
10   IT'S GONNA TAKE A MIRACLE   Deniece Williams

June 19, 1982
1   EBONY AND IVORY   Paul McCartney & Stevie Wonder
2   DON'T YOU WANT ME   Human League
3   ROSANNA   Toto
4   OTHER WOMAN   Ray Parker, Jr.
5   ALWAYS ON MY MIND   Willie Nelson
6   HEAT OF THE MOMENT   Asia
7   CRIMSON AND CLOVER   Joan Jett
8   LET IT WHIP   Dazz Band
9   HURTS SO GOOD   John Cougar
10   IT'S GONNA TAKE A MIRACLE   Deniece Williams

June 26, 1982
1   EBONY AND IVORY   Paul McCartney & Stevie Wonder
2   DON'T YOU WANT ME   Human League
3   ROSANNA   Toto
4   HEAT OF THE MOMENT   Asia
5   ALWAYS ON MY MIND   Willie Nelson
6   HURTS SO GOOD   John Cougar
7   CRIMSON AND CLOVER   Joan Jett
8   LET IT WHIP   Dazz Band
9   LOVE'S BEEN A LITTLE BIT HARD ON ME   Juice Newton
10   OTHER WOMAN   Ray Parker, Jr.

July 3, 1982
1   DON'T YOU WANT ME   Human League
2   ROSANNA   Toto
3   EBONY AND IVORY   Paul McCartney & Stevie Wonder
4   HEAT OF THE MOMENT   Asia
5   HURTS SO GOOD   John Cougar
6   ALWAYS ON MY MIND   Willie Nelson
7   LET IT WHIP   Dazz Band
8   LOVE'S BEEN A LITTLE BIT HARD ON ME   Juice Newton
9   EYE OF THE TIGER   Survivor
10   CAUGHT UP IN YOU   38 Special

July 10, 1982
1   DON'T YOU WANT ME   Human League
2   ROSANNA   Toto
3   HURTS SO GOOD   John Cougar
4   HEAT OF THE MOMENT   Asia
5   EYE OF THE TIGER   Survivor
6   LET IT WHIP   Dazz Band
7   LOVE'S BEEN A LITTLE BIT HARD ON ME   Juice Newton
8   EBONY AND IVORY   Paul McCartney & Stevie Wonder
9   TAINTED LOVE   Soft Cell *
10   CAUGHT UP IN YOU   38 Special
     *Note: * Stayed on the "Hot 100" for 42 weeks.*

July 17, 1982
1   DON'T YOU WANT ME   Human League
2   ROSANNA   Toto
3   HURTS SO GOOD   John Cougar
4   EYE OF THE TIGER   Survivor
5   LET IT WHIP   Dazz Band
6   HOLD ME   Fleetwood Mac
7   LOVE'S BEEN A LITTLE BIT HARD ON ME   Juice Newton
8   TAINTED LOVE   Soft Cell *
9   ONLY THE LONELY   Motels
10   CAUGHT UP IN YOU   38 Special
     *Note: * Stayed on the "Hot 100" for 42 weeks.*

July 24, 1982
1   EYE OF THE TIGER   Survivor
2   ROSANNA   Toto
3   HURTS SO GOOD   John Cougar
4   HOLD ME   Fleetwood Mac
5   LET IT WHIP   Dazz Band
6   ABRACADABRA   Steve Miller Band
7   DON'T YOU WANT ME   Human League
8   TAINTED LOVE   Soft Cell *
9   ONLY THE LONELY   Motels
10   KEEP THE FIRE BURNIN'   REO Speedwagon
     *Note: * Stayed on the "Hot 100" for 42 weeks.*

July 31, 1982
1   EYE OF THE TIGER   Survivor
2   ROSANNA   Toto
3   HURTS SO GOOD   John Cougar
4   HOLD ME   Fleetwood Mac
5   ABRACADABRA   Steve Miller Band
6   HARD TO SAY I'M SORRY   Chicago
7   DON'T YOU WANT ME   Human League
8   EVEN THE NIGHTS ARE BETTER   Air Supply
9   ONLY THE LONELY   Motels
10   KEEP THE FIRE BURNIN'   REO Speedwagon

August 7, 1982
1 EYE OF THE TIGER   Survivor
2 HURTS SO GOOD   John Cougar
3 ABRACADABRA   Steve Miller Band
4 HOLD ME   Fleetwood Mac
5 HARD TO SAY I'M SORRY   Chicago
6 ROSANNA   Toto
7 EVEN THE NIGHTS ARE BETTER   Air Supply
8 KEEP THE FIRE BURNIN'   REO Speedwagon
9 ONLY THE LONELY   Motels
10 DON'T YOU WANT ME   Human League

August 14, 1982
1 EYE OF THE TIGER   Survivor
2 HURTS SO GOOD   John Cougar
3 ABRACADABRA   Steve Miller Band
4 HOLD ME   Fleetwood Mac
5 HARD TO SAY I'M SORRY   Chicago
6 EVEN THE NIGHTS ARE BETTER   Air Supply
7 KEEP THE FIRE BURNIN'   REO Speedwagon
8 ROSANNA   Toto
9 VACATION   Go-Go's
10 WASTED ON THE WAY   Crosby, Stills & Nash

August 21, 1982
1 EYE OF THE TIGER   Survivor
2 HURTS SO GOOD   John Cougar
3 ABRACADABRA   Steve Miller Band
4 HOLD ME   Fleetwood Mac
5 HARD TO SAY I'M SORRY   Chicago
6 EVEN THE NIGHTS ARE BETTER   Air Supply
7 KEEP THE FIRE BURNIN'   REO Speedwagon
8 VACATION   Go-Go's
9 WASTED ON THE WAY   Crosby, Stills & Nash
10 TAKE IT AWAY   Paul McCartney

August 28, 1982
1 EYE OF THE TIGER   Survivor
2 HURTS SO GOOD   John Cougar
3 ABRACADABRA   Steve Miller Band
4 HOLD ME   Fleetwood Mac
5 HARD TO SAY I'M SORRY   Chicago
6 EVEN THE NIGHTS ARE BETTER   Air Supply
7 KEEP THE FIRE BURNIN'   REO Speedwagon
8 VACATION   Go-Go's
9 WASTED ON THE WAY   Crosby, Stills & Nash
10 TAKE IT AWAY   Paul McCartney

September 4, 1982
1 ABRACADABRA   Steve Miller Band
2 EYE OF THE TIGER   Survivor
3 HARD TO SAY I'M SORRY   Chicago
4 HOLD ME   Fleetwood Mac
5 EVEN THE NIGHTS ARE BETTER   Air Supply
6 YOU SHOULD HEAR HOW SHE TALKS ABOUT YOU
   Melissa Manchester
7 HURTS SO GOOD   John Cougar
8 VACATION   Go-Go's
9 WASTED ON THE WAY   Crosby, Stills & Nash
10 TAKE IT AWAY   Paul McCartney

September 11, 1982
1 HARD TO SAY I'M SORRY   Chicago
2 EYE OF THE TIGER   Survivor
3 ABRACADABRA   Steve Miller Band
4 JACK AND DIANE   John Cougar

John Cougar
Jack's pre-Mellencamp ode to Diane is a #1 hit in October.

5 EVEN THE NIGHTS ARE BETTER   Air Supply
6 YOU SHOULD HEAR HOW SHE TALKS ABOUT YOU
   Melissa Manchester
7 HOLD ME   Fleetwood Mac
8 HURTS SO GOOD   John Cougar
9 WASTED ON THE WAY   Crosby, Stills & Nash
10 TAKE IT AWAY   Paul McCartney

September 18, 1982
1 HARD TO SAY I'M SORRY   Chicago
2 ABRACADABRA   Steve Miller Band
3 EYE OF THE TIGER   Survivor
4 JACK AND DIANE   John Cougar
5 YOU SHOULD HEAR HOW SHE TALKS ABOUT YOU
   Melissa Manchester
6 EVEN THE NIGHTS ARE BETTER   Air Supply
7 HOLD ME   Fleetwood Mac
8 HURTS SO GOOD   John Cougar
9 EYE IN THE SKY   Alan Parsons Project
10 TAKE IT AWAY   Paul McCartney

September 26, 1982
1 ABRACADABRA   Steve Miller Band
2 JACK AND DIANE   John Cougar
3 HARD TO SAY I'M SORRY   Chicago
4 EYE OF THE TIGER   Survivor
5 YOU SHOULD HEAR HOW SHE TALKS ABOUT YOU
   Melissa Manchester
6 EYE IN THE SKY   Alan Parsons Project
7 WHO CAN IT BE NOW   Men At Work
8 SOMEBODY'S BABY   Jackson Browne
9 HURTS SO GOOD   John Cougar
10 LOVE IS IN CONTROL   Donna Summer

October 2, 1982

1 JACK AND DIANE   John Cougar
2 ABRACADABRA   Steve Miller Band
3 HARD TO SAY I'M SORRY   Chicago
4 EYE OF THE TIGER   Survivor
5 EYE IN THE SKY   Alan Parsons Project
6 EYE OF THE TIGER   Survivor   ect
7 WHO CAN IT BE NOW   Men At Work
8 SOMEBODY'S BABY   Jackson Browne
9 I KEEP FORGETTIN'   Michael McDonald
10 HURTS SO GOOD   John Cougar

October 9, 1982

1 JACK AND DIANE   John Cougar
2 ABRACADABRA   Steve Miller Band
3 HARD TO SAY I'M SORRY   Chicago
4 EYE IN THE SKY   Alan Parsons Project
5 WHO CAN IT BE NOW   Men At Work
6 EYE OF THE TIGER   Survivor
7 I KEEP FORGETTIN'   Michael McDonald
8 SOMEBODY'S BABY   Jackson Browne
9 YOU CAN DO MAGIC   America
10 I RAN   A Flock of Seagulls

October 16, 1982

1 JACK AND DIANE   John Cougar
2 WHO CAN IT BE NOW   Men At Work
3 EYE IN THE SKY   Alan Parsons Project
4 HARD TO SAY I'M SORRY   Chicago
5 ABRACADABRA   Steve Miller Band
6 I KEEP FORGETTIN'   Michael McDonald
7 SOMEBODY'S BABY   Jackson Browne
8 YOU CAN DO MAGIC   America
9 HEART ATTACK   Olivia Newton-John
10 I RAN   A Flock of Seagulls

October 23, 1982

1 JACK AND DIANE   John Cougar
2 WHO CAN IT BE NOW   Men At Work
3 EYE IN THE SKY   Alan Parsons Project
4 I KEEP FORGETTIN'   Michael McDonald
5 UP WHERE WE BELONG   Joe Cocker & Jennifer Warnes
6 HEART ATTACK   Olivia Newton-John
7 SOMEBODY'S BABY   Jackson Browne
8 YOU CAN DO MAGIC   America
9 I RAN   A Flock of Seagulls
10 ABRACADABRA   Steve Miller Band

October 30, 1982

1 WHO CAN IT BE NOW   Men At Work
2 JACK AND DIANE   John Cougar
3 EYE IN THE SKY   Alan Parsons Project
4 I KEEP FORGETTIN'   Michael McDonald
5 UP WHERE WE BELONG   Joe Cocker & Jennifer Warnes
6 HEART ATTACK   Olivia Newton-John
7 SOMEBODY'S BABY   Jackson Browne
8 YOU CAN DO MAGIC   America
9 I RAN   A Flock of Seagulls
10 HEARTLIGHT   Neil Diamond

November 6, 1982

1 UP WHERE WE BELONG   Joe Cocker & Jennifer Warnes
2 WHO CAN IT BE NOW   Men At Work
3 HEART ATTACK   Olivia Newton-John
4 I KEEP FORGETTIN'   Michael McDonald
5 JACK AND DIANE   John Cougar
6 EYE IN THE SKY   Alan Parsons Project
7 HEARTLIGHT   Neil Diamond
8 YOU CAN DO MAGIC   America
9 GLORIA   Laura Branigan
10 TRULY   Lionel Richie

November 13, 1982

1 UP WHERE WE BELONG   Joe Cocker & Jennifer Warnes
2 TRULY   Lionel Richie
3 HEART ATTACK   Olivia Newton-John
4 GLORIA   Laura Branigan
5 HEARTLIGHT   Neil Diamond
6 WHO CAN IT BE NOW   Men At Work
7 JACK AND DIANE   John Cougar
8 YOU CAN DO MAGIC   America
9 I KEEP FORGETTIN'   Michael McDonald
10 MUSCLES   Diana Ross

November 20, 1982

1 UP WHERE WE BELONG   Joe Cocker & Jennifer Warnes
2 TRULY   Lionel Richie
3 HEART ATTACK   Olivia Newton-John
4 GLORIA   Laura Branigan
5 HEARTLIGHT   Neil Diamond
6 WHO CAN IT BE NOW   Men At Work
7 MICKEY   Toni Basil
8 MANEATER   Daryl Hall & John Oates
9 STEPPIN' OUT   Joe Jackson
10 MUSCLES   Diana Ross

November 27, 1982

1 TRULY   Lionel Richie
2 GLORIA   Laura Branigan
3 HEART ATTACK   Olivia Newton-John
4 UP WHERE WE BELONG   Joe Cocker & Jennifer Warnes
5 HEARTLIGHT   Neil Diamond
6 MICKEY   Toni Basil
7 MANEATER   Daryl Hall & John Oates
8 STEPPIN' OUT   Joe Jackson
9 THE GIRL IS MINE   Michael Jackson & Paul McCartney
10 MUSCLES   Diana Ross

December 4, 1982

1 TRULY   Lionel Richie
2 GLORIA   Laura Branigan
3 MICKEY   Toni Basil
4 MANEATER   Daryl Hall & John Oates
5 HEARTLIGHT   Neil Diamond
6 UP WHERE WE BELONG   Joe Cocker & Jennifer Warnes
7 STEPPIN' OUT   Joe Jackson
8 THE GIRL IS MINE   Michael Jackson & Paul McCartney
9 DIRTY LAUNDRY   Don Henley
10 MUSCLES   Diana Ross

December 11, 1982

1 MICKEY   Toni Basil
2 GLORIA   Laura Branigan
3 MANEATER   Daryl Hall & John Oates
4 TRULY   Lionel Richie
5 THE GIRL IS MINE   Michael Jackson & Paul McCartney
6 STEPPIN' OUT   Joe Jackson
7 DIRTY LAUNDRY   Don Henley
8 SEXUAL HEALING   Marvin Gaye
9 ROCK THIS TOWN   Stray Cats
10 MUSCLES   Diana Ross

Men At Work

Hard work pays off for this Aussie band straight from ''Down Under''—three weeks on top (Jan. 15-29).

December 18, 1982
1. MANEATER   Daryl Hall & John Oates
2. MICKEY   Toni Basil
3. GLORIA   Laura Branigan
4. THE GIRL IS MINE   Michael Jackson & Paul McCartney
5. TRULY   Lionel Richie
6. STEPPIN' OUT   Joe Jackson
7. DIRTY LAUNDRY   Don Henley
8. SEXUAL HEALING   Marvin Gaye
9. ROCK THIS TOWN   Stray Cats
10. MUSCLES   Diana Ross

December 25, 1982
1. MANEATER   Daryl Hall & John Oates
2. MICKEY   Toni Basil
3. THE GIRL IS MINE   Michael Jackson & Paul McCartney
4. DIRTY LAUNDRY   Don Henley
5. GLORIA   Laura Branigan
6. STEPPIN' OUT   Joe Jackson
7. SEXUAL HEALING   Marvin Gaye
8. DOWN UNDER   Men At Work
9. ROCK THIS TOWN   Stray Cats
10. TRULY   Lionel Richie

January 1, 1983
NO SURVEY

January 8, 1983
1. MANEATER   Daryl Hall & John Oates
2. THE GIRL IS MINE   Michael Jackson & Paul McCartney
3. DIRTY LAUNDRY   Don Henley
4. DOWN UNDER   Men At Work
5. SEXUAL HEALING   Marvin Gaye
6. MICKEY   Toni Basil
7. GLORIA   Laura Branigan
8. STEPPIN' OUT   Joe Jackson
9. ROCK THIS TOWN   Stray Cats
10. TRULY   Lionel Richie

January 15, 1983
1. DOWN UNDER   Men At Work
2. THE GIRL IS MINE   Michael Jackson & Paul McCartney
3. DIRTY LAUNDRY   Don Henley
4. MANEATER   Daryl Hall & John Oates
5. SEXUAL HEALING   Marvin Gaye
6. MICKEY   Toni Basil
7. AFRICA   Toto
8. BABY, COME TO ME   Patti Austin & James Ingram
9. ROCK THE CASBAH   Clash
10. HEARTBREAKER   Dionne Warwick

January 22, 1983
1. DOWN UNDER   Men At Work
2. THE GIRL IS MINE   Michael Jackson & Paul McCartney
3. DIRTY LAUNDRY   Don Henley
4. SEXUAL HEALING   Marvin Gaye
5. AFRICA   Toto
6. MANEATER   Daryl Hall & John Oates
7. BABY, COME TO ME   Patti Austin & James Ingram
8. ROCK THE CASBAH   Clash
9. MICKEY   Toni Basil
10. HEARTBREAKER   Dionne Warwick

January 29, 1983
1 DOWN UNDER   Men At Work
2 AFRICA   Toto
3 SEXUAL HEALING   Marvin Gaye
4 DIRTY LAUNDRY   Don Henley
5 THE GIRL IS MINE   Michael Jackson & Paul McCartney
6 MANEATER   Daryl Hall & John Oates
7 BABY, COME TO ME   Patti Austin & James Ingram
8 ROCK THE CASBAH   Clash
9 SHAME ON THE MOON   Bob Seger
10 YOU AND I   Eddie Rabbitt & Crystal Gayle

February 5, 1983
1 AFRICA   Toto
2 DOWN UNDER   Men At Work
3 SEXUAL HEALING   Marvin Gaye
4 BABY, COME TO ME   Patti Austin & James Ingram
5 SHAME ON THE MOON   Bob Seger
6 MANEATER   Daryl Hall & John Oates
7 DIRTY LAUNDRY   Don Henley
8 ROCK THE CASBAH   Clash
9 YOU AND I   Eddie Rabbitt & Crystal Gayle
10 YOU CAN'T HURRY LOVE   Phil Collins

February 12, 1983
1 DOWN UNDER   Men At Work
2 BABY, COME TO ME   Patti Austin & James Ingram
3 SEXUAL HEALING   Marvin Gaye
4 SHAME ON THE MOON   Bob Seger
5 AFRICA   Toto
6 MANEATER   Daryl Hall & John Oates
7 YOU AND I   Eddie Rabbitt & Crystal Gayle
8 ROCK THE CASBAH   Clash
9 STRAY CAT STRUT   Stray Cats
10 YOU CAN'T HURRY LOVE   Phil Collins

February 19, 1983
1 BABY, COME TO ME   Patti Austin & James Ingram
2 DOWN UNDER   Men At Work
3 SHAME ON THE MOON   Bob Seger
4 STRAY CAT STRUT   Stray Cats
5 AFRICA   Toto
6 BILLIE JEAN   Michael Jackson *
7 YOU AND I   Eddie Rabbitt & Crystal Gayle
8 DO YOU REALLY WANT TO HURT ME   Culture Club
9 HUNGRY LIKE A WOLF   Duran Duran
10 YOU CAN'T HURRY LOVE   Phil Collins
    Note: * First hit single from the best-selling album of all time,
      "Thriller," establising the megastar status of Michael
      Jackson.

February 26, 1983
1 BABY, COME TO ME   Patti Austin & James Ingram
2 SHAME ON THE MOON   Bob Seger
3 STRAY CAT STRUT   Stray Cats
4 BILLIE JEAN   Michael Jackson *
5 DO YOU REALLY WANT TO HURT ME   Culture Club
6 HUNGRY LIKE A WOLF   Duran Duran
7 YOU AND I   Eddie Rabbitt & Crystal Gayle
8 DOWN UNDER   Men At Work
9 WE'VE GOT TONIGHT   Kenny Rogers & Sheena Easton
10 PASS THE DUTCHIE   Musical Youth
    Note: * First hit single from the best-selling album of all time,
      "Thriller," establising the megastar status of Michael
      Jackson.

March 5, 1983
1 BILLIE JEAN   Michael Jackson *
2 SHAME ON THE MOON   Bob Seger
3 STRAY CAT STRUT   Stray Cats
4 DO YOU REALLY WANT TO HURT ME   Culture Club
5 HUNGRY LIKE A WOLF   Duran Duran
6 BABY, COME TO ME   Patti Austin & James Ingram
7 YOU AND I   Eddie Rabbitt & Crystal Gayle
8 WE'VE GOT TONIGHT   Kenny Rogers & Sheena Easton
9 BACK ON THE CHAIN GANG   Pretenders
10 PASS THE DUTCHIE   Musical Youth
    Note: * First hit single from the best-selling album of all time,
      "Thriller," establising the megastar status of Michael
      Jackson.

March 12, 1983
1 BILLIE JEAN   Michael Jackson *
2 SHAME ON THE MOON   Bob Seger
3 STRAY CAT STRUT   Stray Cats
4 DO YOU REALLY WANT TO HURT ME   Culture Club
5 HUNGRY LIKE A WOLF   Duran Duran
6 BACK ON THE CHAIN GANG   Pretenders
7 YOU ARE   Lionel Richie
8 WE'VE GOT TONIGHT   Kenny Rogers & Sheena Easton
9 BABY, COME TO ME   Patti Austin & James Ingram
10 SEPARATE WAYS (WORLDS APART)   Journey
    Note: * First hit single from the best-selling album of all time,
      "Thriller," establising the megastar status of Michael
      Jackson.

March 19, 1983
1 BILLIE JEAN   Michael Jackson *

Michael Jackson
Mega-star status begins with the #1 ``Billie Jean'' (Mar. 5).

2   SHAME ON THE MOON   Bob Seger
3   DO YOU REALLY WANT TO HURT ME   Culture Club
4   HUNGRY LIKE A WOLF   Duran Duran
5   BACK ON THE CHAIN GANG   Pretenders
6   YOU ARE   Lionel Richie
7   WE'VE GOT TONIGHT   Kenny Rogers & Sheena Easton
8   SEPARATE WAYS (WORLDS APART)   Journey
9   ONE ON ONE   Daryl Hall & John Oates
10   MR. ROBOTO   Styx
Note: * First hit single from the best-selling album of all time, "Thriller," establising the megastar status of Michael Jackson.

March 26, 1983
1   BILLIE JEAN   Michael Jackson *
2   DO YOU REALLY WANT TO HURT ME   Culture Club
3   HUNGRY LIKE A WOLF   Duran Duran
4   YOU ARE   Lionel Richie
5   BACK ON THE CHAIN GANG   Pretenders
6   WE'VE GOT TONIGHT   Kenny Rogers & Sheena Easton
7   MR. ROBOTO   Styx
8   SEPARATE WAYS (WORLDS APART)   Journey
9   ONE ON ONE   Daryl Hall & John Oates
10   TWILIGHT ZONE   Golden Earring
Note: * First hit single from the best-selling album of all time, "Thriller," establising the megastar status of Michael Jackson.

April 2, 1983
1   BILLIE JEAN   Michael Jackson *
2   DO YOU REALLY WANT TO HURT ME   Culture Club
3   HUNGRY LIKE A WOLF   Duran Duran
4   YOU ARE   Lionel Richie
5   BACK ON THE CHAIN GANG   Pretenders
6   WE'VE GOT TONIGHT   Kenny Rogers & Sheena Easton
7   MR. ROBOTO   Styx
8   SEPARATE WAYS (WORLDS APART)   Journey
9   ONE ON ONE   Daryl Hall & John Oates
10   TWILIGHT ZONE   Golden Earring
Note: * First hit single from the best-selling album of all time, "Thriller," establising the megastar status of Michael Jackson.

April 9, 1983
1   BILLIE JEAN   Michael Jackson *
2   DO YOU REALLY WANT TO HURT ME   Culture Club
3   HUNGRY LIKE A WOLF   Duran Duran
4   COME ON EILEEN   Dexy's Midnight Runners
5   MR. ROBOTO   Styx
6   WE'VE GOT TONIGHT   Kenny Rogers & Sheena Easton
7   ONE ON ONE   Daryl Hall & John Oates
8   SEPARATE WAYS (WORLDS APART)   Journey
9   JEOPARDY   Greg Kihn Band
10   BEAT IT   Michael Jackson
Note: * First hit single from the best-selling album of all time, "Thriller," establising the megastar status of Michael Jackson.

April 16, 1983
1   BILLIE JEAN   Michael Jackson *
2   COME ON EILEEN   Dexy's Midnight Runners
3   MR. ROBOTO   Styx
4   JEOPARDY   Greg Kihn Band
5   BEAT IT   Michael Jackson
6   HUNGRY LIKE A WOLF   Duran Duran
7   ONE ON ONE   Daryl Hall & John Oates
8   SEPARATE WAYS (WORLDS APART)   Journey

9   DER KOMMISSAR   After The Fire
10   DO YOU REALLY WANT TO HURT ME   Culture Club
Note: * First hit single from the best-selling album of all time, "Thriller," establishing the megastar status of Michael Jackson.

April 23, 1983
1   COME ON EILEEN   Dexy's Midnight Runners
2   BEAT IT   Michael Jackson
3   MR. ROBOTO   Styx
4   JEOPARDY   Greg Kihn Band
5   BILLIE JEAN   Michael Jackson *
6   DER KOMMISSAR   After The Fire
7   ONE ON ONE   Daryl Hall & John Oates
8   SEPARATE WAYS (WORLDS APART)   Journey
9   LET'S DANCE   David Bowie
10   SHE BLINDED ME WITH SCIENCE   Thomas Dolby
Note: * First hit single from the best-selling album of all time, "Thriller," establising the megastar status of Michael Jackson.

April 30, 1983
1   BEAT IT   Michael Jackson
2   COME ON EILEEN   Dexy's Midnight Runners
3   JEOPARDY   Greg Kihn Band
4   MR. ROBOTO   Styx
5   DER KOMMISSAR   After The Fire
6   LET'S DANCE   David Bowie
7   BILLIE JEAN   Michael Jackson *
8   SHE BLINDED ME WITH SCIENCE   Thomas Dolby
9   OVERKILL   Men At Work
10   LITTLE RED CORVETTE   Prince
Note: * First hit single from the best-selling album of all time, "Thriller," establising the megastar status of Michael Jackson.

May 7, 1983
1   BEAT IT   Michael Jackson
2   JEOPARDY   Greg Kihn Band
3   LET'S DANCE   David Bowie
4   COME ON EILEEN   Dexy's Midnight Runners
5   DER KOMMISSAR   After The Fire
6   OVERKILL   Men At Work
7   SHE BLINDED ME WITH SCIENCE   Thomas Dolby
8   MR. ROBOTO   Styx
9   LITTLE RED CORVETTE   Prince
10   I WON'T HOLD YOU BACK   Toto

May 14, 1983
1   BEAT IT   Michael Jackson
2   LET'S DANCE   David Bowie
3   JEOPARDY   Greg Kihn Band
4   OVERKILL   Men At Work
5   SHE BLINDED ME WITH SCIENCE   Thomas Dolby
6   COME ON EILEEN   Dexy's Midnight Runners
7   FLASHDANCE   Irene Cara
8   LITTLE RED CORVETTE   Prince
9   SOLITAIRE   Laura Branigan
10   DER KOMMISSAR   After The Fire

May 21, 1983
1   LET'S DANCE   David Bowie
2   BEAT IT   Michael Jackson
3   FLASHDANCE   Irene Cara
4   OVERKILL   Men At Work
5   SHE BLINDED ME WITH SCIENCE   Thomas Dolby
6   LITTLE RED CORVETTE   Prince

Irene Cara

Film title-song spells flashy #1 chart status for Irene (May 28).

7	SOLITAIRE Laura Branigan
8	JEOPARDY Greg Kihn Band
9	MY LOVE Lionel Richie
10	TIME Culture Club

May 28, 1983
1   FLASHDANCE   Irene Cara
2   LET'S DANCE   David Bowie
3   BEAT IT   Michael Jackson
4   OVERKILL   Men At Work
5   SHE BLINDED ME WITH SCIENCE   Thomas Dolby
6   LITTLE RED CORVETTE   Prince
7   SOLITAIRE   Laura Branigan
8   TIME   Culture Club
9   MY LOVE   Lionel Richie
10   STRAIGHT FROM THE HEART   Bryan Adams

June 4, 1983
1   FLASHDANCE   Irene Cara
2   LET'S DANCE   David Bowie
3   OVERKILL   Men At Work
4   TIME   Culture Club
5   SHE BLINDED ME WITH SCIENCE   Thomas Dolby
6   BEAT IT   Michael Jackson
7   MY LOVE   Lionel Richie
8   LITTLE RED CORVETTE   Prince
9   SOLITAIRE   Laura Branigan
10   STRAIGHT FROM THE HEART   Bryan Adams

June 11, 1983
1   FLASHDANCE   Irene Cara
2   LET'S DANCE   David Bowie

3   TIME   Culture Club
4   OVERKILL   Men At Work
5   MY LOVE   Lionel Richie
6   BEAT IT   Michael Jackson
7   SHE BLINDED ME WITH SCIENCE   Thomas Dolby
8   ALWAYS SOMETHING THERE TO REMIND ME   Naked Eyes
9   DON'T LET IT END   Styx
10   AFFAIR OF THE HEART   Rick Springfield

June 18, 1983
1   FLASHDANCE   Irene Cara
2   TIME   Culture Club
3   LET'S DANCE   David Bowie
4   ELECTRIC AVENUE   Eddy Grant
5   OVERKILL   Men At Work
6   MY LOVE   Lionel Richie
7   DON'T LET IT END   Styx
8   ALWAYS SOMETHING THERE TO REMIND ME   Naked Eyes
9   AFFAIR OF THE HEART   Rick Springfield
10   FAMILY MAN   Daryl Hall & John Oates

June 25, 1983
1   FLASHDANCE   Irene Cara
2   TIME   Culture Club
3   ELECTRIC AVENUE   Eddy Grant
4   EVERY BREATH YOU TAKE   Police
5   LET'S DANCE   David Bowie
6   FAMILY MAN   Daryl Hall & John Oates
7   DON'T LET IT END   Styx
8   NEVER GONNA LET YOU GO   Sergio Mendes
9   AFFAIR OF THE HEART   Rick Springfield
10   TOO SHY   Kajagoogoo

July 2, 1983
1   FLASHDANCE   Irene Cara
2   ELECTRIC AVENUE   Eddy Grant
3   EVERY BREATH YOU TAKE   Police
4   TIME   Culture Club
5   NEVER GONNA LET YOU GO   Sergio Mendes
6   DON'T LET IT END   Styx
7   TOO SHY   Kajagoogoo
8   FAMILY MAN   Daryl Hall & John Oates
9   WANNA BE STARTIN' SOMETHING   Michael Jackson
10   SHE'S A BEAUTY   Tubes

July 9, 1983
1   EVERY BREATH YOU TAKE   Police
2   ELECTRIC AVENUE   Eddy Grant
3   FLASHDANCE   Irene Cara
4   NEVER GONNA LET YOU GO   Sergio Mendes
5   TOO SHY   Kajagoogoo
6   WANNA BE STARTIN' SOMETHING   Michael Jackson
7   TIME   Culture Club
8   COME DANCING   Kinks
9   DON'T LET IT END   Styx
10   OUR HOUSE   Madness

July 16, 1983
1   EVERY BREATH YOU TAKE   Police
2   ELECTRIC AVENUE   Eddy Grant
3   FLASHDANCE   Irene Cara
4   NEVER GONNA LET YOU GO   Sergio Mendes
5   WANNA BE STARTIN' SOMETHING   Michael Jackson
6   COME DANCING   Kinks

7 TOO SHY   Kajagoogoo
8 OUR HOUSE   Madness
9 IS THERE SOMETHING I SHOULD KNOW   Duran Duran
10 TIME   Culture Club

July 23, 1983
1 EVERY BREATH YOU TAKE   Police
2 ELECTRIC AVENUE   Eddy Grant
3 FLASHDANCE   Irene Cara
4 NEVER GONNA LET YOU GO   Sergio Mendes
5 WANNA BE STARTIN' SOMETHING   Michael Jackson
6 COME DANCING   Kinks
7 OUR HOUSE   Madness
8 IS THERE SOMETHING I SHOULD KNOW   Duran Duran
9 STAND BACK   Stevie Nicks
10 SHE WORKS HARD FOR THE MONEY   Donna Summer

July 30, 1983
1 EVERY BREATH YOU TAKE   Police
2 ELECTRIC AVENUE   Eddy Grant
3 FLASHDANCE   Irene Cara
4 NEVER GONNA LET YOU GO   Sergio Mendes
5 IS THERE SOMETHING I SHOULD KNOW   Duran Duran
6 SWEET DREAMS (ARE MADE OF THIS)   Eurythmics
7 WANNA BE STARTIN' SOMETHING   Michael Jackson
8 SHE WORKS HARD FOR THE MONEY   Donna Summer
9 STAND BACK   Stevie Nicks
10 OUR HOUSE   Madness

August 6, 1983
1 EVERY BREATH YOU TAKE   Police
2 SWEET DREAMS (ARE MADE OF THIS)   Eurythmics
3 SHE WORKS HARD FOR THE MONEY   Donna Summer
4 IS THERE SOMETHING I SHOULD KNOW   Duran Duran
5 FLASHDANCE   Irene Cara
6 ELECTRIC AVENUE   Eddy Grant
7 MANIAC   Michael Sembello
8 NEVER GONNA LET YOU GO   Sergio Mendes
9 STAND BACK   Stevie Nicks
10 WANNA BE STARTIN' SOMETHING   Michael Jackson

August 13, 1983
1 EVERY BREATH YOU TAKE   Police
2 SWEET DREAMS (ARE MADE OF THIS)   Eurythmics
3 SHE WORKS HARD FOR THE MONEY   Donna Summer
4 MANIAC   Michael Sembello
5 IS THERE SOMETHING I SHOULD KNOW   Duran Duran
6 STAND BACK   Stevie Nicks
7 FLASHDANCE   Irene Cara
8 IT'S A MISTAKE   Men At Work
9 NEVER GONNA LET YOU GO   Sergio Mendes
10 FASCINATION   Human League

August 20, 1983
1 EVERY BREATH YOU TAKE   Police
2 SWEET DREAMS (ARE MADE OF THIS)   Eurythmics
3 SHE WORKS HARD FOR THE MONEY   Donna Summer
4 MANIAC   Michael Sembello
5 STAND BACK   Stevie Nicks
6 IT'S A MISTAKE   Men At Work
7 IS THERE SOMETHING I SHOULD KNOW   Duran Duran
8 FASCINATION   Human League
9 PUTTIN' ON THE RITZ   Taco *
10 I'LL TUMBLE 4 YA   Culture Club
   Note: * A fifty-three year span since this song first became a
      hit in 1930.

August 27, 1983
1 EVERY BREATH YOU TAKE   Police
2 SWEET DREAMS (ARE MADE OF THIS)   Eurythmics
3 MANIAC   Michael Sembello
4 SHE WORKS HARD FOR THE MONEY   Donna Summer
5 PUTTIN' ON THE RITZ   Taco *
6 IT'S A MISTAKE   Men At Work
7 STAND BACK   Stevie Nicks
8 FASCINATION   Human League
9 I'LL TUMBLE 4 YA   Culture Club
10 CHINA GIRL   David Bowie
   Note: * A fifty-three year span since this song first became a
      hit in 1930.

September 3, 1983
1 SWEET DREAMS (ARE MADE OF THIS)   Eurythmics
2 MANIAC   Michael Sembello
3 EVERY BREATH YOU TAKE   Police
4 PUTTIN' ON THE RITZ   Taco *
5 SHE WORKS HARD FOR THE MONEY   Donna Summer
6 THE SAFETY DANCE   Men Without Hats
7 TELL HER ABOUT IT   Billy Joel
8 IT'S A MISTAKE   Men At Work
9 I'LL TUMBLE 4 YA   Culture Club
10 HUMAN NATURE   Michael Jackson
   Note: * A fifty-three year span since this song first became a
      hit in 1930.

September 10, 1983
1 MANIAC   Michael Sembello
2 SWEET DREAMS (ARE MADE OF THIS)   Eurythmics
3 THE SAFETY DANCE   Men Without Hats
4 PUTTIN' ON THE RITZ   Taco *
5 TELL HER ABOUT IT   Billy Joel
6 EVERY BREATH YOU TAKE   Police
7 SHE WORKS HARD FOR THE MONEY   Donna Summer
8 TOTAL ECLIPSE OF THE HEART   Bonnie Tyler
9 HUMAN NATURE   Michael Jackson
10 I'LL TUMBLE 4 YA   Culture Club
   Note: * A fifty-three year span since this song first became a
      hit in 1930.

September 17, 1983
1 MANIAC   Michael Sembello
2 TELL HER ABOUT IT   Billy Joel
3 THE SAFETY DANCE   Men Without Hats
4 TOTAL ECLIPSE OF THE HEART   Bonnie Tyler
5 SWEET DREAMS (ARE MADE OF THIS)   Eurythmics
6 EVERY BREATH YOU TAKE   Police
7 HUMAN NATURE   Michael Jackson
8 PUTTIN' ON THE RITZ   Taco *
9 MAKING LOVE OUT OF NOTHING AT ALL   Air Supply
10 DON'T CRY   Asia
   Note: * A fifty-three year span since this song first became a
      hit in 1930.

September 24, 1983
1 TELL HER ABOUT IT   Billy Joel
2 TOTAL ECLIPSE OF THE HEART   Bonnie Tyler
3 THE SAFETY DANCE   Men Without Hats
4 MANIAC   Michael Sembello
5 MAKING LOVE OUT OF NOTHING AT ALL   Air Supply
6 SWEET DREAMS (ARE MADE OF THIS)   Eurythmics
7 HUMAN NATURE   Michael Jackson
8 PUTTIN' ON THE RITZ   Taco *
9 (SHE'S) SEXY & 17   Stray Cats
10 DON'T CRY   Asia

Bonnie Tyler

Bonnie's ``Total Eclipse of the Heart'' spent the month of October eclipsing other #1-slot contenders.

Note: * A fifty-three year span since this song first became a hit in 1930.

October 1, 1983

1. TOTAL ECLIPSE OF THE HEART   Bonnie Tyler
2. TELL HER ABOUT IT   Billy Joel
3. THE SAFETY DANCE   Men Without Hats
4. MAKING LOVE OUT OF NOTHING AT ALL   Air Supply
5. (SHE'S) SEXY & 17   Stray Cats
6. KING OF PAIN   Police
7. TRUE   Spandau Ballet
8. MANIAC   Michael Sembello
9. ISLANDS IN THE STREAM   Kenny Rogers & Dolly Parton
10. FAR FROM OVER   Frank Stallone

October 8, 1983

1. TOTAL ECLIPSE OF THE HEART   Bonnie Tyler
2. MAKING LOVE OUT OF NOTHING AT ALL   Air Supply
3. KING OF PAIN   Police
4. TRUE   Spandau Ballet
5. (SHE'S) SEXY & 17   Stray Cats
6. ISLANDS IN THE STREAM   Kenny Rogers & Dolly Parton
7. TELL HER ABOUT IT   Billy Joel
8. THE SAFETY DANCE   Men Without Hats
9. ONE THING LEADS TO ANOTHER   Fixx
10. FAR FROM OVER   Frank Stallone

October 15, 1983

1. TOTAL ECLIPSE OF THE HEART   Bonnie Tyler
2. MAKING LOVE OUT OF NOTHING AT ALL   Air Supply
3. KING OF PAIN   Police
4. TIME   Culture Club
5. ISLANDS IN THE STREAM   Kenny Rogers & Dolly Parton
6. ONE THING LEADS TO ANOTHER   Fixx
7. ALL NIGHT LONG   Lionel Richie
8. THE SAFETY DANCE   Men Without Hats
9. TELL HER ABOUT IT   Billy Joel
10. (SHE'S) SEXY & 17   Stray Cats

October 22, 1983

1. TOTAL ECLIPSE OF THE HEART   Bonnie Tyler
2. MAKING LOVE OUT OF NOTHING AT ALL   Air Supply
3. ISLANDS IN THE STREAM   Kenny Rogers & Dolly Parton
4. TRUE   Spandau Ballet
5. ALL NIGHT LONG   Lionel Richie
6. ONE THING LEADS TO ANOTHER   Fixx
7. KING OF PAIN   Police
8. DELIRIOUS   Prince
9. BURNING DOWN THE HOUSE   Talking Heads
10. TELEFONE (LONG DISTANCE LOVE AFFAIR)   Sheena Easton

October 29, 1983

1. ISLANDS IN THE STREAM   Kenny Rogers & Dolly Parton
2. TOTAL ECLIPSE OF THE HEART   Bonnie Tyler
3. ALL NIGHT LONG   Lionel Richie
4. TRUE   Spandau Ballet
5. ONE THING LEADS TO ANOTHER   Fixx
6. MAKING LOVE OUT OF NOTHING AT ALL   Air Supply
7. KING OF PAIN   Police
8. DELIRIOUS   Prince
9. TELEFONE (LONG DISTANCE LOVE AFFAIR)   Sheena Easton
10. UPTOWN GIRL   Billy Joel

November 5, 1983

1. ISLANDS IN THE STREAM   Kenny Rogers & Dolly Parton
2. ALL NIGHT LONG   Lionel Richie
3. TOTAL ECLIPSE OF THE HEART   Bonnie Tyler
4. ONE THING LEADS TO ANOTHER   Fixx
5. UPTOWN GIRL   Billy Joel
6. SAY SAY SAY   Paul McCartney & Michael Jackson
7. MAKING LOVE OUT OF NOTHING AT ALL   Air Supply
8. DELIRIOUS   Prince
9. TELEFONE (LONG DISTANCE LOVE AFFAIR)   Sheena Easton
10. TRUE   Spandau Ballet

November 12, 1983

1. ALL NIGHT LONG   Lionel Richie
2. ISLANDS IN THE STREAM   Kenny Rogers & Dolly Parton
3. UPTOWN GIRL   Billy Joel
4. SAY SAY SAY   Paul McCartney & Michael Jackson
5. TOTAL ECLIPSE OF THE HEART   Bonnie Tyler
6. ONE THING LEADS TO ANOTHER   Fixx
7. CUM ON FEEL THE NOIZE   Quiet Riot
8. DELIRIOUS   Prince
9. MAKING LOVE OUT OF NOTHING AT ALL   Air Supply
10. SUDDENLY LAST SUMMER   Motels

November 19, 1983

1. ALL NIGHT LONG   Lionel Richie
2. SAY SAY SAY   Paul McCartney & Michael Jackson
3. UPTOWN GIRL   Billy Joel
4. ISLANDS IN THE STREAM   Kenny Rogers & Dolly Parton
5. CUM ON FEEL THE NOIZE   Quiet Riot
6. TOTAL ECLIPSE OF THE HEART   Bonnie Tyler
7. LOVE IS A BATTLEFIELD   Pat Benatar
8. ONE THING LEADS TO ANOTHER   Fixx
9. SUDDENLY LAST SUMMER   Motels
10. SAY IT ISN'T SO   Daryl Hall & John Oates

November 26, 1983

1. ALL NIGHT LONG   Lionel Richie
2. SAY SAY SAY   Paul McCartney & Michael Jackson
3. UPTOWN GIRL   Billy Joel
4. ISLANDS IN THE STREAM   Kenny Rogers & Dolly Parton
5. CUM ON FEEL THE NOIZE   Quiet Riot
6. LOVE IS A BATTLEFIELD   Pat Benatar
7. SAY IT ISN'T SO   Daryl Hall & John Oates
8. HEART AND SOUL   Huey Lewis & The News
9. CRUMBLIN' DOWN   John Cougar Mellencamp
10. P.Y.T. (PRETTY YOUNG THING)   Michael Jackson

December 3, 1983

1. ALL NIGHT LONG   Lionel Richie
2. SAY SAY SAY   Paul McCartney & Michael Jackson
3. UPTOWN GIRL   Billy Joel
4. ISLANDS IN THE STREAM   Kenny Rogers & Dolly Parton
5. SAY IT ISN'T SO   Daryl Hall & John Oates
6. LOVE IS A BATTLEFIELD   Pat Benatar
7. CUM ON FEEL THE NOIZE   Quiet Riot
8. HEART AND SOUL   Huey Lewis & The News
9. CRUMBLIN' DOWN   John Cougar Mellencamp
10. CHURCH OF THE POISON MIND   Culture Club

December 10, 1983

1. SAY SAY SAY   Paul McCartney & Michael Jackson
2. ALL NIGHT LONG   Lionel Richie
3. UPTOWN GIRL   Billy Joel
4. SAY IT ISN'T SO   Daryl Hall & John Oates

Your Hit Parade & American Top Ten Hits

5 LOVE IS A BATTLEFIELD   Pat Benatar
6 ISLANDS IN THE STREAM   Kenny Rogers & Dolly Parton
7 UNION OF THE SNAKE   Duran Duran
8 CUM ON FEEL THE NOIZE   Quiet Riot
9 CRUMBLIN' DOWN   John Cougar Mellencamp
10 CHURCH OF THE POISON MIND   Culture Club

December 17, 1983
1 SAY SAY SAY   Paul McCartney & Michael Jackson
2 SAY IT ISN'T SO   Daryl Hall & John Oates
3 ALL NIGHT LONG   Lionel Richie
4 UPTOWN GIRL   Billy Joel
5 UNION OF THE SNAKE   Duran Duran
6 LOVE IS A BATTLEFIELD   Pat Benatar
7 OWNER OF A LONELY HEART   Yes
8 ISLANDS IN THE STREAM   Kenny Rogers & Dolly Parton
9 TWIST OF FATE   Olivia Newton-John
10 CHURCH OF THE POISON MIND   Culture Club

December 24, 1983
1 SAY SAY SAY   Paul McCartney & Michael Jackson
2 SAY IT ISN'T SO   Daryl Hall & John Oates
3 UNION OF THE SNAKE   Duran Duran
4 OWNER OF A LONELY HEART   Yes
5 ALL NIGHT LONG   Lionel Richie
6 UPTOWN GIRL   Billy Joel
7 LOVE IS A BATTLEFIELD   Pat Benatar
8 TWIST OF FATE   Olivia Newton-John
9 UNDERCOVER OF THE NIGHT   Rolling Stones
10 BREAK MY STRIDE   Matthew Wilder

January 7, 1984
1 SAY SAY SAY   Paul McCartney & Michael Jackson
2 SAY IT ISN'T SO   Daryl Hall & John Oates
3 UNION OF THE SNAKE   Duran Duran
4 OWNER OF A LONELY HEART   Yes
5 TWIST OF FATE   Olivia Newton-John
6 TALKING IN YOUR SLEEP   Romantics
7 BREAK MY STRIDE   Matthew Wilder
8 I GUESS THAT'S WHY THEY CALL IT THE BLUES   Elton John
9 UNDERCOVER OF THE NIGHT   Rolling Stones
10 ALL NIGHT LONG   Lionel Richie

January 14, 1984
1 SAY SAY SAY   Paul McCartney & Michael Jackson
2 OWNER OF A LONELY HEART   Yes
3 SAY IT ISN'T SO   Daryl Hall & John Oates
4 UNION OF THE SNAKE   Duran Duran
5 TWIST OF FATE   Olivia Newton-John
6 TALKING IN YOUR SLEEP   Romantics
7 BREAK MY STRIDE   Matthew Wilder
8 I GUESS THAT'S WHY THEY CALL IT THE BLUES   Elton John
9 KARMA CHAMELEON   Culture Club
10 RUNNING WITH THE NIGHT   Lionel Richie

January 21, 1984
1 OWNER OF A LONELY HEART   Yes
2 SAY SAY SAY   Paul McCartney & Michael Jackson
3 KARMA CHAMELEON   Culture Club
4 TALKING IN YOUR SLEEP   Romantics
5 BREAK MY STRIDE   Matthew Wilder
6 I GUESS THAT'S WHY THEY CALL IT THE BLUES   Elton John
7 TWIST OF FATE   Olivia Newton-John
8 JOANNA   Kool & The Gang

9 RUNNING WITH THE NIGHT   Lionel Richie
10 SAY IT ISN'T SO   Daryl Hall & John Oates

January 28, 1984
1 OWNER OF A LONELY HEART   Yes
2 KARMA CHAMELEON   Culture Club
3 TALKING IN YOUR SLEEP   Romantics
4 I GUESS THAT'S WHY THEY CALL IT THE BLUES   Elton John
5 BREAK MY STRIDE   Matthew Wilder
6 JOANNA   Kool & The Gang
7 SAY SAY SAY   Paul McCartney & Michael Jackson
8 RUNNING WITH THE NIGHT   Lionel Richie
9 TWIST OF FATE   Olivia Newton-John
10 THAT'S ALL   Genesis

February 4, 1984
1 KARMA CHAMELEON   Culture Club
2 OWNER OF A LONELY HEART   Yes
3 TALKING IN YOUR SLEEP   Romantics
4 JOANNA   Kool & The Gang
5 BREAK MY STRIDE   Matthew Wilder
6 I GUESS THAT'S WHY THEY CALL IT THE BLUES   Elton John
7 RUNNING WITH THE NIGHT   Lionel Richie
8 THAT'S ALL   Genesis
9 THINK OF LAURA   Christopher Cross
10 PINK HOUSES   John Cougar Mellencamp

February 11, 1984
1 KARMA CHAMELEON   Culture Club
2 JOANNA   Kool & The Gang
3 TALKING IN YOUR SLEEP   Romantics
4 OWNER OF A LONELY HEART   Yes
5 JUMP   Van Halen
6 THAT'S ALL   Genesis
7 RUNNING WITH THE NIGHT   Lionel Richie
8 PINK HOUSES   John Cougar Mellencamp
9 THINK OF LAURA   Christopher Cross
10 I GUESS THAT'S WHY THEY CALL IT THE BLUES   Elton John

February 18, 1984
1 KARMA CHAMELEON   Culture Club
2 JUMP   Van Halen
3 JOANNA   Kool & The Gang
4 99 LUFTBALLOONS   Nena
5 TALKING IN YOUR SLEEP   Romantics
6 THAT'S ALL   Genesis
7 THRILLER   Michael Jackson
8 OWNER OF A LONELY HEART   Yes
9 GIRLS JUST WANT TO HAVE FUN   Cyndi Lauper
10 LET THE MUSIC PLAY   Shannon

February 25, 1984
1 JUMP   Van Halen
2 KARMA CHAMELEON   Culture Club
3 99 LUFTBALLOONS   Nena
4 GIRLS JUST WANT TO HAVE FUN   Cyndi Lauper
5 THRILLER   Michael Jackson
6 JOANNA   Kool & The Gang
7 NOBODY TOLD ME   John Lennon
8 LET THE MUSIC PLAY   Shannon
9 WRAPPED AROUND YOUR FINGER   Police
10 AN INNOCENT MAN   Billy Joel

362

Boy George
February is Culture Club's #1 month with ``Karma Chameleon.''

Eddie Van Halen
Eddie and friends jump up to the #1 slot on February 25.

Kenny Loggins
Another movie title-song takes over at #1 (Mar. 31).

Prince
``When Doves Cry'' was #1 for a month—any tears shed? (Jul. 7).

March 3, 1984
1. JUMP   Van Halen
2. 99 LUFTBALLOONS   Nena
3. GIRLS JUST WANT TO HAVE FUN   Cyndi Lauper
4. THRILLER   Michael Jackson
5. NOBODY TOLD ME   John Lennon
6. KARMA CHAMELEON   Culture Club
7. SOMEBODY'S WATCHING ME   Rockwell
8. WRAPPED AROUND YOUR FINGER   Police
9. LET THE MUSIC PLAY   Shannon
10. I WANT A NEW DRUG   Huey Lewis & The News

March 10, 1984
1. JUMP   Van Halen
2. GIRLS JUST WANT TO HAVE FUN   Cyndi Lauper
3. 99 LUFTBALLOONS   Nena
4. THRILLER   Michael Jackson
5. SOMEBODY'S WATCHING ME   Rockwell
6. NOBODY TOLD ME   John Lennon
7. I WANT A NEW DRUG   Huey Lewis & The News
8. HERE COMES THE RAIN AGAIN   Eurythmics
9. FOOTLOOSE   Kenny Loggins
10. KARMA CHAMELEON   Culture Club

March 17, 1984
1. JUMP   Van Halen
2. GIRLS JUST WANT TO HAVE FUN   Cyndi Lauper
3. SOMEBODY'S WATCHING ME   Rockwell
4. 99 LUFTBALLOONS   Nena
5. FOOTLOOSE   Kenny Loggins
6. THRILLER   Michael Jackson
7. I WANT A NEW DRUG   Huey Lewis & The News
8. HERE COMES THE RAIN AGAIN   Eurythmics
9. NOBODY TOLD ME   John Lennon
10. NEW MOON ON MONDAY   Duran Duran

March 24, 1984
1. JUMP   Van Halen
2. SOMEBODY'S WATCHING ME   Rockwell
3. GIRLS JUST WANT TO HAVE FUN   Cyndi Lauper
4. FOOTLOOSE   Kenny Loggins
5. HERE COMES THE RAIN AGAIN   Eurythmics
6. I WANT A NEW DRUG   Huey Lewis & The News
7. 99 LUFTBALLOONS   Nena
8. AUTOMATIC   Pointer Sisters
9. ADULT EDUCATION   Daryl Hall & John Oates
10. GOT A HOLD ON ME   Christine McVie

March 31, 1984
1. FOOTLOOSE   Kenny Loggins
2. SOMEBODY'S WATCHING ME   Rockwell
3. JUMP   Van Halen
4. HERE COMES THE RAIN AGAIN   Eurythmics
5. GIRLS JUST WANT TO HAVE FUN   Cyndi Lauper
6. I WANT A NEW DRUG   Huey Lewis & The News
7. AGAINST ALL ODDS   Phil Collins
8. AUTOMATIC   Pointer Sisters
9. ADULT EDUCATION   Daryl Hall & John Oates
10. MISS ME BLIND   Culture Club

April 7, 1984
1. FOOTLOOSE   Kenny Loggins
2. SOMEBODY'S WATCHING ME   Rockwell
3. AGAINST ALL ODDS   Phil Collins
4. HERE COMES THE RAIN AGAIN   Eurythmics
5. JUMP   Van Halen
6. AUTOMATIC   Pointer Sisters
7. MISS ME BLIND   Culture Club
8. ADULT EDUCATION   Daryl Hall & John Oates
9. GIRLS JUST WANT TO HAVE FUN   Cyndi Lauper
10. HELLO   Lionel Richie

April 14, 1984
1. FOOTLOOSE   Kenny Loggins
2. AGAINST ALL ODDS   Phil Collins
3. SOMEBODY'S WATCHING ME   Rockwell
4. HELLO   Lionel Richie
5. AUTOMATIC   Pointer Sisters
6. MISS ME BLIND   Culture Club
7. HERE COMES THE RAIN AGAIN   Eurythmics
8. HOLD ME NOW   Thompson Twins
9. ADULT EDUCATION   Daryl Hall & John Oates
10. JUMP   Van Halen

April 21, 1984
1. AGAINST ALL ODDS   Phil Collins
2. FOOTLOOSE   Kenny Loggins
3. HELLO   Lionel Richie
4. HOLD ME NOW   Thompson Twins
5. MISS ME BLIND   Culture Club
6. AUTOMATIC   Pointer Sisters
7. SOMEBODY'S WATCHING ME   Rockwell
8. LOVE SOMEBODY   Rick Springfield
9. HERE COMES THE RAIN AGAIN   Eurythmics
10. THEY DON'T KNOW   Tracey Ullman

April 28, 1984
1. AGAINST ALL ODDS   Phil Collins
2. HELLO   Lionel Richie
3. FOOTLOOSE   Kenny Loggins
4. HOLD ME NOW   Thompson Twins
5. MISS ME BLIND   Culture Club
6. LOVE SOMEBODY   Rick Springfield
7. YOU MIGHT THINK   Cars
8. THEY DON'T KNOW   Tracey Ullman
9. AUTOMATIC   Pointer Sisters
10. TO ALL THE GIRLS I'VE LOVED BEFORE   Julio Iglesias & Willie Nelson

May 5, 1984
1. AGAINST ALL ODDS   Phil Collins
2. HELLO   Lionel Richie
3. HOLD ME NOW   Thompson Twins
4. FOOTLOOSE   Kenny Loggins
5. LOVE SOMEBODY   Rick Springfield
6. TO ALL THE GIRLS I'VE LOVED BEFORE   Julio Iglesias & Willie Nelson
7. YOU MIGHT THINK   Cars
8. THEY DON'T KNOW   Tracey Ullman
9. LET'S HEAR IT FOR THE BOYS   Deniece Williams
10. MISS ME BLIND   Culture Club

May 12, 1984
1. HELLO   Lionel Richie
2. AGAINST ALL ODDS   Phil Collins
3. HOLD ME NOW   Thompson Twins
4. LET'S HEAR IT FOR THE BOYS   Deniece Williams
5. LOVE SOMEBODY   Rick Springfield
6. TO ALL THE GIRLS I'VE LOVED BEFORE   Julio Iglesias & Willie Nelson
7. YOU MIGHT THINK   Cars
8. FOOTLOOSE   Kenny Loggins
9. OH SHERRIE   Steve Perry

10   TIME AFTER TIME   Cyndi Lauper

May 19, 1984
1. HELLO   Lionel Richie
2. LET'S HEAR IT FOR THE BOYS   Deniece Williams
3. AGAINST ALL ODDS   Phil Collins
4. HOLD ME NOW   Thompson Twins
5. TO ALL THE GIRLS I'VE LOVED BEFORE   Julio Iglesias & Willie Nelson
6. TIME AFTER TIME   Cyndi Lauper
7. LOVE SOMEBODY   Rick Springfield
8. OH SHERRIE   Steve Perry
9. YOU MIGHT THINK   Cars
10. FOOTLOOSE   Kenny Loggins

May 26, 1984
1. LET'S HEAR IT FOR THE BOYS   Deniece Williams
2. HELLO   Lionel Richie
3. TIME AFTER TIME   Cyndi Lauper
4. AGAINST ALL ODDS   Phil Collins
5. OH SHERRIE   Steve Perry
6. TO ALL THE GIRLS I'VE LOVED BEFORE   Julio Iglesias & Willie Nelson
7. THE REFLEX   Duran Duran
8. SISTER CHRISTIAN   Night Ranger
9. BREAKDANCE   Irene Cara
10. HOLD ME NOW   Thompson Twins

June 2, 1984
1. LET'S HEAR IT FOR THE BOYS   Deniece Williams
2. TIME AFTER TIME   Cyndi Lauper
3. HELLO   Lionel Richie
4. OH SHERRIE   Steve Perry
5. THE REFLEX   Duran Duran
6. SISTER CHRISTIAN   Night Ranger
7. AGAINST ALL ODDS   Phil Collins
8. THE HEART OF ROCK 'N ROLL   Huey Lewis & The News
9. BREAKDANCE   Irene Cara
10. TO ALL THE GIRLS I'VE LOVED BEFORE   Julio Iglesias & Willie Nelson

June 9, 1984
1. TIME AFTER TIME   Cyndi Lauper
2. LET'S HEAR IT FOR THE BOYS   Deniece Williams
3. OH SHERRIE   Steve Perry
4. THE REFLEX   Duran Duran
5. SISTER CHRISTIAN   Night Ranger
6. THE HEART OF ROCK 'N ROLL   Huey Lewis & The News
7. HELLO   Lionel Richie
8. BREAKDANCE   Irene Cara
9. SELF CONTROL   Laura Branigan
10. JUMP   Van Halen

June 16, 1984
1. TIME AFTER TIME   Cyndi Lauper
2. THE REFLEX   Duran Duran
3. LET'S HEAR IT FOR THE BOYS   Deniece Williams
4. OH SHERRIE   Steve Perry
5. SISTER CHRISTIAN   Night Ranger
6. THE HEART OF ROCK 'N ROLL   Huey Lewis & The News
7. SELF CONTROL   Laura Branigan
8. JUMP   Van Halen
9. DANCING IN THE DARK   Bruce Springsteen
10. BORDERLINE   Madonna

June 23, 1984
1. THE REFLEX   Duran Duran
2. TIME AFTER TIME   Cyndi Lauper
3. LET'S HEAR IT FOR THE BOYS   Deniece Williams
4. DANCING IN THE DARK   Bruce Springsteen
5. SELF CONTROL   Laura Branigan
6. THE HEART OF ROCK 'N ROLL   Huey Lewis & The News
7. JUMP   Van Halen
8. WHEN DOVES CRY   Prince
9. OH SHERRIE   Steve Perry
10. EYES WITHOUT A FACE   Billy Idol

June 30, 1984
1. THE REFLEX   Duran Duran
2. DANCING IN THE DARK   Bruce Springsteen
3. WHEN DOVES CRY   Prince
4. SELF CONTROL   Laura Branigan
5. JUMP   Van Halen
6. THE HEART OF ROCK 'N ROLL   Huey Lewis & The News
7. TIME AFTER TIME   Cyndi Lauper
8. EYES WITHOUT A FACE   Billy Idol
9. LET'S HEAR IT FOR THE BOYS   Deniece Williams
10. ALMOST PARADISE   Mike Reno & Ann Wilson

July 7, 1984
1. WHEN DOVES CRY   Prince
2. DANCING IN THE DARK   Bruce Springsteen
3. JUMP   Van Halen
4. SELF CONTROL   Laura Branigan
5. THE REFLEX   Duran Duran
6. EYES WITHOUT A FACE   Billy Idol
7. TIME AFTER TIME   Cyndi Lauper
8. ALMOST PARADISE   Mike Reno & Ann Wilson
9. THE HEART OF ROCK 'N ROLL   Huey Lewis & The News
10. LEGS   ZZ Top

July 14, 1984
1. WHEN DOVES CRY   Prince
2. DANCING IN THE DARK   Bruce Springsteen
3. JUMP (FOR MY LOVE)   Pointer Sisters
4. EYES WITHOUT A FACE   Billy Idol
5. THE REFLEX   Duran Duran
6. SELF CONTROL   Laura Branigan
7. GHOSTBUSTERS   Ray Parker, Jr.
8. ALMOST PARADISE   Mike Reno & Ann Wilson
9. THE HEART OF ROCK 'N ROLL   Huey Lewis & The News
10. LEGS   ZZ Top

July 21, 1984
1. WHEN DOVES CRY   Prince
2. DANCING IN THE DARK   Bruce Springsteen
3. GHOSTBUSTERS   Ray Parker, Jr.
4. EYES WITHOUT A FACE   Billy Idol
5. JUMP (FOR MY LOVE)   Pointer Sisters
6. STATE OF SHOCK   Jacksons
7. ALMOST PARADISE   Mike Reno & Ann Wilson
8. LEGS   ZZ Top
9. SAD SONGS (SAY SO MUCH)   Elton John
10. INFATUATION   Rod Stewart

July 28, 1984
1. WHEN DOVES CRY   Prince
2. GHOSTBUSTERS   Ray Parker, Jr.
3. DANCING IN THE DARK   Bruce Springsteen
4. STATE OF SHOCK   Jacksons
5. EYES WITHOUT A FACE   Billy Idol

6 INFATUATION   Rod Stewart
7 SAD SONGS (SAY SO MUCH)   Elton John
8 LEGS   ZZ Top
9 WHAT'S LOVE GOT TO DO WITH IT   Tina Turner
10 JUMP (FOR MY LOVE)   Pointer Sisters

August 4, 1984
1 WHEN DOVES CRY   Prince
2 GHOSTBUSTERS   Ray Parker, Jr.
3 STATE OF SHOCK   Jacksons
4 DANCING IN THE DARK   Bruce Springsteen
5 WHAT'S LOVE GOT TO DO WITH IT   Tina Turner
6 INFATUATION   Rod Stewart
7 SAD SONGS (SAY SO MUCH)   Elton John
8 STUCK ON YOU   Lionel Richie
9 BREAKIN'...THERE'S NO STOPPING US   Ollie & Jerry
10 I CAN DREAM ABOUT YOU   Dan Hartman

August 11, 1984
1 GHOSTBUSTERS   Ray Parker, Jr.
2 WHEN DOVES CRY   Prince
3 STATE OF SHOCK   Jacksons
4 WHAT'S LOVE GOT TO DO WITH IT   Tina Turner
5 SAD SONGS (SAY SO MUCH)   Elton John
6 STUCK ON YOU   Lionel Richie
7 DANCING IN THE DARK   Bruce Springsteen
8 I CAN DREAM ABOUT YOU   Dan Hartman
9 INFATUATION   Rod Stewart
10 SUNGLASSES AT NIGHT   Corey Hart

August 18, 1984
1 GHOSTBUSTERS   Ray Parker, Jr.
2 WHAT'S LOVE GOT TO DO WITH IT   Tina Turner
3 STATE OF SHOCK   Jacksons
4 WHEN DOVES CRY   Prince
5 STUCK ON YOU   Lionel Richie
6 I CAN DREAM ABOUT YOU   Dan Hartman
7 MISSING YOU   John Waite
8 SAD SONGS (SAY SO MUCH)   Elton John
9 SUNGLASSES AT NIGHT   Corey Hart
10 IF EVER YOU'RE IN MY ARMS AGAIN   Peabo Bryson

August 25, 1984
1 GHOSTBUSTERS   Ray Parker, Jr.
2 WHAT'S LOVE GOT TO DO WITH IT   Tina Turner
3 STUCK ON YOU   Lionel Richie
4 WHEN DOVES CRY   Prince
5 MISSING YOU   John Waite
6 I CAN DREAM ABOUT YOU   Dan Hartman
7 STATE OF SHOCK   Jacksons
8 SUNGLASSES AT NIGHT   Corey Hart
9 SHE BOP   Cyndi Lauper
10 IF EVER YOU'RE IN MY ARMS AGAIN   Peabo Bryson

September 1, 1984
1 WHAT'S LOVE GOT TO DO WITH IT   Tina Turner
2 MISSING YOU   John Waite
3 STUCK ON YOU   Lionel Richie
4 GHOSTBUSTERS   Ray Parker, Jr.
5 WHEN DOVES CRY   Prince
6 SHE BOP   Cyndi Lauper
7 SUNGLASSES AT NIGHT   Corey Hart
8 LET'S GO CRAZY   Prince
9 IF THIS IS IT   Huey Lewis & The News
10 IF EVER YOU'RE IN MY ARMS AGAIN   Peabo Bryson

September 8, 1984
1 WHAT'S LOVE GOT TO DO WITH IT   Tina Turner
2 MISSING YOU   John Waite
3 SHE BOP   Cyndi Lauper
4 GHOSTBUSTERS   Ray Parker, Jr.
5 STUCK ON YOU   Lionel Richie
6 LET'S GO CRAZY   Prince
7 IF THIS IS IT   Huey Lewis & The News
8 THE WARRIOR   Scandal
9 SUNGLASSES AT NIGHT   Corey Hart
10 DRIVE   Cars

September 15, 1984
1 WHAT'S LOVE GOT TO DO WITH IT   Tina Turner
2 MISSING YOU   John Waite
3 SHE BOP   Cyndi Lauper
4 LET'S GO CRAZY   Prince
5 STUCK ON YOU   Lionel Richie
6 IF THIS IS IT   Huey Lewis & The News
7 DRIVE   Cars
8 THE WARRIOR   Scandal
9 GHOSTBUSTERS   Ray Parker, Jr.
10 THE GLAMOROUS LIFE   Sheila E.

September 22, 1984
1 MISSING YOU   John Waite
2 LET'S GO CRAZY   Prince
3 SHE BOP   Cyndi Lauper
4 WHAT'S LOVE GOT TO DO WITH IT   Tina Turner
5 DRIVE   Cars
6 IF THIS IS IT   Huey Lewis & The News
7 THE WARRIOR   Scandal
8 THE GLAMOROUS LIFE   Sheila E.
9 I JUST CALLED TO SAY I LOVE YOU   Stevie Wonder
10 CRUEL SUMMER   Bananarama

September 29, 1984
1 LET'S GO CRAZY   Prince
2 MISSING YOU   John Waite
3 DRIVE   Cars
4 SHE BOP   Cyndi Lauper
5 I JUST CALLED TO SAY I LOVE YOU   Stevie Wonder
6 WHAT'S LOVE GOT TO DO WITH IT   Tina Turner
7 THE WARRIOR   Scandal
8 THE GLAMOROUS LIFE   Sheila E.
9 CRUEL SUMMER   Bananarama
10 COVER ME   Bruce Springsteen

October 6, 1984
1 LET'S GO CRAZY   Prince
2 I JUST CALLED TO SAY I LOVE YOU   Stevie Wonder
3 DRIVE   Cars
4 MISSING YOU   John Waite
5 SHE BOP   Cyndi Lauper
6 HARD HABIT TO BREAK   Chicago
7 THE GLAMOROUS LIFE   Sheila E.
8 LUCKY STAR   Madonna
9 THE WARRIOR   Scandal
10 COVER ME   Bruce Springsteen

October 13, 1984
1 I JUST CALLED TO SAY I LOVE YOU   Stevie Wonder
2 LET'S GO CRAZY   Prince
3 DRIVE   Cars
4 HARD HABIT TO BREAK   Chicago
5 LUCKY STAR   Madonna

6   CARIBBEAN QUEEN   Billy Ocean
7   MISSING YOU   John Waite
8   COVER ME   Bruce Springsteen
9   THE GLAMOROUS LIFE   Sheila E.
10 SHE BOP   Cyndi Lauper

October 20, 1984
1   I JUST CALLED TO SAY I LOVE YOU   Stevie Wonder
2   CARIBBEAN QUEEN   Billy Ocean
3   HARD HABIT TO BREAK   Chicago
4   LUCKY STAR   Madonna
5   LET'S GO CRAZY   Prince
6   DRIVE   Cars
7   COVER ME   Bruce Springsteen
8   ON THE DARK SIDE   John Cafferty
9   PURPLE RAIN   Prince
10 I'M SO EXCITED   Pointer Sisters

October 27, 1984
1   I JUST CALLED TO SAY I LOVE YOU   Stevie Wonder
2   CARIBBEAN QUEEN   Billy Ocean
3   HARD HABIT TO BREAK   Chicago
4   PURPLE RAIN   Prince
5   LUCKY STAR   Madonna
6   WAKE ME UP BEFORE YOU GO-GO   Wham!
7   ON THE DARK SIDE   John Cafferty
8   LET'S GO CRAZY   Prince
9   I'M SO EXCITED   Pointer Sisters
10 SOME GUYS HAVE ALL THE LUCK   Rod Stewart

November 3, 1984
1   CARIBBEAN QUEEN   Billy Ocean
2   I JUST CALLED TO SAY I LOVE YOU   Stevie Wonder
3   PURPLE RAIN   Prince
4   HARD HABIT TO BREAK   Chicago
5   WAKE ME UP BEFORE YOU GO-GO   Wham!
6   LUCKY STAR   Madonna
7   ON THE DARK SIDE   John Cafferty
8   BLUE JEAN   David Bowie
9   BETTER BE GOOD TO ME   Tina Turner
10 I FEEL FOR YOU   Chaka Khan

November 10, 1984
1   CARIBBEAN QUEEN   Billy Ocean
2   I JUST CALLED TO SAY I LOVE YOU   Stevie Wonder
3   PURPLE RAIN   Prince
4   WAKE ME UP BEFORE YOU GO-GO   Wham!
5   I FEEL FOR YOU   Chaka Khan
6   OUT OF TOUCH   Daryl Hall & John Oates
7   BETTER BE GOOD TO ME   Tina Turner
8   BLUE JEAN   David Bowie
9   HARD HABIT TO BREAK   Chicago
10 DESERT MOON   Dennis DeYoung

November 17, 1984
1   WAKE ME UP BEFORE YOU GO-GO   Wham!
2   PURPLE RAIN   Prince
3   CARIBBEAN QUEEN   Billy Ocean
4   I FEEL FOR YOU   Chaka Khan
5   I JUST CALLED TO SAY I LOVE YOU   Stevie Wonder
6   OUT OF TOUCH   Daryl Hall & John Oates
7   BETTER BE GOOD TO ME   Tina Turner
8   STRUT   Sheena Easton
9   ALL THROUGH THE NIGHT   Cyndi Lauper
10 PENNY LOVER   Lionel Richie

November 24, 1984
1   WAKE ME UP BEFORE YOU GO-GO   Wham!
2   PURPLE RAIN   Prince
3   I FEEL FOR YOU   Chaka Khan
4   OUT OF TOUCH   Daryl Hall & John Oates
5   BETTER BE GOOD TO ME   Tina Turner
6   CARIBBEAN QUEEN   Billy Ocean
7   STRUT   Sheena Easton
8   ALL THROUGH THE NIGHT   Cyndi Lauper
9   PENNY LOVER   Lionel Richie
10 I JUST CALLED TO SAY I LOVE YOU   Stevie Wonder

December 1, 1984
1   WAKE ME UP BEFORE YOU GO-GO   Wham!
2   OUT OF TOUCH   Daryl Hall & John Oates
3   I FEEL FOR YOU   Chaka Khan
4   PURPLE RAIN   Prince
5   BETTER BE GOOD TO ME   Tina Turner
6   ALL THROUGH THE NIGHT   Cyndi Lauper
7   WILD BOYS   Duran Duran
8   PENNY LOVER   Lionel Richie
9   STRUT   Sheena Easton
10 NO MORE LONELY NIGHTS   Paul McCartney

December 8, 1984
1   OUT OF TOUCH   Daryl Hall & John Oates
2   WAKE ME UP BEFORE YOU GO-GO   Wham!
3   I FEEL FOR YOU   Chaka Khan
4   WILD BOYS   Duran Duran
5   ALL THROUGH THE NIGHT   Cyndi Lauper
6   NO MORE LONELY NIGHTS   Paul McCartney
7   SEA OF LOVE   Honeydrippers
8   PENNY LOVER   Lionel Richie
9   COOL IT NOW   New Edition
10 OUT OF TOUCH   Daryl Hall & John Oates

December 15, 1984
1   WILD BOYS   Duran Duran
2   OUT OF TOUCH   Daryl Hall & John Oates
3   LIKE A VIRGIN   Madonna
4   I FEEL FOR YOU   Chaka Khan
5   SEA OF LOVE   Honeydrippers
6   NO MORE LONELY NIGHTS   Paul McCartney
7   COOL IT NOW   New Edition
8   WAKE ME UP BEFORE YOU GO-GO   Wham!
9   WE BELONG   Pat Benatar
10 ALL THROUGH THE NIGHT   Cyndi Lauper

December 22, 1984
1   LIKE A VIRGIN   Madonna
2   WILD BOYS   Duran Duran
3   OUT OF TOUCH   Daryl Hall & John Oates
4   SEA OF LOVE   Honeydrippers
5   COOL IT NOW   New Edition
6   WE BELONG   Pat Benatar
7   I FEEL FOR YOU   Chaka Khan
8   NO MORE LONELY NIGHTS   Paul McCartney
9   ALL I NEED   Jack Wagner
10 VALOTTE   Julian Lennon

January 5, 1985
1   LIKE A VIRGIN   Madonna
2   WILD BOYS   Duran Duran
3   SEA OF LOVE   Honeydrippers
4   COOL IT NOW   New Edition
5   WE BELONG   Pat Benatar

6   ALL I NEED   Jack Wagner
7   OUT OF TOUCH   Daryl Hall & John Oates
8   RUN TO YOU   Bryan Adams
9   YOU'RE THE INSPIRATION   Chicago
10   VALOTTE   Julian Lennon

January 12, 1985

1   LIKE A VIRGIN   Madonna
2   ALL I NEED   Jack Wagner
3   WILD BOYS   Duran Duran
4   SEA OF LOVE   Honeydrippers
5   WE BELONG   Pat Benatar
6   YOU'RE THE INSPIRATION   Chicago
7   RUN TO YOU   Bryan Adams
8   LOVE IT NOW   New Edition
9   VALOTTE   Julian Lennon
10   BORN IN THE USA   Bruce Springsteen

January 19, 1985

1   LIKE A VIRGIN   Madonna
2   ALL I NEED   Jack Wagner
3   YOU'RE THE INSPIRATION   Chicago
4   I WANNA KNOW WHAT LOVE IS   Foreigner
5   EASY LOVER   Philip Bailey & Phil Collins
6   RUN TO YOU   Bryan Adams
7   WILD BOYS   Duran Duran
8   WE BELONG   Pat Benatar
9   BORN IN THE USA   Bruce Springsteen
10   CARELESS WHISPER   Wham!

January 26, 1985

1   LIKE A VIRGIN   Madonna
2   I WANT TO KNOW WHAT LOVE IS   Foreigner
3   YOU'RE THE INSPIRATION   Chicago
4   EASY LOVER   Philip Bailey & Phil Collins
5   CARELESS WHISPER   Wham!
6   ALL I NEED   Jack Wagner
7   RUN TO YOU   Bryan Adams
8   THE BOYS OF SUMMER   Don Henley
9   LOVER BOY   Billy Ocean
10   I WOULD DIE 4 U   Prince & The Revolution

February 2, 1985

1   I WANT TO KNOW WHAT LOVE IS   Foreigner
2   EASY LOVER   Philip Bailey & Phil Collins
3   CARELESS WHISPER   Wham!
4   YOU'RE THE INSPIRATION   Chicago
5   LOVER BOY   Billy Ocean
6   THE BOYS OF SUMMER   Don Henley
7   LIKE A VIRGIN   Madonna
8   I WOULD DIE 4 U   Prince & The Revolution
9   METHOD OF MODERN LOVE   Daryl Hall & John Oates
10   NEUTRON DANCE   The Pointer Sisters

February 9, 1985

1   I WANT TO KNOW WHAT LOVE IS   Foreigner
2   EASY LOVER   Philip Bailey & Phil Collins
3   CARELESS WHISPER   Wham!
4   LOVER BOY   Billy Ocean
5   THE BOYS OF SUMMER   Don Henley
6   YOU'RE THE INSPIRATION   Chicago
7   METHOD OF MODERN LOVE   Daryl Hall & John Oates
8   NEUTRON DANCE   The Pointer Sisters
9   LIKE A VIRGIN   Madonna
10   I WOULD DIE 4 U   Prince & The Revolution

February 16, 1985

1   CARELESS WHISPER   Wham!
2   I WANT TO KNOW WHAT LOVE IS   Foreigner
3   EASY LOVER   Philip Bailey & Phil Collins
4   LOVER BOY   Billy Ocean
5   METHOD OF MODERN LOVE   Daryl Hall & John Oates
6   NEUTRON DANCE   The Pointer Sisters
7   CAN'T FIGHT THIS FEELING   REO Speedwagon
8   THE HEAT IS ON   Glenn Frey
9   THE BOYS OF SUMMER   Don Henley
10   CALIFORNIA GIRLS   David Lee Roth

February 23, 1985

1   CARELESS WHISPER   Wham!
2   LOVER BOY   Billy Ocean
3   EASY LOVER   Philip Bailey & Phil Collins
4   CAN'T FIGHT THIS FEELING   REO Speedwagon
5   I WANT TO KNOW WHAT LOVE IS   Foreigner
6   NEUTRON DANCE   The Pointer Sisters
7   THE HEAT IS ON   Glenn Frey
8   CALIFORNIA GIRLS   David Lee Roth
9   METHOD OF MODERN LOVE   Daryl Hall & John Oates
10   SUGAR WALLS   Sheena Easton

March 2, 1985

1   CARELESS WHISPER   Wham!
2   CAN'T FIGHT THIS FEELING   REO Speedway
3   CALIFORNIA GIRLS   David Lee Roth
4   THE HEAT IS ON   Glenn Frey
5   LOVER BOY   Billy Ocean
6   NEUTRON DANCE   The Pointer Sisters
7   I WANT TO KNOW WHAT LOVE IS   Foreigner
8   EASY LOVER   Philip Bailey & Phil Collins
9   SUGAR WALLS   Sheena Easton
10   THE OLD MEN DOWN THE ROAD   John Forgerty

March 9, 1985

1   CAN'T FIGHT THIS FEELING   REO Speedway
2   CARELESS WHISPER   Wham!
3   THE HEAT IS ON   Glenn Frey
4   CALIFORNIA GIRLS   David Lee Roth
5   MATERIAL GIRL   Madonna
6   TOO LATE FOR GOODBYE   Julian Lennon
7   NEUTRON DANCE   The Pointer Sisters
8   I WANNA KNOW WHAT LOVE IS   Foreigner
9   SUGAR WALLS   Sheena Easton
10   MISLED   Kool & The Gang

March 16, 1985

1   CAN'T FIGHT THIS FEELING   REO Speedwagon
2   THE HEAT IS ON   Glenn Frey
3   MATERIAL GIRL   Madonna
4   CALIFORNIA GIRLS   David Lee Roth
5   ONE MORE NIGHT   Phil Collins
6   TOO LATE FOR GOODBYE   Julian Lennon
7   CARELESS WHISPER   Wham!
8   LOVER GIRL   Teena Marie
9   PRIVATE DANCER   Tina Turner
10   RELAX   Frankie Goes To Hollywood

March 23, 1985

1   CAN'T FIGHT THIS FEELING   REO Speedwagon
2   MATERIAL GIRL   Madonna
3   ONE MORE NIGHT   Phil Collins
4   THE HEAT IS ON   Glenn Frey
5   TOO LATE FOR GOODBYE   Julian Lennon

Madonna
Odds-on pick for the biggest all-around female ``star'' of the decade,
Madonna starts to act ``Like A Virgin''—at least for her five weeks at #1 (Dec. 22, 1984).

6 LOVER GIRL   Teena Marie
7 PRIVATE DANCER   Tina Turner
8 HIGH ON YOU   Survivor
9 ONLY THE YOUNG   Journey
10 RELAX   Frankie Goes To Hollywood

March 30, 1985
1 ONE MORE NIGHT   Phil Collins
2 MATERIAL GIRL   Madonna
3 CAN'T FIGHT THIS FEELING   REO Speedwagon
4 LOVER GIRL   Teena Marie
5 WE ARE THE WORLD   USA For Africa
6 TOO LATE FOR GOODBYE   Julian Lennon
7 PRIVATE DANCER   Tina Turner
8 HIGH ON YOU   Survivor
9 CRAZY FOR YOU   Madonna
10 NIGHTSHIFT   Commodores

April 6, 1985
1 ONE MORE NIGHT   Phil Collins
2 WE ARE THE WORLD   USA For Africa
3 MATERIAL GIRL   Madonna
4 CRAZY FOR YOU   Madonna
5 LOVER GIRL   Teena Marie
6 CAN'T FIGHT THIS FEELING   REO Speedwagon
7 NIGHTSHIFT   Commodores
8 I'M ON FIRE   Bruce Springsteen
9 RHYTHM OF THE NIGHT   DeBarge
10 TOO LATE FOR GOODBYE   Julian Lennon

April 13, 1985
1 WE ARE THE WORLD   USA For Africa
2 ONE MORE NIGHT   Phil Collins
3 CRAZY FOR YOU   Madonna
4 NIGHTSHIFT   Commodores
5 MATERIAL GIRL   Madonna
6 I'M ON FIRE   Bruce Springsteen
7 RHYTHM OF THE NIGHT   DeBarge
8 LOVER GIRL   Teena Marie
9 OBSESSION   Animotion
10 MISSING YOU   Diana Ross

April 20, 1985
1 WE ARE THE WORLD   USA For Africa
2 CRAZY FOR YOU   Madonna
3 NIGHTSHIFT   Commodores
4 ONE MORE NIGHT   Phil Collins
5 RHYTHM OF THE NIGHT   DeBarge
6 I'M ON FIRE   Bruce Springsteen
7 OBSESSION   Animotion
8 DON'T YOU FORGET ABOUT ME   Simple Minds
9 ONE NIGHT IN BANGKOK   Murray Head
10 MISSING YOU   Diana Ross

April 27, 1985
1 WE ARE THE WORLD   USA For Africa
2 CRAZY FOR YOU   Madonna
3 RHYTHM OF THE NIGHT   DeBarge
4 NIGHTSHIFT   Commodores
5 DON'T YOU FORGET ABOUT ME   Simple Minds
6 ONE NIGHT IN BANGKOK   Murray Head
7 OBSESSION   Animotion
8 SOME LIKE IT HOT   Power Station
9 I'M ON FIRE   Bruce Springsteen
10 ALL SHE WANTS TO DO IS DANCE   Don Henley

May 4, 1985
1 WE ARE THE WORLD   USA For Africa
2 CRAZY FOR YOU   Madonna
3 RHYTHM OF THE NIGHT   DeBarge
4 DON'T YOU FORGET ABOUT ME   Simple Minds
5 ONE NIGHT IN BANGKOK   Murray Head
6 OBSESSION   Animotion
7 SOME LIKE IT HOT   Power Station
8 NIGHTSHIFT   Commodores
9 ALL SHE WANTS TO DO IS DANCE   Don Henley
10 SMOOTH OPERATOR   Sade

May 11, 1985
1 CRAZY FOR YOU   Madonna
2 WE ARE THE WORLD   USA For Africa
3 DON'T YOU FORGET ABOUT ME   Simple Minds
4 RHYTHM OF THE NIGHT   DeBarge
5 ONE NIGHT IN BANGKOK   Murray Head
6 SOME LIKE IT HOT   Power Station
7 SMOOTH OPERATOR   Sade
8 EVERYTHING SHE WANTS   Wham
9 OBSESSION   Animotion
10 EVERYBODY WANTS TO RULE THE WORLD   Tears For
    Fears

May 18, 1985
1 DON'T YOU FORGET ABOUT ME   Simple Minds
2 CRAZY FOR YOU   Madonna
3 ONE NIGHT IN BANGKOK   Murray Head
4 EVERYTHING SHE WANTS   Wham
5 SMOOTH OPERATOR   Sade
6 SOME LIKE IT HOT   Power Station
7 RHYTHM OF THE NIGHT   DeBarge
8 WE ARE THE WORLD   USA For Africa
9 EVERYBODY WANTS TO RULE THE WORLD   Tears For
    Fears
10 AXEL F   Harold Faltermeer

May 25, 1985
1 EVERYTHING SHE WANTS   Wham
2 DON'T YOU FORGET ABOUT ME   Simple Minds
3 EVERYBODY WANTS TO RULE THE WORLD   Tears For
    Fears
4 AXEL F   Harold Faltermeer
5 SMOOTH OPERATOR   Sade
6 CRAZY FOR YOU   Madonna
7 ONE NIGHT IN BANGKOK   Murray Head
8 SUDDENLY   Billy Ocean
9 SOME LIKE IT HOT   Power Station
10 THINGS CAN ONLY GET BETTER   Howard Jones

June 1, 1985
1 EVERYTHING SHE WANTS   Wham
2 EVERYBODY WANTS TO RULE THE WORLD   Tears For
    Fears
3 AXEL F   Harold Faltermeer
4 DON'T YOU FORGET ABOUT ME   Simple Minds
5 SUDDENLY   Billy Ocean
6 SMOOTH OPERATOR   Sade
7 HEAVEN   Bryan Adams
8 THINGS CAN ONLY GET BETTER   Howard Jones
9 IN MY HOUSE   Mary Jane Girls
10 FRESH   Kool & The Gang

June 8, 1985
1 EVERYBODY WANTS TO RULE THE WORLD   Tears For
    Fears

370

2   EVERYTHING SHE WANTS   Wham
3   AXEL F   Harold Faltermeer
4   SUDDENLY   Billy Ocean
5   HEAVEN   Bryan Adams
6   THINGS CAN ONLY GET BETTER   Howard Jones
7   IN MY HOUSE   Mary Jane Girls
8   DON'T YOU FORGET ABOUT ME   Simple Minds
9   FRESH   Kool & The Gang
10 WALKING ON SUNSHINE   Katrina & The Waves

June 15, 1985
1   EVERYBODY WANTS TO RULE THE WORLD   Tears For
     Fears
2   HEAVEN   Bryan Adams
3   AXEL F   Harold Faltermeer
4   SUDDENLY   Billy Ocean
5   THINGS CAN ONLY GET BETTER   Howard Jones
6   SUSSUDIO   Phil Collins
7   IN MY HOUSE   Mary Jane Girls
8   EVERYTHING SHE WANTS   Wham
9   ANGEL   Madonna
10 WALKING ON SUNSHINE   Katrina & The Waves

June 22, 1985
1   HEAVEN   Bryan Adams
2   SUSSUDIO   Phil Collins
3   EVERYBODY WANTS TO RULE THE WORLD   Tears For
     Fears
4   RASPBERRY BERET   Prince
5   A VIEW TO A KILL   Duran Duran
6   ANGEL   Madonna
7   IN MY HOUSE   Mary Jane Girls
8   THINGS CAN ONLY GET BETTER   Howard Jones
9   WALKING ON SUNSHINE   Katrina & The Waves
10 THE SEARCH IS OVER   Survivor

July 6, 1985
1   SUSSUDIO   Phil Collins
2   A VIEW TO A KILL   Duran Duran
3   RASPBERRY BERET   Prince
4   HEAVEN   Bryan Adams
5   THE SEARCH IS OVER   Survivor
6   WOULD I LIE TO YOU   Eurythmics
7   YOU GIVE GOOD LOVE   Whitney Houston
8   EVERYTIME YOU GO AWAY   Paul Young
9   VOICES CARRY   Til Tuesday
10 ANGEL   Madonna

July 13, 1985
1   A VIEW TO A KILL   Duran Duran
2   SUSSUDIO   Phil Collins
3   RASPBERRY BERET   Prince
4   THE SEARCH IS OVER   Survivor
5   WOULD I LIE TO YOU   Eurythmics
6   EVERYTIME YOU GO AWAY   Paul Young
7   YOU GIVE GOOD LOVE   Whitney Houston
8   VOICES CARRY   Til Tuesday
9   GLORY DAYS   Bruce Springsteen
10 THE GOONIES 'R' GOOD ENOUGH   Cyndi Lauper

July 20, 1985
1   A VIEW TO A KILL   Duran Duran
2   RASPBERRY BERET   Prince
3   EVERYTIME YOU GO AWAY   Paul Young
4   YOU GIVE GOOD LOVE   Whitney Houston
5   SUSSUDIO   Phil Collins
6   THE SEARCH IS OVER   Survivor

Phil Collins
Ex-Genesis drummer is a #1 solo success with ``Sussudio'' (July 6).

Sting
This now-solo ex-Police vocalist charts Top 10 in July and August.

7 IF YOU LOVE SOMEBODY SET THEM FREE   Sting
8 GLORY DAYS   Bruce Springsteen
9 SHOUT   Tears For Fears
10 WOULD I LIE TO YOU   Eurythmics

July 27, 1985

1 EVERYTIME YOU GO AWAY   Paul Young
2 SHOUT   Tears For Fears
3 YOU GIVE GOOD LOVE   Whitney Houston
4 A VIEW TO A KILL   Duran Duran
5 IF YOU LOVE SOMEBODY SET THEM FREE   Sting
6 GLORY DAYS   Bruce Springsteen
7 RASPBERRY BERET   Prince
8 SENTIMENTAL STREET   Night Ranger
9 NEVER SURRENDER   Corey Hart
10 BANG A GONG   Power Station

August 3, 1985

1 SHOUT   Tears For Fears
2 EVERYTIME YOU GO AWAY   Paul Young
3 IF YOU LOVE SOMEBODY SET THEM FREE   Sting
4 YOU GIVE GOOD LOVE   Whitney Houston
5 GLORY DAYS   Bruce Springsteen
6 NEVER SURRENDER   Corey Hart
7 THE POWER OF LOVE   Huey Lewis & The News
8 SENTIMENTAL STREET   Night Ranger
9 BANG A GONG   Power Station
10 WHO'S HOLDING DONNA NOW   DeBarge

August 10, 1985

1 SHOUT   Tears For Fears
2 EVERYTIME YOU GO AWAY   Paul Young
3 IF YOU LOVE SOMEBODY SET THEM FREE   Sting
4 NEVER SURRENDER   Corey Hart
5 THE POWER OF LOVE   Huey Lewis & The News
6 WHO'S HOLDING DONNA NOW   DeBarge
7 GLORY DAYS   Bruce Springsteen
8 FREEWAY OF LOVE   Aretha Franklin
9 BANG A GONG   Power Station
10 YOU GIVE GOOD LOVE   Whitney Houston

August 17, 1985

1 SHOUT   Tears For Fears
2 THE POWER OF LOVE   Huey Lewis & The News
3 NEVER SURRENDER   Corey Hart
4 IF YOU LOVE SOMEBODY SET THEM FREE   Sting
5 FREEWAY OF LOVE   Aretha Franklin
6 EVERYTIME YOU GO AWAY   Paul Young
7 MAN IN MOTION   John Parr
8 WHO'S HOLDING DONNA NOW   DeBarge
9 SUMMER OF '69   Bryan Adams
10 WE DON'T NEED ANOTHER HERO   Tina Turner

August 24, 1985

1 THE POWER OF LOVE   Huey Lewis & The News
2 SHOUT   Tears For Fears
3 NEVER SURRENDER   Corey Hart
4 MAN IN MOTION   John Pace
5 FREEWAY OF LOVE   Aretha Franklin
6 WE DON'T NEED ANOTHER HERO   Tina Turner
7 SUMMER OF '69   Bryan Adams
8 IF YOU LOVE SOMEBODY SET THEM FREE   Sting
9 EVERYTIME YOU GO AWAY   Paul Young
10 WHAT ABOUT LOVE   Heart

August 31, 1985

1 THE POWER OF LOVE   Huey Lewis & The News
2 MAN IN MOTION   John Parr
3 FREEWAY OF LOVE   Aretha Franklin
4 WE DON'T NEED ANOTHER HERO   Tina Turner
5 SUMMER OF '69   Bryan Adams
6 SHOUT   Tears For Fears
7 NEVER SURRENDER   Corey Hart
8 CHERISH   Kool & The Gang
9 YOU'RE ONLY HUMAN   The Human League
10 MONEY FOR NOTHING   Dire Straits

September 7, 1985

1 MAN IN MOTION   John Parr
2 THE POWER OF LOVE   Huey Lewis & The News
3 WE DON'T NEED ANOTHER HERO   Tina Turner
4 FREEWAY OF LOVE   Aretha Franklin
5 SUMMER OF '69   Bryan Adams
6 MONEY FOR NOTHING   Dire Straits
7 CHERISH   Kool & The Gang
8 DON'T LOSE MY NUMBER   Phil Collins
9 YOU'RE ONLY HUMAN   The Human League
10 POP LIFE   Prince & The Revolution

September 14, 1985

1 ST. ELMO'S FIRE   Man In Motion
2 WE DON'T NEED ANOTHER HERO   Tina Turner
3 MONEY FOR NOTHING   Dire Straits
4 CHERISH   Kool & The Gang
5 THE POWER OF LOVE   Huey Lewis & The News
6 DON'T LOSE MY NUMBER   Phil Collins
7 FREEWAY OF LOVE   Aretha Franklin
8 FREEDOM   Wham!
9 POP LIFE   Prince & The Revolution
10 INVINCIBLE   Pat Benatar

September 21, 1985

1 MONEY FOR NOTHING   Dire Straits
2 CHERISH   Kool & The Gang
3 ST. ELMO'S FIRE   Man In Motion
4 WE DON'T NEED ANOTHER HERO   Tina Turner
5 DON'T LOSE MY NUMBER   Phil Collins
6 FREEDOM   Wham!
7 POP LIFE   Prince & The Revolution
8 THE POWER OF LOVE   Huey Lewis & The News
9 OH SHEILA   Ready For The World
10 DRESS YOU UP   Madonna

September 28, 1985

1 MONEY FOR NOTHING   Dire Straits
2 CHERISH   Kool & The Gang
3 FREEDOM   Wham!
4 DON'T LOSE MY NUMBER   Phil Collins
5 OH SHEILA   Ready For The World
6 DRESS YOU UP   Madonna
7 TAKE ON ME   A-Ha
8 ST. ELMO'S FIRE   Man In Motion
9 SAVING ALL MY LOVE FOR YOU   Whitney Houston
10 LONELY OL' NIGHT   John Cougar Mellencamp

October 5, 1985

1 MONEY FOR NOTHING   Dire Straits
2 CHERISH   Kool & The Gang
3 OH SHEILA   Ready For The World
4 TAKE ON ME   A-Ha
5 DRESS YOU UP   Madonna

Starship

Jefferson Airplane to Jefferson Starship to Starship to #1 hit—``We Built This City'' tops the charts (Nov. 16).

6 SAVING ALL MY LOVE FOR YOU Whitney Houston
7 FREEDOM Wham!
8 LONELY OL' NIGHT John Cougar Mellencamp
9 DANCING IN THE STREET Mick Jagger & David Bowie
10 PART-TIME LOVER Stevie Wonder

October 12, 1985
1 OH SHEILA Ready For The World
2 MONEY FOR NOTHING Dire Straits
3 TAKE ON ME A-Ha
4 SAVING ALL MY LOVE FOR YOU Whitney Houston
5 PART-TIME LOVER Stevie Wonder
6 LONELY OL' NIGHT John Cougar Mellencamp
7 DANCING IN THE STREET Mick Jagger & David Bowie
8 CHERISH Kool & The Gang
9 MIAMI VICE THEME Jan Hammer
10 DRESS YOU UP Madonna

October 19, 1985
1 TAKE ON ME A-Ha
2 SAVING ALL MY LOVE FOR YOU Whitney Houston
3 PART-TIME LOVER Stevie Wonder
4 OH SHEILA Ready For The World
5 MIAMI VICE THEME Jan Hammer
6 LONELY OL' NIGHT John Cougar Mellencamp
7 MONEY FOR NOTHING Dire Straits
8 DANCING IN THE STREET Mick Jagger & David Bowie
9 FORTRESS AROUND YOUR HEART Sting
10 HEAD OVER HEELS Tears For Fears

October 26, 1985
1 SAVING ALL MY LOVE FOR YOU Whitney Houston

2 PART-TIME LOVER Stevie Wonder
3 TAKE ON ME A-Ha
4 MIAMI VICE THEME Jan Hammer
5 HEAD OVER HEELS Tears For Fears
6 OH SHEILA Ready For The World
7 LONELY OL' NIGHT John Cougar Mellencamp
8 FORTRESS AROUND YOUR HEART Sting
9 I'M GOIN' DOWN Bruce Springsteen
10 YOU BELONG TO THE CITY Glenn Frey

November 2, 1985
1 PART-TIME LOVER Stevie Wonder
2 MIAMI VICE THEME Jan Hammer
3 SAVING ALL MY LOVE FOR YOU Whitney Houston
4 HEAD OVER HEELS Tears For Fears
5 TAKE ON ME A-Ha
6 YOU BELONG TO THE CITY Glenn Frey
7 WE BUILT THIS CITY Starship
8 FORTRESS AROUND YOUR HEART Sting
9 LOVIN' EVERY MINUTE OF IT Loverboy
10 BE NEAR ME ABC

November 9, 1985
1 MIAMI VICE THEME Jan Hammer
2 PART-TIME LOVER Stevie Wonder
3 HEAD OVER HEELS Tears For Fears
4 YOU BELONG TO THE CITY Glenn Frey
5 WE BUILT THIS CITY Starship
6 SAVING ALL MY LOVE FOR YOU Whitney Houston
7 SEPARATE LIVES (THEME FROM "WHITE NIGHTS") Phil Collins & Marilyn Martin
8 TAKE ON ME A-Ha

9 BE NEAR ME   ABC
10 LAY YOUR HANDS ON ME   The Thompson Twins

November 16, 1985
1 WE BUILT THIS CITY   Starship
2 YOU BELONG TO THE CITY   Glenn Frey
3 MIAMI VICE THEME   Jan Hammer
4 HEAD OVER HEELS   Tears For Fears
5 PART-TIME LOVER   Stevie Wonder
6 SEPARATE LIVES (THEME FROM "WHITE NIGHTS")   Phil Collins & Marilyn Martin
7 BROKEN WINGS   Mr. Mister
8 NEVER   Heart
9 BE NEAR ME   ABC
10 LAY YOUR HANDS ON ME   The Thompson Twins

November 23, 1985
1 WE BUILT THIS CITY   Starship
2 YOU BELONG TO THE CITY   Glenn Frey
3 SEPARATE LIVES (THEME FROM "WHITE NIGHTS")   Phil Collins & Marilyn Martin
4 BROKEN WINGS   Mr. Mister
5 NEVER   Heart
6 LAY YOUR HANDS ON ME   The Thompson Twins
7 HEAD OVER HEELS   Tears For Fears
8 MIAMI VICE THEME   Jan Hammer
9 WHO'S ZOOMIN' WHO   Aretha Franklin
10 PART-TIME LOVER   Stevie Wonder

November 30, 1985
1 SEPARATE LIVES (THEME FROM "WHITE NIGHTS")   Phil Collins & Marilyn Martin
2 WE BUILT THIS CITY   Starship
3 BROKEN WINGS   Mr. Mister
4 YOU BELONG TO THE CITY   Glenn Frey
5 NEVER   Heart
6 LAY YOUR HANDS ON ME   The Thompson Twins
7 WHO'S ZOOMIN' WHO   Aretha Franklin
8 ELECTION DAY   Arcadia
9 PARTING ALL THE TIME   Eddie Murphy
10 SLEEPING BAG   ZZ Top

December 7, 1985
1 BROKEN WINGS   Mr. Mister
2 SEPARATE LIVES (THEME FROM "WHITE NIGHTS")   Phil Collins & Marilyn Martin
3 WE BUILT THIS CITY   Starship
4 NEVER   Heart
5 SAY YOU, SAY ME (TITLE SONG FROM "WHITE NIGHTS")   Lionel Richie
6 YOU BELONG TO THE CITY   Glenn Frey
7 ELECTION DAY   Arcadia
8 WHO'S ZOOMIN' WHO   Aretha Franklin
9 PARTY ALL THE TIME   Eddie Murphy
10 SLEEPING BAG   ZZ Top

December 14, 1985
1 BROKEN WINGS   Mr. Mister
2 SEPARATE LIVES (THEME FROM "WHITE NIGHTS")   Phil Collins & Marilyn Martin
3 SAY YOU, SAY ME (TITLE SONG FROM "WHITE NIGHTS")   Lionel Richie
4 PARTY ALL THE TIME   Eddie Murphy
5 NEVER   Heart
6 ELECTION DAY   Arcadia
7 ALIVE AND KICKING   Simple Minds

8 SLEEPING BAG   ZZ Top
9 I MISS YOU   Klymaxx
10 WE BUILT THIS CITY   Starship

December 21, 1985
1 SAY YOU, SAY ME (TITLE SONG FROM "WHITE NIGHTS")   Lionel Richie
2 BROKEN WINGS   Mr. Mister
3 PARTY ALL THE TIME   Eddie Murphy
4 ALIVE AND KICKING   Simple Minds
5 SEPARATE LIVES (THEME FROM "WHITE NIGHTS")   Phil Collins & Marilyn Martin
6 ELECTION DAY   Arcadia
7 I MISS YOU   Klymaxx
8 THAT'S WHAT FRIENDS ARE FOR   Dionne & Friends
9 SMALL TOWN   John Cougar Mellencamp
10 SLEEPING BAG   ZZ Top

December 28, 1985
1 SAY YOU, SAY ME (TITLE SONG FROM "WHITE NIGHTS")   Lionel Richie
2 PARTY ALL THE TIME   Eddie Murphy
3 ALIVE AND KICKING   Simple Minds
4 THAT'S WHAT FRIENDS ARE FOR   Dionne & Friends
5 I MISS YOU   Klymaxx
6 SMALL TOWN   John Cougar Mellencamp
7 BROKEN WINGS   Mr. Mister
8 SEPARATE LIVES (THEME FROM "WHITE NIGHTS")   Phil Collins & Marilyn Martin
9 TONIGHT SHE COMES   The Cars
10 ELECTION DAY   Arcadia

January 11, 1986
1 SAY YOU, SAY ME (TITLE SONG FROM "WHITE NIGHTS")   Lionel Richie
2 PARTY ALL THE TIME   Eddie Murphy
3 THAT'S WHAT FRIENDS ARE FOR   Dionne & Friends
4 ALIVE AND KICKING   Simple Minds
5 I MISS YOU   Klymaxx
6 SMALL TOWN   John Cougar Mellencamp
7 TONIGHT SHE COMES   The Cars
8 TALK TO ME   Stevie Nicks
9 BROKEN WINGS   Mr. Mister
10 WALK OF LIFE   Dire Straits

January 18, 1986
1 THAT'S WHAT FRIENDS ARE FOR   Dionne & Friends
2 SAY YOU, SAY ME (TITLE SONG FROM "WHITE NIGHTS")   Lionel Richie
3 PARTY ALL THE TIME   Eddie Murphy
4 ALIVE AND KICKING   Simple Minds
5 I MISS YOU   Klymaxx
6 SMALL TOWN   John Cougar Mellencamp
7 TALK TO ME   Stevie Nicks
8 BURNING HEART   Survivor
9 WALK OF LIFE   Dire Straits
10 TONIGHT SHE COMES   The Cars

January 25, 1986
1 THAT'S WHAT FRIENDS ARE FOR   Dionne & Friends
2 SAY YOU, SAY ME (TITLE SONG FROM "WHITE NIGHTS")   Lionel Richie
3 BURNING HEART   Survivor
4 TALK TO ME   Stevie Nicks
5 I'M YOUR MAN   Wham!
6 MY HOMETOWN   Bruce Springsteen

7   WALK OF LIFE   Dire Straits
8   I MISS YOU   Klymaxx
9   PARTY ALL THE TIME   Eddie Murphy
10 SPIES LIKE US   Paul McCartney

February 1, 1986

1   THAT'S WHAT FRIENDS ARE FOR   Dionne & Friends
2   BURNING HEART   Survivor
3   I'M YOUR MAN   Wham!
4   TALK TO ME   Stevie Nicks
5   SAY YOU, SAY ME (TITLE SONG FROM "WHITE NIGHTS")
    Lionel Richie
6   MY HOMETOWN   Bruce Springsteen
7   WHEN THE GOING GETS TOUGH ("JEWEL OF THE NILE"
    THEME)   Billy Ocean
8   SPIES LIKE US   Paul McCartney
9   WALK OF LIFE   Dire Straits
10 GO HOME   Stevie Wonder

February 8, 1986

1   THAT'S WHAT FRIENDS ARE FOR   Dionne & Friends
2   BURNING HEART   Survivor
3   I'M YOUR MAN   Wham!
4   WHEN THE GOING GETS TOUGH ("JEWEL OF THE NILE"
    THEME)   Billy Ocean
5   HOW WILL I KNOW   Whitney Houston
6   KYRIE   Mr. Mister
7   SPIES LIKE US   Paul McCartney
8   TALK TO ME   Stevie Nicks
9   LIVING IN AMERICA   James Brown
10 CONGA   Miami Sound Machine

February 15, 1986

1   HOW WILL I KNOW   Whitney Houston
2   WHEN THE GOING GETS TOUGH ("JEWEL OF THE NILE"
    THEME)   Billy Ocean
3   BURNING HEART   Survivor
4   KYRIE   Mr. Mister
5   THAT'S WHAT FRIENDS ARE FOR   Dionne & Friends
6   I'M YOUR MAN   Wham!
7   LIVING IN AMERICA   James Brown
8   THE SWEETEST TABOO   Sade
9   SARA   Starship
10 CONGA   Miami Sound Machine

February 22, 1986

1   HOW WILL I KNOW   Whitney Houston
2   KYRIE   Mr. Mister
3   WHEN THE GOING GETS TOUGH ("JEWEL OF THE NILE"
    THEME)   Billy Ocean
4   SARA   Starship
5   LIVING IN AMERICA   James Brown
6   THE SWEETEST TABOO   Sade
7   LIFE IN A NORTHERN TOWN   The Dream Academy
8   SILENT RUNNING   Mike + The Mechanics
9   BURNING HEART   Survivor
10 THAT'S WHAT FRIENDS ARE FOR   Dionne & Friends

March 1, 1986

1   KYRIE   Mr. Mister
2   HOW WILL I KNOW   Whitney Houston
3   SARA   Starship
4   LIVING IN AMERICA   James Brown
5   THE SWEETEST TABOO   Sade
6   WHEN THE GOING GETS TOUGH ("JEWEL OF THE NILE"
    THEME)   Billy Ocean

7   LIFE IN A NORTHERN TOWN   The Dream Academy
8   SILENT RUNNING   Mike + The Mechanics
9   SECRET LOVERS   Atlantic Starr
10 THESE DREAMS   Heart

March 8, 1986

1   KYRIE   Mr. Mister
2   SARA   Starship
3   HOW WILL I KNOW   Whitney Houston
4   THESE DREAMS   Heart
5   SECRET LOVERS   Atlantic Starr
6   SILENT RUNNING   Mike + The Mechanics
7   THE SWEETEST TABOO   Sade
8   LIVING IN AMERICA   James Brown
9   LIFE IN A NORTHERN TOWN   The Dream Academy
10 KING FOR A DAY   Thompson Twins

March 15, 1986

1   SARA   Starship
2   THESE DREAMS   Heart
3   KYRIE   Mr. Mister
4   SECRET LOVERS   Atlantic Starr
5   HOW WILL I KNOW   Whitney Houston
6   R.O.C.K. IN THE U.S.A. (A SALUTE TO 60S ROCK)   John
    Cougar Mellencamp
7   ROCK ME AMADEUS   Falco
8   SILENT RUNNING   Mike + The Mechanics
9   KING FOR A DAY   Thompson Twins
10 NIKITA   Elton John

March 22, 1986

1   THESE DREAMS   Heart
2   SARA   Starship
3   SECRET LOVERS   Atlantic Starr
4   ROCK ME AMADEUS   Falco
5   R.O.C.K. IN THE U.S.A. (A SALUTE TO 60S ROCK)   John
    Cougar Mellencamp
6   KYRIE   Mr. Mister
7   NIKITA   Elton John
8   KING FOR A DAY   Thompson Twins
9   WHAT YOU NEED   INXS
10 KISS   Prince & The Revolution

March 29, 1986

1   ROCK ME AMADEUS   Falco
2   THESE DREAMS   Heart
3   SECRET LOVERS   Atlantic Starr
4   R.O.C.K. IN THE U.S.A. (A SALUTE TO 60S ROCK)   John
    Cougar Mellencamp
5   KISS   Prince & The Revolution
6   WHAT YOU NEED   INXS
7   NIKITA   Elton John
8   SARA   Starship
9   LET'S GO ALL THE WAY   Sly Fox
10 THIS COULD BE THE NIGHT   Loverboy

April 5, 1986

1   ROCK ME AMADEUS   Falco
2   R.O.C.K. IN THE U.S.A. (A SALUTE TO 60S ROCK)   John
    Cougar Mellencamp
3   KISS   Prince & The Revolution
4   SECRET LOVERS   Atlantic Starr
5   THESE DREAMS   Heart
6   WHAT YOU NEED   INXS
7   MANIC MONDAY   Bangles
8   LET'S GO ALL THE WAY   Sly Fox

9   ADDICTED TO LOVE   Robert Palmer
10   NIKITA   Elton John

April 12, 1986
1   ROCK ME AMADEUS   Falco
2   KISS   Prince & The Revolution
3   MANIC MONDAY   Bangles
4   R.O.C.K. IN THE U.S.A. (A SALUTE TO 60S ROCK)   John Cougar Mellencamp
5   WHAT YOU NEED   INXS
6   ADDICTED TO LOVE   Robert Palmer
7   LET'S GO ALL THE WAY   Sly Fox
8   WEST END GIRLS   Pet Shop Boys
9   HARLEM SHUFFLE   The Rolling Stones
10   TENDER LOVE   Force M.D.'s

April 19, 1986
1   KISS   Prince & The Revolution
2   MANIC MONDAY   Bangles
3   ADDICTED TO LOVE   Robert Palmer
4   ROCK ME AMADEUS   Falco
5   WEST END GIRLS   Pet Shop Boys
6   WHAT YOU NEED   INXS
7   LET'S GO ALL THE WAY   Sly Fox
8   HARLEM SHUFFLE   The Rolling Stones
9   WHY CAN'T THIS BE LOVE   Van Halen
10   TENDER LOVE   Force M.D.'s

April 26, 1986
1   KISS   Prince & The Revolution
2   ADDICTED TO LOVE   Robert Palmer
3   WEST END GIRLS   Pet Shop Boys
4   MANIC MONDAY   Bangles
5   WHY CAN'T THIS BE LOVE   Van Halen
6   HARLEM SHUFFLE   The Rolling Stones
7   ROCK ME AMADEUS   Falco
8   WHAT HAVE YOU DONE FOR ME LATELY   Janet Jackson
9   YOUR LOVE   The Outfield
10   TAKE ME HOME   Phil Collins

May 2, 1986
1   ADDICTED TO LOVE   Robert Palmer
2   WEST END GIRLS   Pet Shop Boys
3   KISS   Prince & The Revolution
4   WHY CAN'T THIS BE LOVE   Van Halen
5   HARLEM SHUFFLE   The Rolling Stones
6   WHAT HAVE YOU DONE FOR ME LATELY   Janet Jackson
7   GREATEST LOVE OF ALL   Whitney Houston
8   YOUR LOVE   The Outfield
9   TAKE ME HOME   Phil Collins
10   MANIC MONDAY   Bangles

May 10, 1986
1   WEST END GIRLS   Pet Shop Boys
2   ADDICTED TO LOVE   Robert Palmer
3   GREATEST LOVE OF ALL   Whitney Houston
4   WHY CAN'T THIS BE LOVE   Van Halen
5   WHAT HAVE YOU DONE FOR ME LATELY   Janet Jackson
6   YOUR LOVE   The Outfield
7   TAKE ME HOME   Phil Collins
8   BAD BOY   Miami Sound Machine
9   HARLEM SHUFFLE   The Rolling Stones
10   IF YOU LEAVE   Orchestral Manoevres In The Dark

May 17, 1986
1   GREATEST LOVE OF ALL   Whitney Houston

2   WEST END GIRLS   Pet Shop Boys
3   WHY CAN'T THIS BE LOVE   Van Halen
4   WHAT HAVE YOU DONE FOR ME LATELY   Janet Jackson
5   LIVE TO TELL   Madonna
6   YOUR LOVE   The Outfield
7   TAKE ME HOME   Phil Collins
8   BAD BOY   Miami Sound Machine
9   IF YOU LEAVE   Orchestral Manoevres In The Dark
10   ADDICTED TO LOVE   Robert Palmer

May 24, 1986
1   GREATEST LOVE OF ALL   Whitney Houston
2   LIVE TO TELL   Madonna
3   ON MY OWN   Patti Labelle & Michael McDonald
4   WEST END GIRLS   Pet Shop Boys
5   IF YOU LEAVE   Orchestral Manoevres In The Dark
6   WHAT HAVE YOU DONE FOR ME LATELY   Janet Jackson
7   TAKE ME HOME   Phil Collins
8   BAD BOY   Miami Sound Machine
9   I CAN'T WAIT   Nu Shooz
10   ALL I NEED IS A MIRACLE   Jack Wagner

May 31, 1986
1   GREATEST LOVE OF ALL   Whitney Houston
2   LIVE TO TELL   Madonna
3   ON MY OWN   Patti Labelle & Michael McDonald
4   IF YOU LEAVE   Orchestral Manoevres In The Dark
5   I CAN'T WAIT   Nu Shooz
6   ALL I NEED IS A MIRACLE   Jack Wagner
7   SOMETHING ABOUT YOU   Level 42
8   IS IT LOVE   Mr. Mister
9   BE GOOD TO YOURSELF   Journey
10   WHAT HAVE YOU DONE FOR ME LATELY   Janet Jackson

June 7, 1986
1   LIVE TO TELL   Madonna
2   ON MY OWN   Patti Labelle & Michael McDonald
3   GREATEST LOVE OF ALL   Whitney Houston
4   I CAN'T WAIT   Nu Shooz
5   ALL I NEED IS A MIRACLE   Jack Wagner
6   IF YOU LEAVE   Orchestral Manoevres In The Dark
7   SOMETHING ABOUT YOU   Level 42
8   CRUSH ON YOU   The Jets
9   THERE'LL BE SAD SONGS (TO MAKE YOU CRY)   Billy Ocean
10   A DIFFERENT CORNER   George Michael

June 14, 1986
1   ON MY OWN   Patti Labelle & Michael McDonald
2   LIVE TO TELL   Madonna
3   I CAN'T WAIT   Nu Shooz
4   THERE'LL BE SAD SONGS (TO MAKE YOU CRY)   Billy Ocean
5   CRUSH ON YOU   The Jets
6   GREATEST LOVE OF ALL   Whitney Houston
7   A DIFFERENT CORNER   George Michael
8   NO ONE IS TO BLAME   Howard Jones
9   ALL I NEED IS A MIRACLE   Jack Wagner
10   SOMETHING ABOUT YOU   Level 42

June 21, 1986
1   ON MY OWN   Patti Labelle & Michael McDonald
2   THERE'LL BE SAD SONGS (TO MAKE YOU CRY)   Billy Ocean
3   CRUSH ON YOU   The Jets
4   LIVE TO TELL   Madonna

5 I CAN'T WAIT   Nu Shooz
6 NO ONE IS TO BLAME   Howard Jones
7 A DIFFERENT CORNER   George Michael
8 HOLDING BACK THE YEARS   Simply Red
9 WHO'S JOHNNY ("SHORT CIRCUIT" THEME)   El Debarge
10 NOTHING AT ALL   Heart

June 28, 1986
1 ON MY OWN   Patti Labelle & Michael McDonald
2 THERE'LL BE SAD SONGS (TO MAKE YOU CRY)   Billy Ocean
3 CRUSH ON YOU   The Jets
4 HOLDING BACK THE YEARS   Simply Red
5 NO ONE IS TO BLAME   Howard Jones
6 WHO'S JOHNNY ("SHORT CIRCUIT" THEME)   El Debarge
7 A DIFFERENT CORNER   George Michael
8 INVISIBLE TOUCH   Genesis
9 NASTY   Janet Jackson
10 SLEDGEHAMMER   Peter Gabriel

July 5, 1986
1 THERE'LL BE SAD SONGS (TO MAKE YOU CRY)   Billy Ocean
2 HOLDING BACK THE YEARS   Simply Red
3 WHO'S JOHNNY ("SHORT CIRCUIT" THEME)   El Debarge
4 NO ONE IS TO BLAME   Howard Jones
5 NASTY   Janet Jackson
6 INVISIBLE TOUCH   Genesis
7 CRUSH ON YOU   The Jets
8 ON MY OWN   Patti Labelle & Michael McDonald
9 SLEDGEHAMMER   Peter Gabriel
10 DANGER ZONE   Kenny Loggins

July 12, 1986
1 HOLDING BACK THE YEARS   Simply Red
2 INVISIBLE TOUCH   Genesis
3 THERE'LL BE SAD SONGS (TO MAKE YOU CRY)   Billy Ocean
4 NASTY   Janet Jackson
5 WHO'S JOHNNY ("SHORT CIRCUIT" THEME)   El Debarge
6 SLEDGEHAMMER   Peter Gabriel
7 DANGER ZONE   Kenny Loggins
8 NO ONE IS TO BLAME   Howard Jones
9 YOUR WILDEST DREAMS   The Moody Blues
10 TUFF ENUFF   The Fabulous Thunderbirds

July 19, 1986
1 INVISIBLE TOUCH   Genesis
2 SLEDGEHAMMER   Peter Gabriel
3 NASTY   Janet Jackson
4 DANGER ZONE   Kenny Loggins
5 HOLDING BACK THE YEARS   Simply Red
6 WHO'S JOHNNY ("SHORT CIRCUIT" THEME)   El Debarge
7 GLORY OF LOVE (THEME FROM "THE KARATE KID PART II")   Peter Cetera
8 THERE'LL BE SAD SONGS (TO MAKE YOU CRY)   Billy Ocean
9 YOUR WILDEST DREAMS   The Moody Blues
10 LOVE TOUCH (THEME FROM "LEGAL EAGLES")   Rod Stewart

July 26, 1986
1 SLEDGEHAMMER   Peter Gabriel
2 DANGER ZONE   Kenny Loggins
3 INVISIBLE TOUCH   Genesis
4 NASTY   Janet Jackson

5 GLORY OF LOVE (THEME FROM "THE KARATE KID PART II")   Peter Cetera
6 PAPA DON'T PREACH   Madonna
7 LOVE TOUCH (THEME FROM "LEGAL EAGLES")   Rod Stewart
8 MAD ABOUT YOU   Belinda Carlisle
9 HOLDING BACK THE YEARS   Simply Red
10 MODERN WOMAN (FROM "RUTHLESS PEOPLE")   Billy Joel

August 2, 1986
1 GLORY OF LOVE (THEME FROM "THE KARATE KID PART II")   Peter Cetera
2 SLEDGEHAMMER   Peter Gabriel
3 DANGER ZONE   Kenny Loggins
4 PAPA DON'T PREACH   Madonna
5 INVISIBLE TOUCH   Genesis
6 MAD ABOUT YOU   Belinda Carlisle
7 LOVE TOUCH (THEME FROM "LEGAL EAGLES")   Rod Stewart
8 NASTY   Janet Jackson
9 WE DON'T HAVE TO TAKE OUR CLOTHES OFF   Jermaine Stewart
10 OPPORTUNITIES   Pet Shop Boys

August 9, 1986
1 GLORY OF LOVE (THEME FROM "THE KARATE KID PART II")   Peter Cetera
2 PAPA DON'T PREACH   Madonna
3 MAD ABOUT YOU   Belinda Carlisle
4 SLEDGEHAMMER   Peter Gabriel
5 WE DON'T HAVE TO TAKE OUR CLOTHES OFF   Jermaine Stewart
6 LOVE TOUCH (THEME FROM "LEGAL EAGLES")   Rod Stewart
7 DANGER ZONE   Kenny Loggins
8 HIGHER LOVE   Steve Winwood
9 VENUS   Bananarama
10 RUMORS   Timex Social Club

August 16, 1986
1 PAPA DON'T PREACH   Madonna
2 GLORY OF LOVE (THEME FROM "THE KARATE KID PART II")   Peter Cetera
3 MAD ABOUT YOU   Belinda Carlisle
4 HIGHER LOVE   Steve Winwood
5 WE DON'T HAVE TO TAKE OUR CLOTHES OFF   Jermaine Stewart
6 VENUS   Bananarama
7 DANCING ON THE CEILING   Lionel Richie
8 RUMORS   Timex Social Club
9 TAKE MY BREATH AWAY (LOVE THEME FROM "TOP GUN")   Berlin
10 EDGE OF HEAVEN   Bryan Adams

August 23, 1986
1 PAPA DON'T PREACH   Madonna
2 HIGHER LOVE   Steve Winwood
3 VENUS   Bananarama
4 MAD ABOUT YOU   Belinda Carlisle
5 GLORY OF LOVE (THEME FROM "THE KARATE KID PART II")   Peter Cetera
6 DANCING ON THE CEILING   Lionel Richie
7 TAKE MY BREATH AWAY (LOVE THEME FROM "TOP GUN")   Berlin
8 WE DON'T HAVE TO TAKE OUR CLOTHES OFF   Jermaine Stewart

9   RUMORS   Timex Social Club
10   EDGE OF HEAVEN   Bryan Adams

August 30, 1986
1   HIGHER LOVE   Steve Winwood
2   VENUS   Bananarama
3   PAPA DON'T PREACH   Madonna
4   TAKE MY BREATH AWAY (LOVE THEME FROM "TOP GUN")   Berlin
5   DANCING ON THE CEILING   Lionel Richie
6   FRIENDS AND LOVERS   Carl Anderson & Gloria Loring
7   SWEET FREEDOM (THEME FROM "RUNNING SCARED")   Wham!
8   RUMORS   Timex Social Club
9   STUCK WITH YOU   Huey Lewis & The News
10   MAD ABOUT YOU   Belinda Carlisle

September 6, 1986
1   VENUS   Bananarama
2   TAKE MY BREATH AWAY (LOVE THEME FROM "TOP GUN")   Berlin
3   HIGHER LOVE   Steve Winwood
4   DANCING ON THE CEILING   Lionel Richie
5   FRIENDS AND LOVERS   Carl Anderson & Gloria Loring
6   STUCK WITH YOU   Huey Lewis & The News
7   SWEET FREEDOM (THEME FROM "RUNNING SCARED")   Wham!
8   WORDS GET IN THE WAY   Miami Sound Machine
9   PAPA DON'T PREACH   Madonna
10   WALK THIS WAY   Run D.M.C.

September 13, 1986
1   TAKE MY BREATH AWAY (LOVE THEME FROM "TOP GUN")   Berlin
2   DANCING ON THE CEILING   Lionel Richie
3   STUCK WITH YOU   Huey Lewis & The News
4   FRIENDS AND LOVERS   Carl Anderson & Gloria Loring
5   VENUS   Bananarama
6   HIGHER LOVE   Steve Winwood
7   SWEET FREEDOM (THEME FROM "RUNNING SCARED")   Wham!
8   WORDS GET IN THE WAY   Miami Sound Machine
9   WALK THIS WAY   Run D.M.C.
10   BABY LOVE   Regina

September 20, 1986
1   STUCK WITH YOU   Huey Lewis & The News
2   DANCING ON THE CEILING   Lionel Richie
3   FRIENDS AND LOVERS   Carl Anderson & Gloria Loring
4   TAKE MY BREATH AWAY (LOVE THEME FROM "TOP GUN")   Berlin
5   WORDS GET IN THE WAY   Miami Sound Machine
6   WALK THIS WAY   Run D.M.C.
7   VENUS   Bananarama
8   DON'T FORGET ME (WHEN I'M GONE)   Glass Tiger
9   DREAMTIME   Daryl Hall
10   BABY LOVE   Regina

September 27, 1986
1   STUCK WITH YOU   Huey Lewis & The News
2   FRIENDS AND LOVERS   Carl Anderson & Gloria Loring
3   DANCING ON THE CEILING   Lionel Richie
4   WALK THIS WAY   Run D.M.C.
5   DON'T FORGET ME (WHEN I'M GONE)   Glass Tiger
6   DREAMTIME   Daryl Hall
7   WHEN I THINK OF YOU   Janet Jackson
8   TWO OF HEARTS   Stacey Q

9   TAKE MY BREATH AWAY (LOVE THEME FROM "TOP GUN")   Berlin
10   LOVE ZONE   Billy Ocean

October 4, 1986
1   STUCK WITH YOU   Huey Lewis & The News
2   FRIENDS AND LOVERS   Carl Anderson & Gloria Loring
3   WHEN I THINK OF YOU   Janet Jackson
4   DON'T FORGET ME (WHEN I'M GONE)   Glass Tiger
5   DREAMTIME   Daryl Hall
6   TWO OF HEARTS   Stacey Q
7   THROWING IT ALL AWAY   Genesis
8   WALK THIS WAY   Run D.M.C.
9   TYPICAL MALE   Tina Turner
10   DANCING ON THE CEILING   Lionel Richie

October 11, 1986
1   WHEN I THINK OF YOU   Janet Jackson
2   DON'T FORGET ME (WHEN I'M GONE)   Glass Tiger
3   TWO OF HEARTS   Stacey Q
4   THROWING IT ALL AWAY   Genesis
5   TYPICAL MALE   Tina Turner
6   STUCK WITH YOU   Huey Lewis & The News
7   HEARTBEAT   Don Johnson
8   FRIENDS AND LOVERS   Carl Anderson & Gloria Loring
9   TRUE COLORS   Cyndi Lauper
10   DREAMTIME   Daryl Hall

October 18, 1986
1   WHEN I THINK OF YOU   Janet Jackson
2   TYPICAL MALE   Tina Turner
3   TRUE COLORS   Cyndi Lauper
4   THROWING IT ALL AWAY   Genesis
5   HEARTBEAT   Don Johnson
6   TWO OF HEARTS   Stacey Q
7   DON'T FORGET ME (WHEN I'M GONE)   Glass Tiger
8   I DIDN'T MEAN TO TURN YOU ON   Robert Palmer
9   ALL CRIED OUT   Lisa Lisa & Cult Jam With Full Force
10   A MATTER OF TRUST   Billy Joel

October 25, 1986
1   TRUE COLORS   Cyndi Lauper
2   TYPICAL MALE   Tina Turner
3   WHEN I THINK OF YOU   Janet Jackson
4   I DIDN'T MEAN TO TURN YOU ON   Robert Palmer
5   HEARTBEAT   Don Johnson
6   AMANDA   Boston
7   THROWING IT ALL AWAY   Genesis
8   ALL CRIED OUT   Lisa Lisa & Cult Jam With Full Force
9   HUMAN   The Human League
10   SWEET LOVE   Anita Baker

November 1, 1986
1   TRUE COLORS   Cyndi Lauper
2   TYPICAL MALE   Tina Turner
3   I DIDN'T MEAN TO TURN YOU ON   Robert Palmer
4   AMANDA   Boston
5   HUMAN   The Human League
6   TRUE BLUE   Madonna
7   WHEN I THINK OF YOU   Janet Jackson
8   SWEET LOVE   Anita Baker
9   TAKE ME HOME TONIGHT   Eddie Money
10   ALL CRIED OUT   Lisa Lisa & Cult Jam With Full Force

November 8, 1986
1   AMANDA   Boston

2 I DIDN'T MEAN TO TURN YOU ON   Robert Palmer
3 TRUE COLORS   Cyndi Lauper
4 HUMAN   The Human League
5 TRUE BLUE   Madonna
6 TAKE ME HOME TONIGHT   Eddie Money
7 YOU GIVE LOVE A BAD NAME   Bon Jovi
8 TYPICAL MALE   Tina Turner
9 WORD UP   Cameo
10 THE RAIN   Oran "Juice" Jones

November 15, 1986
1 AMANDA   Boston
2 HUMAN   The Human League
3 TRUE BLUE   Madonna
4 TAKE ME HOME TONIGHT   Eddie Money
5 YOU GIVE LOVE A BAD NAME   Bon Jovi
6 I DIDN'T MEAN TO TURN YOU ON   Robert Palmer
7 WORD UP   Cameo
8 THE NEXT TIME I FALL   Peter Cetera with Amy Grant
9 THE RAIN   Oran "Juice" Jones
10 TRUE COLORS   Cyndi Lauper

November 22, 1986
1 HUMAN   The Human League
2 AMANDA   Boston
3 TRUE BLUE   Madonna
4 YOU GIVE LOVE A BAD NAME   Bon Jovi
5 TAKE ME HOME TONIGHT   Eddie Money
6 WORD UP   Cameo
7 THE NEXT TIME I FALL   Peter Cetera with Amy Grant
8 HIP TO BE SQUARE   Huey Lewis & The News
9 THE WAY IT IS   Bruce Hornsby & The Range

10 LOVE WILL CONQUER ALL   Lionel Richie

November 29, 1986
1 YOU GIVE LOVE A BAD NAME   Bon Jovi
2 HUMAN   The Human League
3 TRUE BLUE   Madonna
4 THE NEXT TIME I FALL   Peter Cetera with Amy Grant
5 HIP TO BE SQUARE   Huey Lewis & The News
6 WORD UP   Cameo
7 AMANDA   Boston
8 THE WAY IT IS   Bruce Hornsby & The Range
9 LOVE WILL CONQUER ALL   Lionel Richie
10 WALK LIKE AN EGYPTIAN   Bangles

December 6, 1986
1 THE NEXT TIME I FALL   Peter Cetera with Amy Grant
2 YOU GIVE LOVE A BAD NAME   Bon Jovi
3 HIP TO BE SQUARE   Huey Lewis & The News
4 THE WAY IT IS   Bruce Hornsby & The Range
5 WALK LIKE AN EGYPTIAN   Bangles
6 WORD UP   Cameo
7 EVERYBODY HAVE FUN TONIGHT   Wang Chung
8 HUMAN   The Human League
9 LOVE WILL CONQUER ALL   Lionel Richie
10 TO BE A LOVER   Billy Idol

December 13, 1986
1 THE WAY IT IS   Bruce Hornsby & The Range
2 WALK LIKE AN EGYPTIAN   Bangles
3 HIP TO BE SQUARE   Huey Lewis & The News
4 THE NEXT TIME I FALL   Peter Cetera with Amy Grant
5 EVERYBODY HAVE FUN TONIGHT   Wang Chung

The Bangles
One of the more successful eighties female bands, this #1 group walked ``Like An Egyptian'' for three weeks (Dec. 20).

6 YOU GIVE LOVE A BAD NAME   Bon Jovi
7 TO BE A LOVER   Billy Idol
8 NOTORIOUS   Duran Duran
9 SHAKE YOU DOWN   Gregory Abbott
10 STAND BY ME   Ben E. King

December 20, 1986
1 WALK LIKE AN EGYPTIAN   Bangles
2 THE WAY IT IS   Bruce Hornsby & The Range
3 EVERYBODY HAVE FUN TONIGHT   Wang Chung
4 NOTORIOUS   Duran Duran
5 SHAKE YOU DOWN   Gregory Abbott
6 TO BE A LOVER   Billy Idol
7 HIP TO BE SQUARE   Huey Lewis & The News
8 C'EST LA VIE   Robbie Nevil
9 STAND BY ME   Ben E. King
10 THE NEXT TIME I FALL   Peter Cetera with Amy Grant

December 27, 1986
1 WALK LIKE AN EGYPTIAN   Bangles
2 EVERYBODY HAVE FUN TONIGHT   Wang Chung
3 NOTORIOUS   Duran Duran
4 SHAKE YOU DOWN   Gregory Abbott
5 THE WAY IT IS   Bruce Hornsby & The Range
6 C'EST LA VIE   Robbie Nevil
7 CONTROL   Janet Jackson
8 WAR   Bruce Springsteen & The E Street Band
9 STAND BY ME   Ben E. King
10 DON'T GET ME WRONG   The Pretenders

January 3, 1987
NO SURVEY

Huey Lewis
Huey and the News climb ``Jacob's Ladder'' to #1 (Mar. 14).

January 10, 1987
1 WALK LIKE AN EGYPTIAN   Bangles
2 NOTORIOUS   Duran Duran
3 SHAKE YOU DOWN   Gregory Abbott
4 EVERYBODY HAVE FUN TONIGHT   Wang Chung
5 C'EST LA VIE   Robbie Nevil
6 CONTROL   Janet Jackson
7 THE WAY IT IS   Bruce Hornsby & The Range
8 WAR   Bruce Springsteen & The E Street Band
9 AT THIS MOMENT   Billy Vera & The Beaters
10 IS THIS LOVE   Survivor

January 17, 1987
1 SHAKE YOU DOWN   Gregory Abbott
2 C'EST LA VIE   Robbie Nevil
3 NOTORIOUS   Duran Duran
4 WALK LIKE AN EGYPTIAN   Bangles
5 AT THIS MOMENT   Billy Vera & The Beaters
6 CONTROL   Janet Jackson
7 OPEN YOUR HEART   Madonna
8 LAND OF CONFUSION   Genesis
9 IS THIS LOVE   Survivor
10 EVERYBODY HAVE FUN TONIGHT   Wang Chung

January 24, 1987
1 AT THIS MOMENT   Billy Vera & The Beaters
2 C'EST LA VIE   Robbie Nevil
3 SHAKE YOU DOWN   Gregory Abbott
4 OPEN YOUR HEART   Madonna
5 CONTROL   Janet Jackson
6 LAND OF CONFUSION   Genesis
7 SOMEDAY   Glass Tiger
8 CHANGE OF HEART   Cyndi Lauper
9 IS THIS LOVE   Survivor
10 VICTORY   Kool & The Gang

January 31, 1987
1 AT THIS MOMENT   Billy Vera & The Beaters
2 OPEN YOUR HEART   Madonna
3 C'EST LA VIE   Robbie Nevil
4 LAND OF CONFUSION   Genesis
5 CHANGE OF HEART   Cyndi Lauper
6 CONTROL   Janet Jackson
7 SOMEDAY   Glass Tiger
8 SHAKE YOU DOWN   Gregory Abbott
9 LIVIN' ON A PRAYER   Bon Jovi
10 TOUCH ME   Samantha Fox

February 7, 1987
1 OPEN YOUR HEART   Madonna
2 AT THIS MOMENT   Billy Vera & The Beaters
3 LIVIN' ON A PRAYER   Bon Jovi
4 CHANGE OF HEART   Cyndi Lauper
5 TOUCH ME   Samantha Fox
6 LAND OF CONFUSION   Genesis
7 KEEP YOUR HANDS TO YOURSELF   Georgia Satellites
8 SOMEDAY   Glass Tiger
9 WILL YOU STILL LOVE ME?   Chicago
10 WE'RE READY   Boston

February 14, 1987
1 LIVIN' ON A PRAYER   Bon Jovi
2 OPEN YOUR HEART   Madonna
3 CHANGE OF HEART   Cyndi Lauper
4 TOUCH ME   Samantha Fox
5 KEEP YOUR HANDS TO YOURSELF   Georgia Satellites

6   WILL YOU STILL LOVE ME?   Chicago
7   AT THIS MOMENT   Billy Vera & The Beaters
8   JACOB'S LADDER   Huey Lewis & The News
9   WE'RE READY   Boston
10 BALLERINA GIRL   Lionel Richie

February 21, 1987
1   LIVIN' ON A PRAYER   Bon Jovi
2   KEEP YOUR HANDS TO YOURSELF   Georgia Satellites
3   WILL YOU STILL LOVE ME?   Chicago
4   JACOB'S LADDER   Huey Lewis & The News
5   TOUCH ME   Samantha Fox
6   YOU GOT IT ALL   The Jets
7   BALLERINA GIRL   Lionel Richie
8   OPEN YOUR HEART   Madonna
9   LOVE YOU DOWN   Ready For The World
10 CHANGE OF HEART   Cyndi Lauper

February 28, 1987
1   LIVIN' ON A PRAYER   Bon Jovi
2   JACOB'S LADDER   Huey Lewis & The News
3   KEEP YOUR HANDS TO YOURSELF   Georgia Satellites
4   WILL YOU STILL LOVE ME?   Chicago
5   YOU GOT IT ALL   The Jets
6   SOMEWHERE OUT THERE (FROM "AN AMERICAN TAIL")
      Linda Ronstadt & James Ingram
7   RESPECT YOURSELF   Bruce Willis
8   (YOU GOTTA) FIGHT FOR YOUR RIGHT (TO PARTY)
      Beastie Boys
9   BIG TIME   Peter Gabriel
10 BALLERINA GIRL   Lionel Richie

March 7, 1987
1   LIVIN' ON A PRAYER   Bon Jovi
2   JACOB'S LADDER   Huey Lewis & The News
3   YOU GOT IT ALL   The Jets
4   SOMEWHERE OUT THERE (FROM "AN AMERICAN TAIL")
      Linda Ronstadt & James Ingram
5   RESPECT YOURSELF   Bruce Willis
6   KEEP YOUR HANDS TO YOURSELF   Georgia Satellites
7   (YOU GOTTA) FIGHT FOR YOUR RIGHT (TO PARTY!)
      Beastie Boys
8   BIG TIME   Peter Gabriel
9   MANDOLIN RAIN   Bruce Hornsby & The Range
10 LET'S WAIT AWHILE   Janet Jackson

March 14, 1987
1   JACOB'S LADDER   Huey Lewis & The News
2   SOMEWHERE OUT THERE (FROM "AN AMERICAN TAIL")
      Linda Ronstadt & James Ingram
3   LET'S WAIT AWHILE   Janet Jackson
4   LIVIN' ON A PRAYER   Bon Jovi
5   LEAN ON ME   Club Nouveau
6   MANDOLIN RAIN   Bruce Hornsby & The Range
7   RESPECT YOURSELF   Bruce Willis
8   BIG TIME   Peter Gabriel
9   YOU GOT IT ALL   The Jets
10 NOTHING'S GONNA STOP US NOW   Starship

March 21, 1987
1   LEAN ON ME   Club Nouveau
2   LET'S WAIT AWHILE   Janet Jackson
3   NOTHING'S GONNA STOP US NOW   Starship
4   MANDOLIN RAIN   Bruce Hornsby & The Range
5   SOMEWHERE OUT THERE (FROM "AN AMERICAN TAIL")
      Linda Ronstadt & James Ingram
6   TONIGHT, TONIGHT, TONIGHT   Genesis

Samantha Fox
``Touch Me'' took Sam into the Top 10 on January 31.

7   JACOB'S LADDER   Huey Lewis & The News
8   RESPECT YOURSELF   Bruce Willis
9   COME GO WITH ME   Expose
10 BIG TIME   Peter Gabriel

March 28, 1987
1   LEAN ON ME   Club Nouveau
2   NOTHING'S GONNA STOP US NOW   Starship
3   LET'S WAIT AWHILE   Janet Jackson
4   TONIGHT, TONIGHT, TONIGHT   Genesis
5   MANDOLIN RAIN   Bruce Hornsby & The Range
6   SOMEWHERE OUT THERE (FROM "AN AMERICAN TAIL")
      Linda Ronstadt & James Ingram
7   COME GO WITH ME   Expose
8   THE FINAL COUNTDOWN   Europe
9   DON'T DREAM IT'S OVER   Crowded House
10 I KNEW YOU WERE WAITING (FOR ME)   Aretha Franklin &
      George Michael

April 4, 1987
1   NOTHING'S GONNA STOP US NOW   Starship
2   LEAN ON ME   Club Nouveau
3   TONIGHT, TONIGHT, TONIGHT   Genesis
4   LET'S WAIT AWHILE   Janet Jackson
5   COME GO WITH ME   Expose
6   I KNEW YOU WERE WAITING (FOR ME)   Aretha Franklin &
      George Michael
7   DON'T DREAM IT'S OVER   Crowded House
8   THE FINAL COUNTDOWN   Europe
9   MANDOLIN RAIN   Bruce Hornsby & The Range
10 LET'S GO!   Wang Chung

April 11, 1987

1. NOTHING'S GONNA STOP US NOW   Starship
2. LEAN ON ME   Club Nouveau
3. I KNEW YOU WERE WAITING (FOR ME)   Aretha Franklin & George Michael
4. TONIGHT, TONIGHT, TONIGHT   Genesis
5. DON'T DREAM IT'S OVER   Crowded House
6. COME GO WITH ME   Expose
7. SIGN 'O' THE TIMES   Prince
8. MIDNIGHT BLUE   Lou Gramm
9. LET'S GO!   Wang Chung
10. THE FINER THINGS   Steve Winwood

April 18, 1987

1. I KNEW YOU WERE WAITING (FOR ME)   Aretha Franklin & George Michael
2. NOTHING'S GONNA STOP US NOW   Starship
3. DON'T DREAM IT'S OVER   Crowded House
4. SIGN 'O' THE TIMES   Prince
5. MIDNIGHT BLUE   Lou Gramm
6. LOOKING FOR A NEW LOVE   Jody Watley
7. LEAN ON ME   Club Nouveau
8. THE FINER THINGS   Steve Winwood
9. COME GO WITH ME   Expose
10. (I JUST) DIED IN YOUR ARMS   Cutting Crew

April 25, 1987

1. I KNEW YOU WERE WAITING (FOR ME)   Aretha Franklin & George Michael
2. DON'T DREAM IT'S OVER   Crowded House
3. SIGN 'O' THE TIMES   Prince
4. LOOKING FOR A NEW LOVE   Jody Watley
5. (I JUST) DIED IN YOUR ARMS   Cutting Crew
6. NOTHING'S GONNA STOP US NOW   Starship
7. LA ISLA BONITA   Madonna
8. THE FINER THINGS   Steve Winwood
9. MIDNIGHT BLUE   Lou Gramm
10. WITH OR WITHOUT YOU   U2

May 2, 1987

1. (I JUST) DIED IN YOUR ARMS   Cutting Crew
2. LOOKING FOR A NEW LOVE   Jody Watley
3. DON'T DREAM IT'S OVER   Crowded House
4. LA ISLA BONITA   Madonna
5. SIGN 'O' THE TIMES   Prince
6. WITH OR WITHOUT YOU   U2
7. I KNEW YOU WERE WAITING (FOR ME)   Aretha Franklin & George Michael
8. THE FINER THINGS   Steve Winwood
9. NOTHING'S GONNA STOP US NOW   Starship
10. STONE LOVE   Kool & The Gang

May 9, 1987

1. (I JUST) DIED IN YOUR ARMS   Cutting Crew
2. LOOKING FOR A NEW LOVE   Jody Watley
3. WITH OR WITHOUT YOU   U2
4. LA ISLA BONITA   Madonna
5. DON'T DREAM IT'S OVER   Crowded House
6. SIGN 'O' THE TIMES   Prince
7. HEAT OF THE NIGHT   Bryan Adams
8. THE LADY IN RED   Chris De Burgh
9. BIG LOVE   Fleetwood Mac
10. I KNEW YOU WERE WAITING (FOR ME)   Aretha Franklin & George Michael

May 16, 1987

1. WITH OR WITHOUT YOU   U2
2. LOOKING FOR A NEW LOVE   Jody Watley
3. (I JUST) DIED IN YOUR ARMS   Cutting Crew
4. LA ISLA BONITA   Madonna
5. THE LADY IN RED   Chris De Burgh
6. HEAT OF THE NIGHT   Bryan Adams
7. BIG LOVE   Fleetwood Mac
8. TALK DIRTY TO ME   Poison
9. YOU KEEP ME HANGIN' ON   Kim Wilde
10. ALWAYS   Atlantic Starr

May 23, 1987

1. WITH OR WITHOUT YOU   U2
2. LOOKING FOR A NEW LOVE   Jody Watley
3. THE LADY IN RED   Chris De Burgh
4. YOU KEEP ME HANGIN' ON   Kim Wilde
5. (I JUST) DIED IN YOUR ARMS   Cutting Crew
6. HEAT OF THE NIGHT   Bryan Adams
7. BIG LOVE   Fleetwood Mac
8. ALWAYS   Atlantic Starr
9. LA ISLA BONITA   Madonna
10. TALK DIRTY TO ME   Poison

May 30, 1987

1. WITH OR WITHOUT YOU   U2
2. YOU KEEP ME HANGIN' ON   Kim Wilde
3. THE LADY IN RED   Chris De Burgh
4. ALWAYS   Atlantic Starr
5. BIG LOVE   Fleetwood Mac
6. HEAD TO TOE   Lisa Lisa & Cult Jam
7. RIGHT ON TRACK   The Breakfast Club
8. HEAT OF THE NIGHT   Bryan Adams
9. I KNOW WHAT I LIKE   Huey Lewis & The News
10. WANTED DEAD OR ALIVE   Bon Jovi

June 6, 1987

1. YOU KEEP ME HANGIN' ON   Kim Wilde
2. ALWAYS   Atlantic Starr
3. HEAD TO TOE   Lisa Lisa & Cult Jam
4. THE LADY IN RED   Chris De Burgh
5. WITH OR WITHOUT YOU   U2
6. IN TOO DEEP   Genesis
7. WANTED DEAD OR ALIVE   Bon Jovi
8. BIG LOVE   Fleetwood Mac
9. DIAMONDS   Herb Alpert
10. I WANNA DANCE WITH SOMEBODY (WHO LOVES ME)   Whitney Houston

June 13, 1987

1. ALWAYS   Atlantic Starr
2. YOU KEEP ME HANGIN' ON   Kim Wilde
3. HEAD TO TOE   Lisa Lisa & Cult Jam
4. IN TOO DEEP   Genesis
5. I WANNA DANCE WITH SOMEBODY (WHO LOVES ME)   Whitney Houston
6. THE LADY IN RED   Chris De Burgh
7. WANTED DEAD OR ALIVE   Bon Jovi
8. DIAMONDS   Herb Alpert
9. WITH OR WITHOUT YOU   U2
10. JUST TO SEE HER   Smokey Robinson

June 20, 1987

1. HEAD TO TOE   Lisa Lisa & Cult Jam
2. ALWAYS   Atlantic Starr
3. I WANNA DANCE WITH SOMEBODY (WHO LOVES ME)   Whitney Houston

Atlantic Starr
Thirteen proves a lucky number for this quartet—``Always'' is #1 on June 13.

4	IN TOO DEEP Genesis
5	DIAMONDS Herb Alpert
6	ALONE Heart
7	WANTED DEAD OR ALIVE Bon Jovi
8	YOU KEEP ME HANGIN' ON Kim Wilde
9	SONGBIRD Kenny G.
10	JUST TO SEE HER Smokey Robinson

June 27, 1987
1 I WANNA DANCE WITH SOMEBODY (WHO LOVES ME)   Whitney Houston
2 HEAD TO TOE   Lisa Lisa & Cult Jam
3 IN TOO DEEP   Genesis
4 ALONE   Heart
5 ALWAYS   Atlantic Starr
6 SONGBIRD   Kenny G.
7 SHAKESDOWN   Bob Seger
8 DIAMONDS   Herb Alpert
9 JUST TO SEE HER   Smokey Robinson
10 WANTED DEAD OR ALIVE   Bon Jovi

July 4, 1987
1 I WANNA DANCE WITH SOMEBODY (WHO LOVES ME)   Whitney Houston
2 ALONE   Heart
3 SHAKEDOWN (FROM "BEVERLY HILLS COP II")   Bob Seger
4 HEAD TO TOE   Lisa Lisa & Cult Jam
5 SONGBIRD   Kenny G.
6 IN TOO DEEP   Genesis
7 DON'T DISTURB THIS GROOVE   The System
8 JUST TO SEE HER   Smokey Robinson
9 POINT OF NO RETURN   Expose
10 FUNKYTOWN   Pseudo Echo

July 11, 1987
1 ALONE   Heart
2 I WANNA DANCE WITH SOMEBODY (WHO LOVES ME)   Whitney Houston
3 SHAKEDOWN (FROM "BEVERLY HILLS COP II")   Bob Seger
4 SONGBIRD   Kenny G.
5 DON'T DISTURB THIS GROOVE   The System
6 POINT OF NO RETURN   Expose
7 FUNKYTOWN   Pseudo Echo
8 SOMETHING SO STRONG   Crowded House
9 HEAD TO TOE   Lisa Lisa & Cult Jam
10 I STILL HAVEN'T FOUND WHAT I'M LOOKING FOR   U2

July 18, 1987
1 ALONE   Heart
2 SHAKEDOWN (FROM "BEVERLY HILLS COP II")   Bob Seger
3 I WANNA DANCE WITH SOMEBODY (WHO LOVES ME)   Whitney Houston
4 DON'T DISTURB THIS GROOVE   The System
5 POINT OF NO RETURN   Expose
6 FUNKYTOWN   Pseudo Echo
7 I STILL HAVEN'T FOUND WHAT I'M LOOKING FOR   U2
8 SOMETHING SO STRONG   Crowded House
9 I WANT YOUR SEX (FROM "BEVERLY HILLS COP II")   George Michael
10 RHYTHM IS GONNA GET YOU   Gloria Estefan & Miami Sound Machine

383

July 25, 1987
1 ALONE   Heart
2 SHAKEDOWN (FROM "BEVERLY HILLS COP II")   Bob Seger
3 I STILL HAVEN'T FOUND WHAT I'M LOOKING FOR   U2
4 I WANNA DANCE WITH SOMEBODY (WHO LOVES ME)   Whitney Houston
5 I WANT YOUR SEX (FROM "BEVERLY HILLS COP II")   George Michael
6 RHYTHM IS GONNA GET YOU   Gloria Estefan & Miami Sound Machine
7 SOMETHING SO STRONG   Crowded House
8 HEART AND SOUL   T'Pau
9 DON'T DISTURB THIS GROOVE   The System
10 POINT OF NO RETURN   Expose

August 1, 1987
1 SHAKEDOWN (FROM "BEVERLY HILLS COP II")   Bob Seger
2 I STILL HAVEN'T FOUND WHAT I'M LOOKING FOR   U2
3 ALONE   Heart
4 I WANT YOUR SEX (FROM "BEVERLY HILLS COP II")   George Michael
5 RHYTHM IS GONNA GET YOU   Gloria Estefan & Miami Sound Machine
6 HEART AND SOUL   T'Pau
7 CROSS MY BROKEN HEART (FROM "BEVERLY HILLS COP II")   The Jets
8 LUKA   Suzanne Vega
9 I WANNA DANCE WITH SOMEBODY (WHO LOVES ME)   Whitney Houston
10 WOT'S IT TO YA   Robbie Nevil

August 8, 1987
1 I STILL HAVEN'T FOUND WHAT I'M LOOKING FOR   U2
2 I WANT YOUR SEX (FROM "BEVERLY HILLS COP II")   George Michael
3 SHAKEDOWN (FROM "BEVERLY HILLS COPS II")   Bob Seger
4 HEART AND SOUL   T'Pau
5 LUKA   Suzanne Vega
6 RHYTHM IS GONNA GET YOU   Gloria Estefan & Miami Sound Machine
7 WHO'S THAT GIRL   Madonna
8 CROSS MY BROKEN HEART (FROM "BEVERLY HILLS COP II")   The Jets
9 ALONE   Heart
10 WOT'S IT TO YA   Robbie Nevil

August 15, 1987
1 I STILL HAVEN'T FOUND WHAT I'M LOOKING FOR   U2
2 WHO'S THAT GIRL   Madonna
3 I WANT YOUR SEX (FROM "BEVERLY HILLS COP II")   George Michael
4 LUKA   Suzanne Vega
5 LA BAMBA   Los Lobos
6 HEART AND SOUL   T'Pau
7 DON'T MEAN NOTHING   Richard Marx
8 CROSS MY BROKEN HEART (FROM "BEVERLY HILLS COP II")   The Jets
9 ONLY IN MY DREAMS   Debbie Gibson
10 RHYTHM IS GONNA GET YOU   Gloria Estefan & Miami Sound Machine

August 22, 1987
1 WHO'S THAT GIRL   Madonna
2 LA BAMBA   Los Lobos
3 LUKA   Suzanne Vega
4 DON'T MEAN NOTHING   Richard Marx
5 I WANT YOUR SEX (FROM "BEVERLY HILLS COP II")   George Michael
6 I STILL HAVEN'T FOUND WHAT I'M LOOKING FOR   U2
7 ONLY IN MY DREAMS   Debbie Gibson
8 ROCK STEADY   The Whispers
9 HEART AND SOUL   T'Pau
10 I JUST CAN'T STOP LOVING YOU   Michael Jackson with Siedah Garrett

August 29, 1987
1 LA BAMBA   Los Lobos
2 WHO'S THAT GIRL   Madonna
3 DON'T MEAN NOTHING   Richard Marx
4 LUKA   Suzanne Vega
5 ONLY IN MY DREAMS   Debbie Gibson
6 I JUST CAN'T STOP LOVING YOU   Michael Jackson with Siedah Garrett
7 ROCK STEADY   The Whispers
8 DIDN'T WE ALMOST HAVE IT ALL   Whitney Houston
9 IT'S NOT OVER ('TIL IT'S OVER)   Starship
10 CAN'T WE TRY   Dan Hill (Duet with Vonda Shepard)

September 5, 1987
1 LA BAMBA   Los Lobos
2 I JUST CAN'T STOP LOVING YOU   Michael Jackson with Siedah Garrett
3 WHO'S THAT GIRL   Madonna
4 ONLY IN MY DREAMS   Debbie Gibson
5 DIDN'T WE ALMOST HAVE IT ALL   Whitney Houston
6 DON'T MEAN NOTHING   Richard Marx
7 CAN'T WE TRY   Dan Hill (Duet with Vonda Shepard)
8 HERE I GO AGAIN   Whitesnake
9 ROCK STEADY   The Whispers
10 DOING IT ALL FOR MY BABY   Huey Lewis & The News

September 12, 1987
1 LA BAMBA   Los Lobos
2 I JUST CAN'T STOP LOVING YOU   Michael Jackson with Siedah Garrett
3 DIDN'T WE ALMOST HAVE IT ALL   Whitney Houston
4 HERE I GO AGAIN   Whitesnake
5 ONLY IN MY DREAMS   Debbie Gibson
6 CAN'T WE TRY   Dan Hill (Duet with Vonda Shepard)
7 DOING IT ALL FOR MY BABY   Huey Lewis & The News
8 WHEN SMOKEY SINGS   ABC
9 WHO'S THAT GIRL   Madonna
10 I HEARD A RUMOUR (FROM "DISORDERLIES")   Bananarama

September 19, 1987
1 I JUST CAN'T STOP LOVING YOU   Michael Jackson with Siedah Garrett
2 DIDN'T WE ALMOST HAVE IT ALL   Whitney Houston
3 LA BAMBA   Los Lobos
4 HERE I GO AGAIN   Whitesnake
5 WHEN SMOKEY SINGS   ABC
6 DOING IT ALL FOR MY BABY   Huey Lewis & The News
7 CAN'T WE TRY   Dan Hill (Duet with Vonda Shepard)
8 I HEARD A RUMOUR (FROM "DISORDERLIES")   Bananarama
9 LOST IN EMOTION   Lisa Lisa & Cult Jam
10 TOUCH OF GREY   Grateful Dead

September 26, 1987
1 DIDN'T WE ALMOST HAVE IT ALL   Whitney Houston

2 HERE I GO AGAIN   Whitesnake
3 I JUST CAN'T STOP LOVING YOU   Michael Jackson with Siedah Garrett
4 I HEARD A RUMOUR (FROM "DISORDERLIES")   Bananarama
5 LOST IN EMOTION   Lisa Lisa & Cult Jam
6 WHEN SMOKEY SINGS   ABC
7 CARRIE   Europe
8 LA BAMBA   Los Lobos
9 TOUCH OF GREY   Grateful Dead
10 U GOT THE LOOK   Prince

October 3, 1987

1 DIDN'T WE ALMOST HAVE IT ALL   Whitney Houston
2 HERE I GO AGAIN   Whitesnake
3 LOST IN EMOTION   Lisa Lisa & Cult Jam
4 I HEARD A RUMOUR (FROM "DISORDERLIES")   Bananarama
5 CARRIE   Europe
6 U GOT THE LOOK   Prince
7 WHO WILL YOU RUN TO   Heart
8 WHEN SMOKEY SINGS   ABC
9 PAPER IN FIRE   John Cougar Mellencamp
10 ONE HEARTBEAT   Smokey Robinson

October 10, 1987

1 HERE I GO AGAIN   Whitesnake
2 LOST IN EMOTION   Lisa Lisa & Cult Jam
3 CARRIE   Europe
4 I HEARD A RUMOUR (FROM "DISORDERLIES")   Bananarama
5 U GOT THE LOOK   Prince
6 DIDN'T WE ALMOST HAVE IT ALL   Whitney Houston
7 WHO WILL YOU RUN TO   Heart
8 BAD   Michael Jackson
9 PAPER IN FIRE   John Cougar Mellencamp
10 CASANOVA   Levert

October 17, 1987

1 LOST IN EMOTION   Lisa Lisa & Cult Jam
2 U GOT THE LOOK   Prince
3 CARRIE   Europe
4 BAD   Michael Jackson
5 CAUSING A COMMOTION   Madonna
6 HERE I GO AGAIN   Whitesnake
7 WHO WILL YOU RUN TO   Heart
8 CASANOVA   Levert
9 PAPER IN FIRE   John Cougar Mellencamp
10 I HEARD A RUMOUR (FROM "DISORDERLIES")   Bananarama

October 24, 1987

1 BAD   Michael Jackson
2 CAUSING A COMMOTION   Madonna
3 U GOT THE LOOK   Prince
4 LOST IN EMOTION   Lisa Lisa & Cult Jam
5 I THINK WE'RE ALONE NOW   Tiffany
6 CASANOVA   Levert
7 MONY MONY   Billy Idol
8 LET ME BE THE ONE   Expose
9 LITTLE LIES   Fleetwood Mac
10 CARRIE   Europe

October 31, 1987

1 BAD   Michael Jackson
2 CAUSING A COMMOTION   Madonna
3 I THINK WE'RE ALONE NOW   Tiffany

4 MONY MONY   Billy Idol
5 CASANOVA   Levert
6 LITTLE LIES   Fleetwood Mac
7 LET ME BE THE ONE   Expose
8 U GOT THE LOOK   Prince
9 BREAKOUT   Swing Out Sister
10 BRILLIANT DISGUISE   Bruce Springsteen

November 7, 1987

1 I THINK WE'RE ALONE NOW   Tiffany
2 CAUSING A COMMOTION   Madonna
3 MONY MONY   Billy Idol
4 LITTLE LIES   Fleetwood Mac
5 BAD   Michael Jackson
6 (I'VE HAD) THE TIME OF MY LIFE   Bill Medley and Jennifer Warnes
7 BREAKOUT   Swing Out Sister
8 BRILLIANT DISGUISE   Bruce Springsteen
9 LET ME BE THE ONE   Expose
10 IT'S A SIN   Pet Shop Boys

November 14, 1987

1 I THINK WE'RE ALONE NOW   Tiffany
2 MONY MONY   Billy Idol
3 (I'VE HAD) THE TIME OF MY LIFE   Bill Medley and Jennifer Warnes
4 LITTLE LIES   Fleetwood Mac
5 HEAVEN IS A PLACE ON EARTH   Belinda Carlisle
6 BREAKOUT   Swing Out Sister
7 BRILLIANT DISGUISE   Bruce Springsteen
8 CAUSING A COMMOTION   Madonna
9 IT'S A SIN   Pet Shop Boys
10 SHOULD'VE KNOWN BETTER   Richard Marx

November 21, 1987

1 MONY MONY   Billy Idol
2 (I'VE HAD) THE TIME OF MY LIFE   Bill Medley and Jennifer Warnes
3 HEAVEN IS A PLACE ON EARTH   Belinda Carlisle
4 I THINK WE'RE ALONE NOW   Tiffany
5 BRILLIANT DISGUISE   Bruce Springsteen
6 BREAKOUT   Swing Out Sister
7 SHOULD'VE KNOWN BETTER   Richard Marx
8 LITTLE LIES   Fleetwood Mac
9 I'VE BEEN IN LOVE BEFORE   Cutting Crew
10 FAITH   George Michael

November 28, 1987

1 (I'VE HAD) THE TIME OF MY LIFE   Bill Medley and Jennifer Warnes
2 HEAVEN IS A PLACE ON EARTH   Belinda Carlisle
3 MONY MONY   Billy Idol
4 SHOULD'VE KNOWN BETTER   Richard Marx
5 FAITH   George Michael
6 BRILLIANT DISGUISE   Bruce Springsteen
7 I THINK WE'RE ALONE NOW   Tiffany
8 WE'LL BE TOGETHER   Sting
9 I'VE BEEN IN LOVE BEFORE   Cutting Crew
10 SHAKE YOUR LOVE   Debbie Gibson

December 5, 1987

1 HEAVEN IS A PLACE ON EARTH   Belinda Carlisle
2 (I'VE HAD) THE TIME OF MY LIFE   Bill Medley and Jennifer Warnes
3 FAITH   George Michael
4 SHOULD'VE KNOWN BETTER   Richard Marx
5 IS THIS LOVE   Whitesnake

6 SHAKE YOUR LOVE   Debbie Gibson
7 WE'LL BE TOGETHER   Sting
8 SO EMOTIONAL   Whitney Houston
9 THE ONE I LOVE   R.E.M.
10 DON'T YOU WANT ME   Jody Watley

December 12, 1987

1 FAITH   George Michael
2 HEAVEN IS A PLACE ON EARTH   Belinda Carlisle
3 SHOULD'VE KNOWN BETTER   Richard Marx
4 (I'VE HAD) THE TIME OF MY LIFE   Bill Medley and
    Jennifer Warnes
5 IS THIS LOVE   Whitesnake
6 SHAKE YOUR LOVE   Debbie Gibson
7 SO EMOTIONAL   Whitney Houston
8 WE'LL BE TOGETHER   Sting
9 DON'T YOU WANT ME   Jody Watley
10 GOT MY MIND SET ON YOU   George Harrison

December 19, 1987

1 FAITH   George Michael
2 IS THIS LOVE   Whitesnake
3 SO EMOTIONAL   Whitney Houston
4 SHAKE YOUR LOVE   Debbie Gibson
5 GOT MY MIND SET ON YOU   George Harrison
6 DON'T YOU WANT ME   Jody Watley
7 HEAVEN IS A PLACE ON EARTH   Belinda Carlisle
8 CATCH ME (I'M FALLING)   Pretty Poison
9 VALERIE   Steve Winwood
10 WE'LL BE TOGETHER   Sting

December 26, 1987

1 FAITH   George Michael
2 SO EMOTIONAL   Whitney Houston
3 IS THIS LOVE   Whitesnake
4 GOT MY MIND SET ON YOU   George Harrison
5 SHAKE YOUR LOVE   Debbie Gibson
6 DON'T YOU WANT ME   Jody Watley
7 THE WAY YOU MAKE ME FEEL   Michael Jackson
8 CATCH ME (I'M FALLING)   Pretty Poison
9 CHERRY BOMB   John Cougar Mellencamp
10 NEED YOU TONIGHT   INXS

January 9, 1988

1 SO EMOTIONAL   Whitney Houston
2 GOT MY MIND SET ON YOU   George Harrison
3 FAITH   George Michael
4 IS THIS LOVE   Whitesnake
5 THE WAY YOU MAKE ME FEEL   Michael Jackson
6 NEED YOU TONIGHT   INXS
7 SHAKE YOUR LOVE   Debbie Gibson
8 CHERRY BOMB   John Cougar Mellencamp
9 TELL IT TO MY HEART   Taylor Dayne
10 DON'T YOU WANT ME   Jody Watley

January 16, 1988

1 GOT MY MIND SET ON YOU   George Harrison
2 SO EMOTIONAL   Whitney Houston
3 THE WAY YOU MAKE ME FEEL   Michael Jackson
4 NEED YOU TONIGHT   INXS
5 COULD'VE BEEN   Tiffany
6 HAZY SHADE OF WINTER   Bangles
7 CANDLE IN THE WIND   Elton John
8 TELL IT TO MY HEART   Taylor Dayne
9 FAITH   George Michael
10 IS THIS LOVE   Whitesnake

January 23, 1988

1 THE WAY YOU MAKE ME FEEL   Michael Jackson
2 NEED YOU TONIGHT   INXS
3 COULD'VE BEEN   Tiffany
4 GOT MY MIND SET ON YOU   George Harrison
5 HAZY SHADE OF WINTER   Bangles
6 CANDLE IN THE WIND   Elton John
7 TELL IT TO MY HEART   Taylor Dayne
8 SEASONS CHANGE   Expose
9 SO EMOTIONAL   Whitney Houston
10 I WANT TO BE YOUR MAN   Roger

January 30, 1988

1 NEED YOU TONIGHT   INXS
2 COULD'VE BEEN   Tiffany
3 HAZY SHADE OF WINTER   Bangles
4 THE WAY YOU MAKE ME FEEL   Michael Jackson
5 SEASONS CHANGE   Expose
6 I WANT TO BE YOUR MAN   Roger
7 GOT MY MIND SET ON YOU   George Harrison
8 HUNGRY EYES (FROM "DIRTY DANCING")   Eric Carmen
9 CANDLE IN THE WIND   Elton John
10 TELL IT TO MY HEART   Taylor Dayne

February 6, 1988

1 COULD'VE BEEN   Tiffany
2 HAZY SHADE OF WINTER   Bangles
3 NEED YOU TONIGHT   INXS
4 SEASONS CHANGE   Expose
5 I WANT TO BE YOUR MAN   Roger
6 HUNGRY EYES (FROM "DIRTY DANCING")   Eric Carmen
7 WHAT HAVE I DONE TO DESERVE THIS?   Pet Shop Boys
    & Dusty Springfield
8 SAY YOU WILL   Foreigner
9 TUNNEL OF LOVE   Bruce Springsteen
10 I COULD NEVER TAKE THE PLACE OF YOUR MAN   Prince

February 13, 1988

1 COULD'VE BEEN   Tiffany
2 SEASONS CHANGE   Expose
3 I WANT TO BE YOUR MAN   Roger
4 HUNGRY EYES (FROM "DIRTY DANCING")   Eric Carmen
5 WHAT HAVE I DONE TO DESERVE THIS?   Pet Shop Boys
    & Dusty Springfield
6 NEED YOU TONIGHT   INXS
7 HAZY SHADE OF WINTER   Bangles
8 SAY YOU WILL   Foreigner
9 DON'T SHED A TEAR   Paul Carrack
10 SHE'S LIKE THE WIND   Patrick Swayze (Featuring Wendy
    Fraser)

February 20, 1988

1 SEASONS CHANGE   Expose
2 WHAT HAVE I DONE TO DESERVE THIS?   Pet Shop Boys
    & Dusty Springfield
3 COULD'VE BEEN   Tiffany
4 FATHER FIGURE   George Michael
5 HUNGRY EYES (FROM "DIRTY DANCING")   Eric Carmen
6 SAY YOU WILL   Foreigner
7 SHE'S LIKE THE WIND   Patrick Swayze (Featuring Wendy
    Fraser)
8 NEVER GONNA GIVE YOU UP   Rick Astley
9 DON'T SHED A TEAR   Paul Carrack
10 I WANT TO BE YOUR MAN   Roger

George Michael

February 27 finds ``Father Figure'' at the top of the pop.

February 27, 1988
1   FATHER FIGURE   George Michael
2   WHAT HAVE I DONE TO DESERVE THIS?   Pet Shop Boys & Dusty Springfield
3   SHE'S LIKE THE WIND   Patrick Swayze (Featuring Wendy Fraser)
4   HUNGRY EYES (FROM "DIRTY DANCING")   Eric Carmen
5   NEVER GONNA GIVE YOU UP   Rick Astley
6   SEASONS CHANGE   Expose
7   SAY YOU WILL   Foreigner
8   I GET WEAK   Belinda Carlisle
9   DON'T SHED A TEAR   Paul Carrack
10   CAN'T STAY AWAY FROM YOU   Gloria Estefan & Miami Sound Machine

March 6, 1988
1   FATHER FIGURE   George Michael
2   NEVER GONNA GIVE YOU UP   Rick Astley
3   SHE'S LIKE THE WIND   Patrick Swayze (Featuring Wendy Fraser)
4   I GET WEAK   Belinda Carlisle
5   WHAT HAVE I DONE TO DESERVE THIS?   Pet Shop Boys & Dusty Springfield
6   CAN'T STAY AWAY FROM YOU   Gloria Estefan & Miami Sound Machine
7   JUST LIKE PARADISE   David Lee Roth
8   ENDLESS SUMMER NIGHTS   Richard Marx
9   THE MAN IN THE MIRROR   Michael Jackson
10   I FOUND SOMEONE   Cher

March 12, 1988
1   NEVER GONNA GIVE YOU UP   Rick Astley

2   FATHER FIGURE   George Michael
3   SHE'S LIKE THE WIND   Patrick Swayze (Featuring Wendy Fraser)
4   I GET WEAK   Belinda Carlisle
5   ENDLESS SUMMER NIGHTS   Richard Marx
6   JUST LIKE PARADISE   David Lee Roth
7   THE MAN IN THE MIRROR   Michael Jackson
8   OUT OF THE BLUE   Debbie Gibson
9   I WANT HER   Keith Sweat
10   CAN'T STAY AWAY FROM YOU   Gloria Estefan & Miami Sound Machine

March 19, 1988
1   NEVER GONNA GIVE YOU UP   Rick Astley
2   I GET WEAK   Belinda Carlisle
3   FATHER FIGURE   George Michael
4   THE MAN IN THE MIRROR   Michael Jackson
5   ENDLESS SUMMER NIGHTS   Richard Marx
6   SHE'S LIKE THE WIND   Patrick Swayze (Featuring Wendy Fraser)
7   OUT OF THE BLUE   Debbie Gibson
8   JUST LIKE PARADISE   David Lee Roth
9   I WANT HER   Keith Sweat
10   GET OUTTA MY DREAMS, GET INTO MY CAR   Billy Ocean

March 26, 1988
1   THE MAN IN THE MIRROR   Michael Jackson
2   ENDLESS SUMMER NIGHTS   Richard Marx
3   NEVER GONNA GIVE YOU UP   Rick Astley
4   OUT OF THE BLUE   Debbie Gibson
5   GET OUTTA MY DREAMS, GET INTO MY CAR   Billy Ocean
6   I GET WEAK   Belinda Carlisle
7   I WANT HER   Keith Sweat
8   FATHER FIGURE   George Michael
9   ROCKET 2 U   The Jets
10   HYSTERIA   Def Leppard

April 2, 1988
1   THE MAN IN THE MIRROR   Michael Jackson
2   ENDLESS SUMMER NIGHTS   Richard Marx
3   GET OUTTA MY DREAMS, GET INTO MY CAR   Billy Ocean
4   OUT OF THE BLUE   Debbie Gibson
5   I WANT HER   Keith Sweat
6   ROCKET 2 U   The Jets
7   DEVIL INSIDE   INXS
8   NEVER GONNA GIVE YOU UP   Rick Astley
9   GIRLFRIEND   Pebbles
10   WHERE DO BROKEN HEARTS GO   Whitney Houston

April 9, 1988
1   GET OUTTA MY DREAMS, GET INTO MY CAR   Billy Ocean
2   THE MAN IN THE MIRROR   Michael Jackson
3   OUT OF THE BLUE   Debbie Gibson
4   DEVIL INSIDE   INXS
5   WHERE DO BROKEN HEARTS GO   Whitney Houston
6   ROCKET 2 U   The Jets
7   ENDLESS SUMMER NIGHTS   Richard Marx
8   GIRLFRIEND   Pebbles
9   I WANT HER   Keith Sweat
10   WISHING WELL   Terence Trent D'Arby

April 16, 1988
1   GET OUTTA MY DREAMS, GET INTO MY CAR   Billy Ocean
2   DEVIL INSIDE   INXS
3   WHERE DO BROKEN HEARTS GO   Whitney Houston
4   THE MAN IN THE MIRROR   Michael Jackson
5   WISHING WELL   Terence Trent D'Arby

6 GIRLFRIEND Pebbles
7 ROCKET 2 U The Jets
8 ANGEL Aerosmith
9 I SAW HIM STANDING THERE Tiffany
10 SOME KIND OF LOVE Jody Watley

April 23, 1988
1 WHERE DO BROKEN HEARTS GO Whitney Houston
2 DEVIL INSIDE INXS
3 GET OUTTA MY DREAMS, GET INTO MY CAR Billy Ocean
4 WISHING WELL Terence Trend D'Arby
5 GIRLFRIEND Pebbles
6 ANGEL Aerosmith
7 I SAW HIM STANDING THERE Tiffany
8 ANYTHING FOR YOU Gloria Estefan & Miami Sound Machine
9 PINK CADILLAC Natalie Cole
10 PROVE YOUR LOVE Taylor Dayne

April 30, 1988
1 WHERE DO BROKEN HEARTS GO Whitney Houston
2 WISHING WELL Terence Trent D'Arby
3 ANGEL Aerosmith
4 DEVIL INSIDE INXS
5 ANYTHING FOR YOU Gloria Estefan & Miami Sound Machine
6 GET OUTTA MY DREAMS, GET INTO MY CAR Billy Ocean
7 PINK CADILLAC Natalie Cole
8 PROVE YOUR LOVE Taylor Dayne
9 I SAW HIM STANDING THERE Tiffany
10 GIRLFRIEND Pebbles

May 7, 1988
1 WISHING WELL Terence Trent D'Arby
2 ANYTHING FOR YOU Gloria Estefan & Miami Sound Machine
3 ANGEL Aerosmith
4 WHERE DO BROKEN HEARTS GO Whitney Houston
5 PINK CADILLAC Natalie Cole
6 ALWAYS ON MY MIND Pet Shop Boys
7 PROVE YOUR LOVE Taylor Dayne
8 SHATTERED DREAMS Johnny Hates Jazz
9 ELECTRIC BLUE Icehouse
10 NAUGHTY GIRLS (NEED LOVE TOO) Samantha Fox

May 14, 1988
1 ANYTHING FOR YOU Gloria Estefan & Miami Sound Machine
2 SHATTERED DREAMS Johnny Hates Jazz
3 WISHING WELL Terence Trent D'Arby
4 ONE MORE TRY George Michael
5 PINK CADILLAC Natalie Cole
6 ALWAYS ON MY MIND Pet Shop Boys
7 ANGEL Aerosmith
8 NAUGHTY GIRLS (NEED LOVE TOO) Samantha Fox
9 ELECTRIC BLUE Icehouse
10 I DON'T WANT TO LIVE WITHOUT YOU Foreigner

May 21, 1988
1 ANYTHING FOR YOU Gloria Estefan & Miami Sound Machine
2 ONE MORE TRY George Michael
3 SHATTERED DREAMS Johnny Hates Jazz
4 ALWAYS ON MY MIND Pet Shop Boys
5 NAUGHTY GIRLS (NEED LOVE TOO) Samantha Fox
6 I DON'T WANT TO LIVE WITHOUT YOU Foreigner
7 ELECTRIC BLUE Icehouse

8 WAIT White Lion
9 EVERYTHING YOUR HEART DESIRES Daryl Hall & John Oates
10 TWO OCCASIONS The Deele

May 28, 1988
1 ONE MORE TRY George Michael
2 SHATTERED DREAMS Johnny Hates Jazz
3 ANYTHING FOR YOU Gloria Estefan & Miami Sound Machine
4 NAUGHTY GIRLS (NEED LOVE TOO) Samantha Fox
5 I DON'T WANT TO LIVE WITHOUT YOU Foreigner
6 ALWAYS ON MY MIND Pet Shop Boys
7 EVERYTHING YOUR HEART DESIRES Daryl Hall & John Oates
8 TOGETHER FOREVER Rick Astley
9 WAIT White Lion
10 PIANO IN THE DARK Brenda Russell featuring Joe Esposito

June 4, 1988
1 ONE MORE TRY George Michael
2 SHATTERED DREAMS Johnny Hates Jazz
3 NAUGHTY GIRLS (NEED LOVE TOO) Samantha Fox
4 EVERYTHING YOUR HEART DESIRES Daryl Hall & John Oates
5 TOGETHER FOREVER Rick Astley
6 PIANO IN THE DARK Brenda Russell Featuring Joe Esposito
7 FOOLISH BEAT Debbie Gibson
8 I DON'T WANT TO LIVE WITHOUT YOU Foreigner
9 MAKE IT REAL The Jets
10 ANYTHING FOR YOU Gloria Estefan & Miami Sound Machine

June 11, 1988
1 ONE MORE TRY George Michael
2 TOGETHER FOREVER Rick Astley
3 EVERYTHING YOUR HEART DESIRES Daryl Hall & John Oates
4 SHATTERED DREAMS Johnny Hates Jazz
5 NAUGHTY GIRLS (NEED LOVE TOO) Samantha Fox
6 FOOLISH BEAT Debbie Gibson
7 MAKE IT REAL The Jets
8 DIRTY DIANA Michael Jackson
9 CIRCLE IN THE SAND Belinda Carlisle
10 THE VALLEY ROAD Bruce Hornsby & The Range

June 18, 1988
1 TOGETHER FOREVER Rick Astley
2 ONE MORE TRY George Michael
3 FOOLISH BEAT Debbie Gibson
4 DIRTY DIANA Michael Jackson
5 MAKE IT REAL The Jets
6 EVERYTHING YOUR HEART DESIRES Daryl Hall & John Oates
7 CIRCLE IN THE SAND Belinda Carlisle
8 THE VALLEY ROAD Bruce Hornsby & The Range
9 THE FLAME Cheap Trick
10 ALPHABET ST. Prince

June 25, 1988
1 FOOLISH BEAT Debbie Gibson
2 DIRTY DIANA Michael Jackson
3 TOGETHER FOREVER Rick Astley
4 MAKE IT REAL The Jets

5   THE FLAME   Cheap Trick
6   THE VALLEY ROAD   Bruce Hornsby & The Range
7   ONE MORE TRY   George Michael
8   ALPHABET ST.   Prince
9   NEW SENSATION   INXS
10   POUR SOME SUGAR ON ME   Def Leppard

July 2, 1988
1   DIRTY DIANA   Michael Jackson
2   FOOLISH BEAT   Debbie Gibson
3   THE FLAME   Cheap Trick
4   MAKE IT REAL   The Jets
5   THE VALLEY ROAD   Bruce Hornsby & The Range
6   MERCEDES BOY   Pebbles
7   POUR SOME SUGAR ON ME   Def Leppard
8   NOTHIN' BUT A GOOD TIME   Poison
9   NEW SENSATION   INXS
10   TOGETHER FOREVER   Rick Astley

July 9, 1988
1   THE FLAME   Cheap Trick
2   MERCEDES BOY   Pebbles
3   POUR SOME SUGAR ON ME   Def Leppard
4   NEW SENSATION   INXS
5   DIRTY DIANA   Michael Jackson
6   NOTHIN' BUT A GOOD TIME   Poison
7   FOOLISH BEAT   Debbie Gibson
8   HOLD ON TO THE NIGHTS   Richard Marx
9   THE VALLEY ROAD   Bruce Hornsby & The Range
10   NITE AND DAY   Al B. Shure!

July 16, 1988
1   THE FLAME   Cheap Trick
2   MERCEDES BOY   Pebbles
3   POUR SOME SUGAR ON ME   Def Leppard
4   NEW SENSATION   INXS
5   HOLD ON TO THE NIGHTS   Richard Marx
6   ROLL WITH IT   Steve Winwood
7   NITE AND DAY   Al B. Shure!
8   HANDS TO HEAVEN   Bryan Adams
9   MAKE ME LOSE CONTROL   Eric Carmen
10   NOTHIN' BUT A GOOD TIME   Poison

July 23, 1988
1   HOLD ON TO THE NIGHTS   Richard Marx
2   POUR SOME SUGAR ON ME   Def Leppard
3   NEW SENSATION   INXS
4   ROLL WITH IT   Steve Winwood
5   THE FLAME   Cheap Trick
6   HANDS TO HEAVEN   Bryan Adams
7   MAKE ME LOSE CONTROL   Eric Carmen
8   MERCEDES BOY   Pebbles
9   SIGN YOUR NAME   Terence Trent D'Arby
10   RUSH HOUR   Jane Wiedlin

July 30, 1988
1   ROLL WITH IT   Steve Winwood
2   HOLD ON TO THE NIGHTS   Richard Marx
3   HANDS TO HEAVEN   Bryan Adams
4   POUR SOME SUGAR ON ME   Def Leppard
5   MAKE ME LOSE CONTROL   Eric Carmen
6   SIGN YOUR NAME   Terence Trent D'Arby
7   NEW SENSATION   INXS
8   1-2-3   Gloria Estefan & Miami Sound Machine
9   RUSH HOUR   Jane Wiedlin
10   I DON'T WANNA GO ON WITH YOU LIKE THAT   Elton John

August 6, 1988
1   ROLL WITH IT   Steve Winwood
2   HANDS TO HEAVEN   Bryan Adams
3   HOLD ON TO THE NIGHTS   Richard Marx
4   MAKE ME LOSE CONTROL   Eric Carmen
5   SIGN YOUR NAME   Terence Trent D'Arby
6   1-2-3   Gloria Estefan & Miami Sound Machine
7   I DON'T WANNA GO ON WITH YOU LIKE THAT   Elton John
8   I DON'T WANNA LIVE WITHOUT YOUR LOVE   Chicago
9   POUR SOME SUGAR ON ME   Def Leppard
10   MONKEY   George Michael

August 13, 1988
1   ROLL WITH IT   Steve Winwood
2   HANDS TO HEAVEN   Bryan Adams
3   MAKE ME LOSE CONTROL   Eric Carmen
4   SIGN YOUR NAME   Terence Trent D'Arby
5   1-2-3   Gloria Estefan & Miami Sound Machine
6   I DON'T WANNA GO ON WITH YOU LIKE THAT   Elton John
7   I DON'T WANNA LIVE WITHOUT YOUR LOVE   Chicago
8   MONKEY   George Michael
9   HOLD ON TO THE NIGHTS   Richard Marx
10   JUST GOT PAID   Johnny Kemp

August 20, 1988
1   ROLL WITH IT   Steve Winwood
2   MONKEY   George Michael
3   1-2-3   Gloria Estefan & Miami Sound Machine
4   I DON'T WANNA GO ON WITH YOU LIKE THAT   Elton John
5   MAKE ME LOSE CONTROL   Eric Carmen
6   I DON'T WANNA LIVE WITHOUT YOUR LOVE   Chicago
7   HANDS TO HEAVEN   Bryan Adams
8   SIGN YOUR NAME   Terence Trent D'Arby
9   SWEET CHILD O'MINE   Guns N' Roses
10   FAST CAR   Tracy Chapman

August 27, 1988
1   MONKEY   George Michael
2   I DON'T WANNA GO ON WITH YOU LIKE THAT   Elton John
3   I DON'T WANNA LIVE WITHOUT YOUR LOVE   Chicago
4   SWEET CHILD O'MINE   Guns N' Roses
5   SIMPLY IRRESISTIBLE   Robert Palmer
6   FAST CAR   Tracy Chapman
7   ROLL WITH IT   Steve Winwood
8   PERFECT WORLD   Huey Lewis & The News
9   LOVE WILL SAVE THE DAY   Whitney Houston
10   1-2-3   Gloria Estefan & Miami Sound Machine

September 3, 1988
1   MONKEY   George Michael
2   SWEET CHILD O'MINE   Guns N' Roses
3   SIMPLY IRRESISTIBLE   Robert Palmer
4   I DON'T WANNA GO ON WITH YOU LIKE THAT   Elton John
5   I DON'T WANNA LIVE WITHOUT YOUR LOVE   Chicago
6   PERFECT WORLD   Huey Lewis & The News
7   FAST CAR   Tracy Chapman
8   WHEN IT'S LOVE   Van Halen
9   IF IT ISN'T LOVE   New Edition
10   I'LL ALWAYS LOVE YOU   Taylor Dayne

September 10, 1988
1 SWEET CHILD O'MINE   Guns N' Roses
2 SIMPLY IRRESISTIBLE   Robert Palmer
3 PERFECT WORLD   Huey Lewis & The News
4 MONKEY   George Michael
5 WHEN IT'S LOVE   Van Halen
6 FAST CAR   Tracy Chapman
7 I'LL ALWAYS LOVE YOU   Taylor Dayne
8 IF IT ISN'T LOVE   New Edition
9 DON'T WORRY, BE HAPPY (FROM "COCKTAIL")   Bobby McFerrin
10 NOBODY'S FOOL (THEME FROM "CADDYSHACK II")   Kenny Loggins

September 17, 1988
1 SWEET CHILD O'MINE   Guns N' Roses
2 SIMPLY IRRESISTIBLE   Robert Palmer
3 PERFECT WORLD   Huey Lewis & The News
4 DON'T WORRY, BE HAPPY (FROM "COCKTAIL")   Bobby McFerrin
5 I'LL ALWAYS LOVE YOU   Taylor Dayne
6 WHEN IT'S LOVE   Van Halen
7 IF IT ISN'T LOVE   New Edition
8 NOBODY'S FOOL (THEME FROM "CADDYSHACK II")   Kenny Loggins
9 LOVE BITES   Def Leppard
10 IT WOULD TAKE A STRONG STRONG MAN   Rick Astley

September 24, 1988
1 DON'T WORRY, BE HAPPY (FROM "COCKTAIL")   Bobby McFerrin
2 SWEET CHILD O' MINE   Guns N' Roses
3 I'LL ALWAYS LOVE YOU   Taylor Dayne
4 SIMPLY IRRESISTIBLE   Robert Palmer
5 LOVE BITES   Def Leppard
6 PERFECT WORLD   Huey Lewis & The News
7 ONE GOOD WOMAN   Peter Cetera
8 IF IT ISN'T LOVE   New Edition
9 NOBODY'S FOOL (THEME FROM "CADDYSHACK II")   Kenny Loggins
10 DON'T BE CRUEL   Cheap Trick

October 1, 1988
1 DON'T WORRY, BE HAPPY (FROM "COCKTAIL")   Bobby McFerrin
2 LOVE BITES   Def Leppard
3 I'LL ALWAYS LOVE YOU   Taylor Dayne
4 ONE GOOD WOMAN   Peter Cetera
5 RED RED WINE   UB40
6 DON'T BE CRUEL   Cheap Trick
7 SWEET CHILD O' MINE   Guns N' Roses
8 I HATE MYSELF FOR LOVING YOU   Joan Jett And The Blackhearts
9 SIMPLY IRRESISTIBLE   Robert Palmer
10 WHAT'S ON YOUR MIND (PURE ENERGY)   Information Society

October 8, 1988
1 LOVE BITES   Def Leppard
2 RED RED WINE   UB40
3 DON'T WORRY, BE HAPPY (FROM "COCKTAIL")   Bobby McFerrin
4 DON'T BE CRUEL   Cheap Trick
5 ONE GOOD WOMAN   Peter Cetera
6 GROOVY KIND OF LOVE   Phil Collins
7 I'LL ALWAYS LOVE YOU   Taylor Dayne

8 I HATE MYSELF FOR LOVING YOU   Joan Jett And The Blackhearts
9 WHAT'S ON YOUR MIND (PURE ENERGY)   Information Society
10 PLEASE DON'T GO GIRL   New Kids On The Block

October 15, 1988
1 RED RED WINE   UB40
2 LOVE BITES   Def Leppard
3 GROOVY KIND OF LOVE   Phil Collins
4 DON'T BE CRUEL   Cheap Trick
5 WHAT'S ON YOUR MIND (PURE ENERGY)   Information Society
6 DON'T WORRY, BE HAPPY (FROM "COCKTAIL")   Bobby McFerrin
7 DON'T YOU KNOW WHAT THE NIGHT CAN DO?   Steve Winwood
8 PLEASE DON'T GO GIRL   New Kids On The Block
9 WILD, WILD WEST   The Escape Club
10 I HATE MYSELF FOR LOVING YOU   Joan Jett And The Blackhearts

October 22, 1988
1 GROOVY KIND OF LOVE   Phil Collins
2 RED RED WINE   UB40
3 WHAT'S ON YOUR MIND (PURE ENERGY)   Information Society
4 LOVE BITES   Def Leppard
5 WILD, WILD WEST   The Escape Club
6 KOKOMO (FROM THE "COCKTAIL" SOUNDTRACK)   The Beach Boys
7 DON'T YOU KNOW WHAT THE NIGHT CAN DO?   Steve Winwood
8 DON'T BE CRUEL   Bobby Brown
9 NEVER TEAR US APART   INXS
10 THE LOCO-MOTION   Kylie Minogue

October 29, 1988
1 GROOVY KIND OF LOVE   Phil Collins
2 KOKOMO (FROM THE "COCKTAIL" SOUNDTRACK)   The Beach Boys
3 WILD, WILD WEST   The Escape Club
4 RED RED WINE   UB40
5 WHAT'S ON YOUR MIND (PURE ENERGY)   Information Society
6 DON'T YOU KNOW WHAT THE NIGHT CAN DO?   Steve Winwood
7 THE LOCO-MOTION   Kylie Minogue
8 NEVER TEAR US APART   Inxs
9 ONE MOMENT IN TIME   Whitney Houston
10 BAD MEDICINE   Bon Jovi

November 5, 1988
1 KOKOMO (FROM "COCKTAIL")   The Beach Boys
2 WILD, WILD WEST   The Escape Club
3 GROOVY KIND OF LOVE   Phil Collins
4 THE LOCO-MOTION   Kylie Minogue
5 BAD MEDICINE   Bon Jovi
6 ONE MOMENT IN TIME   Whitney Houston
7 NEVER TEAR US APART   Inxs
8 DESIRE   U2
9 RED RED WINE   UB40
10 WHAT'S ON YOUR MIND (PURE ENERGY)   Information Society

November 12, 1988
1 WILD, WILD WEST   The Escape Club

2 KOKOMO (FROM THE "COCKTAIL" SOUNDTRACK) The Beach Boys
3 THE LOCO-MOTION Kylie Minogue
4 BAD MEDICINE Bon Jovi
5 ONE MOMENT IN TIME Whitney Houston
6 DESIRE U2
7 GROOVY KIND OF LOVE Phil Collins
8 BABY, I LOVE YOUR WAY/FREEBIRD MEDLEY Will To Power
9 KISSING A FOOL George Michael
10 NEVER TEAR US APART Inxs

November 19, 1988
1 BAD MEDICINE Bon Jovi
2 WILD, WILD WEST The Escape Club
3 THE LOCO-MOTION Kylie Minogue
4 DESIRE U2
5 KOKOMO (FROM THE "COCKTAIL" SOUNDTRACK) The Beach Boys
6 BABY, I LOVE YOUR WAY/FREEBIRD MEDLEY Will To Power
7 KISSING A FOOL George Michael
8 HOW CAN I FALL? Breathe
9 LOOK AWAY Chicago
10 ONE MOMENT IN TIME Whitney Houston

November 26, 1988
1 BAD MEDICINE Bon Jovi
2 BABY I LOVE YOUR WAY/FREEBIRD MEDLEY Will To Power
3 DESIRE U2
4 HOW CAN I FALL? Breathe
5 KISSING A FOOL George Michael
6 LOOK AWAY Chicago
7 I DON'T WANT YOUR LOVE Duran Duran
8 WILD, WILD WEST The Escape Club
9 GIVING YOU THE BEST THAT I GOT Anita Baker
10 THE LOCO-MOTION Kylie Minogue

December 3, 1988
1 BABY, I LOVE YOUR WAY/FREEBIRD MEDLEY Will To Power
2 LOOK AWAY Chicago
3 HOW CAN I FALL? Breathe
4 I DON'T WANT YOUR LOVE Duran Duran
5 DESIRE U2
6 GIVING YOU THE BEST THAT I GOT Anita Baker
7 WAITING FOR A STAR TO FALL Boy Meets Girl
8 BAD MEDICINE Bon Jovi
9 KISSING A FOOL George Michael
10 EVERY ROSE HAS ITS THORN Poison

December 10, 1988
1 LOOK AWAY Chicago
2 BABY, I LOVE YOUR WAY/FREEBIRD MEDLEY Will To Power
3 HOW CAN I FALL? Breathe
4 I DON'T WANT YOUR LOVE Duran Duran
5 GIVING YOU THE BEST THAT I GOT Anita Baker
6 EVERY ROSE HAS ITS THORN Poison
7 WAITING FOR A STAR TO FALL Boy Meets Girl
8 MY PREROGATIVE Bobby Brown
9 WELCOME TO THE JUNGLE Guns N' Roses
10 WALK ON WATER Eddie Money

December 17, 1988
1 LOOK AWAY Chicago

2 EVERY ROSE HAS ITS THORN Poison
3 GIVING YOU THE BEST THAT I GOT Anita Baker
4 MY PREROGATIVE Bobby Brown
5 WAITING FOR A STAR TO FALL Boy Meets Girl
6 BABY, I LOVE YOUR WAY/FREEBIRD MEDLEY Will To Power
7 I DON'T WANT YOUR LOVE Duran Duran
8 HOW CAN I FALL? Breathe
9 WELCOME TO THE JUNGLE Guns N' Roses
10 WALK ON WATER Eddie Money

December 24, 1988
1 EVERY ROSE HAS ITS THORN Poison
2 MY PREROGATIVE Bobby Brown
3 LOOK AWAY Chicago
4 GIVING YOU THE BEST THAT I GOT Anita Baker
5 WAITING FOR A STAR TO FALL Boy Meets Girl
6 TWO HEARTS Phil Collins
7 WELCOME TO THE JUNGLE Guns N' Roses
8 IN YOUR ROOM Bangles
9 WALK ON WATER Eddie Money
10 DON'T RUSH ME Taylor Dayne

January 7, 1989
1 EVERY ROSE HAS ITS THORN Poison
2 MY PREROGATIVE Bobby Brown
3 TWO HEARTS Phil Collins
4 GIVING YOU THE BEST THAT I GOT Anita Baker
5 IN YOUR ROOM Bangles
6 DON'T RUSH ME Taylor Dayne
7 WAITING FOR A STAR TO FALL Boy Meets Girl
8 LOOK AWAY Chicago
9 ARMAGEDDON IT Def Leppard
10 SMOOTH CRIMINAL Michael Jackson

January 14, 1989
1 MY PREROGATIVE Bobby Brown
2 TWO HEARTS Phil Collins
3 EVERY ROSE HAS ITS THORN Poison
4 DON'T RUSH ME Taylor Dayne
5 ARMAGEDDON IT Def Leppard
6 IN YOUR ROOM Bangles
7 SMOOTH CRIMINAL Michael Jackson
8 I REMEMBER HOLDING YOU Boys Club
9 PUT A LITTLE LOVE IN YOUR HEART Annie Lennox & Al Green
10 THE WAY YOU LOVE ME Karyn White

January 21, 1989
1 TWO HEARTS Phil Collins
2 DON'T RUSH ME Taylor Dayne
3 ARMAGEDDON IT Def Leppard
4 MY PREROGATIVE Bobby Brown
5 WHEN I'M WITH YOU Sheriff
6 EVERY ROSE HAS ITS THORN Poison
7 SMOOTH CRIMINAL Michael Jackson
8 THE WAY YOU LOVE ME Karyn White
9 WHEN THE CHILDREN CRY White Lion
10 PUT A LITTLE LOVE IN YOUR HEART Annie Lennox & Al Green

January 28, 1989
1 TWO HEARTS Phil Collins
2 WHEN I'M WITH YOU Sheriff
3 ARMAGEDDON IT Def Leppard
4 DON'T RUSH ME Taylor Dayne
5 WHEN THE CHILDREN CRY White Lion

6   STRAIGHT UP   Paula Abdul
7   BORN TO BE MY BABY   Bon Jovi
8   THE WAY YOU LOVE ME   Karyn White
9   WILD THING   Tone Loc
10   ALL THIS TIME   Tiffany

February 4, 1989
1   WHEN I'M WITH YOU   Sheriff
2   STRAIGHT UP   Paula Abdul
3   WHEN THE CHILDREN CRY   White Lion
4   BORN TO BE MY BABY   Bon Jovi
5   WILD THING   Tone Loc
6   ARMAGEDDON IT   Def Leppard
7   THE WAY YOU LOVE ME   Karyn White
8   DON'T RUSH ME   Taylor Dayne
9   ALL THIS TIME   Tiffany
10   TWO HEARTS   Phil Collins

February 11, 1989
1   STRAIGHT UP   Paula Abdul
2   WHEN I'M WITH YOU   Sheriff
3   WILD THING   Tone Loc
4   BORN TO BE MY BABY   Bon Jovi
5   WHEN THE CHILDREN CRY   White Lion
6   ALL THIS TIME   Tiffany
7   THE LOVER IN ME   Sheena Easton
8   I WANNA HAVE SOME FUN   Samantha Fox
9   SHE WANTS TO DANCE WITH ME   Rick Astley
10   WALKING AWAY   Information Society

February 18, 1989
1   STRAIGHT UP   Paula Abdul
2   WILD THING   Tone Loc
3   BORN TO BE MY BABY   Bon Jovi
4   LOST IN YOUR EYES   Debbie Gibson
5   THE LOVER IN ME   Sheena Easton
6   WHEN I'M WITH YOU   Sheriff
7   SHE WANTS TO DANCE WITH ME   Rick Astley
8   WHAT I AM   Edie Brickell & New Bohemians
9   WALKING AWAY   Information Society
10   YOU GOT IT (THE RIGHT STUFF)   New Kids On The Block

February 25, 1989
1   STRAIGHT UP   Paula Abdul
2   LOST IN YOUR EYES   Debbie Gibson
3   WILD THING   Tone Loc
4   THE LOVER IN ME   Sheena Easton
5   BORN TO BE MY BABY   Bon Jovi
6   SHE WANTS TO DANCE WITH ME   Rick Astley
7   YOU GOT IT (THE RIGHT STUFF)   New Kids On The Block
8   WHAT I AM   Edie Brickell & New Bohemians
9   THE LIVING YEARS   Mike + The Mechanics
10   WALKING AWAY   Information Society

March 4, 1989
1   LOST IN YOUR EYES   Debbie Gibson
2   THE LOVER IN ME   Sheena Easton
3   STRAIGHT UP   Paula Abdul
4   THE LIVING YEARS   Mike + The Mechanics
5   YOU GOT IT (THE RIGHT STUFF)   New Kids On The Block
6   WILD THING   Tone Loc
7   WHAT I AM   Edie Brickell & New Bohemians
8   RONI   Bobby Brown
9   SURRENDER TO ME (FROM "TEQUILA SUNRISE")   Ann
     Wilson & Robin Zander
10   PARADISE CITY   Guns N' Roses

March 11, 1989
1   LOST IN YOUR EYES   Debbie Gibson
2   THE LIVING YEARS   Mike + The Mechanics
3   YOU GOT IT (THE RIGHT STUFF)   New Kids On The Block
4   RONI   Bobby Brown
5   PARADISE CITY   Guns N' Roses
6   SURRENDER TO ME (FROM "TEQUILA SUNRISE")   Ann
     Wilson & Robin Zander
7   GIRL YOU KNOW IT'S TRUE   Milli Vanilli
8   THE LOVER IN ME   Sheena Easton
9   MY HEART CAN'T TELL YOU NO   Rod Stewart
10   STRAIGHT UP   Paula Abdul

March 18, 1989
1   LOST IN YOUR EYES   Debbie Gibson
2   THE LIVING YEARS   Mike + The Mechanics
3   RONI   Bobby Brown
4   GIRL YOU KNOW IT'S TRUE   Milli Vanilli
5   PARADISE CITY   Guns N' Roses
6   ETERNAL FLAME   Bangles
7   MY HEART CAN'T TELL YOU NO   Rod Stewart
8   THE LOOK   Roxette
9   YOU GOT IT (THE RIGHT STUFF)   New Kids On The Block
10   DON'T TELL ME LIES   Breathe

March 25, 1989
1   THE LIVING YEARS   Mike + The Mechanics
2   ETERNAL FLAME   Bangles
3   GIRL YOU KNOW IT'S TRUE   Milli Vanilli
4   THE LOOK   Roxette
5   MY HEART CAN'T TELL YOU NO   Rod Stewart
6   LOST IN YOUR EYES   Debbie Gibson
7   SHE DRIVES ME CRAZY   Fine Young Cannibals
8   WALK THE DINOSAUR   Was (Not Was)
9   RONI   Bobby Brown
10   YOU'RE NOT ALONE   Chicago

April 1, 1989
1   ETERNAL FLAME   Bangles
2   GIRL YOU KNOW IT'S TRUE   Milli Vanilli
3   THE LOOK   Roxette
4   MY HEART CAN'T TELL YOU NO   Rod Stewart
5   THE LIVING YEARS   Mike + The Mechanics
6   SHE DRIVES ME CRAZY   Fine Young Cannibals
7   WALK THE DINOSAUR   Was (Not Was)
8   STAND   R.E.M.
9   DREAMIN'   Vanessa Williams
10   LOST IN YOUR EYES   Debbie Gibson

April 8, 1989
1   THE LOOK   Roxette
2   ETERNAL FLAME   Bangles
3   GIRL YOU KNOW IT'S TRUE   Milli Vanilli
4   SHE DRIVES ME CRAZY   Fine Young Cannibals
5   LIKE A PRAYER   Madonna
6   STAND   R.E.M.
7   MY HEART CAN'T TELL YOU NO   Rod Stewart
8   DREAMIN'   Vanessa Williams
9   WALK THE DINOSAUR   Was (Not Was)
10   FUNKY COLD MEDINA   Tone Loc

April 15, 1989
1   SHE DRIVES ME CRAZY   Fine Young Cannibals
2   THE LOOK   Roxette
3   LIKE A PRAYER   Madonna
4   ETERNAL FLAME   Bangles

5 GIRL YOU KNOW IT'S TRUE   Milli Vanilli
6 STAND   R.E.M.
7 FUNKY COLD MEDINA   Tone Loc
8 SUPERWOMAN   Karyn White
9 YOU GOT IT   Roy Orbison
10 YOUR MAMA DON'T DANCE   Poison

April 22, 1989
1 LIKE A PRAYER   Madonna
2 SHE DRIVES ME CRAZY   Fine Young Cannibals
3 THE LOOK   Roxette
4 FUNKY COLD MEDINA   Tone Loc
5 I'LL BE THERE FOR YOU   Bon Jovi
6 STAND   R.E.M.
7 HEAVEN HELP ME   Deon Estus
8 GIRL YOU KNOW IT'S TRUE   Milli Vanilli
9 ETERNAL FLAME   Bangles
10 SECOND CHANCE   Thirty Eight Special

April 29, 1989
1 LIKE A PRAYER   Madonna
2 I'LL BE THERE FOR YOU   Bon Jovi
3 FUNKY COLD MEDINA   Tone Loc
4 SHE DRIVES ME CRAZY   Fine Young Cannibals
5 HEAVEN HELP ME   Deon Estus
6 THE LOOK   Roxette
7 SECOND CHANCE   Thirty Eight Special
8 REAL LOVE   Jody Watley
9 AFTER ALL (LOVE THEME FROM "CHANCES ARE")   Cher & Peter Cetera
10 FOREVER YOUR GIRL   Paula Abdul

May 6, 1989
1 LIKE A PRAYER   Madonna
2 I'LL BE THERE FOR YOU   Bon Jovi
3 REAL LOVE   Jody Watley
4 FUNKY COLD MEDINA   Tone Loc
5 FOREVER YOUR GIRL   Paula Abdul
6 SECOND CHANCE   Thirty Eight Special
7 AFTER ALL (LOVE THEME FROM "CHANCES ARE")   Cher & Peter Cetera
8 SOLDIER OF LOVE   Donny Osmond
9 ROOM TO MOVE   Animotion
10 SHE DRIVES ME CRAZY   Fine Young Cannibals

May 13, 1989
1 I'LL BE THERE FOR YOU   Bon Jovi
2 LIKE A PRAYER   Madonna
3 REAL LOVE   Jody Watley
4 FOREVER YOUR GIRL   Paula Abdul
5 SOLDIER OF LOVE   Donny Osmond
6 AFTER ALL (LOVE THEME FROM "CHANCES ARE")   Cher & Peter Cetera
7 SECOND CHANCE   Thirty Eight Special
8 ROCK ON (FROM "DREAM A LITTLE DREAM")   Michael Damian
9 PATIENCE   Guns N' Roses
10 WIND BENEATH MY WINGS (FROM "BEACHES")   Bette Midler

May 20, 1989
1 FOREVER YOUR GIRL   Paula Abdul
2 REAL LOVE   Jody Watley
3 I'LL BE THERE FOR YOU   Bon Jovi
4 SOLDIER OF LOVE   Donny Osmond
5 ROCK ON (FROM "DREAM A LITTLE DREAM")   Michael Damian

6 PATIENCE   Guns N' Roses
7 WIND BENEATH MY WINGS (FROM "BEACHES")   Bette Midler
8 AFTER ALL (LOVE THEME FROM "CHANCES ARE")   Cher & Peter Cetera
9 EVERY LITTLE STEP   Bobby Brown
10 LIKE A PRAYER   Madonna

May 27, 1989
1 FOREVER YOUR GIRL   Paula Abdul
2 REAL LOVE   Jody Watley
3 ROCK ON (FROM "DREAM A LITTLE DREAM")   Michael Damian
4 SOLDIER OF LOVE   Donny Osmond
5 PATIENCE   Guns N' Roses
6 WIND BENEATH MY WINGS (FROM "BEACHES")   Bette Midler
7 I'LL BE LOVING YOU (FOREVER)   New Kids On The Block
8 EVERY LITTLE STEP   Bobby Brown
9 I'LL BE THERE FOR YOU   Bon Jovi
10 CLOSE MY EYES FOREVER   Lita Ford (Duet With Ozzy Osbourne)

June 3, 1989
1 ROCK ON (FROM "DREAM A LITTLE DREAM")   Michael Damian
2 SOLDIER OF LOVE   Donny Osmond
3 WIND BENEATH MY WINGS (FROM "BEACHES")   Bette Midler
4 PATIENCE   Guns N' Roses
5 I'LL BE LOVING YOU (FOREVER)   New Kids On The Block
6 EVERY LITTLE STEP   Bobby Brown
7 REAL LOVE   Jody Watley
8 FOREVER YOUR GIRL   Paula Abdul
9 BUFFALO STANCE   Neneh Cherry
10 CLOSE MY EYES FOREVER   Lita Ford (Duet With Ozzy Osbourne)

June 10, 1989
1 WIND BENEATH MY WINGS (FROM "BEACHES")   Bette Midler
2 I'LL BE LOVING YOU (FOREVER)   New Kids On The Block
3 EVERY LITTLE STEP   Bobby Brown
4 ROCK ON (FROM "DREAM A LITTLE DREAM")   Michael Damian
5 BUFFALO STANCE   Neneh Cherry
6 PATIENCE   Guns N' Roses
7 SATISFIED   Richard Marx
8 SOLDIER OF LOVE   Donny Osmond
9 CLOSE MY EYES FOREVER   Lita Ford
10 WHERE ARE YOU NOW?   Jimmy Harnen With Synch

June 17, 1989
1 I'LL BE LOVING YOU (FOREVER)   New Kids On The Block
2 WIND BENEATH MY WINGS (FROM "BEACHES")   Bette Midler
3 EVERY LITTLE STEP   Bobby Brown
4 SATISFIED   Richard Marx
5 BUFFALO STANCE   Neneh Cherry
6 BABY DON'T FORGET MY NUMBER   Milli Vanilli
7 GOOD THING   Fine Young Cannibals
8 CLOSE MY EYES FOREVER   Lita Ford (Duet With Ozzy Osbourne)
9 THIS TIME I KNOW IT'S FOR REAL   Donna Summer
10 CRY   Waterfront

June 24, 1989
1. SATISFIED   Richard Marx
2. I'LL BE LOVING YOU (FOREVER)   New Kids On The Block
3. BUFFALO STANCE   Neneh Cherry
4. BABY DON'T FORGET MY NUMBER   Milli Vanilli
5. GOOD THING   Fine Young Cannibals
6. WIND BENEATH MY WINGS (FROM "BEACHES")   Bette Midler
7. THIS TIME I KNOW IT'S FOR REAL   Donna Summer
8. EVERY LITTLE STEP   Bobby Brown
9. MISS YOU LIKE CRAZY   Natalie Cole
10. CRY   Waterfront

July 1, 1989
1. BABY DON'T FORGET MY NUMBER   Milli Vanilli
2. GOOD THING   Fine Young Cannibals
3. SATISFIED   Richard Marx
4. BUFFALO STANCE   Neneh Cherry
5. IF YOU DON'T KNOW ME BY NOW   Simply Red
6. EXPRESS YOURSELF   Madonna
7. THIS TIME I KNOW IT'S FOR REAL   Donna Summer
8. I DROVE ALL NIGHT   Cyndi Lauper
9. MISS YOU LIKE CRAZY   Natalie Cole
10. I'LL BE LOVING YOU (FOREVER)   New Kids On The Block

July 8, 1989
1. GOOD THING   Fine Young Cannibals
2. BABY DON'T FORGET MY NUMBER   Milli Vanilli
3. IF YOU DON'T KNOW ME BY NOW   Simply Red
4. EXPRESS YOURSELF   Madonna
5. TOY SOLDIERS   Martika
6. I DROVE ALL NIGHT   Cyndi Lauper
7. MISS YOU LIKE CRAZY   Natalie Cole
8. SATISFIED   Richard Marx
9. BUFFALO STANCE   Neneh Cherry
10. WHAT YOU DON'T KNOW   Expose

July 15, 1989
1. IF YOU DON'T KNOW ME BY NOW   Simply Red
2. EXPRESS YOURSELF   Madonna
3. GOOD THING   Fine Young Cannibals
4. TOY SOLDIERS   Martika
5. BABY DON'T FORGET MY NUMBER   Milli Vanilli
6. BATDANCE (FROM "BATMAN")   Prince
7. MISS YOU LIKE CRAZY   Natalie Cole
8. WHAT YOU DON'T KNOW   Expose
9. THE DOCTOR   The Doobie Brothers
10. SO ALIVE   Love And Rockets

July 22, 1989
1. TOY SOLDIERS   Martika
2. EXPRESS YOURSELF   Madonna
3. IF YOU DON'T KNOW ME BY NOW   Simply Red
4. BATDANCE (FROM "BATMAN")   Prince
5. SO ALIVE   Love And Rockets
6. ON OUR OWN (FROM "GHOSTBUSTERS II")   Bobby Brown
7. GOOD THING   Fine Young Cannibals
8. WHAT YOU DON'T KNOW   Expose
9. LAY YOUR HANDS ON ME   Bon Jovi
10. BABY DON'T FORGET MY NUMBER   Milli Vanilli

July 29, 1989
1. TOY SOLDIERS   Martika

Simply Red
Simply the #1 song on July 15—"If You Don't Know Me By Now."

2 BATDANCE (FROM "BATMAN") Prince
3 EXPRESS YOURSELF Madonna
4 SO ALIVE Love And Rockets
5 ON OUR OWN (FROM "GHOSTBUSTERS II") Bobby Brown
6 IF YOU DON'T KNOW ME BY NOW Simply Red
7 LAY YOUR HANDS ON ME Bon Jovi
8 ONCE BITTEN TWICE SHY Great White
9 I LIKE IT Dino
10 RIGHT HERE WAITING Richard Marx

August 5, 1989
1 BATDANCE (FROM "BATMAN") Prince
2 ON OUR OWN (FROM "GHOSTBUSTERS II") Bobby Brown
3 SO ALIVE Love And Rockets
4 RIGHT HERE WAITING Richard Marx
5 TOY SOLDIERS Martika
6 ONCE BITTEN TWICE SHY Great White
7 LAY YOUR HANDS ON ME Bon Jovi
8 I LIKE IT Dino
9 COLD HEARTED Paula Abdul
10 IF YOU DON'T KNOW ME BY NOW Simply Red

August 12, 1989
1 RIGHT HERE WAITING Richard Marx
2 ON OUR OWN (FROM "GHOSTBUSTERS II") Bobby Brown
3 BATDANCE (FROM "BATMAN") Prince
4 SO ALIVE Love And Rockets
5 ONCE BITTEN TWICE SHY Great White
6 COLD HEARTED Paula Abdul
7 I LIKE IT Dino
8 LAY YOUR HANDS ON ME Bon Jovi
9 DON'T WANNA LOSE YOU Gloria Estefan
10 TOY SOLDIERS Martika

August 19, 1989
1 RIGHT HERE WAITING Richard Marx
2 ON OUR OWN (FROM "GHOSTBUSTERS II") Bobby Brown
3 COLD HEARTED Paula Abdul
4 DON'T WANNA LOSE YOU Gloria Estefan
5 ONCE BITTEN TWICE SHY Great White
6 HANGIN' TOUGH New Kids On The Block
7 I LIKE IT Dino
8 BATDANCE (FROM "BATMAN") Prince
9 SECRET RENDEZVOUS Karyn White
10 SO ALIVE Love And Rockets

August 26, 1989
1 RIGHT HERE WAITING Richard Marx
2 COLD HEARTED Paula Abdul
3 HANGIN' TOUGH New Kids On The Block
4 DON'T WANNA LOSE YOU Gloria Estefan
5 ON OUR OWN (FROM "GHOSTBUSTERS II") Bobby Brown
6 SECRET RENDEZVOUS Karyn White
7 ONCE BITTEN TWICE SHY Great White
8 THE END OF THE INNOCENCE Don Henley
9 FRIENDS Jody Watley With Eric B. & Rakim
10 ANGEL EYES The Jeff Healey Band

September 2, 1989
1 COLD HEARTED Paula Abdul
2 RIGHT HERE WAITING Richard Marx
3 HANGIN' TOUGH New Kids On The Block

4 DON'T WANNA LOSE YOU Gloria Estefan
5 ANGEL EYES The Jeff Healey Band
6 HEAVEN Warrant
7 SECRET RENDEZVOUS Karyn White
8 SHOWER ME WITH YOUR LOVE Surface
9 THE END OF THE INNOCENCE Don Henley
10 FRIENDS Jody Watley With Eric B. & Rakim

September 9, 1989
1 HANGIN' TOUGH New Kids On The Block
2 COLD HEARTED Paula Abdul
3 DON'T WANNA LOSE YOU Gloria Estefan
4 HEAVEN Warrant
5 RIGHT HERE WAITING Richard Marx
6 SHOWER ME WITH YOUR LOVE Surface
7 GIRL I'M GONNA MISS YOU Milli Vanilli
8 ANGEL EYES The Jeff Healey Band
9 IF I COULD TURN BACK TIME Cher
10 18 AND LIFE Skid Row

September 16, 1989
1 DON'T WANNA LOSE YOU Gloria Estefan
2 GIRL I'M GONNA MISS YOU Milli Vanilli
3 HEAVEN Warrant
4 HANGIN' TOUGH New Kids On The Block
5 SHOWER ME WITH YOUR LOVE Surface
6 COLD HEARTED Paula Abdul
7 IF I COULD TURN BACK TIME Cher
8 18 AND LIFE Skid Row
9 ANGEL EYES The Jeff Healey Band
10 CHERISH Madonna

September 23, 1989
1 GIRL I'M GONNA MISS YOU Milli Vanilli
2 HEAVEN Warrant
3 IF I COULD TURN BACK TIME Cher
4 18 AND LIFE Skid Row
5 CHERISH Madonna
6 DON'T WANNA LOSE YOU Gloria Estefan
7 SHOWER ME WITH YOUR LOVE Surface
8 MISS YOU MUCH Janet Jackson
9 HANGIN' TOUGH New Kids On The Block
10 COLD HEARTED Paula Abdul

September 30, 1989
1 GIRL I'M GONNA MISS YOU Milli Vanilli
2 HEAVEN Warrant
3 IF I COULD TURN BACK TIME Cher
4 CHERISH Madonna
5 MISS YOU MUCH Janet Jackson
6 18 AND LIFE Skid Row
7 ONE Bee Gees
8 KISSES ON THE WIND Neneh Cherry
9 DON'T WANNA LOSE YOU Gloria Estefan
10 LOVE SONG The Cure

October 7, 1989
1 MISS YOU MUCH Janet Jackson
2 CHERISH Madonna
3 GIRL I'M GONNA MISS YOU Milli Vanilli
4 HEAVEN Warrant
5 IF I COULD TURN BACK TIME Cher
6 MIXED EMOTIONS Rolling Stones
7 LOVE SONG The Cure
8 18 AND LIFE Skid Row
9 BUST A MOVE Young M.C.
10 IT'S NO CRIME Babyface

October 14, 1989
1 MISS YOU MUCH   Janet Jackson
2 CHERISH   Madonna
3 GIRL I'M GONNA MISS YOU   Milli Vanilli
4 LOVE SONG   The Cure
5 MIXED EMOTIONS   Rolling Stones
6 SOWING THE SEEDS OF LOVE   Tears For Fears
7 BUST A MOVE   Young M.C.
8 HEAVEN   Warrant
9 LISTEN TO YOUR HEART   Roxette
10 IT'S NO CRIME   Babyface

October 21, 1989
1 MISS YOU MUCH   Janet Jackson
2 LOVE SONG   The Cure
3 SOWING THE SEEDS OF LOVE   Tears For Fears
4 LISTEN TO YOUR HEART   Roxette
5 MIXED EMOTIONS   Rolling Stones
6 COVER GIRL   New Kids On The Block
7 LOVE IN AN ELEVATOR   Aerosmith
8 IT'S NO CRIME   Babyface
9 BUST A MOVE   Young M.C.
10 WHEN I LOOKED AT HIM   Expose

October 28, 1989
1 MISS YOU MUCH   Janet Jackson
2 SOWING THE SEEDS OF LOVE   Tears For Fears
3 LISTEN TO YOUR HEART   Roxette
4 COVER GIRL   New Kids On The Block
5 LOVE IN AN ELEVATOR   Aerosmith
6 DR. FEELGOOD   Motley Crue
7 IT'S NO CRIME   Babyface
8 BUST A MOVE   Young M.C.
9 WHEN I SEE YOU SMILE   Bad English
10 ROCK WIT'CHA   Bobby Brown

November 4, 1989
1 LISTEN TO YOUR HEART   Roxette
2 COVER GIRL   New Kids On The Block
3 MISS YOU MUCH   Janet Jackson
4 SOWING THE SEEDS OF LOVE   Tears For Fears
5 WHEN I SEE YOU SMILE   Bad English
6 LOVE IN AN ELEVATOR   Aerosmith
7 ROCK WIT'CHA   Bobby Brown
8 DR. FEELGOOD   Motley Crue
9 (IT'S JUST) THE WAY THAT YOU LOVE ME   Paula Abdul
10 LOVE SHACK   The B-52's

November 11, 1989
1 WHEN I SEE YOU SMILE   Bad English
2 LISTEN TO YOUR HEART   Roxette
3 COVER GIRL   New Kids On The Block
4 BLAME IT ON THE RAIN   Milli Vanilli
5 (IT'S JUST) THE WAY THAT YOU LOVE ME   Paula Abdul
6 LOVE SHACK   The B-52's
7 MISS YOU MUCH   Janet Jackson
8 SOWING THE SEEDS OF LOVE   Tears For Fears
9 DIDN'T I (BLOW YOUR MIND)   New Kids On The Block
10 ROCK WIT'CHA   Bobby Brown

November 18, 1989
1 WHEN I SEE YOU SMILE   Bad English
2 BLAME IT ON THE RAIN   Milli Vanilli
3 LOVE SHACK   The B-52's
4 (IT'S JUST) THE WAY THAT YOU LOVE ME   Paula Abdul
5 LISTEN TO YOUR HEART   Roxette
6 WE DIDN'T START THE FIRE   Billy Joel
7 ANGELIA   Richard Marx
8 DIDN'T I (BLOW YOUR MIND)   New Kids On The Block
9 POISON   Alice Cooper
10 BACK TO LIFE   Soul II Soul (Featuring Caron Wheeler)

November 25, 1989
1 BLAME IT ON THE RAIN   Milli Vanilli
2 WHEN I SEE YOU SMILE   Bad English
3 LOVE SHACK   The B-52's
4 (IT'S JUST) THE WAY THAT YOU LOVE ME   Paula Abdul
5 WE DIDN'T START THE FIRE   Billy Joel
6 ANGELIA   Richard Marx
7 POISON   Alice Cooper
8 BACK TO LIFE   Soul II Soul (Featuring Caron Wheeler)
9 DON'T KNOW MUCH   Linda Ronstadt (Featuring Aaron Neville)
10 ANOTHER DAY IN PARADISE   Phil Collins

December 9, 1989
1 WE DIDN'T START THE FIRE   Billy Joel
2 ANOTHER DAY IN PARADISE   Phil Collins
3 BLAME IT ON THE RAIN   Milli Vanilli
4 (IT'S JUST) THE WAY THAT YOU LOVE ME   Paula Abdul
5 DON'T KNOW MUCH   Linda Ronstadt (Featuring Aaron Neville)
6 BACK TO LIFE   Soul II Soul (Featuring Caron Wheeler)
7 ANGELIA   Richard Marx
8 WITH EVERY BEAT OF MY HEART   Taylor Dayne
9 LOVE SHACK   The B-52's
10 PUMP UP THE JAM   Technotronic Featuring Felly

December 16, 1989
1 WE DIDN'T START THE FIRE   Billy Joel
2 ANOTHER DAY IN PARADISE   Phil Collins
3 DON'T KNOW MUCH   Linda Ronstadt (Featuring Aaron Neville)
4 BACK TO LIFE   Soul II Soul (Featuring Caron Wheeler)
5 WITH EVERY BEAT OF MY HEART   Taylor Dayne
6 BLAME IT ON THE RAIN   Milli Vanilli
7 PUMP UP THE JAM   Technotronic Featuring Felly
8 RHYTHM NATION   Janet Jackson
9 LIVING IN SIN   Bon Jovi
10 JUST LIKE JESSE JAMES   Cher

December 23, 1989
1 ANOTHER DAY IN PARADISE   Phil Collins
2 DON'T KNOW MUCH   Linda Ronstadt (Featuring Aaron Neville)
3 WE DIDN'T START THE FIRE   Billy Joel
4 RHYTHM NATION   Janet Jackson
5 WITH EVERY BEAT OF MY HEART   Taylor Dayne
6 BACK TO LIFE   Soul II Soul (Featuring Caron Wheeler)
7 PUMP UP THE JAM   Technotronic Featuring Felly
8 JUST LIKE JESSE JAMES   Cher
9 THIS ONE'S FOR THE CHILDREN   New Kids On The Block
10 LIVING IN SIN   Bon Jovi

The Nineties

January 6, 1990
1. ANOTHER DAY IN PARADISE   Phil Collins
2. RHYTHM NATION   Janet Jackson
3. DON'T KNOW MUCH   Linda Ronstadt (Featuring Aaron Neville)
4. PUMP UP THE JAM   Technotronic Featuring Felly
5. WITH EVERY BEAT OF MY HEART   Taylor Dayne
6. HOW AM I SUPPOSED TO LIVE WITHOUT YOU   Michael Bolton
7. THIS ONE'S FOR THE CHILDREN   New Kids On The Block
8. JUST LIKE JESSE JAMES   Cher
9. WE DIDN'T START THE FIRE   Billy Joel
10. EVERYTHING   Jody Watley

January 13, 1990
1. ANOTHER DAY IN PARADISE   Phil Collins
2. RHYTHM NATION   Janet Jackson
3. PUMP UP THE JAM   Technotronic Featuring Felly
4. HOW AM I SUPPOSED TO LIVE WITHOUT YOU   Michael Bolton
5. DON'T KNOW MUCH   Linda Ronstadt (Featuring Aaron Neville)
6. EVERYTHING   Jody Watley
7. THIS ONE'S FOR THE CHILDREN   New Kids On The Block
8. JUST LIKE JESSE JAMES   Cher
9. WITH EVERY BEAT OF MY HEART   Taylor Dayne
10. JUST BETWEEN YOU AND ME   Lou Gramm

January 20, 1990
1. HOW AM I SUPPOSED TO LIVE WITHOUT YOU   Michael Bolton
2. PUMP UP THE JAM   Technotronic Featuring Felly
3. ANOTHER DAY IN PARADISE   Phil Collins
4. EVERYTHING   Jody Watley
5. DOWNTOWN TRAIN   Rod Stewart
6. RHYTHM NATION   Janet Jackson
7. JUST BETWEEN YOU AND ME   Lou Gramm
8. FREE FALLIN'   Tom Petty
9. TWO TO MAKE IT RIGHT   Seduction
10. LOVE SONG   Tesla

January 27, 1990
1. HOW AM I SUPPOSED TO LIVE WITHOUT YOU   Michael Bolton
2. PUMP UP THE JAM   Technotronic Featuring Felly
3. DOWNTOWN TRAIN   Rod Stewart
4. EVERYTHING   Jody Watley
5. TWO TO MAKE IT RIGHT   Seduction
6. JUST BETWEEN YOU AND ME   Lou Gramm
7. FREE FALLIN'   Tom Petty
8. OPPOSITES ATTRACT   Paula Abdul (Duet With The Wild Pair)
9. I REMEMBER YOU   Skid Row
10. ANOTHER DAY IN PARADISE   Phil Collins

February 3, 1990
1. HOW AM I SUPPOSED TO LIVE WITHOUT YOU   Michael Bolton
2. OPPOSITES ATTRACT   Paula Abdul (Duet With The Wild Pair)
3. DOWNTOWN TRAIN   Rod Stewart
4. TWO TO MAKE IT RIGHT   Seduction
5. JANIE'S GOT A GUN   Aerosmith
6. I REMEMBER YOU   Skid Row
7. FREE FALLIN'   Tom Petty
8. PUMP UP THE JAM   Technotronic Featuring Felly
9. JUST BETWEEN YOU AND ME   Lou Gramm
10. EVERYTHING   Jody Watley

February 10, 1990
1. OPPOSITES ATTRACT   Paula Abdul (Duet With The Wild Pair)
2. TWO TO MAKE IT RIGHT   Seduction
3. DOWNTOWN TRAIN   Rod Stewart
4. JANIE'S GOT A GUN   Aerosmith
5. HOW AM I SUPPOSED TO LIVE WITHOUT YOU   Michael Bolton
6. WHAT KIND OF MAN WOULD I BE?   Chicago
7. DANGEROUS   Roxette
8. I REMEMBER YOU   Skid Row
9. ESCAPADE   Janet Jackson
10. ALL OR NOTHING   Milli Vanilli

February 17, 1990
1. OPPOSITES ATTRACT   Paula Abdul (Duet With The Wild Pair)
2. TWO TO MAKE IT RIGHT   Seduction
3. ESCAPADE   Janet Jackson
4. DANGEROUS   Roxette
5. JANIE'S GOT A GUN   Aerosmith
6. WHAT KIND OF MAN WOULD I BE?   Chicago
7. ALL OR NOTHING   Milli Vanilli
8. DOWNTOWN TRAIN   Rod Stewart
9. TELL ME WHY   Expose
10. WE CAN'T GO WRONG   The Cover Girls

February 24, 1990
1. OPPOSITES ATTRACT   Paula Abdul (Duet With The Wild Pair)
2. ESCAPADE   Janet Jackson
3. DANGEROUS   Roxette
4. ALL OR NOTHING   Milli Vanilli
5. WHAT KIND OF MAN WOULD I BE?   Chicago
6. ROAM   The B-52's
7. TWO TO MAKE IT RIGHT   Seduction
8. HERE WE ARE   Gloria Estefan
9. WE CAN'T GO WRONG   The Cover Girls
10. PRICE OF LOVE   Bad English

March 3, 1990
1. ESCAPADE   Janet Jackson
2. DANGEROUS   Roxette
3. OPPOSITES ATTRACT   Paula Abdul (Duet With The Wild Pair)
4. ROAM   The B-52's
5. ALL OR NOTHING   Milli Vanilli
6. HERE WE ARE   Gloria Estefan
7. PRICE OF LOVE   Bad English
8. WE CAN'T GO WRONG   The Cover Girls

Stevie Ray Vaughan, 1954-1990
Blues guitarist Stevie Ray Vaughan and three other musicians were killed in a plane crash in 1990,
an event echoing the loss of Buddy Holly, Ritchie Valens and J. P. Richardson (The Big Bopper) in February of 1959.

The day the music died—again....

Motley Crue
One of the few heavy metal bands to enter the Top 10, ``Without You'' is with us April 21-28.

9 BLACK VELVET   Alannah Myles
10 NO MORE LIES   Michel'le

March 10, 1990
1 ESCAPADE   Janet Jackson
2 DANGEROUS   Roxette
3 ROAM   The B-52's
4 BLACK VELVET   Alannah Myles
5 PRICE OF LOVE   Bad English
6 OPPOSITES ATTRACT   Paula Abdul (Duet With The Wild Pair)
7 NO MORE LIES   Michel'le
8 HERE WE ARE   Gloria Estefan
9 I GO TO EXTREMES   Billy Joel
10 LOVE WILL LEAD YOU BACK   Taylor Dayne

March 17, 1990
1 ESCAPADE   Janet Jackson
2 BLACK VELVET   Alannah Myles
3 ROAM   The B-52's
4 LOVE WILL LEAD YOU BACK   Taylor Dayne
5 PRICE OF LOVE   Bad English
6 I GO TO EXTREMES   Billy Joel
7 NO MORE LIES   Michel'le
8 I WISH IT WOULD RAIN DOWN   Phil Collins
9 JUST A FRIEND   Biz Markie
10 C'MON AND GET MY LOVE   D-Mob Introducing Cathy Dennis

March 24, 1990
1 BLACK VELVET   Alannah Myles
2 LOVE WILL LEAD YOU BACK   Taylor Dayne

3 ESCAPADE   Janet Jackson
4 ROAM   The B-52's
5 I WISH IT WOULD RAIN DOWN   Phil Collins
6 I'LL BE YOUR EVERYTHING   Tommy Page
7 ALL AROUND THE WORLD   Lisa Stansfield
8 I GO TO EXTREMES   Billy Joel
9 KEEP IT TOGETHER   Madonna
10 GET UP! (BEFORE THE NIGHT IS OVER)   Technotronic

March 31, 1990
1 BLACK VELVET   Alannah Myles
2 LOVE WILL LEAD YOU BACK   Taylor Dayne
3 I WISH IT WOULD RAIN DOWN   Phil Collins
4 I'LL BE YOUR EVERYTHING   Tommy Page
5 ALL AROUND THE WORLD   Lisa Stansfield
6 DON'T WANNA FALL IN LOVE   Jane Child
7 ESCAPADE   Janet Jackson
8 KEEP IT TOGETHER   Madonna
9 GET UP! (BEFORE THE NIGHT IS OVER)   Technotronic
10 HERE AND NOW   Luther Vandross

April 7, 1990
1 LOVE WILL LEAD YOU BACK   Taylor Dayne
2 I'LL BE YOUR EVERYTHING   Tommy Page
3 ALL AROUND THE WORLD   Lisa Stansfield
4 I WISH IT WOULD RAIN DOWN   Phil Collins
5 BLACK VELVET   Alannah Myles
6 DON'T WANNA FALL IN LOVE   Jane Child
7 GET UP! (BEFORE THE NIGHT IS OVER)   Technotronic
8 HERE AND NOW   Luther Vandross
9 NOTHING COMPARES 2 U   Sinead O'Connor
10 FOREVER   Kiss

April 14, 1990
1 I'LL BE YOUR EVERYTHING   Tommy Page
2 DON'T WANNA FALL IN LOVE   Jane Child
3 ALL AROUND THE WORLD   Lisa Stansfield
4 NOTHING COMPARES 2 U   Sinead O'Connor
5 LOVE WILL LEAD YOU BACK   Taylor Dayne
6 I WANNA BE RICH   Calloway
7 HERE AND NOW   Luther Vandross
8 GET UP! (BEFORE THE NIGHT IS OVER)   Technotronic
9 FOREVER   Kiss
10 BLACK VELVET   Alannah Myles

April 21, 1990
1 NOTHING COMPARES 2 U   Sinead O'Connor
2 DON'T WANNA FALL IN LOVE   Jane Child
3 ALL AROUND THE WORLD   Lisa Stansfield
4 I WANNA BE RICH   Calloway
5 I'LL BE YOUR EVERYTHING   Tommy Page
6 HERE AND NOW   Luther Vandross
7 HOW CAN WE BE LOVERS   Michael Bolton
8 FOREVER   Kiss
9 WITHOUT YOU   Motley Crue
10 WHOLE WIDE WORLD (FROM "TRUE LOVE")   A'me Lorain

April 28, 1990
1 NOTHING COMPARES 2 U   Sinead O'Connor
2 DON'T WANNA FALL IN LOVE   Jane Child
3 I WANNA BE RICH   Calloway
4 ALL AROUND THE WORLD   Lisa Stansfield
5 HOW CAN WE BE LOVERS   Michael Bolton
6 WHIP APPEAL   Babyface
7 HERE AND NOW   Luther Vandross
8 WITHOUT YOU   Motley Crue
9 WHOLE WIDE WORLD (FROM "TRUE LOVE")   A'me Lorain
10 ALL I WANNA DO IS MAKE LOVE TO YOU   Heart

May 5, 1990
1 NOTHING COMPARES 2 U   Sinead O'Connor
2 I WANNA BE RICH   Calloway
3 HOW CAN WE BE LOVERS   Michael Bolton
4 VOGUE   Madonna
5 ALL I WANNA DO IS MAKE LOVE TO YOU   Heart
6 DON'T WANNA FALL IN LOVE   Jane Child
7 WHIP APPEAL   Babyface
8 ALL AROUND THE WORLD   Lisa Stansfield
9 WHAT IT TAKES   Aerosmith
10 ALRIGHT   Janet Jackson

May 12, 1990
1 NOTHING COMPARES 2 U   Sinead O'Connor
2 VOGUE   Madonna
3 I WANNA BE RICH   Calloway
4 ALL I WANNA DO IS MAKE LOVE TO YOU   Heart
5 HOW CAN WE BE LOVERS   Michael Bolton
6 HOLD ON   Wilson Phillips
7 SENDING ALL MY LOVE   Linear
8 ALRIGHT   Janet Jackson
9 WHAT IT TAKES   Aerosmith
10 POISON   Bell Biv Devoe

May 19, 1990
1 VOGUE   Madonna
2 NOTHING COMPARES 2 U   Sinead O'Connor
3 ALL I WANNA DO IS MAKE LOVE TO YOU   Heart
4 HOLD ON   Wilson Phillips
5 SENDING ALL MY LOVE   Linear
6 ALRIGHT   Janet Jackson
7 I WANNA BE RICH   Calloway
8 POISON   Bell Biv Devoe
9 IT MUST HAVE BEEN LOVE (FROM "PRETTY WOMAN")   Roxette
10 WHAT IT TAKES   Aerosmith

May 26, 1990
1 VOGUE   Madonna
2 ALL I WANNA DO IS MAKE LOVE TO YOU   Heart
3 NOTHING COMPARES 2 U   Sinead O'Connor
4 HOLD ON   Wilson Phillips
5 ALRIGHT   Janet Jackson
6 POISON   Bell Biv Devoe
7 SENDING ALL MY LOVE   Linear
8 IT MUST HAVE BEEN LOVE (FROM "PRETTY WOMAN")   Roxette
9 U CAN'T TOUCH THIS   M.C. Hammer
10 THIS OLD HEART OF MINE   Rod Stewart With Ronald Isley

June 2, 1990
1 VOGUE   Madonna
2 ALL I WANNA DO IS MAKE LOVE TO YOU   Heart
3 HOLD ON   Wilson Phillips
4 ALRIGHT   Janet Jackson
5 POISON   Bell Biv Devoe
6 IT MUST HAVE BEEN LOVE (FROM "PRETTY WOMAN")   Roxette
7 NOTHING COMPARES 2 U   Sinead O'Connor
8 SENDING ALL MY LOVE   Linear
9 U CAN'T TOUCH THIS   M.C. Hammer
10 OOH LA LA (I CAN'T GET OVER YOU)   Perfect Gentlemen

Hammer
``U Can't Touch This'' feels its way into the Top 10 (May 26).

June 9, 1990
1 HOLD ON   Wilson Phillips
2 VOGUE   Madonna
3 POISON   Bell Biv Devoe
4 ALL I WANNA DO IS MAKE LOVE TO YOU   Heart
5 IT MUST HAVE BEEN LOVE (FROM "PRETTY WOMAN")   Roxette
6 ALRIGHT   Janet Jackson
7 SENDING ALL MY LOVE   Linear
8 STEP BY STEP   New Kids On The Block
9 U CAN'T TOUCH THIS   M.C. Hammer
10 NOTHING COMPARES 2 U   Sinead O'Connor

June 16, 1990
1 IT MUST HAVE BEEN LOVE (FROM "PRETTY WOMAN")   Roxette
2 HOLD ON   Wilson Phillips
3 POISON   Bell Biv Devoe
4 STEP BY STEP   New Kids On The Block
5 VOGUE   Madonna
6 ALL I WANNA DO IS MAKE LOVE TO YOU   Heart
7 ALRIGHT   Janet Jackson
8 U CAN'T TOUCH THIS   M.C. Hammer
9 READY OR NOT   After 7
10 DO YOU REMEMBER?   Phil Collins

June 23, 1990
1 IT MUST HAVE BEEN LOVE (FROM "PRETTY WOMAN")   Roxette
2 STEP BY STEP   New Kids On The Block
3 POISON   Bell Biv Devoe
4 HOLD ON   Wilson Phillips
5 DO YOU REMEMBER?   Phil Collins
6 VOGUE   Madonna
7 READY OR NOT   After 7
8 HOLD ON   En Vogue
9 U CAN'T TOUCH THIS   M.C. Hammer
10 I'LL BE YOUR SHELTER   Taylor Dayne

June 30, 1990
1 STEP BY STEP   New Kids On The Block
2 IT MUST HAVE BEEN LOVE (FROM "PRETTY WOMAN")   Roxette
3 POISON   Bell Biv Devoe
4 DO YOU REMEMBER?   Phil Collins
5 HOLD ON   Wilson Phillips
6 HOLD ON   En Vogue
7 READY OR NOT   After 7
8 I'LL BE YOUR SHELTER   Taylor Dayne
9 SHE AIN'T WORTH IT   Glenn Medeiros Featuring Bobby Brown
10 CRADLE OF LOVE (FROM "FORD FAIRLANE")   Billy Idol

July 7, 1990
1 STEP BY STEP   New Kids On The Block
2 IT MUST HAVE BEEN LOVE (FROM "PRETTY WOMAN")   Roxette
3 SHE AIN'T WORTH IT   Glenn Medeiros Featuring Bobby Brown
4 POISON   Bell Biv Devoe
5 HOLD ON   En Vogue
6 DO YOU REMEMBER?   Phil Collins
7 I'LL BE YOUR SHELTER   Taylor Dayne
8 CRADLE OF LOVE (FROM "FORD FAIRLANE")   Billy Idol
9 HOLD ON   Wilson Phillips
10 RUB YOU THE RIGHT WAY   Johnny Gill

July 14, 1990
1 STEP BY STEP   New Kids On The Block
2 SHE AIN'T WORTH IT   Glenn Medeiros Featuring Bobby Brown
3 HOLD ON   En Vogue
4 I'LL BE YOUR SHELTER   Taylor Dayne
5 CRADLE OF LOVE (FROM "FORD FAIRLANE")   Billy Idol
6 IT MUST HAVE BEEN LOVE (FROM "PRETTY WOMAN")   Roxette
7 RUB YOU THE RIGHT WAY   Johnny Gill
8 ENJOY THE SILENCE   Depeche Mode
9 THE POWER   Snap
10 POISON   Bell Biv Devoe

July 21, 1990
1 SHE AIN'T WORTH IT   Glenn Medeiros Featuring Bobby Brown
2 HOLD ON   En Vogue
3 CRADLE OF LOVE (FROM "FORD FAIRLANE")   Billy Idol
4 RUB YOU THE RIGHT WAY   Johnny Gill
5 VISION OF LOVE   Mariah Carey
6 STEP BY STEP   New Kids On The Block
7 THE POWER   Snap
8 GIRLS NITE OUT   Tyler Collins
9 ENJOY THE SILENCE   Depeche Mode
10 WHEN I'M BACK ON MY FEET AGAIN   Michael Bolton

July 28, 1990
1 SHE AIN'T WORTH IT   Glenn Medeiros Featuring Bobby Brown
2 VISION OF LOVE   Mariah Carey
3 CRADLE OF LOVE (FROM "FORD FAIRLANE")   Billy Idol
4 RUB YOU THE RIGHT WAY   Johnny Gill
5 HOLD ON   En Vogue
6 THE POWER   Snap
7 GIRLS NITE OUT   Tyler Collins
8 WHEN I'M BACK ON MY FEET AGAIN   Michael Bolton
9 ENJOY THE SILENCE   Depeche Mode
10 HANKY PANKY   Madonna

August 4, 1990
1 VISION OF LOVE   Mariah Carey
2 CRADLE OF LOVE (FROM "FORD FAIRLANE")   Billy Idol
3 RUB YOU THE RIGHT WAY   Johnny Gill
4 THE POWER   Snap
5 SHE AIN'T WORTH IT   Glenn Medeiros Featuring Bobby Brown
6 GIRLS NITE OUT   Tyler Collins
7 WHEN I'M BACK ON MY FEET AGAIN   Michael Bolton
8 IF WISHES CAME TRUE   Sweet Sensation
9 HOLD ON   En Vogue
10 UNSKINNY BOP   Poison

August 11, 1990
1 VISION OF LOVE   Mariah Carey
2 THE POWER   Snap
3 RUB YOU THE RIGHT WAY   Johnny Gill
4 CRADLE OF LOVE (FROM "FORD FAIRLANE")   Billy Idol
5 IF WISHES CAME TRUE   Sweet Sensation
6 COME BACK TO ME   Janet Jackson
7 UNSKINNY BOP   Poison
8 KING OF WISHFUL THINKING (FROM "PRETTY WOMAN")   Go West
9 SHE AIN'T WORTH IT   Glenn Medeiros Featuring Bobby Brown
10 DO ME!   Bell Biv Devoe

August 18, 1990
1 VISION OF LOVE   Mariah Carey
2 COME BACK TO ME   Janet Jackson
3 IF WISHES CAME TRUE   Sweet Sensation
4 THE POWER   Snap
5 UNSKINNY BOP   Poison
6 BLAZE OF GLORY (FROM "YOUNG GUNS II")   Jon Bon Jovi
7 DO ME!   Bell Biv Devoe
8 HAVE YOU SEEN HER   M.C. Hammer
9 CRADLE OF LOVE (FROM "FORD FAIRLANE")   Billy Idol
10 KING OF WISHFUL THINKING (FROM "PRETTY WOMAN")   Go West

August 25, 1990
1 VISION OF LOVE   Mariah Carey
2 COME BACK TO ME   Janet Jackson
3 IF WISHES CAME TRUE   Sweet Sensation
4 UNSKINNY BOP   Poison
5 BLAZE OF GLORY (FROM "YOUNG GUNS II")   Jon Bon Jovi
6 RELEASE ME   Wilson Phillips
7 DO ME!   Bell Biv Devoe
8 HAVE YOU SEEN HER   M.C. Hammer
9 JERK OUT   The Time
10 EPIC   Faith No More

September 1, 1990
1 IF WISHES CAME TRUE   Sweet Sensation
2 BLAZE OF GLORY (FROM "YOUNG GUNS II")   Jon Bon Jovi
3 UNSKINNY BOP   Poison
4 RELEASE ME   Wilson Phillips
5 DO ME!   Bell Biv Devoe
6 COME BACK TO ME   Janet Jackson
7 HAVE YOU SEEN HER   M.C. Hammer
8 VISION OF LOVE   Mariah Carey
9 JERK OUT   The Time
10 TONIGHT   New Kids On The Block

September 8, 1990
1 BLAZE OF GLORY (FROM "YOUNG GUNS II")   Jon Bon Jovi
2 RELEASE ME   Wilson Phillips
3 DO ME!   Bell Biv Devoe
4 UNSKINNY BOP   Poison
5 IF WISHES CAME TRUE   Sweet Sensation
6 HAVE YOU SEEN HER   M.C. Hammer
7 TONIGHT   New Kids On The Block
8 (CAN'T LIVE WITHOUT YOUR) LOVE AND AFFECTION   Nelson
9 EPIC   Faith No More
10 COME BACK TO ME   Janet Jackson

September 15, 1990
1 RELEASE ME   Wilson Phillips
2 BLAZE OF GLORY (FROM "YOUNG GUNS II")   Jon Bon Jovi
3 DO ME!   Bell Biv Devoe
4 HAVE YOU SEEN HER   M.C. Hammer
5 UNSKINNY BOP   Poison
6 (CAN'T LIVE WITHOUT YOUR) LOVE AND AFFECTION   Nelson
7 THIEVES IN THE TEMPLE   Prince
8 IF WISHES CAME TRUE   Sweet Sensation
9 TONIGHT   New Kids On The Block
10 CLOSE TO YOU   Maxi Priest

September 22, 1990
1 RELEASE ME   Wilson Phillips
2 BLAZE OF GLORY (FROM "YOUNG GUNS II")   Jon Bon Jovi
3 DO ME!   Bell Biv Devoe
4 (CAN'T LIVE WITHOUT YOUR) LOVE AND AFFECTION   Nelson
5 CLOSE TO YOU   Maxi Priest
6 THIEVES IN THE TEMPLE   Prince
7 SOMETHING HAPPENED ON THE WAY TO HEAVEN   Phil Collins
8 PRAYING FOR TIME   George Michael
9 HAVE YOU SEEN HER   M.C. Hammer
10 UNSKINNY BOP   Poison

September 29, 1990
1 (CAN'T LIVE WITHOUT YOUR) LOVE AND AFFECTION   Nelson
2 CLOSE TO YOU   Maxi Priest
3 RELEASE ME   Wilson Phillips
4 BLAZE OF GLORY (FROM "YOUNG GUNS II")   Jon Bon Jovi
5 PRAYING FOR TIME   George Michael
6 SOMETHING HAPPENED ON THE WAY TO HEAVEN   Phil Collins
7 DO ME!   Bell Biv Devoe
8 THIEVES IN THE TEMPLE   Prince
9 OH GIRL   Paul Young
10 MY, MY, MY   Johnny Gill

October 6, 1990
1 CLOSE TO YOU   Maxi Priest
2 PRAYING FOR TIME   George Michael
3 (CAN'T LIVE WITHOUT YOUR) LOVE AND AFFECTION   Nelson
4 SOMETHING HAPPENED ON THE WAY TO HEAVEN   Phil Collins
5 I DON'T HAVE THE HEART   James Ingram
6 BLAZE OF GLORY (FROM "YOUNG GUNS II")   Jon Bon Jovi
7 ICE ICE BABY   Vanilla Ice
8 OH GIRL   Paul Young
9 DO ME!   Bell Biv Devoe
10 RELEASE ME   Wilson Phillips

October 13, 1990
1 PRAYING FOR TIME   George Michael
2 CLOSE TO YOU   Maxi Priest
3 I DON'T HAVE THE HEART   James Ingram
4 ICE ICE BABY   Vanilla Ice
5 BLACK CAT   Janet Jackson
6 (CAN'T LIVE WITHOUT YOUR) LOVE AND AFFECTION   Nelson
7 ROMEO   Dino
8 SOMETHING HAPPENED ON THE WAY TO HEAVEN   Phil Collins
9 EVERYBODY EVERYBODY   Black Box
10 OH GIRL   Paul Young

October 20, 1990
1 I DON'T HAVE THE HEART   James Ingram
2 BLACK CAT   Janet Jackson
3 PRAYING FOR TIME   George Michael
4 ICE ICE BABY   Vanilla Ice
5 CLOSE TO YOU   Maxi Priest
6 ROMEO   Dino
7 GIVING YOU THE BENEFIT   Pebbles

8 EVERYBODY EVERYBODY   Black Box
9 CAN'T STOP   After 7
10 (CAN'T LIVE WITHOUT YOUR) LOVE AND AFFECTION
    Nelson

October 29, 1990
1 BLACK CAT   Janet Jackson
2 I DON'T HAVE THE HEART   James Ingram
3 ICE ICE BABY   Vanilla Ice
4 GIVING YOU THE BENEFIT   Pebbles
5 LOVE TAKES TIME   Mariah Carey
6 CAN'T STOP   After 7
7 CLOSE TO YOU   Maxi Priest
8 PRAYING FOR TIME   George Michael
9 SUICIDE BLONDE   Inxs
10 EVERYBODY EVERYBODY   Black Box

November 3, 1990
1 ICE ICE BABY   Vanilla Ice
2 BLACK CAT   Janet Jackson
3 LOVE TAKES TIME   Mariah Carey
4 GIVING YOU THE BENEFIT   Pebbles
5 I DON'T HAVE THE HEART   James Ingram
6 PRAY   M.C. Hammer
7 CAN'T STOP   After 7
8 MORE THAN WORDS CAN SAY   Alias
9 SUICIDE BLONDE   Inxs
10 CHERRY PIE   Warrant

November 10, 1990
1 LOVE TAKES TIME   Mariah Carey
2 PRAY   M.C. Hammer
3 ICE ICE BABY   Vanilla Ice
4 GIVING YOU THE BENEFIT   Pebbles
5 I DON'T HAVE THE HEART   James Ingram
6 MORE THAN WORDS CAN SAY   Alias
7 BLACK CAT   Janet Jackson
8 GROOVE IS IN THE HEART   Deee-Lite
9 KNOCKIN' BOOTS   Candyman
10 SOMETHING TO BELIEVE IN   Poison

November 17, 1990
1 LOVE TAKES TIME   Mariah Carey
2 PRAY   M.C. Hammer
3 MORE THAN WORDS CAN SAY   Alias
4 GROOVE IS IN THE HEART   Deee-Lite
5 I'M YOUR BABY TONIGHT   Whitney Houston
6 ICE ICE BABY   Vanilla Ice
7 SOMETHING TO BELIEVE IN   Poison
8 BECAUSE I LOVE YOU (THE POSTMAN SONG)   Stevie B
9 I DON'T HAVE THE HEART   James Ingram
10 FROM A DISTANCE   Bette Midler

November 24, 1990
1 LOVE TAKES TIME   Mariah Carey
2 MORE THAN WORDS CAN SAY   Alias
3 I'M YOUR BABY TONIGHT   Whitney Houston
4 GROOVE IS IN THE HEART   Deee-Lite
5 BECAUSE I LOVE YOU (THE POSTMAN SONG)   Stevie B
6 SOMETHING TO BELIEVE IN   Poison
7 FROM A DISTANCE   Bette Midler
8 PRAY   M.C. Hammer
9 FEELS GOOD   Tony! Toni! Tone!
10 KNOCKIN' BOOTS   Candyman

December 1, 1990
1 I'M YOUR BABY TONIGHT   Whitney Houston
2 LOVE TAKES TIME   Mariah Carey
3 BECAUSE I LOVE YOU (THE POSTMAN SONG)   Stevie B
4 GROOVE IS IN THE HEART   Deee-Lite
5 FROM A DISTANCE   Bette Midler
6 SOMETHING TO BELIEVE IN   Poison
7 MORE THAN WORDS CAN SAY   Alias
8 THE WAY YOU DO THE THINGS YOU DO   UB40
9 IMPULSIVE   Wilson Phillips
10 FEELS GOOD   Tony! Toni! Tone!

December 8, 1990
1 BECAUSE I LOVE YOU (THE POSTMAN SONG)   Stevie B
2 I'M YOUR BABY TONIGHT   Whitney Houston
3 FROM A DISTANCE   Bette Midler
4 SOMETHING TO BELIEVE IN   Poison
5 LOVE TAKES TIME   Mariah Carey
6 GROOVE IS IN THE HEART   Deee-Lite
7 IMPULSIVE   Wilson Phillips
8 THE WAY YOU DO THE THINGS YOU DO   UB40
9 TOM'S DINER   DNA Featuring Suzanne Vega
10 JUSTIFY MY LOVE   Madonna

December 15, 1990
1 BECAUSE I LOVE YOU (THE POSTMAN SONG)   Stevie B
2 FROM A DISTANCE   Bette Midler
3 I'M YOUR BABY TONIGHT   Whitney Houston
4 JUSTIFY MY LOVE   Madonna
5 IMPULSIVE   Wilson Phillips
6 THE WAY YOU DO THE THINGS YOU DO   UB40
7 TOM'S DINER   DNA Featuring Suzanne Vega
8 SOMETHING TO BELIEVE IN   Poison
9 FREEDOM   George Michael
10 HIGH ENOUGH   Damn Yankees

December 22, 1990
1 BECAUSE I LOVE YOU (THE POSTMAN SONG)   Stevie B
2 JUSTIFY MY LOVE   Madonna
3 FROM A DISTANCE   Bette Midler
4 IMPULSIVE   Wilson Phillips
5 TOM'S DINER   DNA Featuring Suzanne Vega
6 HIGH ENOUGH   Damn Yankees
7 I'M YOUR BABY TONIGHT   Whitney Houston
8 FREEDOM   George Michael
9 THE WAY YOU DO THE THINGS YOU DO   UB40
10 SENSITIVITY   Ralph Tresvant

January 5, 1991
1 JUSTIFY MY LOVE   Madonna
2 BECAUSE I LOVE YOU (THE POSTMAN SONG)   Stevie B
3 FROM A DISTANCE   Bette Midler
4 HIGH ENOUGH   Damn Yankees
5 TOM'S DINER   DNA Featuring Suzanne Vega
6 IMPULSIVE   Wilson Phillips
7 LOVE WILL NEVER DO (WITHOUT YOU)   Janet Jackson
8 SENSITIVITY   Ralph Tresvant
9 THE FIRST TIME   Surface
10 I'M YOUR BABY TONIGHT   Whitney Houston

January 12, 1991
1 JUSTIFY MY LOVE   Madonna
2 BECAUSE I LOVE YOU (THE POSTMAN SONG)   Stevie B
3 HIGH ENOUGH   Damn Yankees
4 LOVE WILL NEVER DO (WITHOUT YOU)   Janet Jackson
5 FROM A DISTANCE   Bette Midler

6   TOM'S DINER   DNA Featuring Suzanne Vega
7   THE FIRST TIME   Surface
8   SENSITIVITY   Ralph Tresvant
9   IMPULSIVE   Wilson Phillips
10 GONNA MAKE YOU SWEAT   C&C Music Factory Feat.
     Freedom Williams

January 19, 1991
1   LOVE WILL NEVER DO (WITHOUT YOU)   Janet Jackson
2   JUSTIFY MY LOVE   Madonna
3   HIGH ENOUGH   Damn Yankees
4   THE FIRST TIME   Surface
5   SENSITIVITY   Ralph Tresvant
6   GONNA MAKE YOU SWEAT   C&C Music Factory Feat.
     Freedom Williams
7   PLAY THAT FUNKY MUSIC   Vanilla Ice
8   BECAUSE I LOVE YOU (THE POSTMAN SONG)   Stevie B
9   AFTER THE RAIN   Nelson
10 FROM A DISTANCE   Bette Midler

January 26, 1991
1   THE FIRST TIME   Surface
2   LOVE WILL NEVER DO (WITHOUT YOU)   Janet Jackson
3   GONNA MAKE YOU SWEAT   C&C Music Factory Feat.
     Freedom Williams
4   SENSITIVITY   Ralph Tresvant
5   HIGH ENOUGH   Damn Yankees
6   JUSTIFY MY LOVE   Madonna
7   PLAY THAT FUNKY MUSIC   Vanilla Ice
8   AFTER THE RAIN   Nelson
9   I'M NOT IN LOVE   Will To Power
10 JUST ANOTHER DREAM   Cathy Dennis

February 2, 1991
1   THE FIRST TIME   Surface
2   GONNA MAKE YOU SWEAT   C&C Music Factory Feat.
     Freedom Williams
3   LOVE WILL NEVER DO (WITHOUT YOU)   Janet Jackson
4   SENSITIVITY   Ralph Tresvant
5   PLAY THAT FUNKY MUSIC   Vanilla Ice
6   AFTER THE RAIN   Nelson
7   I'M NOT IN LOVE   Will To Power
8   ALL THE MAN THAT I NEED   Whitney Houston
9   JUST ANOTHER DREAM   Cathy Dennis
10 HIGH ENOUGH   Damn Yankees

February 9, 1991
1   GONNA MAKE YOU SWEAT   C&C Music Factory Feat.
     Freedom Williams
2   THE FIRST TIME   Surface
3   ALL THE MAN THAT I NEED   Whitney Houston
4   PLAY THAT FUNKY MUSIC   Vanilla Ice
5   LOVE WILL NEVER DO (WITHOUT YOU)   Janet Jackson
6   AFTER THE RAIN   Nelson
7   SENSITIVITY   Ralph Tresvant
8   I'M NOT IN LOVE   Will To Power
9   ONE MORE TRY   Timmy T.
10 I'LL GIVE ALL MY LOVE TO YOU   Keith Sweat

February 16, 1991
1   GONNA MAKE YOU SWEAT   C&C Music Factory Feat.
     Freedom Williams
2   ALL THE MAN THAT I NEED   Whitney Houston
3   ONE MORE TRY   Timmy T.
4   THE FIRST TIME   Surface
5   SOMEDAY   Mariah Carey

6   WHERE DOES MY HEART BEAT NOW   Celine Dion
7   I'LL GIVE ALL MY LOVE TO YOU   Keith Sweat
8   DISAPPEAR   Inxs
9   PLAY THAT FUNKY MUSIC   Vanilla Ice
10 LOVE WILL NEVER DO (WITHOUT YOU)   Janet Jackson

February 23, 1991
1   ALL THE MAN THAT I NEED   Whitney Houston
2   GONNA MAKE YOU SWEAT   C&C Music Factory Feat.
     Freedom Williams
3   ONE MORE TRY   Timmy T.
4   SOMEDAY   Mariah Carey
5   WHERE DOES MY HEART BEAT NOW   Celine Dion
6   THE FIRST TIME   Surface
7   WICKED GAME   Chris Isaak
8   I'LL GIVE ALL MY LOVE TO YOU   Keith Sweat
9   DISAPPEAR   Inxs
10 I SAW RED   Warrant

March 2, 1991
1   ALL THE MAN THAT I NEED   Whitney Houston
2   SOMEDAY   Mariah Carey
3   ONE MORE TRY   Timmy T.
4   WHERE DOES MY HEART BEAT NOW   Celine Dion
5   GONNA MAKE YOU SWEAT   C&C Music Factory Feat.
     Freedom Williams
6   WICKED GAME   Chris Isaak
7   SHOW ME THE WAY   Styx
8   ALL THIS TIME   Sting
9   AROUND THE WAY GIRL   L.L. Cool J
10 COMING OUT OF THE DARK   Gloria Estefan

March 9, 1991
1   SOMEDAY   Mariah Carey
2   ONE MORE TRY   Timmy T.
3   ALL THE MAN THAT I NEED   Whitney Houston
4   WHERE DOES MY HEART BEAT NOW   Celine Dion
5   SHOW ME THE WAY   Styx
6   ALL THIS TIME   Sting
7   GONNA MAKE YOU SWEAT   C&C Music Factory Feat.
     Freedom Williams
8   THIS HOUSE   Tracie Spencer
9   COMING OUT OF THE DARK   Gloria Estefan
10 WICKED GAME   Chris Isaak

March 16, 1991
1   SOMEDAY   Mariah Carey
2   ONE MORE TRY   Timmy T.
3   SHOW ME THE WAY   Styx
4   COMING OUT OF THE DARK   Gloria Estefan
5   ALL THIS TIME   Sting
6   THIS HOUSE   Tracie Spencer
7   ALL THE MAN THAT I NEED   Whitney Houston
8   GET HERE   Oleta Adams
9   WHERE DOES MY HEART BEAT NOW   Celine Dion
10 HOLD YOU TIGHT   Tara Kemp

March 23, 1991
1   ONE MORE TRY   Timmy T.
2   SOMEDAY   Mariah Carey
3   COMING OUT OF THE DARK   Gloria Estefan
4   THIS HOUSE   Tracie Spencer
5   GET HERE   Oleta Adams
6   HOLD YOU TIGHT   Tara Kemp
7   YOU'RE IN LOVE   Wilson Phillips
8   I'VE BEEN THINKING ABOUT YOU   Londonbeat

Gloria Estefan
``Coming Out Of The Dark'' peaks at #1 for two weeks (Mar. 30-Apr. 6).

Tesla
``Signs'' is a tenth-slot Top 10 hit for another no-slouch Platinum-favored metal band (Mar 30).

9   RESCUE ME   Madonna
10   SADENESS PART I   Enigma

March 30, 1991
1   COMING OUT OF THE DARK   Gloria Estefan
2   ONE MORE TRY   Timmy T.
3   THIS HOUSE   Tracie Spencer
4   HOLD YOU TIGHT   Tara Kemp
5   I'VE BEEN THINKING ABOUT YOU   Londonbeat
6   SOMEDAY   Mariah Carey
7   YOU'RE IN LOVE   Wilson Phillips
8   SADENESS PART I   Enigma
9   GET HERE   Oleta Adams
10   SIGNS   Tesla

April 6, 1991
1   COMING OUT OF THE DARK   Gloria Estefan
2   I'VE BEEN THINKING ABOUT YOU   Londonbeat
3   YOU'RE IN LOVE   Wilson Phillips
4   HOLD YOU TIGHT   Tara Kemp
5   YOU'RE IN LOVE   Wilson Phillips
6   ONE MORE TRY   Timmy T.
7   BABY BABY   Amy Grant
8   SIGNS   Tesla
9   THIS HOUSE   Tracie Spencer
10   IESHA   Another Bad Creation

April 13, 1991
1   I'VE BEEN THINKING ABOUT YOU   Londonbeat
2   YOU'RE IN LOVE   Wilson Phillips
3   HOLD YOU TIGHT   Tara Kemp
4   BABY BABY   Amy Grant
5   SADENESS PART I   Enigma
6   JOYRIDE   Roxette
7   RICO SUAVE   Gerardo
8   COMING OUT OF THE DARK   Gloria Estefan
9   IESHA   Another Bad Creation
10   SIGNS   Tesla

April 20, 1991
1   YOU'RE IN LOVE   Wilson Phillips
2   BABY BABY   Amy Grant
3   I'VE BEEN THINKING ABOUT YOU   Londonbeat
4   HOLD YOU TIGHT   Tara Kemp
5   JOYRIDE   Roxette
6   SADENESS PART I   Enigma
7   RICO SUAVE   Gerardo
8   I LIKE THE WAY (THE KISSING GAME)   Hi-Five
9   CRY FOR HELP   Rick Astley
10   HERE WE GO   C&C Music Factory Feat. Freedom
Williams & Zelma Davis

April 27, 1991
1   BABY BABY   Amy Grant
2   JOYRIDE   Roxette
3   YOU'RE IN LOVE   Wilson Phillips
4   I LIKE THE WAY (THE KISSING GAME)   Hi-Five
5   HERE WE GO   C&C Music Factory Feat. Freedom
Williams & Zelma Davis
6   I'VE BEEN THINKING ABOUT YOU   Londonbeat
7   CRY FOR HELP   Rick Astley
8   TOUCH ME (ALL NIGHT LONG)   Cathy Dennis
9   I TOUCH MYSELF   Divinyls
10   HOLD YOU TIGHT   Tara Kemp

May 4, 1991
1   BABY BABY   Amy Grant
2   JOYRIDE   Roxette
3   I LIKE THE WAY (THE KISSING GAME)   Hi-Five
4   HERE WE GO   C&C Music Factory Feat. Freedom
Williams & Zelma Davis
5   TOUCH ME (ALL NIGHT LONG)   Cathy Dennis
6   I TOUCH MYSELF   Divinyls
7   CRY FOR HELP   Rick Astley
8   RHYTHM OF MY HEART   Rod Stewart
9   YOU'RE IN LOVE   Wilson Phillips
10   I DON'T WANNA CRY   Mariah Carey

May 11, 1991
1   JOYRIDE   Roxette
2   BABY BABY   Amy Grant
3   I LIKE THE WAY (THE KISSING GAME)   Hi-Five
4   HERE WE GO   C&C Music Factory Feat. Freedom
Williams & Zelma Davis
5   TOUCH ME (ALL NIGHT LONG)   Cathy Dennis
6   I TOUCH MYSELF   Divinyls
7   RHYTHM OF MY HEART   Rod Stewart
8   I DON'T WANNA CRY   Mariah Carey
9   MORE THAN WORDS   Extreme
10   CRY FOR HELP   Rick Astley

May 18, 1991
1   I LIKE THE WAY (THE KISSING GAME)   Hi-Five
2   TOUCH ME (ALL NIGHT LONG)   Cathy Dennis
3   HERE WE GO   C&C Music Factory Feat. Freedom
Williams & Zelma Davis
4   I TOUCH MYSELF   Divinyls

Amy Grant
Amy's ``Baby Baby'' is #1 as April turns to May.

5   RHYTHM OF MY HEART   Rod Stewart
6   JOYRIDE   Roxette
7   BABY BABY   Amy Grant
8   I DON'T WANNA CRY   Mariah Carey
9   MORE THAN WORDS   Extreme
10 I WANNA SEX YOU UP (FROM "NEW JACK CITY")   Color
    Me Badd

May 25, 1991
1   I DON'T WANNA CRY   Mariah Carey
2   TOUCH ME (ALL NIGHT LONG)   Cathy Dennis
3   MORE THAN WORDS   Extreme
4   I LIKE THE WAY (THE KISSING GAME)   Hi-Five
5   RHYTHM OF MY HEART   Rod Stewart
6   I TOUCH MYSELF   Divinyls
7   HERE WE GO   C&C Music Factory Feat. Freedom
    Williams & Zelma Davis
8   I WANNA SEX YOU UP (FROM "NEW JACK CITY")   Color
    Me Badd
9   LOVE IS A WONDERFUL THING   Michael Bolton
10 SILENT LUCIDITY   Queensryche

June 1, 1991
1   I DON'T WANNA CRY   Mariah Carey
2   MORE THAN WORDS   Extreme
3   I WANNA SEX YOU UP (FROM "NEW JACK CITY")   Color
    Me Badd
4   LOVE IS A WONDERFUL THING   Michael Bolton
5   RUSH RUSH   Paula Abdul
6   I LIKE THE WAY (THE KISSING GAME)   Hi-Five
7   LOSING MY RELIGION   R.E.M.
8   TOUCH ME (ALL NIGHT LONG)   Cathy Dennis
9   SILENT LUCIDITY   Queensryche
10 RHYTHM OF MY HEART   Rod Stewart

June 8, 1991
1   MORE THAN WORDS   Extreme
2   I WANNA SEX YOU UP (FROM "NEW JACK CITY")   Color
    Me Badd
3   RUSH RUSH   Paula Abdul
4   I DON'T WANNA CRY   Mariah Carey
5   LOVE IS A WONDERFUL THING   Michael Bolton
6   LOSING MY RELIGION   R.E.M.
7   I LIKE THE WAY (THE KISSING GAME)   Hi-Five
8   UNBELIEVABLE   EMF
9   MIRACLE   Whitney Houston
10 POWER OF LOVE/LOVE POWER   Luther Vandross

June 15, 1991
1   RUSH RUSH   Paula Abdul
2   I WANNA SEX YOU UP (FROM "NEW JACK CITY")   Color
    Me Badd
3   MORE THAN WORDS   Extreme
4   LOVE IS A WONDERFUL THING   Michael Bolton
5   LOSING MY RELIGION   R.E.M.
6   I DON'T WANNA CRY   Mariah Carey
7   UNBELIEVABLE   EMF
8   POWER OF LOVE/LOVE POWER   Luther Vandross
9   STRIKE IT UP   Black Box
10 I LIKE THE WAY (THE KISSING GAME)   Hi-Five

June 22, 1991
1   RUSH RUSH   Paula Abdul
2   I WANNA SEX YOU UP (FROM "NEW JACK CITY")   Color
    Me Badd
3   MORE THAN WORDS   Extreme

Paula Abdul

This energetic singer/dancer rushes to #1 in mid-June.

4   LOSING MY RELIGION   R.E.M.
5   LOVE IS A WONDERFUL THING   Michael Bolton
6   UNBELIEVABLE   EMF
7   POWER OF LOVE/LOVE POWER   Luther Vandross
8   STRIKE IT UP   Black Box
9   I DON'T WANNA CRY   Mariah Carey
10 RIGHT HERE, RIGHT NOW   Jesus Jones

June 29, 1991
1   RUSH RUSH   Paula Abdul
2   I WANNA SEX YOU UP (FROM "NEW JACK CITY")   Color
    Me Badd
3   UNBELIEVABLE   EMF
4   POWER OF LOVE/LOVE POWER   Luther Vandross
5   LOSING MY RELIGION   R.E.M.
6   MORE THAN WORDS   Extreme
7   RIGHT HERE, RIGHT NOW   Jesus Jones
8   LOVE IS A WONDERFUL THING   Michael Bolton
9   STRIKE IT UP   Black Box
10 PLAYGROUND   Another Bad Creation

July 6, 1991
1   RUSH RUSH   Paula Abdul
2   UNBELIEVABLE   EMF
3   I WANNA SEX YOU UP (FROM "NEW JACK CITY")   Color
    Me Badd
4   POWER OF LOVE/LOVE POWER   Luther Vandross
5   RIGHT HERE, RIGHT NOW   Jesus Jones
6   MORE THAN WORDS   Extreme
7   PLACE IN THIS WORLD   Michael W. Smith
8   GYPSY WOMAN (SHE'S HOMELESS)   Crystal Waters
9   LOSING MY RELIGION   R.E.M.
10 HERE I AM (COME AND TAKE ME)   UB40

July 13, 1991
1 RUSH RUSH   Paula Abdul
2 UNBELIEVABLE   EMF
3 RIGHT HERE, RIGHT NOW   Jesus Jones
4 I WANNA SEX YOU UP (FROM "NEW JACK CITY")   Color Me Badd
5 POWER OF LOVE/LOVE POWER   Luther Vandross
6 PLACE IN THIS WORLD   Michael W. Smith
7 HERE I AM (COME AND TAKE ME)   UB40
8 PIECE OF MY HEART   Tara Kemp
9 P.A.S.S.I.O.N.   Rhythm Syndicate
10 GYPSY WOMAN (SHE'S HOMELESS)   Crystal Waters

July 20, 1991
1 UNBELIEVABLE   EMF
2 RUSH RUSH   Paula Abdul
3 RIGHT HERE, RIGHT NOW   Jesus Jones
4 (EVERYTHING I DO) I DO IT FOR YOU (FROM "ROBIN HOOD")   Bryan Adams
5 P.A.S.S.I.O.N.   Rhythm Syndicate
6 I WANNA SEX YOU UP (FROM "NEW JACK CITY")   Color Me Badd
7 PIECE OF MY HEART   Tara Kemp
8 PLACE IN THIS WORLD   Michael W. Smith
9 SUMMERTIME   D.J. Jazzy Jeff & The Fresh Prince
10 HERE I AM (COME AND TAKE ME)   UB40

July 27, 1991
1 (EVERYTHING I DO) I DO IT FOR YOU (FROM "ROBIN HOOD")   Bryan Adams
2 RIGHT HERE, RIGHT NOW   Jesus Jones
3 UNBELIEVABLE   EMF
4 P.A.S.S.I.O.N.   Rhythm Syndicate
5 SUMMERTIME   D.J. Jazzy Jeff & The Fresh Prince
6 RUSH RUSH   Paula Abdul
7 PIECE OF MY HEART   Tara Kemp
8 EVERY HEARTBEAT   Amy Grant
9 IT AIN'T OVER 'TIL IT'S OVER   Lenny Kravitz
10 TEMPTATION   Corina

August 3, 1991
1 (EVERYTHING I DO) I DO IT FOR YOU (FROM "ROBIN HOOD")   Bryan Adams
2 P.A.S.S.I.O.N.   Rhythm Syndicate
3 RIGHT HERE, RIGHT NOW   Jesus Jones
4 SUMMERTIME   D.J. Jazzy Jeff & The Fresh Prince
5 EVERY HEARTBEAT   Amy Grant
6 IT AIN'T OVER 'TIL IT'S OVER   Lenny Kravitz
7 UNBELIEVABLE   EMF
8 TEMPTATION   Corina
9 FADING LIKE A FLOWER (EVERY TIME YOU LEAVE)   Roxette
10 I'LL BE THERE   The Escape Club

August 10, 1991
1 (EVERYTHING I DO) I DO IT FOR YOU (FROM "ROBIN HOOD")   Bryan Adams
2 P.A.S.S.I.O.N.   Rhythm Syndicate
3 EVERY HEARTBEAT   Amy Grant
4 SUMMERTIME   D.J. Jazzy Jeff & The Fresh Prince
5 IT AIN'T OVER 'TIL IT'S OVER   Lenny Kravitz
6 TEMPTATION   Corina
7 FADING LIKE A FLOWER (EVERY TIME YOU LEAVE)   Roxette
8 I'LL BE THERE   The Escape Club
9 RIGHT HERE, RIGHT NOW   Jesus Jones
10 WIND OF CHANGE   Scorpions

August 17, 1991
1 (EVERYTHING I DO) I DO IT FOR YOU (FROM "ROBIN HOOD")   Bryan Adams
2 EVERY HEARTBEAT   Amy Grant
3 IT AIN'T OVER 'TIL IT'S OVER   Lenny Kravitz
4 SUMMERTIME   D.J. Jazzy Jeff & The Fresh Prince
5 FADING LIKE A FLOWER (EVERY TIME YOU LEAVE)   Roxette
6 TEMPTATION   Corina
7 P.A.S.S.I.O.N.   Rhythm Syndicate
8 I'LL BE THERE   The Escape Club
9 WIND OF CHANGE   Scorpions
10 3 A.M. ETERNAL   The KLF

August 24, 1991
1 (EVERYTHING I DO) I DO IT FOR YOU (FROM "ROBIN HOOD")   Bryan Adams
2 IT AIN'T OVER 'TIL IT'S OVER   Lenny Kravitz
3 EVERY HEARTBEAT   Amy Grant
4 FADING LIKE A FLOWER (EVERY TIME YOU LEAVE)   Roxette
5 SUMMERTIME   D.J. Jazzy Jeff & The Fresh Prince
6 TEMPTATION   Corina
7 WIND OF CHANGE   Scorpions
8 THE PROMISE OF A NEW DAY   Paula Abdul
9 3 A.M. ETERNAL   The KLF
10 I CAN'T WAIT ANOTHER MINUTE   Hi-Five

August 31, 1991
1 (EVERYTHING I DO) I DO IT FOR YOU (FROM "ROBIN HOOD")   Bryan Adams

Bryan Adams
Bryan's ``Everything I Do'' peaked at #1 (July 27).

2 FADING LIKE A FLOWER (EVERY TIME YOU LEAVE)   Wind Of Change
3 IT AIN'T OVER 'TIL IT'S OVER   Lenny Kravitz
4 WIND OF CHANGE   Scorpions
5 THE PROMISE OF A NEW DAY   Paula Abdul
6 EVERY HEARTBEAT   Amy Grant
7 3 A.M. ETERNAL   The KLF
8 I CAN'T WAIT ANOTHER MINUTE   Hi-Five
9 MOTOWNPHILLY   Boyz II Men
10 THINGS THAT MAKE YOU GO HMMMM...   C&C Music Factory/F. Williams

September 7, 1991
1 (EVERYTHING I DO) I DO IT FOR YOU (FROM "ROBIN HOOD")   Bryan Adams
2 THE PROMISE OF A NEW DAY   Paula Abdul
3 MOTOWNPHILLY   Boyz II Men
4 THINGS THAT MAKE YOU GO HMMMM...   C&C Music Factory/ F. Williams
5 3 A.M. ETERNAL   The KLF
6 I ADORE MI AMOR   Color Me Badd
7 CRAZY   Seal
8 WIND OF CHANGE   Scorpions
9 TIME, LOVE AND TENDERNESS   Michael Bolton
10 I CAN'T WAIT ANOTHER MINUTE   Hi-Five

September 14, 1991
1 THE PROMISE OF A NEW DAY   Paula Abdul
2 I ADORE MI AMOR   Color Me Badd
3 (EVERYTHING I DO) I DO IT FOR YOU (FROM "ROBIN HOOD")   Bryan Adams
4 MOTOWNPHILLY   Boyz II Men
5 THINGS THAT MAKE YOU GO HMMMM...   C&C Music Factory/F. Williams
6 GOOD VIBRATIONS   Marky Mark & The Funky Bunch/ Loleatta Holloway
7 TIME, LOVE AND TENDERNESS   Michael Bolton
8 CRAZY   Seal
9 TOO MANY WALLS   Cathy Dennis
10 3 A.M. ETERNAL   The KLF

September 21, 1991
1 I ADORE MI AMOR   Color Me Badd
2 GOOD VIBRATIONS   Marky Mark & The Funky Bunch/ Loleatta Holloway
3 MOTOWNPHILLY   Boyz II Men
4 THINGS THAT MAKE YOU GO HMMMM...   C&C Music Factory/F. Williams
5 THE PROMISE OF A NEW DAY   Paula Abdul
6 (EVERYTHING I DO) I DO IT FOR YOU (FROM "ROBIN HOOD")   Bryan Adams
7 TIME, LOVE AND TENDERNESS   Michael Bolton
8 TOO MANY WALLS   Cathy Dennis
9 LOVE OF A LIFETIME   Firehouse
10 THE MOTOWN SONG   Rod Stewart

September 28, 1991
1 I ADORE MI AMOR   Color Me Badd
2 GOOD VIBRATIONS   Marky Mark & The Funky Bunch/ Loleatta Holloway
3 MOTOWNPHILLY   Boyz II Men
4 EMOTIONS   Mariah Carey
5 LOVE OF A LIFETIME   Firehouse
6 THINGS THAT MAKE YOU GO HMMMM...   C&C Music Factory/F. Williams
7 TIME, LOVE AND TENDERNESS   Michael Bolton
8 DO ANYTHING   Natural Selection

9 SOMETHING TO TALK ABOUT   Bonnie Raitt
10 SHINY HAPPY PEOPLE   R.E.M.

October 5, 1991
1 GOOD VIBRATIONS   Marky Mark & The Funky Bunch/ Loleatta Holloway
2 I ADORE MI AMOR   Color Me Badd
3 EMOTIONS   Mariah Carey
4 DO ANYTHING   Natural Selection
5 LOVE OF A LIFETIME   Firehouse
6 ROMANTIC   Karyn White
7 SOMETHING TO TALK ABOUT   Bonnie Raitt
8 MOTOWNPHILLY   Boyz II Men
9 HOLE HEARTED   Extreme
10 SHINY HAPPY PEOPLE   R.E.M.

October 12, 1991
1 EMOTIONS   Mariah Carey
2 GOOD VIBRATIONS   Marky Mark & The Funky Bunch/ Loleatta Holloway
3 DO ANYTHING   Natural Selection
4 I ADORE MI AMOR   Color Me Badd
5 ROMANTIC   Karyn White
6 SOMETHING TO TALK ABOUT   Bonnie Raitt
7 HOLE HEARTED   Extreme
8 LOVE OF A LIFETIME   Firehouse
9 MOTOWNPHILLY   Boyz II Men
10 EVERYBODY PLAYS THE FOOL   Aaron Neville

October 19, 1991
1 EMOTIONS   Mariah Carey
2 DO ANYTHING   Natural Selection
3 ROMANTIC   Karyn White
4 HOLE HEARTED   Extreme
5 SOMETHING TO TALK ABOUT   Bonnie Raitt
6 GOOD VIBRATIONS   Marky Mark & The Funky Bunch/ Loleatta Holloway
7 I ADORE MI AMOR   Color Me Badd
8 EVERYBODY PLAYS THE FOOL   Aaron Neville
9 CAN'T STOP THIS THING WE STARTED   Bryan Adams
10 LOVE...THY WILL BE DONE   Martika

October 26, 1991
1 EMOTIONS   Mariah Carey
2 DO ANYTHING   Natural Selection
3 ROMANTIC   Karyn White
4 HOLE HEARTED   Extreme
5 CAN'T STOP THIS THING WE STARTED   Bryan Adams
6 CREAM   Prince And The N.P.G.
7 REAL REAL REAL   Jesus Jones
8 SOMETHING TO TALK ABOUT   Bonnie Raitt
9 GOOD VIBRATIONS   Marky Mark & The Funky Bunch/ Loleatta Holloway
10 O.P.P.   Naughty By Nature

November 2, 1991
1 ROMANTIC   Karyn White
2 EMOTIONS   Mariah Carey
3 CREAM   Prince And The N.P.G.
4 DO ANYTHING   Natural Selection
5 CAN'T STOP THIS THING WE STARTED   Bryan Adams
6 HOLE HEARTED   Extreme
7 REAL REAL REAL   Jesus Jones
8 O.P.P.   Naughty By Nature
9 DON'T WANT TO BE A FOOL   Luther Vandross
10 THE ONE AND ONLY   Chesney Hawkes

Luther Vandross

This Grammy winner is nobody's fool—he's Top 10 (Nov. 2).

November 9, 1991
1   CREAM   Prince And The N.P.G.
2   ROMANTIC   Karyn White
3   CAN'T STOP THIS THING WE STARTED   Bryan Adams
4   REAL REAL REAL   Jesus Jones
5   WHEN A MAN LOVES A WOMAN   Michael Bolton
6   O.P.P.   Naughty By Nature
7   EMOTIONS   Mariah Carey
8   IT'S SO HARD TO SAY GOODBYE TO YESTERDAY   Boyz II Men
9   DO ANYTHING   Natural Selection
10   SET THE NIGHT TO MUSIC   Roberta Flack With Maxi Priest

November 16, 1991
1   CREAM   Prince And The N.P.G.
2   CAN'T STOP THIS THING WE STARTED   Bryan Adams
3   WHEN A MAN LOVES A WOMAN   Michael Bolton
4   IT'S SO HARD TO SAY GOODBYE TO YESTERDAY   Boyz II Men
5   SET ADRIFT ON MEMORY BLISS   P.M. Dawn
6   SET THE NIGHT TO MUSIC   Roberta Flack With Maxi Priest
7   O.P.P.   Naughty By Nature
8   THAT'S WHAT LOVE IS FOR   Amy Grant
9   ROMANTIC   Karyn White
10   DON'T CRY   Guns N' Roses

November 23, 1991
1   WHEN A MAN LOVES A WOMAN   Michael Bolton
2   CREAM   Prince And The N.P.G.
3   SET ADRIFT ON MEMORY BLISS   P.M. Dawn
4   IT'S SO HARD TO SAY GOODBYE TO YESTERDAY   Boyz II Men
5   CAN'T STOP THIS THING WE STARTED   Bryan Adams
6   SET THE NIGHT TO MUSIC   Roberta Flack With Maxi Priest
7   THAT'S WHAT LOVE IS FOR   Amy Grant
8   BLOWING KISSES IN THE WIND   Paula Abdul
9   I WONDER WHY   Curtis Stigers
10   DON'T CRY   Guns N' Roses

November 30, 1991
1   SET ADRIFT ON MEMORY BLISS   P.M. Dawn
2   WHEN A MAN LOVES A WOMAN   Michael Bolton
3   BLACK OR WHITE   Michael Jackson
4   IT'S SO HARD TO SAY GOODBYE TO YESTERDAY   Boyz II Men
5   CREAM   Prince And The N.P.G.
6   BLOWING KISSES IN THE WIND   Paula Abdul
7   ALL 4 LOVE   Color Me Badd
8   O.P.P.   Naughty By Nature
9   DO ANYTHING   Natural Selection
10   CAN'T STOP THIS THING WE STARTED   Bryan Adams

December 7, 1991
1   BLACK OR WHITE   Michael Jackson
2   WHEN A MAN LOVES A WOMAN   Michael Bolton
3   SET ADRIFT ON MEMORY BLISS   P.M. Dawn
4   IT'S SO HARD TO SAY GOODBYE TO YESTERDAY   Boyz II Men
5   ALL 4 LOVE   Color Me Badd
6   BLOWING KISSES IN THE WIND   Paula Abdul
7   CREAM   Prince And The N.P.G.
8   CAN'T LET GO   Mariah Carey
9   THAT'S WHAT LOVE IS FOR   Amy Grant
10   O.P.P.   Naughty By Nature

December 14, 1991
1   BLACK OR WHITE   Michael Jackson
2   IT'S SO HARD TO SAY GOODBYE TO YESTERDAY   Boyz II Men
3   SET ADRIFT ON MEMORY BLISS   P.M. Dawn
4   WHEN A MAN LOVES A WOMAN   Michael Bolton
5   ALL 4 LOVE   Color Me Badd
6   BLOWING KISSES IN THE WIND   Paula Abdul
7   CAN'T LET GO   Mariah Carey
8   FINALLY   Ce Ce Peniston
9   THAT'S WHAT LOVE IS FOR   Amy Grant
10   WILDSIDE   Marky Mark & The Funky Bunch

December 21, 1991
1   BLACK OR WHITE   Michael Jackson
2   IT'S SO HARD TO SAY GOODBYE TO YESTERDAY   Boyz II Men
3   ALL 4 LOVE   Color Me Badd
4   SET ADRIFT ON MEMORY BLISS   P.M. Dawn
5   WHEN A MAN LOVES A WOMAN   Michael Bolton
6   CAN'T LET GO   Mariah Carey
7   BLOWING KISSES IN THE WIND   Paula Abdul
8   FINALLY   Ce Ce Peniston
9   2 LEGIT 2 QUIT   Hammer
10   WILDSIDE   Marky Mark & The Funky Bunch

January 4, 1992
1   BLACK OR WHITE   Michael Jackson
2   IT'S SO HARD TO SAY GOODBYE TO YESTERDAY   Boyz II Men
3   ALL 4 LOVE   Color Me Badd
4   CAN'T LET GO   Mariah Carey

5   SET ADRIFT ON MEMORY BLISS   P.M. Dawn
6   FINALLY   Ce Ce Peniston
7   WHEN A MAN LOVES A WOMAN   Michael Bolton
8   2 LEGIT 2 QUIT   Hammer
9   BLOWING KISSES IN THE WIND   Paula Abdul
10   WILDSIDE   Marky Mark & The Funky Bunch

January 11, 1992
1   BLACK OR WHITE   Michael Jackson
2   ALL 4 LOVE   Color Me Badd
3   CAN'T LET GO   Mariah Carey
4   IT'S SO HARD TO SAY GOODBYE TO YESTERDAY   Boyz II Men
5   2 LEGIT 2 QUIT   Hammer
6   SMELLS LIKE TEEN SPIRIT   Nirvana
7   ADDAMS GROOVE   Hammer
8   DON'T LET THE SUN GO DOWN ON ME   George Michael/Elton John
9   FINALLY   Ce Ce Peniston
10   WILDSIDE   Marky Mark & The Funky Bunch

January 18, 1992
1   BLACK OR WHITE   Michael Jackson
2   ALL 4 LOVE   Color Me Badd
3   CAN'T LET GO   Mariah Carey
4   DON'T LET THE SUN GO DOWN ON ME   George Michael/Elton John
5   FINALLY   Ce Ce Peniston
6   DIAMONDS AND PEARLS   Prince And The N.P.G.
7   I LOVE YOUR SMILE   Shanice
8   IT'S SO HARD TO SAY GOODBYE TO YESTERDAY   Boyz II Men
9   SMELLS LIKE TEEN SPIRIT   Nirvana
10   ADDAMS GROOVE   Hammer

January 25, 1992
1   ALL 4 LOVE   Color Me Badd
2   CAN'T LET GO   Mariah Carey
3   DON'T LET THE SUN GO DOWN ON ME   George Michael/Elton John
4   BLACK OR WHITE   Michael Jackson
5   FINALLY   Ce Ce Peniston
6   DIAMONDS AND PEARLS   Prince And The N.P.G.
7   I LOVE YOUR SMILE   Shanice
8   SMELLS LIKE TEEN SPIRIT   Nirvana
9   MYSTERIOUS WAYS   U2
10   I'M TOO SEXY   Right Said Fred

February 1, 1992
1   DON'T LET THE SUN GO DOWN ON ME   George Michael/Elton John
2   I LOVE YOUR SMILE   Shanice
3   ALL 4 LOVE   Color Me Badd
4   DIAMONDS AND PEARLS   Prince And The N.P.G.
5   CAN'T LET GO   Mariah Carey
6   I'M TOO SEXY   Right Said Fred
7   FINALLY   Ce Ce Peniston
8   SMELLS LIKE TEEN SPIRIT   Nirvana
9   BLACK OR WHITE   Michael Jackson
10   TELL ME WHAT YOU WANT ME TO DO   Tevin Campbell

February 8, 1992
1   I'M TOO SEXY   Right Said Fred
2   I LOVE YOUR SMILE   Shanice
3   DON'T LET THE SUN GO DOWN ON ME   George Michael/Elton John

4   DIAMONDS AND PEARLS   Prince And The N.P.G.
5   ALL 4 LOVE   Color Me Badd
6   SMELLS LIKE TEEN SPIRIT   Nirvana
7   CAN'T LET GO   Mariah Carey
8   TO BE WITH YOU   Mr. Big
9   FINALLY   Ce Ce Peniston
10   TELL ME WHAT YOU WANT ME TO DO   Tevin Campbell

February 15, 1992
1   I'M TOO SEXY   Right Said Fred
2   I LOVE YOUR SMILE   Shanice
3   DIAMONDS AND PEARLS   Prince And The N.P.G.
4   DON'T LET THE SUN GO DOWN ON ME   George Michael/Elton John
5   TO BE WITH YOU   Mr. Big
6   ALL 4 LOVE   Color Me Badd
7   TELL ME WHAT YOU WANT ME TO DO   Tevin Campbell
8   REMEMBER THE TIME   Michael Jackson
9   SMELLS LIKE TEEN SPIRIT   Nirvana
10   CAN'T LET GO   Mariah Carey

February 22, 1992
1   I'M TOO SEXY   Right Said Fred
2   TO BE WITH YOU   Mr. Big
3   I LOVE YOUR SMILE   Shanice
4   DIAMONDS AND PEARLS   Prince And The N.P.G.
5   REMEMBER THE TIME   Michael Jackson
6   DON'T LET THE SUN GO DOWN ON ME   George Michael/Elton John
7   TELL ME WHAT YOU WANT ME TO DO   Tevin Campbell
8   SMELLS LIKE TEEN SPIRIT   Nirvana
9   ALL 4 LOVE   Color Me Badd
10   FINALLY   Ce Ce Peniston

February 29, 1992
1   TO BE WITH YOU   Mr. Big
2   I'M TOO SEXY   Right Said Fred
3   I LOVE YOUR SMILE   Shanice
4   REMEMBER THE TIME   Michael Jackson
5   DIAMONDS AND PEARLS   Prince And The N.P.G.
6   TELL ME WHAT YOU WANT ME TO DO   Tevin Campbell
7   DON'T LET THE SUN GO DOWN ON ME   George Michael/Elton John
8   MASTERPIECE   Atlantic Starr
9   SMELLS LIKE TEEN SPIRIT   Nirvana
10   ALL 4 LOVE   Color Me Badd

March 7, 1992
1   TO BE WITH YOU   Mr. Big
2   I'M TOO SEXY   Right Said Fred
3   REMEMBER THE TIME   Michael Jackson
4   I LOVE YOUR SMILE   Shanice
5   SAVE THE BEST FOR LAST   Vanessa Williams
6   TEARS IN HEAVEN   Eric Clapton
7   DIAMONDS AND PEARLS   Prince And The N.P.G.
8   MASTERPIECE   Atlantic Starr
9   TELL ME WHAT YOU WANT ME TO DO   Tevin Campbell
10   GOOD FOR ME   Amy Grant

March 14, 1992
1   TO BE WITH YOU   Mr. Big
2   I'M TOO SEXY   Right Said Fred
3   REMEMBER THE TIME   Michael Jackson
4   SAVE THE BEST FOR LAST   Vanessa Williams
5   TEARS IN HEAVEN   Eric Clapton
6   I LOVE YOUR SMILE   Shanice

411

7 MASTERPIECE Atlantic Starr
8 TELL ME WHAT YOU WANT ME TO DO Tevin Campbell
9 DIAMONDS AND PEARLS Prince And The N.P.G.
10 GOOD FOR ME Amy Grant

March 21, 1992
1 SAVE THE BEST FOR LAST Vanessa Williams
2 TO BE WITH YOU Mr. Big
3 TEARS IN HEAVEN Eric Clapton
4 REMEMBER THE TIME Michael Jackson
5 I'M TOO SEXY Right Said Fred
6 MASTERPIECE Atlantic Starr
7 I LOVE YOUR SMILE Shanice
8 GOOD FOR ME Amy Grant
9 I CAN'T DANCE Genesis
10 BREAKIN' MY HEART (PRETTY BROWN EYES) Mint Condition

March 28, 1992
1 SAVE THE BEST FOR LAST Vanessa Williams
2 TEARS IN HEAVEN Eric Clapton
3 REMEMBER THE TIME Michael Jackson
4 TO BE WITH YOU Mr. Big
5 I'M TOO SEXY Right Said Fred
6 MASTERPIECE Atlantic Starr
7 BREAKIN' MY HEART (PRETTY BROWN EYES) Mint Condition
8 I CAN'T DANCE Genesis
9 I LOVE YOUR SMILE Shanice
10 MAKE IT HAPPEN Mariah Carey

April 4, 1992
1 SAVE THE BEST FOR LAST Vanessa Williams
2 TEARS IN HEAVEN Eric Clapton
3 REMEMBER THE TIME Michael Jackson
4 MASTERPIECE Atlantic Starr
5 TO BE WITH YOU Mr. Big
6 I'M TOO SEXY Right Said Fred
7 BREAKIN' MY HEART (PRETTY BROWN EYES) Mint Condition
8 MAKE IT HAPPEN Mariah Carey
9 I CAN'T DANCE Genesis
10 BEAUTY AND THE BEAST Celine Dion And Peabo Bryson

April 11, 1992
1 SAVE THE BEST FOR LAST Vanessa Williams
2 TEARS IN HEAVEN Eric Clapton
3 MASTERPIECE Atlantic Starr
4 REMEMBER THE TIME Michael Jackson
5 MAKE IT HAPPEN Mariah Carey
6 BREAKIN' MY HEART (PRETTY BROWN EYES) Mint Condition
7 I CAN'T DANCE Genesis
8 I'M TOO SEXY Right Said Fred
9 AIN'T 2 PROUD 2 BEG TLC
10 BOHEMIAN RHAPSODY Queen

April 18, 1992
1 SAVE THE BEST FOR LAST Vanessa Williams
2 TEARS IN HEAVEN Eric Clapton
3 JUMP Kris Kross
4 BOHEMIAN RHAPSODY Queen
5 MASTERPIECE Atlantic Starr
6 MAKE IT HAPPEN Mariah Carey
7 AIN'T 2 PROUD 2 BEG TLC
8 MY LOVIN' (YOU'RE NEVER GONNA GET IT) En Vogue

9 BEAUTY AND THE BEAST Celine Dion And Peabo Bryson
10 BREAKIN' MY HEART (PRETTY BROWN EYES) Mint Condition

April 25, 1992
1 JUMP Kris Kross
2 SAVE THE BEST FOR LAST Vanessa Williams
3 TEARS IN HEAVEN Eric Clapton
4 BOHEMIAN RHAPSODY Queen
5 MY LOVIN' (YOU'RE NEVER GONNA GET IT) En Vogue
6 AIN'T 2 PROUD 2 BEG TLC
7 MAKE IT HAPPEN Mariah Carey
8 MASTERPIECE Atlantic Starr
9 HAZARD Richard Marx
10 LIVE AND LEARN Joe Public

May 2, 1992
1 JUMP Kris Kross
2 SAVE THE BEST FOR LAST Vanessa Williams
3 TEARS IN HEAVEN Eric Clapton
4 BOHEMIAN RHAPSODY Queen
5 MY LOVIN' (YOU'RE NEVER GONNA GET IT) En Vogue
6 AIN'T 2 PROUD 2 BEG TLC
7 MAKE IT HAPPEN Mariah Carey
8 LIVE AND LEARN Joe Public
9 EVERYTHING ABOUT YOU Ugly Kid Joe
10 HAZARD Richard Marx

May 9, 1992
1 JUMP Kris Kross
2 BOHEMIAN RHAPSODY Queen
3 SAVE THE BEST FOR LAST Vanessa Williams
4 TEARS IN HEAVEN Eric Clapton
5 MY LOVIN' (YOU'RE NEVER GONNA GET IT) En Vogue
6 LIVE AND LEARN Joe Public
7 AIN'T 2 PROUD 2 BEG TLC
8 UNDER THE BRIDGE Red Hot Chili Peppers
9 EVERYTHING ABOUT YOU Ugly Kid Joe
10 MAKE IT HAPPEN Mariah Carey

May 16, 1992
1 JUMP Kris Kross
2 MY LOVIN' (YOU'RE NEVER GONNA GET IT) En Vogue
3 BOHEMIAN RHAPSODY Queen
4 SAVE THE BEST FOR LAST Vanessa Williams
5 LIVE AND LEARN Joe Public
6 UNDER THE BRIDGE Red Hot Chili Peppers
7 TEARS IN HEAVEN Eric Clapton
8 AIN'T 2 PROUD 2 BEG TLC
9 EVERYTHING ABOUT YOU Ugly Kid Joe
10 ONE U2

May 23, 1992
1 JUMP Kris Kross
2 MY LOVIN' (YOU'RE NEVER GONNA GET IT) En Vogue
3 UNDER THE BRIDGE Red Hot Chili Peppers
4 LIVE AND LEARN Joe Public
5 BOHEMIAN RHAPSODY Queen
6 TEARS IN HEAVEN Eric Clapton
7 SAVE THE BEST FOR LAST Vanessa Williams
8 AIN'T 2 PROUD 2 BEG TLC
9 EVERYTHING ABOUT YOU Ugly Kid Joe
10 IN THE CLOSET Michael Jackson

May 30, 1992
1 JUMP Kris Kross

2 MY LOVIN' (YOU'RE NEVER GONNA GET IT)   En Vogue
3 UNDER THE BRIDGE   Red Hot Chili Peppers
4 LIVE AND LEARN   Joe Public
5 BABY GOT BACK   Sir Mix-A-Lot
6 IN THE CLOSET   Michael Jackson
7 DAMN I WISH I WAS YOUR LOVER   Sophie B. Hawkins
8 AIN'T 2 PROUD 2 BEG   TLC
9 BOHEMIAN RHAPSODY   Queen
10 SAVE THE BEST FOR LAST   Vanessa Williams

June 6, 1992
1 JUMP   Kris Kross
2 UNDER THE BRIDGE   Red Hot Chili Peppers
3 MY LOVIN' (YOU'RE NEVER GONNA GET IT)   En Vogue
4 I'LL BE THERE   Mariah Carey
5 BABY GOT BACK   Sir Mix-A-Lot
6 LIVE AND LEARN   Joe Public
7 DAMN I WISH I WAS YOUR LOVER   Sophie B. Hawkins
8 IN THE CLOSET   Michael Jackson
9 IF YOU ASKED ME TO   Celine Dion
10 AIN'T 2 PROUD 2 BEG   TLC

June 13, 1992
1 JUMP   Kris Kross
2 I'LL BE THERE   Mariah Carey
3 UNDER THE BRIDGE   Red Hot Chili Peppers
4 BABY GOT BACK   Sir Mix-A-Lot
5 MY LOVIN' (YOU'RE NEVER GONNA GET IT)   En Vogue
6 DAMN I WISH I WAS YOUR LOVER   Sophie B. Hawkins
7 LIVE AND LEARN   Joe Public
8 IF YOU ASKED ME TO   Celine Dion
9 IN THE CLOSET   Michael Jackson

10 THE BEST THINGS IN LIFE ARE FREE   Luther Vandross
    and Janet Jackson

June 20, 1992
1 I'LL BE THERE   Mariah Carey
2 BABY GOT BACK   Sir Mix-A-Lot
3 JUMP   Kris Kross
4 UNDER THE BRIDGE   Red Hot Chili Peppers
5 MY LOVIN' (YOU'RE NEVER GONNA GET IT)   En Vogue
6 DAMN I WISH I WAS YOUR LOVER   Sophie B. Hawkins
7 IF YOU ASKED ME TO   Celine Dion
8 ACHY BREAKY HEART   Billy Ray Cyrus *
9 TENNESSEE   Arrested Development
10 THE BEST THINGS IN LIFE ARE FREE   Luther Vandross
    and Janet Jackson
   Note: * A #1 song on the country charts, and only the
           second country single to go Platinum ("Elvira" was the
           first, in mid-1981).

June 27, 1992
1 I'LL BE THERE   Mariah Carey
2 BABY GOT BACK   Sir Mix-A-Lot
3 UNDER THE BRIDGE   Red Hot Chili Peppers
4 JUMP   Kris Kross
5 DAMN I WISH I WAS YOUR LOVER   Sophie B. Hawkins
6 MY LOVIN' (YOU'RE NEVER GONNA GET IT)   En Vogue
7 IF YOU ASKED ME TO   Celine Dion
8 ACHY BREAKY HEART   Billy Ray Cyrus *
9 TENNESSEE   Arrested Development
10 THE BEST THINGS IN LIFE ARE FREE   Luther Vandross
    and Janet Jackson
   Note: * A #1 song on the country charts, and only the

Kris Kross
This little duo took a big jump to an eight-week stay at #1 beginning April 25.

Red Hot Chili Peppers

``Under The Bridge'' peaked at #2 in June but couldn't bump the lingering Kris Kross effort then on top.

second country single to go Platinum ("Elvira" was the first, in mid-1981).

July 4, 1992
1 BABY GOT BACK   Sir Mix-A-Lot
2 I'LL BE THERE   Mariah Carey
3 UNDER THE BRIDGE   Red Hot Chili Peppers
4 JUMP   Kris Kross
5 IF YOU ASKED ME TO   Celine Dion
6 DAMN I WISH I WAS YOUR LOVER   Sophie B. Hawkins
7 ACHY BREAKY HEART   Billy Ray Cyrus *
8 MY LOVIN' (YOU'RE NEVER GONNA GET IT)   En Vogue
9 TENNESSEE   Arrested Development
10 WISHING ON A STAR   The Cover Girls
   Note: * A #1 song on the country charts, and only the second country single to go Platinum ("Elvira" was the first, in mid-1981).

July 11, 1992
1 BABY GOT BACK   Sir Mix-A-Lot
2 I'LL BE THERE   Mariah Carey
3 UNDER THE BRIDGE   Red Hot Chili Peppers
4 IF YOU ASKED ME TO   Celine Dion
5 DAMN I WISH I WAS YOUR LOVER   Sophie B. Hawkins
6 ACHY BREAKY HEART   Billy Ray Cyrus *
7 JUMP   Kris Kross
8 TENNESSEE   Arrested Development
9 MY LOVIN' (YOU'RE NEVER GONNA GET IT)   En Vogue
10 WISHING ON A STAR   The Cover Girls
   Note: * A #1 song on the country charts, and only the second country single to go Platinum ("Elvira" was the first, in mid-1981).

July 18, 1992
1 BABY GOT BACK   Sir Mix-A-Lot
2 I'LL BE THERE   Mariah Carey
3 UNDER THE BRIDGE   Red Hot Chili Peppers
4 ACHY BREAKY HEART   Billy Ray Cyrus *
5 BABY-BABY-BABY   TLC
6 TENNESSEE   Arrested Development
7 THIS USED TO BE MY PLAYGROUND   Madonna
8 IF YOU ASKED ME TO   Celine Dion
9 WISHING ON A STAR   The Cover Girls
10 JUST ANOTHER DAY   Jon Secada
   Note: * A #1 song on the country charts, and only the second country single to go Platinum ("Elvira" was the first, in mid-1981).

July 25, 1992
1 BABY GOT BACK   Sir Mix-A-Lot
2 THIS USED TO BE MY PLAYGROUND   Madonna
3 BABY-BABY-BABY   TLC
4 ACHY BREAKY HEART   Billy Ray Cyrus *
5 I'LL BE THERE   Mariah Carey
6 JUST ANOTHER DAY   Jon Secada
7 LIFE IS A HIGHWAY   Tom Cochran
8 UNDER THE BRIDGE   Red Hot Chili Peppers
9 WISHING ON A STAR   The Cover Girls
10 IF YOU ASKED ME TO   Celine Dion
   Note: * A #1 song on the country charts, and only the second country single to go Platinum ("Elvira" was the first, in mid-1981).

August 1, 1992
1 BABY GOT BACK   Sir Mix-A-Lot

2 THIS USED TO BE MY PLAYGROUND   Madonna
3 BABY-BABY-BABY   TLC
4 ACHY BREAKY HEART   Billy Ray Cyrus *
5 JUST ANOTHER DAY   Jon Secada
6 NOVEMBER RAIN   Guns N' Roses
7 LIFE IS A HIGHWAY   Tom Cochran
8 END OF THE ROAD (FROM "BOOMERANG")   Boyz IIMen**
9 GIVING HIM SOMETHING HE CAN FEEL   En Vogue
10 WISHING ON A STAR   The Cover Girls
   Note: * A #1 song on the country charts, and only the
      second country single to go Platinum ("Elvira" was the
      first, in mid-1981).
         ** Second longest reign at #1 in chart history,
      eclipsing Nat King Cole's "Too Young" (August 1951).

August 8, 1992
1 THIS USED TO BE MY PLAYGROUND   Madonna
2 BABY GOT BACK   Sir Mix-A-Lot
3 BABY-BABY-BABY   TLC
4 END OF THE ROAD (FROM "BOOMERANG")   Boyz II
   Men *
5 NOVEMBER RAIN   Guns N' Roses
6 ACHY BREAKY HEART   Billy Ray Cyrus **
7 JUST ANOTHER DAY   Jon Secada
8 LIFE IS A HIGHWAY   Tom Cochran
9 GIVING HIM SOMETHING HE CAN FEEL   En Vogue
10 TOO FUNKY   George Michael
   Note: * Second longest reign at #1 in chart history, eclipsing
      Nat King Cole's "Too Young" (August 1951).
         ** A #1 song on the country charts, and only the
      second country single to go Platinum ("Elvira" was the
      first, in mid-1981).

Axl Rose
``November Rain'' begins in August for a Top 10 Guns N' Roses.

August 15, 1992
1 END OF THE ROAD (FROM "BOOMERANG")   Boyz II
   Men *
2 BABY-BABY-BABY   TLC
3 THIS USED TO BE MY PLAYGROUND   Madonna
4 BABY GOT BACK   Sir Mix-A-Lot
5 NOVEMBER RAIN   Guns N' Roses
6 JUST ANOTHER DAY   Jon Secada
7 LIFE IS A HIGHWAY   Tom Cochran
8 GIVING HIM SOMETHING HE CAN FEEL   En Vogue
9 ACHY BREAKY HEART   Billy Ray Cyrus **
10 MOVE THIS   Technotronic (featuring Ya Kid K)
   Note: * Second longest reign at #1 in chart history, eclipsing
      Nat King Cole's "Too Young" (August 1951).
         ** A #1 song on the country charts, and only the
      second country single to go Platinum ("Elvira" was the
      first, in mid-1981).

August 29, 1992
1 END OF THE ROAD (FROM "BOOMERANG")   Boyz II
   Men *
2 BABY-BABY-BABY   TLC
3 NOVEMBER RAIN   Guns N' Roses
4 THIS USED TO BE MY PLAYGROUND   Madonna
5 BABY GOT BACK   Sir Mix-A-Lot
6 HUMPIN' AROUND   Bobby Brown
7 GIVING HIM SOMETHING HE CAN FEEL   En Vogue
8 JUST ANOTHER DAY   Jon Secada
9 STAY   Shakespear's Sister
10 LIFE IS A HIGHWAY   Tom Cochran
   Note: * Second longest reign at #1 in chart history, eclipsing
      Nat King Cole's "Too Young" (August 1951).

September 5, 1992
1 END OF THE ROAD (FROM "BOOMERANG")   Boyz II
   Men *
2 BABY-BABY-BABY   TLC
3 NOVEMBER RAIN   Guns N' Roses
4 HUMPIN' AROUND   Bobby Brown
5 THIS USED TO BE MY PLAYGROUND   Madonna
6 MOVE THIS   Technotronic (featuring Ya Kid K)
7 STAY   Shakespear's Sister
8 BABY GOT BACK   Sir Mix-A-Lot
9 GIVING HIM SOMETHING HE CAN FEEL   En Vogue
10 JUST ANOTHER DAY   Jon Secada
   Note: * Second longest reign at #1 in chart history, eclipsing
      Nat King Cole's "Too Young" (August 1951).

September 12, 1992
1 END OF THE ROAD (FROM "BOOMERANG")   Boyz II
   Men *
2 BABY-BABY-BABY   TLC
3 HUMPIN' AROUND   Bobby Brown
4 NOVEMBER RAIN   Guns N' Roses
5 STAY   Shakespear's Sister
6 GIVING HIM SOMETHING HE CAN FEEL   En Vogue
7 SOMETIMES LOVE JUST AIN'T ENOUGH   Patty Smyth
8 JUST ANOTHER DAY   Jon Secada
9 JUMP AROUND   House Of Pain
10 MOVE THIS   Technotronic (featuring Ya Kid K)
   Note: * Second longest reign at #1 in chart history, eclipsing
      Nat King Cole's "Too Young" (August 1951).

September 19, 1992
1 END OF THE ROAD (FROM "BOOMERANG")   Boyz II
   Men *

2   BABY-BABY-BABY   TLC
3   HUMPIN' AROUND   Bobby Brown
4   STAY   Shakespear's Sister
5   NOVEMBER RAIN   Guns N' Roses
6   SOMETIMES LOVE JUST AIN'T ENOUGH   Patty Smyth
7   JUMP AROUND   House Of Pain
8   JUST ANOTHER DAY   Jon Secada
9   THE ONE   Elton John
10   SHE'S PLAYING HARD TO GET   Hi-Five
     Note: * Second longest reign at #1 in chart history, eclipsing
          Nat King Cole's "Too Young" (August 1951).

September 26, 1992

1   END OF THE ROAD (FROM "BOOMERANG")   Boyz II
     Men *
2   SOMETIMES LOVE JUST AIN'T ENOUGH   Patty Smyth
3   BABY-BABY-BABY   TLC
4   HUMPIN' AROUND   Bobby Brown
5   NOVEMBER RAIN   Guns N' Roses
6   STAY   Shakespear's Sister
7   JUMP AROUND   House Of Pain
8   JUST ANOTHER DAY   Jon Secada
9   SHE'S PLAYING HARD TO GET   Hi-Five
10   PLEASE DON'T GO   K.W.S.
     Note: * Second longest reign at #1 in chart history, eclipsing
          Nat King Cole's "Too Young" (August 1951).

October 3, 1992

1   END OF THE ROAD (FROM "BOOMERANG")   Boyz II
     Men *
2   SOMETIMES LOVE JUST AIN'T ENOUGH   Patty Smyth
3   HUMPIN' AROUND   Bobby Brown
4   BABY-BABY-BABY   TLC
5   JUMP AROUND   House Of Pain
6   SHE'S PLAYING HARD TO GET   Hi-Five
7   NOVEMBER RAIN   Guns N' Roses
8   PLEASE DON'T GO   K.W.S.
9   JUST ANOTHER DAY   Jon Secada
10   STAY   Shakespear's Sister
     Note: * Second longest reign at #1 in chart history, eclipsing
          Nat King Cole's "Too Young" (August 1951).

October 10, 1992

1   END OF THE ROAD (FROM "BOOMERANG")   Boyz II
     Men *
2   SOMETIMES LOVE JUST AIN'T ENOUGH   Patty Smyth
3   JUMP AROUND   House Of Pain
4   HUMPIN' AROUND   Bobby Brown
5   BABY-BABY-BABY   TLC
6   SHE'S PLAYING HARD TO GET   Hi-Five
7   PLEASE DON'T GO   K.W.S.
8   PEOPLE EVERYDAY   Arrested Development
9   WHEN I LOOK INTO YOUR EYES   Firehouse
10   I'D DIE WITHOUT YOU (FROM "BOOMERANG")   P.M.
     Dawn
     Note: * Second longest reign at #1 in chart history, eclipsing
          Nat King Cole's "Too Young" (August 1951).

October 17, 1992

1   END OF THE ROAD (FROM "BOOMERANG")   Boyz II
     Men *
2   SOMETIMES LOVE JUST AIN'T ENOUGH   Patty Smyth
3   JUMP AROUND   House Of Pain
4   HUMPIN' AROUND   Bobby Brown
5   SHE'S PLAYING HARD TO GET   Hi-Five
6   PLEASE DON'T GO   K.W.S.
7   I'D DIE WITHOUT YOU (FROM "BOOMERANG")   P.M.
     Dawn

8   WHEN I LOOK INTO YOUR EYES   Firehouse
9   BABY-BABY-BABY   TLC
10   PEOPLE EVERYDAY   Arrested Development
     Note: * Second longest reign at #1 in chart history, eclipsing
          Nat King Cole's "Too Young" (August 1951).

October 24, 1992

1   END OF THE ROAD (FROM "BOOMERANG")   Boyz II
     Men *
2   SOMETIMES LOVE JUST AIN'T ENOUGH   Patty Smyth
3   EROTICA   Madonna
4   I'D DIE WITHOUT YOU (FROM "BOOMERANG")   P.M.
     Dawn
5   JUMP AROUND   House Of Pain
6   HOW DO YOU TALK TO AN ANGEL   The Heights
7   SHE'S PLAYING HARD TO GET   Hi-Five
8   WHEN I LOOK INTO YOUR EYES   Firehouse
9   PEOPLE EVERYDAY   Arrested Development
10   PLEASE DON'T GO   K.W.S.
     Note: * Second longest reign at #1 in chart history, eclipsing
          Nat King Cole's "Too Young" (August 1951).

October 31, 1992

1   END OF THE ROAD (FROM "BOOMERANG")   Boyz II
     Men *
2   SOMETIMES LOVE JUST AIN'T ENOUGH   Patty Smyth
3   I'D DIE WITHOUT YOU (FROM "BOOMERANG")   P.M.
     Dawn
4   HOW DO YOU TALK TO AN ANGEL   The Heights
5   EROTICA   Madonna
6   JUMP AROUND   House Of Pain
7   SHE'S PLAYING HARD TO GET   Hi-Five
8   FREE YOUR MIND   En Vogue
9   RHYTHM IS A DANCER   Snap
10   PEOPLE EVERYDAY   Arrested Development
     Note: * Second longest reign at #1 in chart history, eclipsing
          Nat King Cole's "Too Young" (August 1951).

November 7, 1992

1   END OF THE ROAD (FROM "BOOMERANG")   Boyz II
     Men *
2   HOW DO YOU TALK TO AN ANGEL   The Heights
3   I'D DIE WITHOUT YOU (FROM "BOOMERANG")   P.M.
     Dawn
4   SOMETIMES LOVE JUST AIN'T ENOUGH   Patty Smyth
5   EROTICA   Madonna
6   JUMP AROUND   House Of Pain
7   RHYTHM IS A DANCER   Snap
8   RUMP SHAKER   Wreckx-N-Effect
9   REAL LOVE   Mary J. Blige
10   WHAT ABOUT YOUR FRIENDS   TLC
     Note: * Second longest reign at #1 in chart history, eclipsing
          Nat King Cole's "Too Young" (August 1951).

November 14, 1992

1   HOW DO YOU TALK TO AN ANGEL   The Heights
2   END OF THE ROAD (FROM "BOOMERANG")   Boyz II
     Men *
3   I'D DIE WITHOUT YOU (FROM "BOOMERANG")   P.M.
     Dawn
4   IF I EVER FALL IN LOVE   Shai
5   SOMETIMES LOVE JUST AIN'T ENOUGH   Patty Smyth
6   RUMP SHAKER   Wreckx-N-Effect
7   RHYTHM IS A DANCER   Snap
8   WHAT ABOUT YOUR FRIENDS   TLC
9   EROTICA   Madonna
10   JUMP AROUND   House Of Pain

Whitney Houston

``I Will Always Love You'' is a phenomenal, record-breaking #1 smash beginning November 28.

Note: * Second longest reign at #1 in chart history, eclipsing Nat King Cole's "Too Young" (August 1951).

November 21, 1992

1   HOW DO YOU TALK TO AN ANGEL   The Heights
2   IF I EVER FALL IN LOVE   Shai
3   I'D DIE WITHOUT YOU (FROM "BOOMERANG")   P.M. Dawn
4   END OF THE ROAD (FROM "BOOMERANG")   Boyz II Men *
5   RUMP SHAKER   Wreckx-N-Effect
6   RHYTHM IS A DANCER   Snap
7   WHAT ABOUT YOUR FRIENDS   TLC
8   SOMETIMES LOVE JUST AIN'T ENOUGH   Patty Smyth
9   REAL LOVE   Mary J. Blige
10   JUMP AROUND   House Of Pain
Note: * Second longest reign at #1 in chart history, eclipsing Nat King Cole's "Too Young" (August 1951).

November 28, 1992

1   I WILL ALWAYS LOVE YOU (FROM "THE BODYGUARD")   Whitney Houston *
2   HOW DO YOU TALK TO AN ANGEL   The Heights
3   IF I EVER FALL IN LOVE   Shai
4   RUMP SHAKER   Wreckx-N-Effect
5   I'D DIE WITHOUT YOU (FROM "BOOMERANG")   P.M. Dawn
6   END OF THE ROAD (FROM "BOOMERANG")   Boyz II Men **
7   RHYTHM IS A DANCER   Snap
8   REAL LOVE   Mary J. Blige
9   WHAT ABOUT YOUR FRIENDS   TLC

10   GOOD ENOUGH   Bobby Brown
Note: * Written by Dolly Parton, now the longest reign at #1 in chart history.
    ** Second longest reign at #1 in chart history, eclipsing Nat King Cole's "Too Young" (August 1951).

December 5, 1992

1   I WILL ALWAYS LOVE YOU (FROM "THE BODYGUARD")   Whitney Houston *
2   IF I EVER FALL IN LOVE   Shai
3   RUMP SHAKER   Wreckx-N-Effect
4   HOW DO YOU TALK TO AN ANGEL   The Heights
5   I'D DIE WITHOUT YOU (FROM "BOOMERANG")   P.M. Dawn
6   RHYTHM IS A DANCER   Snap
7   REAL LOVE   Mary J. Blige
8   GOOD ENOUGH   Bobby Brown
9   WHAT ABOUT YOUR FRIENDS   TLC
10   END OF THE ROAD (FROM "BOOMERANG")   Boyz II Men **
Note: * Written by Dolly Parton, now the longest reign at #1 in chart history.
    ** Second longest reign at #1 in chart history, eclipsing Nat King Cole's "Too Young" (August 1951).

December 12, 1992

1   I WILL ALWAYS LOVE YOU (FROM "THE BODYGUARD")   Whitney Houston *
2   IF I EVER FALL IN LOVE   Shai
3   RUMP SHAKER   Wreckx-N-Effect
4   IN THE STILL OF THE NITE (FROM "THE JACKSONS")   Boyz II Men

5   HOW DO YOU TALK TO AN ANGEL   The Heights
6   I'D DIE WITHOUT YOU (FROM "BOOMERANG")   P.M.
     Dawn
7   RHYTHM IS A DANCER   Snap
8   GOOD ENOUGH   Bobby Brown
9   REAL LOVE   Mary J. Blige
10   WHAT ABOUT YOUR FRIENDS   TLC
     Note: * Written by Dolly Parton, now the longest reign at #1
     in chart history.

December 19, 1992

1   I WILL ALWAYS LOVE YOU (FROM "THE BODYGUARD")
     Whitney Houston *
2   IF I EVER FALL IN LOVE   Shai
3   RUMP SHAKER   Wreckx-N-Effect
4   IN THE STILL OF THE NITE (FROM "THE JACKSONS")
     Boyz II Men
5   I'D DIE WITHOUT YOU (FROM "BOOMERANG")   P.M.
     Dawn
6   HOW DO YOU TALK TO AN ANGEL   The Heights
7   RHYTHM IS A DANCER   Snap
8   GOOD ENOUGH   Bobby Brown
9   REAL LOVE   Mary J. Blige
10   WHAT ABOUT YOUR FRIENDS   TLC
     Note: * Written by Dolly Parton, now the longest reign at #1
     in chart history.

December 26, 1992

1   I WILL ALWAYS LOVE YOU (FROM "THE BODYGUARD")
     Whitney Houston *
2   RUMP SHAKER   Wreckx-N-Effect
3   IF I EVER FALL IN LOVE   Shai
4   IN THE STILL OF THE NITE (FROM "THE JACKSONS")
     Boyz II Men
5   I'D DIE WITHOUT YOU (FROM "BOOMERANG")   P.M.
     Dawn
6   RHYTHM IS A DANCER   Snap
7   GOOD ENOUGH   Bobby Brown
8   SAVING FOREVER FOR YOU (FROM "BEVERLY HILLS
     90210")   Shanice
9   HOW DO YOU TALK TO AN ANGEL   The Heights
10   REAL LOVE   Mary J. Blige
     Note: * Written by Dolly Parton, now the longest reign at #1
     in chart history.

January 2, 1993

1   I WILL ALWAYS LOVE YOU (FROM "THE BODYGUARD")
     Whitney Houston *
2   RUMP SHAKER   Wreckx-N-Effect
3   IF I EVER FALL IN LOVE   Shai
4   IN THE STILL OF THE NITE (FROM "THE JACKSONS")
     Boyz II Men
5   RHYTHM IS A DANCER   Snap
6   I'D DIE WITHOUT YOU (FROM "BOOMERANG")   P.M.
     Dawn
7   SAVING FOREVER FOR YOU (FROM "BEVERLY HILLS
     90210")   Shanice
8   GOOD ENOUGH   Bobby Brown
9   WHAT ABOUT YOUR FRIENDS   TLC
10   REAL LOVE   Mary J. Blige
     Note: * Written by Dolly Parton, now the longest reign at #1
     in chart history.

January 9, 1993

1   I WILL ALWAYS LOVE YOU (FROM "THE BODYGUARD")
     Whitney Houston *
2   RUMP SHAKER   Wreckx-N-Effect

3   IF I EVER FALL IN LOVE   Shai
4   IN THE STILL OF THE NITE (FROM "THE JACKSONS")
     Boyz II Men
5   I'D DIE WITHOUT YOU (FROM "BOOMERANG")   P.M.
     Dawn
6   RHYTHM IS A DANCER   Snap
7   SAVING FOREVER FOR YOU (FROM "BEVERLY HILLS
     90210")   Shanice
8   GOOD ENOUGH   Bobby Brown
9   WHAT ABOUT YOUR FRIENDS   TLC
10   REAL LOVE   Mary J. Blige
     Note: * Written by Dolly Parton, now the longest reign at #1
     in chart history.

January 16, 1993

1   I WILL ALWAYS LOVE YOU (FROM "THE BODYGUARD")
     Whitney Houston *
2   IF I EVER FALL IN LOVE   Shai
3   IN THE STILL OF THE NITE (FROM "THE JACKSONS")
     Boyz II Men
4   RUMP SHAKER   Wreckx-N-Effect
5   SAVING FOREVER FOR YOU (FROM "BEVERLY HILLS
     90210")   Shanice
6   RHYTHM IS A DANCER   Snap
7   I'D DIE WITHOUT YOU (FROM "BOOMERANG")   P.M.
     Dawn
8   GOOD ENOUGH   Bobby Brown
9   WHAT ABOUT YOUR FRIENDS   TLC
10   DEEPER AND DEEPER   Madonna
     Note: * Written by Dolly Parton, now the longest reign at #1
     in chart history.

January 23, 1993

1   I WILL ALWAYS LOVE YOU (FROM "THE BODYGUARD")
     Whitney Houston *
2   IF I EVER FALL IN LOVE   Shai
3   IN THE STILL OF THE NITE (FROM "THE JACKSONS")
     Boyz II Men
4   RUMP SHAKER   Wreckx-N-Effect
5   SAVING FOREVER FOR YOU (FROM "BEVERLY HILLS
     90210")   Shanice
6   RHYTHM IS A DANCER   Snap
7   GOOD ENOUGH   Bobby Brown
8   DEEPER AND DEEPER   Madonna
9   A WHOLE NEW WORLD (ALADDIN'S THEME)   Peabo
     Bryson and Regina Belle
10   I'D DIE WITHOUT YOU (FROM "BOOMERANG")   P.M.
     Dawn
     Note: * Written by Dolly Parton, now the longest reign at #1
     in chart history.

January 30, 1993

1   I WILL ALWAYS LOVE YOU (FROM "THE BODYGUARD")
     Whitney Houston *
2   IF I EVER FALL IN LOVE   Shai
3   IN THE STILL OF THE NITE (FROM "THE JACKSONS")
     Boyz II Men
4   SAVING FOREVER FOR YOU (FROM "BEVERLY HILLS
     90210")   Shanice
5   RUMP SHAKER   Wreckx-N-Effect
6   A WHOLE NEW WORLD (ALADDIN'S THEME)   Peabo
     Bryson and Regina Belle
7   DEEPER AND DEEPER   Madonna
8   GOOD ENOUGH   Bobby Brown
9   RHYTHM IS A DANCER   Snap
10   7   Prince and The New Power Generation
     Note: * Written by Dolly Parton, now the longest reign at #1
     in chart history.

February 6, 1993
1. I WILL ALWAYS LOVE YOU (FROM "THE BODYGUARD") Whitney Houston *
2. IF I EVER FALL IN LOVE Shai
3. A WHOLE NEW WORLD (ALADDIN'S THEME) Peabo Bryson and Regina Belle
4. IN THE STILL OF THE NITE (FROM "THE JACKSONS") Boyz II Men
5. SAVING FOREVER FOR YOU (FROM "BEVERLY HILLS 90210") Shanice
6. RUMP SHAKER Wreckx-N-Effect
7. ORDINARY WORLD Duran Duran
8. 7 Prince and The New Power Generation
9. DEEPER AND DEEPER Madonna
10. MR. WENDAL Arrested Development
   Note: * Written by Dolly Parton, now the longest reign at #1 in chart history.

February 13, 1993
1. I WILL ALWAYS LOVE YOU (FROM "THE BODYGUARD") Whitney Houston *
2. A WHOLE NEW WORLD (ALADDIN'S THEME) Peabo Bryson and Regina Belle
3. IF I EVER FALL IN LOVE Shai
4. SAVING FOREVER FOR YOU (FROM "BEVERLY HILLS 90210") Shanice
5. ORDINARY WORLD Duran Duran
6. IN THE STILL OF THE NITE (FROM "THE JACKSONS") Boyz II Men
7. MR. WENDAL Arrested Development
8. 7 Prince and The New Power Generation
9. RUMP SHAKER Wreckx-N-Effect
10. I'M EVERY WOMAN (FROM "THE BODYGUARD") Whitney Houston
   Note: * Written by Dolly Parton, now the longest reign at #1 in chart history.

February 20, 1993
1. I WILL ALWAYS LOVE YOU (FROM "THE BODYGUARD") Whitney Houston *
2. A WHOLE NEW WORLD (ALADDIN'S THEME) Peabo Bryson and Regina Belle
3. ORDINARY WORLD Duran Duran
4. I'M EVERY WOMAN (FROM "THE BODYGUARD") Whitney Houston
5. SAVING FOREVER FOR YOU (FROM "BEVERLY HILLS 90210") Shanice
6. MR. WENDAL Arrested Development
7. IF I EVER FALL IN LOVE Shai
8. 7 Prince and The New Power Generation
9. IN THE STILL OF THE NITE (FROM "THE JACKSONS") Boyz II Men
10. HIP HOP HOORAY Naughty By Nature
   Note: * Written by Dolly Parton, now the longest reign at #1 in chart history.

February 27, 1993
1. I WILL ALWAYS LOVE YOU (FROM "THE BODYGUARD") Whitney Houston *
2. A WHOLE NEW WORLD (ALADDIN'S THEME) Peabo Bryson and Regina Belle
3. ORDINARY WORLD Duran Duran
4. I'M EVERY WOMAN (FROM "THE BODYGUARD") Whitney Houston
5. NUTHIN' BUT A "G" THANG Dr. Dre
6. MR. WENDAL Arrested Development
7. 7 Prince and The New Power Generation
8. SAVING FOREVER FOR YOU (FROM "BEVERLY HILLS 90210") Shanice
9. HIP HOP HOORAY Naughty By Nature
10. INFORMER Snow
   Note: * Written by Dolly Parton, now the longest reign at #1 in chart history.

March 6, 1993
1. A WHOLE NEW WORLD (ALADDIN'S THEME) Peabo Bryson and Regina Belle
2. I WILL ALWAYS LOVE YOU (FROM "THE BODYGUARD") Whitney Houston *
3. ORDINARY WORLD Duran Duran
4. INFORMER Snow
5. NUTHIN' BUT A "G" THANG Dr. Dre
6. I'M EVERY WOMAN (FROM "THE BODYGUARD") Whitney Houston
7. MR. WENDAL Arrested Development
8. HIP HOP HOORAY Naughty By Nature
9. DON'T WALK AWAY Jade
10. BED OF ROSES Bon Jovi
   Note: * Written by Dolly Parton, now the longest reign at #1 in chart history.

March 13, 1993
1. INFORMER Snow
2. A WHOLE NEW WORLD (ALADDIN'S THEME) Peabo Bryson and Regina Belle
3. NUTHIN' BUT A "G" THANG Dr. Dre
4. ORDINARY WORLD Duran Duran
5. I'M EVERY WOMAN (FROM "THE BODYGUARD") Whitney Houston
6. FREAK ME Silk
7. I WILL ALWAYS LOVE YOU (FROM "THE BODYGUARD") Whitney Houston *
8. MR. WENDAL Arrested Development
9. DON'T WALK AWAY Jade
10. BED OF ROSES Bon Jovi
   Note: * Written by Dolly Parton, now the longest reign at #1 in chart history.

March 20, 1993
1. INFORMER Snow
2. NUTHIN' BUT A "G" THANG Dr. Dre
3. FREAK ME Silk
4. A WHOLE NEW WORLD (ALADDIN'S THEME) Peabo Bryson and Regina Belle
5. I'M EVERY WOMAN (FROM "THE BODYGUARD") Whitney Houston
6. ORDINARY WORLD Duran Duran
7. DON'T WALK AWAY Jade
8. MR. WENDAL Arrested Development
9. I HAVE NOTHING (FROM "THE BODYGUARD") Whitney Houston
10. BED OF ROSES Bon Jovi

March 27, 1993
1. INFORMER Snow
2. FREAK ME Silk
3. NUTHIN' BUT A "G" THANG Dr. Dre
4. DON'T WALK AWAY Jade
5. ORDINARY WORLD Duran Duran
6. I HAVE NOTHING (FROM "THE BODYGUARD") Whitney Houston
7. I'M EVERY WOMAN (FROM "THE BODYGUARD") Whitney Houston

8 A WHOLE NEW WORLD (ALADDIN'S THEME) Peabo Bryson and Regina Belle
9 MR. WENDAL Arrested Development
10 BED OF ROSES Bon Jovi

April 3, 1993

1 INFORMER Snow
2 FREAK ME Silk
3 NUTHIN' BUT A "G" THANG Dr. Dre
4 I HAVE NOTHING (FROM "THE BODYGUARD") Whitney Houston
5 DON'T WALK AWAY Jade
6 I'M EVERY WOMAN (FROM "THE BODYGUARD") Whitney Houston
7 ORDINARY WORLD Duran Duran
8 MR. WENDAL Arrested Development
9 CAT'S IN THE CRADLE Ugly Kid Joe
10 BED OF ROSES Bon Jovi

April 10, 1993

1 INFORMER Snow
2 FREAK ME Silk
3 NUTHIN' BUT A "G" THANG Dr. Dre
4 I HAVE NOTHING (FROM "THE BODYGUARD") Whitney Houston
5 DON'T WALK AWAY Jade
6 CAT'S IN THE CRADLE Ugly Kid Joe
7 TWO PRINCES Spin Doctors
8 LOVE IS (FROM "BEVERLY HILLS, 90210") Vanessa Williams/Brian McKnight
9 MR. WENDAL Arrested Development
10 BED OF ROSES Bon Jovi

April 17, 1993

1 INFORMER Snow
2 FREAK ME Silk
3 NUTHIN' BUT A "G" THANG Dr. Dre
4 I HAVE NOTHING (FROM "THE BODYGUARD") Whitney Houston
5 DON'T WALK AWAY Jade
6 LOVE IS (FROM "BEVERLY HILLS, 90210") Vanessa Williams/Brian McKnight
7 CAT'S IN THE CRADLE Ugly Kid Joe
8 TWO PRINCES Spin Doctors
9 I'M SO INTO YOU SWV
10 COMFORTER Shai

April 24, 1993

1 INFORMER Snow
2 FREAK ME Silk
3 NUTHIN' BUT A "G" THANG Dr. Dre
4 I HAVE NOTHING (FROM "THE BODYGUARD") Whitney Houston
5 DON'T WALK AWAY Jade
6 LOVE IS (FROM "BEVERLY HILLS, 90210") Vanessa Williams/Brian McKnight
7 I'M SO INTO YOU SWV
8 TWO PRINCES Spin Doctors
9 CAT'S IN THE CRADLE Ugly Kid Joe
10 DITTY Paperboy

May 1, 1993

1 FREAK ME Silk
2 INFORMER Snow
3 NUTHIN' BUT A "G" THANG Dr. Dre
4 I HAVE NOTHING (FROM "THE BODYGUARD") Whitney Houston

5 LOVE IS (FROM "BEVERLY HILLS, 90210") Vanessa Williams/Brian McKnight
6 DON'T WALK AWAY Jade
7 I'M SO INTO YOU SWV
8 TWO PRINCES Spin Doctors
9 LOOKING THROUGH PATIENT EYES P.M. Dawn
10 DITTY Paperboy

May 8, 1993

1 FREAK ME Silk
2 THAT'S THE WAY LOVE GOES Janet Jackson
3 INFORMER Snow
4 LOVE IS (FROM "BEVERLY HILLS, 90210") Vanessa Williams/Brian McKnight
5 I HAVE NOTHING (FROM "THE BODYGUARD") Whitney Houston
6 NUTHIN' BUT A "G" THANG Dr. Dre
7 DON'T WALK AWAY Jade
8 I'M SO INTO YOU SWV
9 LOOKING THROUGH PATIENT EYES P.M. Dawn
10 DITTY Paperboy

May 15, 1993

1 THAT'S THE WAY LOVE GOES Janet Jackson
2 FREAK ME Silk
3 LOVE IS (FROM "BEVERLY HILLS, 90210") Vanessa Williams/Brian McKnight
4 INFORMER Snow
5 I HAVE NOTHING (FROM "THE BODYGUARD") Whitney Houston
6 NUTHIN' BUT A "G" THANG Dr. Dre
7 KNOCKIN' DA BOOTS H-Town
8 I'M SO INTO YOU SWV
9 LOOKING THROUGH PATIENT EYES P.M. Dawn
10 DON'T WALK AWAY Jade

May 22, 1993

1 THAT'S THE WAY LOVE GOES Janet Jackson
2 FREAK ME Silk
3 KNOCKIN' DA BOOTS H-Town
4 LOVE IS (FROM "BEVERLY HILLS, 90210") Vanessa Williams/Brian McKnight
5 NUTHIN' BUT A "G" THANG Dr. Dre
6 I'M SO INTO YOU SWV
7 LOOKING THROUGH PATIENT EYES P.M. Dawn
8 WEAK SWV
9 I HAVE NOTHING (FROM "THE BODYGUARD") Whitney Houston
10 INFORMER Snow

May 29, 1993

1 THAT'S THE WAY LOVE GOES Janet Jackson
2 FREAK ME Silk
3 KNOCKIN' DA BOOTS H-Town
4 WEAK SWV
5 LOVE IS (FROM "BEVERLY HILLS, 90210") Vanessa Williams/Brian McKnight
6 LOOKING THROUGH PATIENT EYES P.M. Dawn
7 I'M SO INTO YOU SWV
8 NUTHIN' BUT A "G" THANG Dr. Dre
9 I HAVE NOTHING (FROM "THE BODYGUARD") Whitney Houston
10 DON'T WALK AWAY Jade

June 5, 1993

1 THAT'S THE WAY LOVE GOES Janet Jackson

420

2 FREAK ME   Silk
3 KNOCKIN' DA BOOTS   H-Town
4 WEAK   SWV
5 LOVE IS (FROM "BEVERLY HILLS, 90210")   Vanessa
   Williams/Brian McKnight
6 I'M SO INTO YOU   SWV
7 LOOKING THROUGH PATIENT EYES   P.M. Dawn
8 SHOW ME LOVE   Robin S.
9 HAVE I TOLD YOU LATELY (FROM "UNPLUGGED")   Rod
   Stewart
10 BAD BOYS (THEME FROM "COPS")   Inner Circle

June 12, 1993
1 THAT'S THE WAY LOVE GOES   Janet Jackson
2 FREAK ME   Silk
3 KNOCKIN' DA BOOTS   H-Town
4 WEAK   SWV
5 SHOW ME LOVE   Robin S.
6 LOOKING THROUGH PATIENT EYES   P.M. Dawn
7 I'M SO INTO YOU   SWV
8 BAD BOYS (THEME FROM "COPS")   Inner Circle
9 HAVE I TOLD YOU LATELY (FROM "UNPLUGGED")   Rod
   Stewart
10 COME UNDONE   Duran Duran

June 19, 1993
1 THAT'S THE WAY LOVE GOES   Janet Jackson
2 WEAK   SWV
3 KNOCKIN' DA BOOTS   H-Town
4 FREAK ME   Silk
5 HAVE I TOLD YOU LATELY (FROM "UNPLUGGED")   Rod
   Stewart
6 SHOW ME LOVE   Robin S.
7 COME UNDONE   Duran Duran
8 BAD BOYS (THEME FROM "COPS")   Inner Circle
9 LOOKING THROUGH PATIENT EYES   P.M. Dawn
10 I'M SO INTO YOU   SWV

June 26, 1993
1 THAT'S THE WAY LOVE GOES   Janet Jackson
2 WEAK   SWV
3 KNOCKIN' DA BOOTS   H-Town
4 FREAK ME   Silk
5 HAVE I TOLD YOU LATELY (FROM "UNPLUGGED")   Rod
   Stewart
6 SHOW ME LOVE   Robin S.
7 COME UNDONE   Duran Duran
8 WHOOMP! (THERE IT IS)   Tag Team
9 DRE DAY   Dr. Dre
10 BAD BOYS (THEME FROM "COPS")   Inner Circle

July 3, 1993
1 THAT'S THE WAY LOVE GOES   Janet Jackson
2 WEAK   SWV
3 KNOCKIN' DA BOOTS   H-Town
4 WHOOMP! (THERE IT IS)   Tag Team
5 HAVE I TOLD YOU LATELY (FROM "UNPLUGGED")   Rod
   Stewart
6 SHOW ME LOVE   Robin S.
7 CAN'T HELP FALLING IN LOVE (FROM "SLIVER")   UB40
8 DRE DAY   Dr. Dre
9 COME UNDONE   Duran Duran
10 I'LL NEVER GET OVER YOU (GETTING OVER ME)
   Expose

July 10, 1993
1 WEAK   SWV
2 THAT'S THE WAY LOVE GOES   Janet Jackson
3 WHOOMP! (THERE IT IS)   Tag Team
4 CAN'T HELP FALLING IN LOVE (FROM "SLIVER")   UB40
5 KNOCKIN' DA BOOTS   H-Town
6 SHOW ME LOVE   Robin S.
7 HAVE I TOLD YOU LATELY (FROM "UNPLUGGED")   Rod
   Stewart
8 DRE DAY   Dr. Dre
9 I'LL NEVER GET OVER YOU (GETTING OVER ME)
   Expose
10 COME UNDONE   Duran Duran

July 17, 1993
1 WEAK   SWV
2 CAN'T HELP FALLING IN LOVE (FROM "SLIVER")   UB40
3 WHOOMP! (THERE IT IS)   Tag Team
4 THAT'S THE WAY LOVE GOES   Janet Jackson
5 KNOCKIN' DA BOOTS   H-Town
6 HAVE I TOLD YOU LATELY (FROM "UNPLUGGED")   Rod
   Stewart
7 SHOW ME LOVE   Robin S.
8 I'LL NEVER GET OVER YOU (GETTING OVER ME)
   Expose
9 I'M GONNA BE (500 MILES)   The Proclaimers
10 DRE DAY   Dr. Dre

July 24, 1993
1 CAN'T HELP FALLING IN LOVE (FROM "SLIVER")   UB40
2 WEAK   SWV
3 WHOOMP! (THERE IT IS)   Tag Team
4 THAT'S THE WAY LOVE GOES   Janet Jackson
5 KNOCKIN' DA BOOTS   H-Town
6 SHOW ME LOVE   Robin S.
7 SLAM   Onyx
8 I'LL NEVER GET OVER YOU (GETTING OVER ME)
   Expose
9 I'M GONNA BE (500 MILES)   The Proclaimers
10 HAVE I TOLD YOU LATELY (FROM "UNPLUGGED")   Rod
   Stewart

July 31, 1993
1 CAN'T HELP FALLING IN LOVE (FROM "SLIVER")   UB40
2 WHOOMP! (THERE IT IS)   Tag Team
3 WEAK   SWV
4 I'M GONNA BE (500 MILES)   The Proclaimers
5 SLAM   Onyx
6 THAT'S THE WAY LOVE GOES   Janet Jackson
7 LATELY   Jodeci
8 SHOW ME LOVE   Robin S.
9 KNOCKIN' DA BOOTS   H-Town
10 I'LL NEVER GET OVER YOU (GETTING OVER ME)
   Expose

August 7, 1993
1 CAN'T HELP FALLING IN LOVE (FROM "SLIVER")   UB40
2 WHOOMP! (THERE IT IS)   Tag Team
3 WEAK   SWV
4 I'M GONNA BE (500 MILES)   The Proclaimers
5 SLAM   Onyx
6 LATELY   Jodeci
7 IF I HAD NO LOOT   Tony! Toni! Tone!
8 THAT'S THE WAY LOVE GOES   Janet Jackson
9 SHOW ME LOVE   Robin S.
10 I DON'T WANNA FIGHT (FROM "WHAT'S LOVE GOT TO DO
   WITH IT")   Tina Turner

Mariah Carey

In September-October, ``Dreamlover'' spends eight weeks at #1 for this vocally-gifted songstress.

August 14, 1993
1. CAN'T HELP FALLING IN LOVE (FROM "SLIVER")   UB40
2. WHOOMP! (THERE IT IS)   Tag Team
3. WEAK   SWV
4. I'M GONNA BE (500 MILES)   The Proclaimers
5. SLAM   Onyx
6. LATELY   Jodeci
7. IF I HAD NO LOOT   Tony! Toni! Tone!
8. RUNAWAY TRAIN   Soul Asylum
9. I DON'T WANNA FIGHT (FROM "WHAT'S LOVE GOT TO DO WITH IT")   Tina Turner
10. IF   Janet Jackson

August 21, 1993
1. CAN'T HELP FALLING IN LOVE (FROM "SLIVER")   UB40
2. WHOOMP! (THERE IT IS)   Tag Team
3. I'M GONNA BE (500 MILES)   The Proclaimers
4. SLAM   Onyx
5. LATELY   Jodeci
6. WEAK   SWV
7. IF I HAD NO LOOT   Tony! Toni! Tone!
8. RUNAWAY TRAIN   Soul Asylum
9. DREAMLOVER   Mariah Carey
10. IF   Janet Jackson

August 28, 1993
1. CAN'T HELP FALLING IN LOVE (FROM "SLIVER")   UB40
2. WHOOMP! (THERE IT IS)   Tag Team
3. DREAMLOVER   Mariah Carey
4. LATELY   Jodeci
5. RUNAWAY TRAIN   Soul Asylum
6. I'M GONNA BE (500 MILES)   The Proclaimers
7. IF   Janet Jackson
8. SLAM   Onyx
9. IF I HAD NO LOOT   Tony! Toni! Tone!
10. WEAK   SWV

September 4, 1993
1. CAN'T HELP FALLING IN LOVE (FROM "SLIVER")   UB40
2. DREAMLOVER   Mariah Carey
3. WHOOMP! (THERE IT IS)   Tag Team
4. LATELY   Jodeci
5. RUNAWAY TRAIN   Soul Asylum
6. IF   Janet Jackson
7. RIGHT HERE (HUMAN NATURE)/DOWNTOWN   SWV
8. WILL YOU BE THERE (FROM "FREE WILLY")   Michael Jackson
9. I'M GONNA BE (500 MILES)   The Proclaimers
10. IF I HAD NO LOOT   Tony! Toni! Tone!

September 11, 1993
1. DREAMLOVER   Mariah Carey
2. CAN'T HELP FALLING IN LOVE (FROM "SLIVER")   UB40
3. WHOOMP! (THERE IT IS)   Tag Team
4. IF   Janet Jackson
5. RUNAWAY TRAIN   Soul Asylum
6. RIGHT HERE (HUMAN NATURE)/DOWNTOWN   SWV
7. WILL YOU BE THERE (FROM "FREE WILLY")   Michael Jackson
8. LATELY   Jodeci
9. THE RIVER OF DREAMS   Billy Joel
10. IF I HAD NO LOOT   Tony! Toni! Tone!

September 18, 1993
1 DREAMLOVER Mariah Carey
2 WHOOMP! (THERE IT IS) Tag Team
3 CAN'T HELP FALLING IN LOVE (FROM "SLIVER") UB40
4 IF Janet Jackson
5 RIGHT HERE (HUMAN NATURE)/DOWNTOWN SWV
6 THE RIVER OF DREAMS Billy Joel
7 RUNAWAY TRAIN Soul Asylum
8 WILL YOU BE THERE (FROM "FREE WILLY") Michael Jackson
9 LATELY Jodeci
10 BABY I'M YOURS Shai

September 25, 1993
1 DREAMLOVER Mariah Carey
2 WHOOMP! (THERE IT IS) Tag Team
3 RIGHT HERE (HUMAN NATURE)/DOWNTOWN SWV
4 CAN'T HELP FALLING IN LOVE (FROM "SLIVER") UB40
5 IF Janet Jackson
6 THE RIVER OF DREAMS Billy Joel
7 WILL YOU BE THERE (FROM "FREE WILLY") Michael Jackson
8 RUNAWAY TRAIN Soul Asylum
9 LATELY Jodeci
10 BABY I'M YOURS Shai

October 2, 1993
1 DREAMLOVER Mariah Carey
2 RIGHT HERE (HUMAN NATURE)/DOWNTOWN SWV
3 WHOOMP! (THERE IT IS) Tag Team
4 THE RIVER OF DREAMS Billy Joel
5 IF Janet Jackson
6 CAN'T HELP FALLING IN LOVE (FROM "SLIVER") UB40
7 WILL YOU BE THERE (FROM "FREE WILLY") Michael Jackson
8 ANOTHER SAD LOVE SONG Toni Braxton
9 RUNAWAY TRAIN Soul Asylum
10 BABY I'M YOURS Shai

October 9, 1993
1 DREAMLOVER Mariah Carey
2 RIGHT HERE (HUMAN NATURE)/DOWNTOWN SWV
3 WHOOMP! (THERE IT IS) Tag Team
4 THE RIVER OF DREAMS Billy Joel
5 IF Janet Jackson
6 CAN'T HELP FALLING IN LOVE (FROM "SLIVER") UB40
7 ANOTHER SAD LOVE SONG Toni Braxton
8 WILL YOU BE THERE (FROM "FREE WILLY") Michael Jackson
9 I'D DO ANYTHING FOR LOVE (BUT I WON'T DO THAT) Meat Loaf
10 RUNAWAY TRAIN Soul Asylum

October 16, 1993
1 DREAMLOVER Mariah Carey
2 RIGHT HERE (HUMAN NATURE)/DOWNTOWN SWV
3 THE RIVER OF DREAMS Billy Joel
4 WHOOMP! (THERE IT IS) Tag Team
5 JUST KICKIN' IT Xscape
6 I'D DO ANYTHING FOR LOVE (BUT I WON'T DO THAT) Meat Loaf
7 IF Janet Jackson
8 ALL THAT SHE WANTS Ace Of Base
9 ANOTHER SAD LOVE SONG Toni Braxton
10 HEY MR. D.J. Zhane

Billy Joel
``River Of Dreams'' peaks at #3 on October 16.

October 23, 1993
1 DREAMLOVER Mariah Carey
2 JUST KICKIN' IT Xscape
3 I'D DO ANYTHING FOR LOVE (BUT I WON'T DO THAT) Meat Loaf
4 ALL THAT SHE WANTS Ace Of Base
5 THE RIVER OF DREAMS Billy Joel
6 RIGHT HERE (HUMAN NATURE)/DOWNTOWN SWV
7 WHOOMP! (THERE IT IS) Tag Team
8 HEY MR. D.J. Zhane
9 IF Janet Jackson
10 ANNIVERSARY Tony! Toni! Tone!

October 30, 1993
1 DREAMLOVER Mariah Carey
2 I'D DO ANYTHING FOR LOVE (BUT I WON'T DO THAT) Meat Loaf
3 ALL THAT SHE WANTS Ace Of Base
4 JUST KICKIN' IT Xscape
5 THE RIVER OF DREAMS Billy Joel
6 HEY MR. D.J. Zhane
7 WHOOMP! (THERE IT IS) Tag Team
8 RIGHT HERE (HUMAN NATURE)/DOWNTOWN SWV
9 AGAIN Janet Jackson
10 ANNIVERSARY Tony! Toni! Tone!

November 6, 1993
1 I'D DO ANYTHING FOR LOVE (BUT I WON'T DO THAT) Meat Loaf
2 ALL THAT SHE WANTS Ace Of Base
3 JUST KICKIN' IT Xscape
4 AGAIN Janet Jackson

5   DREAMLOVER   Mariah Carey
6   HEY MR. D.J.   Zhane
7   GANGSTA LEAN   DRS
8   THE RIVER OF DREAMS   Billy Joel
9   WHOOMP! (THERE IT IS)   Tag Team
10   ANNIVERSARY   Tony! Toni! Tone!

November 13, 1993
1   I'D DO ANYTHING FOR LOVE (BUT I WON'T DO THAT)
     Meat Loaf
2   ALL THAT SHE WANTS   Ace Of Base
3   AGAIN   Janet Jackson
4   JUST KICKIN' IT   Xscape
5   GANGSTA LEAN   DRS
6   DREAMLOVER   Mariah Carey
7   SHOOP   Salt-N-Pepa
8   HEY MR. D.J.   Zhane
9   WHOOMP! (THERE IT IS)   Tag Team
10   ANNIVERSARY   Tony! Toni! Tone!

November 20, 1993
1   I'D DO ANYTHING FOR LOVE (BUT I WON'T DO THAT)
     Meat Loaf
2   AGAIN   Janet Jackson
3   ALL THAT SHE WANTS   Ace Of Base
4   GANGSTA LEAN   DRS
5   JUST KICKIN' IT   Xscape
6   SHOOP   Salt-N-Pepa
7   PLEASE FORGIVE ME   Bryan Adams
8   HERO   Mariah Carey
9   HEY MR. D.J.   Zhane
10   DREAMLOVER   Mariah Carey

November 27, 1993
1   I'D DO ANYTHING FOR LOVE (BUT I WON'T DO THAT)
     Meat Loaf
2   AGAIN   Janet Jackson
3   ALL THAT SHE WANTS   Ace Of Base
4   GANGSTA LEAN   DRS
5   SHOOP   Salt-N-Pepa
6   JUST KICKIN' IT   Xscape
7   HERO   Mariah Carey
8   PLEASE FORGIVE ME   Bryan Adams
9   WHOOMP! (THERE IT IS)   Tag Team
10   HEY MR. D.J.   Zhane

December 4, 1993
1   I'D DO ANYTHING FOR LOVE (BUT I WON'T DO THAT)
     Meat Loaf
2   AGAIN   Janet Jackson
3   ALL THAT SHE WANTS   Ace Of Base
4   SHOOP   Salt-N-Pepa
5   GANGSTA LEAN   DRS
6   HERO   Mariah Carey
7   JUST KICKIN' IT   Xscape
8   PLEASE FORGIVE ME   Bryan Adams
9   BREATHE AGAIN   Toni Braxton
10   CAN WE TALK   Tevin Campbell

December 11, 1993
1   AGAIN   Janet Jackson
2   I'D DO ANYTHING FOR LOVE (BUT I WON'T DO THAT)
     Meat Loaf
3   ALL THAT SHE WANTS   Ace Of Base
4   HERO   Mariah Carey
5   SHOOP   Salt-N-Pepa

6   GANGSTA LEAN   DRS
7   JUST KICKIN' IT   Xscape
8   BREATHE AGAIN   Toni Braxton
9   PLEASE FORGIVE ME   Bryan Adams
10   ALL FOR LOVE   Bryan Adams/Rod Stewart/Sting

December 18, 1993
1   AGAIN   Janet Jackson
2   ALL THAT SHE WANTS   Ace Of Base
3   HERO   Mariah Carey
4   I'D DO ANYTHING FOR LOVE (BUT I WON'T DO THAT)
     Meat Loaf
5   SHOOP   Salt-N-Pepa
6   GANGSTA LEAN   DRS
7   ALL FOR LOVE   Bryan Adams/Rod Stewart/Sting
8   BREATHE AGAIN   Toni Braxton
9   PLEASE FORGIVE ME   Bryan Adams
10   SAID I LOVED YOU...BUT I LIED   Michael Bolton

December 25, 1993
1   HERO   Mariah Carey
2   AGAIN   Janet Jackson
3   ALL THAT SHE WANTS   Ace Of Base
4   I'D DO ANYTHING FOR LOVE (BUT I WON'T DO THAT)
     Meat Loaf
5   ALL FOR LOVE   Bryan Adams/Rod Stewart/Sting
6   GANGSTA LEAN   DRS
7   SHOOP   Salt-N-Pepa
8   BREATHE AGAIN   Toni Braxton
9   WHAT'S MY NAME?   Snoop Doggy Dogg
10   SAID I LOVED YOU...BUT I LIED   Michael Bolton

January 1, 1994
1   HERO   Mariah Carey
2   AGAIN   Janet Jackson
3   ALL THAT SHE WANTS   Ace Of Base
4   ALL FOR LOVE   Bryan Adams/Rod Stewart/Sting
5   I'D DO ANYTHING FOR LOVE (BUT I WON'T DO THAT)
     Meat Loaf
6   BREATHE AGAIN   Toni Braxton
7   GANGSTA LEAN   DRS
8   WHAT'S MY NAME?   Snoop Doggy Dogg
9   SAID I LOVED YOU...BUT I LIED   Michael Bolton
10   SHOOP   Salt-N-Pepa

January 8, 1994
1   HERO   Mariah Carey
2   ALL FOR LOVE   Bryan Adams/Rod Stewart/Sting
3   ALL THAT SHE WANTS   Ace Of Base
4   AGAIN   Janet Jackson
5   GANGSTA LEAN   DRS
6   BREATHE AGAIN   Toni Braxton
7   WHOOMP! (THERE IT IS)   Tag Team
8   WHAT'S MY NAME?   Snoop Doggy Dogg
9   I'D DO ANYTHING FOR LOVE (BUT I WON'T DO THAT)
     Meat Loaf
10   SAID I LOVED YOU...BUT I LIED   Michael Bolton

January 15, 1994
1   HERO   Mariah Carey
2   ALL FOR LOVE   Bryan Adams/Rod Stewart/Sting
3   ALL THAT SHE WANTS   Ace Of Base
4   AGAIN   Janet Jackson
5   BREATHE AGAIN   Toni Braxton
6   GANGSTA LEAN   DRS
7   SAID I LOVED YOU...BUT I LIED   Michael Bolton

Michael Bolton

Bolton's ``Said I Loved You'' peaks at #6 (Jan. 22).

8	WHOOMP! (THERE IT IS) Tag Team
9	CAN WE TALK Tevin Campbell
10	WHAT'S MY NAME? Snoop Doggy Dogg

January 22, 1994
1 ALL FOR LOVE   Bryan Adams/Rod Stewart/Sting
2 HERO   Mariah Carey
3 BREATHE AGAIN   Toni Braxton
4 AGAIN   Janet Jackson
5 ALL THAT SHE WANTS   Ace Of Base
6 SAID I LOVED YOU...BUT I LIED   Michael Bolton
7 PLEASE FORGIVE ME   Bryan Adams
8 SHOOP   Salt-N-Pepa
9 CAN WE TALK   Tevin Campbell
10 THE POWER OF LOVE   Celine Dion

January 29, 1994
1 ALL FOR LOVE   Bryan Adams/Rod Stewart/Sting
2 HERO   Mariah Carey
3 BREATHE AGAIN   Toni Braxton
4 THE POWER OF LOVE   Celine Dion
5 AGAIN   Janet Jackson
6 SAID I LOVED YOU...BUT I LIED   Michael Bolton
7 ALL THAT SHE WANTS   Ace Of Base
8 PLEASE FORGIVE ME   Bryan Adams
9 SHOOP   Salt-N-Pepa
10 CAN WE TALK   Tevin Campbell

February 5, 1994
1 ALL FOR LOVE   Bryan Adams/Rod Stewart/Sting
2 HERO   Mariah Carey
3 THE POWER OF LOVE   Celine Dion

4 BREATHE AGAIN   Toni Braxton
5 THE SIGN   Ace Of Base
6 ALL THAT SHE WANTS   Ace Of Base
7 SAID I LOVED YOU...BUT I LIED   Michael Bolton
8 AGAIN   Janet Jackson
9 PLEASE FORGIVE ME   Bryan Adams
10 SHOOP   Salt-N-Pepa

February 12, 1994
1 THE POWER OF LOVE   Celine Dion
2 ALL FOR LOVE   Bryan Adams/Rod Stewart/Sting
3 BREATHE AGAIN   Toni Braxton
4 HERO   Mariah Carey
5 THE SIGN   Ace Of Base
6 WHATTA MAN   Salt-N-Pepa featuring En Vogue
7 GETTO JAM   Domino
8 LINGER   The Cranberries
9 SAID I LOVED YOU...BUT I LIED   Michael Bolton
10 ALL THAT SHE WANTS   Ace Of Base

February 19, 1994
1 THE POWER OF LOVE   Celine Dion
2 ALL FOR LOVE   Bryan Adams/Rod Stewart/Sting
3 THE SIGN   Ace Of Base
4 BREATHE AGAIN   Toni Braxton
5 WHATTA MAN   Salt-N-Pepa featuring En Vogue
6 HERO   Mariah Carey
7 WITHOUT YOU/NEVER FORGET YOU   Mariah Carey
8 UNDERSTANDING   Xscape
9 GETTO JAM   Domino
10 SO MUCH IN LOVE   All-4-One

February 26, 1994
1 THE POWER OF LOVE   Celine Dion
2 THE SIGN   Ace Of Base
3 WHATTA MAN   Salt-N-Pepa featuring En Vogue
4 ALL FOR LOVE   Bryan Adams/Rod Stewart/Sting
5 BREATHE AGAIN   Toni Braxton
6 WITHOUT YOU/NEVER FORGET YOU   Mariah Carey
7 HERO   Mariah Carey
8 SO MUCH IN LOVE   All-4-One
9 UNDERSTANDING   Xscape
10 NOW AND FOREVER   Richard Marx

March 5, 1994
1 THE POWER OF LOVE   Celine Dion
2 THE SIGN   Ace Of Base
3 WHATTA MAN   Salt-N-Pepa featuring En Vogue
4 WITHOUT YOU/NEVER FORGET YOU   Mariah Carey
5 BREATHE AGAIN   Toni Braxton
6 ALL FOR LOVE   Bryan Adams/Rod Stewart/Sting
7 SO MUCH IN LOVE   All-4-One
8 NOW AND FOREVER   Richard Marx
9 CANTALOOP (FLIP FANTASIA)   US3
10 HERO   Mariah Carey

March 12, 1994
1 THE SIGN   Ace Of Base
2 THE POWER OF LOVE   Celine Dion
3 WHATTA MAN   Salt-N-Pepa featuring En Vogue
4 WITHOUT YOU/NEVER FORGET YOU   Mariah Carey
5 SO MUCH IN LOVE   All-4-One
6 BUMP N' GRIND   R. Kelly
7 BREATHE AGAIN   Toni Braxton
8 NOW AND FOREVER   Richard Marx
9 CANTALOOP (FLIP FANTASIA)   US3
10 ALL FOR LOVE   Bryan Adams/Rod Stewart/Sting

425

March 19, 1994
1 THE SIGN   Ace Of Base
2 THE POWER OF LOVE   Celine Dion
3 WITHOUT YOU/NEVER FORGET YOU   Mariah Carey
4 WHATTA MAN   Salt-N-Pepa featuring En Vogue
5 BUMP N' GRIND   R. Kelly
6 SO MUCH IN LOVE   All-4-One
7 NOW AND FOREVER   Richard Marx
8 BREATHE AGAIN   Toni Braxton
9 GIN AND JUICE   Snoop Doggy Dogg
10 BECAUSE OF LOVE   Janey Jackson

March 26, 1994
1 THE SIGN   Ace Of Base
2 BUMP N' GRIND   R. Kelly
3 WITHOUT YOU/NEVER FORGET YOU   Mariah Carey
4 THE POWER OF LOVE   Celine Dion
5 WHATTA MAN   Salt-N-Pepa featuring En Vogue
6 SO MUCH IN LOVE   All-4-One
7 NOW AND FOREVER   Richard Marx
8 GIN AND JUICE   Snoop Doggy Dogg
9 CANTALOOP (FLIP FANTASIA)   US3
10 BREATHE AGAIN   Toni Braxton

April 2, 1994
1 THE SIGN   Ace Of Base
2 BUMP N' GRIND   R. Kelly
3 WITHOUT YOU/NEVER FORGET YOU   Mariah Carey
4 THE POWER OF LOVE   Celine Dion
5 WHATTA MAN   Salt-N-Pepa featuring En Vogue
6 SO MUCH IN LOVE   All-4-One
7 NOW AND FOREVER   Richard Marx
8 MMM MMM MMM MMM   Crash Test Dummies
9 GIN AND JUICE   Snoop Doggy Dogg
10 CANTALOOP (FLIP FANTASIA)   US3

April 9, 1994
1 BUMP N' GRIND   R. Kelly
2 THE SIGN   Ace Of Base
3 WITHOUT YOU/NEVER FORGET YOU   Mariah Carey
4 THE POWER OF LOVE   Celine Dion
5 SO MUCH IN LOVE   All-4-One
6 WHATTA MAN   Salt-N-Pepa featuring En Vogue
7 MMM MMM MMM MMM   Crash Test Dummies
8 NOW AND FOREVER   Richard Marx
9 THE MOST BEAUTIFUL GIRL IN THE WORLD   Prince
10 STREETS OF PHILADELPHIA (FROM "PHILADELPHIA")
      Bruce Springsteen

April 16, 1994
1 BUMP N' GRIND   R. Kelly
2 THE SIGN   Ace Of Base
3 WITHOUT YOU/NEVER FORGET YOU   Mariah Carey
4 MMM MMM MMM MMM   Crash Test Dummies
5 THE POWER OF LOVE   Celine Dion
6 SO MUCH IN LOVE   All-4-One
7 WHATTA MAN   Salt-N-Pepa featuring En Vogue
8 THE MOST BEAUTIFUL GIRL IN THE WORLD   Prince
9 NOW AND FOREVER   Richard Marx
10 STREETS OF PHILADELPHIA (FROM "PHILADELPHIA")
      Bruce Springsteen

April 23, 1994
1 BUMP N' GRIND   R. Kelly
2 THE SIGN   Ace Of Base
3 WITHOUT YOU/NEVER FORGET YOU   Mariah Carey
4 MMM MMM MMM MMM   Crash Test Dummies
5 SO MUCH IN LOVE   All-4-One
6 THE MOST BEAUTIFUL GIRL IN THE WORLD   Prince
7 THE POWER OF LOVE   Celine Dion
8 WHATTA MAN   Salt-N-Pepa featuring En Vogue
9 STREETS OF PHILADELPHIA (FROM "PHILADELPHIA")
      Bruce Springsteen
10 NOW AND FOREVER   Richard Marx

April 30, 1994
1 BUMP N' GRIND   R. Kelly
2 THE SIGN   Ace Of Base
3 THE MOST BEAUTIFUL GIRL IN THE WORLD   Prince
4 WITHOUT YOU/NEVER FORGET YOU   Mariah Carey
5 MMM MMM MMM MMM   Crash Test Dummies
6 THE POWER OF LOVE   Celine Dion
7 SO MUCH IN LOVE   All-4-One
8 NOW AND FOREVER   Richard Marx
9 RETURN TO INNOCENCE   Enigma
10 LOSER   Beck

May 7, 1994
1 THE SIGN   Ace Of Base
2 BUMP N' GRIND   R. Kelly
3 THE MOST BEAUTIFUL GIRL IN THE WORLD   Prince
4 RETURN TO INNOCENCE   Enigma
5 WITHOUT YOU/NEVER FORGET YOU   Mariah Carey
6 MMM MMM MMM MMM   Crash Test Dummies
7 I'LL REMEMBER (FROM "WITH HONORS")   Madonna
8 BABY I LOVE YOUR WAY (FROM "REALITY BITES")   Big
      Mountain
9 THE POWER OF LOVE   Celine Dion
10 NOW AND FOREVER   Richard Marx

May 14, 1994
1 THE SIGN   Ace Of Base
2 BUMP N' GRIND   R. Kelly
3 THE MOST BEAUTIFUL GIRL IN THE WORLD   Prince
4 I'LL REMEMBER   Madonna
5 RETURN TO INNOCENCE   Enigma
6 BABY I LOVE YOUR WAY (FROM "REALITY BITES")   Big
      Mountain
7 MMM MMM MMM MMM   Crash Test Dummies
8 I SWEAR   All-4-One
9 WITHOUT YOU/NEVER FORGET YOU   Mariah Carey
10 I'M READY   Tevin Campbell

Chart Milestones Trivia Quiz

1. Name the oldest person to ever have a #1 record?
2. Who are the only three father/daughter pairings to have #1 hit records—separately, not duets—in their singing careers?
3. Name the only music industry mother and son to have writtensongs that turned into #1 records.
4. The first #1 hit from Britain did not bring on the British Invasion, but it did hit #1 in the States before it did in England. What was it?
5. Name the group that had five #2 singles but never peaked at #1?
6. What was the shortest song ever to be pressed on a 45rpm record?
7. Only two songs have been back-to-back #1 songs during the rock era. Name the songs.
8. Name Elvis Presley's first #1 hit.
9. The melody of the Confederate folk song Aura Lee, with new lyrics, became another #1 hit for Elvis. What was the new song title?
10. The second-longest reign at #1 by a male artist in the rock era is held by what artist and what song?
11. Until recently, the longest reign at #1 by a female artist in the rock era was shared by two artists. Name them and their hit songs.
12. "Young Love" was a huge crossover hit for Sonny James, but the #1 pop version actually belongs to who?
13. Name the first rock singer to write and sing a song that reached #1. What was the song?
14. Buddy Holly had only one #1 song. What was it?
15. Who did the first music video? When? What was the song?
16. The beginning of a great change in the music industry occurred in May 1958. What happened?
17. Name the rock song with the oldest lyrics.
18. What was the shortest country single?
19. What song made the biggest one-week jump in chart history?
20. The longest country song—dedicated to a country music icon—was over seven minutes long. What was the song?
21. Name the longest rock song ever written.
22. A patriotic tune about America's possible demise—a big seller on both the pop and country charts—was the second longest country single. What was the song? How long was it?
23. Most experts agree that this song marks the dividing point between the "Big Band" era and the Rock era. Name the song.
24. Name the person that most rock experts agree coined the term "rock-and-roll" to describe an emerging musical style. (Hint: the Rock & Roll Hall of Fame was established in the city with which he is associated.)
25. The song called "Rock & Roll" was a hit song in what year?
26. Name the first "rock-and-roll" record to ever make the charts.
27. What was the title of Peter, Paul & Mary's only #1 record?
28. Who was the first female star to have a #1 song in the Rock era?
29. Who sang the only Italian-language record to make #1 on the American charts? What was the song?
30. At what age did Frankie Avalon record his first record for the RCA subsidiary label, X Records.
31. The theme from "A Threepenny Opera" became this singer's biggest hit. Name the singer and the song.
32. What was the first country single to win a Grammy?
33. Name the only song that entered the Hot 100, dropped off, and returned to go all the way to #1
34. Who sang the first rock "tragedy" song?
35. Mitch Miller turned down this sixteen-year-old girl and told her music publisher to save his money. She went on to become the big-

gest-selling female vocalist of the Rock era. Who is she?

36. Name the only song to have hit #1 on two different occasions (1960, and again in 1962).

37. The shortest #1 single of the rock era with a one-word title was recorded in a now-defunct TV studio in Columbia, South Carolina. What was the song, and who recorded it?

38. The first version of Elvis Presley's #1 hit "Are You Lonesome Tonight" was also a hit for the person who originally recorded it. Can you name that person?

39. Name the first "girl group" to top the charts.

40. What was Elvis Presley's biggest-selling single?

41. Who was the first artist to carry a Lennon-McCartney song onto the Hot 100 (aside from The Beatles)?

42. Who is the only artist to have five #1 hits from the same album?

43. On April 4, 1964, an event in chart history unequaled to this day occurred. What happened?

44. Which popular vocalist has had seven consecutive #1 hits?

45. What was the only song to hit #1 from a position outside of the Top 10?

46. How old was Paul Anka when he wrote his first #1 hit? Name the song.

47. The Platters' recording of "Twilight Time" marked a departure for the entire music industry. Why?

48. The first "true" gold record was issued by RCA in 1941. What was it?

49. The first million-selling pop song was released in 1927. Name the song and the person who recorded it.

50. The first country song to be awarded a gold record was a patriotic tune from World War II by Elton Britt. Can you name it?

51. Who is the only singer to ever garner two Grammys in a single year for two different songs?

52. Which record was first awarded Platinum status?

53. What country singer recorded and charted only novelty hits?

54. Which country singer has had the most Hot 100 pop hits?

55. Name the singer who had over 65 hit songs, but never reached #1 on the charts.

56. What was Chuck Berry's first #1 record?

57. Which singer has had the largest number of charted records?

58. Who had the most #1 records in the Rock Era?

59. Name the first and only country singer to have a #1 country hit in French.

60. After a re-write of the lyrics, an old South African folk song became a #1 hit on the American charts. What was the original title, and what song did it become?

Honor Roll of Hits
• Singles •

Frank Sinatra

"The Voice" not only accounted for six of the all-time favorites listed in this section (as vocalist
for the Tommy Dorsey Orchestra and as a soloist), he also did a stint as one of the Hit Parade regulars.

Top 10 "Your Hit Parade" Hits, 1935-1955

TOP 10 "YOUR HIT PARADE" HITS OF 1935

1. IN A LITTLE GYPSY TEA ROOM - Bob Crosby Orch. (VR: Frank Tennille)
2. RED SAILS IN THE SUNSET - Guy Lombardo Orch. (VR: Carmen Lombardo)
3. CHEEK TO CHEEK - Fred Astaire
4. ON TREASURE ISLAND - Tommy Dorsey Orch. (VR: Edythe Wright)
5. I'M IN THE MOOD FOR LOVE - Little Jack Little (VR: Little Jack Little)
6. CHASING SHADOWS - Dorsey Brothers Orch. (VR: Bob Eberle)
7. IN THE MIDDLE OF A KISS - Hal Kemp Orch. (VR: Bob Allen)
8. LULLABY OF BROADWAY - Dorsey Brothers Orch. (VR: Bob Crosby)
9. EAST OF THE SUN - Tom Coakley Orch. (VR: Carl Ravazza)
10. YOU ARE MY LUCKY STAR - Eddy Duchin Orch. (VR: Lew Sherwood)

TOP 10 "YOUR HIT PARADE" HITS OF 1936

1. DID I REMEMBER - Shep Fields Orch. (VR: Charles Chester)
2. THE WAY YOU LOOK TONIGHT - Fred Astaire
3. IN THE CHAPEL IN THE MOONLIGHT - Shep Fields Orch.
4. IS IT TRUE WHAT THEY SAY ABOUT DIXIE - Jimmy Dorsey Orch. (VR: Bob Eberle)
5. THESE FOOLISH THINGS - Benny Goodman Orch. (VR: Helen Ward)
6. LOST - Guy Lombardo Orch. (VR: Carmen Lombardo)
7. ALONE - Tommy Dorsey Orch. (VR: Cliff Weston)
8. GOODY GOODY - Benny Goodman Orch. (VR: Helen Ward)
9. WHEN DID YOU LEAVE HEAVEN - Guy Lombardo Orch. (VR: Carmen Lombardo)
10. LIGHTS OUT - Eddy Duchin Orch. (VR: Lew Sherwood)

TOP 10 "YOUR HIT PARADE" HITS OF 1937

1. SEPTEMBER IN THE RAIN - Guy Lombardo Orch. (VR: Carmen Lombardo)
2. IT LOOKS LIKE RAIN IN CHERRY BLOSSOM LANE - Guy Lombardo Orch. (VR: Carmen Lombardo)
3. THAT OLD FEELING - Shep Fields Orch. (VR: Bob Goday)
4. PENNIES FROM HEAVEN - Bing Crosby
5. BOO HOO - Guy Lombardo Orch. (VR: Carmen Lombardo)
6. SAILBOAT IN THE MOONLIGHT - Guy Lombardo Orch. (VR: Carmen Lombardo)
7. ONCE IN A WHILE - Tommy Dorsey Orch. (VR: Jack Leonard)
8. WHISPERS IN THE DARK - Bob Crosby Orch. (VR: Kay Weber)
9. IT'S DE-LOVELY - Eddy Duchin Orch. (VR: Jerry Cooper)
10. VIENI, VIENI - Rudy Vallee

TOP 10 "YOUR HIT PARADE" HITS OF 1938

1. MY REVERIE - Larry Clinton Orch. (VR: Bea Wain)
2. I'VE GOT A POCKETFUL OF MIRACLES - Bing Crosby
3. MUSIC, MAESTRO, PLEASE - Tommy Dorsey Orch. (VR: Edythe Wright)
4. A-TISKET, A-TASKET - Ella Fitzgerald with Chuck Webb Orch.
5. SAYS MY HEART - Red Norvo Orch. (VR: Mildred Bailey)
6. TI PI TIN - Horace Heidt Orch. (VR: Lysbeth Hughes & Larry Cotton)
7. PLEASE BE KIND - Red Norvo Orch. (VR: Mildred Bailey)
8. LOVE WALKED IN - Sammy Kay Orch. (VR: Tommy Ryan)
9. I LET A SONG GO OUT OF MY HEART - Duke Ellington Orch.
10. THANKS FOR THE MEMORY - Shep Fields Orch. (VR: Bob Goday)

TOP 10 "YOUR HIT PARADE" HITS OF 1939

1. SOUTH OF THE BORDER - Shep Fields Orch. (VR: Hal Derwin)
2. DEEP PURPLE - Larry Clinton Orch. (VR: Bea Wain)
3. SCATTERBRAIN - Frankie Masters Orch. (VR: Frankie Masters)
4. OVER THE RAINBOW - Glenn Miller Orch. (VR: Ray Eberly)
5. WISHING - Glenn Miller Orch. (VR: Ray Eberly)
6. AND THE ANGELS SING - Benny Goodman Orch. (VR: Martha Tilton)
7. MOON LOVE - Glenn Miller Orch. (VR: Ray Eberly)
8. STAIRWAY TO THE STARS - Glenn Miller Orch. (VR: Ray Eberly)
9. THE BEER BARREL POLKA - Will Glahe Musette
10. JEEPERS CREEPERS - Al Donohue Orch. (VR: Paula Kelly)

TOP 10 "YOUR HIT PARADE" HITS OF 1940

1. WOODPECKER SONG - Glenn Miller Orch. (VR: Marion Hutton)
2. I'LL NEVER SMILE AGAIN - Tommy Dorsey Orch. (VR: Frank Sinatra)
3. THERE I GO - Vaughn Monroe Orch. (VR: Vaughn Monroe)
4. CARELESS - Glenn Miller Orch. (VR: Ray Eberly)
5. WHEN YOU WISH UPON A STAR - Glenn Miller Orch. (VR: Ray Eberly)
6. IMAGINATION - Glenn Miller Orch. (VR: Ray Eberly)
7. ONLY FOREVER - Bing Crosby
8. PRACTICE MAKES PERFECT - Bob Chester Orch. (VR: Al Stuart)
9. ALL THE THINGS YOU ARE - Tommy Dorsey Orch. (VR: Jack Leonard)
10. INDIAN SUMMER - Tommy Dorsey Orch. (VR: Jack Leonard)

TOP 10 "YOUR HIT PARADE" HITS OF 1941

1. I HEAR A RHAPSODY - Charlie Barnet Orch. (VR: Bob Carroll)
2. INTERMEZZO - Guy Lombardo Orch.

3.   FRENESI - Artie Shaw Orch.
4.   AMAPOLA - Jimmy Dorsey Orch. (VR: Bob Eberle and Helen O'Connell)
5.   MARIA ELENA - Jimmy Dorsey Orch. (VR: Bob Eberle)
6.   TONIGHT WE LOVE - Freddy Martin Orch.
7.   I DON'T WANT TO SET THE WORLD ON FIRE - Horace Heidt Orch. (VR: Larry Cotton, Donna Wood & the Don Juans)
8.   MY SISTER AND I - Jimmy Dorsey Orch. (VR: Bob Eberle)
9.   YOU AND I - Glenn Miller Orch. (VR: Ray Eberly)
10. YOURS - Jimmy Dorsey Orch. (VR: Bob Eberle and Helen O'Connell)

TOP 10 "YOUR HIT PARADE" HITS OF 1942

1.   WHITE CHRISTMAS - Bing Crosby
2.   THE WHITE CLIFFS OF DOVER - Kay Kyser Orch. (VR: Harry Babbitt)
3.   SLEEPY LAGOON - Harry James Orch.
4.   ELMER'S TUNE - Glenn Miller Orch. (VR: Ray Eberly)
5.   MY DEVOTION - Charlie Spivak Orch. (VR: Garry Stevens)
6.   HE WEARS A PAIR OF SILVER WINGS - Kay Kyser Orch. (VR: Harry Babbitt)
7.   JINGLE, JANGLE, JINGLE - Kay Kyser Orch. (VR: Julie Conway & Harry Babbitt)
8.   ONE DOZEN ROSES - Dick Jurgens Orch. (VR: Buddy Moreno)
9.   DON'T SIT UNDER THE APPLE TREE - Glenn Miller Orch. (VR: Marion Hutton, Tex Beneke & Modernaires)
10. BLUES IN THE NIGHT - Woody Herman Orch. (VR: Woody Herman)

TOP 10 "YOUR HIT PARADE" HITS OF 1943

1.   PEOPLE WILL SAY WE'RE IN LOVE - Bing Crosby
2.   YOU'LL NEVER KNOW - Dick Haymes
3.   PAPER DOLL - Mills Brothers
4.   AS TIME GOES BY - Rudy Vallee
5.   THERE ARE SUCH THINGS - Tommy Dorsey Orch. (VR: Frank Sinatra & Pied Pipers)
6.   SUNDAY, MONDAY OR ALWAYS - Bing Crosby
7.   COMIN' IN ON A WING AND A PRAYER - Song Spinners
8.   IN THE BLUE OF THE EVENING - Tommy Dorsey Orch. (VR: Frank Sinatra)
9.   I'VE HEARD THAT SONG BEFORE - Harry James Orch. (VR: Helen Forrest)
10. WHITE CHRISTMAS - Bing Crosby

TOP 10 "YOUR HIT PARADE" HITS OF 1944

1.   I'LL BE SEEING YOU - Bing Crosby
2.   MY HEART TELLS ME - Glen Gray Orch. (VR: Eugenie Baird)
3.   LONG AGO AND FAR AWAY - Helen Forrest & Dick Haymes
4.   I'LL GET BY - Harry James Orch. (VR: Dick Haymes)
5.   I WALK ALONE - Dinah Shore
6.   AMOR - Bing Crosby
7.   SWINGING ON A STAR - Bing Crosby
8.   I LOVE YOU - Bing Crosby
9.   SHOO, SHOO, BABY - Andrews Sisters
10. THE TROLLEY SONG - Pied Pipers

TOP 10 "YOUR HIT PARADE" HITS OF 1945

1.   TILL THE END OF TIME - Perry Como
2.   DREAM - Pied Pipers
3.   IF I LOVED YOU - Perry Como
4.   DON'T FENCE ME IN - Bing Crosby & Andrews Sisters
5.   SENTIMENTAL JOURNEY - Les Brown Orch. (VR: Doris Day)
6.   IT'S BEEN A LONG, LONG TIME - Harry James Orch. (VR: Kitty Kallen)
7.   MY DREAMS ARE GETTING BETTER ALL THE TIME - Pied Pipers
8.   ON THE ATCHISON, TOPEKA AND THE SANTA FE - Johnny Mercer
9.   LAURA - Woody Herman Orch.
10. ACCENTUATE THE POSITIVE - Johnny Mercer

TOP 10 "YOUR HIT PARADE" HITS OF 1946

1.   THEY SAY IT'S WONDERFUL - Frank Sinatra
2.   THE GYPSY - Ink Spots
3.   SYMPHONY - Freddy Martin Orch. (VR: Clyde Rogers)
4.   TO EACH HIS OWN - Eddy Howard Orch. (VR: Eddy Howard)
5.   OH, WHAT IT SEEMED TO BE - Frankie Carle Orch. (VR: Marjorie Hughes)
6.   OLE BUTTERMILK SKY - Kay Kyser Orch. (VR: Mike Douglas & Campus Kids)
7.   FIVE MINUTES MORE - Frank Sinatra
8.   ALL THROUGH THE DAY - Perry Como
9.   I CAN'T BEGIN TO TELL YOU - Bing Crosby with Carmen Cavallaro Orch.
10. IT MIGHT AS WELL BE SPRING - Sammy Kaye Orch. (VR: Billy Williams)

TOP 10 "YOUR HIT PARADE" HITS OF 1947

1.   PEG O MY HEART - Harmonicats
2.   THE ANNIVERSARY SONG - Dinah Shore
3.   NEAR YOU - Francis Craig Orch. (VR: Bob Lamm)
4.   LINDA - Buddy Clark with Ray Noble Orch.
5.   FOR SENTIMENTAL REASONS - Nat King Cole
6.   I WISH I DIDN'T LOVE YOU SO - Vaughn Monroe Orch. (VR: Vaughn Monroe)
7.   M'AMSELLE - Art Lund
8.   THAT'S MY DESIRE - Sammy Kaye Orch. (VR: Don Cornell)
9.   HEARTACHES - Ted Weems Orch. (Whistling solo: Elmore Cannon)
10. HOW SOON - Jack Owens

TOP 10 "YOUR HIT PARADE" HITS OF 1948

1.   BALLERINA - Vaughn Monroe Orch. (VR: Vaughn Monroe)
2.   I'M LOOKING OVER A FOUR LEAF CLOVER - Art Mooney Orch. (VR: Ensemble)
3.   MANANA - Peggy Lee
4.   NATURE BOY - Nat King Cole
5.   WOODY WOODPECKER SONG - Kay Kyser Orch. (VR: Gloria Wood & Campus Kids)
6.   NOW IS THE HOUR - Bing Crosby
7.   MY HAPPINESS - Jon & Sandra Steele
8.   A TREE IN THE MEADOW - Margaret Whiting
9.   YOU CAN'T BE TRUE, DEAR - Ken Griffin Orch. (VR: Jerry Wayne)
10. LITTLE WHITE LIES - Dick Haymes

TOP 10 "YOUR HIT PARADE" HITS OF 1949

1. BUTTONS AND BOWS - Dinah Shore
2. A LITTLE BIRD TOLD ME - Evelyn Knight
3. CRUISING DOWN THE RIVER - Russ Morgan Orch. (VR: The Skyliners)
4. CRUISING DOWN THE RIVER - Blue Barron Orch. (VR: Ensemble)
5. RIDERS IN THE SKY - Vaughn Monroe (VR: Vaughn Monroe)
6. SOME ENCHANTED EVENING - Perry Como
7. YOU'RE BREAKING MY HEART - Vic Damone
8. THAT LUCKY OLD SUN - Frankie Laine
9. MULE TRAIN - Frankie Laine
10. ALL I WANT FOR CHRISTMAS - Spike Jones Orch. (VR: George Rock)

TOP 10 "YOUR HIT PARADE" HITS OF 1950

1. GOODNIGHT IRENE - The Weavers
2. IT ISN'T FAIR - Sammy Kaye Orch. (VR: Don Cornell)
3. THE THIRD MAN THEME - Alton Karas
4. MULE TRAIN - Frankie Laine
5. MONA LISA - Nat King Cole
6. MUSIC, MUSIC, MUSIC - Teresa Brewer
7. I WANNA BE LOVED - Andrews Sisters
8. IF I KNEW YOU WERE COMIN' I'D'VE BAKED A CAKE - Eileen Barton
9. I CAN DREAM, CAN'T I? - Tommy Dorsey Orch. (VR: Jack Leonard)
10. MY FOOLISH HEART - Gordon Jenkins Orch. (VR: Eileen Wilson)

TOP 10 "YOUR HIT PARADE" HITS OF 1951

1. TENNESSEE WALTZ - Patti Page
2. HOW HIGH THE MOON - Les Paul & Mary Ford
3. TOO YOUNG - Nat King Cole
4. BE MY LOVE - Mario Lanza
5. BECAUSE OF YOU - Tony Bennett
6. ON TOP OF OLD SMOKEY The Weavers (VR: Terry Gilkyson)
7. IF - Perry Como
8. SIN (IT'S NO) - Eddy Howard Orch. (VR: Eddy Howard)
9. COME ON-A MY HOUSE - Rosemary Clooney
10. MOCKING BIRD HILL - Les Paul & Mary Ford

TOP 10 "YOUR HIT PARADE" HITS OF 1952

1. CRY - Johnnie Ray
2. BLUE TANGO - Leroy Anderson Orch.
3. ANYTIME - Eddie Fisher
4. DELICADO - Percy Faith Orch.
5. KISS OF FIRE - Georgia Gibbs
6. WHEEL OF FORTUNE - Kay Starr
7. TELL ME WHY - Four Aces
8. I'M YOURS - Eddie Fisher
9. HERE IN MY HEART - Al Martino
10. AUF WIEDERSEHN, SWEETHEART - Vera Lynn

TOP 10 "YOUR HIT PARADE" HITS OF 1953

1. SONG FROM MOULIN ROUGE - Percy Faith Orch.
2. TILL I WALTZ AGAIN WITH YOU - Teresa Brewer
3. APRIL IN PORTUGAL - Les Baster Orch.
4. VAYA CON DIOS - Les Paul & Mary Ford
5. I'M WALKING BEHIND YOU - Eddie Fisher
6. I BELIEVE - Frankie Laine
7. YOU, YOU, YOU - Ames Brothers
8. DOGGIE IN THE WINDOW - Patti Page
9. WHY DON'T YOU BELIEVE ME - Joni James
10. PRETEND - Nat King Cole

TOP 10 "YOUR HIT PARADE" HITS OF 1954

1. LITTLE THINGS MEAN A LOT - Kitty Kallen
2. HEY THERE - Rosemary Clooney
3. WANTED - Perry Como
4. YOUNG AT HEART - Frank Sinatra
5. SH-BOOM - Crew Cuts
6. THREE COINS IN THE FOUNTAIN - Four Aces
7. THE LITTLE SHOEMAKER - Gaylords
8. OH, MY PAPA - Eddie Fisher
9. SECRET LOVE - Doris Day
10. HAPPY WANDERER - Frankie Weir

TOP 10 "YOUR HIT PARADE" HITS OF 1955

1. CHERRY PINK AND APPLE BLOSSOM WHITE - Perez Prado
2. ROCK AROUND THE CLOCK - Bill Haley & Comets
3. AUTUMN LEAVES - Roger Williams Orch.
4. YELLOW ROSE OF TEXAS - Mitch Miller
5. LOVE IS A MANY-SPLENDORED THING - Four Aces
6. SIXTEEN TONS - Tennessee Ernie Ford
7. THE BALLAD OF DAVY CROCKETT - Bill Hayes
8. SINCERELY - McGuire Sisters
9. MOMENTS TO REMEMBER - Four Lads
10. UNCHAINED MELODY - Les Baster Orch.

Little Richard

``Long Tall Sally'' was Richard Penniman's first Top 10 hit at #6 *Billboard*. ``Your Hit Parade'' snubbed the song,
leaving it out of its Top 7. Can you imagine a Hit Parade regular trying to perform this song? The cast just
could not adjust to the extremes that popular music was beginning to take,
and that spelled the beginning of the end for ``Your Hit Parade.''

Billboard Top 20 Pop Singles, 1955-1993

TOP 20 POP SINGLES OF 1955

POS.   TITLE - ARTIST - LABEL
1. CHERRY PINK & APPLE BLOSSOM WHITE - Perez Prado - RCA
2. ROCK AROUND THE CLOCK - Bill Haley & his Comets - Decca
3. SINCERELY - McGuire Sisters - Coral
4. YELLOW ROSE OF TEXAS - Mitch Miller - Columbia
5. SIXTEEN TONS - Tennessee Ernie Ford - Capitol
6. LOVE IS A MANY SPLENDORED THING - Four Aces - Decca
7. BALLAD OF DAVY CROCKETT - Bill Hayes - Cadence
8. AUTUMN LEAVES - Roger Williams - Kapp
9. LET ME GO LOVER - Joan Weber - Columbia
10. HEARTS OF STONE - Fontane Sisters - Dot
11. DANCE WITH ME HENRY - Georgia Gibbs - Mercury
12. LEARNIN' THE BLUES - Frank Sinatra - Capitol
13. AIN'T THAT A SHAME - Pat Boone - Dot
14. MOMENTS TO REMEMBER - Four Lads - Columbia
15. UNCHAINED MELODY - Les Baxter - Capitol *
16. ONLY YOU - Platters - Mercury
17. LOVE & MARRIAGE - Frank Sinatra - Capitol
18. KO KO MO - Perry Como - RCA
19. A BLOSSOM FELL - Nat King Cole - Capitol
20. HARD TO GET - Gisele MacKenzie - X
    *Another version by Al Hibbler.

TOP 20 POP SINGLES OF 1956

POS.   TITLE - ARTIST - LABEL
1. SINGING THE BLUES - Guy Mitchell - Columbia
2. DON'T BE CRUEL/HOUND DOG - Elvis Presley - RCA
3. THE WAYWARD WIND - Gogi Grant - ERA
4. HEARTBREAK HOTEL - Elvis Presley - RCA
5. THE GREEN DOOR - Jim Lowe - Dot
6. THE POOR PEOPLE OF PARIS - Les Baxter - Capitol
7. LISBON ANTIGUA - Nelson Riddle - Capitol
8. MEMORIES ARE MADE OF THIS - Dean Martin - Capitol
9. LOVE ME TENDER - Elvis Presley - RCA
10. JUST WALKING IN THE RAIN - Johnny Ray - Columbia
11. ROCK & ROLL WALTZ - Kay Starr - RCA
12. QUE SERA SERA - Doris Day - Columbia *
13. MOONGLOW (THEME FROM PICNIC) - Morris Stoloff - Decca
14. TRUE LOVE - Bing Crosby & Grace Kelly - Capitol
15. CANADIAN SUNSET - Hugo Winterhalter - RCA
16. BLUEBERRY HILL - Fats Domino - Imperial
17. HONKY TONK - Bill Doggett - King
18. MY PRAYER - Platters - Mercury
19. IT'S ALMOST TOMORROW - Dream Weavers - Decca **
20. THE GREAT PRETENDER - Platters - Mercury
    *Also known by WHATEVER WILL BE, WILL BE.
    **Also a hit for "Your Hit Parade" star Snooky Lanson.

TOP 20 POP SINGLES OF 1957

POS.   TITLE - ARTIST - LABEL
1. LOVE LETTERS IN THE SAND - Pat Boone - Dot
2. ALL SHOOK UP - Elvis Presley - RCA
3. TAMMY - Debbie Reynolds - Coral
4. SO RARE - Jimmy Dorsey - Fraternity
5. TEDDY BEAR - Elvis Presley - RCA
6. JAILHOUSE ROCK - Elvis Presley - RCA
7. YOUNG LOVE - Tab Hunter - Dot *
8. BYE BYE LOVE - Everly Brothers - Cadence
9. LITTLE DARLIN' - Diamonds - Mercury
10. SEARCHIN' - Coasters - Atco
11. WAKE UP LITTLE SUSIE - Everly Brothers - Cadence
12. HONEYCOMB - Jimmie Rodgers - Roulette
13. CHANCES ARE/TWELFTH OF NEVER - Johnny Mathis - Columbia
14. COME GO WITH ME - Del Vikings - Dot
15. IT'S NOT FOR ME TO SAY - Johnny Mathis - Columbia
16. DIANA - Paul Anka - ABC Paramount
17. ROUND & ROUND - Perry Como - RCA
18. YOU SEND ME - Sam Cooke - Keen
19. WHOLE LOTTA SHAKIN' GOIN ON - Jerry Lee Lewis - Sun
20. A WHITE SPORT COAT - Marty Robbins - Columbia
    *Also a hit for Sonny James, whose version overall remains the most popular.

TOP 20 POP SINGLES OF 1958

POS.   TITLE - ARTIST - LABEL
1. IT'S ALL IN THE GAME - Tommy Edwards - MGM
2. AT THE HOP - Danny & The Juniors - Singular *
3. TO KNOW HIM IS TO LOVE HIM - Teddy Bears - Dore
4. TEQUILA - Champs - Challenge
5. WITCH DOCTOR - David Seville - Liberty
6. APRIL LOVE - Pat Boone - Dot
7. TOM DOOLEY - Kingston Trio - Capitol
8. ALL I HAVE TO DO IS DREAM - Everly Brothers - Cadence
9. VOLARE (NEL BLU DIPINTO DI BLU) - Dominico Mudogno - Decca
10. SUGARTIME - McGuire Sisters - Coral
11. IT'S ONLY MAKE BELIEVE - Conway Twitty - MGM
12. SAIL ALONG SILVERY MOON - Billy Vaughn - Dot
13. BIRD DOG - Everly Brothers - Cadence
14. PATRICIA - Perez Prado - RCA
15. CATCH A FALLING STAR - Perry Como - RCA
16. PURPLE PEOPLE EATER - Sheb Wooley - MGM
17. PEGGY SUE - Buddy Holly - Coral
18. LITTLE STAR - Elegants - Apt
19. CHANTILLY LACE - Big Bopper - Mercury
20. HE'S GOT THE WHOLE WORLD IN HIS HANDS - Laurie London - Capitol
    *Also released on ABC Paramount.

TOP 20 POP SINGLES OF 1959

POS.   TITLE - ARTIST - LABEL
1. MACK THE KNIFE - Bobby Darin - Atco
2. BATTLE OF NEW ORLEANS - Johnny Horton - Columbia
3. VENUS - Frankie Avalon - Chancellor
4. MR. BLUE - Fleetwoods - Dolton
5. SMOKE GETS IN YOUR EYES - Platters - Mercury
6. LONELY BOY - Paul Anka - ABC Paramount
7. STAGGER LEE - Lloyd Price - ABC Paramount
8. DONNA - Ritchie Valens - Del-Fi

Buddy Holly & The Crickets

Bigger than life following his death in a plane crash in 1959, Buddy had only one #1 record—``That'll Be The Day'' (1958).

9.   A LOVER'S QUESTION - Clyde McPhatter - Atlantic
10. THE THREE BELLS - Browns - RCA
11. HEARTACHES BY THE NUMBER - Guy Mitchell - Columbia
12. MY HEART IS AN OPEN BOOK - Carl Dobkins, Jr. - Decca
13. COME SOFTLY TO ME - Fleetwoods - Liberty
14. DREAM LOVER - Bobby Darin - Atco
15. 16 CANDLES - Crest - Coed
16. PUT YOUR HEAD ON MY SHOULDER - Paul Anka - ABC Paramount
17. SLEEP WALK - Santo & Johnny - Canadian-American
18. PERSONALITY - Lloyd Price - ABC Paramount
19. DON'T YOU KNOW - Della Reese - RCA
20. SEA OF LOVE - Phil Philips - Mercury

TOP 20 POP SINGLES OF 1960

POS. TITLE - ARTIST - LABEL
1.   THEME FROM A SUMMER PLACE - Percy Faith - Columbia
2.   IT'S NOW OR NEVER - Elvis Presley - RCA
3.   HE'LL HAVE TO GO - Jim Reeves - RCA
4.   I'M SORRY - Brenda Lee - Decca
5.   ARE YOU LONESOME TONIGHT - Elvis Presley - RCA *
6.   THE TWIST - Chubby Checker - Parkway
7.   RUNNING BEAR - Johnny Preston - Mercury
8.   EVERYBODY'S SOMEBODY'S FOOL - Connie Francis - MGM
9.   CATHY'S CLOWN - Everly Brothers - Warner Bros.
10. NORTH TO ALASKA - Johnny Horton - Columbia
11. EL PASO - Marty Robbins - Columbia
12. STUCK ON YOU - Elvis Presley - RCA
13. LAST DATE - Floyd Cramer - RCA
14. MY HEART HAS A MIND OF ITS OWN - Connie Francis - MGM

15. TEEN ANGEL - Mark Dinning - MGM
16. SAVE THE LAST DANCE FOR ME - The Drifters - Atlantic
17. SIXTEEN REASONS - Connie Stevens - Warner Bros.
18. ONLY THE LONELY - Roy Orbison - Monument
19. GREENFIELDS - Brothers Four - Columbia
20. SWEET NOTHINS' - Brenda Lee - Decca
     *Crossed over into 1961.

TOP 20 POP SINGLES OF 1961

POS. TITLE - ARTIST - LABEL
1.   TOSSIN' & TURNIN' - Bobby Lewis - Beltone
2.   BIG BAD JOHN - Jimmy Dean - Columbia
3.   EXODUS - Ferrante & Teicher - United Artist
4.   WONDERLAND BY NIGHT - Bert Kaempfert - Decca
5.   RUNAWAY - Del Shannon - Big Top
6.   WILL YOU LOVE ME TOMORROW - Shirelles - Scepter
7.   TRAVELIN' MAN - Ricky Nelson - Imperial
8.   PONY TIME - Chubby Checker - Parkway
9.   CALCUTTA - Lawrence Welk - Dot
10. RUNAROUND SUE - Dion - Laurie
11. THE LION SLEEPS TONIGHT - Tokens - RCA
12. BRISTOL STOMP - Dovells - Parkway
13. PLEASE MR. POSTMAN - Marvelettes - Tamla
14. DEDICATED TO THE ONE I LOVE - Shirelles - Scepter
15. BLUE MOON - Marcells - Colpix
16. MICHAEL - Highwaymen - United Artist
17. MOTHER IN LAW - Ernie K-Doe - Minit
18. QUARTER TO THREE - Gary U.S. Bonds - Legrand
19. RUN TO HIM - Bobby Vee - Liberty
20. RUNNING SCARED - Roy Orbison - Monument

TOP 20 POP SINGLES OF 1962

POS. TITLE - ARTIST - LABEL
1. THE TWIST - Chubby Checker - Parkway
2. I CAN'T STOP LOVING YOU - Ray Charles - ABC Paramount
3. BIG GIRLS DON'T CRY - Four Seasons - Vee Jay
4. LIMBO ROCK - Chubby Checker - Parkway
5. PEPPERMINT TWIST - Joey Dee & Starliters - Roulette
6. ROSES ARE RED - Bobby Vinton - Epic
7. STRANGER ON THE SHORE - Mr. Acker Bilk - Atco
8. SHERRY - Four Seasons - Vee Jay
9. RETURN TO SENDER - Elvis Presley - RCA
10. JOHNNY ANGEL - Shelley Fabares - Colpix
11. MASHED POTATO TIME - Dee Dee Sharp - Cameo
12. THE STRIPPER - David Rose - MGM
13. TELSTAR - Tornadoes - London
14. SOLDIER BOY - Shirelles - Scepter
15. HE'S A REBEL - Crystals - Philles
16. HEY! BABY - Bruce Channell - Smash
17. THE WANDERER - Dion - Laurie
18. DUKE OF EARL - Gene Chandler - Vee Jay
19. THE LOCOMOTION - Little Eva - Dimension
20. RAMBLIN' ROSE - Nat King Cole - Capitol

TOP 20 POP SINGLES OF 1963

POS. TITLE - ARTIST - LABEL
1. SUGAR SHACK - Jimmy Gilmer & Fireballs - Dot
2. DOMINIQUE - Singing Nun - Philips
3. HE'S SO FINE - Chiffons - Laurie
4. BLUE VELVET - Bobby Vinton - Epic
5. HEY PAULA - Paul & Paula - Philips
6. GO AWAY LITTLE GIRL - Steve Lawrence - Columbia
7. LOUIE LOUIE - Kingsmen - Wand
8. MY BOYFRIEND'S BACK - Angels - Smash
9. FINGERTIPS PT. 2 - Stevie Wonder - Tamla
10. SUKIYAKI - Kyu Sakamoto - Capitol
11. END OF THE WORLD - Skeeter Davis - RCA
12. RHYTHM OF THE RAIN - Cascades - Valiant
13. I WILL FOLLOW HIM - Little Peggy March - RCA
14. WALK LIKE A MAN - Four Seasons - Vee Jay
15. I'M LEAVIN' IT UP TO YOU - Dale & Grace - Montel *
16. IT'S MY PARTY - Lesley Gore - Mercury
17. SURFIN USA - Beach Boys - Capitol
18. SURF CITY - Jan & Dean - Liberty
19. WALK RIGHT IN - Rooftop Singers - Vanguard
20. PUFF (THE MAGIC DRAGON) - Peter, Paul & Mary - Warner Bros.

*Also on Michele Records.

TOP 20 POP SINGLES OF 1964

POS. TITLE - ARTIST - LABEL
1. I WANT TO HOLD YOUR HAND - Beatles - Capitol
2. HELLO, DOLLY! - Louis Armstrong - Kapp
3. SHE LOVES YOU - Beatles - Swan
4. OH, PRETTY WOMAN - Roy Orbison - Monument
5. I GET AROUND - Beach Boys - Capitol
6. MY GUY - Mary Wells - Motown
7. COME SEE ABOUT ME - Supremes - Motown
8. BABY LOVE - Supremes - Motown
9. THERE! I'VE SAID IT AGAIN - Bobby Vinton - Epic
10. EVERYBODY LOVES SOMEBODY - Dean Martin - Reprise
11. MR. LONELY - Bobby Vinton - Epic
12. A HARD DAY'S NIGHT - Beatles - Capitol
13. WHERE DID OUR LOVE GO - Supremes - Motown
14. I FEEL FINE - Beatles - Capitol
15. DO WAH DIDDY DIDDY - Manfred Mann - Ascot
16. CAN'T BUY ME LOVE - Beatles - Capitol
17. CHAPEL OF LOVE - Dixie Cups - Red Bird
18. SHE'S NOT THERE - Zombies - Parrot
19. LAST KISS - J. Frank Wilson & Cavaliers - Josie
20. WE'LL SING IN THE SUNSHINE - Gale Garnett - RCA

TOP 20 POP SINGLES OF 1965

POS. TITLE - ARTIST - LABEL
1. (I CAN'T GET NO) SATISFACTION - Rolling Stones - London
2. YOU'VE LOST THAT LOVIN' FEELIN' - Righteous Brothers - Philles
3. WOOLY BULLY - Sam The Sham & The Pharaohs - MGM
4. DOWNTOWN - Petula Clark - Warner Bros.
5. I CAN'T HELP MYSELF - Four Tops - Motown
6. MRS. BROWN YOU'VE GOT A LOVELY DAUGHTER - Herman's Hermits - MGM
7. HELP - Beatles - Capitol
8. LET'S HANG ON - Four Seasons - Philips
9. TURN! TURN! TURN! - The Byrds - Columbia
10. MY GIRL - Temptations - Motown
11. YESTERDAY - The Beatles - Capitol
12. I GOT YOU BABE - Sonny & Cher - Atco
13. THIS DIAMOND RING - Gary Lewis & Playboys - Liberty
14. STOP IN THE NAME OF LOVE - Supremes - Motown
15. GET OFF OF MY CLOUD - Rolling Stones - London
16. HELP ME RHONDA - Beach Boys - Capitol
17. YOU WERE ON MY MIND - We Five - A&M
18. KING OF THE ROAD - Roger Miller - Smash
19. THE "IN" CROWD - Ramsey Lewis Trio - Argo
20. THE BIRDS & THE BEES - Jewel Akens - Era

TOP 20 POP SINGLES OF 1966

POS. TITLE - ARTIST - LABEL
1. I'M A BELIEVER - Monkees - Colgems
2. BALLAD OF THE GREEN BERET - SSgt. Barry Sadler - RCA
3. WINCHESTER CATHEDRAL - New Vaudeville Band - Fontana
4. 96 TEARS - ? & The Mysterians - Cameo
5. SOUL & INSPIRATION - Righteous Brothers - Verve
6. GOOD VIBRATIONS - Beach Boys - Capitol
7. DEVIL WITH A BLUE DRESS ON/GOOD GOLLY MISS MOLLY - Mitch Ryder & Detroit Wheels - New Voice
8. LAST TRAIN TO CLARKSVILLE - Monkees - Colgems
9. REACH OUT I'LL BE THERE - Four Tops - Motown
10. THESE BOOTS ARE MADE FOR WALKIN' - Nancy Sinatra - Reprise
11. YOU CAN'T HURRY LOVE - Supremes - Motown
12. WE CAN WORK IT OUT - Beatles - Capitol
13. CHERISH - The Association - Valiant
14. CALIFORNIA DREAMIN' - Mamas & Papas - Dunhill
15. POOR SIDE OF TOWN - Johnny Rivers - Imperial
16. MONDAY MONDAY - Mamas & Papas - Dunhill
17. STRANGERS IN THE NIGHT - Frank Sinatra - Reprise
18. GOOD LOVIN' - Young Rascals - Atlantic
19. BORN FREE - Roger Williams - Kapp
20. YOU KEEP ME HANGIN' ON - Supremes - Motown

TOP 20 POP SINGLES OF 1967

POS. TITLE - ARTIST - LABEL
1. TO SIR WITH LOVE - Lulu - Epic
2. ODE TO BILLIE JOE - Bobbie Gentry - Capitol
3. LIGHT MY FIRE - Doors - Electra
4. WINDY - The Association - Warner Bros.
5. THE LETTER - Box Tops - Mala
6. SOMETHIN' STUPID - Frank & Nancy Sinatra - Reprise
7. DAYDREAM BELIEVER - Monkees - Colgems
8. HAPPY TOGETHER - Turtles - White Whale
9. INCENSE & PEPPERMINT - Strawberry Alarm Clock - Uni
10. GROOVIN' - Young Rascals - Atlantic
11. I HEARD IT THROUGH THE GRAPEVINE - Gladys Knight & Pips - Soul
12. CAN'T TAKE MY EYES OFF YOU - Frankie Valli - Philips
13. LITTLE BIT O SOUL - Music Explosion - Laurie
14. THE RAIN, THE PARK, & OTHER THINGS - Cowsills - MGM
15. COME BACK WHEN YOU GROW UP - Bobby Vee - Liberty
16. RESPECT - Aretha Franklin - Atlantic
17. HELLO GOODBYE - Beatles - Capitol
18. NEVER MY LOVE - The Association - Warner Bros.
19. TELL IT LIKE IT IS - Aaron Neville - Par-Lo
20. I WAS MADE TO LOVE HER - Stevie Wonder - Tamla

TOP 20 POP SINGLES OF 1968

POS. TITLE - ARTIST - LABEL
1. HEY JUDE - Beatles - Apple
2. I HEARD IT THROUGH THE GRAPEVINE - Marvin Gaye - Tamla
3. LOVE IS BLUE - Paul Mauriat - Philips
4. HONEY - Bobby Goldsboro - United Artist
5. LOVE CHILD - Diana Ross & The Supremes - Motown
6. (SITTIN' ON) THE DOCK OF THE BAY - Otis Redding - Volt
7. PEOPLE GOT TO BE FREE - Rascals - Atlantic
8. THIS GUY'S IN LOVE WITH YOU - Herb Alpert - A&M
9. JUDY IN DISGUISE - John Fred & Playboy Band - Paula
10. WOMAN, WOMAN - Union Gap - Columbia
11. MRS. ROBINSON - Simon & Garfunkel - Columbia
12. TIGHTEN UP - Archie Bell & Drells - Atlantic
13. HELLO, I LOVE YOU - Doors - Electra
14. HARPER VALLEY P.T.A. - Jeannie C. Riley - Plantation
15. YOUNG GIRL - Gary Puckett & Union Gap - Columbia
16. THOSE WERE THE DAYS - Mary Hopkin - Apple
17. WICHITA LINEMAN - Glen Campbell - Capitol
18. CRY LIKE A BABY - Box Tops - Mala
19. FOR ONCE IN MY LIFE - Stevie Wonder - Tamla
20. LITTLE GREEN APPLES - O.C. Smith - Columbia *
    *Original hit by Roger Miller.

TOP 20 POP SINGLES OF 1969

POS. TITLE - ARTIST - LABEL
1. SUGAR SUGAR - Archies - Calendar
2. AQUARIAS/LET THE SUNSHINE IN - 5th Dimension - Soul City
3. HONKY TONK WOMEN - Rolling Stones - London
4. EVERYDAY PEOPLE - Sly & Family Stone - Epic
5. CRIMSON & CLOVER - Tommy James & Shondells - Roulette
6. GET BACK - Beatles - Apple
7. IN THE YEAR 2525 - Zager & Evans - RCA
8. DIZZY - Tommy Roe - ABC
9. I CAN'T GET NEXT TO YOU - Temptations - Gordy
10. COME TOGETHER/SOMETHING - Beatles - Apple
11. LEAVING ON A JET PLANE - Peter, Paul & Mary - Warner Bros.
12. WEDDING BELL BLUES - 5th Dimension - Soul City
13. NA NA HEY HEY KISS HIM GOODBYE - Steam - Fontana
14. ROMEO & JULIET (THEME) - Henry Mancini - RCA
15. HAIR - Cowsills - MGM
16. CRYSTAL BLUE PERSUASION - Tommy James & Shondells - Roulette
17. SUSPICIOUS MINDS - Elvis Presley - RCA
18. DOWN ON THE CORNER - C.C.R. - Fantasy
19. BUILD ME UP BUTTERCUP - The Foundations - UNI
20. HOT FUN IN THE SUMMERTIME - Sly & Family Stone - Epic

TOP 20 POP SINGLES OF 1970

POS. TITLE - ARTIST - LABEL
1. RAINDROPS KEEP FALLING ON MY HEAD - B.J. Thomas - Scepter
2. I'LL BE THERE - Jackson 5 - Motown
3. BRIDGE OVER TROUBLED WATER - Simon & Garfunkel - Columbia
4. I THINK I LOVE YOU - Partridge Family - Bell
5. CLOSE TO YOU - Carpenters - A&M
6. MY SWEET LORD - George Harrison - Apple
7. LET IT BE - Beatles - Apple
8. AMERICAN WOMAN - Guess Who - RCA
9. WAR - Edwin Starr - Gordy
10. I WANT YOU BACK - Jackson 5 - Motown
11. TEARS OF A CLOWN - Smokey Robinson & Miracles - Tamla
12. WE'VE ONLY JUST BEGUN - Carpenters - A&M
13. BAND OF GOLD - Freda Payne - Invictus
14. AIN'T NO MOUNTAIN HIGH ENOUGH - Diana Ross - Motown
15. MAMA TOLD ME - Three Dog Night - Dunhill
16. MAKE IT WITH YOU - Bread - Electra
17. ABC - Jackson 5 - Motown
18. SPIRIT IN THE SKY - Norman Greenbaum - Reprise
19. EVERYTHING IS BEAUTIFUL - Ray Stevens - Barnaby
20. CANDIDA - Dawn - Bell

TOP 20 POP SINGLES OF 1971

POS. TITLE - ARTIST - LABEL
1. JOY TO THE WORLD - Three Dog Night - Dunhill
2. MAGGIE MAY - Rod Stewart - Mercury *
3. IT'S TOO LATE - Carole King - Ode **
4. KNOCK THREE TIMES - Dawn - Bell
5. BRAND NEW KEY - Melanie - Neighborhood
6. INDIAN RESERVATION - The Raiders - Columbia
7. ONE BAD APPLE - Osmonds - MGM
8. GO AWAY LITTLE GIRL - Donny Osmond - MGM
9. JUST MY IMAGINATION - Temptations - Gordy
10. GYPSYS, TRAMPS & THIEVES - Cher - Kapp
11. TAKE ME HOME COUNTRY ROADS - John Denver - RCA
12. FAMILY AFFAIR - Sly & Family Stone - Epic
13. HOW CAN YOU MEND A BROKEN HEART - Bee Gees - Atco
14. ME & BOBBY MCGEE - Janis Joplin - Columbia
15. YOU'VE GOT A FRIEND - James Taylor - Warner Bros.
16. UNCLE ALBERT - Paul & Linda McCartney - Apple
17. GROOVE ME - King Floyd - Chimneyville
18. THEME FROM SHAFT - Isaac Hayes - Enterprise
19. MR. BIG STUFF - Jean Knight - Stax
20. SUPERSTAR - Carpenters - A&M
    *Flip side REASON TO BELIEVE.
    **Flip side I FEEL THE EARTH MOVE.

The Partridge Family
``I Think I Love You'' is one of 1970's Top 20 Pop.

Diana Ross
Diana's ``Ain't No Mountain High Enough'' rides high in 1973.

TOP 20 POP SINGLES OF 1972

POS. TITLE - ARTIST - LABEL
1. FIRST TIME EVER I SAW YOUR FACE - Roberta Flack - Atlantic
2. AMERICAN PIE - Don McLean - United Artist
3. ALONE AGAIN NATURALLY - Gilbert O' Sullivan - MAM
4. WITHOUT YOU - Nilsson - RCA
5. I CAN SEE CLEARLY NOW - Johnny Nash - Epic
6. I GOTCHA - Joe Tex - Dial
7. THE CANDY MAN - Sammy Davis, Jr. - MGM
8. I AM WOMAN - Helen Reddy - Capitol
9. BABY DON'T GET HOOKED ON ME - Mac Davis - Columbia
10. LEAN ON ME - Bill Withers - Sussex
11. HORSE WITH NO NAME - America - Warner Bros.
12. ME & MRS. JONES - Billy Paul - PIR
13. BRANDY - Looking Glass - Epic
14. NIGHTS IN WHITE SATIN - Moody Blues - Deram
15. LET'S STAY TOGETHER - Al Green - Hi
16. I'LL TAKE YOU THERE - Staple Singers - Stax
17. DADDY DON'T YOU WALK SO FAST - Wayne Newton - Chelsea
18. OH GIRL - Chi-lites - Brunswick
19. HEART OF GOLD - Neil Young - Reprise
20. (IF LOVIN' YOU IS WRONG) I DON'T WANT TO BE RIGHT - Luther Ingram - Ko-Ko

TOP 20 POP SINGLES OF 1973

POS. TITLE - ARTIST - LABEL
1. TIE A YELLOW RIBBON AROUND THE OLE OAK TREE - Dawn - Bell
2. LET'S GET IT ON - Marvin Gaye - Tamla
3. WHY ME - Kris Kristofferson - Monument
4. MY LOVE - Paul McCartney & Wings - Apple
5. CROCODILE ROCK - Elton John - MCA
6. THE MOST BEAUTIFUL GIRL - Charlie Rich - Epic
7. KEEP ON TRUCKIN' Eddie Kendricks - Tamla
8. BAD BAD LEROY BROWN - Jim Croce - ABC
9. MIDNIGHT TRAIN TO GEORGIA - Gladys Knight & Pips
10. YOU'RE SO VAIN - Carly Simon - Electra
11. TOUCH ME IN THE MORNING - Diana Ross - Motown
12. TOP OF THE WORLD - Carpenters - A&M *
13. NIGHT THE LIGHTS WENT OUT IN GEORGIA - Vicki Lawrence - Bell
14. KILLING ME SOFTLY WITH HIS SONG - Roberta Flack - Atlantic
15. WILL IT GO ROUND IN CIRCLES - Billy Preston - A&M
16. HALF BREED - Cher - MCA
17. BROTHER LOUIE - Stories - Kama Sutra
18. PLAYGROUND IN MY MIND - Clint Holmes - Epic
19. DELTA DAWN - Helen Reddy - Capitol **
20. LITTLE WILLIE - Sweet - Bell

*Cover of Lynn Anderson's country hit.
**Cover of Tanya Tucker's first hit song in 1972.

TOP 20 POP SINGLES OF 1974

POS. TITLE - ARTIST - LABEL
1. THE WAY WE WERE - Barbra Streisand - Columbia
2. SEASONS IN THE SUN - Terry Jacks - Bell
3. BENNIE & THE JETS - Elton John - MCA
4. THE JOKER - Steve Miller Band - Capitol
5. LOVE'S THEME - Love Unlimited Orchestra - 20th Century
6. YOU MAKE ME FEEL BRAND NEW - Stylistics - Avco

7. SHOW & TELL - Al Wilson - Rocky Road
8. THEN CAME YOU - Dionne Warwick & Spinners - Atlantic
9. THE STREAK - Ray Stevens - Barnaby
10. UNTIL YOU COME BACK TO ME - Aretha Franklin - Atlantic
11. JUNGLE BOOGIE - Kool & The Gang - De-Lite
12. TSOP - MFSB - PIR
13. SPIDERS & SNAKES - Jim Stafford - MGM
14. THE LOCO-MOTION - Grand Funk - Capitol
15. YOU HAVEN'T DONE NOTHING - Stevie Wonder - Tamla
16. COME & GET YOUR LOVE - Redbone - Epic
17. HOOKED ON A FEELING - Blue Swede - EMI
18. DANCING MACHINE - Jackson Five - Motown
19. BAND ON THE RUN - Paul McCartney & Wings - Apple
20. SUNSHINE ON MY SHOULDERS - John Denver - RCA

TOP 20 POP SINGLES OF 1975

POS. TITLE - ARTIST - LABEL
1. RHINESTONE COWBOY - Glen Campbell - Capitol
2. PHILADELPHIA FREEDOM - Elton John Band - MCA
3. LOVE WILL KEEP US TOGETHER - Captain & Tennille - A&M
4. FEELINGS - Morris Albert - RCA
5. I'M SORRY/CALYPSO - John Denver - RCA
6. BEFORE THE NEXT TEARDROP FALLS - Freddie Fender - ABC
7. ONE OF THESE NIGHTS - Eagles - Asylum
8. SHINING STAR - Earth, Wind & Fire - Columbia
9. THAT'S THE WAY (I LIKE IT) - K.C. & Sunshine Band - TK
10. FLY, ROBIN FLY - Silver Convention - Midland Int.
11. FAME - David Bowie - RCA
12. ANOTHER SOMEBODY DONE SOMEBODY WRONG SONG - B.J. Thomas - ABC
13. LADY MARMALADE - Labelle - Epic
14. LOVIN' YOU - Minnie Riperton - Epic
15. JIVE TALKIN' - Bee Gees - RSO
16. ISLAND GIRL - Elton John - MCA
17. THANK GOD I'M A COUNTRY BOY - John Denver - RCA
18. BEST OF MY LOVE - Eagles - Asylum
19. SKY HIGH - Jigsaw - Chelsea
20. BLACK WATER - Doobie Brothers - Warner Bros.

TOP 20 POP SINGLES OF 1976

POS. TITLE - ARTIST - LABEL
1. TONIGHT'S THE NIGHT - Rod Stewart - Warner Bros.
2. PLAY THAT FUNKY MUSIC - Wild Cherry - Epic
3. A FIFTH OF BEETHOVEN - Walter Murphy - Private Stock
4. SILLY LOVE SONGS - Wings - Apple
5. LOVE MACHINE PT. 1 - The Miracles - Tamla
6. I WRITE THE SONGS - Barry Manilow - Arista
7. DISCO DUCK PT. 1 - Rick Dees - RSO
8. KISS & SAY GOODBYE - Manhattans - Columbia
9. DECEMBER 1963 - Four Seasons - Warner Bros.
10. LOVE IS ALIVE - Gary Wright - Warner Bros.
11. IF YOU LEAVE ME NOW - Chicago - Columbia
12. THE RUBBERBAND MAN - Spinners - Atlantic
13. SHAKE YOUR BOOTY - K.C. & Sunshine Band - TK
14. DISCO LADY - Johnnie Taylor - Columbia
15. I'D REALLY LOVE TO SEE YOU TONIGHT - England Dan & John Ford Coley - Big Tree
16. DON'T GO BREAKING MY HEART - Elton John & Kiki Dee - Rocket
17. SARA SMILE - Daryl Hall & John Oates - RCA
18. LOVE SO RIGHT - Bee Gees - RSO
19. MISTY BLUE - Dorothy Moore - Malaco *
20. BOOGIE FEVER - Sylvers - Capitol
*Remake of 1966 country hit by Wilma Burgess.

TOP 20 POP SINGLES OF 1977

POS. TITLE - ARTIST - LABEL
1. YOU LIGHT UP MY LIFE - Debby Boone - Warner/Curb
2. I JUST WANT TO BE YOUR EVERYTHING - Andy Gibb - RSO
3. HOW DEEP IS YOUR LOVE - Bee Gees - RSO
4. BEST OF MY LOVE - Emotions - Columbia
5. LOVE THEME FROM A STAR IS BORN - Barbra Streisand - Columbia
6. DON'T IT MAKE MY BROWN EYES BLUE - Crystal Gayle - United Artist
7. I LIKE DREAMIN' - Kenny Nolen - 20th Century
8. DON'T LEAVE ME THIS WAY - Thelma Houston - Tamla
9. ANGEL IN YOUR ARMS - Hot - Big Tree
10. BOOGIE NIGHTS - Heatwave - Epic
11. I'M YOUR BOOGIE MAN - K.C. & Sunshine Band - TK
12. YOU MAKE ME FEEL LIKE DANCIN' - Leo Sayer - Warner Bros.
13. TORN BETWEEN TWO LOVERS - Mary MacGregor - Ariola America
14. UNDERCOVER ANGEL - Alan O' Day - Pacific
15. HOTEL CALIFORNIA - Eagles - Asylum
16. HIGHER & HIGHER - Rita Coolidge - A&M
17. DANCING QUEEN - Abba - Atlantic
18. CAR WASH - Rose Royce - MCA
19. THAT'S ROCK 'N' ROLL - Shaun Cassidy - Warner Bros.
20. FLY LIKE AN EAGLE - Steve Miller Band - Capitol

TOP 20 POP SINGLES OF 1978

POS. TITLE - ARTIST - LABEL
1. NIGHT FEVER - Bee Gees - RSO *
2. STAYING ALIVE - Bee Gees - RSO
3. SHADOW DANCING - Andy Gibb - RSO
4. I GO CRAZY - Paul Davis - Bang
5. (LOVE IS) THICKER THAN WATER - Andy Gibb - RSO
6. KISS YOU ALL OVER - Exile - Warner/Curb
7. BABY COME BACK - Player - RSO
8. BOOGIE OOGIE OOGIE - Taste of Honey - Capitol
9. HOT CHILD IN THE CITY - Nick Gilder - Chrysalis
10. I LOVE THE NIGHTLIFE - Alicia Bridges - Polydor
11. EMOTION - Samantha Sang - Private Stock
12. LAY DOWN SALLY - Eric Clapton - RSO
13. MCARTHUR PARK - Donna Summer - Casablanca
14. YOU'RE THE ONE THAT I WANT - John Travolta & Olivia Newton-John - RSO
15. JUST THE WAY YOU ARE - Billy Joel - Columbia
16. YOU NEEDED ME - Anne Murray - Capitol
17. THREE TIMES A LADY - Commodores - Motown
18. GREASE - Frankie Valli - RSO
19. WE ARE THE CHAMPIONS - Queen - Electra
20. IF I CAN'T HAVE YOU - Yvonne Ellman - RSO
*RSO label has nine songs in Top 20 in this, the Year of Disco & Dance.

TOP 20 POP SINGLES OF 1979

POS. TITLE - ARTIST - LABEL
1. MY SHARONA - The Knack - Capitol
2. LE FREAK - Chic - Atlantic
3. Y.M.C.A. - Village People - Casablanca
4. HOT STUFF - Donna Summer - Casablanca
5. I WILL SURVIVE - Gloria Gaynor - Polydor
6. BAD GIRLS - Donna Summer - Casablanca
7. DO YA THINK I'M SEXY - Rod Stewart - Warner Bros.

440

8. REUNITED - Peaches & Herb - Polydor
9. SAD EYES - Robert John - EMI America
10. POP MUZIK - M - Sire
11. RING MY BELL - Anita Ward - Juana
12. RISE - Herb Alpert - A&M
13. STILL - The Commodores - Motown
14. I'LL NEVER LOVE THIS WAY AGAIN - Dionne Warwick - Arista
15. ESCAPE - Rupert Holmes - Infinity
16. TRAGEDY - Bee Gees - RSO
17. TOO MUCH HEAVEN - Bee Gees - RSO
18. FIRE - Pointer Sisters - Planet
19. BABE - Styx - A&M
20. GOOD TIMES - Chic - Atlantic

TOP 20 POP SINGLES OF 1980

POS. TITLE - ARTIST - LABEL
1. CALL ME - Blondie - Chrysalis
2. LADY - Kenny Rogers - Liberty
3. ANOTHER ONE BITES THE DUST - Queen - Electra
4. UPSIDE DOWN - Diana Ross - Motown
5. ANOTHER BRICK IN THE WALL - Pink Floyd - Columbia
6. DO THAT TO ME ONE MORE TIME - Captain & Tennille - Casablanca
7. ROCK WITH YOU - Michael Jackson - Epic
8. WOMAN IN LOVE - Barbra Streisand - Columbia
9. CRAZY LITTLE THING CALLED LOVE - Queen - Electra
10. MAGIC - Olivia Newton-John - MCA
11. STARTING OVER - John Lennon - Geffen
12. COMING UP - Paul McCartney & Wings - Columbia
13. IT'S STILL ROCK & ROLL TO ME - Billy Joel - Columbia
14. FUNKYTOWN - Lipps Inc. - Casablanca
15. CRUISIN' - Smokey Robinson - Tamla
16. ALL OUT OF LOVE - Air Supply - Arista
17. LITTLE JEANNIE - Elton John - MCA
18. THE ROSE - Bette Midler - Atlantic
19. RIDE LIKE THE WIND - Christopher Cross - Warner Bros.
20. MORE THAN I COULD SAY - Leo Sayer - Warner Bros.

TOP 20 POP SINGLES OF 1981

POS. TITLE - ARTIST - LABEL
1. PHYSICAL - Olivia Newton-John - MCA
2. BETTE DAVIS EYES - Kim Carnes - EMI America
3. ENDLESS LOVE - Diana Ross & Lionel Ritchie - Motown
4. JESSIE'S GIRL - Rick Springfield - RCA
5. WAITING FOR A GIRL LIKE YOU - Foreigner - Atlantic
6. CELEBRATION - Kool & The Gang - De-Lite
7. QUEEN OF HEARTS - Juice Newton - Capitol
8. KEEP ON LOVING YOU - REO Speedwagon - Epic
9. 9 TO 5 - Dolly Parton - RCA
10. ARTHUR'S THEME - Christopher Cross - Warner Bros.
11. I LOVE A RAINY NIGHT - Eddie Rabbitt - Electra
12. GREATEST AMERICAN HERO - Joey Scarbury - Electra
13. ELVIRA - Oak Ridge Boys - MCA
14. START ME UP - Rolling Stones - Rolling Stone
15. THE TIDE IS HIGH - Blondie - Chrysalis
16. WOMAN - John Lennon - Geffen
17. BEING WITH YOU - Smokey Robinson - Tamla
18. KISS ON MY LIST - Hall & Oates - RCA
19. SLOW HAND - Pointer Sisters - Planet
20. LOVE ON THE ROCKS - Neil Diamond - Columbia

TOP 20 POP SINGLES OF 1982

POS. TITLE - ARTIST - LABEL
1. EYE OF THE TIGER - Survivor - Scotti Bros.
2. CENTERFOLD - J. Geils Band - EMI America
3. I LOVE ROCK & ROLL - Joan Jett & Blackhearts - Boardwalk
4. EBONY & IVORY - Paul McCartney & Stevie Wonder - Columbia
5. HURTS SO GOOD - John Cougar - Riva
6. DON'T YOU WANT ME - Human League - A&M
7. ABRACADABRA - Steve Miller Band - Capitol
8. GLORIA - Laura Branigan - Atlantic
9. MANEATER - Hall & Oates - RCA
10. JACK & DIANE - John Cougar - Riva
11. HARD TO SAY I'M SORRY - Chicago - Columbia
12. HARDEN MY HEART - Quarterflash - Geffen
13. MICKEY - Toni Basil - Chrysalis
14. ROSANNA - Toto - Columbia
15. UP WHERE WE BELONG - Joe Cocker & Jennifer Warnes - Island
16. CHARIOTS OF FIRE - Vangelis - Polydor
17. I CAN'T GO FOR THAT - Hall & Oates - RCA
18. WHO CAN IT BE NOW? - Men At Work - Columbia
19. EYE IN THE SKY - Alan Parsons Project - Arista
20. TAINTED LOVE - Soft Cell - Sire *
*On the Hot 100 43 weeks

TOP 20 POP SINGLES OF 1983

POS. TITLE - ARTIST - LABEL
1. EVERY BREATH YOU TAKE - The Police - A&M
2. FLASHDANCE - WHAT A FEELING - Irene Cara - Casablanca
3. BILLIE JEAN - Michael Jackson - Epic
4. SAY SAY SAY - Paul McCartney & Michael Jackson - Columbia
5. TOTAL ECLIPSE OF THE HEART - Bonnie Tyler - Columbia
6. BEAT IT - Michael Jackson - Epic
7. ALL NIGHT LONG - Lionel Ritchie - Motown
8. DOWN UNDER - Men At Work - Columbia
9. ISLANDS IN THE STREAM - Kenny Rogers & Dolly Parton - RCA
10. SHAME ON THE MOON - Bob Seger - Capitol
11. BABY COME TO ME - Patti Austin & James Ingram - Qwest
12. YOU & I - Eddie Rabbitt & Crystal Gayle - Electra
13. DO YOU REALLY WANT TO HURT ME - Culture Club - Virgin
14. SWEET DREAMS - Eurythmics - RCA
15. MANIAC - Michael Sembello - Casablanca
16. SHE WORKS HARD FOR THE MONEY - Donna Summer - Mercury
17. UPTOWN GIRL - Billy Joel - Columbia
18. MAKING LOVE OUT OF NOTHING AT ALL - Air Supply - Arista
19. LET'S DANCE - David Bowie - EMI America
20. AFRICA - Toto - Columbia

TOP 20 POP SINGLES OF 1984

POS. TITLE - ARTIST - LABEL
1. WHEN DOVES CRY - Prince - Warner Bros.
2. WHAT'S LOVE GOT TO DO WITH IT - Tina Turner - Capitol
3. JUMP - Van Halen - Warner Bros.
4. KARMA CHAMELEON - Culture Club - Epic/Virgin
5. AGAINST ALL ODDS - Phil Collins - Atlantic
6. HELLO - Lionel Ritchie - Motown
7. FOOTLOOSE - Kenny Loggins - Columbia

Stevie Wonder
``I Just Called To Say I Love You'' hits the Top 20 Pop for 1984.

Tina Turner
Love had everything to do with Tina's #2 Top 20 Pop spot (1984).

Steve Winwood
``Higher Love'' is lower Top 20 Pop, but it's there in 1986.

Rick Astley
Watch for ``Never Gonna Give You Up'' in 1988's Top 20 Pop.

8. OWNER OF A LONELY HEART - Yes - Atco
9. LIKE A VIRGIN - Madonna - Sire
10. GHOSTBUSTERS - Ray Parker, Jr. - Arista
11. WAKE ME UP BEFORE YOU GO GO - Wham - Columbia
12. I JUST CALLED TO SAY I LOVE YOU - Stevie Wonder - Tamla
13. MISSING YOU - John Waite - EMI America
14. I FEEL FOR YOU - Chaka Khan - Warner Bros.
15. OUT OF TOUCH - Hall & Oates - RCA
16. LET'S HEAR IT FOR THE BOY - Deniece Williams - Columbia
17. CARRIBEAN QUEEN - Billy Ocean - Jive
18. TALKING IN YOUR SLEEP - The Romantics - Nemperor
19. GIRLS JUST WANT TO HAVE FUN - Cyndi Lauper - Portrait
20. DANCING IN THE DARK - Bruce Springsteen - Columbia

TOP 20 POP SINGLES OF 1985

POS. TITLE - ARTIST - LABEL
1. CARELESS WHISPER - Wham - Columbia
2. SEPARATE LIVES - Phil Collins & Marilyn Martin - Atlantic
3. I WANT TO KNOW WHAT LOVE IS - Foreigner - Atlantic
4. MONEY FOR NOTHING - Dire Straights - Warner Bros.
5. WE ARE THE WORLD - USA For Africa - Columbia
6. BROKEN WINGS - Mr. Mister - RCA
7. EVERYBODY WANTS TO RULE THE WORLD - Tears for Fears - Mercury
8. WE BUILT THIS CITY - Starship - Grunt
9. POWER OF LOVE - Huey Lewis & News - Chrysalis
10. CRAZY FOR YOU - Madonna - Geffen
11. EASY LOVER - Philip Bailey with Phil Collins - Columbia
12. EVERYTIME YOU GO AWAY - Paul Young - Columbia
13. CAN'T FIGHT THIS FEELING - REO Speedwagon - Epic
14. SEA OF LOVE - Honeydrippers - Es Paranza
15. TAKE ON ME - A-Ha - Warner Bros.
16. PARTY ALL THE TIME - Eddie Murphy - Columbia
17. DON'T YOU (FORGET ABOUT ME) - Simple Minds - A&M
18. THE HEAT IS ON - Glen Frey - MCA
19. I MISS YOU - Klymaxx - MCA
20. SHOUT - Tears for Fears - Mercury

TOP 20 POP SINGLES OF 1986

POS. TITLE - ARTIST - LABEL
1. THAT'S WHAT FRIENDS ARE FOR - Dionne & Friends - Arista
2. SAY YOU, SAY ME - Lionel Ritchie - Motown
3. WALK LIKE AN EGYPTIAN - Bangles - Columbia
4. ON MY OWN - Patti LaBelle & Michael McDonald - MCA
5. HOW WILL I KNOW - Whitney Houston - Arista
6. YOU GIVE LOVE A BAD NAME - Bon Jovi - Mercury
7. GREATEST LOVE OF ALL - Whitney Houston - Arista
8. FRIENDS & LOVERS - Gloria Loring & Carl Anderson - Carrere
9. KYRIE - Mr. Mister - RCA
10. NEXT TIME I FALL - Peter Cetera & Amy Grant - Full Moon
11. BURNING HEART - Survivor - Scotti Bros.
12. SECRET LOVE - Atlantic Starr - A&M
13. STUCK WITH YOU - Huey Lewis & News - Chrysalis
14. ROCK ME AMADEUS - Falco - A&M
15. WHEN I THINK OF YOU - Janet Jackson - A&M
16. WEST END GIRLS - Pet Shop Boys - EMI America
17. ADDICTED TO LOVE - Robert Palmer - Island
18. GLORY OF LOVE - Peter Cetera - Full Moon
19. HUMAN - Human League - A&M
20. HIGHER LOVE - Steve Winwood - Island

TOP 20 POP SINGLES OF 1987

POS. TITLE - ARTIST - LABEL
1. FAITH - George Michael - Columbia
2. LIVIN' ON A PRAYER - Bon Jovi - Mercury
3. ALONE - Heart - Capitol
4. HERE I GO AGAIN - Whitesnake - Geffen
5. C'EST LA VIE - Robbie Nevil - Manhattan
6. NOTHING'S GONNA STOP US NOW - Starship - Grunt
7. LA BAMBA - Los Lobos - Slash
8. SHAKE YOU DOWN - Gregory Abbott - Columbia
9. HEAVEN IS A PLACE ON EARTH - Belinda Carlisle - MCA
10. (I'VE HAD) THE TIME OF MY LIFE - Bill Medley & Jennifer Warnes - RCA
11. WITH OR WITHOUT YOU - U2 - Island
12. AT THIS MOMENT - Billy Vera & Beaters - Rhino
13. ONLY IN YOUR DREAMS - Debbie Gibson - Atlantic
14. DON'T DREAM IT'S OVER - Crowded House - Capitol
15. THE LADY IN RED - Chris DeBurgh - A&M
16. HEART AND SOUL - T'Pau - Virgin
17. ALWAYS - Atlantic Starr - Warner Bros.
18. KEEP YOUR HANDS TO YOURSELF - Georgia Satellites - Electra
19. I THINK WE'RE ALONE NOW - Tiffany - MCA
20. I WANNA DANCE WITH SOMEBODY - Whitney Houston - Arista

TOP 20 POP SINGLES OF 1988

POS. TITLE - ARTIST - LABEL
1. LOOK AWAY - Chicago - Reprise
2. NEED YOU TONIGHT - INXS - Atlantic
3. ROLL WITH IT - Steve Winwood - Virgin
4. EVERY ROSE HAS ITS THORN - Poison - Enigma
5. GOT MY MIND SET ON YOU - George Harrison - Dark Horse
6. SO EMOTIONAL - Whitney Houston - Arista
7. SEASONS CHANGE - Expose - Arista
8. BABY, I LOVE YOUR WAY - Will To Power - Epic
9. COULD'VE BEEN - Tiffany - MCA
10. NEVER GONNA GIVE YOU UP - Rick Astley - RCA
11. SWEET CHILD O' MINE - Guns n' Roses - Geffen
12. GET OUTA MY DREAMS, GET INTO MY CAR - Billy Ocean - Jive
13. THE FLAME - Cheap Trick - Epic
14. GIVING YOU THE BEST THAT I GOT - Anita Baker - Electra
15. WAITING FOR A STAR TO FALL - Boy Meets Girl - RCA
16. HANDS TO HEAVEN - Breathe - A&M
17. HOW CAN I FALL - Breathe - A&M
18. ANYTHING FOR YOU - Gloria Estefan - Epic
19. WISHING WELL - Terence Trent D'Arby - Epic
20. HUNGRY EYES - Eric Carmen - RCA

TOP 20 POP SINGLES OF 1989

POS. TITLE - ARTIST - LABEL
1. ANOTHER DAY IN PARADISE - Phil Collins - Atlantic
2. MISS YOU MUCH - Janet Jackson - A&M
3. BUST A MOVE - Young M.C. - Delicious Vinyl
4. DON'T KNOW MUCH - Linda Ronstadt & Aaron Neville - Electra
5. STRAIGHT UP - Paula Abdul - Virgin
6. BACK TO LIFE - Soul To Soul - Virgin
7. WIND BENEATH MY WINGS - Bette Midler - Atlantic
8. WE DIDN'T START THE FIRE - Billy Joel - Columbia
9. BLAME IT ON THE RAIN - Milli Vanilli - Arista *
10. LOVE SHACK - B-52's - Reprise

11. LOST IN YOUR EYES - Debbie Gibson - Atlantic
12. RIGHT HERE WAITING - Richard Marx - EMI
13. FOREVER YOUR GIRL - Paula Abdul - Virgin
14. COLD HEARTED - Paula Abdul - Virgin
15. SHE DRIVES ME CRAZY - Fine Young Cannibals - I.R.S.
16. ONCE BITTEN TWICE SHY - Great White - Capitol
17. GIRL YOU KNOW IT'S TRUE - Milli Vanilli - Arista *
18. I'LL BE THERE FOR YOU - Bon Jovi - Mercury
19. I'LL BE LOVING YOU - New Kids On The Block - Columbia
20. YOU GOT IT - New Kids On The Block - Columbia

*Give these guys some credit. The CD wasn't that bad, and they sold a lot of records. Their singles position remain intact.

TOP 20 POP SINGLES OF 1990

POS. TITLE - ARTIST - LABEL
1. LOVE TAKES TIME - Mariah Carey - Columbia
2. VISION OF LOVE - Mariah Carey - Columbia
3. BECAUSE I LOVE YOU - Stevie B - LMR
4. NOTHING COMPARES - Sinead O' Connor - Ensign
5. HOLD ON - Wilson Philips - SBK
6. IT MUST HAVE BEEN LOVE - Roxette - EMI
7. FROM A DISTANCE - Bette Midler - Atlantic
8. POISON - Bell Biv De Voe - MCA
9. CLOSE TO YOU - Maxi Priest - Charisma
10. BLACK VELVET - Alannah Miles - Atlantic
11. VOGUE - Madonna - Sire
12. HOW AM I SUPPOSED TO LIVE WITHOUT YOU - Michael Bolton - Columbia
13. HOLD ON - En Vogue - Atlantic
14. PUMP UP THE JAM - Technotronic/f Felly - SBK
15. CRADLE OF LOVE - Billy Idol - Chrysalis
16. DO ME - Bell Biv De Voe - MCA
17. OPPOSITES ATTRACT - Paula Abdul - Virgin
18. I DON'T HAVE THE HEART - James Ingram - Warner Bros.
19. SENDING ALL MY LOVE - Linear - Atlantic
20. LOVE & AFFECTION - Nelson - DGC

TOP 20 POP SINGLES OF 1991

POS. TITLE - ARTIST - LABEL
1. (EVERYTHING I DO) I DO IT FOR YOU - Bryan Adams - A&M
2. I WANNA SEX YOU UP - Color Me Badd - Giant
3. RUSH RUSH - Paula Abdul - Virgin
4. BABY BABY - Amy Grant - A&M
5. GONNA MAKE YOU SWEAT - C & C Music Factory - Columbia
6. ONE MORE TRY - Timmy T - Quality
7. UNBELIEVABLE - EMF - EMI
8. THE FIRST TIME - Surface - Columbia
9. MORE THAN WORDS - Extreme - A&M
10. I LIKE THE WAY - Hi-Five - Jive
11. MOTOWNPHILLY - Boyz II Men - Motown
12. SOMEDAY - Mariah Carey - Columbia
13. HIGH ENOUGH - Damn Yankees - Warner Bros.
14. ALL THE MAN I NEED - Whitney Houston - Arista
15. RIGHT HERE, RIGHT NOW - Jesus Jones - SBK
16. I ADORE MI AMOR - Color Me Badd - Giant
17. LOVE WILL NEVER DO - Janet Jackson - A&M
18. GOOD VIBRATIONS - Marky Mark & The Funky Bunch - Interscope
19. JUSTIFY MY LOVE - Madonna - Sire
20. EMOTIONS - Mariah Carey - Columbia

TOP 20 POP SINGLES OF 1992

POS. TITLE - ARTIST - LABEL
1. END OF THE ROAD ("FROM BOOMERANG") - Boyz II Men - Biv 10
2. BABY GOT BACK - Sir Mix-A-Lot - Def American
3. JUMP - Kris Kross - Ruffhouse
4. SAVE THE BEST FOR LAST - Vanessa Williams - Wing
5. BABY-BABY-BABY - TLC - LaFace
6. TEARS IN HEAVEN - Eric Clapton - Reprise
7. MY LOVIN' (YOU'RE NEVER GONNA GET IT) - En Vogue - Atco EastWest
8. UNDER THE BRIDGE - Red Hot Chili Peppers - Warner Bros.
9. ALL FOR LOVE - Color Me Badd - Giant
10. JUST ANOTHER DAY - John Secada - SBK
11. I LOVE YOUR SMILE - Shanice - Motown
12. TO BE WITH YOU - Mr. Big - Atlantic
13. I'M TOO SEXY - Right Said Fred - Charisma
14. BLACK OR WHITE - Michael Jackson - Epic
15. ACHY BREAKY HEART - Billy Ray Cyrus - Mercury
16. I'LL BE THERE - Mariah Carey - Columbia
17. NOVEMBER RAIN - Guns N' Roses - Geffen
18. LIFE IS A HIGHWAY - Tom Cochrane - Capitol
19. REMEMBER THE TIME - Michael Jackson - Epic
20. FINALLY - CeCe Peniston - A&M

TOP 20 POP SINGLES OF 1993

POS. TITLE - ARTIST - LABEL
1. I WILL ALWAYS LOVE YOU (FROM THE BODYGUARD) - Whitney Houston - Arista
2. WHOOMP! (THERE IT IS) - Tag Team - Life
3. CAN'T HELP FALLING IN LOVE (FROM SLIVER) - UB40 - Virgin
4. THAT'S THE WAY LOVE GOES - Janet Jackson - Virgin
5. FREAK ME - Silk - Keia
6. WEAK - SWV - RCA
7. IF I EVER FALL IN LOVE - Sjai - Gasoline Alley
8. DREAMLOVER - Mariah Carey - Columbia
9. RUMP SHAKER - Wreckx-N-Effect - MCA
10. INFORMER - Snow - EastWest
11. NUTHIN' BUT A G THANG - Dr. Dre - Death Row
12. IN THE STILL OF THE NITE (FROM THE JACKSONS) - Boyz II Men - Motown
13. DON'T WALK AWAY - Jade - Giant
14. KNOCKIN' DA BOOTS - H-Town - Luke
15. LATELY - Jadeci - Uptown
16. DAZZEY DUKS - Duice - TMR
17. SHOW ME LOVE - Robin S. - Big Beat
18. A WHOLE NEW WORLD (ALADDIN'S THEME) - Peabo Bryson & Regina Belle - Columbia
19. IF - Janet Jackson - Virgin
20. I'M SO INTO IT - SWV - RCA

Billboard Top 20 Easy Listening Singles, 1966-1993

TOP 20 EASY LISTENING SINGLES OF 1966

POS.   TITLE - ARTIST - LABEL
1.   BORN FREE - Roger Williams - Kapp
2.   STRANGERS IN THE NIGHT - Frank Sinatra - Reprise
3.   THE WHEEL OF HURT - Margaret Whiting - London
4.   THE IMPOSSIBLE DREAM - Jack Jones - Kapp
5.   SOMEWHERE MY LOVE - Ray Conniff & Singers - Columbia
6.   CRYING TIME - Ray Charles - ABC
7.   IN THE ARMS OF LOVE - Andy Williams - Columbia
8.   IT WAS A VERY GOOD YEAR - Frank Sinatra - Reprise
9.   BALLAD OF THE GREEN BERETS - S/Sgt. Barry Sadler - RCA Victor
10.   I WANT TO GO WITH YOU - Eddy Arnold - RCA Victor
11.   SPANISH EYES - Al Martino - Capitol
12.   CALL ME - Chris Montez - A&M
13.   THE MORE I SEE YOU - Chris Montez - A&M
14.   SUMMER SAMBA - Walter Wanderley - Verve
15.   LARA'S THEME - Roger Williams - Kapp
16.   A TIME FOR LOVE - Tony Bennett - Columbia
17.   SUMMER WIND - Frank Sinatra - Reprise
18.   MAS QUE NADA - Sergio Mendes & Brasil '66 - A&M
19.   MY LOVE - Petula Clark - Warner Bros.
20.   ZORBA THE GREEK - Herb Alpert & the Tijuana Brass - A&M

TOP 20 EASY LISTENING SINGLES OF 1967

POS.   TITLE - ARTIST - LABEL
1.   SOMETHIN' STUPID - Nancy Sinatra & Frank Sinatra - Reprise
2.   MY CUP RUNNETH OVER - Ed Ames - RCA Victor
3.   LADY - Jack Jones - Kapp
4.   IT MUST BE HIM - Vikki Carr - Liberty
5.   THE WORLD WE KNEW - Frank Sinatra - Reprise
6.   WHEN THE SNOW IS ON THE ROSES - Ed Ames - RCA Victor
7.   MARY IN THE MORNING - Al Martino - Capitol
8.   STOP! AND THINK IT OVER - Perry Como - RCA Victor
9.   CASINO ROYALE - Herb Alpert & the Tijuana Brass - A&M
10.   MORE THAN THE EYE CAN SEE - Al Martino - Capitol
11.   MUSIC TO WATCH GIRLS BY - Bob Crewe Generation - Dyno Voice
12.   I'LL TAKE CARE OF YOUR CARES - Frankie Lane - ABC
13.   TIME, TIME - Ed Ames - RCA Victor
14.   MORE THAN A MIRACLE - Roger Williams - Kapp
15.   DON'T SLEEP IN THE SUBWAY - Petula Clark - Warner Bros.
16.   ABANDA - Herb Alpert & the Tijuana Brass - A&M
17.   MORE AND MORE - Andy Williams - Columbia
18.   YOU ONLY LIVE TWICE - Nancy Sinatra - Reprise
19.   IN THE CHAPEL IN THE MOONLIGHT - Dean Martin - Reprise
20.   IT'S SUCH A PRETTY WORLD TODAY - Andy Russell - Capitol

TOP 20 EASY LISTENING SINGLES OF 1968

POS.   TITLE - ARTIST - LABEL
1.   LOVE IS BLUE - Paul Mauriat - Philips
2.   THIS GUY'S IN LOVE WITH YOU - Herb Alpert - A&M
3.   THE GOOD, THE BAD & THE UGLY - Hugo Montenegro - RCA Victor
4.   THE FOOL ON THE HILL - Sergio Mendes & Brasil '66 - A&M
5.   CLASSICAL GAS - Mason Williams - Warner Bros./Seven Arts
6.   THOSE WERE THE DAYS - Mary Hopkin - Apple
7.   TURN AROUND, LOOK AT ME - Vogues - Reprise
8.   LOOK OF LOVE - Sergio Mendes & Brasil '66 - A&M
9.   HONEY - Bobby Goldsboro - United Artists
10.   SOUL COAXING (AME CALINE) - Raymond Lefevre - 4 Corners of the World
11.   MASTER JACK - Four Jacks & a Jill - RCA Victor
12.   A MAN WITHOUT LOVE - Engelbert Humperdinck - Parrot
13.   SWEET MEMORIES - Andy Williams - Columbia
14.   MY SPECIAL ANGEL - Vogues - Reprise
15.   HANG 'EM HIGH - Hugo Montenegro - RCA Victor
16.   DREAM A LITTLE DREAM OF ME - Mama Cass - Dunhill
17.   DON'T GIVE UP - Petula Clark - Warner Bros./Seven Arts
18.   AUTUMN OF MY LIFE - Bobby Goldsboro - United Artists
19.   CAB DRIVER - Mills Brothers - Dot
20.   DO YOU KNOW THE WAY TO SAN JOSE - Dionne Warwick - Scepter

TOP 20 EASY LISTENING SINGLES OF 1969

POS.   TITLE - ARTIST - LABEL
1.   HURT SO BAD - Lettermen - Capitol
2.   LOVE THEME FROM ROMEO & JULIET - Henry Mancini & His Ork. - RCA
3.   I'VE GOTTA BE ME - Sammy Davis, Jr. - Reprise
4.   YOU GAVE ME A MOUNTAIN - Frankie Lane - ABC
5.   WITH PEN IN HAND - Vikki Carr - Liberty
6.   JEAN - Oliver - Crewe
7.   SEATTLE - Perry Como - RCA
8.   HAPPY HEART - Andy Williams - Columbia
9.   MY WAY - Frank Sinatra - Reprise
10.   GALVESTON - Glen Campbell - Capitol
11.   I'LL NEVER FALL IN LOVE AGAIN - Tom Jones - Parrot
12.   JOHNNY ONE TIME - Brenda Lee - Decca
13.   AQUARIUS/LET THE SUNSHINE IN - Fifth Dimension - Soul City
14.   SWEET CAROLINE - Neil Diamond - Uni
15.   THIS GIRL'S IN LOVE WITH YOU - Dionne Warwick - Scepter
16.   LOVE (CAN MAKE YOU HAPPY) - Mercy - Sundi
17.   LOVE ME TONIGHT - Tom Jones - Parrot
18.   WEDDING BELL BLUES - Fifth Dimension - Soul City
19.   PUT A LITTLE LOVE IN YOUR HEART - Jackie DeShannon - Imperial
20.   IS THAT ALL THERE IS? - Peggy Lee - Capitol

TOP 20 EASY LISTENING SINGLES OF 1970

POS.   TITLE - ARTIST - LABEL
1.   CLOSE TO YOU - Carpenters - A&M
2.   SNOWBIRD - Anne Murray - Capitol
3.   WE'VE ONLY JUST BEGUN - Carpenters - A&M
4.   BRIDGE OVER TROUBLED WATER - Simon & Garfunkel - Columbia

5. EVERYTHING IS BEAUTIFUL - Ray Stevens - Barnaby
6. I JUST CAN'T HELP BELIEVING - B. J. Thomas - Scepter
7. I'LL NEVER FALL IN LOVE AGAIN - Dionne Warwick - Scepter
8. LET IT BE - Beatles - Apple
9. FOR THE LOVE OF HIM - Bobbi Martin - United Artists
10. RAINDROPS KEEP FALLING ON MY HEAD - B. J. Thomas - Scepter
11. COME SATURDAY MORNING - Sandpipers - A&M
12. RAINY NIGHT IN GEORGIA - Brook Benton - Cotillion
13. WITHOUT LOVE (THERE IS NOTHING) - Tom Jones - Parrot
14. SONG FROM M*A*S*H - Al DeLory - Capitol
15. DAUGHTER OF DARKNESS - Tom Jones - Parrot
16. A SONG OF JOY - Miguel Rios - A&M
17. MAKE IT WITH YOU - Bread - Elektra
18. CRACKLIN' ROSIE - Neil Diamond - Uni
19. AIRPORT LOVE THEME - Vincent Bell - Decca
20. IT'S ONLY MAKE BELIEVE - Glen Campbell - Capitol

TOP 20 EASY LISTENING SINGLES OF 1971

POS. TITLE - ARTIST - LABEL
1. IT'S TOO LATE - Carole King - Ode
2. LOVE STORY (WHERE DO I BEGIN) - Andy Williams - Columbia
3. THE NIGHT THEY DROVE OLD DIXIE DOWN - Joan Baez - Vanguard
4. RAINY DAYS & MONDAYS - Carpenters - A&M
5. IF NOT FOR YOU - Olivia Newton-John - Uni
6. IF - Bread - Elecktra
7. SUPERSTAR - Carpenters - A&M
8. FOR ALL WE KNOW - Carpenters - A&M
9. THEME FROM LOVE STORY - Henry Mancini - RCA
10. ME & YOU & A DOG NAMED BOO - Lobo - Big Tree
11. WATCHING SCOTTY GROW - Bobby Goldsboro - United Artists
12. NEVER MY LOVE - Fifth Dimension - Bell
13. PEACE TRAIN - Cat Stevens - A&M
14. TAKE ME HOME COUNTRY ROADS - John Denver - RCA
15. HOW CAN YOU MEND A BROKEN HEART - Bee Gees - Atco
16. HELP ME MAKE IT THROUGH THE NIGHT - Sammi Smith - Mega
17. BEGINNINGS - Chicago - Columbia
18. HE'S SO FINE - Jody Miller - Epic
19. FOLLOW ME - Mary Travers - Warner Bros.
20. YOU'VE GOT A FRIEND - James Taylor - Warner Bros.

TOP 20 EASY LISTENING SINGLES OF 1972

POS. TITLE - ARTIST - LABEL
1. SONG SUNG BLUE - Neil Diamond - Uni
2. ALONE AGAIN (NATURALLY) - Gilbert O'Sullivan - MAM
3. BABY DON'T GET HOOKED ON ME - Mac Davis - Columbia
4. WITHOUT YOU - Nilsson - RCA
5. THE FIRST TIME EVER I SAW YOUR FACE - Roberta Flack - Atlantic
6. CANDY MAN - Sammy Davis, Jr. - MGM
7. ALL I EVER NEED IS YOU - Sonny & Cher - Kapp
8. GARDEN PARTY - Rick Nelson & the Stone Canyon Band - Decca
9. AMERICAN PIE - Don McLean - United Artists
10. CHERISH - David Cassidy - Bell
11. (LAST NIGHT) I DIDN'T GET TO SLEEP AT ALL - 5th Dimension - Bell

12. HURTING EACH OTHER - Carpenters - A&M
13. POPCORN - Hot Butter - Musicor
14. DON'T SAY YOU DON'T REMEMBER - Beverly Bremers - Scepter
15. NICE TO BE WITH YOU - Gallery - Sussex
16. EVERY DAY OF MY LIFE - Bobby Vinton - Epic
17. I CAN SEE CLEARLY NOW - Johnny Nash - Epic
18. JOY - Apollo 100 - Mega
19. MORNING HAS BROKEN - Cat Stevens - A&M
20. DADDY DON'T YOU WALK SO FAST - Wayne Newton - Chelsea

TOP 20 EASY LISTENING SINGLES OF 1973

POS. TITLE - ARTIST - LABEL
1. DELTA DAWN - Helen Reddy - Capitol
2. AND I LOVE HER SO - Perry Como - RCA
3. LOVES ME LIKE A ROCK - Paul Simon - Columbia
4. TIE A YELLOW RIBBON 'ROUND THE OLE OAK TREE - Tony Orlando & Dawn - Bell
5. SAY, HAS ANYBODY SEEN MY SWEET GYPSY ROSE - Dawn - Bell
6. SING - Carpenters - A&M
7. BOOGIE WOOGIE BUGLE BOY - Bette Midler - Atlantic
8. MY LOVE - Paul McCartney & Wings - Apple
9. YOU ARE THE SUNSHINE OF MY LIFE - Stevie Wonder - Tamla
10. YESTERDAY ONCE MORE - Carpenters - A&M
11. DANNY'S SONG - Anne Murray - Capitol
12. CLAIR - Gilbert O'Sullivan - MAM
13. DANIEL - Elton John - MCA
14. DAISY A DAY - Jud Strunk - MGM
15. TOUCH ME IN THE MORNING - Diana Ross - Motown
16. MY MARIA - B. W. Stevenson - RCA
17. ALL I KNOW - Garfunkel - Columbia
18. BAD, BAD LEROY BROWN - Jim Croce - ABC
19. I'M COMIN' HOME - Johnny Mathis - Columbia
20. ROCKY MOUNTAIN HIGH - John Denver - RCA

TOP 20 EASY LISTENING SINGLES OF 1974

POS. TITLE - ARTIST - LABEL
1. LAST TIME I SAW HIM - Diana Ross - Motown
2. THE WAY WE WERE - Barbra Streisand - Columbia
3. ERES TU (TOUCH THE WIND) - Mocedades - Tara
4. LEAVE ME ALONE (RUBY RED DRESS) - Helen Reddy - Capitol
5. ANNIE'S SONG - John Denver - RCA
6. LOVE'S THEME - Love Unlimited Orchestra - 20th Century
7. TIME IN A BOTTLE - Jim Croce - ABC
8. YOU AND ME AGAINST THE WORLD - Helen Reddy - Capitol
9. THE ENTERTAINER - Marvin Hamlisch - MCA
10. SUNSHINE ON MY SHOULDER - John Denver - RCA
11. HELP ME - Joni Mitchell - Asylum
12. SEASONS IN THE SUN - Terry Jacks - Bell
TIE. SUNDOWN - Gordon Lightfoot - Reprise
14. YOU WON'T SEE ME - Anne Murray - Capitol
15. A VERY SPECIAL LOVE SONG - Charlie Rich - Epic
16. TSOP - MFSB - Philly International
17. THE MOST BEAUTIFUL GIRL - Charlie Rich - Epic
18. PLEASE COME TO BOSTON - Dave Loggins - Epic
19. LET ME BE THERE - Olivia Newton-John - MCA
20. IF YOU LOVE ME (LET ME KNOW) - Olivia Newton-John - MCA

Roger Whittaker
``The Last Farewell'' was Roger's only hello to Top 20 EL (1975).

TOP 20 EASY LISTENING SINGLES OF 1975

POS. TITLE - ARTIST - LABEL - (DIST. LABEL)
1. MIDNIGHT BLUE - Melissa Manchester - Arista
2. AT SEVENTEEN - Janis Ian - Columbia
3. MANDY - Barry Manilow - Bell - (Arista)
4. RHINESTONE COWBOY - Glen Campbell - Capitol
5. (HEY WON'T YOU PLAY) ANOTHER SOMEBODY DONE SOMEBODY WRONG SONG - B. J. Thomas - ABC
6. PLEASE MR. PLEASE - Olivia Newton-John - MCA
7. LOVE WILL KEEP US TOGETHER - Captain & Tennille - A&M
8. FEELINGS - Morris Albert - RCA
9. ANGIE BABY - Helen Reddy - Capitol
10. I'M SORRY - John Denver - RCA
11. THE LAST FAREWELL - Roger Whittaker - RCA
12. BEST OF MY LOVE - Eagles - Asylum
13. EVERYTIME YOU TOUCH ME (I GET HIGH) - Charlie Rich - Epic - (Columbia)
14. LAUGHTER IN THE RAIN - Neil Sedaka - MCA
15. HAVE YOU NEVER BEEN MELLOW - Olivia Newton-John - MCA
16. PLEASE MR. POSTMAN - Carpenters - A&M
17. WISHING YOU WERE HERE - Chicago - Columbia
18. FALLIN' IN LOVE - Hamilton, Joe Frank & Reynolds - Playboy
19. WILDFIRE - Michael Murphey - Epic - (Columbia)
20. HOW SWEET IT IS (TO BE LOVED BY YOU) - James Taylor - Warner Bros.

TOP 20 EASY LISTENING SINGLES OF 1976

POS. TITLE - ARTIST - LABEL - (DIST. LABEL)
1. PALOMA BLANCA - George Baker Selection - Warner Bros.
2. I'D REALLY LOVE TO SEE YOU TONIGHT - England Dan & John Ford Coley - Big Tree - (Atlantic)
3. 50 WAYS TO LEAVE YOUR LOVER - Paul Simon - Columbia
4. LET IT SHINE/HE AIN'T HEAVY...HE'S MY BROTHER - Olivia Newton-John - MCA
5. I WRITE THE SONGS - Barry Manilow - Arista
6. IF YOU KNOW WHAT I MEAN - Neil Diamond - Columbia
7. FLY AWAY - John Denver - RCA
8. MY LITTLE TOWN - Simon & Garfunkel - Columbia
9. YOU'LL NEVER FIND ANOTHER LOVE - Lou Rawls - Philadelphia International - (Epic)
10. THERE'S A KIND OF HUSH (ALL OVER THE WORLD) - Carpenters - A&M
11. SHOWER THE PEOPLE - James Taylor - Warner Bros.
12. MOONLIGHT FEELS RIGHT - Starbuck - Private Stock
13. TODAY'S THE DAY - America - Warner Bros.
14. I'M EASY - Keith Carradine - ABC
15. IF YOU LEAVE ME NOW - Chicago - Columbia
16. COME ON OVER - Olivia Newton-John - MCA
17. DON'T STOP BELIEVIN' - Olivia Newton-John - MCA
18. BREAKIN' UP IS HARD TO DO - Neil Sedaka - Rocket - (MCA)
19. TIMES OF YOUR LIFE - Paul Anka - United Artists
20. FERNANDO - Abba - Atlantic

TOP 20 EASY LISTENING SINGLES OF 1977

POS. TITLE - ARTIST - LABEL
1. NOBODY DOES IT BETTER - Carly Simon - Elektra
2. LOVE THEME FROM "A STAR IS BORN" - Barbra Streisand - Columbia
3. IT'S SAD TO BELONG - England Dan & John Ford Coley - Big Tree
4. MY HEART BELONGS TO ME - Barbra Streisand - Columbia
5. SOUTHERN NIGHTS - Glen Campbell - Capitol
6. ON AND ON - Stephen Bishop - ABC
7. LOOKS LIKE WE MADE IT - Barry Manilow - Arista
8. MARGARITAVILLE - Jimmy Buffet - ABC
9. HELLO STRANGER - Yvonne Elliman - RSO
10. HANDY MAN - James Taylor - Columbia
11. RIGHT TIME OF THE NIGHT - Jennifer Warnes - Arista
12. YOU'RE MY WORLD - Helen Reddy - Capitol
13. DON'T WORRY BABY - B. J. Thomas - MCA
14. JUST A SONG BEFORE I GO - Crosby/Stills/Nash - Atlantic
15. AFTER THE LOVIN' - Engelbert Humperdinck - Epic
16. HIGHER & HIGHER - Rita Coolidge - A&M
17. SAY YOU'LL STAY UNTIL TOMORROW - Tom Jones - Epic
18. SAM - Olivia Newton-John - MCA
19. TORN BETWEEN TWO LOVERS - Mary Macgregor - Ariola America
20. WHEN I NEED YOU - Leo Sayer - Warner Bros.

TOP 20 EASY LISTENING SINGLES OF 1978

POS. TITLE - ARTIST - LABEL
1. WE'LL NEVER HAVE TO SAY GOODBYE AGAIN - England Dan & John Ford Coley - Big Tree
2. HOW DEEP IS YOUR LOVE - Bee Gees - RSO
3. JUST THE WAY YOU ARE - Billy Joel - Columbia
4. (WHAT A) WONDERFUL WORLD - Art Garfunkel with James Taylor & Paul Simon - Columbia

Anne Murray
This Canadian's easy-to-listen-to voice put five songs in the Top 20 EL in the seventies, capped off with one in 1980.

5. BLUER THAN BLUE - Michael Johnson - EMI-America
6. THREE TIMES A LADY - Commodores - Motown
7. FOOL (IF YOU THINK IT'S OVER) - Chris Rea - United Artists
8. IF EVER I SEE YOU AGAIN - Roberta Flack - Atlantic
9. EVEN NOW - Barry Manilow - Arista
10. YOU NEEDED ME - Anne Murray - Capitol
11. FEELS SO GOOD - Chuck Mangione - A&M
12. GOODBYE GIRL - David Gates - Elektra
13. CAN'T SMILE WITHOUT YOU - Barry Manilow - Arista
14. SONGBIRD - Barbra Streisand - Columbia
15. TOO MUCH, TOO LITTLE, TOO LATE - Johnny Mathis & Deniece Williams - Columbia
16. YOU'RE THE LOVE - Seals & Crofts - Warner Bros.
17. LADY LOVE - Lou Rawls - P.I.R.
18. LOVE IS IN THE AIR - John Paul Young - Scotti Bros.
19. BEFORE MY HEART FINDS OUT - Gene Cotton - Ariola
20. TALKING IN YOUR SLEEP - Crystal Gayle - United Artists

TOP 20 ADULT CONTEMPORARY SINGLES OF 1979

POS. TITLE - ARTIST - LABEL
1. TIME PASSAGES - Al Stewart - Arista
2. CRAZY LOVE - Poco - ABC
3. LEAD ME ON - Maxine Nightingale - Windsong
4. SHADOWS IN THE MOONLIGHT - Anne Murray - Capitol
5. MORNING DANCE - Spyro Gyra - Infinity
6. LOVE IS THE ANSWER - England Dan & John Ford Coley - Big Tree
7. JUST WHEN I NEEDED YOU MOST - Randy Vanwarmer - Bearsville
8. DIFFERENT WORLDS - Maureen McGovern - Warner/Curb
9. LOTTA LOVE - Nicolette Larson - Warner Bros.
10. SHE BELIEVES IN ME - Kenny Rogers - United Artists
11. I'LL NEVER LOVE THIS WAY AGAIN - Dionne Warwick - Arista
12. THE GAMBLER - Kenny Rogers - United Artists
13.. MAMA CAN'T BUY YOU LOVE - Elton John - MCA
14. WHEN YOU'RE IN LOVE WITH A BEAUTIFUL WOMAN - Dr. Hook - Capitol
15. RISE - Herb Alpert - A&M
16. WHERE WERE YOU WHEN I WAS FALLING IN LOVE - Lobo - Warner/Curb
17. THIS MOMENT IN TIME - Engelbert Humperdinck - Epic
18. MAIN EVENT - Barbra Streisand - Columbia
19. (OUR LOVE) DON'T THROW IT ALL AWAY - Andy Gibb - RSO
20. PROMISES - Eric Clapton - RSO

TOP 20 ADULT CONTEMPORARY SINGLES OF 1980

POS. TITLE - ARTIST - LABEL
1. LOST IN LOVE - Air Supply - Arista
2. YOU'RE ONLY LONELY - J. D. Souther - Columbia
3. THE ROSE - Bette Midler - Atlantic
4. BROKEN HEARTED ME - Anne Murray - Capitol
5. ALL THINGS ARE POSSIBLE - Dan Peek - Lamb & Lion
6. WHERE WERE YOU WHEN I WAS FALLING IN LOVE - Lobo - MCA
7. SEND ONE YOUR LOVE - Stevie Wonder - Tamla
8. LEAD ME ON - Maxine Nightingale - Windsong
9. RISE - Herb Alpert - A&M
10. WITH YOU I'M BORN AGAIN - Billy Preston & Syreeta - Tamla

11. DIFFERENT WORLDS - Maureen McGovern - Warner/Curb
12. GIVE IT ALL YOU GOT - Chuck Mangione - A&M
13. WHEN I WANTED YOU - Barry Manilow - Arista
14. YES, I'M READY - Teri De Sario w/K.C. - Casablanca
15. THIS NIGHT WON'T LAST FOREVER - Michael Johnson - EMI-America
16. DEJA VU - Dionne Warwick - Arista
17. AFTER THE LOVE HAS GONE - Earth, Wind, & Fire - ARC/Columbia
18. LONGER - Dan Fogelberg - Full Moon/Epic
19. DON'T FALL IN LOVE WITH A DREAMER - Kenny Rogers w/ Kim Carnes - United Artists
20. DO THAT TO ME ONE MORE TIME - Captain & Tennille - Casablanca

TOP 20 ADULT CONTEMPORARY SINGLES OF 1981

POS. TITLE - ARTIST - LABEL
1. I DON'T NEED YOU - Kenny Rogers - Liberty
2. WHAT KIND OF FOOL - Barbra Streisand & Barry Gibb - Columbia
3. ARTHUR'S THEME - Christopher Cross - Warner Bros.
4. ENDLESS LOVE - Diana Ross & Lionel Richie Jr. - Motown
5. I LOVE A RAINY NIGHT - Eddie Rabbitt - Elektra
6. SUKIYAKI - A Taste Of Honey - Capitol
7. ANGEL OF THE MORNING - Juice Newton - Capitol
8. AMERICA - Neil Diamond - Capitol
9. 9 TO 5 - Dolly Parton - RCA
10. THE WINNER TAKES IT ALL - Abba - Atlantic
11. HOW BOUT US - Champaign - Columbia
12. QUEEN OF HEARTS - Juice Newton - Capitol

Ronnie Milsap
Two songs in 1981 and one in 1982 is solid Top 20 EL status.

13. MORNING TRAIN - Sheena Easton - EMI-America
14. NO GETTIN' OVER ME - Ronnie Milsap - RCA
15. TOUCH ME WHEN WE'RE DANCING - Carpenters - A&M
16. THE ONE THAT YOU LOVE - Air Supply - Arista
17. HERE I AM - Air Supply - Arista
18. JUST THE TWO OF US - Grover Washington Jr. - Elektra
19. STEP BY STEP - Eddie Rabbitt - Elektra
20. SMOKEY MOUNTAIN RAIN - Ronnie Milsap - RCA

TOP 20 ADULT CONTEMPORARY SINGLES OF 1982

POS. TITLE - ARTIST - LABEL
1. ANY DAY NOW - Ronnie Milsap - RCA
2. CHARIOTS OF FIRE - Vangelis - Polydor
3. EBONY AND IVORY - Paul McCartney & Stevie Wonder - Columbia
4. YESTERDAY'S SONGS - Neil Diamond - Columbia
5. EVEN THE NIGHTS ARE BETTER - Air Supply - Arista
6. HARD TO SAY I'M SORRY - Chicago - Full Moon/Warner Bros.
7. THROUGH THE YEARS - Kenny Rogers - Liberty
8. ALWAYS ON MY MIND - Willie Nelson - Columbia
9. LOVE WILL TURN YOU AROUND - Kenny Rogers - Liberty
10. KEY LARGO - Bertie Higgins - Family
11. SHANGHAI BREEZES - John Denver - RCA
12. PERSONALLY - Karla Bonoff - Columbia
13. WASTED ON THE WAY - Crosby/Stills/Nash - Atlantic
14. LOVE'S BEEN A LITTLE BIT HARD ON ME - Juice Newton - Capitol
15. THE OLD SONGS - Barry Manilow - Arista
16. LEADER OF THE BAND - Dan Fogelberg - Full Moon/Epic
17. THE SWEETEST THING - Juice Newton - Capitol
18. TAKE ME DOWN - Alabama - RCA
19. BLUE EYES - Elton John - Geffen
20. MAKING LOVE - Roberta Flack - Atlantic

TOP 20 ADULT CONTEMPORARY SINGLES OF 1983

POS. TITLE - ARTIST - LABEL
1. YOU ARE - Lionel Richie - Motown
2. NEVER GONNA LET YOU GO - Sergio Mendes - A&M
3. ALL TIME HIGH - Rita Coolidge - A&M
4. TRULY - Lionel Richie - Motown
5. MY LOVE - Lionel Richie - Motown
6. BABY COME TO ME - Patti Austin with James Ingram - Qwest
7. ALL THIS LOVE - DeBarge - Gordy
8. IT MIGHT BE YOU - Stephen Bishop - Warner Bros.
9. THE GIRL IS MINE - Michael Jackson & Paul McCartney - Epic
10. HOW AM I SUPPOSED TO LIVE WITHOUT YOU - Laura Branigan - Atlantic
11. I WON'T HOLD YOU BACK - Toto - Columbia
12. YOU AND I - Eddie Rabbitt with Crystal Gayle - Elektra
13. HOLD ME 'TIL THE MORNIN' COMES - Paul Anka - Columbia
14. SHAME ON THE MOON - Bob Seger & the Silver Bullet Band - Capitol
15. MAKE LOVE STAY - Dan Fogelberg - Full Moon/Epic
16. HEARTBREAKER - Dionne Warwick - Arista
17. FLASHDANCE...WHAT A FEELING - Irene Cara - Casablanca
18. MORNIN' - Al Jarreau - Warner Bros.

19. TELL HER ABOUT IT - Billy Joel - Columbia
20. AFRICA - Toto - Columbia

TOP 20 ADULT CONTEMPORARY SINGLES OF 1984

POS. TITLE - ARTIST - LABEL
1. IF EVER YOU'RE IN MY ARMS AGAIN - Peabo Bryson - Elektra
2. HELLO - Lionel Richie - Motown
3. STUCK ON YOU - Lionel Richie - Motown
4. TIME AFTER TIME - Cyndi Lauper - Portrait
5. SAD SONGS (SAY SO MUCH) - Elton John - Geffen
6. THE LONGEST TIME - Billy Joel - Columbia
7. LEAVE A TENDER MOMENT ALONE - Billy Joel - Columbia
8. READ 'EM AND WEEP - Barry Manilow - Arista
9. GOT A HOLD ON ME - Christine McVie - Warner Bros.
10. ALMOST OVER YOU - Sheena Easton - EMI-America
11. JOANNA - Kool & the Gang - De-Lite
12. I JUST CALLED TO SAY I LOVE YOU - Stevie Wonder - Motown
13. DRIVE - Cars - Elektra
14. BELIEVE IN ME - Dan Fogelberg - Full Moon/Epic
15. ALMOST PARADISE...LOVE THEME FROM "FOOT-LOOSE" - Mike Reno & Ann Wilson - Columbia
16. I GUESS THAT'S WHY THEY CALL IT THE BLUES - Elton John - Geffen
17. THE WAY HE MAKES ME FEEL - Barbra Streisand - Columbia
18. THIS WOMAN - Kenny Rogers - RCA
19. THINK OF LAURA - Christopher Cross - Warner Bros.
20. AN INNOCENT MAN - Billy Joel - Columbia

TOP 20 ADULT CONTEMPORARY SINGLES OF 1985

POS. TITLE - ARTIST - LABEL
1. CHERISH - Kool & the Gang - De-Lite
2. EVERYTIME YOU GO AWAY - Paul Young - Columbia
3. THE SEARCH IS OVER - Survivor - Scotti Bros.
4. CARELESS WHISPER - Wham! Featuring George Michael - Columbia
5. ONE MORE NIGHT - Phil Collins - Atlantic
6. SUDDENLY - Billy Ocean - Jive
7. YOU'RE THE INSPIRATION - Chicago - Full Moon/Warner Bros.
8. WHO'S HOLDING DONNA NOW - DeBarge - Gordy
9. ALL I NEED - Jack Wagner - Qwest
10. SMOOTH OPERATOR - Sade - Portrait
11. MISSING YOU - Diana Ross - RCA
12. DO WHAT YOU DO - Jermaine Jackson - Arista
13. RHYTHM OF THE NIGHT - DeBarge - Gordy
14. TOO LATE FOR GOODBYES - Julian Lennon - Atlantic
15. AXEL F - Harold Faltermeyer - MCA
16. SAVING ALL MY LOVE FOR YOU - Whitney Houston - Arista
17. NIGHTSHIFT - Commodores - Motown
18. YOU'RE ONLY HUMAN (SECOND WIND) - Billy Joel - Columbia
19. FOOLISH HEART - Steve Perry - Columbia
20. CRAZY FOR YOU - Madonna - Geffen

TOP 20 ADULT CONTEMPORARY SINGLES OF 1986

POS. TITLE - ARTIST - LABEL
1. THAT'S WHAT FRIENDS ARE FOR - Dionne & Friends - Arista
2. SAY YOU, SAY ME - Lionel Richie - Motown
3. YOUR WILDEST DREAMS - The Moody Blues - Polydor
4. GLORY OF LOVE (THEME FROM "THE KARATE KID PART II") - Peter Cetera - Warner Bros.
5. WORDS GET IN THE WAY - Miami Sound Machine - Epic
6. THERE'LL BE SAD SONGS (TO MAKE YOU CRY) - Billy Ocean - Jive
7. GREATEST LOVE OF ALL - Whitney Houston - Arista
8. THESE DREAMS - Heart - Capitol
9. ON MY OWN - Patti LaBelle & Michael McDonald - MCA
10. FRIENDS AND LOVERS - Carl Anderson & Gloria Loring - Carrere
11. STUCK WITH YOU - Huey Lewis & The News - Chrysalis
12. LIVE TO TELL - Madonna - Sire
13. HOLDING BACK THE YEARS - Simply Red - Elektra
14. SARA - Starship - Grunt
15. NO ONE IS TO BLAME - Howard Jones - Elektra
16. THE SWEETEST TABOO - Sade - Portrait
17. NIKITA - Elton John - Geffen
18. GO HOME - Stevie Wonder - Tamla
19. HOW WILL I KNOW - Whitney Houston - Arista
20. SECRET LOVERS - Atlantic Starr - A&M

TOP 20 ADULT CONTEMPORARY SINGLES OF 1987

POS. TITLE - ARTIST - LABEL
1. CAN'T WE TRY - Dan Hill (Duet with Vonda Shepard) - Columbia
2. SOMEWHERE OUT THERE (FROM "AN AMERICAN TAIL") - Linda Ronstadt & James Ingram - MCA
3. WILL YOU STILL LOVE ME? - Chicago - Warner Bros.
4. BALLERINA GIRL - Lionel Richie - Motown
5. THIS IS THE TIME - Billy Joel - Columbia
6. LOVE IS FOREVER - Billy Ocean - Jive
7. DIDN'T WE ALMOST HAVE IT ALL - Whitney Houston - Arista
8. MANDOLIN RAIN - Bruce Hornsby & The Range - RCA
9. I WANNA DANCE WITH SOMEBODY (WHO LOVES ME) - Whitney Houston - Arista
10. SONGBIRD - Kenny G. - Arista
11. BACK IN THE HIGHLIFE AGAIN - Steve Winwood - Island
12. JUST TO SEE HER - Smokey Robinson - Motown
13. ONE HEARTBEAT - Smokey Robinson - Motown
14. YOU GOT IT ALL - The Jets - MCA
15. IN TOO DEEP - Genesis - Atlantic
16. I JUST CAN'T STOP LOVING YOU - Michael Jackson with Siedah Garrett - Epic
17. ALWAYS - Atlantic Starr - Warner Bros.
18. LOVE POWER - Dionne Warwick & Jeffrey Osborne - Arista
19. THE WAY IT IS - Bruce Hornsby & The Range - RCA
20. THE FINER THINGS - Steve Winwood - Island

TOP 20 ADULT CONTEMPORARY SINGLES OF 1988

POS. TITLE - ARTIST - LABEL
1. CAN'T STAY AWAY FROM YOU - Gloria Estefan & Miami Sound Machine - Epic
2. WHERE DO BROKEN HEARTS GO - Whitney Houston - Arista
3. GOT MY MIND SET ON YOU - George Harrison - Dark Horse
4. HANDS TO HEAVEN - Breathe - A&M
5. ANYTHING FOR YOU - Gloria Estefan & Miami Sound Machine - Epic
6. MAKE ME LOSE CONTROL - Eric Carmen - Arista
7. HUNGRY EYES (FROM "DIRTY DANCING") - Eric Carmen - Arista
8. NEVER GONNA GIVE YOU UP - Rick Astley - RCA
9. I DON'T WANNA GO ON WITH YOU LIKE THAT - Elton John - MCA
10. NEVER THOUGHT (THAT I COULD LOVE) - Dan Hill - Columbia
11. THE VALLEY ROAD - Bruce Hornsby & The Range - RCA
12. (I'VE HAD) THE TIME OF MY LIFE - Bill Medley & Jennifer Warnes - RCA
13. I LIVE FOR YOUR LOVE - Natalie Cole - EMI
14. SHE'S LIKE THE WIND - Patrick Swayze Featuring Wendy Fraser - RCA
15. ENDLESS SUMMER NIGHTS - Richard Marx - EMI
16. I'LL ALWAYS LOVE YOU - Taylor Dayne - Arista
17. MAKE IT REAL - The Jets - MCA
18. I DON'T WANT TO LIVE WITHOUT YOU - Foreigner - Atlantic
19. ROLL WITH IT - Steve Winwood - Virgin
20. ONE MORE TRY - George Michael - Columbia

TOP 20 ADULT CONTEMPORARY SINGLES OF 1989

POS. TITLE - ARTIST - LABEL
1. SECOND CHANCE - Thirty Eight Special - A&M
2. IF YOU DON'T KNOW ME BY NOW - Simply Red - Elektra
3. TWO HEARTS - Phil Collins - Atlantic
4. WIND BENEATH MY WINGS - Bette Midler - Atlantic
5. AFTER ALL - Cher & Peter Cetera - Geffen
6. RIGHT HERE WAITING - Richard Marx - EMI
7. DON'T WANNA LOSE YOU - Gloria Estefan - Epic
8. THE LIVING YEARS - Mike + The Mechanics - Atlantic
9. MISS YOU LIKE CRAZY - Natalie Cole - EMI
10. YOU GOT IT - Roy Orbison - Virgin
11. EVERLASTING LOVE - Howard Jones - Elektra
12. THE END OF THE INNOCENCE - Don Henley - Geffen
13. WAITING FOR A STAR TO FALL - Boy Meets Girl - RCA
14. SILHOUETTE - Kenny G. - Arista
15. SOUL PROVIDER - Michael Bolton - Columbia
16. DREAMIN' - Vanessa Williams - Wing
17. THIS TIME I KNOW IT'S FOR REAL - Donna Summer - Atlantic
18. MY HEART CAN'T TELL YOU NO - Rod Stewart - Warner Bros.
19. ETERNAL FLAME - Bangles - Columbia
20. ONE - Bee Gees - Warner Bros.

TOP 20 ADULT CONTEMPORARY SINGLES OF 1990

POS. TITLE - ARTIST - LABEL
1. DO YOU REMEMBER? - Phil Collins - Atlantic
2. HERE WE ARE - Gloria Estefan - Epic
3. I DON'T HAVE THE HEART - James Ingram - Warner Bros.
4. HOW AM I SUPPOSED TO LIVE WITHOUT YOU - Michael Bolton - Columbia

5. VISION OF LOVE - Mariah Carey - Columbia
6. OH GIRL - Paul Young - Columbia
7. LOVE WILL LEAD YOU BACK - Taylor Dayne - Arista
8. SACRIFICE - Elton John - MCA
9. ALL MY LIFE - Linda Ronstadt Featuring Aaron Neville - Elektra
10. CLUB AT THE END OF THE STREET - Elton John - MCA
11. ANOTHER DAY IN PARADISE - Phil Collins - Atlantic
12. HOLD ON - Wilson Phillips - SBK
13. RELEASE ME - Wilson Phillips - SBK
14. HERE AND NOW - Luther Vandross - Epic
15. CUTS BOTH WAYS - Gloria Estefan - Epic
16. IT MUST HAVE BEEN LOVE - Roxette - EMI
17. THIS OLD HEART OF MINE - Rod Stewart - Warner Bros.
18. DOWNTOWN TRAIN - Rod Stewart - Warner Bros.
19. WHAT KIND OF MAN WOULD I BE? - Chicago - Reprise
20. COME BACK TO ME - Janet Jackson - A&M

TOP 20 ADULT CONTEMPORARY
SINGLES OF 1991

POS. TITLE - ARTIST - LABEL
1. (EVERYTHING I DO) I DO IT FOR YOU - Bryan Adams - A&M
2. BABY BABY - Amy Grant - A&M
3. ALL THE MAN THAT I NEED - Whitney Houston - Arista
4. CRY FOR HELP - Rick Astley - RCA
5. LOVE IS A WONDERFUL THING - Michael Bolton - Columbia
6. YOU'RE IN LOVE - Wilson Phillips - SBK
7. WHERE DOES MY HEART BEAT NOW - Celine Dion - Epic
8. COMING OUT OF THE DARK - Gloria Estefan - Epic
9. RUSH RUSH - Paula Abdul - Captive
10. I DON'T WANNA CRY - Mariah Carey - Columbia
11. EVERY HEARTBEAT - Amy Grant - A&M
12. RHYTHM OF MY HEART - Rod Stewart - Warner Bros.
13. THE FIRST TIME - Surface - Columbia
14. THE MOTOWN SONG - Rod Stewart - Warner Bros.
15. CAN'T FORGET YOU - Gloria Estefan - Epic
16. GET HERE - Oleta Adams - Fontana
17. EVERYBODY PLAYS THE FOOL - Aaron Neville - A&M
18. MORE THAN WORDS - Extreme - A&M
19. YOU GOTTA LOVE SOMEONE - Elton John - MCA
20. POWER OF LOVE/LOVE POWER - Luther Vandross - Epic

TOP 20 ADULT CONTEMPORARY
SINGLES OF 1992

POS. TITLE - ARTIST - LABEL
1. SAVE THE BEST FOR LAST - Vanessa Williams - Wing
2. HOLD ON MY HEART - Genesis - Atlantic
3. IF YOU ASKED ME TO - Celine Dion - Epic
4. THE ONE - Elton John - MCA
5. TEARS IN HEAVEN - Eric Clapton - Reprise
6. RESTLESS HEART - Peter Cetera - WArner Bros.
7. BEAUTY AND THE BEAST - Celine Dion/Peabo Bryson - Epic
8. JUST ANOTHER DAY - Jon Secada - SBK
9. HAZARD - Richard Marx - Capitol
10. MISSING YOU NOW - Michael Bolton - Columbia
11. CAN'T LET GO - Mariah Carey - Columbia
12. I WILL REMEMBER YOU - Amy Grant - A&M
13. SOMETIMES LOVE JUST AIN'T ENOUGH - Patty Smyth - MCA
14. MASTERPIECE - Atlantic Starr -Reprise
15. TAKE THIS HEART - Richard Marx - Capitol
16. KEEP COMING BACK - Richard Marx - Capitol
17. I CAN'T MAKE YOU LOVE ME - Bonnie Raitt - Capitol
18. WHAT BECOMES OF THE BROKENHEARTED - Paul Young - MCA
19. NOT THE ONLY ONE - Bonnie Raitt - Capitol
20. DON'T LET THE SUN GO DOWN ON ME - George Michael/ Elton John - Columbia

TOP 20 ADULT CONTEMPORARY
SINGLES OF 1993

POS. TITLE - ARTIST - LABEL
1. LOVE IS - Vanessa Williams & Brian McKnight - Giant
2. I DON'T WANNA FIGHT - Tina Turner - Virgin
3. I'LL NEVER GET OVER YOU (Getting OVER ME) - Expose - Arista
4. I SEE YOUR SMILE - Gloria Estefan - Epic
5. HAVE I TOLD YOU LATELY - Rod Stewart - Warner Bros.
6. A WHOLE NEW WORLD - Peabo Bryson & Regina Belle - Columbia
7. FIELDS OF GOLD - Sting - A&M
8. FOREVER IN LOVE - Kenny G - Arista
9. THE RIVER OF DREAMS - Billy Joel - Columbia
10. DON'T TAKE AWAY MY HEAVEN - Aaron Neville - A&M
11. WHEN SHE CRIES - Restless Heart - RCA
12. TELL ME WHAT YOU DREAM - Restless Heart & W. Hill - Novus
13. SIMPLE LIFE - Elton John - MCA
14. ANGEL - Jon Secada - SBK
15. BY THE TIME THIS NIGHT IS OVER - Kenny G & Peabo Bryson - Arista
16. DREAMLOVER - Mariah Carey - Columbia
17. I HAVE NOTHING - Whitney Houston - Arista
18. I WILL ALWAYS LOVE YOU - Whitney Houston - Arista
19. NEVER A TIME - Genesis - Atlantic
20. I'M FREE - Jon Secada - SBK

George D. Hay

The "Solemn Ol' Judge"—the man who named the "Grand Ole Opry" in 1927.

Bradley Kinkaid

A pioneer folk-country singer in the thirties, Kinkaid's most popular tune was "The Letter Edged In Black."

A few of
Country's
Pre-Chart
Pioneers....

Jimmie Rodgers

The Father of Country Music, the "Singing Brakeman" began his recording career in 1927. Known for his "Blue Yodels," two of his hits were "Waitin' For A Train" and "T For Texas." He died May 26, 1933

Minnie Pearl

Grand Ole Opry mainstay and one of the world's best-loved comedy performers, Minnie has been an Opry regular since 1940.

The Carter Family

One of country music's most influential groups, the Carters began their long, successful career in Bristol, Tennessee, in 1927. Two of their hits were "Wildwood Flower" and "I'm Thinking Tonight Of My Blue Eyes."

Bob Wills

Bob began his recording career in 1932. Hits included ``San Antonio Rose'' and Cotton-Eyed Joe.'' His ``New Spanish Two-Step'' was #1 in 1946. He died in 1975.

Al Dexter

Best remembered for his ``Pistol Packin' Mama,'' Al also had three hits in 1946—including the #2 ``Guitar Polka''—and one in 1947. Dexter died in 1984.

Elton Britt

One of the world's greatest yodelers, and recipient of Country Music's first Gold Record (``There's A Star Spangled Banner Waving Somewhere''), Elton also recorded country's longest single—``The Jimmie Rodgers Blues''—in 1968. He died in 1972.

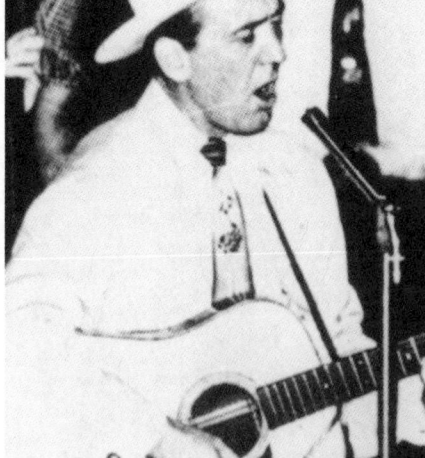

Roy Acuff

The King of Country Music, his ``Wabash Cannonball'' is a country classic, although on the original version (1936) he sang only the train effects. The vocal itself was by Sam ``Dynamite'' Hatcher.

Red Foley

Foley had a string of hits in the late forties and early fifties (five Top 20 songs in 1950 alone), including the #2 ``Chattanooga Shoe-Shine Boy''.

Billboard Top 20 Country Singles, 1946-1993

TOP 20 COUNTRY SINGLES OF 1946

POS. TITLE - ARTIST - LABEL
1. NEW SPANISH TWO STEP - Bob Wills - Columbia
2. GUITAR POLKA - Al Dexter - Columbia
3. DIVORCE ME C.O.D. - Merle Travis - Capitol
4. ROLY-POLY - Bob Wills - Columbia
5. SIOUX CITY SUE - Zeke Manners - RCA Victor
6. WINE, WOMEN AND SONG - Al Dexter - Columbia
7. SOMEDAY (YOU'LL WANT ME TO WANT YOU) - Elton Britt - RCA Victor
8. CINCINNATI LOU - Merle Travis - Capitol
9. SIOUX CITY SUE - Hoosier Hot Shots - Decca
10. THAT'S HOW MUCH I LOVE YOU - Eddy Arnold - RCA Victor
11. SIOUX CITY SUE - Dick Thomas - National
12. HONEY, DO YOU THINK IT'S WRONG? - Al Dexter - Columbia
13. I WISH I HAD NEVER MET SUNSHINE - Gene Autry - Columbia
14. DETOUR - Spade Cooley - Columbia
15. NO VACANCY - Merle Travis - Capitol
16. DRIVIN' NAILS IN MY COFFIN - Floyd Tillman - Columbia
    HAVE I TOLD YOU LATELY THAT I LOVE YOU? - Gene Autry - Columbia
    RAINBOW AT MIDNIGHT - Ernest Tubb - Decca
17. YOU CAN'T BREAK MY HEART - Spade Cooley - Columbia
    FILIPINO BABY - Ernest Tubb - Decca

TOP 20 COUNTRY SINGLES OF 1947

POS. TITLE - ARTIST - LABEL
1. SMOKE, SMOKE, SMOKE (THAT CIGARETTE) - Tex Williams - Capitol
2. IT'S A SIN - Eddy Arnold - RCA Victor
3. SO ROUND, SO FIRM, SO FULLY PACKED - Merle Travis - Capitol
4. WHAT IS LIFE WITHOUT LOVE - Eddy Arnold - RCA Victor
5. I'LL HOLD YOU IN MY HEART - Eddy Arnold - RCA Victor
6. TIMTAYSHUN - Red Ingle-Jo Stafford - Capitol
7. NEW JOLIE BLONDE - Red Foley - Decca
8. RAINBOW AT MIDNIGHT - Ernest Tubb - Decca
9. NEW PRETTY BLONDE - Moon Mullican - King
10. DIVORCE ME C.O.D. - Merle Travis - Capitol
11. SUGAR MOON - Bob Wills - Columbia
12. TO MY SORROW - Eddy Arnold - RCA Victor
13. FILIPINO BABY - Ernest Tubb - Decca
14. THAT'S WHAT I LIKE ABOUT THE WEST - Tex Williams - Capitol
15. JOLE BLON - Roy Acuff - Columbia
16. DOWN AT THE ROADSIDE INN - Al Dexter - Columbia
    FEUDIN' AND FIGHTIN' - Dorothy Shay - Columbia
    NEVER TRUST A WOMAN - Red Foley - Decca

TOP 20 COUNTRY SINGLES OF 1948

POS. TITLE - ARTIST - LABEL
1. BOUQUET OF ROSES - Eddy Arnold - RCA Victor
2. ANYTIME - Eddy Arnold - RCA Victor
3. JUST A LITTLE LOVIN' - Eddy Arnold - RCA Victor
4. TEXARKANA BABY - Eddy Arnold - RCA Victor
5. ONE HAS MY NAME - Jimmy Wakely - Capitol
6. HUMPTY DUMPTY HEART - Hank Thompson - Capitol
7. LIFE GETS TEE-JUS DON'T IT? - Carson Robison - MGM
8. SWEETER THAT THE FLOWERS - Moon Mullican - King
9. DECK OF CARDS - T. Texas Tyler - Four Star
10. MY DADDY IS ONLY A PICTURE - Eddy Arnold - RCA Victor
11. TENNESSEE WALTZ - Pee Wee King - RCA Victor
12. SUSPICION - Tex Williams - Capitol
13. TENNESSEE SATURDAY NIGHT - Red Foley - Decca
14. TENNESSEE WALTZ - Cowboy Copas - King
15. I LOVE YOU SO MUCH IT HURTS - Jimmy Wakely - Capitol
16. SEAMAN BLUES - Ernest Tubb - Decca
17. I'LL HOLD YOU IN MY HEART - Eddy Arnold - RCA Victor
    A HEART FULL OF LOVE - Eddy Arnold - RCA Victor
19. FOREVER IS ENDING TODAY - Ernest Tubb - Decca
20. BLUE SHADOWS ON THE TRAIL - Roy Rogers & Sons of the Pioneers - RCA Victor
20. COOL WATER - Sons of the Pioneers - RCA Victor (tie)

TOP 20 COUNTRY SINGLES OF 1949

POS. TITLE - ARTIST - LABEL
1. LOVESICK BLUES - Hank Williams - MGM
2. DON'T ROB ANOTHER MAN'S CASTLE - Eddy Arnold - RCA Victor
3. I'M THROWING RICE - Eddy Arnold - RCA Victor
4. SLIPPING AROUND - Margaret Whiting & Jimmy Wakely - Capitol
5. WEDDING BELLS - Hank Williams - MGM
6. CANDY KISSES - George Morgan - Columbia
7. WHY DON'T YOU HAUL OFF? - Wayne Raney - King
8. BOUQUET OF ROSES - Eddy Arnold - RCA Victor
9. I LOVE YOU SO MUCH IT HURTS - Jimmy Wakely - Capitol
10. TENNESSEE SATURDAY NIGHT - Red Foley - Decca
11. THE ECHO OF YOUR FOOTSTEPS - Eddy Arnold - RCA Victor
12. ONE HAS MY NAME - Jimmy Wakely - Capitol
13. ONE KISS TOO MANY - Eddy Arnold - RCA Victor
14. SLIPPING AROUND - Ernest Tubb - Decca
15. TENNESSEE BORDER - Red Foley - Decca
16. A HEART FULL OF LOVE - Eddy Arnold - RCA Victor
17. BLUES STAY AWAY FROM ME - Delmore Brothers - King
18. I'M BITIN' MY FINGERNAILS - Ernest Tubb & Andrews Sisters - Decca
19. PLEASE DON'T LET ME LOVE YOU - George Morgan - Columbia
20. LET'S SAY GOODBYE LIKE WE SAID HELLO - Ernest Tubb - Decca

TOP 20 COUNTRY SINGLES OF 1950

POS. TITLE - ARTIST - LABEL
1. I'M MOVIN' ON - Hank Snow - RCA Victor
2. CHATTANOOGA SHOE-SHINE BOY - Red Foley - Decca
3. I'LL SAIL MY SHIP ALONE - Moon Mullican - King
4. WHY DON'T YOU LOVE ME? - Hank Williams - MGM
5. LONG GONE LONESOME BLUES - Hank Williams - MGM
6. GOODNIGHT, IRENE - Red Foley & Ernest Tubb - Decca
7. CUDDLE BUGGIN' BABY - Eddy Arnold - RCA Victor

Merle Travis

Merle had three Top 20 hits in 1946, and two in 1947.

Ernest Tubb

The ``Texas Troubadour'' was Honky Tonk music at its finest. His signature, self-penned song was ``Walkin' The Floor Over You.''

Eddy Arnold

The #1 country singles artist of all time, Eddy had seven Top 20 hits in 1948 alone—including positions #1 through #4.

Hank Williams

Considered the greatest country singer of all time, Hank Sr. had #1 hits in 1949, 1951 (``Cold, Cold Heart''), and 1953.

---

8. (REMEMBER ME) I'M THE ONE - Stuart Hamblen - Columbia
9. BIRMINGHAM BOUNCE - Red Foley - Decca
10. LOVEBUG ITCH - Eddy Arnold - RCA Victor
11. MISSISSIPPI - Red Foley - Decca
12. THROW YOUR LOVE MY WAY - Ernest Tubb - Decca
13. I LOVE YOU BECAUSE - Ernest Tubb - Decca
14. CINCINNATI DANCING PIG - Red Foley - Decca
15. I'LL NEVER BE FREE - Tennessee Ernie & Kay Starr - Capitol
16. LET'S GO TO CHURCH - Margaret Whiting & Jimmy Wakely - Capitol
17. ENCLOSED ONE BROKEN HEART - Eddy Arnold - RCA Victor
18. ANGEL WITH THE DIRTY FACE - Eddy Arnold - RCA Victor
19. WHY SHOULD I CRY OVER YOU? - Eddy Arnold - RCA Victor
20. SLIPPING AROUND - Margaret Whiting & Jimmy Wakely - Capitol

TOP 20 COUNTRY SINGLES OF 1951

POS. TITLE - ARTIST - LABEL
1. COLD, COLD HEART - Hank Williams - MGM
2. I WANT TO BE WITH YOU ALWAYS - Lefty Frizzell - Columbia
3. ALWAYS LATE - Lefty Frizzell - Columbia
4. RHUMBA BOOGIE - Hank Snow - RCA Victor
5. I WANNA PLAY HOUSE WITH YOU - Eddy Arnold - RCA Victor
6. THERE'S BEEN A CHANGE IN ME - Eddy Arnold - RCA Victor
7. SHOTGUN BOOGIE - Tennessee Ernie - Capitol
8. HEY, GOOD LOOKIN' - Hank Williams - MGM
9. MOM AND DAD'S WALTZ - Lefty Frizzell - Columbia
10. GOLDEN ROCKET - Hank Snow - RCA Victor
11. I'M MOVIN' ON - Hank Snow - RCA Victor
12. KENTUCKY WALTZ - Eddy Arnold - RCA Victor
13. SLOW POKE - Pee Wee King - RCA Victor
14. LET'S LIVE A LITTLE - Carl Smith - Columbia
15. I LOVE YOU A THOUSAND WAYS - Lefty Frizzell - Columbia
16. POISON LOVE - Johnnie and Jack - RCA Victor
17. DOWN THE TRAIL OF ACHING HEARTS - Hank Snow - RCA Victor
18. BLUEBIRD ISLAND - Hank Snow - RCA Victor
19. PEACE IN THE VALLEY - Red Foley - Decca
20. MISTER MOON - Carl Smith - Columbia

TOP 20 COUNTRY & WESTERN SINGLES OF 1952

POS. TITLE - ARTIST - LABEL
1. WILD SIDE OF LIFE - Hank Thompson - Capitol
2. LET OLD MOTHER NATURE HAVE HER WAY - Carl Smith - Columbia
3. JAMBALAYA - Hank Williams - MGM
4. IT WASN'T GOD WHO MADE HONKY TONK ANGELS - Kitty Wells - Decca
5. SLOW POKE - Pee Wee King - Victor
6. INDIAN LOVE CALL - Slim Whitman - Imperial
7. WONDERIN' - Webb Pierce - Decca
8. DON'T JUST STAND THERE - Carl Smith - Columbia
9. ALMOST - George Morgan - Columbia
10. GIVE ME MORE, MORE, MORE OF YOUR KISSES - Lefty Frizzell - Columbia
11. HALF AS MUCH - Hank Williams - MGM
12. EASY ON THE EYES - Eddy Arnold - Victor

13. GOLD RUSH IS OVER - Hank Snow - Victor
14. ARE YOU TEASING ME - Carl Smith - Columbia
15. FULL TIME JOB - Eddy Arnold - Victor
16. MISSING IN ACTION - Ernest Tubb - Decca
17. WAITING IN THE LOBBY OF YOUR HEART - Hank Thompson - Capitol
18. TOO OLD TO CUT THE MUSTARD - Red Foley & Ernest Tubb - Decca
19. DON'T STAY AWAY - Lefty Frizzell - Columbia
20. THAT HEART BELONGS TO ME - Webb Pierce - Decca

TOP 20 COUNTRY & WESTERN SINGLES OF 1953

POS. TITLE - ARTIST - LABEL
1. KAW-LIGA - Hank Williams - MGM
2. YOUR CHEATING HEART - Hank Williams - MGM
3. NO HELP WANTED - Carlisles - Mercury
4. DEAR JOHN LETTER - Jean Sheperd & Ferlin Huskey - Capitol
5. HEY, JOE - Carl Smith - Columbia
6. MEXICAN JOE - Jim Reeves - Abbott
7. I FORGOT MORE THAN YOU'LL EVER KNOW - Davis Sisters - RCA Victor
8. IT'S BEEN SO LONG - Webb Pierce - Decca
9. TAKE THESE CHAINS FROM MY HEART - Hank Williams - MGM
10. FOOL SUCH AS I - Hank Snow - Victor
11. EDDY'S SONG - Eddy Arnold - Victor
12. LAST WALTZ - Webb Pierce - Decca
13. RUB-A-DUB-DUB - Hank Thompson - Capitol
14. I'LL NEVER GET OUT OF THIS WORLD ALIVE - Hank Williams - MGM
15. BUMMING AROUND - T. Texas Tyler - Decca
16. THAT ROUND DOG IN THE WINDOW - Homer & Jethro - Victor
17. CRYING IN THE CHAPEL - Rex Allen - Decca
18. JAMBALAYA - Hank Williams - MGM *
19. DEATH OF HANK WILLIAMS - Jack Cardwell - King
20. CARRIBEAN - Mitchell Torok - Abbott

*Carried over from 1952.

TOP 20 COUNTRY & WESTERN SINGLES OF 1954

POS. TITLE - ARTIST - LABEL
1. I DON'T HURT ANYMORE - Hank Snow - Victor
2. ONE BY ONE - Kitty Wells & Red Foley - Decca
3. SLOWLY - Webb Pierce - Decca
4. EVEN THO - Webb Pierce - Decca
5. I REALLY DON'T WANT TO KNOW - Eddy Arnold - Victor
6. MORE AND MORE - Webb Pierce - Decca
7. YOU BETTER NOT DO THAT - Tommy Collins - Capitol
8. THERE STANDS THE GLASS - Webb Pierce - Decca
9. ROSE MARIE - Slim Whitman - Imperial
10. I'LL BE THERE - Ray Price - Columbia
11. BIMBO - Jim Reeves - Abbott
12. THIS IS THE THANKS I GET - Eddy Arnold - Victor
13. THIS OLE HOUSE - Stuart Hamblen - Victor
14. SPARKLING BROWN EYES - Webb Pierce - Decca
15. LOOKING BACK TO SEE - Goldie Hill & Justin Tubb - Decca
16. SECRET LOVE - Slim Whitman - Imperial
17. BACK UP BUDDY - Carl Smith - Columbia
18. WAKE UP IRENE - Hank Thompson - Capitol
19. RELEASE ME - Ray Price - Columbia
20. GOODNIGHT, SWEETHEART, GOODNIGHT - Johnnie & Jack - Victor

TOP 20 COUNTRY & WESTERN SINGLES OF 1955

POS. TITLE - ARTIST - LABEL
1. IN THE JAILHOUSE NOW - Webb Pierce - Decca
2. MAKING BELIEVE - Kitty Wells - Decca
3. I DON'T CARE - Webb Pierce - Decca
4. LOOSE TALK - Carl Smith - Columbia
5. SATISFIED MIND - P. Wagoner - Victor
6. CATTLE CALL - Eddy Arnold & Hugo Winterhalter - Victor
7. LIVE FAST, LOVE HARD AND DIE YOUNG - Faron Young - Capitol
8. IF YOU AIN'T LOVIN' - Faron Young - Capitol
9. YELLOW ROSES - Hank Snow - Victor
10. I'VE BEEN THINKING - Eddy Arnold - Victor
11. MORE AND MORE - Webb Pierce - Decca
12. LOVE, LOVE, LOVE - Webb Pierce - Decca
13. SATISFIED MIND - Red & Betty Foley - Decca
14. BALLAD OF DAVY CROCKETT - Tennessee Ernie - Capitol
15. JUST CALL ME LONESOME - Eddy Arnold - Victor
16. THERE SHE GOES - Carl Smith - Columbia
17. ARE YOU MINE? - Ginny Wright & Tom Tall - Fabor
18. SATISFIED MIND - J. Shepard - Capitol
19. LET ME GO, LOVER - Hank Snow - Victor
20. ALL RIGHT - Faron Young - Capitol

TOP 20 COUNTRY & WESTERN SINGLES OF 1956

POS. TITLE - ARTIST - LABEL
1. CRAZY ARMS - Ray Price - Columbia
2. HEARTBREAK HOTEL - Elvis Presley - Victor
3. I WALK THE LINE - Johnny Cash - Sun
4. BLUE SUEDE SHOES - Carl Perkins - Sun
5. SEARCHING - Kitty Wells - Decca
6. I WANT YOU, I NEED YOU, I LOVE YOU - Elvis Presley - Victor
7. DON'T BE CRUEL - Elvis Presley - Victor
8. WHY BABY WHY - Red Sovine & Webb Pierce - Decca
9. I FORGOT TO REMEMBER TO FORGET - Elvis Presley - Victor
10. SINGING THE BLUES - Marty Robbins - Columbia
11. HOUND DOG - Elvis Presley - Victor
12. YOU AND ME - Red Foley & Kitty Wells - Decca
13. SWEET DREAMS - Faron Young - Capitol
14. SO DOGGONE LONESOME - Johnny Cash - Sun
15. SIXTEEN TONS - Tennessee Ernie - Capitol
16. LOVE LOVE LOVE - Webb Pierce - Decca
17. I DON'T BELIEVE YOU'VE MET MY BABY - Louvin Brothers - Capitol
18. I TAKE THE CHANCE - J.E. & Maxine Brown - Victor
19. BLACKBOARD OF MY HEART - Hank Thompson - Capitol
20. BE-BOP-A-LULA - Gene Vincent - Capitol

TOP 20 COUNTRY & WESTERN SINGLES OF 1957

POS. TITLE - ARTIST - LABEL
1. GONE - Ferlin Husky - Capitol
2. FRAULEIN - Bobby Helms - Decca
3. BYE BYE LOVE - Everly Brothers - Cadence
4. A WHITE SPORT COAT - Marty Robbins - Columbia
5. YOUNG LOVE - Sonny James - Capitol
6. FOUR WALLS - Jim Reeves - RCA Victor
7. THERE YOU GO/TRAIN OF LOVE - Johnny Cash - Sun
8. WAKE UP LITTLE SUSIE - Everly Brothers - Cadence
9. GONNA FIND ME A BLUEBIRD - Marvin Rainwater - MGM
10. JAILHOUSE ROCK - Elvis Presley - RCA Victor
11. SINGING THE BLUES - Marty Robbins - Columbia
12. WHOLE LOTTA SHAKIN' GOIN' ON - Jerry Lee Lewis - Sun
13. TEDDY BEAR/LOVING YOU - Elvis Presley - RCA Victor
14. HONKY TONK SONG - Webb Pierce - Decca
15. MY SPECIAL ANGEL - Bobby Helms - Decca
16. ALL SHOOK UP - Elvis Presley - RCA Victor
17. MY SHOES KEEP WALKING BACK TO YOU - Ray Price - Columbia
18. WALKIN' AFTER MIDNIGHT - Patsy Cline - Decca
19. GEISHA GIRL - Hank Locklin - RCA Victor
20. I'M TIRED - Webb Pierce - Decca

TOP 20 COUNTRY & WESTERN SINGLES OF 1958

POS. TITLE - ARTIST - LABEL
1. OH, LONESOME ME/I CAN'T STOP LOVING YOU - Don Gibson - RCA Victor
2. JUST MARRIED/STAIRWAY OF LOVE - Marty Robbins - Columbia
3. GUESS THINGS HAPPEN THAT WAY/COME IN, STRANGER - Johnny Cash - Sun
4. CITY LIGHTS/INVITATION TO THE BLUES - Ray Price - Columbia
5. DON'T/I BEG OF YOU - Elvis Presley - RCA Victor
6. THE WAYS OF A WOMAN IN LOVE/YOU'RE THE NEAREST THING TO HEAVEN - Johnny Cash - Sun
7. BALLAD OF A TEENAGE QUEEN - Johnny Cash - Sun
8. SEND ME THE PILLOW YOU DREAM ON - Hank Locklin - RCA Victor
9. BLUE, BLUE DAY - Don Gibson - RCA Victor
10. ALONE WITH YOU - Faron Young - Capitol
    BLUE BOY - Jim Reeves - RCA Victor
12. BIRD DOG/DEVOTED TO YOU - Everly Brothers - Cadence
13. ALL I HAVE TO DO IS DREAM - Everly Brothers - Cadence
14. THE STORY OF MY LIFE - Marty Robbins - Columbia
15. I CAN'T STOP LOVING YOU - Kitty Wells - Decca
16. GEISHA GIRL - Hank Locklin - RCA Victor
17. HARD HEADED WOMAN/DON'T ASK ME WHY - Elvis Presley - RCA Victor
18. IT'S A LITTLE MORE LIKE HEAVEN - Hank Locklin - RCA Victor
19. GREAT BALLS OF FIRE - Jerry Lee Lewis - Sun
20. SECRETLY - Jimmie Rodgers - Roulette

TOP 20 COUNTRY & WESTERN SINGLES OF 1959

POS. TITLE - ARTIST - LABEL
1. BATTLE OF NEW ORLEANS - Johnny Horton - Columbia
2. THE THREE BELLS - The Browns - RCA Victor
3. HEARTACHES BY THE NUMBER - Ray Price - Columbia
4. WATERLOO - Stonewall Jackson - Columbia
5. DON'T TAKE YOUR GUNS TO TOWN - Johnny Cash - Columbia
6. WHITE LIGHTNING - George Jones - Mercury
7. COUNTRY GIRL - Faron Young - Capitol
8. I AIN'T NEVER - Webb Pierce - Decca
9. WHEN IT'S SPRINGTIME IN ALASKA - Johnny Horton - Columbia
10. BILLY BAYOU - Jim Reeves - RCA Victor
11. HOME - Jim Reeves - RCA Victor
12. BIG MIDNIGHT SPECIAL - Wilma Lee & Stoney Cooper - Hickory
13. I'M IN LOVE AGAIN - George Morgan - Columbia
14. COUNTRY MUSIC IS HERE TO STAY - Simon Crum - Capitol
15. COME WALK WITH ME - Wilma Lee & Stoney Cooper - Hickory

16. WHO CARES - Don Gibson - RCA Victor
17. LIFE TO GO - Stonewall Jackson - Columbia
18. I GOT STRIPES - Johnny Cash - Columbia
19. TENNESSEE STUD - Eddy Arnold - RCA Victor
20. BLACK LAND FARMER - Frankie Miller - Starday

TOP 20 COUNTRY & WESTERN SINGLES OF 1960

POS. TITLE - ARTIST - LABEL
1. HE'LL HAVE TO GO - Jim Reeves - RCA Victor
2. PLEASE HELP ME, I'M FALLING - Hank Locklin - RCA Victor
3. ALABAM' - Cowboy Copas - Starday
4. EL PASO - Marty Robbins - Columbia
5. ONE MORE TIME - Ray Price - Columbia
6. JUST ONE TIME - Don Gibson - RCA Victor
7. ABOVE AND BEYOND - Buck Owens - Capitol
8. THE SAME OLD ME - Ray Price - Columbia
9. ANOTHER - Roy Drusky - Decca
10. ON THE WINGS OF A DOVE - Ferlin Husky - Capitol
11. I CAN'T HELP YOU (I'M FALLING TOO) - Skeeter Davis - RCA Victor
12. ANYMORE - Roy Drusky - Decca
13. I'M GETTING BETTER - Jim Reeves - RCA Victor
14. NO LOVE HAVE I - Webb Pierce - Decca
15. EXCUSE ME (I THINK I'VE GOT A HEARTACHE - Buck Owens - Capitol
16. WISHFUL THINKING - Wynn Stewart - Challenge
17. YOU'RE THE ONLY GOOD THING - George Morgan - Columbia
18. RIVERBOAT - Faron Young - Capitol
19. AMIGO'S GUITAR - Kitty Wells - Decca
20. HEART TO HEART TALK - Bob Wills & Tommy Duncan - Liberty

TOP 20 COUNTRY & WESTERN SINGLES OF 1961

POS. TITLE - ARTIST - LABEL
1. I FALL TO PIECES - Patsy Cline - Decca
2. FOOLIN' AROUND - Buck Owens - Capitol
3. WINDOW UP ABOVE - George Jones - Mercury
4. TENDER YEARS - George Jones - Mercury
5. THREE HEARTS IN A TANGLE - Roy Drusky - Decca
6. HELLO WALLS - Faron Young - Capitol
7. DON'T WORRY - Marty Robbins - Columbia
8. HEARTBREAK U.S.A. - Kitty Wells - Decca
9. SEA OF HEARTBREAK - Don Gibson - RCA Victor
10. ON THE WINGS OF A DOVE - Ferlin Husky - Capitol
11. SWEET LIPS - Webb Pierce - Decca
12. I'LL JUST HAVE ANOTHER CUP OF COFFEE - Claude Gray - Mercury
13. I MISSED ME - Jim Reeves - RCA Victor
14. HILLBILLY HEAVEN - Tex Ritter - Capitol
15. HEART OVER MIND - Ray Price - Columbia
16. UNDER THE INFLUENCE OF LOVE - Buck Owens - Capitol
17. NORTH TO ALASKA - Johnny Horton - Columbia
18. WALK ON BY - Leroy Van Dyke - Mercury
19. MY EARS SHOULD BURN - Claude Gray - Mercury
20. BEGGAR TO A KING - Hank Snow - RCA Victor

TOP 20 COUNTRY & WESTERN SINGLES OF 1962

POS. TITLE - ARTIST - LABEL
1. WOLVERTON MOUNTAIN - Claude King - Columbia
2. MISERY LOVES COMPANY - Porter Wagoner - RCA Victor
3. SHE THINKS I STILL CARE - George Jones - United Artists

The Sunny Side of Life
by Skeeter Davis

[Everybody loves Skeeter Davis, especially me. As a very special treat, I asked her to write something about her long career in music especially for readers of this book. It certainly is clear from her enthusiasm how music has affected her life, which she's managed to stay on the sunny side of since early childhood. —**Bruce Elrod**]

I love music—country music, pop music, and rock-and-roll! I even like jazz and some classical, so I guess you can call me a MUSIC LOVER! I love music!

Now, I sing and make music and travel all over the world, and feel so blessed to have such a wonderful, successful career doing something I love so much. I've had Top Ten songs in the country and pop market, having "The End Of The World" become #1 in both fields and even charting in rhythm-and-blues in 1963, so I've really been so blessed!!

I say "blessed" because I started singing and recording in 1953 and, as a Christian, I always give God the "glory and honor for all good things," so I've never felt that luck had anything to do with it. I appreciate all the fans and all the wonderful disc jockeys and music industry for their help in my success, and I thank God that I came from a small town in Kentucky, where my mother and daddy and my three brothers and three sisters all gathered around the radio listening to the Carter Family singing every day.

That was an important time in my life, and I believe where my love for the music began. I started when I was about ten years old—singing "Keep On The Sunny Side Of Life," along with Mother Maybelle, A.P. and Sarah. It is not a bad philosophy in that song, and it struck a chord in this little girl's heart. I still remember and I still "Keep On....," etc. I love having a book around that gives all the information about songs that I love and everyone else loves! We can't let the music die!

I can't think of anything better for our hearts than music! music! music! So I hope that this book will have you singing as you are reminded of all the great songs and records and artists. If you need a little harmony on "Keep On The Sunny Side Of Life," call me!!

Love, Skeeter Davis

Jim Reeves

Jim had 80 charted records before his death in July 1964,
including two #1 country chart-toppers in 1960 and 1964.

Patsy Cline

Born Virginia Hensley, Patsy's ``I Fall To Pieces'' was a #1 country
hit in 1961. She died in a plane crash on March 5, 1963.

Bill Anderson

Born in Columbia, South Carolina, ``Whispering Bill'' had over
75 charted records, and two #1 country hits (1963, 1969).

Roger Miller

A pioneer country crossover artist, Roger's
``King Of The Road'' won six Grammys in 1965.

4. CHARLIE'S SHOES - Billy Walker - Columbia
5. ADIOS AMIGO - Jim Reeves - RCA Victor
6. A WOUND TIME CAN'T ERASE - Stonewall Jackson - Columbia
7. SHE'S GOT YOU - Patsy Cline - Decca
8. WALK ON BY - Leroy Van Dyke - Mercury
9. TROUBLE'S BACK IN TOWN - Wilburn Brothers - Decca
10. LOSING YOUR LOVE - Jim Reeves - RCA Victor
11. A LITTLE HEARTACHE - Eddy Arnold - RCA Victor
12. LONESOME NUMBER ONE - Don Gibson - RCA Victor
13. THE COMEBACK - Faron Young - Capitol
14. THAT'S MY PA - Sheb Wooley - MGM
15. A LITTLE BITTY TEAR - Burl Ives - Decca
16. DEVIL WOMAN - Marty Robbins - Columbia
17. MAMA SANG A SONG - Bill Anderson - Decca
18. ALLA MY LOVE - Webb Pierce - Decca
19. EVERYBODY BUT ME - Ernest Ashworth - Hickory
20. I CAN MEND YOUR BROKEN HEART - Don Gibson - RCA Victor

TOP 20 COUNTRY & WESTERN SINGLES OF 1963

POS. TITLE - ARTIST - LABEL
1. LOVE'S GONNA LIVE HERE - Buck Owens - Capitol
2. STILL - Bill Anderson - Decca
3. ACT NATURALLY - Buck Owens - Capitol
4. RING OF FIRE - Johnny Cash - Columbia
5. WE MUST HAVE BEEN OUT OF OUR MINDS - George Jones & Melba Montgomery - United Artists
6. LONESOME 7-7203 - Hawkshaw Hawkins - King
7. TALK BACK TREMBLING LIPS - Ernest Ashworth - Hickory
8. ABILENE - George Hamilton IV - RCA Victor
9. DON'T LET ME CROSS OVER - Carl Butler - Columbia
10. SIX DAYS ON THE ROAD - Dave Dudley - Golden Wing
11. YOU COMB HER HAIR - George Jones - United Artists
12. THE END OF THE WORLD - Skeeter Davis - RCA Victor
13. IS THIS ME? - Jim Reeves - RCA Victor
14. SECOND-HAND ROSE - Roy Drusky - Decca
15. BALLAD OF JED CLAMPETT - Lester Flatt & Roy Scruggs - Columbia
16. GUILTY - Jim Reeves - RCA Victor
17. MAKE THE WORLD GO AWAY - Ray Price - Columbia
18. FROM A JACK TO A KING - Ned Millar - Fabor
19. THE YELLOW BANDANA - Faron Young - Mercury
19. DETROIT CITY - Bobby Bare - RCA Victor (Tie)
20. NOT WHAT I HAD IN MIND - George Jones - United Artists

TOP 20 COUNTRY & WESTERN SINGLES OF 1964

POS. TITLE - ARTIST - LABEL
1. I GUESS I'M CRAZY - Jim Reeves - RCA *
2. MY HEART SKIPS A BEAT - Buck Owens - Capitol *
3. I DON'T CARE - Buck Owens - Capitol *
4. ONCE A DAY - Connie Smith - RCA * *#
5. UNDERSTAND YOUR MAN - Johnny Cash - Columbia *
6. DANG ME - Roger Miller - Smash *
7. SAGINAW, MICHIGAN - Lefty Frizzell - Columbia *
8. TOGETHER AGAIN - Buck Owens - Capitol *
9. B.J. THE D.J. - Stonewall Jackson - Columbia
10. YOU'RE THE ONLY WORLD I KNOW - Sonny James - Capitol *
11. BURNING MEMORIES - Ray Price - Columbia
12. WELCOME TO MY WORLD - Jim Reeves - RCA *
13. MEMORY #1 - WEBB PIERCE - Decca
14. CROSS THE BRAZOS AT WACO - Billy Walker - Columbia *
15. THE RACE IS ON - George Jones - United Artists *

16. WINE, WOMEN & SONG - Loretta Lynn - Decca
17. COWBOY IN THE CONTINENTAL SUIT - Marty Robbins - Columbia *
18. BALLAD OF IRA HAYES - Johnny Cash - Columbia *
19. FOUR STRONG WINGS - Bobby Bare - RCA *
20. CHUG A LUG - Roger Miller - Smash *

(Expanded listing. See *Editor's Note* below.)

21. I DON'T LOVE YOU ANYMORE - Charlie Louvin - Capitol
22. DON'T BE ANGRY - Stonewall Jackson - Columbia
23. PASSWORD - Kitty Wells - Decca
24. I LOVE TO DANCE WITH ANNIE - Ernest Ashworth - Hickory
25. IT AIN'T ME BABE - Johnny Cash - Columbia *
26. MILLERS CAVE - Bobby Bare - RCA *
27. SECOND FIDDLE - Jean Sheppard - Capitol
28. SORROW ON THE ROCKS - Porter Wagoner - RCA
29. KEEPING UP WITH THE JONSES - Margie Singleton/Faron Young - Mercury
30. MOLLY - Eddy Arnold - RCA
31. LONG GONE LONESOME BLUES - Hank Williams Jr. - MGM*#
32. YOUR HEART TURNED LEFT - George Jones - United Artists
33. FIVE LITTLE FINGERS - Bill Anderson - Decca *
34. THE LUMBERJACK - Hal Willia - Sims *
35. BALTIMORE - Sonny James - Capitol *
36. MAD - Dave Dudley - Mercury
37. THIS WHITE CIRCLE ON MY FINGER - Kitty Wells - Decca
38. CIRCUMSTANCES - Billy Walker - Columbia
39. LOOKING FOR MORE IN '64 - Jim Nesbitt - Chart
40. LOVE IS NO EXCUSE - Jim Reeves/Dottie West - RCA *
41. PLEASE TALK TO MY HEART - Ray Price - Columbia
42. GO CAT GO/LONESOME #1 - Norma Jean - RCA **

Hank Williams, Jr.

``Bocephus'' first hit the charts—#5—in 1964 with a Hank Sr. hit, ``Long Gone Lonesome Blues''—#31 for the year (above).

461

43. PEEL ME A NANNER - Roy Drusky - Mercury
44. I THANK MY LUCKY STARS - Eddy Arnold - RCA
45. ME - Bill Anderson - Decca
46. BAD NEWS - Johnny Cash - Columbia
47. GONNA GET ALONG WITHOUT YOU - Skeeter Davis - RCA *+
48. ONE OF THESE DAYS - Marty Robbins - Columbia *
49. HERE COMES MY BABY - Dottie West - RCA *
50. LET'S GO ALL THE WAY - Norma Jean - RCA
    *Also hit the pop chart.
    **Counting the flip side (Moss Rose - Bill Anderson - BMI), this single would tie for the #6 position.
    +Merle Haggard's first Top 10 hit.
    ++Flip side also hit #1: "Together Again" (ranked #8 above).
    #Hank Jr.'s first appearance.
    ##Connie Smith's first appearance. First country single to be translated into French; made #1 in Quebec, Canada.

Editor's Note: Billboard did not calculate rankings for the 1964 year-end country singles charts; additionally, several omissions from the alphabetical listing that was compiled have been noted. Running its charts from October to October, *Billboard* failed to place several all-time biggest hits from the November-December period in either the preceding or the following year. After extensive research, this listing has been corrected and ranked as completely as possible. To provide users of this volume with all of the information resulting from our efforts, the 1964 year-end listings above have been expanded from 20 to 50 songs.

Many of the songs on the 1964 country singles charts also hit the pop charts, something that would not occur again with even one truly country song until "Elvira" (Oak Ridge Boys) in 1981 and "Achy Breaky Heart" (Billy Ray Cyrus) in 1992 (excluded are "Islands In The Stream," "Always On My Mind," and "To All The Girls I've Loved Before," which were pop-oriented).

Buck Owens

Buck has had 88 charted records and 23 #1 Country hits, including 1965's "I've Got A Tiger By The Tail." Co-host of TV's "Hee-Haw" (1969-1986), he is still actively recording.

TOP 20 COUNTRY & WESTERN SINGLES OF 1965

POS. TITLE - ARTIST - LABEL
1. MAKE THE WORLD GO AWAY - Eddy Arnold - RCA *
2. I'VE GOT A TIGER BY THE TAIL - Buck Owens - Capitol *++
3. KING OF THE ROAD - Roger Miller - Smash *
4. BEFORE YOU GO - Buck Owens - Capitol *
5. BEHIND THE TEAR - Sonny James - Capitol *
6. THE BRIDGE WASHED OUT - Warner Mack - Decca
7. THE FIRST THING EVERY MORNING - Jimmy Dean - Columbia *
8. YES MR. PETERS - Roy Drusky/Priscilla Mitchell - Mercury
9. IS IT REALLY OVER? - Jim Reeves - RCA *
10. MAY THE BIRD OF PARADISE FLY UP YOU NOSE - Little Jimmy Dickens - Columbia *
11. BUCKAROO - Buck Owens Buckaroos - Capitol *
12. HELLO VIETNAM - Johnny Wright - Decca
13. WHAT'S HE DOING IN MY WORLD - Eddy Arnold - RCA *
14. THIS IS IT - Jim Reeves - RCA *
15. GIRL ON THE BILLBOARD - Del Reeves - United Artists *
16. RIBBON OF DARKNESS - Marty Robbins - Columbia *
17. SITTIN' IN AN ALL NITE CAFE - Warner Mack - Decca
18. QUEEN OF THE HOUSE - Jody Miller - Capitol *#
19. ORANGE BLOSSOM SPECIAL - Johnny Cash - Columbia *
20. ODE TO THE LITTLE BROWN SHACK OUT BACK - Billy Edd Wheeler - Kapp *

(Expanded listing. See *Editor's Note* below.)
21. HAPPY BIRTHDAY - Loretta Lynn - Decca
22. ENGINE ENGINE #9 - Roger Miller - Smash *
23. BLUE KENTUCKY GIRL - Loretta Lynn - Decca
24. THEN & ONLY THEN - Connie Smith - RCA ** ##
25. YAKETY AXE - Chet Atkins - RCA *
26. I WON'T FORGET YOU - Jim Reeves - RCA *
27. I CAN'T REMEMBER - Connie Smith - RCA
28. ALL OF MY FRIENDS ARE GONNA BE STRANGERS - Merle Haggard - Capitol +
29. A TOMBSTONE EVERY MILE - Dick Curless - Tower
30. TIGER WOMAN - Claude King - Columbia *
31. TRUCK DRIVIN' SON OF A GUN - Dave Dudley - Mercury *
32. WALK TALL - Faron Young - Mercury
33. THE OTHER WOMAN - Ray Price - Columbia
34. 10 LITTLE BOTTLES - Johnny Bond - Starday *
35. WILD AS A WILDCAT - Charlie Walker - Epic
36. I'LL KEEP HOLDING ON - SONNY JAMES - Capitol *
37. MATAMOROS - Billy Walker - Columbia
38. IT'S ALRIGHT - Bobby Bare - RCA *
39. HICKTOWN - Tennessee Ernie Ford - Capitol
40. SEE THE BIG MAN CRY - Charlie Louvin - Capitol
41. THINGS HAVE GONE TO PIECES - George Jones - Musicor
42. THE WISHING WELL - Hank Snow - RCA
43. THREE A.M. - Bill Anderson - Decca
44. DO WHAT YOU DO DO WELL - Ned Miller - Fabor *
45. ALL OF MY FRIENDS ARE GONNA BE STRANGERS - Roy Drusky - Mercury
    *Also hit the pop chart.
    **Double-sided hit.
    + First hit the pop charts in 1956 for Patience & Prudence.
    ++Written from an Exxon (Esso) commercial.
    #Answer to Roger Miller's "King Of The Road."
    ##Flip side: "Tiny Blue Transistor Radio."

Country Music, Then & Now

by Warner Mack

Country music in 1957 when I started was just beginning to accept what we called "rockabilly." I remember the first recording session I did for MCA/Decca. I recorded two Hank Williams-type songs with steel guitar and fiddle. I also recorded a song called "Is It Wrong (For Loving You)" where the lead guitar and piano were more out front, along with a rockabilly song called "Rock-A-Chicka," which had some great rockin'-type pickin' by the great Hank "Sugarfoot" Garland. These last two songs were reviewed in *Billboard* as pop records, although by today's standards both would be reviewed as country all the way.

Country music today has a lot of different sounds—country rock, country pop, easy listening country—but the one I love the most is traditional country, which is what I call down-to-earth. The songs that tell the truth about the different feelings that are part of love, and also the true stories of life and living.

I think Elvis Presley had more to do with changing country music than anyone, because when Elvis came along country took a tremendous nose dive in popularity and almost died entirely. I know that I suffered through those years, and there were some hard times. Just about everyone began to change their style to try and sell to the pop side, because country simply was not selling. Of course we had the older crowd that loved us and our music, but could not buy enough records to keep the traditional side of country alive. Young people were buying, though, so that's the way the record companies started going. I remember Eddy Arnold, Ray Price and others with the big band sound, with the violin sections and the whole works. I even tried it myself, but couldn't make it with that kind of sound. One of the big differences is that the drums are brought out much more than when I started in 1957. Also, the technical side of making sound is so much better now. It's amazing how electronics has improved through the years; FM radio has also helped to project the sound.

Unfortunately, though—from my point of view—country music today simply has not changed from what it became in the late fifties and sixties. I hear

Warner Mack

A country music legend, Warner began his career in 1957. In 1965, he had a #1 country hit with "The Bridge Washed Out." He now records for this author's label, Lost Gold Records. He had a Top 10 Indy release in 1992, "Bring Your Own Blues."

people who say, oh, I can't stand the way country is now, but most of those people are talkers, not buyers of records. Record companies just can't stay in business by relying on big talkers; they have to have people who buy their products—young people do, and young people by-and-large don't go for traditional country.

I do think that traditional country is bigger now than it has been in years, though. There are eight or ten traditional country singers now who are really selling records, and putting out some good country songs, the kind I like to think I was singing when I was hot and on the charts in the sixties and seventies.

Country music will only get bigger and better—I don't think anyone can stop it now—and I'm proud to have been a part of it, then and now.

Warner Mack (aka, Warner McPherson)

Editor's Note: Billboard did not calculate rankings for the 1965 year-end country singles charts; additionally, several omissions from the alphabetical listing that was compiled have been noted. Running its charts from October to October, Billboard failed to place several all-time biggest hits from the November-December period in either the preceding or the following year. A good example of this was the omission of Little Jimmy Dickens' "May The Bird Of Paradise Fly Up Your Nose." Also, in 1965 Billboard listed only forty-one songs (the chart covered only the first eight months of the year).After extensive research, this listing has been corrected and ranked as completely as possible. To provide users of this volume with all of the information resulting from our efforts, the 1965 year-end chart listings above have been expanded from forty-one to forty-five songs.

Many of the songs on the 1965 country singles charts also hit the pop charts, something that would not occur again with even one truly country song until "Elvira" (Oak Ridge Boys) in 1981 and "Achy Breaky Heart" (Billy Ray Cyrus) in 1992 (excluded are "Islands In The Stream," "Always On My Mind," and "To All The Girls I've Loved Before," which were pop-oriented).

TOP 20 COUNTRY & WESTERN SINGLES OF 1966

POS. TITLE - ARTIST - LABEL
1. ALMOST PERSUADED - David Houston - Epic
2. WAITIN' IN YOUR WELFARE LINE - Buck Owens - Capitol
3. I LOVE YOU DROPS - Bill Anderson - Decca
4. YOU AIN'T WOMAN ENOUGH - Loretta Lynn - Decca
5. THINK OF ME - Buck Owens - Capitol
6. TIPPY TOEING - Harden Trio - Columbia
7. TAKE GOOD CARE OF HER - Sonny James - Capitol
8. DON'T TOUCH ME - Jeannie Seely - Monument
9. DISTANT DRUMS - Jim Reeves - RCA Victor
10. WOULD YOU HOLD IT AGAINST ME - Dottie West - RCA Victor
11. A MILLION AND ONE - Billy Walker - Monument
12. SWINGIN' DOORS - Merle Haggard - Capitol
13. I WANT TO GO WITH YOU - Eddy Arnold - RCA Victor
14. BLUE SIDE OF LONESOME - Jim Reeves - RCA Victor
15. ROOM IN YOUR HEART - Sonny James - Capitol
16. THE STREETS OF BALTIMORE - Bobby Bare - RCA Victor
17. THE ONE ON THE R IGHT IS ON THE LEFT - Johnny Cash - Columbia
18. GIDDYUP GO - Red Sovine - Starday
19. EVIL ON YOUR MIND - Jan Howard - Decca
20. SNOWFLAKE - Jim Reeves - RCA Victor

TOP 20 COUNTRY & WESTERN SINGLES OF 1967

POS. TITLE - ARTIST - LABEL
1. ALL THE TIME - Jack Greene - Decca
2. WALK THROUGH THIS WORLD WITH ME - George Jones - Musicor
3. IT'S SUCH A PRETTY WORLD TODAY - Wynn Stewart - Capitol
4. I'LL NEVER FIND ANOTHER YOU - Sonny James - Capitol
5. WHERE DOES THE GOOD TIMES GO - Buck Owens - Capitol
6. I DON'T WANNA PLAY HOUSE - Tammy Wynette - Epic
7. YOUR GOOD GIRL'S GONNA GO BAD - Tammy Wynette - Epic
8. THERE GOES MY EVERYTHING - Jack Greene - Decca
9. IT'S THE LITTLE THINGS - Sonny James - Capitol
10. MY ELUSIVE DREAMS - David Houston & Tammy Wynette - Epic
11. NEED YOU - Sonny James - Capitol

12. SAM'S PLACE - Buck Owens - Capitol
13. WITH ONE EXCEPTION - David Houston - Epic
14. LONELY AGAIN - Eddy Arnold - RCA Victor
15. LAURA (WHAT'S HE GOT THAT I AIN'T GOT?) - Leon Ashley - Ashley
16. TURN THE WORLD AROUND - Eddy Arnold - RCA Victor
17. COLD, HARD FACTS OF LIFE - Porter Wagoner - RCA Victor
18. BRANDED MAN - Merle Haggard - Capitol
19. POP A TOP - Jim Edward Brown - RCA Victor
20. YOUR TENDER LOVING CARE - Buck Owens - Capitol

TOP 20 COUNTRY & WESTERN SINGLES OF 1968

POS. TITLE - ARTIST - LABEL
1. FOLSOM PRISON BLUES - Johnny Cash - Columbia
2. SKIP A ROPE - Henson Cargill - Monument
3. MAMA TRIED (THE BALLAD FROM "KILLERS THREE") - Merle Haggard - Capitol
4. WORLD OF OUR OWN - Sonny James - Capitol
5. I WANNA LIVE - Glen Campbell - Capitol
6. ONLY DADDY THAT'LL WALK THE LINE - Waylon Jennings - RCA Victor
7. HEAVEN SAYS HELLO - Sonny James - Capitol
8. HONEY - Bobby Goldsboro - United Artists
9. HARPER VALLEY PTA - Jeannie C. Riley - Plantation
10. WILD WEEKEND - Bill Anderson - Decca
11. FIST CITY - Loretta Lynn - Decca
12. THE LEGEND OF BONNIE AND CLYDE - Merle Haggard - Capitol *
13. IMAGE OF ME - Conway Twitty - Decca
14. TAKE ME TO YOUR WORLD - Tammy Wynette - Epic
15. ALREADY IT'S HEAVEN - David Houston - Epic
16. NEXT IN LINE - Conway Twitty - Decca
17. WITH PEN IN HAND - Johnny Darrell - United Artists
18. SING ME BACK HOME - Merle Haggard - Capitol
19. THEN YOU CAN TELL ME GOODBYE - Eddy Arnold - RCA Victor
20. YOU'VE JUST STEPPED IN (FROM STEPPING OUT ON ME) - Loretta Lynn - Decca
   *The flip side was "Today I Started Loving You Again," which overtook the popularity of "Bonnie & Clyde" in later years.

Editor's Note: "For Loving You" (Decca) by Bill Anderson & Jan Howard, a #1 hit for four weeks, should be shown as a tie for the #3 position above. "Stand By Your Man" (Epic) by Tammy Wynette, lisyed as #38 on Billboard's yearend Top 50, should actually be a tie for the #5 position above--a huge pop crossover hit and Tammy's biggest-ever record. "Wichita Lineman" (Capitol) by Glen Campbell, should be #6 above. Another huge pop crossover hit, it is not even listed in Billboard's year-end Top 50 country singles.

TOP 20 COUNTRY & WESTERN SINGLES OF 1969

POS. TITLE - ARTIST - LABEL
1. MY LIFE - Bill Anderson - Decca
2. DADDY SANG BASS - Johnny Cash - Columbia
3. I'LL SHARE MY WORLD WITH YOU - George Jones - Musicor
4. HUNGRY EYES - Merle Haggard & the Strangers - Capitol
5. STATUE OF A FOOL - Jack Greene - Decca
6. (MARGIE'S AT) THE LINCOLN PARK INN - Bobby Bare - RCA
7. ONLY THE LONELY - Sonny James - Capitol
8. I LOVE YOU MORE TODAY - Conway Twitty - Decca

Johnny Cash

``The Man In Black'' is a true Country living legend, a superstar with more pop hits—39 in all—than any other country artist.
Out of a total of 140 charted records, 11 went to #1 and another 33 went Top 10.
Johnny's ``Folsom Prison Blues'' was #1 in the Top 20 Country in 1965.

9. DARLING, YOU KNOW I WOULDN'T LIE - Conway Twitty - Decca
10. THE WAYS TO LOVE A MAN - Tammy Wynette - Epic
11. ALL I HAVE TO OFFER YOU (IS ME) - Charley Pride - RCA
12. MY WOMAN'S GOOD TO ME - David Houston - Epic
13. RINGS OF GOLD - Dottie West & Don Gibson - RCA
14. GOODTIME CHARLIE - Del Reeves - United Artists
15. KAW-LIGA - Charley Pride - RCA
16. GAMES PEOPLE PLAY - Freddy Weller - Columbia
17. ONE HAS MY NAME (THE OTHER HAS MY HEART) - Jerry Lee Lewis - Smash
18. SINCE I MET YOU BABY - Sonny James - Capitol
19. WHO'S GONNA MOW MY GRASS - Buck Owens & His Buckaroos - Capitol
20. JOHNNY B. GOODE - Buck Owens & His Buckaroos - Capitol

Editor's Note: "A Boy Named Sue" (Columbia) by Johnny Cash, a huge crossover pop hit (peaked at #2), gold record, and #1 country hit for five weeks, ended up as #24 on Billboard's year-end country Top 50. It should actually tie for the #1 ranking above. "Okie From Muskogee" (Capitol) by Merle Haggard, was left off the year-end Top 50 country singles list; this big crossover pop hit qualifies for a #2 position tie above. "(I'm So) Afraid Of Losing You Again" (RCA) by Charley Pride, also left of the year-end list, should tie for #7 above.

TOP 20 COUNTRY SINGLES OF 1970

POS. TITLE - ARTIST - LABEL
1. HELLO DARLIN' - Conway Twitty - Decca
2. FOR THE GOOD TIMES/GRAZIN' IN GREENER PASTURES - Ray Price - Columbia
3. TENNESSEE BIRDWALK - Jack Blanchard & Misty Morgan - Wayside
4. DON'T KEEP ME HANGIN' ON - Sonny James - Capitol
5. IS ANYBODY GOIN' TO SAN ANTONE? - Charley Pride - RCA
6. WONDER COULD I LIVE THERE ANYMORE - Charley Pride - RCA
7. IT'S JUST A MATTER OF TIME - Sonny James - Capitol
8. MY LOVE - Sonny James - Capitol
9. FIGHTIN' SIDE OF ME - Merle Haggard & the Strangers - Capitol
10. HE LOVES ME ALL THE WAY - Tammy Wynette - Epic
11. MY WOMAN, MY WOMAN, MY WIFE - Marty Robbins - Columbia
12. THERE MUST BE MORE TO LOVE THAN THIS - Jerry Lee Lewis - Mercury
13. ALL FOR THE LOVE OF SUNSHINE - Hank Williams Jr. - MGM
14. SUNDAY MORNING COMING DOWN - Johnny Cash - Columbia
15. WHEN A MAN LOVES A WOMAN - Billy Walker - MGM.
16. POOL SHARK - Dave Dudley - Mercury
17. A WEEK IN A COUNTY JAIL - Tom T. Hall - Mercury
18. I DO MY SWINGING AT HOME - David Houston - Epic
19. SHE'S A LITTLE BIT COUNTRY - George Hamilton IV - RCA
20. HEART OVER MIND - Mel Tillis - Kapp

Editor's Note: "Coal Miner's Daughter" on Decca, undoubtedly Loretta Lynn's biggest hit and title song of the movie, should have been ranked #6 above. "End-lessly" (Capitol) by Sonny James, a number 1 song for three weeks, should have ranked #11.

TOP 20 COUNTRY SINGLES OF 1971

POS. TITLE - ARTIST - LABEL
1. EASY LOVING - Freddie Hart - Capitol
2. I WON'T MENTION IT AGAIN - Ray Price - Columbia
3. HELP ME MAKE IT THROUGH THE NIGHT - Sammi Smith - Mega
4. YEAR THAT CLAYTON DELANEY DIED - Tom T. Hall - Mercury
5. WHEN YOU'RE HOT, YOU'RE HOT - Jerry Reed - RCA
6. EMPTY ARMS - Sonny James - Capitol
7. I'M JUST ME - Charley Pride - RCA
8. HOW CAN I UNLOVE YOU - Lynn Anderson - Columbia
9. GOOD LOVIN' (MAKES IT RIGHT) - Tammy Wynette - Epic (CBS)
10. HOW MUCH MORE CAN SHE STAND - Conway Twitty - Decca
11. ROSE GARDEN - Lynn Anderson - Columbia *
12. YOU'RE MY MAN - Lynn Anderson - Columbia
13. I'D RATHER LOVE YOU - Charley Pride - RCA
14. AFTER THE FIRE IS GONE - Conway Twitty & Loretta Lynn - Decca (MCA)
15. QUITS - Bill Anderson - Decca (MCA)
16. I'D RATHER BE SORRY - Ray Price - Columbia
17. JUST ONE TIME - Connie Smith - RCA
18. RUBY (ARE YOU MAD) - Buck Owens - Capitol
19. WE SURE CAN LOVE EACH OTHER - Tammy Wynette - Epic (CBS)
20. BRIGHT LIGHTS, BIG CITY - Sonny James - Capitol

*Went to #3 on the Hot 100 pop charts.

Editor's Note: "Rose Garden" (Columbia) by Lynn Anderson was one of the biggest records of the year, and should rank #1 on this list in place of "Easy Lovin'."

TOP 20 COUNTRY SINGLES OF 1972

POS. TITLE - ARTIST - LABEL
1. MY HANG UP IS YOU - Freddie Hart - Capitol
2. THE HAPPIEST GIRL IN THE WHOLE U.S.A. - Donna Fargo - Dot (Famous)
3. IT'S FOUR IN THE MORNING - Faron Young - Mercury
4. IT'S GONNA TAKE A LITTLE BIT LONGER - Charley Pride - RCA
5. IF YOU LEAVE ME TONIGHT I'LL CRY - Jerry Wallace - Decca (MCA) *
6. CAROLYN - Merle Haggard & the Strangers - Capitol
7. KISS AN ANGEL GOOD MORNING - Charley Pride - RCA
8. CHANTILLY LACE/THINK ABOUT IT DARLIN' - Jerry Lee Lewis - Mercury
9. ONE'S ON THE WAY - Loretta Lynn - Decca (MCA)
10. WOMAN (SENSUOUS WOMAN - Don Gibson - Hickory
11. I AIN'T NEVER - Mel Tillis - MGM
12. ELEVEN ROSES - Hank Williams Jr. - MGM
13. BLESS YOUR HEART - Freddie Hart - Capitol
14. I CAN'T STOP LOVING YOU - Conway Twitty - Decca (MCA)
15. FUNNY FACE - Donna Fargo - Dot (Famous)
16. WHEN THE SNOW IS ON THE ROSES - Sonny James - Columbia
17. (LOST HER LOVE) ON OUR LAST DATE - Conway Twitty - Decca (MCA)
18. MADE IN JAPAN - Buck Owens & His Buckeroos- Capitol **
19. I'M GONNA KNOCK AT YOUR DOOR - Billy "Crash" Craddock - Capitol
20. GOOD HEARTED WOMAN - Waylon Jennings - RCA

Conway Twitty

One of Country's greatest, Conway had over 65 Top 10 hits before his recent death. ``Hello Darlin''' was #1 Top 20 in 1970.

Ray Price

Another Country superstar, Ray has charted over 120 records in his career. His songs were #2 Top 20 Country hits in 1970 and '71.

Tammy Wynette

One of Country's greatest female singers, Tammy's 1973 duet with George Jones—``We're Gonna Hold On''—went to #1.

Merle Haggard

With 100 charted songs, Merle ranks as one of the top five Country entertainers of all time. He was #2 in the 1974 Top 20 list.

*From Rod Serling's "Night Gallery" TV series ("The Tune In Dan's Cafe").

**A preview of things to come.

TOP 20 COUNTRY SINGLES OF 1973

POS. TITLE - ARTIST - LABEL
1. YOU'VE NEVER BEEN THIS FAR BEFORE - Conway Twitty - MCA
2. BEHIND CLOSED DOORS - Charlie Rich - Epic (Columbia)
3. SATIN SHEETS - Jeanne Pruett - MCA
4. TEDDY BEAR SONG - Barbara Fairchild - Columbia
5. AMANDA - Don Williams - JMI
6. YOU'RE THE BEST THING THAT'S EVER HAPPENED TO ME - Ray Price - Columbia
7. WHY ME - Kris Kristofferson - Monument (Columbia)
8. EVERYBODY'S HAD THE BLUES - Merle Haggard - Capitol
9. SHE NEEDS SOMEONE TO HOLD HER - Conway Twitty - MCA
10. THE LORD KNOWS I'M DRINKING - Cal Smith - MCA
11. WHAT'S YOUR MAMA'S NAME - Tanya Tucker - Columbia
12. SHE'S GOT TO BE A SAINT - Ray Price - Columbia
13. LOVE IS THE FOUNDATION - Loretta Lynn - MCA
14. KIDS SAY THE DARNDEST THINGS - Tammy Wynette - Epic (Columbia)
15. RATED X - Loretta Lynn - MCA
16. TRIP TO HEAVEN - Freddie Hart - Capitol
17. DON'T FIGHT THE FEELINGS OF LOVE - Charley Pride - RCA
18. OLD DOGS, CHILDREN & WATERMELON WINE - Tom T. Hall - Mercury (Phonogram)
19. COME LIVE WITH ME - Roy Clark - Dot (Famous)
20. YOU ALWAYS COME BACK (TO HURTING ME) - Johnny Rodriguez - Mercury (Phonogram)

Editor's Note: "The Most Beautiful Girl!" (Epic) by Charlie Rich, one of the biggest country hits of all time, should have been ranked among the top three above. (Although listed as #45 in the Top 50 Country Singles list for 1974, that rank should be in a yearly crossover as it had already peaked at #1 in 1973.) "Paper Roses" (MGM) by Marie Osmond should rank at #8 above; it peaked at #1 for two weeks on *Billboard*'s country charts, at #5 on the Hot 100, and was certified gold. "We're Gonna Hold On" (Epic) by George Jones and Tammy Wynette (their first #1 duo hit) was #1 for two weeks and should rank #10 above.

TOP 20 COUNTRY SINGLES OF 1974

POS. TITLE - ARTIST - LABEL
1. THERE WON'T BE ANYMORE - Charlie Rich - RCA
2. IF WE MAKE IT THROUGH DECEMBER - Merle Haggard - Capitol
3. I LOVE - Tom T. Hall - Mercury (Phonogram)
4. THE GRAND TOUR - George Jones - Epic (Columbia)
5. RUB IT IN - Billy "Crash" Craddock - ABC
6. JOLENE - Dolly Parton - RCA
7. MARIE LAVEAU - Bobby Bare - RCA *
8. A VERY SPECIAL LOVE SONG - Charlie Rich - Epic (Columbia)
9. IF YOU LOVE ME (LET ME KNOW) - Olivia Newton-John - MCA
10. ANOTHER LONELY SONG - Tammy Wynette - Epic (Columbia)
11. MIDNIGHT, ME & THE BLUES - Mel Tillis - MGM
12. WORLD OF MAKE BELIEVE - Bill Anderson - MCA
13. WOULD YOU LAY WITH ME (IN A FIELD OF STONE) - Tanya Tucker - Columbia

14. I WOULDN'T WANT TO LIVE IF YOU DIDN'T LOVE ME - Don Williams - ABC/Dot
15. THERE'S A HONKY TONK "ANGEL" - Conway Twitty - MCA
16. NO CHARGE - Melba Montgomery - Elektra
17. I'M STILL LOVING YOU - Joe Stampley - ABC/Dot
18. IS IT WRONG (FOR LOVING YOU) - Sonny James - Columbia
19. YOU CAN'T BE A BEACON (IF YOUR LIGHT DON'T SHINE) - Donna Fargo - ABC/Dot
20. (JEANNIE MARIE) YOU WERE A LADY - Tommy Overstreet - ABC/Dot

*Flipside: "The Mermaid."

TOP 20 COUNTRY SINGLES OF 1975

POS. TITLE - ARTIST - LABEL
1. RHINESTONE COWBOY - Glen Campbell - Capitol *
2. RECONSIDER ME - Narvel Felts - ABC/Dot
3. BLUE EYES CRYING IN THE RAIN - Willie Nelson - Columbia
4. LOVE IN THE HOT AFTERNOON - Gene Watson - Capitol
5. WASTED DAYS & WASTED NIGHTS - Freddy Fender - ABC/Dot
6. FEELIN'S - Loretta Lynn & Conway Twitty - MCA
7. IT'S TIME TO PAY THE FIDDLER - Cal Smith - MCA
8. YOU'RE MY BEST FRIEND - Don Williams - ABC/Dot
9. WRONG ROAD AGAIN - Crystal Gayle - United Artists
10. LIZZIE & THE RAINMAN - Tanya Tucker - MCA
11. DAYDREAMS ABOUT NIGHT THINGS - Ronnie Milsap - RCA
12. BEFORE THE NEXT TEARDROP FALLS - Freddy Fender - ABC/Dot **
13. WINDOW UP ABOVE - Mickey Gilley - Playboy

Waylon Jennings

Waylon has had over 90 charted hits, and was #1 Top 20 Country in 1977 with "Luckenbach, Texas."

14. TRYIN' TO BEAT THE MORNING HOME - T.G. Sheppard - Melodyland (Motown)
15. DEVIL IN THE BOTTLE - T.G. Sheppard - Melodyland (Motown)
16. I'M NOT LISA - Jessi Colter - Capitol
17. TOUCH THE HAND - Conway Twitty - MCA
18. I CAN'T HELP IT (I'M STILL IN LOVE WITH YOU) - Linda Ronstadt - Capitol
19. (HEY WON'T YOU PLAY) ANOTHER SOMEBODY DONE SOMEBODY WRONG SONG - B.J. Thomas - ABC
20. JUST GET UP AND CLOSE THE DOOR - Johnny Rodriguez - Mercury (Phonogram)
   *#1 Hot 100 pop song.
   **#1 Hot 100 pop song.

Editor's Note: "I Can Help" (Monument) by Billy Swan was a #1 country hit in December 1974, a #1 pop hit and a million seller, and should have ranked as #10 above since its chart history crossed over into 1975.

TOP 20 COUNTRY SINGLES OF 1976

POS. TITLE - ARTIST - LABEL
1. CONVOY - C.W. McCall - MGM *
2. GOOD HEARTED WOMAN - Waylon Jennings & Willie Nelson - RCA
3. THE DOOR IS ALWAYS OPEN - Dave and Sugar - RCA
4. I'LL GET OVER YOU - Crystal Gayle - United Artists
5. TEDDY BEAR - Red Sovine - Starday
6. EL PASO CITY - Marty Robbins - Columbia
7. (I'M A) STAND BY MY WOMAN MAN - Ronnie Milsap - RCA
8. I DON'T WANT TO HAVE TO MARRY YOU - Jim Ed Brown & Helen Cornelius - RCA
9. ONE PIECE AT A TIME - Johnny Cash - Columbia
10. STRANGER - Johnny Duncan - Columbia **
11. BROKEN LADY - Larry Gatlin - Monument
12. ALL THESE THINGS - Joe Stampley - ABC/Dot
13. FASTER HORSES (THE COWBOY AND THE POET) - Tom T. Hall - Mercury
14. TILL THE RIVERS ALL RUN DRY - Don Williams - ABC/Dot
15. DON'T THE GIRLS ALL GET PRETTIER AT CLOSING TIME - Mickey Gilley - Playboy
16. GOLDEN RING - George Jones & Tammy Wynette - Playboy
17. DRINKING MY BABY (OFF MY MIND) - Eddie Rabbitt - Elektra
18. IF YOU'VE GOT THE MONEY I'VE GOT THE TIME - Willie Nelson - Lone Star
19. SAY IT AGAIN - Don Williams - ABC/Dot
20. SOMETIMES - Bill Anderson & Mary Lou Turner - MCA
   *#1 Hot 100 pop song (the CB radio craze sweeps America).
   **With Janie Fricke.

TOP 20 COUNTRY SINGLES OF 1977

POS. TITLE - ARTIST - LABEL
1. LUCKENBACH, TEXAS (BACK TO THE BASICS OF LOVE) - Waylon Jennings - RCA
2. DON'T IT MAKE MY BROWN EYES BLUE - Crystal Gayle - United Artists
3. LUCILLE - Kenny Rogers - United Artists
4. HEAVEN'S JUST A SIN AWAY - Kendalls - Ovation
5. IT WAS ALMOST LIKE A SONG - Ronnie Milsap - RCA
6. ROLLING WITH THE FLOW - Charlie Rich - Epic
7. SHE'S PULLING ME BACK AGAIN - Mickey Gilley - Playboy
8. SOUTHERN NIGHTS - Glen Campbell - Capitol

9. WAY DOWN/PLEDGING MY LOVE - Elvis Presley - RCA
10. SHE'S GOT ME - Loretta Lynn - MCA
11. NEAR YOU - George Jones & Tammy Wynette - Epic
12. SOME BROKEN HEARTS NEVER MEND - Don Williams - ABC/Dot
13. PLAY GUITAR PLAY - Conway Twitty - MCA
14. IT COULDN'T HAVE BEEN BETTER - Johnny Duncan - Columbia *
15. THAT WAS YESTERDAY - Donna Fargo - Warner Bros.
16. I'LL BE LEAVIN' ALONE - Charley Pride - RCA Victor
17. DAYTIME FRIENDS - Kenny Rogers - United Artists
18. PAPER ROSIE - Gene Watson - Capitol
19. THINKIN' OF A RENDEZVOUS -Johnny Duncan - Columbia **
20. I'VE ALREADY LOVED YOU IN MY MIND - Conway Twitty - MCA
   * and **With Janie Fricke.

TOP 20 COUNTRY SINGLES OF 1978

POS. TITLE - ARTIST - LABEL
1. MAMAS DON'T LET YOUR BABIES GROW UP TO BE COWBOYS/ICAN GET OFF ON YOU - Waylon Jennings & Willie Nelson - RCA
2. HERE YOU COME AGAIN - Dolly Parton - RCA
3. ONLY ONE LOVE IN MY LIFE - Ronnie Milsap - RCA
4. I'VE ALWAYS BEEN CRAZY - Waylon Jennings - RCA
5. HEARTBREAKER - Dolly Parton - RCA
6. TAKE THIS JOB AND SHOVE IT - Johnny Paycheck - Epic
7. DON'T BREAK THE HEART THAT LOVES YOU - Margo Smith - Warner Bros.
8. EVERYTIME TWO FOOLS COLLIDE - Kenny Rogers & Dottie West - United Artists
9. DO YOU KNOW YOU ARE MY SUNSHINE - Statler Brothers - Mercury
10. SOMEONE LOVES YOU HONEY - Charley Pride - RCA
11. TALKING IN YOUR SLEEP - Crystal Gayle - United Artists
12. OUT OF MY HEAD AND BACK IN MY BED - Loretta Lynn - MCA
13. IT'S ALL WRONG, BUT IT'S ALRIGHT/TWO DOORS DOWN - Dolly Parton - RCA
14. WHAT A DIFFERENCE YOU MADE IN MY LIFE - Ronnie Milsap - RCA
15. GEORGIA ON MY MIND - Willie Nelson - Columbia
16. SHE CAN PUT HER SHOES UNDER MY BED (ANYTIME) - Johnny Duncan - Columbia
17. IT ONLY HURTS FOR A LITTLE WHILE - Margo Smith - Warner Bros.
18. HEARTS ON FIRE - Eddie Rabbitt - Elektra
19. LOVE OR SOMETHING LIKE IT - Kenny Rogers - United Artists
20. MIDDLE AGE CRAZY - Jerry Lee Lewis - Mercury

TOP 20 COUNTRY SINGLES OF 1979

POS. TITLE - ARTIST - LABEL
1. I JUST FALL IN LOVE AGAIN - Anne Murray - Capitol
2. IF I SAID YOU HAD A BEAUTIFUL BODY WOULD YOU HOLD IT AGAINST ME - Bellamy Brothers - Warner/Curb
3. AMANDA - Waylon Jennings - RCA
4. EVERY WHICH WAY BUT LOOSE - Eddie Rabbitt - Elektra
5. GOLDEN TEARS - Dave & Sugar - RCA
6. SHE BELIEVES IN ME - Kenny Rogers - United Artists
7. THE GAMBLER - Kenny Rogers - United Artists
8. YOU'RE THE ONLY ONE - Dolly Parton - RCA
9. SLEEPING SINGLE IN A DOUBLE BED - Barbara Mandrell - ABC

A rare publicity photo of now-superstar Randy Travis.

Randy Traywick
by Al Ward

When 17-year-old Randy Traywick steps on stage to sing a song such as "The Only Hell My Mama Ever Raised," it's a story he's lived, and the emotion in his voice tells an audience: he's been there.

The emotion comes through just as strong as his new record, a story of unfulfilled love, "Dreaming."

Raised in rural North Carolina, Randy's story has been told many times--except for the ending.

A rebellious teenager, Randy Tarywick feel in with a wild crowd, and sought escape in daring escapades and alcohol. He had many scrapes with the law from his early teens until a year ago. Then, a kindly judge recognized a kid worth saving. He was released into the custody of a woman who not only served as a guardian but as a manager. She recognized his potential as a performer.

Once a singer in his country church, Randy's talent is natural. He's able to capture the mood and emotion of a song and transmit it to his audience as thoroughly as most singers with many more years of experience. Because of that, Randy has been compared to artists such as Waylon Jennings and Conway Twitty. Just listening to Randy, as with Jennings and Twitty, one feels he knows the stories he's telling from experience; one gets the impression he's lived more than is possible to pack into 17 years.

The ending of Randy's story is different only because his guardian recognized his true potential and because Randy decided he wanted to become a man those who love him could be proud of.

"Dreaming" is only the first of many hit records you'll hear from Randy Traywick. Remember him!

Al Ward (1978)

Editor's Note: From the Paula Records publicity files. Courtesy Stan Lewis.

10. WHY HAVE YOU LEFT THE ONE YOU LEFT ME FOR - Crystal Gayle - United Artists
11. LAST CHEATER'S WALTZ - T.G. Sheppard - Warner/Curb
12. NOBODY LIKES SAD SONGS - Ronnie Milsap - RCA
13. JUST GOOD OL' BOYS - Moe Bandy & Joe Stampley - Columbia
14. WHERE DO I PUT HER MEMORY - Charley Pride - RCA
15. ALL I EVER NEED IS YOU - Kenny Rogers & Dottie West - United Artists
16. BACKSIDE OF THIRTY - John Conlee - ABC
17. LADY LAY DOWN - John Conlee - ABC
18. SUSPICIONS - Eddie Rabbitt - Elektra
19. (IF LOVING YOU IS WRONG) I DON'T WANT TO BE RIGHT - Barbara Mandrell - MCA
20. I MAY NEVER GET TO HEAVEN - Conway Twitty - MCA

Editor's Note: "All The Gold In California" (Columbia) by the Gatlin Brothers peaked at #1 for two weeks in October 1979, and should have ranked as #10 above. "You Decorated My Life" (United Artists) by Kenny Rogers, which was a #1 country hit for two weeks in November 1979 and peaked at #7 in the pop charts, should rank as #7 above.

TOP 20 COUNTRY SINGLES OF 1980

POS. TITLE - ARTIST - LABEL
1. MY HEART/SILENT NIGHT (AFTER THE FIGHT) - Ronnie Milsap - RCA
2. ONE DAY AT A TIME - Cristy Lane - United Artists
3. HE STOPPED LOVING HER TODAY - George Jones - Epic
4. DANCIN' COWBOYS - Bellamy Brothers - Warner/Curb
5. TENNESSEE RIVER - Alabama - RCA
6. BAR ROOM BUDDIES - Merle Haggard & Clint Eastwood - Elektra
7. TRUE LOVE WAYS - Mickey Gilley - Epic
8. COWARD OF THE COUNTY - Kenny Rogers - United Artists
9. COWBOYS AND CLOWNS - Ronnie Milsap - RCA
10. STAND BY ME - Mickey Gilley - Asylum *
11. TRYING TO LOVE TWO WOMEN - Oak Ridge Boys - MCA
12. I'LL BE COMING BACK FOR MORE - T.G. Sheppard - Warner/Curb
13. MY HEROES HAVE ALWAYS BEEN COWBOYS - Willie Nelson - Columbia
14. LOOKIN' FOR LOVE - Johnny Lee - Asylum **
15. WHY DON'T YOU SPEND THE NIGHT - Ronnie Milsap - RCA
16. LOVE ME OVER AGAIN - Don Williams - MCA
17. A LESSON IN LEAVIN' - Dottie West - United Artists
18. DRIVIN' MY LIFE AWAY - Eddie Rabbitt - Elektra
19. I AIN'T LIVING LONG LIKE THIS - Waylon Jennings - RCA
20. HAPPY BIRTHDAY DARLIN' - Oak Ridge Boys - MCA
    * and **The year of the "Urban Cowboy."
    ***#1 Hot 100 pop song.

Editor's Note: All of the following songs, some of the biggest country hits of all time (some were also huge pop hits) peaked at #1 during 1980, and did not cross over into 1981. They should all have ranked in *Billboard's* Top 50 Country Singles list, but were left out for some reason:

"Could I Have This Dance" (Capitol) by Anne Murray
"I Believe In You" (MCA) by Don Williams
"If You Change Your Mind" (Columbia) by Crystal Gayle
"Lady" (Liberty) by Kenny Rogers ***
"On The Road Again" (Columbia) by Willie Nelson
"Smoky Mountain Rain" (RCA) by Ronnie Milsap
"Theme From 'Dukes Of Hazzard' " (RCA) by Waylon Jennings
"Why Lady Why" (RCA) by Alabama

Barbara Mandrell

This multi-talented Country and Pop star's ``Sleeping Single In A Double Bed'' was #9 Top 20 Country in 1979.

Eddie Rabbitt

Elvis recorded this singer/songwriter's ``Kentucky Rain,'' and he was on his way. Eddie scored a #4 Top 20 Country in 1979.

TOP 20 COUNTRY SINGLES OF 1981

POS. TITLE - ARTIST - LABEL
1. FIRE AND SMOKE - Earl Thomas Conley - Sunbird
2. NO GETTIN' OVER ME - Ronnie Milsap - RCA
3. SEVEN YEAR ACHE - Rosanne Cash - Columbia
4. I DON'T NEED YOU - Kenny Rogers - Liberty
5. PARTY TIME - T.G. Sheppard - Warner/Curb
6. BUT YOU KNOW I LOVE YOU - Dolly Parton - RCA
7. MIDNIGHT HAULER/SCRATCH MY BACK - Razzy Bailey - RCA
8. FRIENDS - Razzy Bailey - RCA
9. FEELS SO RIGHT - Alabama - RCA
10. TOO MANY LOVERS - Crystal Gayle - Columbia
11. ANGEL FLYING TOO CLOSE TO THE GROUND - Willie Nelson - Columbia
12. I LOVE A RAINY NIGHT - Eddie Rabbitt - Elektra
13. IT'S A LOVELY, LOVELY WORLD - Gail Davies - Warner Bros.
14. OLDER WOMEN - Ronnie McDowell - Epic
15. I KEEP COMING BACK - Razzy Bailey - RCA
16. WHO'S CHEATING WHO - Charly McClain - Epic
17. BLESSED ARE THE BELIEVERS - Anne Murray - Capitol
18. YOU'RE THE REASON GOD MADE OKLAHOMA - David Frizzell & Shelly West - Warner/Viva
19. DON'T WAIT ON ME - Statler Brothers - Mercury
20. STEP BY STEP - Eddie Rabbitt - Elektra

Editor's Note: ``Elvira'' (MCA) by the Oak Ridge Boys, country's hottest-selling-ever single and the only platinum country single until ``Achy Breaky Heart'' in 1992, should have ranked #1 above, a major gaff on the part of *Billboard* statisticians. ``Never Been So Loved (In All My Life)'' (RCA) by Charley Pride, a #1 country hit for two weeks, should have ranked #5. All of the following peaked at #1 and should have ranked in the year-end Top 50 Country Singles list:

``All My Rowdy Friends'' (Warner Bros.) by Hank Williams Jr.
``Fancy Free'' (MCA) by the Oak Ridge Boys
``My Baby Thinks He's A Train'' (Columbia) by Rosanne Cash
``Still Doin' Time'' (Epic) by George Jones

TOP 20 COUNTRY SINGLES OF 1982

POS. TITLE - ARTIST - LABEL
1. ALWAYS ON MY MIND - Willie Nelson - Columbia
2. NOBODY - Sylvia - RCA
3. WHAT'S FOREVER FOR - Michael Murphey - Liberty
4. CRYING MY HEART OUT OVER YOU - Ricky Skaggs - Epic
5. I'M GONNA HIRE A WINO TO DECORATE YOUR HOME - David Frissell - Warner/Viva
6. JUST TO SATISFY YOU - Waylon Jennings & Willie Nelson - RCA
7. SHE GOT THE GOLDMINE (I GOT THE SHAFT) - Jerry Reed - RCA
8. IF YOU'RE THINKING YOU WANT A STRANGER - George Strait - MCA
9. A COUNTRY BOY CAN SURVIVE - Hank Williams Jr. - Elektra/Curb
10. SHE LEFT LOVE ALL OVER ME - Razzy Bailey - RCA
11. 'TIL YOU'RE GONE - Barbara Mandrell - MCA
12. LORD, I HOPE THIS DAY IS GOOD - Don Williams - MCA
13. BIG CITY - Merle Haggard - Epic
14. YOU'RE THE BEST BREAK THIS OLD HEART EVER HAD - Ed Bruce - MCA
15. FOOL HEARTED MEMORY - George Strait - MCA
16. I'M NOT THAT LONELY YET - Reba McEntire - Mercury

Willie Nelson

Willie first recorded for Bellaire Records, a Texas label. It wasn't until 1975 when ``Blue Eyes Crying In The Rain'' hit big that Willie started down the road of super-stardom. His familiar ``Always On My Mind'' was the #1 Top 20 Country hit in 1982.

17. THE CLOWN - Conway Twitty - Elektra
18. LOVE WILL TURN YOU AROUND - Kenny Rogers - Liberty
19. DANCING YOUR MEMORY AWAY - Charly McClain - Epic
20. SLOW HAND - Conway Twitty - Elektra

Editor's Note: "You & I" (Elektra) by Eddie Rabbitt and Crystal Gayle, a #1 country and #7 pop hit, should have ranked #4 above. "Love In The First Degree" (RCA) by Alabama, #1 country and #15 pop, should have ranked #7. "Wild & Blue" (Warner Bros.) by John Anderson, #1 country for two weeks, should have ranked #9. "War Is Hell" (Warner Bros.) by T.G. Sheppard

TOP 20 COUNTRY SINGLES OF 1983

POS. TITLE - ARTIST - LABEL
1. JOSE CUERVO - Shelly West - Warner/Viva
2. YOU'RE GONNA TUIN MY BAD REPUTATION - Ronnie McDowell - Epic
3. WHATEVER HAPPENED TO OLD-FASHIONED LOVE - B.J. Thomas - Cleveland Int'l/Epic
4. HE'S A HEARTACHE (LOOKING FOR A PLACE TO HAPPEN) - Janie Fricke - Columbia
5. A FIRE I CAN'T PUT OUT - George Strait - MCA
6. PANCHO & LEFTY - Willie Nelson & Merle Haggard - Epic
7. YOU'RE THE FIRST TIME I'VE THOUGHT ABOUT LEAVING - Reba McIntyre - Mercury
8. I'M ONLY IN IT FOR THE LOVE - John Conlee - MCA
9. SWINGIN' - John Anderson - Warner Bros.
10. NIGHT GAMES - Charley Pride - RCA
11. I ALWAYS GET LUCKY WITH YOU - George Jones - Epic
12. YOU'RE LOVE'S ON THE LINE - Earl Thomas Conley - RCA
13. I WOULDN'T CHANGE YOU IF I COULD - Ricky Skaggs - Epic
14. HEY BARTENDER - Johnny Lee - Full Moon/Asylum
15. FAKIN' LOVE - T.G. Sheppard & Karen Brooks - Warner Bros.
16. LOST IN THE FEELING - Conway Twitty - Warner Bros.
17. COMMON MAN - John Conlee - MCA
18. NEW LOOK FROM AN OLD LOVER - B.J. Thomas - Columbia
19. YOU TAKE ME FOR GRANTED - Merle Haggard - Epic
20. FOOL FOR YOUR LOVE - Mickey Gilley - Epic

Editor's Note: "Islands In The Stream" (RCA) by Kenny Rogers and Dolly Parton, #1 country and #1 platinum pop hit, should have ranked #1 above. All of the following peaked at #1 and should have ranked in the year-end Top 50 Country Singles, but appeared neither on the 1983 nor the 1984 lists:

"Black Sheep" (Warner Bros.) by John Anderson
"Holding Her & Loving You" (RCA) by Earl Thomas Conley
"Houston" (RCA) by Ronnie Milsap
"A Little Good News" (Capitol) by Anne Murray
"One Of A Kind Pair Of Fools" (MCA) by Barbara Mandrell
"Somebody's Gonna Love You" (MCA) by Lee Greenwood
"Tell Me A Lie" (Columbia) by Janie Fricke

TOP 20 COUNTRY SINGLES OF 1984

POS. TITLE - ARTIST - LABEL
1. TO ALL THE GIRLS I'VE LOVED BEFORE - Julio Iglesias & Willie Nelson - Columbia
2. I CAN TELL BY THE WAY YOU DANCE (YOU'RE GONNA LOVE ME TONIGHT) - Vern Gosdin - Compleat
3. MAMA HE'S CRAZY - The Judds - RCA
4. I DON'T WANNA BE A MEMORY - Exile - Epic

5. ELIZABETH - The Statlers - Mercury
6.* YOU'RE GETTIN' TO ME AGAIN - Jim Glaser - Noble Vision
   I'VE BEEN AROUND ENOUGH TO KNOW - John Schneider - MCA (tie)
7. I GOT MEXICO - Eddy Raven - RCA
8. LET'S FALL TO PIECES TOGETHER - George Strait - MCA
9. JUST ANOTHER WOMAN IN LOVE - Anne Murray - Capitol
10. ANGEL IN DISGUISE - Earl Thomas Conley - RCA
11. I DON'T KNOW A THING ABOUT LOVE - Conway Twitty - Warner Bros.
12. LONG HARD ROAD (THE SHARECROPPER'S DREAM) - Nitty Gritty Dirt Band - Warner Bros.
13. MONA LIS LOST HER SMILE - David Allan Coe - Columbia
14. THAT'S THE THING ABOUT LOVE - Don Williams - MCA
15. IF YOU'RE GONNA PLAY IN TEXAS - Alabama - RCA
16. STILL LOSING YOU - Ronnie Milsap - RCA
17. WOKE UP IN LOVE - Exile - Epic
18. SOMEBODY'S NEEDIN' SOMEBODY - Conway Twitty - Warner Bros.
19. TENNESSEE HOMESICK BLUES - Dolly Parton - RCA
20. UNCLE PEN - Ricky Skaggs - Sugar Hill/Epic

Editor's Note: "Why Not Me" (RCA) by The Judds, #1 for two weeks, should have ranked #5 above. All of the following peaked at #1 and should have ranked in the year-end Top 50 Country Singles list:

"Chance Of Lovin' You" (RCA) by Earl Thomas Conley
"Nobody Loves You Like I Do" (Capitol) by Anne Murray & Dave Loggins
"You Could've Heard A Heartbreak" (Warner Bros.) by Johnny Lee
"Your Heart's Not In It" (Columbia) by Janie Fricke

TOP 20 COUNTRY SINGLES OF 1985

POS. TITLE - ARTIST - LABEL
1. LOST IN THE FIFTIES TONIGHT (IN THE STILL OF THE NIGHT) - Ronnie Milsap - RCA
2. DIXIE ROAD - Lee Greenwood - MCA
3. REAL LOVE - Dolly Parton with Kenny Rogers - RCA
4. RADIO HEART - Charly McClain - Epic
5. HIGHWAYMAN - Waylon Jennings, Willie Nelson, Johnny Cash, Kris Kristofferson - Columbia
6. SHE'S SINGLE AGAIN - Janie Fricke - Columbia
7. I'M FOR LOVE - Hank Williams Jr. - Warner/Curb
8. MODERN DAY ROMANCE - Nitty Gritty Dirt Band - Warner Bros.
9. FALLIN' IN LOVE - Sylvia - RCA
10. FORGIVING YOU WAS EASY - Willie Nelson - Columbia
11. I DON'T KNOW WHY YOU DON'T WANT ME - Rosanne Cash - Columbia
12. BABY'S GOT HER BLUE JEANS ON - Mel McDaniel - Capitol
13. SHE'S A MIRACLE - Exile - Epic
14. MEET ME IN MONTANA - Marie Osmond with Dan Seals - Capitol/Curb
15. LOVE IS ALIVE - The Judds - RCA/Curb
16. DRINKIN' AND DREAMIN' - Waylon Jennings - RCA
17. LITTLE THINGS - Oak Ridge Boys - RCA
18. SEVEN SPANISH ANGELS - Ray Charles with Willie Nelson - Columbis
19. HONOR BOUND - Earl Thomas Conley - RCA
20. SHE KEEPS THE HOME FIRES BURNING - Ronnie Milsap - RCA

TOP 20 COUNTRY SINGLES OF 1986

POS. TITLE - ARTIST - LABEL
1. NEVER BE YOU - Rosanne Cash - Columbia
2. TOO MUCH ON MY HEART - Statler Brothers - Mercury
3. I DON'T MIND THE THORNS (IF YOU'RE THE ROSE) - Lee Greenwood - MCA
4. HAVE MERCY - The Judds - RCA/Curb
5. I'LL NEVER STOP LOVING YOU - Gary Morris - Warner Bros.
6. MORNING DESIRE - Kenny Rogers - RCA
7. YOU CAN DREAM OF ME - Steve Wariner - MCA
8. WHOEVER'S IN NEW ENGLAND - Reba McEntire - MCA
9. UNTIL I MET YOU - Judy Rodman - MTM
10. ON THE OTHER HAND - Randy Travis - Warner Bros. *
11. BOP - Dan Seals - EMI America
12. JUST ANOTHER LOVE - Tanya Tucker - Capitol
13. EVERYTHING THAT GLITTERS (IS NOT GOLD) - Dan Seals - EMI America
14. STRONG HEART - T.G. Sheppard - Columbia
15. ONE LOVE AT A TIME - Tanya Tucker - Capitol
16. THERE'S NO STOPPING YOUR HEART - Marie Osmond - Capitol/Curb
17. LONELY ALONE - Forester Sisters - Warner Bros.
18. I COULD GET USED TO YOU - Exile - Epic
19. WHAT'S A MEMORY LIKE YOU (DOING IN A LOVE LIKE THIS) - John Schneider - MCA
20. NOBODY FALLS LIKE A FOOL - Earl Thomas Conley - RCA
*Hit the charts twice: 1985 (peaked at #67); 1986 (#1).

Editor's Note: "Diggin' Up Bones" (Warner Bros.) by Randy Travis should actually have ranked #10 above.

Rosanne Cash

Oldest daughter of Johnny Cash, Rosanne began her career in 1979. She has had ten #1 singles. Her ``Never Be You'' was the #1 Top 20 Country hit in 1986.

TOP 20 COUNTRY SINGLES OF 1987

POS. TITLE - ARTIST - LABEL
1. GIVE ME WINGS - Michael Johnson - RCA
2. HALF PAST FOREVER (TILL I'M BLUE IN THE HEART) - T.G. Sheppard - Columbia
3. WHAT AM I GONNA DO ABOUT YOU - Reba McEntire - MCA
4. FISHIN' IN THE DARK - Nitty Gritty Dirt Band - Warner Bros.
5. THE MOON IS STILL OVER HER SHOULDER - Michael Johnson - RCA
6. CRY MYSELF TO SLEEP - The Judds - RCA/Curb
7. YOU AGAIN - Forester Sisters - Warner Bros.
8. SOMEBODY LIED - Ricky Van Shelton - Columbia
9. THE WAY WE MAKE A BROKEN HEART - Rosanne Cash - Columbia
10. IT TAKES A LITTLE RAIN - Oak Ridge Boys - MCA
11. HELL AND HIGH WATER - T. Graham Brown - Capitol
12. YOU STILL MOVE ME - Dan Seals - EMI America
13. THIS CRAZY LOVE - Oak Ridge Boys - MCA
14. FOREVER AND EVER, AMEN - Randy Travis - Warner Bros.
15. MORNIN' RIDE - Lee Greenwood - MCA
16. FALLIN' FOR YOUR FOR YEARS - Conway Twitty - Warner Bros.
17. ONE PROMISE TOO LATE - Reba McEntire - MCA
18. CAN'T STOP MY HEART FROM LOVING YOU - The O'Kanes - Columbia
19. LOVE ME LIKE YOU USED TO - Tanya Tucker - Capitol
20. DON'T GO TO STRANGERS - T. Graham Brown - Capitol

Editor's Note: "Forever And Ever, Amen" (Warner Bros.) by Randy Travis, the first country single to stay at #1 for three weeks since 1980, deserves more than the #14 year-end ranking above. This should be the year's #1 country single.

TOP 20 COUNTRY SINGLES OF 1988

POS. TITLE - ARTIST - LABEL
1. DON'T CLOSE YOUR EYES - Keith Whitley - RCA
2. IF YOU CHANGE YOUR MIND - Rosanne Cash - Columbia
3. SET 'EM UP JOE - Vern Gosdin - Columbia
4. STRONG ENOUGH TO BEND - Tanya Tucker - Capitol
5. BLUEST EYES IN TEXAS - Restless Heart - RCA
6. IT'S SUCH A SMALL WORLD - Rodney Crowell & Rosanne Cash - Columbia
7. I COULDN'T LEAVE YOU IF I TRIED - Rodney Crowell - Columbia
8. IF IT DON'T COME EASY - Tanya Tucker - Capitol
9. I'M GONNA GET YOU - Eddy Raven - RCA
10. JOE KNOWS HOW TO LIVE - Eddy Raven - RCA
11. ADDICTED - Dan Seals - Capitol
12. DARLENE - T. Graham Brown - Capitol
13. WE BELIEVE IN HAPPY ENDINGS - Earl Thomas Conley with Emmylou Harris - RCA
14. I WANNA DANCE WITH YOU - Eddie Rabbitt - RCA
15. TOO GONE TOO LONG - Randy Travis - Warner Bros.
16. I SHOULD BE WITH YOU - Steve Wariner - MCA
17. A LITTLE BIT LOVE - Patty Loveless - MCA
18. I'LL ALWAYS COME BACK - K.T. Oslin - RCA
19. EIGHTEEN WHEELS AND A DOZEN ROSES - Kathy Mattea - Mercury
20. STREETS OF BAKERSFIELD - Dwight Yoakam & Buck Owens - Reprise

Editor's Note: The following songs held the #1 position for two weeks each, yet the first two are ranked at #19 and #38 on *Billboard*'s year-end Top 50 Country Singles list, and the last

Tanya Tucker

Tanya had two songs in the Top 20 Country in 1988, ``Strong Enough To Bend'' (#4) and ``If It Don't Come Easy'' (#8).

two are not ranked at all. All should be ranked in the top ten above:

``Eighteen Wheels & A Dozen Roses'' (Mercury) by Kathy Mattea
``I Told You So'' (Warner Bros.) by Randy Travis
``I'll Leave This World Loving You'' (Columbia) by Ricky Van Shelton
``When You Say Nothing At All'' (RCA) by Keith Whitley

TOP 20 COUNTRY SINGLES OF 1989

POS. TITLE - ARTIST - LABEL
1. BETTER MAN - Clint Black - RCA
2. KILLIN' TIME - Clint Black - RCA
3. SHE'S GOT A SINGLE THING IN MIND - Conway Twitty - MCA
4. LOVIN' ONLY ME - Ricky Skaggs - Epic
5. I GOT DREAMS - Steve Wariner - MCA
6. ABOVE AND BEYOND - Rodney Crowell - Columbia
7. I'M NO STRANGER TO THE RAIN - Keith Whitley - RCA
8. LET ME TELL YOU ABOUT LOVE - The Judds - Curb/RCA
9. WHAT'S GOING ON IN YOUR WORLD - George Strait - MCA
10. NOTHING I CAN DO ABOUT IT NOW - Willie Nelson - Columbia
11. LOVE OUT LOUD - Earl Thomas Conley - RCA
12. LIVING PROOF - Ricky Van Shelton - Columbia
13. HIGH COTTON - Alabama - RCA
14. I WONDER DO YOU THINK OF ME - Roasanne Cash - Columbia
15. CATHY'S CLOWN - Reba McEntire - MCA
16. I DON'T WANT TO SPOIL THE PARTY - Rosanne Cash - Columbia

17. WHERE DID I GO WRONG - Steve Wariner - MCA
18. IN A LETTER TO YOU - Eddy Raven - Universal
19. SUNDAY IN THE SOUTH - Shenandoah - Columbia
20. ARE YOU EVER GONNA LOVE ME - Holly Dunn - Warner Bros.

TOP 20 COUNTRY SINGLES OF 1990

POS. TITLE - ARTIST - LABEL
1. NOBODY'S HOME - Clint Black - RCA
2. HARD ROCK BOTTOM OF YOUR HEART - Randy Travis - Warner Bros.
3. ON SECOND THOUGHT - Eddie Rabbitt - Capitol
4. LOVE WITHOUT END, AMEN - George Strait - MCA
5. WALKIN' AWAY - Clint Black - RCA
6. I'VE CRIED MY LAST TEAR FOR YOU - Ricky Van Shelton - Columbia
7. NO MATTER HOW HIGH - Oak Ridge Boys - MCA
8. HELP ME HOLD ON - Travis Tritt - Warner Bros.
9. CHAINS - Patty Loveless - MCA
10. HERE IN THE REAL WORLD - Alan Jackson - Arista
11. SOUTHERN STAR - Alabama - RCA
12. LOVE ON ARRIVAL - Dan Seals - Capitol
13. THE DANCE - Garth Brooks - Capitol
14. FIVE MINUTES - Lorrie Morgan - RCA
15. I'M OVER YOU - Keith Whitley - RCA
16. SEEIN' MY FATHER IN ME - Paul Overstreet - RCA
17. MY ARMS STAY OPEN ALL NIGHT - Tanya Tucker - Capitol
18. JUKEBOX IN MY MIND - Alabama - RCA
19. STATUE OF A FOOL - Ricky Van Shelton - Columbia
20. NOT COUNTING YOU - Garth Brooks - Capitol

Lorrie Morgan

Lorrie had a #14 Top 20 Country hit in 1990 with ``Five Minutes,'' along with a #5 Top 20 Country album.

TOP 20 COUNTRY SINGLES OF 1991

POS. TITLE - ARTIST - LABEL
1. DON'T ROCK THE JUKEBOX - Alan Jackson - Arista
2. I'VE COME TO EXPECT IT FROM YOU - George Strait - MCA
3. FOREVER'S AS FAR AS I'LL GO - Alabama - RCA
4. THE THUNDER ROLLS - Garth Brooks - Capitol
5. IN A DIFFERENT LIGHT - Doug Stone - Epic
6. BROTHER JUKEBOX - Mark Chesnutt - MCA
7. YOU KNOW ME BETTER THAN THAT - George Strait - MCA
8. DOWN HOME - Alabama - RCA
9. UNANSWERED PRAYERS - Garth Brooks - Capitol
10. IF I KNOW ME - George Strait - MCA
11. I'D LOVE YOU ALL OVER AGAIN - Alan Jackson - Arista
12. DADDY'S COME AROUND - Paul Overstreet - RCA
13. WALK ON FAITH - Mike Reid - Columbia
14. LOVING BLIND - Clint Black - RCA
15. TWO OF A KIND, WORKIN' ON A FULL HOUSE - Garth Brooks - Capitol
16. MEET IN THE MIDDLE - Diamond Rio - Arista
17. RUMOR HAS IT - Reba McEntire - MCA
18. SHE'S IN LOVE WITH THE BOY - Trisha Yearwood - MCA
19. I AM A SIMPLE MAN - Ricky Van Shelton - Columbia
20. HERE WE ARE - Alabama - RCA

TOP 20 COUNTRY SINGLES OF 1992

POS. TITLE - ARTIST - LABEL
1. I SAW THE LIGHT - Wynonna - Curb/MCA
2. ACHY BREAKY HEART - Billy Ray Cyrus - Mercury
3. IS THERE LIFE OUT THERE - Reba McEntire - MCA
4. WHAT SHE'S DOING NOW -Garth Brooks - Liberty
5. WE TELL OURSELVES - Clint Black - RCA
6. DALLAS - Alan Jackson - Arista
7. BOOT SCOOTIN' BOOGIE - Brooks & Dunn - Arista
8. I STILL BELIEVE IN YOU - Vince Gill - MCA
9. NEON MOON - Brooks & Dunn - Arista
10. SOME GIRLS DO - Sawyer Brown - Curb
11. I'LL THINK OF SOMETHING - Mark Chesnutt - MCA
12. LOVE'S GOT A HOLD ON YOU - Alan Jackson - Arista
13. BETTER CLASS OF LOSERS - Randy Travis - Warner Bros.
14. A JUKEBOX WITH A COUNTRY SONG - Doug Stone - Epic
15. I FEEL LUCKY - Mary-Chapin Carpenter - Columbia
16. STRAIGHT TEQUILA NIGHT - John Anderson - BNA
17. BORN COUNTRY - Alabama - RCA
18. SHE IS HIS ONLY NEED - Wynonna - Curb/MCA
19. TAKE A LITTLE TRIP - Alabama - RCA
20. PAST THE POINT OF RESCUE - Hal Ketchum - Curb

TOP 20 COUNTRY SINGLES OF 1993

POS. TITLE - ARTIST - LABEL
1. CHATTAHOOCHEE - Alan Jackson - Arista
2. WHAT'S IT ALL ABOUT - Clay Walker - Giant
3. CAN'T BREAK IT TO MY HEART - Tracy Lawrence - Atlantic

George Strait
Among many hits, George was #2 Top 20 Country in 1992 with ``I've Come To Expect It Of You.''

4. THANK GOD FOR YOU - Sawyer Brown - Curb
5. ONE MORE LAST CHANCE - Vince Gill - MCA
6. EASY COME, EASY GO - George Strait - MCA
7. AIN'T GOING DOWN (TIL THE SUN COMES UP) - Garth Brooks - Liberty
8. IT SURE IS MONDAY - Mark Chesnutt - MCA
9. I LOVE THE WAY YOU LOVE ME - John Michael Montgomery - Atlantic
10. WHY DIDN'T I THINK OF THAT - Doug Stone - Epic
11. IN THE HEART OF A WOMAN - Billy Ray Cyrus - Mercury
12. BLAME IT ON YOUR HEART - Patty Loveless - Epic
13. PROP ME UP BESIDE THE JUKEBOX (IF I DIE) - Joe Diffie - Epic
14. ALIBIS - Tracy Lawrence - Atlantic
15. AIN'T THAT LONELY YET - Dwight Yoakam - Reprise
16. HOLDIN' HEAVEN - Tracy Byrd - MCA
17. A THOUSAND MILES FROM NOWHERE - Dwight Yoakam - Reprise
18. MONEY IN THE BANK - John Anderson - BNA
19. A BAD GOODBYE - Clint Black with Wynonna - RCA
20. NO TIME TO KILL - Clint Black - RCA

Billboard Top 20 Rhythm & Blues Singles, 1946-1993

TOP 20 RHYTHM & BLUES SINGLES OF 1946

POS.	TITLE - ARTIST - LABEL
1.	HEY-BA-BA-RE-BOP - Lionel Hampton - Decca
2.	CHOO CHOO CH'BOOGIE - Louis Jordan - Decca
3.	STONE COLD DEAD IN THE MARKET - Louis Jordan & Ella Fitzgerald - Decca
4.	THE GYPSY - Ink Spots - Decca
5.	R.M. BLUES - Roy Milton - Juke Box/Specialty
6.	BUZZ ME - Louis Jordan - Decca
7.	DRIFTING BLUES - Johnny Moore & His Three Blazers - Philo
8.	SALT PROK, W. VA. - Louis Jordan - Decca
9.	I KNOW - The Jubilaires & Andy Kirk Orch. - Decca
10.	AIN'T THAT JUST LIKE A WOMAN? - Louis Jordan - Decca
11.	DON'T WORRY 'BOUT THAT MULE - Louis Jordan - Decca
12.	ROUTE 66 - King Cole Trio - Capitol
13.	BEWARE - Louis Jordan - Decca
14.	RECONVERSION BLUES - Louis Jordan - Decca
15.*	DON'T BE A BABY, BABY - Mills Brothers - Decca
	THAT CHICK'S TOO YOUNG TO FRY - Louis Jordan - Decca (*Tie)
16.*	I'VE GOT A RIGHT TO CRY - Joe Liggins & His Honeydrippers - Exclusive
	DON'T LET THE SUN CATCH YOU CRYIN' - Louis Jordan - Decca
	I KNOW WHO THREW THE WHISKEY IN THE WELL - Bull Moose Jackson - Queen (*Three-way tie)
17.*	I'VE GOT A RIGHT TO CRY - Erskine Hawkins - Victor
	TANYA - Joe Liggins & His Honeydrippers - Exclusive (*Tie)

TOP 20 RHYTHM & BLUES SINGLES OF 1947

POS.	TITLE - ARTIST - LABEL
1.	AIN'T NOBODY HERE BUT US CHICKENS - Louis Jordan - Decca
2.	BOOGIE WOOGIE BLUE PLATE - Louis Jordan - Decca
3.	I WANT TO BE LOVED - Savannah Churchill - Manor
4.	JACK, YOU'RE DEAD - Louis Jordan - Decca
5.	OLD MAID BOOGIE - Eddie Vinson Orch. - Mercury
6.	SNATCH AND GRAB IT - Julie Lee & Her Boy Friends - Capitol Americana
7.	LET THE GOOD TIMES ROLL - Louis Jordan - Decca
8.	TEXAS AND PACIFIC - Louis Jordan - Decca
9.	HE'S A REAL GONE GUY - Nellie Lutcher - Capitol Americana
10.	HURRY ON DOWN - Nellie Lutcher - Capitol Americana
11.	NEW ORLEANS BLUES - Johnny Moore's Three Blazers - Exclusive
12.	I WANT TO BE LOVED - Lionel Hampton - Decca
13.	ACROSS THE VALLEY FROM THE ALAMO - Mills Brothers - Decca
14.	OPEN THE DOOR, RICHARD - Louis Jordan - Decca
15.	OPEN THE DOOR, RICHARD - Dusty Fletcher - National
16.	OPEN THE DOOR, RICHARD - Jack McVea - Black & White
17.*	HAWK'S BOOGIE - Erskine Hawkins - Victor
	SINCE I FELL FOR YOU - Paul Gayten Trio - DeLuxe (*Tie)
18.	AIN'T THAT JUST LIKE A WOMAN - Louis Jordan - Decca
19.*	OPEN THE DOOR, RICHARD - Count Basie - Victor
	THAT'S MY DESIRE - Frankie Laine - Mercury (*Tie)

TOP 20 RHYTHM & BLUES SINGLES OF 1948

POS.	TITLE - ARTIST - LABEL
1.	LONG GONE - Sonny Thompson - Miracle
2.	GOOD ROCKIN' TONIGHT - Wynonie Harris - King
3.	TOMORROW NIGHT - Lonnie Johnson - King
4.	PRETTY MAMA BLUES - Ivory Joe Hunter - 4 Star
5.	I CAN'T GO WITHOUT YOU - Bull Moose Jackson - King
6.	MESSIN' AROUND - Memphis Slim - Miracle
7.	MY HEART BELONGS TO YOU - Arbee Stidham - Victor
8.	CORN BREAD - Hal Singer Sextette - Savoy
9.	RUN, JOE - Louis Jordan - Decca
10.	BLUES AFTER HOURS - Pee Wee Crayton - Modern
11.	NATURE BOY - King Cole - Capitol
12.	ALL MY LOVE BELONGS TO YOU - Bull Moose Jackson - King
13.	LATE FREIGHT - Sonny Thompson - Miracle
14.*	SEND FOR ME IF YOU NEED ME - The Ravens - National
	AM I ASKING TOO MUCH? - Dinah Washington - Mercury (*Tie)
15.	HOP, SKIP AND JUMP - Roy Milton - Specialty
16.	KING SIZE PAPA - Julie Lee - Capitol
17.	LONG ABOUT MIDNIGHT - Roy Brown - DeLuxe
18.	IT'S TOO SOON TO KNOW - The Orioles - Natural
19.	IT'S TOO SOON TO KNOW - Dinah Washington - Mercury

TOP 20 RHYTHM & BLUES SINGLES OF 1949

POS.	TITLE - ARTIST - LABEL
1.	THE HUCKLEBUCK - Paul Williams - Savoy
2.	TROUBLE BLUES - Charles Brown - Aladdin
3.	SATURDAY NIGHT FISH FRY - Louis Jordan & Tympany Five - Decca
4.	AIN'T NOBODY'S BUSINESS - Jimmy Witherspoon - Supreme
5.	LITTLE GIRL, DON'T CRY - Bull Moose Jackson - King
6.	TELL ME SO - The Orioles - Jubilee
7.	DRINKIN' WINE, SPO-DEE-O-DEE - Stick McHee & Buddies - Atlantic
8.	HOLD ME, BABY - Amos Milburn - Aladdin
9.	CHICKEN SHACK BOOGIE - Amos Milburn - Aladdin
10.	BOOGIE CHILLIN' - John Lee Hooker - Modern
11.	BABY, GET LOST - Dinah Washington - Mercury
12.	ROCKIN' AT MIDNIGHT - Roy Brown - DeLuxe
13.	WRAPPED UP IN A DREAM - Do Ray & Me - Commodore
14.	BEWILDERED - Amos Milburn - Aladdin
15.	ALL SHE WANTS TO DO IS ROCK - Wynonie Harris - King
16.	BEWILDERED - Red Miller Trio - Bullet
17.	CLOSE YOUR EYES - Herb Lance - Sittin' In
18.	DRINKIN' WINE, SPO-DEE-O-DEE - Wynonie Harris - King
19.	THE HUCKLEBUCK - Roy Milton - Specialty
20.	CONFESSION BLUES - Maxine Trio - Downbeat

TOP 20 RHYTHM & BLUES SINGLES OF 1950

POS.	TITLE - ARTIST - LABEL
1.	PINK CHAMPAGNE - Joe Liggins - Specialty
2.	DOUBLE CROSSING BLUES - Johnny Otis, Little Esther, Mel Walker - Savoy
3.	I NEED YOU SO - Ivory Joe Hunter - MGM

4. HARD LUCK BLUES - Roy Brown - DeLuxe
5. CUPID'S BOOGIE - Little Esther, Johnny Otis, Mel Walker - Savoy
6. I ALMOST LOST MY MIND - Ivory Joe Hunter - MGM
7. WELL. OH, WELL - Tiny Bradshaw - King
8. BLUE LIGHT BOOGIE - Louis Jordan - Decca
9. FOR YOU MY LOVE - Larry Darnell - Regal
10. MISTRUSTIN' BLUES - Johnny Otis, Little Esther, Mel Walker - Savoy
11. EVERYDAY I HAVE THE BLUES - Lowell Fulson - Swingtime
12. BLUE SHADOWS - Lowell Fulson - Swingtime
13. ANYTIME, ANYPLACE, ANYWHERE - Joe Morris - Atlantic
14. WHY DO THINGS HAPPEN TO ME? - Roy Hawkins - Modern
15. MONA LISA - Nat King Cole - Capitol
16. I WANNA BE LOVED - Dinah Washington - Mercury
17. PLEASE SEND ME SOMEONE TO LOVE - Percy Mayfield - Specialty
18. I LOVE MY BABY - Larry Darnell - Regal
19. SATURDAY NIGHT FISH FRY - Louis Jordan - Decca
20. CRY, CRY, CRY - Ed Wiley - Sittin' In

TOP 20 RHYTHM & BLUES SINGLES OF 1951

POS. TITLE - ARTIST - LABEL
1. SIXTY MINUTE MAN - Dominoes - Federal
2. BLACK NIGHT - Charles Brown - Aladdin
3. TEARDROPS FROM MY EYES - Ruth Brown - Atlantic
4. CHAINS OF LOVE - Joe Turner - Atlantic
5. DON'T YOU KNOW I LOVE YOU - Clovers - Atlantic
6. PLEASE SEND ME SOMEONE TO LOVE - Percy Mayfield - Specialty
7. I'M WAITING JUST FOR YOU - Lucky Millinder - King
8. GLORY OF LOVE - Five Keys - Aladdin
9. ROCKET 88 - Jackie Brenston - Chess
10. ROCKIN' BLUES - Johnny Otis, Mel Walker - Savoy
11. BAD, BAD WHISKEY - Amos Milburn - Aladdin
12. FOOL, FOOL, FOOL - Clovers - Atlantic
13. LOST LOVE - Percy Mayfield - Specialty
14. I'M IN THE MOOD - John Lee Hooker - Modern
15. I GOT LOADED - "Peppermint" Harris - Aladdin
16. ANYTIME, ANYPLACE, ANYWHERE - Joe Morris - Atlantic
17. TOO YOUNG - Nat "King" Cole - Capitol
18. RED'S BOOGIE - Piano Red - Victor
19. SEVEN LONG DAY'S - Charles Brown - Aladdin
20. DO SOMETHING FOR ME - Dominoes - Federal

TOP 20 RHYTHM & BLUES SINGLES OF 1952

POS. TITLE - ARTIST - LABEL
1. LAWDY, MISS CLAWDY - Lloyd Price - Specialty
2. HAVE MERCY, BABY - Dominoes - Federal
3. FIVE, TEN, FIFTEEN HOURS - Ruth Brown - Atlantic
4. GOIN' HOME - Fats Domino - Imperial
5. NIGHT TRAIN - Jimmy Forrest - United
6. MY SONG - Johnny Ace - Duke
7. ONE MINT JULEP - Clovers - Atlantic
8. TING A LING - Clovers - Atlantic
9. THREE O'CLOCK BLUES - B.B. King - RPM
10. JUKE - Little Walter - Checker
11. NO MORE DOGGIN' - Roscoe Gordon - RPM
12. YOU KNOW I LOVE YOU - B.B. King - RPM
13. MARY JO - Four Blazers - Atlantic
14. BOOTED - Roscoe Gordon - Chess/RPM
15. FIVE LONG YEARS - Eddie Boyd - Job

16. HEAVENLY FATHER - Edna McGriff - Jubilee
17. CALL OPERATOR 210 - Floyd Dixon - Aladdin
18. FLAMINGO - Earl Bostic - King
19. CRY - Johnnie Ray - Okeh
20. MOODY, MOOD FOR LOVE - King Pleasure - Prestige

TOP 20 RHYTHM & BLUES SINGLES OF 1953

POS. TITLE - ARTIST - LABEL
1. (MAMA) HE TREATS YOUR DAUGHTER MEAN - Ruth Brown - Atlantic
2. SHAKE A HAND - Faye Adams - Herald
3. HOUND DOG - Willie Mae Thornton - Peacock
4. CRYING IN THE CHAPEL - Orioles - Jubilee
5. CLOCK - Johnny Ace - Duke
6. I DON'T KNOW - Willie Mabon - Chess
7. GOOD LOVIN' - Clovers - Atlantic
8. BABY, DON'T DO IT - Five Royales - Apollo
9. HELP ME, SOMEBODY - Five Royales - Apollo
10. PLEASE LOVE ME - B.B. King - RPM
11. GOING TO THE RIVER - Fats Domino - Imperial
12. CRAWLIN' - Clovers - Atlantic
13. LET ME GO HOME, WHISKEY - Amos Milburn - Aladdin
14. I WANNA KNOW - Du Droppers - RCA Victor
15. I'M MAD - Willie Mabon - Chess
16. TOO MUCH LOVIN' - Five Royales - Apollo
17. SOFT - Tiny Bradshaw - King
18. RED TOP - King Pleasure - Prestige
19. CROSS MY HEART - Johnny Ace - Duke
20. DON'T DECEIVE ME - Chuck Willis - Okeh

TOP 20 RHYTHM & BLUES SINGLES OF 1954

POS. TITLE - ARTIST - LABEL
1. WORK WITH ME, ANNIE - Midnighters - Federal
2. HONEY LOVE - Drifters - Atlantic
3. WHAT A DREAM - Ruth Brown - Atlantic
4. YOU'LL NEVER WALK ALONE - Roy Hamilton - Epic
5. SHAKE, RATTLE AND ROLL - Joe Turner - Atlantic
6. THINGS THAT I USED TO DO - Guitar Slim - Specialty
7. HURTS ME TO MY HEART - Faye Adams - Herald
8. ANNIE HAD A BABY - Midnighters - Federal
9. LOVEY DOVEY - Clovers - Atlantic
10. SEXY WAYS - Midnighters - Federal
11. MONEY, HONEY - Drifters - Atlantic
12. SH-BOOM - Chords - Cat
13. DIDN'T WANT TO DO IT - Spiders - Imperial
14. I'LL BE TRUE - Faye Adams - Federal
15. HONEY, HUSH - Joe Turner - Atlantic
16. JUST MAKE LOVE TO ME - Muddy Waters - Chess
17. LITTLE MAMA - Clovers - Atlantic
18. SUCH A NIGHT - Drifters - Atlantic
19. YOU'RE STILL MY BABY - Chuck Willis - Okeh
20. GOODNIGHT, SWEETHEART, GOODNIGHT - Spaniels - Vee Jay

TOP 20 RHYTHM & BLUES SINGLES OF 1955

POS. TITLE - ARTIST - LABEL
1. PLEDGING MY LOVE - Johnny Ace - Duke
2. AIN'T THAT A SHAME - Fats Domino - Imperial
3. MAYBELLENE - Chuck Berry - Chess
4. EARTH ANGEL - Penguins - Dootone
5. I'VE GOT A WOMAN - Ray Charles - Atlantic
6. WALLFLOWER - Etta James - Modern

Chuck Berry

Chuck was in the Top 20 R&B lists as early as1955, but it took until 1972 before he was in the overall Top 10 (with ``My Ding-A-Ling'').

Ray Charles

Ray's signature song—``Georgia On My Mind''—was Top 20 R&B in 1960. He's also had eight other Top 20 R&B hits.

7. ONLY YOU - Platters - Mercury
8. MY BABE - Little Walter - Chess
9. SINCERELY - Moonglows - Chess
10. UNCHAINED MELODY - Roy Hamilton - Epic
11. HEARTS OF STONE - Charms - DeLuxe
12. TWEEDLE DEE - LaVern Baker - Atlantic
13. EVERYDAY - Count Basie - Clef
14. IT'S LOVE, BABY - Larry Brooks - Excello
15. FLIP, FLOP AND FLY - Joe Turner - Atlantic
16. DON'T BE ANGRY - Nappy Brown - Savoy
17. BO DIDDLEY - Bo Diddley - Checker
18. WHAT'CHA GONNA DO? - Drifters - Atlantic
19. UNCHAINED MELODY - Al Hibbler - Decca
20. STORY UNTOLD - Nutmegs - Herald

TOP 20 RHYTHM & BLUES SINGLES OF 1956

POS. TITLE - ARTIST - LABEL
1. HONKY TONK - Bill Doggett - King
2. I'M IN LOVE AGAIN - Fats Domino - Imperial
3. LONG TALL SALLY - Little Richard - Specialty
4. FEVER - Little Willie John - King
5. GREAT PRETENDER - Platters - Mercury
6. WHY DO FOOLS FALL IN LOVE - Teen Agers - Gee
7. I WANT YOU TO BE MY GIRL - Teen Agers - Gee
8. MY PRAYER - Platters - Mercury
9. BLUE SUEDE SHOES - Carl Perkins - Sun
10. LET THE GOOD TIMES ROLL - Shirley & Lee - Aladdin
11. RIP IT UP - Little Richard - Specialty
12. TUTTI FRUITTI - Little Richard - Specialty
13. DROWN IN MY OWN TEARS - Ray Charles - Atlantic
14. DON'T BE CRUEL - Elvis Presley - Victor
15. TREASURE OF LOVE - Clyde McPhatter - Atlantic
16. EDDIE MY LOVE - Teen Queens - RPM
17. PLEASE PLEASE PLEASE - James Brown - Federal
18. SPEEDOO - Cadillacs - Josie
19. HEARTBREAK HOTEL - Elvis Presley - Victor
20. IT'S TOO LATE - Chuck Willis - Atlantic

TOP 20 RHYTHM & BLUES SINGLES OF 1957

POS. TITLE - ARTIST - LABEL
1. JAILHOUSE ROCK / TREAT ME NICE - Elvis Presley - RCA Victor
2. SEARCHIN' / YOUNG BLOOD - Coasters - Atco
3. YOU SEND ME - Sam Cooke - Keen
4. WAKE UP LITTLE SUSIE - Everly Brothers - Cadence
5. ALL SHOOK UP - Elvis Presley - RCA Victor
6. BLUE MONDAY - Fats Domino - Imperial
7. HONEYCOMB - Jimmie Rodgers - Roulette
8. DIANA - Paul Anka - ABC-Paramount
9. SILHOUETTES - Rays - Caneo
10. COME GO WITH ME - Del Vikings - Dot
11. I'M WALKIN' - Fats Domino - Imperial
12. LOVE IS STRANGE - Mickey & Sylvia - Vik
13. SEND FOR ME - Nat "King" Cole - Capitol
14. SHORT FAT FANNIE - Larry Williams - Specialty
15. SCHOOL DAY - Chuck Berry - Chess
16. LITTLE DARLIN' - Diamonds - Mercury
17. THAT'LL BE THE DAY - Crickets - Brunswick
18. LUCILLE - Little Richard - Specialty
19.* WHOLE LOTTA SHAKIN' GOIN' ON - Jerry Lee Lewis - Sun
     BLUEBERRY HILL - Fats Domino - Imperial (*Tie)

TOP 20 RHYTHM & BLUES SINGLES OF 1958

POS. TITLE - ARTIST - LABEL
1. WHAT AM I LOVING FOR / HANG UP MY ROCK & ROLL SHOES - Chuck Willis - Atlantic
2. ROCK-IN' ROBIN - Bobby Day - Class
3. DON'T / I BEG OF YOU - Elvis Presley - RCA Victor
4. LOOKING BACK / DO I LIKE IT - Nat "King" Cole - Capitol
5. ALL I HAVE TO DO IS DREAM - Everly Brothers - Cadence
6. IT'S ALL IN THE GAME - Tommy Edwards - MGM
7. JUST A DREAM - Jimmy Clanton - Ace
8. YAKETY YAK - Coasters - Atco
9. WITCH DOCTOR - David Seville - Liberty
10. LITTLE STAR - Elegants - Apt
11. TEQUILA - Champs - Challenge
12.* WIN YOUR LOVE FOR ME - Sam Cooke - Keen
     BIRD DOG / DEVOTED TO YOU - Everly Brothers - Cadence (*Tie)
13. TWILIGHT TIME - Platters - Mercury
14. MY TRUE LOVE / LEROY - Jack Scott - Carlton
15. AT THE HOP - Danny & The Juniors - ABC-Paramount
16. GET A JOB - Silhouettes - Ember
17. POOR LITTLE FOOL - Ricky Nelson - Imperial
18. TEARS ON MY PILLOW - Little Anthony & The Imperials - End
19. PATRICIA - Prez Prado - RCA Victor

TOP 20 RHYTHM & BLUES SINGLES OF 1959

POS. TITLE - ARTIST - LABEL
1. STAGGER LEE - Lloyd Price - ABC-Paramount
2. IT'S JUST A MATTER OF TIME - Brook Benton - Mercury
3. KANSAS CITY - Wilbert Harrison - Fury
4. LONELY TEARDROPS - Jackie Wilson - Brunswick
5. PERSONALITY - Lloyd Price - ABC-Paramount
6. I CRIED A TEAR - LaVern Baker - Atlantic
7. TRY ME (I NEED YOU) - James Brown & The Famous Flames - Federal
8. THERE GOES MY BABY - Drifters - Atlantic
9. WHAT'D I SAY - Ray Charles - Atlantic
10. THANK YOU PRETTY BABY - Brook Benton - Mercury
11. THERE IS SOMETHING ON YOUR MIND - Big Jay McNeely - Swingin'
12. YOU'RE SO FINE - Falcons - Unart
13. I LOVES YOU PORGY - Nina Simone - Bethlehem
14. SO FINE - Fiestas - Old Town
15. (NIGHT TIME IS) THE RIGHT TIME - Ray Charles - Atlantic
16. I'M GONNA GET MARRIED - Lloyd Price - ABC-Paramount
17. CHARLIE BROWN - Coasters - Atco
18. SMOKE GETS IN YOUR EYES - Platters - Mercury
19. POISON IVY - Coasters - Atco
20. 16 CANDLES - Crests - Coed

TOP 20 RHYTHM & BLUES SINGLES OF 1960

POS. TITLE - ARTIST - LABEL
1. KIDDIO - Brook Benton - Mercury
2. BABY - Brook Benton & Dinah Washington - Mercury
3. FOOL IN LOVE - Ike & Tina Turner - Sue
4. THE TWIST - Chubby Checker - Parkway
5. CHAIN GANG - Sam Cooke - RCA Victor
6. MONEY - Barrett Strong - Anna
7. LET'S GO, LET'S GO, LET'S GO - Hank Ballard & The Midnighters - King
8. FINGER POPPIN' TIME - Hank Ballard & The Midnighters - King

LaVern Baker
Miss Baker's Top 20 R&B charters were in 1955 and 1959.

9. A WOMAN, A LOVER, A FRIEND - Jackie Wilson - Brunswick
10. SAVE THE LAST DANCE FOR ME - Drifters - Atlantic
11. DOGGIN' AROUND - Jackie Wilson - Brunswick
12. GEORGIA ON MY MIND - Ray Charles - ABC-Paramount
13. THIS BITTER EARTH - Dinah Washington - Mercury
14. FANNIE MAE - Buster Brown - Fire
15. HE WILL BREAK YOUR HEART - Jerry Butler - Vee Jay
16. A ROCKIN' GOOD WAY - Dinah Washington - Mercury
17. MY DEAREST DARLING - Etta James - Argo
18. WHITE SILVER SANDS - Bill Black's Combo - Hi
19. THERE'S SOMETHING ON YOUR MIND - Bobby Marchan - Fire
20. ALL I COULD DO WAS CRY - Etta James - Argo

TOP 20 RHYTHM & BLUES SINGLES OF 1961

POS. TITLE - ARTIST - LABEL
1. TOSSIN' AND TURNIN' - Bobby Lewis - Beltone
2. IT'S GONNA WORK OUT FINE - Ike & Tina Turner - Sue
3. DON'T CRY NO MORE - Bobby Bland - Duke
4. HIDEAWAY - Freddy King - Federal
5. SHOP AROUND - Miracles - Tamla
6. MY TRUE STORY - Jive Five - Beltone
7. I LIKE IT LIKE THAT - Chris Kenner - Instant
8. STAND BY ME - Ben E. King - Atco
9. MOTHER-IN-LAW - Ernie K-Doe - Minit
10. ALL IN MY MIND - Maxine Brown - Nomar
11. I PITY THE FOOL - Bobby Bland - Duke
12. EVERY BEAT OF MY HEART - Pips - Vee Jay
13. BABY, YOU'RE RIGHT - James Brown - King
14. LAST NIGHT - Mar-Keys - Satellite
15. FOR MY BABY - Brook Benton - Mercury
16. BOLL WEEVIL SONG - Brook Benton - Mercury
17. HIT THE ROAD JACK - Ray Charles - ABC-Paramount
18. I DON'T MIND - James Brown - King
19. YA-YA - Lee Dorsey - Fury
20. (WILL YOU LOVE ME) TOMORROW - Shirelles - Scepter

TOP 20 RHYTHM & BLUES SINGLES OF 1962

POS. TITLE - ARTIST - LABEL
1. SOUL TWIST - King Curtis - Enjoy
2. I CAN'T STOP LOVING YOU - Ray Charles - ABC-Paramount
3. TWIST AND SHOUT - Isley Brothers - Wand
4. BRING IT ON HOME TO ME - Sam Cooke - RCA Victor
5. LOST SOMEONE - James Brown & The Famous Flames - King
6. MASHED POTATO TIME - Dee Dee Sharp - Cameo
7. ANY DAY NOW - Chuck Jackson - Wand
8. SNAP YOUR FINGERS - Joe Henderson - Todd
9. PARTY LIGHTS - Claudine Clark - Chancellor
10. YOU'LL LOSE A GOOD THING - Barbara Lynn - Jamie
11. THE DUKE OF EARL - Gene (Duke of Earl) Chandler - Vee Jay
12. TWISTIN' THE NIGHT AWAY - Sam Cooke - RCA Victor
13. SOMETHING'S GOT A HOLD ON ME - Etta James - Argo
14. I KNOW - Barbara George - AFO
15. Soldier Boy - Shirelles - Scepter
16. I NEED YOUR LOVIN' - Don Gardner & Dee Dee Ford - Fire
17. NIGHT TRAIN - James Brown & The Famous Flames - King
18. THE ONE WHO REALLY LOVES YOU - Mary Wells - Motown
19. THE TWIST - Chubby Checker - Parkway
20. DON'T PLAY THAT SONG - Ben E. King - Atco

TOP 20 RHYTHM & BLUES SINGLES OF 1963

POS. TITLE - ARTIST - LABEL
1. PART TIME LOVE - Little Johnny Taylor - Galaxy
2. MOCKINGBIRD - Inez Foxx - Symbol
3. BABY WORKOUT - Jackie Wilson - Brunswick
4. FINGERTIPS (PART II) - Little Stevie Wonder - Motown
5. HEAT WAVE - Martha & The Vandellas - Gordy
6. PRIDE AND JOY - Marvin Gaye - Tamla
7. THE LOVE OF MY MAN - Theola Gilgore - Serock
8. CRY BABY - Garnett Mimms & The Enchanters - United Artists
9. YOU'VE REALLY GOT A HOLD ON ME - Miracles - Tamla
10. HELLO STRANGER - Barbara Lewis - Atlantic
11. JUST ONE LOOK - Doris Troy - Atlantic
12. THE MONKEY TIME - Major Lance - Okeh
13. THAT'S THE WAY LOVE IS - Bobby Bland - Duke
14. OUR DAY WILL COME - Ruby & The Romantics - Kapp
15. HE'S SO FINE - Chiffons - Laurie
16. IF YOU WANNA BE HAPPY - Jimmy Soul - S.P.Q.R.
17. TWO LOVERS - Mary Wells - Motown
18. EASIER SAID THAN DONE - Essex - Roulette
19. MICKEY'S MONKEY - Miracles - Tamla
20. HEY PAULA - Paul & Paula - Philips

TOP 20 RHYTHM & BLUES SINGLES OF 1964

POS. TITLE - ARTIST - LABEL
1. BABY LOVE - Supremes - Motown
2. CHAPEL OF LOVE - Dixie Cups- Red Bird
3. MY GUY - Mary Wells - Motown
4. WHERE DID OUR LOVE GO - Supremes - Motown

481

James Brown
A man with 14 Top 20 R&B hits, and 95 charted singles in all.

5. COME SEE ABOUT ME - Supremes - Motown
6. DANCING IN THE STREET - Martha & The Vandellas - Gordy
7. LET IT BE ME - Betty Everette & Jerry Butler - Vee Jay
8. C'MON AND SWIM - Bobby Freeman - Josie
9. UM UM UM UM UM - Major Lance - Okeh
10. SHOOP SHOOP SONG - Betty Everette - Vee Jay
11. GOIN OUT OF MY HEAD - Little Anthony & The Imperials - DCP
12. THE JERK - Larks - Money
13. AMEN - Impressions - ABC
14. WHAT KIND OF FOOL - Tams - ABC
15. THE WAY YOU DO THE THINGS YOU DO - Temptations - Gordy
16. BABY I NEED YOUR LOVING - Four Tops - Motown
17. KEEP ON PUSHING - Impressions - ABC
18. GOOD NEWS - Sam Cooke - RCA
19. NITTY GRITTY - Shirley Ellis - Congress
20. QUICKSAND - Martha & The Vandellas - Gordy *
    *Carry over from 1963.

Editor's Note: There were no r&b charts published by *Billboard* in 1964. This computer-generated list was prepared especially for this book.

TOP 20 RHYTHM & BLUES SINGLES OF 1965

POS. TITLE - ARTIST - LABEL
1. I CAN'T HELP MYSELF - Four Tops - Motown

2. IN THE MIDNIGHT HOUR - Wilson Pickett - Atlantic
3. SHOTGUN - Jr. Walker & The All Stars - Soul
4. I DO LOVE YOU - Billy Stewart - Chess

5. YES, I'M READY - Barbara Mason - Arctic
6. PAPA'S GOT A BRAND NEW BAG - James Brown - King
7. THE TRACK OF MY TEARS - Miracles - Tamla
8. WE'RE GONNA MAKE IT - Little Milton - Checker
9. TONIGHT'S THE NIGHT - Solomon Burke - Atlantic
10. I'LL BE DOGGONE - Marvin Gaye - Tamla
11. NOTHING CAN STOP ME - Gene Chandler - Constellation
12. DON'T MESS UP A GOOD THING - Fontella Bass & Bobby McClure - Checker
13. MY GIRL - Temptations - Gordy
14. STOP IN THE NAME OF LOVE - Supremes - Motown
15. OO WEE BABY I LOVE YOU - Fred Hughes - Vee Jay
16. NOWHERE TO RUN - Martha & The Vandellas - Gordy
17. SINCE I LOST MY BABY - Temptations - Gordy
18. IT'S A MAN DOWN THERE - G.L. Crockett - Brothers
19. OOO BABY BABY - Miracles - Tamla
20. BABY I'M YOURS - Barbara Lewis - Atlantic

TOP 20 RHYTHM & BLUES SINGLES OF 1966

POS. TITLE - ARTIST - LABEL
1. HOLD ON! I'M COMIN' - Sam & Dave - Stax
2. COOL JERK - Capitols - Karen
3. BABY SCRATCH MY BACK - Slim Harpo - Excello
4. AIN'T TOO PROUD TO BEG - Temptations - Gordy
5. BAREFOOTIN' - Robert Parker - Nola
6. 634-5789 - Wilson Pickett - Atlantic
7. UP TIGHT - Stevie Wonder - Tamla
8. WHEN A WOMAN LOVES A MAN - Percy Sledge - Atlantic
9. WHAT BECOMES OF THE BROKENHEARTED - Jimmy Ruffin - Soul
10. BEAUTY IS ONLY SKIN DEEP - Temptations - Gordy
11. LOVE MAKES THE WORLD GO ROUND - Deon Jackson - Carla
12. KNOCK ON WOOD - Eddie Floyd - Stax
13. LOVE IS A HURTIN' THING - Lou Rawls - Capitol
14. OPEN THE DOOR TO YOUR HEART - Darrell Banks - Revilot
15. DON'T MESS WITH BILL - Marvelettes - Tamla
16. I LOVE YOU 1000 TIMES - Platters - Mercury
17. SUNNY - Bobby Hebb - Philips
18. WADE IN THE WATER - Ramsey Lewis - Cadet
19. (I'M A) ROAD RUNNER - Jr. Walker & The All Stars - Soul
20. GOING TO A GO-GO - Miracles - Tamla

TOP 20 RHYTHM & BLUES SINGLES OF 1967

POS. TITLE - ARTIST - LABEL
1. RESPECT - Aretha Franklin - Atlantic
2. SOUL MAN - Sam & Dave - Stax
3. I NEVER LOVED A MAN THE WAY I LOVE YOU - Aretha Franklin - Atlantic
4. MAKE ME YOURS - Bettye Swann - Money
5. I WAS MADE TO LOVE HER - Stevie Wonder - Tamla
6. COLD SWEAT - James Brown & The Famous Flames - King
7. ARE YOU LONELY FOR ME - Freddie Scott - Shout
8. TELL ME LIKE IT IS - Aaron Neville - Parlo
9. SWEET SOUL MUSIC - Arthur Conley - Atco
10. (YOUR LOVE KEEPS LIFTING ME) HIGHER AND HIGHER - Jackie Wilson - Brunswick
11. MERCY, MERCY, MERCY - Cannonball Adderley - Capitol
12. BABY I LOVE YOU - Aretha Franklin - Atlantic
13. JIMMY MACK - Martha & The Vandellas - Gordy
14. SOUL FINGER - Bar-Kays - Volt
15. GET ON UP - Esquires - Bunky
16. THE HUNTER GETS CAPTURED BY THE GAME - Marvelettes - Tamla

17. LOVE IS HERE AND NOW YOU'RE GONE - Diana Ross & The Supremes - Motown
18. STAND BY ME - Spyder Turner - MGM
19. HIP-HUG-HER - Booker T & The M.G.'s - Stax
20. EXPRESSWAY TO YOUR HEART - Soul Survivors - Crimson

TOP 20 RHYTHM & BLUES SINGLES OF 1968

POS. TITLE - ARTIST - LABEL
1. SAY IT LOUD—I'M BLACK AND I'M PROUD - James Brown - King
2. SLIP AWAY - Clarence Carter - Atlantic
3. (SITTIN' ON THE) DOCK OF THE BAY - Otis Redding - Volt
4. GRAZING IN THE GRASS - Hugh Masekela - Uni
5. YOU'RE ALL I NEED TO GET BY - Marvin Gaye & Tammi Terrell - Tamla
6. STAY IN MY CORNER - Dells - Cadet
7. WE'RE A WINNER - Impressions - ABC
8. I WISH IT WOULD RAIN - Temptations - Gordy
9. TIGHTEN UP - Archie Bell & The Drells - Atlantic
10. LOVER'S HOLIDAY - Peggy Scott & JoJo Benson - SSS International
11. (SWEET SWEET BABY) SINCE YOU'VE BEEN GONE - Aretha Franklin - Atlantic
12. THINK - Aretha Franklin - Atlantic
13. CHAIN OF FOOLS - Aretha Franklin - Atlantic
14. COWBOYS TO GIRLS - Intruders - Gamble
15. DANCE TO THE MUSIC - Sly & The Family Stone - Epic
16. NEVER GIVE YOU UP - Jerry Butler - Mercury
17. THE HORSE - Cliff Nobles & Co. - Phil L.A. of Soul
18. GIRL WATCHER - O'Kaysions - ABC
19. LOVE MAKES A WOMAN - Barbara Acklin - Brunswick
20. LA LA MEANS I LOVE YOU - Delfonics - Philly Groove

TOP 20 RHYTHM & BLUES SINGLES OF 1969

POS. TITLE - ARTIST - LABEL
1. WHAT DOES IT TAKE TO WIN YOUR LOVE - Jr. Walker & The All Stars - Soul
2. I CAN'T GET NEXT TO YOU - Temptations - Gordy
3. MOTHER POPCORN, PART I - James Brown - KIng
4. TOO BUSY THINKING ABOUT MY BABY - Marvin Gaye - Tamla
5. IT'S YOUR THING - Isley Brothers - T-Neck
6. ONLY THE STRONG SURVIVE - Jerry Butler - Mercury
7. CHOKIN' KIND - Joe Simon - Sound Stage 7
8. HOT FUN IN THE SUMMERTIME - Sly & The Family Stone - Epic
9. JEALOUS KIND OF FELLOW - Garland Green - Uni
10. GRAZING IN THE GRASS - Friends of Distinction - RCA
11. SHARE YOUR LOVE WITH ME - Aretha Franklin - Atlantic
12. RUNAWAY CHILD, RUNNING WILD - Temptations - Gordy
13. CHOICE OF COLORS - Impressions - Custom
14. THAT'S THE WAY LOVE IS - Marvin Gaye - Tamla
15. YOUR GOOD THING (IS ABOUT TO END) - Lou Rawls - Capitol
16. OH, WHAT A NIGHT - Dells - Cadet
17. CAN I CHANGE MY MIND - Tyrone Davis - Dakar
18. EVERYDAY PEOPLE - Sly & The Family Stone - Epic
19. BABY, I'M FOR REAL - Originals - Soul
20. COLOR HIM FATHER - Winstons - Metromedia

TOP 20 RHYTHM & BLUES SINGLES OF 1970

POS. TITLE - ARTIST - LABEL
1. I'LL BE THERE - Jackson 5 - Motown
2. LOVE ON A TWO WAY STREET - Moments - Stang
3. SIGNED, SEALED, DELIVERED (I'M YOURS) - Stevie Wonder - Motown
4. THE LOVE YOU SAVE - Jackson 5 - Motown
5. THANK YOU (FALLETIN ME BE MICE ELF AGIN) - Sly & The Family Stone - Epic
6. RAINY DAY IN GEORGIA - Brook Benton - Cotillion
7. BALL OF CONFUSON (THAT'S THE WAY THE WORLD IS TODAY) - Temptations - Gordy
8. TURN BACK THE HANDS OF TIME - Tyrone Davis - Dakar
9. COLE, COOKE & REDDING / SUGAR, SUGAR - Wilson Pickett - Atlantic
10. EXPRESS YOURSELF - Charles Wright & The Watts 103rd Street Rhythm Band - Warner Bros.
11. STEAL AWAY - Johnnie Taylor - Stax
12. PSYCHEDELIC SHACK - Temptations - Gordy
13. IT'S A SHAME - Spinners - V.I.P.
14. CALL ME - Aretha Franklin - Atlantic
15. PATCHES - Clarence Carter - Atlantic
16. DIDN'T I (BLOW YOUR MIND THIS TIME) - Delfonics - Philly Groove
17. GROOVY SITUATION - Gene Chandler - Mercury
18. ABC - Jackson 5 - Motown
19. I WANT YOU BACK - Jackson 5 - Motown
20. DON'T PLAY THAT SONG - Aretha Franklin - Atlantic

TOP 20 RHYTHM & BLUES SINGLES OF 1971

POS. TITLE - ARTIST - LABEL
1. MR. BIG STUFF - Jean Knight - Stax
2. WHAT'S GOING ON - Marvin Gaye - Tamla
3. WANT ADS - Honey Cone - Hot Wax
4. TIRED OF BEING ALONE - Al Green - Hi
5. SPANISH HARLEM - Aretha Franklin - Atlantic
6. JUST MY IMAGINATION (RUNNING AWAY WITH ME) - Temptations - Gordy
7. BRIDGE OVER TROUBLED WATER - Aretha Franklin - Atlantic
8. THIN LINE BETWEEN LOVE AND HATE - Persuaders - Atco
9. NEVER CAN SAY GOODBYE - Jackson 5 - Motown
10. MAKE IT FUNKY, PART 1 - James Brown - Polydor
11. GROOVE ME - King Floyd - Chimneyville
12. TRAPPED BY A THING CALLED LOVE - Denise LaSalle - Westbound
13. DON'T KNOCK MY LOVE - Wilson Pickett - Atlantic
14. STICK-UP - Honey Cone - Hot Wax
15. (DO THE) PUSH & PULL, PART 1 - Rufus Thomas - Stax
16. MERCY MERCY ME (THE ECOLOGY) - Marvin Gaye - Tamla
17. SMILING FACES SOMETIMES - Undisputed Truth - Gordy
18. SHE'S NOT JUST ANOTHER WOMAN - 8th Day - Invictus
19. WATCHA SEE IS WATCHA GET - Dramatics - Volt
20. THE LOVE WE HAD (STAYS IN MIND) - Dells - Cadet

TOP 20 RHYTHM & BLUES SINGLES OF 1972

POS. TITLE - ARTIST - LABEL
1. LET'S STAY TOGETHER - Al Green - Hi
2. I'LL TAKE YOU THERE - Staple Singers - Stax
3. IF LOVING YOU IS WRONG, I DON'T WANT TO BE RIGHT - Luther Ingram - Koko

4. IN THE RAIN - Dramatics - Volt
5. OH GIRL - Chi-Lites - Brunswick
6. BACK STABBERS - O'Jay's - Philadelphia International
7. THAT'S THE WAY I FEEL ABOUT 'CHA - Bobby Womack - United Artists
8. EVERYBODY PLAYS THE FOOL - Main Ingredient - RCA
9. DO THE FUNKY PENGUIN - Rufus Thomas - Stax
10. I GOTCHA - Joe Tex - Dial
11. YOU SAID A BAD WORD - Joe Tex - Dial
12. CLEAN UP WOMAN - Betty Wright - Alston
13. LEAN ON ME - Bill Withers - Sussex
14. OUTA-SPACE - Billy Preston - A&M
15. GOODFOOT PART I - James Brown - Polydor
16. WOMAN'S GOTTA HAVE IT - Bobby Womack - United Artists
17. DAY DREAMING - Aretha Franklin - Atlantic
18. POWER OF LOVE - Joe Simon - Spring
19. LOOK WHAT YOU DONE FOR ME - Al Green - Hi
20. FREDDIE'S DEAD - Curtis Mayfield - Custom

TOP 20 RHYTHM & BLUES SINGLES OF 1973

POS. TITLE - ARTIST - LABEL
1. LET'S GET IT ON - Marvin Gaye - Tamla
2. SUPERSTITION - Stevie Wonder - Tamla
3. NEITHER ONE OF US (WANTS TO BE THE FIRST TO SAY GOODBYE) - Gladys Knight & The Pips - Soul
4. ME AND MRS. JONES - Billy Paul - Philadelphia International
5. WHY CAN'T WE LIVE TOGETHER - Timmy Thomas - Glades
6. ONE OF A KIND (LOVE AFFAIR) - Spinners - Atlantic
7. LOVE TRAIN - O'Jay's - Philadelphia International
8. DOING IT TO DEATH - Fred Wesley & The JB's - People
9. MIDNIGHT TRAIN TO GEORGIA - Gladys Knight & The Pips - Buddah
10. LOVES JONES - Brighter Side of Darkness - 20th Century
11. I'M GONNA LOVE YOU JUST A LITTLE MORE - Barry White - 20th Century
12. COULD IT BE I'M FALLING IN LOVE - Spinners - Atlantic
13. MASTERPIECE - Temptations - Gordy
14. NATURAL HIGH - Bloodstone - London
15. PILLOW TALK - Sylvia - Vibration
16. THAT LADY - Isley Brothers - T-Neck
17. GIVE YOUR BABY A STANDING OVATION - Dells - Cadet
18. KEEP ON TRUCKIN' - Eddie Kendricks - Tamla
19. IF YOU WANT ME TO STAY - Sly & The Family Stone - Epic
20. THE WORLD IS A GHETTO - War - United Artists

TOP 20 RHYTHM & BLUES SINGLES OF 1974

POS. TITLE - ARTIST - LABEL
1. FEEL LIKE MAKING LOVE - Roberta Flack - Atlantic
2. BOOGIE DOWN - Eddie Kendricks - Tamla
3. JUNGLE BOOGIE - Kool and the Gang - De-Lite
4. BEST THING THAT EVER HAPPENED TO ME - Gladys Knight & The Pips
5. LOOKIN' FOR LOVE - Bobby Womack - United Artists
6. ROCK YOUR BABY - George McCrae - TK
7. THE PAYBACK - James Brown - Polydor
8. MIGHTY LOVE, PART 1 - Spinners - Atlantic
9. DANCING MACHINE - Jackson 5 - Motown
10. SEXY MAMA - Moments - Stang
11. PUT YOUR HANDS TOGETHER - O'Jay's - Philadelphia International
12. ROCK THE BOAT - Hues Corporation - RCA
13. TSOP - MFSB - Philadelphia International

14. I'M IN LOVE - Aretha Franklin - Atlantic
15. CAN'T GET ENOUGH OF YOUR LOVE, BABE - Barry White - 20th Century
16. TRYING TO HOLD ON TO MY WOMAN - Lamont Dozier - ABC
17. OUTSIDE WOMAN - Bloodstone - London
18. BE THANKFUL FOR WHAT YOU GOT - William DeVaughn - Roxbury
19. TELL ME SOMETHING GOOD - Rufus featuring Chaka Khan - ABC
20. LIVIN' FOR YOU - Al Green - Hi

TOP 20 RHYTHM & BLUES SINGLES OF 1975

POS. TITLE - ARTIST - LABEL
1. FIGHT THE POWER, PT. 1 - Isley Brothers - T-Neck
2. FIRE - Ohio Players - Mercury
3. GET DOWN TONIGHT - K.C. & The Sunshine Band - TK
4. LOVE WON'T LET ME WAIT - Major Harris - Atlantic
5. I BELONG TO YOU - Love Unlimited - 20th Century
6. LOOK AT ME (I'M IN LOVE) - Moments - Stang
7. THE HUSTLE - Van McCoy & The Soul City Symphony - Avco
8. ROCKIN' CHAIR - Gwen McCrae - Cat
9. PICK UP THE PIECES - Average White Band - Atlantic
10. SHINING STAR - Earth, Wind & Fire - Columbia
11. YOUR LOVE - Graham Central Station - Warner Bros.
12. GET DOWN, GET DOWN (GET ON THE FLOOR) - Joe Simon - Spring
13. BABY THAT'S BACKATCHA - Smokey Robinson - Tamla
14. L-O-V-E (LOVE) - Al Green - Hi
15. THIS WILL BE - Natalie Cole - Capitol
16. GIVE THE PEOPLE WHAT THEY WANT - O'Jay's - Philadelphia International
17. BOOGIE ON REGGAE WOMAN - Stevie Wonder - Tamla
18. I FEEL A SONG IN MY HEART - Gladys Knight & The Pips - Buddah
19. YOU'RE THE FIRST, THE LAST, MY EVERYTHING - Barry White - 20th Century
20. SOONER OR LATER - Impressions - Custom

TOP 20 RHYTHM & BLUES SINGLES OF 1976

POS. TITLE - ARTIST - LABEL
1. DISCO LADY - Johnnie Taylor - Columbia
2. SOMETHING HE CAN FEEL - Aretha Franklin - Atlantic
3. KISS AND SAY GOODBYE - Manhattans - Columbia
4. (SHAKE, SHAKE, SHAKE) SHAKE YOUR BOOTY - K.C. & The Sunshine Band - TK
5. YOU'LL NEVER FIND ANOTHER LOVE LIKE MINE - Lou Rawls - Philadelphia International
6. GETAWAY - Earth, Wind & Fire - Columbia
7. MISTY BLUE - Dorothy Moore - Malaco
8. SING A SONG - Earth, Wind & Fire - Columbia
9. SWEET THING - Rufus featuring Chaka Khan - ABC
10. BOOGIE FEVER - Sylvers - Capitol
11. WAKE UP EVERYBODY (PT. 1) - Harold Melvin & The Bluenotes - Philadelphia International
12. PLAY THAT FUNKY MUSIC - Wild Cherry - Epic/Sweet City
13. YOUNG HEARTS RUN FREE - Candi Staton - Warner Bros.
14. TURNING POINT - Tyrone Davis - Dakar
15. SOPHISTICATED LADY (SHE'S A DIFFERENT LADY) - Natalie Cole - Capitol
16. HEAVEN MUST BE MISSING AN ANGEL (PT. 1) - Tavares - Capitol
17. WHO'D SHE COO - Ohio Players - Mercury

18. I LOVE MUSIC (PT. 1) - O'Jay's - Philadelphia International
19. GET UP OFFA THAT THING - James Brown - Polydor
20. LIVIN' FOR THE WEEKEND/STAIRWAY TO HEAVEN - O'Jay's - Philadelphia International

TOP 20 RHYTHM & BLUES SINGLES OF 1977

POS. TITLE - ARTIST - LABEL
1. FLOAT ON - Floaters - ABC
2. I'VE GOT LOVE ON MY MIND - Natalie Cole - Capitol
3. GOT TO GIVE IT UP - Marvin Gaye - Tamla
4. I WISH - Stevie Wonder - Tamla
5. BEST OF MY LOVE - Emotions - Columbia
6. DAZZ - Brick - Bang
7. TRYING TO LOVE TWO - William Bell - Mercury
8. IT'S ECSTASY WHEN YOU LAY DOWN NEXT TO ME - Barry White - 20th Century
9. STRAWBERRY LETTER 23 - Brothers Johnson - A&M
10. SLIDE - Slave - Cotillion
11. GOOD THING MAN - Frank Lucas - ICA
12. DON'T LEAVE ME THIS WAY - Thelma Houston - Tamla
13. CAR WASH - Rose Royce - MCA
14. EASY - Commodores - Motown
15. SUNSHINE - Enchantment - Roadshow
16. FREE - Deniece Williams - Columbia
17. AIN'T GONNA BUMP NO MORE (WITH NO BIG FAT WOMAN) - Joe Tex - Epic
18. GLORIA - Enchantment - Roadshow
19. I BELIEVE YOU - Dorothy Moore - United Artists
20. SOMETIMES - Facts of Life - Kayvette

TOP 20 RHYTHM & BLUES SINGLES OF 1978

POS. TITLE - ARTIST - LABEL
1. SERPENTINE FIRE - Earth, Wind & Fire - Columbia
2. USE TA BE MY GIRL - O'Jay's - P.I.R.
3. TOO MUCH, TOO LITTLE, TOO LATE - Johnny Mathis & Deniece Williams - Columbia
4. FLASHLIGHT - Parliament - Casablanca
5. ONE NATION UNDER GROOVE - Funkadelic - Warner Bros.
6. OUR LOVE - Natalie Cole - Capitol
7. BOOGIE OOGIE OOGIE - A Taste of Honey - Capitol
8. YOU AND I - Rick James - Gordy
9. CLOSE THE DOOR - Teddy Pendergrass - P.I.R.
10. FFUN - Con Funk Shun - Mercury
11. THE CLOSER I GET TO YOU - Roberta Flack with Donny Hathaway
12. GET OFF - Foxy - Dash
13. TAKE ME TO THE NEXT PHASE - Isley Brothers - T-Neck
14. WHICH WAY IS UP - Stargard - MCA
15. THREE TIMES A LADY - Commodores - Motown
16. STUFF LIKE THAT - Quincy Jones - A&M
17. BOOTZILLA - Bootsy's Rubber Band - Warner Bros.
18. IT'S YOU THAT I NEED - Enchantment - United Artists
19. DANCE WITH ME - Peter Brown - Drive
20. HOLDING ON - L.T.D. - A&M

TOP 20 RHYTHM & BLUES SINGLES OF 1979

POS. TITLE - ARTIST - LABEL
1. GOOD TIMES - Chic - Atlantic
2. RING MY BELL - Anita Ward - Juana
3. DON'T STOP TIL YOU GET ENOUGH - Michael Jackson - Epic
4. BUSTIN' LOOSE - Chuck Brown & The Soul Searchers - Source

5. LE FREAK - Chic - Atlantic
6. AQUA BOOGIE - Parliament - Casablanca
7. REUNITED - Peaches & Herb - Polydor
8. I GOT MY MIND MADE UP - Instant Funk - Salsoul
9. I'M EVERY WOMAN - Chaka Khan - Warner Bros.
10. DISCO NIGHTS - G.Q. - Arista
11. ONE NATION UNDER GROOVE - Funkadelic - Warner Bros.
12. SHAKE YOUR BODY - The Jacksons - Epic
13. AIN'T NO STOPPIN' US NOW - McFadden & Whitehead - P.I.R.
14. TURN OFF THE LIGHTS - Teddy Pendergrass - P.I.R.
15. GOT TO BE REAL - Cheryl Lynn - Columbia
16. BAD GIRLS - Donna Summer - Casablanca
17. WHAT CHA GONNA DO WITH MY LOVIN' - Stephanie Mills - 20th Century
18. WHY LEAVE US ALONE - Five Special - Elektra
19. DO YOU WANNA GO PARTY - K.C. & The Sunshine Band - TK
20. YOU'RE GONNA MAKE ME LOVE SOMEBODY ELSE - The Jones Girls - P.I.R.

TOP 20 RHYTHM & BLUES SINGLES OF 1980

POS. TITLE - ARTIST - LABEL
1. LET'S GET SERIOUS - Jermaine Jackson - Motown
2. ROCK WITH YOU - Michael Jackson - Epic
3. TAKE YOUR TIME - The S.O.S. Band - Tabu
4. THE SECOND TIME AROUND - Shalamar - Solar
5. AND THE BEAT GOES ON - The Whispers - Solar
6. ONE IN A MILLION YOU - Larry Graham - Warner Bros.
7. DO YOU LOVE WHAT YOU FEEL - Rufus/Chaka Khan - MCA
8. DON'T SAY GOODNIGHT - Isley Brothers - T-Neck
9. I WANNA BE YOUR LOVER - Prince - Warner Bros.
10. LADIES NIGHT - Kool & The Gang - De-Lite
11. CRUISIN' - Smokey Robinson - Tamla
12. SPECIAL LADY - Ray, Goodman & Brown - Polydor
13. STOMP - The Brothers Johnson - A&M
14. SHINING STAR - Manhattans - Columbia
15. FUNKYTOWN - Lipps Inc. - Casablanca
16. KNEE DEEP - Funkadelic - Warner Bros.
17. GIVE ME THE NIGHT - George Benson - Warner Bros./ Qwest
18. SWEET SENSATION - Stephanie Mills - 20th Century
19. UPSIDE DOWN - Diana Ross - Motown
20. ALL NIGHT THING - The Invisible Man's Band - Mango

TOP 20 RHYTHM & BLUES SINGLES OF 1981

POS. TITLE - ARTIST - LABEL
1. ENDLESS LOVE - Diana Ross & Lionel Richie, Jr. - Motown
2. MASTER BLASTER - Stevie Wonder - Tamla
3. GIVE IT TO ME BABY - Rick James - Gordy
4. DON'T STOP THE MUSIC - Yarbrough & Peoples - Mercury
5. BEING WITH YOU - Smokey Robinson - Tamla
6. DOUBLE DUTCH BUS - Frankie Smith - WMOT
7. CELEBRATION - Kool & The Gang - De-Lite
8. SUKIYAKI - A Taste of Honey - Capitol
9. WHAT CHA' GONNA DO FOR ME - Chaka Khan - Warner Bros.
10. FANTASTIC VOYAGE - Lakeside - Solar
11. A WOMAN NEEDS LOVE - Ray PArker Jr. & Raydio - Arista
12. BURN RUBBER - Gap Band - Mercury
13. HOW 'BOUT US - Champaign - Columbia
14. IT'S A LOVE THING - The Whispers - Solar
15. WATCHING YOU - Slave - Cotillion

16. JUST THE TWO OF US - Grover Washington Jr. - Elektra
17. TWO HEARTS - Stephanie Mills - 20th Century
18. FREAKY DANCIN' - Cameo - Chocolate City
19. SHE'S A BAD MAMA JAMA - Carl Carlton - 20th Century
20. MAGIC MAN - Robert Winters & Fall - Buddah

TOP 20 RHYTHM & BLUES SINGLES OF 1982

POS. TITLE - ARTIST - LABEL
1. THAT GIRL - Stevie Wonder - Tamla
2. LET'S GROOVE - Earth, Wind & Fire - ARC/Columbia
3. LET IT WHIP - Dazz Band - Motown
4. LOVE COME DOWN - Evelyn King - RCA
5. JUMP TO IT - Aretha Franklin - Arista
6. AND I'M TELLING YOU I'M NOT GOING - Jennifer Holliday - Geffen
7. EARLY IN THE MORNING - The Gap Band - Total Experience
8. CALL ME - Skyy - Salsoul
9. IF IT AIN'T ONE THING IT'S ANOTHER - Richard "Dimples" Fields - Boardwalk
10. I REALLY DON'T NEED NO LIGHT - Jeffrey Osborne - A&M
11. FORGET ME NOTS - Patrice Rushen - Elektra
12. IT'S GONNA TAKE A MIRACLE - Deniece Williams - ARC/Columbia
13. DANCE FLOOR - Zapp - Warner Bros.
14. STREET CORNER - Ashford & Simpson - Capitol
15. WE GO A LONG WAY BACK - Bloodstone - T-Neck
16. TURN YOUR LOVE AROUND - George Benson - Warner Bros.
17. THE OTHER WOMAN - Ray Parker Jr. - Arista
18. LET THE FEELING FLOW - Peabo Bryson - Capitol
19. ONE HUNDRED WAYS - Quincy Jones featuring James Ingram - A&M
20. TAKE MY HEART - Kool & The Gang - De-Lite

TOP 20 RHYTHM & BLUES SINGLES OF 1983

POS. TITLE - ARTIST - LABEL
1. SEXUAL HEALING - Marvin Gaye - Columbia
2. BILLIE JEAN - Michael Jackson - Epic
3. JUICY FRUIT - Mtume - Epic
4. COLD BLOODED - Rick James - Gordy
5. ATOMIC DOG - George Clinton - Capitol
6. THE GIRL IS MINE - Michael Jackson & Paul McCartney - Epic
7. SHE WORKS HARD FOR THE MONEY - Donna Summer - Mercury
8. SAVE THE OVERTIME FOR ME - Gladys Knight & The Pips - Columbia
9. OUTSTANDING - The Gap Band - Total Experience
10. I LIKE IT - DeBarge - Gordy
11. BABY COME TO ME - Patti Austin with James Ingram - Qwest
12. TRY AGAIN - Champaign - Columbia
13. YOU ARE - Lionel Richie - Motown
14. BEAT IT - Michael Jackson - Epic
15. FLASHDANCE...WHAT A FEELING - Irene Cara - Casablanca
16. BETCHA SHE DON'T LOVE YOU - Evelyn King - RCA
17. JUST BE GOOD TO ME - S.O.S. Band - Tabu
18. BETWEEN THE SHEETS - Isley Brothers - T-Neck
19. GOT TO BE THERE - Chaka Khan - Warner Bros.
20. GET IT RIGHT - Aretha Franklin - Arista

TOP 20 RHYTHM & BLUES SINGLES OF 1984

POS. TITLE - ARTIST - LABEL
1. WHEN DOVES CRY - Prince & The Revolution - Warner Bros.
2. IF ONLY YOU KNEW - Patti LaBelle - Philadelphia International
3. WHAT'S LOVE GOT TO DO WITH IT - Tina Turner - Capitol
4. SHE'S STRANGE - Cameo - Atlanta Artists
5. TIME WILL REVEAL - DeBarge - Gordy
6. CARIBBEAN QUEEN - Billy Ocean - Jive/Arista
7. HELLO - Lionel Richie - Motown
8. JOANNA - Kool & The Gang - De-Lite
9. LET THE MUSIC PLAY - Shannon - Mirage
10. DON'T LOOK ANY FURTHER - Dennis Edwards - Gordy
11. LET'S HEAR IT FOR THE BOY - Deneice Williams - Columbia
12. SOMEBODY'S WATCHING ME - Rockwell - Motown
13. YOU, ME AND HE - Mtume - Epic
14. GHOSTBUSTERS - Ray Parker Jr. - Arista
15. LOVELITE - O'Bryan - Capitol
16. ENCORE - Cheryl Lynn - Columbia
17. DON'T WASTE YOUR TIME - Yarbrough & Peoples - Total Experience
18. ALL NIGHT LONG (ALL NIGHT) - Lionel Richie - Motown
19. SAY SAY SAY - Paul McCartney & Michael Jackson - Columbia
20. TAXI - J. Blackfoot - Sound Town

TOP 20 RHYTHM & BLUES SINGLES OF 1985

POS. TITLE - ARTIST - LABEL
1. ROCK ME TONIGHT - Freddie Jackson - Capitol
2. YOU GIVE GOOD LOVE - Whitney Houston - Arista
3. MISSING YOU - Diana Ross - RCA
4. NIGHTSHIFT - Commodores - Motown
5. SAVING ALL MY LOVE FOR YOU - Whitney Houston - Arista
6. IN MY HOUSE - Mary Jane Girls - Gordy
7. FREEWAY OF LOVE - Aretha Franklin - Arista
8. SOLID - Ashford & Simpson - Capitol
9. OH SHEILA - Ready for the World - MCA
10. GOTTA GET YOU HOME TONIGHT - Eugene Wilde - Philly World
11. (NO MATTER HOW HIGH I GET) I'LL STILL BE LOOKIN' UP TO YOU - Wilton Felder with Bobby Womack - MCA
12. HANGIN' ON A STRING - Loose Ends - MCA/Virgin
13. CHERISH - Kool & The Gang - De-Lite
14. MR. TELEPHONE MAN - New Edition - MCA
15. FRESH - Kool & The Gang - De-Lite
16. MISLED - Kool & The Gang - De-Lite
17. YOU ARE MY LADY - Freddie Jackson - Capitol
18. RHYTHM OF THE NIGHT - DeBarge - Gordy
19. OPERATOR - Midnight Star - Solar
20. TREAT HER LIKE A LADY - Temptations - Gordy

TOP 20 RHYTHM & BLUES SINGLES OF 1986

POS. TITLE - ARTIST - LABEL
1. ON MY OWN - Patti LaBelle & Michael McDonald - MCA
2. DO ME BABY - Mellisa Morgan - Capitol
3. SECRET LOVERS - Atlantic Starr - A&M
4. THAT'S WHAT FRIENDS ARE FOR - Dionne & Friends - Arista
5. NASTY - Janet Jackson - A&M

6. KISS - Prince & The Revolution - Paisley Park
7. RUMORS - Timex Social Club - Jay
8. THERE'LL BE SAD SONGS (TO MAKE YOU CRY) - Billy Ocean - Jive
9. I HAVE LEARNED TO RESPECT THE POWER OF LOVE - Stephanie Mills - MCA
10. I CAN'T WAIT - Nu Shooz - Atlantic
11. SAY YOU, SAY ME - Lionel Richie - Motown
12. YOUR SMILE - Rene & Angela - Mercury
13. WHAT HAVE YOU DONE FOR ME LATELY - Janet Jackson - A&M
14. ALL CRIED OUT - Lisa Lisa & Cult Jam with Full Force - Columbia
15. DON'T SAY NO TONIGHT - Eugene Wilde - Philly World
16. THE RAIN - Oran "Juice" Jones (Def Jam/Columbia
17. WORD UP - Cameo - Atlanta Artists
18. CLOSER THAN CLOSE - Jean Carne - Omni
19. SWEET LOVE - Anita Baker - Elektra
20. THE FINEST - The S.O.S. Band - Tabu

TOP 20 RHYTHM & BLUES SINGLES OF 1987

POS. TITLE - ARTIST - LABEL
1. STOP TO LOVE - Luther Vandross - Epic
2. ALWAYS - Atlantic Starr - Warner Bros.
3. AS WE LAY - Shirley Murdock - Elektra
4. VICTORY - Kool & The Gang - Mercury
5. CONTROL - Janet Jackson - A&M
6. CASANOVA - Levert - Atlantic
7. LOVE YOU DOWN - Ready for the World - MCA
8. LOOKING FOR A NEW LOVE - Jody Watley
9. JUST TO SEE HER - Smokey Robinson - Motown
10. LOVE IS A HOUSE - Force M.D.'s - Tommy Boy
11. GIRLFRIEND - Bobby Brown - MCA
12. I FEEL GOOD ALL OVER - Stephanie Mills - MCA
13. HAVE YOU EVER LOVED SOMEBODY - Freddie Jackson - Capitol
14. FALLING - Melba Moore - Capitol
15. DON'T DISTURB THIS GROOVE - The System - Atlantic
16. CANDY - Cameo - Atlanta Artists
17. HAPPY - Surface - Columbia
18. THERE'S NOTHING BETTER THAN LOVE - Luther Vandross with Gregory Hines - Epic
19. JIMMY LEE - Aretha Franklin - Arista
20. DIAMONDS - Herb Alpert featuring Janet Jackson - A&M

TOP 20 RHYTHM & BLUES SINGLES OF 1988

POS. TITLE - ARTIST - LABEL
1. I WANT HER - Keith Sweat - Vintertainment
2. GIRLFRIEND - Pebbles - MCA
3. JUST GOT PAID - Johnny Kenp - Columbia
4. I WANT TO BE YOUR MAN - Roger - Reprise
5. TWO OCCASIONS - The Deele - Solar
6. LOVE CHANGES - Kashif & Meli'sa Morgan - Arista
7. NITE AND DAY - Al B. Surel - Warner Bros.
8. MY FOREVER LOVE - LeVert - Atlantic
9. JOY - Teddy Pendergrass - Elektra
10. LOVE OVERBOARD - Gladys Knight & The Pips - MCA
11. IF YOU CAN DO IT: I CAN TOO!! - Meli'sa Morgan - Capitol
12. NICE 'N' SLOW - Freddie Jackson - Capitol
13. WISHING WELL - Trence Trent D'Arby - Columbia
14. MAKE IT LAST FOREVER - Keith Sweat - (Duet with Jacci McGhee) - Vintertainment
15. DA'BUTT (FROM THE FILM "SCHOOL DAZE") - E.U. - EMI
16. OFF ON YOUR OWN GIRL - Al B. Sure! - Warner Bros.

17. THE WAY YOU MAKE ME FEEL - Michael Jackson - Epic
18. TO PROVE MY LOVE - Michael Cooper - Warner Bros.
19. MAMACITA - Troop - Atlantic
20. MERCEDES BOY - Pebbles - MCA

TOP 20 RHYTHM & BLUES SINGLES OF 1989

POS. TITLE - ARTIST - LABEL
1. SUPERWOMAN - Karyn White - Warner Bros.
2. KEEP ON MOVIN' - Soul II Soul featuring Caron Wheeler - Virgin
3. SO GOOD - Al Jarreau - Reprise
4. SHOWER ME WITH YOUR LOVE - Surface - Columbia
5. DON'T MAKE ME OVER - Sybil - Next Plateau
6. SOMETHING IN THE WAY (YOU MAKE ME FEEL) - Stephanie Mills - MCA
7. BABY COME TO ME - Regina Belle - Columbia
8. LOVE SAW IT - Karyn White - Warner Bros.
9. WILD THING - Tone Loc - Deliscious Vinyl
10. START OF A ROMANCE - Skyy - Atlantic
11. BACK TO LIFE - Soul II Soul featuring Caron Wheeler - Virgin
12. ME, MYSELF AND I - De La Soul - Tommy Boy
13. DREAMIN' - Vanessa Williams - Wing
14. CONGRATULATIONS - Vesta - A&M
15. CLOSER THAN FRIENDS - Surface - Columbia
16. REMEMBER THE FIRST TIME - Eric Gamble - Orpheus
17. SPEND THE NIGHT (CE SOIR) - The Isley Brothers - Warner Brothers
18. CAN U READ MY LIPS - Z'Looke - Orpheus
19. MY FANTASY (FROM "DO THE RIGHT THING") - Teddy Riley featuring Guy - Motown

Jazzie B of Soul II Soul
Soul II Soul had two Top 20 R&B hits in 1989.

20. IT'S NO CRIME - Babyface - Solar

TOP 20 R&B SINGLES OF 1990

POS. TITLE - ARTIST - LABEL
1. HOLD ON - En Vogue - Atlantic
2. MAKE IT LIKE IT IS - Regina Belle - Columbia
3. REAL LOVE - Skyy - Atlantic
4. FEELS GOOD - Tony! Toni! Tone! - Wing
5. VISIONS OF LOVE - Mariah Carey - Columbia
6. ALL AROUND THE WORLD - Lisa Stanfield - Arista
7. I'LL BE GOOD TO YOU - Quincy Jones featuring Ray Charles & Chaka Khan - Qwest
8. MY, MY, MY - Johnny Gill - Motown
9. READY OR NOT - After 7 - Virgin
10. POISON - Bell Biv Devoe - MCA
11. SPREAD MY WINGS - Troop - Atlantic
12. EVERYBODY EVERYBODY - Black Box - RCA
13. TENDER LOVER - Babyface - Solar
14. LOVE UNDER NEW MANAGEMENT - Miki Howard - Atlantic
15. LIES - En Vogue - Atlantic
16. MAKE YOU SWEAT - Keith Sweat - Vintertainment
17. RUB YOU THE RIGHT WAY - Johnny Gill - Motown
18. CRAZY - The Boys - Motown
19. WHY YOU GET FUNKY ON ME (FROM "HOUSE PARTY") - Today - Motown
20. LET'S GET IT ON - By All Means - Island

TOP 20 R&B SINGLES OF 1991

POS. TITLE - ARTIST - LABEL
1. WRITTEN ALL OVER YOUR FACE - Rude Boys - Atlantic
2. LOVE MAKES THINGS HAPPEN - Pebbles - MCA
3. GONNA MAKE YOU SWEAT - C&C Music Factory - Columbia
4. I LIKE THE WAY (THE KISSING GAME) - Hi-Five - Jive
5. CAN YOU STOP THE RAIN - Peabo Bryson - Columbia
6. HOW CAN I EASE THE PAIN - Lisa Fischer - Elektra
7. LET THE BEAT HIT 'EM - Lisa Lisa & Cult Jam - Columbia
8. THE FIRST TIME - Surface - Columbia
9. I CAN'T WAIT ANOTHER MINUTE - Hi-Five - Jive
10. SOMETHING IN MY HEART - Michel'le - Ruthless
11. IT NEVER RAINS (IN SOUTHERN CALIFORNIA) - Tony! Toni! Tone! - Wing
12. ADDICTIVE LOVE - BeBe & CeCe Winans - Capitol
13. LOVE ME DOWN - Freddie Jackson - Capitol
14. BABY I'M READY - LeVert - Atlantic
15. DO ME AGAIN - Freddie Jackson - Capitol
16. YOU DON'T HAVE TO WORRY - En Vogue - Atlantic
17. ONLY HUMAN - Jeffrey Osborne - Arista
18. ALL THE MAN I NEED - Whitney Houston - Arista
19. I'LL GIVE ALL MY LOVE TO YOU - Keith Sweat - Vintertainment
20. WRAP MY BODY TIGHT - Johnny Gill - Motown

TOP 20 R&B SINGLES OF 1992

POS. TITLE - ARTIST - LABEL
1. COME & TALK TO ME - Jodeci - Uptown
2. HONEY LOVE - R. Kelly & Public Announcement - Jive
3. YOU REMIND ME (FROM "STRICTLY BUSINESS") - Mary J. Blige - Uptown
4. END OF THE ROAD (FROM "BOOMERANG") - Boyz II Men - Biv 10
5. TELL ME WHAT YOU WANT ME TO DO - Tevin Campbell - Qwest
6. BREAKIN' MY HEART (PRETTY BROWN EYES) - Mint Condition - Perspective
7. BABY-BABY-BABY - TLC - LaFace
8. SOMEBODY LOVES YOU BABY (YOU KNOW WHO IT IS) - Patti LaBelle - MCA
9. TENNESSEE - Arrested Development - Chrysalis
10. STAY - Jodeci - Uptown
11. ALL WOMAN - Lisa Stansfield - Arista
12. I LOVE YOUR SMILE - Shanice - Motown
13. PEOPLE EVERYDAY - Arrested Development - Chrysalis
14. KEEP IT COMIN' - Keith Sweat - Elektra
15. WHY ME BABY - Keith Sweat - Elektra
16. UHH AHH - Boyz II Men - Motown
17. DON'T BE AFRAID (FROM "JUICE") - Aaron Hall - Soul
18. REMEMBER THE TIME - Michael Jackson - Epic
19. SLOW DANCE (HEY MR. DJ) - R. Kelly & Public Announcement - Jive
20. HERE I GO AGAIN - Glenn Jones - Atlantic

TOP 20 R&B SINGLES OF 1993

POS. TITLE - ARTIST - LABEL
1. I WILL ALWAYS LOVE YOU (FROM "THE BODYGUARD") - Whitney Houston - Arista
2. KNOCKIN' DA BOOTS - H-Town - Luke
3. THAT'S THE WAY LOVE GOES - Janet Jackson - Virgin
4. FREAK ME - Silk - Keia
5. IF EVER I FALL IN LOVE - Shai - Gasoline Alley
6. WEAK - SWV - RCA
7. I'M SO INTO YOU - SWV - RCA
8. DON'T WALK AWAY - Jade - Giant
9. WHOOMP! THERE IT IS - Tag Team - Life
10. RUMP SHAKER - Wreckx-N-Effect - MCA
11. NUTHIN BUT A G THANG - Dr. Dre - Death Row/Interscope
12. LATELY - Jodeci - Uptown
13. SOMETHING'S GOIN' ON - UNV - Maverick/Sire
14. SO ALONE - Men At Large - EastWest
15. ANOTHER SAD LOVE SONG - Toni Braxton - LaFace
16. JUST KICKIN' IT - Xscape - So So Def
17. RIGHT HERE (HUMAN NATURE / DOWNTOWN - SWV - RCA
18. CRY NO MORE - II D Extreme - Gasoline Alley
19. HEY MR. D.J. - Zhane - Flavor Unit
20. DREAMLOVER - Mariah Carey - Columbia

Rhythm-and-Blues Trivia Quiz

1. To what name did Darlene Love answer during the mid-fifties when she sang as a member of The Echoes?
2. Who is Elias McDaniel?
3. What is Ray Charles' last name?
4. By what name do we know Gary Anderson?
5. What do the B's stand for in B.B. King?
6. Who was the fourth Isely brother, killed in an accident before they began their recording career?
7. Besides her mother, Cissy Drinkard, name three other musical females in Whitney Houston's extended family.

8. Jean Terrell replaced Diana Ross in the Supremes, but what is her non-musical claim to fame?
9. What is the origin of the name of Memphis' Stax label?
10. How was the infamous Fame studios named?
11. From which Chi-town group did Big Dee Irwin hail?
12. Before Chryssie Hind's band there was a black Pretenders. Who was it's lead singer?

13. What was his big solo hit and its later hit re-make?
14. What was the early integrated r&b act that was forced to appear on television without its black members?
15. What was the name of the black group that originally recorded the 1954 Crew Cuts hit, "Sh-Boom"?
16. Name two members of the Bronx quintet The Hearts who enjoyed hits after leaving the group.
17. What two hitmakers emerged from The Falcons?
18. Who was Larry "Short Fat Fanny" Williams pattered after?
19. Name the four consecutive "dogs" recorded by Rufus Thomas in 1963.
20. What sixties pop singer was mistakenly booked on the r&b/chitlin circuit in the deep South?
21. What was the name of Frankie Lymon's brother Lewis' group?
22. Who were the two lead singers for The Impressions?
23. What was The Bobbettes hit record and its follow-up?
24. Who performed backing vocals on Joey Dee & The Starlighters Scepter recording, "Face Of An Angel"?
25. By what name did The Chiffons earlier appear?
26. What were the two precursors to The Blue Belles?
27. From which group did The Mirettes emerge?
28. What were the two groups Minnie Riperton sang in before her tragically short-lived solo career?
29. Who was Motown's first white female artist?
30. What was the name of her answer song and its hit counterpart?
31. With what four women did Marvin Gaye duet?
32. Who were Judy Clay's two male partners?
33. Who was Otis Redding's female "sparring" partner?

34. What song/singer inspired Otis Redding's "Pain In Her Heart"?
35. By what name did Jimi Hendrix earlier perform?
36. Who was Jimi Hendrix' "Foxey Lady"?
37. Who first recorded the Big Brother/Janis Joplin hit, "Piece Of My Heart"?
38. Who recorded the original version of The Rolling Stones' first Top Ten hit, "Time Is On My Side."
39. Who were James & Bobby Purify?
40. "Girl Watcher" was a smash for what blue-eyed soul group?
41. What was the first song to simultaneoulsy reach the number one spot on both the pop and r&b charts?
42. Name the song that became both an instrumental hit in 1968 and a vocal hit in 1969, as well as the artists who recorded each.
43. Name the five cover songs recorded by Wilson Pickett in 1969 and their original artists.
44. Who performed the 1969 and 1970 remakes of the 1958 Chantels hit, "Maybe"?
45. What was the basis for Otis Redding protege Arthur Conley's "Sweet Soul Music"?
46. What was the title of Conley's 1969 tribute to his mentor?
47. What was the title of Jean Knight's follow-up to her smash, "Mr. Big Stuff"?
48. When and what was fifties phenomenon Chuck Berry's first number one hit?
49. In what real-life tragedy was Gloria "Tainted Love" Jones involved?
50. For what crime did Chuck Berry serve time in a prison camp?

Jimi Hendrix
Another artist who became bigger than life following his death. Signature song ``Purple Haze'' peaked at only #65, and Jimi had only one overall Top 20 hit—``All Along The Watchtower.'' (Want more? See question #35.)

Billboard Top 20 Rap Singles, 1989-1993

TOP 20 RAP SINGLES OF 1989

POS.	TITLE - ARTIST - LABEL
1.	SELF DESTRUCTION - The Stop The Violence Movement - Jive
2.	ME MYSELF AND I - De La Soul - Tommy Boy
3.	BUST A MOVE - Young M.C. - Delicious Vinyl
4.	FIGHT THE POWER - Public Enemy - Motown
5.	IT'S FUNKY ENOUGH - The D.O.C. - Ruthless
6.	CHILDREN'S STORY - Slick Rick - Def Jam
7.	EXPRESS YOURSELF - N.W.A. - Ruthless
8.	TURN THIS MUTHA OUT - M.C. Hammer - Capitol
9.	ROLLIN' WITH KID 'N Play - Kid 'N Play - Select
10.	WE GOT OUR THANG - Heavy D. & The Boyz - Uptown
11.	SMOOTH OPERATOR - Big Daddy Kane - Cold Chillin'
12.	FUNKY DIVIDENDS - Three Times Dope - Arista
13.	THEY WANT MONEY - Kool Moe Dee - Jive
14.	THE MAN WE ALL KNOW AND LOVE - Kwame - Atlantic
15.	ME SO HORNY - The 2 Live Crew - Skywalker
16.	FUNKY COLD MEDINA - Tone Loc - Delicious Vinyl
17.	I'M THAT TYPE OF GUY - L.L. Cool J - Def Jam
18.	THEY PUT ME IN THE MIX - M.C. Hammer - Capitol
19.	GIRL YOU KNOW IT'S TRUE - Milli Vanilli - Arista
20.	PUMP IT UP - M.C. Hammer - Capitol

TOP 20 RAP SINGLES OF 1990

POS.	TITLE - ARTIST - LABEL
1.	EXPRESSION - Salt-N-Pepa - Next Plateau
2.	THE HUMPTY DANCE - Digital Underground - Tommy Boy
3.	BUDDY - De La Soul - Tommy Boy
4.	THE POWER - Snap - Arista
5.	CALL ME D-NICE - D-Nice - Jive
6.	BEEPERS - Sir Mix-A-Lot - Nastymix
7.	MURDER RAP - Above The Law - Ruthless
8.	OWNLEE EUE - Kwame & A New Beginning - Atlantic
9.	FUNHOUSE - Kid 'N Play - Select
10.	ME SO HORNY - The 2 Live Crew - Skywalker
11.	NEW JACK SWING - Wrecks-N-Effect - Sound of New York
12.	WE'RE ALL IN THE SAME GANG - The West Coast Rap All-Stars - Warner Bros.
13.	THE BOOMIN' SYSTEM - L.L. Cool J - Def Jam
14.	TREAT THEM LIKE THEY WANT TO BE TREATED - Father MC - Uptown
15.	THE POWER - Power Jam featuring Chill Rob G - Wild Pitch
16.	LET THE RHYTHM HIT 'EM - Eric B. & Rakim - MCA
17.	AMERIKKKA'S MOST WANTED - Ice Cube - Priority
18.	911 IS A JOKE - Public Enemy - Def Jam
19.	WELCOME TO THE TERRORDOME - Public Enemy - Def Jam
20.	PUMP IT HOTTIE - Redhead Kingpin & The F.B.I. - Virgin

D.J. Jazzy Jeff & The Fresh Prince

''Summertime'' spent three weeks at #4 in the overall Top 10, as well as being a Top 20 Rap hit (1991).

TOP 20 RAP SINGLES OF 1991

POS. TITLE - ARTIST - LABEL
1. TREAT 'EM RIGHT - Chubb Rock - Select
2. AROUND THE WAY GIRL - L.L. Cool J - Def Jam
3. I'LL DO 4 YOU - Father M.C. - Uptown
4. LOOKING AT THE FRONT DOOR - Main Source - Wild Pitch
5. O.P.P. - Naughty By Nature - Tommy Boy
6. MIND PLAYING TRICKS ON ME - Geto Boys - Rap-A-Lot
7. GOLD DIGGER - EPMD - RAL
8. YOU CAN'T PLAY WITH MY YO-YO - Yo-Yo Feat, Ice Cube - EastWest
9. STOMPIN' IN THE 90'S - Yo-Yo - Atlantic
10. DADDY'S LITTLE GIRL - Nikki D - Def Jam
11. THE CHUBBSTER - Chubb Rock - Select
12. F-CK COMPTON - Tim Dog - Ruffhouse
13. I GOT TO HAVE IT - ED O.G. & DA Bulldogs - PWL America
14. MAMA SAID KNOCK YOU OUT - L.L. Cool J - Def Jam
15. BORN AND RAISED IN COMPTON - DJ Quik - Profile
16. SUMMERTIME - D.J. Jazzy Jeff & The Fresh Prince - Jive
17. THE GHETTO - Too Short - Jive
18. HOMEY DON'T PLAY DAT - Terminator X - P.R.O. Division
19. YOUR MOM'S IN MY BUSINESS - K-Solo - Atlantic
20. GROWIN' UP IN THE HOOD - Compton's Most Wanted - Qwest

TOP 20 RAP SINGLES OF 1992

POS. TITLE - ARTIST - LABEL
1. THE PHUNCKY FEEL ONE/HOW COULD I JUST KILL A MAN - Cypress Hill - Ruffhouse
2. THEY WANT EFX - Das EFX - Atco EastWest
3. JUMP - Kris Kross - Ruffhouse
4. TENNESSEE - Arrested Development - Chrysalis
5. THEY REMINISCE OVER YOU - Pete Rock & C.L. Smooth - Elektra
6. JUST THE TWO OF US - Chubb Rock - Select
7. THE CHOICE IS YOURS - Black Sheep - Mercury
8. CROSSOVER - EPMD - RAL/Chaos
9. TAKE IT PERSONAL - Gang Starr - Chrysalis
10. PEOPLE EVERYDAY - Arrested Development - Chrysalis
11. 360 DEGREES (WHAT GOES AROUND) - Grand Puba - Elektra
12. OOCHIE COOCHIE - M.C. Brains - Motown
13. SOMETIMES I RHYME SLOW - Nice & Smooth - RAL
14. POOR GEORGIE - MC Lyte - First Priority
15. WARM IT UP - Kris Kross - Ruffhouse
16. MIC CHECKA - Das EFX - Atco EastWest
17. GROOVE WITH IT - Big Daddy Kane - Cold Chillin'/Reprise
18. EVER SO CLEAR - Bushwick Bill - Rap-A-Lot
19. SHUT 'EM DOWN - Public Enemy - Def Jam
20. HAND ON THE PUMP - Cypress Hill - Ruffhouse

TOP 20 RAP SINGLES OF 1993

POS. TITLE - ARTIST - LABEL
1. WE GETZ BUZY/HEAD OR GUT - Illegal -
2. REBIRTH OF SLICK (COOL LIKE DAT) - Digable Planets - Pendulum
3. I GOT A MAN - Positive K - Island
4. CHIEF ROCKA - Lords Of The Underground - Pendulum
5. INFORMER - Snow - EastWest
6. NUTHIN' BUT A G THANG - Dr. Dre - Death Row/Interscope
7. RUFFNECK - MC Lyte - First Priority
8. THROW YOUR GUNS - Onyx - RAL/Chaos
9. PUNKS JUMP UP TO GET BEAT DOWN - Brand Nubian - Elektra
10. LOTS OF LOVIN - Pete Rock & C.L. Smooth - Elektra
11. PASSIN' ME BY - The Pharcyde - Delicious Vinyl
12. ALRIGHT - Kris Kross featuring Supercat - Ruffhouse
13. SLAM - Onyx - RAL/Chaos
14. INSANE IN THE BRAIN - Cypress Hill - Ruffhouse
15. WICKED - Ice Cube - Priority
16. WHOOT, THERE IT IS - 95 South - Wrap
17. DOWN WITH THE KING - Run-D.M.C. - Profile
18. FUNKY CHILD - Lords Of The Underground - Pendulum
19. FLOW JOE - Fat Joe - Violator
20. LET ME ROLL - Scarface - Rap-A-Lot

Billboard Top 20 Alternative Rock Tracks, 1988-1993

TOP 20 ALTERNATIVE ROCK TRACKS OF 1988

POS. TITLE - ARTIST - LABEL
1. PEEK-A-BOO - Siouxsie & The Banshees - Geffen
2. WHAT I AM - Edie Brickell & New Bohemians - Geffen
3. DESIRE - U2 - Island
4. ALL THAT MONEY WANTS - Psychedelic Furs - Columbia
5. PUT THIS LOVE TO THE TEST - Jon Astley - Atlantic
6. BACK ON THE BREADLINE - Hunters & Collectors - I.R.S.
7. CAROLYN'S FINGERS - Cocteau Twins - 4 A.D.
8. I'VE GOT A FEELING - The Screaming Tribesmen - Rykodisc
9. THE KILLING JAR - Siouxsie & The Banshees - Geffen
10. JUST PLAY MUSIC! - Big Audio Dynamite - Columbia
    Editor's Note: First year of coverage limited to ten tracks.

TOP 20 ALTERNATIVE ROCK TRACKS OF 1989

POS. TITLE - ARTIST - LABEL
1. SO ALIVE - Love & Rockets - RCA
2. FASCINATION STREET - The Cure - Elektra
3. GOOD THING - Fine Young Cannibals - I.R.S.
4. STAND - R.E.M. - Warner Bros.
5. LOVE SONG - The Cure - Elektra
6. I'LL BE YOU - The Replacements - Sire
7. THE MAYOR OF SIMPLETON - XTC - Geffen
8. CHARLOTTE ANNE - Julian Cope - Island
9. ANGEL OF HARLEM - U2 - Island
10. DIRTY BLVD. - Lou Reed - Sire
11. SWEET JANE - Cowboy Junkies - RCA
12. HERE COMES YOUR MAN - Pixies - Elektra
13. ORANGE CRUSH - R.E.M. - Warner Bros.
14. SHE DRIVES ME CRAZY - Fine Young Cannibals - I.R.S.
15. FISHERMAN'S BLUES - The Waterboys - Ensign
16. VERONICA - Elvis Costello - Warner Bros.
17. COME ANYTIME - Hoodoo Gurus - RCA
18. DISAPPOINTED - Public Image Ltd. - Virgin
19. BETWEEN SOMETHING AND NOTHING - The Ocean Blue - Sire
20. NIGHTMARES - Violent Femmes - Slash

TOP 20 ALTERNATIVE ROCK TRACKS OF 1990

POS. TITLE - ARTIST - LABEL
1. CUTS YOU UP - Peter Murphy - Beggar's Banquet
2. POLICY OF TRUTH - Depeche Mode - Sire
3. HERE'S WHERE THE STORY ENDS - The Sundays - Rough Trade
4. METROPOLIS - The Church - Arista
5. THE EMPEROR'S NEW CLOTHES - Sinead O'Connor - Ensign
6. NOTHING COMPARES 2 U - Sinead O'Connor - Ensign
7. NO MYTH - Michael Penn - RCA
8. HEAD ON - The Jesus And Mary Chain - Warner Bros.
9. LOVE AND ANGER - Kate Bush - Columbia
10. WAY DOWN NOW - World Party - Ensign
11. JOEY - Concrete Blonde - I.R.S.
12. I'M FREE - The Soup Dragons - Big Life
13. PROUD TO FALL - Ian McCulloch - Sire
14. STANDING THERE - The Creatures - Geffen
15. FORGOTTEN YEARS - Midnight Oil - Columbia
16. JEALOUS - Gene Loves Jezebel - Beggar's Banquet
17. I DON'T KNOW WHY I LOVE YOU - The House Of Love - Mercury
18. ENJOY THE SILENCE - Depeche Mode - Sire
19. HOUSE - The Psychedelic Furs - Columbia
20. BLUE SKY MINE - Midnight Oil - Columbia

TOP 20 ALTERNATIVE ROCK TRACKS OF 1991

POS. TITLE - ARTIST - LABEL
1. RUSH - Big Audio Dynamite II - Columbia
2. KISS THEM FOR ME - Siouxsie and The Banshees - Geffen
3. GET THE MESSAGE - Electronic - Warner Bros.
4. UNTIL SHE COMES - The Psychedelic Furs - Columbia
5. RIGHT HERE, RIGHT NOW - Jesus Jones - SBK
6. MORE - Sisters Of Mercy - Elektra
7. SEE THE LIGHTS - Simple Minds - A&M
8. THIS LOVE - Daniel Ash - RCA
9. LOSING MY RELIGION - R.E.M. - Warner Bros.
10. THERE SHE GOES - The La's - London
11. SO YOU THINK YOU'RE IN LOVE - Robyn Hitchcock - A&M
12. KINKY AFRO - Happy Mondays - Elektra
13. AMERICAN MUSIC - Violent Femmes - Slash
14. I TOUCH MYSELF - Divinlys - Virgin
15. THEN - The Charlatans UK - Beggar's Banquet
16. SATISFIED - Squeeze - Reprise
17. NIGHT AND DAY - U2 - Chrysalis
18. ALL THIS TIME - Sting - A&M
19. UNBELIEVABLE - EMF - EMI
20. WALKING DOWN MADISON - Kirsty MacColl - Charisma

TOP 20 ALTERNATIVE ROCK TRACKS OF 1992

POS. TITLE - ARTIST - LABEL
1. ONE - U2 - Island
2. WEIRDO - The Charlatans - Beggar's Banquet
3. FRIDAY I'M IN LOVE - The Cure - Fiction
4. COME AS YOU ARE - Nirvana - DGC
5. FAR GONE AND OUT - The Jesus And Mary Chain - Def American
6. HIT - The Sugarcubes - Elektra
7. MYSTERIOUS WAYS - U2 - Island
8. TOMORROW - Morrissey - Sire
9. DIGGING IN THE DIRT - Peter Gabriel - Geffen
10. INTO THE FIRE - Sarah McLachlan - Nettwerk
11. UNDER THE BRIDGE - Red Hot Chili Peppers - Warner Bros.
12. CARIBBEAN BLUE - Enya - Reprise
13. BLOOD MAKES NOISE - Suzanne Vega - A&M
14. NOT ENOUGH TIME - INXS - Atlantic
15. TEEN ANGST (WHAT THE WORLD NEEDS NOW) - Cracker - Virgin
16. BORN OF FRUSTRATION - James - Fontana
17. THE BALLAD OF PETER PUMPKINHEAD - XTC - Geffen
18. DIVINE THING - The Soup Dragons - Big Life
19. BAD LUCK - Social Distortion - Epic
20. MIDLIFE CRISIS - Faith No More - Slash

The Charlatans UK
One of the biggest bands on the modern rock charts,
this group scored in the 1991 and 1992 Top 20 alternative category.

TOP 20 ALTERNATIVE ROCK TRACKS OF 1993

POS. TITLE - ARTIST - LABEL
1. REGRET - New Order - Qwest
2. NO RAIN - Blind Melon - Capitol
3. BREAK IT DOWN AGAIN - Tears For Fears - Mercury
4. CREEP - Radiohead - Capitol
5. FEED THE TREE - Belly - Sire
6. SOUL TO SQUEEZE - Red Hot Chili Peppers - Warner Bros.
7. PETS - Porno For Pyros - Warner Bros.
8. CANDY EVERYBODY WANTS - 10,000 Maniacs - Elektra
9. WALKING IN MY SHOES - Depeche Mode - Mule/Sire
10. HEART-SHAPED BOX - Nirvana - DGC
11. CANNONBALL - The Breeders - 4 A.D.
12. MY SISTER - The Juliana Hatfield Three - Mammoth
13. I FEEL YOU - Depeche Mode - Mule/Sire
14. ARE YOU GONNA GO MY WAY - Lenny Kravitz - Virgin
15. DOGS OF LUST - The The - Epic
16. THE DEVIL YOU KNOW - Jesus Jones - SBK
17. LOW - Cracker - Virgin
18. PLUSH - Stone Temple Pilots - Atlantic
19. HUMAN BEHAVIOUR - Bjork - Elektra
20. BELIEVE - Lenny Kravitz - Virgin

RIAA Sales Certifications
Gold, Platinum & Multi-Platinum Singles, 1958-1994

This listing cites performer name, titles of singles certified, and year of certification. Certifications are Gold unless same-year Gold and Platinum certifcation occurred—(G, P). If year of Platinum certifcation differs, the latter certification year is given thusly—(G, P - 1991). If Multi-Platinum status was awarded, level of certification is indicated in a note. Includes all singles formats: 45rpm, cassette and CD. (Data provided courtesy of the Recording Industry Association of America.)

A

AALIYAH
Back & Forth - 1994
ABBA
Dancing Queen - 1977
Take A Chance On Me - 1978
ABBOTT, GREGORY
Shake You Down - 1992 (G,P)
ABDUL, PAULA
Cold Hearted - 1989
Forever Your Girl - 1989
Opposites Attract - 1990
Rush Rush - 1991
Straight Up - 1989 (G, P)
ACE OF BASE
All That She Wants - 1993 (G,P)
Don't Turn Around - 1994
The Sign - 1994 (G,P)
ADAMS, BRYAN
Can't Stop This Thing We Started - 1991
(Everything I Do) I Do For You - 1991 (G, P*)
*Triple platinum as of 09/12/91
ADAMS, BRYAN, ROD STEWART & STING
All For Love - 1994 (G, P)
AEROSMITH
Cryin' - 1993
Love In An Elevator - 1989
AFTER 7
Can't Stop - 1991
Ready Or Not - 1990
AIR SUPPLY
All Out Of Love - 1980
Making Love Out Of Nothing At All - 1983
The One That You Love - 1981
ALICE IN CHAINS
Sap - 1994
ALL 4 ONE
I Swear - 1994
So Much In Love - 1994
ALPERT, HERB
Rise - 1979
ALPERT, HERB & THE TIJUANA BRASS
This Guy's In Love With You - 1968
AMERICA
A Horse With No Name - 1972
THE AMERICAN BREED
Bend Me, Shape Me - 1968
ANDERSON, JOHN
Swingin' - 1983
ANDERSON, LYNN
Rose Garden - 1971

ANDREA TRUE CONNECTION
More, More, More - 1976
ANKA, PAUL
(You're) Having My Baby - 1974
ANOTHER BAD CREATION
Iesha - 1991
THE ARCHIES
Jingle, Jangle - 1970
Sugar, Sugar - 1969
ARRESTED DEVELOPMENT
Mr. Wendal - 1993
People Everyday - 1992
Tennessee - 1992
THE ASSOCIATION
Cherish - 1966
Never My Love - 1967
Windy - 1967
ASTLEY, RICK
Never Gonna Give You Up - 1989
ATLANTIC STARR
Masterpiece - 1992
AUSTIN, PATTY & JAMES INGRAM
Baby Come To Me - 1983
AUTRY, GENE
Rudolph, The Red-Nosed Reindeer - 1969
AVERAGE WHITE BAND
Pick Up The Pieces - 1975

B

B.T. EXPRESS
Do It ('til You're Satisfied) - 1974
Express - 1975
BACHMAN-TURNER OVERDRIVE
You Ain't Seen Nothing Yet - 1974
BAD COMPANY
Rock 'N Roll Fantasy - 1990
BAD ENGLISH
When I See You Smile - 1989
BADFINGER
Day After Day - 1972
BAEZ, JOAN
The Night They Drove Old Dixie Down - 1971
BAILEY, PHILIP
Easy Lover (Duet with Phil Collins) - 1985
BAMBAATA, A./SOUL SONIC FORCE
Planet Rock - 1982
BAND AID
Do They Know It's Christmas? - 1984
BANGLES
Eternal Flame - 1989
Walk Like An Egyptian - 1989
BASE, ROB & D.J. E-Z ROCK

It Takes Two - 1989 (G, P)
BASIL, TONI
Mickey - 1982 (G, P - 1983)
BAY CITY ROLLERS
Saturday Night - 1975
THE BEACH BOYS
Kokomo - 1989 (G, P)
THE BEACH BOYS
Good Vibrations - 1966
I Get Around - 1982
BEAR EDWARD
Last Song - 1973
THE BEATLES
All You Need Is Love - 1967
Ballad Of John & Yoko - 1969
Can't Buy Me Love - 1964
Eight Days A Week - 1965
Get Back - 1969
A Hard Day's Night - 1964
Hello Goodbye - 1967
Help! - 1965
Hey Jude - 1968
I Feel Fine - 1964
I Want To Hold Your Hand - 1964
Lady Madonna - 1968
Let It Be - 1970
Nowhere Man - 1966
Paperback Writer - 1966
Penny Lane - 1967
Something - 1969
We Can Work It Out - 1966
Yellow Submarine - 1966
Yesterday - 1965
BECK
Loser - 1994
BEE GEES
How Can You Mend A Broken Heart - 1971
How Deep Is Your Love - 1977
Jive Talkin' - 1975
Lonely Days - 1971
Love So Right - 1976
Love You Inside Out - 1979
Night Fever - 1978 (G, P)
Stayin' Alive - 1978 (G, P)
Too Much Heaven - 1978 (G, P - 1979)
Tragedy - 1979 (G, P)
You Should Be Dancing - 1976
BELL & JAMES
Livin' It Up - 1979
BELL, ARCHIE & THE DRELLS
Tighten Up - 1968
BELL BIV DEVOE
Poison - 1990 (G, P)

BELL, WILLIAM
Tryin' To Love Two - 1977
BELLE, REGINA & PEABO BRYSON
A Whole New World - 1993
THE BELLS
Stay Awhile - 1971
BENATAR, PAT
Hit Me With Your Best Shot - 1981
Love Is A Battlefield - 1989
BENTON, BROOK
Rainy Night In Georgia - 1970
BERLIN
Take My Breath Away - 1992
BERRY, CHUCK
My Ding-A-Ling - 1972
B-52'S
Love Shack - 1989
Roam - 1990
BIG MOUNTAIN
Baby, I Love Your Way - 1994
BILK, MR. ACKER
Stranger On The Shore - 1967
BISHOP, ELVIN
Fooled Around And Fell In Love - 1976
BLIGE, MARY
Real Love - 1992
You Remind Me - 1992
BLONDIE
Call Me - 1980
Heart Of Glass - 1979
Rapture - 1981
The Tide Is High - 1981
BLOOD, SWEAT & TEARS
And When I Die - 1970
Spinning Wheel - 1969
You Make Me So Very Happy - 1969
BLOODSTONE
Natural High - 1973
BLOW, KURTIS
The Breaks (12") - 1980
BLUE MAGIC
Sideshow - 1974
BLUE SWEDE
Hooked On A Feeling - 1974
BLUES IMAGE
Ride Captain Ride - 1970
BOLTON, MICHAEL
Said I Loved You, But I Lied - 1993
BON JOVI, JON
Blaze Of Glory - 1990 (G,P)
BOOKER T. & THE M.G.'S
Green Onions - 1967
BOONE, DEBBY
You Light Up My Life - 1977 (G, P)
BOWIE, DAVID
Fame - 1975
Let's Dance - 1983
THE BOX TOPS
Cry Like A Baby - 1968
The Letter - 1967
BOYZ II MEN
End Of The Road - 1992 (G, P)
In The Still Of The Nite - 1993 (G, P)
It's So Hard To Say Goodbye To
Yesterday - 1991
Motownphilly - 1991 (G, P)
BRANIGAN, LAURA
Gloria - 1983

BRAXTON, TONI
Another Sad Love Song - 1993
Breathe Again - 1993
You Mean The World To Me - 1994
BREAD
Baby I'm A Want You - 1972
Make It With You - 1970
BRIDGES, ALICIA
I Love The Nightlife - 1978
BRIGHTER SIDE OF DARKNESS
Love Jones - 1973
BROOKLYN BRIDGE
The Worst That Could Happen - 1969
BROTHERS JOHNSON
I'll Be Good To You - 1977
Strawberry Letter 23 - 1977
BROWN, BOBBY
Don't Be Cruel - 1989
Every Little Step - 1989
Good Enough - 1993
Humpin' Around - 1992
My Prerogative - 1989
On Our Own - 1989 (G, P)
Rock Wit'cha - 1989
BROWN, CHUCK/SOUL SEARCHERS
Bustin' Loose - 1979
BROWN, JAMES
Get On The Good Foot - 1972
The Payback - 1974
BROWNSVILLE STATION
Smokin' In The Boys Room - 1974
BUCKNER & GARCIA
Pac-Man Fever - 1982
BURDON, ERIC & WAR
Spill The Wine - 1970
BUTLER, JERRY
Only The Strong Survive - 1969
BUTLER, JERRY & BRENDA LEE EAGER
Ain't Understanding Mellow - 1972

C

C & C MUSIC FACTORY
Gonna Make You Sweat (Everybody
Dance Now) - 1990 (G, P - 1991)
Here We Go - 1991
Things That Make You Go Hmmmm...
- 1991
CALLOWAY
I Wanna Be Rich - 1990
CAMPBELL, GLEN
Galveston- 1969
Rhinestone Cowboy - 1975
Southern Nights - 1977
Wichita Lineman - 1969
CAMPBELL, TEVIN
Can We Talk? - 1993
Round And Round - 1991
Tell Me What You Want Me To Do
- 1992
CANDYMAN
Knockin' Boots - 1990 (G, P)
CAPTAIN & TENNILLE
Do That To Me One More Time - 1980
Lonely Night (Angel Face) - 1976
Love Will Keep Us Together - 1975
Muskrat Love - 1976
Shop Around - 1976

The Way I Want To Touch You - 1975
CARA, IRENE
Flashdance...What A Feeling - 1983
CAREY, MARIAH
Dreamlover - 1993 (G, P)
Emotions - 1991
Hero - 1993 (G, P)
Love Takes Time - 1990
Someday - 1991
Vision Of Love - 1990
Without You - 1994
CARLTON, CARL
She's A Bad Mama Jama - 1981
CARMEN, ERIC
All By Myself - 1976
CARNES, KIM
Bette Davis Eyes - 1981
CARPENTERS
For All We Know - 1971
Hurting Each Other - 1972
Please Mr. Postman - 1975
Rainy Days & Mondays - 1971
Sing - 1973
Superstar - 1971
(They Long To Be) Close To You
- 1970
Top Of The World - 1973
We've Only Just Begun - 1970
Yesterday Once More - 1973
CARTER, CLARENCE
Patches - 1970
Slip Away - 1968
Too Weak To Fight - 1969
CASH, JOHNNY
A Boy Named Sue - 1969
CASSIDY, DAVID
Cherish - 1971
CASSIDY, SHAUN
Da Doo Ron Ron - 1977
Hey Deanie - 1978
That's Rock 'N Roll - 1977
CHAIRMEN OF THE BOARD
Give Me Just A Little More Time
- 1970
THE CHAKACHAS
Jungle Fever - 1972
CHANDLER, GROOVY
Groovy Situation - 1970
CHAPIN, HARRY
Cat's In The Cradle - 1974
CHARLIE DANIELS BAND
The Devil Went Down To Georgia
- 1989
CHARLES, RAY
I Can't Stop Loving You - 1962
CHARLIE DANIELS BAND
The Devil Went Down In Georgia
- 1979
CHEAP TRICK
I Want You To Want Me - 1979
CHER
Dark Lady - 1974
Gypsies, Tramps & Thieves - 1971
Half Breed - 1973
If I Could Turn Back Time - 1989
Take Me Home - 1979
CHER & PETER CETERA
After All - 1989

CHERRY, NENEH
Buffalo Stance - 1989
CHIC
Dance, Dance, Dance - 1978
Le Freak - 1978 (G, P)
Good Times - 1979
I Want Your Love - 1979
CHICAGO
Hard To Say I'm Sorry - 1982
If You Leave Me Now - 1976
Just You And Me - 1974
Look Away (Come In From The Night) - 1989
Saturday In The Park - 1972
CHICAGO BEARS SHUFFLIN' CREW
Superbowl Shuffle - 1986
CHILD, JANE
Don't Wanna Fall In Love - 1990
CHRISTIE, LOU
Lightnin' Strikes - 1966
CLAPTON, ERIC
I Shot The Sheriff - 1974
Lay Down Sally - 1978
Tears In Heaven - 1992 (G, P)
CLARK, PETULA
Downtown - 1965
CLASSICS IV
Stormy - 1969
CLIMAX
Precious & Few - 1972
CLUB NOUVEAU
Lean On Me - 1987
COCHRANE, TOM
Life Is A Highway - 1992
COCKER, JOE & JENNIFER WARNES
Up Where We Belong - 1989 (G, P)
COFFEY, G./DETROIT GUITAR BAND
Scorpio - 1971
COLE, NATALIE
I've Got Love On My Mind - 1977
Our Love - 1978
Unforgettable - 1991
COLLINS, PHIL
Against All Odds (Take Another Look At Me Now) - 1984
Another Day In Paradise - 1989
A Groovy Kind Of Love - 1989
In The Air Tonight - 1991
One More Night - 1990
Sussudio - 1990
COLOR ME BADD
All 4 Love - 1992
I Adore Mi Amor - 1991
I Wanna Sex You Up - 1991 (G, P*)
*Double platinum as of 06/27/91
COMO, PERRY
Catch A Falling Star - 1958
CONLEY, ARTHUR
Sweet Soul Music - 1967
CONTI, BILL
Gonna Fly Now (Theme From "Rocky") - 1977
COOLIDGE, RITA
We're All Alone - 1978
(Your Love Has Lifted Me) Higher & Higher - 1977
COOLIO
Fantastic Voyage - 1994

COOPER, ALICE
I Never Cry - 1977
Poison - 1989
CORNELIUS BROTHERS/SISTER ROSE
To Late To Turn Back Now - 1972
Treat Her Like A Lady - 1971
COUGAR, JOHN
Hurts So Bad - 1982
Jack & Diane - 1982
THE COWSILLS
Hair - 1969
The Rain, The Park & Other Things - 1967
THE CRANBERRIES
Linger - 1994
CRASH TEST DUMMIES
MMM, MMM, MMM, MMM - 1994
CRAZY WORLD OF ARTHUR BROWN
Fire - 1968
CREAM
Sunshine Of Your Love - 1968
CREEDENCE CLEARWATER REVIVAL
Bad Moon Rising - 1990
Down On The Corner - 1990
Green River - 1990
Have You Ever Seen The Rain - 1971
Lookin' Out My Back Door - 1990
Proud Mary - 1990
Susie Q - 1990
Sweet Hitch-hiker - 1990
Travelin' Band - 1970
Up Around The Bend - 1970
Who'll Stop The Rain - 1990 (G, P)
CROCE, JIM
Bad, Bad Leroy Brown - 1973
Time In A Bottle - 1974
CROSS, CHRISTOPHER
Arthur's Theme (The Best You Can Do) - 1982
CULTURE CLUB
Karma Chameleon - 1984
Mr. Vain - 1994
CUMMINGS, BURTON
Stand Tall - 1977
CYPRESS HILL
Insane In The Brain - 1993
CYRUS, BILLY RAY
Achy Breaky Heart - 1992 (G, P)
CULTURE CLUB
Karma Chameleon - 1984

D

D.N.A. FEATURING SUZANNE VEGA
Tom's Diner - 1990
D.R.S.
Gangsta Lean - 1993 (G, P)
DA BEAT
Funkdafied - 1994
D'ARBY, TERENCE TRENT
Wishing Well - 1991
DAMIAN, MICHAEL
Rock On - 1989
DAMN YANKEES
High Enough - 1991
DAS EFX
They Want EFX - 1992
DAVIS, MAC
Baby Don't Get Hooked On Me - 1972

DAVIS, SAMMY, JR.
Candy Man - 1972
DAVIS, TYRONE
Can I Change My Mind - 1969
Turn Back The Hands Of Time - 1970
DAYNE, TAYLOR
I'll Always Love You - 1989
Love Will Lead You Back - 1990
Tell It To My Heart - 1989
DE LA SOUL
Me, Myself & I - 1989
DEAN, JIMMY
Big Bad John - 1961
I.O.U. - 1976
DEEE-LITE
Groove Is In The Heart - 1990
DEEP PURPLE
Smoke On The Water - 1973
DEES, RICK/HIS CAST OF IDIOTS
Disco Duck - 1976 (G, P)
DE FRANCO FAMILY
Heartbeat—It's A Lovebeat - 1973
THE DELFONICS
(Didn't I) Blow Your Mind Thus Time - 1970
THE DELLS
Give Your Body A Standing Ovations - 1973
DENVER, JOHN
Annie's Song - 1974
Back Home Again - 1975
Have You Ever Seen The Rain - 1971
I'm Sorry - 1975
Sunshine On My Shoulder - 1974
Thank God I'm A Country Boy - 1975
DEPECHE MODE
Enjoy The Silence - 1990
I Feel You - 1993
Personal Jesus - 1990 (G, P)
DE SARIO, TERI & KC
Yes, I'm Ready - 1980
DE SHANNON, JACKIE
Put A Little Love In Your Heart - 1969
DE VAUGHN, WILLIAM
Be Thankful For What You Got - 1974
DEVO
Whip It - 1980
DEVORZON, B. & P. BORKIN, JR.
Nadia's Theme ("The Young & The Restless") - 1977
DIAMOND, NEIL
Cracklin' Rose - 1970
Holly Holy - 1969
Song Sung Blue - 1972
Sweet Caroline - 1969
DIGABLE PLANETS
Rebirth Of Slick (Cool Like Dat) - 1993
DIGITAL UNDERGROUND
The Humpty Dance - 1990 (G, P)
Kiss You Back - 1992
DINO
I Like It - 1989
DION
Abraham, Martin & John - 1969
DION, CELINE
The Power Of Love - 1994 (G, P)
DION, CELINE AND PEABO BRYSON
Beauty And The Beast - 1992

DJ JAZZY JEFF & FRESH PRINCE
Boom! Shake The Room - 1993
Parents Just Don't Understand - 1989
Ring My Bell - 1991
Summertime - 1991 (G, P)

DOMINO
Ghetto Jam - 1994

DONALDSON, BO & THE HEYWOODS
Billy Don't Be A Hero - 1974

DONOVAN
Mellow Yellow - 1967

DOOBIE BROTHERS
Black Water - 1975
What A Fool Believes - 1979

THE DOORS
Hello, I Love You - 1968
Light My Fire - 1967
Touch Me - 1969

DOUGLAS, CARL
Kung Fu Fighting - 1974

DR. DRE
Dre Day - 1993
Nuthin' But A 'G' Thang - 1993 (G, P)

DR. HOOK
The Cover Of Rolling Stone - 1973
Only Sixteen - 1976
Sexy Eyes - 1980
Sharing The Night Together - 1978
Sylvia's Mother - 1972
When You're In Love With A Beautiful
Woman - 1979

DUICE
Dazzey Duks - 1993 (G, P*)
*Double platinum as of 01/27/94

DURAN DURAN
Hungry Like A Wolf - 1993
Ordinary World - 1993
The Reflex - 1993
The Wild Boys - 1993

E

EAGAN, WALTER
Magnet & Steel - 1978

EAGLES
Heartache Tonight - 1980
Hotel California - 1977
New Kid In Town - 1977

EARTH, WIND & FIRE
After The Love Has Gone - 1979
Boogie Wonderland - 1979
Getaway - 1976
Got To Get You Into My Life - 1978
Let's Groove - 1982
September - 1979
Shining Star - 1975
Sing A Song - 1976

EASTON, SHEENA
Morning Train - 1981

EDGAR WINTER GROUP
Frankenstein - 1973

EDISON LIGHTHOUSE
Love Grows (Where My Rosemary
Goes) - 1970

EDWARDS, JONATHAN
Sunshine - 1972

EDWIN HAWKINS' SINGERS
Oh Happy Day - 1969

EIGHT DAY
She's Not Just Another Woman
- 1971

ELECTRIC LIGHT ORCHESTRA
Don't Bring Me Down - 1979
I'm Alive - 1980
Telephone Line - 1977

ELLIMAN, YVONNE
If I Can't Have You - 1978

ELMO AND PATSY
Grandma Got Run Over By A
Reindeer - 1989

EMF
Unbelievable - 1991

EMOTIONS
Best Of My Love - 1977

EN VOGUE
Free Your Mind - 1992
Giving Him Something He Can Feel
- 1992
Hold On - 1990 (G, P)
My Lovin' - 1992

ENGLAND DAN & JOHN FORD COLEY
I'd Really Love To See You Tonight
- 1976

ENIGMA
Return To Innocence - 1994
Sadness, Part I - 1991

EPMD
Crossover - 1992

ESCAPE CLUB
I'll Be There - 1991
Wild, Wild, West - 1989

ESSEX, DAVID
Rock On - 1974

**ESTEFAN, GLORIA & MIAMI SOUND
MACHINE**
Anything For You - 1989
Bad Boy - 1989
Conga - 1989
Don't Wanna Lose You - 1989

EURYTHMICS
Sweet Dreams (Are Made Of This)
- 1983

EXILE
Kiss You All Over - 1978

EXPOSE
I'll Never get Over You (Getting Over
Me) - 1993
What You Don't Know - 1989

EXTREME II
More Than Words - 1991

F

FAITH NO MORE
Epic - 1990

FAITH, PERCY
Theme From A Summer Place - 1962

FARGO, DONNA
Funny Face - 1973
Happiest Girl In The Whole U.S.A.
- 1972

FATHER M.C.
I'll Do For You - 1991

FENDER, FREDDY
Before The Next Teardrop Falls
- 1975

Wasted Days & Wasted Nights - 1975

FIFTH DIMENSION
Aquarius/Let The Sun Shine In - 1991
Last Night I Didn't Get To Sleep At All
- 1991
One Less Bell To Answer - 1991
Stoned Soul Picnic - 1991
Wedding Bell Blues - 1991

FINE YOUNG CANNIBALS
She Drives Me Crazy - 1989

FIREHOUSE
Love Of A Lifetime - 1991

FIVE MAN ELECTRICAL BAND
Signs - 1971

FLACK, ROBERTA
Feel Like Makin' Love - 1974
The First Time Ever I Saw Your Face
- 1972
Killing Me Softly With His Song - 1973

FLACK, ROBERTA/DONNY HATHAWAY
The Closer I Get To You - 1978
Where Is The Love - 1972

FLEETWOOD MAC
Dreams - 1977

THE FLOATERS
Float On - 1977

FLYING MACHINE
Smile A Little Smile For Me - 1969

FORD, LITA
Close My Eyes Forever - 1989

FOREIGNER
Double Vision - 1978
Hot Blooded - 1978
I Want To Know What Love Is - 1985
Waiting For A Girl Like You - 1982

FOUNDATIONS
Build Me Up Buttercup - 1969

4 NON BLONDES
What's Up - 1993

THE FOUR SEASONS
December, 1963 (Oh, What A Night)
- 1976
Rag Doll - 1964

THE FOUR TOPS
Ain't No Woman - 1973

FOX, SAMANTHA
I Wanna Have Some Fun - 1989

FRANKIE GOES TO HOLLYWOOD
Relax - 1989

FRANKLIN, ARETHA
Baby I Love You - 1967
Bridge Over Troubled Waters - 1971
Chain Of Fools - 1968
Day Dreaming - 1972
Don't Play That Song - 1970
I Never Loved A Man The Way I Love
You - 1967
I Say A Little Prayer - 1968
Respect - 1967
Rock Steady - 1971
See Saw - 1969
Since You've Been Gone - 1968
Spanish Harlem - 1971
Think - 1968
Until You Come Back To Me - 1974

FRED, JOHN & THE PLAYBOYS
Judy In Disguise With Glasses - 1968

FRESH DOUG E. & GET FRESH CREW
The Show (12") - 1986
FRIENDS OF DISTINCTION
Going In Circles - 1969
Grazin' In The Grass - 1969
FRIJID PINK
House Of The Rising Sun - 1970
FUNKADELIC
One Nation Under A Groove - 1978
FU-SCHNICKENS (WITH S. O'NEAL)
What's Up Doc? (Can We Rock)
- 1993

G

G.Q.
Disco Nights (Rock Freak) - 1979
GALLERY
Nice To Be With You - 1972
GAYE, MARVIN
Sexual Healing - 1982
GAYLE, CRYSTAL
Don't It Make My Brown Eyes Blue
- 1977
GAYNOR, GLORIA
I Will Survive - 1979 (G, P)
GENTRY, BOBBY
Ode To Billy Joe - 1967
GERARDO
Rico Suave - 1991
GETO BOYS
Mind Playing Tricks On Me 1991
GIBB, ANDY
An Everlasting Love - 1978
I Just Want To Be Your Everything
- 1977
Love Is Thicker Than Water - 1978
(Our Love) Don't Throw It Away - 1979
Shadow Dancing - 1978 (G, P)
GIBSON, DEBBIE
Electric Youth - 1989
Lost In Your Eyes - 1989
Only In My Dreams - 1989
Shake Your Love - 1989
GILDER, NICK
Hot Child In The City - 1978 (G, P
- 1979)
GILL, JOHNNY
Rub You The Right Way - 1990
GILMER, JIM & THE FIREBALLS
Sugar Shack - 1963
THE GO-GO's
We Got The Beat - 1982
GOLDSBORO, BOBBY
Honey - 1968
GOODMAN, DICKIE
Mr. Jaws - 1975
GRAHAM, LARRY
One In A Million - 1980
GRAND FUNK RAILROAD
The Loco-Motion - 1974
We're An American Band - 1973
GRANT, EDDY
Electric Avenue - 1989
THE GRASSROOTS
Midnight Confession - 1968
GRAY, DOBIE
Drift Away - 1973

GREAT WHITE
Once Bitten, Twice Shy - 1989
GREAVES, R.B.
Take A Letter To Mama - 1969
GREEN, AL
Call Me (Come Back Home) - 1973
Here I Am (Come & Take Me Away)
- 1973
I'm Still In Love With You - 1972
Let's Stay Together - 1972
Look What You've Done To Me - 1972
Sha-La-La (Make Me Happy) - 1975
Tired Of Being Alone - 1971
You Ought To Be With Me - 1972
GREEN JELLY
Three Little Pigs - 1993
GREENBAUM, NORMAN
Spirit In The Sky - 1970
GROSS, HENRY
Shannon - 1976
GUESS WHO
American Woman - 1970
Laughing - 1969
These Eyes - 1969
GUNS 'N ROSES
Don't Cry - 1989
November Rain - 1992
Patience - 1989
Sweet Child O' Mine - 1989
You Could Be Mine - 1991

H

HADDAWAY
What Is Love - 1993
HALL & OATES
I Can't Go For That (No Can Do)
- 1982
Kiss On My List - 1981
Maneater - 1983
Private Eyes - 1981
Rich Girl - 1977
Sara Smile - 1976
HAMILTON, JOE FRANK & REYNOLDS
Don't Pull Your Love - 1971
Fallin' In Love - 1975
HAMMER
Addams Groove - 1992
Bumps Ana A Bump - 1994
Too Legit To Quit - 1992 (G, P)
HAMMER, M.C.
Have You Seen Here - 1990
Pray - 1990
HAMMOND, ALBERT
It Never Rains In Southern California
- 1973
HANCOCK, HERBIE
Rockit - 1990
HARRIS, MAJOR
Love Won't Let Me Wait - 1975
HARRISON, GEORGE
My Sweet Lord - 1970
HART, FREDDIE
Easy Loving - 1971
HARTMAN, DAN
Instant Replay - 1979
HEART
All I Wanna Do Is Make Love To You
- 1990

HEATWAVE
Always & Forever - 1978
Boogie Nights - 1977 (G, P)
The Groove Line - 1978
HEAVY D AND THE BOYZ
Now That We Found Love - 1991
HEBB, BOBBY
Sunny - 1966
THE HEIGHTS
How Do You Talk To An Angel - 1992
HENLEY, DON
Dirty Laundry - 1983
HERMAN'S HERMITS
I'm Henry The VIII, I Am - 1965
Mrs. Brown, You've Got A Lovely
Daughter - 1965
There's A Kind Of Hush - 1967
HERNANDEZ, PATRICK
Born To Be Alive - 1979
HI-FIVE
I Like The Way - 1991
HILL, DAN
Sometimes When We Touch - 1978
HOLLIES
The Air That I Breathe - 1974
Long Cool Woman (In A Black Dress)
- 1972
HOLLY, BUDDY & THE CRICKETS
That'll Be The Day - 1969
HOLMAN, EDDIE
Hey There Lonely Girl - 1970
HOLMES, CLINT
Playground In The Mind - 1973
HOLMES, RUPERT
Escape (The Pina Colada Song)
- 1980
HONEY CONE
Stick-Up - 1971
Want Ads - 1971
HOPKIN, MARY
Those Were The Days - 1968
HORTON, JOHNNY
Battle Of New Orleans - 1966
HOT
Angel In Your Arms - 1977
HOT CHOCOLATE
Every One's A Winner - 1979
You Sexy Thing - 1976
HOUSE OF PAIN
Jump Around - 1992 (G, P)
HOUSTON, WHITNEY
All The Man That I Need - 1990
I Have Nothing - 1993
I Wanna Dance With Somebody (Who
Loves Me) - 1987 (G, P - 1989)
I Will Always Love You - 1992 (G, P*)
*Triple platinum as of 12/29/92;
Quad-platinum as of 01/12/93
I'm Every Woman - 1993
I'm Your Baby Tonight - 1990
The Star Spangled Banner - 1991
H-TOWN
Knockin' The Boots - 1993
HUES CORPORATION
Rock The Boat - 1974
HUMAN LEAGUE
Don't You Want Me - 1982

HUMPERDINCK, ENGELBERT
After The Lovin' - 1977
HYLAND, BRIAN
Gypsy Woman - 1971

I

ICE CUBE
Check Yo Self - 1993 (G, P)
It Was A Good Day - 1993
Wicked/U Ain't Gonna Take My Life
- 1993
IDOL, BILLY
Cradle Of Love - 1990
IGLESIAS, JULIO AND WILLIE NELSON
To All The Girls I've Loved Before
- 1992
THE INDEPENDENTS
Leaving Me - 1973
INFORMATION SOCIETY
What's On Your Mind (Pure Energy)
- 1989
INNER CIRCLE
Bad Boys - 1993
INSTANT FUNK
I Got My Mind Made Up (You Can
Get It Girl) - 1979
THE INTRUDERS
Cowboys To Girls - 1968
INXS
Suicide Blonde - 1990
ISAAK, CHRIS
Wicked Game - 1991
ISLEY BROTHERS
Fight The Power Part I - 1975
It's Your Thing - 1969
That Lady - 1973

J

J. GEILS BAND
Centerfold - 1982
Freeze Frame - 1982
J.J. FAD
Supersonic - 1989
JACKS, TERRY
Seasons In The Sun - 1974
JACKSON, ALAN
Chattahoochee - 1993
JACKSON, JANET
Again - 1993 (G, P)
Alright - 1990
Any Time, Any Place - 1994
Black Cat - 1990
Control - 1990
Escapade- 1990
If - 1993
Love Will Never Do (Without You)
- 1991
Miss You Much - 1989 (G, P)
Nasty - 1990
Rhythm Nation - 1990
That's The Way Love Goes - 1993
(G, P)
What Have You Done For Me Lately
- 1990
When I Think Of You - 1990
JACKSON, MICHAEL
Beat It - 1989 (G, P)

Billie Jean - 1989 (G, P)
Black Or White - 1992 (G, P)
Don't Stop 'Til You Get Enough
- 1979 (G, P - 1989)
I Just Can't Stop Loving You - 1987
In The Closet - 1992
Off The Wall - 1989
Remember The Time - 1992
Rock With You - 1989
She's Out Of My Life - 1989
Thriller - 1989 (G, P)
Will You Be There? - 1993
JACKSON, MICHAEL & PAUL
McCARTNEY
Say Say Say - 1983 (G, P - 1992)
JACKSON, REBBIE
Centipede - 1992
THE JACKSONS
Enjoy Yourself - 1989
Shake Your Body - 1979 (G, P)
State Of Shock - 1984
JADE
Don't Walk Away - 1993
JAGGERZ
The Rapper - 1970
JAMES, TOMMY & THE SHONDELLS
Hanky Panky - 1966
JAY & THE AMERICANS
This Magic Moment - 1969
JENNINGS, WAYLON
Theme From "The Dukes Of Hazard"
- 1980
JETT, JOAN & THE BLACKHEARTS
I Love Rock 'N' Roll - 1982 (G, P)
JIMMY CASTOR BUNCH
Troglodyte - 1972
JIVE BUNNY AND THE MIXMASTERS
Swing The Mood - 1989
JODECI
Come And Talk To Me - 1992
Cry For You - 1994
Lately - 1993
JOEL, BILLY
It's Still Rock 'N' Roll To Me - 1980
Just The Way You Are - 1978
My Life - 1978
Uptown Girl - 1984
We Didn't Start The Fire - 1989
JOHN, ELTON
Bennie & The Jets - 1974
Crocodile Rock - 1973
Don't Let The Sun Go Down On Me
- 1974
Goodbye Yellow Brick Road - 1974
Island Girl - 1975
Little Jeannie - 1980
Lucy In The Sky With Diamonds
- 1975
Mama Can't Buy You Love - 1979
Philadelphia Freedom - 1975
Someone Saved My Life Tonight
- 1975
Sorry Seems To Be The Hardest Word
- 1977
JOHN, ELTON & KIKI DEE
Don't Go Breaking My Heart - 1976
JOHN, ROBERT
The Lion Sleeps Tonight - 1972

Sad Eyes - 1979
JOHNS, SAMMY
Chevy Van - 1975
JONES GIRLS
You're Gonna Make Me Love
Somebody Else - 1979
JONES, ORAN "JUICE"
The Rain - 1991
JONES, QUINCY
The Secret Garden - 1990
JONES, TOM
I'll Never Fall In Love Again - 1969
She's A Lady - 1971
Without Love - 1970

K

K7
Come Baby Come - 1993
K.W.S.
Please Don't Go - 1992
KANSAS
Carry On Wayward Son - 1990
Dust In The Wind - 1978
KELLEY, R.
Bump And Grind - 1994 (G, P)
Sex Me, Parts 1 & 2 - 1993
Your Body's Callin' - 1994
KEMP, JOHNNY
Just Got Paid - 1989
KEMP, TARA
Hold You Tight - 1991
KHAN, CHAKA
I Feel For You - 1984
KIM, ANDY
Baby, I Love You - 1969
Rock Me Gently - 1974
KING, CAROLE
It's Too Late - 1971
KING, EVELYN "CHAMPAGNE"
I Don't Know If It's Right - 1979
Shame - 1978
KING FLOYD
Groove Me - 1971
KINGSTON TRIO
Tom Dooley - 1959
KISS
Beth - 1977
I Was Made For Loving You - 1979
KIX
Don't Close Your Eyes - 1990
THE KLF
3 a.m. Eternal - 1991
THE KNACK
My Sharona - 1979
KNIGHT, GLADYS & THE PIPS
The Best Thing That Ever Happened
To Me - 1974
Midnight Train To Georgia - 1973
On & On - 1974
KOOL & THE GANG
Celebration - 1981 (G, P)
Cherish - 1989
Get Down - 1989
Hollywood Swinging - 1974
Joanna - 1989
Jungle Boogie - 1974
Ladies Night - 1979

Too Hot - 1989

KRISS KROSS
Alright - 1993
Jump - 1992 (G, P*)
*Double platinum as of 05/19/92
Warm It Up - 1992

KRISTOFFERSON, KRIS
Why Me - 1973

KYPER
Tic-Tac-Toe - 1990

L

L.A. STYLE
James Brown Is Dead - 1992

L.L. COOL J
Around The Way Girl - 1991
Going Back To Cali - 1991
I'm That Type Of Guy - 1989
Mama Said Knock You Out - 1991

L.T.D.
Back In Love Again - 1977

LA BELLE
Lady Marmalade - 1975

LABELLE, PATTI & MICHAEL MCDONALD
On My Own - 1986

LA SALLE, DENISE
Trapped By A Thing Called Love - 1971

LAUPER, CYNDI
Girls Just Want To Have Fun - 1989
She Bop - 1989
Time After Time - 1989

LAWRENCE, VICKI
The Night The Lights Went Out In Georgia - 1973

LED ZEPPELIN
Whole Lotta Love - 1970

LEE, JOHNNY
Lookin' For Love - 1980

LEMON PIPERS
Green Tambourine - 1968

LENNON, JOHN
Instant Karma - 1979
Starting Over - 1980
Woman - 1981

LEVERT
Casanova - 1989

LEWIS, GARY
This Diamond Ring - 1967

LEWIS, HUEY & THE NEWS
I Want A New Drug - 1989
Power Of Love - 1989

LIGHTFOOT, GORDON
Sundown - 1974

LINDSAY, MARK
Arizona - 1970

LINEAR
Sending All My Love - 1990

LIPPS, INC.
Funkytown - 1980 (G, P)

LISA LISA AND CULT JAM
All Cried Out - 1991
Head To Toe - 1991
I Wonder If I Take You Home - 1991
Let The Beat Hit 'Em - 1991
Lost In Emotion - 1992

LOBO
I'd Love You To Want Me - 1972

LOEB, LISA
Stay - 1994

LOGGINS & MESSINA
Your Mama Don't Dance - 1973

LOGGINS, KENNY
Footloose 1984

LONDON BEAT
I've Been Thinking About You - 1991

LONDON, LAURIE
He's Got The Whole World In His Hands - 1958

LOOKING GLASS
Brandy - 1972

LOVE UNLIMITED
Love's Theme - 1974
Walking In The Rain With The One I Love - 1972

LOVIN' SPOONFUL
Summer In The City - 1966

LULU
To Sir With Love - 1967

LYNN, CHERYL
Got To Be Real - 1979

M

M
Pop Muzik - 1979

M/A/R/R/S
Pump Up The Volume - 1988

MFSB
TSOP - 1974

MACGREGOR, BYRON
Americans - 1974

MACGREGOR, MARY
Torn Between Two Lovers - 1977

MAD COBRA
Flex - 1992

MADONNA
Angel/Into The Groove (12") - 1985
Crazy For You - 1985
Erotica - 1992
Express Yourself - 1989
Hanky Panky - 1990
I'll Remember (Theme From "With Honors") - 1994
Justify My Love - 1991 (G, P)
Keep It Together - 1990
Like A Prayer - 1989 (G, P)
Like A Virgin - 1985
Rescue Me - 1991
This Used To Be My Playground - 1992
Vogue - 1990 (G, P*)
*Double platinum as of 06/28/90

MAIN INGREDIENT
Everybody Plays The Fool - 1972
Just Don't Want To Be Lonely - 1974

THE MAMAS & THE PAPAS
California Dreamin' - 1966
Monday, Monday - 1966

MANCINI, HENRY
Love Theme From "Romeo & Juliet" - 1969

MANFRED MANN'S EARTH BAND
Blinded By The Light - 1977

THE MANHATTANS
Kiss & Say Goodbye - 1976 (G, P)
Shining Star - 1980

MANILOW, BARRY
Can't Smile Without You - 1978
Copacabana - 1978
I Write The Songs - 1976
Looks Like We Made It - 1977
Mandy - 1975

MARKIE, BIZ
Just A Friend - 1990 (G, P)

MARKY MARK AND THE FUNKY BUNCH
Good Vibrations - 1991
Wildside - 1991

MARTIKA
Toy Soldiers - 1989

MARTIN, DEAN
Everybody Loves Somebody - 1964

MARTIN, STEVE
King Tut - 1978

MARX, RICHARD
Right Here Waiting - 1989 (G, P)

MASEKELA, HUGH
Grazing In The Grass - 1968

MATHIS, JOHNNY/DENIECE WILLIAMS
Too Much, Too Little, Too Late - 1978

MAURIAT, PAUL
Love Is Blue - 1968

MAYFIELD, CURTIS
Freddie's Dead - 1972
Super Fly - 1973

MCBRAINS
Oochie Coochie - 1992

MCCALL, C.W.
Convoy - 1975

MCCANN, PETER
Do You Wanna Make Love - 1977

MCCARTNEY, PAUL & LINDA
Live & Let Die - 1973
My Love - 1973
Uncle Albert/Admiral Halsey - 1971

MCCARTNEY, PAUL AND MICHAEL JACKSON
Say Say Say - 1992 (P)

MCCARTNEY, PAUL & WINGS
Band On The Run - 1974
Coming Up - 1980
Good Night Tonight - 1979
Let 'Em In - 1976
Listen To What The Man Said - 1975
Silly Love Songs - 1976

MCCARTNEY, PAUL/STEVIE WONDER
Ebony & Ivory - 1982

MCCOO, MARILYN & BILLY DAVIS
You Don't Have To Be A Star - 1976

MCCOY, VAN
The Hustle - 1975

MCDOWELL, RONNIE
The King Is Gone - 1977

MCFADDIN & WHITEHEAD
Ain't No Stoppin' Us Now - 1979 (G, P)

MCFERRIN, BOBBY
Don't Worry Be Happy - 1989

MCGOVERN, MAUREEN
The Morning After - 1973

MCGRAW, TIM
Don't Take The Girl - 1994
Indian Outlaw - 1994

MCLEAN, DON
American Pie - 1972
MEAD, SISTER JANET
The Lord's Prayer - 1974
MEAT LOAF
I'd Do Anything For Love (But I Won't Do That) - 1993 (G, P)
Two Out Of Three Ain't Bad - 1978
MECO
Star Wars Theme/Cantina Band - 1977 (G, P)
MEDEIROS, GLENN FEATURING B. BROWN
She Ain't Worth It - 1990
MEDLEY, BILL & JENNIFER WARNES
(I've Had) The Time Of My Life - 1989
MEL & TIM
Back Field In Motion - 1969
MELANIE
Brand New Key - 1971
MELLOW MAN ACE
Mentirosa - 1990
MELVIN, HAROLD & THE BLUE NOTES
If You Don't Know Me By Now - 1972
The Love I Lost - 1973
MEN AT WORK
Down Under - 1983
MERCY
Love Can Make You Happy - 1969
METALLICA
Enter Sandman - 1991
One - 1990
MICHAEL, GEORGE
Don't Let The Sun Go Down On Me - 1992
Faith - 1989
Freedom - 1991
I Want Your Sex - 1989 (G, P)
One More Try - 1989
Too Funky - 1992
MICHEL'LE
No More Lies - 1990
MIDLER, BETTE
From A Distance - 1990 (G, P)
The Rose - 1980
Wind Beneath My Wings - 1989 (G, P - 1991)
MILLER, ROGER
King Of The Road - 1965
MILLI VANILLI
Baby Don't Forget My Number - 1989
Blame It On The Rain - 1989 (G, P - 1990)
Girl I'm Gonna Miss You - 1989
Girl You Know It's True - 1989 (G, P)
MILLS, FRANK
Music Box Dancer - 1979
MILLS, STEPHANIE
Never Knew Love Like This Before - 1981
MINOGUE, KYLIE
The Loco-Motion - 1993
MINT CONDITION
Breakin' My Heart - 1992
THE MOMENTS
Love On A Two-Way Street - 1970
THE MONKEES
Daydream Believer - 1967

I'm A Believer - 1966
Last Train To Clarksville - 1966
A Little Bit Me, A Little Bit You - 1967
Pleasant Valley Sunday - 1967
Valleri - 1968
MOODY BLUES
Nights In White Satin - 1972
MOORE, JACKIE
Precious, Precious - 1971
MORRIS, ALBERT
Feelings - 1975
MOTLEY CRUE
Dr. Feelgood - 1989
MOUTH & McNEAL
How Do You Do - 1972
MR. BIG
To Be With You - 1992
MTUME
Juicy Fruit - 1983
MUNGO JERRY
In The Summertime - 1970
MURPHEY, MICHAEL
Wildfire - 1975
MURPHY, EDDIE
Party All The Time - 1985
MURPHY, W./THE BIG APPLE BAND
A Fifth Of Beethoven - 1976
MURRAY, ANNE
Snowbird - 1970
You Needed Me - 1978
MUSIC EXPLOSION
Little Bit O' Soul - 1967
MYLES, ALANNAH
Black Velvet - 1990

N

N 2 DEEP
Back To The Hotel - 1992
NASH, JOHNNY
I Can See Clearly Now - 1972
NAUGHTON, DAVID
Makin' It - 1979
NAUGHTY BY NATURE
Hip Hop Hooray - 1993 (G, P)
O.P.P. - 1991 (G, P*)
*Double platinum as of 03/31/92
NAZARETH
Love Hurts - 1976
NELSON
(Can't Live Without Your) Love And Affection - 1990
NELSON, RICK
Garden Party - 1972
Travelin' Man - 1977
NELSON, TERRY
The Battle Hymn Of Lt. Calley - 1971
NELSON, WILLIE
Always On My Mind - 1991 (G, P)
NENA
99 Luft Balloons - 1984
NEW EDITION
Cool It Now - 1985
NEW KIDS ON THE BLOCK
Cover Girl - 1989
Hangin' Tough - 1989 (G, P)
I'll Be Loving You Forever - 1989
Step By Step - 1990 (G, P)

This One's For The Children - 1990
You Got It (The Right Stuff) - 1989
NEW SEEKERS
I'd Like To Teach The World To Sing - 1972
NEW VAUDEVILLE BAND
Winchester Cathedral - 1966
NEWMAN, RANDY
Short People - 1978
NEWTON, JUICE
Angel Of The Morning - 1981
Queen Of Hearts - 1981
NEWTON, WAYNE
Daddy Don't You Walk So Fast - 1972
NEWTON-JOHN, OLIVIA
Have You Never Been Mellow - 1975
Hopelessly Devoted To You - 1978
I Honestly Love You - 1974
If You Love Me (Let Me Know) - 1974
Let Me Be There - 1974
A Little More Love - 1979
Magic - 1980
Physical - 1981 (G, P - 1982)
Please Mister Please - 1975
NICHOLAS, PAUL
Heaven On The 7th Floor - 1977
NIGHTINGALE, MAXINE
Lead Me On - 1979
Right Back Where I Started From - 1976
NILSSON
Without You - 1972
1910 FRUITGUM COMPANY
Indian Giver - 1969
1,2,3, Red Light - 1968
Simon Says - 1968
95 SOUTH
Whoot, There It Is - 1993 (G, P)
NIRVANA
Smells Like Teen Spirit - 1992 (G, P)
NOBLES, CLIFF & COMPANY
The Horse - 1968
NOLAN, KENNY
I Like Dreamin' - 1977
NU SHOOZ
I Can't Wait - 1992

O

OAK RIDGE BOYS
Elvira - 1981 (G, P - 1982)
OCEAN
Put Your Hand In The Hand - 1971
OCEAN, BILLY
Caribbean Queen - 1984
O'CONNOR, SINEAD
Nothing Compares 2 U - 1990 (G, P)
O'DAY, ALAN
Undercover Angel - 1977
OHIO EXPRESS
Chewy, Chewy - 1969
Yummy, Yummy, Yummy - 1968
OHIO PLAYERS
Fire - 1975
Funky Worm - 1973
Love Rollercoaster - 1976
Skin Tight - 1974
THE O'KAYSIONS
Girl Watcher - 1968

Abba
``Take A Chance On Me''

The Beatles
``I Want To Hold Your Hand''

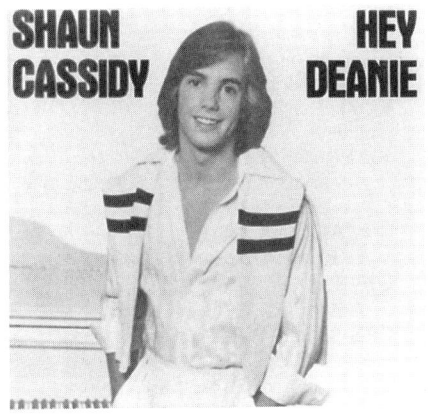

Shaun Cassidy
``Hey Deanie''

Don Henley
``Dirty Laundry''

Joan Jett
``I Love Rock 'N Roll''

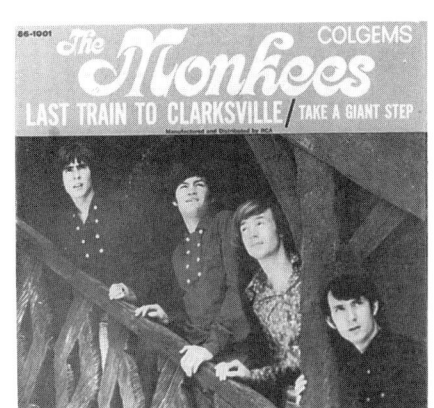

The Monkees
``Last Train To Clarksville''

Donny Osmond
``The Twelfth Of Never''

The Righteous Brothers
``Soul & Inspiration''

The Young Rscals
``Groovin' ''

O'JAYS
Backstabbers - 1972
For The Love Of Money - 1974
I Love Music - 1976
Love Train - 1973
Use To Be My Girl - 1978

OLIVER
Jean - 1969

100 PROOF
Somebody Has Been Sleeping In My
Bed - 1970

O'NEAL, SHAQVILLE
I Know I Got Skillz - 1993

ONYX
Slam - 1993 (G, P)

ORBISON, ROY
Oh, Pretty Woman - 1964

ORLANDO, TONY & DAWN
Candida - 1970
He Don't Love You (Like I Do) - 1975
Knock Three Times - 1970
Say, Has Anybody Seen My Sweet
Gypsy Rose - 1973
Tie A Yellow Ribbon Round The Old
Oak Tree - 1973

OSMOND, DONNY
Go Away Little Girl - 1971
Hey Girl - 1972
Puppy Love - 1972
Sweet & Innocent - 1971
Twelfth Of Never - 1973

OSMOND, DONNY & MARIE
I'm Leaving It (All) Up To You - 1974

OSMOND, MARIE
Paper Roses - 1973

THE OSMONDS
Down By The Lazy River - 1972
One Bad Apple - 1971
Yo-Yo - 1971

O'SULLIVAN, GILBERT
Alone Again (Naturally) - 1972
Get Down - 1973

OUTKAST
Player's Ball -1994

P

P.M. DAWN
I'd Die Without You - 1992
Set Adrift On Memory Bliss - 1991

PAGE, TOMMY
I'll Be Your Everything - 1990

PALMER, ROBERT
Addicted To Love - 1989

PAPER LACE
The Night Chicago Died - 1974

PAPERBOY
Ditty - 1993 (G, P)

PARKER, RAY, JR.
Ghostbusters - 1984

PARLIAMENT
Flash Light - 1978
Tear The Roof Off The Sucker - 1976

PARTNERS IN KRYME
Turtle Power - 1990

PARTON, DOLLY
Here You Go Again - 1978
9 To 5 - 1981

PARTRIDGE FAMILY
Doesn't Somebody Want To Be
Wanted - 1971
I Think I Love You - 1970

PAUL & PAULA
Hey Paula - 1963

PAUL, BILLY
Me & Mrs. Jones - 1972

PAYNE, FREDA
Band Of Gold - 1970
Bring The Boys Home - 1971

PEACHES & HERB
Reunited - 1979 (G, P)
Shake Your Groove Thing - 1979

PENDERGRASS, TEDDY
Close The Door - 1978

PENISTON, CE CE
Finally - 1992

PEOPLES CHOICE
Do It Any Way You Wanna - 1975

THE PERSUADERS
Thin Line Between Love & Hate - 1971

PETER, PAUL & MARY
Jet Plane - 1969

PICKETT, BOBBY
Monster Mash - 1973

PICKETT, WILSON
Don't Knock My Love - 1971
Don't Let The Green Grass Fool You
- 1971

PILOT
Magic - 1975

PINK FLOYD
Another Brick In The Wall (Part II)
- 1980

PLAYER
Baby Come Back - 1978

POINTER SISTERS
Fire - 1979
He's So Shy - 1980
Slowhand - 1981

POISON
Every Rose Has Its Thorn - 1989
Something To Believe In - 1991
Unskinny Bop - 1990

POLICE
Every Breath You Take - 1983

POPPY FAMILY
Which Way You Goin' Billy - 1970

POSITIVE K
I Got A Man - 1993

PRADO, PEREZ
Patricia - 1958

PRESLEY, ELVIS
Ain't That Loving You Babe - 1992
All Shook Up - 1992 (G, P*)
*Double platinum as of 03/27/92
Are You Lonesome Tonight - 1983
(G, P* - 1992*)
*Double platinum as of 03/27/92
A Big Hunk O' Love - 1992
Blue Christmas - 1992
Bossa Nova Baby - 1992
Burning Love - 1972 (G, P - 1992)
Can't Help Falling In Love - 1962
(G, P - 1992)
Clean Up Your Backyard - 1992
Crying In The Chapel - 1986 (G, P
- 1992)

Devil In Disguise - 1992
Don't - 1983 (G, P - 1992)
Don't Cry Daddy - 1970 (G, P - 1992)
A Fool Such As I - 1983 (G, P - 1992)
Frankie And Johnny - 1992
Good Luck Charm - 1992 (G, P)
Hard Headed Woman - 1958
(G, P - 1992)
Heartbreak Hotel - 1992
Hound Dog/Don't Be Cruel
- 1992 (G, P*)
*Double platinum as of 03/27/92
I Feel So Bad - 1992
I Got Stung - 1983 (G, P - 1992)
I Want You, I Need You, I Love You
- 1992 (G, P)
I'm Yours - 1992
I've Lost You - 1992
If I Can Dream - 1992
In The Ghetto - 1969 (G, P - 1992)
It's Now Or Never - 1992
Jailhouse Rock - 1992 (G, P*)
*Double platinum as of 03/27/92
Kentucky Rain - 1992 (G, P)
Kissin' Cousins - 1992
Love Me Tender - 1992 (G, P*)
*Double platinum as of 03/27/92
(Marie's The Name Of) His Latest
Flame - 1992
My Way - 1978
One Broken Heart - 1992
Puppet On A String - 1992
Really Don't Want To Know - 1992
Return To Sender - 1983 (G, P - 1992)
Separate Ways - 1992
She's Not You - 1992
Stuck On You - 1992 (G, P)
Surrender - 1992 (G, P)
Suspicious Minds - 1969 (G, P - 1992)
Teddy Bear - 1992 (G, P)
Tell Me Why - 1992
Too Much - 1992 (G, P)
Viva Las Vegas - 1992
Way Down - 1977
Wear My Ring Around Your Neck
- 1983 (P - 1992)
The Wonder Of You - 1970
You Don't Have To Say You Love Me
- 1992

PRESTON, BILLY
Nothing From Nothing - 1974
Outa-Space - 1972
Space Race - 1973
Will It Go Round In Circles - 1973

PRETTY POISON
Catch Me (I'm Falling) - 1989

PRIDE, CHARLEY
Kiss An Angel Good Mornin' - 1972

PRIEST, MAXI
Close To You - 1990

PRINCE
Batdance - 1989 (G, P)
I Wanna Be Your Lover - 1980
Let's Go Crazy - 1984
The Most Beautiful Girl In The World
- 1994
Partyman - 1989
Thieves In The Temple - 1990

When Doves Cry - 1984 (G, P)
PRINCE & NEW POWER GENERATION
Cream - 1992
Gett Off - 1991
7 - 1993
PRINCE & THE REVOLUTION
Kiss - 1986
Purple Rain - 1984
THE PROCLAIMERS
I'm Gonna Be (500 Miles) - 1993
PUBLIC ENEMY
Can't Truss It - 1991
PUCKETT, GARY & THE UNION GAP
Lady Willpower - 1968
Over You - 1968
Woman, Woman - 1968
Young Girl - 1968

Q

QUARTERFLASH
Harden My Heart - 1993
QUATRO, SUZIE/CHRIS NORMAN
Stumblin' In - 1979
QUEEN
Another One Bites The Dust
- 1980 (G, P)
Bohemian Rhapsody - 1976
Crazy Little Thing Called Love - 1980
The Show Must Go On - 1992
We Are The Champions - 1978 (G, P)
? & THE MYSTERIANS
96 Tears - 1966
QUIET RIOT
Cum On Feel The Noize - 1983

R

R.E.M.
Losing My Religion - 1991
R.E.O. SPEEDWAGON
Can't Fight This Feeling - 1989
Keep On Loving You - 1981 (G, P -
1989)
Take It On The Run - 1989
RABBITT, EDDIE
Drivin' My Life Away - 1981
I Love A Rainy Night - 1981
RAFFERTY, GERRY
Baker Street - 1978
RAIDERS
Indian Reservation - 1971
RANKS, SHABBA
Slow And Sexy - 1992
THE RASCALS
Beautiful Morning - 1968
People Got To Be Free - 1968
THE RASPBERRIES
Go All The Way - 1972
RAWLS, LOU
You'll Never Find Another Love Like
Mine - 1976
RAY, GOODMAN & BROWN
Special Lady - 1980
RAYDIO
Jack & Jill - 1978
RED HOT CHILI PEPPERS
Under The Bridge - 1992
REDBONE
Come & Get Your Love - 1974

REDDING, OTIS
(Sittin' On) The Dock Of The Bay
- 1968
REDDY, HELEN
Angie Baby - 1975
Delta Dawn - 1973
I Am Woman - 1972
Leave Me Alone (Ruby Red Dress)
- 1974
REED, JERRY
Amos Moses - 1971
RHYTHM HERITAGE
Theme From S.W.A.T. - 1976
RICH, CHARLIE
Behind Closed Doors - 1973
The Most Beautiful Girl - 1973
RICHARD, CLIFF
Devil Woman - 1976
RICHIE, LIONEL
All Night Long - 1983
Hello - 1984
Say You, Say Me - 1986
Truly - 1982
RIGHT SAID FRED
I'm Too Sexy - 1992
RIGHTEOUS BROTHERS
Soul & Inspiration - 1966
Unchained Melody - 1991 (G, P)
RILEY, JEANNIE C.
Harper Valley P.T.A. - 1968
RIPERTON, MINNIE
Lovin' You - 1975
RIVERS, JOHNNY
Rockin' Pneumonia & The Boogie
Woogie Flu - 1973
Swayin' To The Music - 1977
ROBIN S
Show Me Love - 1993
ROBINSON, SMOKEY
Being With You - 1981
ROCKWELL
Somebody's Watching Me - 1984
ROE. TOMMY
Dizzy - 1969
Jam Up & Jelly Tight - 1970
Sheila - 1969
Sweet Pea - 1969
ROGERS, KENNY
Coward Of The County - 1980
Lady - 1980
Lucille - 1977
She Believes In Me - 1979
ROGERS, KENNY (with DOLLY PAR-TON)
Islands In The Stream - 1983 (G, P)
THE ROLLING STONES
Angie - 1973
Honky Tonk Woman - 1969
(I Can't Get No) Satisfaction - 1965
Miss You - 1978
Ruby Tuesday - 1967
RONSTADT, LINDA
Blue Bayou - 1990
Don't Know Much - 1989
RONSTADT, LINDA & JAMES INGRAM
Somewhere Out There - 1992
ROSE ROYCE
Car Wash - 1976 (G, P)

ROSS, DIANA
Upside Down - 1981
ROSS, DIANA & LIONEL RICHIE
Endless Love - 1981 (G, P)
ROXETTE
It Must Have Been Love - 1990
The Look - 1989
THE ROYAL GUARDSMEN
Snoopy Vs. The Red Baron - 1967
RUFUS
Sweet Thing - 1976
Tell Me Something Good - 1974
RUN-D.M.C.
Down With The King - 1993
Walk This Way - 1993

S

S.O.S. BAND
Take Your Time (Do It Right)
- 1980 (G, P)
S.W.V.
I'm So Into You - 1993
Right There (Human Nature)/
Downtown - 1993
Weak - 1993 (G, P)
SADLER, SSGT. BARRY
Ballad Of The Green Berets - 1966
SAIGON KICK
Love Is On The Way - 1993
SALT 'N PEPA
Do You Want Me - 1991
Expressions - 1990
Let's Talk About Sex - 1991
Push It - 1988 (G, P - 1989)
Shoop - 1993
Whatta Man - 1994 (G, P)
SAM & DAVE
Soul Man - 1967
SAM THE SHAM & THE PHAROAHS
Lil' Red Riding Hood - 1966
Wooly Bully - 1965
SANG, SAMAMTHA
Emotion - 1978 (G, P)
SAYER, LEO
More Than I Can Say - 1980
When I Need You - 1977
You Make Me Feel Like Dancing
- 1976
SCAGGS, BOZ
Lowdown - 1976
SCARBURY, JOEY
Theme From "Greatest American
Hero" - 1981
SCORPIONS
Wind Of Change - 1991
SEBASTIAN, JOHN
Welcome Back - 1976
SECADA, JOHN
Just Another Day - 1992
SEDAKA, NEIL
Bad Blood - 1975
SEDUCTION
Two To Make It Right - 1990
THE SEEKERS
Georgy Girl - 1967
SHAI
Comforter - 1993
If I Ever Fall In Love - 1992 (G, P)

SHAKESPEAR'S SISTER
Stay - 1992
SHALAMAR
Second Time Around - 1980
SHANNON
Let The Music Play - 1984
SHERIFF
When I'm With You - 1989
SHERMAN, BOBBY
Easy Come, Easy Go - 1970
Julie, Do You Love Me - 1970
La La La (If I Had You) - 1970
Little Women - 1969
SHOCKING BLUE
Venue - 1970
SILK
Freak Me - 1993
SILVER CONVENTION
Fly, Robin, Fly - 1975
Get Up & Boogie - 1976
SIMON & GARFUNKEL
Bridge Over Troubled Waters - 1970
Cecilia - 1970
Mrs. Robinson - 1968
Sounds Of Silence - 1966
SIMON, CARLY
Jessie - 1980
Nobody Does It Better - 1977
You're So Vain - 1973
SIMON, JOE
The Chokin' Kind - 1969
Drowning In The Sea Of Love - 1972
Power Of Love - 1972
SIMON, PAUL
50 Ways To Leave Your Lover - 1976
Loves Me Like A Rock - 1973
SIMPLY RED
If You Don't Know Me By Now - 1989
SINATRA, FRANK & NANCY
Somethin' Stupid - 1967
SINATRA, NANCY
Sugartown - 1967
These Boots Are Made For Walkin'
- 1966
SIR MIX-A-LOT
Baby Got Back - 1992 (G, P*)
*Double platinum as of 07/30/92
SISTER SLEDGE
We Are Family - 1979
SKID ROW
18 And Life - 1989
SLEDGE, PERCY
When A Man Loves A Woman
SLY & THE FAMILY STONE
Everyday People - 1969
Family Affair - 1971
If You Want Me To Stay - 1973
Thank You (Fallettinme Be Mice Elf
Again) - 1970
SMITH, FRANKIE
Double Dutch Bus (7") - 1981
Double Dutch Bus (12") - 1981
SMITH, O.C.
Little Green Apples - 1968
SMITH, REX
You Take My Breath Away - 1979
SMITH, SAMMI
Help Me Make It Through The Night
- 1971

SMYTH, PATTI
Sometimes Love Just Ain't Enough
- 1992
SNAP
Ooops Up - 1990
The Power - 1990 (G, P)
Rhythm Is A Dancer - 1992
SNOOP DOGGY DOG
Gin And Juice - 1994
What's My Name? - 1994
SNOW
Informer - 1993
SOHO
Hippychick - 1990
SONNY & CHER
I Got You Babe - 1965
SOUL, DAVID
Don't Give Up On Us - 1977
SOUL ASYLUM
Runaway Train - 1993
SOUL TO SOUL
Back To Life - 1989 (G, P)
Keep On Movin' - 1989 (G, P)
SOVINE, RED
Teddy Bear - 1976
SPINNERS
Could It Be I'm Falling In Love - 1973
I'll Be Around - 1972
One Of A Kind (Love Affair) - 1973
The Rubberband Man - 1976
They Just Can't Stop It - 1975
Workin' My Way Back To You - 1980
SPRINGFIELD, RICK
Jessie's Girl - 1981
SPRINGSTEEN, BRUCE
Dancin' In The Dark - 1992 (G, P)
Santa Claus Is Coming To Town
- 1992
Streets Of Philadelphia - 1994
STAFFORD, JIM
Spiders & Snakes - 1974
STAIRSTEPS
O-O-H Child - 1970
STANSFIELD, LISA
All Around The World - 1990 (G, P)
STAPLE SINGERS
If You're Ready - 1973
Let's Do It Again - 1975
STARLAND VOCAL BAND
Afternoon Delight - 1976
STARR, RINGO
It Don't Come Easy - 1971
Photograph - 1973
You're Sixteen - 1974
STARS ON
Stars On 45 - 1981
STARSHIP
Nothing's Gonna Stop Us Now - 1989
We Built This City - 1989
STEAM
Na Na Hey Hey Kiss Him Goodbye
- 1969
STEVE MILLER BAND
Abracadabra - 1982
Fly Like An Eagle - 1977
The Joker - 1974
STEPPENWOLF
Born To Be Wild - 1968

STEVENS, RAY
Everything Is Beautiful - 1970
Gitarzan - 1969
The Streak - 1974
STEVIE B
Because I Love You - 1990
STEWART, AMII
Knock On Wood - 1979 (G, P)
STEWART, ROD
Do Ya Think I'm Sexy - 1979 (G, P)
Have I Told You Lately - 1993
Maggie May - 1971
Tonight's The Night (Gonna Be Alright)
- 1976
You're In My Heart - 1978
"THE STING" (SOUNDTRACK)
The Entertainer - 1974
STOP THE VIOLENCE MOVEMENT
Self-Destruction - 1989
STORIES
Brother Louie - 1973
STRAWBERRY ALARM CLOCK
Incense & Peppermints - 1967
STREISAND, BARBRA
Evergreen (Theme From "A Star Is
Born") - 1977
Main Event - 1979
No More Tears (Enough Is Enough)
(7") - 1980
The Way We Were - 1974
Woman In Love - 1980
STREISAND, BARBRA/BARRY GIBB
Guilty - 1981
STREISAND, BARBRA/NEIL DIAMOND
You Don't Bring Me Flowers - 1978
THE STYLISTICS
Betcha By Golly, Wow - 1972
Break Up To Make Up - 1973
You Are Everything - 1972
You Make Me Feel Brand New - 1974
STYX
Babe - 1980
Mr. Roboto - 1983
SUMMER, DONNA
Bad Girls - 1979 (G, P)
Dim All The Lights - 1979
Heaven Knows - 1979
Hot Stuff - 1979 (G, P)
I Feel Love - 1977
Last Dance - 1978
Love To Love You Baby - 1976
MacArthur Park - 1978
No More Tears (Enough Is Enough)
(12") - 1980
On The Radio - 1980
This Time I Know It's For Real - 1989
The Wanderer - 1980
SURFACE
The First Time - 1991
Shower Me With Your Love - 1989
SURVIVOR
Eye Of The Tiger - 1982 (G, P)
SWAN, BILLY
I Can Help - 1974
SWEAT, KEITH
I Want Her - 1989
Make You Sweat - 1990

SWEET
Fox On The Run - 1976
Little Willie - 1973

SYBIL
Don't Make Me Over - 1989

SYLVERS
Boogie Fever - 1976
Hot Line - 1977

SYLVIA
Nobody - 1982
Pillow Talk - 1973

T

TLC
Ain't 2 Proud 2 Beg - 1992 (G, P)
Baby Baby Baby - 1992 (G, P)
What About Your Friends - 1992

TACO
Puttin' On The Ritz - 1983

TAG TEAM
Whoomp! (There It Is) - 1993 (G, P*)
*Triple platinum as of 01/27/94;
quad-platinum as of 02/24/94

A TASTE OF HONEY
Boogie Oogie Oogie - 1978 (G, P)
Sukiyaki - 1981

TAVARES
Heaven Must Be Missing An Angel
- 1976

TAYLOR, JAMES
You've Got A Friend - 1971

TAYLOR, JAMES & CARLY SIMON
Mockingbird - 1974

TAYLOR, JOHNNY
Disco Lady - 1976 (G, P)
I Believe In You (You Believe In Me)
- 1973
Who's Making Love - 1968

TEARS FOR FEARS
Shout - 1989

TECHNOTRONIC
Get Up - 1990
Pump Up The Jam - 1989 (G, P)

10 CC
The Things We Do For Love - 1977

TESLA
Love Song - 1990

TEX, JOE
Ain't Gonna Bump No More - 1977
I Gotcha - 1972
Skinny Legs And All - 1968

3RD BASE
Pop Goes The Weasel - 1991

THOMAS, B.J.
Another Somebody Done Somebody
Wrong Song - 1975
Hooked On A Feeling - 1969
Raindrops Keep Falling On My Head
- 1969

THREE DEGREES
When Will I See You Again - 1974

THREE DOG NIGHT
Black & White - 1972
Joy To The World - 1971
Mama Told Me Not To Come - 1970
An Old Fashioned Love Song - 1971
One - 1969
Shambala - 1973

The Show Must Go On - 1974

THE TIME
Jerk Out - 1990

TIMMY T
One More Try - 1991 (G, P)

THE TOKENS
The Lion Sleeps - 1962
Hold The Line - 1979

TONE LOC
Funky Cold Medina - 1989 (G, P)
Wild Thing - 1989 (G, P*)
*Double platinum as of 02/03/89

TONY! TONI! TONE!
Anniversary - 1993
Feels Good - 1990
If I Had No Loot - 1993

TOTO
Africa - 1991
Hold The Line - 1979
Rosanna - 1991

THE TOYS
A Lover's Concerto - 1965

TRAVOLTA, JOHN/OLIVIA NEWTON-JOHN
Summer Nights - 1978
You're The One That I Want
- 1978 (G, P)

TRESVANT, RALPH
Sensitivity - 1991

TURNER, IKE & TINA
Proud Mary - 1971

TURNER, TINA
What's Love Got To Do With It - 1984

THE TURTLES
Happy Together - 1967

TUTONE, TOMMY
867-5309/Jenny - 1991

12 GAUGE
Dunkie Butt - 1994

THE 2 LIVE CREW
Me So Horny - 1989

THE 2 LIVE CREW, FEATURING LUKE
Banned In The U.S.A - 1990

2 IN A ROOM
Wiggle It - 1990

2 PAC
I Get Around - 1993
Keep Ya Head Up - 1993

TYLER, BONNIE
It's A Heartache - 1978
Total Eclipse Of The Heart - 1983

U

U2
Desire - 1989

UB-40
Can't Help Falling In Love - 1993
(G, P*)
Red Red Wine - 1989
The Way You Do The Things You Do
- 1991

USA FOR AFRICA
We Are The World - 1985 (G, P*)
*Quadruple platinum as of 04/01/85

US3
Cantaloop - 1994

UGLY KID JOE
Cats In The Cradle - 1993

V

VALLI, FRANKIE
Can't Take My Eyes Off Of You
- 1967
Grease - 1978 (G, P)
My Eyes Adored You - 1975

VAN HALEN
Jump - 1984

VANDROSS, LUTHER
Here And Now - 1990

VANILLA ICE
Ice Ice Baby - 1990 (G, P)
Play That Funky Music - 1991

VANITY FAIR
Hitchin' A Ride - 1970

VANWARMER, RANDY
Just When I Needed You Most - 1979

VARIOUS ARTISTS
Aladdin - 1993
Alice In Wonderland - 1993 (G, P)
Aristocats - 1993
Bambi - 1988 (G, P* - 1993)
*Triple platinum as of 01/13/93
Beauty And The Beast Read-A-Long
- 1993
Brer Rabbit And The Tar Baby - 1985
Cinderella - 1983 (G, P - 1993*)
*Triple platinum as of 01/13/93
Dumbo - 1983 (G, P - 1993*)
*Double platinum as of 01/13/93
E.T.: The Extra-Terrestrial - 1983
The Empire Strikes Back - 1982
The Fox And The Hound - 1983
The Hobbit - 1985
It's A Small World - 1983 (G, P
- 1993*)
*Double platinum as of 01/13/93
The Jungle Book - 1984
Lady And The Tramp - 1983
The Little Mermaid Read-A-Long
- 1990
Mary Poppins - 1983
Mickey's Christmas Carol - 1989
Mother Goose Rhymes - 1985
101 Dalmations - 1989 (G, P*)
*Double platinum as of 01/13/93
Peter Pan - 1983
Pete's Dragon - 1983
Pinocchio - 1983
Rescuers - 1984
Return Of The Jedi - 1983
Robin Hood - 1984
Sleeping Beauty - 1983
Snow White - 1988
Star Wars - 1984 (G, P)
The Three Little Pigs - 1983
Voices That Care - 1992
Winnie The Pooh And The Blustery
Day - 1985
Winnie The Pooh And The Honeytree
- 1988
Winnie the Pooh & Tigger Too - 1983
The Wizard Of Oz - 1985

VEE, BOBBY & THE STRANGERS
Come Back When You Grow Up
- 1967

VERA, BILLY & THE BEATERS
At This Moment - 1989

VILLAGE PEOPLE
In The Navy - 1979
Macho Man - 1978
Y.M.C.A. - 1978 (G, P - 1979)
VINTON, BOBBY
I Love How You Love Me - 1968
My Melody Of Love - 1974
Roses Are Red - 1962
THE VOGUES
Turn Around, Look At Me - 1968

W

WAR
Cisco Kid - 1973
Slippin' Into Darkness - 1972
Summer - 1976
Why Can't We Be Friends - 1975
The World Is A Ghetto - 1973
WARRANT
Heaven - 1989
WARREN G & NATE DOGG
Regulate - 1994
WARWICK, DIONNE
I Say A Little Prayer - 1968
I'll Never Love This Way Again - 1979
WARWICK, DIONNE & FRIENDS
That's What Friends Are For - 1986
WARWICK, DIONNE & THE SPINNERS
Then Came You - 1974
WATERS, CRYSTAL
Gypsy Woman (She's Homeless) - 1991
WATLEY, JODY
Real Love - 1989
WEISSBERG, ERIC
Dueling Banjos - 1973
WELK, LAWRENCE
Calcutta - 1961
WESLEY, FRED & THE JB's
Doin' It To Death - 1973
WEST COAST RAP ALL STARS
We're All The Same Gang - 1990

WHAM!
Careless Whisper - 1985
Everything She Wants - 1992
Wake Me Up Before You Go - 1984
THE WHISPERS
And The Beat Goes On - 1980
WHITE, BARRY
Can't Get Enough Of Your Love, Babe - 1974
I'm Gonna Love You Just A Little Bit More Baby - 1973
It's Ecstasy When You Lay Down Next To Me - 1977
Never, Never Gonna Give Ya Up - 1974
You're The First, The Last, My Everything - 1974
WHITE, KARYN
Superwoman - 1989
The Way You Love Me - 1989
WILD CHERRY
Play That Funky Music - 1976 (G, P)
WILL TO POWER
Baby I Love Your Way - 1989
WILLIAMS, DENIECE
Let's Hear It For The Boy - 1992
WILLIAMS, VANESSA
Save The Best For Last - 1992
WILSON, AL
Show & Tell - 1973
WILSON, MARY
Telephone Man - 1977
WILSON PHILLIPS
Hold On - 1990
Release Me - 1990
WINSTONS
Color Him Father - 1969
WITHERS, BILL
Ain't No Sunshine - 1971
Lean On Me - 1972
Use Me - 1972
WOMACK, BOBBY & PEACE
Harry Hippie - 1973

Lookin' For A Love - 1974
WONDER, STEVIE
I Just Called To Say I Love You - 1984
WRECKX 'N' EFFECT
Rump Shaker - 1992 (G, P)
*Double platinum as of 01/22/93
WRIGHT, BETTY
Clean Up Woman - 1971
WRIGHT, GARY
Dream Weaver - 1976

X

XSCAPE
Just Kickin' It - 1993 (G, P)
Understanding - 1994

Y

YANKOVIC, "WEIRD AL"
Eat It - 1989
YARBROUGH & PEOPLES
Don't Stop The Music - 1981
YOUNG HOLT UNLIMITED
Soulful Strut - 1969
YOUNG M.C.
Bust A Move - 1989 (G, P - 1990)
YOUNG, NEIL
Heart Of Gold - 1972
YOUNG, PAUL
Every Time You Go Away - 1990
YOUNG RASCALS
Groovin' - 1967
YOUNGBLOODS
Get Together - 1969

Z

ZAGER & EVANS
In The Year 2525 - 1969
ZHANE
Hey Mr. D.J. - 1993
ZOMBIES
Time Of The Season - 1969

Honor Roll of Hits
• Albums •

Herb Alpert
Tijuana Brass fans well remember the heady days of Herb Alpert's back-to-back album blitz.
Herb and the Brass had five—count 'em—Top 20 Pop LPs in 1966 (including the #1 ``Whipped Cream And Other Delights''),
and followed that up with four Top 20 marks in the 1967 list.

Billboard Top 20 Pop Albums, 1956-1993

TOP 20 POP ALBUMS OF 1956

POS.   TITLE - ARTIST - LABEL
1. CALYPSO - Harry Belafonte - RCA Victor
2. MY FAIR LADY - Original Cast - Columbia
3. THE KING AND I - Soundtrack - Capitol
4. THE EDDY DUCHIN STORY - Soundtrack - Decca
5. ELVIS PRESLEY - Elvis Presley - RCA Victor
6. HIGH SOCIETY - Soundtrack - Capitol
7. SONGS FOR SWINGON' LOVERS - Frank Sinatra - Capitol
8. BELAFONTE - Harry Belafonte - RCA Victor
9. THE PLATTERS - Platters - Mercury
10. OKLAHOMA! - Soundtrack - Capitol
11. ELVIS - Elvis Presley - RCA Victor
12. CAROUSEL - Soundtrack - Capitol
13. SAY IT WITH MUSIC - Lawrence Welk - Coral
14. FOUR FRESHMEN AND FIVE TROMBONES - Four Freshmen - Capitol
15. BUBBLES IN THE WINE - Lawrence Welk - Coral
16. SOLO MOOD - Paul Weston - Columbia
17. FRESHMAN FAVORITES - Four Freshmen - Capitol
18. THE COLE PORTER SONG BOOK - Ella Fitzgerald - Verve
19. HOWDY - Pat Boone - Dot
20. MISTY MISS CHRISTY - June Christy - Capitol

TOP 20 POP ALBUMS OF 1957

POS.   TITLE - ARTIST - LABEL
1. MY FAIR LADY - Original Cast - Columbia
2. HYMNS - Tennessee Ernie Ford - Capitol
3. OKLAHOMA! - Soundtrack - Capitol
4. AROUND THE WORLD IN 80 DAYS - Soundtrack - Decca
5. THE KING AND I - Soundtrack - Capitol
6. CALYPSO - Harry Belafonte - RCA Victor
7. LOVE IS THE THING - Nat King Cole - Capitol
8. THE EDDY DUCHIN STORY - Soundtrack - Decca
9. SONGS OF THE FABULOUS FIFTIES - Roger Williams - Kapp
10. FILM ENCORES - Mantovani - London
11. LOVING YOU - Elvis Presley - RCA Victor
12. ELVIS - Elvis Presley - RCA Victor
13. AN EVENING WITH HARRY BELAFONTE - Harry Belafonte - RCA Victor
14. JERRY LEWIS JUST SINGS - Jerry Lewis - Decca
15. A SWINGIN' AFFAIR - Frank Sinatra - Capitol
16. BELAFONTE - Harry Belafonte - RCA Victor
17. STEADY DATE WITH TOMMY SANDS - Tommy Sands - Capitol
18. SPIRITUALS - Tennessee Ernie Ford - Capitol
19. WHERE ARE YOU? - Frank Sinatra - Capitol
20. WONDERFUL, WONDERFUL - Johnny Mathis - Columbia

TOP 20 POP ALBUMS OF 1958

POS.   TITLE - ARTIST - LABEL
1. MY FAIR LADY - Original Cast - Columbia
2. THE MUSIC MAN - Original Cast - Capitol
3. JOHNNY'S GREATEST HITS - Johnny Mathis - Columbia
4. SOUTH PACIFIC - Soundtrack - RCA Victor
5. COME FLY WITH ME - Frank Sinatra - Capitol
6. AROUND THE WORLD IN 80 DAYS - Soundtrack - Decca
7. WARM - Johnny Mathis - Columbia
8. SOUTH PACIFIC - Original Cast - Columbia
9. RICKY - Ricky Nelson - Imperial
10. THE KING AND I - Soundtrack - Capitol
11. HYMNS - Tennessee Ernie Ford - Capitol
12. OKLAHOMA! - Soundtrack - Capitol
13. TCHAIKOVSKY: PIANO CONCERTO NO.1 - Van Cliburn - RCA Victor
14. PAT'S GREAT HITS - Pat Boone - Dot
15. FILM ENCORES - Mantovani - London
16. THE LATE, LATE SHOW - Dakota Staton - Capitol
17. GIGI - Soundtrack - MGM
18. ELVIS' GOLDEN RECORDS - Elvis Presley - RCA Victor
19. SING ALONG WITH MITCH - Mitch Miller - Columbia
20. PAL JOEY - Soundtrack - Capitol

TOP 20 POP ALBUMS OF 1959

POS.   TITLE - ARTIST - LABEL
1. MUSIC FROM "PETER GUNN" - Henry Mancini - RCA Victor
2. GIGI - Soundtrack - MGM
3. SOUTH PACIFIC - Soundtrack - RCA Victor
4. FROM THE HUNGRY I - Kingston Trio - Capitol
5. THE KINGSTON TRIO AT LARGE - Kingston Trio - Capitol
6. SING ALONG WITH MITCH - Mitch Miller - Columbia
7. INSIDE SHELLEY BERMAN - Shelley Berman - Verve
8. EXOTICA, VOL. 1 - Martin Denny - Liberty
9. MY FAIR LADY - Original Cast - Columbia
10. FLOWER DRUM SONG - Original Cast - Columbia
11.* JOHNNY'S GREATEST HITS - Johnny Mathis - Columbia
    COME DANCE WITH ME - Frank Sinatra - Capitol (*Tie)
12. THE KINGSTON TRIO - Kingston Trio - Capitol
13. THE MUSIC MAN - Original Cast - Capitol
14. OPEN FIRE, TWO GUITARS - Johnny Mathis - Columbia
15. MORE SING ALONG WITH MITCH - Mitch Miller - Columbia
16. MORE JOHNNY'S GREATEST HITS - Johnny Mathis - Columbia
17. TCHAIKOVSKY: PIANO CONCERTO NO.1 - Van Cliburn - RCA Victor
18. FILM ENCORES - Mantovani - London
19. HAVE TWANGY GUITAR, WILL TRAVEL - Duane Eddy - Jamie

TOP 20 POP ALBUMS OF 1960

POS.   TITLE - ARTIST - LABEL
1. THE SOUND OF MUSIC - Original Cast - Columbia
2. INSIDE SHELLEY BERMAN - Shelley Berman - Verve
3. THE BUTTON-DOWN MIND OF BOB NEWHART - Bob Newhart - Warner Bros.
4. SIXTY YEARS OF MUSIC AMERICA LOVES BEST, VOL. I - Various Artists - RCA Victor
5. HERE WE GO AGAIN - Kingston Trio - Capitol
6. SOLD OUT - Kingston Trio - Capitol
7. HEAVENLY - Johnny Mathis - Columbia
8. SOUTH PACIFIC - Soundtrack - RCA Victor
9. FAITHFULLY - Johnny Mathis - Columbia
10. OUTSIDE SHELLEY BERMAN - Shelley Berman - Verve
11. STRING ALONG - Kingston Trio - Capitol

12. BELAFONTE AT CARNEGIE HALL - Harry Belafonte - RCA Victor
13. THEME FROM "A SUMMER PLACE" - Billy Vaughn - Dot
14. ELVIS IS BACK - Elvis Presley - RCA Victor
15. ITALIAN FAVORITES - Connie Francis - MGM
16. FROM THE HUNGRY I - Kingston Trio - Capitol
17. FABULOUS FABIAN - Fabian - Chancellor
18. NICE AND EASY - Frank Sinatra - Capitol
19. ENCORE OF GOLDEN HITS - Platters - Mercury
20. THE KINGSTON TRIO AT LARGE - Kingston Trio - Capitol

TOP 20 POP ALBUMS OF 1961 (Monaural)

POS. TITLE - ARTIST - LABEL
1. CAMELOT - Original Cast - Columbia
2. GREAT MOTION PICTURE THEMES - Various Artists - United Artists
3. NEVER ON SUNDAY - Soundtrack - United Artists
4. THE SOUND OF MUSIC - Original Cast - Columbia
5. EXODUS - Soundtrack - RCA Victor
6. KNOCKERS UP - Rusty Warren - Jubilee
7. G.I. BLUES - Elvis Presley/Soundtrack - RCA Victor
8. SING ALONG WITH MITCH - Mitch Miller - Columbia
9. CALCUTTA - Lawrence Welk - Dot
10. TONIGHT IN PERSON - Limeliters - RCA Victor
11. THE BUTTON-DOWN MIND OF BOB NEWHART - Bob Newhart - Warner Bros.
12. JOHNNY'S GREATEST HITS - Johnny Mathis - Columbia
13. MAKE WAY - Kingston Trio - Capitol
14. ENCORE OF GOLDEN HITS - Platters - Mercury
15. BELAFONTE AT CARNEGIE HALL - Harry Belafonte - RCA Victor
16. THE BUTTON-DOWN MIND STRIKES BACK - Bob Newhart - Warner Bros.
17. MUSIC FROM EXODUS AND OTHER GREAT THEMES - Mantovani - London
18. ALL THE WAY - Frank Sinatra - Capitol
19. PAUL ANKA SINGS HIS BIG 15 - Paul Anka - ABC-Paramount
20. THE KINGSTON TRIO - Kingston Trio - Capitol

TOP 20 POP ALBUMS OF 1961 (Stereo)

POS. TITLE - ARTIST - LABEL
1. THE SOUND OF MUSIC - Original Cast - Columbia
2. CALCUTTA - Lawrence Welk - Dot
3. EXODUS - Soundtrack - RCA Victor
4. CAMELOT - Original Cast - Columbia
5. GREAT MOTION PICTURE THEMES - Various Artists - United Artists
6. MUSIC FROM "EXODUS" AND OTHER GREAT THEMES - Mantovani - London
7. BELAFONTE AT CARNEGIE HALL - Harry Belafonte - RCA Victor
8. SING ALONG WITH MITCH - Mitch Miller - Columbia
9. PERSUASIVE PERCUSSION - Terry Snyder & The All Stars - Command
10. PROVOCATIVE PERCUSSION - Enoch Light & The Light Brigade - Command
11. THE BUTTON-DOWN MIND OF BOB NEWHART - Bob Newhart - Warner Bros.
12. G.I. BLUES - Elvis Presley/Soundtrack - RCA Victor
13. MAKE WAY - Kingston Trio - Capitol
14. ENCORE OF GOLDEN HITS - Platters - Mercury
15. ALL THE WAY - Frank Sinatra - Capitol
16. HAPPY TIMES SING ALONG WITH MITCH - Mitch Miller - Columbia

17. TV SING ALONG WITH MITCH - Mitch Miller - Columbia
18. TONIGHT IN PERSON - Limeliters - RCA Victor
19. CARNIVAL - Original Cast - MGM
20. NEVER ON SUNDAY - Soundtrack - United Artists

TOP 20 POP ALBUMS OF 1962 (Monaural)

POS. TITLE - ARTIST - LABEL
1. WEST SIDE STORY - Soundtrack - Columbia
2. BREAKFAST AT TIFFANY'S Henry Mancini - RCA Victor
3. BLUE HAWAII - Elvis Presley/Soundtrack - RCA Victor
4. WEST SIDE STORY - Original Cast - Columbia
5. THE SOUND OF MUSIC - Original Cast - Columbia
6. TIME OUT - Dave Brubeck - Columbia
7. CAMELOT - Original Cast - Columbia
8. YOUR TWIST PARTY - Chubby Checker - Parkway
9. KNOCKERS UP - Rusty Warren - Jubilee
10. JUDY AT CARNEGIE HALL - Judy Garland - Capitol
11. JOAN BAEZ, VOL. 2 - Joan Baez - Vanguard
12. MY FAIR LADY - Original Cast - Columbia
13. DOIN' THE TWIST AT THE PEPPERMINT LOUNGE - Joey Dee & The Starliters - Roulette
14. JOHNNY'S GREATEST HITS - Johnny Mathis - Columbia
15. DO THE TWIST - Ray Charles - Atlantic
16. MOON RIVER - Lawrence Welk - Dot
17. THE TWIST - Chubby Checker - Parkway
18. A SONG FOR YOUNG LOVE - Lettermen - Capitol
19. OLDIES BUT GOODIES - Various Artists - Original Sound
20. JUMP UP CALYPSO - Harry Belafonte - RCA Victor

TOP 20 POP ALBUMS OF 1962 (Stereo)

POS. TITLE - ARTIST - LABEL
1. WEST SIDE STORY - Soundtrack - Columbia
2. BREAKFAST AT TIFFANY'S Henry Mancini - RCA Victor
3. STEREO 35MM - Enoch Light & His Orchestra - Command
4. CAMELOT - Original Cast - Columbia
5. THE SOUND OF MUSIC - Original Cast - Columbia
6. BLUE HAWAII - Elvis Presley/Soundtrack - RCA Victor
7. JUDY AT CARNEGIE HALL - Judy Garland - Capitol
8. WEST SIDE STORY - Original Cast - Columbia
9. TIME OUT - Dave Brubeck - Columbia
10. MOON RIVER - Lawrence Welk - Dot
11. MODERN SOUNDS IN COUNTRY AND WESTERN MUSIC - Ray Charles - ABC-Paramount
12. STRANGER ON THE SHORE - Mr. Acker Bilk - Atco
13. PERSUASIVE PERCUSSION - Terry Snyder & The All Stars - Command
14. NO STRINGS - Original Cast - Capitol
15. COLLEGE CONCERT - Kingston Trio - Capitol
16. TIME FURTHER OUT - Dave Brubeck Quartet - Columbia
17. SOUTH PACIFIC - Soundtrack - RCA Victor
18. THE STRIPPER AND OTHER FUN SONGS FOR THE FAMILY - David Rose and His Orchestra - MGM
19. WEST SIDE STORY - Ferrante & Teicher - United Artists
20. STEREO 35MM VOL. 2 - Enoch Light & His Orchestra - Command

TOP 20 POP ALBUMS OF 1963

POS. TITLE - ARTIST - LABEL
1. WEST SIDE STORY - Soundtrack - Columbia
2. PETER, PAUL AND MARY - Peter, Paul & Mary - Warner Bros.
3. MOVING - Peter, Paul & Mary - Warner Bros.

4. JOAN BAEZ IN CONCERT - Joan Baez - Vanguard
5. I LEFT MY HEART IN SAN FRANCISCO - Tony Bennett - Columbia
6. MOON RIVER AND OTHER GREAT MOVIE THEMES - Andy Williams - Columbia
7. LAWRENCE OF ARABIA - Soundtrack - Colpix
8. DAYS OF WINE AND ROSES - Andy Williams - Columbia
9. OLIVER - Original Cast - RCA Victor
10. MODERN SOUNDS IN COUNTRY AND WESTERN MUSIC, VOL. 2 - Ray Charles - ABC-Paramount
11. MODERN SOUNDS IN COUNTRY AND WESTERN MUSIC, VOL. 1 - Ray Charles - ABC-Paramount
12. THE BEST OF THE KINGSTON TRIO - Kingston Trio - Capitol
13. JAZZ SAMBA - Stan Getz & Charlie Byrd - Verve
14. ROY ORBISON'S GREATEST HITS - Roy Orbison - Monument
15. THE BARBRA STREISAND ALBUM - Barbra Streisand - Columbia
16. SONGS I SING ON THE JACKIE GLEASON SHOW - Frank Fontaine - ABC-Paramount
17. BYE BYE BIRDIE - Soundtrack - Columbia
18. THE SOUND OF MUSIC - Original Cast - Columbia
19. THE FIRST FAMILY - Vaughn Meader - Cadence
20. MY SON, THE FOLK SINGER - Allan Sherman - Warner Bros.

TOP 20 POP ALBUMS OF 1964

POS. TITLE - ARTIST - LABEL
1. HELLO, DOLLY! - Original Cast - RCA Victor
2. IN THE WIND - Peter, Paul & Mary - Warner Bros.
3. HONEY ON THE HORN - Al Hirt - RCA Victor
4. THE BARBRA STREISAND ALBUM - Barbra Streisand - Columbia
5. WEST SIDE STORY - Soundtrack - Columbia
6. PETER, PAUL AND MARY - Peter, Paul & Mary - Warner Bros.
7. THE SECOND BARBRA STREISAND ALBUM - Barbra Streisand - Warner Bros.
8. MEET THE BEATLES - Beatles - Capitol
9. THE THIRD BARBRA STREISAND ALBUM - Barbra Streisand - Columbia
10. MOON RIVER AND OTHER GREAT MOVIE THEMES - Andy Williams - Columbia
11. LOUIE LOUIE - Kingsmen - Wand
12. CATCH A RISING STAR - John Gary - RCA Victor
13. INTRODUCING THE BEATLES - Beatles - Vee Jay
14. DAYS OF WINE AND ROSES - Andy Williams - Columbia
15. FUNNY GIRL - Original Cast - Capitol
16. BACH'S GREATEST HITS - Swingle Singers - Philips
17. THE PINK PANTHER - Henry Mancini & His Orchestra - RCA Victor
18. MOVING - Peter, Paul & Mary - Warner Bros.
19. HELLO, DOLLY! - Louis Armstrong - Kapp
20. I LEFT MY HEART IN SAN FRANCISCO - Tony Bennett - Columbia

TOP 20 POP ALBUMS OF 1965

POS. TITLE - ARTIST - LABEL
1. MARY POPPINS - Soundtrack - Vista
2. BEATLES '65 - Beatles - Capitol
3. THE SOUND OF MUSIC - Soundtrack - RCA Victor
4. MY FAIR LADY - Soundtrack - Columbia
5. FIDDLER ON THE ROOF - Original Cast - RCA Victor
6. GOLDFINGER - Soundtrack - United Artists
7. HELLO, DOLLY! - Original Cast - RCA Victor
8. DEAR HEART - Andy Williams - Columbia
9. INTRODUCING HERMAN'S HERMITS - Herman's Hermits - MGM
10. BEATLES VI - Beatles - Capitol
11. PETER, PAUL AND MARY IN CONCERT - Peter, Paul & Mary - Warner Bros.
12. TODAY - New Christy Minstrels - Columbia
13. ON TOUR - Herman's Hermits - MGM
14. NY NAME IS BARBRA - Barbra Streisand - Columbia
15. BLUE MIDNIGHT - Bert Kaempfert & His Orchestra - Decca
16. RAMBLIN' ROSE - Nat King Cole - Capitol
17. FUNNY GIRL - Original Cast - Capitol
18. WHERE DID OUR LOVE GO - Supremes - Motown
19. PEOPLE - Barbra Streisand - Columbia
20. GETZ/GILBERTO - Stan Getz & Joao Gilberto - Verve

TOP 20 POP ALBUMS OF 1966

POS. TITLE - ARTIST - LABEL
1. WHIPPED CREAM AND OTHER DELIGHTS - Herb Alpert's Tijuana Brass - A&M
2. THE SOUND OF MUSIC - Soundtrack - RCA Victor
3. GOING PLACES - Herb Alpert & The Tijuana Brass - A&M
4. RUBBER SOUL - Beatles - Capitol
5. WHAT NOW MY LOVE - Herb Alpert & The Tijuana Brass - A&M
6. IF YOU CAN BELIEVE YOUR EYES AND EARS - Mamas & The Papas - Dunhill
7. DR. ZHIVAGO - Soundtrack - MGM
8. REVOLVER - Beatles - Capitol
9. COLOR ME BARBRA - Barbra Streisand - Columbia
10. BALLADS OF THE GREEN BERETS - S/Sgt. Barry Sadler - RCA Victor
11. SOUTH OF THE BORDER - Herb Alpert's Tijuana Brass - A&M
12. STRANGERS IN THE NIGHT - Frank Sinatra - Reprise
13. THE BEST OF THE ANIMALS - Animals - MGM
14. LONELY BULL - Herb Alpert & The Tijuana Brass - A&M
15. BIG HITS (HIGH TIDE AND GREEN GRASS) - Rolling Stones - London
16. SEPTEMBER OF MY YEARS - Frank Sinatra - Reprise
17. YESTERDAY AND TODAY - Beatles - Capitol
18. FIDDLER ON THE ROOF - Original Cast - RCA Victor
19. MY FAIR LADY - Soundtrack - Columbia
20. MAN OF LA MANCHA - Original Cast - Kapp

TOP 20 POP ALBUMS OF 1967

POS. TITLE - ARTIST - LABEL
1. MORE OF THE MONKEES - Monkees - Colgems
2. THE MONKEES - Monkees - Colgems
3. DR. ZHIVAGO - Soundtrack - MGM
4. THE SOUND OF MUSIC - Soundtrack - RCA Victor
5. THE TEMPTATION'S GREATEST HITS - Temptations - Gordy
6. A MAN AND A WOMAN - Soundtrack - United Artists
7. S.R.O. - Herb Alpert & The Tijuana Brass - A&M
8. WHIPPED CREAM AND OTHER DELIGHTS - Herb Alpert's Tijuana Brass - A&M
9. GOING PLACES - Herb Alpert & The Tijuana Brass - A&M
10. SGT. PEPPER'S LONELY HEARTS CLUB BAND - Beatles - Capitol
11. WHAT NOW MY LOVE - Herb Alpert & The Tijuana Brass - A&M

12. WONDERFULNESS - Bill Cosby - Warner Bros.
13. MAN OF LA MANCHA - Original Cast - Kapp
14. SERGIO MENDES AND BRASIL '66 - Sergio Mendes & Brasil '66 - A&M
15. COLLECTIONS - Young Rascals - Atlantic
16. BILL COSBY IS A VERY FUNNY FELLOW, RIGHT? - Bill Cosby - Warner Bros.
17. BORN FREE - Roger Williams - Kapp
18. THAT'S LIFE - Frank Sinatra - Reprise
19. WHY IS THERE AIR? - Bill Cosby - Warner Bros.
20. THE BEST OF THE ANIMALS - Animals - MGM

TOP 20 POP ALBUMS OF 1968

POS. TITLE - ARTIST - LABEL
1. ARE YOU EXPERIENCED? - Jimi Hendrix Experience - Reprise
2. THE GRADUATE - Simon & Garfunkel/Soundtrack - Columbia
3. DISRAELI GEARS - Cream - Atco
4. MAGICAL MYSTERY TOUR - Beatles/Soundtrack - Capitol
5. DIANA ROSS AND THE SUPREMES' GREATEST HITS - Diana Ross & The Supremes - Motown
6. SGT. PEPPER'S LONELY HEARTS CLUB BAND - Beatles - Capitol
7. DOORS - Doors - Elektra
8. PARSLEY, SAGE, ROSEMARY AND THYME - Simon & Garfunkel - Columbia
9. VANILLA FUDGE - Vanilla Fudge - Atco
10. BLOOMING HITS - Paul Mauriat & His Orchestra - Philips
11. BOOKENDS - Simon & Garfunkel - Columbia
12. BY THE TIME I GET TO PHOENIX - Glen Campbell - Capitol
13. LADY SOUL - Aretha Franklin - Atlantic
14. THE SOUND OF MUSIC - Soundtrack - RCA Victor
15. THE TEMPTATIONS' GREATEST HITS - Temptations - Gordy
16. DIONNE WARWICK'S GOLDEN HITS, PART I - Dionne Warwick - Scepter
17. FAREWELL TO THE FIRST GOLDEN ERA - Mamas & The Papas - Dunhill
18. THE FOUR TOPS' GREATEST HITS - Four Tops - Motown
19. WILDFLOWERS - Judy Collins - Elektra
20. CAMELOT - Soundtrack - Warner Bros.-7 Arts

TOP 20 POP ALBUMS OF 1969

POS. TITLE - ARTIST - LABEL
1. IN-A-GADDA-DA-VIDA - Iron Butterfly - Atco
2. HAIR - Original Cast - RCA
3. BLOOD, SWEAT AND TEARS - Blood, Sweat & Tears - Columbia
4. BAYOU COUNTRY - Creedence Clearwater Revival - Fantasy
5. LED ZEPPELIN - Led Zeppelin - Atlantic
6. JOHNNY CASH AT FOLSOM PRISON - Johnny Cash - Columbia
7. FUNNY GIRL - Soundtrack - Columbia
8. THE BEATLES ("THE WHITE ALBUM") - Beatles - Apple
9. DONOVAN'S GREATEST HITS - Donovan - Epic
10. THE ASSOCIATION'S GREATEST HITS - Association - Warner Bros.-7 Arts
11. ROMEO AND JULIET - Soundtrack - Capitol
12. THREE DOG NIGHT - Three Dog Night - Dunhill
13. HELP YOURSELF - Tom Jones - Parrot
14. CLOUD NINE - Temptations - Gordy
15. TOM JONES LIVE - Tom Jones - Parrot

16. OLIVER - Soundtrack - Colgems
17. FEVER ZONE - Tom Jones - Parrot
18. NASHVILLE SKYLINE - Bob Dylan - Columbia
19. WICHITA LINEMAN - Glen Campbell - Capitol
20. BALL - Iron Butterfly - Atco

TOP 20 POP ALBUMS OF 1970

POS. TITLE - ARTIST - LABEL
1. BRIDGE OVER TROUBLED WATER - Simon & Garfunkel - Columbia
2. LED ZEPPELIN II - Led Zeppelin - Atlantic
3. CHICAGO - Chicago - Columbia
4. ABBEY ROAD - Beatles - Apple
5. SANTANA - Santana - Columbia
6. GET READY - Rare Earth - Rare Earth
7. EASY RIDER - Soundtrack - Dunhill
8. BUTCH CASSIDY AND THE SUNDANCE KID - Soundtrack - A&M
9. JOE COCKER! - Joe Cocker - A&M
10. THREE DOG NIGHT WAS CAPTURED LIVE AT THE FORUM - Three Dog Night - Dunhill
11. DEJA VU - Crosby, Stills, Nash & Young - Atlantic
12. WILLIE AND THE POOR BOYS - Creedence Clearwater Revival - Fantasy
13. BLOOD, SWEAT AND TEARS - Blood, Sweat & Tears - Columbia
14. HAIR - Original Cast - RCA
15. SWEET BABY JAMES - James Taylor - Warner Bros.
16. IN-A-GADDA-DA-VIDA - Iron Butterfly - Atco
17. AMERICAN WOMAN - Guess Who - RCA
18. GRAND FUNK - Grand Funk Railroad - Capitol
19. CROSBY, STLLS, AND NASH - Crosby Stills & Nash - Atlantic
20. RAINDROPS KEEP FALLING ON MY HEAD - B.J. Thomas - Scepter

TOP 20 POP ALBUMS OF 1971

POS. TITLE - ARTIST - LABEL
1. JESUS CHRIST SUPERSTAR - Various Artists - Decca
2. TAPESTRY - Carole King - Ode
3. CLOSE TO YOU - Carpenters - A&M
4. PEARL - Janis Joplin - Columbia
5. ABRAXAS - Santana - Columbia
6. THE PARTRIDGE FAMILY ALBUM - Partridge Family - Bell
7. SWEET BABY JAMES - James Taylor - Warner Bros.
8. TEA FOR THE TILLERMAN - Cat Stevens - A&M
9. GREATEST HITS - Sly & The Family Stone - Epic
10. CHICAGO III - Chicago - Columbia
11. CHAPTER TWO - Roberta Flack - Atlantic
12. NATURALLY - Three Dog Night - Dunhill
13. PARANOID - Black Sabbath - Warner Bros.
14. GOLDEN BISQUITS - Three Dog Night - Dunhill
15. CHICAGO TRANSIT AUTHORITY - Chicago Transit Authority - Columbia
16. LIVE ALBUM - Grand Funk Railroad - Capitol
17. TO BE CONTINUED - Isaac Hayes - Enterprise
18. ALL THINGS MUST PASS - George Harrison - Apple
19. CHICAGO II - Chicago - Columbia
20. AFTER THE GOLD RUSH - Neil Young - Reprise

TOP 20 POP ALBUMS OF 1972

POS.   TITLE - ARTIST - LABEL
1.   HARVEST - Neil Young - Reprise
2.   TAPESTRY - Carole King - Ode
3.   AMERICAN PIE - Don McLean - United Artists
4.   TEASER AND THE FIRECAT - Cat Stevens - A&M
5.   HOT ROCKS 1964-71 - Rolling Stones - London
6.   KILLER - Alice Cooper - Warner Bros.
7.   FIRST TAKE - Roberta Flack - Atlantic
8.   AMERICA - America - Warner Bros.
9.   MUSIC - Carole King - Ode
10.   MADMAN ACROSS THE WATER - Elton John - Uni
11.   ALL DAY MUSIC - War - United Artists
12.   LET'S STAY TOGETHER - Al Green - Hi
13.   BABY I'M-A WANT YOU - Bread - Elektra
14.   LED ZEPPELIN - Led Zeppelin - Atlantic
15.   EAT A PEACH - Allman Brothers - Capricorn
16.   THE CONCERT FOR BANGLA DESH - George Harrison & Friends - Apple
17.   QUIET FIRE - Roberta Flack - Atlantic
18.   FRAGILE - Yes - Atlantic
19.   FIDDLER ON THE ROOF - Soundtrack - United Artists
20.   NILSSON SCHMILSSON - Nilsson - RCA

TOP 20 POP ALBUMS OF 1973

POS.   TITLE - ARTIST - LABEL
1.   THE WORLD IS A GHETTO - War - United Artists
2.   SUMMER BREEZE - Seals & Crofts - Warner Bros.
3.   TALKING BOOK - Stevie Wonder - Tamla
4.   NO SECRETS - Carly Simon - Elektra
5.   LADY SINGS THE BLUES - Diana Ross - Motown
6.   THEY ONLY COME OUT AT NIGHT - Edgar Winter Group - Epic
7.   I AM WOMAN - Helen Reddy - Capitol
8.   DON'T SHOOT ME, I'M ONLY THE PIANO PLAYER - Elton John - MCA
9.   I'M STILL IN LOVE WITH YOU - Al Green - Hi
10.   SEVENTH SOJOURN - Moody Blues - Threshold
11.   DARK SIDE OF THE MOON - Pink Floyd - Harvest
12.   HOT AUGUST NIGHT - Neil Diamond - MCA
13.   LOGGINS AND MESSINA - Loggins & Messina - Columbia
14.   CATCH BULL AT FOUR - Cat Stevens - A&M
15.   BILLION DOLLAR BABIES - Alice Cooper - Warner Bros.
16.   CAN'T BUY A THRILL - Steely Dan - ABC
17.   THE CAPTAIN AND ME - Doobie Brothers - Warner Bros.
18.   THE BEST FO BREAD - Bread - Elektra
19.   WHO DO WE THINK WE ARE! - Deep Purple - Warner Bros.
20.   ROCKY MOUNTAIN HIGH - John Denver - RCA

TOP 20 POP ALBUMS OF 1974

POS.   TITLE - ARTIST - LABEL
1.   GOODBYE YELLOW BRICK ROAD - Elton John - MCA
2.   JOHN DENVER'S GREATEST HITS - John Denver - RCA
3.   BAND ON THE RUN - Paul McCartney & Wings - Apple
4.   INNERVISIONS - Stevie Wonder - Tamla
5.   YOU DON'T MESS AROUND WITH JIM - Jim Croce - ABC
6.   AMERICAN GRAFFITI - Soundtrack - MCA
7.   IMAGINATION - Gladys Knight & The Pips - Buddah
8.   BEHIND CLOSED DOORS - Charlie Rich - Epic
9.   THE STING - Soundtrack - MCA
10.   TRES HOMBRES - ZZ Top - London
11.   DARK SIDE OF THE MOON - Pink Floyd - Harvest
12.   BACHMAN-TURNER OVERDRIVE II - Bachman-Turner Overdrive - Mercury

13.   COURT AND SPARK - Joni Mitchell - Asylum
14.   SUNDOWN - Gordon Lightfoot - Reprise
15.   MARIA MULDAUR - Maria Muldaur - Reprise
16.   I GOT A NAME - Jim Croce - ABC
17.   BRAIN SALAD SURGERY - Emerson, Lake & Palmer - Manticore
18.   SHIP AHOY - O'Jay's - Philadelphia International
19.   FULL SAIL - Loggins & Messina - Columbia
20.   WILD & PEACEFUL - Kool & The Gang - De-Lite

TOP 20 POP ALBUMS OF 1975

POS.   TITLE - ARTIST - LABEL
1.   ELTON JOHN—GREATEST HITS - Elton John - MCA
2.   JOHN DENVER'S GREATEST HITS - John Denver - RCA
3.   THAT'S THE WAY OF THE WORLD - Earth, Wind & Fire - Columbia
4.   BACK HOME AGAIN - John Denver - RCA
5.   PHOEBE SNOW - Phoebe Snow - Shelter
6.   HEART LIKE A WHEEL - Linda Ronstadt - Asylum
7.   CAPTAIN FANTASTIC AND THE BROWN DIRT COWBOY - Elton John - MCA
8.   AN EVENING WITH JOHN DENVER - John Denver - RCA
9.   AWB - Average White Band - Atlantic
10.   ON THE BORDER - Eagles - Asylum
11.   PERFECT ANGEL - Minnie Riperton - Epic
12.   BETWEEN THE LINES - Janis Ian - Columbia
13.   HAVE YOU EVER BEEN MELLOW - Olivia Newton-John - MCA
14.   BLUE SKY—NIGHT THUNDER - Michael Murphey - Epic
15.   PHYSICAL GRAFFITI - Led Zeppelin - Swan Song
16.   A SONG FOR YOU - Temptations - Gordy
17.   WAR CHILD - Jethro Tull - Chrysalis
18.   TOMMY - Soundtrack - Polydor
19.   I FEEL A SONG - Gladys Knight & The Pips - Buddah
20.   YOUNG AMERICANS - David Bowie - RCA

TOP 20 POP ALBUMS OF 1976

POS.   TITLE - ARTIST - LABEL
1.   FRAMPTON COMES ALIVE - Peter Frampton - A&M
2.   FLEETWOOD MAC - Fleetwood Mac - Warner Bros.
3.   WINGS AT THE SPEED OF SOUND - Wings - Capitol
4.   GREATEST HITS 1971-1975 - Eagles - Asylum
5.   CHICAGI IX—CHICAGO'S GREATEST HITS - Chicago - Columbia
6.   THE DREAM WEAVER - Gary Wright - Warner Bros.
7.   DESIRE - Bob Dylan - Columbia
8.   A NIGHT AT THE OPERA - Queen - Elektra
9.   HISTORY—AMERICA'S GREATEST HITS - America - Warner Bros.
10.   GRATITUDE - Earth, Wind & Fire - Columbia
11.   FACE THE MUSIC - Electric Light Orchestra - United Artists
12.   BRASS CONSTRUCTION - Brass Construction - United Artists
13.   TRYIN' TO GET THE FEELIN' - Barry Manilow - Arista
14.   STILL CRAZY AFTER ALL THESE YEARS - Paul Simon - Columbia
15.   TOYS IN THE ATTIC - Aerosmith - Columbia
16.   RED OCTOPUS - Jefferson Starship - Grunt
17.   SILK DEGREES - Boz Scaggs - Columbia
18.   FOOL FOR THE CITY - Foghat - Bearsville
19.   BREEZIN' - George Benson - Warner Bros.
20.   ERIC CARMEN - Eric Carmen - Arista

TOP 20 POP ALBUMS OF 1977

POS. TITLE - ARTIST - LABEL
1. RUMOURS - Fleetwood Mac - Warner Bros.
2. SONGS IN THE KEY OF LIFE - Stevie Wonder - Tamla
3. A STAR IS BORN - Barbra Streisand/Kris Kristofferson/ Soundtrack - Columbia
4. HOTEL CALIFORNIA - Eagles - Asylum
5. BOSTON - Boston - Epic
6. A NEW WORLD RECORD - Electric Light Orchestra - United Artists
7. PART 3 - K.C. & The Sunshine Band - TK
8. SILK DEGREES - Boz Scaggs - Columbia
9. NIGHT MOVES - Bob Seger & The Silver Bullet Band - Capitol
10. FLEETWOOD MAC - Fleetwood Mac - Warner Bros.
11. FLY LIKE AN EAGLE - Steve Miller Band - Capitol
12. THEIR GREATEST HITS 1971-1975 - Eagles - Asylum
13. BIGGER THAN BOTH OF US - Daryl Hall & John Oates - RCA
14. FRAMPTON COMES ALIVE - Peter Frampton - A&M
15. THIS ONE'S FOR YOU - Barry Manilow - Arista
16. ENDLESS FLIGHT - Leo Sayer - Warner Bros.
17. LEFTOVERTURE - Kansas - Kirshner
18. YEAR OF THE CAT - Al Stewart - Janus
19. ROCK AND ROLL OVER - Kiss - Casablanca
20. GREATEST HITS - Linda Ronstadt - Asylum

TOP 20 POP ALBUMS OF 1978

POS. TITLE - ARTIST - LABEL
1. SATURDAY NIGHT FEVER - Bee Gees/Various Artists/ Soundtrack - RSO
2. GREASE - John Tavolta/Olivia Newton-John/Soundtrack - RSO
3. RUMOURS - Fleetwood Mac - Warner Bros.
4. THE STRANGER - Billy Joel - Columbia
5. AJA - Steely Dan - ABC
6. FEELS SO GOOD - Chuck Mangione - A&M
7. THE GRAND ILLUSION - Styx - A&M
8. SIMPLE DREAMS - Linda Ronstadt - Asylum
9. POINT OF KNOW RETURN - Kansas - Kirshner
10. SLOWHAND - Eric Clapton - RSO
11. RUNNING ON EMPTY - Jackson Browne - Asylum
12. ALL 'N' ALL - Earth, Wind & Fire - Columbia
13. BAT OUT OF HELL - Meat Loaf - Cleveland International
14. FOOT LOOSE AND FANCY FREE - Rod Stewart - Warner Bros.
15. FANTASY LOVE AFFAIR - Peter Brown - Drive
16. EVEN NOW - Barry Manilow - Arista
17. FRENCH KISS - Bob Welch - Capitol
18. OUT OF THE BLUE - Electric Light Orchestra - Jet
19. FOREIGNER - Foreigner - Atlantic
20. HERE YOU COME AGAIN - Dolly PArton - RCA

TOP 20 POP ALBUMS OF 1979

POS. TITLE - ARTIST - LABEL
1. 52nd STREET - Billy Joel - Columbia
2. SPIRITS HAVING FLOWN - Bee Gees - RSO
3. MINUTE BY MINUTE - Doobie Brothers - Warner Bros.
4. CARS - Cars - Elektra
5. BREAKFAST IN AMERICA - Supertramp - A&M
6. LIVE AND MORE - Donna Summer - Casablanca
7. PIECES OF EIGHT - Styx - A&M
8. BAD GIRLS - Donna Summer - Columbia
9. PARALLEL LINES - Blondie - Chrysalis
10. BLONDES HAVE MORE FUN - Rod Stewart - Warner Bros.
11. THE GAMBLER - Kenny Rogers - United Artists
12. CRUISIN' - Village People - Casablanca
13. CHEAP TRICK AT BUDOKAN - Cheap Trick - Epic
14. STRANGER IN TOWN - Bob Seger & The Silver Bullet Band - Capitol
15. VAN HALEN - Van Halen - Warner Bros.
16. GET THE KNACK - Knack - Capitol
17. 2 HOT - Peaches & Herb - Polydor/MVP
18. THE STRANGER - Billy Joel - Columbia
19. TOTO - Toto - Columbia
20. GREASE - Soundtrack - RSO

TOP 20 POP ALBUMS OF 1980

POS. TITLE - ARTIST - LABEL
1. THE WALL - Pink Floyd - Columbia
2. THE LONG RUN - Eagles - Asylum
3. OFF THE WALL - Michael Jackson - Epic
4. GLASS HOUSES - Billy Joel - Columbia
5. DAMN THE TORPEDOES - Tom Petty & The Heartbreakers - Backstreet
6. AGAINST THE WIND - Bob Seger & The Silver Bullet Band - Capitol
7. IN THE HEAT OF THE NIGHT - Pat Benatar - Chrysalis
8. EAT TO THE BEAT - Blondie - Chrysalis
9. IN THROUGH THE OUT DOOR - Led Zeppelin - Swan Song
10. KENNY - Kenny Rogers - United Artists
11. LADIES' NIGHT - Kool & The Gang - De-Lite
12. THE ROSE - Bette Midler/Soundtrack - Atlantic
13. CORNERSTONE - Styx - A&M
14. ON THE RADIO—GREATEST HITS, VOL. ONE AND TWO - Donna Summer - Casablanca
15. PHOENIX - Dan Fogelberg - Full Moon/Epic
16. KEEP THE FIRE - Kenny Loggins - Columbia
17. CHRISTOPHER CROSS - Christopher Cross - Warner Bros.
18. THE GAMBLER - Kenny Rogers - United Artists
19. PRETENDERS - Pretenders - Sire
20. TUSK - Fleetwood Mac - Warner Bros.

TOP 20 POP ALBUMS OF 1981

POS. TITLE - ARTIST - LABEL
1. HI INFIDELITY - REO Speedwagon - Epic
2. DOUBLE FANTASY - John Lennon & Yoko Ono - Geffen
3. GREATEST HITS - Kenny Rogers - Liberty
4. CHRISTOPHER CROSS - Christopher Cross - Warner Bros.
5. CRIMES OF PASSION - Pat Benatar - Chrysalis
6. PARADISE THEATRE - Styx - A&M
7. BACK IN BLACK - AC/DC - Atlantic
8. VOICES - Daryl Hall & John Oates - RCA
9. ZENYATTA MONDATTA - Police - A&M
10. THE RIVER - Bruce Springsteen - Columbia
11. THE TURN OF A FRIENDLY CARD - Alan Parsons Project - Arista
12. GUILTY - Barbra Streisand - Columbia
13. WINELIGHT - Grover Washington, Jr. - Elektra
14. THE JAZZ SINGER - Neil Diamond/Soundtrack - Capitol
15. MISTAKEN IDENTITY - Kim Carnes - EMI America
16. GREATEST HITS - Doors - Elektra
17. ARC OF A DIVER - Steve Winwood - Island
18. MOVING PICTURES - Rush - Mercury
19. CELEBRATE - Kool & The Gang - De-Lite
20. FACE VALUE - Phil Collins - Atlantic

The Police

Each year from 1981-1984, the Police occupied a Top 20 Pop album slot—``Synchronicity'' extended its stay from 1983 into 1984.

TOP 20 POP ALBUMS OF 1982

POS.	TITLE - ARTIST - LABEL
1.	ASIA - Asia - Geffen
2.	BEAUTY AND THE BEAT - Go-Go's - I.R.S.
3.	4 - Foreigner - Atlantic
4.	AMERICAN FOOL - John Cougar - Riva
5.	FREEZE-FRAME - J. Geils Band - EMI America
6.	ESCAPE - Journey - Columbia
7.	GET LUCKY - Loverboy - Columbia
8.	BELLA DONNA - Stevie Nicks - Modern
9.	CHARIOTS OF FIRE - Vangelis/Soundtrack - Polydor
10.	GHOST IN THE MACHINE - Police - A&M
11.	TATTOO YOU - Rolling Stones - Rolling Stones
12.	ABACAB - Genesis - Atlantic
13.	HOOKED ON CLASSICS - Royal Philharmonic Orchestra conducted by Louis Clark - RCA
14.	SOMETHING SPECIAL - Kool & The Gang - De-Lite
15.	PHYSICAL - Olivia Newton-John - MCA
16.	PRIVATE EYES - Daryl Hall & John Oates - RCA
17.	DIARY OF A MADMAN - Ozzy Osbourne - Jet
18.	FEELS SO RIGHT - Alabama - RCA
19.	THE INNOCENT AGE - Dan Fogelberg - Full Moon/Epic
20.	QUARTERFLASH - Quarterflash - Geffen

TOP 20 POP ALBUMS OF 1983

POS.	TITLE - ARTIST - LABEL
1.	THRILLER - Michael Jackson - Epic
2.	BUSINESS AS USUAL - Men At Work - Columbia
3.	SYNCHRONICITY - Police - A&M
4.	H2O - Daryl Hall & John Oates - RCA
5.	1999 - Prince - Warner Bros.
6.	LIONEL RICHIE - Lionel Richie - Motown
7.	JANE FONDA'S WORKOUT RECORD - Jane Fonda - Columbia
8.	PYROMANIA - Def Leppard - Mercury
9.	KISSING TO BE CLEVER - Culture Club - Virgin/Epic
10.	OLIVIA'S GREATEST HITS, VOL. 2 - Olivia Newton-John - MCA
11.	TOTO IV - Toto - Columbia
12.	FRONTIERS - Journey - Columbia
13.	RIO - Duran Duran - Capitol
14.	BUILT FOR SPEED - Stray Cats - EMI America
15.	CUTS LIKE A KNIFE - Bryan Adams - A&M
16.	GET NERVOUS - Pat Benatar - Chrysalis
17.	THE DISTANCE - Bob Seger & The Silver Bullet Band - Capitol
18.	GET LUCKY - Loverboy - Columbia
19.	MOUNTAIN MUSIC - Alabama - RCA
20.	FLASHDANCE - Soundtrack - Casablanca

TOP 20 POP ALBUMS OF 1984

POS.	TITLE - ARTIST - LABEL
1.	THRILLER - Michael Jackson - Epic
2.	SPORTS - Huey Lewis & The News - Chrysalis
3.	CAN'T SLOW DOWN - Lionel Richie - Motown
4.	AN INNOCENT MAN - Billy Joel - Columbia
5.	COLOUR BY NUMBERS - Culture Club - Virgin/Epic
6.	1984 - Van Halen - Warner Bros.
7.	ELIMINATOR - ZZ Top - Warner Bros.
8.	SYNCHRONICITY - Police - A&M
9.	FOOTLOOSE - Soundtrack - Columbia

10. SEVEN AND THE RAGGED TIGER - Duran Duran - Capitol
11. SHE'S SO UNUSUAL - Cyndi Lauper - Portrait
12. HEARTBREAK CITY - Cars - Elektra
13. WHAT'S NEW - Linda Ronstadt - Asylum
14. BREAK OUT - Pointer Sisters - Planet
15. MIDNIGHT MADNESS - Night Ranger - Camel/MCA
16. REBEL YELL - Billy Idol - Chrysalis
17. MADONNA - Madonna - Sire
18. SHOUT AT THE DEVIL - Motley Crue - Elektra
19. UH-HUH - John Cougar Mellencamp - Riva
20. THE BIG CHILL - Soundtrack - Motown

TOP 20 POP ALBUMS OF 1985

POS.   TITLE - ARTIST - LABEL
1. BORN IN THE U.S.A. - Bruce Springsteen - Columbia
2. RECKLESS - Bryan Adams - A&M
3. LIKE A VIRGIN - Madonna - Sire
4. MAKE IT BIG - Wham! - Columbia
5. PRIVATE DANCER - Tina Turner - Capitol
6. NO JACKET REQUIRED - Phil Collins - Atlantic
7. BEVERLY HILLS COP - Various Artists/Soundtrack - MCA
8. SUDDENLY - Billy Ocean - Jive
9. PURPLE RAIN - Prince & The Revolution - Warner Bros.
10. SONGS FROM THE BIG CHAIR - Tears For Fears - Mercury
11. CENTERFIELD - John Fogerty - Warner Bros.
12. EMERGENCY - Kool & The Gang - De-Lite
13. BUILDING THE PERFECT BEAST - Don Henley - Geffen
14. SPORTS - Huey Lewis & The News - Chrysalis
15. VITAL SIGNS - Survivor - Scotti Bros.
16. BREAK OUT - Pointer Sisters - Planet
17. BIG BAM BOOM - Daryl Hall & John Oates - RCA
18. WHEELS ARE TURNING - REO Speedwagon - Epic
19. THE UNFORGETTABLE FIRE - U2 - Island
20. AGENT PROVOCATEUR - Foreigner - Atlantic

TOP 20 POP ALBUMS OF 1986

POS.   TITLE - ARTIST - LABEL
1. WHITNEY HOUSTON - Whitney Houston - Arista
2. HEART - Heart - Capitol
3. SCARECROW - John Cougar Mellencamp - Riva
4. AFTERBURNER - ZZ Top - Warner Bros.
5. BROTHERS IN ARMS - Dire Straits - Warner Bros.
6. CONTROL - Janet Jackson - A&M
7. WELCOME TO THE REAL WORLD - Mr. Mister - RCA
8. PROMISE - Sade - Portrait
9. NO JACKET REQUIRED - Phil Collins - Atlantic
10. PRIMITIVE LOVE - Miami Sound Machine - Epic
11. RIPTIDE - Robert Palmer - Island
12. THE BROADWAY ALBUM - Barbra Streisand - Columbia
13. KNEE DEEP IN THE HOOPLA - Starship - Grunt
14. 5150 - Van Halen - Warner Bros.
15. LISTEN LIKE THIEVES - INXS - Atlantic
16. BORN IN THE U.S.A. - Bruce Springsteen - Columbia
17. PLAY DEEP - The Outfield - Columbia
18. IN SQUARE CIRCLE - Stevie Wonder - Tamla
19. SONGS FROM THE BIG CHAIR - Tears For Fears - Mercury
20. MIKE & THE MECHANICS - Mike & The Mechanics - Atlantic

TOP 20 POP ALBUMS OF 1987

POS.   TITLE - ARTIST - LABEL
1. SLIPPERY WHEN WET - Bon Jovi - Mercury
2. GRACELAND - Paul Simon - Warner Bros.

Bruce Springsteen
Bruce had four Top 20 LPs, including "Born In The U.S.A" (1986).

3. LICENSED TO ILL - Beastie Boys - Def Jam
4. THE WAY IT IS - Bruce Hornsby & The Range - RCA
5. CONTROL - Janet Jackson - A&M
6. THE JOSHUA TREE - U2 - Island
7. FORE! - Huey Lewis & The News - Chrysalis
8. NIGHT SONGS - Cinderella - Mercury
9. RAPTURE - Anita Baker - Elektra
10. INVISIBLE TOUCH - Genesis - Atlantic
11. TRUE BLUE - Madonna - Sire
12. THE FINAL COUNTDOWN - Europe - Epic
13. LOOK WHAT THE CAT DRAGGED IN - Poison - Enigma
14. BACK IN THE HIGHLIFE - Steve Winwood - Island
15. DUOTONES - Kenny G. - Arista
16. WHITESNAKE - Whitesnake - Geffen
17. THIRD STAGE - Boston - MCA
18. DANCING ON THE CEILING - Lionel Richie - Motown
19. GIVE ME THE REASON - Luther Vandross - Epic
20. JUST LIKE THE FIRST TIME - Freddie Jackson - Capitol

TOP 20 POP ALBUMS OF 1988

POS.   TITLE - ARTIST - LABEL
1. FAITH - George Michael - Columbia
2. DIRTY DANCING - Soundtrack - RCA
3. HYSTERIA - Def Leppard - Mercury
4. KICK - INXS - Atlantic
5. BAD - Michael Jackson - Epic
6. APPETITE FOR DESTRUCTION - Guns N' Roses - Geffen
7. OUT OF THE BLUE - Debbie Gibson - Atlantic
8. RICHARD MARX - Richard Marx - EMI
9. TIFFANY - Tiffany - MCA
10. PERMANENT VACATION - Aerosmith - Geffen

11. THE HARDLINE ACCORDING TO TERENCE TRENT D'ARBY - Terence Trent D'Arby - Columbia
12. WHITNEY - Whitney Houston - Arista
13. LET IT LOOSE - Gloria Estefan & Miami Sound Machine - Epic
14. THE LONESOME JUBILEE - John Cougar Mellencamp - Mercury
15. WHENEVER YOU NEED SOMEBODY - Rick Astley - RCA
16. TUNNEL OF LOVE - Bruce Springsteen - Columbia
17. HEAVEN ON EARTH - Belinda Carlisle - MCA
18. MORE DIRTY DANCING - Soundtrack - RCA
19. WHITESNAKE - Whitesnake - Geffen
20. NOW AND ZEN - Robert Plant - EsParanza

TOP 20 POP ALBUMS OF 1989

POS.	TITLE - ARTIST - LABEL
1.	DON'T BE CRUEL - Bobby Brown - MCA
2.	HANGIN' TOUGH - New Kids On The Block - Columbia
3.	FOREVER YOUR GIRL - Paula Abdul - Virgin
4.	NEW JERSEY - Bon Jovi - Mercury
5.	APPETITE FOR DESTRUCTION - Gubs N' Roses - Geffen
6.	THE RAW & THE COOKED - Fine Young Cannibals - I.R.S.
7.	G N' R LIES - Guns N' Roses - Geffen
8.	TRAVELING WILBURYS - Traveling Wilburys - Wilbury
9.	HYSTERIA - Def Leppard - Mercury
10.	GIRL YOU KNOW IT'S TIME - Milli Vanilli - Arista
11.	SKID ROW - Skid Row - Atlantic
12.	LIKE A PRAYER - Madonna - Sire
13.	VIVID - Living Colour - Epic
14.	BEACHES - Soundtrack - Atlantic
15.	WINGER - Winger - Atlantic

16. ELECTRIC YOUTH - Debbie Gibson - Atlantic
17. GIVING YOU THE BEST THAT I GOT - Anita Baker - Elektra
18. SHOOTING RUBBERBANDS AT THE STARS - Edie Brickell & New Bohemians - Geffen
19. FULL MOON FEVER - Tom Petty - MCA
20. OPEN UP AND SAY...AHH! - Poison - Enigma

TOP 20 POP ALBUMS OF 1990

POS.	TITLE - ARTIST - LABEL
1.	JANET JACKSON'S RHYTHM NATION 1814 - Janet Jackson - A&M
2.	...BUT SERIOUSLY - Phil Collins - Atlantic
3.	SOUL PROVIDER - Michael Bolton - Columbia
4.	PUMP - Aerosmith - Geffen
5.	PLEASE HAMMER DON'T HURT 'EM - M.C. Hammer - Capitol
6.	FOREVER YOUR GIRL - Paula Abdul - Virgin
7.	DR. FEELGOOD - Motley Crue - Elektra
8.	THE END OF INNOCENCE - Don Henley - Geffen
9.	COSMIC THING - The B-52's - Reprise
10.	STORM FRONT - Billy Joel - Columbia
11.	GIRL YOU KNOW IT'S TRUE - Milli Vanilli - Arista
12.	POISON - Bell Biv Devoe - MCA
13.	HANGIN' TOUGH - New Kids On The Block - Columbia
14.	CRY LIKE A RAINSTORM, HOWL LIKE THE WIND - Linda Ronstadt (featuring Aaron Neville) - Elektra
15.	WILSON PHILLIPS - Wilson Phillips - SBK
16.	NICK OF TIME - Bonnie Raitt - Capitol
17.	VIOLATOR - Depeche Mode - Sire
18.	PRETTY WOMAN - Soundtrack - EMI
19.	I DO NOT WANT WHAT I HAVEN'T GOT - Sinead O'Connor - Ensign

Poison

Heavy metal's Poison scored twice with Top 20 Pop albums: 1987 (#13) and 1989 (#20).

20.   CAN'T FIGHT FATE - Taylor Dayne - Arista

TOP 20 POP ALBUMS OF 1991

POS.   TITLE - ARTIST - LABEL
1.   MARIAH CAREY - Mariah Carey - Columbia
2.   NO FENCES - Garth Brooks - Capitol
3.   SHAKE YOUR MONEY MAKER - The Black Crowes - Def American
4.   GONNA MAKE YOU SWEAT - C&C Music Factory - Columbia
5.   WILSON PHILLIPS - Wilson Phillips - SBK
6.   TO THE EXTREME - Vanilla Ice - SBK
7.   PLEASE HAMMER DON'T HURT 'EM - Hammer - Capitol
8.   THE IMMACULATE COLLECTION - Madonna - Sire
9.   EMPIRE - Queensryche - EMI
10.   I'M YOUR BABY TONIGHT - Whitney Houston - Arista
11.   OUT OF TIME - R.E.M. - Warner Bros.
12.   THE RAZORS EDGE - AC/DC - Atco
13.   MAMA SAID KNOCK YOU OUT - L.L. Cool J - Def Jam
14.   TIME, LOVE AND TENDERNESS - Michael Bolton - Columbia
15.   HEART IN MOTION - Amy Grant - A&M
16.   SOME PEOPLE'S LIVES - Bette Midler - Atlantic
17.   CRAZY WORLD - Scorpions - Mercury
18.   SPELLBOUND - Paula Abdul - Captive
19.   PUT YOURSELF IN MY SHOES - Clint Black - RCA
20.   COOLIN' AT THE PLAYGROUND YA' KNOW - Another BAd Creation - Motown

TOP 20 POP ALBUMS OF 1992

POS.   TITLE - ARTIST - LABEL
1.   ROPIN' THE WIND - Garth Brooks - Liberty
2.   DANGEROUS - Michael Jackson - Epic
3.   NEVERMIND - Nirvana - DGC
4.   SOME GAVE ALL - Billy Ray Cyrus - Mercury
5.   ACHTUNG BABY - U2 - Island
6.   NO FENCES - Garth Brooks - Liberty

7.   METALLICA - Metallica - Elektra
8.   TIME, LOVE AND TENDERNESS - Michael Bolton - Columbia
9.   TOO LEGIT TO QUIT - Hammer - Capitol
10.   TOTALLY CROSSED OUT - Kris Kross - Ruffhouse
11.   TEN - Pearl Jam - Epic Associated
12.   COOLEYHIGHHARMONY - Boyz II Men - Motown
13.   WE CAN'T DANCE - Genesis - Atlantic
14.   BLOOD SUGAR SEX MAGIK - Red Hot Chili Peppers - Warner Bros.
15.   ADRENALIZE - Def Leppard - Mercury
16.   LUCK OF THE DRAW - Bonnie Raitt - Capitol
17.   USE YOUR ILLUSION I - Guns N' Roses - Geffen
18.   UNFORGETTABLE - Natalie Cole - Elektra
19.   C.M.B. - Color Me Bad - Giant/Reprise
20.   USE YOUR ILLUSION II - Guns N' Roses - Geffen

TOP 20 POP ALBUMS OF 1993

POS.   TITLE - ARTIST - LABEL
1.   THE BODYGUARD - Soundtrack - Arista
2.   BREATHLESS - Kenny G - Arista
3.   UNPLUGGED - Eric Clapton - Duck/Reprise
4.   JANET - Janet Jackson - Virgin
5.   SOME GAVE ALL - Billy Ray Cyrus - Mercury
6.   THE CHRONIC - Dr. Dre - Death Row/Interscope
7.   POCKET FULL OF KRYPTONITE - Soin Doctors - Epic
8.   TEN - Pearl Jam - Epic
9.   THE CHASE - Garth Brooks - Liberty
10.   CORE - Stone Temple Pilots - Atlantic
11.   TIMELESS (THE CLASSICS) - Michael Bolton - Columbia
12.   LOVE DELUXE - Sade - Epic
13.   PURE COUNTRY (SOUNDTRACK) - George Strait - MCA
14.   GET A GRIP - Aerosmith - Geffen
15.   VS. - Pearl Jam - Epic
16.   IT'S ABOUT TIME - SWV - RCA
17.   IN PIECES - Garth Brooks - Liberty
18.   SLEEPLESS IN SEATTLE - Soundtrack - Epic Soundtrax
19.   IT'S YOUR CALL - Reba McEntire - MCA
20.   ALADDIN - Soundtrack - Epic Soundtrax

Billboard Top 20 Country Albums, 1965-1993

TOP 20 COUNTRY ALBUMS OF 1965

POS.	TITLE - ARTIST - LABEL
1.	I'VE GOT A TIGER BY THE TAIL - Buck Owens - Capitol
2.	CONNIE SMITH - Connie Smith - RCA Victor
3.	THE JIM REEVES WAY - Jim Reeves - RCA Victor
4.	RETURN OF ROGER MILLER - Roger Miller - Smash
5.	I DON'T CARE - Buck Owens & His Buckeroos - Capitol
6.	YOU'RE THE ONLY WORLD I KNOW - Sonny James - Capitol
7.	THE FABULOUS SOUND OF FLATT & SCRUGGS - Lester Flatt & Earl Scruggs - Columbia
8.	THE BEST OF JIM REEVES - Jim Reeves - RCA Victor
9.	TOGETHER AGAIN/MY HEART SKIPS A BEAT - Buck Owens & His Buckeroos - Capitol
10.	THE EASY WAY - Eddy Arnold - RCA Victor
11.	THE RACE IS ON - George Jones - United Artists
12.	THE THIRD TIME AROUND - Roger Miller - Smash
13.	GEORGE JONES & GENE PITNEY - George Jones & Gene Pitney - Musicor
14.	THE BEST OF BUCK OWENS - Buck Owens - Capitol
15.	ORANGE BLOSSOM SPECIAL - Johnny Cash - Columbia
16.	BURNING MEMORIES - Kitty Wells - Decca
17.	LOVE LIFE - Ray Price - Columbia
18.	BITTER TEARS - Johnny Cash - Columbia
19.	I'LL KEEP HOLDIN' ON (JUST TO YOUR LOVE) - Sonny James - Capitol
20.	BEFORE YOU GO/NO ONE BUT YOU - Buck Owens - Capitol

TOP 20 COUNTRY ALBUMS OF 1966

POS.	TITLE - ARTIST - LABEL
1.	MY WORLD - Eddy Arnold - RCA Victor
2.	ROLL OUT THE RED CARPET FOR BUCK OWENS & HIS BUCKEROOS - Buck Owens & His Buckeroos - Capitol
3.	DISTANT DRUMS - Jim Reeves - RCA Victor
4.	I WANT TO GO WITH YOU - Eddy Arnold - RCA Victor
5.	CARNEGIE HALL CONCERT WITH BUCK OWENS & HIS BUCKEROOS - Buck Owens & His Buckeroos - Capitol
6.	BEHIND THE TEAR - Sonny James - Capitol
7.	ROGER MILLER/GOLDEN HITS - Roger Miller - Smash
8.	I LIKE 'EM COUNTRY - Loretta Lynn - Decca
9.	I LOVE YOU DROPS - Bill Anderson - Decca
10.	THE LAST WORLD IN LONESOME IS ME - Eddy Arnold - RCA Victor
11.	CUTE 'N' COUNTRY - Connie Smith - RCA Victor
12.	DUST ON MOTHER'S BIBLE - Buck Owens & His Buckeroos - Capitol
13.	THE OTHER WOMAN - Ray Price - Columbia
14.	ALMOST PERSUADED - David Houston - Epic
15.	YOU AIN'T WOMAN ENOUGH - Loretta Lynn - Decca
16.	THE COUNTRY TOUCH - Warner Mack - Decca
17.	ANOTHER BRIDGE TO BURN - Ray Price - Columbia
18.	I'M A PEOPLE - George Jones - Musicor
19.	MISS SMITH GOES TO NASHVILLE - Connie Smith - RCA Victor
20.	PRETTY MISS NORMA JEAN - Norma Jean - RCA Victor

TOP 20 COUNTRY ALBUMS OF 1967

POS.	TITLE - ARTIST - LABEL
1.	THERE GOES MY EVERYTHING - Jack Greene - Decca
2.	THE BEST OF EDDY ARNOLD - Eddy Arnold - RCA Victor
3.	TOUCH MY HEART - Ray Price - Columbia
4.	LONELY AGAIN - Eddy Arnold - RCA Victor
5.	ALL THE TIME - Jack Greene - Decca
6.	SOMEBODY LIKE ME - Eddy Arnold - RCA Victor
7.	DON'T COME HOME A DRINKIN' - Loretta Lynn - Decca
8.	OPEN UP YOUR HEART - Buck Owens & His Buckeroos - Capitol
9.	THE BEST OF SONNY JAMES - Sonny James - Capitol
10.	DANNY BOY - Ray Price - Columbia
11.	I'M A LONESOME FUGITIVE - Merle Haggard - Capitol
12.	YOURS SINCERELY - Jim Reeves - RCA Victor
13.	JOHNNY CASH'S GREATEST HITS, VOL. I - Johnny Cash - Columbia
14.	SWINGING DOORS - Merle Haggard - Capitol
15.	IT'S SUCH A PRETTY WORLD TODAY - Wynn Stewart - Capitol
16.	COLD HARD FACTS OF LIFE - Porter Wagoner - RCA Victor
17.	TURN THE WORLD AROUND - Eddy Arnold - RCA Victor
18.	BUCK OWENS & HIS BUCKEROOS IN JAPAN - Buck Owens & His Buckeroos - Capitol

Connie Smith

One of Country's legendary female artists, Connie has had 72 charted hits, the biggest being ``Once A Day'' —#1 for eight weeks! Connie has had twenty Top 10 singles, and her namesake LP was #2 Top 20 in 1965.

521

George Jones

The #2 Country singles artist of all time—with over 160 charted hits—George had two Top 20 albums in 1965.

19. YOU AIN'T WOMAN ENOUGH - Loretta Lynn - Decca
20. NEED YOU - Sonny James - Capitol

TOP 20 COUNTRY ALBUMS OF 1968

POS.	TITLE - ARTIST - LABEL
1.	BY THE TIME I GET TO PHOENIX - Glen Campbell - Capitol
2.	GENTLE ON MY MIND - Glen Campbell - Capitol
3.	PROMISES PROMISES - Lynn Anderson - Chart
4.	BEST OF EDDY ARNOLD - Eddy Arnold - RCA Victor
5.	HEY LITTLE ONE - Glen Campbell - Capitol
6.	THE COUNTRY WAY - Charley Pride - RCA Victor
7.	HONEY - Bobby Goldsboro - United Artists
8.	NEW PLACE IN THE SUN - Glen Campbell - Capitol
9.	EVERLOVIN' WORLD OF EDDY ARNOLD - Eddy Arnold - RCA Victor
10.	JOHNNY CASH AT FOLSOM PRISON - Johnny Cash - Columbia
11.	THE ROMANTIC WORLD OF EDDY ARNOLD - Eddy Arnold - RCA Victor
12.	MAKE MINE COUNTRY - Charley Pride - RCA Victor
13.	ANOTHER PLACE, ANOTHER TIME - Jerry Lee Lewis - Smash
14.	TOUCH OF SADNESS - Jim Reeves - RCA Victor
15.	LEGEND OF BONNIE AND CLYDE - Merle Haggard - Capitol
16.	LORETTA LYNN'S GREATEST HITS - Loretta Lynn - Decca
17.	IT TAKES PEOPLE LIKE YOU TO MAKE PEOPLE LIKE ME - Buck Owens & His Buckeroos - Capitol
18.	FIST CITY - Loretta Lynn - Decca
19.	SING ME BACK HOME - Merle Haggard - Capitol

20. BEST OF BUCK OWENS, VOL. 2 - Buck Owens & His Buckeroos - Capitol

TOP 20 COUNTRY ALBUMS OF 1969

POS.	TITLE - ARTIST - LABEL
1.	WICHITA LINEMAN - Glen Campbell - Capitol
2.	JOHNNY CASH AT FOLSOM PRISON - Johnny Cash - Columbia
3.	STAND BY YOUR MAN - Tammy Wynette - Epic
4.	JEWELS - Waylon Jennings - RCA
5.	CHARLEY PRIDE IN PERSON - Charley Pride - RCA
6.	YOUR SQUAW IS ON THE WARPATH - Loretta Lynn - Decca
7.	THE SENSATIONAL CHARLEY PRIDE - Charley Pride - RCA
8.	JOHNNY CASH AT SAN QUENTIN - Johnny Cash - Columbia
9.	SAME TRAIN, DIFFERENT TIME - Merle Haggard - Capitol
10.	GALVESTON - Glen Campbell - Capitol
11.	JUST THE TWO OF US - Dolly Parton & Porter Wagoner - RCA
12.	CARROLL COUNTY ACCIDENT - Porter Wagoner - RCA
13.	GENTLE ON MY MIND - Glen Campbell - Capitol
14.	BOBBIE GENTRY & GLEN CAMPBELL - Bobbie Gentry & Glen Campbell - Capitol
15.	HOLY LAND - Johnny Cash - Columbia
16.	IT'S A SIN - Marty Robbins - Columbia

Norma Jean

Norma Jean was a regular on Porter Wagoner's TV show from 1960 to 1967; following her departure, she was replaced by a little known singer named Dolly Parton. She has had a very successful recording career at RCA, with over twenty albums to her credit—one of them in the Top 20 in 1966.

Marty Robbins

Well known for crossover hits like "Singing The Blues" and "A White Sport Coat," two of Marty's albums were Top 20 Country in 1969, and one in 1970.

17. FROM ELVIS IN MEMPHIS - Elvis Presley - RCA
18. HALL OF FAME, VOL. I - Jerry Lee Lewis - Smash
19. SONGS MY FATHER LEFT ME - Hank Williams, Jr. - MGM
20. I WALK ALONE - Marty Robbins - Columbia

TOP 20 COUNTRY ALBUMS OF 1970

POS.   TITLE - ARTIST - LABEL
1. THE BEST OF CHARLEY PRIDE - Charley Pride - RCA
2. OKIE FROM MUSKOGEE - Merle Haggard & The Strangers - Capitol
3. JUST PLAIN CHARLEY - Charley Pride - RCA
4. TAMMY WYNETTE'S GREATEST HITS - Tammy Wynette - Epic
5. HELLO, I'M JOHNNY CASH - Johnny Cash - Columbia
6. CHARLEY PRIDE'S 10TH ALBUM - Charley Pride - RCA
7. FIGHTIN' SIDE OF ME - Merle Haggard & The Strangers - Capitol
8. TAMMY'S TOUCH - Tammy Wynette - Epic
9. THE WAYS TO LOVE A MAN - Tammy Wynette - Epic
10. MY WOMAN, MY WOMAN, MY WIFE - Marty Robbins - Columbia
11. THE BEST OF JERRY LEE LEWIS - Jerry Lee Lewis - Smash
12. JOHNNY CASH AT SAN QUENTIN - Johnny Cash - Columbia
13. HELLO DARLIN' - Conway Twitty - Decca
14. THE WORLD OF JOHNNY CASH - Johnny Cash - Columbia
15. BABY, BABY - David Houston - Epic
16. HANK WILLIAMS' GREATEST HITS - Hank Williams - MGM

17. TO SEE MY ANGEL CRY/WHEN SHE STARTED TO STOP LOVING YOU - Conway Twitty - Decca
18. STORY SONGS OF THE TRAINS & RIVERS - Johnny Cash & The Tennessee Two - Sun
19. PORTER WAYNE & DOLLY REBECCA - Porter Wagoner & Dolly Parton - RCA
20. WINGS UPON YOUR HORNS - Loretta Lynn - Decca

TOP 20 COUNTRY ALBUMS OF 1971

POS.   TITLE - ARTIST - LABEL
1. ROSE GARDEN - Lynn Anderson - Columbia
2. FOR THE GOOD TIMES - Ray Price - Columbia
3. I WON'T MENTION IT AGAIN - Ray Price - Columbia
4. HAG - Merle Haggard - Capitol
5. YOU'RE MY MAN - Lynn Anderson - Columbia
6. FROM ME TO YOU - Charley Pride - RCA
7. WHEN YOU'RE HOT, YOU'RE HOT - Jerry Reed - RCA
8. HELP ME MAKE IT THROUGH THE NIGHT - Sammi Smith - Mega
9. I'M JUST ME - Charley Pride - RCA
10. MAN IN BLACK - Johnny Cash - Columbia
11. DID YOU THINK TO PRAY - Charley Pride - RCA
12. WE ONLY MAKE BELIEVE - Conway Twitty & Loretta Lynn - Decca
13. GLEN CAMPBELL'S GREATEST HITS - Glen Campbell - Capitol
14. BED OF ROSES - Statler Brothers - Mercury
15. COAL MINER'S DAUGHTER - Loretta Lynn - Decca
16. 15 YEARS AGO - Conway Twitty - Decca
17. SNOWBIRD - Anne Murray - Capitol

Lynn Anderson

Lynn started out as a regular on—of all places—the "Lawrence Welk Show." She went on to have over fifty charted hits.

18. POEMS, PRAYERS & PROMISES - John Denver - RCA
19. ELVIS COUNTRY - Elvis Presley - RCA
20. HOW MUCH MORE CAN SHE STAND - Conway Twitty - Decca

TOP 20 COUNTRY ALBUMS OF 1972

POS. TITLE - ARTIST - LABEL
1. BEST OF CHARLEY PRIDE, VOL. 2 - Charley Pride - RCA
2. CHARLEY PRIDE SINGS HEART SONGS - Charley Pride - RCA
3. EASY LOVING - Freddie Hart - Capitol
4. FOR THE GOOD TIMES - Ray Price - Columbia
5. REAL McCOY - Charlie McCoy - Monument
6. HAPPIEST GIRL IN THE WHOLE U.S.A. - Donna Fargo - Dot
7. CRY - Lynn Anderson - Columbia
8. A SUNSHINY DAY WITH CHARLEY PRIDE - Charley Pride - RCA
9. HOW CAN I UNLOVE YOU - Lynn Anderson - Columbia
10. WE GO TOGETHER - Tammy Wynette & George Jones - Epic
11. LET ME TELL YOU ABOUT A SONG - Merle Haggard - Capitol
12. MY HANG UP IS YOU - Freddie Hart - Capitol
13. TO GET TO YOU - Jerry Wallace - Decca
14. A THING CALLED LOVE - Johnny Cash - Columbia
15. SHE'S ALL I GOT - Johnny Paycheck - Epic
16. LEAD ME ON - Conway Twitty & Loretta Lynn - Decca
17. THE JOHNNY CASH COLLECTION: HIS GREATEST HITS VOL. 2 - Johnny Cash - Columbia
18. BLESS YOUR HEART - Freddie Hart - Capitol
19. RANGER'S WALTZ - Mom & Dads - GNP
20. THE KILLER ROCK'S ON - Jerry Lee Lewis - Mercury

TOP 20 COUNTRY ALBUMS OF 1973

POS. TITLE - ARTIST - LABEL
1. BEHIND CLOSED DOORS - Charlie Rich - Epic
2. INTRODUCING - Johnny Rodriguez - Mercury
3. SATIN SHEETS - Jeanne Pruett - MCA
4. ALOHA FROM HAWAII VIA SATELLITE - Elvis Presley - RCA
5. ENTERTAINER OF THE YEAR - Loretta Lynn - MCA
6. CHARLIE McCOY - Charlie McCoy - Monument
7. THE BEST OF MERLE HAGGARD - Merle Haggard - Capitol
8. THE HAPPIEST GIRL IN THE WHOLE U.S.A. - Donna Fargo - Dot
9. SONG OF LOVE - Charley Pride - RCA
10. JESUS WAS A CAPRICORN - Kris Kristofferson - Monument
11. THE RHYMER & OTHER FIVE & DIMERS - Tom T. Hall - Mercury
12. GOT THE ALL OVERS FOR YOU - Freddie Hart - Capitol
13. IT'S NOT LOVE (BUT IT'S NOT BAD) - Merle Haggard - Capitol
14. I'VE FOUND SOMEONE OF MY OWN - Cal Smith - MCA
15. DELIVERANCE/SOUNDTRACK - Eric Weissberg & Steve Mandell - Warner Bros.
16. WHAT'S YOUR MAMA'S NAME? - Tanya Tucker - Columbia
17. GOOD TIME CHARLIE - Charlie McCoy - Monument
18. SUPERPICKER - Roy Clark - Dot
19. SHE NEEDS SOMEONE TO HOLD HER - Conway Twitty - MCA
20. ROY CLARK LIVE - Roy Clark - Dot

Kris Kristofferson

Rhodes scholar, film star, composer and singer, Kris has a solid body of album work to his credit (one of which was #10 Top 20 Country in 1973).

TOP 20 COUNTRY ALBUMS OF 1974

POS. TITLE - ARTIST - LABEL
1. BEHIND CLOSED DOORS - Charlie Rich - Epic
2. LET ME BE THERE - Olivia Newton-John - MCA
3. VERY SPECIAL LOVE SONGS - Charlie Rich - Epic
4. THERE WON'T BE ANYMORE - Charlie Rich - Epic
5. IF YOU LOVE ME LET ME KNOW - Olivia Newton-John - MCA
6. YOU'VE NEVER BEEN THIS FAR BEFORE/BABY'S GONE - Conway Twitty - MCA
7. A LEGENDARY PERFORMER VOL. I - Elvis Presley - RCA
8. STOP & SMELL THE ROSES - Mac Davis - Columbia
9. SPIDERS & SNAKES - Jim Stafford - MGM
10. BACK HOME AGAIN - John Denver - RCA
11. AMAZING LOVE - Charlie Pride - RCA
12. WHERE MY HEART IS - Ronnie Milsap - RCA
13. WE'RE GONNA HOLD ON - George Jones & Tammy Wynette - Epic
14. FOR THE PEOPLE IN THE LAST HARD TOWN - Tom T. Hall - Mercury
15. COUNTRY PARTNERS - Loretta Lynn & Conway Twitty - MCA
16. THIS TIME - Waylon Jennings - RCA
17. BOBBY BARE SINGS LULLABYS, LEGENDS & LIES - Bobby Bare - RCA
18. COUNTRY BUMPKIN - Cal Smith - MCA
19. NEW SUNRISE - Brenda Lee - MCA
20. ROY CLARK'S FAMILY ALBUM - Roy Clark - ABC/Dot

TOP 20 COUNTRY ALBUMS OF 1975

POS.   TITLE - ARTIST - LABEL
1. BACK HOME AGAIN - John Denver - RCA
2. HEART LIKE A WHEEL - Linda Ronstadt - Capitol
3. BEFORE THE NEXT TEARDROP FALLS - Freddy Fender - ABC/Dot
4. HAVE YOU NEVER BEEN MELLOW - Olivia Newton-John - MCA
5. I'M JESSI COLTER - Jessi Colter - Capitol
6. MERLE HAGGARD & THE STRANGERS - Merle Haggard - Capitol
7. AN EVENING WITH JOHN DENVER - John Denver - RCA
8. KEEP MOVIN' ON - Merle Haggard - Capitol
9. LINDA ON MY MIND - Conway Twitty - MCA
10. SONGS OF FOX HOLLOW - Tom T. Hall - Mercury
11. IT'S TIME TO PAY THE FIDDLER - Cal Smith - MCA
12. IF YOU LOVE ME LET ME KNOW - Olivia Newton-John - MCA
13. THE RAMBLIN' MAN - Waylon Jennings - RCA
14. REDHEADED STRANGER - Willie Nelson - Columbia
15. DON WILLIAMS, VOL. III - Don Williams - ABC/Dot
16. CITY LIGHTS - Mickey Gilley - Playboy
17. GREATEST HITS, VOL. I - Billy "Crash" Craddock - ABC
18. OUT OF HAND - Gary Stewart - RCA
19. PHONE CALL FROM GOD - Jerry Jordan - MCA
20. SONGS ABOUT LADIES & LOVE - Johnny Rodriguez - Mercury

TOP 20 COUNTRY ALBUMS OF 1976

POS.   TITLE - ARTIST - LABEL
1. THE SOUND IN YOUR MIND - Willie Nelson - Columbia
2. BLACK BEAR ROAD - C.W. McCall - MGM
3. WANTED: THE OUTLAWS - Waylon Jennings, Willie Nelson, Jessi Colter, Tompall Glaser - RCA
4. ELITE HOTEL - Emmylou Harris - Warner Bros.
5. ARE YOU READY FOR THE COUNTRY - Waylon Jennings - RCA
6. SOMEBODY LOVES YOU - Crystal Gayle - United Artists
7. FROM ELVIS PRESLEY BOULEVARD, MEMPHIS, TENNESSEE - Elvis Presley - RCA
8. HARMONY - Don Williams - ABC/Dot
9. WINDSONG - John Denver - RCA
10. ARE YOU READY FOR FREDDY - Freddy Fender - ABC/Dot
11. PRISONER IN DISGUISE - Linda Ronstadt - Asylum
12. 20-20 VISION - Ronnie Milsap - RCA
13. REDHEADED STRANGER - Willie Nelson - Columbia
14. IT'S ALL IN THE MOVIES - Merle Haggard - Capitol
15. UNITED TALENT - Loretta Lynn & Conway Twitty - MCA
16. NIGHT THINGS - Ronnie Milsap - RCA
17. GILLEY'S GREATEST HITS, VOL. I - Mickey Gilley - Playboy
18. TWITTY - Conway Twitty - MCA
19. DREAMING MY DREAMS - Waylon Jennings - RCA
20. CLEARLY LOVE - Olivia Newton-John - MCA

TOP 20 COUNTRY ALBUMS OF 1977

POS.   TITLE - ARTIST - LABEL
1. OL' WAYLON - Waylon Jennings - RCA
2. LUXURY LINER - Emmylou Harris - Warner Bros.
3. MOODY BLUE - Elvis Presley - RCA
4. KENNY ROGERS - Kenny Rogers - United Artists
5. WAYLON LIVE - Waylon Jennings - RCA

6. CRYSTAL - Crystal Gayle - United Artists
7. SOUTHERN NIGHTS - Glen Campbell - Capitol
8. GREATEST HITS - Linda Ronstadt - Asylum
9. CHANGES IN LATITUDE-CHANGES IN ATTITUDES - Jimmy Buffet - ABC
10. NEW HARVEST..FIRST GATHERING - Dolly Parton - RCA
11. CONWAY TWITTY'S GREATEST HITS VOLUME II - Conway Twitty - MCA
12. ARE YOU READY FOR THE COUNTRY - Waylon Jennings - RCA
13. THE TROUBLEMAKER - Willie Nelson - Columbia
14. THE BEST OF CHARLEY PRIDE, VOL. III - Charley Pride - RCA
15. RONNIE MILSAP LIVE - Ronnie Milsap - RCA
16. VISIONS - Don Williams - ABC/Dot
17. GILLEY'S SMOKIN' - Mickey Gilley - Playboy
18. SOMEBODY SOMEWHERE - Loretta Lynn - MCA
19. FARGO COUNTRY - Donna Fargo - Warner Bros.
20. SHE'S JUST AN OLD LOVE TURNED MEMORY - Charley Pride - RCA

TOP 20 COUNTRY ALBUMS OF 1978

POS.   TITLE - ARTIST - LABEL
1. STARDUST - Willie Nelson - Columbia
2. HERE YOU COME AGAIN - Dolly Parton - RCA
3. WAYLON & WILLIE - Waylon Jennings & Willie Nelson - RCA
4. HEARTBREAKER - Dolly Parton - RCA
5. ELVIS IN CONCERT - Elvis Presley - RCA

Tom T. Hall

Country music's storyteller and author of a book on songwriting, Tom penned ``Harper Valley P.T.A.'' for Jeannie C. Riley. Tom had a #10 Top 20 Country album in 1975.

6. SIMPLE DREAMS - Linda Ronstadt - Asylum
7. TEN YEARS OF GOLD - Kenny Rogers - United Artists
8. TAKE THIS JOB AND SHOVE IT - Johnny Paycheck - Epic
9. WE MUST BELIEVE IN MAGIC - Crystal Gayle - United Artists
10. HEAVEN'S JUST A SIN AWAY - The Kendalls - Ovation
11. Y'ALL COME BACK SALOON - Oak Ridge Boys - ABC
12. IT WAS ALMOST A SONG - Ronnie Milsap - RCA
13. THE BEST OF THE STATLER BROTHERS - Statler Brothers - Mercury
14. QUARTER MOON IN A TEN CENT TOWN - Emmylou Harris - Warner Bros.
15. LOVE IS JUST A GAME - Larry Gatlin - Monument
16. DAYTIME FRIENDS - Kenny Rogers - United Artists
17. EVERYTIME TWO FOOLS COLLIDE - Kenny Rogers & Dottie West - United Artists
18. LET'S KEEP IT THAT WAY - Anne Murray - Capitol
19. GREATEST HITS - Linda Ronstadt - Asylum
20. ENTERTAINERS..ON AND OFF THE ROAD - Statler Brothers - Mercury

TOP 20 COUNTRY ALBUMS OF 1979

POS. TITLE - ARTIST - LABEL
1. THE GAMBLER - Kenny Rogers - United Artists
2. GREATEST HITS - Waylon Jennings - RCA
3. I'VE ALWAYS BEEN CRAZY - Waylon Jennings - RCA
4. STARDUST - Willie Nelson - Columbia
5. WILLIE & FAMILY LIVE - Willie Nelson - Columbia
6. WHEN I DREAM - Crystal Gayle - United Artists
7. EXPRESSIONS - Don Williams - MCA
8. TEN YEARS OF GOLD - Kenny Rogers - United Artists
9. LET'S KEEP IT THAT WAY - Anne Murray - Capitol
10. HEARTBREAKER - Dolly Parton - RCA
11. NEW KIND OF FEELING - Anne Murray - Capitol
12. TNT - Tanya Tucker - MCA
13. MOODS - Barbara Mandrell - MCA
14. TOTALLY HOT - Olivia Newton-John - MCA
15. MILLION MILE REFLECTIONS - Charlie Daniels Band - Epic
16. ROSE COLORED GLASSES - John Conlee - MCA
17. THE BEST OF THE STATLER BROTHERS - Statler Brothers - Mercury
18. PROFILE/BEST OF EMMYLOU HARRIS - Emmylou Harris - Warner Bros.
19. CLASSICS - Kenny Rogers & Dottie West - United Artists
20. LARRY GATLIN'S GREATEST HITS - Larry Gatlin - Monument

TOP 20 COUNTRY ALBUMS OF 1980

POS. TITLE - ARTIST - LABEL
1. KENNY - Kenny Rogers - United Artists
2. GREATEST HITS - Waylon Jennings - RCA
3. THE GAMBLER - Kenny Rogers - United Artists
4. STRAIGHT AHEAD - Larry Gatlin & The Gatlin Brothers Band - Columbia
5. STARDUST - Willie Nelson - Columbia
6. TEN YEARS OF GOLD - Kenny Rogers - United Artists
7. WHISKEY BENT AND HELL BOUND - Hank Williams, Jr. - Elektra/Curb
8. FAMILY TRADITION - Hank Williams, Jr. - Elektra/Curb
9. MISS THE MISSISSIPPI - Crystal Gayle - Columbia
10. 3/4 LONELY - T.G. Sheppard - Warner/Curb
11. GIDEON - Kenny Rogers - United Artists
12. URBAN COWBOY - Soundtrack - Asylum
13. THE BEST OF EDDIE RABBITT - Eddie Rabbitt - Elektra

14. THE OAK RIDGE BOYS HAVE ARRIVED - Oak Ridge Boys - MCA
15. THE BEST OF DON WILLIAMS, VOL. II - Don Williams - MCA
16. BLUE KENTUCKY GIRL - Emmylou Harris - Warner Bros.
17. CLASSIC CRYSTAL - Crystal Gayle - United Artists
18. THERE'S A LITTLE BIT OF HANK IN ME - Charley Pride - RCA
19. MILLION MILE REFLECTIONS - The Charlie Daniels Band - Epic
20. WHAT GOES AROUND, COMES AROUND - Waylon Jennings - RCA

TOP 20 COUNTRY ALBUMS OF 1981

POS. TITLE - ARTIST - LABEL
1. 9 TO 5 - Dolly Parton - RCA
2. GREATEST HITS - Kenny Rogers - Liberty
3. FEELS SO RIGHT - Alabama - RCA
4. HORIZONS - Eddie Rabbitt - Elektra
5. GREATEST HITS - Ronnie Milsap - MCA
6. I AM WHAT I AM - George Jones - Epic
7. GREATEST HITS - Waylon Jennings - RCA
8. GREATEST HITS - Anne Murray - Capitol
9. GREATEST HITS - Oak Ridge Boys - MCA
10. I BELIEVE IN YOU - Don Williams - MCA
11. HONEYSUCKLE ROSE - Soundtrack - Columbia
12. ROWDY - Hank Williams, Jr. - Elektra
13. MY HOME'S IN ALABAMA - Alabama - RCA
14. SEVEN YEAR ACHE - Rosanne Cash - Columbia
15. THE BEST OF EDDIE RABBITT - Eddie Rabbitt - Elektra
16. BACK TO THE BARROOMS - Merle Haggard - MCA
17. LOOKIN' FOR LOVE - Johnny Lee - Asylum
18. JUICE - Juice Newton - Capitol
19. LOVE IS FAIR - Barbara Mandrell - MCA
20. SOMEWHERE OVER THE RAINBOW - Willie Nelson - Columbia

TOP 20 COUNTRY ALBUMS OF 1982

POS. TITLE - ARTIST - LABEL
1. ALWAYS ON MY MIND - Willie Nelson - Columbia
2. FEELS SO RIGHT - Alabama - RCA
3. MOUNTAIN MUSIC - Alabama - RCA
4. WILLIE NELSON'S GREATEST HITS (AND SOME THAT WILL BE) - Willie Nelson - Columbia
5. BIG CITY - Merle Haggard - Epic
6. THE PRESSURE IS ON - Hank Williams, Jr. - Elektra/Curb
7. WAITIN' FOR THE SUN TO SHINE - Ricky Skaggs - Epic
8. MY HOME'S IN ALABAMA - Alabama - RCA
9. FANCY FREE - Oak Ridge Boys - MCA
10. GREATEST HITS - Kenny Rogers - Liberty
11. BOBBIE SUE - Oak Ridge Boys - MCA
12. STEP BY STEP - Eddie Rabbitt - Elektra
13. SOUTHERN COMFORT - Conway Twitty - Elektra
14. STILL THE SAME OLE ME - George Jones - Epic
15. JUICE - Juice Newton - Capitol
16. BET YOUR HEART ON ME - Johnny Lee - Full Moon/Asylum
17. I AM WHAT I AM - George Jones - Epic
18. STRAIT COUNTRY - George Strait - MCA
19. BLACK ON BLACK - Waylon Jennings - RCA
20. GREATEST HITS - Oak Ridge Boys - MCA

The Judds
Among other album hits, this mother-daughter team had the #2 Top 20 Country LP in 1985.

TOP 20 COUNTRY ALBUMS OF 1983

POS. TITLE - ARTIST - LABEL
1. MOUNTAIN MUSIC - Alabama - RCA
2. THE CLOSER YOU GET - Alabama - RCA
3. PANCHO AND LEFTY - Willie Nelson & Merle Haggard - Epic
4. HIGHWAYS AND HEARTACHES - Ricky Skaggs - Epic
5. ALWAYS ON MY MIND - Willie Nelson - Columbia
6. HANK WILLIAMS JR.'S GREATEST HITS - Hank Williams, Jr. - Elektra
7. GREATEST HITS - Bellamy Brothers - Warner/Curb
8. WILD AND BLUE - John Anderson - Warner Bros.
9. FEELS SO RIGHT - Alabama - RCA
10. IT AIN'T EASY - Janie Fricke - Columbia
11. AMERICAN MADE - Oak Ridge Boys - MCA
12. GOING WHERE THE LONELY GO - Merle Haggard - Epic
13. WILLIE NELSON'S GREATEST HITS (AND SOME THAT WILL BE) - Willie Nelson - Columbia
14. MY HOME'S IN ALABAMA - Alabama - RCA
15. RADIO ROMANCE - Eddie Rabbitt - Elektra
16. SOMEBODY'S GONNA LOVE YOU - Lee Greenwood - MCA
17. TRUE LOVE - Crystal Gayle - Elektra
18. STRONG WEAKNESS - Bellamy Brothers - Warner/Curb
19. JUST SYLVIA - Sylvia - RCA
20. WAITIN' FOR THE SUN TO SHINE - Ricky Skaggs - Epic

TOP 20 COUNTRY ALBUMS OF 1984

POS. TITLE - ARTIST - LABEL
1. DON'T CHEAT IN OUR HOMETOWN - Ricky Skaggs - Sugar Hill/Epic
2. RIGHT OR WRONG - George Strait - MCA
3. DON'T MAKE IT EASY FOR ME - Earl Thomas Conley - RCA
4. ROLL ON - Alabama - RCA
5. DELIVER - Oak Ridge Boys - MCA
6. WITHOUT A SONG - Willie Nelson - Columbia
7. MAN OF STEEL - Hank Williams, Jr. - Warner/Curb
8. CAGE THE SONGBIRD - Crystal Gayle - Warner Bros.
9. EYES THAT SEE IN THE DARK - Kenny Rogers - RCA
10. THE CLOSER YOU GET - Alabama - RCA
11. IN MY EYES - John Conlee - MCA
12. SOMEBODY'S GONNA LOVE YOU - Lee Greenwood - MCA
13. MAJOR MOVES - Hank Williams, Jr. - Warner/Curb
14. GREATEST HITS, VOL. II - Eddie Rabbitt - Warner Bros.
15. EXILE - Exile - Epic
16. MOVIN' TRAIN - Kendalls - Mercury
17. PANCHO AND LEFTY - Willie Nelson & Merle Haggard - Epic
18. IT TAKES BELIEVERS - Mickey Gilley & Charly McClain - Epic
19. THAT'S THE WAY LOVE GOES - Merle Haggard - Epic
20. THE MAN IN THE MIRROR - Jim Glaser - Noble Vision

TOP 20 COUNTRY ALBUMS OF 1985

POS. TITLE - ARTIST - LABEL
1. 40 HOUR WEEK - Alabama- RCA
2. WHY NOT ME - The Judds- RCA/Curb
3. DOES FORT WORTH EVER CROSS YOUR MIND - George Strait - MCA
4. COUNTRY BOY - Ricky Skaggs - Epic
5 FREINDSHIP - Ray Charles - Columbia.

11. GREATEST HITS, VOLUME II - Hank Williams, Jr. - Warner/Curb
12. FIVE-O - Hank Williams, Jr. - Warner/Curb
13. HANG ON TO YOUR HEART - Exile - Epic
14. WON'T BE BLUE ANYMORE - Dan Seals - EMI-America
15. PARDNERS IN RHYME - The Statler Brothers - Mercury
16. #7 - George Strait - MCA
17. 40 HOUR WEEK - Alabama - RCA
18. WHY NOT ME - The Judds - RCA/Curb
19. STORMS OF LIFE - Randy Travis - Warner Bros.
20. GREATEST HITS VOL. 2 - Ronnie Milsap - RCA

TOP 20 COUNTRY ALBUMS OF 1987

POS. TITLE - ARTIST - LABEL
1. STORMS OF LIFE - Randy Travis - Warner Bros.
2. OCEAN FRONT PROPERTY - George Strait - MCA
3. WHEELS - Restless Heart - RCA
4. THE TOUCH - Alabama - RCA
5. GUITARS, CADILLACS, ETC., ETC. - Dwight Yoakam - Reprise
6. HEART LAND - The Judds - RCA/Curb
7. ALWAYS & FOREVER - Randy Travis - Warner Bros.
8. WHAT AM I GONNA DO ABOUT YOU - Reba McEntire - MCA
9. WINE COLORED ROSES - George Jones - Epic
10. TRIO - Dolly Parton, Linda Ronstadt, Emmylou Harris - Warner Bros.
11. HANK LIVE - Hank Williams, Jr. - Warner/Curb
12. SWEETHEARTS OF THE RODEO - Sweethearts of the Rodeo - Columbia
13. TOO MANY TIMES - Earl Thomas Conley - RCA
14. HILLBILLY DELUXE - Dwight Yoakam - Reprise
15. ROCKIN' WITH THE RHYTHM - The Judds - RCA/Curb
16. THE O'KANES - The O'Kanes - Columbia
17. GREATEST HITS - Alabama - RCA
18. GUITAR TOWN - Steve Earle - MCA
19. WALK THE WAY THE WIND BLOWS - Kathy Mattea - Mercury
20. GREATEST HITS - Reba McEntire - MCA

TOP 20 COUNTRY ALBUMS OF 1988

POS. TITLE - ARTIST - LABEL
1. ALWAYS & FOREVER - Randy Travis - Warner Bros.
2. WILD EYED DREAM - Ricky Van Shelton - Columbia
3. BO'S LADIES - K.T. Oslin - RCA
4. BORN TO BOOGIE - Hank Williams, Jr. - Warner Bros.
5. GREATEST HITS, VOL. 2 - George Strait - MCA
6. KING'S RECORD SHOP - Rosanne Cash - Columbia
7. THE ROYAL TREATMENT - Billy Joe Royal - Atlantic America
8. IF YOU AIN'T LOVING YOU AIN'T LIVIN' - George Strait - MCA
9. THE LAST ONE TO KNOW - Reba McEntire - MCA
10. JUST US - Alabama - RCA
11. STORMS OF LIFE - Randy Travis - Warner Bros.
12. GREATEST HITS - Reba McEntire - MCA
13. REBA - Reba McEntire - MCA
14. HIGHWAY 101 - Highway 101 - Warner Bros.
15. HILLBILLY DELUXE - Dwight Yoakam - Reprise
16. CHILL FACTOR - Merle Haggard - Epic
17. HEART LAND - The Judds - RCA/Curb
18. UNTASTED HONEY - Kathy Mattea - Mercury
19. CHISELED IN STONE - Vern Gosdin - Columbia
20. TRIO - Dolly Parton, Linda Ronstadt, Emmylou Harris - Warner Bros.

Reba McEntire

Reba has had at least one—and sometimes two and three—Top 20 Country albums every year since 1986.

6 KENTUCKY HEARTS - Exile - Epic.
7. FIVE-O - Hank Williams Jr. - Warner/Curb
8. TREADIN' WATER - Earl Thomas Conley - RCA
9. ME AND PAUL - Willie Nelson - Columbia
10. GREATEST HITS 2 - The Oak Ridge Boys - MCA
11. GEORGE STRAIT'S GREATEST HITS - George Strait - MCA
12. GREATEST HITS VOL. 2 - Ronnie Milsap - RCA
13. SAWYER BROWN - Sawyer Brown - Capitol/Curb
14. HEART OVER MIND - Anne Murray - Capitol
15. ATLANTA BLUE - The Statler Brothers - Mercury
16. ROLL ON - Alabama - RCA
17. STEP ON OUT - The Oak Ridge Boys - MCA
18. TOO GOOD TO STOP NOW - John Schneider - MCA
19. PARDNERS IN RHYME - The Statler Brothers - Mercury
20. HIGHWAYMAN - Waylon Jennings, Willie Nelson, Johnny Cash, Kris Kristofferson - Columbia

TOP 20 COUNTRY ALBUMS OF 1986

POS. TITLE - ARTIST - LABEL
1. ROCKIN' WITH THE RHYTM - The Judds - RCA/Curb
2. GREATEST HITS - Earl Thomas Conley - RCA
3. GREATEST HITS - Alabama - RCA
4. SOMETHING SPECIAL - George Strait - MCA
5. GUITARS, CADILLACS, ETC., ETC. - Dwight Yoakam - Reprise
6. LIVE IN LONDON - Ricky Skaggs - Epic
7. RHYTHM AND ROMANCE - Rosanne Cash - Columbia
8. WHOEVER'S IN NEW ENGLAND - Reba McEntire - MCA
9. SHAKIN' - Sawyer Brown - Capitol/Curb
10. STREAMLINE - Lee Greenwood - MCA

Ricky Van Shelton
Ricky had the #2 Top 20 Country LP in 1988—and #1 in 1989!

Clint Black
Clint's ``Killin' Time'' LP was #1 Top 20 Country in 1990.

Kathy Mattea
Kathy had the #8 Top 20 Country album of 1990.

Travis Tritt
Travis had three Top 20 Country albums—in 1990, '91 and '92.

Taken backstage at the Grand Ole Opry in 1989, Garth had just finished singing his first hit—``Much Too Young To Feel This Damn Old''—and graciously consented to a photo with the author's son Chris (left) and Brian O'Neill Terry, an aspiring artist for Sing Me Records.

Garth Brooks

What can we say? The #1 and #2 Country albums in 1991, the #1 in 1992 (one of five in the Top 20—none lower than #11), and another six in the Top 20 Country in 1993, including the #2 position.

Collin Raye

A newcomer on the Country scene, Collin had the
#19 Top 20 Country album in 1992.

TOP 20 COUNTRY ALBUMS OF 1989

POS.   TITLE - ARTIST - LABEL
1. LOVING PROOF - Ricky Van Shelton - Columbia
2. OLD 8 X 10 - Randy Travis - Warner Bros.
3. THIS WOMAN - K.T. Oslin - RCA
4. GREATEST HITS III - Hank Williams, Jr. - Warner/Curb
5. GREATEST HITS - The Judds - RCA/Curb
6. BEYOND THE BLUE NEON - George Strait - MCA
7. DIAMONDS & DIRT - Rodney Crowell - Columbia
8. BUENAS NOCHES FROM A LONELY ROOM - Dwight Yoakam - Reprise
9. ALWAYS & FOREVER - Randy Travis - Warner Bros.
10. REBA - Reba McEntire - MCA
11. HONKY TONK ANGEL - Patty Loveless - MCA
12. SOUTHERN STAR - Alabama - RCA
13. RIVER OF TIME - The Judds - Curb/RCA
14. DON'T CLOSE YOUR EYES - Keith Whitley - RCA
15. SWEET SIXTEEN - Reba McEntire - MCA
16. KILLIN' TIME - Clint Black - RCA
17. 80'S LADIES - K.T. Oslin - RCA
18. THE ROAD NOT TAKEN - Shenandoah - Columbia
19. WILD EYE DREAM - Ricky Van Shelton - Columbia
20. STRONG ENOUGH TO BEND - Tanya Tucker - Capitol

TOP 20 COUNTRY ALBUMS OF 1990

POS.   TITLE - ARTIST - LABEL
1. KILLIN' TIME - Clint Black - RCA
2. NO HOLDIN' BACK - Randy Travis - Warner Bros.
3. PICKIN' ON NASHVILLE - The Kentucky Headhunters - Mercury
4. GARTH BROOKS - Garth Brooks - Capitol
5. LEAVE THE LIGHT ON - Lorrie Morgan - RCA
6. RVS III - Ricky Van Shelton - Columbia
7. SIMPLE MAN - The Charlie Daniels Band - Epic
8. WILLOW IN THE WIND - Kathy Mattea - Mercury
9. THE BOYS ARE BACK - Sawyer Brown - Capitol/Curb
10. REBA LIVE - Reba McEntire - MCA
11. COUNTRY CLUB - Travis Tritt - Warner Bros.
12. HERE IN THE REAL WORLD - Alan Jackson - Arista
13. LONE WOLF - Hank Williams, Jr. - Warner/Curb
14. WHITE LIMOZEEN - Dolly Parton - Columbia
15. ALWAYS & FOREVER - Randy Travis - Warner Bros.
16. ABSOLUTE TORCH AND TWANG - k.d. lang & the reclines - Sire
17. GREATEST HITS III - Hank Williams, Jr. - Warner/Curb
18. THE ROAD NOT TAKEN - Shenandoah - Columbia
19. FAST MOVIN' TRAIN - Restless Heart - RCA
20. I WONDER DO YOU THINK OF ME - Keith Whitley - RCA

TOP 20 COUNTRY ALBUMS OF 1991

POS.   TITLE - ARTIST - LABEL
1. NO FENCES - Garth Brooks - Capitol
2. GARTH BROOKS - Garth Brooks - Capitol
3. PUT YOURSELF IN MY SHOES - Clint Black - RCA
4. RUMOR HAS IT - Reba McEntire - MCA
5. HERE IN THE REAL WORLD - Alan Jackson - Arista
6. KILLIN' TIME - Clint Black - RCA
7. PICKIN' ON NASHVILLE - The Kentucky Headhunters - Mercury
8. LOVE CAN BUILD A BRIDGE - The Judds - Curb/RCA
9. WHEN I CALL YOUR NAME - Vince Gill - MCA
10. COUNTRY CLUB - Travis Tritt - Warner Bros.
11. HEROES AND FRIENDS - Randy Travis - Warner Bros.
12. IF THERE WAS A WAY - Dwight Yoakam - Reprise
13. EAGLE WHEN SHE FLIES - Dolly Parton - Columbia
14. PASS IT ON DOWN - Alabama - RCA
15. TOO COLD AT HOME - Mark Chesnutt - MCA
16. RVS III - Ricky Van Shelton - Columbia
17. DON'T ROCK THE JUKEBOX - Alan Jackson - Arista
18. LOVE IN A SMALLTOWN - K.T. Oslin - RCA
19. GREATEST HITS - Keith Whitley - RCA
20. A COLLECTION OF HITS - Kathy Mattea - Mercury

TOP 20 COUNTRY ALBUMS OF 1992

POS.   TITLE - ARTIST - LABEL
1. ROPIN' THE WIND - Garth Brooks - Liberty
2. SOME GAVE ALL - Billy Ray Cyrus - Mercury
3. NO FENCES - Garth Brooks - Liberty
4. THE CHASE - Garth Brooks - Liberty
5. GARTH BROOKS - Garth Brooks - Liberty
6. WYNONNA - Wynonna - Curb/MCA
7. FOR MY BROKEN HEART - Reba McEntire - MCA
8. BRAND NEW MAN - Brooks & Dunn - Arista
9. IT'S ALL ABOUT TO CHANGE - Travis Tritt - Warner Bros.
10. DON'T ROCK THE JUKEBOX - Alan Jackson - Arista
11. BEYOND THE SEASON - Garth Brooks - Liberty
12. POCKET FULL OF GOLD - Vince Gill - MCA
13. TRISHA YEARWOOD - Trisha Yearwood - MCA
14. SOMETHING IN RED - Lorrie Morgan - RCA
15. WHAT DO I DO WITH ME - Tanya Tucker - Liberty
16. SEMINOLE WIND - John Anderson - BNA
17. THE HARD WAY - Clint Black - RCA
18. PAST THE POINT OF RESCUE - Hal Ketchum - Curb
19. ALL I CAN BE - Collin Raye - Epic

Billy Ray Cyrus

Billy Ray's ``Achy Breaky Heart'' (1992) was only the second truly Country hit single to go Platinum. His debut album ``Some Gave All'' was #2 Country in 1992, and #1 in 1993.

20. DIAMOND RIO - Diamond Rio - Arista

TOP 20 COUNTRY ALBUMS OF 1993

POS.   TITLE - ARTIST - LABEL
1. SOME GAVE ALL - Billy Ray Cyrus - Mercury
2. THE CHASE - Garth Brooks - Liberty
3. PURE COUNTRY (SOUNDTRACK) - George Strait - MCA
4. IN PIECES - Garth Brooks - Liberty
5. IT'S OUR CALL - Reba McEntire - MCA
6. A LOT ABOUT LIVIN' (AND A LITTLE 'BOUT LOVE) - Alan Jackson - Arista
7. BRAND NEW MAN - Brooks & Dunn - Arista
8. I STILL BELIEVE IN YOU - Vince Gill - MCA
9. NO FENCES - Garth Brooks - Liberty
10. HARD WORKIN' MAN - Brooks & Dunn - Arista
11. COME ON COME ON - Mary Chapin Carpenter - Columbia
12. WYBONNA - Wynonna - Curb/MCA
13. ROPIN' THE WIND - Garth Brooks - Liberty
14. LIFE'S A DANCE - John Michael Montgomery - Atlantic
15. BEYOND THE SEASON - Garth Brooks - Liberty
16. IT WON'T BE THE LAST - Billy Ray Cyrus - Mercury
17. TELL ME WHY - Wynonna - Curb/MCA
18. THIS TIME - Dwight Yoakam - Reprise
19. ALIBIS - Tracy Lawrence - Atlantic
20. GARTH BROOKS - Garth Brooks - Liberty

Billboard Top 20 Classical Albums, 1969-1993

TOP 20 CLASSICAL ALBUMS OF 1969

POS.   TITLE - ARTIST - LABEL
1. TRANS-ELECTRONIC MUSIC PRODUCTIONS, INC., PRESENTS SWITCHED-ON BACH - Walter Carlos/Benjamin Folkman - Columbia
2. 2001: A SPACE ODYSSEY - Soundtrack - MGM
3. MOZART: CONCERTOS 17 & 21 (ELVIRA MADIGAN) - Anda/Camarata Academica of the Salzburg Mozarteum (Anda) - DGG
4. MY FAVORITE CHOPIN - Van Cliburn - RCA
5. TCHAIKOVSKY: 1812 OVERTURE - New Philharmonic Orchestra (Buketoff) - RCA
6. UP, UP AND AWAY - Boston Pops (Fielder) - RCA
7. BERNSTEIN'S GREATEST HITS - New York Philharmonic (Bernstein) - Columbia
8. BELLINI & DONIZETTI HEROINES - Beverly Sills/Vienna Volksoper Orch. (Jalas) - Westminster
9. R. STRAUSS; ALSO SPRACH ZARATHUSTRA - Philadelphia Orchestra (Ormandy) - Columbia
10. SELECTIONS FROM 2001: A SPACE ODYSSEY - Philadelphia Orchestra (Ormandy)/New York Philharmonic (Bernstein) - Columbia
11. HOROWITZ ON TELEVISION - Vladimir Horowitz - Columbia
12. ROYAL FAMILY OF OPERA (3 LPS) - Various Artists - London
13. GRIEG: CONCERTO IN A MINOR/LIZST: CONCERTO NO. 1 - Van Cliburn/Philadelphia Orchestra (Ormandy) - RCA
14. GLORY OF GABRIELLI - E. Power Biggs/Various Artists - Columbia
15. CHOPIN'S GREATEST HITS - Various Artists - Columbia
16. GOUNOD: ROMEO & JULIET (3 LPS) - Freni & Corelli/Various Artists/Paris Opera Orchestra (Lombard) - Angel/Capitol
17. BACH'S GREATEST HITS - Various Artists - Columbia
18. R. STRAUSS: ALSO SPRACH ZARATHUSTRA - Chicago Symphony (Reiner) - RCA
19. E. POWER BIGGS' GREATEST HITS - E. Power Biggs - Columbia
20. CHOPIN: SONATAS NO. 2 & 3 - Van Cliburn - RCA

TOP 20 CLASSICAL ALBUMS OF 1970

POS.   TITLE - ARTISTS - LABEL
1. TRANS-ELECTRONIC MUSIC PRODUCTIONS, INC., PRESENTS SWITCHED-ON BACH - Walter Carlos/Benjamin Folkman - Columbia
2. TRANS-ELECTRONIC MUSIC PRODUCTIONS, INC., PRESENTS THE WELL-TEMPERED SYNTHESIZER - Walter Carlos - Columbia
3. 2001: A SPACE ODYSSEY - Soundtrack - MGM
4. MY FAVORITE CHOPIN - Van Cliburn - RCA
5. SCENES & ARIAS FROM FRENCH OPERA - Beverly Sills - Westminster
6. MOZART: CONCERTOS NOS. 17 & 21 (ELVIRA MADIGAN) - Anda/Camarata of the Salzburg Mozarteum Academica (Anda) - DGG
7. BACH'S GREATEST HITS - Various Artists - Columbia
8. R. STRAUSS: DER ROSENKAVALIET (4 LPS) - Crespin/Donath/Various Artists/Vienna Philharmonic (Solti) - London

9. R. STRAUSS: ALSO SPRACH ZARATHUSTRA - Philadelphia Orchestra (Ormandy) - Columbia
10. A TEBALDI FESTIVAL (2 LPS) - Renata Tebaldi - London
11. CHOPIN'S GREATEST HITS - Various Artists - Columbia
12. SELECTIONS FROM 2001: A SPACE ODYSSEY - Philadelphia Orchestra (Ormandy)/New York Philharmonic (Bernstein) - Columbia
13. BELLINI & DONIZETTI HEROINES - Beverly Sills/Vienna Volksoper (Jalas) - Westminster
14. R. STRAUSS: ALSO SPRACH ZARATHUSTRA - Berlin Philharmonic (Boehm) - DGG
15. MISSA LUBA - Troubadours Du Roi Bafouin - Phillips
16. DONIZETTI: ROBERTO DEVEREUX (3 LPS) - Beverly Sills/Wolff/Various Artists/Royal Philharmonic/Ambrosian Opera Chorus (MacKerras) - Westminster
17. A KARAJAN FESTIVAL (2 LPS) - Berlin Philharmonic (Karajan) - DGG
18. E. POWER BIGGS' GREATEST HITS - E. Power Biggs - Columbia
19. MOONDOG (Louis Thomas Hardin) - 60 New York Studio Musicians (Hardin) - Columbia
20. VAUGHN-WILLIAMS: SEA SYMPHONY (2 LPS) - Sheila Armstrong/John Carol Case/London Philharmonic & Chorus (Boult) - Angel

TOP 20 CLASSICAL ALBUMS 0F 1971

POS.   TITLE - ARTIST - LABEL
1. TRANS-ELECTRONIC MUSIC PRODUCTIONS, INC., PRESENTS SWITCHED-ON BACH - Walter Carlos/Benjamin Folkman - Columbia
2. TCHAIKOVSKY: 1812 OVERTURE - Los Angeles Philharmonic (Mehta) - London
3. BEETHOVEN'S GREATEST HITS - Various Artists - Columbia
4. TRANS-ELECTRONIC MUSIC PRODUCTIONS, INC., PRESENTS THE WELL-TEMPERED SYNTHESIZER - Walter Carlos - Columbia
5. MOZART: CONCERTOS 17 & 21 (ELVIRA MADIGAN) - Anda/Camarata of the Salzburg Mozarteum Academia (Anda) - DGG
6. 2001: A SPACE ODYSSEY - Soundtrack - MGM
7. BACH'S GREATEST HITS - Various Artists - Columbia
8. THE CHOPIN I LOVE - Artur Rubinstein - RCA Red Seal
9. MY FAVORITE ENCORES - Van Cliburn - RCA Red Seal
10. MASSENET: MANON (4 LPS) - Sills/Gedda/Souzay/Various/New Philharmonia (Rudel) - ABC
11. DONIZETTI: LUCIA DI LAMERMOOR (3 LPS) - Sills/Birgonzi/Various Artists/London Symphony (Schippers) - ABC/ATS 200006/3
12. MY FAVORITE CHOPIN - Van Cliburn - RCA Red Seal
13. TCHAIKOVSKY: 1812 OVERTURE/BEETHOVEN: WELLINGTON'S VICTORY - Various/Philadelphia Orchestra (Ormandy) - RCA Red Seal
14. HOLST: THE PLANETS - Boston Symphony (Steinberg) - DGG
15. STRAUSS: ALSO SPRACH ZARATHUSTRA - Philadelphia Orchestra (Ormandy) - Columbia
16. BACH LIVE AT FILLMORE EAST - Virgil Fox - Decca
17. TCHAIKOVSKY: 1812 OVERTURE - Mormon Tabernacle Choir/Philadelphia Orchestra (Ormandy) - Columbia

18. HEIFETZ ON TV - Jasha Heifetz - RCA Red Seal
19. BERLIOZ: LES TROYENS (5 LPS) - Vickers/Veasey/ Various/New Philharmonia (Bonynge) - Philips
20. SINFONIAS - Waldo de los Rios - United Artists

TOP 20 CLASSICAL ALBUMS OF 1972

POS.	TITLE - ARTIST - LABEL
1.	MASS - Leonard Bernstein - Columbia
2.	SWITCHED-ON BACH - Walter Carlos/Benjamin Folkman - Columbia
3.	THE CHOPIN I LOVE - Artur Rubenstein - RCA Red Seal
4.	MY FAVORITE CHOPIN - Van Cliburn - RCA Red Seal
5.	BACH LIVE AT THE FILLMORE EAST - Virgil Fox - Decca/ MCA
6.	HOLST: THE PLANETS - Boston Symphony - DGG
7.	A CLOCKWORK ORANGE - Soundtrack - Warner Bros.
8.	VERDI: LA TRAVIATA - Sills/Gedda/Panera/Alldis Choir (Deccato) - Angel/Capitol
9.	2001: A SPACE ODYSSEY - Soundtrack - MGM
10.	WELL TEMPERED SYNTHESIZER - Walter Carlos - Columbia
11.	HOLST: THE PLANETS - Los Angeles Philharmonic (Mehta) - London
12.	SINFONIAS - Waldo de los Rios - United Artists
13.	TCHAIKOVSKY: 1812 OVERTURE/BEETHOVEN: WELLINGTON'S VICTORY - Various Artists/Philadelphia Orchestra (Ormandy) - RCA Red Seal
14.	HEAVY ORGAN - Virgil Fox - Decca/MCA
15.	HIGHLIGHTS/METROPOLITAN OPERA GALA VOL. 1 HONORING SIR RUDOLF BING - Various Artists - DGG
16.	MAHLER: 8TH SYMPHONY - Chicago Symphony (Solti) - London
17.	DONIZETTI: MARIA STUARTI - Sills/Farrell/Burrows/Quilico (Ceccat) - ABC
18.	WAGNER: DIE MEISTERSINGER VON NURNBERG - Adam/Donath/Dresden State Opera (Von Karajan) - Angel/ Capitol
19.	PAGANINI: VIOLIN CONCERTO #3 - Henryk Szering - Philips/Mercury
20.	VERDI: I LOMBARDI - Royal Philharmonic & Chorus (Gardelli) - Philips/Mercury

TOP 20 CLASSICAL ALBUMS OF 1973

POS.	TITLE - ARTIST - LABEL
1.	SCOTT JOPLIN: PIANO RAGS, VOL. I - Joshua Rifkin - Nonesuch
2.	SCOTT JOPLIN: THE RED BACK BOOK - Gunther Schuller - Angel
3.	SCOTT JOPLIN: PIANO RAGS, VOL. II - Joshua Rifkin - Nonesuch
4.	TRANS-ELECTRONIC MUSIC PRODUCTIONS, INC., SWITCHED-ON BACH - Walter Carlos/Benjamin Folkman - Columbia
5.	THE SEA HAWK - National Philharmonic Orchestra of London (Gerhardt) - RCA
6.	MAHLER: 8TH SYMPHONY - Chicago Symphony Orchestra (Solti) - London
7.	2001: A SPACE ODYSSEY - Soundtrack - MGM
8.	BEETHOVEN: SYMPHONY #9 - Chicago Symphony Orchestra (Solti) - London
9.	BIZET: CARMEN - M. Horn/J. McCraken/L. Bernstein - DGG
10.	VERDI: RIGOLETTO - Sutherland/Pavarotti (London Symphony) - London
11.	SONGS BY STEPHEN FOSTER - Stephen Foster - Nonesuch

12. BACH: BRANDENBERG CONCERTOS - Ristenpart - Nonesuch
13. BERNSTEIN: MASS - L. Bernstein - Columbia
14. VERDI: ATTILA - Royal Philharmonic (Gardelli) - Phillips
15. VERDI: GIOVANNA D'ARCO - Cabelle/Domingo - Angel
16. BERNSTEIN: SYMPHONIC DANCES FORM WEST SIDE STORY RUSSO: THREE PIECES FOR BLUES BAND & ORCHESTRA - Siegel Schwall Band/San Francisco Symphony Orchestra (Ozawa) - DGG
17. MAX STEINER: NOW VOYAGER - National Philharmonic (Gerhardt) - RCA
18. ANNA BOLENA - Beverly Sills - ABC
19. BACH: COMPLETE FLUTE SONATAS - Odyssey
20. THE CHOPIN I LOVE - Artur Rubenstein - RCA Red Seal

TOP 20 CLASSICAL ALBUMS OF 1974

POS.	TITLE - ARTIST - LABEL
1.	SCOTT JOPLIN: THE RED BACK BOOK - Gunther Schuller - Angel
2.	PUCCINI: TURANDOT - Sutherland/Pavarotti/Caballe/ Chiaurov/Krause/Pears/Mehta - London
3.	SCOTT JOPLIN: PIANO RAGS, VOL. 1 - Joshua Rifkin - Nonesuch
4.	SCOTT JOPLIN: PIANO RAGS, VOL. 2 - Joshua Rifkin - Nonesuch
5.	PIANO MUSIC BY GEORGE GERSHWIN - William Bolcom - Nonesuch
6.	SWITCHED-ON BACH - Carlos/Folkman - Columbia
7.	BACH: FLUTE SONATAS (COMPLETE) - Rampal - Odyssey
8.	BACH: BRANDENBURG CONCERTOS - Ristenpart - Nonesuch
9.	MAHLER: 8TH SYMPHONY - Chicago Symphony Orchestra (Solti) - London
10.	CLASSIC FILM SCORES FOR BETTE DAVIS - National Philharmonic of London (Gerhardt) - RCA
11.	PRIMO TENORE - Luciano Pavarotti - London
12.	SWITCHED-ON BACH II - Walter Carlos - Columbia
13.	RACHMININOFF: VESPERS - U.S.S.R. Russian Chorus & Soloists - Melodiya
14.	PUCCINI: LA BOHEME - Pavarotti/Freni/Von Karajan - London
15.	THE CHRISTOPHER PARKENING ALBUM - Christopher Parkening - Angel
16.	BEETHOVEN: SYMPHONY #9 - Chicago Symphony Orchestra (Solti) - London
17.	KING OF THE HIGH C'S - Luciano Pavarotti - London
18.	PROKOFIEV: ROMEO AND JULIET (COMPLETE BALLET) - Cleveland Orchestra (Maazel) - Nonesuch
19.	E. POWER BIGGS PLAYS SCOTT JOPLIN - E. Power Biggs - Columbia
20.	VERDI: I VESPRI SILICIANI - Arroyo/Domingo/Milnes/ Raimondi/New Philharmonia/Levine - RCA

TOP 20 CLASSICAL ALBUMS OF 1975

POS.	TITLE - ARTIST - LABEL
1.	SNOWFLAKES ARE DANCING: THE NEWEST SOUNDS OF DEBUSSY - Isao Tomita - RCA Red Seal
2.	STRAVINSKY: RITE OF SPRING - Chicago Symphony (Solti) - London
3.	BERLIOZ: SYMPHONIE FANTASTIQUE - Chicago Symphony (Solti) - London
4.	KING OF THE HIGH C'S - Luciano Pavarotti - London
5.	ORFF: CARMINA BURANA - Cleveland Orchestra & Chorus (Thomas) - Columbia

6. SCOTT JOPLIN: THE RED BACK BOOK - New England Conservatory Ragtime Ensemble (Schuller) - Angel/Capitol
7. PAVAROTTI IN CONCERT - Luciano Pavarotti/Orchestra di Teatro Communale Bologna (Bonynge) - London
8. SCOTT JOPLIN: PIANO RAGS, VOL. 1 - Joshua Rifkin - Nonesuch/Elektra
9. SCOTT JOPLIN: PIANO RAGS, VOL. 3 - Joshua Rifkin - Nonesuch/Elektra
10. ALBINONI: ADAGIO & OTHER PIECES - Academy of St. Martin-in-the-Fields (Marriner) - Angel/Capitol
11. ROSSINI: THE SIEGE OF CORINTH - London Symphony Orchestra (Schippers) - Angel/Capitol
    BACH: FLUTE SONATAS (COMPLETE) - Rampal - Odyssey/Columbia
13. SCOTT JOPLIN: PIANO RAGS, VOL. 1 & 2 - Joshua Rifkin - Nonesuch/Elektra
14. AFTER THE BALL: A TREASURY OF TURN-OF-THE-CENTURY POPULAR SONGS - Joan Morris/William Bolcom - Nonesuch/Elektra
15. MOUSSORGSKY: PICTURES AT AN EXHIBITION - Isao Tomita - RCA Red Seal
16. SCOTT JOPLIN: PIANO RAGS, VOL. 2 - Joshua Rifkin - Nonesuch/Elektra
17. HAYDN: COMPLETE SYMPHONIES, VOL. 9 - Philharmonia Hungarica (Dorati) - London
18. PUCCINI: MADAME BUTTERFLY - Vienna Philharmonic (Freni)/Pavarotti (Karajan) - London
19. BELLINI: I PURITANI - London Symphony Orchestra (Bonynge)/Sutherland/Pavarotti - London
20. SCOTT JOPLIN: THE EASY WINNERS - Perlman/Previn - Angel/Capitol

TOP 20 CLASSICAL ALBUMS OF 1976

POS. COMPOSER: TITLE - ARTIST - LABEL
1. PACHELBEL KANON: THE RECORD THAT MADE IT FAMOUS AND OTHER BAROQUE FAVORITES - Stuttgart Chamber Orchestra (Munchinger) - London
2. BEETHOVEN: SYMPHONY NO. 5 - Vienna Philharmonic Orchestra (Kleiber) - DGG/Polydor
3. LUCIANO PAVAROTTI: THE WORLD'S FAVORITE TENOR ARIAS - Luciano Pavarotti - London
4. SNOWFLAKES ARE DANCING: THE NEWEST SOUNDS OF DEBUSSY - Isao Tomita - RCA Red Seal
5. BEETHOVEN: NINE SYMPHONIES - Chicago Symphony Orchestra (Solti) - London
6. BEVERLY SILLS: MUSIC OF VICTOR HERBERT - Beverly Sills - Angel/Capitol
7. 19TH CENTURY AMERICAN BALLROOM MUSIC (1840-1860) - Smithsonian Social Orchestra & Quadrille Band (Weaver)/Camerata Chorus of Washington - Nonesuch/Elektra
8. JOAN SUTHERLAND & LUCIANO PAVAROTTI: DUETS FROM LUCIA DI LAMMERMOOR - Joan Sutherland & Luciano Pavarotti - London
9. JEAN-PEIRRE RAMPAL & CLAUDE BOLLING: SUITE FOR FLUTE & JAZZ PIANO - Rampal & Bolling - Columbia
10. THE LEGENDARY LAZAR BERMAN PLAYS LISZT - Lazar Berman - Melodiya/Columbia
11. GERSHWIN: PORGY AND BESS - Cleveland Orchestra & Chorus (Maazel) - London
12. BEVERLY SILLS: PLAISIR D'AMOUR - Columbia Symphony Orchestra (Davis) - Philips/Phonogram
13. KORNGOLD: DIE TOTE STADT - Bavarian Radio Chorus & Munich Radio Orchestra (Leinsdorf) - RCA Red Seal
14. SIBELIUS: SYMPHONY # 5 & SYMPHONY # 7 - Boston Symphony Orchestra (Davis) - Philips/Phonogram

15. SCOTT JOPLIN'S TREEMONISHA/ORIGINAL CAST RECORDING - Houston Grand Opera (Schuller) - DGG/Polydor
16. LISZT: SONATA IN B MINOR - Lazar Berman - Melodiya/Columbia
17. CHOPIN: 24 PRELUDES OP. 28 - Maurizio Pollini - DGG/Polydor
18. PAVAROTTI IN CONCERT - Luciano Pavarotti - London
19. R. STRAUSS: ALSO SPRACH ZARATHUSTRA - Chicago Symphony Orchestra (Solti) - London
20. ANDRE WATTS PLAYS GEORGE GERSHWIN - Andre Watts - Columbia

TOP 20 CLASSICAL ALBUMS OF 1977

POS. TITLE - ARTIST - LABEL
1. THE GREAT PAVAROTTI - Luciano Pavarotti - London
2. SUITE FOR FLUTE AND JAZZ PIANO - Jean-Pierre Rampal & Claude Bolling - Columbia
3. HOLST: THE PLANETS - Isao Tomita - RCA Red Seal
4. CARUSO: A LEGENDARY PREFORMER - Caruso - RCA Red Seal
5. BOLLING: CONCERTO FOR CLASSIC GUITAR AND JAZZ PIANO - Lagoya - RCA
6. PACHELBEL CANON: TWO SUITES; FASCH: TWO SYMPHONIES - Paillard Chamber Orchestra (Andre) - RCA
7. GERSHWIN: PORGY AND BESS - Houston Opera Co. - RCA Red Seal
8. LUCIANO PAVAROTTI: THE WORLD'S FAVORITE TENOR ARIAS - Luciano Pavarotti - London
9. BEETHOVEN: SYMPHONY NO. 5 - Vienna Philharmonic Orchestra (Kleiber) - DGG/Polydor
10. RAVEL: BOLERO - Chicago Symphony Orchestra (Solti) - London
11. THE CONCERT OF THE CENTURY - Columbia
12. MEYERBEER: LE PROPHETE - Horne/Royal Philharmonic (Lewis) - Columbia
13. GO FOR BAROQUE - Paillard Chamber Orchestra - RCA Victrola
14. MAHLER: SYMPHONY NO. 9 - Chicago Symphony Orchestra (Solti) - DGG/Polydor
    PARKENING & THE GUITAR: MUSIC OF TWO CENTURIES - Parkening - Angel/Capitol
16. VAUDEVILLE: SONGS OF THE GREAT LADIES OF THE MUSICAL STAGE - Morris/Bolcom - Nonesuch/Elektra
17. PACHELBEL CANON: THE RECORD THAT MADE IT FAMOUS AND OTHER BAROQUE FAVORITES - Stuttgart Chamber Orchestra (Munchinger) - London
18. PUCCINI: TOSCA - Montserrat Caballe/Carreras/Royal Opera House Covent Garden (Gardell) - Philips/Phonogram
19. PAVAROTTI IN CONCERT - Luciano Pavarotti - London
20. THE HOROWITZ CONCERTS 1975-1976 - Horowitz - RCA Red Seal

TOP 20 CLASSICAL ALBUMS OF 1978

POS. TITLE - ARTIST - LABEL
1. VERDI: IL TROVATORE - Sutherland/Horne/Pavarotti/Bonynge - London
2. GREATEST HITS OF 1720 - Kapp - Columbia
3. STAR WARS & CLOSE ENCOUNTERS - Los Angeles Philharmonic (Zubin Mehta) - London
4. JEAN-PIERRE RAMPAL & CLAUDE BOLLING: SUITE FOR FLUTE & JAZZ PIANO - Rampal & Bolling - Columbia

5.   SUTHERLAND & PAVAROTTI: OPERATIC DUETS - Sutherland & Pavarotti - London
6.   PACHELBEL KANON: TWO SUITES; FASCH: TWO SYMPHONIES - Paillard Chamber Orchestra (Andre) - RCA
7.   MAHLER: SYMPHONY NO. 9 - Chicago Symphony Orchestra (Giulini) - DG/Polydor
8.   THE WORLD'S FAVORITE TENOR ARIAS - Luciano Pavarotti - London
9.   THE GREAT PAVAROTTI - Luciano Pavarotti - London
10.   GOLDEN JUBILEE RECITAL: 1977-1978 - RCA
11.   GERSHWIN: PORGY AND BESS - Houston Opera Company - RCA Red Seal
12.   RACHMANINOFF: CONCERTO NO. 3 - Berman/Abbado - Columbia
13.   BEETHOVEN: COMPLETE SYMPHONIES - Berlin Philharmonic (Von Karajan) - DG/Polydor
14.   GRANADOS: GOYESCAS - De Larrocha - London
15.   BACH: BRANDENBURG CONCERTOS - Leonhardt - ABC
16.   DONIZETTI: LA FAVORITA - London
17.   VERDI: LA TRAVIATA - Cotrubus/Domingo/Milnes/Kleiter - DG/Polydor
18.   CHOPIN POLONAISES - Pollini - DG/Polydor
19.* RAMPAL: SAKURA - Rampal/Laskine - Columbia
      RAVEL: BOLERO - Chicago Symphony Orchestra (Solti) - London (*Tie)

TOP 20 CLASSICAL ALBUMS OF 1979

POS. TITLE - ARTIST - LABEL
1.   ANNIE'S SONG - James Galway/National Philharmonic Orchestra (Gerhardt) - RCA
2.   BRAVO PAVAROTTI - Luciano Pavarotti - London
3.   HITS FROM LINCOLN CENTER - Luciano Pavarotti - London
4.   SUITE FOR FLUTE & JAZZ PIANO - Claude Bolling - Zukerman
5.   PACHELBEL: KANON - Paillard Chamber Orchestra (Andre) - RCA
6.   SUITE FOR FLUTE & JAZZ PIANO - Jean-Pierre Rampal & Laskine - Columbia
7.   UP IN CENTRAL PARK - Beverly Sills/Milnes - Angel
8.   RAMPAL: JAPANESE MELODIES FOR FLUTE & HARP - Jean-Pierre Rampal & Laskine - Columbia
9.   RACHMANINOFF: CONCERTO #3 - Horowitz/New York Philharmonic (Ormandy) - RCA
10.   DONIZETTI: DON PASQUALE - Sills/Kraus/Gramm/Caldwell - Angel
11.   VERDI: OTELLO - Domingo/Scotto/Milnes (Levine) - RCA
12.   MASCAGNI: CAVALLERIA RUSTICANA; LEONCAVALLO: PAGLIACCI - Pavarotti/Freni/Varady/Cappuccilli/Wixell/National Philharmonic Orchestra (Gavazzeni/Patane) - London
13.   LUCIANO PAVAROTTI: THE WORLD'S FAVORITE TENOR ARIAS - Luciano Pavarotti - London
14.   VIRTUOSO VIOLINIST - Itzhak Perlman/Pittsburgh Symphony Royal Philharmonic (Previn/Foster) - Angel
15.   PETER GRIMES - Britten/Davis - Philips
16.   HOROWITZ: GOLDEN JUBILEE RECITAL 1977/1978 - Horowitz - RCA
17.   JULIAN BREAM & JOHN WILLIAMS LIVE - Julian Bream & John Williams - RCA
18.* GERSHWIN: MANHATTAN - Soundtrack (Mehta) - Columbia
      GERSHWIN SONGS - Morris Bolcom - Nonesuch
      LEHAR: THE MERRY WIDOW - New York City Opera (Rudel) - Angel (*Three-way tie)

TOP 20 CLASSICAL ALBUMS OF 1980

POS. TITLE - ARTIST - LABEL
1.   O SOLE MIO: NEOPOLITAN SONGS - Pavarotti - London
2.   ANNIE'S SONG - Galway/National Philharmonic Association (Gerhardt) - RCA
3.   BRAVO PAVAROTTI - Pavarotti - London
4.   PACHELBEL: KANON - Paillard Chamber Orchestra - RCA
5.   HITS FROM LINCOLN CENTER - Pavarotti - London
6.   TCHAIKOVSKY: VIOLIN CONCERTO - Perlman/Philadelphia Orchestra (Ormandy) - Angel
7.   SONG OF THE SEASHORE - James Galway - RCA
8.   TCHAIKOVSKY: 1812 OVERTURE - Cincinnati Orchestra (Kunzel) - Telarc Digital
9.   BRAHMS: FOUR SYMPHONIES - Chicago Symphony (Solti) - London
10.   PAVAROTTI'S GREATEST HITS - Pavarotti - London
11.   MUSIC OF TELEMANN: GALWAY - Galway - RCA ARL
12.   NEW YEAR'S IN VIENNA - Boscovsky/Vienna Philharmonic - London Digital
13.   DEBUSSY: IMAGES - London Symphony (Previn) - Angel Digital
14.   STRAUSS: THE EGYPTIAN HELEN - Detroit Symphony Orchestra (Dorati) - London
15.   THE GREATEST HITS OF 1721 - Philharmonic Virtuosi (Kapp) - CBS
16.   MOUSSORGSKY: PICTURES AT AN EXHIBITION - Cleveland Orchestra - Telarc Digital
17.   JEAN-PIERRE RAMPAL & CLAUDE BOLLING: SUITE FOR FLUTE & JAZZ PIANO - Rampal & Bolling - CBS
18.   HANDEL: ARIODANTE - Baker/English Chamber Orchestra - Philips
19.   BERG: LULU - Orchestre de L'Opera de Paris - DG
20.   BOLLING: GUITAR & JAZZ CONCERTO - Romero & Shearing - Angel Digital

TOP 20 CLASSICAL ALBUMS OF 1981

POS. TITLE - ARTIST - LABEL
1.   PAVAROTTI'S GREATEST HITS - Pavarotti - London
2.   JEAN-PIERRE RAMPAL & CLAUDE BOLLING: SUITE FOR FLUTE & JAZZ PIANO - Rampal & Bolling - CBS
3.   O SOLE MIO: NEOPOLITAN SONGS - Pavarotti - London
4.   PACHELBEL: KANON - Paillard Chamber Orchestra - RCA
5.   BOLLING: SUITE FOR FLUTE, GUITAR & JAZZ PIANO - Rampal/Bolling/Lagoya - CBS
6.   ANNIE'S SONG - Galway/National Philharmonic Orchestra (Gerhardt) - RCA
7.   HITS FROM LINCOLN CENTER - Pavarotti - London
8.   PAVAROTTI: VERISIMO ARIAS - Pavarotti - London
9.   BRAVO PAVAROTTI - Pavarotti - London
10.   A DIFFERENT KIND OF BLUES - Perlman & Previn - Angel
11.   POPS IN SPACE - Boston Pops (Williams) - Philips
12.   PAVAROTTI'S GREATEST HITS, VOL. 2 - Pavarotti - London
13.   SONGS OF THE SEASHORE - James Galway - RCA
14.   60TH ANNIVERSARY GALA - Stern/Perlman/Zukerman/New York Philharmonic (Mehta) - CBS
15.   BRAHMS: DOUBLE CONCERTO - Perlman/Rostropovich - Angel
16.   MOZART: SYMPHONIES, VOL. IV - Academy of Ancient Music (Hogwood) - L'Oiseau Lyre
17.   SOMETIMES WHEN WE TOUCH - Cleo Laine & James Galway - RCA
18.   BRAHMS: VIOLIN CONCERTO - Perlman - Angel
19.   MOZART: THE MAGIC FLUTE - Karajan - DG
20.   VIVALDI: FOUR SEASONS - Academy of St. Martin (Brown) - Philips

TOP 20 CLASSICAL ALBUMS OF 1982

POS. TITLE - ARTIST - LABEL
1. PACHELBEL: CANON - Paillard Chamber Orchestra - RCA
2. THE UNKNOWN KURT WEILL - Teresa Stratas - Nonesuch
3. BEETHOVEN: VIOLIN CONCERTOS IN D - Perlman (Giulini) - Angel
4. SUITE FOR FLUTE & JAZZ PIANO - Rampal/Bolling - CBS Masterworks
5. 60TH ANNIVERSARY GALA - Stern/Perlman/Zukerman/New York Philharmonic (Mehta) - CBS Masterworks
6. O SOLE MIO: NEAPOLITAN SONGS - Luciano Pavarotti - London
7. HOLST: THE PLANETS - Karajan - Deutsche Grammophon
8. PACHELBEL: CANON - Academy of Ancient Music (Hogwood) - L'Oiseau Lyre
9. PAVAROTTI'S GREATEST HITS - Luciano Pavarotti - London
10. BEETHOVEN: COMPLETE SYMPHONIES - Berlin Philharmonic (Karajan) - DG Bargain Box
11. LIVE FROM LINCOLN CENTER - Sutherland/Horne & Pavarotti/New York City Opera Orchestra (Bonynge) - London
12. ANNIE'S SONG - James Galway/National Philharmonic Orchestra (Gerhardt) - RCA
13. MAHLER: SYMPHONY NO. 2 - Solti - London
14. BOLLING: TOOT SUITE FOR TRUMPET & JAZZ PIANO - Andre Bolling - CBS
15. A LITTLE STREET MUSIC - The Cambridge Buskers - Deutsche Grammophon
16. PLACIDO DOMINGO GALA OPERATIC CONCERT - Placido Domingo (Giulini) - Deutsche Grammophon
17. PLACIDO DOMINGO SINGS TANGOS - Placido Domingo - Deutsche Grammophon
18. PICNIC SUITE - Bolling/Rampal/Lagoya - CBS Masterworks
19. THE TANGO PROJECT - Schimmel/Sahl/Jurtis - Nonesuch
20. VIVALDO: THE FOUR SEASONS - Karajan - Deutsche Grammophon

TOP 20 CLASSICAL ALBUMS OF 1983

POS. TITLE - ARTIST - LABEL
1. BACH: GOLDBERG VARIATIONS - Glenn Gould - CBS
2. PACHELBEL: KANON - Paillard Chamber Orchestra - RCA
3. PERHAPS LOVE - Placido Domingo - CBS
4. VIVALDI: THE FOUR SEASONS - Pinnock - Deutsche Grammophon
5. PACHELBEL: CANON - Academy of Ancient Music (Hogwood) - L'Oiseau Lyre
6. IN CONCERT AT THE MET - Price/Horne (Levine) - RCA
7. MY LIFE FOR A SONG - Placido Domingo - CBS
8. CANTELOUBE: SONGS OF THE AUVERGNE - Te Kanawa/ English Chamber Orchestra (Tate) - London
9. MOZART: ARIAS - Te Kanawa (Davis) - Philips
10. GLADRAGS - Labeque Sisters - Angel
11. SUITE FOR FLUTE & JAZZ PIANO - Jean-Pierre Rampal & Claude Bolling - CBS
12. AISLE SEAT - Boston Pops (Williams) - Philips
13. GALA CONCERT AT THE ROYAL ALBERT HALL - Pavarotti - London
14. HIGH, BRIGHT, LIGHT & CLEAR - Canadian Brass - RCA
15. BEETHOVEN: SYMPHONIES NOS. 5 & 6 - Philharmonia Orchestra (Ashkenazy) - London
16. THE TANGO PROJECT - Schimmel/Sahl/Kurtis - Nonesuch
17. MOZART: SYMPHONIES, VOLUME 6 - Academy of Ancient Music (Hogwood) - L'Oiseau Lyre
18. STRAUSS: FOUR LAST SONGS - Popp/London Philharmonic (Tennstedt) - Angel

19. BOLLING: SUITE FOR CHAMBER ORCHESTRA AND JAZZ PIANO TRIO - English Chamber Orchestra/Bolling (Rampal) - CBS
20. VERDI & PUCCINI: ARIAS - Te Kanawa/London Philharmonic Orchestra (Pritchard) - CBS

TOP 20 CLASSICAL ALBUMS OF 1984

POS. TITLE - ARTIST - LABEL
1. PACHELBEL: KANON - Paillard Chamber Orchestra - RCA Red Seal
2. HAYDN/HUMMEL/L. MOZART: TRUMPET CONCERTOS - Marsalis/National Philharmonic Orchestra (Leppard) - CBS Masterworks
3. BACH: GOLDBERG VARIATIONS - Glenn Gould - CBS Masterworks
4. STRAUSS: FOUR LAST SONGS - Jessye Norman (Masur) - Philips
5. MAMMA - Luciano Pavarotti - London
6. NOCTURNE - James Galway - RCA Red Seal
7. CANTELOUBE: SONGS OF THE AUVERGNE - Te Kanawa/ English Chamber Orchestra (Tate) - London
8. BOLLING: SUITE FOR CELLO & JAZZ PIANO TRIO - Claude Bolling/Yo-Yo Ma - CBS Masterworks
9. BACH: UNACCOMPANIED CELLO SUITES - Yo-Yo Ma - CBS Masterworks
10. HANDEL: WATER MUSIC - English Concert (Pinnock) - Archiv
11. COME TO THE FAIR - Kiri Te Kanawa - Angel
12. RAMPAL/BOLLING: SUITE FOR FLUTE AND JAZZ PIANO - Jean-Pierre Rampal/Claude Bolling - CBS Masterworks
13. MATTINATA - Luciano Pavarotti - London
14. SUNDAY IN THE PARK WITH GEORGE - Original Broadway Cast - RCA
15. HUBERMAN FESTIVAL, LIVE - Mintz/Perlman/Zukerman/ Stern/Israel Philharmonic Orchestra (Mehta) - Deutsche Grammophon
16. BEETHOVEN: CELLO SONATAS NOS. 3 & 5 - Yo-Yo Ma/ Emanuel Ax - CBS Masterworks
17. DVORAK: SYMPHONY NO. 9 ("NEW WORLD") - Chicago Symphony Orchestra (Solti) - London
18. MOZART ARIAS - Kiri Te Kanawa (Davis) - Philips
19. PACHELBEL: CANON - Academy of Ancient Music (Hogwood) - L'Oiseau Lyre
20. MAHLER: SYMPHONY NO. 9 - Chicago Symphony Orchestra (Solti) - London

TOP 20 CLASSICAL ALBUMS OF 1985

POS. TITLE - ARTIST - LABEL
1. AMADEUS - Neville Marriner - Fantasy
2. MOZART: REQUIEM - Academy of Ancient Music (Hogwood) - L'Oiseau Lyre
3. WEBER: REQUIEM - Domingo/Brightman (Maazel) - RCA
4. BERNSTEIN: WEST SIDE STORY - Te Kanawa/Carreras (Bernstein) - Deutsche Grammophon
5. HAYDN/HUMMEL/L. MOZART: TRUMPET CONCERTOS - Wynton Marsalis/National Philharmonic Orchestra (Leppard) - CBS
6. MAMMA - Luciano Pavarotti (Mancini) - London
7. PACHELBEL: CANON/FASCH: TRUMPET CONCERTO - Paillard Chamber Orchestra - RCA
8. THE BEST OF WOLFGANG AMADEUS MOZART - Neville Marriner - Philips
9. WITH A SONG IN MY HEART - Jessye Norman/Boston Pops (Williams) - Philips

10. GERSHWIN: AN AMERICAN IN PARIS - Labeque Sisters - Angel
11. BAROQUE SOLOS AND DUETS - Wynton Marsalis/Edita Gruberova - CBS
12. BIZET: CARMEN (EXCERPTS) - Migenes-Johnson/Domingo (Maazel) - Erato
13. AVE MARIA - Kiri Te Kanawa - Philips
14. IN THE PINK - James Galway/Henry Mancini - RCA
15. GERSHWIN: RHAPSODY IN BLUE - Michael Tilson-Thomas - CBS
16. BEVERLY SILLS SINGS VERDI - Beverly Sills - Angel
17. CANTELOUBE: SONGS OF THE AUVERGNE, VOL. 2 - Te Kanawa/English Chamber Orchestra - London
18. BACH: GOLDBERG VARIATIONS - Glenn Gould - CBS
19. MUSIC OF WOLFGANG AMADEUS MOZART - Various Artists - Angel
20. BOULEZ CONDUCTS ZAPPA: THE PERFECT STRANGER - Pierre Boulez/Frank Zappa - Angel

TOP 20 CLASSICAL ALBUMS OF 1986

POS. TITLE - ARTIST - LABEL
1. HOROWITZ: THE LAST ROMANTIC - Vladimir Horowitz - DG
2. AMADEUS SOUNDTRACK - Neville Marriner - Fantasy
3. GERSHWIN: RHAPSODY IN BLUE - Los Angeles Philharmonic - Thom/CBS
4. PLEASURES OF THEIR COMPANY - Kathleen Battle/ Christopher Parkening - Angel
5. WEBBER: REQUIEM - Domingo/Brightman (Maazel) - Angel
6. TOMASI/JOLIVET: TRUMPET CONCERTOS - Wynton Marsalis - CBS
7. MUSIC OF WOLFGANG AMADEUS MOZART - Various Artists - Angel

8. ROMANCE FOR SAXOPHONE - Branford Marsalis - CBS
9. THE DESERT MUSIC - Steve Reich - Nonesuch
10. GLASS: SATYAGRAHA - Philip Glass - CBS
11. HAYDN/HUMMEL/L. MOZART: TRUMPET CONCERTOS - Wynton Marsalis/National Philharmonic Orchestra - CBS
12. MORE MUSIC FROM AMADEUS - Neville Marriner - Fantasy
13. COPLAND: BILLY THE KID/RODEO - Saint Louis Symphony (Slatkin) - Angel
14. PACHELBEL: CANON/FASCH: TRUMPET CONCERTO - Paillard Chamber Orchestra - RCA
15. BEETHOVEN: SYMPHONIES 1 & 2 - Academy of Ancient Music (Hogwood) - L'Oiseau Lyre
16. VIVALDI: THE FOUR SEASONS - Itzhak Perlman - Angel
17. PRESENTING APRILE MILLO - Aprile Millo - Angel
18. MISHIMA SOUNDTRACK - Philip Glass - Nonesuch
19. HOROWITZ: THE STUDIO RECORDINGS - Vladimir Horowitz - DG
20. THE BEST OF WOLFGANG AMADEUS MOZART - Neville Marriner - Philips

TOP 20 CLASSICAL ALBUMS OF 1987

POS. TITLE - ARTIST - LABEL
1. HOROWITZ IN MOSCOW - Vladimir Horowitz - DG
2. PLEASURES OF THEIR COMPANY - Kathleen Battle/ Christopher Parkening - Angel
3. KATHLEEN BATTLE SINGS MOZART - Kathleen Battle - Angel
4. HOROWITZ: THE STUDIO RECORDINGS - Vladimir Horowitz - DG
5. CARNIVAL - Wynton Marsalis - CBS
6. HOROWITZ: THE LAST ROMANTIC - Vladimir Horowitz - DG

Wynton Marsalis
This enormously successful trumpet soloist had more than ten Top 20 classical albums between 1984 and 1993.

7. DVORAK: CELLO CONCERTO - Yo-Yo Ma - CBS
8. POPS IN LOVE - Boston Pops (Williams) - Philips
9. HOLST: THE PLANETS - Montreal Symphony (Dutoit) - London
10. VIENNA, CITY OF MY DREAMS - Placido Domingo - Angel
11. AMADEUS SOUNDTRACK - Neville Marriner - Fantasy
12. VERDI: OTELLO - Placido Domingo - Angel
13. TCHAIKOVSKY: PIANO CONCERTO NO. 1 - Barry Douglas - RCA
14. ROMANCES FOR SAXOPHONE - Branford Marsalis - CBS
15. GROFE: GRAND CANYON SUITE - Cincinnati Pops (Kunzel) - Telarc
16. WHITE MAN SLEEPS - The Kronos Quartet - Nonesuch
17. SALZBURG RECITAL - Kathleen Battle - DG
18. ANNIVERSARY - Luciano Pavarotti - London
19. ADAMS: THE CHAIRMAN DANCES - San Francisco Symphony (De Waart) - Nonesuch
20. THE KRONOS QUARTET - The Kronos Quartet - Nonesuch

TOP 20 CLASSICAL ALBUMS OF 1988

POS. TITLE - ARTIST - LABEL
1. HOROWITZ PLAYS MOZART - Vladimir Horowitz - DG
2. BAROQUE MUSIC FOR TRUMPETS - Wynton Marsalis - CBS
3. HOROWITZ IN MOSCOW - Vladimir Horowitz - DG
4. MENDELSSOHN: VIOLIN CONCERTO - Nadja Salerno-Sonnenberg - Angel
5. BEETHOVEN: SYMPHONY NO. 9 - London Classical Players (Norrington) - Angel
6. THE MOVIES GO TO THE OPERA - Various Artists - Angel
7. BEETHOVEN: PIANO CONCERTO NO. 5 - Murray Perahia - CBS
8. WAGNER: THE 'RING' WITHOUT WORDS - Berlin Philharmonic (Maazel) - Telarc
9. THE ACADEMY PLAYS OPERA - Academy of St. Martin-in-the-Fields - Angel
10. BRAHMS: DOUBLE CONCERTO Isaac Stern/Yo-Yo Ma - CBS
11. VERDI: REQUIEM - Dunn/Curry/Hadley/Pishka (Shaw) - Telarc
12. GLASS: AKHNATEN - Stuttgart State Opera (Davies) - CBS
13. BACH: CHACONNE/PARTITA/CELLO SUITE - Andres Segovia - MCA
14. CHOPIN: SELECTIONS FROM THE COLLECTION - Arthur Rubinstein - RCA
15. HOLST: THE PLANETS - Boston Pops (Williams) - Philips
16. POPS IN LOVE - Boston Pops (Williams) - Philips
17. CARNAVAL - Wynton Marsalis - CBS
18. FINZI: CLARINET CONCERTO - English String Orchestra (Boughton) - Nimbus
19. WHITE MAN SLEEPS - The Kronos Quartet - Nonesuch
20. RODRIGO/PONCE/TORROBA - Andres Segovia - MCA

TOP 20 CLASSICAL ALBUMS OF 1989

POS. TITLE - ARTIST - LABEL
1. THE MOVIES GO TO THE OPERA - Various Artists - Angel
2. VERDI & PUCCININ: ARIAS - Kiri Te Kanawa - CBS
3. PAVAROTTI AT CARNEGIE HALL - Luciano Pavarotti - London
4. WAGNER: THE 'RING' WITHOUT WORDS - Berlin Philharmonic (Maazel) - Telarc
5. BERLIOZ: SYMPHONIE FANTASTIQUE - London Classical Players (Norrington) - Angel
6. PORTRAIT OF WYNTON MARSALIS - Wynton Marsalis - CBS

7. BARBER/BRITTEN: CELLO CONCERTOS - Yo-Yo Ma - CBS
8. BEETHOVEN: SYMPHONY NO. 3 - London Classical Players (Norrington) - Angel
9. HOROWITZ AT HOME - Vladimir Horowitz - DG
10. BEETHOVEN: SYMPHONIES 1 & 6 - London Classical Players (Norrington) - Angel
11. WINTER WAS HARD - Kronos Quartet - Nonesuch
12. MAHLER: SYMPHONY NO. 2 - London Symphony (Kaplan) - MCA
13. MAHLER: SYMPHONY NO. 1 - Concertgebouw Orchestra (Bernstein) - DG
14. HOROWITZ IN MOSCOW - Vladimir Horowitz - DG
15. PART: PASSIO - Hilliard Ensemble - ECM
16. REICH: DIFFERENT TRAINS - Kronos Quartet - Nonesuch
17. HANSON: SYMPHONIES 1 & 2 - Seattle Symphony (Schwarz) - Delos
18. LIVE IN TOKYO 1988 - Kathleen Battle/Placido Domingo - DG
19. VERDI: REQUIEM - Dunn/Curry/Hadley/Pishka (Shaw) - Telarc
20. LUCIANO PAVAROTTI CONCERT - Luciano Pavarotti - CBS

TOP 20 CLASSICAL ALBUMS OF 1990

POS. TITLE - ARTIST - LABEL
1. HOROWITZ AT HOME - Vladimir Horowitz - DG
2. HOROWITZ: THE LAST RECORDING - Vladimir Horowitz - Sony Classical
3. HOROWITZ IN MOSCOW - Vladimir Horowitz - DG
4. BEETHOVEN: SYMPHONY NO. 9 - Leonard Bernstein - DG
5. TUTTO PAVAROTTI - Luciano Pavarotti - London
6. HANDEL: ARIAS - Kathleen Battle - Angel
7. VERDI & PUCCINI: ARIAS - Kiri Te Kanawa - Sony Classical
8. THE MOVIES GO TO THE OPERA - Various Artists - Angel
9. BLACK ANGELS - Kronos Quartet - Nonesuch
10. BEETHOVEN: 9 SYMPHONIES - Aturo Toscanini - RCA
11. TCHAIKOVSKY & VERDI ARIAS - Dmitri Hvorostovsky - Philips
12. BARTOK: 6 STRING QUARTETS - Emerson String Quartet - DG
13. THE SUNDAY BRUNCH ALBUM - Various Artists - Sony Classical
14. CHOPIN: PIANO CONCERTOS 1 & 2 - Murray Perahia - Sony Classical
15. BRAHMS/BRUCH: VIOLIN CONCERTOS - Nadja Salerno-Sonnenberg - Angel
16. CLASSICS OF THE SILVER SCREEN - Cincinnati Pops (Kunzel) - Telarc
17. DEBUSSY: 12 ETUDES - Mitsuko Uchida - Philips
18. BEETHOVEN: SYMPHONIES 4 & 5 - London Classical Players (Norrington) - Angel
19. CARRERAS DOMINGO PAVAROTTI: IN CONCERT - Carreras/Domingo/Pavarotti (Mehta) - London
20. VIVALDI: CELLO CONCERTOS - Ofra Harnoy - RCA

TOP 20 CLASSICAL ALBUMS OF 1991

POS. TITLE - ARTIST - LABEL
1. IN CONCERT - Carreras/Domingo/Pavarotti (Mehta) - London
2. HOROWITZ: THE LAST RECORDING - Vladimir Horowitz - Sony Classical
3. PIAZZOLLA: FIVE TANGO SENSATIONS - Kronos Quartet - Nonesuch
4. BEETHOVEN: SYMPHONY NO. 9 - Leonard Bernstein - DG
5. BLACK ANGELS - Kronos Quartet - Nonesuch

6. ITZHAK PERLMAN: LIVE IN RUSSIA - Itzhak Perlman - Angel
7. MIDORI: LIVE AT CARNEGIE HALL - Midori - Sony Classical
8. CORIGLIANO: SYMPHONY NO. 1 - Chicago Symphony (Barenboim) - Erato
9. BERNSTEIN: CANDIDE - Hadley/Anderson/Green/Ludwig (Bernstein) - DG
10. BRAHMS: THE 3 VIOLIN SONATAS - Itzhak Perlman/David Barenboim - Sony Classical
11. RUSSIAN ROMANCES - Dmitri Hvorostovsky - Philips
12. RACHMANINOFF: VESPERS - Robert Shaw Festival Singers - Telarc
13. BRAHMS: CONCERTO IN D - Kennedy/London Philharmonic (Tennstedt) - Angel
14. HANSON CONDUCTS HANSON: SYMPHONIES 1 & 2 - Eastman-Rochester Orchestra - Mercury
15. CARNEGIE HALL DEBUT CONCERT - Evgeny Kissin - RCA
16. VIVALDI: THE FOUR SEASONS - Nadja Salerno-Sonnenberg - Angel
17. IVES: SYMPHONY NO. 2 - New York Philharmonic (Bernstein) - DG
18. THE ALDEBURGH RECITAL - Murray Perahia - Sony Classical
19. VIVALDI: THE FOUR SEASONS - Nigel Kennedy/English Chamber Orchestra - Angel
20. DINNER FOR TWO - Various Artists - Sony Classical

TOP 20 CLASSICAL ALBUMS OF 1992

POS. TITLE - ARTIST - LABEL
1. IN CONCERT - Carreras, Domingo, Pavarotti (Mehta) - London
2. BAROQUE DUET - Kathleen Battle, Wynton Marsalis - Sony Classical
3. PIECES OF AFRICA - Kronos Quartet - Nonesuch
4. THE BACH ALBUM - Kathleen Battle, Itzhak Perlman - DG
5. MCCARTNEY/DAVIS: LIVERPOOL ORATORIO - Te Kanawa, Hadley, Royal Liverpool Philharmonic (Davis) - EMI Classics
6. GORECKI: SYMPHONY NO. 3 - Upshaw, London Sinfonietta (Zinman) - Nonesuch
7. MOZART: ARIAS - Cecilia Bartoli - London
8. FAVORITE ARIAS BY WORLD'S FAVORITE... - Carreras, Domingo, Pavarotti - Sony Classical
9. CORIGLIANO: SYMPHONY NO. 1 - Chicago Symphony (Barenboim) - Erato
10. ROSSINI HEROINES - Cecilia Bartoli - London
11. THE BELLS OF ST. GENEVIEVE - Various Artists - RCA

12. PART: MISERERE - Hilliard Ensemble - ECM
13. BERNSTEIN: CANDIDE - Hadley, Anderson, Green, Ludwig (Bernstein) - DG
14. KATHLEEN BATTLE AT CARNEGIE HALL - Kathleen Battle - DG
15. PAVAROTTI IN HYDE PARK - Luciano Pavarotti - London
16. HOROWITZ THE POET - Vladimir Horowitz - DG
17. SWITCHED-ON BACH 2000 - Wendy Carlos - Telarc
18. TOGETHER - Placido Domingo, Itzhak Perlman - EMI Classics
19. FROM THE OFFICIAL BARCELONA GAMES CEREMONY - Domingo, Carreras, Caballe - RCA
20. GALA LIRICA - Domingo, Carreras, Caballe - RCA

TOP 20 CLASSICAL ALBUMS OF 1993

POS. TITLE - ARTIST - LABEL
1. IF YOU LOVE ME - Cecilia Bartoli - London
2. GORECKI: SYMPHONY NO. 3 - Upshaw, London Sinfonietta (Zinman) - Nonesuch
3. IN CONCERT - Carreras, Domingo, Pavarotti (Mehta) - London
4. TOUS LES MATINS DU MONDE - Jordi Savall - Valois
5. AN ENGLIS LADYMASS - Anonymous Four - Harmonia Mundi (France)
6. BAROQUE DUET - Kathleen Battle, Wynton Marsalis - Sony Classical
7. KATHLEEN BATTLE AT CARNEGIE HALL - Kathleen Battle - DG
8. PHILIP GLASS: LOW SYMPHONY - Brooklyn Philharmonic (Davies) - Point Music
9. ROSSINI HEROINES - Cecilia Bartoli - London
10. HOROWITZ: DISCOVERED TREASURES - Vladimir Horowitz - Sony Classical
11. OPERA'S GREATEST MOMENTS - Various Artists - RCA
12. HEAVY CLASSIX - Various Artists - Angel
13. MOZART: ARIAS - Cecilia Bartoli - London
14. SHASTAKOVICH: 24 PRELUDES & FUGUES - Keith Jarrett - ECM
15. AMORE - Luciano Pavarotti - London
16. THE REINER SOUND - CSO/Reiner - RCA
17. BRAHMS: CELLO SONATAS - Yo-Yo Ma, Emanuel Ax - Sony Classical
18. SENSUAL CLASSICS - Various Artists - Teldec
19. THE LAST RECITAL FOR ISRAEL - Arthur Rubinstein - RCA
20. IT AIN'T NECESSARILY SO - Nadja Salerno-Sonnenberg - EMI Classics

Billboard Top 20 Gospel Albums, 1980-1993

TOP 20 GOSPEL ALBUMS OF 1980

Top Inspirational Albums
POS. TITLE - ARTIST - LABEL
1. MUSIC MACHINE - Candle - Birdwing
2. ONE MORE SONG FOR YOU - The Imperials - DaySpring
3. MY FATHER'S EYES - Amy Grant - Myrrh
4. GOT TO TELL SOMEBODY - Don Francisco - New Pax
5. HEED THE CALL - The Imperials - DaySpring
6. FORGIVEN - Don Francisco - New Pax
7. BULLFROGS AND BUTTERFLIES - Candle - Birdwing
8. YOU GAVE ME LOVE - B.J. Thomas - Myrrh
9. NEVER THE SAME - Evie Tornquist - Word
10. ROAR OF LOVE - Second Chapter of Acts - Sparrow

Top Spiritual Albums
POS. TITLE - ARTIST - LABEL
1. LOVE ALIVE II - Walter Hawkins & The Love Center Choir - Light
2. IT'S A NEW DAY - James Cleveland - Savoy
3. CHANGING TIME - Mighty Clouds of Joy - Epic
4. I DON'T FEEL NOWAYS TIRED - James Cleveland & The Salem Inspirational Choir - Savoy
5. I'LL BE THINKING OF YOU - Andrae Crouch - Light
6. PLEASE BE PATIENT WITH ME - Albertina Walker with James Cleveland - Savoy
7. LORD, LET ME BE AN ISTRUMENT - J.C. & The Charles Fold Singers - Savoy
8. WHAT A WONDERFUL SAVIOR - Donald Vails & The Voice of Deliverance - Savoy
9. LEGENDARY GENTLEMAN - Jackson Southernaires - Malaco
10. BECAUSE HE LIVES - International Mass Choir of Churches - New Birth

TOP 20 GOSPEL ALBUMS OF 1981

Top Inspirational Albums
POS. TITLE - ARTIST - LABEL
1. IN HIS TIME, PRAISE IV - Maranatha Singers - Maranatha
2. HEED THE CALL - The Imperials - DaySpring
3. MY FATHER'S EYES - Amy Grant - Myrrh
4. ONE MORE SONG FOR YOU - The Imperials - DaySpring
5. NEVER ALONE - Amy Grant - Myrrh
6. BULLFROGS AND BUTTERFLIES - Candle - Birdwing
7. FORGIVEN - Don Francisco - New Pax
8. PRIORITY - The Imperials - DaySpring
9. MUSIC MACHINE - Candle - Birdwing
10. AMY GRANT - Amy Grant - Myrrh

Top Spiritual Albums
POS. TITLE - ARTIST - LABEL
1. TRAMAINE (WORD) - Tramaine Hawkins - Light
2. IT'S A NEW DAY - James Cleveland & The Southern California Community Choir - Savoy
3. PLEASE BE PATIENT WITH ME - Albertina Walker with James Cleveland - Savoy
4. THE LORD WILL MAKE A WAY - Al Green - Myrrh
5. LOVE ALIVE II - Walter Hawkins & The Love Center Choir - Light

6. EVERYONE'S ALRIGHT - Dr. Charles G. Hayes & The Cosmopolitan Church of Prayer - Savoy
7. REJOICE - Shirley Caesar - Myrrh
8. I'LL BE THINKING OF YOU - Andrae Crouch - Light
9. THE LORD IS MY LIGHT - New Jerusalem Baptist Choir Church - Savoy
10. THE HAWKINS FAMILY LIVE - The Hawkins Family - Light

TOP 20 GOSPEL ALBUMS OF 1982

Top Inspirational Albums
POS. TITLE - ARTIST - LABEL
1. AMAZING GRACE - B.J. Thomas - Myrrh
2. PRIORITY - The Imperials - DaySpring
3. BULLFROGS AND BUTTERFLIES - Candle - Birdwing
4. JONI'S SONG - Joni Eareckson - Word
5. HEARTS OF FIRE - Sweet Comfort Band - Light
6. AMY GRANT IN CONCERT, VOL. I - Amy Grant - Myrrh
7. MY FATHER'S EYES - Amy Grant - Myrrh
8. UNFAILING LOVE - Evie Tornquist - Word
9. IN HIS TIME, PRAISE IV - Maranatha Singers - Maranatha
10. MUSIC MACHINE - Candle - Birdwing

Top Spiritual Albums
POS. TITLE - ARTIST - LABEL
1. IS MY LIVING IN VAIN - The Clark Sisters - New Birth
2. WHERE IS YOUR FAITH - James Cleveland & The Southern California Community Choir - Savoy
3. CLOUDBURST - The Mighty Clouds of Jou - Myrrh
4. TRUE VICTORY - Pentecostal Choir - Savoy
5. THE LORD WILL MAKE A WAY - Al Green - Myrrh
6. 20th ANNIVERSARY ALBUM - James Cleveland & The World's Greatest Choirs - Savoy
7. THE HAWKINS FAMILY LIVE - The Hawkins Family - Light
8. IT'S A NEW DAY - James Cleveland & The Southern California Community Choir - Savoy
9. THE LORD IS MY LIGHT - New Jerusalem Baptist Choir Church - Savoy
10. GO - Shirley Caesar - Myrrh

TOP 20 GOSPEL ALBUMS OF 1983

Top Inspirational Albums
POS. TITLE - ARTIST - LABEL
1. AGE TO AGE - Amy Grant - Myrrh
2. SONG FOR THE SHEPHERD - Keith Green - Pretty Good
3. MORE POWER TO YA - Petra - Star Song
4. STAND BY THE POWER - The Imperials - DaySpring
5. LIFT UP THE LORD - Sandi Patti - Impact
6. I'LL NEVER STOP LOVING YOU - Leon Patillo - Word
7. A SONG IN THE NIGHT - Silverwind - Sparrow
8. AEROBIC CELEBRATION - Various Artists - Benson
9. AMAZING GRACE - B.J. Thomas - Myrrh
10. THE VERY BEST OF THE IMPERIALS - The Imperials - DaySpring

Top Spiritual Albums
POS. TITLE - ARTIST - LABEL
1. IT'S GONNA RAIN - Rev. Milton Brunson - Myrrh

2. YOU BROUGHT THE SUNSHINE - The Clark Sisters - Sound Of Gospel
3. LORD, YOU KEEP ON PROVING YOURSELF TO ME - Florida Mass Choir - Savoy
4. PRECIOUS LORD - Al Green - Myrrh
5. TOUCH OF CLASS - Jackson Southernaires - Malaco
6. THE JOY OF THE LORD IS MY STRENGTH - Douglas Miller & The Rue Way Choir - (C.O.G.I.C.) GosPearl
7. RICHARD SMALLWOOD SINGERS - Richard Smallwood Singers - Onyx
8. UNCLOUDY DAY - Myrna Summers - Savoy
9. WHEN IT RAINS IT POURS - Rev. Barnes & Sister Brown - A.I.R.
10. I FEEL LIKE GOING DOWN - Keith Pringle - Hope Song

TOP 20 GOSPEL ALBUMS OF 1984

Top Inspirational Albums

POS. TITLE - ARTIST - LABEL
1. AGE TO AGE - Amy Grant - Myrrh
2. MORE THAN WONDERFUL - Sandi Patti - Impact
3. STRAIGHT AHEAD - Amy Grant - Myrrh
4. NOT OF THIS WORLD - Petra - Star Song
5. MORE POWER TO YA - Petra - Star Song
6. THE MICHAEL W. SMITH PROJECT - Michael W. Smith - Reunion
7. MICHAEL W. SMITH II - Michael W. Smith - Reunion
8. SURRENDER - Debby Boone - Lamb and Lion
9. THE SKY'S THE LIMIT - Leon Patillo - Myrrh
10. THE PRODIGAL SON - Keith Green - Pretty Good

Top Spiritual Albums

POS. TITLE - ARTIST - LABEL
1. WE SING PRAISES - Sandra Crouch - Light
2. ROUGH SIDE OF THE MOUNTAIN - Rev. F.C. Barnes & Sister Brown - Atlanta Int'l
3. PEACE BE STILL - Vanessa Bell Armstrong - Onyx
4. THIS TOO WILL PASS - James Cleveland & The Charles Fold Choir - Savoy
5. JESUS I LOVE CALLING YOUR NAME - Shirley Caesar - Word
6. SING AND SHOUT - The Mighty Clouds of Joy - Myrrh
7. I'LL RISE AGAIN - Al Green Myrrh
8. PSALMS - The Richard Smallwood Singers - Onyx
9. FEEL THE SPIRIT - The Williams Brothers - Myrrh
10. I STILL LOVE THE NAME JESUS - Douglas Miller - GosPearl

TOP 20 GOSPEL ALBUMS OF 1985

Top Inspirational Albums

POS. TITLE - ARTIST - LABEL
1. STRAIGHT AHEAD - Amy Grant - Myrrh
2. SONGS FROM THE HEART - Sandi Patti - Impact
3. MORE THAN WONDERFUL - Sandi Patti - Impact
4. BEAT THE SYSTEM - Petra - Star Song
5. AGE TO AGE - Amy Grant - Myrrh
6. UNGUARDED - Amy Grant - Myrrh
7. COMING ON STRONG - Carman - Myrrh
8. LET THE WIND BLOW - The Imperials - Myrrh
9. MICHAEL W. SMITH II - Michael W. Smith - Reunion
10. THE SKY'S THE LIMIT - Leon Patillo - Myrrh

Top Spiritual Albums

POS. TITLE - ARTIST - LABEL
1. CHOSEN - Vanessa Bell Armstrong - Onyx
2. NO TIME TO LOSE - Andrae Crouch - Light
3. LOVE ALIVE III - Walter Hawkins - Light
4. TOMORROW - The Winans - Light
5. BLESSED - The Williams Brothers - Malaco
6. ROUGH SIDE OF THE MOUNTAIN - Rev. F.C. Barnes & Sister Brown - Atlanta Int'l
7. SAILIN' - Shirley Caesar - Word
8. PERFECT PEACE - Keith Pringle - Heartwarming
9. MADE IN MISSISSIPPI - Jackson Southernaires - Malaco
10. WHAT HE'S DONE FOR ME - Rev. Clay Evans & The Fellowship Choir - Savoy

TOP 20 GOSPEL ALBUMS OF 1986

Top Inspirational Albums

POS. TITLE - ARTIST - LABEL
1. UNGUARDED - Amy Grant - Myrrh
2. HYMNS JUST FOR YOU - Sandi Patti - Impact
3. MORNING LIKE THIS - Sandi Patti - Word
4. SONGS FROM THE HEART - Sandi Patti - Impact
5. AGE TO AGE - Amy Grant - Word
6. THE CHAMPION - Carman - Word
7. MEDALS - Russ Taff - Myrrh
8. STRAIGHT AHEAD - Amy Grant - Myrrh
9. MORE THAN WONDERFUL - Sandi Patti - Impact
10. SOLDIERS UNDER COMMAND - Stryper - Enigma

Top Spiritual Albums

POS. TITLE - ARTIST - LABEL
1. DEDICATED - Nicholas - Command
2. WE'RE WAITING - Sandra Crouch - Light
3. LET MY PEOPLE GO - The Winans - Qwest
4. BLESSED - The Williams Brothers - Malaco
5. LOVE ALIVE III - Walter Hawkins - Light
6. HAVE MERCY - Edwin Hawkins - Birthright
7. CELEBRATION - Shirley Caesar - Word
8. UNSPEAKABLE JOY - Douglas Miller - Light
9. THERE IS HOPE - Rev. Milton Brunson & The Thompson Community Choir - Rejoice
10. THE SEARCH IS OVER - Tramaine - A&M

TOP 20 GOSPEL ALBUMS OF 1987

Top Inspirational Albums

POS. TITLE - ARTIST - LABEL
1. MORNING LIKE THIS - Sandi Patti - Word
2. THE COLLECTION - Amy Grant - Myrrh
3. HYMNS JUST FOR YOU - Sandi Patti - Impact
4. FOR GOD AND GOD ALONE - Steve Green - Sparrow
5. TO HELL WITH THE DEVIL - Stryper - Enigma
6. THE BIG PICTURE - Michael W. Smith - Reunion
7. BACK TO THE STREET - Petra - Star Song
8. THIS YEAR'S MODEL - The Imperials - Myrrh
9. THE CHAMPION - Carman - Myrrh
10. HYMNS - Second Chapter of Acts - Live Oaks

Top Spiritual Albums

POS. TITLE - ARTIST - LABEL
1. I'M ENCOURAGED - Rev. Thomas A. Whitfield & Co. - Sound of Gospel
2. HAND AND HAND - The Williams Brothers - Malaco
3. SOUL SURVIVOR - Al Green - A&M

Stryper
Heavy metal's Gospel Kings, Stryper had Top 10 Inspirational albums in 1986 and 1987.

Petra
Rock gospel at its best—Petra had at least one Top 10 Inspirational album every year between 1983 and 1992.

Famous Hymn Histories

ABIDE WITH ME

The words of this poignant hymn were the supplications of a man approaching death. Rev. Henry Lyte, vicar of Lower Brixham in Devonshire, was fifty-four at the time and in failing health. He made plans to spend the winter in Italy and, as September came and the date of his departure approached, he insisted on preaching once more to his people. That evening, he gave a relative the words and music he had written; it was this hymn. He died the following November 4, 1847.

AMAZING GRACE

John Newton lived a rough and adventurous life. He west to sea at an early age with his sea captain father, was kidnapped and badly treated, later became a sea captain himself. When he was seventeen, he fell in love with a young Christian girl, Mary Kattlet. He continued his seafaring ways, but during a violent storm he remembered Mary's teachings and turned to God. This hymn was written as a result of the experience. He returned to England, where he and Mary were married. He later became a minister, wrote many hymns, and served God until he died at 82.

HOLY, HOLY, HOLY

Reginald Heber took the title and part of the stanzas of this majestic hymn from the last words of the Bible—Revelations, Chapter 4. He wrote it when he was twenty-six, and a young vicar for a village church in England. Born of wealth and culture, Heber was a very early Bible student. At only five years of age, he could recite many Bible verses. He devoted his life to serving God. He wrote more than sixty hymns, but this is the best known. He died while serving as a missionary in India in 1826.

HOW GREAT THOU ART

While walking through a thunderstorm from a church meeting two miles away, a young minister, Reverend Carl Boberg, was inspired to write the poem of nine verses. Several years later it was sung to the tune of an old Swedish folk melody and later translated into several different languages. An English missionary, the Reverend Stuart K. Hine came across it in 1927, translated it into English, and added a fourth verse. It was published in 1954 and has since become one of the most beloved hymns in America.

IN THE SWEET BY AND BY

Sanford F. Bennett wrote the words to this beloved hymn in his drugstore in Elkhorn, Wisconsin, shortly after the close of the Civil War. The composer of the melody, Joseph P. Webster, came into the store. Bennett noticed he appeared dejected and asked "What's wrong now?" Webster replied, "It's no matter. It will be all right in the by and by." Bennett picked up a prescription pad and wrote—"by and by...in the sweet by and by." In less than thirty minutes he had the completed poem and handed it to Webster. The musician's eyes twinkled as he took paper and pen and wrote the notes. Taking his violin, Webster, Bennett, and two friends sang the song together. It was first published in 1868.

JUST A CLOSER WALK WITH THEE

"Just A Closer Walk With Thee," one of America's favorite spirituals, has been a difficult hymn to trace to its origins. As far as the words are concerned, there appears to be no record as to who the author was, but at to the person responsible for it becoming a beloved hymn, there is no doubt. Robert Emmett Winsett, a native of Tennessee, took the words to the hymn, edited the last stanza, and arranged the music.

Winsett, born in 1886, began singing sacred music in his childhood and for more than thirty-two years was one of the South's leading music publishers. He was also the writer of many songs, including: "Jesus Passed This Way Before," "Lift Me Up Above The Shadows," and "I'll Be There Anyway."

A MIGHTY FORTRESS

This is the most well-known and beloved of Martin Luther's compositions (he wrote 37 hymns during his busy lifetime of reforming the Church). This hymn was written in 1529 when the Lutheran movement underwent its severest persecution. Based on Psalm 46: "God is our Refuge and our Strength," it did much to encourage the persecuted and fearful of that day. It became known as the Marseillaise of the Reformation.

THE OLD RUGGED CROSS

"Just like seeing John 3:16 leave the printed page." This has been the apt description of this beloved gospel hymn. A minister, George Bennard, wrote both the words and music in 1913. When he sang it for friends, they encouraged him to publish it, and it has since become one of our most well-known hymns.

ONWARD CHRISTIAN SOLDIERS

In a small village in England in 1865, a Whitmonday celebration was planned in which the school children would march to a neighboring village. Rev. Sabine Baring-Gould was to lead them. He looked in vain for suitable marching music, then sat up all night writing the words of this song to be sung to an old tune. Later, Sir Arthur Sullivan, a famous musician, wrote the stirring march music to complete the song as we know it today.

ROCK OF AGES

This great hymn grew out of a rainstorm and an argument. Its writer, Augustus M. Toplady, was caught in a sudden thunderstorm while walking, and took cover in the cleft of a large rock. As the thunder rolled above and the lightning flashed, he realized how safe he was under the rock. Toplady, an ordained priest in the Church of England, was also in conflict with the Calvinistic theology of the day, and these words also reflect his convictions that man is saved by God's actions and not by his own works. The music was written by Thomas Hastings.

WHAT A FRIEND WE HAVE IN JESUS

When Joseph Scriven's lovely young fiancee was drowned the day before they were to be married, he reacted not with bitterness and anger. Instead he turned to God for solace and comfort. Out of this experience, he wrote the words of this hymn. He left Ireland in 1845 to settle in Porthope, Ontario, Canada, where he spent his life ministering to the needy and distressed.

WHEN THE ROLL IS CALLED UP YONDER

This hymn was written in 1893 by James M. Black and first appeared in "Songs Of The Soul," compiled in 1894 by the author and composer and Joseph F. Berry. Black says he wrote the words after attending a consecration service one evening where members answered the roll call by repeating Scripture texts. Failure of one person to answer with Scripture caused him to say: "O God, when my own name is called up yonder, may I be there to respond." After he arrived home, he sat down and composed the three stanzas in fifteen minutes. He then went to the piano and composed the music. Not a word of the poem nor a note of the melody was ever changed.

Editor's Note: Special thanks to Word Records, publisher of "America's Best Loved Hymns," from which these histories are drawn.

4. THERE IS HOPE - Rev. Milton Brunson & The Thompson Community Choir - Rejoice
5. LOOK UP AND LIVE - New Jersy Mass Choir - Light
6. GIVE US PEACE - Edwin Hawkins & Music & Arts Seminar Mass Choir - Birthright
7. GO TELL SOMEBODY - Commissioned - Light
8. A LOVE LIKE THIS - Nicholas - Command
9. FOLLOWING JESUS - Vanessa Bell Armstrong - Muscle Shoals Sound
10. HEART AND SOUL - The Clark Sisters - Rejoice

TOP 20 GOSPEL ALBUMS OF 1988

Top Inspirational Albums
POS. TITLE - ARTIST - LABEL
1. THE COLLECTION - Amy Grant - Myrrh
2. THIS MEANS WAR - Petra - Star Song
3. MORNING LIKE THIS - Sandi Patti - Word
4. MAKE HIS PRAISE GLORIOUS - Sandi Patti - Word
5. RUSS TAFF - Russ Taff - Myrrh
6. RADICALLY SAVED - Carman - Benson
7. HYMNS JUST FOR YOU - Sandi Patti - Impact
8. THE LIVE SET - Michael W. Smith - Reunion
9. LEAD ME ON - Amy Grant - Myrrh
10. THE FATHER HATH PROVIDED - Larnelle Harris - Impact

Top Spiritual Albums
POS. TITLE - ARTIST - LABEL
1. IF I BE LIFTED - Rev. Milton Brunson & The Thompson Community Singers - Rejoice
2. ONE LORD, ONE FAITH, ONE BAPTISM - Aretha Franklin - Arista
3. DECISIONS - The Winans - Qwest
4. LIVE IN CHICAGO - Shirley Caesar - Rejoice
5. LIVE IN MIAMI FLORIDA - Florida Mass Choir - Rejoice
6. SHOW ME THE WAY - New Jerusalem Baptist Church Choir - Sound of Gospel
7. HOLD UP THE LIGHT - The New Jersey Mass Gospel Choir - Light
8. HALLELUJAH IS THE ... - T. Wright & J. Ferrell & The Lighthouse Choir - Sound of Gospel
9. A LOVE LIKE THIS - Nicholas - Command
10. VANESSA BELL ARMSTRONG - Vanessa Bell Armstrong - Jive

TOP 20 GOSPEL ALBUMS OF 1989

Top Inspirational Albums
POS. TITLE - ARTIST - LABEL
1. LEAD ME ON - Amy Grant - A&M
2. I 2 (EYE) - Michael W. Smith - Word
3. SANDI PATTI AND THE FRIENDSHIP COMPANY - Sandi Patti - Word
4. MAKE HIS PRAISE GLORIOUS - Sandi Patti - Word
5. RADICALLY SAVED - Carman - Benson
6. ON FIRE - Petra - Star Song
7. HEAVEN - BeBe & CeCe Winans - Sparrow
8. THANK YOU - Ray Boltz - Diadem
9. TAKE 6 - Take 6 - Reunion
10. THE COLLECTION - Amy Grant - Myrrh

Top Spiritual Albums
POS. TITLE - ARTIST - LABEL
1. LIVE IN CHICAGO - Shirley Caesar - Rejoice
2. AVAILABLE TO YOU - Rev. Milton Brunson - Rejoice

3. HEAVEN - BeBe & CeCe Winans - Sparrow
4. LET THE HOLY SPIRIT LEAD YOU - Florida Mass Choir - Malaco
5. NO GREATER LOVE - Keith Pringle & Pentecostal Community Choir - Savoy
6. WE'RE GONNA MAKE IT - Myrna Summers & Rev. Timothy Wright - Savoy
7. TAKE 6 - Take 6 - Reunion
8. GIVE HIM THE GLORY! - L.A. Mass Choir - Light
9. FREE SPIRIT VOL. 2 - Rev. Charkes Nicks Jr. - Sound of Gospel
10. THE JOY THAT FLOODS MY SOUL - Tramaine Hawkins - Sparrow

TOP 20 GOSPEL ALBUMS OF 1990

Top Contemporary Christian Albums
POS. TITLE - ARTIST - LABEL
1. REVIVAL IN THE LAND - Carman - Benson
2. PETRA PRAISE: THE ROCK CRIES OUT - Petra - DaySpring
3. MORE TO THIS LIFE - Steve Curtis Chapman - Sparrow
4. I 2 (EYE) - Michael W. Smith - Reunion
5. THE FINEST MOMENTS - Sandi Patti - Word
6. THE WAY HOME - Russ Taff - Myrrh
7. BEYOND BELIEF - Petra - Word
8. THE COLLECTION - Amy Grant - Myrrh
9. ACAPELLA PROJECT II - Glad - Benson
10. THE MISSION - Steve Green - Sparrow

Top Gospel Albums
POS. TITLE - ARTIST - LABEL
1. MISSISSIPPI MASS CHOIR - Mississippi Mass Choir - Malaco
2. CAN'T HOLD BACK - L.A. Mass Choir - Light
3. I REMEMBER MAMA - Shirley Caesar - Word
4. OPEN OUR EYES - Milton Brunson - Rejoice
5. RETURN - The Winans - Warner Alliance
6. HAVING CHURCH - Rev. James Cleveland/Southern California Community Choir - Savoy
7. HOLD ON, HELP IS ON THE WAY - Georgia Mass Choir - Savoy
8. CAN'T YOU SEE ... - Rev. F.C. Barnes & Co. with Debra and Geraldine Barnes - Atlanta Int'l
9. WAIT ON HIM - New Life Community Choir featuring John P. Kee - Tyscot
10. SAINTS IN PRAISE VOL. I - The West Angeles C.O.G.I.C. - Sparrow

TOP 20 GOSPEL ALBUMS OF 1991

Top Contemporary Christian Albums
POS. TITLE - ARTIST - LABEL
1. GO WEST YOUNG MAN - Michael W. Smith - Reunion
2. ANOTHER TIME ANOTHER PLACE - Sandi Patti - Word
3. HEART IN MOTION - Amy Grant - Word
4. FOR THE SAKE OF THE CALL - Steven Curtis Chapman - Sparrow
5. BEYOND BELIEF - Petra - Word
6. NU THANG - D.C. Talk - Forefront
7. REVIVAL IN THE LAND - Carman - Benson
8. RADICALLY SAVED - Carman - Benson
9. DIFFERENT LIFESTYLES - BeBe & CeCe Winans - Sparrow
10. SO MUCH 2 SAY - Take 6 - Warner Alliance

Sandi Patti
Gospel's #1 female vocalist with eighteen Top 10 Inspirational albums, including four in one year (1986).

Steve Green
Steve had Top 10 Inspirational Lps in 1987, 1990 and 1993.

Steven Curtis Chapman
Two Top 10 Inspirational albums in 1992 are part of Steve's total of five chart-toppers.

Tramaine Hawkins
Tramaine has three Top 10 Spiritual albums—one was #1 in 1981.

Top Gospel Albums
POS. TITLE - ARTIST - LABEL
1. LIVE WITH MISSISSIPPI MASS CHOIR - Rev. James Moore - Malaco
2. LIVE - Tramaine Hawkins - Sparrow
3. LOVE ALIVE IV - Walter Hawkins - Malaco
4. HE'S RIGHT ON TIME: LIVE FROM LOS ANGELES - Daryl Coley - Sparrow
5. PHENOMENON - Rance Allen - Bellmark
6. HAVING CHURCH - Rev. James Cleveland/Southern California Community Choir - Savoy
7. PRAY FOR ME - Mighty Clouds of Joy - Word
8. WAIT ON THE LORD - Lamora Park Young Adult Choir - Bellmark
9. SAINTS IN PRAISE - West Angeles C.O.G.I.C. - Sparrow
10. WASH ME - New Life Community Choir featuring John P. Kee - Tyscot

TOP 20 GOSPEL ALBUMS OF 1992

Top Contemporary Christian Albums
POS. TITLE - ARTIST - LABEL
1. ADDICTED TO JESUS - Carman - Benson
2. HEART IN MOTION - Amy Grant - Myrrh
3. GO WEST YOUNG MAN - Michael W. Smith - Reunion
4. UNSEEN POWER - Petra - DaySpring
5. MICHAEL ENGLISH - Michael English - Warner Alliance
6. FOR THE SAKE OF THE CALL - Steven Curtis Chapman - Sparrow
7. DIFFERENT LIFESTYLES - BeBe & CeCe Winans - Sparrow
8. SANCTUARY - Twila Paris - Starsong
9. GREAT ADVENTURE - Steven Curtis Chapman - Sparrow
10. ANOTHER TIME ANOTHER PLACE - Sandi Patti - Word

Top Gospel Albums
POS. TITLE - ARTIST - LABEL
1. GOD GETS THE GLORY - Mississippi Mass Choir - Malaco
2. MY MIND IS MADE UP - Rev. Milton Brunson & The Thompson Community Singers - Word
3. HE'S WORKING IT OUT FOR YOU - Shirley Caesar - Word
4. DIFFERENT LIFESTYLES - BeBe & CeCe Winans - Sparrow
5. I'M GLAD ABOUT IT - Rev. Timothy Wright & The Chicago Interdenominational Mass Choir - Savoy
6. WASH ME - New Life Community Choir featuring John P. Kee - Tyscot
7. LIVE - Dorothy Norwood/Northern California G.M.W.A. Mass Choir - Malaco
8. HE LIVES - Shun Pace Rhodes - Savoy
9. ALIVE & SATISFIED - Thomas Whitfield - Benson
10. THROUGH THE STORM - Yolanda Adams - Tribute

TOP 20 GOSPEL ALBUMS OF 1993

Top Contemporary Christian Albums
POS. TITLE - ARTIST - LABEL
1. FREE AT LAST - D.C. Talk - Forefront
2. CHANGE YOUR WORLD - Michael W. Smith - Reunion
3. GREAT ADVENTURE - Steven Curtis Chapman - Sparrow
4. THE BASICS OF LIFE - 4 Him - Benson
5. HOPE - Michael English - Warner Alliance
6. HEART THAT KNOWS YOU - Twila Paris - Starsong
7. LEVOYAGE - Sandi Patti - Word
8. ABSOLUTE BEST - Carman - Sparrow
9. HYMNS: A PORTRAIT OF CHRIST - Steve Green - Sparrow
10. MERCY - Bryan Duncan - Myrrh

Top Gospel Albums
POS. TITLE - ARTIST - LABEL
1. WE WALK BY FAITH - John P. Kee & New Life Community Choir - Tyscot
2. I'M GOING THROUGH - Rev. Clay Evans - Savoy
3. I SING BECAUSE I'M HAPPY - Georgia Mass Choir - Savoy
4. WHEN THE MUSIC STOPS - Daryl Coley - Sparrow
5. U KNOW - The Anointed Pace Sisters - Savoy
6. MY MIND IS MADE UP - Rev. Milton Brunson & The Thompson Community Singers - Word
7. IT REMAINS TO BE SEEN - Mississippi Mass Choir - Malaco
8. SEND YOUR ANOINTING - TM Mass Youth Choir - TM
9. A SONGWRITER'S POINT OF VIEW - Tri-City Singers - Gospo-Centric
10. I'LL NEVER FORGET - Dr. Charles G. Hayes/Cosmopolitan Church of Prayer Choir - Savoy

Top 20 Old Time Gospel Classics

1. IN THE SWEET BY AND BY
2. SHALL WE GATHER AT THE RIVER
3. BRINGING IN THE SHEAVES
4. WHEN THE ROLL IS CALLED UP YONDER
5. OLD TIME RELIGION
6. I SHALL NOT BE MOVED
7. BEULAH LAND
8. BRIGHTEN THE CORNER WHERE YOU ARE
9. LIFE'S RAILWAY TO HEAVEN
10. PRECIOUS MEMORIES
11. I'LL FLY AWAY
12. FARTHER ALONG
13. HALLELUJAH! WE SHALL RISE
14. DO LORD
15. VICTORY IN JESUS
16. OH HOW I LOVE JESUS
17. WILL THERE BE ANY STARS
18. THE UNCLOUDY DAY
19. LILY OF THE VALLEY
20. COME UNTO ME

Top 20 Gospel Classics

1. ONWARD CHRISTIAN SOLDIERS
2. BLESSED ASSURANCE
3. HE LIVES
4. STANDING ON THE PROMISES
5. JESUS SAVES
6. LEANING ON THE EVERLASTING ARMS
7. STAND UP, STAND UP FOR JESUS
8. LOVE LIFTED ME
9. BLESSED BE THY NAME
10. POWER IN THE BLOOD
11. COUNT YOUR BLESSINGS
12. JESUS LOVES ME
13. ARE YOU WASHED IN THE BLOOD
14. HE KEEPS ME SINGING
15. WHEN WE ALL GET TO HEAVEN
16. SOFTLY AND TENDERLY
17. PRECIOUS MEMORIES
18. THERE IS A FOUNTAIN
19. REVIVE US AGAIN
20. WHISPERING HOPE

Editor's Note: Differences in the popularity of certain hymns often takes on a regional character. For example, "Beulah Land"—familiar to viewers of "The Waltons" and "The Doll Maker"—are more popular in mountain areas. "Bringing In The Sheaves" is more western in character, and has probably been the most widely sung hymn in TV and movie westerns.

Top 30 Country Gospel Songs

1. WINGS OF A DOVE - Ferlin Husky
2. WHY ME - Kris Kristofferson
3. OH HAPPY DAY - Glen Campbell
4. HE'S ALIVE - Dolly Parton
5. JESUS TAKE A HOLD - Merle Haggard
6. THE UNCLOUDY DAY - Willie Nelson
7. I SAW THE LIGHT - Hank Williams, Sr.
8. IT IS NO SECRET - Stuart Hamblen
9. ONE DAY AT A TIME - Christy Lane
10. YOU CAN'T BE A BEACON - Donna Fargo
11. PEACE IN THE VALLEY - Red Foley
12. DID YOU THINK TO PRAY - Charlie Pride
13. TURN YOUR RADIO ON - Ray Stevens
14. THE SEEKER - Dolly Parton
15. I KNEW JESUS BEFORE HE WAS A SUPERSTAR - Glen Campbell
16. THIS OLE HOUSE - Sturat Hamblen
17. ME AND JESUS - Tom T. Hall
18. COMIN' FOR TO CARRY ME HOME - Dolly Parton
19. BATTLE HYMN OF THE REPUBLIC - Wanda Jackson
20. I DON'T DESERVE A MANSION - Charlie Pride
21. ONE DAY AT A TIME - Marilyn Sellers
22. THE WONDERS YOU PERFORM - Tammy Wynette
23. TILL THE LAST LEAF SHALL FALL - Sonny James
24. PEACE IN THE VALLEY - Elvis Presley
25. EVOLUTION AND THE BIBLE - Hugh X. Lewis
26. SUNRISE - Slim Whitman
27. LOVE LIFTED ME - Ray Stevens
28. TAKE MY HAND PRECIOUS LORD - Jim Reeves
29. COME ON HOME - Bobby Goldsboro
30. VICTORY IN JESUS - Burl Ives

Top 20 Pop & Rock Gospel Songs

1. HE'S GOT THE WHOLE WORLD IN HIS HAND - Laurie London

2. DOMINIQUE - Singing Nun
3. TURN TURN TURN - Byrds
4. EVERYTHING IS BEAUTIFUL - Ray Stevens
5. PUT YOUR HAND IN THE HAND - Ocean
6. THE LORDS PRAYER - Sister Janet Meade
7. SPIRIT IN THE SKY - Norman Greenberg
8. OH HAPPY DAY - Edwin Hawkins Singers
9. WHY ME - Kris Kristofferson
10. MORNING HAS BROKEN - Cat Stevens
11. REV. MR. BLACK - Kingston Trio
12. AMAZING GRACE - Judy Collins
13. SHADRACK - Brook Benton
14. JESUS IS A SOUL MAN - Lawrence Reynolds
15. ONE DAY AT A TIME - Marilyn Sellers
16. PEACE IN THE VALLEY - Elvis Presley
17. ANGELS - Amy Grant
18. OH HAPPY DAY - Glen Campbell
19. DEAR MR. JESUS - POWER SOURCE (SHARON)
20. LOVE IN ANY LANGUAGE - Sandi Patti

Editor's Note: The place of "Jesus Christ Superstar" was difficult to determine owing to lingering controversy over the words and lyrics.

Mahalia Jackson
One of black Gospel's greatest vocalists.

Top 15 Sprituals

1. HE'S GOT THE WHOLE WORLD IN HIS HANDS
2. AMEN
3. WHEN THE SAINTS GO MARCHING IN
4. SWING LOW, SWEET CHARIOT
5. STANDIN' IN THE NEED OF PRAYER
6. DOWN BY THE RIVERSIDE
7. GET ON BOARD LITTLE CHILDREN
8. SWING DOWN CHARIOT
9. JOSHUA FIT THE BATTLE
10. I WANT TO BE READY
11. WHEN GOD DIPS HIS LOVE IN MY HEART
12. NOAH FOUND GRACE
13. I KNOW THE LORD LAID HIS HANDS ON ME
14. GO DOWN MOSES
15. STAND BY ME

Top 20 Hymn Classics

1. HOW GREAT THOU ART *
2. AMAZING GRACE
3. THE OLD RUGGED CROSS
4. THE LORDS PRAYER
5. ROCK OF AGES
6. A MIGHTY FORTRESS IS OUR GOD
7. FAITH OF OUR FATHERS
8. HOLY, HOLY, HOLY
9. WHAT A FRIEND WE HAVE IN JESUS
10. JUST AS I AM
11. ALL HAIL THE POWER
12. SWEET HOUR OF PRAYER
13. O FOR A THOUSAND TONGUES
14. JUST A CLOSER WALK WITH THEE
15. ABIDE WITH ME
16. IN THE GARDEN
17. BEYOND THE SUNSET
18. COME THOU ALMIGHTY GOD
19. WE'RE MARCHING TO ZION
20. GREAT IS THY FAITHFULNESS

Editor's Note: *Shea's version of "How Great Thou Art" is considered the #1 gospel hit of all time.

George Beverly Shea
A mainstay in Billy Graham's crusades, Shea's signature song—``How Great Thou Art''—was released by RCA in 1956.

Billboard Top 20 Jazz Albums, 1969-1993

TOP 20 JAZZ ALBUMS OF 1969

POS.	TITLE - ARTIST - LABEL
1.	FOOL ON THE HILL - Sergio Mendes & Brasil '66 - A&M
2.	SOULFUL STRUT - Young-Holt Unlimited - Brunswick
3.	MEMPHIS UNDERGROUND - Herbie Mann - Atlantic
4.	A DAY IN THE LIFE - Wes Montgomery - A&M
5.	MOTHER NATURE'S SON - Ramsey Lewis - Cadet
6.	HOT BUTTERED SOUL - Isaac Hayes - Enterprise/Stax
7.	STONE SOUL - Mongo Santamaria - Columbia
8.	ROAD SONG - Wes Montgomery - A&M
9.	THE WORM - Jimmy McGriff - Solid State
10.	MERCY, MERCY - Buddy Rich Big Band - World Pacific
11.	SILVER CYCLES - Eddie Harris - Atlantic
12.	SAY IT LOUD - Lou Donaldson - Blue Note
13.	AQUARIUS - Charlie Byrd - Columbia
14.	CRYSTAL ILLUSIONS - Sergio Mendes & Brasil '66 - A&M
15.	BUDDY & SOUL - Buddy Rich Big Band - World Pacific
16.	MOOG: THE ELECTRIC ECLECTICS OF DICK HYMAN - Dick Hyman - Command
17.	KARMA - Pharoah Sanders - Impulse/ABC
18.	HIGH VOLTAGES - Eddie Harris - Atlantic
19.	MILES DAVIS' GREATEST HITS - Miles Davis - Columbia
20.	THE GREATEST BYRD - Charlie Byrd - Columbia

TOP 20 JAZZ ALBUMS OF 1970

POS.	TITLE - ARTIST - LABEL
1.	SWISS MOVEMENT - Les McCann & Eddie Harris - Atlantic
2.	ISAAC HAYES MOVEMENT - Isaac Hayes - Enterprise
3.	HOT BUTTERED SOUL - Isaac Hayes - Enterprise
4.	WALKING IN SPACE - Quincy Jones - A&M
5.	BITCHES BREW - Miles Davis - Columbia
6.	MEMPHIS UNDERGROUND - Herbie Mann - Atlantic
7.	COUNTRY PREACHER - Cannonball Adderley - Capitol
8.	WES MONTGOMERY'S GREATEST HITS - Wes Montgomery - A&M
9.	BEST OF RAMSEY LEWIS - Ramsey Lewis - Cadet
10.	BLACK TALK - Charles Earland - Prestige
11.	GULA MATARI - Quincy Jones - A&M
12.	YE ME LE - Sergio Mendes & Brasil '66 - A&M
13.	BUDDY & SOUL - Buddy Rich Big Band - World Pacific
14.	BEST OF HERBIE MANN - Herbie Mann - Atlantic
15.	IN A SILENT WAY - Miles Davis - Columbia
16.	CHAPTER TWO - Roberta Flack - Atlantic
17.	HERBIE MANN LIVE AT THE WHISKEY A GO GO - Herbie Mann - Atlantic
18.	JEWELS OF THOUGHT - Pharoah Sanders - Impulse
19.	CRYSTAL ILLUSIONS - Sergio Mendes & Brasil '66 - A&M
20.	STONE FLUTE - Herbie Mann - Embryo

TOP 20 JAZZ ALBUMS OF 1971

POS.	TITLE - ARTIST - LABEL
1.	TO BE CONTINUED - Isaac Hayes - Enterprise/Stax-Volt
2.	BITCHES BREW - Miles Davis - Columbia
3.	CHAPTER TWO - Roberta Flack - Atlantic
4.	MILES DAVIS AT FILLMORE - Miles Davis - Columbia
5.	ISAAC HAYES MOVEMENT - Isaac Hayes - Enterprise/Stax-Volt
6.	SUGAR - Stanley Turrentine - CTI
7.	SECOND MOVEMENT - Eddie Harris & Les McCann - Atlantic
8.	JACK JOHNSON - Jack Johnson - Miles Davis soundtrack
9.	MEMPHIS TWO STEP - Herbie Mann - Embryo/Atlantic
10.	TJADER - Cal Tjader - Fantasy
11.	STRAIGHT LIFE - Freddie Hubbard - CTI
12.	B. B. KING LIVE AT COOK COUNTY JAIL - B. B. King - ABC
13.	THEM CHANGES - Ramsey Lewis - Cadet
14.	BRIDGE OVER TROUBLED WATER - Paul Desmond - A&M
15.	OLD SOCKS, NEW SHOES..NEW SOCKS, OLD SHOES - Jazz Crusaders - Chisa/Motown
16.	DON ELLIS AT FILLMORE - Don Ellis - Columbia
17.	GULA MATARI - Quincy Jones - A&M
18.	BLACK DROPS - Charles Earland - Prestige/Fantasy
19.	M. F. HORN - Maynard Horn - Columbia
20.	LIVING BLACK - Charles Earland - Prestige/Fantasy

TOP 20 JAZZ ALBUMS OF 1972

POS.	TITLE - ARTIST - LABEL
1.	SMACKWATER JACK - Quincy Jones - A&M
2.	SHAFT SOUNDTRACK - Isaac Hayes - MGM (Enterprise/Stax-Volt)
3.	PUSH PUSH - Herbie Mann - Embryo/Atlantic
4.	BLACK MOSES - Isaac Hayes - Enterprise/Stax-Volt
5.	UPENDO NI PAMAJOS - Ramsey Lewis Trio - Columbia
6.	CRUSADERS I - Blue Thumb/Famous
7.	GROVER WASHINGTON, JR. - Grover Washington, Jr. - Inner City Blues/Kudu/CTI
8.	QUIET FIRE - Roberta Flack - Atlantic
9.	A DIFFERENT DRUMMER - Buddy Rich - RCA
10.	TODAY - Stan Kenton - Phase 4/London
11.	FIRST TAKE - Roberta Flack - Atlantic
12.	BUDDY RICH IN LONDON - Buddy Rich - RCA
13.	SOUL ZODIAC - Nat Adderly - Capitol
14.	THE AGE OF STEAM - Gerry Mulligan - A&M
15.	MISSISSIPPI GAMBLER - Herbie Mann - Atlantic
16.	TEARS OF JOY - Don Ellis - Columbia
17.	SUN SHIP - John Coltrane - Impulse
18.	BITCHES BREW - Miles Davis - Columbia
19.	ALL THE KING'S HORSES - Grover Washington, Jr. - Kudu/CTI
20.	VISIONS - Grant Green - Blue Note

TOP 20 JAZZ ALBUMS OF 1973

POS.	TITLE - ARTIST - LABEL
1.	BLACK BYRD - Donald Byrd - Blue Note
2.	SECOND CRUSADE - Crusaders - Blue Thumb
3.	PRELUDE/DEODATO - Deodato - CTI
4.	SUNFLOWER - Milt Jackson - CTI
5.	YOU'VE GOT IT BAD, GIRL - Quincy Jones - A&M
6.	SWEETNIGHTER - Weather Report - Columbia
7.	ON THE CORNER - Miles Davis - Columbia
8.	TALK TO THE PEOPLE - Les McCann - Atlantic
9.	SEXTANT - Herbie Hancock - Columbia
10.	M. F. HORN - Maynard Ferguson - Columbia
11.	STRANGE FRUIT - Billie Holiday - Atlantic

Top 40 Favorite Songs of Jazz Musicians

1. AIREGIN	23. LIKE SOMEONE IN LOVE
2. ALL THE THINGS YOU ARE	24. LUSH LIFE
3. APRIL IN PARIS	25. MAY-REH (ALL GOD'S CHILLIN' GOT RHYTHM)
4. BAUBLES, BANGLES & BEADS	26. MOONLIGHT IN VERMONT
5. BILLIE'S BOUNCE (BLUES)	27. OLEO (I GOT RYHTHM)
6. BLUESETTE	28. ONE NOTE SAMBA
7. DONNA LEE (INDIANA)	29. PENSATIVA
8. DON'T GET AROUND MUCH ANYMORE	30. 'ROUND MIDNIGHT
9. GETTIN' SENTIMENTAL OVER YOU	31. SATIN DOLL
10. GREEN DOLPHIN STREET	32. SLOW BOAT TO CHINA
11. I LET A SONG GO OUT OF MY HEART	33. SOME TIME AGO
12. I LOVE YOU	34. SOMEDAY MY PRINCE WILL COME
13. I REMEMBER YOU	35. THE SONG IS YOU
14. I'LL REMEMBER APRIL	36. STELLA BY STARLIGHT
15. IN A MELLOW TONE	37. STOMPIN' AT THE SAVOY
16. IN A SENTIMENTAL MOOD	38. STRAIGHT, NO CHASER (BLUES)
17. INDIAN SUMMER	39. TIME AFTER TIME
18. INVITATIONS	40. THE WAY YOU LOOK TONIGHT
19. IT MIGHT AS WELL BE SPRING	41. YARDBIRD SUITE
20. JORDU	
21. JOY SPRING	
22. JUST IN TIME	

Editor's Note: Alphabetical; songs not ranked. Survey conducted by Terry Rosen.

12.	SKY DIVE - Freddie Hubbard - CTI
13.	DEODATO 2 - Deodato - CTI
14.	SOUL BOX - Grover Washington, Jr. - Kudu
15.	MORNING STAR - Hubert Laws - CTI
16.	ALL THE KING'S HORSES - Grover Washington, Jr. - Kudu
17.	HOLD ON, I'M COMIN' - Herbie Mann - Atlantic
18.	LIVE AT MONTREUX - Les McCann - Atlantic
19.	CHERRY - Stanley Turrentine with Milt Jackson - CTI
20.	CARNEGIE HALL - Hubert Laws - CTI

TOP 20 JAZZ ALBUMS OF 1974

POS.	TITLE - ARTIST - LABEL
1.	HEADHUNTERS - Herbie Hancock - Columbia
2.	SPECTRUM - Billy Cobham - Atlantic
3.	BLACK BYRD - Donald Byrd - Blue Note
4.	SWEETNIGHTER - Weather Report - Columbia
5.	LIGHT AS A FEATHER - Chick Corea - Polydor
6.	CLOSER TO IT! - Brian Auger's Oblivion Express - RCA
7.	2 - Deodato - CTI
8.	BODY TALK - George Benson - CTI
9.	DON'T MESS WITH MR. T - Stanley Turrentine - CTI
10.	BLACKS & BLUES - Bobbi Humphrey - Blue Note
11.	SUPERSAX PLAYS BYRD - Supersax - Capitol
12.	SOUL BOX - Grover Washington, Jr. - Kudu
13.	STREET LADY - Donald Byrd - Blue Note
14.	BODY HEAT - Quincy Jones - A&M
15.	YOU'VE GOT IT BAD, GIRL - Quincy Jones - A&M
16.	MR. BOJANGLES - Sonny Stitt - Cadet
17.	CROSSWINDS - Billy Cobham - Atlantic
18.	LAYERS - Les McCann - Atlantic
19.	UNSUNG HEROES - Crusaders - ABC/Blue Thumb
20.	LAND OF MAKE BELIEVE - Chuck Mangione - Mercury

TOP 20 JAZZ ALBUMS OF 1975

POS.	TITLE - ARTIST - LABEL
1.	PIECES OF DREAMS - Stanley Turrentine - Fantasy
2.	MISTER MAGIC - Grover Washington, Jr. - Kudu
3.	BAD BENSON - George Benson - CTI
4.	SUN GODDESS - Ramsey Lewis - Columbia
5.	SOUTHERN COMFORT - Crusaders - ABC/Blue Thumb
6.	BODY HEAT - Quincy Jones - A&M
7.	THRUST - Herbie Hancock - Columbia
8.	FLYING START - Blackbyrds - Fantasy
9.	STEPPING INTO TOMORROW - Donald Byrd - Blue Note
10.	EXPANSIONS - Lonnie Liston Smith & The Cosmic Echoes - Flying Dutchman
11.	TWO - Bob James - CTI
12.	CHASE AWAY THE CLOUDS - Chuck Mangione - A&M
13.	NO MYSTERY - Return To Forever Featuring Chick Corea - Polydor
14.	IN THE POCKET - Stanley Turrentine - Fantasy
15.	SATIN DOLL - Bobbi Humphrey - Blue Note
16.	ONE - Bob James - CTI
17.	LAND OF MAKE BELIEVE - Chuck Mangione - Mercury
18.	DISCOTHEQUE - Herbie Mann - Atlantic
19.	WHERE HAVE I KNOWN YOU BEFORE - Return To Forever Featuring Chick Corea - Polydor
20.	IS IT IN - Eddie Harris - Atlantic

TOP 20 JAZZ ALBUMS OF 1976

POS.	TITLE - ARTIST - LABEL
1.	BREEZIN' - George Benson - Warner Bros.
2.	FEEL SO GOOD - Grover Washington, Jr. - Kudu
3.	KOLN CONCERT - Keith Jarrett - ECM
4.	TOUCH - John Klemmer - ABC/Blue Thumb
5.	CITY LIFE - Blackbyrds - Fantasy

6. PLACES & SPACES - Donald Byrd - Blue Note
7. PRESSURE SENSITIVE - Ronnie Laws - Blue Note
8. JOURNEY TO LOVE - Stanley Clarke - Nemperor
9. THE LEPRECHAUN - Chick Corea - Polydor
10. LOOK OUT FOR #1 - Brothers Johnson - A&M
11. MAN-CHILD - Herbie Hancock - Columbia
12. MYSTIC VOYAGE - Roy Ayers Ubiquity - Polydor
13. ROMANTIC WARRIOR - Return To Forever - Columbia
14. THOSE SOUTHERN KNIGHTS - Crusaders - ABC/Blue Thumb
15. YOU ARE MY STARSHIP - Norman Connors - Buddah
16. NEW YORK CONNECTION - Tom Scott - Ode
17. MISTER MAGIC - Grover Washington, Jr. - Kudu
18. HARD WORK - John Handy - ABC/Impulse
19. OPEN YOUR EYES YOU CAN FLY - Flora Purim - Milestone
20. FLY WITH THE WIND - McCoy Tyner - Milestone

TOP 20 JAZZ ALBUMS OF 1977

POS. TITLE - ARTIST - LABEL
1. IN FLIGHT - George Benson - Warner Bros.
2. FREE AS THE WIND - Crusaders - ABC/Blue Thumb
3. BREEZIN' - George Benson - Warner Bros.
4. IMAGINARY VOYAGE - Jean-Luc Ponty - Atlantic
5. HEAVY WEATHER - Weather Report - Columbia
6. A SECRET PLACE - Grover Washington, Jr. - Kudu (Motown)
7. CALIENTE - Gato Barbieri - A&M
8. CONQUISTADOR - Maynard Ferguson - Columbia
9. MAIN SQUEEZE - Chuck Mangione - A&M
10. FRIENDS & STRANGERS - Ronnie Laws - Blue Note
11. FOUR - Bob James - CTI (Motown)
12. SCHOOL DAYS - Stanley Clarke - Nemperor
13. I HEARD THAT/THE MUSICAL WORLD OF QUINCY JONES - Quincy Jones - A&M
14. UNFINISHED BUSINESS - Blackbyrds - Fantasy
15. MY SPANISH HEART - Chick Corea - Polydor
16. LIFESTYLE - John Klemmer - ABC
17. BAREFOOT - John Klemmer - ABC
18. THE MAN WITH THE SAD FACE - Stanley Turrentine - Fantasy
19. VIBRATIONS - Roy Ayers Ubiquity - Polydor
20. V.S.O.P. - Herbie Hancock - Columbia

TOP 20 JAZZ ALBUMS OF 1978

POS. TITLE - ARTIST - LABEL
1. FEELS SO GOOD - Chuck Mangione - A&M
2. WEEKEND IN L.A. - George Benson - Warner Bros.
3. IMAGES - Crusaders - ABC
4. LIVE AT THE BIJOU - Grover Washington, Jr. - Kudu (Motown)
5. RAINBOW SEEKER - Joe Sample - ABC
6. SOUND...AND STUFF LIKE THAT - Quincy Jones - A&M
7. HEADS - Bob James - Tappan Zee
8. MAGIC IN YOUR EYES - Earl Klugh - United Artists
9. CHILDREN OF SANCHEZ - Chuck Mangione - A&M
10. SAY IT WITH SILENCE - Hubert Laws - Columbia
11. LOOK TO THE RAINBOW - AL JARREAU LIVE IN EUROPE - Al Jarreau - Warner Bros.
12. SUNLIGHT - Herbie Hancock - Columbia
13. ELECTRIC GUITARIST - John McLaughlin - Columbia
14. ARABESQUE - John Klemmer - ABC
15. CASINO - Al DiMeola - Columbia
16. FREESTYLE - Bobbi Humphrey - Epic
17. LOVE ISLAND - Deodato - Warner Bros.

18. MODERN MAN - Stanley Clarke - Nemperor
19. LOVELAND - Lonnie Liston Smith - Columbia
20. PAT METHENY - Pat Metheny - ECM/Warner Bros.

TOP 20 JAZZ ALBUMS OF 1979

POS. TITLE - ARTIST - LABEL
1. STREET LIFE - Crusaders - MCA
2. LIVIN' INSIDE YOUR LOVE - George Benson - Warner Bros.
3. TOUCHDOWN - Bob James - Tappan-Zee/Columbia
4. REED SEED - Grover Washington, Jr. - Motown
5. PAT METHENY - Pat Metheny - ECM
6. CARMEL - Joe Sample - ABC
7. CHILDREN OF SANCHEZ - Chuck Mangione - A&M
8. MR. GONE - Weather Report - Columbia
9. FLAME - Ronnie Laws - United Artists
10. MORNING DANCE - Spyro Gyra - Infinity
11. ANGIE - Angela Bofill - GRP/Arista
12. ALL FLY HOME - Al Jarreau - Warner Bros.
13. PARADISE - Grover Washington, Jr. - Elektra
14. FEETS DON'T FAIL ME NOW - Herbie Hancock - Columbia
15. HEART STRING - Earl Klugh - United Artists
16. FEELS SO GOOD - Chuck Mangione - A&M
17. NEW CHAUTAUQUA - Pat Metheny Group - ECM
18. COSMIC MESSENGER - Jean-Luc Ponty - Atlantic
19. PATRICE - Patrice Rushen - Elektra
20. SECRETS - Gil Scott-Heron & Brian Jackson - Arista

TOP 20 JAZZ ALBUMS OF 1980

POS. TITLE - ARTIST - LABEL
1. STREET LIFE - Crusaders - MCA
2. ONE ON ONE - Bob James & Earl Klugh - Tappan-Zee/Columbia
3. MORNING DANCE - Spyro Gyra - MCA
4. CATCHING THE SUN - Spyro Gyra - MCA
5. ANGEL OF THE NIGHT - Angela Bofill - Arista/GRP
6. RISE - Herb Alpert - A&M
7. HEART STRING - Earl Klugh - Arista/GRP
8. AMERICAN GARAGE - Pat Metheny Group - ECM
9. SKYLARKIN' - Grover Washington, Jr. - Motown
10. LUCKY SEVEN - Bob James - Tappan-Zee/Columbia
11. PIZZAZZ - Patrice Rushen - Elektra
12. 8:30 - Weather Report - ARC/Columbia
13. A TASTE FOR PASSION - Jean-Luc Ponty - Atlantic
14. BROWNE SUGAR - Tom Browne - Arista/GRP
15. HIROSHIMA - Hiroshima - Arista
16. WATER SIGN - Jeff Lorber Fusion - Arista
17. FUN AND GAMES - Chuck Mangione - A&M
18. EVERY GENERATION - Ronnie Laws - United Artists
19. HIDEAWAY - David Sanborn - Warner Bros.
20. I WANNA PLAY FOR YOU - Stanley Clarke - Nemperor

TOP 20 JAZZ ALBUMS OF 1981

POS. TITLE - ARTIST - LABEL
1. WINELIGHT - Grover Washington, Jr. - Elecktra
2. BREAKIN' AWAY - Al Jarreau - Warner Bros.
3. GIVE ME THE NIGHT - George Benson - Warner Bros.
4. VOYEUR - David Sanborn - Warner Bros.
5. 80/81 - Pat Metheny - ECM
6. LATE NIGHT GUITAR - Earl Klugh - Liberty
7. CARNAVAL - Spyro Gyra - MCA
8. MOUNTAIN DANCE - Dave Grusin - Arista/GRP
9. RIT - Lee Ritenour - Elektra

Grover Washington, Jr.

Grover had twenty-two Top 20 Jazz albums
between 1972 and 1992—his LP ''Winelight'' was #1 in 1981.

10.	NIGHT PASSAGE - Weather Report - ARC/Columbia
11.	THE MAN WITH THE HORN - Miles Davis - Columbia
12.	THE CLARKE/DUKE PROJECT - Stanley Clarke/George Duke - Epic
13.	THIS TIME - Al Jarreau - Warner Bros.
14.	INHERIT THE WIND - Wilton Felder - MCA
15.	THE DUDE - Quincy Jones - A&M
16.	AS FALLS WICHITA SO FALLS WICHITA FALLS - Pat Metheny & Lyle Mays - ECM
17.	FAMILY - Hubert Laws - Columbia
18.	CIVILIZED EVIL - Jean-Luc Ponty - Atlantic
19.	HIDEAWAY - David Sanborn - Warner Bros.
20.	VOICES IN THE RAIN - Joe Sample - MCA

TOP 20 JAZZ ALBUMS OF 1982

POS.	TITLE - ARTIST - LABEL
1.	BREAKIN' AWAY - Al Jarreau - Warner Bros.
2.	COME MORNING - Grover Washington, Jr. - Elektra
3.	MYSTICAL ADVENTURE - Jean-Luc Ponty - Atlantic
4.	THE GEORGE BENSON COLLECTION - George Benson - Warner Bros.
5.	OFFRAMP - Pat Metheny Group - ECM
6.	THE DUDE - Quincy Jones - A&M
7.	CRAZY FOR YOU - Earl Klugh - Liberty
8.	FREETIME - Spyro Gyra - MCA
9.	REFLECTIONS - Gil Scott-Heron - Arista
10.	WYNTON MARSALIS - Wynton Marsalis - Columbia
11.	AS FALLS WICHITA SO FALLS WICHITA FALLS - Pat Metheny & Lyle Mays - ECM
12.	SOMETHING ABOUT YOU - Angela Bofill - Arista

13.	AS WE SPEAK - David Sanborn - Warner Bros.
14.	SOLID GROUND - Ronnie Laws - Liberty
15.	ELECTRIC RENDEZVOUS - Al DiMeola - Columbia
16.	OBJECTS OF DESIRE - Michael Franks - Warner Bros.
17.	STANDING TALL - Crusaders - MCA
18.	WINELIGHT - Grover Washington, Jr. - Elektra
19.	SLEEPWALK - Larry Carlton - Warner Bros.
20.	A LADY AND HER MUSIC - Lena Horne - Qwest

TOP 20 JAZZ ALBUMS OF 1983

POS.	TITLE - ARTIST - LABEL
1.	TWO OF A KIND - Bob James & Earl Klugh - Capitol
2.	JARREAU - Al Jarreau - Warner Bros.
3.	AS WE SPEAK - David Sanborn - Warner Bros.
4.	OFFRAMP - Pat Metheny Group - ECM
5.	IN YOUR EYES - George Benson - Warner Bros.
6.	BREAKIN' AWAY - Al Jarreau - Warner Bros.
7.	DECEMBER - George Winston - Windham Hill
8.	INCOGNITO - Spyro Gyra - MCA
9.	THE BEST IS YET TO COME - Grover Washington, Jr. - Elektra
10.	WINTER INTO SPRING - George Winston - Windham Hill
11.	CASINO LIGHTS - Various Artists - Warner Bros.
12.	HANDS DOWN - Bob James - Tappan Zee/Columbia
13.	THE GEORGE BENSON COLLECTION - George Benson - Warner Bros.
14.	LOW RIDE - Earl Klugh - Capitol
15.	DAVE GRUSIN AND THE N.Y./L.A. DREAM BAND - Dave Grusin & the N.Y./L.A. Dream Band - GRP
16.	AUTUMN - George Winston - Windham Hill
17.	THE HUNTER - Joe Sample - MCA
18.	RIT/2 - Lee Ritenour - Elektra
19.	OFF THE TOP - Jimmy Smith - Musician
20.	PROCESSION - Weather Report - Columbia

TOP 20 JAZZ ALBUMS OF 1984

POS.	TITLE - ARTIST - LABEL
1.	BACKSTREET - David Sanborn - Warner Bros.
2.	THINK OF ONE - Wynton Marsalis - Columbia
3.	FUTURE SHOCK - Herbie Hancock - Columbia
4.	DECEMBER - George Winston - Windham Hill
5.	AUTUMN - George Winston - Windham Hill
6.	WISHFUL THINKING - Earl Klugh - Capitol
7.	WHAT'S NEW - Linda Ronstadt - Asylum
8.	PASSIONFRUIT - Michael Franks - Warner Bros.
9.	IN YOUR EYES - George Benson - Warner Bros.
10.	JARREAU - Al Jarreau - Warner Bros.
11.	ACCESS ALL AREAS - Spyro Gyra - MCA
12.	IMAGINE THIS - Pieces Of A Dream - Elektra
13.	WINTER INTO SPRING - George Winston - Windham Hill
14.	GHETTO BLASTER - Crusaders - MCA
15.	INDIVIDUAL CHOICE - Jean-Luc Ponty - Atlantic
16.	G FORCE - Kenny G - Arista
17.	DECOY - Miles Davis - Columbia
18.	REJOICING - Pat Metheny - ECM
19.	FOXIE - Bob James - Columbia
20.	SHADOWDANCE - Shadowfax - Windham Hill

TOP 20 JAZZ ALBUMS OF 1985

POS.	TITLE - ARTIST - LABEL
1.	HOT HOUSE FLOWERS - Wynton Marsalis - Columbia
2.	MAGIC TOUCH - Stanley Jordan - Blue Note

3. FIRST CIRCLE - Pat Metheny Group - ECM
4. STRAIGHT TO THE HEART - David Sanborn - Warner Bros.
5. 20/20 - George Benson - Warner Bros.
6. DANCING IN THE SUN - George Howard - TBA
7. HIGH CRIME - Al Jarreau - Warner Bros.
8. WHITE WINDS - Andreas Vollenweider - Columbia
9. DECEMBER - George Winston - Windham Hill
10. AMERICAN EYES - Rare Silk - Palo Alto
11. INSIDE MOVES - Grover Washington, Jr. - Elektra
12. YOU'RE UNDER ARREST - Miles Davis - Columbia
13. SODA FOUNTAIN SHUFFLE - Earl Klugh - Warner Bros.
14. DIAMOND LIFE - Sade - Portrait
15. HARLEQUIN - Dave Grusin & Lee Ritenour - GRP
16. OPEN MIND - Jean-Luc Ponty - Atlantic
17. ALTERNATING CURRENTS - Spyro Gyra - MCA
18. NIGHT SONGS - Earl Klugh - Capitol
19. NIGHT LINES - Dave Grusin - GRP
20. SKIN DIVE - Michael Franks - Warner Bros.

TOP 20 JAZZ ALBUMS OF 1986

POS. TITLE - ARTIST - LABEL
1. MAGIC TOUCH - Stanley Jordan - Blue Note
2. BLACK CODES (FROM THE UNDERGROUND) - Wynton Marsalis - Columbia
3. LOVE WILL FOLLOW - George Howard - TBA
4. VOCALESE - The Manhattan Transfer - Atlantic
5. HARLEQUIN - Dave Grusin & Lee Ritenour - GRP
6. ALONE/BUT NEVER ALONE - Larry Carlton - MCA
7. DOUBLE VISION - Bob James/David Sanborn - Warner Bros.
8. ANOTHER PLACE - Hiroshima - Epic
9. DANCING IN THE SUN - George Howard - TBA
10. PROMISE - Sade - Portrait
11. SKIN DIVE - Michael Franks - Warner Bros.
12. ALTERNATING CURRENTS - Spyro Gyra - MCA
13. STILL WARM - John Scofield - Gramavision
14. BREAKOUT - Spyro Gyra - MCA
15. CANYON - Paul Winter - Living Music
16. SHADES - Yellowjackets - MCA
17. DOWN TO THE MOON - Andreas Vollenweider - CBS Masterworks
18. ACOUSTICITY - David Grisman - Zebra/Acoustic
19. DECEMBER - George Winston - Windham Hill
20. THIS SIDE UP - David Benoit - Spindletop

TOP 20 JAZZ ALBUMS OF 1987

POS. TITLE - ARTIST - LABEL
1. THE OTHER SIDE OF ROUND MIDNIGHT - Dexter Gordon - Blue Note
2. MICHAEL BRECKER - Michael Brecker - MCA/Impulse
3. ROUND MIDNIGHT - Soundtrack - Columbia
4. J MOOD - Wynton Marsalis - Columbia
5. ROYAL GARDEN BLUES - Branford Marsalis - Columbia
6. DIGIGAL DUKE - The Duke Ellington Orchestra - GRP
7. CIVILIZATION - Tony Williams - Blue Note
8. GOOD MORNING KISS - Carmen Lundy - Black Hawk/Aspen
9. POWER OF THREE - Michel Petrucciani - Blue Note
10. 10TH AVENUE - Patrick Williams' New York Band - Soundwings
11. TO BIRD WITH LOVE - Eddie Daniels - GRP
12. BOLLING: SUITE FOR FLUTE & JAZZ PIANO TRIO NO. 2 - Claude Bolling & Jean-Pierre Rampal - CBS Masterworks
13. QUARTET WEST - Charlie Haden - Verve

14. IRRESISTIBLE FORCES - Jack DeJohnette's Special Edit - MCA/Impulse
15. PHANTOM NAVIGATOR - Wayne Shorter - Columbia
16. DIANE SCHUUR - COUNT BASIE ORCHESTRA - Diane Schuur & Count Basie Orchestra - GRP
17. STANDARD TIME - Wynton Marsalis - Columbia
18. YOU'RE THE ONE - Henry Johnson - MCA/Impulse
19. STATE OF THE TENOR: LIVE AT THE VILLAGE VANGUARD, VOL. II - Joe Henderson - Blue Note
20. BRAZILIAN ROMANCE - Sarah Vaughan - CBS Masterworks

TOP 20 CONTEMPORARY JAZZ ALBUMS OF 1988

POS. TITLE - ARTIST - LABEL
1. DIANNE REEVES - Dianne Reeves - Blue Note
2. TIME AND TIDE - Basia - Epic
3. SIMPLE PLEASURES - Bobby McFerrin - EMI
4. GO - Hiroshima - Epic
5. DOLPHIN SMILES - Steve Kindler & Teja Bell - Global Pacific
6. STILL LIFE (TALKING) - Pat Metheny Group - Geffen
7. AND YOU KNOW THAT! - Kirk Whalum - Columbia
8. STORIES WITHOUT WORDS - Spyro Gyra - MCA
9. CLOSE-UP - David Sanborn - Reprise
10. BRASIL - The Manhattan Transfer - Atlantic Jazz
11. REFLECTIONS - George Howard - MCA
12. RITES OF SUMMER - Spyro Gyra - MCA
13. IF THIS BASS COULD ONLY TALK - Stanley Clarke - Portrait
14. KILIMANJARO - Rippingtons Featuring Russ Freeman - Passport Jazz
15. EVERY STEP OF THE WAY - David Benoit - GRP
16. COLLABORATION - George Benson & Earl Klugh - Warner Bros.
17. DUOTONES - Kenny G - Arista
18. THE GIFT OF TIME - Jean-Luc Ponty - Columbia
19. PORTRAIT - Lee Ritenour - GRP
20. POLITICS - Yellowjackets - MCA

TOP 20 JAZZ ALBUMS OF 1988

POS. TITLE - ARTISTS - LABEL
1. DIANE SCHUUR - COUNT BASIE ORCHESTRA - Diane Schuur & Count Basie Orchestra - GRP
2. EVERY NIGHT - Joe Williams - Verve
3. STANDARD TIME - Wynton Marsalis - Columbia
4. RENAISSANCE - Branford Marsalis - Columbia
5. ELLA IN ROME - THE BIRTHDAY CONCERT - Ella Fitzgerald - Verve
6. SYMPHONIC DREAMS - Gerry Mulligan - Projazz
7. LOOK WHAT I GOT - Betty Carter - Verve
8. THE VILLAGE - Henry Butler - MCA/Impulse
9. MICHAEL BRECKER - Michael Brecker - MCA/Impulse
10. VIRGIN BEAUTY - Ornette Coleman & Prime Time - Portrait
11. BRAZILIAN ROMANCE - Sarah Vaughan - CBS Masterworks
12. STILL LIVE - Keith Jarrett - ECM
13. KALEIDOSCOPE - Mike Metheny - MCA/Impulse
14. LIVE AT BLUES ALLEY - Wynton Marsalis - Columbia
15. BORDERTOWN - Bennie Wallace - Blue Note
16. TRIBUTE TO COUNT BASIE - Gene Harris - Concord Jazz
17. THEN AND NOW - Grover Washington, Jr. - Columbia
18. NIGHTWIND - Mike Lawrence - Optimism
19. CROSS CURRENTS - Eliane Elias - Blue Note/Denon
20. RANDOM ABSTRACT - Branford Marsalis - Columbia

TOP 20 JAZZ ALBUMS OF 1989

POS.   TITLE - ARTIST - LABEL
1.   BLUE SKIES - Cassandra Wilson - JMT
2.   MICHEL CAMILO - Michel Camilo - Portrait
3.   TALKIN' BOUT YOU - Diane Schuur - GRP
4.   IN A SENTIMENTAL MOOD - Dr. John - Warner Bros.
5.   THE TRUTH IS SPOKEN HERE - Marcus Roberts - Novus
6.   BIRD - The Original Recordings Of Charlie Parker - Verve/
     Norrington/Angel
7.   CHICK COREA AKOUSTIC BAND - Chick Corea Akoustic
     Band - GRP
8.   CHET BAKER SINGS AND PLAYS (FROM "LET'S GET
     LOST") - Chet Baker - Novus
9.   LOOK WHAT I GOT - Betty Carter - Verve
10. THE MAJESTY OF THE BLUES - Wynton Marsalis -
     Columbia
11. TENDERLY - George Benson - Warner Bros.
12. BIRD - Soundtrack - Columbia
13. TRIO JEEPY - Branford Marsalis - Columbia
14. REVELATIONS - McCoy Tyner - Blue Note
15. IN GOOD COMPANY - Joe Williams - Verve Digital
16. THEN AND NOW - Grover Washington, Jr. - Columbia
17. 20 - Harry Connick, Jr. - Columbia
18. MUSIC FROM "WHEN HARRY MET SALLY..." - Harry
     Connick, Jr. - Columbia
19. ORIGINAL BIRD: THE BEST OF BIRD ON SAVOY - Parker
     - Savoy Jazz
20. THE MEN IN MY LIFE - Lena Horne - Three Cheri

TOP 20 CONTEMPORARY JAZZ ALBUMS OF 1989

POS.   TITLE - ARTIST - LABEL
1.   SILHOUETTE - Kenny G - Arista
2.   SPELLBOUND - Joe Sample - Warner Bros.
3.   HEART'S HORIZON - Al Jarreau - Reprise
4.   EAST - Hiroshima - Epic
5.   AMANDLA - Miles Davis - Warner Bros.
6.   SIMPLE PLEASURES - Bobby McFerrin - EMI
7.   LETTER FROM HOME - Pat Metheny - Geffen
8.   FESTIVAL - Lee Ritenour - GRP
9.   CLOSE-UP - David Sanborn - Reprise
10. PENSYL SKETCHES #1 - Kim Pensyl - Optimism
11. REAL LIFE STORY - Terri Lyne Carrington - Verve Forecast
12. TOURIST IN PARADISE - Rippingtons Featuring Russ
     Freeman - GRP
13. LOVE WARRIORS - Tuck & Patti - Windham Hill
14. AT LAST - Lou Rawls - Blue Note
15. ON SOLID GROUND - Larry Carlton - MCA
16. WHISPERS AND PROMISES - Earl Klugh - Warner Bros.
17. POINT OF VIEW - Spyro Gyra - MCA
18. TIME AND TIDE - Basia - Epic
19. DON'T TRY THIS AT HOME - Michael Brecker - Impulse
20. URBAN DAYDREAMS - David Benoit - GRP

TOP 20 JAZZ ALBUMS 0F 1990

POS.   TITLE - ARTIST - LABEL
1.   MUSIC FROM "WHEN HARRY MET SALLY..." - Harry
     Connick, Jr. - Columbia
2.   WAITING FOR SPRING - David Benoit - GRP
3.   ON FIRE - Michael Camilo - Epic
4.   STANDARD TIME VOL 3 - THE RESOLUTION OF RO-
     MANCE - Wynton Marsalis - Columbia

5.   REMEMBRANCE - The Harper Brothers - Verve
6.   DEEP IN THE SHED - Marcus Roberts - Novus
7.   MOOD INDIGO - Frank Morgan - Antilles
8.   WE ARE IN LOVE - Harry Connick, Jr. - Columbia
9.   REUNION - Gary Burton - GRP
10. PARALLEL REALITIES - Jack De Johnette - MCA
11. STOLEN MOMENTS - Lee Ritenour - GRP
12. TIME ON MY HANDS - John Scofield - Blue Note
13. APASIANADO - Stan Getz - A&M
14. MY FAVORITE SONGS: THE LAST GREAT CONCERT -
     Chet Baker - Enja
15. LOFTY'S ROACH SOUFFLE - Harry Connick, Jr. - Columbia
16. QUESTION AND ANSWER - Pat Metheny - Geffen
17. THE FABULOUS BAKER BOYS - Soundtrack - GR
18. CARMEN SINGS MONK - Carmen McRae - Novus
19. ELIANE ELIAS PLAYS JOBIM - Eliane Elias - Blue Note
20. MUSIC FROM "MO' BETTER BLUES" - Branford Marsalis
     Quartet/Terence Blanchard - Columbia

TOP 20 CONTEMPORARY JAZZ ALBUMS OF 1990

POS.   TITLE - ARTIST - LABEL
1.   LONDON WARSAW NEW YORK - Basia - Epic
2.   LIVE - Kenny G - Arista
3.   BACK ON THE BLOCK - Quincy Jones - Qwest
4.   TOKYO BLUE - Najee - EMI
5.   TIME OUT OF MIND - Grover Washington, Jr. - Columbia
6.   CORNUCOPIA - Stanley Jordan - Blue Note
7.   NEVER TOO FAR - Dianne Reeves - EMI
8.   HAPPY ANNIVERSARY, CHARLIE BROWN - Various Artists -
     GRP

Branford Marsalis
Jay Leno's bandmaster has had seven Top 20 LPs since 1987.

9. RICH AND POOR - Rany Crawford - Warner Bros.
10. FAST FORWARD - Spyro Gyra Featuring Jay Beckenstein - GRP
11. BLUE PACIFIC - Michael Franks - Reprise
12. MIGRATION - Dave Grusin - GRP
13. LOVE IS GONNA GETCHA - Patti Austin - GRP
14. PERSONAL - George Howard - MCA
15. LIVE AT THE ROYAL FESTIVAL HALL - John McLaughlin Trio - JMT
16. UPTOWNSHIP - Hugh Masekela - RCA
17. PENSYL SKETCHES #2 - Kim Pensyl - Optimism
18. AT LAST - Lou Rawls - Blue Note
19. LOVE GODDESS - Lonnie Liston Smith - Startrak
20. INSIDE OUT - Chick Corea Elektric Band - GRP

TOP 20 JAZZ ALBUMS OF 1991

POS.	TITLE - ARTIST - LABEL
1.	WE ARE IN LOVE - Harry Connick, Jr. - Columbia
2.	YOU WON'T FORGET ME - Shirley Horn - Verve
3.	UNFORGETTABLE - Natalie Cole - Elektra
4.	ROOTS REVISITED - Maceo Parker - Verve
5.	I REMEMBER - Dianne Reeves - Blue Note
6.	ALONE WITH THREE GIANTS - Marcus Roberts - Novus
7.	STANDARD TIME VOL. 2 INTIMACY CALLING - Wynton Marsalis - Columbia
8.	ARTISTRY - The Harper Brothers - Verve
9.	DROPPIN' THINGS - Betty Carter - Verve
10.	ANOTHER HAND - David Sanborn - Elektra Musician
11.	FREDDIE FREELOADER - Jon Hendricks And Friends - Denon
12.	SARAH-DEDICATED TO YOU - Carmen McRae - Novus
13.	A LOVESOME THING - Frank Morgan - Antilles
14.	AFRICAN EXCHANGE STUDENT - Kenny Garrett - Atlantic
15.	NEW YORK REUNION - McCoy Tyner - Chesky
16.	ALIVE - Chick Corea Akoustic Band - GRP
17.	THICK IN THE SOUTH - Wynton Marsalis - Columbia
18.	PART III - Joey DeFrancesco - Columbia
19.	SERENITY - Stan Getz - Emarcy
20.	PUBLIC EYE - Roy Hargrove - Novus

TOP 20 CONTEMPORARY JAZZ ALBUMS OF 1991

POS.	TITLE - ARTIST - LABEL
1.	ASHES TO ASHES - Joe Sample - Warner Bros.
2.	HEALING THE WOUNDS - The Crusaders - GRP
3.	PURE SCHUUR - Diane Schuur - GRP
4.	DREAM COME TRUE - Gerald Albright - Atlantic
5.	GREENHOUSE - Yellowjackets - GRP
6.	LISTEN LOVE - Jon Lucien - Mercury
7.	MEDICINE MUSIC - Bobby McFerrin - EMI
8.	DAVE KOZ - Dave Koz - Capitol
9.	MIDNIGHT IN SAN JUAN - Earl Klugh - Warner Bros.
10.	LOVE AND UNDERSTANDING - George Howard - GRP
11.	SO MUCH 2 SAY - Take 6 - Reprise
12.	INNER MOTION - David Benoit - GRP
13.	DREAM - Tuck & Patti - Windham Hill Jazz
14.	TCHOKOLA - Jean-Luc Ponty - Epic
15.	SAXUALITY - Candy Dulfer - Arista
16.	FLIGHT OF THE COSMIC HIPPO - Bela Fleck & The Flecktones - Warner Bros.
17.	COLLECTION - Spyro Gyra - GRP
18.	IT'S SUPPOSED TO BE FUN - Lou Rawls - Blue Note
19.	CURVES AHEAD - The Rippingtons - GRP
20.	PLAYING WITH FIRE - Sam Riney - Spindletop

Al Di Meola

Al's ``Kiss My Axe'' was the #2 Contemporary Jazz LP in 1992.

TOP 20 JAZZ ALBUMS OF 1992

POS.	TITLE - ARTIST - LABEL
1.	HERE'S TO LIFE - Shirley Horn - Verve
2.	LUSH LIFE - Joe Henderson - Verve
3.	THE GERSHWIN CONNECTION - Dave Grusin - GRP
4.	YOU GOTTA PAY THE BAND - Abbey Lincoln featuring Stan Getz - Verve
5.	BLUE LIGHT, RED LIGHT - Harry Connick, Jr. - Columbia
6.	IN TRIBUTE - Diane Schuur - GRP
7.	GRP ALL-STAR BIG BAND - GRP All-Star Big Band - GRP
8.	BLUE INTERLUDE - Wynton Marsalis Septet - Columbia
9.	UNFORGETTABLE - Natalie Cole - Elektra
10.	GOIN' BACK TO NEW ORLEANS - Dr. John - Warner Bros.
11.	THE VIBE - Roy Hargrove - Novus
12.	LIVE AT BIRDLAND - Gerald Albright - Atlantic
13	PLAY - Bobby McFerrin & Chick Corea - Blue Note.
14.	THE BEAUTIFUL ONES ARE NOT YET BORN - Branford Marsalis - Columbia
15.	THE EARL KLUGH TRIO VOLUME ONE - Earl Klugh Trio - Warner Bros.
16.	ALL THE WAY - Jimmy Scott - Sire
17.	THE CURE - Keith Jarrett Trio - ECM
18.	HAUNTED HEART - Charlie Haden Quartet West - Verve
19.	DINGO - Miles Davis & Michel Legrand - Warner Bros.
20.	AS SERENITY APPROACHES - Marcus Roberts - Novus

TOP 20 CONTEMPORARY JAZZ ALBUMS OF 1992

POS.	TITLE - ARTIST - LABEL
1.	FOURPLAY - Fourplay - Warner Bros.

2. KISS MY AXE - Al DiMeola Project - Tomato
3. UPFRONT - David Sanborn - Elektra
4. ON THE TOWN - Richard Elliot - Manhattan
5. NEXT EXIT - Grover Washington, Jr. - Columbia
6. SHADOWS - David Benoit - GRP
7. DOO BOP - Miles Davis - Warner Bros.
8. HEAVEN AND EARTH - Al Jarreau - Reprise
9. DO I EVER CROSS YOUR MIND - George Howard - GRP
10. WITH MY LOVER BESIDE ME - Nancy Wilson - Columbia
11. SECRET STORY - Pat Metheny - Geffen
12. STUCK ON YOU - Bobby Caldwell - Sin-Drome
13. LIVE WIRES - Yellowjackets - GRP
14. JUST AN ILLUSION - Najee - EMI
15. KEEP IT RIGHT THERE - Marion Meadows - Novus
16. EVERETTE HARP - Everette Harp - Manhattan
17. OASIS - Eric Marienthal - GRP
18. COOL - Bob James/Earl Klugh - Warner Bros.
19. A LONG STORY - Elaine Elias - Manhattan
20. QUE ALEGRIA - John McLaughlin Trio - Verve

TOP 20 JAZZ ALBUMS OF 1993

POS. TITLE - ARTIST - LABEL
1. SO NEAR, SO FAR - Joe Henderson - Verve
2. INVITATION - Joe Sample - Warner Bros.
3. PERFECTLY FRANK - Tony Bennett - Columbia
4. TAKE A LOOK - Natalie Cole - Elektra
5. 25 - Harry Connick Jr. - Columbia
6. HOMAGE TO DUKE - Dave Grusin - GRP
7. LETTER TO EVAN - David Benoit - GRP
8. IT'S GOT TO BE FUNKY - Horace Silver - Columbia
9. I HEARD YOU TWICE THE FIRST TIME - Branford Marsalis - Columbia
10. JOSHUA REDMAN - Joshua Redman - Warner Bros.
11. LIVE AT MONTREUX - Miles Davis & Quincy Jones - Warner Bros.

12. HAUNTED HEART - Charlie Haden Quartet West - Verve
13. BYE BYE BLACKBIRD - Keith Jarrett Trio - ECM
14. LOVE SONGS - Diane Schuur - GRP
15. RENDEZVOUS - Michel Camilo - Columbia
16. YOU MUST BELIEVE IN SPRING - Frank Morgan - Antilles
17. DEVIL'S GOT YOUR TONGUE - Abbey Lincoln - Verve
18. A SINGLE WOMAN - Nina Simone - Elektra
19. PORTRAIT OF THE BLUES - Lou Rawls - Manhattan
20. RHYTHM OF THE EARTH - Jackie McLean - Antilles

TOP 20 CONTEMPORARY JAZZ ALBUMS OF 1993

POS. TITLE - ARTIST - LABEL
1. BREATHLESS - Kenny G - Arista
2. WES BOUND - Lee Ritenour - GRP
3. SNAPSHOT - George Duke - Warner Bros.
4. THE JAZZMASTERS - Jazzmasters featuring Paul Hardcastle - JVC
5. LOVE REMEMBERS - George Benson - Warner Bros.
6. WORTH WAITING FOR - Jeff Lorber - Verve Forecast
7. DRAGONFLY SUMMER - Michael Franks - Reprise
8. SOUL EMBRACE - Richard Elliot - Manhattan
9. CACHE - Kirk Whalum - Columbia
10. LUCKY MAN - Dave Koz - Capitol
11. COOL - Bob James/Earl Klugh - Warner Brothers
12. LIFE ON PLANET GROOVE - Maceo Parker - Verve
13. BETWEEN THE SHEETS - Fourplay - Warner Bros.
14. WEEKEND IN MONACO - The Rippingtons - GRP
15. JUST BETWEEN US - Norman Brown - MoJazz
16. LIKE A RIVER - Yellowjackets - GRP
17. WHEN SUMMER COMES - George Howard - GRP
18. ON A ROLL - Fattburger - Sin-Drome
19. THE ROAD TO YOU - Pat Metheny - Geffen
20. STRAIGHT TO THE POINT - Art Porter - Verve Forecast

Billboard Top 120 Heavy Metal Albums, 1968-1994

AC/DC
    BACK IN BLACK - 1980
    DIRTY DEEDS DONE DIRT CHEAP - 1981
    FOR THOSE ABOUT TO ROCK - 1981
    LIVE - 1994
    THE RAZOR'S EDGE - 1992

ALICE COOPER
    TRASH - 1989
    WELCOME TO MY NIGHTMARE - 1975

ALICE IN CHAINS
    JAR OF FLIES - 1994

BIG HEAD TOAD & THE MONSTERS
    SISTER SWEETLY - 1994

BLACK SABBATH
    MASTER OF REALITY - 1971
    PARANOID - 1970

BLUE CHEER
    NINCEBUS ERUPTUM - 1968

BLUE OYSTER CULT
    AGENTS OF FORTUNE - 1976

CANDLEBOX
    CANDLEBOX - 1994

CINDERELLA
    LONG COLD WINTER - 1988
    NIGHT SONGS - 1986

DEEP PURPLE
    BURN - 1974
    FIREBALL - 1971
    HOUSE OF BLUE LIGHT - 1987

    MACHINE HEAD - 1972
    MADE IN JAPAN - 1973
    PERFECT STRANGERS - 1984
    SHADES OF - 1968
    STORMBRINGER - 1974
    WHO DO WE THINK THEY ARE - 1973

DEF LEPPARD
    ADRENALIZE - 1993
    HIGH 'N' DRY - 1981
    HYSTERIA - 1987
    PYROMANIA - 1983
    RETROACTIVE - 1993

FIREHOUSE
    FIREHOUSE - 1991

GUNS N' ROSES
    APPETITE FOR DESTRUCTION - 1987
    ILLUSION 1 & 2 - 1991
    SPHAGETTI INCIDENT - 1993

JIMI HENDRIX
    EXPERIENCE - 1969

IRON MAIDEN
    FEAR OF THE DARK - 1992
    LIVE AFTER DEATH - 1985
    NUMBER OF THE BEAST - 1982
    PIECE OF MIND - 1983
    POWER SLAVE - 1984
    SEVENTH SON OF SEVENTH SON - 1988
    SOMEWHERE IN TIME - 1986

Def Leppard
Five Top 40 Metal albums in ten years puts this band right up there with the best.

Heavy Metal Trivia Quiz

1. Guitarist Ace Frehley was an original member of which heavy metal group?
2. Soloist Lita Ford and second guitarist/vocalist Joan Jett were originally part of this Kim Fowley all-girl teenage band. What was the name of the band?
3. Who was the guitarist for the 1982 Kiss album CREATURES OF THE NIGHT?
4. Which easily amused and excitable member of Motley Crue is now the husband of actress Heather Locklear of "T.J. Hooker" and "Firestarter" fame?
5. By what professional name does Frank Carlton Sterafino Ferrano go by? (Hint: He's a member of Motley Crue.)
6. Before the formation of Megadeth, which group was lead singer Dave Mustaine a part of?
7. Before joining Whitesnake, David Coverdale replaced Ian Gillan as the lead singer in which group?
8. What was the name of the band in which Carmine Appice and bassist Tim Bogert played before their stints in Vanilla Fudge and Beck, Bogert & Appice?
9. Name the band in which Blackie Lawless performed before joining W.A.S.P.
10. Who was the drummer for the Michigan-based band The Iguanas in 1964?
11. The Swiss thrash band Hellhammer eventually evolved into a group with another name. Name the later group.
12. This group's first single was "Stick To Your Guns" b/w "Toast Of The Town." Name the group.
13. Besides haircut styles and a fondness for Misfits t-shirts, what do the groups Metallica, Exodus, Testament and Death Angel have in common?
14. Name the country superstar who released his tribute to Kiss—"Hard Luck Woman"—in July 1994.
15. The single "St. Valentine's Day Massacre" features two English metal bands performing together. Name the bands.
16. Known primarily as the bassist of this famous group, his first solo album was called SMASH YOUR HEAD AGAINST THE WALL. Name the performer and the group.
17. They jokingly refer to themselves as lesbian dopeheads on mopeds. What's the real name of their group?
18. What is Ozzy Osbourne's manager's name?
19. Can you name the release—song and group—regarded as the first Heavy Metal single?
20. Name the guitarist on Ozzy Osbourne's album THE ULTIMATE SIN.

Editor's Note: Metal trivia by Chris Elrod and John D. "Treis" Williams.

Metallica

In addition to two other LPs, this group's namesake album was also a Top 40 Heavy Metal hit in 1994.

Motorhead
Only one Top 40 album, but a very popular metal band despite its lack of top-of-the-chart successes.

JUDAS PRIEST
PAINKILLER - 1990
KINGDOM COME
KINGDOM COME - 1988
KISS
ALIVE - 1975
ALIVE II - 1977
DESTROYER - 1976
DYNASTY - 1979
LOVE GUN - 1977
LED ZEPPELIN
CODA - 1982
HOUSES OF THE HOLY - 1973
IN THROUGH THE DOOR - 1979
LED ZEPPELIN - 1969
LED ZEPPELIN II - 1969
LED ZEPPELIN III - 1970
LED ZEPPELIN IV - 1971
PHYSICAL GRAFFITI - 1987
PRESENCE - 1976
MEGADETH
SO FAR SO GOOD - 1988
METALLICA
AND JUSTICE FOR ALL - 1988
MASTER OF PUPPETS - 1986
METALLICA - 1994
MOTLEY CRUE
DECADE OF DECADENCE - 1991
GIRLS GIRLS GIRLS - 1987
MOTLEY CRUE - 1994
SHOUT AT THE DEVIL - 1983
THEATRE OF PAIN - 1985
TOO FAST FOR LOVE - 1982

MOTORHEAD
NO REMORSE - 1982
NIRVANA
IN UTERO - 1994
NEVERMIND - 1991
TED NUGENT
GREAT GONZOS (Best of) - 1981
OZZY OSBOURNE
BARK AT THE MOON - 1983
DIARY OF A MADMAN - 1981
NO MORE TEARS - 1993
NO REST FOR THE WICKED - 1988
SPEAK TO THE DEVIL - 1982
TRIBUTE - 1987
ULTIMATE SIN - 1986
PANTERA
FAR BEYOND DRIVEN - 1994
PEARL JAM
TEN - 1993
VS. - 1994
POISON
FLESH & BLOOD - 1991
LOOK WHAT THE CAT DRAGGED IN - 1987
OPEN UP & SAY, AHH! - 1988
QUEENSRYCHE
EMPIRE - 1991
QUIET RIOT
CONDITION CRITICAL - 1984
METAL HEALTH - 1983
SCORPIONS
BLACKOUT - 1984
LOVE AT FIRST STING - 1984
SAVAGE AMUSEMENT - 1988

WORLDWIDE - 1985

SKID ROW
SKID ROW - 1989
SLAVE TO THE GRIND - 1991

SLAUGHTER
STICK IT TO YA - 1990
WILD LIFE - 1992

SMASHING PUMPKINS
SIAMESE DREAM - 1994

PAUL STANLEY
PAUL STANLEY - 1978

STONE TEMPLE PILOTS
PURPLE - 1994

STRYPER
IN GOD WE TRUST - 1988
TO HELL WITH THE DEVIL - 1986

TESLA
GREAT RADIO CONTROVERSY - 1992

TWISTED SISTER
BIG HITS & NASTY CUTS - 1992

UGLY KID JOE
AMERICAS LEAST WANTED - 1993

URIAH HEEP
DEMONS & WIZARDS - 1972
URIAH HEEP LIVE - 1973

VAN HALEN
DIVER DOWN - 1982
FAIR WARNING - 1981
5150 - 1986
1984 - 1984
OU812 - 1988
VAN HALEN - 1976
VAN HALEN II - 1979
WOMEN AND CHILDREN FIRST - 1980

WARRANT
DIRTY ROTTEN FILTHY STINKING RICH - 1989

WHITESNAKE
BEST OF - 1994
SLIDE IT IN - 1984
SLIP OF THE TONGUE - 1989
WHITESNAKE - 1987

Editor's Note: Alphabetical; not ranked. Derived from the *Billboard* Top 200 LP chart. Albums had to reach #40 or higher to make this list, resulting in few albums for otherwise very popular metal groups such as Motorhead and Judas Priest.

Groups like Aerosmith, Rush, etc., regarded as essentially Hard Rock, are not included in this list.

Research by Chris Elrod.

Proud Father's Note: Chris was born Feb. 15, 1972. "Let's Stay Together" by Al Green was #1. The war in Viet Nam was coming to an end, Nixon was president, the "hippy" years were giving way to more conservative, conventional ways. Baby Boomers were growing up and starting families.

Chris has been an inspiration to his Dad in preparing this book. He's proofread behind me, and many a night we've worked till sunrise. He's had his wild ways, which have included a preoccupation with the lifestyle surrounding Heavy Metal music—drugs, violence, and Satanic verse.

A year ago Chris made the decision, on his own, to become a Christian. His knowledge of Heavy Metal music has borne the fruit of this section of the book. For once I don't worry about him any more; the music—other than Stryper (Christian Metal)—and the lifestyle have become part of his past.

CHRIS ELROD
"For those young people reading these particular pages,
drugs and alcohol are not the answers to life.
Put faith in the Creator that gave you life.
It'll change you forever."

Billboard Top 20 New Age Albums, 1989-1993

TOP 20 NEW AGE ALBUMS OF 1989

POS.	TITLE - ARTIST - LABEL
1.	CRISTOFORI'S DREAM - David Lanz - Narada
2.	DEEP BREAKFAST - Ray Lynch - Music West
3.	DANCING WITH THE LION - Andreas Vollenweider - Columbia
4.	WATERMARK - Enya - Geffen
5.	WINDHAM HILL SAMPLER '89 - Various Artists - Windham Hill
6.	NO BLUE THING - Ray Lynch - Music West
7.	CHAMELEON DAYS - Yanni - Private Music
8.	OPTICAL RACE - Tangerine Dream - Private Music
9.	DOLPHIN SMILES - Steven Kindler & Teja Bell - Global Pacific
10.	ISLAND - David Arkenstone - Narada Equinox
11.	THE NARADA COLLECTION TWO - Narada Artists - Narada
12.	DECEMBER - George Winston - Windham Hill
13.	THE NARADA COLLECTION - Narada Artists - Narada
14.	WORLD DANCE - DO'AH - Global Pacific
15.	RIVERS GONNA RISE - Patrick O'Hearn - Private Music
16.	PASSION - Peter Gabriel - Geffen
17.	NEVERLAND - Suzanne Ciani - Private Music
18.	A WINTER'S SOLSTICE, VOL. II - Windham Hill Artists - Windham Hill
19.	A JOURNEY HOME - Georgia Kelly with Dusan Dogdanovich - Global Pacific
20.	WINTER INTO SPRING - George Winston - Windham Hill

TOP 20 NEW AGE ALBUMS OF 1990

POS.	TITLE - ARTIST - LABEL
1.	NO BLUE THING - Ray Lynch - Music West
2.	DANCING WITH THE LION - Andreas Vollenweider - Columbia
3.	YELLOWSTONE: THE MUSIC OF NATURE - Mannheim Steamroller - American Gramophone
4.	CRISTOFORI'S DREAM - David Lanz - Narada
5.	NOUVEAU FLAMENCO - Ottmar Liebert - Higher Octave
6.	REFLECTIONS OF PASSION - Yanni - Private Music
7.	CITIZEN OF TIME - David Arkenstone - Narada
8.	KOJIKI - Kitaro - Geffen
9.	WATERMARK - Enya - Geffen
10.	NIKI NANA - Yanni - Private Music
11.	DEEP BREAKFAST - Ray Lynch - Music West
12.	EL DORADO - Patrick O'Hearn - Private Music
13.	ACROSS A RAINBOW SEA - Steven Kindler - Global Pacific
14.	GARDEN CITY - John Tesh - Cypress
15.	FOREVER BLUE SKY - Bruce Becvar - Shining Star
16.	THE NARADA COLLECTION TWO - Narada Artists - Narada
17.	THE ODD GET EVEN - Shadowfax - Private Music
18.	WINDHAM HILL SAMPLER '89 - Various Artists - Windham Hill
19.	THEMES - Vangelis - Polydor
20.	DECEMBER - George Winston - Windham Hill

TOP 20 NEW AGE ALBUMS OF 1991

POS.	TITLE - ARTIST - LABEL
1.	REFLECTIONS OF PASSION - Yanni - Private Music
2.	NOUVEAU FLAMENCO - Ottmar Liebert - Higher Octave
3.	SKYLINE FIREDANCE - David Lanz - Narada
4.	AT THE EDGE - Mickey Hart - Ryko
5.	FRESH AIRE 7 - Mannheim Steamroller - American Gramophone
6.	IN THE WAKE OF THE WIND - David Arkenstone - Narada
7.	THE NARADA WILDERNESS COLLECTION - Various Artists - Narada
8.	BORRASCA - Ottmar Liebert - Higher Octave
9.	BLUES FROM THE RAIN FOREST - Merl Saunders - Sumerlone
10.	THE CITY - Vangelis - Atlantic
11.	TAPROOT - Michael Hedges - Windham Hill
12.	STRATA - Robert Rich & Steve Roach - Hearts of Space
13.	SHELL GAME - Don Harriss - Sonic Atmospheres
14.	NARADA COLLECTION THREE - Various Artists - Narada
15.	DISTANT FIELDS - Gary Lamb - Golden Gate
16.	WINDHAM HILL: THE FIRST TEN YEARS - Various Artists - Windham Hill
17.	WATERMARK - Enya - Geffen
18.	THE PIPER'S RHYTHM - Spencer Brewer - Narada
19.	DESERT MOON SONG - Dean Evenson - Soundings of the Planet
20.	LIVE IN AMERICA - Kitaro - Geffen

TOP 20 NEW AGE ALBUMS OF 1992

POS.	TITLE - ARTIST - LABEL
1.	SHEPHERD MOONS - Enya - Reprise
2.	SUMMER - George Winston - Windham Hill
3.	SOLO PARA TI - Ottmar Liebert & Luna Negra - Epic

David Lanz
``Skyline Firedance'' was the #3 New Age album in 1991.

Ottmar Liebert

Liebert's sensational 1991 hit ``Nouveau Flamenco'' (#2) continues to be one of the best-selling New Age LPs.

4. RETURN TO THE HEART - David Lanz - Narada
5. WATERMARK - Enya - Geffen
6. DARE TO DREAM - Yanni - Private Music
7. BORRASCA - Ottmar Liebert - Higher Octave
8. ROCKOON - Tangerine Dream - Miramar
9. NOUVEAU FLAMENCO - Ottmar Liebert - Higher Octave
10. BOOK OF ROSES - Andreas Vollenweider - Columbia
11. THE VISIT - Loreena McKennitt - Warner Bros.
12. YONNONDIO - Peter Buffett - Narada
13. IN CELEBRATION OF LIFE - Yanni - Private Music
14. DREAM - Kitaro - Geffen
15. A CHILDHOOD REMEMBERED - Various Artists - Narada
16. CANYON DREAMS - Tangerine Dream - Miramar
17. THE SPIRIT OF OLYMPIA - David Arkenstone / Kostia - Narada
18. INDIGO - Patrick O'Hearn - Private Nusic
19. AUTUMN DREAMS - Danny Wright - Nichols-Wright
20. REFLECTIONS OF PASSION - Yanni - Private Music

TOP 20 NEW AGE ALBUMS OF 1993

POS. TITLE - ARTIST - LABEL
1. SHEPHERD MOONS - Enya - Reprise
2. WATERMARK - Enya - Geffen
3. IN MY TIME - Yanni - Private Music
4. SOLO PARA TI - Ottmar Liebert & Luna Negra - Epic
5. MRS. CROWE'S BLUE WALTZ - Adrian Legg - Relativity
6. THE VISIT - Loreena McKennitt - Warner Bros.

7. CURTAIN CALL - Danny Wright - Moulin D'Or
8. NARADA DECADE - Various Artists - Narada
9. MY FOOLISH HEART - Liz Story - Windham Hill
10. NOUVEAU FLAMENCO - Ottmar Liebert - Higher Octave
11. ACOUSTIC HIGHWAY - Craig Chaquico - Higher Octave
12. CELTIC ODYSSEY - Various Artists - Narada
13. TUBULAR BELLS - Mike Oldfield - Reprise
14. THE LONDON CONCERT - Christopher Franke - Varese Sarabande
15. THE IMPRESSIONISTS: A WINDHAM HILL SAMPLER - Various Artists - Windham Hill
16. HOURS BETWEEN NIGHT AND DAY - Ottmar Liebert & Luna Negra - Epic
17. SUMMER - George Winston - Windham Hill
18. ROMANCE - Chip Davis - American Gramophone
19. CUSCO 2000 - Cusco - Higher Octave
20. MONTEREY NIGHTS - John Tesh - GTS

Billboard Top 25 Soundtracks & Original Cast Albums

1. WEST SIDE STORY
2. SOUTH PACIFIC
3. SATURDAY NIGHT FEVER
4.* PURPLE RAIN (Prince)
    THE BODYGUARD
5. BLUE HAWAII (Elvis Presley)
6. DIRTY DANCING
7. LOVE ME OR LEAVE ME (Doris Day)
8. THE SOUND OF MUSIC (Original cast)
9. MY FAIR LADY (Original cast)
10. MARY POPPINS
11. EXODUS
12. A HARD DAY'S NIGHT (The Beatles)
13. HAIR (Original cast)
14. THE MUSIC MAN (Original cast)
15. BREAKFAST AT TIFFANY'S (Henry Mancini)
16. GREASE
17. MIAMI VICE (TV soundtrack)
18. AROUND THE WORLD IN 80 DAYS
19. GIGI
20. MUSIC FROM PETER GUNN (TV soundtrack)
21. G.I. BLUES (Elvis Presley)
22. FOOTLOOSE
23. LOVING YOU (Elvis Presley)
24. THE GRADUATE (Simon & Garfunkel)
25. HELP (The Beatles)
    *Tie.

Miscellaneous Trivia Quiz #2

1. Johnny Ace of "Pledging My Love" fame died Christmas Eve 1954 after playing what deadly game?
2. RCA wouldn't release this Elvis song, so another young man got very lucky and took it to the top of the charts. Name the singer and the song.
3. Name country music's all-time #1 performer.
4. This English lad of thirteen had his only Gold Record hit spiritual in 1958. Who is he?
5. Who is Harold Jenkins?
6. Herbert Khaury sang a novelty song about a spring flower. What was Herbert's stage name?
7. What is the best selling rock record of all time?
8. Who had a hit with "The Twist" before Chubby Checker?
9. Name the album with the longest run on the charts.
10. The second longest run on the album charts belongs to what LP?
11. Name the longest-running country album.
12. This group started out as The Juvenairs. What did they become?
13. Her grandfather thought she was such an active youngster that he nicknamed her after a mosquito. Who is she?
14. What song holds the record for the most weeks on the rock charts?
15. The most weeks on all charts?
16. The Gladiolas on Excello Records had a very minor hit with a song that became The Diamonds' biggest hit. Can you name the song and the lead singer of The Gladiolas?
17. Who are The Rinky Dinks?
18. Name the performer with the most Top 40 "cover" hits.
19. This country artist actually served time in San Quentin prison. Who is he?
20. Mickey Dolenz appeared in this fifties TV show, and resurfaced in "The Monkees" in the late sixties. What was Mickey's first series called?
21. What populat TV game show host had a big hit with a song called "Deck of Cards"? (Hint: he was a Memphis disc jockey in the late fifties, one of the first to play Elvis' first recordings.)
22. Who is the all-time Grammy winner?
23. Who is the Rev. Richard Penniman?
24. Johnny Dee is actually a more famous songwriter than singer. What's Johnny's real name?
25. How old was Brenda Lee when she recorded her first hit single?
26. Before hitting the Big Time, this singer was part of the Chad Mitchell Trio. Can you name him?
27. This country superstar was once a member of the Pozo-Seco Singers. Know his name?
28. This superstar was once a New Christy Minstrel. Name him.
29. If country singer Norma Jean had not called it quits, this superstar might not have made her mark. Who is she?
30. Who are regarded as "The King" and "The Queen" of country music?
31. Peter Best once played drums in this group. Name them.
32. This star of the TV series "The Real McCoys" also had a successful recording career. Can you name him?
33. Chuck Connor's "The Rifleman" series also shared its cast credits with a recording artist. Who is he?
34. Actress/singer Annette once had a job that required her to wear big ears? What did she do?
35. Who is America's #1 disco star?
36. Who is Len Slye?
37. Who was Dick Weston?
38. Who is Sarah Ophelia Colley?
39. Mickey Gilley and Rev. Jimmy Swaggart have an equally famous cousin. Name him.
40. "The Ballad Of Davy Crockett" was a monster hit for this singer, who went on to become a popular actor on the TV daytime soap "Days Of Our Lives." Can you name him?
41. Which Everly Brothers' song was banned from broadcast by some radio stations for having

suggestive lyrics?

42. Paul Wynn released this novelty tune in 1946, but had to wait until 1975 before it became a hit. What was its title, and under what stage name did he sing it?

43. George Jones released his first "rock" record under a different name. What did he call himself?

44. Who created The Henhouse Five Plus Two?

45. Can you give the real name of "Orion," an Elvis sound-alike?

46. Who replaced Sam Cooke as lead singer of The Soul Stirrers?

47. Black music's all-time #1 singer is?

48. He called his music "Western Bop." Who was he?

49. Other than "Your Hit Parade," on what other series did Gisele MacKenzie appear?

50. Audrey Brown had a huge hit about "wind." What name did she record under?

51. What was the first theme song of the TV show "Happy Days"?

52. Who is considered the "Father of Rock and Roll"?

53. What country superstar played baseball for the St. Louis Cardinals?

54. What duo is known as the "Sweethearts of the Blues"?

55. Ross Bagdasarian came up with the idea of recording human voices, and then speeding up the playback and re-recording it. He released the records under what name?

56. Name the group that started out as The Primettes?

57. Who was the original lead vocalist of The Tokens, of "Lion Sleeps Tonight" fame?

58. Give the real names of the duo who first called themselves Tom & Jerry.

59. Two superstar groups developed out of a group called The Mugwumps? Name the groups.

60. The Golliwogs became what superstar group?

61. Reginald Dwight is this English superstar's real name. Who is he?

62. Name the country superstar who started out as a backup guitarist for Tennessee Ernie Ford, Sonny James, and Tommy Sands.

63. Where, of all places, was Jewish country star Kinky Friedman born?

64. Name the group in which Glen Campbell started his career.

65. This female songstress was first a member of a group called The Stone Poneys. Who is she? (Hint: She's gone all the way from rock-and-roll to "torch" songs to singing in Spanish.)

66. On what cartoon character did The Royal Guardsmen depend for much of their chart success?

67. Name the recording artist played the Pete Nolan character on the TV series "Rawhide."

68. What country singer sacrificed his own recording contract to further his songwriting career?

69. Who was known as "The Hillbilly Shakespeare"?

70. This tall, lanky Kentuckian first recorded for Oak Records, where his first album was a flop. The album was later released by Reprise, and he's now a country suoerstar. Who is he?

71. Songwriter Sylvia Dee wrote "Too Young" for Nat King Cole in 1951. In 1961, Sylvia presented Skeeter Davis with a song which had taken forty years to complete. What was the song?

72. What was the real name of "Bill Parsons" of "All American Boy" fame?

73. Who is known as "The Polish Prince"?

74. This Columbia, South Carolina, native's biggest hit was a "sultry" Christmas song released in 1953. Who is she?

75. Rick Derringer was also a lead singer for what group?

76. "The Fat Man" was this singer's first big hit, resulting in his nickname. Who is he?

77. Name the most popular singing group of the fifties.

78. Two major rock stars have the distinction of having never appeared on "American Bandstand." One is Elvis Presley. Who is the other (of "Be Bop Baby" fame)?

79. Roy Orbison's guitar player in the early sixties became a recording star in his own right. Who is he?

80. This bluegrass duo created the theme song for the TV series "The Beverly Hillbillies." Name them.
81. This country superstar started as a bass guitarist for Ray Price. Who is he?
82. Name the country music legend who is still with us because he gave up his seat on a small plane to The Big Bopper, who, with Buddy Holly and Richie Valens, died when the plane crashed.
83. This folk singer worked as a writer for the Communist *Daily Worker*, but his most favorite composition is sung across America in schools, political rallies, and even churches. Name the singer and the song.
84. This classical folk recording artist, once a pro football player, played "Big Daddy" on the silver screen. Can you name him?
85. At age four, Jimmie Loden won a talent contest. Legend has it that Kate Smith was in the audience, gave him a silver dollar, and predicted a great career for him. A country superstar, what name do we know him by?
86. When he first started making records, he was driving a truck for $35 a week. Name him.
87. When this supergroup went broke, Johnny Cash made them a loan and Paul Simon used them as backup on his smash hit "Slip Sliding Away." The rest is history. (Hint: The Lord works in mysterious ways.)
88. The son of a conservative Protestant minister, he became one of the leading exponents of "shock rock." Who is he?
89. Who was once Tommy Scott, "The Twisting Vocalist"?
90. This performer was affectionately known as "Pearl." Who was she?
91. This Oxford University graduate is the author of two (unpublished) novels. His biggest record was a self-penned gospel song which hit #1 country and stayed on the pop charts for 38 weeks. Who is he?
92. What group was a "spinoff" of Joey Dee's band, The Starlighters?
93. This group got its name from a box of tissues. Who are they?
94. Led Zeppelin emerged from what rock group?
95. Name the first successful Heavy Metal rock band.
96. Singer Johnny Cymbal had a 1968 hit under another name. What was the name and what was the hit?
97. This folk singer started out as a classical pianist. Who is she?
98. He was once the lead vocalist of a band called "The System." Who is he?
99. What group was once known as The Buffalo Chips?
100. This singer, turned down by countless record companies, wrote a lengthy chronicle of sixties rock music history that went on to become one of the biggest songs of the sixties. Name him.

Hits in Special Categories

The History of "Carolina Beach Music"
by Marion Carter

Since time began man has felt a strange attraction to the open sea. By means of the oceans, he's traveled and explored, spreading his ideas and skills around the globe. The sea has also provided mankind with food in abundance. More recently in man's history, it has also provided entertainment—an outlet for enjoyment and recreation. The ocean beach is a wonderful world of sunshine, sand, and surf, one that gives rise to its own lifestyle and music. Many still call such music "rhythm-and-blues" or "rock-and-roll." In the South, though—particularly the Carolinas—the music you listen and dance to at the beach is generally called "Beach Music" (or, as in South Carolina, "Shag Music").

How *did* southern beach music come into being?

The southern beach generation began to explode in the fifties. The reasons were fairly simple: this was the first post-war generation of youth that had the time and the money to spend on leisure at the seashore—and spend they did. Unlike northern beach-goers, who would drive to the beach for a day, southerners saved up their money in order to go to the beach for several days, a week, or in some cases even the entire summer. When these people began to invade the shorefront, they brought with them a whole new social order complete with its own language, dress, and music.

Oddly enough, what was being played on jukeboxes at the beach wasn't the current string of radio hits of the time, but the forbidden fruit of rhythm-and-blues—music that best suited the happy, carefree mood of the shore, by and large music to dance to. But why was this music the choice of southerners more than beach-goers in other parts of the country? Mainly because most of the rhythm-and-blues acts of the early fifties grew up and performed in the South; their music was Southern in origin. It had strong gospel roots, and it was the music of the working class. Music the audience could relate to, in word and melody. And the undercurrent for it all was rhythm—dancing rhythm.

The earliest hits at the beach were just that: beach hits. Few radio stations would play them; in fact, they could generally be described as the underground sounds of the era because about the only place they could be heard were on personal phonographs or on the jukeboxes at beach pavillions. There were a couple of reasons for this. There wasn't really a widely developed broadcast

Billy Ward & The Dominoes
``Sixty Minute Man'' is the all-time #1 Beach Music favorite.

outlet for these tunes, many of which were branded as being of Negro origin—"race" music. In addition, the bawdy lyrical content of many of the records kept them off the radio altogether. "Work With Me Baby" and "Big Ten Inch"—what's going on here? Mild nowadays, but in 1954? And so it was in those early years.

But what about beach music today?

The tag "Beach Music" only came into general use only around 1964 or 1965, when the somewhat seasonal and shorebound nature of the phenomenon was found to be rather widespread after all. You'll discover that it is truly not only a particular sound, but an idiom, a particular lifestyle that defines "Beach Music" these days. Since the early years, the beach scene has gone through countless permutations in style and substance, incorporating virtually every type of music imaginable. So much so, in fact, that, in the Carolinas, songs are categorized as either beach or shag songs.

All "shag" songs must have an accompanying beat which accomodates the South Carolina state dance, the

"Shag." Many "Beach Music" songs also employ this particular beat and rhythm, but not necessarily all. "Beach Music" songs are still more identified with their true r&b roots and project a certain aura that is hard to pin down. Only through repeated listenings do you begin to develop a feel for what makes a classic "beach" tune. Whatever the case, the Carolina music movement—like California "surf" genre before it—has grown from its infancy in the late forties into a force to be reckoned with on the national and even international music scenes.

Marion Carter (Repete Records)

The Drifters
What true Beach Music fan can remember a summer without hearing "Under The Boardwalk"?

Top 40 Beach Music Songs

1. SIXTY MINUTE MAN - Dominoes
2. MS. GRACE - Tymes
3. GREEN EYES - Ravens
4. NIP SIP - Clovers
5. MY GIRL - Temptations
6. UNDER THE BOARDWALK - Drifters
7. THANK YOU JOHN - Willie Tee
8. (YOU'RE MORE THAN A NUMBER IN MY) LITTLE RED BOOK - Drifters
9. STAY - Maurice Williams
10. WITH THIS RING - Platters
11. BRENDA - O.C. Smith
12. ONE MINT JULEP - Clovers
13. COOL ME OUT - Lamont Dozier
14. HELLO STRANGER - Barbara Lewis
15. 39-21-46 - Showmen
16. SUMMERTIME'S CALLING ME - Catalinas
17. FAT BOY - Billy Stewart
18. PARTY TIME MAN - Futures
19. IT STARTED WITH A KISS - Hot Chocolate
20. I LOVE YOU 1000 TIMES - Platters
21. WORK WITH ME ANNIE - Midnighters
22. I'M JUST THINKING ABOUT (COOLIN' IT) - Jerry Butler
23. LADY SOUL - Temptations
24. A QUIET PLACE - Garnett Mimms
25. RAINY DAY BELLS - Globetrotters
26. BE YOUNG, BE FOOLISH, BE HAPPY - Tams
27. I LOVE BEACH MUSIC - Embers
28. CAROLINA GIRLS - Chairmen of the Board
29. ZING! WENT THE STRINGS OF MY HEART - Coasters
30. I'VE GOT SAND IN MY SHOES - Drifters
31. BABY I NEED YOUR LOVING - Four Tops
32. HIGHER AND HIGHER - Jackie Wilson
33. AIN'T NO BIG THING - Radiants
34. MEET ME WITH YOUR BLACK DRAWERS ON - Gloria Hardiman
35. I DO LOVE YOU - Billy Stewart
36. HEY BABY - Bruce Channel
37. GIVE ME JUST A LITTLE MORE TIME - Chairmen of the Board
38. WHITE CLIFFS OF DOVER - Checkers
39. GOIN' BACK TO LOUISIANA - Delbert McClinton
40. I JUST CAN'T GET YOU OUT OF MY MIND - Four Tops

Editor's Note: The Top 40 of all time, compiled from a survey of dj's, radio stations, record shop owners and customers, collectors and beach music dancers themselves. Courtesy of the Wax Museum, 1505 Elizabeth Ave., Charlotte, NC 28204.

Top Shag Music Songs

1. BE WITH THE ONE YOU LOVE - Dramatics
2. BEAUTICIAN BLUES - B.B. King
3. BLUES IS ALRIGHT - Little Milton
4. BOOGIE THE JOINT - Buddy Skipper
5. BOOGIE WOOGIE KING - Jimmy Liggins
6. BOP - Dan Seals
7. BUT IT'S ALRIGHT - J.J. Jackson
8. CAN WE SLIP AWAY AGAIN? - Clarence Carter
9. CLUB SAVOY - Rockin' Louie
10. COLD WOMAN - Big Twist & Mellow Fellows
11. COWBOYS TO GIRLS - Philly Cream
12. DARLENE - Big Al Downing
13. DO IT - Delbert McClinton
14. DO YOU BELIEVE IN LOVE AT FIRST SIGHT - Dionne Warwick
15. DOCTOR'S ORDERS - Carol Douglas
16. DR. CC - Clarence Carter
17. FANNY MAE - KoKo Taylor
18. FLAMIN' MAMIE - KoKo Taylor
19. FLIM FLAM MAN - Laura Mayo
20. GOIN' TO NEW ORLEANS - Rockin' Tabby
21. GONNA GET ALONG WITHOUT YOU - Viola Wills
22. GROOVY PEOPLE - Lou Rawls
23. GUNNING FOR LOVE - Controllers
24. HALLELUJAH I LOVE HER SO - Ray Charles
25. HEAVEN MUST BE MISSIN' AN ANGEL - Tavares
26. HEY THERE - Mills Brothers
27. HOLD BACK THE NIGHT - Trammps
28. I CRY JUST A LITTLE BIT - Shakin' Stevens
29. I HATE HATE - Razzy Bailey
30. IF IT DON'T FIT, DON'T FORCE IT - K. Patterson
31. IT STARTED WITH A KISS - Hot Chocolate
32. JAZZY LADY - Richard Fields
33. JIMMIE MACK - Sheena Easton
34. JIMMY LEE - Aretha Franklin
35. JOHNNY B. GOODE - Elton John
36. JUST A GIGOLO - David Lee Roth
37. JUST ONE STEP - Little Milton
38. KEEP YOUR PANTS ON - Denise LaSalle
39. KNOCKIN' ON YOUR DOOR - John Fogerty
40. L.O.D./LOVE REALLY HURTS WITHOUT YOU - Billy Ocean
41. LAST CALL FOR ALCOHOL - Moore/Dynamic Upsetters
42. LET ME TAKE YOU TO THE SUN - Delegation
43. LET'S GO SOMEWHERE AND MAKE LOVE - Jackie Moore
44. LOVE DON'T COME NO STRONGER - Jeff Perry
45. LOVE MAKES A WOMAN - Barbara Acklin
46. LUCKY CHARM - Stray Cats
47. MAN IN LOVE - Eric Clapton
48. MEMORY - Menage
49. MY BOY LOLLIPOP - Millie Small
50. MY EVER CHANGING MOODS - Style Council
51. NOBODY BUT YOU - Marcel Evans
52. OO EE BABY - Mojo Blues Band
53. POISON IVEY - Willie Mabon
54. PUT IT WHERE YOU WANT IT - Gary Bass
55. RED LIGHT - Linda Clifford
56. RESCUE ME - Fontella Bass
57. SEACRUISE - Mojo Blues Band
58. SHA LA LA - Al Green
59. SHE FELT SO GOOD - Jimmie McCracklin
60. SHOO DOO FU FU OOH - Lenny Williams
61. SHOULD I DO IT - Pointer Sisters
62. SICK AND TIRED - Lulu Reed
63. SING BABY SING - Stylistics
64. SOMEBODY'S EYES - Viola Wills
65. STEP BY STEP/COME GET DOWN - Joe Simon
66. STORMY WEATHER - Viola Wills
67. SUPER LOVE/SHE'S A MIRACLE - Exile
68. SUSPICIOUS MINDS - Candi Staton
69. TEN WAYS OF LOVING YOU - Lenny Williams
70. (THEY CALL IT) MR. DOLLAR'S - Bradford/Bell
71. THIS OLD HEART OF MINE - Isley Brothers
72. TOUCHING IN THE DARK - Walter Jackson
73. TRYIN' TO LIVE MY LIFE WITHOUT YOU - F. Henry
74. WELL-A-WIGGY - Weather Girls
75. WHAT YOU DO TO ME - Carl Wilson
76. WITHOUT YOU I CRY - Candi Staton
77. YOU ARE - Stylistics
78. YOU BRING OUT THE BOOGIE - Sonny Terry
79. YOU'RE THE REASON - Viola Wills

Editor's Note: The Shag is South Carolina's state dance; it can be danced to country, r&b, and rock 'n' roll. This list of "shaggable" music was compiled by Seaco Music, one of South Carolina's oldest record stores; alphabetical order, not ranked.

The Five Satins

Although it has charted on three different occasions and has reportedly sold millions of copies, The Five Satins' "Still" has never risen higher than #24 on the *Billboard* charts.

Top 10 Doo Wop Singles

1. IN THE STILL OF THE NIGHT
2. EARTH ANGEL
3. 16 CANDLES
4. I ONLY HAVE EYES FOR YOU
5. MY TRUE LOVE
6. DADDY'S HOME
7. TEN COMMANDMENTS OF LOVE
8. TEAR DROPS
9. A THOUSAND MILES AWAY
10. BEEN SO LONG

Bill Monroe
The father of Bluegrass music.

Flatt & Scruggs
Tunes by Bluegrass legends Lester Flatt and Earl Scruggs occupy three of the Top 5 positions.

Top 50 Bluegrass Singles

1	ROCKY TOP - Osborne Brothers	29.	MOLLY & TENBROOKS - Bill Monroe
2.	FOGGY MOUNTAIN BREAKDOWN - Flatt & Scruggs*	30.	HEAVEN - Flatt & Scruggs
3.	ORANGE BLOSSOM SPECIAL - Stanley Brothers	31.	I'LL STILL WRITE YOUR NAME IN THE SAND - Mac Wiseman
4.	ROLL IN MY SWEET BABY'S ARMS - Flatt & Scruggs	32.	I WOULDN'T CHANGE YOU IF I COULD - Jim Eanes
5.	SALTY DOG BLUES - Flatt & Scruggs	33.	GRAND OLE OPRY SONG - Jimmy Martin
6.	FOX ON THE RUN - Country Gentlemen	34.	DARK HOLLOW - Various Artists
7.	DUELING BANJOS - Eric Weissberg**	35.	I WONDER HOW THE OLD FOLKS ARE AT HOME - Mac Wiseman
8.	UNCLE PEN - Bill Monroe	36.	RUBY - Osborne Brothers
9.	LEGEND OF THE REBEL SOLDIER - Country Gentlemen	37.	LITTLE GEORGIA ROSE - Seldom Scene
10.	BLUE MOON OF KENTUCKY - Bill Monroe	38.	WILL YOU MISS ME - Ralph Stanley
11.	WHITE DOVE - Stanley Brothers	39.	A FACE IN THE CROWD - Larry Sparks
12.	MULESKINNER BLUES - Bill Monroe	40.	SPARKLING BROWN EYES - Joe Val
13.	BRINGING MARY HOME - Country Gentlemen	41.	SALLY GOODIN' - Various Artists
14.	SUNNY SIDE OF THE MOUNTAIN - Jimmy Martin	42.	LOVE COME HOME - Reno & Smiley
15.	RIDER - Seldom Scene	43.	HIT PARADE OF LOVE - Jimmy Martin
16.	WILDWOOD FLOWER - Carter Family	44.	CITY OF NEW ORLEANS - Seldom Scene
17.	DOING MY TIME - Flatt & Scruggs	45.	TENNESSEE - Jimmy Martin
18.	OLD HOME PLACE - J.D. Crowe	46.	KEEP ON THE SUNNY SIDE - Mac Wiseman
19.	RANK STRANGER - Stanley Brothers	47.	AIR MAIL SPECIAL - Jim & Jesse
20.	PARADISE - Seldom Scene	48.	SHUCKIN' THE CORN - Flatt & Scruggs
21.	CRIPPLE CREEK - Various Artists	49.	JERUSALEM RIDGE - Bill Monroe
22.	I KNOW YOU'RE MARRIED - Reno & Smiley	50.	FREEBORN MAN - Jimmy Martin
23.	SITTING ON TOP OF THE WORLD - Various Artists		*Editor's Note:* List compiled by Chet Rhodes (Manager, Record Depot Distributors) and Gary B. Reid (Rebel Records).
24.	LOVE OF THE MOUNTAINS - Larry Sparks		
25.	RAWHIDE - Bill Monroe		*From the movie "Bonnie & Clyde."
26.	TENNESSEE STUD - Doc Watson		**From the movie "Deliverance."
27.	LITTLE MAGGIE - Ralph Stanley		
28.	HOME SWEET HOME - Reno & Smiley		

Mac Wiseman
Three of Mac's recordings made the all-time Top 20 Bluegrass.

The Stanley Brothers
Need we say more than the words ``Orange Blossom Special''?

The Osborne Brothers ∨
The Osbornes boast the most popular Bluegrass tune of all time.

Jimmy Martin
Appropriate to this volume, Jimmy's five Top 20
Bluegrass songs include ``Hit Parade of Love.''

Top 10 Comedy Acts On Record

1950s & 1960s

1. STAN FREBERG
2. BROTHER DAVE GARDNER
3. MOMS MOBLEY
4. RUSTY WARREN
5. REDD FOXX
6. HOMER & JETHRO
7. ALLAN SHERMAN
8. THE BICKERSONS
9. JOSE JIMENEZ
10. DICKIE GOODMAN

1970s, 1980s & 1990s

1. EDDIE MURPHY
2. GEORGE CARLIN
3. FLIP WILSON
4. RICHARD PRYOR
5. RODNEY DANGERFIELD
6. SAM KINISON
7. BETTE MIDLER
8. ANDREW DICE CLAY
9. LEWIS GRIZZARD
10. SMOTHERS BROTHERS

Top 100 Instrumental Hits

1. CHERRY PINK & APPLE BLOSSOM WHITE - Perez Prado
2. THEME FROM A SUMMER PLACE - Henry Mancini
3. POOR PEOPLE OF PARIS - Les Baxter
4. LOVE IS BLUE - Paul Mauriat
5. AUTUMN LEAVES - Roger Williams
6. CRAZY OTTO MEDLEY - Johnny Maddox
7.* A FIFTH OF BEETHOVEN - Walter Murphy
   CANADIAN SUNSET - Hugo Winterhalter
8. PATRICIA - Perez Prado
9. TEQUILA - Champs
10. LOVE'S THEME - Love Unlimited Orchestra
11.* RISE - Herb Alpert
    FRANKENSTEIN - Edgar Winter Group
12. TSOP - MFSB
13. CALCUTTA - Lawrence Welk
14. THEME FROM ROCKY - Bill Conti
15. THEME FROM STAR WARS - Meco
16. FLY ROBIN FLY - Silver Convention
17. PICK UP THE PIECES - Average White Band
18. THE HUSTLE - Van McCoy
19. THEME FROM ROMEO AND JULIET - Henry Mancini
20. GRAZING IN THE GRASS - Hugh Masakela
21. ALSO SPRACH ZARATHUSTRA (2001) - Deodato
22. MUSIC BOX DANCER - Frank Mills
23. GREEN ONIONS - Booker T. & The M.G.'s
24. SCORPIO - Dennis Coffey
25. THE HORSE - Cliff Nobles & Co.
26. STRANGER ON THE SHORE - Mr. Acker Bilk
27. MOONGLOW AND THEME FROM PICNIC - Morris Stoloff
28. LISBON ANTIGUA - Nelson Riddle
29. WONDERLAND BY NIGHT - Bert Kaempfert
30. TELSTAR - Tornados
31. CHARIOTS OF FIRE - Vangelis
32. HAPPY ORGAN - Dave "Baby" Cortez
33. SLEEP WALK - Santo & Johnny
34. THEME FROM S.W.A.T. - Rhythm Heritage
35. MELODY OF LOVE - Billy Vaughn
36. HONKY TONK - Bill Doggett
37. WIPE OUT - Surfaris **
38. EXODUS - Ferrante & Teicher
39. LAST DATE - Floyd Cramer
40. RAUNCHY - Bill Justis
41. WALK DPN'T RUN - Ventures
42. THE GOOD, THE BAD, AND THE UGLY - Hugo Montenegro
43. OUTA SPACE - Billy Preston
44. APACHE - Jordan Ingmann
45. CLASSICAL GAS - Mason Williams
46. DUELING BANJOS - Eric Weisberg
47. WASHINGTON SQUARE - Village Stompers
48. MIDNIGHT IN MOSCOW - Kenny Ball
49. TOPSY II - Cozy Cole
50. WHEELS - String Alongs
51. THE ENTERTAINER - Marvin Hamblish
52. SOULFUL STRUT - Young Holt Unlimited
53. NO MATTER WHAT SHAPE (YOUR STOMACH'S IN) - T. Bones +
54. OUT OF LIMITS - Marketts
55. MOONGLOW AND THEME FROM PICNIC - George Gates
56. FEELS SO GOOD - Chuck Mangione
57. IN THE MOOD - Ernie Fields
58. JAVA - Al Hirt
59. SPACE RIDE - Billy Preston
60. QUIET VILLAGE - Martin Denny
61. BECAUSE THEY'RE YOUNG - Duane Eddy
62. RAUNCHY - Ernie Freeman
63. TEEN BEAT - Sandy Nelson
64. ON THE REBOUND - Floyd Cramer
65. PIPELINE - Chantays
66. HAWAII FIVE-O - Ventures
67. SAIL ALONG SILVERY MOON - Billy Vaughn
68. RED RIVER ROCK - Johnny & The Hurricanes
69. THE IN CROWD - Ramsey Lewis
70. GUITAR BOOGIE SHUFFLE - Virtues
71. MEMPHIS - Lonnie Mack
72. THE HAPPY WHISTER - Don Robertson
73. REBEL ROUSER - Duane Eddy ++
74. LONELY BULL - Herb Alpert & The Tijuana Brass
75. MARIA ELENA - Los Indios Trabajaros
76. JOY - Apollo 100
77. TIME IS TIGHT - Booker T. & The M.G.'s
78. SHIFTING WHISPERING SANDS - Billy Vaughn
79. A TASTE OF HONEY - Herb Alpert & The Tijuana Brass
80. LET THERE BE DRUMS - Sandy Nelson
81. TUBULAR BELLS - Mike Oldfield
82. ROCK & ROLL PART 2 - Gary Glitter
83. MELODY OF LOVE - David Carroll
84. NADIA'S THEME - Barry DeVorzon & Perry Boykin
85. PETER GUNN - Ray Anthony
86. THEME FROM A THREE PENNY OPERA - Dick Hyman Trio
87. WILD WEEKEND - Rebels
88. ASIA MINOR - Kokomo @
89. ONE MINT JULEP - Ray Charles
90. TONIGHT - Ferrante & Teicher
91. WALK DON'T RUN '64 - Ventures
92. POPCORN - Hot Butter
93. FORTY MILES OF BAD ROAD - Duane Eddy
94. WHITE SILVER SANDS - Bill Black's Combo @@
95. HANG 'EM HIGH - Booker T. & The M.G.'s
96. HOCUS POCUS - Focus
97. THEME FROM "THE APARTMENT" - Ferrante & Teicher

Duane Eddy

Music's all-time instrumental hitmaker.

98. MANHATTAN SPIRITUAL - Reg Owen
99. HOOKED ON CLASSICS - Royal Philharmonic Orchestra
100. MIDNIGHT COWBOY - Ferrante & Teiche101.
101. CAST YOUR FATE TO THE WIND - Sounds Orchestral
102. NEAR YOU - Roger Williams
103. DYNOMITE PT. 1 - Bazuka
104. ROCKFORD FILES - Mike Post
105. HILL STREET BLUES - Mike Post
106. RINKY DINK - Dave "Baby" Cortez
107. PERCOLATOR TWIST - Billy Joe & Checkmates
108. THEME FROM "STAR WARS" - John Williams
109. WATERMELON MAN - Manto Santemaria
110. SHISH KEBAB - Ralph Marterie
111. SOFT SUMMER BREEZE - Eddie Heywood
112. DO IT ANY WAY YOU WANNA - People's Choice
113. THEME FROM "A THREE PENNY OPERA" - Richard Hayman & Jan August
114. RED ROSES FOR A BLUE LADY - Bert Kaempfert
115. DON'T BE CRUEL - Bill Black's Combo
116. AMAZING GRACE - Royal Scots Dragoon Guards
117. MERCY, MERCY, MERCY - Cannonball Adderley
118. ZORBA THE GREEK - Herb Alpert & The Tijuana Brass
119. HANG ON SLOOPY - Ramsey Lewis Trio
120. AROUND THE WORLD IN 80 DAYS - Mantovani
121. DANCE WITH THE GUITAR MAN - Duane Eddy
122. A WALK IN THE BLACK FOREST - Horst Jankowski

Editor's Note: All songs listed peaked between #1 and #12. Number 123 on the list would be "Around The World In 80 Days" by Victor Young, which rode a flip side vocal version of the song by Bing Crosby to #13.

The shortest record ever made was an instrumental: Les Paul & Mary Ford's "Magic Melody Part II" (Capitol RPM PRO 234).

*Tie.
**Hit the charts twice.
⁺Alka Seltzer jingle.
⁺⁺The #1 instrumentalist of the rock & roll era.
@Jimmy Wisner.
@@Bill of Scotty & Bill, Elvis Presley's backup band.

Top 200 Novelty Singles

1. THE PURPLE PEOPLE EATER - Sheb Wooley
2. THE STREAK - Ray Stevens
3. DISCO DUCK - Rick Dees
4. A BOY NAMED SUE - Johnny Cash
5. MONSTER MASH - Bobby "Boris" Pickett
6. WITCH DOCTOR - David Seville
7. ITSY BITSY TEENIE WEENIE YELLOW POLKA DOT BIKINI - Brian Hyland
8. SPIDERS & SNAKES - Jim Stafford
9. MY DING A LING - Chuck Berry
10. CHIPMUNK SONG - David Seville
11. ALLEY OOP - Hollywood Argyles
12. SHORT PEOPLE - Randy Newman
13. ALL AMERICAN BOY - Bill Parsons (Bobby Bare)
14. THE JOLLY GREEN GIANT - Kingsmen
15. MR. CUSTER - Larry Verne
16. PEPINO THE ITALIAN MOUSE - Lou Monte
17. SPEEDY GONZALEZ - Pat Boone
18. CHANTILLY LACE - Big Bopper
19. TROGLODYTE - Jimmy Castor Bunch
20. MAY THE BIRD OF PARADISE FLY UP YOUR NOSE - Little Jimmy Dickens
21. AMOS MOSES - Jerry Reed
22. GITARZAN - Ray Stevens
23. CONVENTION 72 - Delegates
24. CHARLIE BROWN - Coasters
25. SNOOPY VS. RED BARON - Royal Guardsmen
26. SHE GOT THE GOLDMINE (I GOT THE SHAFT) - Jerry Reed
27. WOULD JESUS WEAR A ROLEX ON HIS TELEVISION SHOW - Ray Stevens

Sheb Wooley

``Purple People Eater'' stays the all-time #1 novelty record.

28. HELLO MUDDAH, HELLO FADDAH - Allan Sherman
29. TIE ME KANGAROO DOWN - Rolf Harris
30. ALONG CAME JONES - Coasters
31. ALVIN'S HARMONICA - Chipmunks
32. SWINGIN' - John Anderson
33. THEY'RE COMING TO TAKE ME AWAY, HA HA - Napoleon IV
34. BEEP BEEP - Playmates
35. KOOKIE KOOKIE (LEND ME YOUR COMB) - Edward Byrnes
36. SURFIN' BIRD - Trashmen
37. THE BIRD - Jerry Reed
38. AHAB THE ARAB - Ray Stevens
39. PAC MAN FEVER - Buckner & Garcia
40. ATTITUDE ADJUSTMENT - Hank Williams Jr.
41. FLYING SAUCER I & II - Buchanan & Goodman
42. DOES YOUR CHEWING GUM LOSE ITS FLAVOR ON THE BEDPOST OVERNIGHT - Lonnie Donegan
43. COVER OF ROLLING STONE - Dr. Hook (Original)
    COVER OF MUSIC CITY NEWS - Buck Owens (Country)
44. BABY SITTIN' BOOGIE - Buzz Clifford
45. DINNER WITH DRAC - John Zacherie
46. MR. JAWS - Dickie Goodman
47. WILDWOOD WEED - Jim Stafford
48. LITTLE OLD MAN - Bill Cosby
49. DANG ME - Roger Miller
50. LET'S THINK ABOUT LIVING - Bob Luman
51. WHO PUT THE BOMP IN THE BOMP BOMP BOMP - Barry Mann
52. WESTERN MOVIES - Olympics
53. TRANSFUSION - Nervous Norvus
54. YOGI - Ivy League
55. HERE COMES THE JUDGE - Shorty Long
56. LIFE IS A ROCK (BUT THE RADIO ROLLED ME) - Reunion
57. HOT ROD LINCOLN - Commander Cody & His Lost Planet Airmen
58. UNEASY RIDER - Charlie Daniels Band
59. GIMME DAT DING - Pipkins
60. JUNK FOOD JUNKIE - Larry Groce
61. CHUG-A-LUG - Roger Miller
62. EARACHE MY EYE - Cheech & Chong
63. WHEN YOU'RE HOT YOU'RE HOT - Jerry Reed
64. HAUNTED HOUSE - Gene Simmons
65. MY GIRL BILL - Jim Stafford
66. BATTLE OF KOOKAMONGA - Homer & Jethro
67. DO WACKA DO - Roger Miller
68. ON TOP OF SPAGHETTI - Tom Glaser
69. UH ON PT. 2 - Nutty Squirrels
70. STAND BY ME - Spyder Turner
71. ALLEY OOP - Dante & The Evergreens
72. FUNKY WORM - Ohio Players
73. RETURN OF RED BARON - Royal Guardsmen
74. TIP TOE THRU THE TULIPS - Tiny Tim
75. DEAD SKUNK - Loudon Wainwright III
76. BERTHA BUTT BOOGIE - Jimmy Castor Bunch
77. THE CURLY SHUFFLE - Jump N Saddle Band
78. TAKE OFF - Bob & Doug McKenzie
79. KING TUT - Steve Martin
80. THE ASTRONAUT - Jose Jimenez
81. FLYING SAUCER II - Buchanan & Goodman
82. TELEPHONE MAN - Meri Wilson
83. MY BOOMERANG WON'T COME BACK - Charlie Drake
84. POPCORN SONG - Cliffie Stone
85. STRANDED IN THE JUNGLE - Cadets
86. LITTLE BLUE MAN - Betty Johnson
87. THE WHITE KNIGHT - Cletus Maggard
88. BASKETBALL JONES - Cheech & Chong
89. LITTLE EGYPT - Coasters
90. LITTLE SPACE GIRL - Jesse Lee Turner

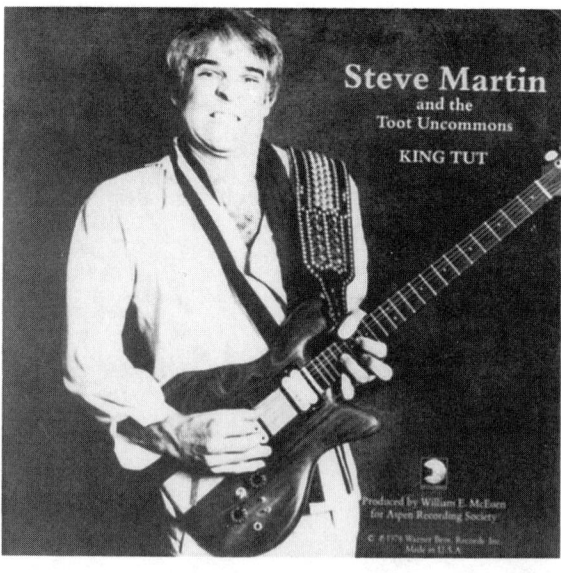

Steve Martin
Steve's "King Tut" ranks #79 on the Novelty hit parade.

91. WILD THING - Senator Bobby
92. DELAWARE - Perry Como
93. BLACK SUPERMAN (MAHAMMAD ALI) - Johnny Wakelin
94. ONE PIECE AT A TIME - Johnny Cash
95. CHILDREN'S MARCHING SONG - Mitch Miller
96. RUBBER DUCKIE - Ernie
97. RAGTIME COWBOY JOE - Chipmunks
98. IN THE MOOD - Henhouse Five Plus Two (Ray Stevens)
99. YELLOW ROSE OF TEXAS - Stan Freberg
100. ONCE YOU UNDERSTAND - Think
101. HARRY THE HAIRY APE - Ray Stevens
102. LEADER OF THE LAUNDROMAT - Detergents
103. HERE COMES THE JUDGE - Pigmeat Markham
104. THE MERMAID/MARIE LAVEAU - Bobby Bare
105. IN THE MIDDLE OF THE HOUSE - Vaughn Monroe
106. THE THING - Phil Harris
107. OH SUSANNA - Singing Dogs
108. TENNESSEE BIRDWALK - Blanchard & Morgan
109. ODE TO THE LITTLE BROWN SHACK - Billy Edd Wheeler
110. SHIMMY SHIMMY KO KO POP - Little Anthony & The Imperials
111. SISTER MARY ELEPHANT - Cheech & Chong
112. I GOT A WIFE - Mark IV
113. YOUR BULLDOG DRINKS CHAMPAGNE - Jim Stafford
114. APE CALL - Nervous Norvus
115. SATURDAY MORNING CONFUSION - Bobby Russell
116. BIRD ON MY HEAD - David Seville
117. KANSAS CITY STAR - Roger Miller
118. I GOT STONED AND I MISSED IT - Jim Stafford
119. JOHN AND MARSHA - Stan Freberg
120. MAKE YOURSELF COMFORTABLE - Andy Griffith
121. CRAZY DOWNTOWN - Allan Sherman
122. BANANA BOAT DAY O - Stan Freberg
123. HOT ROD LINCOLN - Johnny Bond
124. RUNNIN' BARE - Jim Nesbitt
125. IT'S HARD TO BE HUMBLE - Mac Davis
126. ALONG CAME JONES - Ray Stevens
127. HIGH SCHOOL U.S.A. - Tommy Facenda
128. THANK GOD AND GREYHOUND - Roy Clark
129. TEN LITTLE BOTTLES - Johnny Bond

130. MISSISSIPPI SQUIRREL REVIVAL - Ray Stevens
131. BIG BOPPER'S WEDDING - Big Bopper
132. JEREMIAH PEABODY'S POLY UNSATURATED QUICK DISSOLVING FAST ACTING OLEASANT TASTING GREEN AND PURPLE PILLS - Ray Stevens
133. BAD MAN BLUNDER - KIngston Trio
134. BALLAD OF IRVING - Frank Gallup
135. LOOKIN' FOR MORE IN '64 - Jim Nesbitt
136. YOU NEVER CALLED ME BY MY NAME - David Allen Coe
137. RUTHLESS/YOU CAN'T HAVE YOUR KATE AND EDITH TOO - Statler Brothers
138. THE CLASS - Chubby Checker
139. ALMOST PERSUADED #2 - Ben Colder
140. SWAMP WITCH - Jim Stafford
141. YOU CAN't ROLLER SKATE IN A BUFFALO HERD - Roger Miller
142. ANDY AND CLEOPATRA - Andy Griffith
143. ALVIN TWIST - Chipmunks
144. ENERGY CRISIS - Dickie Goodman
145. THE MUMMY - Bob McFadden
146. A TIGER IN MY TANK - Jim Nesbitt
147. I'M A NUT - Leroy Pullins
148. MOTHER IN LAW - Jim Nesbitt
149. MY TOOT TOOT - Rockin Sydney (Country); Jean Knight (Pop)
150. SUPER FLY MEETS SHAFT - John & Ernest
151. RIP VAN WINKLE - Devotions
152. MURPHY'S LAW - Cheri
153. RUBBER BISQUIT - Blues Brothers
154. BEANS IN MY EARS - Serendipity Singers
155. BEN CRAZY - Dickie Goodman
156. I LOVE ONIONS - Susan Christie
157. BRIDGET THE MIDGET - Ray Stevens
158. THE PTL HAS GONE TO HELL (SO WHERE DO I SEND MY MONEY) - Rev. Needmore & The Almighty Bucks
159. WHEN THE SHIP HIT THE SAND - Little Jimmy Dickens

Archie Campbell
Four of Archie's hits made the Top 200 list.

160. TRUCKLOAD OF STARVIN' KANGAROOS - Little Jimmy Dickens
161. BIG BRUCE - Steve Greenberg
162. DROPKICK ME JESUS (THROUGH THE GOAL POST OF LIFE) - Bobby Bare
163. ONE ON RIGHT IS ON LEFT - Johnny Cash
164. PEEL ME A NANNER - Roy Drusky
165. BALLAD OF JIM & TAMMY - Sheb Wooley
166. ROCK AROUND MOTHER GOOSE - Barry Gordon
167. HUMPHREY THE CAMEL - Blanchard & Morgan
168. BATMAN AND HIS GRANDMOTHER - Dickie Goodman
169. MY UNCLE USED TO LOVE ME BUT SHE DIED - Roger Miller
170. KONG - Dickie Goodman
171. SNEAKY SNAKE - Tom T. Hall
172. COON HUNTIN' STORY - Jerry Clower
173. HERE COME THE RATTLESNAKES - Wendy Bagnell
174. WORLD'S BIGGEST WHOPPER - Junior Samples
175. HOUND DOG IN THE WINDER - Homer & Jethro
176. CHICKEN FEED - Bobbi Staff
177. CUZ YORE SO SWEET - Simon Crum (Ferlin Husky)
178. BUTTERBEANS - Little David Wilkins
179. THE COCKFIGHT - Archie Campbell
180. WATERGRATE - Dickie Goodman
181. FREDDIE FEELGOOD AND HIS FUNKY LITTLE FIVE PIECE BAND - Ray Stevens
182. DERN YA - Ruby Wright
183. THEY AIN'T MAKIN' JEWS LIKE JESUS ANYMORE - Kinky Friedman & The Texas Jewboys
184. BIG FANNY - Neil Ray
185. PUT YOUR BISQUITS IN THE OVEN AND YOUR BUNS IN THE BED - Kinky Friedman
186. PFFT! YOU WERE GONE - Archie Campbell *

Tommy Facenda
Tommy's ``High School U.S.A.'' (#127) peaked at #28 in 1959.

187. THE TOUCHABLES - Dickie Goodman
188. REDNECK HIPPIE ROMANCE - Bobby Bare
189. BIG SWEET JOHN - Ben Colder
190. HOW TO CATCH AN AFRICAN SKEETER LIVE - Little Jimmy Dickens
191. GOLF, GOLF, GOLF - Archie Campbell
192. THE TOUCHABLES IN BROOKLYN - Dickie Goodman
193. TOBACCO - George Hamilton IV
194. THAT'S A HEE HAW - Junior Samples
195. MAY THE BIRD OF PARADISE FLY UP YORE SNOOT - Ben Colder
196. DETROIT CITY #2 - Ben Colder
197. MR. PRESIDENT - Dickie Goodman
198. THE HATFIELDS AND THE MCCOYS - Archie Campbell
199. BABY IT'S COLD OUTSIDE - Don Bowman & Skeeter Davis
200. SWEET THANG - Frankie & Johnny
201. ELECTION '84 - Dickie Goodman

Editor's Note: All records were released on 45rpm and/or 78rpm.

Several artists have gained real prominence through their association with the novelty record: David Seville, Dickie Goodman, Ray Stevens, Roger Miller, Little Jimmy Dickens, Jerry Reed, Jim Stafford, and Sheb Wooley (aka Ben Colder).

This list of songs does not include "X-rated" material or "race" records for which, though widely available, no airplay or sales information is available.

*From the TV show "Hee Haw."

Jerry Clower
Clower's classic ``Coon Huntin' Story'' made the list at #172.

Holiday, Seasonal & Patriotic Hits

Top 50 Christmas Hits

1. WHITE CHRISTMAS - Bing Crosby
2. RUDOLPH THE RED NOSED REINDEER - Gene Autry
3. THE LITTLE DRUMMER BOY - Harry Simeon Chorale
4. THE CHRISTMAS SONG - Nat King Cole
5. SILENT NIGHT - Bing Crosby
6. BLUE CHRISTMAS - Elvis Presley
7. JINGLE BELL ROCK - Bobby Helms
8. SILVER BELLS - Earl Grant
   PEACE ON EARTH/LITTLE DRUMMER BOY - David Bowie & Bing Crosby (Tie)
9. PLEASE COME HOME FOR CHRISTMAS - Charles Brown
10. THE CHIPMUNK SONG - Chipmunks
11. JINGLE BELLS - SInging Dogs
12. GRANDMA GOT RUN OVER BY A REINDEER - Elmo And Patsy
13. ROCKING AROUND THE CHRISTMAS TREE - Brenda Lee
14. CHRISTMAS MEDLEY - Salsoul Orchestra
15. FROSTY THE SNOWMAN - Gene Autry
16. I SAW MOMMY KISSING SANTA CLAUS - Jimmy Boyd
17. DO YOU HEAR WHAT I HEAR? - Andy Williams
18. HERE COMES SANTA CLAUS - Gene Autry
19. ALL I WANT FOR CHRISTMAS (IS MY TWO FRONT TEETH) - Spike Jones
20. NUTTIN FOR CHRISTMAS - Barry Gordon
21. MARY'S BOY CHILD - Harry Belafonte
22. JINGLE BELL ROCK - Brenda Lee
23. DO THEY KNOW ITS CHRISTMAS - Band Aid
24. 'TWAS THE NIGHT BEFORE CHRISTMAS - Fred Waring
25. CHRISTMAS IN DIXIE - Alabama
26. WINTER WONDERLAND - Dolly Parton
27. MERRY CHRISTMAS, DARLING - Carpenters
28. MERRY CHRISTMAS, BABY - Charles Brown
29. CHRISTMAS DREAM - Perry Como
30. FELIZ NAVIDAD - Jose Feliciano
31. AN OLD CHRISTMAS CARD - Jim Reeves
32. HAPPY CHRISTMAS (WAR IS OVER) - John Lennon/Yoko Ono
33. IF EVERY DAY WAS LIKE CHRISTMAS - Elvis Presley
34. SHAKE ME I RATTLE - Christy Lane; Marion Worth (2 vers.)
35. COME ON RING THOSE BELLS - Evie
36. CHRISTMAS DRAGNET - Stan Freberg
37. HAPPY BIRTHDAY, JESUS - Mike Douglas
38. LIGHT OF THE STABLE - Judds; Emmylou Harris (2 vers.)
39. SANTA CLAUS IS WATCHING YOU - Ray Stevens
40. MY FAVORITE THINGS - Herb Alpert
41. ANOTHER LONELY CHRISTMAS - Prince
42. PRETTY PAPER - Willie Nelson
43. SANTA LOOKED A LOT LIKE DADDY - Buck Owens
44. LITTLE SAINT NICK - Beach Boys
45. BAREFOOT SANTA CLAUS - Sonny James
46. HOLLY JOLLY CHRISTMAS - Burl Ives
47. MONSTERS HOLIDAY Bobby "Boris" Pickett
48. O HOLY NIGHT - Mario Lanza
49. WINTER WONDERLAND - Andrews Sisters
50. SNOWFLAKE - Jim Reeves

Top 25 Solid Gold Christmas Singles

1. WHITE CHRISTMAS - Bing Crosby
2. SILENT NIGHT - Bing Crosby
3. RUDOLPH THE RED NOSED REINDEER - Gene Autry
4. JINGLE BELL ROCK - Bobby Helms
5. CHIPMUNK SONG - Chipmunks
6. ROCKING AROUND THE CHRISTMAS TREE - Brenda Lee
7. THE LITTLE DRUMMER BOY - Harry Simeon Chorale
8. JINGLE BELLS - Andrews Sisters
9. HERE COMES SANTA CLAUS - Gene Autry
10. I SAW MOMMY KISSING SANTA CLAUS - Jimmy Boyd
11. HAPPY CHRISTMAS (WAR IS OVER) - John Lennon/Yoko Ono
12. THE CHRISTMAS SONG - Nat King Cole
13. ALL I WANT FOR CHRISTMAS (IS MY TWO FRONT TEETH) - Spike Jones
14. BLUE CHRISTMAS - Elvis Presley
15. JINGLE BELLS - Singing Dogs
16. NUTTIN FOR CHRISTMAS - Barry Gordon
17. MARY'S BOY CHILD - Harry Belafonte
18. I'LL BE HOME FOR CHRISTMAS - Bing Crosby
19. IF EVERY DAY WAS LIKE CHRISTMAS - Elvis Presley
20. FROSTY THE SNOWMAN - Gene Autry
21. WHITE CHRISTMAS - Frank Sinatra
22. 'TWAS THE NIGHT BEFORE CHRISTMAS - Fred Waring
23. PLEASE COME HOME FOR CHRISTMAS - Charles Brown
24. DO THEY KNOW ITS CHRISTMAS - Band Aid
25. SILVER BELLS - Earl Grant

Editor's Note: These singles and/or 78's have sold in the multi-millions.

Top 50 Christmas Albums

1. THE LITTLE DRUMMER BOY - Harry Simeon Chorale
2. MERRY CHRISTMAS - Bing Crosby
3. ELVIS CHRISTMAS ALBUM - Elvis Presley
4. MANNHEIM STEAMROLLER CHRISTMAS - Mannheim Steamroller *
5. FRESH AIRE XMAS - Mannheim Steamroller *
6. THE CHRISTMAS SONG - Nat King Cole
7. BEYOND THE SEASON - Garth Brooks *
8. ONCE UPON A CHRISTMAS - Kenny Rogers/Dolly Parton
9. A CHRISTMAS ALBUM - Amy Grant *
10. THE CHRISTMAS ALBUM - Neil Diamond *
11. HOME FOR CHRISTMAS - Amy Grant *
12. ANDY WILLIAMS CHRISTMAS LP (Green) - Andy Williams
13. MERRY CHRISTMAS - Johnny Mathis
14. CHRISTMAS IN AMERICA - Kenny Rogers
15. CHRISTMAS PARTY - Arthur Fiedler & Boston Pops
16. CHRISTMAS SING ALONG WITH MITCH - Mitch Miller
17. A CHRISTMAS ALBUM - Barbra Streisand
18. WHITE CHRISTMAS - John Schneider
19. PERRY SINGS MERRY CHRISTMAS - Perry Como
20. OAK RIDGE BOYS CHRISTMAS - Oak Ridge Boys
21. KENNY ROGERS CHRISTMAS - Kenny Rogers
22. MERRY CHRISTMAS (Red) - Andy Williams
23. CRESCENT CITY CHRISTMAS CARD - Wynton Marsalis *
24. NOEL - Joan Baez
25. LET THERE BE PEACE ON EARTH - Vince Gill *
26. HOME FOR CHRISTMAS - Dolly Parton
27. BILLBOARD'S GREATEST CHRISTMAS HITS, 1955-PRESENT - Various Artists
28. THE STAR CAROL - Tennessee Ernie Ford
29. HOLIDAY SING ALONG WITH MITCH - Mitch Miller
30. JOY TO THE WORLD - Mormon Tabernacle Choir
31. AN OLD TIME CHRISTMAS - Randy Travis *
32. BILLBOARD'S GREATEST CHRISTMAS HITS, 1935-1954 - Various Artists

33. CHRISTMAS WITH THE CHIPMUNKS - Chipmunks
34. ROCKY MOUNTAIN CHRISTMAS - John Denver
CHRISTMAS WITH ANNE MURRAY (Tie)
35. MARIO SINGS CHRISTMAS CAROLS - Mario Lanza
36. CHRISTMAS JOLLIES - Salsoul Orchestra
37. CHRISTMAS WITH CONIFF - Ray Coniff
38. SEASONS GREETINGS - Perry Como
39. CHRISTMAS PORTRAIT - The Carpenters
40. LIGHT OF THE STABLE - Emmylou Harris
41. A CHRISTMAS ALBUM - Frank Sinatra
42. 'TWAS THE NIGHT BEFORE CHRISTMAS - Fred Waring
ROCKIN' AROUND THE CHRISTMAS TREE - Brenda Lee
(Tie)
43. RUDOLPH THE RED NOSED REINDEER - Gene Autry **
44. A HOLLY JOLLY CHRISTMAS - Burl Ives
45. RICKY VAN SHELTON SINGS CHRISTMAS - Ricky Van
Shelton *
46. A CHRISTMAS GIFT FOR YOU - Phil Spector
47. CHRISTMAS MELODIES - Percy Faith
48. WORLD'S MOST BEAUTIFUL CHRISTMAS SONGS - Roger
Whittaker *
49. MEMORIES OF CHRISTMAS - Elvis Presley
50. GREATEST CHRISTMAS NOVELTY - Dr. Demento
Editor's Note: List is current through May 31, 1994. Newer
product (*) may of course eclipse this order of rank.
**Released on 10-inch LP. If standard LP's were
counted, would tie for #2 position.

Top New Years Eve Classics

1. AULD LANG SYNE - Guy Lombardo
2. THERE'LL BE A HOT TIME IN THE OLD TOWN TONIGHT -
Guy Lombardo
3. NEW YEAR'S EVE PARTY - George Thoroughgood & The
Destroyers
4. FUNKY NEW YEAR - The Eagles
5. NEW YEAR'S MEDLEY - Salsoul Orchestra

Top St. Patrick's Day Hits

1. WHEN IRISH EYES ARE SMILING - Bing Crosby
2. TOO RA LOO RA LOO RA - Bing Crosby
3. THE UNICORN - Irish Rovers
4. DANNY BOY - Ray Price
5. MY WILD IRISH ROSE - Hank Locklin
6. AVONDALE - James Galway
7. ROSE OF TRALEE - Bing Crosby
8. GALWAY BAY - Bing Crosby

Top Easter Hits

1. EASTER PARADE - Bing Crosby *
2. PETER COTTONTAIL - Gene Autry **
3. THE OLD RUGGED CROSS - George Beverly Shea
4. WERE YOU THERE - Tennessee Ernie Ford
5. EASTER PARADE - Judy Garland
6. PETER COTTONTAIL - Del Wood

7. EASTER PARADE - Perry Como
8. CHRIST AROSE - George Beverly Shea
9. THE OLD RUGGED CROSS - Jim Nabors
10. WERE YOU THERE - Johnny Cash
11. AT THE CROSS - Tennessee Ernie Ford
12. THEN, NOW AND FOREVER - Barbara Mandrell
*Other versions by Guy Lombardo, Harry James, and
Liberace..
**Other versions by Mervin Shiner, Jimmy Wakely, Johnny Lee
Wills, and Fran Allison..

Favorite Easter Hymns

1. CHRIST AROSE
2. WERE YOU THERE
3. CHRIST THE LORD IS RISEN TODAY
4. I KNOW THAT MY REDEEMER LIVETH
5. GREAT GETTIN UP MORNING
6. AT THE CROSS
7. THE OLD RUGGED CROSS
8. AT CALVARY
9. WE SHALL RISE
10. MUST JESUS BEAR THE CROSS ALONE

Top Mother's Day Hits

1. I.O.U. - Jimmmy Dean *
2. MAMA LIKED THE ROSES - Elvis Presley
3. ROSES FOR MAMA - C.W. McCall
4. MAMA SANG A SONG - Walter Brennan (Pop); Bill Anderson (Country)
5. NO CHARGE - Melba Montgomery
*Platinum single from 1976..

Top Father's Day Hits

1. TO DADDY - Emmylou Harris
2. DADDY'S HANDS - Holly Dunn
3. DADDY DON'T YOU WALK SO FAST - Wayne Newton
4. DADDY'S HOME - Shep & The Limelighters
5. MY DAD - Paul Peterson

Top Halloween Hits

1. MONSTER MASH
2. THE PURPLE PEOPLE EATER
3. GHOSTBUSTERS
4. HAUNTED HOUSE
5. ADDAMS FAMILY THEME
6. SPIDERS & SNAKES
7. DINNER WITH DRAC
8. TWILIGHT ZONE THEME
9. I PUT A SPELL ON YOU
10. QUENTIN'S THEME
11. WITCH DICTOR
12. GHOST IN THE HOUSE

Kate Smith
Kate's version of "God Bless America" is still
the all-time #1 patriotic favorite.

Lee Greenwood
A gigantic leap since the '84 edition of this book—partly
due to Desert Storm—has made "God Bless the U.S.A." #2.

Top 20 Patriotic Songs

1. GOD BLESS AMERICA - Kate Smith
2. GOD BLESS THE U.S.A. - Lee Greenwood
3. THERE'S A STAR SPANGLED BANNER WAVING SOME-
   WHERE - Elton Britt
4. AMERICA - Neil Diamond
5. THIS LAND IS YOUR LAND - Woody Guthrie
6. THE AMERICANS - Gordon Sinclair; Byron McGregor
7. BALLAD OF THE GREEN BERET - S/Sgt. Barry Sadler
8. DAY FOR DECISION - Johnny Sea
9. BATTLE HYMN OF THE REPUBLIC - Mormon Tabernacle
   Choir

10. RAGGED OLD FLAG - Johnny Cash
11. STAR SPANGLED BANNER - Whitney Houston
12. STARS AND STRIPES FOREVER - Boston Pops
13. STAR SPANGLED BANNER - Jose Feliciano
14. THE PLEDGE OF ALLEGIANCE - RED SKELTON
15. AMERICANA - Moe Bandy
16. AMERICAN TRILOGY - Elvis Presley
17. BORN IN THE U.S.A. - Bruce Springsteen
18. U.S. OF A. - Donna Fargo
19. ALL ABOARD THE FREEDOM TRAIN - Merle Haggard
20. STAR SPANGLED BANNER - Billy Ray Cyrus

Music from the Confederate Scrapbook

Official Documentation, Confederate States of America Archives, Lizzie Cary Daniel, 1893

Around five years ago, I obtained a copy of a very rare book entitled *A Confederate Scrapbook*. It was a scrapbook kept during the War Between the States (sometimes referred to as the Civil War) by a teenage girl named Lizzie Cary Daniel. Now, as co-founder of the Southern Heritage Foundation and former member of The Sons of Confederate Veterans--my great, great uncle was named Jeb Stuart, and both my great, great grandfathers proudly served the Confederate States of America--I was naturally very excited about finding this book.

Much to my surprise, I soon found that the book included a listing of the Confederate Top 50 songs, 1860-1865! Before we delve into the list, it should be noted that some of the songs centered around two official holidays declared by President Jefferson Davis: March 10, Southern Thanksgiving (a day of fasting, not feasting), and November 16, set aside as a Day of Worship of God. Now, here they are, ranked according to their appearance in the *Confederate Scrapbook*.

Bruce Elrod

50 Most Popular Songs of the Confederacy

1. DIXIE

    The rallying war song of the South, Dixie was also very popular in the North and was one of Abraham Lincoln's favorite songs. Written in 1859, over 400 variations exist, but Daniel Emment's lyrics remain the most popular. Written by a Northerner, it was a minstrel song for Bryant's Ethiopian Minstrel Troupe in New York City. Bryant's Troupes were in New Orleans at the outbreak of the war, thus the Confederacy adopted Dixie as its own song.

2. THE BONNIE BLUE FLAG

    Considered the Southern national anthem, although never officially adopted as such, this song was written in 1861 by a young actor, Harry McCarthy. First performed in New Orleans, the tune is that of an Irish jig.

3. I'M GOING BACK TO DIXIE (Foster)
4. THE BONNIE BLUE GAL (Arr. "The Bonnie Blue Flag")
5. STONEWALL JACKSON'S WAY

    A song found on the body of a sergeant of the Old Stonewall Brigade at Winchester, Virginia.

6. AURA LEE

    A melody redone by Elvis as "Love Me Tender."

7. LORENA (Composer unknown)
8. THE VALIANT CONSCRIPT (Arr. "Yankee Doodle")
9. GOOBER PEAS (as in peanuts)
10. THE SOUTHERN WAGON (Arr. "Wait For The Wagon")
11. MARYLAND, MY MARYLAND (James Randall)
12. THE SOUTHERN SOLDIER BOY

    Written by Captain G.W. Alexander for a Confederate musical comedy, "The Virginia Cavalier," at Capitol's New Theatre in Richmond, Virginia.

13. GOD SAVE THE SOUTH (Arr. "God Save The Queen")
14. WEEPING SAD AND LONELY (or, WHEN THE CRUEL WAR IS OVER) (Charles Sawyer and Henry Tucker)
15. WHEN JOHNNY COMES MARCHING HOME AGAIN

    Authorship still in question. Equally popular in the North and the South.

16. RIDING A RAID (Jeb Stuart; Arr: Bonnie Dundee)
17. THE REBEL SOLDIER

    Author unknown. Appalachian folk song. The tune made its way west and became "Rye Whiskey."

18. FLIGHT OF DOODLES (Arr: "Root Hog Or Die")

    Flight of Doodles refers to the hasty retreat of the Yankees back to Washington after the Battle of Bull Run.

19. THE VOLUNTEER (Arr: "The Girl I Left Behind")
20. IMOGEN (General J.B. Magruder)
21. THERE'S LIFE IN THE OLD LAND YET (James Randall)
22. I CAN WHIP THE SCOUNDREL
23. THE SOUTHRONS CHANT OF DEFIANCE (C.A. Warfield)
24. IT IS MY COUNTRY'S CALL (Harry McCarthy)
25. GOD BLESS OUR SOUTHERN LAND (Arr: "God Save The Queen")
26. ALLONS ENFANS (Arr: "Marseillaise," A.E. Blackmar)
27. THE CAVALIER'S GLEE (Arr: "Pirate's Glee," Captain Blackford)
28. GAY AND HAPPY (Composer unknown)
29. THE SOUTHERN CROSS (Arr: "Star Spangled Banner," St. George Tucker)
30. RICHMOND IS A HARD ROAD TO TRAVEL

    Dedicated to Northern General Burnside (or, at least, to his frustrated attempts to take Richmond, the song is an arrangement of "Jordan Is A Hard Road To Travel."

31. SONG OF THE EXILE (Arr: "Dixie")
32. THE HOMESPUN DRESS (Arr: "Bonnie Blue Flag," Carrie Sinclair)
33. SONG OF THE SOUTHERN SOLDIER (Barclay & Perkins Drayman)
34. VIRGINIA'S WAR CALL (Composer unknown)
35. SONG OF THE SNOW (Mrs. M.T. Pearson)
36. ADDRESS TO THE WOMEN TO THE SOUTHERN TROOPS (Arr: "Bruce's Address," Mrs. F.H. Cross)
37. MY ORDER (W. Gordon McCabe)
38. THE BATTLE SONG (Unknown)
39. MY SOLDIER (Unknown)
40. WE SWEAR (Unknown)
41. HURRAH (Unknown)
42. A NEW RED, WHITE & BLUE (Jeff Thompson)
43. SOMEBODY'S DARLIN' (Unknown)
44. MUSIC IN CAMP (John Thompson)
45. THE CONQUERED BANNER (Rev. J.A. Ryan, a Catholic priest)
46. FOLD IT UP CAREFULLY (Henry Hart of England)
47. THE SOUTH (Father Ryan)
48. ALL QUIET ALONG THE POTOMAC TO-NIGHT (Unknown)
49. THE FADED GRAY JACKET (Mrs. C.A. Ball)
50. FAREWELL TO THE STAR-SPANGLED BANNER (Unknown)

Other Southern Hits from the Period 1860-1865

COTTON STATES FAREWELL TO YANKEE DOODLE
OUR DEAD (Father Ryan)
THE POOR SOLDIER IN HOLLYWOOD - A SLUMBER SONG (Gillie Cary)
SOUTHERN LAND (Arr: "Dixie")
A SOUTHERN WOMAN'S SONG CHIVALROUS C.S.A. (Arr: "Vive la Copmagnie")
VIRGINIANS (OF THE VALLEY) (Frank Ticnor, M.D.)

Trivia Quiz
Answers

Big Band Trivia
Quiz Answers

1. Frank Sinatra.
2. Jimmy Dorsey's "Maria Elena"/"Green Eyes" (Summer 1941).
3. University of North Carolina at Chapel Hill; Duke University at Durham.
4. "Daddy" (1941); "I'm A Big Girl Now" (1946); "Harbor Lights" (1950).
5. Red Skelton.
6. Billie Holiday.
7. Artie Shaw's "Frenesi."
8. Margaret Whiting.
9. Barry Wood.
10. "Perfidia," January 4, 1941, was announced under the title "Tonight" (as in "Tonight, my heart cries out perfidia.").
11. "There I Go," 1940-41.
12. The wholesale exit of the six ASCAP songs rated in the Top Ten on December 28, 1940, replaced by six EMI songs on January 4, 1941, included the remarkable reappearance of "The Same Old Story," which held #10 twice in September after thirteen weeks off the Hit Parade.
13. Take your pick between "People Will Say We're In Love" (thirty weeks in 1943-44) and "White Christmas," the latter of which was on for fifteen weeks during its first 1942-43 outing but which reappeared for a week or two during many subsequent Christmas seasons.
14. Each was a substantial "big hit" twice during the history of the Hit Parade": "Harbor Lights" in 1937 (11 weeks) and in 1950-51 (18 weeks, including two weeks at #1); "Blueberry Hill" in 1940 (14 weeks) and 1956-57 (12 weeks); "My Prayer" in 1939-40 (14 weeks) and 1956 (11 weeks, including one at #1).
15. Helen O'Connell.
16. University of Wisconsin, Madison.
17. Tommy Dorsey.
18. Shep Fields.
19. Shrewd businessman and topdog at RCA (in 1938), Tommy Dorsey had recorded it and, on hearing the new Clinton band's version, told the brass" "No!"
20. Russ Morgan.
21: Tommy Dorsey.
22. Greta Garbo.
23. Henry Busse.
24. James Petrillo.
25. Everything.
26. Elaine Beatty.
27. Kay Starr.
28. The beloved Bea Wain.
29. James C. Petrillo.
30. By countering Columbia's 33rpm with the 45rpm. The final compromise between the "big two" was popular music on 45rpm and classical music on 33rpm.
31. Not to our knowledge.
32. Uh-huh.
33. Johnny Messner.
34. Jack Fina.
35. Russ Morgan.
36. Total indifference and depressed record sales.
37. Paul Douglas.
38. Skinnay Ennis.
39. Ray Noble.
40. Janet Blair.
41. "Why Don't You Do Right" with Benny Goodman, 1942.
42. Ozzie Nelson.
43. Helen Forrest and "Pal Joey."
44. Fletcher Henderson.
45. Rose Marie.
46. Bette Davis.
47. Benny Goodman.
48. Sammy Kaye.
49. "Rum And Coca Cola" (1945).
50. Bea Wain and Lanny Ross.

Miscellaneous Trivia #1
Quiz Answers

1. Waylon Jennings.
2. Both recorded hit versions of "The Three Bells."
3. He was a barber.
4. Guy Mitchell of "Singing The Blues" fame.
5. George Jones.
6. John Lennon and Paul McCartney.
7. Gary Paxton. The made-up name was adopted to avoid legal hassles.
8. Marvin Gaye.
9. B.B. King.
10. The Blossoms led by Darlene Love sang back-up, with Glen Campbell playing guitar.
11. Ray Charles' recording of "I Can't Stop Loving You."
12. Carole King.
13. The Judds.
14. Michael Jackson; in the former case, with the Jackson 5 (they sang the "Doo Doo Wopsssss"), and alone in the latter.
15. Alabama.
16. Sam "Dynamite" Hatcher. Roy Acuff played only the train effect.
17. Boy George & Culture Club.
18. Al Jolson.
19. Colonel Tom Parker.
20. Sam Cooke.
21. Gene Autry's "Champion."
22. Vernon Dalhart and "The Prisoner Song."
23. Duke Ellington.
24. "Sixteen Tons," by Tennessee Ernie Ford.
25. Dean Martin.
26. $40,000.
27. "The Wayward Wind."
28. Big Mama Thornton.
29. Roy Orbison.
30. Ricky Nelson's "Travelin' Man."
31. The Del Satins.
32. Jimmy Dean.
33. The Four Seasons.
34. The Blossoms.
35. "He's So Fine."
36. "Big Girls Don't Cry."
37. Lesley Gore.
38. The U.S. Marine Corp.
39. Linda McCartney.
40. Clyde Beavers. (Actually, the real title in Japanese is "Ue O Muite Arute," or "I Look Up When I Walk.")
41. "I Want To Hold Your Hand," by The Beatles.
42. "Battle Of New Orleans" by Johnny Horton.
43. "I'm A Honky Tonk Girl," on Zero Records.
44. Mitch Miller.
45. "Wild Side Of Life," by Hank Thompson.
46. Dolly Parton.
47. Garth Brooks.
48. Billy Joel.
49. Ernest Tubb, whose words were mistakenly interpreted as,

shall we say, amorous urgings regarding a "chick."
50. Jimmy C. Newman pioneered with "Future Farmers Of America."
51. Lamar Morris on Boone Records.
52. "Time After Time" by Jack Clement. Those words are the only lyric, repeated over and over.
53. None other than the Godfather of Soul, James Brown.
54. Johnny Paycheck.
55. Gene Pitney.
56. Randy Travis.
57. The Beatles.
58. "There Won't Be No Country Music, There Won't Be No Rock N' Roll, When They Take Away Our Country, They'll Take Away Our Soul," by C.W. McCall (1976).
59. Eric Clapton.
60. Stu Sutcliffe, the original "fifth Beatle."

Chart Milestones
Quiz Answers

1. Louis Armstrong with "Hello Dolly."
2. Pat and Debby Boone; Frank and Nancy Sinatra; Johnny and Rosanne Cash.
3. Mae Axton was one of the co-writers of Elvis' "Heartbreak Hotel," and Hoyt Axton wrote "Joy To The World," the Three Dog Night hit.
4. Mr. Acker Bilk's "Stranger On The Shore."
5. Creedence Clearwater Revival.
6. Les Paul's "Magic Melody, Pt.2" at 00:01—that's one second long.
7. "Lisbon Antigua" and "Poor People Of Paris" from 1956.
8. "Heartbreak Hotel."
9. "Love Me Tender."
10. Guy Mitchell's "Singing The Blues."
11. Debby Boone ("You Light Up My Life") and Olivia Newton-John ("Physical"). Whitney Houston's "I Will Always Love You" broke both records.
12. Actor Tab Hunter.
13. Buddy Knox and "Party Doll."
14. "That'll Be The Day."
15. The Platters singing "Twilight Time" (1958).
16. The advent of stereo recordings.
17. "Turn, Turn, Turn" by The Byrds is based on the Bible's book of Ecclesiastes.
18. "The Shortest Song In The World," by Kenny Price, timed out at 00:17 seconds.
19. "Harper Valley P.T.A." made an amazing 74-point leap in one week.
20. "The Jimmy Rodgers Blues," by Elton Britt.
21. "Hey Jude," by The Beatles.
22. "Day For Decision," by Johnny Sea (5:39).
23. "Rock Around The Clock," by Bill Haley & The Comets.
24. Cleveland disc jockey Alan Freed is credited with the honors, a derivation connected to the 1947 r&b hit "We're Gonna Rock, We're Gonna Roll," by Wild Bill Moore.
25. It was a hit by The Boswell Sisters in 1934.
26. "Crazy, Man, Crazy," by Bill Haley & The Comets (1953).
27. "Leaving On A Jet Plane."
28. Kay Starr, "The Rock & Roll Waltz."
29. Domenico Modugno's "Volare."
30. Frankie was eleven years old.
31. Bobby Darin's "Mack The Knife."
32. "El Paso," by Marty Robbins.
33. "Running Bear," by Johnny Preston.
34. Mark Dinning broke ground with "Teen Angel."

35. Connie Francis.
36. Chubby Checker's "The Twist."
37. "Stay," by Maurice Williams & The Zodiacs.
38. Al Jolson in 1926.
39. The Shirelles.
40. "It's Now Or Never."
41. Del Shannon with "From Me To You" in 1963.
42. Michael Jackson from "Bad" (LP).
43. Songs by The Beatles occupied the top five positions.
44. Whitney Houston.
45. "Tequila," by The Champs went from #12 to #1.
46. Anka wrote "Diana" when he was fifteen.
47. It marked the end of the 78rpm record.
48. Glenn Miller's "Chattanooga Choo Choo."
49. Gene Austin's "My Blue Heaven."
50. "There's A Star spangled Banner Waving Somewhere."
51. David Houston.
52. Iron Butterfly's "In A Gadda Da Vida."
53. Jim Nesbitt.
54. Johnny Cash (48 in all).
55. Fats Domino.
56. "My Ding-A-Ling" (1972).
57. Elvis Presley.
58. The Beatles.
59. Connie Smith ("Once A Day" hit #1 in Quebec, Canada).
60. "Wimoweh" became "The Lion Sleeps Tonight," by The To-

Rhythm-and-Blues
Quiz Answers

1. Darlene Franklin.
2. Bo Diddley.
3. Robinson.
4. Gary U.S. Bonds.
5. "Blues Boy."
6. Vernon Isley. He was the youngest brother.
7. Dionne and Dee Dee Warwick, and Judy Clay.
8. Her brother was a well-known fighter, Ernie Terrell.
9. Stax is an amalgamation of the first two letters of the last last of brother/sister label owners, Jim STewart and Estelle AXton.
10. Fame is an acronym for the Florence Alabama Music Emporium.
11. The Pastels.
12. Jimmy Jones.
13. "Handy Man," which became James Taylor's first Columbia hit in 1977.
14. Joey Dee & The Starlighters.
15. The Chords.
16. Miss Johnnie Richardson teamed up with Joe Rivers as Johnnie & Joe for the hit "Over The Mountain, Across The Sea (written by the lone male Heart, Rex Garvin), and Jeanette "Baby" Washington, with "That's How Heartaches Are Made," a 1963 cross-over hit.
17. Wilson Pickett and Eddie Floyd.
18. Little Richard. Their label, Specialty, hoped Williams would duplicate the irrepressible Richard Penniman's success.
19. "The Dog," "Walking The Dog," "Can Your Monkey Do The Dog?" and "Somebody Stole My Dog."
20. Promoters booked Lou Christie, whom they thought to be a black female.
21. Lewis Lymon & The Teenchords.
22. Jerry Butler and, later, Curtis Mayfield.
23. "Mr. Lee" and "I Shot Mr. Lee."
24. The Shirelles.

25. The Four Pennies.
26. Patti LaBelle and Cindy Birdsong were in The Ordettes, and Sarah Dash and Nona Hendrix came out of The Del Capris.
27. They began as The Ikettes, backing Ike and Tina Turner.
28. The Gems, and Rotary Connection.
29. Debbie Dean.
30. Her directive, "Don't Let Him Shop Around," was in response to The Miracles' smash, "Shop Around."
31. Mary Wells, Kim Weston, Tammi Terrell, and Diana Ross.
32. Billy Vera, a white Atlantic artist, and William Bell, ler Stax label-mate.
33. Carla Thomas; they first squared off in the 1967 hit "Tramp," from their "King & Queen" album.
34. "Ruler Of My Heart," by Irma Thomas.
35. Jimmy James and The Blue Flames.
36. Ronnie Spector.
37. Aretha's sister, Erma Franklin, on the Shout label.
38. Irma Thomas.
39. They were cousins: James Purify and Bobby Dicky.
40. The O'Kaysions, who hailed from North Carolina.
41. The Rascals' "People Got To Be Free."
42. "Grazing In The Grass" by Hugh Masakela in 1968, and The Friends Of Distinction in 1969.
43. "Hey Jude," The Beatles; "Born To Be Wild," Steppenwolf; "Hey Joe," The Leaves; "You Keep Me Hangin' On," Supremes/Vanilla Fudge; and, "Sugar, Sugar," The Archies.
44. Janis Joplin, 1969, and The Three Degrees, 1970.
45. It was an adaptation of Sam Cooke's "Yeah, Man."
46. "Otis Sleep On."
47. "You Think You're Hot Stuff."
48. Not until 1972, with a recording of his long-time signature song, "My Ding-A-Ling."
49. She was behind the wheel when boyfriend Marc Bolan of T-Rex was killed in a car accident.
50. Tax evasion.

Heavy Metal
Quiz Answers

1. Kiss
2. The Runaways
3. Vinnie Vincent (Cusano) of the Vinnie Vincent Invasion.
4. Tommy Lee
5. Nikki Sixx
6. Metallica; Mustaine was lead guitarist.
7. Deep Purple
8. Cactus
9. New York Dolls
10. James Osterberg, better known as Iggy Pop
11. Celtic Frost
12. Motley Crue
13. They all hail from San Francisco.
14. Garth Brooks
15. Motorhead and Girlschool
16. John Entwistle of The Who
17. Gaye Bykers On Acid
18. Sharon Osbourne
19. "Summertime Blues," by Blue Cheer.
20. Jake E. Moore

Miscellaneous Trivia #2
Quiz Answers

1. Russian Roulette.
2. Joe Dowell and "Wooden Heart."
3. Eddy Arnold.
4. Laurie London (He's Got The Whole World In His Hands").
5. Conway Twitty.
6. Tiny Tim (Tip Toe Thru The Tulips").
7. Bill Haley's "Rock Around The Clock" (24 million copies).
8. Hank Ballard.
9. Pink Floyd's "Dark Side Of The Moon."
10. "Johnny Mastis' Greatest Hits."
11. Willie Nelson's "Stardust."
12. Danny & The Juniors.
13. Skeeter Davis
14. "Tainted Love" by Soft Cell.
15. Hank Snow's "I'm Movin' On."
16. "Little Darlin'"; Maurice Williams.
17. Bobby Darin.
18. Donny Osmond.
19. Merle Haggard; no, Johnny Cash played concerts in prisons, he didn't serve time.
20. "Circus Boy."
21. Wink Martindale.
22. Henry Mancini.
23. Little Richard.
24. John D. Loudermilk.
25. Twelve years old.
26. John Denver.
27. Don Williams.
28. Kenny Rogers.
29. Dolly PArton.
30. Roy Acuff; Kitty Wells.
31. The Beatles.
32. Walter Brennan.
33. Johnny Crawford.
34. A Mouseketeer.
35. Donna Summer.
36. Roy Rogers.
37. Len Slye.
38. Minnie Pearl.
39. Jerry Lee Lewis.
40. Bill Hayes.
41. "Wake Up Little Susie."
42. Benny Bell's "Shaving Cream."
43. Thumper Jones.
44. Ray Stevens.
45. Jimmy Ellis.
46. Johnnie Taylor.
47. James Brown.
48. Charles Hardin (Buddy) Holly.
49. "Club 15."
50. Gogi Grant ("The Wayward Wind").
51. "Rock Around The Clock."
52. Bill Haley.
53. Jim Reeves.
54. Shirley & Lee.
55. David Seville & The Chipmunks
56. The Supremes.
57. Neil Sedaka.
58. Simon & Garfunkel.
59. The Mamas & The Papas and The Lovin' Spoonful.
60. Creedence Clearwater Revival.
61. Elton John.

62. Buck Owens.
63. Palestine, Texas.
64. Green River Boys.
65. Linda Ronstadt.
66. "Snoopy," from the cartoon strip "Peanuts."
67. Sheb Wooley of "Purple People Eater" fame.
68. Eddie Rabbit, who penned "Kentucky Rain" for Elvis Presley.
69. Hank Williams Sr.
70. Dwight Yoakum.
71. "The End Of The World."
72. Bobby Bare became Bill Parsons through a record company error.
73. Bobby Vinton.
74. Eartha Kitt.
75. The McCoys.
76. Fats Domino.
77. The Platters.
78. Ricky Nelson.
79. Bobby Goldsboro.
80. Lester Flatt & Earl Scruggs.
81. Willie Nelson.
82. Waylon Jennings.
83. Woody Guthrie; "This Land Is Your Land."
84. Burl Ives.
85. Sonny James.
86. Elvis Presley.
87. The Oak Ridge Boys.
88. Alice Cooper.
89. Tom Jones.
90. Janis Joplin.
91. Kris Kristofferson.
92. The Young Rascals.
93. The Statler Brothers (from Statler Tisues).
94. The Yardbirds.
95. Iron Butterfly.
96. Derek; "Cinnamon."
97. Judy Collins.
98. Bob Seger.
99. Ozark Mountain Daredevils.
100. Don McLean.

Performer &
Song Title Indexes

Performer Index to the Weekly Charts, 1935-1994

Following the performer names below, six-digit numerical citations refer to weekly chart dates. For example: 012481 refers to the listing for the week of January 24, 1981, etc. This index affords an at-a-glance summary of how successful an artist was in reaching the Top Ten.

072967, 080567, 081267, 092367, 093067, 100767, 101467, 102167, 102867, 110467, 111167, 030268

ASTAIRE, FRED 083135, 090735, 092135, 092835, 100535, 101235, 101935, 102635, 110235, 110935, 111635, 112335, 020136, 020836, 021536, 022236, 022936, 030736, 031436, 032136, 032836, 040436, 041136, 041836, 042536, 050236, 050936, 052336, 091936, 092636, 100336, 101036, 101736, 102436, 103136, 110736, 111436, 112136, 112836, 120536, 121236, 121936, 052237, 060537, 061237, 062637, 071037, 112737, 120437, 121137, 121837, 122537, 010138, 011538, 012938, 100138, 100838, 101538, 102238, 102938, 110538, 111238, 111938, 112638

ASTLEY, RICK 022088, 022788, 030588, 031288, 031988, 032688, 040288, 052888, 060488, 061188, 061888, 062588, 070288, 091788, 021189, 021889, 022589, 042091, 042791, 050491, 051191

ATLANTA RHYTHM SECTION 040977, 041677, 042377, 043077, 050777, 051477, 051378, 052078, 052778, 060378

ATLANTIC STARR 030186, 030886, 031586, 032286, 032986, 040586, 051687, 052387, 053087, 060687, 061387, 062087, 062787, 022992, 030792, 031492, 032192, 032892, 040492, 041192, 041892, 042592

AUSTIN, PATTI & JAMES INGRAM 011583, 012283, 012983, 020583, 021283, 021983, 022683, 030583, 031283

AUTRY, GENE 122449, 123149, 010750, 041550, 120250, 120950, 121650, 122350, 123050, 122051, 122751, 010352, 122652

AVALON, FRANKIE 031459, 032159, 032859, 040459, 041159, 041859, 042559, 050259, 050959, 102459, 103159, 110759, 121959, 122659, 010160, 010860, 011560, 012260, 012960, 020560, 021260, 021960

AVERAGE WHITE BAND 012675, 020175, 020875, 021575, 022275, 030175, 030875, 062175, 062875

B

B. T. EXPRESS 110974, 111674, 112374, 113074, 120774, 121474, 122174, 031575, 032275, 032975, 040575, 041275

BABYFACE 100789, 101489, 102189, 102889, 042890, 050590

BACHELORS 062064

BACHMAN-TURNER OVERDRIVE 102674, 110274, 110974, 113074, 120774

BAD COMPANY 101274, 101974, 102674, 110274, 092075, 092775

BAD ENGLISH 102889, 110489, 111189, 111889, 112589, 022490, 030390, 031090, 031790

BADFINGER 032870, 040470, 041170, 041870, 042570, 050270, 120570, 121270, 121970, 122670, 012272, 012972, 020572, 021272

BAEZ, JOAN 091871, 092571, 100271, 100971, 101671, 102371, 103071, 110671

BAILEY, MILDRED 021337, 022737, 031337, 040337, 041037, 041737, 042437, 050837, 051537, 052237, 052937, 060537, 061237, 061937, 090338, 091038, 091738, 092438, 100138, 100838, 101538, 102238, 102938, 110538, 111238, 111938

BAILEY, PHILIP & PHIL COLLINS 011985, 012685, 020285, 020985, 021685, 022385, 030285

BAKER, ANITA 102586, 110186, 112688, 120388, 121088, 121788,

122488, 010789

BAKER, LAVERN 030759

BALIN, MARTY 072581, 080181, 080881, 081581

BALL, KENNY 030262, 030962, 031662, 032362, 040662, 042062

BALLARD, HANK 082660, 090260, 090960, 111860, 112560

BANANARAMA 092284, 092984, 080986, 081686, 082386, 083086, 090686, 091386, 092086, 091287, 091987, 092687, 100387, 101087, 101787

BANGLES 040586, 041286, 041986, 042686, 050286, 112986, 120686, 121386, 122086, 122786, 011087, 011787, 011688, 012388, 013088, 020688, 021388, 122488, 010789, 011489, 031889, 032589, 040189, 040889, 041589, 042289

BARE, BOBBY PARSONS, BILL

BARRY, LEN 103065, 110665, 111365, 112065, 112765, 120465, 121165

BARTON, EILEEN 032550, 040150, 040850, 041550, 042250, 042950, 050650, 051350, 052050, 052750, 060350

BASIL, TONI 112082, 112782, 120482, 121182, 121882, 122582, 010883, 011583, 012283

BASS, FONTELLA 110665, 111365, 112065, 112765, 120465, 121165

BASSEY, SHIRLEY 032065, 032765, 040365

BAY CITY ROLLERS 120675, 121375, 122075, 122775, 010376, 011076, 032776, 040376, 081377, 082077

BAZUKA 080275

BEACH BOYS 050463, 051163, 051863, 052563, 060163, 060863, 091463, 092163, 092863, 120763, 121463, 122163, 122863, 030764, 031464, 032164, 032864, 041364, 062064, 052764, 070464, 071164, 071864, 072564, 080164, 080864, 101764, 102464, 121264, 121964, 122664, 051565, 052265, 052965, 060565, 061265, 061965, 062665, 081465, 082165, 082865, 090465, 091165, 012966, 020566, 021266, 021966, 042366, 043066, 050766, 051466, 052166, 091766, 102466, 111266, 111966, 112666, 120366, 121066, 121766, 122466, 071776, 072476, 073176, 080776, 081476, 082176, 102288, 102988, 110588, 111288, 111988

BEAR, EDWARD 022473, 030373, 031073, 031773, 032473, 033173

BEASTIE BOYS 022887, 030787

BEATLES 012564, 020164, 020864, 021564, 022264, 022964, 030764, 031464, 032164, 032864, 040464, 041164, 041864, 042564, 050264, 050964, 051564, 052364, 060664, 061364, 062064, 072564, 080164, 080864, 081564, 082264, 082964, 090564, 091264, 121264, 121964, 122664, 010265, 010965, 011665, 012365, 030665, 031365, 032065, 032765, 040365, 050565, 051565, 052265, 052965, 060565, 061265, 082165, 082865, 090465, 091165, 091865, 092565, 100265, 100965, 101665, 102365, 103065, 110665, 010166, 010866, 011566, 012266, 012966, 020566, 021266, 030566, 031966, 032666, 040266, 040966, 062566, 070266, 070966, 071666, 072366, 082766, 090366, 090966, 091066, 091766, 092466, 100166, 031167, 031867, 032567, 040167, 040867, 080567, 081267, 081967, 082667, 090267, 090967, 091667, 120967, 121667, 122367, 123067, 010668, 011368, 012068, 012768, 033068, 040668, 041368, 042068, 042768, 050468, 051168, 091468, 092168, 092868, 100568, 101268, 101968, 102668, 110268, 110968, 111668,

112368, 113068, 120768, 121468, 051069, 051769, 052469, 053169, 060769, 061469, 062169, 062869, 070569, 071269, 071969, 072669, 080269, 110169, 110869, 111569, 112269, 112969, 120669, 121369, 122069, 122769, 032170, 032870, 040470, 041170, 041870, 042570, 050270, 050970, 051670, 052370, 053070, 060670, 061370, 062070, 062770, 070470, 071170, 071076, 071776, 072476, 073176, 080776

BEAU BRUMMELS 052965, 060565, 061265

BECK 043094

BEE GEES 092168, 092868, 100568, 101268, 101968, 102668, 012569, 020169, 020869, 010971, 011671, 012371, 013071, 020671, 021371, 022071, 071771, 072471, 073171, 080771, 081471, 082171, 082871, 090471, 091171, 091871, 071975, 072675, 080275, 080975, 081675, 082375, 083075, 090675, 112975, 120675, 121375, 122075, 080776, 081476, 082176, 082876, 090476, 091176, 091876, 102376, 103076, 110676, 111376, 112076, 112776, 120476, 121176, 111277, 111977, 112677, 120377, 121077, 121777, 122477, 010778, 011478, 012178, 012778, 020478, 021178, 021878, 022578, 030478, 031178, 031878, 032578, 040178, 040878, 041578, 042278, 042978, 050678, 051378, 052078, 121678, 122378, 012178, 010679, 011278, 012079, 012779, 020379, 021079, 022479, 030379, 031079, 031779, 032479, 033179, 040779, 041479, 051979, 052679, 060279, 060979, 061679, 093089

BELAFONTE, HARRY 011957, 012657, 020257, 020957, 021657, 022357, 030257, 030957, 031657, 032357, 033057

BELL BIV DEVOE 051290, 051990, 052690, 060290, 060990, 061690, 062390, 063090, 070790, 071490, 081190, 081890, 082590, 090190, 090890, 091590, 092290, 092990, 100690

BELL NOTES 031459, 032159, 032859, 040459

BELL, ARCHIE & THE DRELLS 042768, 050468, 051168, 051868, 052568, 060168, 060868, 061568, 062268, 082468, 083168, 090768

BELL, WILLIAM 043077

BELLAMY BROTHERS 032776, 040376, 041076, 041776, 042476, 050176, 050876

BELLS 042471, 050171, 050871, 051571

BENATAR, PAT 121380, 122080, 122780, 111983, 112683, 120383, 121083, 121783, 122483, 121584, 122284, 010585, 011285, 011985, 091485

BENNETT, TONY 072151, 072851, 080451, 081151, 081851, 082551, 090151, 090851, 091551, 092051, 092751, 100451, 101151, 101851, 102551, 110151, 110851, 111551, 112251, 112951, 120651, 121351, 122051, 111453, 112853, 120553, 121253, 121953, 122653, 010254, 010954, 011654, 012354, 013054, 020654, 021354, 020254, 022754, 030654, 031354, 032054, 032754, 040354, 041054, 090757, 091457, 092157, 092857, 100557, 101957

BENNY GOODMAN ORCH. 071136, 071836, 080136, 080836, 112136, 043038, 050738, 051438, 052138, 052838, 060438, 061138, 061838, 062538, 050942, 052342, 053042, 060642, 061342, 062042, 062742, 070442, 071142, 071842, 072542, 080142, 080842, 032445

BENNY GOODMAN ORCH. (VR: BENNY GOODMAN) 072145, 081145, 081845, 082545, 090145, 090845, 091545, 092245, 092945, 100845, 101345, 102745

BENNY GOODMAN ORCH. (VR: BETTY VAN) 090437, 091137, 091837, 092537, 100237, 100937, 101637

BENNY GOODMAN ORCH. (VR: DOTTIE REID) 090845, 091545, 092245, 092945, 100645, 101345, 102045, 102745, 110345

BENNY GOODMAN ORCH. (VR: ELLA FITZGERALD) 012337, 013037, 020637, 021337, 022037, 022737, 030637, 031337, 032037, 032737

BENNY GOODMAN ORCH. (VR: HELEN FORREST) 042040, 042740, 050440, 052540, 062940, 070640, 071340, 072740, 030643, 031343, 032743, 040343, 041043, 041743, 042443, 050143, 050843, 051543, 052243, 052943, 060543, 061243, 061943, 062643, 071043

BENNY GOODMAN ORCH. (VR: HELEN WARD) 042035, 042735, 050435, 051135, 051835, 071335, 110935, 111635, 112335, 113035, 120735, 121435, 122135, 122835, 010436, 011136, 011836, 012536, 020136, 021536, 022236, 030736, 031436, 032136, 032836, 040436, 041136, 041836, 042536, 050236, 050936, 051636, 052336, 053036, 060636, 061336, 062036, 062736, 070436, 071136, 071836, 072536, 080136, 080836, 081536, 082236, 082936, 090536, 091236, 091936, 101736, 102436, 103136, 110736, 111436, 112136, 112836, 120536, 121236

BENNY GOODMAN ORCH. (VR: LOUISE TOBIN) 112539, 120239, 120939, 121639, 122339, 123039, 010640, 012541, 020141, 020841, 022241, 030141, 030841, 031541, 032241, 032941, 040541, 041241, 041941, 042641, 050341, 051041

BENNY GOODMAN ORCH. (VR: MARGARET MACRAE) 022037, 022737, 030637, 032037, 032737, 041037, 041737

BENNY GOODMAN ORCH. (VR: MARTHA TILTON) 010138, 010838, 011538, 012938, 020538, 021938, 032638, 040238, 082738, 090338, 091038, 091738, 092438, 100138, 100838, 101538, 122438, 123138, 010739, 011439, 012139, 012839, 020439, 021139, 021839, 022539, 042939, 050639, 051339, 052039, 052739, 060339, 061039, 061739, 062439, 070139, 070839, 071539

BENNY GOODMAN ORCH. (VR: MILDRED BAILEY) 020340, 021740, 022440, 030240, 030940, 031640, 032340

BENNY GOODMAN ORCH. (VR: PEGGY LEE) 032142, 032842, 040442, 041142, 041842, 042542, 050242, 050942, 052342, 053042, 060642, 092245, 102045

BENNY GOODMAN ORCH. (VR: PEGGY MANN) 021045

BENSON, GEORGE 082876, 090476, 052778, 060378, 061078, 061778, 083080, 090680, 090380, 092080, 092780, 100480, 101180, 100982, 011682, 012382, 013082, 020682, 021382

BENT FABRIC 092962, 100662, 101362

BENTON, BROOK 032159, 032859, 040459, 041159, 041859, 042559, 112159, 112859, 120559, 121259, 121959, 093060, 040761, 062361, 063061, 070761, 071461, 072161, 072661, 080461, 081161, 110563, 011263, 011963, 022170, 022870, 030770, 031470, 032170

BENTON, BROOK & DINAH WASHING-TON 031160, 031860, 032560, 040160, 040860, 070160, 070860

CAMEO 110886, 111586, 112286, 112986, 120686

CAMPBELL, GLEN 112368, 113068, 120768, 121468, 122168, 122868, 010469, 011169, 011869, 032969, 040569, 041269, 041969, 042669, 050369, 103170, 080975, 081675, 082375, 083075, 090675, 091375, 092075, 092775, 100475, 040277, 040977, 041677, 042377, 043077, 050777, 051477, 052177

CAMPBELL, TEVIN 020192, 020892, 021592, 022292, 022992, 030792, 031492, 120493, 011594, 012294, 012994, 051494

CANDYMAN 111090, 112490

CANNON, FREDDY 062059, 062759, 070459, 071159, 071859, 072559, 122659, 010160, 010860, 011560, 012260, 012960, 020560, 061562, 062262, 062962, 070662, 071362, 072062

CAPITOLS 061866, 062566, 070266, 070966

CAPRIS 021761, 022461, 030361, 031061

CAPTAIN & TENNILLE 061475, 062175, 062875, 070575, 071275, 071975, 110875, 111575, 112975, 120675, 022876, 030676, 031376, 032076, 032776, 040376, 041076, 041776, 060576, 061276, 061976, 062676, 070376, 071076, 071776, 103076, 110676, 111376, 112076, 112776, 120476, 121176, 121876, 111878, 112578, 120879, 121579, 122279, 010580, 011280, 011980, 012680, 020280, 020980, 021680, 022380, 030180, 030880

CARA, IRENE 082380, 083080, 090680, 091380, 092080, 092780, 051483, 052183, 052883, 060483, 061183, 061883, 062583, 070283, 070983, 071683, 072383, 073083, 080683, 081383, 052684, 060284, 060984

CARAVELLS 120763, 121463, 122163, 122863

CAREY, MARIAH 072190, 072890, 080490, 081190, 081890, 082590, 090190, 102990, 110390, 111090, 111790, 112490, 120190, 120890, 021691, 022391, 030291, 030991, 031691, 032391, 033091, 050491, 051191, 051891, 052591, 060191, 060891, 061591, 062291, 092891, 100591, 101291, 101991, 102691, 110291, 110991, 120791, 121491, 122191, 010492, 011192, 011892, 012592, 020192, 020892, 021592, 032892, 040492, 041192, 041892, 042592, 050292, 050992, 060692, 061392, 062092, 062792, 070492, 071192, 071892, 072592, 082193, 082893, 090493, 091193, 091893, 092593, 100293, 100993, 101693, 102393, 103093, 110693, 111393, 112093, 112793, 120493, 121193, 121893, 122593, 010194, 010894, 011594, 012294, 012994, 020594, 021294, 021994, 022694, 030594, 031294, 031994, 032694, 040294, 040994, 041694, 042394, 043094, 050794, 051494

CARLISLE, BELINDA 072686, 080286, 080986, 081686, 082386, 083086, 111487, 112187, 112887, 120587, 121287, 121987, 022788, 030588, 031288, 031988, 032688, 061188, 061888

CARLISLE, UNA MAE 040541, 042641, 050341, 051041, 051741, 052441, 053141, 060741, 061441

CARLTON, CARL 111674, 112374, 113074

CARMEN, ERIC 022176, 022876, 030676, 031376, 032076, 032776, 013088, 020688, 021388, 022088, 022788, 071688, 072388, 073088, 080688, 081388, 082088

CARMICHAEL, HOAGY & CASS DALEY

052750, 060350, 061050, 061750, 062450, 070150

CARNES, KIM 081680, 082380, 083080, 050281, 050981, 051681, 052381, 053081, 060681, 061381, 062081, 062781, 070481, 071181, 071881, 072581, 080181

CARPENTERS 071170, 071870, 072570, 080170, 080870, 081570, 082270, 082970, 090570, 091270, 091970, 101070, 101770, 102470, 103170, 110770, 111470, 112170, 112970, 120570, 030671, 031371, 032071, 032771, 040371, 041071, 041771, 060571, 061271, 061971, 062671, 070371, 071071, 071771, 092571, 100271, 100971, 101671, 102371, 103071, 110671, 111371, 020572, 021272, 021972, 022672, 030472, 031172, 081972, 082672, 090272, 033173, 040173, 041473, 042173, 042873, 050573, 070773, 071473, 072173, 072873, 080473, 081173, 111073, 111173, 112473, 120173, 120873, 121673, 122273, 122973, 010475, 011175, 011875, 012675, 020175, 050375, 051075, 051775, 052475, 053175

CARR, CATHY 051256, 051956, 052656, 060256, 060956, 061656, 062356, 063056, 070756

CARR, VICKI 102167, 102867, 110467, 111167, 111867, 112567

CARRACK, PAUL 021388, 022088, 022788

CARS 020682, 021382, 030682, 031382, 032082, 042884, 050584, 051284, 051984, 090884, 091584, 092284, 092984, 100684, 102084, 122885, 011186, 011886

CARSON, MINDY 042250, 050650

CARTER, CLARENCE 092868, 100568, 101268, 082270, 082970, 090570, 091270, 091970, 092670

CARTER, MEL 082865, 090465

CASCADES 020963, 021663, 022363, 030263, 030963, 031663, 032363, 033063, 040563

CASH, JOHNNY 080969, 081669, 082369, 083069, 090669, 091369, 092069

CASINOS 022567, 030467, 031167, 031867

CASSIDY, DAVID 121871, 122571, 010172, 010872

CASSIDY, SHAUN 062577, 070277, 070977, 071677, 072377, 073077, 080677, 092477, 100177, 100877, 101577, 102277, 102977, 110577, 010778, 011478, 012178

CETERA, PETER 071986, 072686, 080286, 080986, 081686, 082386, 092488, 100188, 100888

CETERA, PETER WITH AMY GRANT 111586, 112286, 112986, 120686, 121386, 122086

CHAD & JEREMY 101064, 101764, 102464

CHAIRMAN OF THE BOARD 030770, 031470, 032170, 032870

CHAKACHAS 032572, 040172, 040872

THE CHAMPS 030858, 031558, 032258, 032958, 040558, 041258, 041958, 042658

CHANDLER, GENE 020262, 020962, 022362, 030262, 030962, 031662, 032362

CHANDLER, KAREN 022853, 030753, 032153

CHANNEL, BRUCE 022362, 030262, 030962, 031662, 032362, 040662

CHANTAYS 042063, 042763, 050463, 051163, 051863

CHAPIN, HARRY 112374, 113074, 120774, 121474, 122174, 122874

CHAPMAN, TRACY 082088, 082788, 090388, 091088

CHARLENE 050182, 050882, 051582, 052282, 052982, 060582

CHARLES, JIMMY 091660, 092360,

093060, 100760, 101460, 102160

CHARLES, RAY 082259, 082959, 090559, 091259, 111160, 111860, 112560, 120260, 050561, 092961, 100661, 102061, 102761, 110361, 110961, 111761, 112461, 052562, 060162, 060862, 061562, 062262, 062962, 070662, 071362, 072062, 072762, 080462, 081162, 081862, 082562, 090162, 090862, 091562, 121562, 122262, 122962, 010563, 052563, 101263, 101963, 102663, 110263, 110963, 020566, 021266, 021966

CHARLIE BARNET ORCH. (VR: BOB CARROLL) 010441, 011141, 011841, 012541, 020141, 020841, 021541, 022241, 030141, 030841, 031541, 032241, 032941, 040541, 041241, 041941

CHARLIE BARENT ORCH. (VR: MARY ANN MCCALL) 060140, 060840, 061540, 062240, 062940, 070640, 071340, 072040, 072740, 080340

CHARLIE DANIELS BAND 081179, 082579, 090179, 090879, 091579, 092279, 092979

CHARLIE SPIVAK ORCH. (VR: GARRY STEVENS) 122041, 010342, 012442, 021442, 082242, 082942, 090542, 091242, 091942, 092642, 100342, 101042, 101742, 102442, 103142, 110742, 111442, 112142, 112842, 120542

CHARLIE SPIVAK ORCH. (VR: JIMMIE SAUNDERS) 042845, 060945, 090145

CHEAP TRICK 070779, 071479, 072179, 072879, 080479, 061888, 062588, 070288, 070988, 071488, 072388, 092488, 100188, 100888, 101588

CHECKER, CHUBBY 082660, 090260, 090960, 091660, 092360, 093060, 100760, 101460, 102160, 102860, 110460, 022461, 030361, 031061, 031761, 032461, 033161, 040761, 041461, 081861, 111061, 111761, 120861, 122261, 122961, 010562, 011262, 011962, 012662, 020262, 020962, 022362, 030262, 030962, 032362, 040662, 042062, 042762, 050462, 051162, 110362, 111762, 112462, 120162, 120862, 121562, 122262, 122962, 010563, 011263, 011963, 012663

CHEECH & CHONG 100574, 101274

CHER 040266, 040966, 041666, 042366, 043066, 050766, 121667, 122367, 101671, 102371, 103071, 110671, 111371, 112071, 112771, 120471, 121171, 031172, 031872, 032572, 092273, 092973, 100373, 101373, 102073, 102773, 110373, 111073, 030588, 090989, 091689, 092389, 093089, 100789, 121689, 122389, 100690, 011390

CHER & PETER CETERA 042989, 050689, 051389, 052089

CHERRY, DON 102850, 110450, 111150, 111850, 112550, 120250, 120950, 020456, 021156, 022556, 030356, 031756

CHERRY, NENEH 060389, 061089, 061789, 062489, 070189, 070889, 093089

CHIC 021178, 021878, 022578, 030478, 031178, 031878, 112578, 120278, 120978, 121678, 122378, 010679, 011379, 012079, 012779, 020379, 021079, 021779, 022479, 030379, 042179, 042879, 050579, 051279, 072179, 072879, 080479, 081179, 082579, 090179, 090879, 091579

CHICAGO 060670, 061370, 082970, 090570, 091270, 091970, 092670, 121270, 121970, 122670, 010271, 010971, 080771, 081471, 082171, 090972, 091672, 092372, 093072, 081873, 090173, 111773, 112473, 120173, 120873, 121673, 122273,

051174, 051874, 052574, 072774, 080374, 081074, 081774, 052475, 053175, 060775, 061875, 091875, 092576, 100276, 100976, 101676, 102376, 103076, 110676, 111376, 110577, 111277, 111977, 112677, 120377, 121077, 073182, 080782, 081482, 082182, 082882, 090482, 091182, 091882, 092682, 100282, 100982, 101682, 100684, 102084, 102784, 110384, 111084, 010585, 011285, 011985, 012685, 020285, 020985, 020787, 021487, 022187, 022887, 080688, 081388, 082088, 082788, 090388, 111988, 112688, 120388, 121088, 121788, 122488, 010789, 032589, 021090, 021790, 022490

CHIFFONS 031663, 032363, 033063, 040563, 041363, 042063, 042763, 050463, 051163, 062963, 070663, 071363, 072063, 062566

CHILD, JANE 033190, 040790, 041490, 042190, 042890, 050590

CHI-LITES 111371, 112071, 112771, 120471, 121171, 121871, 122571, 010172, 051372, 052072, 052772, 060472, 061172, 061772, 062472

CHIPMUNKS 121958, 122658, 010359, 011059, 011759, 012459, 013159, 031459, 032159, 032859, 040459, 041159

THE CHORDETTES 111354, 112054, 112754, 120454, 121154, 121854, 122554, 010155, 010855, 011555, 012255, 012955, 020555, 021255, 021955, 022655, 030555, 031955, 040558, 041258, 041958, 070761, 071461, 072161, 072861, 080461, 081161, 081861, 082561

CHRIS BARBER'S JAZZ BAND 022859, 030759, 031459, 032159

CHRISTIE, LOU 052563, 060163, 060863, 061563, 020566, 021266, 021966, 022666, 030566, 022666, 102569

CLANTON, JIMMY 082258, 082958, 090558, 091258, 091958, 092658, 100358, 012260, 012960, 020560, 021260, 100662

CLAPTON, ERIC 082474, 083174, 090774, 091474, 092174, 022578, 030478, 031178, 031878, 032578, 040178, 040878, 041578, 042278, 042978, 050678, 011379, 012079, 050281, 050981, 031492, 032192, 032892, 040492, 041192, 041892, 042592, 050292, 050992, 051692, 052392

CLARK, BUDDY 030847, 032247, 032947, 040547, 041247, 041947, 042647, 050347, 051047, 051747

CLARK, BUDDY WITH RAY NOBLE ORCH. 032247, 032947, 040547, 041247, 041947, 042647, 050347, 051047, 051747, 052447, 053147, 060747, 061447, 062147, 062847, 070547, 071247, 071947, 011048, 011748, 012448, 013148, 020748, 021448, 022148, 022848

CLARK, CLAUDINE 082562, 090162, 090862

CLARK, DEE 061661, 062361, 063061, 070761, 071461, 072161, 072861

CLARK, PETULA 010965, 011665, 012365, 013065, 020665, 021365, 022065, 022765, 030665, 041065, 041765, 042465, 050165, 050865, 051565, 022765, 012966, 020566, 021266, 021966, 022666, 030566, 082066, 082766, 040167, 040867, 041567, 042267, 042967, 070167, 070867, 071567

CLASH 011583, 012283, 012983, 020583, 021283

CLASSICS IV 012768, 020368, 021068, 021768, 022468, 030268, 120768, 121468, 121268, 122888, 010484, 031569, 032269, 032969, 040569

CLAUDE THORNHILL ORCH. (VR: JIMMY

600

FARRELL) 091837, 092537,
100237, 100937, 101637, 102337,
103037, 110637, 111337, 112037,
112737
CLAY, TOM 073171, 080771, 081471
CLIFF NOBLES & CO. 062968, 070668,
071368, 072068, 072768, 080368
CLIMAX 020572, 021272, 021972,
022672, 030472, 031172, 031872
CLIMAX BLUES BAND 050777, 051477,
052177, 052877, 060477, 061177
CLINE, PATSY 090861, 120161, 120861
CLOONEY, ROSEMARY 042851,
080451, 081151, 081851, 082551,
090151, 090851, 091551, 092051,
100451, 101151, 080752, 081452,
082152, 082952, 090552, 091252,
091952, 092652, 100352, 101052,
101752, 102452, 103152, 073154,
080754, 081454, 082154, 082854,
090454, 091154, 091854, 092554,
100254, 100954, 101654, 102354,
103054, 110654, 111354, 112054,
112754, 120454
CLUB NOUVEAU 031487, 032187,
032887, 040487, 041187, 041887
COASTERS 062758, 070458, 071158,
071858, 072558, 080158, 080858,
081558, 030759, 031459, 032159,
032859, 040459, 041159, 041859,
062759, 070459, 101759, 102459,
111459
COCHRAN, TOM 072592, 080192,
080892, 081592, 082992
COCKER, JOE 032275, 032975, 040575
COCKER, JOE & JENNIFER WARNES
102382, 103082, 110682, 111382,
112082, 112782, 120482
COFFEY, DENNIS 122571, 010172,
010872, 011572, 012272, 012972
COLE, COZY 102458, 103158, 110758,
111458, 112158, 112858, 120558,
121258
COLE, NAT KING 121446, 122146,
122846, 010447, 011147, 011847,
012547, 020147, 020847, 021547,
022247, 030147, 030847, 032247,
032947, 040547, 052248, 052948,
060548, 061248, 061948, 062648,
070348, 071048, 071748, 072448,
071550, 072250, 072950, 080550,
081250, 081950, 082650, 090250,
080950, 091650, 092350, 093050,
100750, 101450, 102150, 102850,
110450, 051951, 052651, 060251,
060951, 061651, 062351, 063051,
070751, 071451, 072151, 072851,
080451, 081151, 081851, 082551,
090151, 090851, 091551, 092051,
092751, 100451, 101851, 081452,
082952, 090552, 091252, 091952,
092652, 100352, 101052, 101752,
102452, 103152, 110752, 032153,
032853, 040453, 041153, 041853,
042553, 050253, 050953, 051653,
052353, 053053, 060653, 061353,
062053, 041754, 050154, 050854,
051554, 052254, 052954, 060554,
061954, 070354, 070955, 071655,
072355, 082055, 082755, 060758,
090862, 091562, 092262, 092962,
100662, 101362, 102062, 060863,
061563, 062263, 062963
COLE, NAT KING WITH STAN KENTON
ORCH. 111150
COLE, NATALIE 110175, 110875,
111575, 112975, 040277, 040977,
041677, 042377, 043077, 050777,
041578, 042278, 042388, 043088,
050788, 051488, 062489, 070189,
070889, 071589
COLLINS, JUDY 122168
COLLINS, PHIL 050579, 051279,
051979, 020583, 021283, 021983,
033184, 040784, 041484, 042184,
042884, 050584, 051284, 051984,
052684, 060284, 031685, 032385,
033085, 040685, 041385, 042085,
061585, 062285, 070685, 071385,
072085, 090785, 091485, 092185,

092885, 042686, 050286, 051086,
051786, 052486, 100888, 101588,
102288, 102988, 110588, 111288,
122488, 010789, 011489, 012189,
012889, 020489, 112589, 120989,
121689, 122389, 010690, 011390,
012090, 012790, 031790, 032490,
033190, 040790, 061690, 062390,
063090, 070790, 092290, 092990,
100690, 101390
COLLINS, PHIL & MARILYN MARTIN
110985, 111685, 112385, 113085,
120785, 121485, 122185, 122885,
122185
COLLINS, TYLER 072190, 072890,
080490
COLOR ME BADD 051891, 052591,
060191, 060891, 061591, 062291,
062991, 070691, 071391, 072091,
090791, 091491, 092191, 092891,
100591, 101291, 101991, 113091,
120791, 121491, 122191, 010492,
011192, 011892, 012592, 020192,
020892, 021592, 022292, 022992
COLTER, JESSI 060775, 061475,
062175, 062875, 070575, 071275
COMMANDER CODY 052772, 060472
COMMODORES 041076, 041776,
042476, 050176, 110676, 111376,
112076, 112776, 080677, 081377,
082077, 082777, 090377, 091077,
100877, 101577, 102277, 102977,
110577, 112677, 120377, 121077,
121777, 122477, 072278, 072978,
080578, 081278, 081978, 082678,
090278, 090978, 091678, 092378,
093078, 091579, 092279, 092979,
100679, 101379, 102079, 102779,
110379, 111079, 111779, 112479,
120179, 120879, 121579, 122279,
010580, 012580, 052480, 053180,
082281, 082981, 090581, 091281,
091981, 092681, 112881, 120581,
121281, 121981, 033085, 040685,
041385, 042085, 042785, 050485
COMO, PERRY 120244, 011345,
021045, 021145, 071445, 072845,
080445, 081145, 081845, 082545,
090145, 090845, 091545, 092245,
092945, 100645, 101345, 102045,
102745, 110345, 111045, 111745,
112445, 120145, 120845, 121545,
122245, 040446, 041346, 042046,
042746, 050446, 051146, 051846,
052546, 060146, 060846, 061546,
062246, 062946, 070646, 071346,
072046, 072746, 080346, 081046,
081746, 082446, 083146, 090746,
091446, 092146, 092846, 100546,
101246, 101946, 102646, 110246,
110946, 061447, 062147, 062847,
070547, 071247, 071947, 072647,
080247, 080947, 081647, 082347,
083047, 090647, 091347, 092047,
092747, 100447, 101147, 101847,
102547, 110147, 112947, 011748,
041048, 051548, 052248, 052948,
060548, 061248, 061948, 062648,
070348, 071048, 071748, 042349,
043049, 050749, 051449, 052149,
052849, 060449, 061149, 061849,
062549, 070249, 070949, 071649,
072349, 073049, 080649, 081349,
082049, 082749, 090349, 091049,
091749, 092449, 100149, 100849,
102249, 111249, 112649, 120349,
121049, 121749, 122449, 123149,
010750, 011450, 012150, 012850,
020450, 021150, 021850, 052050,
052750, 061050, 061750, 062450,
070150, 070850, 071550, 072250,
080550, 081250, 012751, 020351,
021051, 021751, 022451, 030351,
031051, 031751, 032451, 033151,
040751, 041451, 042151, 042851,
050551, 051251, 051951, 052651,
060251, 121952, 122652, 010353,
011053, 011753, 012453, 013153,
020753, 021453, 022153, 022853,
030753, 031453, 032153, 032853,

040453, 041153, 041853, 042553,
060653, 061353, 062753, 070453,
071153, 071853, 072553, 080153,
080853, 081553, 082253, 082953,
090553, 091253, 091953, 092653,
100353, 101053, 101753, 102453,
112153, 120553, 032054, 032754,
040354, 041054, 041754, 042454,
050154, 050854, 051554, 052254,
052954, 060554, 061254, 061954,
062654, 070354, 071054, 102354,
103054, 110654, 111354, 112054,
112754, 120454, 121154, 121854,
010855, 022655, 030555, 031255,
031955, 032655, 040255, 040955,
101555, 033156, 041456, 042156,
042856, 050556, 051256, 051956,
052656, 060256, 060956, 031657,
032357, 033057, 040657, 041357,
042057, 042757, 050457, 051157,
051857, 052557, 060157, 021558,
022258, 030158, 030858, 031558,
032258, 032958, 040558, 041958,
060758, 012371
COMO, PERRY & BETTY HUTTON
111850, 112550, 120250, 120950,
121650, 122350, 123050, 010651,
011351, 012051, 012751, 020351,
021051, 021751, 022451
COMO, PERRY & EDDIE FISHER
073152
CONLEY, ARTHUR 042267, 042967,
050667, 051367, 052067, 052767,
060367
CONNIFF, RAY 073066, 080666,
081166
CONTI, BILL 052177, 052877, 060477,
061177, 061877, 062577, 070277,
070977
CONTOURS 101362, 102062, 110362,
111062
COOKE, SAM 112357, 113057, 120757,
121457, 122157, 122857, 010458,
011158, 091660, 092360, 093060,
100760, 101460, 102160, 102860,
110460, 111160, 032362, 020665,
021365, 022065, 022765
COOKIES 042063, 042763, 050463
COOLIDGE, RITA 073077, 080677,
081377, 082077, 082777, 090377,
091077, 111277, 111977, 112677,
120377, 121077, 121777
COOPER, ALICE 072272, 072972,
080572, 081272, 080677, 081377,
082077, 111889, 112589
CORINA 072791, 080391, 081091,
081791, 082491
CORNELIUS BROTHERS & SISTER ROSE
061271, 061971, 062671, 070371,
071071, 071771, 072471, 062472,
070172, 070872, 071572, 072272,
072972, 080572, 081272
CORNELL, DON 060552, 061952,
062652, 070352, 110654, 100855,
102255, 102955
CORNELL, DON, ALAN DALE & JOHNNY
DESMOND 010954, 011654,
012354, 020654, 021354, 020254,
022754, 030654, 031354
CORTEZ, DAVE "BABY" 050259,
050959, 051659, 052359, 053059,
060659, 061359, 062059
COSBY, BILL 100767, 101467, 102167
COUGAR, JOHN 061982, 062682,
070382, 071082, 071782, 072482,
073182, 080782, 081482, 082182,
082882, 090482, 091182, 091882,
092682, 100282, 100982, 101682,
102382, 103082, 110682, 111382
COUNT BASIE (VR: THELMA CARPEN-
TER) 012045, 042145
THE COVER GIRLS 021790, 022490,
030390, 070492, 071192, 071892,
072592, 080192
COWSILLS 110467, 111167, 111867,
112567, 120267, 120967, 121667,
122367, 071368, 072068, 072768,
041269, 041969, 042669, 050369,
051069, 051769, 052469, 053169,

060769
CRAIG, FRANCIS 022848, 030648,
031348, 032048, 032748, 040348,
041048, 041748, 042448, 050148,
050848
CRAMER, FLOYD 111860, 112560,
120260, 120960, 121660, 122360,
123060, 010561, 011361, 012061,
012761, 020361, 041461, 042161,
042861, 050561, 051261, 051961,
071461, 072161, 072861, 080461
THE CRANBERRIES 021294
CRANE, LES 112771, 120471, 121171
CRASH TEST DUMMIES 040294,
040994, 041694, 042394, 043094,
050794, 051494
CRAWFORD, JOHNNY 062262
CRAZY WORLD OF ARTHUR BROWN
092168, 092868, 100568, 101268,
101968, 102668, 110268, 110968
CREAM 080368, 081068, 081768,
082468, 083168, 110268, 110968,
111668, 112368, 113068
CREEDENCE CLEARWATER REVIVAL
060769, 061469, 062169, 062869,
070569, 071269, 082369, 083069,
090669, 091369, 092069, 092769,
100469, 100369, 112969, 120669,
121369, 122069, 122769, 010370,
011070, 011770, 021470, 022170,
022870, 030770, 031470, 051670,
052370, 053070, 060670, 061370,
090570, 091270, 091970, 092670,
100370, 101070, 101770, 031371,
082171, 082871
CRESTS 012459, 013159, 020759,
021459, 022159, 022859, 030759,
031459
CREW CUTS 073154, 080754, 081454,
082154, 082854, 090454, 091154,
091854, 092554, 100254, 100954,
101654, 091154
CROCE, JIM 082672, 090272, 090972,
070773, 071473, 072173, 072873,
080473, 081173, 081873, 082573,
111773, 121673, 122273, 122973,
010574, 011274, 011974, 012674,
042074, 042774
CROSBY, BING 042935, 042035,
042735, 050435, 051135, 051835,
052535, 090735, 092135, 092835,
100535, 101235, 101935, 102635,
110235, 110935, 040436, 041136,
042536, 050236, 050936, 051636,
052336, 053036, 060636, 061336,
062036, 062736, 070436, 071136,
071836, 072536, 091936, 092636,
100336, 102436, 110736, 111436,
112136, 120536, 121236, 121936,
122636, 010237, 010937, 011637,
012337, 013037, 020637, 021337,
022037, 022737, 041737, 050137,
051537, 052937, 060537, 061237,
061937, 062637, 070337, 071037,
071737, 072437, 073137, 080737,
081437, 092537, 100237, 100937,
101637, 102337, 103037, 110637,
111337, 112037, 112737, 120437,
121137, 121837, 122537, 010138,
010838, 011538, 012238, 012938,
020538, 021238, 021938, 022638,
030538, 031238, 040238, 042338,
050738, 052138, 052838, 060438,
061138, 061838, 073038, 080638,
081338, 082738, 090338, 091038,
091738, 092438, 100138, 100838,
101538, 102238, 102938, 110538,
111238, 111938, 112638, 120338,
121038, 121738, 122438, 123138,
010739, 011439, 012139, 012839,
020439, 021139, 021839, 030439,
031139, 031839, 092339, 100739,
101439, 102139, 102839, 110439,
111139, 111839, 112539, 120239,
120939, 121639, 041340, 042040,
042740, 050440, 051140, 051840,
052540, 060140, 060840, 061540,
062240, 071340, 072040, 072740,
080340, 081040, 081740, 082440,
090740, 091440, 092140, 092840,

100540, 101240, 101940, 102640,
110240, 110940, 111640, 112340,
113040, 120740, 121440, 122140,
122840, 110841, 111541, 112241,
112941, 120641, 121341, 122041,
010342, 011042, 011742, 012442,
013142, 072542, 080842, 081542,
082242, 082942, 090542, 091242,
091942, 092642, 100342, 101042,
101742, 102442, 103142, 110742,
111442, 112142, 112842, 120542,
121242, 121942, 122642, 010243,
010943, 011643, 012343, 013043,
020643, 021343, 022043, 022743,
030643, 031343, 032043, 032743,
040343, 061943, 071743, 072443,
073143, 080743, 081443, 082143,
082843, 090443, 091143, 091843,
092543, 100243, 100943, 101643,
102343, 103043, 110643, 111343,
112043, 112743, 120443, 121143,
121843, 122543, 010144, 010844,
011544, 012244, 012944, 020544,
021944, 030444, 031144, 031844,
032544, 040144, 040844, 041544,
042244, 042944, 050644, 051344,
052044, 052744, 060344, 061044,
061744, 062444, 070144, 070844,
071544, 072244, 072944, 080544,
081244, 081944, 082644, 090244,
090944, 091644, 092344, 093044,
100744, 101444, 102144, 110444,
121644, 122344, 123044, 020345,
032445, 042145, 042845, 050545,
051245, 051945, 052645, 060245,
061645, 063045, 070745, 072145,
072845, 081145, 122245, 122945,
012646, 020246, 020946, 021646,
022346, 030246, 030946, 031646,
032346, 033046, 042746, 051146,
051846, 052546, 060146, 060846,
061546, 062246, 062946, 070646,
071346, 072046, 072746, 122846,
010447, 112247, 122747, 010348,
020748, 021448, 022148, 022848,
030648, 031348, 032048, 032748,
040348, 041048, 041748, 042448,
050148, 050848, 051548, 052248,
052948, 060548, 070348, 122548,
010149, 012249, 012949, 020549,
021249, 021949, 022649, 030549,
031249, 031949, 032649, 040249,
040949, 121049, 121749, 122449,
123149, 010750, 011450, 012150,
012850, 020450, 021150, 021850,
022550, 030450, 031150, 031850,
081950, 082650, 090250, 080950,
091650, 092350, 093050, 100750,
101450, 102150, 102850, 122550,
123050, 093050, 100750, 010651,
012051, 122554, 010155, 031255,
123155, 020158, 020858, 021558,
022258, 030158, 030858, 031558,
032258

CROSBY, BING & AL JOLSON 041947

CROSBY, BING & ANDREWS SISTERS
081244, 081944, 090244, 090944,
091644, 092344, 093044, 100744,
101444, 102144, 102844, 110444,
120244, 120944, 121644, 122344,
123044, 102844, 010645, 011345,
012045, 012745, 020345, 021045,
021745, 022445, 030345, 031045,
031745, 090145, 092945, 101345,
102045, 102745, 110345, 111045,
111745, 112445, 120845, 083146,
090746, 091446, 092146, 092846,
100546, 101246, 101946, 102646,
110246, 110946, 111646, 112346,
113046, 082347, 083047, 010149,
041451, 042151, 042851, 050551,
051251

CROSBY, BING & CONNEE BOSWELL
091038, 091738, 092438, 100138,
100838, 101538, 102238, 102938,
093039, 101439

CROSBY, BING & GARY CROSBY
080550, 081250, 081950, 082650,
090250, 080950, 091650, 092350,

093050, 100750, 101450, 102150

CROSBY, BING & GRACE KELLY
101356, 102756, 110356, 111056,
111756, 112456, 120156, 120856,
121556, 122256, 122956, 010557,
011257, 011957, 012657, 020257,
020957

CROSBY, BING & JANE WYMAN
092751, 110151, 110151

CROSBY, BING & JOHNNY MERCER
100838, 102238

CROSBY, BING WITH CARMEN
CAVALLARO ORCH. 102745,
120145, 120845, 121545, 122245,
122945, 010546, 011246, 011946,
012646, 020246, 020946, 021646,
022346, 030246, 030946, 031646

CROSBY, BING WITH JIMMY DORSEY
ORCH. 090536, 091236, 092636,
100336, 101036, 101736, 102436,
103136, 110736, 041737, 042437,
050137, 050837, 051537, 052237,
052937, 060537, 061237, 061937,
062637, 070337, 071037

CROSBY, STILLS & NASH 082077,
082777, 090377, 081482, 082182,
082882, 090482, 091182

CROSS, CHRISTOPHER 032980,
040580, 041280, 041980, 042680,
050380, 051080, 051780, 052480,
080280, 080980, 081680, 082380,
083080, 090680, 091380, 091281,
091981, 092681, 100381, 101081,
101781, 102481, 103181, 110781,
111481, 112181, 112881, 020484,
021184

CROWDED HOUSE 032887, 040487,
041187, 041887, 042587, 050287,
050987, 071187, 071887, 072587

CRYSTALS 101362, 102062, 110362,
111062, 111762, 112462, 120162,
120862, 022363, 060163, 060863,
061563, 062263, 062963, 091463,
092163, 092863, 100563, 101263

CUFF LINKS 101869, 102569, 110169

CUGAT, XAVIER 010441, 011141,
011841, 012541, 020141, 020841,
021541, 022241, 030141, 030841,
031541, 032241, 032941, 040541,
041241, 041941, 042641

CULTURE CLUB 021983, 022683,
030583, 031283, 031983, 032683,
040283, 040983, 041683, 052183,
052883, 060483, 061183, 061883,
062583, 070283, 070983, 071683,
082083, 082783, 090183, 091083,
101583, 120383, 121083, 121783,
011484, 012184, 012884, 020484,
021184, 021884, 022584, 030384,
031084, 033184, 040784, 041484,
042184, 042884, 050584

CUMMINGS, BURTON 010877, 011577

THE CURE 093089, 100789, 101489,
102189

CUTTING CREW 041887, 042587,
050287, 050987, 051687, 052387,
112187, 112887

CYRKLE 061866, 062566, 070266,
070966, 071666, 072366

CYRUS, BILLY RAY 062092, 062792,
070492, 071192, 071892, 072592,
080192, 080892, 081592

D

D.J. JAZZY JEFF & THE FRESH PRINCE
072091, 072791, 080391, 081091,
081791, 082491

DNA FEATURING SUZANNE VEGA
120890, 121590, 122290, 010591,
011291

DRS 110693, 111393, 112093, 112793,
120493, 121193, 121893, 122593,
010194, 010894, 011594

DADDY DEWDROP 050171, 050871,
051571, 052271, 052971

DALE & GRACE 110963, 111663,
112363, 113063, 120763, 121463,
122163, 022964, 030764

DALE, ALAN 073055, 080655, 081355

DAMIAN, MICHAEL 051389, 052089,
052789, 060389, 061089

DAMN YANKEES 121590, 122290,
010591, 011291, 011991, 012691,
020291

DAMONE, VIC 082049, 082749, 090349,
091049, 091749, 092449, 100149,
100849, 101549, 102249, 102949,
110549, 111249, 112649, 120349,
060256, 061656, 062356, 063056,
070756, 071456, 072156, 072856,
080456, 081156, 081856, 082556,
090156, 090856, 091556

DANA, VIC 040365, 041065

DANIELS, CHARLIE 081173, 081873,
082573

DANNY & THE JUNIORS 010458,
011158, 011858, 020158, 020858,
021558, 022258

D'ARBY, TERENCE TRENT 040988,
041688, 042388 043088, 050788,
051488, 072388, 073088, 080688,
081388, 082088

DARIN, BOBBY 071858, 072558,
080158, 080858, 081558, 052359,
053059, 060659, 061359, 062059,
062759, 070459, 071159, 071859,
072559, 091959, 092659, 100359,
101059, 101759, 102459, 103159,
110759, 111459, 112159, 112859,
120559, 121259, 121959, 122659,
010160, 010860, 011560, 022660,
030460, 031160, 031860, 032560,
040160, 092961, 100661, 102061,
081862, 082562, 090162, 090862,
022363, 030263, 030963, 031663,
032363, 033063, 040563, 062263,
110566, 111266, 111966

DARREN, JAMES 112461, 120161,
120861, 122261, 122941, 010562,
011262, 030962, 031662, 032362,
060162, 060862

DARTELLS 051863, 052563, 060163

DAVE CLARK FIVE 032864, 040464,
041164, 041864, 042564, 050264,
050964, 051664, 052364, 070464,
071164, 071864, 072564, 082264,
082964, 090564, 091264, 091964,
073165, 080765, 091865, 092565,
100265, 100965, 120465, 121165,
121865, 122565, 010166, 010866,
050667, 051367, 052067

DAVIS, MAC 082672, 090272, 090972,
091672, 092372, 093072, 100772,
101472, 102172, 102674, 110274

DAVIS, PAUL 030478, 031178, 031878,
032578, 040178, 042482, 050182,
050882, 051582, 052282, 052982,
060582

DAVIS, SAMMY, JR. 052772, 060472,
061172, 061772, 062472, 070172,
070872

DAVIS, SKEETER 030963, 031663,
032363, 033063, 040563, 041363,
042063, 110263, 110963

DAVIS, TYRONE 042570, 050270,
050970, 051670

DAWN 091970, 092670, 100370,
101070, 101770, 102470, 103170,
110770, 121970, 122670, 010271,
010971, 011671, 012371, 013071,
020671, 021371, 022071, 022771,
040773, 041473, 042173, 042873,
050573, 051273, 051973, 052673,
060273, 060973, 061673, 082573,
090173, 090873, 091573, 101974,
102674, 110274, 041975, 042675,
050375, 051075, 051775, 052475

DAWN, DOLLIE 010138, 010838,
011538, 012238, 012938, 020538,
021238, 021938, 022638, 030538,
031238

DAY, BOBBY 091958, 092658, 100358,
101058, 101758, 102458, 103158,
110758, 111458

DAY, DORIS 072448, 073148, 080748,
081448, 082148, 082848, 090448,
091148, 091848, 092548, 100448,
100948, 101648, 102348, 103048,
110648, 040249, 040949, 041649,

043049, 050749, 051449, 052149,
052849, 060449, 061149, 061849,
062549, 070249, 070949, 071649,
072349, 073049, 080649, 081349,
082049, 082749, 090349, 091749,
043049, 050749, 072851, 080451,
081151, 081851, 082551, 090151,
090851, 091551, 092051, 092751,
100451, 101151, 101851, 102551,
050152, 050852, 051552, 052252,
052952, 060552, 061252, 061952,
012354, 013054, 020654, 021354,
020254, 022754, 030654, 031354,
032054, 032754, 040354, 041054,
041754, 042454, 050154, 050854,
092554, 100254, 100954, 101654,
102354, 103054, 110654, 111354,
112054, 112754, 120454, 121154,
080456, 081156, 081856, 082556,
090156, 090856, 091556, 092256,
092956, 100656, 101356, 102056,
102756, 090558

DAY, DORIS & BUDDY CLARK 073148,
081448, 082148, 082848, 090448,
091148, 091848, 092548, 100248,
101648

DAYNE, TAYLOR 010988, 011688,
012388, 013088, 042388, 043088,
050788, 090388, 091088, 091788,
092488, 100188, 100888, 122488,
010789, 011489, 012189, 012889,
020489, 120989, 121689, 122389,
010690, 011390, 031090, 031790,
032490, 033190, 040790, 041490,
062390, 063090, 070790, 071490

DAZZ BAND 061982, 062682, 070382,
071082, 071782, 072482

DEAN, JIMMY 102061, 102761, 110361,
111061, 111761, 112461, 120161,
120861, 122261, 112461, 050462,
051862, 052562

DEBARGE 040685, 041385, 042085,
042785, 050485, 051185, 051885,
080385, 081085, 081785

DEBARGE, EL 062186, 062886, 070586,
071986

DE BURGH, CHRIS 050987, 051687,
052387, 053087, 060687, 061387

DEE, JOEY & THE STARLITERS
020262, 020962, 022362, 030262,
042062, 042762, 050462, 051162

DEEE-LITE 111090, 111790, 112490,
120190, 120890

THE DEELE 052188

DEEP PURPLE 091468, 092168,
092868, 071473, 072173, 072873,
080473, 081173

DEES, RICK 092576, 100276, 100976,
101676, 102376, 103076, 110676,
111376, 112076, 112776

DEF LEPPARD 032688, 062588,
070288, 070988, 071688, 072388,
073088, 080688, 091788, 092488,
100188, 100888, 101588, 102288,
010789, 011489, 012189, 012889,
020489

DEFRANCO FAMILY 102073, 102773,
110373, 111073, 111773, 112473,
120173

DEKKER, DESMOND & THE ACES
062869

DELEGATES 111172, 111872

DELFONICS 030968, 031668, 032368,
033068, 040668, 032170

DELLS 082468, 083168, 090768,
092769, 100469

DENNIS, CATHY 012691, 020291,
042791, 050491, 051191, 051891,
052591, 060191, 091491, 092191

DENNY, JACK 110450, 111150,
111850, 112550, 120250, 120950,
121650, 122350, 010651, 011351,
012051, 012751

DENNY, MARTIN 052359, 053059,
060659, 061359, 062059, 062759,
070459, 071159, 071859

DENVER, JOHN 072471, 073171,
080771, 081471, 082171, 082871,
090471, 091171, 021773, 022473,
030373, 031073, 030974, 031674,

HOWARD) 080346, 081046, 081746, 082446, 083146, 090746, 091446, 092146, 092846, 100546, 101246, 101946, 102646, 110246, 110946, 111646, 112346, 113046, 120746, 121446, 050347, 051047, 051747, 052447, 053147, 060747, 061447, 062147, 062847, 070547, 071247, 071947, 072647, 080247, 080947, 081647, 082347, 083047, 090647, 072349, 073049, 080649, 081349, 082049, 082749, 091049, 092449, 102551, 110151, 110851, 111551, 112251, 112951, 120651, 121351, 122051, 122751, 010352, 011052, 011752, 012452, 013152, 020752, 021452, 050152, 050852, 051552, 052252, 052952, 060552, 061252, 061952, 062652, 070352, 071052

EDISON LIGHTHOUSE 032170, 032870, 040470, 041170, 041870, 042570, 050270

EDMUNDS, DAVE 013071, 020671, 021371, 022071, 022771

EDWARDS, BOBBY 111761, 112461

EDWARDS, JONATHAN 090471, 091171, 091871, 092571, 100271, 100971, 010172, 010872, 011572, 012272, 012972, 020572

EDWARDS, TOMMY 091258, 091958, 092658, 100358, 101058, 101758, 102458, 103158, 110758, 111458, 112158, 112858, 120558, 121258

EDWIN HAWKINS' SINGERS 052469, 053169, 060769, 061469

EGAN, WALTER 081278, 081978, 082678, 090278

ELECTRIC LIGHT ORCHESTRA 030875, 031575, 021476, 022176, 090377, 091077, 091777, 092477, 100177, 071479, 072179, 072879, 082579, 090179, 090879, 091579, 092279, 092979, 100381, 101081

ELEGANTS 080858, 081558, 082258, 082958, 090558, 091258, 091958, 092658, 100358, 101058, 101758

ELLIMAN, YVONNE 032578, 040178, 040878, 041578, 042278, 042978, 050678, 051378, 052078, 052778

ELLIS, SHIRLEY 010464, 011164, 011864, 012365, 013065, 020665, 021365, 022065, 041765, 042465

EN VOGUE 062390, 063090, 070790, 071490, 072190, 072890, 080490, 041892, 042592, 050292, 050992, 051692, 052392, 053092, 060692, 061392, 062092, 062792, 070492, 071192, 080192, 080892, 081592, 082992, 090592, 091292, 103192

ENGLAND DAN & JOHN FORD COLEY 081476, 082176, 082676, 090476, 091176, 091876, 092576, 100276, 100976, 101676, 121176, 121876, 041578, 042278, 052679, 060279

ENIGMA 032391, 033091, 041391, 042091, 043094, 050794, 051494

ENRIC MADRIGUERA ORCH. (VR: TONY SACCO) 102635, 110235, 110935, 111635, 112335, 113035, 120735, 122135

ERSKINE HAWKINS ORCH. (VR: JIMMIE MITCHELLE) 042443

THE ESCAPE CLUB 101588, 102288, 102988, 110588, 111288, 111988, 112688, 080391, 081091, 081791, 081091

ESSEX 062963, 070663, 071363, 072063, 072763, 080363, 081063, 081763

ESSEX, DAVID 021674, 022374, 030274, 030974, 031674

ESTEFAN, GLORIA 081289, 081989, 082689, 090289, 090989, 091689, 092389, 093089, 022490, 030390, 031090, 030291, 030991, 031691, 032391, 033091, 040691, 041391

ESTEFAN, GLORIA & MIAMI SOUND MACHINE 071887, 072587, 080187, 080887, 081587, 022788,

030588, 031288, 042388, 043088, 050788, 051488, 052188, 052888, 060488, 073088, 080688, 081388, 082088, 082788

ESTUS, DEON 042289, 042989

ETTING, RUTH 050045, 051135, 051835, 052535, 060135, 060835, 061535, 062235, 062935, 070635, 071335

EUROPE 032887, 040487, 092687, 100387, 101087, 101787, 102487

EURYTHMICS 032783, 080683, 081383, 082083, 082783, 090383, 091083, 091783, 092483, 031084, 031784, 032484, 033184, 040784, 041484, 042184, 070685, 071385, 072085

EVELYN "CHAMPAGNE" KING 090278, 090978, 091678

EVERETTE, BETTY 040464, 041164, 041864

EVERLY BROTHERS 062957, 070657, 071357, 072057, 072757, 080357, 081057, 081757, 082457, 101257, 101957, 102657, 110257, 110957, 111657, 112357, 050358, 051058, 051758, 052458, 053158, 060758, 061358, 062058, 062758, 070458, 071158, 071858, 072558, 082258, 082958, 090558, 091258, 091958, 092658, 100358, 101058, 101758, 102458, 103158, 110758, 120558, 121258, 121958, 122658, 010359, 011059, 011759, 091259, 091959, 092659, 100359, 101059, 110259, 102459, 103159, 110759, 022660, 030460, 031160, 031860, 051360, 052060, 052760, 060360, 061060, 061760, 062460, 070160, 070860, 071560, 072260, 100760, 101460, 102860, 031761, 032461, 033161, 022362, 030262, 030962, 031662, 032362, 062262, 101764, 102464, 103164, 110764, 111464

EVERY MOTHER'S SON 070167, 070867, 071567, 072267

EXCITERS 011263, 011963, 012663, 020263

EXILE 090278, 090978, 091678, 092378, 093078, 100778, 101478, 102178, 102878, 110478, 111178, 111878

EXPOSE 032187, 032887, 040487, 041187, 041887, 070487, 071187, 071887, 072587, 102487, 103187, 110787, 012388, 013088, 020688, 021388, 022088, 022788, 070889, 071589, 072289, 102189, 021790, 070393, 071093, 071793

F

FABARES, SHELLEY 032362, 040662, 042062, 042762, 050462, 051162, 051862, 052562

FABIAN 050959, 051659, 071859, 072559, 080159, 080859, 081559

THE FABULOUS THUNDERBIRDS 070586

FAITH NO MORE 082590, 090890

FAITH, PERCY 021960, 022660, 030460, 031160, 031860, 032560, 040160, 040860, 041560, 042260, 042960, 050660, 051360

FALCO 031586, 032286, 032986, 040586, 041286, 041986, 042686

FALTERMEIER, HAROLD 051885, 052585, 060185, 060885, 061585

FAME, GEORGIE 032368, 033068, 040668, 041368, 042068, 042768

FANTASTIC JOHNNY C 121667, 122367, 123067, 010668

FARGO, DONNA 122372, 123072, 010673, 011373

FATS WALLER ORCH. (VR: FATS WALLER) 042735, 072735, 080335, 081035, 081735, 082435, 083135, 090735, 092135, 092835, 100535, 101235, 102635, 110235, 110935, 112335, 113035, 120735, 121435, 122135, 122835, 010436, 011136,

011836, 022236, 022936, 030736, 031436, 032136, 041836, 042536, 050236, 050936, 051636, 052336, 053036, 060636, 061336, 062036, 062736, 070436, 071136, 071836, 072536, 080136, 080836, 081536, 082236, 082936, 090536, 091236, 091936, 092636, 101036, 101736, 102436, 103136, 031337, 041638, 051438, 052138, 112638, 120338, 121038, 121738, 122438, 123138, 010739, 011439, 012139, 012839, 020439, 021139, 032539, 050440, 052540, 060140

FELICIANO, JOSE 081768, 082468, 083168, 090768, 091468

FENDER, FREDDY 041975, 042675, 050375, 051075, 051775, 052475, 053175, 060775, 091375, 092075, 092775

FENDERMEN 070860, 071560, 072260, 072960, 080560, 081260

FERGUSON, JAY 032578, 040178, 040878

FERRANTE & TEICHER 090960, 091660, 092360, 093060, 100760, 101460, 102160, 102860, 110460, 111160, 111860, 112560, 122060, 120960, 122660, 122360, 123060, 010561, 011361, 012061, 012761, 020361, 021061, 021761, 022461, 030361, 031061, 031761, 032461, 120861, 122261, 011770

FERRER, JOSE & ROSEMARY CLOONEY 022754

FIELDS, ERNIE 112859, 120559, 121259, 121959

FIELDS, SHEP 020538

5TH DIMENSION 070867, 071567, 072267, 072967, 071368, 072068, 072768, 080368, 081068, 081768, 082468, 032969, 040569, 041269, 041969, 042669, 050369, 051069, 051769, 052469, 053169, 060769, 101869, 102569, 110169, 110869, 111569, 112269, 112969, 120669, 120570, 121270, 121970, 122670, 010271, 010971, 011671, 012371, 013071, 020671, 061172, 061772, 062472, 112572

FINE YOUNG CANNIBALS 032589, 040189, 040889, 041589, 042289, 042989, 050689, 061789, 062489, 070189, 070889, 071589, 072289

FIREBALLS 030268, 030968

FIREFALL 120476, 121176, 121876

FIREHOUSE 092191, 092891, 100591, 101291, 101092, 101792, 102492

FIRST CLASS 092874, 100574, 101274

FIRST EDITION 030268, 030968, 031668, 032368

FISHER, EDDIE WISH Y, 012452, 013152, 021452, 022152, 022852, 030652, 031352, 032052, 032752, 040352, 041052, 041752, 042452, 050152, 050852, 051552, 052252, 052952, 060552, 061252, 061952, 062652, 070352, 071052, 071752, 072452, 073152, 080752, 081452, 082152, 082952, 090552, 091252, 091952, 092652, 100352, 101052, 101752, 102452, 103152, 110752, 111452, 112152, 112852, 120552, 011053, 011753, 012453, 013153, 020753, 061353, 062053, 062753, 070453, 071153, 071853, 072553, 080153, 080853, 081553, 082253, 082953, 090553, 091953, 092653, 100353, 101753, 103153, 110753, 111453, 112153, 112853, 120553, 121253, 121953, 010954, 011654, 012354, 013054, 020654, 021354, 020254, 022754, 030654, 031354, 032054, 032754, 100954, 101654, 102354, 103054, 110654, 111354, 112054, 112754, 120454, 121154, 121854, 122554, 010155, 010855, 011555, 012255, 012955, 060455, 061155, 061855, 062555, 070255, 070955, 072355, 021856, 112456, 120856, 122256, 122956, 010557

FISHER, MISS TONI 122659, 010160, 010860, 011560, 012260, 012960, 020560

FITZGERALD, ELLA 120845

FITZGERALD, ELLA & THE INK SPOTS 102144, 111144, 111844, 120244, 120944, 121644, 122344, 123044, 010645, 011345, 012045, 012745, 020345, 021045, 020345

FITZGERALD, ELLA WITH CHUCK WEBB ORCH. 080638, 081338, 082038, 082738, 090338, 091038, 091738, 092438, 100138, 100838, 101538, 011439, 012139, 020439, 021139

FIVE AMERICANS 040167, 040867, 041567, 042267, 042967

FIVE MAN ELECTRICAL BAND 081471, 082171, 082871, 090471, 091171

FIVE STAIRSTEPS 071870, 072570, 080170, 080870

FIXX 100883, 101583, 102283, 102983, 110583, 111283, 111983

FLACK, ROBERTA 040172, 040872, 041572, 042272, 042972, 050672, 051372, 052072, 052772, 060472, 061172, 021773, 022473, 030373, 031073, 031773, 032473, 033173, 040773, 041473, 072774, 080374, 081074, 081774, 082474, 083174

FLACK, ROBERTA & DONNY HATHAWAY 071572, 072272, 072972, 080572, 081272, 081972, 041578, 042278, 042978, 050678, 051378, 052078, 052778, 060378

FLACK, ROBERTA WITH MAXI PRIEST 110991, 111691, 112391

FLEETWOOD MAC 031277, 031977, 052177, 052877, 060477, 061177, 061877, 062577, 070277, 082777, 090377, 091077, 091777, 092477, 100177, 121077, 121777, 052877, 102779, 110379, 111079, 111779, 112479, 012680, 020280, 020980, 021680, 022380, 071782, 072482, 073182, 080782, 081482, 082182, 082882, 090482, 091182, 091882, 050987, 051687, 052387, 053087, 060687, 102487, 103187, 110787, 111487, 112187

FLEETWOODS 032859, 040459, 041159, 041859, 042559, 050259, 050959, 051659, 052359, 101059, 101759, 102459, 103159, 110759, 111459, 112159, 112859, 120559, 121259, 121959, 122659, 010160

FLETCHER HENDERSON ORCH. 082236, 091236, 091936, 092636, 101736, 103136

FLOATERS 082777, 090377, 091077, 091777, 092477

A FLOCK OF SEAGULLS 100982, 101682, 102382, 103082

FLOYD, KING 011671, 012371, 013071, 020671, 021371, 022071

FLYING MACHINE 110869, 111569, 112269, 112969

FOCUS 052673, 060273, 060973

FOGELBERG, DAN 020980, 021680, 022380, 030180, 030880, 031580, 032280, 012181, 032881, 101781, 102481, 103181, 110781, 030682, 031382

FOLEY, RED 021150, 021850, 022550, 030450, 031150, 031850, 032550, 040150, 040850

FONTANA, WAYNE & THE MINDBENDERS 041065, 041765, 042465, 050165, 050865

FONTANE SISTERS 012255, 012955, 020555, 021255, 021955, 022655, 030555, 031255, 090355, 091055, 091755, 092455, 100155, 100855, 101555, 102255, 102955, 110555

FORCE M.D.'S 041286, 041986

FORD, LITA 061089

FORD, LITA (DUET WITH OZZY OSBOURNE) 052789, 060389, 061789

FORD, TENNESSEE ERNIE 111955, 112655, 120355, 121055, 121755,

122455, 123155, 010756, 011456,
012156, 012856, 020456, 021156,
021856, 022556
FOREIGNER 052877, 060477, 061177,
061877, 062577, 092477, 100177,
100877, 101577, 102277, 080578,
081278, 081978, 082678, 090278,
090978, 091678, 092378, 102878,
110478, 111178, 111878, 112578,
120278, 082981, 090581, 091281,
091981, 092681, 100381, 101081,
110781, 111481, 112181, 112881,
120581, 121281, 121981, 122681,
010982, 011682, 012382, 013082,
020682, 021382, 011985, 012685,
020285, 020985, 021685, 022385,
030285, 030985, 020688, 021388,
022088, 022788, 051488, 052188,
052888, 060488
FORGERTY, JOHN 030285
FORREST, HELEN 062444, 070144,
070844, 071544, 072944, 080544,
081244, 081944, 082644, 090244,
090944, 091644, 092344, 093044,
100744, 101444
FORREST, HELEN & DICK HAYMES
040844, 041544, 042244, 042944,
050644, 051344, 052044, 052744,
060344, 061044, 061744, 062444,
070144, 070844, 071544, 072244,
072944, 080544, 081244, 081944,
082644, 090244, 090944, 091644,
092344, 093044, 100744, 101444,
102144, 102844, 110444, 111144,
111844, 112544, 120244, 120944,
121644, 122344, 010645, 011345,
021646, 032346, 051846, 061546,
062246, 070646, 071346, 072046,
072746, 081046, 081746, 082446
FORTUNES 100265, 100965
FOUNDATIONS 020169, 020869,
021569, 022269, 030169, 030869,
031569, 032269
FOUR ACES 020752, 021452, 022152,
022852, 030652, 031352, 032052,
032752, 040352, 041052, 060554,
061254, 061954, 062654, 070354,
071054, 071754, 072454, 073154,
080754, 081454, 082154, 082854,
090355, 091055, 091755, 092455,
100155, 100855, 101555, 102255,
102955, 110555, 111255, 111955,
112655, 120355, 121055, 121755,
122455
FOUR KNIGHTS 032054, 032754,
040354, 041054, 041754, 042454,
050154, 050854, 051554, 052254,
052954, 060554, 061254, 062654
FOUR LADS 102955, 110555, 111255,
111955, 112655, 120355, 121055,
121755, 122455, 123155, 010756,
011456, 012156, 030356, 031056,
031756, 032456, 033156, 040756,
041456, 042156, 060256, 060956,
061656, 062356, 063056, 070756,
071456, 072156, 072856
FOUR PREPS 032958, 060758, 061358,
062058, 062758, 070458
FOUR SEASONS 091562, 092262,
092962, 100662, 101362, 102062,
110362, 111062, 111762, 112462,
120162, 120862, 121562, 122262,
122962, 010563, 011263, 020963,
021663, 022363, 030263, 030963,
031663, 032363, 081763, 081763,
082463, 090763, 022264, 022964,
030764, 031464, 032164, 032864,
050264, 050964, 051664, 052364,
070464, 071164, 071864, 072564,
080164, 080864, 081564, 092664,
100364, 111365, 112065, 112765,
120465, 121165, 121865, 122565,
010166, 022666, 030566, 100866,
101566, 012167, 071567, 072267,
072967, 101875, 102575, 110175,
110875, 111575, 112975, 022876,
030676, 031376, 032076, 032776,
040376
FOUR TOPS 060565, 061265, 061965,
062665, 070365, 071065, 071765,

072465, 073165, 080765, 081465,
082165, 082865, 090465, 092466,
100166, 100866, 101566, 102266,
102966, 110566, 010767, 011467,
012167, 012867, 020467, 040167,
040867, 041567, 042267, 042967,
011373, 032473, 033173, 040773,
041473, 042173, 042873
FOUR TUNES 071754, 072454, 080754
FOX, SAMANTHA 013187, 020787,
021487, 022187, 050788, 051488,
052188, 052888, 060488, 061188,
021189
FOXX, INEZ 082463, 090763, 091463
FOXY 110478, 111178
FRAMPTON, PETER 041776, 042476,
050176, 050876, 051576, 111376,
112076, 071677, 072377, 073077,
080677, 081377, 082077
FRANCIS, CONNIE 031558, 032958,
040558, 041258, 041958, 042658,
011059, 011758, 012459, 013159,
020759, 021459, 022159, 022859,
030759, 062759, 070459, 071159,
071859, 072559, 080159, 080859,
010160, 010860, 011560, 012260,
012960, 040160, 040860, 041560,
042260, 061760, 062460, 070160,
070860, 071560, 072260, 072960,
091660, 092360, 093060, 100760,
101460, 102160, 102860, 110460,
111160, 122360, 123060, 010561,
011361, 030361, 031061, 031761,
032461, 033161, 040761, 060261,
060961, 081161, 081861, 082561,
100661, 102761, 110361, 111061,
011262, 011962, 030962, 031662,
032362, 040662, 060862, 061562,
090162, 090862
FRANCIS CRAIG ORCH. (VR: BOB LAMM)
100447, 101147, 101847, 102547,
110147, 110847, 111547, 112247,
112947, 120647, 121347, 122047,
122747, 010348, 011048
FRANCK POURCEL'S FRENCH FIDDLES
060659, 061359
FRANK CHACKSFIELD ORCH. 101753,
102453, 103153, 110753, 111453,
112153, 112853, 120553, 121253,
121953, 122653, 010254, 011654,
013054
FRANK FROBA ORCH. 110444
FRANKE & THE KNOCKOUTS 060681,
061381
FRANKIE CARLE ORCH. (VR: MARJORIE
HUGHES) 021646, 022346,
030246, 030946, 031646, 032346,
033046, 040646, 041346, 042046,
042746, 050446, 051146, 051646,
052546, 060146, 060846, 100546,
101246, 101946, 102646, 110246,
110946, 111646, 112346, 113046,
120746, 121446, 122146, 122846,
010447, 011147
FRANKIE CARLE ORCH. (VR: PAUL
ALLEN) 021045, 021745, 022445,
030345, 031045, 031745, 032445,
033145, 030745, 041445, 042145,
042845, 050545
FRANKIE GOES TO HOLLYWOOD
031685, 032385
FRANKIE MASTERS ORCH. (VR: FRANKIE
MASTERS) 111139, 111839,
112539, 120239, 120939, 121639,
122339, 123039, 010640, 011340,
012040, 012740, 021040, 092840,
010441, 011141, 011841
FRANKIE MASTERS ORCH. (VR: MARION
FRANCIS) 041340
FRANKIE MASTERS ORCH. (VR:
SWINGMASTERS) 030841
FRANKLIN, ARETHA 041567, 042267,
052067, 052767, 060367, 061067,
061767, 062467, 070167, 100867,
110467, 111167, 123067, 010668,
011368, 012068, 012788, 020368,
021068, 031668, 032368, 033068,
040668, 041368, 042068, 042768,
060868, 061568, 062268, 062968,
090768, 091468, 092168, 082871,

090471, 091171, 091871, 092571,
100271, 112771, 120471, 041572,
042272, 042972, 050672, 051372,
020274, 020974, 021674, 022374,
030274, 030974, 081085, 081785,
082485, 083185, 090785, 091485,
112385, 113085, 120785
FRANKLIN, ARETHA & GEORGE
MICHAEL 032887, 040487,
041187, 041887, 042587, 050287,
050987
FRED, JOHN & THE PLAYBOY BAND
123067, 010668, 011368, 012068,
012768, 020368, 021068, 021768
FREDDIE & THE DREAMERS 040365,
041065, 041765, 042465, 050165,
050865
FREDDY MARTIN ORCH. 051835,
052535, 060135, 060835, 062235,
070635, 071335, 080335, 081035,
081735, 082435, 083135, 090735,
092135, 122135, 101141, 101841,
102541, 110141, 110841, 111541,
112241, 112941, 120641, 121341,
122041, 010342, 011042, 011742
FREDDY MARTIN ORCH. (VR: CLYDE
ROGERS) 121545, 122245,
122945, 010546, 011246, 011946,
012646, 020246, 020946, 021646,
022346, 030246, 030946, 031646,
032346, 033046, 040646, 041346,
042046
FREDDY MARTIN ORCH. (VR: EDDIE
STONE) 061441, 062141, 062841,
070541, 071241, 071941, 072641,
080241, 080941, 081641, 082341,
083041, 010342, 011742, 012442,
013142, 020742, 021442, 022142,
022842, 030742, 031442, 032142,
032842, 022142
FREDDY MARTIN ORCH. (VR: ELMER
FELDKAMP) 042035, 050435,
052535, 060135, 060835
FREDDY MARTIN ORCH. (VR: GLENN
HUGHES) 063045, 071346,
072046, 072746, 080346, 081046,
081746, 082446, 083146, 091446,
092146, 092846, 100546, 101246,
101946, 041748, 042448, 050148,
050848, 051548, 052248, 061248,
061948
FREDDY MARTIN ORCH. (VR: MERV
GRIFFIN) 010750, 011450, 012150,
012850
FREDDY MARTIN ORCH. (VR: STUART
WADE) 053042, 071142
FREDDY MARTIN ORCH. (VR: THE
MARTIN MEN) 100447, 101847,
102547, 110147, 110847
FREE 100370, 101070, 101770,
102470, 103170, 110770
FREE MOVEMENT 103071, 110671,
111371
FREEMAN, BOBBY 081564, 082264,
082964, 090564, 091264
FREY, GLENN 021685, 022385, 030285,
030985, 031685, 032385, 102685,
112185, 110985, 111685, 112385,
113085, 120785
FRIEND AND LOVER 062268, 062968,
070668
FRIENDS OF DISTINCTION 041870,
042570, 050270, 050970
FRIJID PINK 040470, 041170

G

G., KENNY 062087, 062787, 070487,
071187
GABRIEL, PETER 062886, 070586,
071986, 072686, 080286, 080986,
022887, 030787, 031487, 032187
GALLERY 060472, 061172, 061772,
062472, 070172
GARDNER, DAVE 081057, 082457
GARFUNKEL, ART 110373, 111073
GARLAND, JUDY 072740, 080340,
081040, 081740, 082440, 090740,
091440, 092140, 092840, 100540,
011946

GARLAND, JUDY & DICK HAYMES
113046, 121446, 122146, 011847
GARLAND, JUDY & GENE KELLY
022043, 022743, 031343, 032043,
032743, 040343, 041043, 041743,
050143
GARNETT, GALE 100364, 101064,
101764, 102464, 103164, 110764
GARRETT, LEIF 021779, 022479
GAYE, MARVIN 011665, 012365,
013065, 020665, 051565, 111365,
112065, 112765, 120465, 120768,
121468, 122168, 122868, 010469,
011169, 011869, 012569, 020169,
020869, 021569, 060769, 061469,
062169, 062869, 070569, 101869,
032071, 032771, 040371, 041071,
041771, 042471, 050171, 050871,
080771, 081471, 082171, 082871,
110671, 111371, 012773, 021073,
081173, 081873, 082573, 090173,
090873, 091573, 092273, 092973,
100673, 101373, 102073, 102773,
110373, 051477, 052177, 052877,
060477, 061177, 061877, 062577,
070277, 070977, 121182, 121882,
122582, 010883, 011583, 012283,
012983, 020583, 021283
GAYE, MARVIN & TAMMI TERRELL
102167, 102867, 110467, 111167,
111867, 012068, 012768, 052568,
060168, 083168, 090768, 091468
GAYLE, CRYSTAL 102977, 110577,
111277, 111977, 112677, 120377,
121077, 121777, 122477
THE GAYLORDS 022153, 022853,
030753, 071754, 072454, 073154,
080754, 081454, 082154, 082854,
090454, 091154, 091854, 092554,
100254
GAYNOR, GLORIA 020379, 021079,
021779, 022479, 030379, 031079,
031779, 032479, 033179, 040779,
041479, 042179, 042879
GEDDES, DAVID 091375, 092075,
092775, 100475
GENE KRUPA ORCH. (VR: ANITA O'DAY)
031541, 032241, 041941, 050341,
060741, 061441, 062141, 062841,
070541, 071241, 071941, 072641,
080241, 080941
GENE KRUPA ORCH. (VR: BUDDY
STEWART) 121545, 122945,
010546, 011246, 011946, 012646,
020246, 020946
GENE KRUPA ORCH. (VR: HOWARD
DULANY) 011841, 012541, 020841,
021541, 022241, 030141, 030841,
031541, 032241, 032941, 040541,
041241, 041941, 042641, 050341
GENESIS 012884, 020484, 021184,
021884, 062886, 070586, 071986,
072686, 080286, 100486, 101186,
101886, 102586, 011787, 012487,
013187, 020787, 032187, 032887,
040487, 041187, 060687, 061387,
062087, 062787, 070487, 032192,
032892, 040492, 041192
GENTRY, BOBBIE 081967, 082667,
090267, 090967, 091667, 092367,
093067, 100767, 101467
GENTRYS 101665, 102365, 103065,
110665
GEORGE, BARBARA 011262, 011962,
012662, 020262, 020962
GEORGIA SATELLITES 020787, 021487,
022187, 022887, 030787
GERARDO 041391, 042091
GERRY & THE PACEMAKERS 062064,
052764, 070464, 071164, 071864,
082264, 082964, 090564, 030665,
031365, 032065, 032765
GETZ, STAN & ASTRUD GILBERTO
071164, 071864, 072564, 080164
GIBB, ANDY 070277, 070977, 071677,
072377, 073077, 080877, 081377,
082077, 082777, 090377, 091077,
091777, 092477, 100177, 100877,
101577, 012778, 020478, 021178,
021878, 022578, 030478, 031178,

031878, 032578, 040178, 040878, 052078, 052778, 060378, 061078, 061778, 070178, 070878, 071578, 072278, 072978, 080578, 081278, 081978, 082678, 090278, 090978, 091678, 092378, 093078, 121678, 122378, 010679, 011379, 021680, 022380, 030180, 030880, 031580, 032280, 032980, 040580

GIBBS, GEORGIA 051552, 052252, 052952, 060552, 061252, 061952, 062652, 070352, 071052, 071752, 072452, 073152, 080752, 082152, 021955, 022655, 030555, 031255, 031955, 032655, 040255, 040955, 041655, 042355, 043055, 050755, 051455, 052155, 052855, 060455, 061155, 062555

GIBSON, DEBBIE 081587, 082287, 082987, 090587, 091287, 112887, 120587, 121287, 121987, 010988, 031288, 031988, 032688, 040288, 040988, 060488, 061188, 061888, 062588, 070288, 070988, 021889, 022589, 030489, 031189, 031889, 032589, 040189

GILDER, NICK 092378, 093078, 100778, 101478, 102178, 102878, 110478, 111178, 111878

GILL, JOHNNY 070790, 071490, 072190, 072890, 080490, 081190, 092990

GILMER, JIMMY & THE FIREBALLS 100563, 101263, 101963, 102663, 110263, 110963, 111663, 112363, 113063, 120763

GLASS TIGER 092086, 092786, 100486, 101186, 101886, 012487, 013187, 020787

GLEN GRAY ORCH. 070139, 070839, 071539, 072239, 072939, 080539, 081239, 081939, 082639, 090239, 090939, 091639, 092339, 093039, 100739

GLEN GRAY ORCH. (VR: CLYDE BURKE) 031839, 032539, 040139, 040839, 041539, 042239, 042939, 050639, 051339, 052039, 052739

GLEN GRAY ORCH. (VR: EUGENIE BAIRD) 111343, 112043, 112743, 120443, 121143, 121843, 122543, 010144, 010844, 011544, 012244, 012944, 020544, 021244, 021944, 022644, 030444, 031144, 031844

GLEN GRAY ORCH. (VR: KENNY SARGENT) 042035, 042735, 050435, 051135, 051835, 052535, 030439, 032539, 042939, 050639, 051140, 051840, 121848

GLEN GRAY ORCH. (VR: PHIL BRITO) 112743

GLEN GRAY ORCH. (VR: SKIP NELSON) 070745

GLENN MILLER ORCH. 093039, 101439, 020340

GLENN MILLER ORCH. (VR: MARION HUTTON) 082639, 091639, 092339, 093039, 100739, 101439, 102139, 102839, 110439, 111139, 040640, 041340, 042040, 042740, 050440, 051140, 051840, 052540, 060140, 060840, 061540, 062240, 062940, 070640, 071340, 072040, 051140, 051840, 010441

GLENN MILLER ORCH. (VR: MARION HUTTON, TEX BENEKE & MODERNAIRES) 042542, 050942, 052342, 053042, 060642, 061342, 062042, 062742, 070442, 071142, 071842

GLENN MILLER ORCH. (VR: RAY EBERLE) 110637, 052039, 052739, 060339, 061039, 061739, 062439, 070139, 070839, 071539, 072239, 072939, 080539, 081239, 081939, 082639, 090239, 090939, 091639, 092339, 093039, 100739, 101439, 102139, 102839, 110439, 111139, 111839, 112539, 120239, 120939, 121639, 122339, 123039, 010640,

011340, 012040, 012740, 020340, 021040, 021740, 022440, 030240, 030940, 031640, 032340, 033040, 040640, 041340, 042040, 042740, 050440, 051140, 051840, 052540, 060140, 060840, 061540, 062240, 062940, 070640, 071340, 072040, 072740, 080340, 081040, 081740, 082440, 090740, 091440, 092140, 092840, 100540, 101240, 101940, 102640, 110240, 110940, 111640, 112340, 113040, 120740, 121440, 122140, 122840, 081641, 082341, 083041, 090641, 091341, 092041, 092741, 100441, 101141, 101841, 102541, 110141, 110141, 110841, 111541, 112241, 112941, 120641, 121341, 122041, 010342, 011042, 011742, 012442, 013142, 020742, 021442, 022142, 022842, 030742, 031442, 032142, 032842, 040442, 041142, 041842, 042542, 050242, 050942, 052342, 053042, 060642, 061342, 080142, 082942, 091242, 092840, 091942, 100342, 101042, 102442, 103142

GLENN MILLER ORCH. (VR: RAY EBERLE & MODERNAIRES) 083041, 090641, 091341, 092041, 092741, 100441, 101141, 101841, 102541, 110141, 110841, 111541, 112241, 092642, 101042, 101742, 102442, 103142, 110742, 111442, 112142, 112842

GLENN MILLER ORCH. (VR: SKIP NELSON) 091942, 102442, 110742, 112142, 112842, 120542, 121242, 121942, 122642, 010243, 010943, 011643, 012343, 013043, 020643, 021343

GLENN MILLER ORCH. (VR: SKIP NELSON & MODERNAIRES) 013043, 020643, 021343, 022743, 030643, 031343, 032043, 032743, 040343, 041043, 041743, 042443, 050143, 050843, 051543, 052243, 052943, 060543

GLENN MILLER ORCH. (VR: TEX BENEKE) 052039, 060339, 061039, 061739, 062439, 070139, 070839, 072239, 072939

GLENN MILLER ORCH. (VR: TEX BENEKE & MODERNAIRES) 090542, 091242, 091942, 092642, 100342, 101042, 101742, 102442, 103142, 110742, 111442

GLENN MILLER ORCH. (VR: TEX BENEKE & MODERNAIRES WITH PAULA KELLY) 112241, 120641, 121341, 122041, 010342, 011042, 011742, 012442, 013142, 020742, 021442, 022142

GLITTER, GARY 090272, 090972, 091672, 092372

GO WEST 081190, 081890

GODFREY, ARTHUR 012448

GO-GO'S 031382, 032082, 032782, 040382, 041082, 041782, 042482, 050182, 050882, 081482, 082182, 082882, 090482

GOLD, ANDREW 052877, 060477, 061177, 061877, 062577

GOLDEN EARRING 032683, 040283

GOLDSBORO, BOBBY 030764, 031464, 040668, 041368, 042068, 042768, 050468, 051168, 051868, 052568, 060168, 060868

GOODMAN, DICKIE 100475, 101175

GORDON JENKINS ORCH. 102144, 102844, 111144, 111844, 112544, 120244, 120944, 123044, 012045, 082848, 090448, 092548, 100248, 100948, 102348, 103048, 110648, 111348, 112048, 112748, 120448, 121148, 121848, 122548, 010849

GORDON JENKINS ORCH. (VR: BETTY BREWER) 102249, 102949, 110549, 111249, 112649, 120349, 121049, 121749, 122449, 123149, 010750, 011450

GORDON JENKINS ORCH. (VR: EILEEN WILSON) 040150, 040850, 041550, 042250, 042950, 050650, 051350, 052050, 052750, 060350, 061050, 061750, 062450, 070150, 070850, 071550, 072250, 072950

GORDON JENKINS ORCH. (VR: STARDUSTERS) 060449, 061149, 062549, 070249, 070949, 071649, 072349, 080649

GORE, LESLEY 052563, 060163, 060863, 061563, 062263, 062963, 070663, 071363, 080363, 081063, 081763, 082463, 111663, 112363, 113063, 120763, 020164, 020864, 021564, 022264, 022964

GRAHAM, LARRY 092080, 092780

GRAMM, LOU 041187, 041887, 042587, 011390, 012090, 012790, 020390

GRAMMAR, BILLY 011759, 012459, 013159, 020759, 021459, 022159

GRAND, EARL 110758, 111458, 112158, 112858

GRAND FUNK 090873, 091573, 092273, 092973, 100673, 101373, 042074, 042774, 050474, 051174, 051874, 052574, 020175, 020875, 021575, 022275, 030175, 052475, 053175, 060775, 061475

GRANT, AMY 040691, 041391, 042091, 042791, 050491, 051191, 051891, 072791, 080391, 081091, 081791, 082491, 083191, 111691, 112391, 120791, 121491, 030792, 031492, 032192

GRANT, EDDY 061883, 062583, 070283, 070983, 071683, 072383, 073083, 080683

GRANT, GOGI 102955, 110555, 111255, 111955, 112655, 060956, 061656, 062356, 063056, 070756, 071456, 072156, 072856, 080456, 081156, 081856, 082556, 090156

GRASS ROOTS 062467, 070167, 070867, 101268, 101968, 102668, 110268, 110968, 072471, 073171

GRATEFUL DEAD 091987, 092687

GRAY, DOBIE 050573, 051273, 051973, 052673

GREAT WHITE 072989, 080589, 081289, 081989, 082689

GREAVES, R. B. 111569, 112269, 112969, 120669, 121369, 122069, 122769

GREEN, AL 010872, 011572, 012272, 012972, 020572, 021272, 021972, 022672, 030472, 042972, 050672, 051372, 052072, 052772, 060472, 081272, 081972, 082672, 090272, 090972, 091672, 112572, 120272, 120972, 121672, 122372, 123072, 010673, 041473, 090873, 091573, 120774, 121474, 122174

GREENBAUM, NORMAN 032870, 040470, 041170, 041870, 042570, 050270, 050970, 051670

GREENE, LORNE 111464, 112164, 112864, 120564, 121264, 121964, 122664

GREG KIHN BAND 040983, 041683, 042383, 043083, 050783, 051483, 052183

GROSS, HENRY 051576, 052276, 052976, 060576, 061276, 061976

GUESS WHO 051769, 052469, 053169, 060769, 061469, 082369, 020770, 021470, 022170, 022870, 041870, 042570, 050270, 050970, 051670, 052370, 053070, 060670, 120570, 121270, 091474, 092174, 092874, 100574

GUNS N' ROSES 082088, 082788, 090388, 091088, 091788, 092488, 100188, 121788, 122488, 030489, 031189, 031889, 051389, 052089, 052789, 060389, 061089, 111691, 112391, 080192, 080892, 081592, 082992, 090592, 091292, 091992, 092692, 100392

GUY LOMBARDO ORCH. 101439,

051041, 051741, 052441, 053141, 060741, 061441, 062141, 062841, 070541, 071241, 071941, 072641, 080241, 080941, 081641, 082341, 083041, 090641, 091341, 100441

GUY LOMBARDO ORCH. (VR: BILLY LEACH) 121843, 011544, 021244

GUY LOMBARDO ORCH. (VR: CARMEN LOMBARDO) 042035, 050435, 051135, 051835, 052535, 060135, 060835, 061535, 062235, 062935, 070635, 100535, 101935, 102635, 110235, 110935, 111635, 112335, 113035, 120735, 121435, 122135, 122835, 110235, 010436, 011136, 011836, 012536, 020136, 020836, 030736, 061237, 061937, 062637, 070337, 071037, 071737, 072437, 073137, 080737, 081437, 082137, 082837, 090437, 091137, 091837, 031238, 031938, 071638, 073038, 080638, 022539, 030439, 031139, 031839, 032539, 040139, 040839, 041539, 042239, 042939, 050639, 051339, 052039, 052739, 061039, 091639, 100739, 032136, 032836, 040436, 041136, 041836, 042536, 050236, 050936, 051636, 052336, 053036, 060636, 061336, 062036, 062736, 091236, 091936, 092636, 100336, 101036, 101736, 102436, 103136, 110736, 111436, 112136, 112836, 122636, 012337, 013037, 020637, 021337, 022037, 022737, 030637, 031337, 032037, 032737, 040337, 041037, 041737, 042437, 050137, 050837, 051537, 052237, 052937, 060537, 061237, 061937, 062637, 070337, 071037, 071737, 072437, 073137, 080737, 081437, 082137, 082837, 090437, 091137, 091837, 092537, 100237, 100937, 051537

GUY LOMBARDO ORCH. (VR: CARMEN LOMBARDO, LARRY OWEN & FRED HENRY) 011439, 012139

GUY LOMBARDO ORCH. (VR: DON RODNEY) 051146, 021547, 030147, 030847, 032247, 032947, 040547, 041247, 041947, 042647, 050347, 051047, 052447, 061149

GUY LOMBARDO ORCH. (VR: DON RODNEY & ROSE MARIE LOMBARDO) 111745

GUY LOMBARDO ORCH. (VR: KENNY GARDNER) 031150, 040150

GUY LOMBARDO ORCH. (VR: KENNY GARDNER & TRIO) 032550, 040150, 040850, 041550, 042250, 042950, 050650, 051350, 052050

GUY LOMBARDO ORCH. (VR: SKIP NELSON) 031144, 040144, 040844, 041544, 042244, 042944, 050644, 051344, 052044, 052744, 060344, 061044, 061744

H

HAINES, CONNIE 061849

HAL KEMP ORCH. 121435, 122135, 122835, 010436, 011136, 011836, 012536, 020136, 020836, 021536, 081536, 082936, 090536, 091236, 091936, 092636, 100336, 101036, 101736, 102436, 103136, 110736, 111436, 112136

HAL KEMP ORCH. (VR: AL HIBBLER) 061039, 061739, 062439, 070139, 070839

HAL KEMP ORCH. (VR: BOB ALLEN) 042735, 051135, 052535, 060135, 060835, 061535, 062235, 062935, 070635, 071335, 072035, 072735, 080335, 081035, 081735, 092835, 071037, 071737, 072437, 073137, 080737, 081437, 082137, 082837, 073038, 082038, 050639, 052039, 052739, 060339

HAL KEMP ORCH. (VR: MAXINE GRAY) 060135, 061535, 062235, 062935, 070635, 071335, 072035, 072735,

080335, 050936, 051636, 060636,
061336, 062036, 062736, 070436,
071136, 071836, 072536, 080136,
080836
HAL KEMP ORCH. (VR: SKINNAY ENNIS)
081035, 082435, 083135, 090735,
092135, 092835, 071136, 072536,
080136, 080836, 081536, 082236,
082936, 090536, 091236, 091936,
092636, 100336, 101036, 101736
HAL MCINTYRE ORCH. (VR: FRANK
LESTER & QUARTET) 091545
HALEY, BILL & COMETS 070955,
071655, 072355, 073055, 080655,
081355, 082055, 082755, 090355,
091055, 091755, 100155
HALL, DARYL 092086, 092786, 100486,
101186
HALL, DARYL & JOHN OATES 052976,
060576, 061276, 061976, 062676,
070376, 071076, 100976, 101676,
102376, 103076, 110676, 031277,
031977, 032677, 040277, 040977,
041677, 032881, 040481, 041181,
041881, 042581, 050281, 050981,
051681, 062081, 062781, 070481,
071181, 071881, 072581, 101081,
101781, 102481, 103181, 110781,
111481, 112181, 112881, 120581,
121981, 122681, 010982, 011682,
012382, 013082, 020682, 021382,
030682, 050882, 051582, 052282,
052982, 112082, 112782, 120482,
121182, 121882, 122582, 010883,
011583, 012283, 012983, 020583,
021283, 031983, 032683, 040283,
040983, 041683, 042383, 061883,
062583, 070283, 111983, 112683,
120383, 121083, 121783, 122483,
010784, 011484, 012184, 032484,
033184, 040784, 041484, 111084,
111784, 112484, 120184, 120884,
121584, 122284, 010585, 020285,
020985, 021685, 022385, 052188,
052888, 060488, 061188, 061888
HAMILTON, JOE FRANK & REYNOLDS
062671, 070371, 071071, 071771,
072471, 073171, 081675, 082375,
083075, 090675, 091375, 092075
HAMILTON, RUSS 090757
HAMLISCH, MARVIN 051174, 051874,
052574, 060174, 060874, 061574,
062274
HAMMER 122191, 010492, 011192,
011892
HAMMER, JAN 101285, 101985,
102685, 112185, 110985, 111685,
112385
HAMMER, M.C. 052690, 060290,
060990, 061690, 062390, 081890,
082590, 090190, 090890, 091590,
092290, 110390, 111090, 111790,
112490
HAMMOND, ALBERT 120272, 120972,
121672, 122372, 123072, 010673
HANNA, PHIL 090944
HAPPENINGS 082066, 082766, 090366,
091066, 091766, 051367, 052067,
052767, 060367, 061067, 061767
HARMONICATS 053147, 062147,
062847, 070547, 071247, 071947,
072647, 080247, 080947, 081647,
082347, 083047, 090647, 091347,
092047, 092747, 100447, 101147,
101847, 102547
HARNEN, JIMMY WITH SYNCH 061089
HARRIS, MAJOR 060775, 061475,
062175, 062875, 070575
HARRIS, PHIL 040646, 041346,
042046, 042746, 050446
HARRIS, RICHARD 060868, 061568,
062268, 062968, 070668
HARRIS, ROLF 070663, 071363,
072063, 072763, 080363, 081063
HARRISON, GEORGE 121270, 121970,
122670, 010271, 010971, 011671,
012371, 013071, 020671, 021371,
032771, 061673, 062373, 063073,
070773, 071473, 072173, 072873,
061381, 062081, 062781, 070481,

071181, 071881, 121287, 121987,
122687, 010988, 011688, 012388,
013088
HARRISON, WILBERT 051659, 052359,
053059, 060659, 061359, 062059,
062759, 070459, 071159
HARRY JAMES ORCH. 050942, 052342,
053042, 060642, 061342, 062042,
062742, 070442, 071142, 071842,
072542, 080142, 080842, 081542,
082242, 082942, 090542, 091242,
102045
HARRY JAMES ORCH. (VR: BUDDY DI
VITO) 012646, 020246, 020946,
021646, 022346, 030246, 030946,
031646, 032346, 033046, 040646,
041346, 101946, 102646, 110246,
110946, 111646, 112346, 120746
HARRY JAMES ORCH. (VR: DICK
HAYMES) 040844, 042244,
042944, 050644, 051344, 052044,
052744, 060344, 061044, 061744,
062444, 070144, 070844, 071544,
072244, 072944, 080544, 081244,
081944, 082644, 090244, 091644
HARRY JAMES ORCH. (VR: FRANK
SINATRA) 071043, 071743,
073143, 080743, 081443, 082143,
082843, 090443, 091143, 091843,
092543, 100243, 101643, 102343
HARRY JAMES ORCH. (VR: HELEN
FORREST) 022142, 030742,
031442, 032142, 032842, 040442,
041142, 041842, 042542, 050242,
050942, 101042, 101742, 112142,
112842, 120542, 121242, 121942,
122642, 010243, 010943, 011643,
012343, 013043, 020643, 021343,
022043, 022743, 030643, 031343,
032043, 032743, 040343, 041043,
041743, 042443, 050143, 050843,
051543, 052243, 052943, 081443,
082843, 090443, 091143, 091843,
092543, 100243, 100943, 101643,
102343, 103043, 110643
HARRY JAMES ORCH. (VR: KITTY
KALLEN) 031745, 032445, 033145,
030745, 041445, 042145, 042845,
050545, 051245, 051945, 052645,
080445, 081145, 110345, 111145,
111745, 112445, 120145, 120845,
121545, 122245, 122945, 010546,
011246, 011646, 012646, 020246
HARRY JAMES ORCH. (VR: MARIAN
MORGAN) 020147
HART, COREY 081184, 081884,
082584, 090184, 090884, 072785,
080385, 081085, 081785, 082485,
083185
HARTMAN, DAN 080484, 081184,
081884, 082584
HAWKES, CHESNEY 110291
HAWKINS, SOPHIE B. 053092, 060692,
061392, 062092, 062792, 070492,
071192
HAYES, BILL 031955, 032655, 040255,
040955, 041655, 042355, 043055,
050755, 051455, 052155, 052855,
060455, 061155, 061855, 070255
HAYES, ISAAC 102371, 103071,
110671, 111371, 112071, 112771,
120471, 121171, 121871
HAYES, RICHARD 010750, 011450,
012150, 012850, 020450, 021150,
021850, 022550
HAYMAN, RICHARD 051653, 053053,
060653, 061353, 062053, 062753,
070453, 071153, 071853, 072553,
080153, 081553
HAYMES, DICK 032043, 041043,
041743, 042443, 050143, 050843,
051543, 052243, 052943, 060543,
061243, 061943, 062643, 070343,
071043, 071743, 072443, 073143,
080743, 081443, 082143, 082843,
090443, 091443, 091843, 092543,
100243, 100943, 101643, 103043,
110643, 120443, 121143, 122543,
122543, 010144, 011544, 012244,
012944, 021944, 060344, 042845,

060945, 061645, 062345, 063045,
070745, 071445, 072145, 072845,
080445, 081145, 081845, 082545,
090145, 090845, 091545, 092245,
092945, 100645, 101345, 102045,
102745, 110345, 111045, 111745,
112445, 120145, 120845, 121545,
122245, 122945, 010546, 011246,
111646, 061948, 062648, 070348,
071048, 071748, 073148, 080748,
073049, 091049, 091749, 092449,
100149, 100849, 101549, 102249,
102949
HEAD, MURRAY 042085, 042785,
050485, 051185, 051885, 052585
HEAD, ROY 100265, 100965, 101665,
102365, 103065
HEART 103076, 110676, 082485,
111685, 112385, 113085, 120785,
121485, 030186, 030886, 031586,
032286, 032986, 040586, 062186,
062087, 062787, 070487, 071187,
071887, 072587, 080187, 080887,
100387, 101087, 101787, 042890,
050590, 051290, 051990, 052690,
060290, 060990, 061690
HEATWAVE 100877, 101577, 102277,
102977, 110577, 111277, 111977,
112677, 120377, 070178, 070878,
071578, 072278, 072978
HEBB, BOBBY 081166, 082066,
082766, 090366, 091066, 091766
THE HEIGHTS 102492, 103192, 110792,
111492, 112192, 112892, 120592,
121292, 121992, 122692
HENDERSON, JOE 070662
HENLEY, DON 120482, 121182,
121882, 122582, 010883, 011583,
012283, 012983, 020583, 012685,
020285, 020985, 021685, 042785,
050485, 082689, 090289
HENRY BUSSE ORCH. (VR: BOB
HANNON) 011637, 012337,
013037, 020637, 021337, 022037,
022737, 013037
HENRY BUSSE ORCH. (VR: MARION
HOLMES) 042035, 042735
HENRY, CLARENCE "FROGMAN"
042161, 042861, 050561, 051261
HENRY KING ORCH. (VR: JOE SUDY)
051636, 052336, 053036, 060636,
061336, 062036, 062736, 070436,
071136, 071836, 072536, 080136,
080836, 081536, 082236, 082936
HERMAN'S HERMITS 031365, 032065,
032765, 040365, 041065, 041765,
042465, 050165, 050865, 051565,
052265, 052965, 060565, 061265,
061965, 062665, 070365, 071065,
071765, 072465, 073165, 080765,
081465, 082165, 101665, 102365,
012266, 012966, 020566, 030566,
031966, 032666, 043066, 050766,
102266, 102966, 110566, 111266,
031867, 032567, 040167, 040867
HI-FIVE 042091, 042791, 050491,
051191, 051891, 052591, 060191,
060891, 061591, 082491, 083191,
090791, 091992, 092692, 100392,
101092, 101792, 102492, 103192
HIGGINS, BERTIE 040382, 041082,
041782, 042482
HIGHWAYMEN 081161, 081861,
082561, 090161, 090861, 091561,
092261, 092961, 100661, 101361
HILL, DAN 020478, 021178, 021878,
022578, 030478, 031178, 031878,
032578
HILL, DAN (DUET WITH VONDA
SHEPARD) 082987, 090587,
091287, 091987
HILLTOPPERS 080853, 081553,
082253, 082953, 090553, 091253,
091953, 092653, 100353, 101053,
021657, 022357, 030257, 030957,
031657, 032357, 033057, 040657,
041357, 042057
HIRT, AL 021564, 022264, 022964,
030764, 031464, 032164
HOLDEN, RON 052760, 061060,
061760

HOLIDAY, BILLIE 073038, 081338,
082038, 082738, 090338, 091038,
091738, 092438
HOLLIES 091066, 091766, 092466,
100166, 120366, 121066, 081267,
030770, 031470, 032170, 032870,
072972, 080572, 081272, 081972,
082672, 090272, 090972, 091672,
071374, 072074, 072774, 080374
HOLLY, BUDDY 122857, 010458,
011158, 011858, 020158
HOLLY, BUDDY & THE CRICKETS
092157, 092857, 100557
HOLLYWOOD ARGYLES 061760,
062460, 070160, 070860, 071560,
072260, 072960, 080560, 081260,
081960
HOLMAN, EDDIE 020770, 021470,
022170, 022870, 030770, 031470
HOLMES, CLINT 060273, 060973,
061673, 062373, 063073, 070773,
071473, 072173
HOLMES, RUPERT 120179, 120879,
121579, 122279, 010580, 011280,
011980, 012680, 020280, 030880,
031580, 032280, 032980, 040580
HONDELLS 103164
HONEY CONE 052271, 052971,
060571, 061271, 061971, 062671,
070371, 071071, 062671
THE HONEYCOMBS 102464, 103164,
110764, 111464, 112164
HONEYDRIPPERS 120884, 121584,
122284, 010585, 011285
HOPKIN, MARY 102668, 110268,
110968, 111668, 112368, 113068,
120768
HORACE HEIDT ORCH. (VR: KING'S MEN
& GLEE CLUB) 031938, 032638,
040238, 040938, 041638, 042338,
043038, 050738, 051438, 052138,
052838
HORACE HEIDT (VR: LARRY COTTON)
072437, 073137, 080737, 012238,
021238, 030538, 031238, 031938,
032638, 060438, 061138, 061838,
062538, 070238, 071638, 072338,
073038
HORACE HEIDT ORCH. (VR: LARRY
COTTON, BOB MCCOY & THE
CHARIOTEERS) 070238
HORACE HEIDT ORCH. (VR: LARRY
COTTON, DONNA WOOD & THE
DON JUANS) 092741, 100441,
101141, 101841, 102541, 110141,
110841, 111541, 112241, 112941,
120641, 121341, 122041, 010342
HORACE HEIDT ORCH. (VR: LYSBETH
HUGHES & LARRY COTTON)
031938, 032638, 040238, 040938,
041638, 042338, 043038, 050738,
051438, 052138, 052838, 060438,
091738
HORACE HEIDT (VR: RONNIE KEMPER)
051741, 053141, 060741, 062841,
070541
HORNSBY, BRUCE & THE RANGE
112286, 112986, 120686, 121386,
122086, 122786, 011687, 030787,
031487, 032187, 032887, 040487,
061188, 061888, 062588, 070288,
070988
HORTON, JOHNNY 053059, 060659,
061359, 062059, 062759, 070459,
071159, 071859, 072559, 080159,
080859, 081559, 082259, 082959,
040860, 041560, 042260, 042960,
050660, 051360, 052060, 052760,
060360, 120260, 120960, 121660,
122360, 123060, 010561, 011361,
012061
HOT 061877, 062577, 070277, 070977,
071677, 072377
HOT BUTTER 093072, 100772, 101472,
102172
HOT CHOCOLATE 041975, 042675,
011776, 012476, 013176, 020776,
021476, 022176, 022876, 030676,
012779, 020379, 021079, 021779
HOUSE OF PAIN 091292, 091992,

092692, 100392, 101092, 101792,
102492, 103192, 110792, 111492,
112192
HOUSTON, THELMA 031977, 032677,
040277, 040977, 041677, 042377,
043077, 050777
HOUSTON, WHITNEY 070685, 071385,
072085, 072785, 080385, 081085,
092885, 100585, 101285, 101985,
102685, 112185, 110985, 020886,
021586, 022286, 030186, 030886,
031586, 050286, 051086, 051786,
052486, 053186, 060786, 061486,
060687, 061387, 062087, 062787,
070487, 071187, 071887, 072587,
080187, 082987, 090587, 091287,
091987, 092687, 100387, 101087,
120587, 121287, 121987, 122687,
010988, 011688, 012388, 040288,
040988, 041688, 042388, 043088,
050788, 082788, 102988, 110588,
111288, 111988, 111790, 112490,
120190, 120890, 121590, 122290,
010591, 020291, 020991, 021691,
022391, 030291, 030991, 031691,
060891, 112892, 120592, 121292,
121992, 122692, 010293, 010993,
011693, 012393, 013093, 020693,
021393, 022093, 022793, 030693,
031393, 032093, 032793, 040393,
041093, 041793, 042493, 050193,
050893, 051593, 052293, 052993
HOWARD, DON 021453, 022153,
022853, 030753, 031453
H-TOWN 051593, 052293, 052993,
060593, 061293, 061993, 062693,
070393, 071093, 071793, 072493,
073193, 071793
HUDSON-DELANGE ORCH. (VR: MARY
MCHUGH) 043038
HUDSON-DELANGE ORCH. (VR: NAN
WYNN) 091137, 091837
HUES CORPORATION 062974,
070674, 071374, 072074, 072774
HUGO WINDERHALTER ORCH. 081156,
081856, 082556, 090156, 090856,
091556, 092256, 092956, 100656,
101356, 102056, 102756
HUMAN BEINZ 020368, 021068,
021768, 022468
HUMAN LEAGUE 052282, 052982,
060582, 061282, 061982, 062682,
070382, 071082, 071782, 072482,
073182, 080782, 081383, 082083,
082783, 083185, 090785, 102586,
110186, 110886, 111586, 112286,
112986, 120686
HUMPERDINCK, ENGLEBERT 052067,
052767, 060367, 061067, 061767,
122576, 010877, 012277
HUNT, PEE WEE 110648, 082953,
090553, 091253, 091953, 092653,
100353, 101053, 101753, 102453,
103153, 110753, 112153, 112853
HUSKEY, FERLIN 050457, 051157,
051857, 052557
HUTTON, BETTY 022346, 030246,
030946, 031646, 032346, 033046,
040646, 041346, 042046
HYLAND, BRIAN 072960, 080560,
081260, 081960, 082660, 090260,
090960, 091660, 071362, 072062,
072762, 080462, 081162, 081862,
111470, 112170, 112970, 120570,
121270

I

IAN, JANIS 082375, 083075, 090675,
091375, 092075, 092775
ICEHOUSE 050788, 051488, 052188
IDES OF MARCH 050270, 050970,
051670, 052370, 053070
IDOL, BILLY 062384, 063084, 070784,
071484, 072184, 072884, 120686,
121386, 122086, 102487, 103187,
110787, 111487, 112187, 112887,
063090, 070790, 071490, 072190,
072890, 080490, 081190, 081890
IFIELD, FRANK 100662, 101362,
102062

IGLESIAS, JULIO & WILLIE NELSON
042884, 050584, 051284, 051984,
052684, 060284
IMPALAS 050259, 050959, 051659,
052359, 053059, 060659, 061359
IMPRESSIONS 102663, 110263,
110963, 111663, 112363, 113063,
071864, 072564, 010265, 010965
INFORMATION SOCIETY 100188,
100888, 101588, 102288, 102988,
110588, 021189, 021889, 022589
INGMANN, JORGEN 032461, 033161,
040761, 041461, 042161, 042861,
050561
INGRAM, JAMES 100690, 101390,
102090, 102990, 110390, 111090,
111790
INGRAM, LUTHER 070872, 071572,
072272, 072972, 080572, 081272,
081972, 082672
INK SPOTS 060339, 061039, 061739,
062439, 070139, 070839, 072239,
091440, 092140, 092840, 100540,
101240, 101940, 102640, 110240,
110940, 111640, 112340, 113040,
120740, 121440, 122140, 122840,
032743, 040343, 041043, 042443,
050143, 050843, 051543, 052243,
052943, 060543, 061243, 061943,
062643, 070343, 071043, 061744,
051146, 051846, 052546, 060146,
060846, 061546, 062246, 062946,
070646, 071346, 072046, 072746,
080346, 081046, 081746, 082446,
083146, 090746, 091446, 092146,
040547, 080247, 080947, 081647,
082347, 083047, 090047, 091347,
092047, 092747
INNER CIRCLE 060593, 061293,
061993, 062693
INTRUDERS 050468, 051168, 051868,
052568, 060168
INXS 032286, 032986, 040586, 041286,
041986, 122687, 010988, 011688,
012388, 013088, 020688, 021388,
040288, 040988, 041688, 042388,
043088, 062588, 070288, 070988,
071688, 072388, 073088, 102288,
102988, 110588, 111288, 102990,
110390, 021691, 022391
IRISH ROVERS 050468, 051168,
051868, 052568
ISAAK, CHRIS 022391, 030291, 030991
ISLEY BROTHERS 041269, 041969,
042669, 050369, 051069, 051769,
052469, 092273, 092973, 100673,
101373, 102073, 102773, 083075,
090675, 091375, 092075, 092775
IVES, BURL 020962, 022362
IVY THREE 092360

J

J. FRANK WILSON 101064, 101764,
102464, 103164, 110764, 111464,
112164, 112864
J. GEILS BAND 010982, 011682,
012382, 013082, 020682, 021382,
030682, 031382, 032082, 032782,
040382, 041082, 041782, 042482,
050182, 050882, 051582
JACK TETER TRIO 020450, 021850
JACKS, TERRY 022374, 030274,
030974, 031674, 032374, 033074,
040674, 041374
JACKSON 5 122769, 010370, 011070,
011770, 012470, 013170, 020770,
021470, 022170, 061370, 062070,
062770, 070470, 071170, 071870,
072570, 080170, 080870, 100370,
101070, 101770, 102470, 103170,
110770, 111470, 112170, 112970,
120570, 121270, 021371, 022071,
022771, 030671, 031371, 042471,
050171, 050871, 051571, 052271,
052971, 060571, 012272, 012972,
042774, 050474, 051174, 051874,
052574, 060174, 060874, 061574,
062274, 011875, 012675
JACKSON, JANET 042686, 050286,

051086, 051786, 052486, 053186,
062886, 070586, 071986, 072686,
080286, 092786, 100486, 101186,
101886, 102586, 110186, 122786,
011087, 011787, 012487, 013187,
030787, 031487, 032187, 032887,
040487, 092389, 093089, 100789,
101489, 102189, 102889, 110489,
111189, 121689, 122389, 010690,
011390, 012090, 021090, 021790,
022490, 030390, 031090, 031790,
032490, 033190, 050590, 051290,
051990, 052690, 060290, 060990,
061690, 081190, 081890, 082590,
090190, 090890, 101390, 102090,
102990, 110390, 111090, 010591,
011291, 011991, 012691, 020291,
020991, 021691, 050893, 051593,
052293, 052993, 060593, 061293,
061993, 062693, 070393, 071093,
071793, 072493, 073193, 080793,
081493, 082193, 082893, 090493,
091193, 091893, 092593, 100293,
100993, 101693, 102393, 103093,
110693, 111393, 112093, 112793,
120493, 121193, 121893, 122593,
010194, 010894, 011594, 012294,
012994, 020594
JACKSON, JANEY 031994
JACKSON, JERMAINE 031073,
031773, 070580, 071280, 071980
JACKSON, JOE 112082, 112782,
120482, 121182, 121882, 122582,
010883
JACKSON, MICHAEL 112071, 112771,
120471, 121171, 121871, 122571,
010172, 010872, 011572, 040172,
040872, 041572, 042272, 042972,
050672, 051372, 052072, 092372,
093072, 100772, 101472, 102172,
102872, 110472, 092979, 100679,
101379, 102079, 102779, 110379,
010580, 011280, 011980, 012680,
020280, 020980, 021680, 022380,
030180, 041280, 041980, 062180,
062880, 021983, 022683, 030583,
031283, 031983, 032683, 040283,
040983, 041683, 042383, 043083,
050783, 051483, 052183, 052883,
060483, 061183, 070283, 070983,
071683, 072383, 073083, 080683,
090383, 091083, 091783, 092483,
112683, 021884, 022584, 030384,
031084, 031784, 110187, 101787,
102487, 103187, 110787, 122687,
010988, 011688, 012388, 013088,
030588, 031288, 031988, 032688,
040288, 040988, 041688, 061188,
061888, 062588, 070288, 070988,
010789, 011489, 012189, 113091,
120791, 121491, 122191, 010492,
011192, 011892, 012592, 020192,
021592, 022292, 022992, 030792,
031492, 032192, 032892, 040492,
041192, 052392, 053092, 060692,
061392, 090493, 091193, 091893,
092593, 100293, 100993
JACKSON, MICHAEL & PAUL
MCCARTNEY 112782, 120482,
121182, 121882, 122582, 010883,
011583, 012283, 012983
JACKSON, MICHAEL WITH SIEDAH
GARRETT 082287, 082987,
090587, 091287, 091987, 092687
JACKSON, STONEWALL 071159,
071859, 072559, 080159, 080859,
081559, 082259
JACKSONS 032870, 040470, 041170,
041870, 042570, 050270, 050970,
051670, 052370, 020577, 021277,
021977, 022677, 051279, 051979,
052679, 060279, 060979, 072184,
072884, 080484, 081184, 081884,
082584
JADE 030693, 031393, 032093, 032793,
040393, 041093, 041793, 042493,
050193, 050893, 051593, 052993,
032093
JAGGER, MICK & DAVID BOWIE
100585, 101285, 101985

JAGGERZ 030770, 031470, 032170,
032870, 040470, 041170
JAMES, JONI 121252, 121952, 122652,
010353, 011053, 011753, 012453,
013153, 020753, 021453, 022153,
022853, 030753, 031453, 032853,
040453, 041153, 041853, 042553,
050253, 050953, 051653, 052353,
053053, 060653, 062053, 062753,
071853, 032655, 040255, 040955,
041655, 042355, 043055, 050755
JAMES, OLGA 042856
JAMES, SONNY 011957, 012657,
020257, 020957, 021657, 022357,
030257, 030957, 031657, 032357,
033057, 040657, 041357
JAMES, TOMMY 071771, 072471,
073171, 080771, 081471, 082171
JAMES, TOMMY & THE SHONDELLS
070266, 070966, 071666, 072366,
073066, 080666, 040867, 041567,
042267, 042967, 050667, 051367,
061767, 060168, 060868, 061568,
062268, 062968, 011169, 011869,
012569, 020169, 020869, 021569,
022269, 030169, 030869, 031569,
032269, 042669, 050369, 051069,
070569, 071269, 071969, 072669,
080269, 080969, 081669, 082369,
083069
JAN & DEAN 070663, 071363, 072063,
072763, 080363, 081063, 011864,
012564, 041864, 042564, 050264,
050964, 051664, 071864, 072564,
080164, 080864, 081564
JAN GARBER ORCH. 010237, 010937,
011637, 020637, 021337, 022737
JAN GARBER ORCH. (VR: FRITZ
HEILBRON) 050435, 051835,
052535, 060135, 062235, 062935,
072035
JAN GARBER ORCH. (VR: LEE BENNETT)
010436, 011136, 011836, 012536,
020136, 020836, 021536, 022236,
022936, 041136, 041836, 042536,
050236, 050936, 051636, 052336,
053036, 060636, 061336, 062336,
062736, 070436, 071136, 092438,
042239
JAN GARBER ORCH. (VR: LEW PALMER)
012536, 020136, 020836, 021536,
022236, 022936, 030736, 031436,
032136, 032836, 040436, 041136,
041836, 042536, 050236
JAY & THE AMERICANS 051162,
051862, 052562, 110764, 111464,
112164, 112864, 071065, 071765,
072465, 073165, 080765, 022269,
030169, 030869, 031569
JAY & THE TECHNIQUES 090267,
090967, 091667, 092367, 093067,
100767
JAYNETTS 092163, 092863, 100563,
101263, 101963
THE JEFF HEALEY BAND 082689,
090289, 090989, 091689
JEFFERSON AIRPLANE 060367,
061067, 061767, 062467, 072967,
080567
JEFFERSON STARSHIP 101175,
101875, 102575, 110175, 110875,
111575, 050678, 051378, 052078,
052778
JELLY BEANS 080864, 081564
THE JETS 060786, 061486, 062186,
062886, 070586, 022187, 022887,
030787, 031487, 080187, 080887,
081587, 032688, 040288, 040988,
041688, 060488, 061188, 061888,
062588, 070288
JETT, JOAN 061282, 061982, 062682
JETT, JOAN & THE BLACKHEARTS
030682, 031382, 032082, 032782,
040382, 041082, 041782, 042482,
050182, 050882, 051582, 100188,
100888, 101588
JIGSAW 111575, 112975, 120675,
121375, 122075
JIMMY CASTOR BUNCH 061772,
062472, 070172, 070872

120558, 121258, 121958, 122658, 010359, 011059, 011759, 012459, 051163, 051863

KINKS 112164, 112864, 120564, 121264, 121964, 013065, 020665, 021365, 022065, 041765, 042465, 050165, 102470, 103170, 110770, 070983, 071683, 072383

KISS 112076, 112776, 120476, 040790, 041490, 042190

KLYMAXX 121485, 122185, 122885, 011186, 011886, 012586

KNACK 080479, 081179, 082579, 090179, 090879, 091579, 092279, 092979, 100679, 101379, 102079

KNIGHT, EVELYN 121148, 121848, 122548, 010149, 010849, 011549, 012249, 012949, 020549, 021249, 021949, 022649, 030549, 031249, 031949, 032649, 040249, 040949, 041649, 042349, 043049, 050749

KNIGHT, JEAN 071071, 071771, 072471, 073171, 080771, 081471, 082171, 082871

KNIGHT, GLADYS & THE PIPS 120267, 120967, 121667, 122367, 123067, 010668, 011368, 012068, 012768, 020671, 021371, 031773, 032473, 033173, 040773, 041473, 042173, 101373, 102073, 102773, 110373, 111073, 111773, 112473, 120173, 010574, 011274, 011974, 012674, 020274, 020974, 040674, 041374, 042074, 042774, 050474, 070674, 071374, 072074

KNOX, BUDDY 032357, 033057, 040657, 041357, 042057, 042757

KOKOMO 040761, 041461, 042161, 042861

KOOL & THE GANG 020974, 021674, 022374, 030274, 030974, 031674, 032374, 062274, 062974, 070674, 122279, 010580, 011280, 011980, 031580, 032280, 032980, 040580, 041280, 013181, 020781, 021481, 022181, 028181, 030781, 031481, 032181, 052282, 052982, 012184, 012884, 020484, 021184, 021884, 022584, 030985, 060185, 060885, 083185, 090785, 091485, 092185, 092885, 100585, 101285, 012487, 050287

KRAMER, BILLY J. WITH THE DAKOTAS 052364, 060664, 061364, 052764, 070464

KRAVITZ, LENNY 072791, 080391, 081091, 081791, 082491, 083191

KRIS KROSS 041892, 042592, 050292, 050992, 051692, 052392, 053092, 060692, 061392, 062092, 062792, 070492, 071192

L

L.L. COOL J 030291

LTD 120377, 121077, 121777, 122477, 010778, 011478

LABELLE 030175, 030875, 031575, 032275, 032975, 040575, 041275

LABELLE, PATTI & MICHAEL MCDONALD 052486, 053186, 060786, 061486, 062186, 062886, 070586, 062886

LAINE, FRANKIE 100149, 100849, 101549, 102249, 102949, 110549, 111249, 112649, 120349, 121049, 121749, 122449, 123149, 040453, 041153, 041853, 042553, 050253, 050953, 051653, 052353, 053053, 060653, 061353, 062053, 062753, 070453, 071153, 071853, 072553, 080153, 080853, 082253, 011456, 020957, 021657, 022357

LAMOUR, DOROTHY 061739, 062439, 070839, 071539

LANCE, MAJOR 091463, 012564, 020164, 020864, 021564, 022264, 022964

LANGFORD, FRANCES 062637

LANZA, MARIO 012751, 020351, 021051, 021751, 022451, 030351, 031051, 031751, 032451, 033151,

040751, 041451, 042151, 042851, 050551, 051251, 051951, 052651, 060251, 060951, 061651, 062351, 063051, 070751, 071451, 072151, 072851, 080451, 081151, 081851, 082551, 090151, 090851, 091551, 092051, 092751, 100451, 101151, 101851, 102551, 110151, 110851, 110752, 111452, 112152, 112852, 120552, 121252, 121952, 122652, 010353, 011053, 011753, 013153, 020753, 021453

LARKS 122664, 010265, 010965, 011665, 012365

LA ROSA, JULIUS 121953

LARRY CLINTON ORCH. (VR: BEA WAIN) 122537, 010138, 010838, 011538, 012238, 012938, 020538, 021238, 021938, 031938, 040238, 040938, 041638, 042338, 043038, 050738, 051438, 052138, 052838, 060438, 061138, 061838, 062538, 070938, 071638, 072338, 073038, 080638, 081338, 082038, 082738, 090338, 091038, 091738, 092438, 100138, 102238, 102938, 110538, 111238, 111938, 112638, 120338, 121038, 121738, 122438, 123138, 010739, 011439, 012139, 012839, 022539, 030439, 031139, 031839, 032539, 040139, 040839, 041539, 042239, 042939, 050639, 051339

LARSON, NICOLETTE 021079, 021779, 022479, 030379

LAUPER, CYNDI 021884, 022584, 030384, 031084, 031784, 032484, 033184, 040784, 051284, 051984, 052684, 060284, 060984, 061684, 062384, 063084, 070784, 082584, 090184, 090884, 091584, 092284, 092984, 100684, 111784, 112484, 120184, 120884, 121584, 071385, 101186, 101886, 102586, 110186, 110886, 111586, 012487, 013187, 020787, 021487, 022187, 070189, 070889

LAWRENCE, STEVE 010160, 011560, 012960, 020560, 021260, 042260, 051261, 051961, 052661, 122262, 122962, 010563, 011263, 011963, 012663, 020263

LAWRENCE, VICKI 033173, 040773, 041473, 042173, 042873, 050573, 051273

LAWRENCE WELK ORCH. 021839, 022539

LAWRENCE WELK ORCH. (VR: WALTER BLOOM) 040839, 042239, 050639, 042239

LAWRENCE WELK ORCH. (VR: WAYNE MARSH) 032544, 050644

LED ZEPPELIN 122769, 010370, 011070, 011770, 012470, 013170, 020770

LEE, BRENDA 032560, 040160, 040860, 041560, 042260, 042960, 050660, 070160, 070860, 071560, 072260, 072960, 080560, 081260, 081960, 082660, 090260, 090960, 102160, 102860, 110460, 111160, 111860, 112560, 021061, 021761, 022461, 051261, 051961, 080461, 081161, 081861, 082561, 090161, 111061, 111761, 112461, 120161, 120861, 020962, 022362, 030262, 030962, 031662, 051862, 052562, 060162, 102062, 110362, 111062, 111762, 112462, 120162, 120862, 051863, 052563, 060163

LEE, CURTIS 081861, 082561, 090161

LEE, DICKEY 091562, 092262, 092962, 100662, 101362, 102062, 110362

LEE, JOHNNY 090680, 091380, 092080, 092780, 100480

LEE, PEGGY 100645, 111745, 122945, 010546, 011246, 092846, 100546, 110246, 032947, 040547, 041247, 041947, 042647, 011048, 011748, 012448, 013148, 020748, 022148, 022848, 030648, 031348, 032048,

032748, 040348, 041048, 041748, 042448, 050148, 050848, 051548, 052248, 052948, 060548, 031348, 032048, 121154, 121854, 122554, 010155, 010855, 011555, 012255, 012955, 020555, 021255, 021955, 082258, 082958

LEFT BANKE 101566, 102266, 102966, 110566

LEMON PIPERS 011368, 012068, 012768, 020368, 021068, 021768, 022468

LENNON, JOHN 032170, 032870, 040470, 041170, 041870, 042570, 050270, 050970, 103071, 110671, 111371, 112071, 112771, 120471, 110274, 110974, 111674, 021575, 022275, 111580, 112280, 112980, 120680, 121380, 122080, 122780, 011081, 011781, 012481, 013181, 020781, 021481, 022181, 032881, 030781, 031481, 032181, 032881, 040481, 041181, 041881, 042581, 052381, 053081, 022584, 030384, 031084, 031784

LENNON, JULIAN 122284, 010585, 011285, 030985, 031685, 032385, 033085, 040685

LENNOX, ANNIE & AL GREEN 011489, 012189

LEO REISMAN ORCH. 072536

LEO REISMAN ORCH. (VR: BENNY DAVIS) 040436, 042536

LEO REISMAN ORCH. (VR: LEE SULLIVAN) 021040, 030240, 030940, 032340

LEONARD, JACK 061243

LEROY ANDERSON ORCH. 061651, 040352, 041052, 041752, 042452, 050152, 050852, 051552, 052252, 052952, 060552, 061252, 061952, 062652, 070352, 071052, 071752, 072452, 073152, 080752, 081452, 082952, 090552

LES BAXTER ORCH. 050253, 050953, 051653, 052353, 053053, 060653, 061353, 062053, 062753, 070453, 071153, 071853, 072553, 080153, 080853, 081553, 110753, 081454, 082154, 082854, 090454, 091154, 091854, 092554, 100254, 100954, 101654, 102354, 103054, 043055, 050755, 051455, 052155, 052855, 060455, 061155, 061855, 062555, 070255, 070955, 071655, 072355, 073055, 080655, 081355, 082055, 082755, 091755, 092455, 100155, 100855, 101555, 102255, 031056, 031756, 032456, 033156, 040756, 041456, 042156, 042856, 050556, 051256, 051956, 052656

LES BROWN ORCH. 020549, 021249, 021949, 022649, 030549, 031249, 031949, 032649, 040249, 040949, 041649

LES BROWN ORCH. (VR: DORIS DAY) 021045, 030345, 031045, 051245, 051945, 052645, 060245, 060945, 061645, 062345, 063045, 070745, 071445, 072145, 072845, 080445, 081145, 081845, 082545, 011946, 033046, 040646, 041346, 042046, 042746, 050446, 051146, 051846, 070646, 080346, 081046, 081746, 082446, 083146, 090746, 091446, 092146, 092846, 100546, 101246, 110946, 112346, 113046, 120746, 121446, 122146, 122846, 010447, 011147, 011847, 012547, 020147, 020847

LESTER, KETTY 040662, 042062, 042762, 042062

LETTERMEN 010562, 011962, 012662, 020368, 021068, 021768, 022468

LEVEL 42 053186, 060786, 061486

LEVERT 101087, 101787, 102487, 103187

LEWIS, BARBARA 061563, 062263, 062963, 070663, 071363

LEWIS, BOBBY 062361, 063061,

070761, 071461, 072161, 072861, 080461, 081161, 081861, 082561, 090161, 090861, 091561

LEWIS, GARY & THE PLAYBOYS 013065, 020665, 021365, 022065, 022765, 030665, 031365, 032065, 032765, 050165, 050865, 051565, 052265, 052965, 073165, 080765, 081465, 082165, 082865, 102365, 103065, 110665, 111365, 102365, 010866, 011566, 012266, 012966, 020566, 040266, 040966, 060466, 061166, 061866

LEWIS, HUEY & THE NEWS 041082, 041782, 042482, 050182, 112683, 120383, 030384, 031084, 031784, 032484, 033184, 060284, 060984, 061684, 062384, 063084, 070784, 071484, 090184, 090884, 091584, 092284, 080385, 081085, 081785, 082485, 083185, 090785, 091485, 092185, 083086, 090686, 091386, 092086, 092786, 100486, 101186, 112286, 112986, 120686, 121386, 122086, 012487, 022887, 030787, 031487, 032187, 053087, 090587, 091287, 091987, 082788, 090388, 091088, 091788, 092488

LEWIS, MONICA 061447

LIGHTFOOT, GORDON 022071, 022771, 030671, 031371, 032071, 060174, 060874, 061574, 062274, 062974, 070674, 071374, 110974, 111674, 103076, 110676, 111376, 112076, 112776, 120476

LIND, BOB 022666, 030566, 031966, 032666

LINDSAY, MARK 021470

LINEAR 051290, 051990, 052690, 060290, 060990

LIPPS, INC. 051780, 052480, 053180, 060780, 061480, 062180, 062880, 070580, 071280

LISA LISA & CULT JAM 053087, 060687, 061387, 062087, 062787, 070487, 071187, 091987, 092687, 100387, 101087, 101787, 102487

LISA LISA & CULT JAM WITH FULL FORCE 101886, 102586, 110186

LITTLE ANTHONY & THE IMPERIALS 092658, 100358, 101058, 101758, 102458, 103158, 110758, 121964, 122664, 010265, 010965, 011665, 031365

LITTLE CAESAR & THE ROMANS 063061

LITTLE EVA 080462, 081162, 081862, 082562, 090162, 090862, 091562, 092262

LITTLE JACK LITTLE (VR: LITTLE JACK LITTLE) 081735, 082435, 083135, 090735, 092135, 092835, 100535, 101235, 101935, 102635, 110235, 120735, 121435, 122135, 122835

LITTLE RIVER BAND 092378, 093078, 100778, 101478, 102178, 102878, 110478, 092378, 040779, 041479, 090879, 091579, 092279, 092979, 100679, 101379, 011980, 101781, 102481, 103181, 110781, 111481, 112181, 030682, 031382

LOBO 050871, 051571, 052271, 052971, 060571, 110472, 111172, 111872, 112572, 120272, 021073, 021773, 022473, 030373

LOCKLIN, HANK 072960, 080560, 081260, 081960, 082660

LOGGINS & MESSINA 123072, 010673, 011373, 012073, 012773

LOGGINS, DAVE 072774, 080374, 081074, 081774

LOGGINS, KENNY 100778, 101478, 102178, 102878, 110478, 111178, 111878, 092780, 100480, 101180, 101880, 102580, 031084, 031784, 032484, 033184, 040784, 041484, 042184, 042884, 050584, 051284, 051984, 070586, 071986, 072686, 080286, 080986, 091088, 091788, 092488

030858, 031558, 032258, 032958
MCKENZIE, SCOTT 062467, 070167,
070867, 071567, 072267
MCLEAN, DON 121871, 122571,
010172, 010872, 011572, 012272,
012972, 020572, 021272, 021972,
022672, 030781, 031481, 032181,
032881, 040481, 041181
MCPHATTER, CLYDE 011059, 012459,
013159, 020759, 040662, 042062,
042762, 050462
MCVIE, CHRISTINE 032484
MEAD, SISTER JANE 033074, 040674,
041374, 042074
MEAT LOAF 100993, 101693, 102393,
103093, 110693, 111393, 112093,
112793, 120493, 121193, 121893,
122593, 010194, 010894
MECO 091777, 092477, 100177,
100877, 101577, 102277, 102977
MEDEIROS, GLENN FEATURING BOBBY
BROWN 063090, 070790, 071490,
072190, 072890, 080490, 081190
MEDLEY, BILL AND JENNIFER WARNES
110787, 111487, 112187, 112887,
120587, 121287
MELANIE 062070, 062770, 070470,
071170, 071870, 072570, 121171,
121871, 122571, 010172, 010872,
011572, 012272, 012972, 020572,
021272
MELLENCAMP, JOHN COUGAR
112683, 120383, 121083, 020484,
021184, 092885, 100585, 101285,
101985, 102685, 122185, 122885,
011186, 011886, 031586, 032286,
032986, 040586, 041286, 100387,
101087, 101787, 122687, 010988
MELTON, JAMES 111144
MELVIN, HAROLD & THE BLUE NOTES
112572, 120272, 120972, 121672,
122372, 112473, 120173, 120873
MEN AT WORK 092682, 100282,
100982, 101682, 102382, 103082,
110682, 111382, 112082, 122582,
010883, 011583, 012283, 012983,
020583, 021283, 021983, 022683,
043083, 050783, 051483, 052183,
052583, 060483, 061183, 061883,
081383, 082083, 082783, 090383
MEN WITHOUT HATS 090383, 091083,
091783, 092483, 100183, 100883,
101583
MENDES, SERGIO 062583, 070283,
070983, 071683, 072383, 073083,
080683, 081383
MENDES, SERGIO & BRASIL '66
061568, 062268, 062968, 070668,
071368
MERCER, JOHNNY 012045, 012745,
020345, 021045, 021745, 022445,
030345, 031045, 031745, 032445,
033145, 030745, 041445, 081845,
082545, 090145, 090845, 091545,
092245, 092945, 100645, 101345,
102045, 102745, 110345, 111045,
111745, 030246, 030946, 031646,
032346, 033046, 040646, 041346,
042046, 042746, 050446, 111646,
112346, 120746, 121446, 122146,
122846, 010447, 011147, 011847,
012547, 020147, 020847, 021547,
022247, 030147, 030847, 032247
MERCER, JOHNNY & JO STAFFORD
033145, 030745, 041445, 042145,
042845, 050545, 051245, 051945,
052645, 060245, 060945, 061645
MERCER, JOHNNY & MARGARET
WHITING 070249, 070949, 071649,
072349, 073049, 080649, 081349
MERCY 051769, 052469, 053169,
060769, 061469, 062169
MERRY MACS 020544, 021244,
021944, 022644, 030444, 031144,
031844, 032544, 040144, 040844,
041544, 082644
MIAMI SOUND MACHINE 020886,
021586, 051686, 051786, 052486,
090686, 091386, 092086
MICHAEL, GEORGE 060786, 061486,

062186, 062886, 071887, 072587,
080187, 080887, 081587, 082287,
112187, 112887, 120587, 121287,
121987, 122687, 010988, 011688,
022088, 022788, 030588, 031288,
031988, 032688, 051488, 052188,
052888, 060488, 061188, 061888,
062588, 080688, 081388, 082088,
082788, 090388, 091088, 111288,
111988, 112688, 120388, 092290,
092990, 100690, 101390, 102090,
102990, 121590, 122290, 080892
MICHAEL, GEORGE/ELTON JOHN
011192, 011892, 012592, 020192,
020892, 021592, 022292, 022992
MICHAELS, LEE 100271, 100971,
101671, 102371, 103071
MICHEL'LE 030390, 031090, 031790
MIDLER, BETTE 072173, 072873,
060780, 061480, 062180, 062880,
070580, 071280, 071980, 072680,
051389, 052089, 052789, 060389,
061089, 061789, 062489, 111790,
112490, 120190, 120890, 121590,
122290, 010591, 011291, 011991
MIKE + THE MECHANICS 022286,
030186, 030886, 031586, 022589,
030489, 031189, 031889, 032589,
040189
MILES, GARRY 072260, 072960,
080560, 081260, 081960, 082660,
090260
MILLER, MITCH 081355, 082055,
082755, 090355, 091055, 091755,
092455, 100155, 100855, 101555,
102255, 102955, 110555, 111255,
020759, 021459, 022159, 022859,
030759, 031459, 032159
MILLER, NED 021663, 022363, 030263
MILLER, ROGER 071864, 072564,
080164, 080864, 103164, 110764,
022765, 030665, 031365, 032065,
032765, 040365, 041065, 060565,
061265, 061965, 121865, 122565,
010166
MILLER, STEVE 021977, 022677,
030577, 031277, 031977, 032677
MILLI VANILLI 031189, 031889, 032589,
040189, 040889, 041589, 042289,
061789, 062489, 070189, 070889,
071589, 072289, 090989, 091689,
092389, 093089, 100789, 101489,
111189, 111889, 112589, 120989,
121689, 121090, 021790, 022490,
030390
MILLS BROTHERS 120338, 121038,
121738, 091143, 091843, 092543,
100243, 100943, 101643, 102343,
103043, 110643, 111343, 112043,
112743, 120443, 121143, 121843,
122543, 010144, 010844, 011544,
012244, 012944, 020544, 021244,
061546, 062246, 062946, 070646,
071346, 072046, 072746, 080346,
081046, 081746, 082446, 083146,
090746, 091446, 092146, 092846,
071247, 071947, 072647, 080247,
080947, 081647, 031850, 041550,
042250, 042950, 032752, 040352,
041052, 041752, 042452, 110752,
111452, 112152, 112852, 120552,
121252, 121952, 122652, 010353,
011053, 011753, 012453, 013153,
020753, 021453, 022153
MILLS, FRANK 040779, 041479,
042179, 042879, 050579
MILLS, STEPHANIE 102580, 110180,
110880, 111580, 112280
MILSAP, RONNIE 081581, 082281,
082981, 090581, 091281, 091981,
092681, 100381
MIMMS, GARNET & THE ENCHANTERS
100563, 101263, 101963, 102663
MINDBENDERS 052166, 052866,
060466, 061166, 061866
MINOGUE, KYLIE 102288, 102988,
110588, 111288, 111988, 112688
MINT CONDITION 032192, 032892,
040492, 041192, 041892
MIRACLES 012761, 020361, 021061,
021761, 022461, 030361, 020963,

021663, 022363, 092163, 092863,
100563, 120967, 121667, 122367,
123067, 010668, 011368, 012068,
030169, 030869, 111470, 112170,
112970, 120570, 121270, 121970,
122670, 010271, 010971, 011671,
021476, 022176, 022876, 030676,
031376, 032076
MITCHELL AYRES ORCH. (VR: MARY
ANN MERCER) 052540, 061540,
062240, 062940, 070640, 071340,
072040, 072740, 080340, 081040,
081740, 082440, 110240
MITCHELL, GUY 011351, 012051,
012751, 020351, 021051, 021751,
022451, 030351, 031051, 031751,
032451, 033151, 040751, 062351,
063051, 070751, 071451, 072151,
072851, 080451, 081151, 081851,
082551, 112456, 120156, 120856,
121556, 122256, 122956, 010557,
011257, 011957, 012657, 020257,
020957, 021657, 022357, 030257,
112159, 112859, 120559, 121259,
121959, 122659, 010160, 010860,
011560, 012260
MITCHELL, JONI 052574, 060174,
060874
MOCEDADES 032374, 033074
MODUGNO, DOMENICO 080858,
081558, 082258, 082958, 090558,
091258, 091958, 092658, 100358,
101058, 101758, 102458, 103158,
091958
MOMENTS 052370, 053070, 060670,
061370, 062070
MONEY, EDDIE 110186, 110886,
111586, 112286, 121088, 121788,
122488
MONKEES 100866, 101566, 102266,
102966, 110566, 111266, 111966,
112666, 121766, 122466, 123166,
010767, 011467, 012167, 012867,
020467, 021167, 021867, 022567,
030467, 040867, 041567, 042267,
042967, 050667, 051367, 080567,
081267, 081967, 082667, 090267,
112567, 120267, 120967, 121667,
122367, 123067, 010668, 011368,
012068, 012768, 030968, 031668,
032368, 033068, 040668
MONTE, LOU 010563, 011263, 011963
MONTENEGRO, HUGO 050468,
051168, 051868, 052568, 060168,
060868, 061568, 020869, 021569
MONTEZ, CHRIS 092262, 092962,
100662, 101362
MOODY BLUES 041765, 101472,
102172, 102872, 110472, 111172,
111872, 112572, 070586, 071986
MOORE, BOB 092961, 102061, 102761,
110361
MOORE, DOROTHY 052276, 052976,
060576, 061276, 061976, 062676,
070376, 071076
MORGAN, AL 101549, 110549
MORGAN, JANE 083157, 090757,
091457, 092157, 092857, 100557,
101257, 101957, 102657, 110257,
110957, 111657, 112357, 113057,
111458
MORGAN, JAYE P. 020555, 021255,
021955, 022655, 030555, 031255,
031955, 032655, 040255, 040955,
100155, 101555, 102255
MORRIS STOLOFF ORCH. 050556,
051256, 051956, 052656, 060256,
060956, 061656, 062356, 063056,
070756, 071456, 072156, 072856,
080456
MORRISON, VAN 093067, 010271
MORSE, ELLA MAE 010844, 012244,
012944, 020544, 021244, 021944,
022644, 030444, 031144, 031844,
070844, 071544, 072244, 072944,
080544, 081244, 041752, 042452,
050152, 050852, 051552, 052252,
060552, 060552, 061252
MOTELS 071782, 072482, 073182,
080782, 111283, 111983

MOTLEY CRUE 102889, 110489,
042190, 042890
MOUTH & MCNEAL 072272, 072972,
080572, 081272
MR. ACKER BILK 042762, 050462,
051162, 051862, 052562, 060162,
060862, 061562, 062262, 062962
MR. BIG 020892, 021592, 022292,
022992, 030792, 031492, 032192,
032892, 040492
MR. MISTER 111685, 112385, 113085,
120785, 121485, 122185, 122885,
011186, 020886, 021586, 022286,
030186, 030886, 031586, 032286,
053186
MULDAUR, MARIA 051174, 051874,
052574, 060174, 060874, 061574
MUNGO JERRY 092769, 100469,
100369, 101869, 102569, 110169,
110869, 081570, 082270, 082970,
090570, 091270, 091970
MURMAIDS 122163, 122863, 010464,
011164, 011864, 012564
MURPHY, EDDIE 113085, 120785,
121485, 122185, 122885, 011186,
011886, 012586
MURPHY, MICHAEL MARTIN 062175,
062875, 070575, 071275
MURPHY, WALTER 082876, 090476,
091176, 091876, 092576, 100276,
100976, 101676, 102376, 103076
MURRAY, ANNE 092670, 100370,
031773, 032473, 033173, 040773,
041473, 042173, 070674, 071374,
072074, 100778, 101478, 102178,
102878, 110478, 111178, 111878,
112578
MUSIC EXPLOSION 061067, 061767,
062467, 070167, 070867, 071567,
072267, 072967, 080567
MUSICAL YOUTH 022683, 030583
MYLES, ALANNAH 030390, 031090,
031790, 032490, 033190, 040790,
041490

N

NAKED EYES 061183, 061883
NAPOLEON XIV 080666, 081166,
082066
NASH, JOHNNY 110268, 110968,
111668, 112368, 113068, 102872,
110472, 111172, 111872, 112572,
120272, 120972, 121672
NATURAL SELECTION 092891, 100591,
101291, 101991, 102691, 110291,
110991, 113091
NAUGHTON, DAVID 070779, 071479,
072179, 072879, 080479, 081179
NAUGHTY BY NATURE 102691,
110291, 110991, 111691, 113091,
120791, 022093, 022793, 030693
NAZARETH 022876, 030676, 031376
NELSON 090890, 091590, 092290,
092990, 100690, 101390, 102090,
011991, 012691, 020291, 020991
NELSON, RICK 040662, 042062,
042762, 050462, 091562, 092962,
092962, 020263, 102172, 102872,
110472, 111172
NELSON, RICKY 071858, 072558,
080158, 080858, 081558, 082258,
082958, 090558, 091258, 091958,
112158, 112858, 120558, 121258,
121958, 122658, 011059, 011059,
011759, 013159, 040459, 041159,
041859, 042559, 050259, 051961,
052661, 060261, 060961, 061661,
062361, 063061, 070761, 020164,
020864, 021564
NELSON RIDDLE ORCH. 012156,
012856, 020456, 021156, 021856,
022556, 030356, 031056, 031756,
032456, 033156, 040756, 041456,
042156, 042856, 050556
NELSON, SANDY 100359, 101059,
101759, 102459, 103159, 110759,
111459, 112159, 120861, 122261,
122961
NELSON, WILLIE 052982, 060582,

PAUL WHITEMAN ORCH. (VR: DURELLE ALEXANDER) 022936, 030736, 032836, 040436, 041136, 041836
PAUL WHITEMAN ORCH. (VR: JOHN HAUSER) 032136, 032836, 041136, 041836, 042536, 050236
PAUL WHITEMAN ORCH. (VR: RAMONA DAVIES) 042035
PAYNE, FREDA 070470, 071170, 071870, 072570, 080170, 080870, 081570, 082270
PEACHES & HERB 050667, 051367, 052067, 031079, 031779, 032479, 033179, 040779, 041479, 042179, 042879, 050579, 051279, 051979, 052679, 060279, 060979, 061679
PEBBLES 040288, 040988, 041688, 042388, 043088, 070288, 070988, 071688, 072388, 102090, 102990, 110390, 111090
PENISTON, CE CE 121491, 122191, 010492, 011192, 011892, 012592, 020192, 020892, 022292
PERCY FAITH ORCH. 062652, 070352, 071052, 071752, 072452, 073152, 080752, 081452, 082152, 050253, 050953, 051653, 052353, 053053, 060653, 061353, 062053, 062753, 070453, 071153, 071853, 072553, 080153, 080853, 081553, 082253, 090553, 091253
PERFECT GENTLEMEN 060290
PERICOLI, EMILIO 062262, 062962, 070662, 071362, 072062
PERKINS, CARL 041456, 042156, 042856, 050556, 051256, 051956, 052656
PERRY, STEVE 051284, 051984, 052684, 060284, 060984, 061684, 062384
PET SHOP BOYS 041286, 041986, 042686, 050286, 051086, 051786, 052486, 080286, 110787, 111487, 050788, 051488, 052188, 052888
PET SHOP BOYS & DUSTY SPRINGFIELD 020688, 021388, 022088, 022788, 030588
PETER & GORDON 052364, 060664, 061364, 062064, 052764, 070464, 071164, 021365, 022065, 022765, 112666, 120366, 121066
PETER, PAUL & MARY 041363, 042063, 042763, 050463, 051163, 051863, 072763, 080363, 081063, 081763, 082463, 090763, 090366, 092367, 093067, 112669, 120669, 121369, 122069, 122769, 010370, 011070, 011770, 012470, 013170
PETER PIPER ORCH. (VR: BLACK PEPPER) 122642, 011643, 013043, 021343, 022043
PETERSEN, PAUL 011963, 012663, 020263
PETERSON, RAY 072260, 080560, 081260, 081960
PETTY, TOM 020280, 020980, 012090, 012790, 020390
PHIL HARRIS ORCH. (VR: PHIL HARRIS) 113035, 120950, 121650, 122350, 123050, 010651, 011351, 012051
PHILLIPS, ESTHER 121562, 122262, 122962
PHILLIPS, PHIL WITH THE TWILIGHTS 081559, 082959, 090559, 091259, 091959, 092659, 100359, 101059
PICKETT, BOBBY "BORIS" 092962, 100662, 101362, 102062, 110362, 111062, 081173
PICKETT, WILSON 090366, 091066, 091766, 091667, 092367, 093067
PIED PIPERS 102844, 110444, 111144, 111844, 120244, 120944, 121644, 122344, 123044, 010645, 011345, 012045, 012745, 031045, 031745, 032445, 030745, 041445, 042145, 042845, 050545, 051245, 051945, 052645, 060245, 060945, 061645, 062345, 063045, 070745, 071445, 072145, 072845, 080445, 081145, 081845, 082545, 090145,

090845, 092245, 092945, 100645, 101345, 102045, 102745, 110345, 111045, 111745, 112445, 120145, 120845, 121545
PILOT 062875, 070575, 071275, 071975, 090675, 091375, 092075, 092775
PINK FLOYD 030180, 030880, 031580, 032280, 032980, 040580, 041280, 041980, 042680, 050380, 051080, 051780
PIPKINS 071870
PIPS 061661, 062361, 063061, 070761, 071461, 072161, 072861
PITNEY, GENE 060862, 061562, 062262, 062962, 101362, 102062, 110362, 111062, 111762, 092664, 100364, 101064, 101764, 120564, 121264, 121964, 092664
THE PLATTERS 120355, 121755, 012856, 020456, 021156, 021856, 022556, 030356, 031056, 031756, 032456, 033156, 040756, 080456, 081156, 081856, 082556, 090156, 090856, 091556, 092256, 092956, 100656, 102056, 042658, 050358, 051058, 051758, 052458, 053158, 060758, 061358, 062058, 062758, 070458, 071158, 121958, 122658, 010359, 011059, 011759, 012459, 013159, 020759, 021459, 022159, 022859, 030759, 040160, 040860
PLAYER 121777, 122477, 010778, 011478, 012178, 012778, 020478, 021178, 021878, 060378, 061078
PLAYMATES 112158, 112858, 120558, 121258, 121958, 122658, 010359, 011059
POINTER SISTERS 020379, 021079, 021779, 022479, 030379, 031079, 031779, 032479, 101880, 102580, 110180, 110880, 111580, 071181, 071881, 072581, 080181, 080881, 081581, 082281, 082981, 090581, 091281, 091981, 032484, 033184, 040784, 041484, 042184, 042884, 071484, 072184, 072884, 102084, 102784, 020285, 020985, 021685, 022385, 030285, 030985
POISON 051687, 052387, 070288, 070988, 071688, 120388, 121088, 121788, 122488, 010789, 011489, 012189, 041889, 081190, 081890, 082590, 090190, 090890, 091590, 092290, 111090, 111790, 112490, 120190, 120890, 121590
POLICE 011781, 012481, 041181, 041881, 042581, 112181, 112881, 120581, 121281, 062583, 070283, 070983, 071683, 072383, 073083, 080683, 081383, 082083, 082783, 090383, 091083, 091783, 100183, 100883, 101583, 102283, 102983, 022584, 030384
PONI-TALES 090558, 091258
POPPY FAMILY 053070, 060670, 061370, 062070, 062770
POST, MIKE 080975, 081675, 111481, 112181
POWER STATION 042785, 050485, 051185, 051885, 052585, 072785, 080385, 081085
POWERS, JOEY 010464, 011164
PRADO, PEREZ 041655, 042355, 043055, 050755, 051455, 052155, 052855, 060455, 061155, 061855, 062555, 070255, 070955, 071655, 072355, 073055, 080455, 071158, 071858, 072558, 080158, 080858, 081558, 082258, 082958, 090558, 091258, 091958, 092658, 100358, 101058, 101758
PRATT & MCCLAIN 051576, 052276, 052976, 060576, 061276
PRESLEY, ELVIS 042856, 050556, 051256, 051956, 052656, 060256, 060956, 061656, 090156, 090856, 091556, 092256, 092956, 070745, 101356, 102056, 102756, 110356, 111056, 111756, 112456, 120156,

120856, 121556, 122256, 122956, 010557, 011257, 011957, 012657, 020257, 021657, 022357, 030257, 030957, 031657, 041357, 042057, 042757, 050457, 051157, 051857, 052557, 060157, 060857, 061557, 062257, 072757, 080357, 081757, 083157, 102657, 110257, 110957, 111657, 112357, 113057, 120757, 122157, 060758, 071158, 071858, 072558, 080158, 080858, 081558, 112858, 120558, 121258, 121958, 122658, 010359, 011059, 011759, 041859, 042559, 050259, 050959, 051659, 072559, 080159, 080859, 081559, 082258, 082959, 090559, 042260, 042960, 050660, 051360, 052060, 052760, 060360, 061060, 061760, 062460, 070160, 080560, 081260, 081960, 082660, 090260, 090960, 091660, 092360, 093060, 100760, 101460, 102160, 102860, 031061, 031761, 032461, 033161, 040761, 041461, 042161, 042861, 060261, 091561, 092261, 092961, 100661, 010562, 011262, 011962, 012682, 020262, 020962, 032362, 040662, 042062, 042762, 050462, 051162, 051862, 052562, 090162, 090862, 091562, 092262, 111062, 111762, 112462, 120162, 120862, 121562, 122262, 122962, 010563, 072763, 080363, 081063, 081763, 082463, 111663, 112363, 052265, 052985, 060565, 061265, 061965, 062665, 070365, 053169, 060769, 061469, 062169, 062869, 101869, 102569, 110169, 110869, 111569, 112269, 011770, 012470, 013170, 062770, 070470, 071170, 093072, 100772, 101472, 102172, 102872, 110472
PRESTON, BILLY 061172, 061772, 062472, 070572, 070872, 071572, 061673, 062373, 063073, 070773, 071473, 072173, 072873, 080473, 110373, 111073, 111773, 112473, 120173, 120873, 090774, 091474, 092174, 092874, 100574, 101274, 101974
PRESTON, BILLY & SYREETA 041280, 041980, 042680, 050380, 051080, 051780
PRESTON, JOHNNY 010860, 011560, 012260, 012960, 020560, 021260, 021960, 022660, 030460, 031160, 031860, 052060, 031860
PRETENDERS 030583, 031283, 031983, 032683, 040283, 122786
PRETTY POISON 121987, 122687
PRICE, LLOYD 013159, 020759, 021459, 022159, 022859, 030759, 031459, 032159, 032859, 053059, 060659, 061359, 062059, 062759, 070459, 071159, 071859, 072559, 080159, 080859, 091259, 091959, 092659, 100359, 101059, 101759
PRIEST, MAXI 091590, 092290, 092990, 100690, 101390, 102090, 102990
PRINCE 043083, 050783, 051483, 052183, 052883, 060483, 102283, 102983, 110583, 111283, 062384, 063084, 070784, 071484, 072184, 072884, 080484, 081184, 081884, 082584, 090184, 090884, 091584, 092284, 092984, 100684, 102084, 102784, 110384, 111084, 111784, 112484, 120184, 062285, 070685, 071385, 072085, 072785, 041187, 041887, 042587, 050287, 050987, 092687, 100387, 101087, 101787, 102487, 103187, 020688, 061888, 062588, 071589, 072289, 072989, 080589, 081289, 081989, 091590, 092290, 092990, 040994, 041694, 042394, 043094, 050794, 051494
PRINCE AND THE NEW POWER GENERATION 102691, 110291, 110991, 111691, 112391, 113091,

120791, 011892, 012592, 020192, 020892, 021592, 022292, 022992, 030792, 031492, 013093, 020693, 021393, 022093, 022793
PRINCE & THE REVOLUTION 012685, 020285, 020985, 090785, 091485, 092185, 032286, 032986, 040586, 041286, 041986, 042686, 050286
THE PROCLAIMERS 071793, 072493, 073193, 080793, 081493, 082193, 082893, 090493
PROCOL HARUM 071567, 072267, 072967, 080567, 081267, 081967, 082667
PSEUDO ECHO 070487, 071187, 071887
PUBLIC, JOE 042592, 050292, 050992, 051692, 052392, 053092, 060892, 061392
PUCKETT, GARY & THE UNION GAP 122367, 123067, 010668, 011368, 012068, 012768, 020368, 021068, 033068, 040668, 041368, 042068, 042768, 050468, 051168, 051868, 070668, 071368, 072068, 072768, 080368, 081068, 101268, 101968, 102668, 110268, 100369
PURE PRAIRIE LEAGUE 071280, 071980
PURIFY, JAMES & BOBBY 111266, 111966, 112666
PURSELL, BILL 033063

Q

QUARTERFLASH 121281, 121981, 122681, 011682, 012382, 013082, 020682, 021382, 010982
QUATRO, SUZI & CHRIS NORMAN 041479, 042179, 042879, 050579, 051279, 051979, 052679
QUEEN 041776, 042476, 050176, 011478, 012178, 012778, 020478, 021178, 021878, 022578, 012680, 020280, 020980, 021680, 022380, 030180, 030880, 031580, 032280, 032980, 040580, 041280, 091380, 092080, 092780, 100480, 101180, 101880, 102580, 110180, 110880, 111580, 112280, 112980, 120680, 121380, 122080, 041192, 041892, 042592

R

R.E.M. 120587, 040189, 040889, 041589, 042289, 060191, 060891, 061591, 062291, 062991, 070691, 092891, 100591
REO SPEEDWAGON 021481, 022181, 032881, 030781, 031481, 032181, 032881, 040481, 041181, 050981, 051681, 052381, 053081, 060681, 061381, 072482, 073182, 080782, 081482, 082182, 082882, 021685, 022385, 031685, 032385, 033085, 040685
RABBITT, EDDIE 091380, 092080, 092780, 100480, 101180, 101880, 012481, 013181, 020781, 021481, 022181, 032881, 030781, 031481, 032181, 091281, 091981, 092681, 100381, 101081, 101781, 102481, 103181
RABBITT, EDDIE & CRYSTAL GAYLE 012983, 020583, 021283, 021983, 022683, 030583
RAFFERTY, GERRY 061078, 061778, 070178, 070878, 071578, 072278, 072978, 080578
RAIDERS 061971, 062671, 070371, 071071, 071771, 072471, 073171, 080771, 081471
RAITT, BONNIE 092891, 100591, 101291, 101991, 102691
RALPH MARTERIE ORCH. 092554, 100254, 100954, 101654, 102354, 110654
RAMONA 092835, 100535, 101235, 102635
RAMSEY LEWIS TRIO 091165, 091865,

031288, 031988
ROXETTE 031889, 032589, 040189,
040889, 041589, 042289, 042989,
101489, 102189, 102889, 110489,
111189, 111889, 021090, 021790,
022490, 030390, 031090, 051990,
052690, 060290, 060990, 061690,
062390, 063090, 070790, 071490,
041391, 042091, 042791, 050491,
051191, 051891, 080391, 081091,
081791, 082491
ROYAL, BILLY JOE 081465, 082165,
082865
ROYAL GUARDSMEN 122466, 123166,
010767, 011467, 012167, 012867,
020467, 021167
ROYAL PHILHARMONIC ORCHESTRA
013082, 020682
RUBY & THE ROMANTICS 030263,
030963, 031663, 032363, 033063,
040563, 041363
RUBY NEWMAN ORCH (VR: BARRY
MCKINLEY) 082936, 091936,
092636, 100336, 101036, 101736,
102436, 103136, 110736, 111436
RUFFIN, DAVID 032969, 040569,
011776, 012476, 013176
RUFFIN, JIMMY 101566, 102266,
102966, 110566, 050380, 051080
RUFUS 081074, 081774, 082474,
083174, 090774, 091474
RUFUS FEATURING CHAKA KHAN
041275, 031376, 032076, 032776,
040376
RUN D.M.C. 090686, 091386, 092086,
092786, 100486
RUNDGREN, TODD 120873, 121673,
122273, 122973
RUSH, MERRILEE 062268, 062968,
070668, 071368
RUSS MORGAN ORCH. 072035,
080335, 081035, 081735, 082435,
083135, 090735, 092835, 101935,
083135, 110736, 111436, 072845
RUSS MORGAN ORCH. (VR: AL
JENNINGS) 101444, 102144,
102844, 110444, 111144, 111844,
112544, 120244, 120944, 121644,
122344, 123044, 010645, 011345,
012045
RUSS MORGAN ORCH. (VR: BERNICE
PARKS) 010838, 011538, 012238,
012938, 020538, 021238, 021938,
022638, 030538, 031238, 031938,
032638
RUSS MORGAN ORCH. (VR: JIMMY
LEWIS) 062637, 070337, 071037,
071737, 072437, 073137, 080737,
081437, 082137, 082837, 100838,
101538, 102938, 110538, 111238,
112638, 120338, 121038
RUSS MORGAN ORCH. (VR: MARJORIE
LEE) 080445
RUSS MORGAN ORCH. (VR: MERT
CURTIS) 040337, 102337, 111337,
121137, 121837
RUSS MORGAN ORCH. (VR: RUSS
MORGAN) 042944, 051344,
052044, 052744, 060344, 061044,
061744, 062444, 070144, 070844,
071544, 072244, 072944, 080544,
120244, 121644, 122344, 123044,
010645, 011345, 012045, 012745,
020345, 021045, 021745, 022445
RUSS MORGAN ORCH. (VR: RUSS
MORGAN & DAVE FRANKLIN)
080737
RUSS MORGAN ORCH. (VR: THE
SKYLARKS) 022649, 030549,
031249, 031949, 032649, 040249,
040949, 041649, 042349, 043049,
050749, 051449, 052149, 052849,
060449, 061149, 061849, 062549,
070249, 070949, 071649, 072349,
073049, 080649, 081349, 082049
RUSS MORGAN ORCH. (VR: THE
SKYLINERS) 022649, 030549,
031249, 031949, 032649, 040249,
040949, 041649, 042349, 043049,
050749, 051449, 052149, 052849,

060449, 061149, 061849, 062549,
070249, 051449
RUSSELL, ANDY 111844, 011847,
012547, 020847, 021547, 022247,
030147, 030847, 032247, 032947,
040547, 041247, 041947
RUSSELL, BRENDA FEATURING JOE
ESPOSITO 052888, 060488
RYDELL, BOBBY 121259, 121959,
122659, 030460, 031160, 031860,
032560, 040160, 040860, 041560,
042260, 042960, 062460, 082660,
090260, 090960, 091660, 092360,
093060, 111762, 122863, 010464,
011164, 011748, 012448, 013148,
020748, 021448, 022148, 022848,
032567
RYDER, MITCH & THE DETROIT WHEELS
012966, 111266, 111966, 112666,
120386, 121066, 121766, 122466,
120366, 030467, 031167, 031867,
032567
RHYTHM SYNDICATE 071391, 072091,
072791, 080391, 081091, 081791

S

S.O.S. BAND 072680, 080280, 080980,
081680, 082380, 083080, 090680
SWV 041793, 042493, 050193, 050893,
051593, 052293, 052993, 060593,
061293, 061993, 062693, 070393,
071093, 071793, 072493, 073193,
080793, 081493, 082193, 082893,
090493, 091193, 091893, 092593,
100293, 100993, 101693, 102393,
103093
SADE 050485, 051185, 051885,
052585, 060185, 021586, 022286,
030186, 030886
SADLER, SSGT. BARRY 021966,
022666, 030566, 031966, 032666,
040266, 040966, 041666
SAFARIS 072960, 080560, 081960
SAKAMOTO, KYU 060863, 061563,
062263, 062963, 070663, 071363,
072063
SALT-N-PEPA 111393, 112093, 112793,
120493, 121193, 121893, 122593,
010194, 012294, 012994, 020594
SALT-N-PEPA FEATURING EN VOGUE
021294, 021994, 022694, 030594,
031294, 031994, 032694, 040294,
040994, 041694, 042394
SAM & DAVE 101467, 102167, 102867,
110467, 111167, 111867, 112567,
120267, 031668, 032368
SAM THE SHAM & THE PHAROAHS
051565, 052265, 052965, 060565,
061265, 061965, 062665, 070365,
071065, 071666, 072366, 073066,
080666, 081166, 082066, 082766
SAMMY KAYE ORCH. (ALLAN FOSTER)
112941, 122041, 011042, 011742
SAMMY KAYE ORCH. (VR: ARTHUR
WRIGHT) 052441, 060741, 061441,
062141
SAMMY KAYE ORCH. (VR: BETTY
BARCLAY) 011147, 012547,
020147, 020847
SAMMY KAYE ORCH. (VR: BILLY
WILLIAMS) 041445, 042845,
050545, 051245, 051945, 052645,
060245, 060945, 062345, 063045,
112445, 120145, 120845, 121545,
122245, 122945, 010546, 011246,
011946, 012646, 020246, 020946,
021646, 022346, 050446, 051146,
051846, 052546, 060146, 060846,
061546, 062246, 062946, 070646,
071346, 072046, 113046, 120746,
121446, 122146, 122846, 010447,
011147, 011847, 012547, 020147,
020847, 021547, 022247, 030147,
030847
SAMMY KAYE ORCH. (VR: CHARLIE
WILSON) 021839, 022539
SAMMY KAYE ORCH. (VR: CHOIR)
062141, 062841, 070541, 071241,
071941, 072641, 080541, 080941,
081641, 082341, 083041, 090641,
091341, 092041, 092741, 021442,

022142, 022842, 030742
SAMMY KAYE ORCH. (VR: DON
CORNELL) 080842, 081542,
082242, 082942, 090542, 091242,
091942, 092642, 100342, 101042,
101742, 102442, 110742, 112842,
062847, 070547, 071247, 071947,
072647, 080247, 080947, 081647,
082347, 083047, 090647, 091347,
092047, 092747, 100447, 110847,
111547, 122047, 122747, 010348,
011048, 011748, 012448, 013148,
020748, 021448, 022148, 022848,
030648, 031348, 032048, 032748,
040348, 081349, 082049, 082749,
090349, 091049, 091749, 092449,
100149, 100849, 101549, 102249,
102949, 110549, 111249, 040150,
040850, 041550, 042250, 042950,
050650, 051350, 052050, 052750,
050350, 061050, 061750
SAMMY KAYE ORCH. (VR: DON
CORNELL & LAURA LESLIE)
052849, 062549
SAMMY KAYE ORCH. (VR: ELAINE
BEATTY) 070442, 071142, 072542
SAMMY KAYE ORCH. (VR: GLEE CLUB)
072338
SAMMY KAYE ORCH. (VR: NANCY
NORMAN) 092642, 100342,
101042, 102442, 111442, 112142,
112842
SAMMY KAYE ORCH. (VR: NANCY
NORMAN & BILLY WILLIAMS)
111045, 112445, 120145, 120845,
121545, 122245, 122945, 010546,
011246, 011946, 012646, 020246,
020946
SAMMY KAYE ORCH. (VR: THE
KAYDETS) 090349, 091049,
091749, 092449
SAMMY KAYE ORCH. (VR: THREE
KAYDETS) 122548, 010149,
010849, 011549, 012249, 012949,
020549, 021249, 021949, 022649,
030549, 031249, 031949, 032649
SAMMY KAYE ORCH. (VR: TOMMY
RYAN) 121837, 122537, 010138,
010838, 011538, 012238, 012938,
020538, 021238, 021938, 022638,
030538, 031238, 040238, 040938,
041638, 042338, 043038, 050738,
051438, 052138, 052838, 060438,
061138, 061838, 062538, 070238,
111238, 111938, 112638, 120338,
121038, 121738, 122438, 123138,
010739, 041340, 042040, 042740,
050440, 051140, 051840, 111640,
112340
SAMMY KAYE ORCH. (VR: TONY ALAMO)
080649, 102150, 102850, 110450,
111150, 111850, 112550, 120250,
120950, 121650, 122350, 123050,
010651, 011351, 012051, 012751,
020351, 021051, 021751
SANDPIPERS 091066, 091766
SANDS, TOMMY 033057
SANFORD/TOWNSEND 091077,
091777
SANG, SAMANTHA 020478, 021178,
021878, 022578, 030478, 031178,
031878, 032578, 040178, 040878
SANTAMARIA, MONGO 050463
SANTANA 031470, 032170, 121270,
121970, 122670, 010271, 010971,
011671, 012371
SANTO & JOHNNY 082959, 090559,
091259, 091959, 092659, 100359,
101059, 101759, 102459
SAYER, LEO 050375, 051075, 121176,
121876, 122576, 010877, 011577,
012277, 012977, 042377, 043077,
050777, 051477, 052177, 052877,
060477, 111580, 112280, 112980,
120680, 121380, 122080, 122780,
011081
SCAGGS, BOZ 090476, 091176,
091876, 092576, 100276, 100976,
101676, 102376
SCANDAL 090884, 091584, 092284,

092984, 100684
SCARBURY, JOEY 070481, 071181,
071881, 072581, 080181, 080881,
081581, 082981, 090581, 082281
SCORPIONS 081091, 081791, 082491,
083191, 090791
SCOTT, JACK 081558, 082258, 082958,
090558, 091258, 091958, 021459,
021960, 022660, 030460, 031160,
031860, 032560, 060360, 061060,
061760, 062460, 070160, 070860,
071560, 090861
SCOTT, LINDA 042861, 050561,
051261, 051961, 052661
SEAL 090791, 091491
SEALS & CROFTS 111872, 112572,
120272, 072873, 080473, 072476,
073176, 082176, 082876
SEARCHERS 010265, 010965, 011665,
012365, 013065, 020665
SEBASTIAN, JOHN 042476, 050176,
050876, 051576, 052276, 052976,
060576
SECADA, JON 071892, 072592,
080192, 080892, 081592, 082992,
090592, 091292, 091992, 092692,
100392
SEDAKA, NEIL 121259, 012761,
020361, 021061, 021761, 022461,
122961, 010562, 011262, 011962,
012662, 020262, 072762, 080462,
081162, 081862, 082562, 090162,
090862, 091562, 110362, 111062,
111762, 112462, 122874, 010475,
011175, 011875, 012675, 020175,
020875, 100475, 101175, 101875,
102575, 110175, 020776, 021476,
022176
SEDUCTION 012090, 012790, 020390,
021090, 021790, 022490
THE SEEKERS 042465, 050165,
050865, 051565, 052265, 052965,
011467, 012167, 012867, 020467,
021167, 021867, 022567, 030467
SEGER, BOB 021977, 022677, 030577,
031277, 031977, 032677, 061778,
070178, 070878, 071578, 072278,
072978, 080578, 041980, 042680,
050380, 051080, 053180, 060780,
061480, 062180, 062880, 070580,
103181, 110781, 111481, 112181,
112881, 012983, 020583, 021283,
021983, 022683, 030583, 031283,
031983, 062787, 070487, 071187,
071887, 072587, 080187, 080887
SEMBELLO, MICHAEL 080683, 081383,
082083, 082783, 090383, 091083,
091783, 092483, 100183
SENSATIONS 030962, 031662, 032362,
040662
SERENDIPITY SINGERS 041164,
041864, 042564, 050264, 050964,
051664
SEVILLE, DAVID 042658, 050358,
051058, 051758, 052458, 053158,
060758, 061358, 062058, 062758,
070458
SHADOWS OF NIGHT 050766, 051466
SHAI 111492, 112192, 112892, 120592,
121292, 121992, 122692, 010293,
010993, 011693, 012393, 013093,
020693, 021393, 022093, 041793,
091893, 092593, 100293
SHAKESPEAR'S SISTER 082992,
090592, 091292, 091992, 092692,
100392
SHALAMAR 030880, 031580, 032280,
032980
SHANGRI-LAS 091264, 091964,
092664, 100364, 101064, 101764,
110764, 111464, 112164, 112864,
120564, 120465, 121165, 121865,
122565
SHANICE 011892, 012592, 020192,
020892, 021592, 022292, 022992,
030792, 031492, 032192, 032892,
122692, 010293, 010993, 011693,
012393, 013093, 020693, 021393,
022093, 022793
SHANNON 021884, 022584, 030384

073066, 080666, 081166, 082066
STACEY Q 092786, 100486, 101186, 101886
STAFFORD, JIM 020274, 020974, 021674, 022374, 030274, 030974, 031674, 081074, 081774, 082474, 083174, 030274
STAFFORD, JO 072944, 080544, 081944, 082644, 090244, 090944, 091644, 092344, 093044, 101444, 102144, 030745, 071445, 090845, 112346, 113046, 120746, 121446, 122146, 122846, 010447, 011147, 011847, 012547, 020147, 080247, 011549, 012949, 021949, 071649, 072349, 081349, 082049, 082749, 090349, 091049, 091749, 092449, 010352, 011052, 011752, 012452, 013152, 020752, 021452, 022152, 022852, 030652, 091252, 091952, 092652, 100352, 101052, 101752, 102452, 103152, 110752, 111452, 112152, 112852, 120552, 121252, 121952, 122652, 010353, 011053, 011753, 012453, 013153, 020753, 021453, 022153, 022853, 030753, 031453, 032153, 032853, 030654, 031354, 032054, 032754, 040354, 041054, 041754, 042454, 050154, 050854, 051554, 052254, 052954, 061954, 112754, 120454, 121154, 121854, 122554, 010155, 010855, 011555, 012255, 012955
STAFFORD, JO & GORDON MACRAE 112748, 120448, 121148, 121848, 122548, 010149, 010849, 011549, 011249, 012949, 020549, 021249, 021949, 012150, 012850, 020450, 021150, 022550, 030450
STAFFORD, TERRY 032864, 040464, 041164, 041864, 042564, 050264, 050964
STALLONE, FRANK 100183, 100883
STAMPEDERS 100971, 101671, 102371
STAN KENTON ORCH. (VR: JUNE CHRISTY) 042046, 042746, 050446, 051146, 051846, 052546, 060146, 060846
STANSFIELD, LISA 032490, 033190, 040790, 041490, 042190, 042890, 050590
STAPLE SINGERS 050672, 051372, 052072, 052772, 060472, 061172, 061772, 062472, 121673, 122273, 111575, 112975, 120675, 121375, 122075, 122775, 010376
STARBUCK 071776, 072476, 073176, 080776
STARLAND VOCAL BAND 061976, 062676, 070376, 071076, 071776, 072476, 073176, 080776, 071076
STARR, EDWIN 041269, 041969, 042669, 081570, 082270, 082970, 090570, 091270, 091970, 092670, 100370
STARR, KAY 110648, 111348, 112048, 112748, 120448, 121148, 121848, 122548, 010149, 010849, 011549, 012249, 012949, 100750, 031352, 032052, 032752, 040352, 041052, 041752, 042452, 050152, 050852, 051552, 031453, 032153, 032853, 040453, 041153, 041853, 042553, 050953, 052353, 070354, 071054, 071754, 072454, 012856, 020456, 021156, 021856, 022556, 030356, 031056, 031756, 032456, 033156, 040756, 041456, 042156, 042856
STARR, RINGO 052271, 052971, 060571, 061271, 061971, 062671, 070371, 050672, 051372, 052072, 111073, 111773, 112473, 120173, 120873, 121673, 011274, 011974, 012674, 020274, 020974, 021674, 022374, 041374, 042074, 042774, 122874, 010475, 011175, 032275, 032975, 040575, 041275, 041975
STARS ON 45 052381, 053081, 060681, 061381, 062081, 062781, 070481, 071181

STARSHIP 112185, 110985, 111685, 112385, 113085, 120785, 121485, 021586, 022286, 030186, 030886, 031586, 032286, 032986, 031487, 032187, 032887, 040487, 041187, 041887, 042587, 050287, 082987
STATLER BROTHERS 010866, 011566
STEALERS WHEEL 042873, 050573, 051273, 051973
STEAM 112269, 112969, 120669, 121369, 122069, 122769, 010370, 011070
STEELE, JON & SANDRA 062648, 070348, 071048, 071748, 072448, 073148, 080748, 081448, 082148, 082848, 090448, 091148, 091848, 092548, 100248, 100948, 101648, 120448
STEELY DAN 021073, 021773, 022473, 072074, 072774, 080374, 021481, 022181
STEPPENWOLF 081768, 082468, 083168, 090768, 091468, 092168, 110968, 111668, 112368, 113068, 120768, 121468, 122168, 041969
STEVE MILLER BAND 121673, 122273, 122973, 010574, 011274, 011974, 012674, 020274, 102376, 103076, 110676, 111376, 112076, 062577, 070277, 070977, 071677, 072482, 073182, 080782, 081482, 082182, 082882, 090482, 091182, 091882, 092682, 100282, 100982, 101882, 102382
STEVENS, CAT 103071, 110671, 111371, 112071, 112771, 052072, 052772, 060472, 061172, 060174, 092874, 100574, 101274
STEVENS, CONNIE 042960, 050660, 051360, 052060, 052760, 060360, 061060
STEVENS, DODIE 040459, 041159, 041859, 042559, 050259, 050959, 051659, 052359
STEVENS, RAY 072762, 080462, 081162, 081862, 082562, 051769, 052469, 053169, 050970, 051670, 052370, 053070, 060670, 061370, 050474, 051174, 051874, 052574, 060174, 060874, 061574, 062274
STEVENSON, B. W. 092973
STEVIE B 111790, 112490, 120190, 120890, 121590, 122290, 010591, 011291, 011991
STEWART, AL 030577, 031277, 112578, 120278, 120978, 121678
STEWART, AMII 033179, 040779, 041479, 042179, 042879, 050579
STEWART, BILLY 082766, 090366
STEWART, JERMAINE 080286, 080986, 081686, 082386
STEWART, JOHN 072179, 072879, 080479, 081179
STEWART, ROD 091171, 091871, 092571, 100271, 100971, 101671, 102371, 103071, 110671, 111371, 112071, 110676, 111376, 112076, 112776, 120476, 121176, 121876, 122576, 010877, 011577, 010778, 011478, 012178, 012778, 020478, 012079, 012779, 020379, 021079, 021779, 022479, 030379, 031079, 031779, 032479, 033179, 040779, 011081, 011781, 012481, 013181, 020781, 021481, 120581, 121281, 121981, 122681, 010982, 072184, 072884, 080484, 081184, 102784, 071986, 072686, 080286, 080986, 031189, 031889, 032589, 040189, 040889, 012090, 012790, 020390, 021090, 021790, 050491, 051191, 051891, 052591, 060191, 092191, 060593, 061293, 061993, 062693, 070393, 071193, 071793, 072493
STEWART, ROD WITH RONALD ISLEY 052690
STIGERS, CURTIS 112391
STING 072085, 072785, 080385, 081085, 081785, 082485, 101985, 102685, 112185, 112887, 120587,

121287, 121987, 030291, 030991, 031691
STORIES 080473, 081173, 081873, 082573, 090173, 090873, 091573, 092273
STORM, GALE 121055, 051857, 052557, 060157, 060857, 061557, 062257, 062957, 070657, 071357
STRAWBERRY ALARM CLOCK 102867, 110467, 111167, 111867, 112567, 120267, 120967, 121667, 122367
STRAY CATS 121182, 121882, 122582, 010883, 021283, 021983, 022683, 030583, 031283, 092483, 100183, 100883, 101583
STREISAND, BARBRA 032864, 040464, 061364, 062064, 052764, 070464, 071164, 010971, 011671, 012371, 013071, 011974, 012674, 020274, 020974, 021974, 022374, 030274, 030974, 031674, 011577, 012977, 020577, 021277, 021977, 022677, 030577, 031277, 031977, 032677, 040277, 040977, 041677, 042377, 070977, 071677, 072377, 073077, 080677, 081377, 072879, 080479, 081179, 082579, 090179, 090879, 100480, 101180, 101880, 102580, 110180, 110880, 111580, 112280, 112980, 120680, 121380
STREISAND, BARBRA & BARRY GIBB 121380, 122080, 122780, 011081, 011781, 012481, 032881, 040481
STREISAND, BARBRA & DONNA SUMMER 110379, 111079, 111779, 112479, 120179, 120879, 121579, 122279
STREISAND, BARBRA & NEIL DIAMOND 111878, 112578, 120278, 120978, 121678, 122378, 010679, 011379, 012079
STRING-A-LONGS 022461, 030361, 031061, 031761, 032461, 033161, 040761, 041461, 042161
STRONG, BENNY 060449
STYLISTICS 012272, 012972, 041572, 042272, 042972, 050672, 051372, 052072, 120972, 121672, 032473, 033173, 040773, 041473, 051874, 052574, 060174, 060874, 061574, 062274, 062974, 070674
STYX 030274, 030974, 031674, 032374, 033074, 040674, 030175, 030875, 031575, 100475, 101175, 101875, 032076, 032776, 040376, 041076, 041776, 042476, 050176, 050876, 011478, 012178, 012778, 110379, 111079, 111779, 112479, 120179, 120879, 121579, 122279, 010580, 011280, 022181, 032881, 030781, 031481, 032181, 032881, 040481, 041181, 041881, 042581, 051681, 052381, 053081, 031983, 032683, 040283, 040983, 041683, 042383, 043083, 050783, 061183, 061883, 062583, 070283, 070983, 030291, 030991, 031691
SUGARLOAF 101070, 101770, 102470, 103170, 110770, 111470, 112170, 112970, 031575, 032275, 032975
SUMMER, DONNA 011076, 011776, 012476, 013176, 020776, 021476, 022176, 101577, 102277, 102977, 110577, 111277, 071578, 072278, 072978, 080578, 081278, 081978, 082678, 102178, 102878, 110478, 111178, 111878, 112578, 120278, 120978, 121678, 030379, 031079, 031779, 032479, 033179, 051279, 051979, 052679, 060279, 060979, 061679, 062379, 063079, 070779, 071479, 072179, 072879, 080479, 081179, 082579, 100679, 101379, 102079, 102779, 110379, 111079, 111779, 112479, 120179, 021680, 022380, 030180, 030880, 031580, 032280, 102580, 110180, 110880, 111580, 112280, 112980, 092682, 072383, 073083, 080683, 081383, 082083, 082783, 090383, 091083,

061789, 062489, 070189
SUPERTRAMP 060279, 060979, 061679, 062379, 063079, 070779, 121579, 122279
SUPREMES 080164, 080864, 081564, 082264, 082964, 090564, 091264, 091964, 092664, 102464, 103164, 110764, 111464, 112164, 112864, 120564, 121264, 121964, 122664, 121264, 010265, 010965, 011665, 012365, 013065, 031365, 032065, 032765, 040365, 041065, 041765, 042465, 050165, 052265, 052965, 060565, 061265, 061965, 111365, 112065, 112765, 120465, 121165, 121865, 021266, 021966, 022666, 030566, 052166, 052866, 082766, 090366, 091066, 091766, 092466, 100166, 100666, 101566, 111266, 111966, 112666, 120366, 121066, 121766, 021167, 021867, 022567, 030467, 031167, 031867, 032567, 042967, 050667, 051367, 052067, 052767, 060367, 082667, 090267, 090967, 091667, 092367, 093067, 100767, 120967, 121667, 110268, 110968, 111668, 112368, 113068, 120768, 121468, 122168, 122868, 010469, 011169, 012669, 121369, 122069, 122769, 010370, 011070, 011770, 012470, 013170, 041870, 121970, 122670, 010271, 010971, 011671
SUPREMES & TEMPTATIONS 122868, 010469, 011169, 011869, 012569, 020169, 020869, 021569
SURFACE 090289, 090989, 091689, 092389, 010591, 011291, 011991, 012691, 020291, 020991, 021691, 022391
SURFARIS 072063, 072763, 080363, 081063, 081763, 082463
SURVIVOR 070382, 071082, 071782, 072482, 073182, 080782, 081482, 082182, 082882, 090482, 091182, 091882, 092682, 100282, 100982, 032385, 033085, 062285, 070685, 071385, 072085, 011886, 012586, 020186, 020886, 021586, 022286, 011087, 011787, 012487
SURVIVOR ECT 100282
SWAN, BILLY 111674, 112374, 113074, 120774, 121474, 122174
SWAYZE, PATRICK (FEATURING WENDY FRASER) 021388, 022088, 022788, 030588, 031288, 031988
SWEAT, KEITH 031288, 031988, 032688, 040288, 040988, 020991, 021691, 022391
SWEET 042173, 042873, 050573, 051273, 051973, 052673, 060273, 092775, 100475, 101175, 101875, 102575, 121375, 122075, 122775, 010376, 011076, 011776, 061778, 070178
SWEET SENSATION 080490, 081190, 081890, 082590, 090190, 090890, 091590
SWING OUT SISTER 103187, 110787, 111487, 112187
SYLVERS 041076, 041776, 042476, 050176, 050876, 051576, 052276, 011577, 012277, 012977, 020577
SYLVIA 051973, 052673, 060273, 060973, 061973, 062373, 063073
SYMS, SYLVIA 062356, 063056, 071456, 072156
SYNDICATE OF SOUND 070966, 071666
THE SYSTEM 070487, 071187, 071887, 072587

T

TLC 041192, 041892, 042592, 050292, 050992, 051692, 052392, 053092, 060692, 071892, 072592, 080192, 080892, 081592, 082992, 090592, 091292, 091992, 092692, 100392, 101092, 101792, 110792, 111492,

TRESVANT, RALPH   122290, 010591, 011291, 011991, 012691, 020291, 020991

TROGGS   070966, 071666, 072366, 073066, 080666, 081166, 082066, 082766, 051868

TROY, DORIS   072763

TUBES   070283

TURNER, IKE & TINA   022269, 030169, 030869, 031569, 032269, 032969, 040569, 031371, 032071, 032771, 040371, 041071

TURNER, SAMMY   081559, 082259, 082959, 090559, 091259, 091959

TURNER, TINA   072884, 080484, 081184, 081884, 082584, 090184, 090884, 091584, 092284, 092984, 110384, 111084, 111784, 112484, 120184, 031685, 032385, 033085, 081785, 082485, 083185, 090785, 091485, 092185, 100486, 101186, 101886, 102586, 110186, 110886, 080793, 081493

TURTLES   031167, 031867, 032567, 040167, 040867, 041567, 042267, 042967, 050667, 061067, 061767, 062467, 070167, 102668, 110268, 110968, 111668, 021569, 022269, 030169

TUTONE, TOMMY   042482, 050182, 050882, 051582, 052282, 052982

TWITTY, CONWAY   102458, 103158, 110758, 111458, 112158, 112858, 120558, 121258, 121958, 122658, 010359, 021260, 021960

TYLER, BONNIE   061078, 061778, 070178, 070878, 071578, 091083, 091783, 092483, 100183, 100883

U

UB40   100188, 100888, 101588, 102288, 102988, 110588, 120190, 120890, 121590, 122290, 070691, 071391, 072091, 070393, 071093, 071793, 072493, 073193, 080793, 081493, 082193, 082893, 090493, 091193, 091893, 092593, 100293, 100993

USA FOR AFRICA   033085, 040685, 041385, 042085, 042785, 050485, 051185, 051885

U.S. BONDS   111860, 112560, 120260, 120960, 121660

US3   030594, 031294, 032694, 040294

U2   042587, 050287, 050987, 051687, 052387, 053087, 060687, 061387, 071187, 071887, 072587, 080187, 080887, 081587, 082287, 110588, 111288, 111988, 112688, 120388, 012592, 051692

UGLY KID JOE   050292, 050992, 051692, 052392, 040393, 041093, 041793, 042493

ULLMAN, TRACEY   042184, 042884, 050584

UNDISPUTED TRUTH   082871, 090471, 091171, 091871, 092571, 100271

V

VALENS, RITCHIE   012459, 013159, 020759, 021459, 022159, 022859, 030759, 031459, 032159, 032859

VALLEE, RUDY   051636, 103037, 110637, 111337, 112037, 112737, 120437, 121137, 121837, 122537, 010138, 010838, 011538, 062538, 070238, 070938, 022842, 032043, 032743, 040343, 041043, 041743, 042443, 050143, 050843, 051543, 052243, 052943, 060543, 061243, 061943, 062643, 070343, 071043, 071743, 072443, 073143, 080743

VALLI, FRANKIE   062467, 070167, 070867, 071567, 072267, 072967, 080567, 081267, 021575, 022275, 030175, 030875, 031575, 032275, 032975, 040575, 071275, 071975, 072675, 072278, 072978, 080578, 081278, 081978, 082678, 090278, 090978

VALLI, JUNE   082953, 091253, 091953, 092653, 100353, 101053, 101753, 102453, 103153, 110753, 111453, 103153, 110753

VANDROSS, LUTHER   033190, 040790, 041490, 042190, 042890, 060891, 061591, 062291, 062991, 070691, 071391, 110291

VAN DYKE, LEROY   120861, 122261, 122961, 010562, 011262, 011962, 012662, 052364, 060664, 061364, 062064

VANGELIS   032782, 040382, 041082, 041782, 042482, 050182, 050882, 051582, 052282

VAN HALEN   021184, 021884, 022584, 030384, 031084, 031784, 032484, 033184, 040784, 041484, 060984, 061684, 062384, 063084, 070784, 041986, 042686, 050286, 051086, 051786, 090388, 091088, 091788

VANILLA ICE   100690, 101390, 102090, 102990, 110390, 111090, 111790, 011991, 012691, 020291, 020991, 021691

VANITY FARE   062070, 062770, 070470, 071170

VANNELLI, GINO   111178, 111878, 112578, 120278, 120978, 121678, 122378, 050281, 050981, 051681, 052381, 053081, 060681, 061381

VANWARMER, RANDY   052679, 060279, 060979, 061679, 062379, 063079

VAUGHN MONROE ORCH. (VR: VAUGHN MONROE)   101940, 102640, 110240, 110940, 111640, 112340, 113040, 120740, 121440, 122140, 122840, 010441, 011141, 011841, 012541, 020141, 020841, 021541, 030141, 101742, 103142, 111442, 112142, 112842, 120542, 121242, 121942, 122642, 010243, 010943, 011643, 012343, 013043, 020643, 021343, 022043, 041743, 050143, 052243, 052943, 060543, 061243, 061943, 062643, 070343, 071043, 071743, 072443, 073143, 080743, 112544, 060945, 061645, 062345, 063045, 070745, 071445, 072845, 080445, 081145, 010546, 011246, 011946, 012646, 020246, 020946, 021646, 022346, 030246, 030946, 031646, 032346, 033046, 091347, 092047, 092747, 100447, 101147, 101847, 102547, 110147, 110847, 111547, 112247, 112947, 120647, 121347, 122047, 122747, 010348, 011048, 011748, 012448, 013148, 020748, 021448, 022148, 022848, 030648, 031348, 032048, 032748, 102348, 112048, 031249, 031949, 032649, 040249, 040949, 041649, 042349, 043049, 050749, 051449, 052149, 052849, 060449, 061149, 061849, 062549, 070249, 070949, 071649, 072349, 073049, 080649, 081349, 091049, 091749, 092449, 100149, 100849, 101549, 102249, 102949, 110549, 111249, 082049, 082749, 092554

VAUGHN, SARAH   011555, 020555, 091259, 091959, 092659, 100359

VEE, BOBBY   102160, 102860, 110460, 111160, 012061, 012761, 020361, 021061, 021561, 092261, 092961, 100661, 102061, 120861, 122261, 122961, 010562, 011262, 011962, 012662, 011263, 011963, 012663, 020263, 020963, 021663, 022363, 090267, 090967, 091667, 092367, 093067, 100767, 101467

VEGA, SUZANNE   080187, 080887, 081587, 082287, 082987

VENTURES   081960, 082660, 090260, 090960, 091660, 092360, 093060, 100760, 101460, 082264, 050369, 051069, 051769

VERA, BILLY & THE BEATERS   011087, 011787, 012487, 013187, 020787, 021487

VERDON, GWEN   051455, 052155, 052855, 060455, 061155, 061855, 062555

VERNE, LARRY   091660, 092360, 093060, 100760, 101460, 102160, 102860, 110460

VICTOR YOUNG ORCH.   042035, 042735, 050435, 051135

VICTOR YOUNG ORCH. (VR: HAL BURKE & TUNE TWISTERS)   042735, 051135, 051835, 052535, 060135, 060835, 061535

VICTOR YOUNG ORCH. (VR: MILTON WATSON)   052535, 060135, 060835

VILLAGE PEOPLE   122378, 010679, 011379, 012079, 012779, 020379, 021079, 021779, 022479, 030379, 031079, 040279, 050579, 051279, 051979, 052679, 060279

VILLAGE STOMPERS   102663, 110263, 110963, 111663, 112363, 113063, 120763

VINCENT LOPEZ ORCH. (VR: JOHNNY MORRIS)   072338

VINTON, BOBBY   062962, 070662, 071362, 072062, 072762, 080462, 081162, 081862, 082562, 090162, 090862, 061563, 062263, 062963, 070663, 071363, 072063, 090763, 091463, 092163, 092863, 100563, 101263, 101963, 102663, 121463, 122163, 122863, 010464, 011164, 011864, 012564, 020164, 020864, 112864, 120564, 121264, 121964, 122664, 010265, 010965, 011665, 012365, 110467, 111167, 111867, 112567, 120267, 121468, 122168, 122868, 011169, 110974, 111674, 112374, 113074, 120774

VIRTUES   041859, 042559, 050259, 050959, 051659, 052359, 053059

THE VOGUES   102365, 103065, 110665, 113165, 112065, 010866, 011566, 012266, 012966, 020566, 021266, 080368, 081068, 081768, 082468, 101268, 101968

W

WADE, ADAM   050561, 051261, 060961, 061661, 062361, 063061, 070761, 071461, 090161, 090861

WADSWORTH MANSION   022071, 022771, 030671

WAGNER, JACK   122284, 010585, 011285, 011985, 012685, 052486, 053186, 060786, 061486

WAITE, JOHN   081884, 082584, 090184, 090884, 091584, 092284, 092984, 100684

WALKER, JR. & THE ALL STARS   032065, 032765, 040365, 041065, 041765, 042465, 071269, 071969, 072669, 080269, 080969, 081669

WALLACE, JERRY   103159, 110759, 111459, 112159, 112859, 120559

WANG CHUNG   120686, 121386, 122086, 122786, 011087, 011787, 040487, 041187

WAR   012773, 021073, 040773, 041473, 042173, 042873, 050573, 051273, 090873, 091573, 080975, 081675, 082375, 083075, 111575, 112975, 120675, 091176, 091876, 092576, 100276

WARD, ANITA   060979, 061679, 062379, 063079, 070779, 071479, 072179, 072879, 080479, 081179

WARNES, JENNIFER   042377, 043077, 050777, 051477

WARRANT   090289, 090989, 091689, 092389, 093089, 100789, 101489, 110390, 022391

WARWICK, DIONNE   020164, 020864, 021564, 052764, 051466, 052166, 111867, 112567, 120267, 120967, 121667, 122367, 021768, 022468, 030268, 030968, 031668, 032368, 033068, 051868, 052568, 060168, 100568, 030869, 031569, 032269,

090669, 091369, 092069, 092769, 012470, 013170, 020770, 021470, 090179, 090879, 091579, 092279, 092979, 100679, 101379, 102079, 102779, 011583, 012283

WARWICK, DIONNE & THE SPINNERS   090774, 091474, 092174, 092874, 100574, 101274, 101974, 102674

WAS (NOT WAS)   032589, 040189, 040889

WASHINGTON, DINAH   082259

WASHINGTON, GROVER & BILL WITHERS   032881, 040481, 041181, 041881, 042581, 050281, 050981, 051681, 052381, 053081, 060681

WATERFRONT   061789, 062489

WATERS, CRYSTAL   070691, 071391

WATLEY, JODY   041887, 042587, 050287, 050987, 051687, 052387, 120587, 121287, 121987, 122687, 010988, 041688, 042989, 050689, 051389, 052089, 052789, 060389, 010690, 011390, 012090, 012790, 020390

WATLEY, JODY WITH ERIC B. & RAKIM   082689, 090289

WAYNE KING ORCH.   101036

WAYNE, THOMAS   032859, 040459, 041159, 041859, 042559

WE FIVE   090465, 091165, 091865, 092565, 100265, 100965

THE WEAVERS   081950, 082650, 090250, 080950, 091650, 092350, 093050, 100750, 101450, 102150, 102850, 110450, 111150, 111850, 112550

THE WEAVERS (VR: TERRY GILKYSON)   050551, 051251, 051951, 052651, 060251, 060951, 061651, 062351, 063051, 070751, 071451, 072151, 072851

THE WEAVERS WITH GORDON JENKINS ORCH.   080550, 090250, 091650

WEIR, FRANKIE   060554, 061254, 062654, 070354, 071054, 071754, 072454, 073154

WEISSBERG, ERIC & STEVE MANDELL   021773, 022473, 030373, 031073, 031773, 032473

WELCH, BOB   122477, 010778, 011478

WELCH, LENNY   121463, 122163, 122863, 010464, 011164

WELK, LAWRENCE   011361, 012061, 012761, 020361, 021061, 021761, 022461, 030361, 031061, 031761, 032461, 033161

WELLS, MARY   060162, 060862, 061562, 011963, 012663, 042564, 050264, 050964, 051564, 052364, 060664, 061364

WET WILLIE   082474

WHAM!   102784, 110384, 111084, 111784, 112484, 120184, 120884, 121584, 011985, 012685, 020285, 020985, 021685, 022385, 030285, 030985, 031685, 051185, 051885, 052585, 060185, 060685, 061585, 091485, 092185, 092885, 100585, 012586, 020186, 020886, 021586, 083086, 090686, 091386

THE WHISPERS   082287, 082987, 090587

WHITCOMB, IAN   071065, 071765, 072465

WHITE, BARRY   060273, 060973, 061673, 062373, 063073, 070773, 122273, 122973, 010574, 011274, 083174, 090774, 091474, 092174, 120774, 121474, 122174, 122874, 010475, 011175, 011875, 041275, 041975, 042675, 102977, 110577, 111277, 111977, 112677

WHITE, KARYN   011489, 012189, 012889, 020489, 041589, 081989, 082689, 090289, 100591, 101291, 101991, 102691, 110291, 110991, 111691

WHITE LION   052188, 052888, 012189, 012889, 020489, 021189

Song Title Index to the Weekly Charts, 1935-1994

Following the song titles below, six-digit numerical citations refer to the song's weekly chartings. For example: 012481 refers to the listing for the week of January 24, 1981, etc. This provides an at-a-glance summary of just how many weeks a song remained on the charts.

112269, 112969, 120669, 121369, 122069
ANGEL 061585, 062285, 070685, 041688, 042388, 043088, 050788, 051488
ANGEL BABY 010561, 012061, 012761, 020361, 021061, 021761
ANGEL EYES 082689, 090289, 090989, 091689
ANGEL IN YOUR ARMS 061877, 062577, 070277, 070977, 071677, 072377
ANGEL OF THE MORNING 062268, 062968, 070668, 071368, 041881, 042581, 050281, 050981, 051681, 052381
ANGELIA 111889, 112589, 120989
ANGIE 100673, 101373, 102073, 102773, 110373, 111073, 111773
ANGIE BABY 113074, 120774, 121474, 122174, 122874, 010475
ANNABELLE 021839, 022539
ANNIE'S SONG 062974, 070674, 071374, 072074, 072774, 080374, 081074
ANNIVERSARY 102393, 103093, 110693, 111393
THE ANNIVERSARY SONG 021547, 022247, 030147, 030847, 032247, 032947, 040547, 041247, 041947, 042647, 050347, 051047, 051747, 052447, 053147, 060747
ANOTHER BRICK IN THE WALL 030180, 030880, 031580, 032280, 032980, 040580, 041280, 041980, 042680, 050380, 051080, 051780
ANOTHER DAY IN PARADISE 112589, 120989, 121689, 122389, 010690, 011390, 012090, 012790, 010690
ANOTHER DAY/OH WOMAN OH WHY 040371, 041071, 041771, 042471, 050171
ANOTHER ONE BITES THE DUST 091380, 092080, 092780, 100480, 101180, 101880, 102580, 101180, 110880, 111580, 112280, 112980, 120680, 121380, 122080
ANOTHER SAD LOVE SONG 100293, 100993, 101693
ANOTHER SATURDAY NIGHT 092874, 100574, 101274
ANSWER ME, MY LOVE 041754, 050154, 050854, 051554, 052254, 052954, 060554, 061954, 070354
ANYONE WHO HAD A HEART 020164, 020864, 021564
ANYTHING FOR YOU 042388, 043088, 050788, 051488, 052188, 052888, 060488
ANYTIME 012452, 013152, 021452, 022152, 022852, 030652, 031352, 032052, 032752, 040352, 041052, 041752, 042452, 050152, 050852, 051552, 052252
APACHE 032461, 033161, 040761, 041461, 042161, 042861, 050561
APPLE BLOSSOM WEDDING 090647, 092747, 110847, 111547
APPLE BLOSSOMS AND CHAPEL BELLS 051140
AN APPLE FOR THE TEACHER 093039, 101439
APPLES PEACHES PUMPKIN PIE 090267, 090967, 091667, 092367, 093067, 100767
APRIL IN PORTUGAL 050253, 050953, 051653, 052353, 053053, 060653, 061353, 062053, 062753, 070453, 071153, 071853, 072553, 080153, 080853, 081553
APRIL LOVE 112357, 113057, 120757, 121457, 122157, 122857, 010458, 011158, 011858, 020158, 020858
APRIL SHOWERS 041247, 041947, 051047, 052447
AQUARIUS/LET THE SUNSHINE IN 032969, 040569, 041269, 041969, 042669, 050369, 051069, 051769, 052469, 053169, 060769
ARE YOU HAVING ANY FUN? 102139,

102839, 110439, 111139, 111839, 112539, 120239
ARE YOU LONESOME TONIGHT? 112560, 120260, 120960, 121660, 122360, 123060, 010561, 011361, 012061, 012761, 020361, 021061, 021761
ARE YOU SINCERE 040558
AREN'T YOU GLAD YOU'RE YOU 012646, 020246, 020946, 021646, 022346, 030246, 030946, 031646, 032346, 033046
ARIZONA 021470
ARMAGEDDON IT 010789, 011489, 012189, 012889, 020489
AROUND THE WAY GIRL 030291
AROUND THE WORLD 062957, 070657, 071357, 072057, 072757, 080357, 081057, 081757, 082457, 083157, 090757, 091457, 092157, 092857, 100557, 101257, 102657
ARTHUR'S THEME 091281, 091981, 092681, 100381, 101081, 101781, 102481, 103181, 110781, 111481, 112181, 112881
AS IF I DIDN'T KNOW 090161, 090861
AS TEARS GO BY 011566, 012266, 012966
AS TIME GOES BY 032043, 032743, 040343, 041043, 041743, 042443, 050143, 050843, 051543, 052243, 052943, 060543, 061243, 061943, 062643, 070343, 071043, 071743, 072443, 073143, 080743
ASIA MINOR 040761, 041461, 042161, 042861
ASK ANYONE WHO KNOWS 080247, 080947, 081647, 082347, 083047, 090647, 091347, 092047, 092747
AT A PERFUME COUNTER 042338
AT LAST 082942, 091242, 091942, 100342, 101042, 102442, 103142
AT LONG LAST LOVE 100838, 101538, 102238, 102938, 110538, 111238
AT SEVENTEEN 082375, 083075, 090675, 091375, 092075, 092775
AT THE BALALAIKA 011340, 012040, 012740, 020340, 021740, 022440, 030240, 030940, 031640, 032340, 040640
AT THE HOP 010458, 011158, 011858, 020158, 020858, 021558, 022258
AT THIS MOMENT 011087, 011787, 012487, 013187, 020787, 021487
A-TISKET, A-TASKET 080638, 081338, 082038, 082738, 090338, 091038, 091738, 092438, 100138, 100838, 101538
ATLANTIS 051069, 051769, 052469, 053169
AUF WIEDERSEHN, SWEETHEART 071752, 072452, 073152, 080752, 081452, 082152, 082952, 090552, 091252, 091952, 092652, 100352, 101052, 101752, 102452, 103152
AUTOMATIC 032484, 033184, 040784, 041484, 042184, 042884
AUTUMN LEAVES 091755, 092455, 100155, 100855, 101555, 102255, 102955, 110555, 111255, 111955, 112655, 120355, 121055, 121755, 122455, 123155, 010756, 011456, 012156, 012856
AUTUMN SERENADE 102045
AXEL F 051885, 052585, 060185, 060885, 061585

B

BABE 110379, 111079, 111779, 112479, 120179, 120879, 121579, 122279, 010580, 011280
BABY 031160, 031860, 032560, 040160, 040860
BABY BABY 040691, 041391, 042091, 042791, 050491, 051191, 051891
BABY BABY DON'T CRY 030169, 030869
BABY COME BACK 121777, 122477, 010778, 011478, 012178, 012778,

020478, 021178, 021878
BABY, COME TO ME 011583, 012283, 012983, 020583, 021283, 021983, 022683, 030583, 031283
BABY DON'T FORGET MY NUMBER 061789, 062489, 070189, 070889, 071589, 072289
BABY DON'T GET HOOKED ON ME 082672, 090272, 090972, 091672, 092372, 093072, 100772, 101472, 102172
BABY DON'T GO 100265, 100965, 101665
BABY FACE 041748, 042448, 050848, 051548, 052248, 052948, 060548, 061248, 061948
BABY GOT BACK 053092, 060692, 061392, 062092, 062792, 070492, 071192, 071892, 072592, 080192, 080892, 081592, 082992, 090592
BABY I LOVE YOU 081967, 082667, 090267, 090967, 091667, 072669, 080269, 080969, 081669
BABY I LOVE YOUR WAY (FROM "REALITY BITES") 050794, 051494
BABY, I LOVE YOUR WAY/FREEBIRD MEDLEY 111288, 111988, 112688, 120388, 121088, 121788
BABY, I NEED YOUR LOVING 022567, 030467, 031167, 031867, 032567
BABY I'M YOURS 091893, 092593, 100293
BABY I'M-A WANT YOU 112071, 112771, 120471, 121171, 121871
BABY, IT'S COLD OUTSIDE 070249, 070949, 071649, 072349, 073049, 080649, 081349
BABY IT'S YOU 020262, 020962, 102569, 110169, 110869, 111569
BABY LOVE 102464, 103164, 110764, 111464, 112164, 112864, 120564, 121264, 091386, 092086
BABY SITTIN' BOOGIE 031061, 031761
BABY, WHAT A BIG SURPRISE 110577, 111277, 111977, 112677, 120377, 121077
BABY WORKOUT 033063, 040563, 041363, 042063, 042763, 050463, 051163
BABY-BABY-BABY 071892, 072592, 080192, 080892, 081592, 082992, 090592, 091292, 091992, 092692, 100392, 101092, 101792
BACK HOME AGAIN 110974, 111674, 112374
BACK IN LOVE AGAIN 120377, 121077, 121777, 122477, 010778, 011478
BACK IN MY ARMS AGAIN 052265, 052965, 060565, 061265, 061965
BACK OFF BOOGALOO 050672, 051372, 052072
BACK ON THE CHAIN GANG 030583, 031283, 031983, 032683, 040283
BACK STABBERS 090272, 090972, 091672, 092372, 093072, 100772, 101472
BACK TO LIFE 111889, 112589, 120989, 121689, 122389
BAD 101087, 101787, 102487, 103187, 110787
BAD, BAD LEROY BROWN 070773, 071473, 072173, 072873, 080473, 081173, 081873, 082573
BAD BLOOD 100475, 101175, 101875, 102575, 110175
BAD BOY 051086, 051786, 052486
BAD BOYS (THEME FROM "COPS") 060593, 061293, 061993, 062693
BAD GIRLS 062379, 063079, 070779, 071479, 072179, 072879, 080479, 081179, 082579
BAD MEDICINE 102988, 110588, 111288, 111988, 112688, 120388
BAD MOON RISING 060769, 061469, 062169, 062869, 070569, 071269
BAD TIME 052475, 053175, 060775, 061475
BAD TO ME 052764, 070464
BAIA 070745
BAKER STREET 061078, 061778,

070178, 070878, 071578, 072278, 072978, 080578
BALI HA'I 052849, 060449, 061149, 061849, 062549, 070249, 070949, 071649, 072349, 073049, 080649, 081349, 082049, 082749, 090349, 091049, 091749
BALL OF CONFUSION 062070, 062770, 070470, 071170, 071870, 072570, 080170, 080870, 081570
THE BALLAD OF BONNIE AND CLYDE 032368, 033068, 040668, 041368, 042068, 042768
THE BALLAD OF DAVY CROCKETT 031955, 032555, 040255, 040955, 041655, 042355, 043055, 050755, 051455, 052155, 052855, 060455, 061155, 061855, 070255
THE BALLAD OF JOHN AND YOKO 071269, 071969, 072669, 080269
THE BALLAD OF THE GREEN BERETS 021966, 022666, 030566, 031966, 032666, 040266, 040966, 041666
BALLERINA 120647, 121347, 122047, 122747, 010348, 011048, 011748, 012448, 013148, 020748, 021448, 022148, 022848, 030648, 031348, 032048, 032748
BALLERINA GIRL 021487, 022187, 022887
BALLROOM BLITZ 092775, 100475, 101175, 101875, 102575
LA BAMBA 081587, 082287, 082987, 090587, 091287, 091987, 092687
BAMBINA 092438
THE BANANA BOAT SONG 011957, 012657, 020257, 020957, 021657, 022357, 030257, 030957, 031657, 032357, 033057
BAND OF GOLD 020456, 021156, 022556, 030356, 031756, 070470, 071170, 071870, 072570, 080170, 080870, 081570, 082270
BAND ON THE RUN 051874, 052574, 060174, 060874, 061574, 062274, 062974
BANG A GONG 030472, 031172, 072785, 080385, 081085
BANG BANG 040266, 040966, 041666, 042366, 043066, 050766
BARBARA ANN 012966, 020566, 021266, 021966
BAREFOOTIN' 061166, 061866, 062566, 070266
BATDANCE (FROM "BATMAN") 071589, 072289, 072989, 080589, 081289, 081989
THE BATTLE OF NEW ORLEANS 053059, 060659, 061359, 062059, 062759, 070459, 071159, 071859, 072559, 080159, 080859, 081559, 082259, 082959
BE ANYTHING 050152, 050852, 051552, 052252, 052952, 060552, 061252, 061952, 062652, 070352, 071052
BE CAREFUL, IT'S MY HEART 072542, 080842, 081542, 082242, 082942, 090542, 091242, 091942, 092642, 100342, 101042, 101742, 102442, 103142, 111442
BE GOOD TO YOURSELF 053186
BE MY BABY 092863, 100563, 101263, 101963, 102663, 110263
BE MY LIFE'S COMPANION 032752, 040352, 041052, 041752, 042452
BE MY LOVE 012751, 020351, 021051, 021751, 022451, 030351, 031051, 031751, 032451, 033151, 040751, 041451, 042151, 042851, 050551, 051251, 051951, 052651, 060251
BE NEAR ME 112185, 110985, 111685
BE THANKFUL FOR WHAT YOU'VE GOT 061574, 062274, 062974
BE TRUE TO YOUR SCHOOL 120763, 121463, 122163, 122863
BEACH BABY 092874, 100574, 101274
BEAST OF BURDEN 110478, 111178
THE BEAT GOES ON 021167, 021867, 022567, 030467

DEEPER AND DEEPER   011693, 012393, 013093, 020693

DELICADO   062652, 070352, 071052, 071752, 072452, 073152, 080752, 081452, 082152

DELIRIOUS   102283, 102983, 110583, 111283

DELTA DAWN   081873, 082573, 090173, 090873, 091573, 092273, 092973, 100673

DESERT MOON   111084

THE DESIDERATA   112771, 120471, 121171

DESIRE   021680, 022380, 030180, 030880, 031580, 032280, 032980, 040580, 110588, 111288, 111988, 112688, 120388

DEVIL INSIDE   040288, 040988, 041688, 042388, 043088

DEVIL MAY CARE   061540, 062940, 070640, 071340

DEVIL OR ANGEL   102160, 102860, 110460, 111160

THE DEVIL WENT DOWN TO GEORGIA   081179, 082579, 090179, 090879, 091579, 092279, 092979

DEVIL WITH A BLUE DRESS ON & GOOD GOLLY MISS MOLLY   111266, 111966, 112666, 120366, 121066, 121766, 122466

DEVIL WOMAN   091876, 092576, 100276, 100976, 101676

DEVOTED TO YOU   091258

DIAMOND GIRL   072873, 080473

DIAMONDS   060687, 061387, 062087, 062787

DIAMONDS AND PEARLS   011892, 012592, 020192, 020892, 021592, 022292, 022992, 030792, 031492

DIANA   090757, 091457, 092157, 092857, 100557, 101257, 101957

DIANE   062064

DICKEY BIRD SONG   041748, 042448, 050148, 050848, 051548, 052248, 061248, 061948

DID I REMEMBER   080836, 081536, 082236, 082936, 090536, 091236, 091936, 092636, 100336, 101036, 101736, 102436, 103136, 110736, 111436, 112136

DID IT IN A MINUTE   050882, 051582, 052282, 052982

DID YOU EVER GET THAT FEELING IN THE MOONLIGHT   120145

DID YOU EVER HAVE TO MAKE UP YOUR MIND?   052866, 060466, 061166, 061866, 062566, 070266

DID YOU MEAN IT?   110736, 111436, 120536

DIDN'T I?   032170

DIDN'T I (BLOW YOUR MIND)   111189, 111889

DIDN'T WE ALMOST HAVE IT ALL   082987, 090587, 091287, 091987, 092687, 100387, 101087

A DIFFERENT CORNER   060786, 061486, 062186, 062886

DIM ALL THE LIGHTS   100679, 101379, 102079, 102779, 110379, 111079, 111779, 112479, 120179

DINNER FOR ONE, PLEASE JAMES   011836, 012536, 020136, 020836, 021536, 022236, 022936, 030736

DIPSY DOODLE   012238, 012938, 020538, 021238, 021938, 022638, 030538, 031238, 031938, 032638

DIRTY DIANA   061188, 061888, 062588, 070288, 070988

DIRTY LAUNDRY   120482, 121182, 121882, 122582, 010883, 011583, 012283, 012983, 020583

DISAPPEAR   021691, 022391

DISCO DUCK PART 1   092576, 100276, 100976, 101676, 102376, 103076, 110676, 111376, 112076, 112776

DISCO LADY   032076, 032776, 040376, 041076, 041776, 042476, 050176, 050876

DITTY   042493, 050193, 050893

DIZZY   030169, 030869, 031569,

032269, 032969, 040569, 041269, 041969, 042669

DO ANYTHING   092891, 100591, 101291, 101991, 102691, 110291, 110991, 113091

DO I LOVE YOU?   021040, 030240, 030940, 032340

DO I WORRY   042641, 050341, 051041, 051741, 052441, 053141, 060741, 061441, 062141, 062841, 070541, 071241, 071941, 072641

DO IT AGAIN   021073, 021773, 022473

DO IT ('TIL YOU'RE SATISFIED)   110974, 111674, 112374, 113074, 120774, 121474, 122174

DO ME!   081190, 081890, 082590, 090190, 090890, 091590, 092290, 092990, 100690

DO NOTHIN' TIL YOU HEAR FROM ME   041544

DO THAT TO ME ONE MORE TIME   120879, 121579, 122279, 010580, 011280, 011980, 012680, 020280, 020980, 021680, 022380, 030180, 030880

DO WAH DIDDY DIDDY   091964, 092664, 100364, 101064, 101764, 102464, 103164, 110764, 111464

DO YOU BELIEVE IN LOVE   041082, 041782, 042482, 050182

DO YOU BELIEVE IN MAGIC   100965, 101665

DO YOU CARE   081641, 082341, 091341, 092041, 092741, 100441, 101141, 101841, 102541, 110141, 110841, 111541, 112241, 092741

DO YOU FEEL LIKE WE DO   111376, 112076

DO YOU KNOW THE WAY TO SAN JOSE?   051868, 052568, 060168

DO YOU KNOW WHAT I MEAN   100271, 100971, 101671, 102371, 103071

DO YOU LOVE ME   101362, 102062, 110362, 111062

DO YOU REALLY WANT TO HURT ME   021983, 022683, 030583, 031283, 031983, 032683, 040283, 040983, 041683

DO YOU REMEMBER?   061690, 062390, 063090, 070790

DO YOU THINK I'M SEXY   012079, 012779, 020379, 021079, 021779, 022479, 030379, 031079, 031779, 032479, 033179, 040779

DO YOU WANNA MAKE LOVE   071677, 072377, 073077, 080677, 081377, 082077

DO YOU WANT TO KNOW A SECRET   041864, 042564, 050264, 050964, 051664

THE DOCTOR   071589

DOCTOR, LAWYER, INDIAN CHIEF   022346, 030246, 030946, 031646, 032346, 033046, 040646, 041346, 042046

DOCTOR MY EYE   042272, 042972, 050672

DOES ANYBODY REALLY KNOW WHAT TIME IT IS   122670, 121970, 122670, 010271, 010971

DOES THE CHEWING GUM LOSE ITS FLAVOR   090861, 091561, 092261, 092961

DOESN'T SOMEBODY WANT TO BE WANTED?   031371, 032071, 032771, 040371, 041071, 041771

DOGGIE IN THE WINDOW   031453, 032153, 032853, 040453, 041153, 041853, 042553, 050253, 050953, 051653, 052353, 053053

DOIN' WHAT COMES NATURALLY   071346, 072046, 072746, 080346, 081046, 081746, 082446, 083146, 091446, 092146, 092846, 100546, 101246, 101946

DOING IT ALL FOR MY BABY   090587, 091287, 091987

DOMINIQUE   112363, 113063, 120763, 121463, 122163, 122863, 010464, 011164, 011864

DOMINO   122051, 122751, 010352, 011052, 011752, 010271

DONNA   012459, 013159, 020759, 021459, 022159, 022859, 030759, 031459, 032159, 032859

DONNA THE PRIMA DONNA   101963, 102663, 110263, 110963

DON'T BE CRUEL   090856, 091556, 092256, 092956, 100656, 101356, 102056, 102756, 110356, 092488, 100188, 100888, 101588, 102288

DON'T BE THAT WAY   043038, 050738, 051438, 052138, 052838, 060438, 061138, 061838, 062538

DON'T BREAK THE HEART THAT LOVES YOU   030962, 031662, 032362, 040662

DON'T BRING ME DOWN   082579, 090179, 090879, 091579, 092279, 092979

DON'T CALL US, WE'LL CALL YOU   031575, 032275, 032975

DON'T CRY   042443, 091783, 092483, 111691, 112391

DON'T CRY DADDY/RUBBERNECKIN'   011770, 012470, 013170

DON'T CRY, JOE   102249, 102949, 110549, 111249, 112649, 120349, 121049, 121749, 122449, 123149, 010750, 011450

DON'T CRY OUT LOUD   033179

DON'T DISTURB THIS GROOVE   070487, 071187, 071887, 072587

DON'T DO ME LIKE THAT   020280, 020980

DON'T DREAM IT'S OVER   032887, 040487, 041187, 041887, 042587, 050287, 050987

DON'T EVER CHANGE   012745

DON'T EXPECT ME TO BE YOUR FRIEND   021073, 021773, 022473, 030373

DON'T FALL IN LOVE WITH A DREAMER   051080, 051780, 052480, 053180, 060780

DON'T FENCE ME IN   120244, 120944, 121644, 122344, 123044, 010645, 011345, 012045, 012745, 020345, 021045, 021745, 022445, 030345, 031045, 031745

DON'T FORBID ME   012657, 020257, 020957, 021657, 022357, 030257, 030957, 031657, 032357

DON'T FORGET ME (WHEN I'M GONE)   092086, 092786, 100486, 101186, 101886

DON'T GET AROUND MUCH ANY MORE   032743, 040343, 041043, 042443, 050143, 050843, 051543, 052243, 052943, 060543, 061243, 061943, 062643, 070343, 071043

DON'T GET ME WRONG   122786

DON'T GIVE UP ON US   031977, 032677, 040277, 040977, 041677, 042377, 043077

DON'T GIVE UP THE SHIP   111635, 112335, 113035, 120735, 121435, 122135

DON'T GO BREAKING MY HEART   072476, 073176, 080776, 081476, 082176, 082876, 090476, 091176

DON'T HANG UP   112462, 120162, 120862, 121562, 122262

DON'T IT MAKE MY BROWN EYES BLUE   102977, 110577, 111277, 111977, 112677, 120377, 121077, 121777, 122477

DON'T JUST STAND THERE   080765, 081465, 082165

DON'T KNOW MUCH   112589, 120989, 121689, 122389, 010690, 011390

DON'T LEAVE ME THIS WAY   031977, 032677, 040277, 040977, 041677, 042377, 043077, 050777

DON'T LET IT END   061183, 061883, 062583, 070283, 070983

DON'T LET THE RAIN COME DOWN   041164, 041864, 042564, 050264, 050964, 051664

DON'T LET THE STARS GET IN YOUR EYES   121952, 122652, 010353,

011053, 011753, 012453, 013153, 020753, 021453, 022153, 022853, 030753, 031453, 032153, 032853, 040453, 041153, 041853, 042553

DON'T LET THE SUN CATCH YOU CRYING   062064, 052764, 070464, 071164, 071864

DON'T LET THE SUN GO DOWN ON ME   071374, 072074, 072774, 080374, 081074, 011192, 011892, 012592, 020192, 020892, 021592, 022292, 022992

DON'T LOOK BACK   091678, 092378, 093078, 100778, 101478, 102178

DON'T LOSE MY NUMBER   090785, 091485, 092185, 092885

DON'T MEAN NOTHING   081587, 082287, 082987, 090587

DON'T MESS WITH BILL   021266, 021966, 022666

DON'T PULL YOUR LOVE   062671, 070371, 071071, 071771, 072471, 073171

DON'T RUSH ME   122488, 010789, 011489, 012189, 012889, 020489

DON'T SAY NOTHING BAD ABOUT MY BABY   042063, 042763, 050463

DON'T SHED A TEAR   021388, 022088, 022788

DON'T SIT UNDER THE APPLE TREE   042542, 050942, 052342, 053042, 060642, 061342, 062042, 062742, 070442, 071142, 071842

DON'T SLEEP IN THE SUBWAY   070167, 070867, 071567

DON'T STAND SO CLOSE TO ME   041181, 041881, 042581

DON'T STOP   082777, 090377, 091077, 091777, 092477, 100177

DON'T STOP BELIEVING   121281, 121981, 122681

DON'T STOP 'TIL YOU GET ENOUGH   092979, 100679, 101379, 102079, 102779, 110379

DON'T SWEETHEART ME   032544, 050644

DON'T TALK TO STRANGERS   040382, 041082, 041782, 042482, 050182, 050882, 051582, 052282, 052982, 060582, 061282

DON'T TELL ME LIES   031889

DON'T THINK TWICE IT'S ALL RIGHT   102663

DON'T WALK AWAY   030693, 031393, 032093, 032793, 040393, 041093, 041793, 042493, 050193, 050893, 051593, 052993

DON'T WANNA FALL IN LOVE   033190, 040790, 041490, 042190, 042890, 050590

DON'T WANNA LOSE YOU   081289, 081989, 082689, 090289, 090989, 091689, 092389, 093089

DON'T WANT TO BE A FOOL   110291

DON'T WORRY   030361, 031061, 031761, 032461, 033161, 040761, 041461

DON'T WORRY, BE HAPPY   091088, 091788, 092488, 100188, 100888, 101588

DON'T WORRY 'BOUT ME   050639, 052039, 052739, 060339, 061039, 061739, 062439, 070139, 070839

DON'T YOU CARE   050667, 051367, 052067

DON'T YOU FORGET ABOUT ME   042085, 042785, 050485, 051185, 051885, 052585, 060185, 060885

DON'T YOU KNOW   103159, 110759, 111459, 112159, 112859, 120559, 121259, 121959, 122659

DON'T YOU KNOW I CARE   012745

DON'T YOU KNOW WHAT THE NIGHT CAN DO?   101588, 102288, 102988

DON'T YOU WANT ME   052282, 052982, 060582, 061282, 061982, 062682, 070382, 071082, 071782, 072482, 073182, 080782, 120587, 121287, 121987, 122687, 010988

THE DOOR IS STILL OPEN TO MY HEART

083075, 090675, 091375, 092075

FAME 090675, 091375, 092075,
092775, 100475, 101175, 082380,
083080, 090680, 091380, 092080,
092780

FAMILY AFFAIR 112071, 112771,
120471, 121171, 121871, 122571,
010172, 010872, 011572

FAMILY MAN 061883, 062583, 070283

FAR AWAY PLACES 010849, 011549,
012249, 012949, 020549, 021249,
021949, 022649, 030549, 031249,
031949, 032649, 040249, 040949,
041649, 042349, 043049, 050749,
051449

FAR FROM OVER 100183, 100883

FAREWELL, MY LOVE 111337, 121137,
121837

FASCINATION 083157, 090757,
091457, 092157, 092857, 100557,
101257, 101957, 102657, 110257,
110957, 111657, 112357, 113057,
081383, 082083, 082783

FAST CAR 082088, 082788, 090388,
091088

FATHER FIGURE 022088, 022788,
030588, 031288, 031988, 032688

FEEL LIKE MAKIN' LOVE 072774,
080374, 081074, 081774, 082474,
083174, 092075, 092775

FEELIN' STRONGER EVERY DAY
081873, 090173

FEELINGS 101875, 102575, 110175,
110875, 111575

FEELS GOOD 112490, 120190

FEELS LIKE THE FIRST TIME 052877,
060477, 061177, 061877, 062577

FEELS SO GOOD 052078, 052778,
060378, 061078, 061778

FELLOW ON A FURLOUGH 090944

FERRY CROSS THE MERSEY 030665,
031365, 032065, 032765

FERRYBOAT SERENADE 101940,
102640, 110240, 110940, 111640,
112340, 113040, 120740, 121440,
122140, 122840

FEUDIN' AND FIGHTIN' 090647,
091347, 092047, 092747, 100447,
101147, 101847, 102547, 110147,
110847, 111547, 112247

FEVER 082258, 082958, 121865,
122565, 010166

FIDDLE DEE DEE 090349, 091049,
091749, 092449

A FIFTH OF BEETHOVEN 082876,
090476, 091176, 091876, 092576,
100276, 100976, 101676, 102376,
103076

50 WAYS TO LEAVE YOUR LOVER
013176, 020776, 021476, 022176,
022876, 030676

FIGHT THE POWER 083075, 090675,
091375, 092075, 092775

THE FINAL COUNTDOWN 032887,
040487

FINALLY 121491, 122191, 010492,
011192, 011892, 012592, 020192,
020892, 022292

A FINE ROMANCE 100336, 101036,
101736, 102436, 103136, 110736,
111436, 112136

THE FINER THINGS 041187, 041887,
042587, 050287

FINGER POPPIN' TIME 082660, 090260,
090960

FINGERTIPS (PART II) 072063, 072763,
080363, 081063, 081763, 082463,
090763

FIRE 092868, 100568, 101268,
101968, 102668, 110268, 110968,
012675, 020175, 020875, 021575,
020379, 021079, 021779, 022479,
030379, 031079, 031779, 032479

FIRE AND RAIN 101770, 102470,
103170, 110770, 111470, 112170,
112970, 120570

FIRE LAKE 041980, 042680, 050380,
051080

THE FIRST TIME 010591, 011291,
011991, 012691, 020291, 020991,

021691, 022391

THE FIRST TIME EVER I SAW YOUR
FACE 040172, 040872, 041572,
042272, 042972, 050672, 051372,
052072, 052772, 060472, 061172

THE FIRST TIME I SAW YOU 073137,
082137, 082837, 090437, 091137,
092537

FIVE FOOT TWO, EYES OF BLUE
060449

FIVE MINUTES MORE 083146, 090746,
091446, 092146, 092846, 100546,
101246, 101946, 102646, 110246,
110946, 111646, 112346, 113046,
120746, 121446

FIVE O'CLOCK WORLD 010866,
011566, 012266, 012966, 020566,
021266

THE FLAME 061888, 062588, 070288,
070988, 071688, 072388

FLASHDANCE 051483, 052183,
052883, 060483, 061183, 061883,
062583, 070283, 070983, 071683,
072383, 073083, 080683, 081383

FLAT FOOT FLOOGEY 070938, 071638,
072338, 073038, 080638, 081338

FLOAT ON 082777, 090377, 091077,
091777, 092477

FLOWERS FOR MADAME 042735,
051135, 051835, 052535, 060135,
061535, 062235

FLOWERS ON THE WALL 010866,
011566

THE FLY 111061, 111761

FLY LIKE AN EAGLE 021977, 022677,
030577, 031277, 031977, 032677

FLY, ROBIN, FLY 111575, 112975,
120675, 121375, 122075, 122775,
010376

FOOL #1 111061, 111761, 112461,
120161, 120861

THE FOOL ON THE HILL 092168,
092868

A FOOL SUCH AS I 041859, 042559,
050259, 050959, 051659

FOOL TO CRY 060576, 061276

FOOLED AROUND AND FELL IN LOVE
042476, 050176, 050876, 051576,
052276, 052976

FOOLISH BEAT 060488, 061188,
061888, 062588, 070288, 070988

FOOLISH LITTLE GIRL 051163, 051863,
052563

FOOLS RUSH IN 062940, 072040,
072740, 080340, 081040, 081740,
082440, 090740

FOOTLOOSE 031084, 031784, 032484,
033184, 040784, 041484, 042184,
042884, 050584, 051284, 051984

FOOTLOOSE AND FANCY FREE
061535, 070635

FOOTSTEPS 042260

FOR ALL WE KNOW 030671, 031371,
032071, 032771, 040371, 041071,
041771

FOR ME AND MY GAL 022043, 022743,
031343, 032043, 032743, 040343,
041043, 041743, 050143

FOR ONCE IN MY LIFE 113068,
120768, 121468, 122168, 122868,
010469, 011169, 011869

FOR SENTIMENTAL REASONS 121446,
122146, 122846, 010447, 011147,
011847, 012547, 020147, 020847,
021547, 022247, 030147, 030847,
032247, 032947, 040547

FOR THE FIRST TIME 103043, 110643,
120443, 121143, 121843, 122543,
010144, 011544, 012244, 012944,
021944

FOR THE LOVE OF MONEY 060874,
061574

FOR WHAT IT'S WORTH 032567,
040167

FOR YOU 121848, 020164, 020864,
021564

FOR YOU, FOR ME, FOREVERMORE
113046, 121446, 122146, 011847

FOR YOUR EYES ONLY 101081,
101781, 102481, 103181, 110781,

FOR YOUR LOVE 061965, 062665,
070365

FOREVER 040790, 041490, 042190

FOREVER AND EVER 040249, 040949,
041649, 042349, 043049, 050749,
051449, 052149, 052849, 060449,
061149, 061849, 062549, 070249,
070949, 071649, 072349, 073049,
080649, 081349, 082049

FOREVER YOUR GIRL 042989, 050689,
051389, 052089, 052789, 060389

FORGET HIM 122863, 010464, 011164,
011864, 012564

FORGIVE ME 052252, 052952, 061252

FORTRESS AROUND YOUR HEART
101985, 102685, 112185

FORTY MILES OF BAD ROAD 080159,
080859, 081559

FOUR WALLS 062257

FOUR WINDS AND THE SEVEN SEAS
080649

FOX ON THE RUN 121375, 122075,
122775, 010376, 011076, 011776

FRANKENSTEIN 050573, 051273,
051973, 052673, 060273, 060973,
061673

FRANKIE 071159

LE FREAK 112578, 120278, 120978,
121678, 122378, 010679, 011379,
012079, 012779, 020379, 021079,
021779, 022479, 030379

FREAK ME 031393, 032093, 032793,
040393, 041093, 041793, 042493,
050193, 050893, 051593, 052293,
052993, 060593, 061293, 061993,
062693

FREDDIE'S DEAD (SUPERFLY) 102872,
110472, 111172, 111872

FREE FALLIN' 012090, 012790, 020390

FREE YOUR MIND 103192

FREEDOM 091485, 092185, 092885,
100585, 121590, 122290

FREEWAY OF LOVE 081085, 081785,
082485, 083185, 090785, 091485

FREEZE FRAME 032782, 040382,
041082, 041782, 042482, 050182,
050882, 051582

FRENESI 120740, 121440, 122140,
122840, 010441, 011141, 011841,
012541, 020141, 020841, 021541,
022241, 030141, 030841, 031541,
032241, 032941, 040541, 041241

FRESH 060185, 060885

A FRIEND OF YOURS 060245, 072145

FRIENDLY PERSUASION 110356,
111056, 111756, 120156, 120856

FRIENDS 082689, 090289

FRIENDS AND LOVERS 083086,
090686, 091386, 092086, 092786,
100486, 101186

FROM A DISTANCE 111790, 112490,
120190, 120890, 121590, 122290,
010591, 011291, 011991

FROM A JACK TO A KING 021663,
022363, 030263

FROM THE TOP OF YOUR HEAD
090735, 092835, 100535, 101235,
101935, 102635, 110935

FROSTY THE SNOWMAN 123050

FULL MOON 050242

FULL MOON AND EMPTY ARMS
052546, 060146, 060846, 062246,
062946

FUN FUN FUN 030764, 031464,
032164, 032864

FUNKY BROADWAY 091667, 092367,
093067

FUNKY COLD MEDINA 040889, 041589,
042289, 042989, 050689

FUNKYTOWN 051780, 052480, 053180,
060780, 061480, 062180, 062880,
070580, 071280, 070487, 071187,
071887

FUNNY FACE 122372, 123072, 010673,
011373

G

G.T.O. 090564, 091264, 091964,
092664, 100364, 101064

A GAL IN CALICO 122146, 122846,

010447, 011147, 011847, 012547,
020147, 020847, 021547, 022247,
030147, 030847, 032247

GALVESTON 032969, 040569, 041269,
041969, 042669, 050369

GALWAY BAY 012249, 012949, 020549,
021249, 021949, 022649, 030549,
031249, 031949, 032649, 040249,
040949

GAME OF LOVE 041065, 041765,
042465, 050165, 050865

GAMES PEOPLE PLAY 101875, 102575,
110175, 110875

GANGSTA LEAN 110693, 111393,
112093, 112793, 120493, 121193,
121893, 122593, 010194, 010894,
011594

GARDEN PARTY 102172, 102872,
110472, 111172

GAUCHO SERENADE 022440, 040640

G'BYE NOW 051741, 053141, 060741,
062841, 070541

THE GENTLEMAN OBVIOUSLY DOESN'T
BELIEVE 101235, 102635

GEORGIA ON MY MIND 031541,
032241, 041941, 050341, 060741,
111160, 111860, 112560, 120260

GEORGY GIRL 011467, 012167,
012867, 020467, 021167, 021867,
022567, 030467

GET A JOB 011858, 020158, 020858,
021558, 022258, 030158, 030858

GET BACK 051069, 051769, 052469,
053169, 060769, 061469, 062169,
062869, 070569

GET CLOSER 072476, 073176, 082176,
082876

GET DANCIN' 020875

GET DOWN 081873, 082573, 090173

GET DOWN, GET DOWN (GET ON THE
FLOOR) 061475, 062175, 062875

GET DOWN ON IT 052282, 052982

GET DOWN TONIGHT 082375, 083075,
090675, 091375

GET HERE 031691, 032391, 033091

GET OFF 110478, 111178

GET OFF OF MY CLOUD 102365,
103065, 110665, 111365, 112065,
112765

GET OUT OF TOWN 012839, 021139

GET OUTTA MY DREAMS, GET INTO MY
CAR 031988, 032688, 040288,
040988, 041688, 042388, 043088

GET READY 060670, 061370, 062070,
062770, 070470

GET TOGETHER 082369, 083069,
090669, 091369, 092069

GET UP AND BOOGIE 050876, 051576,
052276, 052976, 060576, 061276,
061976, 062676, 070376

GET UP! (BEFORE THE NIGHT IS OVER)
032490, 033190, 040790, 041490

GETTO JAM 021294, 021994

GHOSTBUSTERS 071484, 072184,
072884, 080484, 081184, 081884,
082584, 090184, 090884, 091584

GIMME DAT DING 071870

GIMME LITTLE SIGN 100767, 101467,
102167

GIMME SOME LOVIN' 021867, 022567,
030467

GIN AND JUICE 031994, 032694,
040294

GINA 111062, 111762, 112462, 120162

THE GIRL FROM IPANEMA 071164,
071864, 072564, 080164

GIRL I'M GONNA MISS YOU 090989,
091689, 092389, 093089, 100789,
101489

THE GIRL IS MINE 112782, 120482,
121182, 121882, 122582, 010883,
011583, 012283, 012983

A GIRL LIKE YOU 081267, 081967

GIRL WATCHER 092868, 100568,
101268, 101968, 102668

GIRL YOU KNOW IT'S TRUE 031189,
031889, 032589, 040189, 040889,
041589, 042289

GIRL, YOU'LL BE A WOMAN SOON
052767

HAVE YOU FORGOTTEN SO SOON?
120338, 121038, 121738, 010739
HAVE YOU GOT ANY CASTLES, BABY
090437, 091837, 092537, 100237,
100937, 101637, 102337, 103037,
110637, 111337
HAVE YOU NEVER BEEN MELLOW
022275, 030175, 030875, 031575,
032275, 032975, 040575
HAVE YOU SEEN HER 081890, 082590,
090190, 090890, 091590, 092290
HAVE YOU SEEN HER? 111371,
112071, 112771, 120471, 121171,
121871, 122571, 010172
HAVE YOU SEEN YOUR MOTHER, BABY,
STANDING IN THE SHADOW
102966, 110566
HAWAII FIVE-O 050369, 051069,
051769
HAWAIIAN WEDDING SONG 022159,
022859, 030759, 031459, 032159,
032859, 040459, 041159
HAZARD 042592, 050292
HAZY SHADE OF WINTER 011688,
012388, 013088, 020688, 021388
HE 110555, 111955, 112655, 120355,
121055, 121755, 122455, 123155,
010756, 012156, 021156
HE AIN'T HEAVY, HE'S MY BROTHER
030770, 031470, 032170, 032870
HE DON'T LOVE YOU LIKE I LOVE YOU
041975, 042675, 050375, 051075,
051775, 052475
HE WEARS A PAIR OF SILVER WINGS
071842, 072542, 080142, 080842,
081542, 082242, 082942, 090542,
091242, 091942, 092642, 100342,
101042, 101742, 103142
HE WILL BREAK YOUR HEART 120960,
121660, 122360, 123060
HEAD OVER HEELS 101985, 102685,
112185, 110985, 111685, 112385
HEAD TO TOE 053087, 060687,
061387, 062087, 062787, 070487,
071187
HEART 060455, 061155, 061855,
062555, 070255, 070955, 072355
HEART AND SOUL 102238, 102938,
110538, 111238, 111938, 112638,
120338, 121038, 121738, 122438,
112683, 120383, 072587, 080187,
080887, 081587, 082287
HEART ATTACK 101682, 102382,
103082, 110682, 111382, 112082,
112782
HEART FULL OF SOUL 091865, 092565
HEART OF GLASS 040779, 041479,
042179, 042879, 050579, 051279,
051979
HEART OF GOLD 030472, 031172,
031872, 032572, 040172, 040872,
041572, 042272
HEART OF MY HEART 010954, 011654,
012354, 020654, 021354, 022054,
022754, 030654, 031354
THE HEART OF ROCK 'N ROLL 060284,
060984, 061684, 062384, 063084,
070784, 071484
HEARTACHE TONIGHT 102079,
102779, 110379, 111079, 111779,
112479, 120179, 120879, 121579
HEARTACHES 032947, 040547,
041247, 041947, 042647, 050347,
051047, 051747, 052447, 053147,
060747, 061447, 062147, 120161
HEARTACHES BY THE NUMBER
112159, 112859, 120559, 121259,
121959, 122659, 010160, 010860,
011560, 012260
HEARTBEAT 101186, 101886, 102586
HEARTBEAT IT'S A LOVEBEAT 102073,
102773, 110373, 111073, 111773,
112473, 120173
HEARTBREAK HOTEL 042856, 050556,
051256, 051956, 052656, 060256,
060956, 061656
HEARTBREAKER 011583, 012283
HEARTLIGHT 103082, 110682, 111382,
112082, 112782, 120482
HEARTS 072581, 080181, 080881,
081581

HEARTS OF STONE 012255, 012955,
020555, 021255, 021955, 022655,
030555, 031255
THE HEAT IS ON 021685, 022385,
030285, 030985, 031685, 032385
HEAT OF THE MOMENT 060582,
061282, 061982, 062682, 070382,
071082
HEAT OF THE NIGHT 050987, 051687,
052387, 053087
HEAT WAVE 090763, 091463, 092163,
092863, 100563, 101263
HEAT WAVE/LOVE IS A ROSE 110175,
110875, 111575
HEAVEN 060185, 060885, 061585,
062285, 070685, 090289, 090989,
091689, 092389, 093089, 100789,
101489
HEAVEN CAN WAIT 031839, 032539,
040139, 040839, 041539, 042239,
042939, 050639, 051339, 052039,
052739
HEAVEN HELP ME 042289, 042989
HEAVEN HELP US ALL 112970, 120570
HEAVEN IS A PLACE ON EARTH
111487, 112187, 112887, 120587,
121287, 121987
HEAVEN KNOWS 030379, 031079,
031779, 032479, 033179
HEAVEN ON THE 7TH FLOOR 110577,
111277, 111977, 112677, 120377,
121077
HEIGH HO 031938, 032638, 040238,
040938, 041638, 042338, 043038,
050738, 051438, 052138, 052838
HELEN WHEELS 011274
HE'LL HAVE TO GO 021960, 022660,
030460, 031160, 031860, 032560,
040160, 040860, 041560, 042260,
042960, 050660
HE'LL HAVE TO STAY 052760, 060360,
061060, 061760, 062460
HELLO 040784, 041484, 042184,
042884, 050584, 051284, 051984,
052684, 060284, 060984
HELLO AGAIN 030781, 031481, 032181,
032881, 040481
HELLO DOLLY 032164, 032864,
040464, 041164, 041864, 042564,
050264, 050964, 051664, 052364,
060664, 061364
HELLO GOODBYE 120967, 121667,
122367, 123067, 010668, 011368,
012068, 012768
HELLO I LOVE YOU 072068, 072768,
080368, 081068, 081768, 082468,
083168, 090768, 091468
HELLO IT'S ME 120873, 121673,
122273, 122973
HELLO MUDDAH, HELLO FADDUH
081763, 082463, 090763, 091463,
092163
HELLO STRANGER 061563, 062263,
062963, 070663, 071363
HELP 082165, 082865, 090465,
091165, 091865, 092565
HELP ME 052574, 060174, 060874
HELP ME MAKE IT THROUGH THE NIGHT
032071, 032771, 040371
HELP ME RHONDA 051565, 052265,
052965, 060565, 061265, 061965,
062665
HENRY VIII 071765, 072465, 073165,
080765, 081465, 082165
HER ROYAL MAJESTY 030962, 031662,
032362
HERE 051554, 052254
HERE AND NOW 033190, 040790,
041490, 042190, 042890
HERE COMES COOKIE 042035, 042735
HERE COMES THE JUDGE 062968,
070668, 071368
HERE COMES THE RAIN AGAIN
031084, 031784, 032484, 033184,
040784, 041484, 042184
HERE I AM 110781, 111481, 112181,
112881, 120581, 121281
HERE I AM (COME AND TAKE ME)
090873, 091573, 070691, 071391,
072091

HERE I GO AGAIN 090587, 091287,
091987, 092687, 100387, 101087,
101787
HERE I'LL STAY 011549, 012949,
021949
HERE IN MY HEART 061952, 062652,
070352, 071052, 071752, 072452,
082952, 090552
HERE WE ARE 022490, 030390, 031090
HERE WE GO 042091, 042791, 050491,
051191, 051891, 052591
HERE YOU ARE 070442, 071142,
072542
HERE YOU COME AGAIN 121777,
122477, 010778, 011478, 012178
HERE'S LOVE IN YOUR EYES 112136
HERE'S TO ROMANCE 110235,
110935, 111635, 112335
HERNANDO'S HIDEAWAY 061254,
061954, 062654, 070354, 071054,
071754, 072454, 073154, 080754,
081454, 082154, 082854, 090454,
091154
HERO 112093, 112793, 120493,
121193, 121893, 122593, 010194,
010894, 011594, 012294, 012994,
020594, 021294, 021994, 022694,
030594
HE'S A REBEL 101362, 102062,
110362, 111062, 111762, 112462,
120162, 120862
HE'S GOT THE WHOLE WORLD IN HIS
HANDS 041258, 041958, 042658,
050358, 051058, 051758, 060758,
061358, 062058
HE'S HOME FOR A LITTLE WHILE
050545
HE'S MY GUY 101042, 101742
HE'S SO FINE 031663, 032363, 033063,
040563, 041363, 042063, 042763,
050463, 051163
HE'S SO SHY 101880, 102580, 110180,
110880, 111580
HE'S SURE THE BOY I LOVE 022363
HE'S THE GREATEST DANCER 050579,
051279, 051979
HEY! BABY 022362, 030262, 030962,
031662, 032362, 040662
HEY DEANIE 010778, 011478, 012178
HEY GIRL/I KNEW YOU WHEN 122571,
010172, 010872, 011572
HEY, JEALOUS LOVER 121556, 011257
HEY JUDE 091468, 092168, 092868,
100568, 101268, 101968, 102668,
110268, 110968, 111668, 112368,
113068, 120768, 121468
HEY LITTLE COBRA 011864, 012564,
020164, 020864, 021564, 022264
HEY MR. D.J. 101693, 102393, 103093,
110693, 111393, 112093, 112793
HEY NINETEEN 021481, 022181
HEY PAULA 012663, 020263, 020963,
021663, 022363, 030263, 030963,
031663
HEY THERE 073154, 080754, 081454,
082154, 082854, 090454, 091154,
091854, 092554, 100254, 100954,
101654, 102354, 103054, 110654,
111354, 112054
HEY THERE LONELY GIRL 020770,
021470, 022170, 022870, 030770,
031470
HEY WON'T YOU PLAY ANOTHER
SOMEBODY DONE SOMEBODY
WRONG SONG 040575, 041275,
041975, 042675, 050375, 051075,
051775
HI, NEIGHBOR 102541
THE HIGH AND THE MIGHTY 081454,
082154, 082854, 090454, 091154,
091854, 092554, 100254, 100954,
101654, 102354, 103054
HIGH ENOUGH 121590, 122290,
010591, 011291, 011991, 012691,
020291
HIGH ON A WINDY HILL 020141,
020841, 021541, 022241, 030141,
030841, 031541, 032241, 032941,
040541, 041241, 041941, 042641
HIGH ON YOU 032385, 033085

HIGHER AND HIGHER 092367, 093067,
100767, 101467, 073077, 080677,
081377, 082077, 082777, 090377,
091077
HIGHER GROUND 092273, 092973,
100673, 101373, 102073, 102773
HIGHER LOVE 080986, 081686,
082386, 083086, 090686, 091386
HIM 030880, 031580, 032280, 032980,
040580
HIM OR ME, WHAT'S IT TO BE?
052767, 060367, 061067
HIP HOP HOORAY 022093, 022793,
030693
HIP TO BE SQUARE 112286, 112986,
120686, 121386, 122086
HIT ME WITH YOUR BEST SHOT
121380, 122080, 122780
HIT THE ROAD JACK 092961, 100661,
102061, 102761, 110361, 111061,
111761, 112461
HITCHIN' A RIDE 062070, 062770,
070470, 071170
HOCUS POCUS 052673, 060273,
060973
HOLD ME 071782, 072482, 073182,
080782, 081482, 082182, 082882,
090482, 091182, 091882
HOLD ME NOW 041484, 042184,
042884, 050584, 051284, 051984,
052684
HOLD ME, THRILL ME, KISS ME
022853, 030753, 032153, 082865,
090465
HOLD ME TIGHT 110268, 110968,
111668, 112368, 113068
HOLD MY HAND 110654
HOLD ON 051290, 051990, 052690,
060290, 060990, 061690, 062390,
063090, 070790, 071490, 072190,
072890, 080490
HOLD ON TIGHT 100381, 101081
HOLD ON TO MY LOVE 050380, 051080
HOLD ON TO THE NIGHTS 070988,
071688, 072388, 073088, 080688,
081388
HOLD THE LINE 122378, 010679,
011379, 012079, 012779
HOLD TIGHT 040139, 040839, 041539
HOLD WHAT YOU'VE GOT 013065,
020665, 021365
HOLD YOU TIGHT 031691, 032391,
033091, 040691, 041391, 042091,
042791
HOLD YOUR HEAD UP 081972,
082672, 090272
HOLDING BACK THE YEARS 062186,
062886, 070586, 071986, 072686
HOLE HEARTED 100591, 101291,
101991, 102691, 110291
HOLLY HOLY 122069, 122769, 010370
HOLLYWOOD SWINGING 062274,
062974, 070674
HOMESICK, THAT'S ALL 101345
HOMEWARD BOUND 030566, 031966,
032666, 040266
HONEY 040668, 041368, 042068,
042768, 050468, 051168, 051868,
052568, 060168, 060868
HONEY BABE 060455, 061855, 070255,
071655
HONEYCOMB 091457, 092157, 092857,
100557, 101257, 101957, 102657,
110257, 110957, 111657
HONKY CAT 091672, 092372
HONKY TONK WOMAN 080269,
080969, 081669, 082369, 083069,
090669, 091369, 092069, 092769,
100469, 100369
HOOKED ON A FEELING 010469,
011169, 011869, 012569, 020169,
032374, 033074, 040674, 041374,
042074, 042774, 050474
HOOKED ON CLASSICS 013082,
020682
HOOP-DEE-DOO 052050, 052750,
061050, 061750, 062450, 070150,
070850, 071550, 072250, 080550,
081250
HOORAY FOR HAZEL 102966, 110566

I GET SO LONELY 032054, 032754, 040354, 041054, 041754, 042454, 050154, 050854, 051554, 052254, 052954, 060554, 061254, 062654
I GET WEAK 022788, 030588, 031288, 031988, 032688
I GIVE YOU MY WORD 121440, 122140, 122840, 010441, 011141, 011841, 012541, 020141, 020841, 021541, 022241, 030141, 030841
I GO CRAZY 030478, 031178, 031878, 032578, 040178
I GO TO EXTREMES 031090, 031790, 032490
I GO TO PIECES 021365, 022065, 022765
I GOT A NAME 111773
I GOT IT BAD 012442
I GOT RHYTHM 051367, 052067, 052767, 060367, 061067, 061767
I GOT STUNG 112858, 120558, 121258, 121958, 122658
I GOT THE FEELIN' 041368, 042068, 042768, 050468
I GOT THE SUN IN THE MORNING 070646, 080346, 081046, 081746, 082446, 083146, 090746, 091446, 092146, 092846, 100546, 101246
I GOT YOU BABE 080765, 081465, 082165, 082865, 090465, 091165, 091865
I GOT YOU (I FEEL GOOD) 112765, 120465, 121165, 121865, 122565, 010166, 010866
I GOTCHA 032572, 040172, 040872, 041572, 042272, 042972, 050672, 051372, 052072, 052772
I GUESS I'LL HAVE TO DREAM THE REST 083041, 090641, 091341, 092041, 092741, 100441, 101141, 101841, 102541, 110141, 110841, 111541, 112241
I GUESS THAT'S WHY THEY CALL IT THE BLUES 010784, 011484, 012184, 012884, 020484, 021184
I HAD THE CRAZIEST DREAM 121242, 121942, 122642, 010243, 010943, 011643, 012343, 013043, 020643, 021343, 022043, 022743, 030643, 031343, 032043
I HADN'T ANYONE 'TIL YOU 070938, 071638, 072338, 080638, 081338, 082038, 082738
I HATE MYSELF FOR LOVING YOU 100188, 100888, 101588
I HAVE EYES 020439, 021139, 021839, 030439, 031139, 031839
I HAVE NOTHING (FROM "THE BODYGUARD") 032093, 032793, 040393, 041093, 041793, 042493, 050193, 050893, 051593, 052293, 052993
I HEAR A RHAPSODY 010441, 011141, 011841, 012541, 020141, 020841, 021541, 022241, 030141, 030841, 031541, 032241, 032941, 040541, 041241, 041941
I HEAR A SYMPHONY 111365, 112065, 112765, 120465, 121165, 121865
I HEAR YOU KNOCKING 121055, 013071, 020671, 021371, 022071, 022771
I HEARD A RUMOUR (FROM "DISORDERLIES") 091287, 091987, 092687, 100387, 101087, 101787
I HEARD IT THROUGH THE GRAPEVINE 120267, 120967, 121667, 122367, 123067, 010668, 011368, 012068, 012768, 120768, 121468, 122168, 122868, 010469, 011169, 011869, 012569, 020169, 020869, 021569
I HEARD YOU CRIED LAST NIGHT 081443, 082843, 090443, 091143, 091843, 092543, 100243, 100943, 101643, 102343, 103043, 110643
I HONESTLY LOVE YOU 092174, 092874, 100574, 101274, 101974
I JUST CALLED TO SAY I LOVE YOU 092284, 092984, 100684, 102084,

102784, 110384, 111084, 111784, 112484
I JUST CAN'T HELP BELIEVING 082270
I JUST CAN'T STOP LOVING YOU 082287, 082987, 090587, 091287, 091987, 092687
(I JUST) DIED IN YOUR ARMS 041887, 042587, 050287, 050987, 051687, 052387
I JUST WANNA STOP 111178, 111878, 112578, 120278, 120978, 121678, 122378
I JUST WANT TO BE YOUR EVERYTHING 070277, 070977, 071677, 072377, 073077, 080677, 081377, 082077, 082777, 090377, 091077, 091777, 092477, 100177, 100877, 101577
I JUST WANT TO CELEBRATE 090471, 091171, 091871, 092571
I KEEP FORGETTIN' 100282, 100982, 101682, 102382, 103082, 110682, 111382
I KNEW YOU WERE WAITING (FOR ME) 032887, 040487, 041187, 041887, 042587, 050287, 050987
I KNOW 011262, 011962, 012662, 020262, 020962
I KNOW A PLACE 041065, 041765, 042465, 050165, 050865, 051565
(I KNOW) I'M LOSING YOU 122466, 123166, 092670, 100370, 101070
I KNOW NOW 011737, 080737, 081437, 082137, 082837, 090437, 091137, 091837
I KNOW WHAT I LIKE 053087
I LET A SONG GO OUT OF MY HEART 052838, 061838, 062538, 070238, 070938, 071638, 072338, 073038, 080638, 081338, 082038, 082738
I LIKE DREAMIN' 021277, 021977, 022677, 030577, 031277, 031977, 032677
I LIKE IT 072989, 080589, 081289, 081989
I LIKE IT LIKE THAT 080461, 081161, 081861, 082561, 090161, 073165, 080765
I LIKE THE WAY (THE KISSING GAME) 042091, 042791, 050491, 051191, 051891, 052591, 060191, 060891, 061591
I LOVE A RAINY NIGHT 012481, 013181, 020781, 021481, 022181, 032881, 030781, 031481, 032181
I LOVE HOW YOU LOVE ME 102761, 110361, 111061, 121468, 122168, 122868, 011169
I LOVE MUSIC 122775, 010376, 011076, 011776, 012476, 013176
I LOVE PARIS 110753
I LOVE ROCK 'N ROLL 030682, 031382, 032082, 032782, 040382, 041082, 041782, 042482, 050182, 050882, 051582
I LOVE THE NIGHT LIFE 112578, 120278, 120978, 121678, 122378, 010679
I LOVE THE WAY YOU LOVE 041560
I LOVE TO WHISTLE 041638, 051438, 052138
I LOVE YOU 030444, 031144, 031844, 032544, 040144, 040844, 041544, 042244, 042944, 050644, 051344, 052044, 052744, 060344, 061044, 061744, 062444, 070144
I LOVE YOU BECAUSE 052563, 060163, 060863, 061563, 062263
I LOVE YOU MORE AND MORE EVERY DAY 031464, 032164
I LOVE YOUR SMILE 011892, 012592, 020192, 020892, 021592, 022292, 022992, 030792, 031492, 032192, 032892
I MADE IT THROUGH THE RAIN 013181
I MARRIED AN ANGEL 070938, 071638, 072338, 073038, 080638, 081338, 082038
I MISS YOU 121485, 122185, 122885, 011186, 011886, 012586
I MUST SEE ANNIE TONIGHT 011439, 012139

I NEED YOU 070172, 070872
I NEED YOU NOW 100954, 101654, 102354, 103054, 110654, 111354, 112054, 112754, 120454, 121854, 122554, 010155, 010855
I NEED YOUR LOVE TONIGHT 041859, 042559, 050259, 050959
I NEVER KNEW HEAVEN COULD SPEAK 052039, 052739, 060339, 061039, 061739
I NEVER LOVED A MAN THE WAY I LOVE YOU 041567, 042267
I NEVER MENTION YOUR NAME 061243
I POURED MY HEART INTO A SONG 072239, 072939, 080539, 081239, 081939, 082639, 090239, 090939, 091639
I PROMISE YOU 022539
I RAN 100982, 101682, 102382, 103082
I REMEMBER HOLDING YOU 011489
I REMEMBER YOU 040442, 041142, 050242, 100662, 101362, 102062, 012790, 020390, 021090
I SAID MY PAJAMAS 022550, 030450, 031150, 031850, 032550, 040850
I SAW HER AGAIN 072366, 073066, 080666, 081166
I SAW HIM STANDING THERE 041688, 042388, 043088
I SAW MOMMY KISSING SANTA CLAUS 010353
I SAW RED 022391
I SAY A LITTLE PRAYER 111867, 112567, 120267, 120967, 121667, 122367, 100568
I SECOND THAT EMOTION 120967, 121667, 122367, 123067, 010668, 011368, 012068
I SEE A MILLION PEOPLE 110141
I SEE THE MOON 112153
I SEE YOUR FACE BEFORE ME 031238
I SHOT THE SHERIFF 082474, 083174, 090774, 091474, 092174
I SHOULD CARE 051245, 051945, 052645, 060245, 060945, 061645, 062345
I STARTED A JOKE 012569, 020169, 020869
I STILL HAVEN'T FOUND WHAT I'M LOOKING FOR 071187, 071887, 072587, 080187, 080887, 081587, 082287
I STILL LOVE TO KISS YOU GOODNIGHT 112037, 121137, 122537
I SWEAR 051494
I THANK YOU 031668, 032368
I THINK I LOVE YOU 110770, 111470, 112170, 112970, 120570, 121270, 121970, 122670, 010271, 010971, 011671
I THINK WE'RE ALONE NOW 040867, 041567, 042267, 042967, 050667, 051367, 102487, 103187, 110787, 111487, 112187, 112887
I TOUCH MYSELF 042791, 050491, 051191, 051891, 052591
I UNDERSTAND JUST HOW YOU FEEL 071754, 072454, 080754
I WALK ALONE 060552, 061952, 062652, 070352
I WANNA BE LOVED 070850, 071550, 072250, 072950, 080550, 081250, 081950, 082650, 090250
I WANNA BE RICH 041490, 042190, 042890, 050590, 051290, 051990
I WANNA DANCE WITH SOMEBODY (WHO LOVES ME) 060687, 061387, 062087, 062787, 070487, 071187, 071887, 072587, 080187
I WANNA GET NEXT TO YOU 050777, 051477
I WANNA HAVE SOME FUN 021189
I WANNA KNOW WHAT LOVE IS 011985, 030985
I WANNA LOVE HIM SO BAD 080864, 081564
I WANNA SEX YOU UP (FROM "NEW JACK CITY") 051891, 052591, 060191, 060891, 061591, 062291,

062991, 070691, 071391, 072091
I WANT A NEW DRUG 030384, 031084, 031784, 032484, 033184
I WANT HER 031288, 031988, 032688, 040288, 040988
I WANT MY SHARE OF LOVE 041539
I WANT TO BE WANTED 102160, 102860, 110460, 111160, 111860, 112560
I WANT TO BE YOUR MAN 012388, 013088, 020688, 021388, 022088
I WANT TO HOLD YOUR HAND 012564, 020164, 020864, 021564, 022264, 022964, 030764, 031464, 032164, 032864, 040464, 041164
I WANT TO KNOW WHAT LOVE IS 012685, 020285, 020985, 021685, 022385, 030285
I WANT TO WALK YOU HOME 091959, 092659
I WANT YOU BACK 122769, 010370, 011070, 011770, 012470, 013170, 020770, 021470, 022170
I WANT YOU TO WANT ME 070779, 071479, 072179, 072879, 080479
I WANT YOUR LOVE 042179, 042879, 050579, 051279
I WANT YOUR SEX (FROM "BEVERLY HILLS COP II") 071887, 072587, 080187, 080887, 081587, 082287
I WAS LUCKY 042035, 042735, 050435
I WAS MADE FOR DANCING 021779, 022479
I WAS MADE TO LOVE HER 072267, 072967, 080567, 081267, 081967, 082667, 090267
I WENT OUT OF MY WAY 080941
I WENT TO YOUR WEDDING 100352, 101052, 101752, 102452, 103152, 110752, 111452, 112152, 112852, 120552, 121252, 121952
I WILL 121165, 121865
I WILL ALWAYS LOVE YOU (FROM "THE BODYGUARD") 112892, 120592, 121292, 121992, 122692, 010293, 010993, 011693, 012393, 013093, 020693, 021393, 022093, 022793, 030693, 031393
I WILL FOLLOW HIM 041363, 042063, 042763, 050463, 051163, 051863, 052563, 060163
I WILL SURVIVE 020379, 021079, 021779, 022479, 030379, 031079, 031779, 032479, 033179, 040779, 041479, 042179, 042879
I WISH 122576, 010877, 011577, 012277, 012977, 020577, 021277
I WISH I DIDN'T LOVE YOU SO 091347, 092047, 092747, 100447, 101147, 101847, 102547, 110147, 110847, 111547, 112247, 112947, 120647, 121347
I WISH I KNEW 062345, 072845, 080445, 081845, 082545, 090145, 090845, 091545, 092245, 092945, 100645
I WISH I WERE ALADDIN 100535, 110235
I WISH IT WOULD RAIN 021068, 021768, 022468, 030268, 030968, 031668
I WISH IT WOULD RAIN DOWN 031790, 032490, 033190, 040790
I WISHED ON THE MOON 090735, 092135, 092835, 100535, 101235, 101935, 102635
I WONDER, I WONDER, I WONDER 060747, 061447, 062147, 062847, 070547, 071247, 071947, 072647, 080247, 080947, 081647, 082347, 083047, 090647
I WONDER WHAT SHE'S DOING TONIGHT 020368, 021768, 022468, 030268, 030968
I WONDER WHO'S KISSING HER NOW 080947, 081647, 082347, 083047, 090647, 091347, 092047, 092747, 100447, 101147, 101847, 102547, 110147
I WONDER WHY 112391

634

I'M STEPPIN' OUT WITH A MEMORY TONIGHT 070640, 072040

I'M STILL IN LOVE WITH YOU 081272, 081972, 081972, 082672, 090272, 090972, 091672

I'M STONE IN LOVE WITH YOU 120972, 121672

I'M TELLING YOU NOW 040365, 041065, 041765, 042465, 050165, 050865

I'M TOO SEXY 012592, 020192, 020892, 021592, 022292, 022992, 030792, 031492, 032192, 032892, 040492, 041192

I'M WALKIN' 040657, 042057, 042757, 051157, 051857, 052557

I'M WALKING BEHIND YOU 061353, 062053, 062753, 070453, 071153, 071853, 072553, 080153, 080853, 081553, 082253, 082953, 090553, 091953, 092653, 100353, 103153

I'M YOUR BABY TONIGHT 111790, 112490, 120190, 120890, 121590, 122290, 010591

I'M YOUR BOOGIE MAN 051477, 052177, 052877, 060477, 061177, 061877

I'M YOUR MAN 012586, 020186, 020886, 021586

I'M YOUR PUPPET 111266, 111966, 112666

I'M YOURS 052952, 060552, 061252, 061952, 062652, 070352, 071052, 071752, 072452, 073152, 080752, 081452, 082152, 091252, 091952, 081452

IMAGE OF A GIRL 072960, 080560, 081960

IMAGINARY LOVER 051378, 052078, 052778, 060378

IMAGINATION 051840, 052540, 060140, 060840, 061540, 062240, 062940, 070640, 071340, 072040, 072740, 080340, 081040

IMAGINE 103071, 110671, 111371, 112071, 112771, 120471

IMPULSIVE 120190, 120890, 121590, 122290, 010591, 011291

IN A LITTLE GYPSY TEA ROOM 051835, 060135, 060835, 061535, 062235, 062935, 070635, 071335, 072035, 072735, 080335, 081035, 081735, 082435, 083135, 090735

IN AN EIGHTEENTH CENTURY DRAWING ROOM 101439

IN AN OLD DUTCH GARDEN 021040, 021740, 022440, 030240, 030940, 031640, 032340, 033040, 040640, 041340, 042040

IN AND OUT OF LOVE 120967, 121667

THE "IN" CROWD 091165, 091865, 092565, 100265, 100965, 101665

IN DREAMS 033063, 040563, 041363

IN LOVE IN VAIN 051846, 061546, 062246, 070646, 071346, 072046, 072746, 081046, 081746, 082446

IN MY ARMS 071743, 073143, 080743, 082143, 082843, 090443, 091143, 091843, 100243, 100943

IN MY HOUSE 060185, 060885, 061585, 062285

IN THE BLUE OF EVENING 051543, 052943, 060543, 061243, 061943, 062643, 070343, 071043, 071743, 072443, 073143, 080743, 081443, 082143, 082843, 090443, 091143, 091843, 092543

IN THE CHAPEL IN THE MOONLIGHT 111436, 112136, 112836, 120536, 121236, 121936, 122636, 010237, 010937, 011637, 012337, 013037, 020637, 022037, 090454, 091154, 091854

IN THE CLOSET 052392, 053092, 060692, 061392

IN THE COOL, COOL, COOL OF THE EVENING 092751, 101151, 110151

IN THE GHETTO 053169, 060769, 061469, 062169, 062869

IN THE MIDDLE OF A DREAM 072239, 072939, 081239

IN THE MIDDLE OF A KISS 052535, 060135, 060835, 061535, 062235, 062935, 070635, 071335, 072035, 072735, 080335, 081035, 081735

IN THE MIDDLE OF AN ISLAND 090757, 091457, 092157, 092857, 100557, 101957

IN THE MOOD 020340, 112859, 120559, 121259, 121959

IN THE NAVY 042879, 050579, 051279, 051979, 052679, 060279

IN THE RAIN 040872, 041572, 042272, 042972

IN THE STILL OF THE NIGHT 012238

IN THE STILL OF THE NITE (FROM "THE JACKSONS") 121292, 121992, 122692, 010293, 010993, 011693, 012393, 013093, 020693, 021393, 022093

IN THE SUMMERTIME 081570, 082270, 082970, 090570, 091270, 091970

IN THE YEAR 2525 070569, 071269, 071969, 072669, 080269, 080969, 081669, 082369, 083069

IN TOO DEEP 060687, 061387, 062087, 062787, 070487

IN YOUR ROOM 122488, 010789, 011489

INCENSE AND PEPPERMINT 102867, 110467, 111167, 111867, 112567, 120267, 120967, 121667, 122367

INDIAN GIVER 022269, 030869, 031569, 032269, 032969

INDIAN LAKE 071368, 072068, 072768

INDIAN RESERVATION 061971, 062671, 070371, 071071, 071771, 072471, 073171, 080771, 081471

INDIAN SUMMER 122339, 011340, 012040, 012740, 020340, 021040, 021740, 022440, 050143, 030940, 031640, 032340, 033040, 040640

INDIANA WANTS ME 102470, 103170, 110770, 111470, 112170, 112970

INFATUATION 072184, 072884, 080484, 081184

INFORMER 022793, 030693, 031393, 032093, 032793, 040393, 041093, 041793, 042493, 050193, 050893, 051593, 052293

INNER CITY BLUES 110671, 111371

AN INNOCENT MAN 022584

INSTANT KARMA 032170, 032870, 040470, 041170, 041870, 042570, 050270, 050970

INTERMEZZO 051041, 051741, 052441, 053141, 060741, 061441, 062141, 062841, 070541, 071241, 071941, 072641, 080241, 080941, 081641, 082341, 083041, 090641, 091341, 100441

INVINCIBLE 091485

INVISIBLE TOUCH 062886, 070586, 071986, 072686, 080286

IS IT LOVE 053186

IS IT TRUE WHAT THEY SAY ABOUT DIXIE 050936, 051636, 052336, 053036, 060636, 061336, 062036, 062736, 070436, 071136, 071836, 072536, 080136, 080836

IS THERE SOMETHING I SHOULD KNOW 071683, 072383, 073083, 080683, 081383, 082083

IS THIS LOVE 011087, 011787, 012487, 120587, 121287, 121987, 122687, 010988, 011688

IS YOU IS OR IS YOU AIN'T 081244, 081944, 090244, 090944, 091644, 092344, 093044, 100744, 101444, 102144, 102844, 110444

LA ISLA BONITA 042587, 050287, 050987, 051687, 052387

ISLAND GIRL 102575, 110175, 110875, 111575, 112975, 120675

ISLANDS IN THE STREAM 100183, 100883, 101583, 102283, 102983, 110583, 111283, 111983, 112683, 120383, 121083, 121783

ISLE OF CAPRI 042035, 042735, 050435

ISN'T THIS A LOVELY DAY 092135, 092835, 100535, 101235, 101935, 102635, 110235, 110935, 111635

THE ISRAELITES 062869

IT AIN'T ME BABE 091165, 091865, 092565

IT AIN'T OVER 'TIL IT'S OVER 072791, 080391, 081091, 081791, 082491, 083191

IT ALL COMES BACK TO ME NOW 011841, 012541, 020841, 021541, 022241, 030141, 030841, 031541, 032241, 032941, 040541, 041241, 041941, 042641, 050341

IT CAN'T BE WRONG 032043, 041043, 041743, 042443, 050143, 050843, 051543, 052243, 052943, 060543, 061243, 061943, 062643, 070343, 071043, 071743, 072443, 073143, 080743, 081443

IT COULD HAPPEN TO YOU 072944, 080544, 081944, 082644, 090244, 090944, 091644, 092344, 093044, 101444, 102144

IT DON'T COME EASY 052271, 052971, 060571, 061271, 061971, 062671, 070371

IT DON'T MATTER TO ME 111470

IT HAD TO BE YOU 082644, 090244, 090944, 091644, 092344, 093044, 100744, 101444, 102144, 102844, 110444, 111144

IT HURTS TO BE IN LOVE 092664, 100364, 101064, 101764

IT ISN'T FAIR 040150, 040850, 041550, 042250, 042950, 050650, 051350, 052050, 052750, 060350, 061050, 061750

IT KEEPS RIGHT ON A-HURTIN' 060862, 061562, 062262, 062962, 070662, 071362

IT LOOKS LIKE RAIN IN CHERRY BLOSSOM LANE 061237, 061937, 062637, 070337, 071037, 071737, 072437, 073137, 080737, 081437, 082137, 082837, 090437

IT MIGHT AS WELL BE SPRING 112445, 120145, 120845, 121545, 122245, 122945, 010546, 011246, 011946, 012646, 020246, 020946, 021646, 022346

IT MUST BE HIM 102167, 102867, 110467, 111167, 111867, 112567

IT MUST HAVE BEEN LOVE (FROM "PRETTY WOMAN") 051990, 052690, 060290, 060990, 061690, 062390, 063090, 070790, 071490

IT NEVER DAWNED ON ME 110235

IT NEVER RAINS IN SOUTHERN CALIFORNIA 120272, 120972, 121672, 122372, 123072, 010673

IT ONLY HAPPENS WHEN I DANCE WITH YOU 091148

IT ONLY TAKES A MINUTE 102575

IT WOULD TAKE A STRONG STRONG MAN 091788

IT'S A BLUE WORLD 021740, 022440, 030240, 031640, 032340, 033040, 040640, 041340, 042740

IT'S A GOOD DAY 032947, 040547, 041247, 041947, 042647

IT'S A GREAT FEELING 082749, 090349

IT'S A HEARTACHE 061078, 061778, 070178, 070878, 071578

IT'S A HUNDRED TO ONE YOU'RE IN LOVE 102139

IT'S A MAN'S MAN'S MAN'S WORLD 052866, 060466, 061166

IT'S A MARSHMELLOW WORLD 122350, 010651, 012051

IT'S A MISTAKE 081383, 082083, 082783, 090383

IT'S A SIN 110787, 111487

IT'S A SIN TO TELL A LIE 051636, 053036, 060636, 061336, 062036, 062736, 070436, 071136, 071836, 072536, 080136, 080836, 081536, 082236, 082936, 090536

IT'S A WONDERFUL WORLD 060840

IT'S ALL IN THE GAME 091258, 091958,

092658, 100358, 101058, 101758, 102458, 103158, 110758, 111458, 112158, 112858, 120558, 121258

IT'S ALL RIGHT 110263, 110963, 111663, 112363, 113063

IT'S ALMOST TOMORROW 010756, 011456, 012856, 021856

IT'S ALWAYS YOU 051543, 061243, 061943, 062643, 070343, 072443, 080743, 081443, 082143

IT'S AN OLD SOUTHERN CUSTOM 042035, 042735, 050435

IT'S BEEN A LONG, LONG TIME 110345, 111045, 111745, 112445, 120145, 120845, 121545, 122245, 122945, 010546, 011246, 011946, 012646, 020246

IT'S BEEN SO LONG 021536, 022236, 030736, 031436, 032136, 032836, 040436, 041136, 041836, 042536, 050236, 050936

IT'S DANGEROUS TO LOVE LIKE THIS 122135

IT'S DE-LOVELY 112836, 120536, 121236, 121936, 122636, 010237, 010937, 011637, 012337, 013037

IT'S EASY TO REMEMBER 042035, 042735, 050435, 051135, 051835

IT'S ECSTASY WHEN YOU LAY DOWN NEXT TO ME 102977, 110577, 111277, 111977, 112677

IT'S GONNA TAKE A MIRACLE 061282, 061982

IT'S IMPOSSIBLE 012371

IT'S JUST A MATTER OF TIME 032159, 032859, 040459, 041159, 041859, 042559

(IT'S JUST) THE WAY THAT YOU LOVE ME 110489, 111189, 111889, 112589, 120989

IT'S LATE 041159, 042559

IT'S LOVE, LOVE, LOVE 031144, 040144, 040844, 041544, 042244, 042944, 050644, 051344, 052044, 052744, 060344, 061044, 061744

IT'S MAGIC 072448, 073148, 080748, 081448, 082148, 082848, 090448, 091148, 091848, 092548, 100248, 100948, 101648, 102348, 103048, 110648

IT'S MY PARTY 052563, 060163, 060863, 061563, 062263, 062963, 070663, 071363

IT'S MY TURN 012481, 013181, 020781

IT'S NEVER TOO LATE 042239

IT'S NO CRIME 100789, 101489, 102189, 102889

IT'S NOT FOR ME TO SAY 072057, 081757, 082457, 083157

IT'S NOT OVER ('TIL IT'S OVER) 082987

IT'S NOT UNUSUAL 052965, 060565

IT'S NOW OR NEVER 080560, 081260, 081960, 082660, 090260, 090960, 091660, 092360, 093060, 100760, 101460, 102160, 102860

IT'S ONLY A PAPER MOON 120845

IT'S ONLY MAKE BELIEVE 102458, 103158, 110758, 111458, 112158, 112858, 120558, 121258, 121958, 122658, 010359, 103170

IT'S OVER 051664, 052364

IT'S SO EASY 112677, 120377, 121077, 121777, 122477

IT'S SO HARD TO SAY GOODBYE TO YESTERDAY 110991, 111691, 112391, 113091, 120791, 121491, 122191, 010492, 011192, 011892

IT'S STILL ROCK AND ROLL TO ME 061480, 062180, 062880, 070580, 071280, 072080, 072680, 080280, 080980, 081680, 082380

IT'S THE SAME OLD SONG 081465, 082165, 082665, 090465

IT'S TIME TO CRY 122659, 010160, 010860, 011560, 012260

IT'S TOO LATE 060571, 061271, 061971, 062671, 070371, 071071, 071771, 072471, 073171, 080771

IT'S TOO SOON TO KNOW 032258

IT'S UP TO YOU 020263

KISSES ON THE WIND   093089
KISSES SWEETER THAN WINE   121457,
    122857, 010458, 011158, 011858
KISSING A FOOL   111288, 111988,
    112688, 120388
KNOCK, KNOCK, WHO'S THERE?
    082236, 082936, 090536, 091236,
    091936
KNOCK ON WOOD   033179, 040779,
    041479, 042179, 042879, 050579
KNOCK THREE TIMES   121970,
    122670, 010271, 010971, 011671,
    012371, 013071, 020671, 021371,
    022071, 022771
KNOCKIN' BOOTS   111090, 112490
KNOCKIN' DA BOOTS   051593, 052293,
    052993, 060593, 061293, 061993,
    062693, 070393, 071093, 071793,
    072493, 073193
KO KO MO   022655, 030555, 031255,
    031955, 032655, 040255, 040955
KODACHROME   061673, 062373,
    063073, 070773, 071473, 072173,
    072873
KOKOMO (FROM THE "COCKTAIL"
    SOUNDTRACK)   102288, 102988,
    110588, 111288, 111988
DER KOMMISSAR   041683, 042383,
    043083, 050783, 051483
KOOKIE, KOOKIE (LEND ME YOUR
    COMB)   051659, 052359, 053059,
    060659, 061359, 062059
KUNG FU FIGHTING   112374, 113074,
    120774, 121474, 122174, 122874,
    010475, 011175
KYRIE   020886, 021586, 022286,
    030186, 030886, 031586, 032286

L

LA LA LA (IF I HAD YOU)   010370,
    011070
LA LA MEANS I LOVE YOU   030968,
    031668, 032368, 033068, 040668
LADIES NIGHT   010580, 011280,
    011980, 122279
LADY   030175, 030875, 031575,
    040779, 041479, 102580, 110180,
    110880, 111580, 112280, 112980,
    120680, 121380, 122080, 122780,
    011081, 011781
THE LADY FROM 29 PALMS   100447,
    101847, 102547, 110147, 110847
LADY GODIVA   112666, 120366, 121066
LADY IN RED   051835, 060835, 061535,
    062235, 062935, 070635, 071335,
    072035, 072735, 080335, 081035
THE LADY IN RED   050987, 051687,
    052387, 053087, 060687, 061387
LADY MADONNA   033068, 040668,
    041368, 042068, 042768, 050468,
    051168
LADY MARMALADE   030175, 030875,
    031575, 032275, 032975, 040575,
    041275
LADY OF SPAIN   111452, 112152,
    112852, 120552, 011053, 011753,
    012453, 013153, 020753
LADY WILLPOWER   070668, 071368,
    072068, 072768, 080368, 081068
LADY YOU BRING ME UP   082281,
    082981, 090581, 091281, 091981,
    092681
THE LADY'S IN LOVE WITH YOU
    052039, 060339, 061039, 061739,
    062439, 070139, 070839, 072239,
    072939
LAMBETH WALK   100838, 101538,
    102938, 110538, 111238, 112638,
    120338, 121038
THE LAMP IS LOW   080539, 081239,
    082639, 090239, 090939, 091639,
    092339, 093039
LAND OF 1,000 DANCES   090366,
    091066, 091766
LAND OF CONFUSION   011787,
    012487, 013187, 020787
LAROO, LAROO, LILLI BOLERO   050148,
    050848, 051548, 052248, 052948,
    060548

LAST DANCE   071578, 072278, 072978,
    080578, 081278, 081978, 082678
LAST DATE   111860, 112560, 120260,
    120960, 121660, 122360, 123060,
    010561, 011361, 012061, 012761,
    020361
LAST KISS   101064, 101764, 102464,
    103164, 110764, 111464, 112164,
    112864
LAST NIGHT   102839, 111839, 112539,
    120239, 121639, 122339, 080461,
    081161, 081861, 082561, 090161
LAST NIGHT I DIDN'T GET TO SLEEP AT
    ALL   061172, 061772, 062472
LAST SONG   022473, 030373, 031073,
    031773, 032473, 033173
THE LAST TIME   050165, 050865
LAST TRAIN TO CLARKSVILLE   100866,
    101566, 102266, 102966, 110566,
    111266, 111966, 112666
LATE IN THE EVENING   090680, 091380,
    092080, 092780, 100480, 101180,
    101880
LATELY   073193, 080793, 081493,
    082193, 082893, 090493, 091193,
    091893, 092593
LAUGH AT ME   092565, 100265
LAUGHING   082369
LAUGHING ON THE OUTSIDE   050446,
    051146, 051846, 052546, 060146,
    060846, 061546, 062246, 062946,
    070646, 071346, 072046
LAUGHTER IN THE RAIN   122874,
    010475, 011175, 011875, 012675,
    020175, 020875
LAURA   042145, 042845, 050545,
    051245, 051945, 052645, 060245,
    060945, 061645, 062345, 063045,
    070745, 071445, 072145
LAVENDER BLUE   122548, 010149,
    010849, 011549, 012249, 012949,
    020549, 021249, 021949, 022649,
    030549, 031249, 031949, 032649,
    081559, 082259, 082959, 090559,
    091259, 091959
LAY DOWN (CANDLES IN THE RAIN)
    062070, 062770, 070470, 071170,
    071870, 072570
LAY DOWN SALLY   022578, 030478,
    031178, 031878, 032578, 040178,
    040878, 041578, 042278, 042978,
    050678
LAY LADY LAY   083069, 090669, 091369
LAY YOUR HANDS ON ME   110985,
    111685, 112385, 113085, 072289,
    072989, 080589, 081289
LAYLA   080572
LEAD ME ON   082579, 090179, 090879,
    091579, 092279
LEADER OF THE BAND   030682,
    031382
LEADER OF THE PACK   110764,
    111464, 112164, 112864, 120564
LEAN ON ME   061772, 062472, 070172,
    070872, 071572, 072272, 072972,
    031487, 032187, 032887, 040487,
    041187, 041887
LEANIN' ON THE OLD TOP RAIL
    030940, 031640, 033040
LEANING ON THE LAMP POST   043066,
    050766
LEARNIN' THE BLUES   061155, 062555,
    070255, 070955, 071655, 072355,
    073055, 080655, 081355, 082055,
    090355, 091055
LEATHER AND LACE   121981, 122681,
    010982, 011682, 012382, 013082,
    020682
LEAVE ME ALONE   120873, 121673,
    122273, 122973, 010574
LEAVING ON A JET PLANE   112969,
    120669, 121369, 122069, 122769,
    010370, 011070, 011770, 012470,
    013170
LEFT RIGHT OUT OF YOUR HEART
    080158
LEGS   070784, 071484, 072184, 072884
LET EM IN   073176, 080776, 081476,
    082176, 082876, 090476, 091176
LET HER IN   072476

LET IT BE   032170, 032870, 040470,
    041170, 041870, 042570, 050270,
    050970, 051670, 052370, 053070
LET IT BE ME   022660, 030460, 031160,
    031860, 101764, 102464, 103164,
    110764, 111464
LET IT SNOW   010546, 011246, 011946,
    012646, 020246, 020946, 021646,
    022346, 030246, 030946, 031646,
    032346, 033046
LET IT WHIP   061982, 062682, 070382,
    071082, 071782, 072482
LET ME BE THE ONE   102487, 103187,
    110787
LET ME BE THERE   011274, 011974,
    012674, 020274, 020974, 021674,
    022374
LET ME GO, LOVER   121154, 121854,
    122554, 010155, 010855, 011555,
    012255, 012955, 020555, 021255,
    021955
LET ME IN   030962, 031662, 032362,
    040662
LET ME LOVE YOU TONIGHT   100744,
    102844, 120944, 071280, 071980
LET ME OPEN THE DOOR   082380,
    083080
LET ME WHISPER   061138, 061838
LET MY LOVE OPEN THE DOOR
    081680
LET THE LITTLE GIRL DANCE   051360,
    052060
LET THE MUSIC PLAY   021884, 022584,
    030384
LET THERE BE DRUMS   120861,
    122261, 122961
LET THERE BE LOVE   041340, 042040,
    042740, 050440, 051140, 051840
LET YOUR LOVE FLOW   032776,
    040376, 041076, 041776, 042476,
    050176, 050876
LET YOURSELF GO   030736, 031436,
    032136, 032836, 040436, 041136,
    041836, 042536, 050236, 050936,
    052336
LET'S CALL THE WHOLE THING OFF
    052237, 060537
LET'S DANCE   092262, 092962, 100662,
    101362, 042383, 043083, 050783,
    051483, 052183, 052883, 060483,
    061183, 061883, 062583
LET'S DO IT AGAIN   111575, 112975,
    120675, 121375, 122075, 122775,
    010376
LET'S DREAM THIS ONE OUT   030841
LET'S FACE THE MUSIC AND DANCE
    031436, 032836, 040436, 041136,
    041836, 042536, 050236, 050936
LET'S GET IT ON   081173, 081873,
    082573, 090173, 090873, 091573,
    092273, 092973, 100673, 101373,
    102073, 102773, 110373
LET'S GET LOST   041743, 050143,
    052243, 052943, 060543, 061243,
    061943, 062643, 070343, 071043,
    071743, 072443, 073143, 080743
LET'S GET SERIOUS   070580, 071280,
    071980
LET'S GET TOGETHER   100661,
    102761, 110361, 111061
LET'S GO!   040487, 041187
LET'S GO ALL THE WAY   032986,
    040586, 041286, 041986
LET'S GO CRAZY   090184, 090884,
    091584, 092284, 092984, 100684,
    102084, 102784
LET'S GO, LET'S GO, LET'S GO
    111860, 112560
LET'S GROOVE   120581, 121281,
    121981, 122681, 010982, 011682,
    012382, 013082
LET'S HANG ON   111365, 112065,
    112765, 120465, 121165, 121865,
    122565, 010166
LET'S HEAR IT FOR THE BOYS   050584,
    051284, 051984, 052684, 060284,
    060984, 061684, 062384, 063084
LET'S LIVE FOR TODAY   062467,
    070167, 070867
LET'S SAIL TO DREAMLAND   031938

LET'S SING AGAIN   070436, 071836,
    072536, 080136
LET'S STAY TOGETHER   010872,
    011572, 012272, 012972, 020572,
    021272, 021972, 022672, 030472
LET'S SWING IT   062235, 070635,
    071335, 072035, 072735, 080335,
    082435
LET'S TAKE AN OLD FASHIONED WALK
    073049, 082049, 082749, 090349,
    091049, 091749, 100149, 100849,
    102249
LET'S TAKE THE LONG WAY HOME
    030745
LET'S THINK ABOUT LIVIN'   110460
LET'S TWIST AGAIN   081861
LET'S WAIT AWHILE   030787, 031487,
    032187, 032887, 040487
THE LETTER   090967, 091667, 092367,
    093067, 100767, 101467, 102167,
    102867, 053070, 060670, 061370,
    062070
LIAR   082171, 082871, 090471
LIECHTENSTEINER POLKA   011858
LIFE CAN BE BEAUTIFUL   020147
LIFE IN A NORTHERN TOWN   022286,
    030186, 030886
LIFE IS A HIGHWAY   072592, 080192,
    080892, 081592, 082992
LIFE IS A ROCK (BUT THE RADIO
    ROLLED ME)   110974, 111674
LIFE IS A SONG   050435, 051135,
    051835, 052535, 060135, 060835,
    061535, 062235, 062935, 070635,
    071335
LIGHT MY FIRE   071567, 072267,
    072967, 080567, 081267, 081967,
    082667, 090267, 090967, 091768,
    082468, 083168, 090768, 091468,
    092168
LIGHTNIN' STRIKES   020566, 021266,
    021966, 022666, 030566
LIGHTS OUT   010436, 011136, 012536,
    020136, 020836, 021536, 022236,
    022936, 030736, 031436, 032136,
    032836, 040436, 041136, 041836,
    042536
LIKE A PRAYER   040889, 041589,
    042289, 042989, 050689, 051389,
    052089
LIKE A ROLLING STONE   082865,
    090465, 091165, 091865, 092565
LIKE A VIRGIN   121584, 122284,
    010585, 011285, 011985, 012685,
    020285, 020985, 020285
LIL' RED RIDING HOOD   071666,
    072366, 073066, 080666, 081166,
    082066, 082766
LILACS IN THE RAIN   110439, 111139,
    111839, 112539, 120339, 120939,
    121639, 122339, 123039, 010640,
    011340
LIMBO ROCK   110362, 111762, 112462,
    120162, 120862, 121562, 122262,
    122962, 010563, 011263, 011963,
    012663
LINDA   032247, 032947, 040547,
    041247, 041947, 042647, 050347,
    051047, 051747, 052447, 053147,
    060747, 061447, 062147, 062847,
    070547, 071247, 071947
LINGER   021294
LINGER IN MY ARMS A LITTLE LONGER
    092846, 100546, 110246
LION SLEEPS TONIGHT   021972,
    022672, 030472, 031172, 031872,
    032572, 040172, 040872
THE LION SLEEPS TONIGHT   120861,
    122261, 122961, 010562, 011262,
    011962, 012662, 020262, 020962
LIPSTICK ON YOUR COLLAR   062759,
    070459, 071159, 071859, 072559,
    080159, 080859
LISBON ANTIGUA   012156, 012856,
    020456, 021156, 021856, 022556,
    030356, 031056, 031756, 032456,
    033156, 040756, 041456, 042156,
    042856, 050556
LISTEN PEOPLE   030566, 031966,
    032666

042184, 042884, 050584, 051284, 051984

LOVE SONG 093089, 100789, 101489, 102189, 012090

LOVE STORY (WHERE DO I BEGIN) 040371

LOVE TAKES TIME 102990, 110390, 111090, 111790, 112490, 120190, 120890

LOVE THEME FROM "A STAR IS BORN" 011577, 012977, 020577, 021277, 021977, 022677, 030577, 031277, 031977, 032677, 040277, 040977, 041677, 042377

LOVE THEME FROM "ROMEO AND JULIET" 060769, 061469, 062169, 062869, 070569, 071269, 071969, 072669

LOVE...THY WILL BE DONE 101991

LOVE TO LOVE YOU BABY 011076, 011776, 012476, 013176, 020776, 021476, 022176

LOVE TOUCH (THEME FROM "LEGAL EAGLES") 071986, 072686, 080286, 080986

LOVE TRAIN 022473, 030373, 031073, 031773, 032473, 033173

LOVE WALKED IN 040238, 040938, 041638, 042338, 043038, 050738, 051438, 052138, 052838, 060438, 061138, 061838, 062538, 070238

LOVE WILL CONQUER ALL 112286, 112986, 120686

LOVE WILL FIND A WAY 072978, 080578, 081278, 081978, 082678

LOVE WILL KEEP US TOGETHER 061475, 062175, 062875, 070575, 071275, 071975

LOVE WILL LEAD YOU BACK 031090, 031790, 032490, 033190, 040790, 041490

LOVE WILL NEVER DO (WITHOUT YOU) 010591, 011291, 011991, 012691, 020291, 020991, 021691

LOVE WILL SAVE THE DAY 082788

LOVE WON'T LET ME WAIT 060775, 061475, 062175, 062875, 070575

LOVE YOU DOWN 022187

LOVE YOU INSIDE OUT 051979, 052679, 060279, 060979, 061679

LOVE YOU SAVE 061370, 062070, 062770, 070470, 071170, 071870, 072570, 080170, 080870

LOVE YOU SO 052760, 061060, 061760

LOVE ZONE 092786

THE LOVELIEST NIGHT OF THE YEAR 060951, 061651, 062351, 063051, 070751, 071451, 072151, 072851, 080451, 081151, 081851, 082551, 090151, 090851, 091551, 092051, 092751, 100451, 101151, 101851, 102551, 110151, 110851

LOVELIGHT IN THE STARLIGHT 060438, 061138, 061838, 062538, 070238, 071638, 072338

LOVELY LADY 032136, 032836

LOVELY TO LOOK AT 042035, 042735, 050435, 051135, 051835, 052535, 060135, 060835, 061535

A LOVELY WAY TO SPEND AN EVENING 021944, 022644, 031844, 032544, 040144

LOVER BOY 012685, 020285, 020985, 021685, 022385, 030285

LOVER GIRL 031685, 032385, 033085, 040685, 041385

THE LOVER IN ME 021189, 021889, 022589, 030489, 031189

LOVER PLEASE 040662, 042062, 042762, 050462

LOVER'S CONCERTO 101665, 102365, 103065, 110665, 111365, 112065

LOVER'S GOLD 080649

LOVER'S LULLABY 051140, 051840

A LOVER'S QUESTION 011059, 012459, 013159, 020759

LOVERS WHO WANDER 060162, 060862, 061562

LOVE'S BEEN A LITTLE BIT HARD ON ME 062682, 070382, 071082, 071782

LOVES ME LIKE A ROCK 090173, 090873, 091573, 101373

LOVE'S THEME 011974, 012674, 020274, 020974, 021674, 022374, 030274

LOVIN' EVERY MINUTE OF IT 112185

LOVIN' YOU 030875, 031575, 032275, 032975, 040575, 041275, 041975, 042675

LOW RIDER 111575, 112975, 120675

LOWDOWN 090476, 091176, 091876, 092576, 100276, 100976, 101676, 102376

LUCILLE 052177, 052877, 060477, 061177, 061877, 062577

LUCKY STAR 100684, 102084, 102784, 110384

LUCY IN THE SKY WITH DIAMONDS 121474, 122174, 122874, 010475, 011175, 011875

LUKA 080187, 080887, 081587, 082287, 082987

LULLABYE OF BROADWAY 042035, 042735, 050435, 051135, 051835

M

MA BELLE AMIE 022870, 030770, 031470

MACARTHUR PARK 060868, 061568, 062268, 062968, 070668, 102178, 102878, 110478, 111178, 111878, 112578, 120278, 120978, 121678

MACK THE KNIFE 091959, 092659, 100359, 101059, 101759, 102459, 103159, 110759, 111459, 112159, 112859, 120559, 121259, 121959, 122659, 010160, 010860, 011560

MAD ABOUT THE BOY 081735

MAD ABOUT YOU 072686, 080286, 080986, 081686, 082386, 083086

MADELEINE 112941, 122041, 011042, 011742

MAGGIE MAY 091171, 091871, 092571, 100271, 100971, 101671, 102371, 103071, 110671, 111371, 112071

MAGIC 062875, 070575, 071275, 071975, 071280, 071980, 072680, 080280, 080980, 081680, 082380, 083080, 090680

MAGIC CARPET RIDE 110968, 111668, 112368, 113068, 120768, 121468, 122168

MAGIC MAN 103076, 110676

MAGNET AND STEEL 081278, 081978, 082678, 090278

MAIN EVENT 072879, 080479, 081179, 082579, 090179, 090879

MAIRZY DOATS 020544, 021244, 021944, 022644, 030444, 031144, 031844, 032544, 040144, 040844, 041544

MAKE A MOVE ON ME 032082, 032782, 040382, 041082, 041782

MAKE BELIEVE ISLAND 052540, 061540, 062240, 062940, 070640, 071340, 072040, 072740, 080340, 081040, 081740, 082440

MAKE IT HAPPEN 032892, 040492, 041192, 041892, 042592, 050292, 050992

MAKE IT REAL 060488, 061188, 061888, 062588, 070288

MAKE IT WITH YOU 071870, 072570, 080170, 080870, 081570, 082270, 082970, 090570, 091270, 091970

MAKE LOVE TO ME 030654, 031354, 032054, 032754, 040354, 041054, 041754, 042454, 050154, 050854, 051554, 052254, 052954, 061954

MAKE ME LOSE CONTROL 071688, 072388, 073088, 080688, 081388, 082088

MAKE ME SMILE 060670, 061370

MAKE THE WORLD GO AWAY 121865, 122565, 010166

MAKE YOURSELF COMFORTABLE 011555, 020555

MAKIN' IT 070779, 071479, 072179, 072879, 080479, 081179

MAKING LOVE OUT OF NOTHING AT ALL 091783, 092483, 100183, 100883, 101583, 102283, 102983, 110583, 111283

MAMA 040160, 040860, 041560, 042260

MAMA CAN'T BUY YOU LOVE 081179, 082579, 090179

MAMA SAID 052661, 060261, 060961

MAMA, THAT MOON IS HERE AGAIN 020538

MAMA TOLD ME (NOT TO COME) 062070, 062770, 070470, 071170, 071870, 072570, 080170, 080870, 081570

MAMA'S PEARL 021371, 022071, 022771, 030671, 031371

M'AMSELLE 042647, 050347, 051047, 051747, 052447, 053147, 060747, 061447, 062147, 062847, 070547, 071247, 071947, 072647

A MAN AND HIS DREAM 092339, 100739, 101439

MAN IN MOTION 081785, 082485, 083185, 090785

THE MAN IN THE MIRROR 030588, 031288, 031988, 032688, 040288, 040988, 041688

(MAN WHO SHOT) LIBERTY VALANCE 060862, 061562, 062262, 062962

MAN WITH THE MANDOLIN 082639, 091639, 092339, 093039, 100739, 101439, 102139, 102839, 110439, 111139

MANAGUA, NICARAGUA 021547, 030147, 030847, 032247, 032947, 040547, 041247, 041947, 042647, 050347

MANANA 030648, 031348, 032048, 032748, 040348, 041048, 041748, 042448, 050148, 050848

MANDOLIN RAIN 030787, 031487, 032187, 032887, 040487

MANDY 010475, 011175, 011875, 012675, 020175

MANEATER 112082, 112782, 120482, 121182, 121882, 122582, 010883, 011583, 012283, 012983, 020583, 021283

MANHATTAN SERENADE 100342, 101742, 103142, 110742, 111442, 112142, 112842, 120542, 121242, 121942, 122642

MANIAC 080683, 081383, 082083, 082783, 090383, 091083, 091783, 092483, 100183

MANIC MONDAY 040586, 041286, 041986, 042686, 050286

MANY TEARS AGO 122360, 123060, 010561, 011361

MANY TIMES 101753, 103153, 110753, 111453, 112153, 112853, 120553, 121253, 121953

MARGARITAVILLE 070277, 070977, 071677, 072377, 073077

MARIA ELENA 050341, 051041, 051741, 052441, 053141, 060741, 061441, 062141, 062841, 070541, 071241, 071941, 072641, 080241, 080941, 081641, 082341, 083041, 090641, 091341, 092041, 092741

MARIANNE 021657, 022357, 030257, 030957, 031657, 032357, 033057, 040657, 041357, 042057

MARIE ELENA 110263, 110963, 111663, 112363

(MARIE'S THE NAME) HIS LATEST FLAME 091561, 092261

MASHED POTATOE TIME 040662, 042062, 042762, 050462, 051162, 051862, 052562, 060162, 060862

THE MASQUERADE IS OVER 031839, 032539, 040139, 040839, 041539, 042239, 042939, 051339

MASTER BLASTER (JAMMIN') 110180, 110880, 111580, 112280, 112980, 120680, 121380, 122080

MASTERPIECE 022992, 030792, 031492, 032192, 032892, 040492, 041192, 041892, 042592, 042173,

042873

MATERIAL GIRL 030985, 031685, 032385, 033085, 040685, 041385

A MATTER OF TRUST 101886

MAY I NEVER LOVE AGAIN 011141, 011841, 012541, 020141, 021541, 022241

MAYBE 091440, 092140, 092840, 100540, 101240, 101940, 102640, 110240, 110940, 111640, 112340, 113040, 120740, 073152

MAYBE I'M AMAZED 040277

MAYBE IT'S BECAUSE 073049, 091049, 091749, 092449, 100149, 100849, 101549, 102249, 102949

MAYBE YOU'LL BE THERE 082848, 090448, 092548, 100248, 100948, 102348, 103048, 110648, 111348, 112048, 112748, 120448, 121148, 121848, 122548, 010849

ME AND BOBBY MCGEE 022771, 030671, 031371, 032071, 032771, 040371, 041071, 041771

ME AND MRS. JONES 120972, 121672, 122372, 123072, 010673, 011373, 012073, 012773

ME AND MY MELINDA 041842

ME AND THE MOON 081536, 090536, 091236, 091936, 092636, 100336, 101036, 101736, 102436, 103136, 110736, 111436, 112136

ME AND YOU AND A DOG NAMED BOO 050871, 051571, 052271, 052971, 060571

MEAN WOMAN BLUES 101263, 101963, 102663, 110263, 110963, 111663

MEDLEY; STARS ON 45 052381, 053081, 060681, 061381, 062081, 062781, 070481, 071181

MELANCHOLY MOOD 100739, 101439

MELLOW YELLOW 112666, 120366, 121066, 121766, 122466, 123166, 010767

MELODIE D'AMOUR 110257, 111657, 112357, 120757

A MELODY FROM THE SKY 041136, 041836, 042536, 050236, 050936, 051636, 052336, 053036, 060636, 061336, 062036, 062736, 070436, 071136

MELODY OF LOVE 011555, 012255, 012955, 020555, 021255, 021955, 022655, 030555, 031255, 031955, 032655, 040255, 040955, 041655, 042355, 043055, 050755, 051455, 052155, 052855

MEMORIES ARE MADE OF THIS 122455, 123155, 010756, 011456, 012156, 012856, 020456, 021156, 021856, 022556, 030356, 031056, 032456

MEMPHIS 062963, 070663, 071363, 072063, 072763, 080363, 052764, 070464, 071164, 071864, 072564, 080164

MEN IN MY LITTLE GIRL'S LIFE 011566, 012266, 012966, 020566

MERCEDES BOY 070288, 070988, 071688, 072388

MERCY MERCY 080771, 081471, 082171, 082871

MERCY, MERCY, MERCY 072967, 080567, 081267, 081967

THE MERRY-GO-ROUND BROKE DOWN 062637, 063037, 071037, 071737, 072437, 073137, 080737, 081437, 082137, 082837

MESSAGE TO MICHAEL 051466, 052166

METHOD OF MODERN LOVE 020285, 020985, 021685, 022385

MEXICO 092961, 102061, 102761, 110361

MIAMI VICE THEME 101285, 101985, 102685, 112185, 110985, 111685, 112385

MICHAEL 081161, 081861, 082561, 090161, 090861, 091561, 092261, 092961, 100661

MY LITTLE TOWN 120675, 121375
MY LOVE 012966, 020566, 021266, 021966, 022666, 030566, 051973, 052673, 060273, 060973, 061673, 062373, 063073, 070773, 071473, 052183, 052883, 060483, 061183, 061883
MY LOVIN' (YOU'RE NEVER GONNA GET IT) 041892, 042592, 050292, 050992, 051692, 052392, 053092, 060692, 061392, 062092, 062792, 070492, 071192
MY MARGUERITA 070238
MY MARIA 092973
MY MELODY OF LOVE 110974, 111674, 112374, 113074, 120774
MY, MY, MY 092990
MY ONE AND ONLY HIGHLAND FLING 070949
MY OWN 102938, 110538, 111238, 111938, 112638, 121738
MY PRAYER 102839, 110439, 111139, 111839, 112539, 120239, 120939, 121639, 122339, 123039. 010640, 011340, 012040, 012740, 080456, 081156, 081856, 082556, 090156, 090856, 091556, 092256, 092956, 100656, 102056
MY PREROGATIVE 121088, 121788, 122488, 010789, 011489, 012189
MY REVERIE 102238, 110538, 111238, 111938, 112638, 120338, 121038, 121738, 122438, 123138, 010739, 011439, 012139, 012839
MY SHARONA 080479, 081179, 082579, 090179, 090879, 091579, 092279, 092979, 100679, 101379, 102079
MY SHINING HOUR 012244, 022644
MY SISTER AND I 050341, 051041, 051741, 052441, 053141, 060741, 061441, 062141, 062841, 070541, 071241, 071941, 072641, 080241
MY SPECIAL ANGEL 101268, 101968
MY SWEET LORD/ISN'T IT A PITY 121270, 121970, 122670, 010271, 010971, 011671, 012371, 013071, 020671, 021371
MY TRUE LOVE 081558, 082258, 082958, 090558, 091258, 091958, 090861
MY TRUE STORY 091561, 092261
MY TRULY, TRULY FAIR 062351, 063051, 070751, 071451, 072151, 072851, 080451, 081151, 081851, 082551
MY WHOLE WORLD ENDED (THE MOMENT YOU LEFT ME) 032969, 040569
MY WORLD IS EMPTY WITHOUT YOU 021266, 021966, 022666, 030566
MYSTERIOUS WAYS 012592

N

NA NA HEY HEY KISS HIM GOODBYE 112269, 112969, 120669, 121369, 122069, 122769, 010370, 011070
NADIA'S THEME (THE YOUNG AND THE RESTLESS) 112776, 120476, 121176, 121876
NAME GAME 012365, 013065, 020665, 021365, 022065
NASHVILLE CATS 012167, 012867
NASTY 062886, 070586, 071986, 072686, 080286
NATURAL HIGH 072173
A NATURAL WOMAN 102867, 110467, 111167
NATURE BOY 052248, 052948, 060548, 061248, 061948, 062648, 070348, 071048, 071748, 072448
NAUGHTY GIRLS (NEED LOVE TOO) 050788, 051488, 052188, 052888, 060488, 061188
THE NAUGHTY LADY OF SHADY LANE 121154, 121854, 122554, 010155, 010855, 011555, 012255, 012955, 020555, 021255
NAVY BLUE 022264, 022964, 030764,

031464, 032164
NEAR YOU 100447, 101147, 101847, 102547, 110147, 110847, 111547, 112247, 112947, 120647, 121347, 122047, 122747, 010348, 011048, 092658, 100358, 101058, 101758
THE NEARNESS OF YOU 081740, 082440, 090740, 091440
NEED YOU TONIGHT 122687, 010988, 011688, 012388, 013088, 020688, 021388
NEITHER ONE OF US (WANTS TO BE THE FIRST TO SAY GOODBYE) 031773, 032473, 033173, 040773, 041473, 042173
NEUTRON DANCE 020285, 020985, 021685, 022385, 030285, 030985
NEVER 111685, 112385, 113085, 120785, 121485
NEVER BE ANYONE ELSE BUT YOU 040459, 041159, 041859, 042559, 050259
NEVER BEEN TO SPAIN 012972, 020572, 021272, 021972
NEVER CAN SAY GOODBYE 042471, 050171, 050871, 051571, 052271, 052971, 060571, 011875, 012675
NEVER GONNA GIVE YOU UP 022088, 022788, 030588, 031288, 031988, 032688, 040288
NEVER GONNA LET YOU GO 062583, 070283, 070983, 071683, 072383, 073083, 080683, 081383
NEVER IN A MILLION YEARS 050137, 051537, 052237, 052937, 060537, 061237, 061937, 062637, 070337, 071037
NEVER KNEW LOVE LIKE THIS BEFORE 102580, 110180, 110880, 111580, 112280
NEVER MY LOVE 092367, 093067, 100767, 101467, 102167, 102867, 110467, 111167, 101274, 101974
NEVER, NEVER GONNA GIVE YOU UP 122273, 122973, 010574, 011274
NEVER ON SUNDAY 070761, 071461, 072161, 072861, 080461, 081161, 081861, 082561
NEVER SURRENDER 072785, 080385, 081085, 081785, 082485, 083185
NEVER TEAR US APART 102288, 102988, 110588, 111288
NEVERTHELESS 110450, 111150, 111850, 112550, 120250, 120950, 121650, 122350, 010651, 011351, 012051, 012751
NEW KID IN TOWN 012277, 012977, 020577, 021277, 021977, 022677, 030577
NEW MOON AND OLD SERENADE 052739, 060339, 061739, 062439
NEW MOON ON MONDAY 031784
NEW ORLEANS 111860, 112560, 120260, 120960, 121660
NEW SENSATION 062588, 070288, 070988, 071688, 072388, 073088
NEXT DOOR TO AN ANGEL 110362, 111062, 111762, 112462
THE NEXT TIME I FALL 111586, 112286, 112986, 120686, 121386, 122086
NICE TO BE WITH YOU 060472, 061172, 061772, 062472, 070172
NICE WORK IF YOU CAN GET IT 112737, 120437, 121137, 121837, 122537, 010138, 011538, 012938
NIGHT 042960, 050660, 051360, 052060, 052760, 060360, 061060
NIGHT BEFORE CHRISTMAS 122438, 123138
NIGHT CHICAGO DIED 080374, 081074, 081774, 082474, 083174, 090774
NIGHT FEVER 022578, 030478, 031178, 031878, 032578, 040178, 040878, 041578, 042278, 042978, 050678, 051378, 052078
NIGHT HAS A THOUSAND EYES 011263, 011963, 012663, 020263, 020963, 021663, 022363
THE NIGHT IS YOUNG AND YOU'RE SO

BEAUTIFUL 010237, 010937, 011637, 020637, 021337, 022737
NIGHT MOVES 021977, 022677, 030577, 031277, 031977, 032677
THE NIGHT OWL 101781, 102481, 103181, 110781, 111481, 112181
NIGHT THE LIGHTS WENT OUT IN GEORGIA 033173, 040773, 041473, 042173, 042873, 050573, 051273
NIGHT THEY DROVE OLD DIXIE DOWN 091871, 092571, 100271, 100971, 101671, 102371, 103071, 110671
NIGHTINGALE 022275, 030175
NIGHTS ARE FOREVER WITHOUT YOU 121176, 121876
NIGHTS IN WHITE SATIN 101472, 102172, 102872, 110472, 111172, 111872, 112572
NIGHTS ON BROADWAY 112975, 120675, 121375, 122075
NIGHTSHIFT 033085, 040685, 041385, 042085, 042785, 050485
NIKITA 031586, 032286, 032986, 040586
9 TO 5 013181, 020781, 021481, 022181, 032881, 030781, 031481, 032181, 032881
19TH NERVOUS BREAKDOWN 030566, 031966, 032666, 040266, 040966, 041666
98.6 020467, 021167, 021867
99 LUFTBALLOONS 021884, 022584, 030384, 031084, 031784, 032484
96 TEARS 092466, 100166, 100866, 101566, 102266, 102966, 110566, 111266, 111966
NITE AND DAY 070988, 071688
NITTY GRITTY 010464, 011164, 011864
NO CAN DO 111745
NO LOVE, NO NOTHIN' 010844, 012244, 012944, 020544, 021244, 021944, 022644, 030444, 031144, 031844, 021944
NO MATTER WHAT 120570, 121270, 121970, 122670
NO MATTER WHAT SHAPE (YOUR STOMACH'S IN) 011566, 012266, 012966, 020566, 021266, 021966
NO MORE LIES 030390, 031090, 031790
NO MORE LONELY NIGHTS 120184, 120884, 121584, 122284
NO MORE TEARS (ENOUGH IS ENOUGH) 110379, 111079, 111779, 112479, 120179, 120879, 121579, 122279
NO NO SONG 032275, 032975, 040575, 041275, 041975
NO, NOT MUCH 030356, 031056, 031756, 032456, 033156, 040756, 041456, 042156
NO ONE IS TO BLAME 061486, 062186, 062886, 070586, 070586
NO OTHER LOVE 070453, 071153, 071853, 072553, 080153, 080853, 081553, 082253, 082953, 090553, 091253, 091953, 092653, 100353, 101053, 101753, 102453, 112153
NO OTHER ONE 110935, 111635, 112335, 113035, 120735, 121435, 122135, 122835, 010436, 011136, 011836
NO PARTICULAR PLACE TO GO 071164
NO REGRETS 071836, 080136, 080836, 081536, 082236, 082936, 090536, 091236, 091936, 092636, 100336
NO STRINGS 092135, 092835, 100535
NO TIME 020770, 021470, 022170, 022870
NOBODY BUT ME 020368, 021068, 021768, 022468
NOBODY DOES IT BETTER 100177, 100877, 101577, 102277, 102977, 110577, 111277, 111977
NOBODY TOLD ME 022584, 030384, 031084, 031784
NOBODY'S FOOL (THEME FROM "CADDYSHACK II") 091088, 091788, 092488

NORMAN 012662, 020262, 020962, 022362, 030262
NORTH TO ALASKA 120260, 120960, 121660, 122360, 123060, 010561, 011361, 012061
NOTHIN' BUT A GOOD TIME 070288, 070988, 071688
NOTHING AT ALL 062186
NOTHING COMPARES 2 U 040790, 041490, 042190, 042890, 050590, 051290, 051990, 052690, 060290, 060990
NOTHING FROM NOTHING 090774, 091474, 092174, 092874, 100574, 101274, 101974
NOTHING'S GONNA STOP US NOW 031487, 032187, 032887, 040487, 041187, 041887, 042587, 050287
NOTORIOUS 121386, 122086, 122786, 011087, 011787
NOVEMBER RAIN 080192, 080892, 081592, 082992, 090592, 091292, 091992, 092692, 100392
NOW AND FOREVER 022694, 030594, 031294, 031994, 032694, 040294, 040994, 041694, 042394, 043094, 050794
NOW I LAY ME DOWN TO DREAM 101240, 110940
NOW IS THE HOUR 020748, 021448, 022148, 022848, 030648, 031348, 032048, 032748, 040348, 041048, 041748, 042448, 050148, 050848, 051548, 052248, 052948, 060548, 070348
NOW IT CAN BE TOLD 080638, 081338, 082038, 082738, 090338, 091038, 091738, 092438, 100138
NOWHERE MAN 030566, 031966, 032666, 040266, 040966
NOWHERE TO RUN 040365, 041065, 041765
#9 DREAM 021575, 022275
NUMBER TEN LULLABYE LANE 042641, 051041, 052441, 053141
NUTHIN' BUT A "G" THANG 022793, 030693, 031393, 032093, 032793, 040393, 041093, 041793, 042493, 050193, 050893, 051593, 052293, 052993

O

O.P.P. 102691, 110291, 110991, 111691, 113091, 120791
OBSESSION 041385, 042085, 042785, 050485, 051185
ODE TO BILLIE JOE 081967, 082667, 090267, 090967, 091667, 092367, 093067, 100767, 101467
OFF SHORE 010254
OFF THE WALL 041280, 041980
OH 082953, 090553, 091253, 091953, 092653, 100353, 101053, 101753, 102453, 103153, 110753, 112153, 112853
OH, BABE, WHAT WOULD YOU SAY 012073, 012773, 021073, 021773
OH, BUT I DO 011847, 012547, 020147, 020847, 021547, 022247, 030147, 030847, 032247, 032947
OH CAROL 121259
OH GIRL 092990, 100690, 101390, 051372, 052072, 052772, 060472, 061172, 061772, 062472
OH HAPPY DAY 021453, 022153, 022853, 030753, 031453, 022153, 052469, 053169, 060769, 061469
OH, JOHNNY, OH 120939, 121639, 122339, 123039, 010640, 011340, 012040, 012740, 020340, 021040, 021740
OH, LOOK AT ME NOW 032941, 041241, 041941, 042641, 050341, 051041, 051741, 053141
OH, MA, MA 062538, 070238, 070938
OH MY MY 041374, 042074, 042774
OH, MY PAPA 010954, 011654, 012354, 013054, 020654, 021354, 022054, 022754, 030654, 031354, 032054, 032754

PEGGY SUE   122857, 010458, 011158, 011858, 020158

PENNIES FROM HEAVEN   111436, 121236, 121936, 122636, 010237, 010937, 011637, 012337, 013037, 020637, 021337, 022037, 022737

A PENNY A KISS   022451, 030351, 031051

PENNY LANE   031167, 031867, 032567, 040167, 040867

PENNY LOVER   111784, 112484, 120184, 120884

PENNY SERENADE   022539, 030439, 031139, 031839, 032539, 040139, 040839, 041539, 042239, 042939, 051339

PEOPLE   061364, 062064, 052764, 070464, 071164

PEOPLE EVERYDAY   101092, 101792, 102492, 103192

PEOPLE GOT TO BE FREE   081068, 081768, 082468, 083168, 090768, 091468, 092168, 092868, 100568

PEOPLE WILL SAY WE'RE IN LOVE   061943, 071743, 072443, 073143, 080743, 081443, 082143, 082843, 090443, 091143, 091843, 092543, 100243, 100943, 101643, 102343, 103043, 110643, 111343, 112043, 112743, 120443, 121143, 121843, 122543, 010144, 010844, 011544, 012244, 012944

PEPPERMINT TWIST   122961, 010562, 011262, 011962, 012662, 020262, 020962, 022362, 030262

PERCOLATOR (TWIST)   031662

PERFECT WORLD   082788, 090388, 091088, 091788, 092488

PERFIDIA   010441, 011141, 011841, 012541, 020141, 020841, 021541, 022241, 030141, 030841, 031541, 032241, 032941, 040541, 041241, 041941, 042641

PERSONALITY   030246, 030946, 031646, 032346, 033046, 040646, 041346, 042046, 042746, 050446, 053059, 060659, 061359, 062059, 062759, 070459, 071159, 071859, 072559, 080159, 080859

PETER COTTONTAIL   041550

PETITE FLEUR   022859, 030759, 031459, 032159

PHILADELPHIA FREEDOM   032975, 040575, 041275, 041975, 042675, 050375, 051075, 060775, 061475

PHOTOGRAPH   111073, 111773, 112473, 120173, 120873, 121673

PHYSICAL   111481, 112181, 112881, 120581, 121281, 121981, 122681, 010982, 011682, 012382, 013082, 020682, 021382

PIANO IN THE DARK   052888, 060488

PICCOLINO   092835, 101935

PICK UP THE PIECES   012675, 020175, 020875, 021575, 022275, 030175, 030875

PICNIC   051256, 051956, 052656, 060256, 060956, 061656, 062356, 063056, 070756, 071456, 072156, 072856, 080456

PIECE OF MY HEART   071391, 072091, 072791

PIED PIPER   072366, 073066, 080666, 081166, 082066

PILLOW TALK   051973, 052673, 060273, 060973, 061673, 062373, 063073

PINK CADILLAC   042388, 043088, 050788, 051488

PINK HOUSES   020484, 021184

PINK SHOE LACES   040459, 041159, 041859, 042559, 050259, 050959, 051659, 052359

PIPELINE   042063, 042763, 050463, 051163, 051863

PIPENO THE ITALIAN MOUSE   010563, 011263, 011963

PISTOL PACKIN' MAMA   100243, 100943, 101643, 102343, 103043, 110643, 111343, 112043, 112743, 120443, 121143, 121843, 122543, 010144

A PLACE IN THE SUN   121766, 122466, 123166

PLACE IN THIS WORLD   070691, 071391, 072091

PLAY A SIMPLE MELODY   081950, 082650, 090250, 080950, 091650, 092350, 093050, 100750, 101450, 102150, 102850

PLAY THAT FUNKY MUSIC   082876, 090476, 091176, 091876, 092576, 100276, 100976, 101676, 102376, 103076, 100276, 011991, 012691, 020291, 020991, 021691

PLAYBOY   061562, 062262, 062962, 070662

PLAYGROUND   062991

PLAYGROUND IN MY MIND   060273, 060973, 061673, 062373, 063073, 070773, 071473, 072173

PLAYMATES   051140, 052540, 060140, 060840, 061540, 062240, 062940, 070640, 071340, 072040, 072740, 080340

PLEASANT VALLEY SUNDAY   080567, 081267, 081967, 082667, 090267

PLEASE BE KIND   031938, 040238, 040938, 041638, 042338, 043038, 050738, 051438, 052138, 052838, 060438, 061138, 061838

PLEASE BELIEVE ME   012536, 020136, 021536, 022236, 022936, 030736, 031436, 032136, 032836, 040436

PLEASE COME TO BOSTON   072774, 080374, 081474, 081774

PLEASE DON'T GO   111079, 111779, 112479, 120179, 120879, 121579, 122279, 010580, 011280, 011980, 092692, 100392, 101092, 101792, 102492

PLEASE DON'T GO GIRL   100888, 101588

PLEASE FORGIVE ME   112093, 112793, 120493, 121193, 121893, 012294, 012994, 020594

PLEASE HELP ME I'M FALLING   072960, 080560, 081260, 081960, 082660

PLEASE LOVE ME FOREVER   110467, 111167, 111867, 112567, 120267

PLEASE MR. PLEASE   070575, 071275, 071975, 072675, 080275, 080975, 081675, 082375

PLEASE MR. POSTMAN   112461, 120161, 120861, 122261, 122961, 010475, 011175, 011875, 012675, 020175

PLEASE, MR. SUN   022152, 022852, 030652, 031352, 032052, 032752, 040352, 041052, 041752, 042452, 050152, 050852

PLEASE PLEASE ME   022964, 030764, 031464, 032164, 032864, 040464, 041164

POETRY IN MOTION   110460, 111160, 111860, 112560, 120260, 120960, 121660, 122360

POETRY MAN   032275, 032975, 040575, 041275

POINCIANA   030444, 032544, 040144, 040844, 041544, 042244, 042944, 050644, 051344, 052044, 052744

POINT OF NO RETURN   070487, 071187, 071887, 072587

POISON   111889, 112589, 051290, 051990, 052690, 060290, 060990, 061690, 062390, 063090, 070790, 071490

POISON IVY   101759, 102459, 111459

POLK SALAD ANNIE   082369

PONY TIME   022461, 030361, 031061, 031761, 032461, 033161, 040761, 041461

POOR LITTLE FOOL   071858, 072558, 080158, 080858, 081558, 082258, 082958, 090558, 091258, 091958

POOR PEOPLE OF PARIS   031056, 031756, 032456, 033156, 040756, 041456, 042156, 042856, 050556, 051256, 051956, 052656

POOR SIDE OF TOWN   102266, 102966, 110566, 111266, 111966, 112666, 120366

POP CORN   093072, 100772, 101472, 102172

POP EYE (THE HITCHHIKER)   111062

POP LIFE   090785, 091485, 092185

POP MUZIK   100679, 101379, 102079, 102779, 110379, 111079, 111779, 112479, 120179

POPSICLES AND ICICLES   122163, 122863, 010464, 011164, 011864, 012564

PORTRAIT OF MY LOVE   051261, 051961, 052661

POSITIVELY 4TH STREET   102365, 103065, 110665

POUR SOME SUGAR ON ME   062588, 070288, 070988, 071688, 072388, 073088, 080688

POWDER YOUR FACE WITH SUNSHINE   012949, 020549, 021249, 021949, 022649, 030549, 031249, 031949, 032649, 040249, 040949, 041649, 042349, 043049, 050749

THE POWER   071490, 072190, 072890, 080490, 081190, 081890

THE POWER OF LOVE   080385, 081085, 081785, 082485, 083185, 090785, 091485, 092185, 012294, 012994, 020594, 021294, 021994, 022694, 030594, 031294, 031994, 032694, 040294, 040994, 041694, 042394, 043094, 050794

POWER OF LOVE/LOVE POWER   060891, 061591, 062291, 062991, 070691, 071391

PRACTICE MAKES PERFECT   082440, 090740, 091440, 092140, 092840, 100540, 101240, 101940, 102640, 110240, 110940, 111640, 112340, 113040, 010441, 011141

PRAISE THE LORD AND PASS THE AMMUNITION   102442, 103142, 110742, 111442, 112142, 112842, 120542, 121242, 121942, 122642, 010243, 010943

PRAY   110390, 111090, 111790, 112490

PRAYING FOR TIME   092290, 092990, 100690, 101390, 102090, 102990

PRECIOUS AND FEW   020572, 021272, 021972, 022672, 030472, 031172, 031872

PRETEND   032153, 032853, 040453, 041153, 041853, 042553, 050253, 050953, 051653, 052353, 053053, 060653, 061353, 062053

PRETTY BLUE EYES   010160, 011560, 012960, 020560, 021260

PRAISE THE LORD AND PASS THE AMMUNITION   112142

PRETTY KITTY BLUE EYES   082644

PRETTY LITTLE ANGEL EYES   081861, 082561, 090161

PRICE OF LOVE   022490, 030390, 031090, 031790

PRIMROSE LANE   103159, 110759, 111459, 112159, 112859, 120559

PRISONER OF LOVE   051146, 051846, 052546, 060146, 060846, 061546, 062246, 062946, 070646, 071346, 072746, 080346, 081046, 081746, 082446

PRIVATE DANCER   031685, 032385, 033085

PRIVATE EYES   101081, 101781, 102481, 103181, 110781, 111481, 112181, 112881, 120581

PROBLEMS   120558, 121258, 121958, 122658, 010359, 011059, 011759

THE PROMISE OF A NEW DAY   082491, 083191, 090791, 091491, 092191

PROMISES   011379, 012079

PROUD MARY   022269, 030169, 030869, 031569, 032269, 032969, 040569, 031371, 032071, 032771, 040371, 041071

PROVE YOUR LOVE   042388, 043088, 050788

PSYCHEDELIC SHACK   021470, 022170, 022870

PSYCHOTIC REACTION   100866, 101566, 102266

PUFF (THE MAGIC DRAGON)   041363, 042063, 042763, 050463, 051163, 051863

PUMP UP THE JAM   120989, 121689, 122389, 010690, 011390, 012090, 012790, 020390

PUPPY LOVE   032560, 040160, 040860, 041560, 042260, 042960, 031872, 032572, 040172, 040872, 041572

PURPLE PEOPLE EATER   060758, 061358, 062058, 062758, 070458, 071158, 071858, 072558, 080158

PURPLE RAIN   102084, 102784, 110384, 111084, 111784, 112484, 120184

PUT A LITTLE LOVE IN YOUR HEART   080969, 081669, 082369, 083069, 090669, 091369, 011489, 012189

PUT THAT RING ON MY FINGER   122245

PUT YOUR ARMS AROUND ME, HONEY   072443, 082143, 082843, 090443, 091143, 091843, 092543, 100243, 100943, 101643, 102343, 103043, 110643, 111343, 112043, 112743

PUT YOUR HAND IN THE HAND   041771, 042471, 050171, 050871, 051571, 052271, 052971

PUT YOUR HANDS TOGETHER   030274

PUT YOUR HEAD ON MY SHOULDER   092659, 100359, 101059, 101759, 102459, 103159, 110759, 111459, 112159, 112859, 120559, 121259

PUTTIN' ON THE RITZ   082083, 082783, 090383, 091083, 091783, 092483

Q

QUARTER TO THREE   061661, 062361, 063061, 070761, 071461, 072161, 072861, 080461

QUEEN OF HEARTS   080181, 080881, 081581, 082281, 082981, 090581, 091281, 091981, 092681, 100381

QUICKER THAN YOU CAN SAY 'JACK ROBINSON'   122835

R

R.O.C.K. IN THE U.S.A. (A SALUTE TO 60S ROCK)   031586, 032286, 032986, 040586, 041286

RAG DOLL   070464, 071164, 071864, 072564, 080164, 080864, 081564

RAG MOP   022550, 030450, 031150, 031850, 032550

RAGS TO RICHES   111453, 112853, 120553, 121253, 121953, 122653, 010954, 012354, 013054

THE RAIN   110886, 111586

RAIN ON THE ROOF   111966

THE RAIN, THE PARK AND OTHER THINGS   110467, 111167, 111867, 112567, 120267, 120967, 121667, 122367

RAINBOW   090757

RAINDROPS   061661, 062361, 063061, 070761, 071461, 072161, 072861

RAINDROPS KEEP FALLIN' ON MY HEAD   121369, 122069, 122769, 010370, 011070, 011770, 012470, 013170, 020770, 021470, 022170, 022870, 030770

RAINY DAY WOMEN #12 & 35   050766, 051466, 052166, 052866, 060466

RAINY DAYS AND MONDAYS   060571, 061271, 061971, 062671, 070371, 071071, 071771

RAINY NIGHT IN GEORGIA   022170, 022870, 030770, 031470, 032170

RAMBLIN' MAN   092973, 100673, 101373, 102073, 102773, 110373

RAMBLIN' ROSE   090862, 091562, 092262, 092962, 100662, 101362, 102062

EL RANCHO GRANDE   120239, 120939, 121639

THE RAPPER   030770, 031470, 032170, 032870, 040470, 041170

RAPTURE   031481, 032181, 032881, 040481, 041181, 041881, 042581, 050281

070453, 071153, 071853, 072553,
080153, 080853, 081553, 082253,
090553, 091253
SONG SUNG BLUE 061172, 061772,
062472, 070172, 070872, 071572
SONGBIRD 062087, 062787, 070487,
071187
SOON 042935, 042735, 050435,
051135, 052535
SOONER OR LATER 011147, 012547,
020147, 020847, 072471, 073171
SORRY (I RAN ALL THE WAY HOME)
050259, 050959, 051659, 052359,
053059, 060659, 061359
SORRY SEEMS TO BE THE HARDEST
WORD 121876, 122576, 010877,
011577
SOUL MAN 101467, 102167, 102867,
110467, 111167, 111867, 112567,
120267
SOULFUL STRUT 010469, 011169,
011869, 012569, 020169
SOUNDS OF SILENCE 122565,
010166, 010866, 011566, 012266
SOUTH AMERICA, TAKE IT AWAY
083146, 090746, 091446, 092146,
092846, 100546, 101246, 101946,
102646, 110246, 110946, 111646,
112346, 113046
SOUTH OF THE BORDER 102139,
102839, 110439, 111139, 111839,
112539, 120239, 120939, 121639,
122339, 123039, 010640, 011340,
012040, 012740, 020340
SOUTH SEA ISLAND MAGIC 102436,
110736, 111436, 112136, 120536
SOUTH STREET 032363, 033063,
040563, 041363, 042063, 042763
SOUTHERN NIGHTS 040277, 040977,
041677, 042377, 043077, 050777,
051477, 052177
SOWING THE SEEDS OF LOVE 101489,
102189, 102889, 110489, 111189
SPACE RACE 110373, 111073, 111773,
112473, 120173, 120873
SPANISH HARLEM 082871, 090471,
091171, 091871, 092571, 100271
SPARROW IN THE TREETOP 041451,
042151, 042851, 050551, 051251
SPEAK LOW 121843, 011544, 021244
SPEAKING OF HEAVEN 120939,
123039
SPECIAL LADY 040580, 041280,
041980, 042680
SPEEDY GONZALES 072062, 072762,
080462, 081162, 081862
SPIDERS AND SNAKES 020274,
020974, 021674, 022374, 030274,
030974, 031674
SPIES LIKE US 012586, 020186,
020886
SPILL THE WINE 080170, 080870,
081570, 082270, 082970, 090570,
091270
SPINNING WHEEL 062169, 062869,
070569, 071269, 071969, 072669,
080269
SPIRIT IN THE SKY 032870, 040470,
041170, 041870, 042570, 050270,
050970, 051670
SPLISH SPLASH 071858, 072558,
080158, 080858, 081558
SPOOKY 012768, 020368, 021068,
021768, 022468, 030268
ST. ELMO'S FIRE 091485, 092185,
092885
STAGE DOOR CANTEEN 080842,
081542, 082242, 082942, 090542,
091242, 091942, 092642, 100342,
101042, 101742, 102442
STAGGER LEE 013159, 020759,
021459, 022159, 022859, 030759,
031459, 032159, 032859
STAIRWAY TO THE STARS 062439,
070139, 070839, 071539, 072239,
072939, 080539, 081239, 081939,
082639, 090239, 090939
STAND 040189, 040889, 041589,
042289
STAND BACK 072383, 073083, 080683,

081383, 082083, 082783
STAND BY ME 060961, 061661,
062361, 121386, 122086, 122786
STAND TALL 010877, 011577
STANDING IN THE SHADOWS OF LOVE
010767, 011467, 012167, 012867,
020467
STANDING ON THE CORNER 060256,
060956, 061656, 062356, 063056,
070756, 071456, 072156, 072856
STAR EYES 011544, 021244
A STAR FELL OUT OF HEAVEN 081536,
082936, 090536, 091236, 091936,
092636, 100336, 101036, 101736,
102436, 103136
STAR GAZING 072035, 081035, 081735
STARDUST ON THE MOON 082137,
082837, 091137
STARLIT HOUR 030940, 031640,
032340, 033040, 040640, 041340,
042740
START ME UP 092681, 100381,
101081, 101781, 102481, 103181,
110781, 111481, 112181, 112881,
120581
STARTING OVER 111580, 112280,
112980, 120680, 121380, 122080,
122780, 011081, 011781, 012481,
013181, 020781, 021481
STATE OF SHOCK 072184, 072884,
080484, 081184, 081884, 082584
STAY 111160, 111860, 112560, 120260,
120960, 082992, 090592, 091292,
091992, 092692, 100392
STAY AWHILE 042471, 050171, 050871,
051571
STAY IN MY CORNER 082468, 083168,
090768
STAYIN' ALIVE 012178, 012778,
020478, 021178, 021878, 022578,
030478, 031178, 031878, 032578,
040178, 040878, 041578
STEAL AWAY 061480, 062180, 062880,
070580, 071280, 071980, 072680
STEP BY STEP 091281, 091981,
092681, 100381, 101081, 101781,
102481, 103181, 060990, 061690,
062390, 063090, 070790, 071490,
072190
STEPPIN' OUT 112082, 112782,
120482, 121182, 121882, 122582,
010883
STEPPIN' OUT (GONNA BOOGIE
TONIGHT) 101974, 102674,
110274
STILL 060863, 061563, 062263,
102079, 102779, 110379, 111079,
111779, 112479, 120179, 120879,
121579, 122279, 010580, 011280
STILL THE ONE 100276, 100976,
101676, 102376
STILL THE SAME 061778, 070178,
070878, 071578, 072278, 072978,
080578
STOMP! 052480, 053180
STOMPIN' AT THE SAVOY 071136,
071836, 080136, 080836
STONE LOVE 050287
STONED LOVE 121970, 122670,
010271, 010971, 011671
STONED SOUL PICNIC 071368,
072068, 072768, 080368, 081068,
081768, 082468
STONEY END 010971, 011671,
012371, 013071
STOP AND SMELL THE ROSES 102674,
110274
STOP AND THINK IT OVER 022964,
030764
STOP BEATING 'ROUND THE MULBERRY
BUSH 090338, 091738, 092438,
100138, 100838, 101538, 102238,
102938, 110538
STOP DRAGGIN' MY HEART AROUND
082281, 082981, 090581, 091281,
091981, 092681, 100381, 101081,
101781, 102481
STOP! IN THE NAME OF LOVE 031365,
032065, 032765, 040365, 041065,
041765, 042465, 050165

STOP, IT'S WONDERFUL 120939,
010640, 012040
STOP STOP STOP 120366, 121066
STOP, YOU'RE BREAKING MY HEART
080737
STORMY 120768, 121468, 122168,
122868, 010469
STRAIGHT FROM THE HEART 052883,
060483
STRAIGHT UP 012889, 020489, 021189,
021889, 022589, 030489, 031189
STRANGE ENCHANTMENT 061739,
062439, 070839, 071539
STRANGE MUSIC 111144
STRANGER IN PARADISE 121253,
122653, 010254, 010954, 011654,
012354, 013054, 020654, 021354,
022054, 022754, 030654, 031354,
032054, 032754, 040354, 041054
A STRANGER IN TOWN 112445
STRANGER ON THE SHORE 042762,
050462, 051162, 051862, 052562,
060162, 060862, 061562, 062262,
062962
STRANGERS IN THE NIGHT 060466,
061166, 061866, 062566, 070266,
070966, 071666
STRAWBERRY FIELDS FOREVER
040167
STRAWBERRY LETTER #23 082777,
090377, 091077, 091777, 092477,
100177
STRAY CAT STRUT 021283, 021983,
022683, 030583, 031283
THE STREAK 050474, 051174, 051874,
052574, 060174, 060874, 061574,
062274
STREETS OF PHILADELPHIA (FROM
"PHILADELPHIA") 040994,
041694, 042394
STRIKE IT UP 061591, 062291, 062991
THE STRIPPER 062262, 062962,
070662, 071362, 072062, 072762,
080462, 081162
THE STROLL 020858, 021558
STRUT 111784, 112484, 120184
STUCK IN THE MIDDLE WITH YOU
042873, 050573, 051273, 051973
STUCK ON YOU 042260, 042960,
050660, 051360, 052060, 052760,
060360, 061060, 061760, 062460,
070160, 080484, 081184, 081884,
082584, 090184, 090884, 091584
STUCK WITH YOU 083086, 090686,
091386, 092086, 092786, 100486,
101186
STUMBLIN' IN 041479, 042179, 042879,
050579, 051279, 051979, 052679
SUDDENLY 052585, 060185, 060885,
061585
SUDDENLY LAST SUMMER 111283,
111983
SUDDENLY, THERE'S A VALLEY
102955, 110555, 111255, 111955,
112655
SUGAR DADDY 012272, 012972
SUGAR MOON 060758, 061358,
062058, 062758, 070458, 071158
SUGAR SHACK 100563, 101263,
101963, 102663, 110263, 110963,
111663, 112363, 113063, 120763
SUGAR SUGAR 083069, 090669,
091369, 092069, 092769, 100469,
100369, 101869, 102569, 110169,
110869, 111569
SUGAR TOWN 121766, 122466,
123166, 010767, 011467, 012167
SUGAR WALLS 022385, 030285,
030985
SUGARTIME 011858, 020858, 021558,
022258, 030158, 030858, 031558,
032258, 032958
SUICIDE BLONDE 102990, 110390
SUKIYAKI 060863, 061563, 062263,
062963, 070663, 071363, 072063,
050981, 051681, 052381, 053081,
060681, 061381, 062081, 062781
SULTANS OF SWING 031079, 031779,
032479, 033179, 040779, 041479,
042179

SUMMER 091176, 091876, 092576,
100276
SUMMER BREEZE 111872, 112572,
120272
SUMMER IN THE CITY 073066, 080666,
081166, 082066, 082766, 090366,
091066
SUMMER NIGHTS 090978, 091678,
092378, 093078, 100778, 101478,
102178
SUMMER OF '69 081785, 082485,
083185, 090785
A SUMMER SONG 101064, 101764,
102464
SUMMER SOUVENIRS 111938, 112638
SUMMERTIME 082766, 090366,
072091, 072791, 080391, 081091,
081791, 082491
SUNDAY IN THE PARK 043038
SUNDAY, MONDAY, OR ALWAYS
081443, 082143, 082843, 090443,
091143, 091843, 092543, 100243,
100943, 101643, 102343, 103043,
110643, 111343, 112043, 112743,
120443, 121143
SUNDAY WILL NEVER BE THE SAME
062467
SUNDOWN 060174, 060874, 061574,
062274, 062974, 070674, 071374
SUNFLOWER 022649, 030549, 031249,
031949, 032649, 040249, 040949,
041649, 042349, 043049, 050749,
051449, 052149
SUNGLASSES AT NIGHT 081184,
081884, 082584, 090184, 090884
SUNNY 081166, 082066, 082766,
090366, 091066, 091766
SUNRISE SERENADE 070139, 070839,
071539, 072239, 072939, 080539,
081239, 081939, 082639, 090239,
090939, 091639, 092339, 093039,
100739
SUNSHINE 010172, 010872, 011572,
012272, 012972, 020572
SUNSHINE OF YOUR LOVE 080368,
081068, 081768, 082468, 083168
SUNSHINE ON MY SHOULDER 030974,
031674, 032374, 033074, 040674,
041374, 042074
SUNSHINE SUPERMAN 082066,
082766, 090366, 091066, 091766,
092466, 100166
SUPERFLY 123072, 010673, 011373,
012073
SUPERNATURAL THING 041975,
042675
SUPERSTAR 092571, 100271, 100971,
101671, 102371, 103071, 110671,
111371
SUPERSTITION 010673, 011373,
012073, 012773, 021073
SUPERWOMAN 041589
SURE GONNA MISS HER 040266,
040966
SURF CITY 070663, 071363, 072063,
072763, 080363, 081063
SURFER GIRL 091463, 092163, 092863
SURFIN' BIRD 011164, 011864, 012564,
020164, 020864
SURFIN' U.S.A. 050463, 051163,
051863, 052563, 060163, 060863
SURRENDER 072746, 080346, 081046,
081746, 082446, 083146, 090746,
091446, 092146, 092846, 100546,
101246, 101946, 102646, 110246,
031061, 031761, 032461, 033161,
040761, 041461, 042161, 042861
SURRENDER TO ME (FROM "TEQUILA
SUNRISE") 030489, 031189
SUSIE DARLIN' 100358, 101058,
101758
SUSPICION 032864, 040464, 041164,
041864, 042564, 050264, 050964
SUSPICIOUS MINDS 101869, 102569,
110169, 110869, 111569, 112269
SUSSUDIO 061585, 062285, 070685,
071385, 072085
SWAYIN' TO THE MUSIC 102277
SWEARIN' TO GOD 071275, 071975,
072675

(THEME FROM) "VALLEY OF THE DOLLS" 021768, 022468, 030268, 030968, 031668, 032368, 033068

THEN CAME YOU 090774, 091474, 092174, 092874, 100574, 101274, 101974, 102674

THEN HE KISSED ME 091463, 092163, 092863, 100563, 101263

THEN YOU CAN TELL ME GOODBYE 022567, 030467, 031167, 031867

THERE ARE SUCH THINGS 120542, 121242, 121942, 122642, 010243, 010943, 011643, 012343, 013043, 020643, 021343, 022043, 022743, 030643, 031343, 032043, 032743, 040343

THERE GOES MY BABY 080159, 080859, 081559, 082259, 082959, 090559, 091259

THERE GOES THAT SONG AGAIN 120244, 121644, 122344, 123044, 010645, 011345, 012045, 012745, 020345, 021045, 021745, 022445

THERE I GO 101940, 102640, 110240, 110940, 111640, 112340, 113040, 120740, 121440, 122140, 122840, 010441, 011141, 011841, 012541, 020141, 020841, 021541, 030141

THERE, I'VE SAID IT AGAIN 060945, 061645, 062345, 063045, 070745, 071445, 072845, 080445, 081145, 121463, 122163, 122863, 010464, 011164, 011864, 012564, 020164, 020864

THERE MUST BE A WAY 042845, 060945, 090145

THERE WILL NEVER BE ANOTHER YOU 101042, 111442, 112142, 112842

THERE'LL BE SAD SONGS (TO MAKE YOU CRY) 060786, 061486, 062186, 062886, 070586, 071986

THERE'LL BE SOME CHANGES MADE 012541, 020141, 020841, 022241, 030141, 030841, 031541, 032241, 032941, 040541, 041241, 041941, 042641, 050341, 051041

THERE'S A GOLD MINE IN THE SKY 121137, 121837, 122537, 010138, 010838, 011538, 012238, 012938, 020538, 021238, 021938, 022638, 030538, 031238, 040238

THERE'S A KIND OF HUSH (ALL OVER THE WORLD) 031867, 032567, 040167, 040867

THERE'S A LULL IN MY LIFE 051537, 052237, 052937, 060537, 061237, 061937, 062637, 070337, 071737

THERE'S A MOON OUT TONIGHT 021761, 022461, 030361, 031061

THERE'S A SMALL HOTEL 060636, 061336, 062036, 062736, 070436, 071136, 071836, 072536, 080136, 080836

THERE'S A STAR SPANGLED BANNER WAVING SOMEWHERE 121942

THERE'S ALWAYS A HAPPY ENDING 051636

THERE'S HONEY ON THE MOON TONIGHT 072338

THERE'S NO GETTING OVER YOU 081581, 082281, 082981, 090581, 091281, 091981, 092681, 100381

THERE'S NO TOMORROW 050750, 020450, 021150, 021850, 022550, 030450, 031150, 031850, 032550

THERE'S NO YOU 090845

THERE'S SOMETHING IN THE AIR 020637, 021337, 022037

THERE'S 'YES, YES' IN YOUR EYES 072349, 073049, 080649, 081349, 082049, 082749, 091049, 092449

THESE BOOTS ARE MADE FOR WALKIN' 021966, 022666, 030566, 031966, 032666, 040266

THESE DREAMS 030186, 030886, 031586, 032286, 032986, 040586

THESE EYES 051769, 052469, 053169, 060769, 061469

THESE FOOLISH THINGS 062736, 070436, 071136, 071836, 072536,

080136, 080836, 081536, 082236, 082936, 090536, 091236, 091936

THEY CAN'T TAKE THAT AWAY FROM ME 060537, 061237, 062637, 071037

THEY DON'T KNOW 042184, 042884, 050584

(THEY LONG TO BE) CLOSE TO YOU 071170, 071870

THEY SAY 010739, 012839, 020439, 021139, 021839

THEY SAY IT'S WONDERFUL 052546, 060146, 060846, 061546, 062246, 062946, 070646, 071346, 072046, 072746, 080346, 081046, 081746, 082446, 083146, 090746, 091446, 092146, 092846, 100546, 101246, 101946

THEY WERE DOIN' THE MAMBO 092554

THEY'RE COMING TO TAKE ME AWAY HA-HAA 080666, 081166, 082066

THEY'RE EITHER TOO YOUNG OR TOO OLD 101643, 102343, 103043, 110643, 111343, 112043, 112743, 121143, 121843, 122543, 010844, 011544

THIEVES IN THE TEMPLE 091590, 092290, 092990

THE THING 120950, 121650, 122350, 123050, 010651, 011351, 012051

THINGS 081862, 082562, 090162, 090862

THINGS CAN ONLY GET BETTER 052585, 060185, 060885, 061585, 062285

THE THINGS I LOVE 051741, 052441, 053141, 060741, 061441, 062141, 062841, 070541, 071241, 071941, 072641, 080241, 080941, 081641, 082341, 083041, 090641, 091341

THINGS THAT MAKE YOU GO HMMMM... 083191, 090791, 091491, 092191, 092891

THE THINGS WE DID LAST SUMMER 112346, 113046, 120746, 121446, 122146, 122846, 010447, 011147, 011847, 012547, 020147

THE THINGS WE DO FOR LOVE 032677, 040277, 040977, 041677, 042377

THINK 060868, 061568, 062268, 062968

THINK OF LAURA 020484, 021184

THINK TWICE 040761

THINKING OF YOU 102850, 110450, 111150, 111850, 112550, 120250, 120950

THE THIRD MAN THEME 042950, 050650, 051350, 052050, 052750, 060350, 061050, 061750, 062450, 070150, 070850, 071550, 072250, 072950, 081250

THIS CAN'T BE LOVE 122438, 123138, 010739, 011439, 012139, 012839, 020439, 021139, 021839, 022539

THIS CHANGING WORLD 012740, 020340

THIS COULD BE THE NIGHT 032986

THIS DIAMOND RING 013065, 020665, 021365, 022065, 022765, 030665, 031365, 032065, 032765

THIS GIRL IS A WOMAN NOW 100369

THIS GIRL'S IN LOVE WITH YOU 030869, 031569, 032269

THIS GUY'S IN LOVE WITH YOU 060868, 061568, 062268, 062968, 070668, 071368, 072068, 072768

THIS HOUSE 090991, 031691, 032391, 033091, 040691

THIS IS ALWAYS 101946, 102646, 110246, 110946, 111646, 112346, 120746

THIS IS IT 031839, 040139

THIS IS MY SONG 040167, 040867, 041567, 042267, 042967

THIS IS NO DREAM 072939, 080539

THIS IS NO LAUGHING MATTER 122041, 010342, 012442, 021442

THIS IS WORTH FIGHTING FOR

062742, 071842, 080842

THIS LOVE OF MINE 112241, 112941, 120641, 121341, 122041, 010342, 011042, 011742, 012442, 013142, 020742, 021442

THIS MAGIC MOMENT 022269, 030169, 030869, 031569

THIS MASQUERADE 082876, 090476

THIS OLD HEART OF MINE 052690

THIS OLE HOUSE 091854, 100254, 100954, 101654, 102354, 103054, 110654, 111354, 112054, 112754, 120454

THIS ONE'S FOR THE CHILDREN 122389, 010690, 011390

THIS TIME 102761, 110361, 111061, 111761, 112461, 120161

THIS TIME I KNOW IT'S FOR REAL 061789, 062489, 070189

THIS TIME I'M IN IT FOR LOVE 060378, 061078

THIS TIME IT'S REAL 070238, 073038

THIS USED TO BE MY PLAYGROUND 071892, 072592, 080192, 080892, 081592, 082992, 090592

THIS WILL BE 110175, 110875, 111575, 112975

THIS YEAR'S KISSES 022037, 022737, 030637, 032037, 032737, 041037, 041737

THOSE LAZY-HAZY-CRAZY DAYS OF SUMMER 060863, 061563, 062263, 062963

THOSE OLDIES BUT GOODIES (REMIND ME OF YOU) 063061

THOSE WERE THE DAYS 102668, 110268, 110968, 111668, 112368, 113068, 120768

THOUSAND STARS 112560, 120260, 120960, 121660, 122360, 123060, 010561, 011361, 012061

3 A.M. ETERNAL 081791, 082491, 083191, 090791, 091491

THE THREE BELLS 082259, 082959, 090559, 091259, 091959, 092659, 100359, 101059, 101759, 102459, 091959

THREE COINS IN THE FOUNTAIN 060554, 061254, 061954, 062654, 070354, 071054, 071754, 072454, 073154, 080754, 081454, 082154, 082854

THREE LITTLE FISHIES 050639, 051339, 052039, 052739, 060339, 061039, 061739, 062439, 070139

THREE LITTLE SISTERS 060642, 061342, 062042, 062742, 070442, 071142, 071842, 072542, 080142

THREE TIMES A LADY 072278, 072978, 080578, 081278, 081978, 082678, 090278, 090978, 091678, 092378, 093078

THRILLED 061535, 062235, 062935, 070635, 071335, 072035, 072735, 080335

THRILLER 021884, 022584, 030384, 031084, 031784

THROWING IT ALL AWAY 100486, 101186, 101886, 102586

THUNDER ISLAND 032578, 040178, 040878

TI PI TIN 031938, 032638, 040238, 040938, 041638, 042338, 043038, 050738, 051338, 052138, 052838, 060438

TICKET TO RIDE 050865, 051565, 052265, 052965, 060565, 061265

THE TIDE IS HIGH 122780, 011081, 011781, 012481, 013181, 020781, 021481, 022181, 032881

TIE A YELLOW RIBBON ROUND THE OLD OAK TREE 040773, 041473, 042173, 042873, 050573, 051273, 051973, 052673, 060273, 060973, 061673

TIE ME KANGAROO DOWN SPORT 070663, 071363, 072063, 072763, 080363, 081063

TIGER 071859, 072559, 080159, 080859, 081559

TIGHTEN UP 042768, 050468, 051168, 051868, 052568, 060168, 060868, 061568, 062268

TIGHTER TIGHTER 080170, 080870, 081570, 082270

'TIL REVEILLE 080241, 080941, 081641, 082341, 083041, 090641, 091341, 092041, 092741, 100441, 101141, 101841, 102541, 110141, 110841

(TILL) I KISSED YOU 091259, 091959, 092659, 100359, 101059, 101759, 102459, 103159, 110759

TILL I WALTZ AGAIN WITH YOU 012453, 013153, 020753, 021453, 022153, 022853, 030753, 031453, 032153, 032853, 040453, 041153, 041853, 042553, 050253

TILL THE END OF TIME 081845, 082545, 090145, 090945, 091545, 092245, 092945, 100645, 101345, 102045, 102745, 110345, 111045, 111745, 112445, 120145, 120845, 121545, 122245

TIME 052183, 052883, 060483, 061183, 061883, 062583, 070283, 070983, 071683, 101583

TIME AFTER TIME 051747, 052447, 053147, 060747, 051284, 051984, 052684, 060284, 060984, 061684, 062384, 063084, 070784

TIME IN A BOTTLE 121673, 122273, 122973, 010574, 011274, 011974, 012674

TIME IS ON MY SIDE 112164, 112864, 120564, 121264, 121964, 122664, 112864

TIME IS TIGHT 042669, 050369, 051069

TIME, LOVE AND TENDERNESS 090791, 091491, 092191, 092891

TIME OF THE SEASON 031569, 032269, 032969, 040569, 041269, 041969

TIME OF YOUR LIFE 011076, 011776, 012476, 013176, 020776

TIME PASSAGES 112578, 120278, 120978, 121678

TIME WAITS FOR NO ONE 062444, 070144, 070844, 071544, 072944, 080544, 081244, 081944, 082644, 090244, 090944, 091644, 092344, 093044, 100744, 101444

TIME WAS 090641, 092041, 092741, 100441, 101141, 101841, 102541, 110141, 110841, 111541

TIME WON'T LET ME 041666, 042366, 043066

TIN MAN 110274, 110974, 111674, 112374

TINA MARIE 101555

TIRED OF TOEIN' THE LINE 072680, 080280

TIRED OF WAITING FOR YOU 041765, 042465, 050165

TO ALL THE GIRLS I'VE LOVED BEFORE 042884, 050584, 051284, 051984, 052684, 060284

TO BE A LOVER 120686, 121386, 122086

TO BE WITH YOU 020892, 021592, 022292, 022992, 030792, 031492, 032192, 032892, 040492

TO EACH HIS OWN 080346, 081046, 081746, 082446, 083146, 090746, 091446, 092146, 092846, 100546, 101246, 101946, 102646, 110246, 110946, 111646, 112346, 113046, 120746, 121446

TO KNOW HIM IS TO LOVE HIM 111458, 112158, 112858, 120558, 121258, 121958, 122658, 010359, 011059, 011759, 012459

TO MARY WITH LOVE 111436, 112136

TO SIR WITH LOVE 101467, 102167, 102867, 110467, 111167, 111867, 112567, 120267, 120967

TO YOU 080539, 090239, 090939, 093039, 102139

TO YOU, SWEETHEART, ALOHA 021040

TOGETHER 093044, 100744, 102844,

V

VACATION 090162, 090862, 081482, 082182, 082882, 090482

VALERIE 121987

VALLERI 030968, 031668, 032368, 033068, 040668

THE VALLEY ROAD 061188, 061888, 062588, 070288, 070988

VALOTTE 122284, 010585, 011285

VAYA CON DIOS 072553, 080153, 080853, 081553, 082253, 082953, 090553, 091253, 091953, 092653, 100353, 101053, 101753, 102453, 103153, 110753, 111453, 112153, 112853, 120553, 121253, 121953, 122653

VEHICLE 050270, 050970, 051670, 052370, 053070

VENTURA HIGHWAY 120272, 120972, 121672

VENUS 031459, 032159, 032859, 040459, 041159, 041859, 042559, 050259, 050959, 010370, 011070, 011770, 012470, 013170, 020770, 021470, 022170, 022870, 080986, 081686, 082386, 083086, 090686, 091386, 092086

VENUS IN BLUE JEANS 100662

THE VERY THOUGHT OF YOU 112544

VICTORY 012487

LA VIE EN ROSE 090250, 080950, 091650, 092350, 093050, 100750, 101450, 102150, 102850, 110450, 111150, 111850, 112550, 120250

VIENI, VIENI 103037, 110637, 111337, 112037, 112737, 120437, 121137, 121837, 122537, 010138, 010838, 011538

A VIEW TO A KILL 062285, 070685, 071385, 072085, 072785

THE VILLAGE OF ST. BERNADETTE 012960, 020560

VISION OF LOVE 072190, 072890, 080490, 081190, 081890, 082590, 090190

VOGUE 050590, 051290, 051990, 052690, 060290, 060990, 061690, 062390

VOICES CARRY 070685, 071385

VOLARE (NEL BLU DIPINTO DI BLU) 080858, 081558, 082258, 082958, 090558, 091258, 091958, 092658, 100358, 101058, 101758, 102458, 103158, 082660, 090260, 090960, 091660, 092360, 093060

W

WAH HOO 022936, 030736, 032836, 040436, 041136, 041836

WAH-WATUSI 071362, 072062, 072762, 080462, 081162, 081862

WAIT 052188, 052888

WAIT AND SEE 011946

WAITIN' FOR THE TRAIN TO COME IN 100645, 111745, 122945, 010546, 011246

WAITING FOR A GIRL LIKE YOU 110781, 111481, 112181, 112881, 120581, 121281, 121981, 122681, 010982, 011682, 012382, 013082, 020682, 021382

WAITING FOR A STAR TO FALL 120388, 121088, 121788, 122488, 010789

WAKE ME UP BEFORE YOU GO-GO 102784, 110384, 111084, 111784, 112484, 120184, 120884, 121584

WAKE THE TOWN AND TELL THE PEOPLE 082755, 091755, 092455, 100155, 100855, 101555, 102255

WAKE UP AND SING 032836

WAKE UP LITTLE SUSIE 101257, 101957, 102657, 110257, 110957, 111657, 112357

WALK - DON'T RUN '64 082264

WALK AWAY FROM LOVE 011776, 012476, 013176

WALK AWAY RENEE 101566, 102266, 102966, 110566

WALK DON'T RUN 081960, 082660

WALK LIKE A MAN 020963, 021663, 022363, 030263, 030963, 031663, 032363

WALK LIKE AN EGYPTIAN 112986, 120686, 121386, 122086, 122786, 011087, 011787

WALK OF LIFE 011186, 011886, 012586, 020186

WALK ON BY 120861, 122261, 122961, 010562, 011262, 011962, 012662, 052364, 060664, 061364, 062064, 052764

WALK ON WATER 121088, 121788, 122488

WALK RIGHT IN 011963, 012663, 020263, 020963, 021663, 022363, 030263, 030963

WALK THE DINOSAUR 032589, 040189, 040889

WALK THIS WAY 090686, 091386, 092086, 092786, 100486, 012977, 020577

WALKIN' BY THE RIVER 040541, 042641, 050341, 051041, 051741, 052441, 053141, 060741, 061441

WALKIN' MY BABY BACK HOME 071052, 071752, 072452, 073152, 080752, 081452, 082152, 082952, 090552, 091252, 091952, 092652

WALKIN' WITH MY HONEY 112445

WALKING AWAY 021189, 021889, 022589

WALKING IN RHYTHM 042675, 050375, 051075, 051775

WALKING ON SUNSHINE 060885, 061585, 062285

WALKING THE DOG 113063, 120763, 121463

THE WANDERER 020262, 020962, 022362, 030262, 102580, 110180, 110880, 111580, 112280, 112980

WANNA BE STARTIN' SOMETHING 070283, 070983, 071683, 072383, 073083, 080683

WANT ADS 052271, 052971, 060571, 061271, 061971, 062671, 070371, 071071

WANTED 032054, 032754, 040354, 041054, 041754, 042454, 050154, 050854, 051554, 052254, 052954, 060554, 061254, 061954, 062654, 070354, 071054

WANTED DEAD OR ALIVE 053087, 060687, 061387, 062087, 062787

WAR 081570, 082270, 082970, 090570, 091270, 091970, 092670, 100370, 122786, 011087

THE WARRIOR 090884, 091584, 092284, 092984, 100684

WAS IT RAIN 062637

WASHINGTON SQUARE 102663, 110263, 110963, 111663, 112363, 113063, 120763

WASTED DAYS AND WASTED NIGHTS 091375, 092075, 092775

WASTED ON THE WAY 081482, 082182, 082882, 090482, 091182

WATCHING THE WHEELS 052381, 053081

WATERLOO 071159, 071859, 072559, 080159, 080859, 081559, 082259, 081074, 081774, 082474

WATERMELON MAN 050463

WAY BACK HOME 052535, 060135, 060835

WAY DOWN YONDER IN NEW ORLEANS 122659, 010160, 010860, 011560, 012260, 012960, 020560

THE WAY I WANT TO TOUCH YOU 110875, 111575, 112975, 120675

THE WAY IT IS 112286, 112986, 120686, 121386, 122086, 122786, 011087

WAY OF LOVE 031172, 031872, 032572

WAY WE WERE 011974, 012674, 020274, 020974, 021674, 022374, 030274, 030974, 031674

THE WAY YOU DO THE THINGS YOU DO 120190, 120890, 121590, 122290

THE WAY YOU LOOK TONIGHT 091936, 092636, 100336, 101036, 101736, 102436, 103136, 110736, 111436, 112136, 112836, 120536, 121236, 121936

THE WAY YOU LOVE ME 011489, 012189, 012889, 020489

THE WAY YOU MAKE ME FEEL 122687, 010988, 011688, 012388, 013088

THE WAYWARD WIND 060956, 061656, 062356, 063056, 070756, 071456, 072156, 072856, 080456, 081156, 081856, 082556, 090156

(WE AIN'T GOT) NOTHIN' YET 012867, 020467, 021167, 021867, 022567

WE ARE FAMILY 052679, 060279, 060979, 061679, 062379, 063079, 070779

WE ARE THE CHAMPIONS 011478, 012178, 012778, 020478, 021178, 021878, 022578

WE ARE THE WORLD 033085, 040685, 041385, 042085, 042785, 050485, 051185, 051885

WE BELONG 121584, 122284, 010585, 011285, 011985

WE BUILT THIS CITY 112185, 110985, 111685, 112385, 113085, 120785, 121485

WE CAN WORK IT OUT 010166, 010866, 011566, 012266, 012966, 020566, 021266

WE CAN'T GO WRONG 021790, 022490, 030390

WE DIDN'T START THE FIRE 111889, 112589, 120989, 121689, 122389, 010690

WE DON'T HAVE TO TAKE OUR CLOTHES OFF 080286, 080986, 081686, 082386

WE DON'T NEED ANOTHER HERO 081785, 082485, 083185, 090785, 091485, 092185

WE DON'T TALK ANYMORE 010580, 011280, 011980, 012680

WE GOT LOVE 121259, 121959, 122659

WE GOT THE BEAT 031382, 032082, 032782, 040382, 041082, 041782, 042482, 050182, 050882

WE THREE 111640, 112340, 113040, 120740, 121440, 122140, 122840

WEAK 052293, 052993, 060593, 061293, 061993, 062693, 070393, 071093, 071793, 072493, 073193, 080793, 081493, 082193, 082893

WEAR MY RING AROUND YOUR NECK 060758

THE WEDDING 010265, 010965

WEDDING BELL BLUES 101869, 102569, 110169, 110869, 111569, 112269, 112969, 120669

WEEKEND IN NEW ENGLAND 022677, 030577

WELCOME BACK 042476, 050176, 050876, 051576, 052276, 052976, 060576

WELCOME TO THE JUNGLE 121088, 121788, 122488

WE'LL BE TOGETHER 112887, 120587, 121287, 121987

WE'LL NEVER HAVE TO SAY GOODBYE AGAIN 041578, 042278

WE'LL SING IN THE SUNSHINE 100364, 101064, 101764, 102464, 103164, 110764

WE'RE ALL ALONE 111277, 111977, 112677, 120377, 121077, 121777

WE'RE AN AMERICAN BAND 090873, 091573, 092273, 092973, 100673, 101373

WE'RE READY 020787, 021487

WE'RE THE COUPLE OF THE CASTLE 020742

WEST END GIRLS 041286, 041986, 042686, 050286, 051086, 051786, 052486

WEST WIND 030736, 031436

WESTERN UNION 040167, 040867, 041567, 042267, 042967

WE'VE GOT TONIGHT 022683, 030583, 031283, 031983, 032683, 040283, 040983

WE'VE ONLY JUST BEGUN 101070, 101770, 102470, 103170, 111470, 112170, 112970, 120570

WHAT A DIFF'RENCE A DAY MADE 111844

WHAT A DIFF'RENCE A DAY MAKES 082259

WHAT A FOOL BELIEVES 030379, 031079, 031779, 032479, 033179, 040779, 041479, 042179, 042879

WHAT ABOUT LOVE 082485

WHAT ABOUT YOUR FRIENDS 110792, 111492, 112192, 112892, 120592, 121292, 121992, 010293, 010993, 011693

WHAT AM I GONNA DO WITH YOU 041275, 041975, 042675

WHAT BECOMES OF THE BROKEN HEARTED 101566, 102266, 102966, 110566

WHAT DOES IT TAKE (TO WIN YOUR LOVE)? 071269, 071969, 072669, 080269, 080969, 081669

WHAT GOES ON HERE IN MY HEART 082738, 090338, 092438, 100138, 100838, 101538

WHAT HAVE I DONE TO DESERVE THIS? 020688, 021388, 022088, 022788, 030588

WHAT HAVE YOU DONE FOR ME LATELY 042686, 050286, 051086, 051786, 052486, 053186

WHAT HAVE YOU GOT THAT GETS ME 122438, 123138

WHAT I AM 021889, 022589, 030489

WHAT IN THE WORLD'S COME OVER YOU 021960, 022660, 030460, 031160, 031860, 032560

WHAT IS LIFE 032771

WHAT IT TAKES 050590, 051290, 051990

WHAT KIND OF FOOL 021564, 022264, 032881, 040481

WHAT KIND OF MAN WOULD I BE? 021090, 021790, 022490

WHAT THE WORLD NEEDS NOW/ ABRAHAM, MARTIN AND JOHN 073171, 080771, 081471

WHAT THE WORLD NEEDS NOW IS LOVE 070365, 071065, 071765, 072465, 073165

WHAT WILL I TELL MY HEART 030637, 032037, 032737, 040337, 041037, 041737, 042437, 050137, 050837

WHAT WILL MARY SAY 031663, 032363

WHAT YOU DON'T KNOW 070889, 071589, 072289

WHAT YOU NEED 032286, 032986, 040586, 041286, 041986

WHAT YOU WON'T DO FOR LOVE 031779, 032479, 033179

WHATCHA GONNA DO 073077, 080677, 081377, 082077, 082777

WHATCHA SEE IS WHATCHA GET 091871, 092571

WHAT'D I SAY 082259, 082959, 090559, 091259

WHATEVER GETS YOU THRU THE NIGHT 110274, 110974, 111674

WHATEVER LOLA WANTS 051455, 052155, 052855, 060455, 061155, 061855, 062555

WHATEVER WILL BE, WILL BE 080456, 081156, 081856, 082556, 090156, 090856, 091556, 092256, 092956, 100656, 101356, 102056, 102756

WHAT'S GOING ON? 032071, 032771, 040371, 041071, 041771, 042471, 050171, 050871

WHAT'S LOVE GOT TO DO WITH IT 072884, 080484, 081184, 081884, 082584, 090184, 090884, 091584, 092284, 092984

WHAT'S MY NAME? 122593, 010194, 010894, 011594

YOU MUST HAVE BEEN A BEAUTIFUL BABY 121738, 122438, 123138, 010739, 011439, 012139, 012839, 020439, 092961, 100661, 102061

YOU NEEDED ME 100778, 101478, 102178, 102878, 110478, 111178, 111878, 112578

YOU NEVER DONE IT LIKE THAT 111878, 112578

YOU OUGHT TO BE WITH ME 112572, 120272, 120972, 121672, 122372, 123072, 010673

YOU REALLY GOT ME 112164, 112864, 120564, 121264, 121964

YOU RHYME WITH EVERYTHING THAT'S BEAUTIFUL 061243, 070343

YOU SEND ME 112357, 113057, 120757, 121457, 122157, 122857, 010458, 011158

YOU SEXY THING 011776, 012476, 013176, 020776, 021476, 022176, 022876, 030676

YOU SHOULD BE DANCING 080776, 081476, 082176, 082876, 090476, 091176, 091876

YOU SHOULD HEAR HOW SHE TALKS ABOUT YOU 090482, 091182, 091882, 092682

YOU SHOWED ME 021569, 022269, 030169

YOU STARTED ME DREAMING 040436, 041136, 041836, 042536, 050236, 050936, 051636, 052336, 053036, 060636, 061336

YOU TAKE MY BREATH AWAY 062379, 063079

YOU TALK TOO MUCH 111160, 111860

YOU THINK OF EVERYTHING 081040

YOU TOOK THE WORDS RIGHT OUT OF MY HEART 012938, 020538, 021938

YOU TURN ME ON 071065, 071765, 072465

YOU TURNED THE TABLES ON ME 101736, 102436, 103136, 110736, 111436, 112136, 112836, 120536, 121236

YOU WALK BY 010441, 011141, 011841, 012541, 020141, 020841, 021541, 022241, 030141, 030841, 031541, 032241, 032941, 040541, 041241, 041941

YOU WAS 041649

YOU WERE ON MY MIND 090465, 091165, 091865, 092565, 100265, 100965

YOU WERE ONLY FOOLING 110648, 111348, 112048, 112748, 120448, 121148, 121848, 122548, 010149, 010849, 011549, 012249, 012949

YOU WON'T BE SATISFIED 033046, 040646, 041346, 042046, 042746, 050446, 051146, 051846

YOU WON'T SEE ME 070674, 071374, 072074

YOU, YOU DARLING 050440

YOU, YOU, YOU 082253, 082953, 090553, 091253, 091953, 092653, 100353, 101053, 101753, 102453, 103153, 110753, 111453, 112153, 112853, 120553, 121253, 122653, 010254, 010954

YOU'D BE SO NICE TO COME HOME TO 010243, 012343, 013043, 020643, 021343, 022043, 022743, 030643, 031343, 032043, 032743, 040343, 041043, 041743, 042443, 050143

YOU'LL ALWAYS BE THE ONE I LOVE 022247

YOU'LL LOSE A GOOD THING 081162

YOU'LL NEVER FIND ANOTHER LOVE LIKE MINE 080776, 081476, 082176, 082876, 090476, 091176, 091876, 092576

YOU'LL NEVER KNOW 050843, 051543, 052243, 052943, 060543, 061243, 061943, 062643, 070343, 071043, 071743, 072443, 073143, 080743, 081443, 082143, 082843, 090443, 091143, 091843, 092543, 100243, 101643

YOUNG AT HEART 030654, 031354, 032054, 032754, 040354, 041054, 041754, 042454, 050154, 050854, 051554, 052254, 052954, 060554, 061254, 061954, 062654, 071054

YOUNG GIRL 033068, 040668, 041368, 042068, 042768, 050468, 051168, 051868

YOUNG LOVE 011957, 012657, 020257, 020957, 021657, 022357, 030257, 030957, 031657, 032357, 033057, 040657, 041357

YOUNG LOVERS 040563, 041363, 042063, 042763

YOUNG TURKS 120581, 121281, 121981, 122681, 010982

YOUNG WORLD 040662, 042062, 042762, 050462

YOUNGER THAN SPRINGTIME 092449

YOUR CHEATIN' HEART 032853, 040453, 041153, 041853, 042553, 050253, 050953, 051653, 052353, 053053, 060653, 062053, 062753, 071853

YOUR LOVE 042686, 050286, 051086, 051786

YOUR MAMA DON'T DANCE 123072, 010673, 011373, 012073, 012773, 041589

YOUR PRECIOUS LOVE 102167, 102867, 110467, 111167, 111867

YOUR SONG 012371, 013071, 020671, 021371

YOUR WILDEST DREAMS 070586, 071986

YOU'RE A HEAVENLY THING 050435, 051135, 051835

YOU'RE A SWEET LITTLE HEADACHE 030439, 031139, 031839

YOU'RE A SWEETHEART 010138, 010838, 011538, 012238, 012938, 020538, 021238, 021938, 022638, 030538, 031238

YOU'RE ALL I NEED 072735, 080335, 081035, 081735, 082435, 083135, 090735, 092135, 092835

YOU'RE ALL I NEED TO GET BY 083168, 090768, 091468

YOU'RE AN EDUCATION 031938, 040238, 040938, 041638, 042338, 050738, 051438, 052138

YOU'RE BREAKING MY HEART 082049, 082749, 090349, 091049, 091749, 092449, 100149, 100849, 101549, 102249, 102949, 110549, 111249, 112649, 120349

(YOU'RE) HAVING MY BABY 081774, 082474, 083174, 090774, 091474, 092174

YOU'RE IN LOVE 032391, 033091, 040691, 041391, 042091, 042791, 050491

YOU'RE IN MY HEART (THE FINAL ACCLAIM) 010778, 011478, 012178, 012778, 020478

YOU'RE JUST IN LOVE 012751, 020351, 021051, 021751, 022451, 030351, 031051, 031751, 032451, 033151, 040751, 041451, 042151

YOU'RE LAUGHING AT ME 031337

YOU'RE LONELY AND I'M LONELY 062940, 070640

YOU'RE MY EVERYTHING 082667, 090267, 090967, 091667, 092367

(YOU'RE MY) SOUL AND INSPIRATION 032666, 040266, 040966, 041666, 042366, 043066, 050766, 051466

YOU'RE NO GOOD 012675, 020175, 020875, 021575, 022275

YOU'RE NOT ALONE 032589

YOU'RE NOT THE KIND 081536, 082236, 090536, 091236

YOU'RE ONLY HUMAN 083185, 090785

YOU'RE ONLY LONELY 120879, 121579, 122279

YOU'RE SIXTEEN 123060, 010561, 011361, 011274, 011974, 012674, 020274, 020974, 021674, 022374

YOU'RE SO DARN CHARMING 081735, 092835

YOU'RE SO VAIN 122372, 123072, 010673, 011373, 012073, 012773, 021073, 021773, 022473, 030373

(YOU'RE THE) DEVIL IN DISGUISE 072763, 080363, 081063, 081763, 082463

YOU'RE THE FIRST, THE LAST, MY EVERYTHING 120774, 121474, 122174, 122874, 010475, 011175, 011875

YOU'RE THE INSPIRATION 010585, 011285, 011985, 012685, 020285, 020985

YOU'RE THE ONE 102365, 103065, 110665, 111365, 112065

YOU'RE THE ONE THAT I WANT 042978, 050678, 051378, 052078, 052778, 060378, 061078, 061778

YOU'RE THE REASON 111761, 112461

YOU'RE THE REASON I'M LIVING 022363, 030263, 030963, 031663, 032363, 033063, 040563

YOURS 072641, 080241, 080941, 081641, 082341, 083041, 090641, 091341, 092041, 092741, 100441, 101141, 101841, 102541, 110141, 110841, 111541

YOURS AND MINE 091137, 091837

YOURS TRULY IS TRULY YOURS 040436, 042536

YOU'VE GOT A FRIEND 070371, 071071, 071771, 072471, 073171, 080771, 081471, 082171

YOU'VE GOT TO HIDE YOUR LOVE AWAY 112765

YOU'VE GOT YOUR TROUBLES 100265, 100965

YOU'VE LOST THAT LOVIN' FEELING 010965, 011665, 012365, 013065, 020665, 021365, 022065, 022765, 030665

YOU'VE MADE ME SO VERY HAPPY 040569, 041269, 041969, 042669, 050369, 051069

YOU'VE REALLY GOT A HOLD ON ME 020963, 021663, 022363

YO-YO 100271, 100971, 101671, 102371, 103071, 110671, 111371, 112071

YUMMY YUMMY YUMMY 060168, 060868, 061568, 062268, 062968

Z

ZING, ZING, ZOOM, ZOOM 030351

ZIP A DEE DOO DAH 111646, 112346, 120746, 121446, 122146, 122846, 010447, 011147, 011847, 012547, 020147, 122962, 010563, 011263